THE ISLAMIC WORLD

The Islamic World is an outstanding guide to Islamic faith and culture in all its geographical and historical diversity. Written by a distinguished international team of Islamic scholars, it elucidates the history, philosophy and practice of one of the world's great religious traditions. Its grounding in contemporary scholarship makes it an ideal reference source for students and scholars alike.

Edited by Andrew Rippin, a leading scholar of Islam, the volume covers the political, geographical, religious, intellectual, cultural and social worlds of Islam, and offers insight into all aspects of Muslim life including the Qur'an and law, philosophy, science and technology, art, literature, and film and much else. It explores the concept of an 'Islamic' world: what makes it distinctive and how uniform is that distinctiveness across Muslim geographical regions and through history?

Andrew Rippin is Professor of Islamic History and Dean of the Faculty of Humanities, University of Victoria, Canada, and Fellow of the Royal Society of Canada. His publications include *Muslims: Their Religious Beliefs and Practices* (third edition Routledge 2005) and *The Qur'an and its Interpretative Tradition* (2001).

THE ROUTLEDGE WORLDS

THE BABYLONIAN WORLD
Edited by Gwendolyn Leick

THE EGYPTIAN WORLD
Edited by Toby Wilkinson

THE WORLD OF POMPEII
Edited by Pedar W. Foss and John J. Dobbins

THE RENAISSANCE WORLD
Edited by John Jeffries Martin

THE EARLY CHRISTIAN WORLD
Edited by Philip F. Esler

THE GREEK WORLD
Edited by Anton Powell

THE ROMAN WORLD
Edited by John Wacher

THE HINDU WORLD
Edited by Sushil Mittal and Gene Thursby

Forthcoming:

THE VIKING WORLD
Edited by Stefan Brink and Neil Price

THE OTTOMAN WORLD
Edited by Christine Woodhead

THE ELIZABETHAN WORLD
Edited by Susan Doran and Norman Jones

THE BYZANTINE WORLD
Edited by Paul Stephenson

THE ATLANTIC WORLD
Edited by William O'Reilly

THE ISLAMIC WORLD

Andrew Rippin

Routledge
Taylor & Francis Group
LONDON AND NEW YORK

First published 2008 by Routledge
2 Park Square, Milton Park, Abingdon, Oxon OX14 4RN

Simultaneously published in the USA and Canada
by Routledge
270 Madison Ave, New York, NY 10016

Routledge is an imprint of the Taylor & Francis Group, an informa business

Typeset in Sabon by
RefineCatch Limited, Bungay, Suffolk
Printed and bound in Great Britain by
CPI Antony Rowe, Chippenham, Wiltshire

British Library Cataloguing in Publication Data
A catalogue record for this book is available from the British Library

Library of Congress Cataloging in Publication Data
A catalog record for this book has been requested

ISBN10: 0–415–36407–8 (hbk)
ISBN13: 978–0–415–36646–5 (hbk)

CONTENTS

LIST OF ILLUSTRATIONS

Note. The following were reproduced with kind permission. While every effort has been made to trace copyright holders and obtain permission, this has not been possible in all cases. Any omissions brought to our attention will be remedied in future editions.

Maps

Figures

Tables

Text acknowledgements

Chapter 43: based upon "Ibn Khaldun's Understanding of Civilizations and the Dilemmas of Islam and the West Today," Akbar Ahmed, *Middle East Journal*, 56 (1) (Winter 2003): 20–45. Reproduced with permission.

Chapter 44: based upon "Islam and Cultural Issues: Talk given at the Milad Celebrations, University of Victoria, Victoria, BC, June 3, 2001". Reproduced with permission from the Centre for Studies in Religion and Society, University of Victoria.

CONTRIBUTORS

Akbar Ahmed is the Ibn Khaldun Chair of Islamic Studies and Professor of International Relations, The American University, Washington DC. He has held senior administrative positions in Pakistan, and was the Pakistan High Commissioner (Ambassador) to the UK, and is author of *Journey into Islam: The Crisis of Globalization* (Brookings Press, 2007). He is the author of many other books and articles, and a frequent commentator on Islamic affairs in the media.

Kecia Ali is Assistant Professor of Religion at Boston University. Her primary research interests center on marriage in early Islamic jurisprudence but she is also interested in modern appropriations of classical texts. She is the author of *Sexual Ethics and Islam: Feminist Reflections on Qur'an, Hadith, and Jurisprudence* (Oneworld, 2006), and co-author of *Islam: The Key Concepts* (Routledge, 2008). She is currently working on a biography of the jurist al-Shāfi'ī.

John R. Bowen is the Dunbar-Van Cleve Professor in Arts and Sciences at Washington University in St. Louis. He studies problems of pluralism, law, and religion, and in particular contemporary efforts to rethink Islamic norms and law in Asia, Europe, and North America. He has written on Asia in *Islam, Law and Equality in Indonesia: An Anthropology of Public Reasoning* (Cambridge, 2003), and his *Why the French Don't Like Headscarves* (Princeton, 2007) concerns current debates in France on Islam and laïcité. Forthcoming are *Shaping French Islam* (Princeton) and *The New Anthropology of Islam* (Cambridge).

Christopher Buck is author of *Alain Locke: Faith and Philosophy* (Kalimat, 2005), *Paradise and Paradigm: Key Symbols in Persian Christianity and the Bahá'í Faith* (SUNY Press, 1999), *Symbol and Secret: Qur'an Commentary in Bahá'u'lláh's* Kitáb-i Íqán (Kalimat, 1995/2004), and a chapter in *The Blackwell Companion to the Qur'ān* (Blackwell, 2006). He is a Pennsylvania attorney and independent scholar (Ph.D. 1996; JD 2006), having formerly taught at Michigan State University (2000–4), Quincy University (1999–2000), Millikin University (1997–9), and Carleton University (1994–6), where he variously taught American Studies, African American Studies, Islamic Studies, Religious Studies, Argument Theory and Research Writing.

Art Buehler is Senior Lecturer at Victoria University of Wellington, New Zealand. He is a scholar of the phenomenon of transregional Ṣūfī networks and the transmission of Islamic revivalist ideas, and is senior editor of the *Journal of the History of*

Sufism. His two books *Sufi Heirs of the Prophet: The Indian Naqshbandiyya and the Rise of the Mediating Sufi Shaykh* (University of South Carolina Press, 1998) and *Analytical Indexes for the Collected Letters of Ahmad Sirhindi* [in Persian] (Iqbal Academy, 2001) are the result of four years of fieldwork in Indo-Pakistan.

Martin Bunton is an Assistant Professor in the Department of History at the University of Victoria, Canada. His book, *Colonial Land Policies in Palestine, 1917–1936* was published by Oxford University Press in 2007, and he is currently working on a comparison of government land policies in Middle East territories under British rule in the interwar period.

Jeffrey C. Burke is Visiting Assistant Professor of Islamic Studies at the College of the Holy Cross in Worcester, MA. He received his Ph.D. from the Institute of Islamic Studies, McGill University, and has published book chapters, articles, and reviews in leading scholarly works with a focus on women in religious traditions, the history of Islam, and Muslim–Christian relations.

Amila Buturovic is Associate Professor of Humanities and the Noor Fellow in Islamic Studies at York University, Toronto. She holds a Ph.D. in Islamic Studies from McGill University where she specialized in medieval Arabic literature and thought. Her main research interests lie in the intersections between literature and religion, especially in the context of identity formation in the Ottoman and post-Ottoman Balkans. In addition to many articles, she is the author of *Stone Speaker: Medieval Tombstones, Landscape and Bosnian Identity in the Poetry of Mak Dizdar* (Palgrave, 2002) and, with Irvin C. Schick, co-editor of *Women in the Ottoman Balkans* (I. B. Tauris, 2007). Her current research focuses on Muslim funerary inscriptions in Bosnia-Herzegovina.

Simonetta Calderini is Senior Lecturer in Islamic Studies at Roehampton University, London. She received her PhD in Islamic Studies from SOAS, University of London, and her first degree in Oriental Languages and Civilizations from the Oriental Institute, Naples, Italy. She has written a number of books, among which, with Delia Cortese, is *Women and the Fatimids in the World of Islam* (Edinburgh University Press, 2006). Her works on the topics of *tafsīr*, gender studies, contemporary Islam as well as Medieval Ismailism, appear as articles in academic journals and entries in various *Atlases* and *Encyclopedias*. Her current research focuses on classical and modern arguments for and against women *imāms*.

Niall Christie teaches History, Art and Religious Studies at the University of British Columbia and Corpus Christi College, Vancouver. He has published articles on a variety of subjects, including in particular the Muslim response to the crusades and comparisons of holy war preaching in Islam and Christianity. He is currently co-authoring a book on the latter topic.

Elton L. Daniel is a Professor of Islamic and Middle Eastern History at the University of Hawaii-Manoa. He received his Ph.D. from the University of Texas-Austin and has conducted research in Iran, Turkey, Syria, and Egypt. He has served as associate editor of the *Encyclopaedia Iranica* and published many books and articles pertaining to Iran, including *Khurasan under Abbasid Rule* (Bibliotheca Islamica, 1979), *A*

Shi'ite Pilgrimage to Mecca 1885–1886 (University of Texas Press, 1990), and *The History of Iran* (Greenwood, 2001).

Devin DeWeese is Professor of Central Eurasian Studies at Indiana University specializing in the religious history of Islamic Central Asia. He is the author of *Islamization and Native Religion in the Golden Horde* (Pennsylvania State University Press, 1994) and a number of articles on the history of Ṣūfī communities in Central Asia and on the historical process and mythic poetics of Islamization.

Gönül Dönmez-Colin is an independent writer and researcher. She graduated from the American College in Istanbul and the University of Istanbul, Department of Philology and completed her post-graduate studies at the Concordia and McGill Universities in Montreal, Canada. She has taught in Montreal and Hong Kong and has done field research in Iran, Turkey, India and Central Asia. Among her recent books are *Women, Islam and Cinema* (Reaktion Books, 2004), *Cinemas of the Other: A Personal Journey with Filmmakers from the Middle East and Central Asia* (Intellect, 2006), *Cinema of North Africa and the Middle East* (ed.) (Wallflower Press, 2007) and *Turkish Cinema: Identity, Distance and Belonging* (Reaktion Books, 2008). Her work has been translated into nine languages.

Markus Dressler received his Ph.D. from Erfurt University in 2001 and since 2005 he has been an Assistant Professor at Hofstra University. His research focus is on the religion, politics, and history of modern Turkey with a special interest in Turkish Alevism. His monographs include *Die civil Religion der Türkei. Kemalistische und alevitische Atatürk-Rezeption im Vergleich* (Würzburg 1999) and *Die alevitische Religion. Traditionslinien und Neubestimmungen* (Würzburg 2002). He has also written articles and book chapters mainly on Turkish Alevism, religion and politics in Turkey, and on contemporary Sufism.

Michael Frishkopf is Associate Professor of Music at the University of Alberta. He received his doctorate from UCLA's Department of Ethnomusicology in 1999. He has conducted fieldwork primarily in Egypt, and in Ghana. His research and teaching center on Sufi music, sound in Islamic ritual, and the musical traditions of the Arab world and West Africa. Recent articles and book chapters include "Globalization and re-localization of Sufi music in the West" (Routledge), "Nationalism, Nationalization, and the Egyptian music industry" (Asian Music), and "Mediated Qur'anic recitation and the contestation of Islam in contemporary Egypt" (Ashgate). Three books are in progress: *The Sounds of Islam* (Routledge), *Sufism, Ritual, and Modernity in Egypt: Language Performance as an Adaptive Strategy* (Brill) and an edited collection entitled *Music and Media in the Arab World*.

Robert Gleave, who received his Ph.D. in Islamic Studies, University of Manchester, in 1996, is Professor of Arabic Studies at the University of Exeter. He has published extensively on Shiʿism, focusing on Twelver Shīʿī legal hermeneutics. He has strong research interests in Islamic Law, in particular the development of Twelver Shīʿī legal thought, as well as the relationship between theory and practice in Islamic Law, medieval and modern Islamic political theory and the legitimization of violence in Muslim legal works. He is the author of *Inevitable Doubt: Two Theories of Shīʿī Jurisprudence* (Brill, 2000) and editor of *Religion and Society in Qajar Iran*

(RoutledgeCurzon, 2004). More recent works include *Scripturalist Islam: The History and Doctrines of the Akhbari School of Imami Shiʿism* (Brill, 2007), and *Islam and Literalism: A Study of Literal Meaning in Early Muslim Legal Theory* (forthcoming).

Frank Griffel is Associate Professor of Islamic Studies, Yale University. He has published *Shariʿa: Islamic Law in the Contemporary Context*, ed. Frank Griffel and Abbas Amanat (Stanford University Press 2007), *Apostasie und Toleranz im Islam. Die Entwicklung zu al-Gazalis Urteil gegen die Philosophie und die Reaktionen der Philosophen* (Brill, 2000), and translated, introduced, and annotated *Über Rechtgläubigkeit und religiöse Toleranz. Eine Übersetzung der Schrift Das Kriterium der Unterscheidung zwischen Islam und Gottlosigkeit* (Faysal at-tafriqa bayna l-Islam wa-z-zandaqa) (Spur Verlag, 1998).

Paul L. Heck is assistant professor of Islamic Studies in Georgetown University's Theology Department. He is author of *The Construction of Knowledge in Islamic Civilization* (Brill, 2002) and editor of *Sufism and Politics* (Markus Wiener, 2006). His articles treat varied topics, including concepts of *jihād*, the rise of early Kharijism, political thought in Islam, and the role of skepticism in Islam's intellectual heritage.

Marcia K. Hermansen is professor in the Theology department and Director of the Islamic World Studies Program at Loyola University Chicago. Her translation of Shāh Walī Allāh's, *Ḥujjat Allāh al-Bāligha, The Conclusive Argument from God*, was published by Brill in 1996 and in subsequent Pakistani and Indian editions. She was co-editor of the *MacMillan Encyclopedia of Islam and the Muslim World* (2003) and is currently writing *American Sufis* for Oxford University Press. She has contributed numerous scholarly articles on topics such as contemporary Islamic thought, Islam in South Asia, Sufism, Muslims in America, and women and gender in Islam.

Valerie J. Hoffman received her Ph.D. in Arabic and Islamic studies from the University of Chicago in 1986, and is currently Associate Professor in the Department of Religion at the University of Illinois at Urbana-Champaign, where she teaches on all aspects of Islam. She has published *Sufism, Mystics and Saints in Modern Egypt* (University of South Carolina Press, 1995) and a second book, *The Essentials of Ibadi Islam*, is forthcoming with Syracuse University Press. She has also published many articles on various aspects of Islam and made a film for classroom use, "Celebrating the Prophet in the Remembrance of God: Sufi Dhikr in Egypt" (1997). Her current research is on Muslim scholars in nineteenth- and early twentieth-century Oman and East Africa.

Amir Hussain is Associate Professor in the Department of Theological Studies at Loyola Marymount University in Los Angeles. He specializes in the study of contemporary Muslim communities in North America. His latest book is *Oil and Water: Two Faiths, One God* (Copper House, 2006), an introduction to Islam for a North American audience. He has published about Muslims in journals such as *Studies in Religion*, *Method and Theory in the Study of Religion*, and the *Journal of the American Academy of Religion*. He is on the editorial boards of two journals, *Comparative Islamic Studies* and *Contemporary Islam: Dynamics of Muslim Life*.

Zayn Kassam is Associate Professor of Religious Studies at Pomona College, Claremont, California. She has been honored with two Wig Awards for Distinguished Teaching at Pomona College, as well as an American Academy of Religion Excellence in Teaching Award, and has lectured widely on gender issues in the USA, Canada, and Britain. She is the author of the volume on Islam in a series titled *Introduction to the World's Major Religions* published by Greenwood Press (2006), and has published articles on women in Islam, on Islam and violence, and on teaching Islam.

Hussein Keshani is an Assistant Professor of Art History at University of British Columbia-Okanagan in Kelowna, Canada, where he teaches courses in European, Contemporary and Islamic Art. His research focuses on the architectural history of Islamic India during the Sultanate (twelfth to fifteenth century) and late Mughal periods (eighteenth to nineteenth century).

Oliver Leaman teaches at the University of Kentucky and writes on Islamic and Jewish philosophy. His most recent publication is *Islam: The Key Concepts*, with Kecia Ali (Routledge, 2008). He has written and edited a number of previous books and works of reference in the areas of Islamic and Jewish thought and culture, including *Jewish Thought* (Routledge, 2006) and *Islamic Aesthetics: An Introduction* (Edinburgh University Press, 2004).

Michael Lecker is a Professor at the Institute of Asian and African Studies of the Hebrew University, Jerusalem. Among his recent publications are *The "Constitution of Medina": Muhammad's First Legal Document* (Darwin Press, 2004) and *People, Tribes and Society in Arabia around the Time of Muhammad* (Aldershot, 2005). Recently he has worked on prosopography. A demo of his project may be seen at http://micro5.mscc.huji.ac.il:81/JPP/demo; username: jpp-demo; password: guest. His homepage is: http://michael-lecker.net.

James E. Lindsay is Associate Professor of History, Colorado State University. He is the author of *Daily Life in the Medieval Islamic World* (Greenwood, 2005) and the editor of *Ibn ʿAsakir and Early Islamic History* (Darwin Press, 2001). He is the author of several articles on Ibn ʿAsākir (d. 1176) and his *Taʾrīkh madīnat Dimashq*. He is currently working on *"Fight in the Path of God": Ibn ʿAsākir of Damascus and His Contribution to the Jihād Campaign of Sultan Nūr al-Dīn*, co-authored with Suleiman A. Mourad to be published by Ashgate in the "Crusade Texts in Translation" series.

Ebrahim Moosa is Associate Professor of Islamic Studies in the Department of Religion and Director of the Center for Study of Muslim Networks at Duke University. He is the author of *Ghazali and the Poetics of Imagination* (University of North Carolina Press, 2005) and editor of the last manuscript of the late Professor Fazlur Rahman, *Revival and Reform in Islam: A Study of Islamic Fundamentalism* (Oneworld, 2000). Previously he taught at the University of Cape Town's Department of Religious Studies in his native South Africa till 1998 and was Visiting Professor at Stanford University prior to joining Duke in 2001.

Suleiman Ali Mourad received his Ph.D. from Yale University in 2004 and is Associate Professor of Religion at Smith College. His research and publications focus on medieval Islamic history and religious thought, including the Muʿtazilite school's approach and method in Qurʾanic exegesis, the presentation of Jesus in the Qurʾān and Islamic scholarship, Muslim reactions to the Crusades, and the holiness of Jerusalem. He is the author of *Early Islam between Myth and History: al-Ḥasan al-Baṣrī (d. 110H/728CE) and the Formation of His Legacy in Classical Islamic Scholarship* (Brill, 2005), and co-editor of *Jerusalem: Idea and Reality* (Routledge, 2008).

Gordon Nickel is an Assistant Professor of Intercultural Studies for the ACTS seminary consortium at Trinity Western University, Langley, British Columbia, Canada. His Ph.D. dissertation was on the earliest commentaries on the Qurʾān. He has extensive experience of Muslim communities in Pakistan and India.

David Owusu-Ansah is Professor of History at James Madison University in Virginia. He received his master's degree in Islamic Studies at McGill University and a doctorate in African history from Northwestern University. He has published two editions of the *Historical Dictionary of Ghana* (Scarecrow Press, 1995 and 2005) and he is also the author of *Islamic Talismanic Tradition in Nineteenth Century Asante* (Edwin Mellen Press, 1991). He is part of a research project on the modernization of Islamic education in Ghana.

Gabriel Said Reynolds is Assistant Professor of Islamic Studies and Theology at the University of Notre Dame (USA). He is the author of *A Muslim Theologian in the Sectarian Milieu: ʿAbd al-Jabbār and the Critique of Christian Origins* (Brill, 2004) and the editor of *The Qurʾān in Its Historical Context* (Routledge, 2008). Currently he is completing a manuscript on the Qurʾān's conversation with Biblical literature, the result of research in Beirut and Jerusalem during 2006–7.

Andrew Rippin is Professor of Islamic History and Dean of the Faculty of Humanities, University of Victoria, Canada and a Fellow of the Royal Society of Canada. He is the author of *Muslims: their Religious Beliefs and Practices* (3rd edition Routledge, 2005) and *The Qurʾān and its Interpretative Tradition* (Ashgate, 2001); his other works include *Classical Islam: A Sourcebook of Religious Literature* with Norman Calder and Jawid Mojaddedi (Routledge, 2003).

Sajjad H. Rizvi is Senior Lecturer in Islamic Studies at the University of Exeter. A specialist on Islamic intellectual history, he is the author of *Mulla Sadra* (Oxford, 2007) and with Feras Hamza of *Understanding the Word of God* (Oxford, 2008). His current project is a study of Islamic philosophical traditions in India.

Amyn B. Sajoo lectured at Simon Fraser University and held visiting appointments at Cambridge and McGill universities before he joined the Institute of Ismaili Studies in London in 2007. He is the author of *Muslim Ethics* (I. B. Tauris, 2004), and *Pluralism in Old Societies and New States* (Institute of Southeast Asian Studies, 1994) as well as being the contributing editor of *Muslim Modernities: Expressions of the Civil Imagination* (I. B. Tauris, 2008) and of *Civil Society in the Muslim World* (I. B. Tauris, 2002).

George Saliba is Professor of Arabic and Islamic Science at the Department of Middle East and Asian Languages and Cultures at Columbia University. He studies the developments of Islamic planetary theories and their impact on European astronomy. His publications include *Islamic Science and the Making of the European Renaissance* (MIT Press, 2007) and *A History of Arabic Astronomy: Planetary Theories During the Golden Age of Islam* (New York University Press, 1994).

Zeki Saritoprak received his Ph.D. in Islamic Theology from the University of Marmara, Turkey. Currently he is the holder of the Bediüzzaman Said Nursi Chair in Islamic Studies at John Carroll University in Cleveland, Ohio. In addition to presenting at numerous conferences and universities over the years, Dr. Saritoprak is also the author of several books and academic articles in Turkish, English, and Arabic.

Mustafa Shah is a lecturer in the Near and Middle East Department at the School of Oriental and African Studies, London, where he completed both his BA and Ph.D. degrees in the field of Arabic linguistics and Islamic Studies. His principal research and teaching interests include early Arabic linguistic thought, classical Islamic theology and jurisprudence, and, Qur'anic hermeneutics and exegesis. He has published articles on these subjects in the *Journal of Qur'anic Studies* and the *Encyclopaedia of Arabic Language and Linguistics*. He is currently working on a number of monographs including *Religious Dogma and the Synthesis of Early Arabic Linguistic Thought* (Kegan Paul International, 2008) and *Classical Interpretations of the Qur'ān* (I. B. Tauris, 2008).

William Shepard is Associate Professor of Religion Studies (Retired) at the University of Canterbury, in Christchurch, New Zealand. He completed his Ph.D. degree in the comparative study of religion at Harvard University in 1973 and taught in the USA and then New Zealand from 1971 to 1999. His research has been primarily on Islam in the modern world, particularly the writings of Sayyid Quṭb.

David Thomas is Professor of Christianity and Islam at the University of Birmingham. He specializes in the history and theology of Christian–Muslim relations, and has recently published *Muslim–Christian Polemic during the Crusades, the Letter from the People of Cyprus and Ibn Abī Ṭālib al-Dimashqī's Reply* (Brill, 2005), together with R. Ebied, and *The Bible in Arab Christianity* (Brill, 2007). He is editor of the journal *Islam and Christian–Muslim Relations* and senior editor of the texts and studies series "The History of Christian–Muslim Relations".

Nelly Van Doorn-Harder holds the Surjit Patheja Chair in World Religions and Ethics at Valparaiso University. Her areas of study include Islam in Indonesia, the Coptic Orthodox Church, Religion and Gender, and Inter-religious Studies. She is the author of *Women Shaping Islam. Indonesian Muslim Women Reading the Qur'an* (University of Illinois Press, 2006), *Contemporary Coptic Nuns* (University of South Carolina Press, 1995), and *De Koptisch-Orthodoxe Kerk* (Kampen, 2005). She has also co-edited *Between Desert and City: The Coptic Orthodox Church Today* (Wipf and Stock Publishers, 1997), and *Coping with Evil in Religion and Culture: Case Studies* (Editions Ropodi, 2007).

David Waines is Professor Emeritus of Islamic Studies in the Department of Religious Studies, Lancaster University, England. Since retirement he has been Visiting Professor at Leiden University, The Netherlands, teaching and researching his next book on the fourteenth-century Muslim world. His most recent books are *An Introduction to Islam* (Cambridge University Press, 2nd edition, 2003), and editor of *Patterns of Everyday Life* (Ashgate, 2002).

Earle H. Waugh is Professor Emeritus of Religious Studies and Interdisciplinary Studies at the University of Alberta. He has researched and published widely on the history of religions and Islamic Studies. His most recent book *Music, Memory, Religion: Morocco's Mystical Chanters* (University of South Carolina Press, 2005) was short-listed for the prestigious Albert Hourani prize for best book on the Middle East. He is the editor of the journal *Religious Studies and Theology* and was senior editor of the *Gale Encyclopedia of Contemporary Religion* (2005). He is also a consultant for many publications and media organizations including the *New York Times* and the Canadian Broadcasting Corporation. Currently he directs a research institute in culture and medicine at the University.

Neguin Yavari is Assistant Professor of History at the New School, New York. Her biography of Niẓām al-Mulk is forthcoming. Her most recent article on "Mirror for Princes or a Hall of Mirrors: Niẓām al-Mulk's *Siyar al-mulūk* Reconsidered," appeared in *al-Masaq*. Her "Polysemous Texts and Reductionist Readings: Women and Heresy in the *Siyar al-mulūk*," appeared in a collected volume of articles co-edited by her: *Views from the Edge: Essays in Honor of Richard W. Bulliet* (Columbia University Press, 2004).

INTRODUCTION

Andrew Rippin

Within the context of world politics, the Islamic world has taken on a prominence today that can hardly be ignored. In making that simple observation, however, challenging, confusing and misleading terminology is necessarily employed. The precise reference of "the" Islamic world is unclear. The basis upon which that singular category has been created is not immediately evident or sufficiently enunciated. Even if one assumes that the religion of Islam must play a role within the definition of that world, it is immediately apparent there is a problem: it is well known that not everyone in that geographical region is, in fact, Muslim. It is also clear that, even of those who consider themselves Muslims, there are many different manifestations of that faith itself. Further, it may be debated whether the faith itself is, in fact, the defining feature of the interaction of that geographical region with the rest of world. The extent to which the realities of contemporary power structures play a role that overwhelms issues that might be thought to be grounded in religious values does, on many occasions, seem evident. To undertake an investigation of what it is that we mean by "the Islamic world," then, is a task that is both important and complex.

The goal of this volume is to provide an overview of the culture of those who maintained, and continue to maintain, adherence to the religion of Islam in all of its geographical and historical diversity. The notion of diversity provides the main focus for the work as it aims by means of its overall contents to approach an answer to the fundamental question of what we mean by the frequently used phrase that constitutes the title of the book, "the Islamic world." The chapters herein are unified by their common quest for the definition of this phrase. Each essay contributes, through its reflections on its own goal and scope, to the central theme of the volume. Each essay poses the question of what it is within the topic being treated that gives "the Islamic world" meaning and to what extent that meaning is uniform across Muslim-populated countries and through historical eras. The volume in its totality, therefore, attempts to define the topic reflected in the title of the work, while at the same time aiming to provide an authoritative and accessible source of information on topics of relevance, concern and interest.

In attempting to achieve the conceptual goal of the volume, however, it has also become apparent that not every possible approach to the overall conception can be explored within the finite contents of the two covers of a book. Compromises are necessary. It should not be thought that there are no other ways of exploring the notion of "the Islamic world." Indeed, there certainly are further geographical regions to examine, other themes to trace, more concerns to consider. The chapters that make

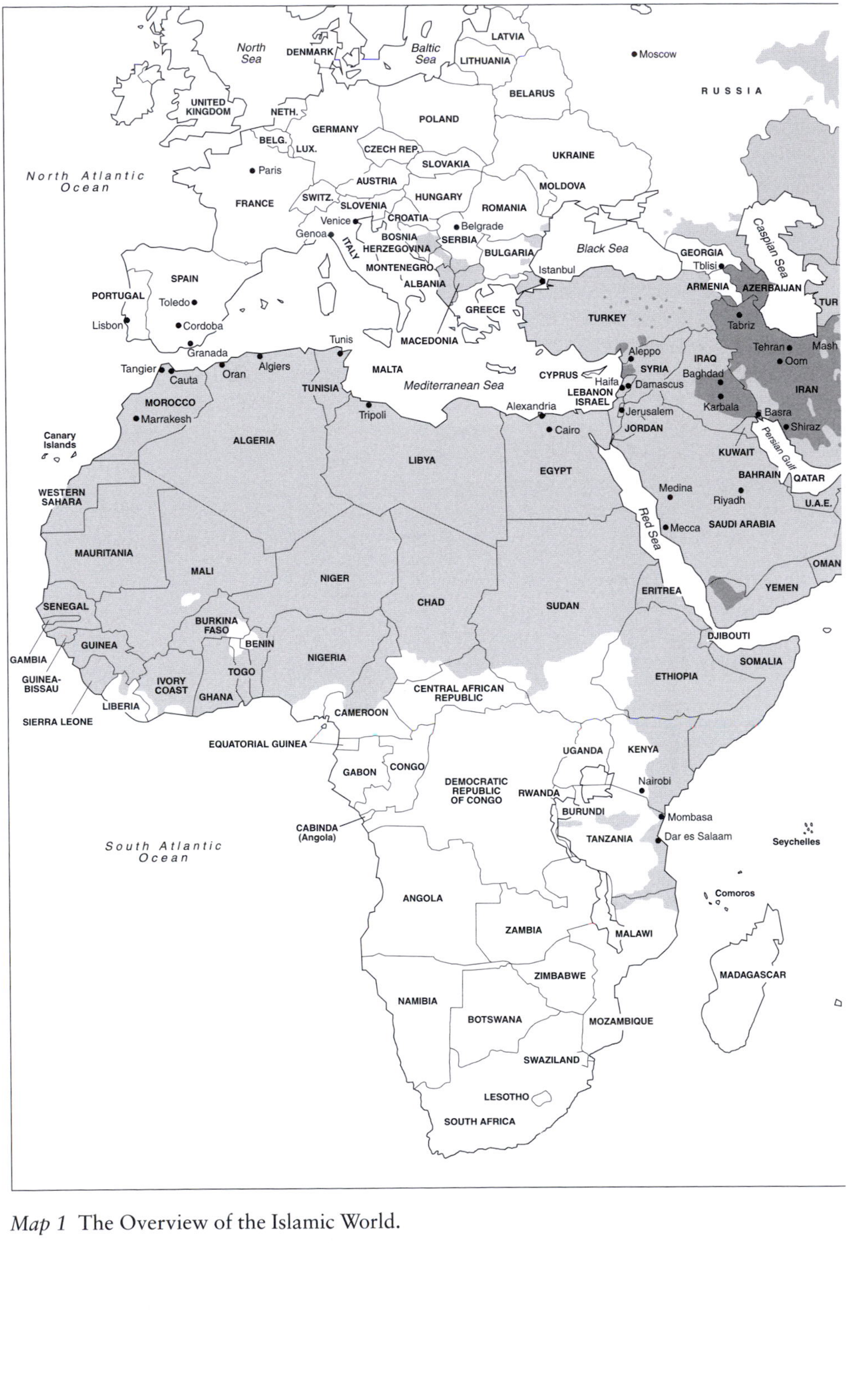

Map 1 The Overview of the Islamic World.

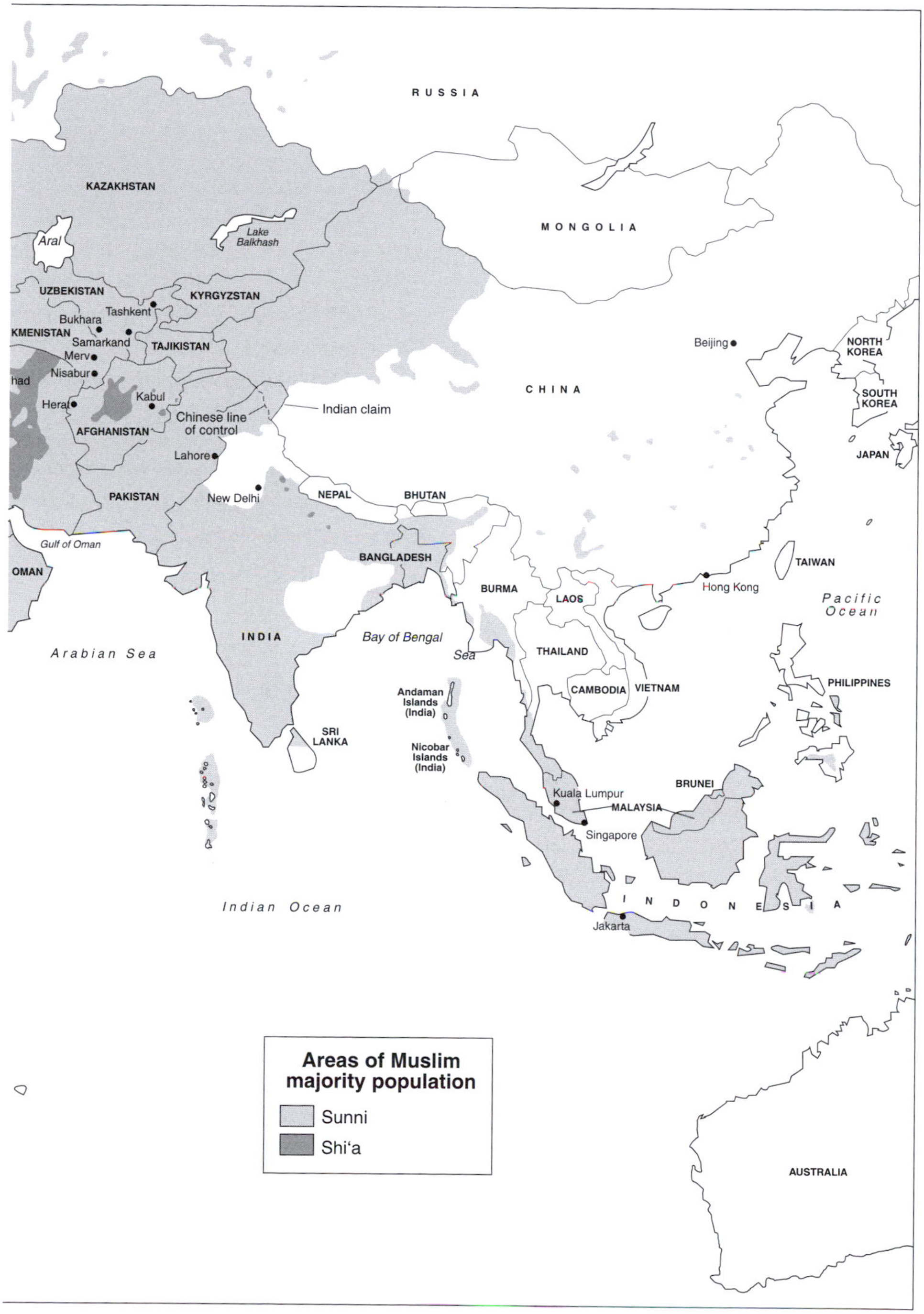
RUSSIA
KAZAKHSTAN
Aral
Lake Balkhash
MONGOLIA
UZBEKISTAN
KYRGYZSTAN
Tashkent
Bukhara
KMENISTAN
Samarkand
TAJIKISTAN
Merv
Nisabur
had
Kabul
Herat
AFGHANISTAN
Chinese line of control
Indian claim
CHINA
Beijing
NORTH KOREA
SOUTH KOREA
JAPAN
Lahore
PAKISTAN
New Delhi
NEPAL
BHUTAN
Gulf of Oman
OMAN
BANGLADESH
TAIWAN
Hong Kong
Pacific Ocean
BURMA
LAOS
INDIA
Bay of Bengal
Arabian Sea
Sea
THAILAND
Andaman Islands (India)
CAMBODIA
VIETNAM
PHILIPPINES
SRI LANKA
Nicobar Islands (India)
BRUNEI
Kuala Lumpur
MALAYSIA
Singapore
Indian Ocean
INDONESIA
Jakarta
Areas of Muslim majority population
Sunni
Shi'a
AUSTRALIA

up this book should be thought of as examples only, as explorations of a concept that continues to need to be refined and defined, and as models of scholarly inquiry into topics which truly know no bounds.

Conception

The approach to the overall task of this volume has been divided into five parts. Geography is used as the initial organizational category in Part I. Each geographical area reflects modern geo-political boundaries; this draws attention immediately to a basic problem in the concept of "the Islamic world" and the need to pay attention to the variability of the "borders" in medieval and modern times. It can be observed that, at each point in history, there is an underlying question concerning the presence of an Islamic identity in each geographical region.

Given that a concept of "Islam" superficially appears to underpin the notion of the Islamic world, Part II covers the fundamentals of the Islamic religion while paying attention to the diversity of thought and manifestation in both history and geography. While Islam is a convenient concept by which to try to define the Islamic world, once again the diversity of its attributes and the features of cultural adaptation do mean that, beyond sharing a limited set of common symbols, the Islamic basis of the Islamic world is a concept which needs to be explored and carefully defined.

In Part III the intellectual world, as it manifests itself in thought about the world beyond (but yet including) the religious sphere, provides the theme by which the manifestation of the Islamic world may be understood. The organization of knowledge on both the theoretical and applied levels as enunciated by leading intellectuals from different time periods provides a measure of how the Islamic world both understood itself and created a tradition of cultural knowledge. Here, too, attention to regional and historical variation is crucial in understanding a concept of "the Islamic world." This part features a sequence of ten biographies of individual Muslims, stretched across time and place to serve as illustrations of the diversity of thought and approach, and also to provide models of biographical treatments in the Islamic context. The world is, in the end, composed of individuals whose lives are interwoven with one another; while ten such lives can hardly be said to be a sufficient selection to allow more than the slightest glimpse of the ways in which individuals involve themselves in the concept of Islam, the sense of the commonality of the venture itself does emerge.

Material culture is often interpreted to provide tangible evidence of the presence of Islam in the world, and that provides the focus of Part IV. The reality is, however, that this is an aspect which is overwhelming in its diversity across the Islamic world and through history. The various manifestations of art, architecture, urban design, music, and literature throughout Islamic history and across the geographical range centrally raise the question of what makes these manifestations Islamic.

Finally, the structuring of society in the context of Islam, founded in Islamic law and finding its expression in a range of historical and geographically conditioned manners, is crucial to providing an understanding of how individual Muslims live their lives as a part of the "Islamic world." The chapters in Part V display the full depth of the issue of the meaning of "the Islamic world" by dealing with those matters that so deeply inhere in assumptions about day-to-day life involving power in its many social organizational aspects. How individuals create and maintain their own sense of identity as Muslims is embedded in the generally unspoken values that ground human existence.

The end result of this compilation of data combined with reflection on the overall definitional theme can hardly be said to point in a single direction. The Islamic world is a dynamic notion, shifting through time, finding its manifestation adjusting to the pressures of the moment. Of course there are symbolic touchstones, especially in the dimensions of human existence we call "religious," but to no extent do those symbols serve to dictate absolutely and uniformly every aspect of life in every circumstance. Pragmatic interpretation influenced by the exchange of ideas across human cultures has allowed the Islamic world to continue to flourish and adapt.

Realization

Bringing together a volume of this type has meant that I have, in my role as editor, encountered many technical issues which have challenged me. The very diversity of the Islamic world creates a complex linguistic universe; the existence of that world over a time period of over 1,400 years defeats any easy notion of cultural uniformity. Dealing with those two facts has meant that I have had to work with a diverse range of authors to contribute to the volume.

To deal with these complexities some basic principles related to the technicalities of our discipline have been employed. Many aspects have made me, as the editor, confront the oft-remarked Arabo-centric nature of so many of our studies; yet I needed to find ways to resolve some basic technical issues and the ways to do so were not always obvious to me. So, once again, in order to deal with diversity in the confines of one book, compromises – but sensible ones, I hope – have been necessary. Place names have not been presented in transliteration, generally preferring a common English form of names where such exist. Names of people, on the other hand, are provided in full transliteration except in the case of most contemporary figures where common spelling is used when possible and where such seems to prevail in common practice. Of course, the point at which someone is "contemporary" is difficult to define. To simplify matters, I have used C. E. Bosworth *The New Islamic Dynasties: A Chronological and Genealogical Manual* (Edinburgh: Edinburgh University Press, 1996) as a source for the spelling of rulers' names: this may, in some situations, suggest an Arabo-centric vision but better that than having the names of people spelled differently in different chapters as dictated by linguistic context (this has proven most troublesome to me in dealing with Turkish matters). Proper nouns received Anglicizing endings (Qur'anic, for example) have not been transliterated, although, as that example shows, the differentiation between *ʿayn* and *hamza* has been maintained. Bosworth's *The New Islamic Dynasties* has also been the source for dates, about which there can certainly be divergence between sources on occasion. Dates are only given in their CE format and not *hijrī*, once again because different time periods and different geographical areas result in a jumble of possible approaches, and they simply needed to be resolved into a single standard to bring uniformity and consistency to this work.

Gratitude

The work on this volume has stretched over several years. I must express my thanks to the contributors for their patience and responsiveness. Amy Laurens, Gemma Dunn and Lalle Pursglove, who handled the details of the volume at Routledge, have been remarkably accommodating; the support of Routledge's Religion editor, Lesley Riddle, has of course been essential.

References

In bringing this work together, many of the authors have used essential reference works in the field to which it is worth drawing attention. These are the tools for anyone who hopes who pursue the study of the Islamic world further.

The Encyclopaedia of Islam is always referenced here in the version on CD-Rom issued by Brill in Leiden in 2004 and called *The Encyclopaedia of Islam I–XII CD-ROM Edition*. The encyclopaedia started out in its first edition 1913–36 which was then reprinted in 1987. A new edition emerged between 1960 and 2004 which is the basis of the CD-Rom. The *Shorter Encyclopaedia of Islam*, first issued in 1953, gathers together articles on religion from the first edition with some updated material. For beginning students issues related to transliteration in the encyclopaedia often create a challenge. The main differences between the Encyclopaedia and this book (and most other scholarly works) are to be seen in the letters represented in this work as "j" (*jīm*) and "q" (*qāf*). For "j" the Encyclopaedia uses "dj," so, for example, an entry for *ḥajj* ("pilgrimage") will be found under *ḥadjdj*, or *jihād* ("holy war") under *djihād*. For "q," the Encyclopaedia uses "k" with a subscript dot, thus intertwining the entries with "k" representing the letter *kāf*. The reader must remember that where "q" is found in a word in this book, the Encyclopaedia entry will have a "k." Examples are *qāḍī/ḳāḍī* ("judge"), *ṭarīqa/ṭarīḳa* ("Ṣūfī brotherhood") and *Qur'ān/Ḳur'ān*. The third edition of the Encyclopaedia started to appear in 2007 and it will avoid some of these problems by using English keywords and a more generally accepted transliteration scheme.

The *Encyclopedia Iranica* (Eisenbrauns, 1982 and ongoing) is partially available freely online (*www.iranica.com*) and is an excellent scholarly resource for topics related to Iran but often with a broader reference. A different transliteration system is employed there too – one more amendable to Persian pronunciation – but some browsing through it will solve most issues.

The *Encyclopedia of the Qur'ān* (Brill, 2000–6) uses English keywords to present a summary of current scholarship on the Qur'ān and many related topics, in alphabetical order.

The *Encyclopedia of Women and Islamic Culture* (Brill, 2003 and ongoing) provides a wide-ranging survey with a significant social-science orientation to its subject; it is organized thematically and by English headings.

C. E. Bosworth *The New Islamic Dynasties: A Chronological and Genealogical Manual* (Edinburgh University Press, 1996) is, as already mentioned, a useful and ready reference for basic historical facts.

Index Islamicus (various publishers since 1958) is a major bibliographical source of periodical and monograph items, available in print and now online, going back in its coverage to the seventeenth century.

Atlas of the Islamic World since 1500 by Francis Robinson (Facts on File, 1982) is an excellent source of maps.

Some internet resources are well worth consideration for research purposes, although the polemical and apologetic nature of many sites means some substantial analysis of many sites is compulsory. One good guide is *www.uga.edu/islam*: maintained by Professor A. Godlas at the University of Georgia, it is by far the best academically oriented site and the place to begin most searches for information.

Another useful site is *www.fordham.edu/halsall/islam/islamsbook.html*, the Fordham University Internet History project, with a significant collection of original and secondary source material in their Medieval Sourcebook.

Part I

THE GEO-POLITICAL ISLAMIC WORLD

1

THE ARAB MIDDLE EAST

Martin Bunton

The Arab Middle East is a term that refers to a region stretching from the Arabian Peninsula to Syria and from Egypt to Iraq. Many important markers point to a special attachment between Islam and this region, among them the importance of the Arabic language and the presence of sites endowed with great religious and cultural significance. The historical commonalities are particularly important: the last century of interactions of political economy and foreign intervention, the four preceding centuries of Ottoman rule, and, prior to that, eight centuries of various types of Arab-Islamic rule. Nonetheless, the difficulties of defining the region as a coherent subject of study must be recognized. On the one hand, it is a complex mosaic of distinct and intersecting identities (embracing significant non-Muslim Arab communities and non-Arab Muslim communities) while on the other hand (as will become evident in this chapter) it is difficult to study the history of the region in isolation from Arab North Africa, or for that matter other neighboring Muslim countries (Turkey, Iran, Sudan, for example).

Most modern politico-religious movements in the Arab Middle East have two outstanding features in common. One is the evident consensus on seeking the necessary solutions to the problems of their state's institutional structures from "golden ages" of early Arab-Islamic empires. A second feature is that, for all its transnational linkages, Islam's Arab core is similar to the rest of the world in that its politics is overwhelmingly determined by local political systems. Here lies a paradox. Whereas the first feature, of a shared "golden age," may encourage conceptualizations of basic, essentialized forms and patterns of religious behavior over the centuries, the second feature of a shared political context pushes one to focus on the very modern and fluid, but also specific, processes of state formation. The more religious movements, in their political manifestations, call for a return to an idealized Muslim community of 1,400 years ago the more they need to be recognized as modern phenomena, who address specific oppositional groups and whose actions are circumscribed by the consolidation and evolution of the modern state. The importance of core rituals can be recognized within a community or nation, united in belief in the message of the Qur'ān, but who otherwise differ on the political, economic or moral organization of that society. This can be seen in the development of the historical caliphate in the Middle East, as well as in the diverse, multilayered and local manifestations of contemporary politico-religious activity.

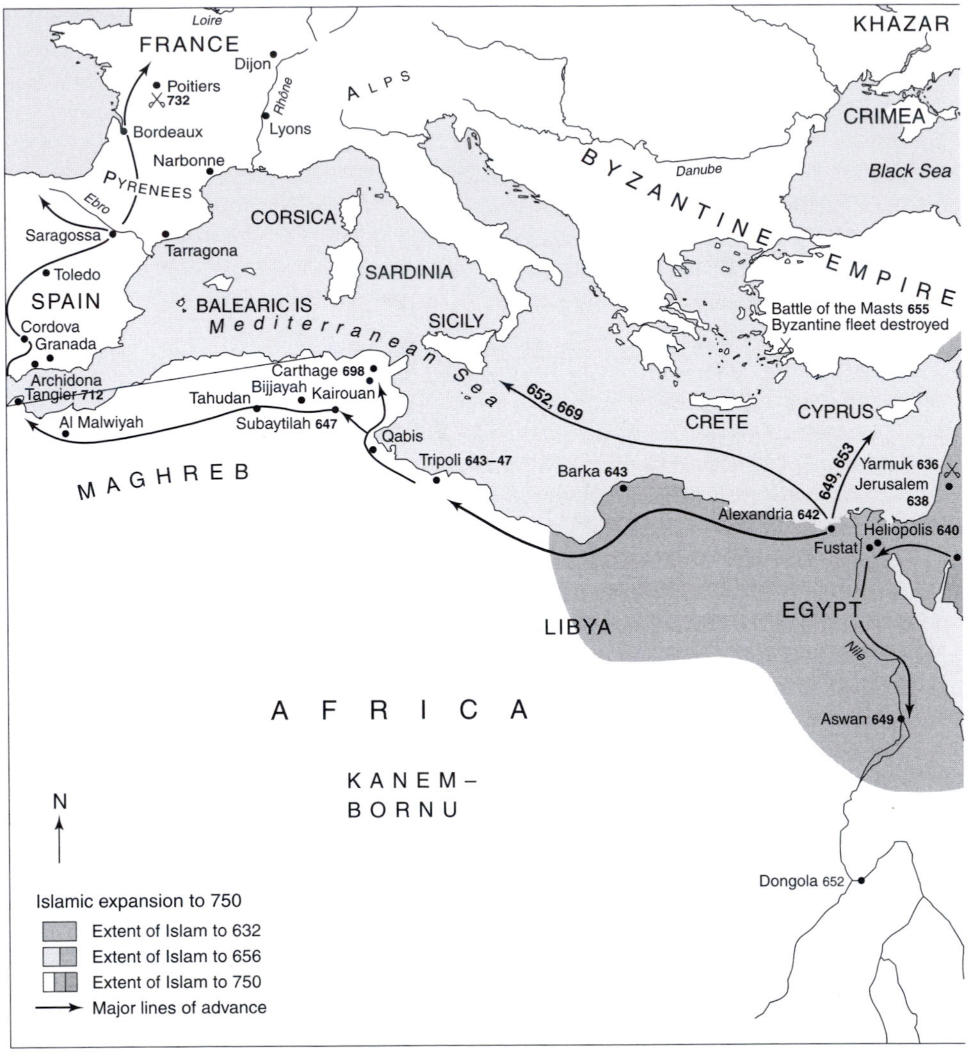

Map 2 Expansion of the Muslim Empire.

Islamic caliphate in the Middle East and North Africa

Upon the Prophet Muḥammad's death in 632, Arab forces first asserted their authority over the Arabian peninsula and then, expanding the Muslim community northwards, wrested control of territories from the weakened or decaying Byzantine and Sasanian empires. Within a decade, Arabs had captured towns in Syria and Mesopotamia and had begun the conquest of Egypt. Subsequent campaigns marched into Tunisia in 670, conquered all of North Africa by 712, and moved into Spain shortly afterwards. The Byzantine empire remained strong enough to check Arab expansion in Europe, ensuring a continually contested frontier between Christendom and Islam. In the east, however, the collapse of Sasanian rule opened the Iranian plateau to Arab forces,

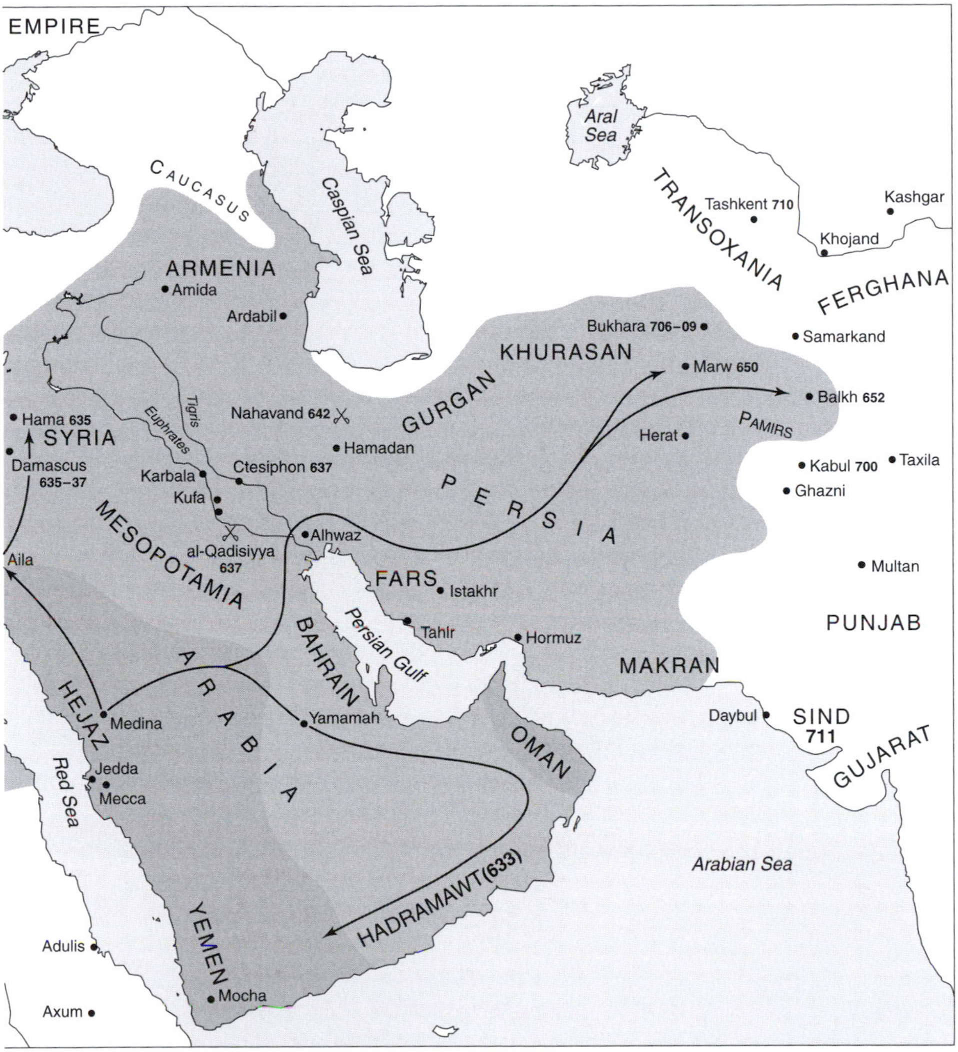

from where they moved into India. Thus was established, in a huge area of multiple ecological zones and political influences, what Ira Lapidus (2002: 34) has described as "the geographical arena for the eventual diffusion of a common culture and a common sociopolitical identity in the name of Islam."

The Arab forces who conquered this massive land mass were a cohesive group, but such an expansive political entity required new, more regional forms of government. In Arabia some confusion over governing the Islamic polity had emerged upon the death of the Prophet, and those disputes over power grew substantially as the community encompassed richer lands in the north. It was a situation that lent itself to the emergence of personal and factional differences, in particular the competition between claims of authority legitimated by closeness to the prophet and claims based upon family nobility and power. In the rush of early conquests, the term caliph (*khalīfa*) came to designate the leader of the Islamic *umma*, and the office became known as the caliphate. The first four caliphs, all recognized for their personal closeness to the prophet, succeeded by acclamation in accordance with tribal custom. But a civil war erupted in 656 when the claim to leadership of ʿAlī ibn Abī Ṭālib, a cousin and son-in-law of Muḥammad, established himself as caliph in Kufa, Iraq, but was unable to impose his authority over the whole community. His claim was contested by Mu'āwiya, the governor of Syria, and in 661, the title of caliph was claimed by the Umayyad dynasty which moved the centre of power from Mecca to Damascus, with its Byzantine administrative legacy.

In 750, one ruling family replaced another in a second civil war as the caliphate was claimed by the Abbasids. The capital was moved to Baghdad, a new city but one that was strategically located on trade routes linking Syria and Egypt with Iran and beyond. For nearly two centuries the Abbasids' elaborate governing structures ruled the Middle East through a broad alliance of interests, bringing together soldiers, landlords, scribes, merchants and others to serve the central regime. Various cultural traditions mingled together under the patronage of the Abbasid rulers, and Baghdad became widely recognized for its artistic and intellectual communities. The Abbasid caliphate enjoyed considerable economic growth, but maintaining centralized authority over such a vast empire eventually overwhelmed it.

Nominally, the capital of Baghdad remained the seat of caliphs until 1258, but the structure of government broke down by the middle of the tenth century. In Baghdad

Figure 1 Aleppo Citadel, Aleppo, Syria, thirteenth century and later. Though dating back to antiquity, the site of Aleppo's imposing citadel, which is surrounded by a deep moat, took its current form in the thirteenth century.

Source: © Photographer Michel Ecochard/Aga Khan Trust for Culture itself, more and more power was exercised by soldiers of Turkish regiments who had served various caliphs. Elsewhere, successor states emerged, ruled by independent dynasties whose influence extended from their capitals to shifting frontiers, not easily demarcated on a map.

One way to approach the political history of the Arabic-speaking peoples from the tenth century on is as a series of regional histories centered around three areas: Iraq (frequently linked to Iran), Egypt (often ruling over parts of Syria and Egypt), and North Africa (where regimes formed at the heart of trading and cultivation networks). Though the caliphate at Baghdad might still be recognized as both a symbolic position and a unifying entity, sultans and emirs elsewhere developed their own regional blends of local and Islamic practices. In this way, weakness and decay in one area of the Islamic Middle East can be understood in a context in which the reinvigoration and enrichment of Islamic traditions happened in other areas. No single political or cultural entity can be said to have embraced the totality of Islam: William Cleveland (2004: 20) emphasizes the continual existence at this time of Islamic pluralism when he asserts that Islamic societies were "diverse and dynamic, not static and monolithic." It is a perspective which stands in contrast to the widespread notion of a rise and fall of an Islamic empire.

Nonetheless, this was the politically fragmented order that came under attack from Christian Europe in the eleventh and twelfth centuries, initiating a troubled relationship in which Islam and the Arab world acquired its problematic place in the European imagination as a threat. In the thirteenth century, the destructive Mongol invasions dealt the caliphate a fatal blow. Southern Iraq became more of a frontier zone, contested between Iran and the more stable orders established by the Mamluks in Cairo and, further west, the Hafsids in Tunis. By the fifteenth century, however, the cumulative effects of population decline, caused by the plague epidemic, and by the increasingly adverse balances of trade with an expanding Europe, had clearly weakened the existing political orders. As a result, neither the Mamluk dynasty nor those in North Africa were able to match the resources of a new and expanding Turkish dynasty which had emerged as a small Anatolian principality in the wake of the Mongol invasions.

Named after its founder, Osman, the Ottoman dynasty came to wield one of the most effective militaries, and navies, of the sixteenth and seventeenth centuries. With the exception of parts of Arabia and Morocco (which developed under a separate dynasty also seeking legitimation by protecting religious law), all the Arab regions of the Middle East and North Africa came to be ruled by the Ottoman empire, with its capital at Istanbul. On its eastern border, a continual seesaw struggle with the rival Safavid empire for control of Iraq meant that Baghdad was conquered in 1534, lost in 1623, and then taken again in 1638. Economic and strategic factors clearly played a key role in the Ottoman defense of the frontier in the Persian Gulf, but the prolonged conflict exposed religious tensions that continue to influence political activity to this day. Whereas the Safavids established Twelver Shiʿism as the official religion, as it consolidated dynastic rule over Iran for the first time since the Sasanians, the Ottoman empire increasingly proclaimed an adherence to Ḥanafī Sunnism.

It should be noted that the Ottomans did make an effort to claim the title of caliph of the Muslim *umma*. Though the caliphate had continued as the centerpiece of Muslim political thought, the idea had, as L. Carl Brown (2000: 36) observes, "long been quite divorced from operative reality." Its use by the Ottoman sultans reflected more of a local claim to authority, a religious sanctioning of power, than a kind of universalist or exclusive authority. Rather than based on the claims of a title, the consolidation of the Ottoman empire as, what Hourani (1991: 221) terms, the "last great expression of the universality of the world of Islam" reflected their place as guardians of the holy cities (thus controlling the pilgrimage routes), protectors of religious law, and defenders of the frontiers. When made, claims to the title were as often as not rooted quite specifically, and strategically, in attempts to bolster their credibility in the eyes of the Great Powers of Europe by playing a pan-Islamic card.

The pragmatic ruling institutions established and maintained by the Ottomans for over 400 years drew together disparate populations from throughout the Middle East. Islamic leaders (*ʿulamāʾ*) were organized into an official hierarchy and religious judges and teachers were appointed throughout the empire, playing an important role that stood parallel to, and equivalent to, the other pillars of the sultan's centralized administration, the military and bureaucratic elite. The Ottoman bureaucracy was one of the most highly developed of any Muslim empire, in large part because of their successful elaboration of the Byzantine political structures they inherited. Despite this, little attempt was made to impose religious doctrine. In addition to the *sharīʿa*, the sultan issued his own orders and regulations, thus creating an institutional dualism between new legal codes and the traditional *sharīʿa* court system, and further entrenching a separation between religion and state.

This separation is a particularly salient feature of the period of legal and administrative reform commonly referred to as the Tanzimat (1839–76). The transformation was instituted as part of a concerted effort to revitalize imperial structures in the face of Europe's relative strength. By the middle of the eighteenth century, the nature of global trading patterns had changed in ways that positioned the Ottoman empire as an importer of manufactured goods and an exporter of raw materials. It was an important marker of the changing balance of power with Europe. The Tanzimat reorganization failed to stop European economic penetration, and political domination predictably increased. Technological advances, particularly in the military, gave an even sharper edge to European influence so that by the nineteenth century actual annexation of Ottoman lands was accelerating. France occupied Algeria in 1830 and Tunisia in 1881, Britain took Cyprus in 1878 and Egypt in 1882.

From this rapid survey of governing structures established by the coalition of Arab nomadic conquerors in the seventh century through to the comprehensive, if pressed, institutional restructuring by Ottoman bureaucratic rulers in the nineteenth century, two significant themes emerge. One is that the multiple ways by which religious law has been separated from the political sphere outweigh the number of examples of the *sharīʿa* actually forming the basis of political structures. One cannot overestimate the importance that the idea of the political organization of earlier Muslim communities has acquired in the Middle East today as a reservoir of political ideas; however, it is equally important to recognize the reality of the diversity of that political behavior over the centuries. Muḥammad's successors were forced from the beginning to build their states and develop their governments through adaptation and borrowing. In this sense, early governing practices emerged in the Middle East that necessarily owed a great deal to the more ancient institutions and cultures into which Islam extended. Gradually the legacies and traditions of Byzantium and Persia were absorbed into the political, administrative and legal structures of Islam. As Albert Hourani writes:

> No doubt this process involved some "adulteration" of law and tradition, the creation of new traditions in order to give a cover of Islamic respectability to what was not Islamic by origin; but it also worked in the opposite way, by the selection of customs and practices, the rejection of some and acceptance of others, and the modification even of those which were accepted, in the light of the teaching of Islam.
>
> (Hourani 1983: 9)

Either way, Islam over the centuries took on what Sami Zubaida (1993: 42–3) describes as "diverse and overlapping forms, many of which bore only a tenuous relation to orthodox, scriptural Islam." The variations are multiple and multilayered: in addition to the improvisations of governing structures, and the diversity of religious manifestations that formed around the question of succession, one can note the conflicting orientations that emerged between the perceived orthodoxy of urban Islam and the heterodoxy of more traditional rural districts.

Recognition of the problems of essentializing Islam, or of simplifying its relation to governance structures, leads to a second important theme revealed by an examination of the caliphate's checkered history: that, in the words of Nazih Ayubi (1991: 156), "the Islamic theory of politics was developed gradually and piecemeal (and mainly in response to social and ideological opposition from various protest movements), by jurists who played the role of the ideologues of rulers." For example, it was the Shīʿī opposition to the right of the caliph to rule that obligated those who accepted the caliph's power to explain the reasons for the caliphate and to elaborate upon its nature. Several twists and turns later, the caliphate would be justified by Ottoman sultans in an attempt to cushion their standing within the boundaries of their empire, but with no claim to be authoritative teachers of Islamic doctrine.

The continuing or renewed presence of religious politics into the twentieth century is therefore to be understood less in terms of essential characteristics of religious belief than by an account of its active reconstruction in particular contexts. It is only by paying attention to specific historical conjunctures that one can understand both the contemporary significance and multiple diversity of Islamic politics.

Islam and the modern state

World War I and the treaties that followed mark the major turning point in the history of the modern Middle East. As noted at the outset, contemporary religious movements are mobilized and organized to impact upon the political practices within a particular context. From the colonial period on this context has been defined by the territorial state, despite the fact that the legitimacy of the state system has remained open to challenge on the grounds of breaking up the Muslim community. Indeed, the postwar secular leaders of Turkey saw the abolishment of the caliphate in 1923 as an essential part of their assault on the *ancien régime*. As for the Arab lands of the defeated Ottoman empire, European powers divided them up between a number of new states, whose borders reflected little adherence to local socio-economic and ethnic realities. Though these impositions left many of the inhabitants feeling betrayed, the implementation of the state system has remained the preeminent political development of the twentieth century.

It is important to recognize that the creation of the state system in the Arab world was not a smooth process. Though centuries of Ottoman rule, and the Tanzimat restructuring in particular, had bequeathed significant administrative frameworks, it was generally open to British and French imperialists to determine such essential features of statehood as borders, administrative and legal systems, flags and capital cities. By incorporating such strategies as divide and rule, and privileging economic systems based on fiscally conservative, export-oriented colonial structures, colonial powers ensured that government institutions and frameworks were slow to develop. Nonetheless, their importance was quickly recognized by the Arab inhabitants. In Iraq for example it was rather remarkable how immediately religious, ethnic and tribal leaders modified their ways of mobilizing constituencies in order to insert themselves into emerging structures of the new state. These ways are perhaps best exemplified in the early issuance of a *fatwā* by certain Shīʿī *ʿulamāʾ* in 1923 condemning the forthcoming elections to the constituent assembly. Far from representing a futile rejection of the tide of political changes, the *fatwā* declaring participation in the elections as unlawful had more to do with the fear of religious leaders that "their representatives would not be elected as the British and Iraqi government were likely to exercise pressures on the voters to choose their own candidates" (Nakash 2003: 79).

In the second half of the twentieth century, Islam came to serve a particularly important role as a medium of opposition to state structures that had become dominated by unpopular regimes. What allowed Islamist movements to attract widespread attention was the political and moral vacuum created by the responses of most governments to increasing economic and political challenges. Two kinds of explanation are needed to understand the significance of this vacuum: one in terms of the weakening of the legitimacy of the existing regimes in the last quarter of the century, the other in terms of the accumulation of legitimacy by the Islamist opposition.

Powerful nationalist critiques were developed by Arab leaders in the interwar years. The rhetoric of national liberation was accompanied by the promise of better education, expansion of social welfare, and a better standard of living than could be supplied by the conservative economic strategies of colonial rulers. When independence came, generally in the wake of the World War II, state structures and governing patterns were transformed by those nationalist leaders who came to monopolize control. To simplify greatly, leaders of the newly independent countries initiated development projects in the 1950s and 1960s aimed at compensating for the inequities of the colonial legacy and distributing the nation's assets more equitably. While features of this administrative expansion were unfolding across the world at this time, they were accentuated in the Middle East by the presence of oil wealth as well as by the agenda of pan-Arabism. Gamal Abdel Nasser (Jamāl ʿAbd al-Nāṣir) was one of the first leaders to expand the state apparatus, and Boumedienne (Abū Madyan) in Algeria, the Baath (Baʿth: Arabic for "resurrection") in Syria and Iraq all sought to build coalitions among the middle and lower classes through the expansion of government services. The monarchies of the Gulf countries successfully maintained power in the hands of ruling families, but the expansion of the state apparatus was a prominent feature there as well.

These projects mostly failed. Their inability to fulfill the promises of national honor, and provide the services of social welfare, subjected Arab regimes to a sustained critique. For some countries the 1967 Arab–Israeli war marked the major rupture. As it was secular modernizers like Nasser who were held responsible for the military humiliation, the defeat discredited the prevailing agendas associated with Arab nationalism and created an ideological vacuum for Islamist ideas to fill. Moreover, huge spending on development projects had resulted in such levels of indebtedness that governments were forced to retreat from their national objectives and reposition the state to allow for greater economic liberalization. Reductions in services and subsidies and rising unemployment, at a time when economies were facing high rates of population growth and urbanization, all contributed to generally lowering the standard of living and widening the gap between rich and poor. The sense of relative deprivation was particularly widespread in the main cities. Rapid urbanization was placing huge strains on urban infrastructure, but the problems – overcrowding, insufficient investment in transportation and utilities, and so on – were left unattended by governments. Families who had left traditional lifestyles of rural villages for the promise of a higher standard of living in the cities were sorely let down.

It is this ideological and political vacuum of the 1970s and 1980s that provides the pertinent context for understanding the successful mobilization of political support by Islamist parties across much of the Arab world. The wrenching economic adjustments rendered the secular, nationalist ideologies vulnerable to attack. The field was open to Islamist ideas. The fact that postwar, state-led development processes tended to be secular and rather imitative meant that the process could be portrayed as inauthentic or alien by Islamists:

> The name of the entire game was modernization. When modernization stumbled, failing to achieve the promised economic development and instead deepening the alienation and dependency, groups that were previously excluded or were promised what was never given, came forward with their alternative ideational system.
>
> (Ayubi 1991: 216)

Islamist movements were particularly well placed to establish broad coalitions of support by filling the many gaps left by retreating governments, strategically building a social base by providing the very services that the various state regimes had withdrawn. Islamic networks in many Arab countries pursued strategies of mobilizing support through the provision of their own welfare programs (ranging from health clinics to kindergartens), articulating new discourses of political legitimacy, and creating a new sense of community responsibility, all of which highlighted the states' failures. In Egypt, for example, the Islamist movement was particularly successful in mobilizing a young professional underclass that had grown significantly in the 1950s and 1960s with Nasser's expansion of university enrollments, but who in large numbers were left unemployed or underemployed by the 1970s. In Algeria the increasing number of unemployed youths hanging around on overcrowded streets acquired the name "hittistes," those who hold up the walls (Bekkar 1997: 286). Engaging with the expanding activities of the mosque provided graduates with a sense of participation at a time when economically, politically and socially they were otherwise excluded. On an ideological level, one can note "the vitality and mobilizing power of an Islamic vocabulary, particularly when it incorporated such themes as nationalism and social justice" (Owen 2004: 164). In this way, Islamist organizations not only filled the infrastructural gaps left by the failure of the state to provide public services, but also fulfilled, in the face of social degeneration, what one scholar has referred to as "the desired promise of a restored moral order" (Wickham 1997: 133).

It is also important to note that the mosque, with its effective networks of services and activities, was one of the few spaces in most Arab countries where neighborhood communities could in fact mobilize and organize against a dominant regime. Part of the reason for the mosque's independence can be explained, again, by the inability of the state to keep up with urban growth and find the resources to appoint an official *imām*, with the result that the Islamist opposition could monopolize the space. However, there is a larger political issue at stake that raises the question of the mosque's privileged status as a place of worship and thus less easily controlled by an authoritarian government. The mosque thus provides an effective network enjoying a degree of separation from state control that the more highly constricted and heavily regulated trade unions and professional associations lack. In organizing and mobilizing this network, Islamist political leaders have regularly exhibited superior campaign organization and financing skills.

The national socioeconomic arena provides the most immediate context for Islamist mobilization in the Arab world in the last quarter of the twentieth century. However, there also was an important international dimension to their success. Two factors in particular need to be highlighted. First, a key role was played by the 1979 Iranian revolution. In putting the Islamist ideas into actual practice, the revolution had ripple effects throughout the Arab world. Arab communities living under dictatorial, Western allied regimes sought inspiration in the overthrow of the Shāh. A second prominent factor was the increased financial weight of Saudi Arabia, flush with oil revenues following the sharp rise in prices in 1973 and 1979. The Saudi monarchy, which had long sought national legitimacy through its association with the religious establishment, sought to further bolster its power by attracting attention as a generous benefactor of charitable institutions throughout the region, and the whole Muslim *umma* for that matter. In addition to the direct support Islamist groups in the Arab world received from Saudi Arabia, Arabs working in the expanding Gulf economies sent home remittances, some of which benefited Islamist movements. Moreover, for "those returning from the El Dorada of oil, social ascent went hand in hand with an intensification of religious practice" (Kepel 2002: 71), as absorbed in the more doctrinaire milieu of the Arabian peninsula.

Conclusions: failures and futures

The terrorist actions of September 11, 2001, shocked many outside observers into focusing on the perils of Islamism in the Middle East. For some observers, this attack, orchestrated by Saudi dissident Osama bin Laden and his Al Qaeda organization, portended a war between Islam and the West. Indeed, the increasing strength of Islamist movements across the Middle East since then – the coming to power of Hamas in Gaza, the increasing assertiveness of Hizbullah in Beirut, the growing alliance between a new Islamist government in Baghdad and an older one with renewed regional ambitions in Tehran – has all brought grist to their mill.

The Arab world itself has, however, witnessed the mobilization of political Islam over decades. While Islamist movements in the Middle East may appear to have numbers on their side – as well as sophisticated political organizations to mobilize that support – their political and ideological agendas must be seen as necessarily diverse, even factious. The deepening division in Iraq between Sunnī and Shīʿī, the two main branches of Islam, is the bloodiest example of the present day. In the political vacuum following the defeat of Saddam Hussein's regime, the clerical hierarchies of the newly dominant Shīʿī Arabs, with 60 percent of the population, sought to assert themselves against Sunnī Arabs, who had ruled Iraq since its creation nearly a century ago. The sectarianism prevailing in Iraq can also be understood as an extreme example of what has been described here as the disintegration of the distributive capacity of the state and the loss of credibility in established structures of political allegiance. Sunnīs and Shīʿīs are divided among themselves, but the articulation over centuries of this major fault line in Islam has certainly sharpened the edge of the communal and geo-strategic conflicts at play. A prolonged conflict risks sucking in neighboring countries, with revolutionary Iran backing the Shīʿīs as a show of regional influence and Saudi Arabia backing Iraqi Sunnīs in response. Or consider two of the best-known religious movements in the Middle East, bin Laden's Al Qaeda and Egypt's Muslim Brotherhood. They share common ideological roots in the historical context and seek inspiration in similarly historical narratives of the glory of Islam, but they diverge greatly over primary aims and tactics. Al Qaeda routinely condemns the ways in which the world of Islam has been subdivided by European colonial powers into rival nations, and publicly laments the 1923 loss of the caliphate's authority. Conversely, Egypt's Muslim Brotherhood (like its offshoot Hamas, as well as Hizbullah and the Islamist governments in Iraq and Iran) all accept the existence of the territorial national state and contest individually for power within those borders.

In addition to Islamist agendas being necessarily diverse, they are also increasingly circumscribed. By the end of the 1990s some analysts in fact argued that, for all the convulsions, the Islamists were a limited force. On the one hand, their overall weakness was in part a result of their initial success in building broad coalitions in opposition to dominating, alienating regimes. The central paradox at the heart of Islamist movements – modern, historically specific political organizations invoking utopian visions of a 1,400 year old community – was difficult to sustain over the long run: Islamist movements proved themselves much more effective at responding to the impact of social and economic problems facing society than they did at proposing concrete solutions or viable alternatives to the prevailing systems. Kepel (2002), for example, emphasizes the challenge faced by Islamist groups who mobilized support across a broad spectrum that included both the young urban poor as well as an older, pious business class. They inevitably found that their social base was simply too disparate and contradictory to sustain. On the other hand, the limits imposed on Islamist groups were a function of the effective responses adopted by the regimes. Despite the repositioning that was occurring in the economic and social spheres, Arab regimes still found the necessary resources to repress movements when they became too threatening. Additionally, they adapted to the changed circumstances and many of them became more Islamic in appearance, harnessing the language of Islam for themselves, and seeking legitimacy from religious leaders: having been steadily marginalized during the nationalist development period, the *ʿulamaʾ* were now being courted for the legitimacy their support would bestow. Though huge obstacles remain on all sides, there appears to be little alternative in the long run to Islamist groups eventually participating in democratic systems.

As a final point, it should be noted that Islamist movements have long been representative of wider movements of defiant self-assertion. The fact that the vast majority of the region's inhabitants are members of the Muslim community, or *umma*, means that they share a common set of foes, as well as a common set of practices and rituals. In the twenty-first century, the perception that a deepening foreign imperialism is dominating the region is becoming an increasingly powerful rallying point. In the shock of the events of September 11, 2001, Muslims across the region joined in condemnation of the outrage and in sympathy with the victims, but then came new polarizing wars in Afghanistan, Lebanon and, above all, Iraq. Meanwhile the enduring conflict between Palestinians and Israelis dragged on. Fuelled by electronic and satellite television images of widespread fighting, populations across the Middle East have been increasingly galvanized by the impulse to resist in the name of Islam what is widely being perceived as a western assault on Muslims. Should international crises abate in the future, Arabs who now primarily assert political manifestations of Islam will perhaps draw upon different senses of association and belonging from the mosaic of distinct and intersecting national, ethnic, tribal, class and religious identities, that have long subjected the Arab world to a complex interplay of centripetal and centrifugal forces.

References and further reading

Ayubi, N. (1991) *Political Islam: Religion and Politics in the Arab World*, London, New York: Routledge.

Bekkar, R. (1997) Interview with H. D. Taïeb, "Taking up Space in Tlemcen: the Islamist Occupation of Urban Algeria," in J. Beinin, J. Stork, eds., *Political Islam: Essays from Middle East Report*, Berkeley: University of California Press, 283–91.

Bromley, S. (1994) *Rethinking Middle East Politics: State Formation and Development*, Oxford: Polity Press.

Brown, L. C. (2000) *Religion and State: The Muslim Approach to Politics*, New York: Columbia University Press.

Cleveland, W. (2004) *A History of the Modern Middle East*, Boulder: Westview Press.

Hourani, A. (1983) *Arabic Thought in the Liberal Age, 1798–1939*, Cambridge: Cambridge University Press.

—— (1991) *A History of the Arab Peoples*, Cambridge, MA: Harvard University Press.

Humphreys, S. (1999) *Between Memory and Desire: The Middle East in a Troubled Age*, Berkeley: University of California Press.

Kepel, G. (2002) *Jihad: the Trail of Political Islam*, Cambridge, MA: Harvard University Press.

Lapidus, I. M. (2002) *A History of Islamic Societies*, 2nd edition, Cambridge: Cambridge University Press.

Lockman, Z. (2004) *Contending Visions of the Middle East: the History and Politics of Orientalism*, Cambridge: Cambridge University Press.

Nakash, Y. (2003) *The Shi'is of Iraq*, Princeton: Princeton University Press.
Owen, R. (2004) *State, Power and Politics in the Making of the Modern Middle East*, 3rd edition, London: Routledge.
Tripp, C. (2000) *A History of Iraq*, Cambridge: Cambridge University Press.
Vergès, M. (1997) "Genesis of a Mobilization: the Young Activists of Algeria's Islamic Salvation Front," in J. Beinin, J. Stork, eds., *Political Islam: Essays from Middle East Report*, Berkeley: University of California Press, 292–305.
Wickham, C. R. (1997) "Islamic Mobilization and Political Change: The Islamist Trend in Egypt's Professional Associations," in J. Beinin, J. Stork, eds., *Political Islam: Essays from Middle East Report*, Berkeley: University of California Press, 120–35.
Zubaida, S. (1993) *Islam, the People and the State: Political Ideas and Movements in the Middle East*, London: I. B. Tauris.

2

WEST AFRICA

David Owusu-Ansah

The story of the coming of Islam to the western sector of Africa has been well told in the historical records. In the decades following the end of World War II when the new generation of Arab and African leaders strived to end colonial rule in their respective countries, they pointed to the historic contacts of the early Muslim trans-Saharan commerce that spread Islam to the region as evidence of a shared past. Again in the late 1970s and through the earlier years of the 1980s, interest in the Afro–Arab relations was revisited – this time, to call for an African–Arabian–Muslim solidarity in support of an Arab/OPEC oil embargo as an economic weapon in the confrontation against the West for its support of Israel in the conflict over the question of Palestine. It was in the spirit of exploring the extent of the Islamic world and for the specific purpose of delineating the nature of Arab–Africa relations that the Beirut Center for Arab Unity Studies and the Arab Thought Forum of Jordan sponsored a conference in Amman in April 1983. The intended purpose of the conference was the same as that of the diplomats: to place stress on, and to remind African leaders of, the historic connection between Africa and Arabia, cemented through the common experience of Islam. Proceedings of the conference were published in 1985 under the title *The Arabs and Africa*. The 717-page work, edited by Khair El-Din Haseeb, included thoughtful presentations on such contemporary topics as "African perspectives on the Arab–Israeli conflict" and "Afro–Arab cooperation." Other contributors stressed the civilizing mission of Arabian culture on Africa.

Expressions regarding Arabia's significant impact on Africa are not new. Informed readers will be reminded of similar representations in Abū' l-Qāsim ibn Ḥawqal al-Nuṣaybī's *Kitab ṣūrat al-arḍ*, the account of the lands in which he traveled. Following his tours of Spain, North Africa, and the Maghreb, the tenth-century Upper Mesopotamia native commented positively about the wealth of Awdaghust and Sijilmasa. Located to the southeastern corner of the territories that now compose the modern African country of Mauritania, Awdaghust's link to market centers of the historic West African kingdom of Ancient Ghana is well known. The gold-smelting town of Sijilmasa, located in the territory that is now part of the modern North African state of Algeria, was also commented upon as having a wealthy commercial population. The importation of gold from the *Bilād al-Sūdān* ("Land of the Blacks") in exchange for Mediterranean goods was identified as the source of the lucrative commerce. But while the great wealth accumulated through trade with that part of Black Africa immediate to the south of the Sahara impressed Ibn Ḥawqal, he was dismissive in his evaluation of the cultures of the *Bilād al-Sūdān*. He justified his position as follows:

> We have not described the land of the Sudan [Blacks] in the west . . . nor other peoples with the same characteristics, because orderly government of kingdoms is based upon religious beliefs, good manners, law and order, and the organization of settled life directed by sound policy. The people lack all these qualities and have no share in them. Their kingdoms, therefore, do not deserve to be dealt with separately as we have dealt with other kingdoms.
>
> (Levtzion and Hopkins 1981: 44)

An observation such as this was consistent with the views of Arabian geographers of a time when Islamic civilization was dominant politically and culturally. From Spain

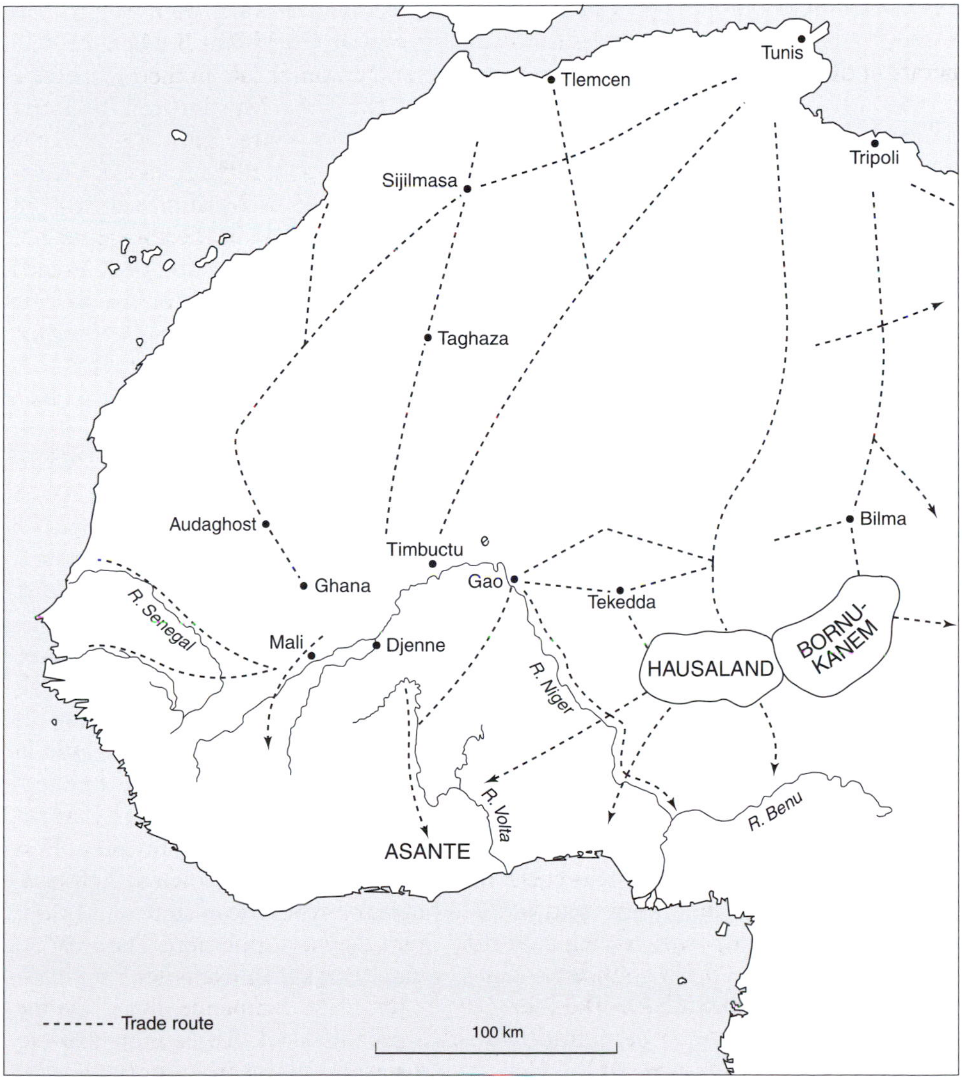

Map 3 Trans-Sahara Trading Networks.

to Persia, Islamic political institutions were viewed as superior. Muslim traders and travelers provided accounts of other lands and, often, Arabian/Islamic values – represented in laws and political and religious institutions – were the standards by which others were evaluated.

There is no doubt that historic contact with the Arabian/Islamic world, as well as with Europe, impacted upon local peoples. However, it would be parochial to argue that those local cultures did not have civilizations of their own; they certainy possessed an understanding of what was historically important. Unlike Ibn Ḥawqal, there are scholars today who see Africans as active participants in the making of history – engaging in rational choices that suited their cultural environments. In other words, while the Arabian-Muslim contacts with West Africa are important to the review of the impact of Islam in West Africa, it is equally relevant that one evaluates how the peoples – as Muslims and non-Muslims – reacted toward the carriers of the religion. This is the material that constitutes the discourse in the history of West Africa as part of the Muslim world.

The history of Islam in West Africa: a narrative

The modern African country that officially retains the name "Sudan" is located to the immediate south of Egypt. However, the Egyptian Sudan is only the easternmost part of the belt that demarcated the *Bilād al-Sūdān* from the Berber and Arab-populated northern sector of the continent. The central section of the Sudanic belt now comprises modern African countries that include Chad, Niger, and the northern region of Nigeria. To the historic Western Sudan are located such modern countries as the Republic of Mali, Burkina Faso, Senegal, Gambia, Guinea, and the southern parts of Mauritania. It is also important to note that while Muslims initially entered West Africa via locations in the Sudanic belt, the history and presence of Islam in the western quarter of the continent reach over to the Atlantic coast.

By the mid-seventh century, Muslim forces under the command of ʿAmr ibn al-ʿĀṣ (d. *c.* 663) had already entered Egypt. In the decades following, they expanded westward to arrive at the northern tip of Morocco and crossed over to Spain early in the eighth century. Spain is mentioned here because Muslim geographers and historians traveling through North African and/or residing in Spain recorded the earliest pieces of information about the *Bilād al-Sūdān*. Toward the end of the eighth century, for example, al-Fazārī from the court of the Abbasid caliph provided information that indicated his knowledge of the gold-producing region of ancient Ghana – a place he identified as located beyond the Maghreb and the Sahara. To borrow E. W. Bovil's restatement of the primary sources, Ghana was also *Bilād al-dhahab* or land of gold where "gold came out of the soil just like carrots growing in the sand" (Bovil 1958: 123). While Bovil stresses the abundance of the gold in the region, to most historians of Africa, it is equally significant that attention be paid to the nature of the traditional political structures that existed during the early period of reporting. For example, it is suggested that al-Yaʿqūbī (d. after 905) provides "the earliest insight into the political history and the dynamics of state-building in West Africa" (Levtzion and Hopkins 1981: 19). In addition to Ghana, al-Kawkaw (Gao) and Malal (Mali) of the Western Sudan, Kanem was also identified as located in the central Sudanic belt. In the tenth-century accounts of Ibn Ḥawqal, the linkage of Ghana and Kawkaw to Awdaghust and Sijilmasa were affirmed. In the eleventh-century description of al-Bakrī, Ghana, Mali, and Gao were presented as the major political societies of the Western Sudan.

The sources supply basic information to aid the reconstruction of the political environment of the region. For example, the rulers of ancient Ghana were favorably disposed toward Muslim traders. According to al-Bakrī's information, Awdaghust was "fifteen days' march from Ghana" and Awdaghust itself "two months' distance from Sijilmasa." Awdaghust and Sijilmasa had "cathedral mosques and many small ones" and the culture was Islamic. Ghana on the other hand was pagan and less sophisticated. For example, the "houses of the inhabitance were constructed from stones and acacia wood," and next to the king's residence was a grove in which the royal dead were buried with their slaves, favorite wives, and dishes. The purpose was to ensure that the dead entered the world of their ancestors' royally (Levtzion and Hopkins 1981: 62–77). The king, when alive, was the link between the ancestors and the mundane world and therefore he guarded traditional customs as a divine monarch. Al-Bakrī described the Ghana countryside as unhealthy, inhospitable to strangers, and therefore not populous. Yet the king could put in the field some "200,000 troops (with) more than 40,000 of them archers", presenting a formidable force compared to its neighbors (Levtzion and Hopkins 1981: 81).

From D. T. Niane's *Epic of Old Mali*, constructed from local oral traditions, we also learn about how Sundiata (Sunjata) of the Keita lineage and founder of the Mali kingdom, was able to bring together various Malinke units to form the single Mali political entity that stretched from the gold-producing area of Bure in the Senegambia region to the Niger. Sundiata was represented in the sources in local terms. He was a nominal Muslim but, most importantly, he was a hunter/warrior king and magician whose knowledge of the spiritual and physical environments legitimized his authority. Even Sunni ʿAlī, founder of the Songhai empire that rose to dominance after the fall of Mali in the fifteenth century, was described as another nominal Muslim who turned to the traditional religion and the legitimacy it provided politically (Hunwick 1985: 72–6). Levtzion makes the apt observation that rulers like Sundiata and Sunni ʿAlī, "founders of empires, are the heroes of national traditions, whereas the exploits of their Muslim successors – Mansa Musa of Mali and Askia Muhammad of Songhay, for example – were recorded by the Arabic sources" (Levtzion and Pouwels 2000: 66). The dichotomy in emphasis is an aspect of the conversation about the place of West Africa in the history of the Muslim world.

Another important point worth noting is that West African knowledge of iron technology and its adoption for military and agricultural uses were significant developments that pre-dated the Arab invasion of North Africa. Turning against their weaker neighbors, the societies in the region that had gained metallurgical mastery successfully expanded and brought others under their control. The consolidation of territories led to the establishment of the more stable political environments necessary for the exchange of thoughts, ideas, and commerce. While the demand for West African gold is an interesting topic to economic historians, Levtzion (1973: 11–15) again argues that these "early economic, social, and political developments were the result of the agricultural revolution [that occurred as a result of the development of West Africa's own knowledge about the uses of] iron." Based on radiocarbon dating and archeological information, historians have reconstructed the Western Sudan as a settled and a cultivated environment where Soninke, Maninke, and Bamana farmers grew "millet, sorghum, and fonio" (Levtzion 1973: 116). The people of the Gambia River basin also fished and produced rice, and the ethnic Fulbe bred cattle.

Peasant cultivation was very important in sustaining the communities. The production of different types of primary products was directly linked to the stimulation of local exchanges and ultimately to the development of long-distance trade. On this subject, Levtzion writes:

> Rice was transported from the Gambia to the hinterland in exchange for iron. Millet and sorghum, grown by Bambara and Maninke of the Savannah, were sent to Timbuktu and Walata for consumption, as well as farther north into the desert as far as the salt mines of Taghaza.
>
> (Levtzion 1973: 117)

The production of primary products and the exchanges associated with agriculture were widespread in West Africa. Early in the sixteenth century, the famous North African traveler Ḥasan ibn Muḥammad al-Wazzān al-Zayyātī (known as Leo Africanus, d. *c.* 1550) observed in Hausaland (now part of Northern Nigeria) that the production of such products as millet, cotton, lemon, and rice was common in the Niger River basin. The Hausa were weavers and some raised goats, sheep, and cattle. Thus, Hausa farmers cultivated their lands, supplied food to markets, and paid taxes in kind. In Hausaland, as in the Western Sudan, slave labor was an important factor of production to supply local markets and distance trade as well as providing for the royal households. Agriculture was therefore the foundation upon which the political structure was built. This notwithstanding, it is again to the demand for West African gold and slaves that the commerce with North African and the Arabian Muslims as well as the spread of Islam in the sub-region have been attributed.

West Africa and the Muslim world: gold, slaves, and Muslim traders

The famous tenth-century Mālikī legal commentator Ibn Abī Zayd (d. 996) wrote in his *Risāla* that "trading in the land of the enemy (*ʿadw*) and to the *Bilād al-Sūdān* is disapproved" (Bercher 1949: 318; Levtzion and Hopkins 1981: 55). According to Wilks (in Levtzion and Pouwels 2000: 95), the paradox of the situation was that even in such early times, trade into the land of the infidels (and especially for the gold of the Western Sudan) had become very "vital to the well-being of *Dar al-Islam*." A way out of the dilemma, as Wilks observed, was for the Muslim traders to deny any direct contacts with Africans in the *Bilād al-Sūdān* and thus "the myth of a silent trade was propagated."

A silent transaction could have been conducted only in a very simple way – that Muslim traders left their goods at known pickup points where the locals came to investigate the value of the goods. Amounts of gold estimated to be equal to the value of the merchandise would be left for the visiting traders to assess as acceptable exchange for the commodities. If satisfied, the transaction was concluded; otherwise, the process continued until satisfactory exchange was arrived at. Scholars are doubtful as to whether the great volume of trade reported to have taken place between

North Africa merchants and the *Bilād al-Sūdān* could have prevailed under conditions of "silent" trading.

If Muslim traders of the tenth century felt compelled to conceal direct commercial relations in the land of the unbelievers, the situation must have changed drastically by the eleventh century when al-Bakrī wrote from Cordoba. Muslim merchants had direct commercial contacts with the *Bilād al-Sūdān* and they carried out their trading activities under the political protection of non-Muslim rulers, at least initially. We learn also of the sensitivity and recognition these local Sudanese rulers granted to their Muslim guests. In both Ghana and pre-Islamic Malal (Mali), Muslim clerics were sought to redress local concerns. Such was the case in Malal (Mali) where a Muslim prayer was said to have ended a protracted drought (al-Bakrī in Levtzion and Hopkins 1981: 82–3). The local chief later accepted Islam as court religion but his people remained pagan. While the rulers of Ancient Ghana were absolutely pagan, and those of Mali in the eleventh century had became nominal Muslims, later administrators of Mali – at least from the fourteenth century onwards – were clearly presented to us as full-fledged Muslims and again while Sunni ʿAlī's commitment to Islam was questioned in the Muslim sources, Askiya Muḥammad who became ruler of Songhay in about 1493 was viewed as a true believer. Both Mansa Mūsā of Mali (d. 1339) and Askiya Muḥammad (d. 1528) performed the *ḥajj* to Mecca in 1324 and the early 1490s respectively. On both occasions, the rulers were accompanied by large entourages – many of them were slaves carrying several pounds of gold not only to fund the travel but also given out as *zakāt*. Indeed, Mansa Mūsā's impressive display of gold was the first by an African ruler in the Muslim world, and just two years after his death Mali was represented on the map of the known world. From this time on, the Western Sudan was also accepted as part of *dār al-Islām* because their rulers had embraced Islam; the *sharīʿa* (especially the Mālikī school of interpretation) became the basis of law, not only in Mali, but later in Songhay and throughout the Muslim communities of West Africa.

The point has already been made that Muslim traders were attracted to the Western Sudan because of the region's gold production, but equally important were the policies that local rulers implemented to sustain supply of the precious metal. We learn from the sources (Levtzion 1973: 115–18) that rulers of both Ghana and Mali "regarded direct authority over the commercial centers [of the Western Sudan] as more important than intrusion into the goldfield areas; they derived their income from controlling the routes to the sources of that precious metal." Yet, in both Ghana and Mali, the accumulation of wealth was also regulated by the policy that "rare nuggets [from an ounce to about a pound] found in the mine were reserved for the king, and only gold dust was left for the people." Thus, royal policy was intended to preserve the market value of the precious metal.

As warrior kings whose military exploits created kingdoms, the exercise of authority that allowed rulers to impose taxes or to claim rights to gold nuggets was not out of the ordinary. In many ways, the trade in gold represented commercial exchanges between local rulers and Muslim merchants. It was the Muslim demand for gold that served to stimulate the commercial activities in West Africa and, hence, the spread of Islam in the region. It was also the security provided by local rulers that made the region attractive to foreign merchants. For example, during his journey to Mali in 1353, the world-traveler Ibn Baṭṭūṭa (d. 1368–9 or 1377) recorded that over 12,000 camels loaded with goods had passed through the copper-producing town of Tekkeda heading towards Mali. At the major Niger-bend city of Timbuktu, Ibn Baṭṭūṭa found evidence of a large and prosperous market where foreign Muslim merchants who died while away from home were buried. The king retained the financial values of the deceased traders' goods until an appropriate relative showed up to make a claim. These were the conditions that made West Africa a favorable environment for the attraction of Muslim merchants and clerics into the region.

Gold from the *Bilād al-Sūdān* was important in sustaining the economy of the Mediterranean world and Europe because the precious metal was used to settle international debt. For example, it has been noted that the Italian merchants of Genoa, Florence, and Venice held favorable trade balances with North Africa from the end of the twelfth century, and as such benefited from the Muslim trade with Africa. Detailed studies (Lopez 1956; Watson 1967) show that European demand for gold increased by the mid-thirteenth century when the metal began to replace silver as currency. Balance of trade that favored the Italian cities, for example, brought them into partnership in the Mediterranean-West African trade and the volume of gold exports from the Western Sudan did reflect an effective politically stable environment as much as throwing light on the existence of a complex socio-economic network across the region.

Even though Mali had collapsed by the late fifteenth century, in its place had emerged Songhay under the leadership of Sunni ʿAlī. At its height, Songhay controlled the territories previously dominated by Ancient Ghana and Mali. Western Sudanese traders expanded their commercial network to the fringes of the Akan forest located to the south of Jenne and areas that are now part of the modern nations of Ghana and Côte d'Ivoire became integrated into the commercial network. From here, kola nuts and more gold were added to the Sudanese exports. Further to the east, the economic activities of the Hausa states (such as Gobir, Katsina and Kano) became increasingly linked to markets in the Western Sudan and goods such as leather produced in Kano and exported to Timbuktu, for example, were traded to Morocco from where they were later sold to European markets as "Moroccan leather."

Trade in slaves was also an essential part of the West African economy. This point is attested to not only with cases from Ancient Ghana, but also from the *Taʾrīkh al-Sūdān* – the seventeenth century accounts by ʿAbd al-Raḥmān al-Saʿīd (also see Hunwick and Troutt Powell 2002 for more documentary evidence on slavery; on the specific nature of the economy of slavery in the Western Sudan, see Willis 1985; Fisher and Fisher 1970). Slave labor for agricultural production and in the craft industry, the holding of slave women as concubines, slaves as porters, and as traders on behalf of their masters are all discussed. Slaves, transported from the *Bilād al-Sūdān*, also labored at the desert salt mines of Bilma and Taghaza. African slaves were bartered for North African/Mediterranean goods and as a result a good number of Sudanese slaves ended up in Morocco and other North African centers. This was the complex and lucrative trade that attracted Arabian merchants to the *Bilād al-Sūdān*, introduced Islam into the region, and consequently transformed West Africa as part of the Muslim world.

Accommodation and political Islam

Trimingham concludes in his numerous writings on the history of Islam in Africa that Muslim merchant activities paved the way and made it possible for the penetration of their holy men to locations hitherto untouched by Islam. The idea of a simultaneous movement of Muslim clerics and merchants into the African hinterlands which Trimingham started to write about in the late 1940s is now supported by several research cases. Cohen (1971), for example, stresses the importance of the clerical presence in the trading caravans that were central to the trans-Saharan commerce. In the first place, the dangers of trans-Saharan travel and the need for security gave birth to the merchant convoys. But the very act of traveling in large numbers also created a need for internal cohesion. Thus, the accompanying holy men were critical to the caravans since they performed standard religious duties for the traveling communities, mediated their conflicts, and even at times predicted opportune moments for the convoys to arrive at market centers. Many of these traveling scholars/clerics settled in the Sudanese commercial centers, conducted schools, and trained students who reproduced new generations of clerics to spread Islam across West Africa. It has also been illustrated how some Muslims, because of their literacy abilities, at times functioned as "medicine men," gaining prestige and influence with non-Muslim rulers or even becoming important political advisors. It was through such contacts that the foundation was laid for conversion.

The classic case of how Muslim merchant/clerics introduced Islam to non-Muslim rulers is the one represented in the accounts of al-Bakrī regarding the conversion of the king of Malal. The example shows that over time, some of the previously non-Muslim rulers accepted the new religion, even when many of the traditional local practices were retained. The scholarly interpretation of the continued retention of aspects of pre-conversion local cultures has been justified in the context of syncretism or the "Africanization" of Islam. Some research (Lewis 1966; Levtzion 1973) points to peaceful conversions due to seeming similarities of traditional African concepts and those of Islam. It is also important to note that in other situations, such as in the case of the Asante of the Akan forest region now part of the modern country of Ghana, conversion never occurred – notwithstanding long periods of contact – and yet Muslims and non-Muslims lived peacefully. In other words, there was never a single reason on its own that fully justified the acceptance or rejection of Islam. There are several historical cases also where Muslims resorted to *jihād* of the sword in defense of Islam, such as the taking over of territories now part of Northern Nigeria by Usuman (ʿUthmān) dan Fodio (1754–1817) or the resistance of Umar Tal to French colonial encroachment in the Senegambia region.

It is not adequate to say that Islam spread peacefully in West Africa or to claim that militant or political Islam was responsible for the transformation of Northern Nigeria, for example. What is relevant to a discussion such as this overview of West Africa as part of the Muslim world is to seek the Islamic-based argument(s) presented by those whose actions and thoughts the historian seeks to reconstruct. Wilks has pointed to what he describes as the "Suwarian attitude [against] *jihād*," a tradition or philosophy that he identifies as having been constructed from the study of three major works: the *Tafsīr al Jalālayn* of al-Maḥallī (d. 1459) and al-Suyūṭī (d. 1505), the *Muwatta*ʾ of Imām Mālik ibn Anas (d. 796) and the *Shifā*ʾ of Qāḍī Iyāḍ ibn Mūsā al-Sabtī (d. 1149). From these sources, al-Ḥajj Salīm Suwārī (d. 1594) developed an interpretive position that was in contrast to the strict prohibition of contacts with non-believers that Ibn Abī Zayd stood for. The Suwarian tradition was a gradualist approach to the spread of Islamic influence; it was also a system of learning known from the *asānīd* or chains of authority (singular: *isnād*) that called for peaceful residency in non-Islamic communities of West Africa. For the peacefully settled Muslim community it was important that the institutions and structures necessary for the consolidation of the Muslim community were well-established. This was needed in order to achieve a stronger, religiously well-preserved and informed Muslim community that would become an example for the non-believers so as to attract them to Islam subsequently. Wilks sums up the Suwarian philosophy of neutrality best when he writes: "It was quietist in rejecting active proselytism (urging that true conversion must occur in God's time and not that of men). And it was compromising, in that it rejected the pursuit of secular office while permitting participation in the political process insofar as the partisan interests of the Muslim community were not jeopardized" (Wilks 2002: 219, 230). To this extent, the Suwarian tradition was broadly accommodative, allowing, if not enjoining, acceptance of the status quo.

As Muslim merchants and clerics spread throughout West Africa, their accommodative attitude with regard to the spread of Islamic ideals made it more possible for them to co-habit with non-Muslims. Hanretta (2005: 483) has cautioned against the temptation of looking under every stone "for the Suwarian influence whether such influence actually existed or not" to explain all instances where failure to wage *jihād* had been advocated. In fact, there are several cases in the history of West Africa where this desire to co-habit with non-Muslims had been coerced and thus accommodation can also be seen as a co-opted strategy for existence. This arises, for example, when believers in the majority Muslim societies of Senegal and Mauritania "negotiated" their relationship with the hegemonic French colonial government from the 1880s through the 1920s. The need to come to terms with or adopt such accommodative relationship with non-Muslim powers was explained in very realistic manner by Muḥammad al-Ghambaʿ, the head of the relatively small but influential Muslim community that resided peacefully among the non-Muslim Asante kingdom of the nineteenth century. In addition to the known adherence of the Muslims in the Asante capital of Kumase to the Suwarian philosophy, they also saw *jihād* as a poor option for spreading Islam in their case because

> the absence of that political co-operation in the north [is] mainly the cause why the southern believers are checked in their efforts to propagate God's worship by dint of arms; for the existing government in the vicinity of the great inland water (the Niger) are supine, and devoid in the energy which distinguished the career of the Arabs.
>
> (Wilks 1966: 325–6)

The above statement allows for several interpretations; among them is the view that accommodation was the strategy of the pragmatic, the weak, the coerced, or even those who became preoccupied with priorities other than "the propagation of God's worship by dint of arms." On the other hand, *jihād* is best resorted to for the purpose of preventing the relaxation of Islamic values or even preventing outright apostasy; but it must be engaged in from a position of strength.

The issues of accommodation and *jihād* in the context of West African Islamic history can best be appreciated in discussions that look at the variety of ways by which secular power has related to religious authority and vice versa. Hunwick (1996) has paid particular attention to state and society relations in the Songhay Empire of the Western Sudan; he focuses on the place of Muslim religious authorities as well as the nature of the tensions that developed between them and the various regimes that held political power (also see Hunwick in Lewis 1966; Hunwick 1985; Kaba 1984). In all these cases, the discourse centered on the basic definition of a Muslim, the determination of the appropriate political and social environment needed for Islam to be fulfilled, as well as the acceptable balance of influence between secular authority and religious leadership.

Tensions between secular power and religious authority have been resolved in a number of ways in the history of Islam. Hunwick (1996) outlines five broad categories of regimes and their secular/religious relations. The first was the situation under which those who held political power kept Muslim judges, teachers, and individuals or groups of religious leaders in check by force. Sunni ʿAlī of Songhay ensured recognition of secular power by executing some of the religious authorities who opposed his administration. On the other hand, dissatisfaction with excessive abuse of state power and the need to preserve the Islamic character of the Muslim state made some religious authorities favor the direct takeover of secular power. Usuman Dan Fodio's successful *jihād* in early nineteenth-century Hausaland led to the establishment of a Muslim state in which the social, economic and state ideology became established on the basis of Islamic law. There was also the case where "a revolutionary alliance between religious authorities and a secular power produced a regime in which the secular authority retained political power, but the religious authority dictated the social and economic agenda" (Hunwick 1996: 177). The most common form of power relation in the history of Islam in West Africa, according to Hunwick (1996: 178–81), was the one under which a situation of equilibrium took shape. Under that system, secular power was recognized to rule. On the other hand, the state allowed religious leaders the independence to perform their religious functions and "did not dictate government policies, but [on moral grounds] might influence it." Finally, the system under which secular power co-opted religious leaders was also widespread in West Africa, first, by the traditional African states, followed by the colonial and then the modern state.

Of the varied systems of relations, the one under which secular power and religious authorities balanced each other in an equilibrium was identified by Hunwick as the normative model because "it is the model set up by the Islamic source texts" – as the Qur'ān enjoins believers to "Obey God and obey the messenger and those among you who have authority" (Hunwick 1996: 179, and Qur'ān 4:59). But while such textual justification is appropriate explanation for recognizing the authority in Muslim states such as Muḥammad Rumfa's sixteenth-century Kano where the Muslim ruler was known to have created a just environment, enforced morally acceptable laws, and allowed Muslim authorities the freedom to operate, there are also several cases in the history of West Africa where leaders of the religious community have justified their recognition of non-Muslim secular political administrations on the basis of this same Qur'anic passage.

In his research on the Muslim community of Korhogo in the northern sector of the modern state of the Côte d'Ivoire, Launay (1996) observes that this tradition of cooperation with non-Muslim authorities had continued to shape twentieth-century clerical perception of secular power. Muslim leaders in that part of French West

Africa made it clear that "politics was not their business" and therefore deferred to French colonial officials. But cooperation with secular powers did not mean the absence of Muslim religious concerns with regards to developments that affected daily life. Clearly, citizens desire stable political environments to pursue their affairs. It was not surprising, then, that the *ʿulamāʾ* supported colonial administrations that guaranteed public safety and allowed them to engage in commerce and the Islamic scholarship needed for the preservation of their religious culture. This was the case even in the Senegambia where the French faced organized Muslim resistance in the earlier days of colonialism. But part of the reason for the successful cooptation of religious authority was the fact that the French brutally suppressed radical elements of the supporters of Islam in the territories; Muslim leaders were carefully watched, but when they accepted French authority, Islam was accommodated. Once the territories were pacified, the French developed policies that recognized religious authority within the local Muslim communities as long as the supremacy of the state was upheld. There was, therefore, an effective cooptation of traditional Muslim leaders whose economic and traditional interests depended on the political protection provided by the colonial state. In this symbiotic relationship, the state counted on Muslim leaders to ensure peace in their communities. If the peace was ever broken by radical Muslim actions, the French were still in a position to suppress any rebellion with brutal force almost in the same manner as Sunni ʿAlī had done in the early phase of the history of the Songhay empire.

In the British colony of Sierra Leone, not only did the government recognize the right of Muslims to pursue private commerce and conduct religious learning, but the state also sought and won the community's approval in the extension of formal western education to Muslim children. The indefatigable Reverend Edward Blyden was instrumental in this effort and was rewarded in 1902 with a colonial appointment as Director of "Mohammedan Education." As articulated in his *Christianity, Islam and the Negro Race* (1888:), Blyden argued that Islam had many characters similar to Christianity. Muslims recognized a monotheistic supreme being, and Islam had a "simple, rigid form of worship and a literate culture [that] were important seeds of civilization." However, Blyden saw the African acceptance of Islam as only the first step in their salvation. The provision of western education to Muslim children was therefore part of the process of Christian conversion. I have not come across any evidence to suggest that Blyden's plan to convert Muslim children succeeded. On the other hand, however, Sierra Leone's Muslims embraced western education and established several modern (English/Arabic) schools. This new generation of educated Muslims joined the civil service and played positive roles in the modern nation-building process. The crisis of the state resulting in the civil war of the 1990s in that country was not due to challenges from Muslim radicals. Rather, the policy of authoritarian centralism and the corruption of the state of affairs during the Siaka Stevens era undermined the trust built into the system.

The clear opposite to the cooptation of traditional Muslim leaders in the cases referred to above is that of Nigeria. Since the late 1970s, thousands have died in the Muslim protest actions against the state as well as in the several incidents of clashes between Muslims and Christians in such northern cities as Katsina. However, the development that attracted the most attention was the sentencing of a woman to die by stoning. Judges of a northern Nigerian Islamic court found her guilty of having a child outside marriage. Even though the verdict was not carried out because of the international attention it generated from human rights organizations, the case still underscored the strength of *sharīʿa* courts in that country.

It must be qualified that Islamic law is applicable only in the predominantly Muslim north but calls have been made by those who protested in the state that such courts be accepted to deal with Muslim cases across the country. In an article on the constitutional treatment of religion and the politics of human rights, Ilesanmi (2001) presents an insightful analysis of the subject of regulating state–society tensions. According to the author, Nigerian Muslims were not the only religious group to call for the injection of religion into national politics. Pentecostal bishops of Nigeria have also argued for a Christian interpretation of the constitution. The religious groups have argued for the need to save the secular state from "moral, socio-economic and political collapse." The refusal of the state to respond to this argument has been seen as equal to subjecting the rest of society to human rights abuses (Ilesanmi 2001: 530–1). While the Muslims are but one of several groups to use the "moral card" in this debate on the need for a religious constitution for Nigeria, they are the loudest advocators of the cause. The strength of their position stems from a successful history of Muslim rule in pre-colonial Nigeria when the *jihād* of the early nineteenth century in the Hausa-speaking north succeeded in uniting the numerous autonomous city-states into one great Islamic legal-based empire. This was the "Muslim Golden Age" in Nigerian history that British colonial rule inherited, preserved in several aspects of its institutions, and transferred as part of civil society to the modern secular state.

Unlike the French in their African territories, British colonial government in Nigeria did not disturb the administrative structure that the Muslim jihadists constructed. Under the policy of indirect rule, the Emirates (these being the chiefly positions held by Muslim leaders) were preserved. By protecting such traditional institutions, the colonial government found an appropriate means of communication with the local rural populations; this was a policy that was justified as cost effective and useful in reducing tension in the territories. The concept of indirect rule was conceived with the purpose of preserving and civilizing traditional rule. In Northern Nigeria, however, the dominant "traditional system" was Islamic and hence the *sharīʿa* survived the colonial period as the foundation upon which local government was managed. Islamic influence survived, it was valued as an important tradition, and the colonial administration relied upon Islamic religious authority for the management of local affairs. It is not surprising, then, that these Muslim leaders have been able to speak out loudly to challenge the authority of the modern secular state. The Islamic institutions are important counter-weights to those of the modern state and in many cases are of immediate relevance to the majority of the people. This is the nature of Nigeria's "Islamic factor."

Observations and conclusions

With the exception of Nigeria, the post-independent governments of West Africa were handed administrations that did not have much to worry about with regards to religious conflicts. The French contained their traditional Muslim leaders and made them subservient to the state inherited by the western educated ruling elite. The result has been a continuation of the relationship that existed in the colonial era. In fact, across West Africa, the preoccupation with nation building focused attention on infrastructure developments and the provision of formal western education. The traditional forms of Islamic learning continue across West Africa, but, where specific state attention had been directed at educating Muslim children, the concern has been how to incorporate aspects of religious instruction into the modern school curriculum. For the most part, the *ʿulamāʾ* have been concerned with local issues of the bread-and-butter type; they are interested in state allocation of hard currency that makes it possible for some of its members to attend the annual *ḥajj* to Mecca, and they are pleased when governments allow them the freedom to handle religious affairs directly associated with their faith. Certainly such concerns do not threaten the state nor are Muslim religious authorities threatened by the state.

Traditional Muslim leaders are equally contained in those countries where Islam is a minority religion. However, there is a current trend whereby the new process of democratization has allowed the younger generation of western-educated Muslims to organize non-governmental organizations (NGOs) to address Muslim concerns. There is evidence, for example, in the rise of NGOs interested in organizing Muslim women, in the reconstruction of mosques, and in the modernization of Muslim schools. One thing common to this new generation of Muslims is the perception that the older generation of Muslim leaders has become traditionalized and hence there is a need for the production of a new and more organic leadership. The traditional leaders are seen as uneducated in the western sense and therefore easily manipulated by politicians. In other words, the former modes by which secular states have sought to accommodate religious authority have now been questioned, though not violently. Such demands by Muslims cannot be interpreted as part of an anti-western tradition. In fact, they definitely are not. Generally, the modern state has managed to strike degrees of accommodation with several Muslim groups in a symbiotic way. It would thus be appropriate to observe that while Islam unites believers in the West African sub-region with the Islamic world by their adherence to the universal faith, reactions to Islam in the history of West Africa have been influenced by local realities. The major problem for the region is the ability of the modern states to be effective providers of citizens' needs. This is especially important since the state, colonial and modern, usurped control of the public sphere by determining the content of national education, economic resources, welfare activities through state-run hospitals and currency exchanges. By assuming control of such otherwise civic spheres, the state weakened the potential for traditional leaders to pose as effective challengers to state power, but it is the state's inability to meet expectations that plants the seed of discontent. In countries such as Nigeria where a strong political Islamic tradition can be called upon, Muslim leaders have used it to suggest an Islamic alternative. In other countries in the region the most effective avenue for Muslim protestation is through Islamic NGOs and human rights organizations. In the years ahead, it will be interesting to see how West African governments democratically address these concerns.

References and further reading

Bercher, L. ed. and trans. (1949) *Ibn Abi Zayd al-Qayrawani: La Risala*, 3rd edition, Algiers: Editions Jules Carbonel.

Blyden, E. W. (1888) *Christianity, Islam and the Negro Race*, London: W. B. Whittingham, 2nd edition.
Bovil, E. W. (1958) *The Golden Trade of the Moors*, London: Oxford University Press.
Brenner, L. (1993) *Muslim Identity and Social Change in Sub-Saharan Africa*, Bloomington, Indiana: Indiana University Press.
—— (2001) *Controlling Knowledge: Religion, Power, and Schooling in a West African Muslim Society*, Bloomington, Indiana: Indiana University Press.
Cohen, A. (1971) "Cultural Strategies in the Organization of Trade Diasporas," in C. Meillassoux, ed., *The Development of Indigenous Trade and Markets in West Africa*, London: Oxford University Press.
Fisher, H. J. (1973) "Conversion Reconsidered: Some Aspects of Religious Conversion in Black Africa," *Africa*, 43: 27–40.
Fisher, A. G. B. and Fisher H. J. (1970) *Slavery and Muslim Society in Africa: the Institution in Saharan and Sudanic Africa, and the Trans-Saharan Trade*, London: C. Hurst.
Hajj, M. A. al- (1968) "A Seventeenth Century Chronicle on the Origins and Missionary Activities of the Wangarawa," *Kano Studies*, 1: 7–42.
Hanretta, S. (2005) "Muslim Histories, African Societies: the Venture of Islamic Studies in Africa," *Journal of African History*, 46: 479–92.
Hunwick, J. O. (1976) *Islam in Africa, Friend or Foe? An Inaugural Lecture Delivered at the University of Ghana, Legon*, Accra: Ghana Universities Press.
—— (1985) *Sharīʿa in Songhay*, Oxford: Oxford University Press.
—— (1996) "Secular Power and Religious Authority in Muslim Society: the Case of Songhay," *Journal of African History*, 37: 175–94.
Hunwick, J. and Troutt Powell, E. (2002) *The African Diaspora in the Mediterranean Lands of Islam*, Princeton: Markus Wiener Publishers.
Ilesanmi, S. (2001) "Constitutional Treatment of Religion and the Politics of Human Rights in Nigeria," *African Affairs*, 100: 529–54.
Kaba, L. (1984) "The Pen, the Sword, and the Crown: Islam and Revolution in Songhay Reconsidered, 1464–1491," *Journal of African History*, 25: 241–56.
—— (2000) "Islam in West Africa: Radicalism and the New Ethic of Disagreement, 1960–1990," in N. Levtzion, R. Pouwels, eds., *The History of Islam in Africa*, Athens: Ohio University Press, 189–208.
Launay, R. (1977) *Traders without Trade: Response to Change in Two Dyula Communities*, London: Cambridge University Press.
—— (1996) "La trahison des clercs? The 'Collaboration' of a Suwarian *ʿalim*," in J. Hunwick, N. Lawler, eds., *The Cloth of Many Colored Silks: Papers on History and Society, Ghanaian and Islamic in Honor of Ivor Wilks*, Evanston: Northwestern University Press, 297–318.
Levtzion, N. (1968) *Muslims and Chiefs in West Africa*, Oxford: Clarendon Press.
—— (1973) *Ancient Ghana and Mali*, London: Methuen.
Levtzion, N., Hoexter, M. and Eisenstadt, S. N. (2002) *The Public Sphere in Muslim Society*, Albany: State University of New York Press.
Levtzion, N. and Hopkins, J. E. P., eds. (1981) *Corpus of Early Arabic Sources for West African History*, Cambridge: Cambridge University Press.
Levtzion, N. and Pouwels, R., eds. (2000) *The History of Islam in Africa*, Athens: Ohio University Press.
Lewis, I. M., ed. (1966) *Islam in Tropical Africa*, London: Oxford University Press.
Lopez, R. S. (1956) "Back to Gold, 1252," *Economic History Review*, 9: 219–40.
Lovejoy, P. E. (1980) "Kola in the History of West Africa," *Cahiers d'études africaines*, 20: 73–8.
McCall, D. F. and Bennett, N. R. (1971) *Aspects of West African Islam*, Boston: Boston University's African Studies Center.

Owusu-Ansah, D. (1991) *A Talismanic Tradition: Muslims in Nineteenth Century Asante*, Lewiston, New York: Edwin Mellen Press.
Robinson, D. (2000) *Paths of Accommodation: Muslim Societies and French Colonial Authorities in Senegal and Mauritania, 1880–1920*, Athens: Ohio University Press.
Sanneh, L. O. (1997) *The Crown and the Turban. Muslims and West African Pluralism*, Boulder, Colorado: Westview Press.
Watson, A. M. (1967) "Back to Gold and Silver," *Economic History Review*, 20: 1–34.
Wilks, I. G. (1966) "The Position of Muslims in Metropolitan Ashanti," in I. M. Lewis, ed., *Islam in Tropical Africa*, London: Oxford University Press, 318–41.
—— (2000) "The Juula and the Expansion of Islam into the Forest," in N. Levtzion, R. Pouwels, eds., *History of Islam in Africa*, Athens: Ohio University Press, 93–115.
—— (2002) " 'Mallams do not Fight with the Heathen': A Note on Suwarian Attitudes to Jihad," *Ghana Studies*, 5: 215–30.
Willis, J. R. (1985) *Slaves and Slavery in Muslim Africa*, London: Frank Cass.

3

EAST AFRICA

Valerie J. Hoffman

East Africa, which includes the Horn of Africa (Ethiopia, Somalia, Eritrea and Djibouti), the Swahili coast and Great Lakes region (Uganda, Kenya, Tanzania, Mozambique, the Democratic Republic of the Congo, Rwanda, Burundi, Zambia, and Malawi), and the island states of the Comoros, Madagascar, Mauritius and Mayotte, is a vast region encompassing tremendously diverse topography and supporting equally diverse lifestyles. The Muslim population of this region numbers today approximately 92 million, or about 26 percent of the entire population of these countries. Islam entered East Africa mainly via seafaring merchants from southern Yemen, particularly in the Horn of Africa, so Muslims are most concentrated along the coast, from Eritrea to northern Mozambique, with the proportion of the Muslim population diminishing as one goes inland. Somalia, which has a long coastline bordering both the Gulf of Aden and the Indian Ocean, is entirely Muslim, and this is nearly the case for Djibouti, a small country at the intersection of the Red Sea and the Gulf of Aden, and for the Comoros, Mayotte, and Zanzibar (the last of which joined with Tanganyika to form the nation of Tanzania in 1964). Nonetheless, the country with by far the largest number of Muslims (over 38 million) is the entirely landlocked state of Ethiopia, where Muslims constitute about half the population, despite Ethiopia's historical identification with Christianity.

Islamization of East Africa

There were interactions between Arabia and the Banadir coast of southern Somalia before Islam: Muḥammad is said to have been born in 570, the "year of the elephant," when Abraha, ruler of the kingdom of Axum in present-day Ethiopia, attacked Mecca; and when the Muslims were persecuted in Mecca, they found asylum in Christian Abyssinia (*c.* 615). Trade across the Indian Ocean fostered exchanges between East Africa, Arabia, Persia, India and Southeast Asia for untold generations. Swahili culture probably developed in towns on the southern Somali coast from the intermarriage of Arab and Persian merchants with local women; although Swahili is a Bantu language, some 30 percent of its vocabulary is Arabic in origin, and there are words of Persian and Hindi origin as well. Some say that Swahili culture pre-dates the Islamization of the Swahili coast, but others say that the earliest Swahili settlements on the east coast were founded in the ninth and tenth centuries. Tradition, coastal chroniclers and Arab geographers suggest that the first settlers came from the Persian Gulf, in a series of waves over several centuries. For decades there has been much discussion among scholars and among the Swahili themselves concerning the "African" or "Asiatic" origin of Swahili culture and the nature of Swahili identity. Many scholars feel that racial prejudice led earlier Western writers to over-emphasize the Arab and Persian role in the development of Swahili culture as well as in the spread of Islam on the Swahili coast. Recent works tend to emphasize the "Africanness" of Swahili civilization and of Islam in East Africa. Nonetheless, a major sub-group of Swahili speakers call themselves "Shirazi," based on putative descent from princes of Shiraz in southern Iran who settled in East Africa in the tenth century. Evidence of a Persian presence is indicated by an inscription in a thirteenth-century mosque in Mogadishu naming its builder as Khusrow ibn Muḥammad al-Shīrāzī, and by the fact that one of the ancient quarters of Mogadishu bears a Persian name; indeed, the word *banādir*, which is applied to the entire southern coast of Somalia, is of Persian origin (Mukhtar 1995: 5). Until the development of African nationalisms in the late 1950s and early 1960s, Arabs often enjoyed political power and religious and cultural prestige in East Africa. Many families claim Arab descent, especially from the Hadramawt region of southeast Yemen; Ḥaḍramī influence in East Africa is palpable, recognizable in family names, the preponderance of the Shāfiʿī school of Sunnī Islam, the extreme importance in Swahili society of *sharīf*-ian descent – descent from the Prophet, and the spiritual linkages that led many Swahili scholars to go to the Hadramawt for study.

Until the 1960s, Swahili identity was strongly linked to Islamic identity – to be a Swahili meant that one was a Muslim. With the adoption of Swahili as a national language in Kenya and Tanzania, however, Swahili identity is now linked to language, not religion. Although Swahili civilization originated in the coastal towns of southern Somalia, Somali-speaking nomads, who appeared in that region around the thirteenth century, gradually eroded the Swahili language in the cities of Warsheikh, Mogadishu and Merka; Swahili has survived only in the southernmost part of the coast, particularly in Brava, where the dialect, Chimbalazi, has incorporated some Somali vocabulary.

Tradition has it that the second caliph, ʿUmar ibn al-Khaṭṭāb (r. 634–44), sent a delegation to various East African settlements that had accepted Islam. This would put the beginnings of East Africa's Islamization very early. Arab sources state that the Umayyad caliph ʿAbd al-Malik ibn Marwān (r. 685–705) sent an army to conquer Mogadishu and Kilwa, but Umayyad and then Abbasid dominance of the Banadir coast ended in 805 when Mogadishu succeeded in establishing an independent sultanate. The East African coast sometimes served as a refuge for sectarian groups of Shīʿa and Ibāḍīs, but Sunnism was the dominant form of Islam, with certain families of Arab ancestry forming a religious aristocracy, monopolizing religious functions and education. Islamization intensified in the Red Sea region when trade revived in the late tenth century as the Fatimids came to power in Egypt and assumed the role of protectors of Muslims in Ethiopia; trading towns like Zeila, on the coast of the Gulf of Aden in what is now northern Somalia, served as centers for the diffusion of Islam. For many centuries, Islam remained a largely coastal and urban phenomenon closely tied to trade. A series of Muslim sultanates arose in the twelfth century along the trade routes, including Mogadishu, Merca and Brava. As Swahili civilization extended southward, Lamu, Pate, Mombasa and Kilwa all became virtual city-states, usually ruled by a family claiming Arab descent. The Ethiopian city of Harar was the only major Islamic center that was inland. Muslim immigrants to northeast Africa were "relatively small groups of traders, adventurers, and refugees" (Trimingham 1952: 33), who married African women and had Muslim children, leading to the gradual development of Muslim genealogies based on an Arab ancestor. Until the thirteenth century, Muslims in the northern trading centers lived under the rule of pagans and the Christian kings of Abyssinia, who did not allow them complete freedom of religion. The earliest known mosque south of the Banadir is in Kizimkazi, on the east coast of Zanzibar, bearing a date of 500 *hijrī* (1107–8). At Kilwa, on the Tanganyikan coast, Muslim-style tombs and stone mosques first appeared in the twelfth and thirteenth centuries. The only other pre-fourteenth-century stone mosque is in Mogadishu, where two mosques bear thirteenth-century dates. Scholars conclude that actual groups of Muslims on the Swahili coast south of Somalia were scarce before 1300 (Pouwels 1978a: 211). From the fourteenth through sixteenth centuries, Islam gradually expanded through trade, particularly from north to south. Many stone towns appeared during this period along the Swahili coast, including Lamu, Gedo, Mombasa, Malindi, and others. This was also the period that the first Ṣūfī order, the Qādiriyya, was introduced to the Banadir coast from Yemen.

By the thirteenth and fourteenth centuries, many nomadic peoples of the Horn of Africa had embraced Islam, including the ʿAfar, Somali and Beja, leaving Abyssinian Christianity "isolated in a sea of Islam" (Trimingham 1952: xv). Islam did not enjoy a comparable spread among rural populations in countries south of Somalia until the nineteenth and twentieth centuries.

Development of Islamic civilization in East Africa

Much of the history of Islam in Ethiopia is marked by struggle and warfare between Muslim principalities and the Christian kingdom of Axum. Between 1529 and 1543, Aḥmad ibn Ibrāhīm of Harar, who took the religious title Imām and is nicknamed *al-Ghāzī* ('the Conqueror"), conquered most of Ethiopia with the moral and military support of the Ottomans, who had conquered Egypt in 1517 and Yemen in 1525, wreaking massive devastation, forcing conversions, and destroying cities and churches. A Portuguese army defeated him in 1543, and by 1555 the Ethiopian state had restored its pre-*jihād* boundaries. The number of Muslims in the Ethiopian highlands increased through Imām Aḥmad's *jihād*, but the region was also laid open to mass migrations of pastoral Oromo (Galla) people. In the late seventeenth century, Emperor Yohannes I ordered Muslims to live separately from Christians in villages and town quarters of their own. Christians could not eat with Muslims, drink from cups they had used, or eat meat they had slaughtered.

Vasco da Gama visited Kilwa in 1498, and within a few years the Portuguese had captured and destroyed both Kilwa and Mombasa, the two greatest Shirazi cities. With the exception of Goa on the west coast of India and Mozambique on the south-eastern coast of Africa, the Portuguese did not acquire large colonies, but they did seize small territories throughout the Indian Ocean and the Persian Gulf where they built forts and garrisons, including Fort Jesus at Mombasa. They were the strongest naval power in the region throughout the sixteenth century, and directly contributed to the decline of Shirazi civilization, as the coastal towns depended on the Indian Ocean trade for their survival. The decline of Shirazi civilization was hastened by population movements in East Africa; Shirazi towns were frequently attacked by African groups moving into their hinterland.

Omani rule in East Africa

In the seventeenth century a new dynasty in Oman challenged Portuguese supremacy in the Indian Ocean. Imām Sulṭān ibn Sayf (r. 1640–80) recaptured the Omani port city of Muscat from the Portuguese in 1651, and in the 1660s and 1670s he attacked Portuguese garrisons in India and the Persian Gulf. Omani immigrants living in Mombasa requested assistance against the Portuguese, so he sent a fleet that attacked and burned Portuguese positions in Mombasa, Pate, Zanzibar and Mozambique, leading to a general revolt against the Portuguese in all the coastal towns. For a time the Portuguese were able to crush the revolts, but in the 1660s Sulṭān was able to capture Mombasa after a long siege. Once he left, however, the Portuguese recaptured Mombasa and severely punished its inhabitants. His son, Sayf ibn Sulṭān I (r. 1692–1711), laid siege to Mombasa again in 1696, but it was not until December 1698 that he was able to capture Fort Jesus. He proceeded to expel the Portuguese from Pemba and Kilwa as well, and returned to Oman, leaving the governorships of the major towns in the hands of important Omani families that lived in them: the Mazrūʿī (Mazrui) family in Mombasa and Pemba, and the Nabhānī family in Lamu and Pate. The Portuguese recaptured Mombasa in 1727, but the Omanis took it back in 1729. The Portuguese harassed Omani merchants and closed their Indian ports to them. The ongoing war between the Portuguese and Omanis from 1650 to about 1730 was "a stand-off, costly and detrimental to both sides" (Risso 1986: 13), but in the eighteenth century Portuguese power declined, and by the nineteenth century their only territory in East Africa was Mozambique.

In the 1740s the Bū Saʿīdī dynasty came to power in Oman. The Mazrūʿīs and Nabhānīs of Mombasa, Lamu, Pate and Pemba refused to recognize the new dynasty, and claimed independence. Only Zanzibar remained loyal to the new Omani sovereign. The rebellion was weakened by rivalry between the two families. The Mazrūʿīs were definitively subdued only in 1837 by Omani ruler Sayyid Saʿīd ibn Sulṭān after a series of battles over many years. It was Sayyid Saʿīd who transferred the capital of the Omani empire from Oman to Zanzibar in 1832. From 1832 to 1856, Zanzibar was the capital of a vast empire that included Oman and the Swahili coast from Mogadishu in Somalia to twelve miles south of the Rovuma River in northern Mozambique. By the early nineteenth century, Muslim traders from the coast, usually with the financial backing of Indian merchants, were taking caravans into the interior to obtain ivory and slaves for export. Towns began to appear along these inland trade routes, from which Islam gradually spread into the interior. Although the exact extent of Omani rule in the interior was defined mainly by the payment of tribute by African chieftains and the appointment of Omani governors of often ambivalent loyalties, Zanzibar's prestige was such that, according to a popular saying, "When one pipes in Zanzibar, they dance on the Lakes." The most important conversions were among the Yao of the eastern side of Lake Malawi in the Portuguese colony of Mozambique, who embraced Islam in the second half of the nineteenth century.

Sayyid Saʿīd encouraged American and European merchants to come to Zanzibar, and in the 1830s and 1840s consuls arrived from the USA, Great Britain, France,

Portugal, Italy, Belgium, Germany, and Austria-Hungary. Sayyid Saʿīd fostered clove cultivation, which became an important staple of Zanzibar's economy. The development of plantation agriculture on the Swahili coast in the nineteenth century caused the pace of the slave trade to increase dramatically, accompanied by warfare and convulsive population displacements throughout the interior.

Most Omani settlers in East Africa belonged to the Ibāḍī sect of Islam, but they did not proselytize; according to Trimingham (1964: 73), the Omanis regarded Ibadism as "a tribal religion" that marked their separateness from and superiority to the indigenous population. Although Omanis took African concubines, and the offspring of such unions were social equals to the offspring born to their Omani wives, the Omanis, unlike the Ḥaḍramīs, remained socially distinct, and did not become fully Swahilized until the twentieth century. A nineteenth-century scholar from Brava who served the sultans of Zanzibar, though claiming Arab ancestry for himself, reserved the word "Arab" for Omanis, who, he wrote, did not know Swahili (Hoffman 2006: 259). Sayyid Saʿīd was determined to make Zanzibar an important center of Islamic scholarship, and for this purpose he invited to Zanzibar not only Ibāḍī scholars, but also Sunnī scholars from various towns along the Swahili coast. The overwhelming majority of the indigenous population of the Swahili coast follows the Shāfiʿī school of Sunnī Islam.

Swahili society during this period consisted of Omani overlords who were Ibāḍī, Baluchi soldiers who were Ḥanafī Sunnīs, Indian merchants who were Ismāʿīlī, Bohora and Hindu, Ḥaḍramī scholars and traders who were Shāfiʿī, and African subjects and slaves who were Shāfiʿī or followed indigenous religions. Ḥaḍramīs intermarried with the local population and became integrated into Swahili society, who were also Shāfiʿī Sunnīs, but the Omanis did so less often, and the Indians formed separate religious and social communities that practiced endogamy and preserved their native languages.

The scholarly class – the *ʿulamāʾ* – was a close-knit group that knew each other personally and recruited from particular families and groups; more than three-quarters of them were of Ḥaḍramī background, though Ḥaḍramīs constituted probably no more than 2 percent of the Sunnī population of East Africa (Nimtz 1980: 20). It is also noteworthy that two of the most important scholars of Zanzibar in the nineteenth century were from the southern Somali town of Brava. Both claimed Arab, though not Ḥaḍramī or *sharīf*-ian, descent.

When Sayyid Saʿīd died in 1856, the British brokered a division of his empire, Oman passing to the rule of one of his sons, and East Africa to another.

European colonialism

European encroachment gradually whittled away Bū Saʿīdī power in East Africa throughout the nineteenth century. The British, who formally took India as a colony in 1857, were the European power that was closest and most influential with the Bū Saʿīdī sultans. In 1868 Ibāḍī religious scholars in Oman led a revolution that overthrew the sultan and replaced him with an Imām of their choosing. The British regarded the Imām's government as fanatical and hostile to their interests; a mixed Omani–Wahhābī–British force killed the Imām in January 1871 and reinstated a sultan. From that point on, British interference in Omani affairs was very significant. Sayyid Saʿīd's son, Barghash, opposed the division of the Omani empire, was sympathetic to Ibāḍī aspirations for a righteous Imamate, and conspired to overthrow his brother, Sayyid Mājid, ruler of Zanzibar from 1856 to 1870. Barghash was exiled to Bombay, where he underwent an apparent change of heart. When he succeeded Mājid in 1870, he conducted an ambitious modernization program, including the introduction of plumbing and electricity. During his reign, steamship, cable, and the opening of the Suez Canal brought East Africa into closer connection with the outside world. An Englishman, Sir Lloyd Matthews, commanded Barghash's army, and the British Resident, Sir John Kirk, was his close ally and confidant. Despite Zanzibar's economic dependence on the slave trade, Kirk convinced Barghash to put a halt to it in 1874 (although slavery as an institution continued into the early twentieth century), and promised to uphold Barghash's interests in East Africa. Barghash made a state visit to England in 1876, and also visited Paris and Berlin before returning to East Africa. Ultimately, however, Great Britain betrayed Barghash's trust. In the "scramble for Africa," the sultan of Zanzibar lost Tanganyika (the mainland portion of present-day Tanzania) to Germany, Kenya to Great Britain, and southern Somalia to Italy. Beyond the sultan's domains, Germany took Rwanda and Burundi, Belgium took the Congo, France took Madagascar, the Comoros and Mayotte, Great Britain took Uganda, Nyasaland (later Malawi), Rhodesia (later Zambia and Zimbabwe), and Mauritius, Italy took Eritrea, and Somalia was divided between Italy, Great Britain and France. Only Ethiopia, under Menelik II, surprised the Western world by defeating Italy in the battle of Adowa in 1896; Ethiopia remained independent, except for a brief period (1936–41) when it was incorporated into the domains of Italian East Africa. In 1890 the British established a protectorate over Zanzibar. After World War I, Germany lost its territories in East Africa: Tanganyika went to Great Britain, and Rwanda and Burundi went to Belgium.

European rulers of East Africa adopted policies that favored Muslims and the spread of Islam: they recognized that Islam represented a high civilization, appointed *qāḍīs*, judges of Islamic law, over urban and rural communities, and extended their jurisdiction to populations with tenuous linkages to Islam. Nonetheless, secular administrators had ultimate authority over Muslim magistrates and restricted the jurisdiction of the *sharīʿa* to marriage, divorce, child custody, and inheritance.

Trimingham believed that Islamization increased dramatically during the colonial period because European power and the suppression of the slave trade brought increased security, allowing Muslim traders greater access to the interior. Nimtz disagrees, arguing that Islam's major expansion in East Africa, particularly during the period from 1916 to 1924, was a militant response to the advent of colonial rule and an effort to bring order to a chaotic situation, and that Islamization progressed most rapidly during periods of upheaval and crisis (Nimtz 1980: 15).

Modern regimes in East Africa

Most sub-Saharan African nations were granted independence in the early 1960s: the Malagasy Republic (formerly Madagascar), the Republic of the Congo (formerly the Belgian Congo, later Zaire, and later still the Democratic Republic of the Congo) and Somalia in 1960, Tanganyika in 1961, Uganda, Rwanda and Burundi in 1962, Kenya and Zanzibar in 1963, Malawi (formerly Nyasaland) and Zambia (formerly Northern Rhodesia) in 1964, Mauritius in 1968. Others did not attain independence until the 1970s: the Comoros and Mozambique in 1975, the latter only after ten years of sporadic warfare, Djibouti in 1977. Mayotte remains a *département* of France.

The post-independence history of this region has been marked by many military coups and wars – both civil wars and interstate wars like the Ogaden conflict between Ethiopia and Somalia. Some of these conflicts are a direct legacy of the arbitrary division of Africa into European spheres of interest in the nineteenth century, while others are the result of government corruption and communist revolutions. Only the most important of these will be described here.

In Ethiopia, Mengistu Haile Mariam led a military coup that deposed Emperor Haile Selassie in 1974 and established a one-party communist state. The ensuing years brought a series of military coups, war with Somalia over the Ogaden province, which the British had given to Ethiopia, severe drought, and displacement of hundreds of thousands of people. Many civilians were deliberately starved by the regime to force them into submission. In 1993, after a thirty-year war for independence, Eritrea seceded from Ethiopia.

Italian Somaliland and British Somaliland joined to form the independent republic of Somalia in 1960, except for Ogaden, which was made part of Ethiopia. Somalia's history has also been marked by military coups. Violence has plagued much of Somalia, especially the capital, Mogadishu, since Mohamed Siad Barre was overthrown in 1991. Although the United Nations recognizes a Transitional National Government, its power is extremely limited. The northern provinces, known as Somaliland and Puntland, are virtually autonomous.

Uganda became an independent nation in 1962. In 1966 Milton Obote overthrew the constitution and declared himself president. He in turn was overthrown in 1971 by Idi Amin, whose rule was marked by ruthless killings that claimed an estimated 300,000 lives, the expulsion of the Indian population, and the collapse of the economy. He was finally ousted by a Tanzanian force aided by Ugandan exiles. Uganda suffered subsequent coups, civil war, and the abduction of children by militias who force them into military service, but it is nonetheless relatively stable and is a major contributor of soldiers to African peacekeeping forces in the region.

Kenya attracted the most British and European settlement in the region, with consequent displacement of the indigenous population, leading to the famous Mau Mau rebellion of the 1950s. Kenya gained independence in December 1963. Although its politics have been authoritarian and sometimes marked by violence, there have been no successful coup attempts, and the government is a parliamentary democracy. The election in 2002 of an opposition candidate to the presidency, Mwai Kibaki, was heralded as a triumph of democracy.

Tanganyika attained full independence from Great Britain in December 1961 under the leadership of Julius Nyerere, who established a system of socialist villages throughout the country. In December 1963 Zanzibar was granted independence as a constitutional monarchy under Sultan Jamshīd ibn ʿAbd Allāh Āl Bū Saʿīdī, but in January 1964 the government was overthrown in a violent coup led by a Ugandan Christian named John Okello, who styled himself "Field Marshall." The Zanzibar revolution, as it is called, was a revolt against Arab and Indian political and economic dominance; although slavery had ended more than a half-century earlier, the Arabs remained a privileged class. Arabs sometimes continued to address blacks as "slave," and held a strong sense of racial superiority. Indians did not have the same political power or social prestige, but they had become the wealthiest segment of society, owning most of the land and businesses. The black African majority was clearly disadvantaged in every way. The leaders of the revolution encouraged black Africans to attack non-blacks; a horrific massacre ensued, in which some ten thousand unarmed civilians were murdered. Thousands of Arabs and Indians fled Zanzibar at this time. The revolutionaries specifically targeted Zanzibar's Islamic heritage, which had been in decline for some time; most of the Arabic manuscripts in the Zanzibar National Archive have been vandalized. Eyewitnesses say that Qur'āns were burned in the streets, although 98 percent of Zanzibar's population was Muslim. Homes were invaded, and people of lighter skin were selected for extermination, often in a hideous fashion, so that no body could remain for burial. Okello allegedly bragged that he personally killed more than 8,000 people. Many Arabs fled to Oman, which remains under Bū Saʿīdī rule to this day and has a large number of Swahili-speaking citizens; even Oman's Grand Muftī, Shaykh Aḥmad ibn Ḥamad al-Khalīlī, is from Zanzibar. Once the revolution was over, Okello went abroad, and his co-conspirators prohibited him from returning to Zanzibar. He was last seen in Uganda in 1971 with Idi Amin, and it is speculated that Amin ordered his assassination, though nothing is known of what happened to him. Zanzibar joined with Tanganyika in April 1964 to form the Republic of Tanzania, although it has its own president and retains some autonomy.

Mozambique attained independence in 1975 after ten years of sporadic warfare against the Portuguese colonial regime. After independence it was plagued by civil war and attacks by the neighboring white-dominated regimes of Rhodesia and South Africa. The civil war ended in 1992, and was followed by a massive resettlement of refugees.

Islamic education and religious functionaries

In the coastal towns many Muslims assiduously observe their religious obligations. In Zanzibar and other towns most children attend Qur'ān school several hours daily in addition to daily attendance at a secular school. The focus of Qur'ān school is memorization of the Qur'ān, but the children also memorize a lengthy poem that praises the Prophet Muḥammad – the famous *mawlid* (*maulidi* in Swahili) of Jaʿfar ibn Ḥasan al-Barzanjī (d. 1765). Like other *mawlid*s, this poem relates that the first thing God created was the "Muḥammadan light," made from a handful of God's own light, and from this all other things were made. The poem then traces the transmission of this light from person to person until the conception of the Prophet, whose gestation is marked by miraculous occurrences. In Swahili towns the Prophet's birthday is celebrated with open-air communal recitation of this *mawlid*. Groups of children also recite it on other important occasions, like weddings.

During the Omani period, the government appointed *qāḍī*s for each Muslim legal school represented in the population. The *ʿulamāʾ* also taught in their homes or in mosques, and some, both Sunnī and Ibāḍī, were influential at court, serving as counselors and ambassadors for the sultans. European expansion in the region encroached upon the authority of the *ʿulamāʾ* as the scope of *sharīʿa* law became more restricted and new schools were built, first by European missionaries, then by colonial governments. In the early twentieth century the British in Zanzibar organized a commission that included Sunnī and Ibāḍī *ʿulamāʾ* as well as British officials, to improve Islamic education and administration. They also introduced the use of Latin letters for writing Swahili, which was formerly written in the Arabic script.

In the twentieth century, Indian and Pakistani Muslims, especially Ismāʿīlīs and Aḥmadīs, played a major role in the expansion of education in East Africa, especially in Kenya and mainland Tanzania. The Ismāʿīlīs generally enjoyed good relations with the Sunnī majority, and did not aim primarily to recruit people to the Ismāʿīlī group, but Sunnīs often perceived the Aḥmadiyya as non-Muslims disguised as Muslims, and therefore their educational activities and translation of the Qurʾān into Swahili were perceived as threatening, and led directly to Sunnī translations of texts into Swahili as well as polemical literature attacking the Aḥmadiyya.

Ṣūfī orders

Many coastal towns had already been Muslim for centuries before the introduction into the region of the Ṣūfī orders – the *ṭuruq* (*ṭarīqa* in the singular), sometimes translated as "brotherhood," but really meaning "way" or "method" of mystical practice. The first Ṣūfī order was the Qādiriyya, introduced from Yemen and the Hadramawt into the coastal towns of Masawwa (in present-day Eritrea), Zayla (in northern Somalia near Djibouti), and Mogadishu in the fifteenth and sixteenth centuries, and into Harar in the highlands of Ethiopia at the beginning of the sixteenth century. Shaykh Uways ibn Muḥammad of Brava spearheaded the spread of the Qādiriyya further south on the coast as far as Zanzibar in the later part of the nineteenth century, and his disciples disseminated it widely in Tanganyika as well. The Qādiriyya's use of music and ecstasy during the public ritual of *dhikr* played an important part in the attraction of this order for ordinary Africans; Shaykh ʿAbd al-ʿAzīz al-Amawī wrote that an African chieftain who witnessed his *dhikr* during one of his journeys on the mainland in 1885 asked to be allowed to convert on the spot, so he could do this *dhikr* (Hoffman 2006: 263). The orders attracted new converts to Islam, facilitated their integration into Muslim society, and met material, social and spiritual needs (Nimtz 1980: 65). Membership was open to anyone, usually even to women, and Africans rapidly ascended to leadership positions in the Qādiriyya. One of Shaykh Uways's most important disciples, ʿUmar al-Qullatayn, played a major role in disseminating the Qādiriyya through Zanzibar and the vicinity of Dar es Salaam, and later served on the Zanzibar Revolutionary Council. During the Omani period, many *ʿulamāʾ* of Zanzibar belonged to the ʿAlawiyya, a Ḥadramī Ṣūfī order founded in the thirteenth century that focuses on the descendants of the Prophet (Bang 2003: 93–115), and had reservations about other Ṣūfī orders. "In their opinion, brotherhood membership was often a substitute for strict adherence to the essential pillars of Sunnī Islam, especially among the less knowledgeable" (Nimtz 1980: 64). Another major international order founded in the thirteenth century, the Shādhiliyya, was introduced to the Swahili coast by a Comorian *shaykh*, Muḥammad Maʿrūf ibn Aḥmad (1853–1905), and is popular in many parts of East Africa, from Uganda to Mozambique.

In the nineteenth century many new Ṣūfī orders were founded, especially in North Africa, often with a reformist message, missionary zeal, political strength, and even militancy. Quite a few of these were founded by disciples of the Moroccan *shaykh*, Sayyid Aḥmad ibn Idrīs (1760–1837), who had acquired fame in Mecca. Among the most important orders spawned by his disciples are the Sanūsiyya in Libya, the

Mirghaniyya or Khatmiyya in Sudan and Eritrea, the Dandarāwiyya in Egypt, and the Ṣāliḥiyya in Somalia. The Sanūsiyya were important in the fight against Italian occupation in Libya and French incursions in Chad, while the Ṣāliḥiyya fought the British in northern Somalia from 1899 to 1920, led by Muḥammad ibn ʿAbd Allāh al-Ḥasan, who claimed to be the expected *Mahdī* (who would restore justice to the world before the day of judgment), and whom the British nicknamed "the Mad Mullah." The Khatmiyya, on the other hand, sided with the Turko-Egyptian government of Sudan against the Sudanese Mahdi in the 1880s. Other orders that appeared in the region in the nineteenth century are the Tījāniyya, founded in Morocco and West Africa in the late eighteenth century, and the Sammāniyya, an eighteenth-century offshoot of the Khalwatiyya. Agricultural settlements associated with a *ṭarīqa* emerged in the nineteenth century, making the order the basis for a new social group.

Saint veneration

Throughout the Muslim world it is believed that saints – men or women who work miracles and are favored by God – intercede with God on behalf of ordinary believers, and are even more powerful after death than in life. Their tombs become places of pilgrimage, and their help is sought by women who wish to bear children, by those who wish healing or justice, or just for the sake of receiving some of their *baraka* – their spiritual power or blessing. Although Muslim scholars who allow such visitations to saints' tombs stress that God alone should be the object of prayer and worship, and that one may pray to God at a saint's tomb in order to incur His favor by virtue of the saint's *baraka*, in reality many people pray directly to the saints. They often make vows, promising that if the saint answers their petition, they will sacrifice an animal in his or her honor and share the food with the poor or with other devotees of the saint. Saint veneration is pervasive, and it is more important in the Horn of Africa than on the Swahili coast, but less significant in mainland Tanzania or Kenya.

Spirit possession cults

Spirit possession cults play an important part in East African religious life. Scholars have tended to see such beliefs and practices as pre-Islamic survivals, but the *zār* spirit possession cult, which originated in Ethiopia, was transmitted into Egypt as recently as the nineteenth century; the standard Islamic belief in *jinn*, who are popularly believed to cause human illnesses and inhabit desolate and dirty places as well as latrines and cemeteries, accords perfectly with ageless beliefs in spirits found in Africa and in other places as well. Trimingham observes that saint veneration predominated in regions where Islam has been long established, but contacts with spirits are more important in recently Islamized parts of East Africa (Trimingham 1952: 256–7).

Spirit possession ceremonies and traditional healing methods often acquire Islamic elements, such as use of Qur'anic verses or the names of God, and their practitioners believe that it is God who works through these ceremonies to heal and help the afflicted. Some of the spirits whose presence is sought in ceremonies like the *zār* or *ngoma ya pepo* are Muslim saints, so the distinction between the world of saints and the world of spirits is not so clear-cut. All over the Muslim world *ʿulamāʾ* and *imāms* perform healing and divination that utilize techniques that from the Western point of view are merely magical; the wearing of protective amulets bearing Qur'anic verses is nearly universal. However, the ʿ*ulamā*ʾ view magic (*siḥr* in Arabic) as something evil and effected through the mediation of *jinn*, whereas prophetic medicine and divination follow sound Islamic methods derived from the Prophet's own practice. The Ibāḍīs of Oman call divination and the writing of Islamic talismans ʿ*ilm al-sirr* – secret knowledge – and it is the subject of a very large portion of the manuscripts written by Muslim scholars in the Zanzibar National Archives, written by both Ibāḍī and Sunnī scholars.

Pre-Islamic practices associated with the agricultural cycle and life cycle are often retained, with some addition of Islamic elements. One traditional practice that many Swahili see as evidence of their Persian ancestry is the celebration of *Norūz*, the New Year. However, the Swahili celebration bears no resemblance to the Persian celebration, despite the use of the name, and appears to be similar to celebrations among the nomadic Somali that they call "the Pharaonic festival." Indeed, the Egyptian celebration of the "new year" in the spring, also called *Norūz* (*nawrūz*) and associated with fertility, is thought to derive from ancient Egyptian fertility rites.

Islamic reformism

Nineteenth-century reform movements in Africa were Ṣūfī-oriented movements seeking to eradicate what were perceived as heretical innovations (*bid*ʿ*a*) in Muslim practice. Scholars of the ʿAlawiyya order introduced new disciplines of Islamic learning on the East African coast in the late 1880s and criticized specific practices of the Qādiriyya Ṣūfī brotherhood such as the *dhikr* with *dufu* (drums) (Loimeier 2003: 249).

In early twentieth-century Zanzibar, scholars were aware of the ideas of the Egyptian scholar Muḥammad ʿAbduh (d. 1905), and two Ibāḍī leaders in Zanzibar founded the first Arabic newspaper there in 1911, with the specific goal of supporting and spreading ʿAbduh's reformism and pan-Islamist ideas. ʿAbduh called his reform Salafī, an adjective related to the word *salaf*, the pious Muslims of the first generation. But rather than wanting a fundamentalist revival of primitive Islam, ʿAbduh wanted to recapture the spirit of innovation and vitality that characterized the early Muslim community, in order to identify Islam with rationalism and reinterpret Islamic law according to its original motive and spirit, but to make it compatible with the modern age.

In the twentieth century, Islamic reformers in East Africa tended to oppose Sufism altogether. Shaykh al-Amīn ibn ʿAlī al-Mazrūʿī (Mazrui) of Mombasa (1890–1947), though a student of the most famous ʿAlawī *shaykh*s in Zanzibar, adopted a more anti-Ṣūfī point of view in the 1930s and became the major inspirer of Islamic reform in East Africa. He became Grand Qāḍī of Kenya, founded several reformist journals, and taught many subsequent reformist scholars (Pouwels 1987: 201–2). He was the first to introduce a distinct anti-*bid*ʿ*a* discourse in East Africa which was directed against Ṣūfī practices. He also stressed the importance of modern (not only Islamic) education that should extend to females, and he wrote texts in Swahili rather than Arabic. His most influential student, ʿAbd Allāh Ṣāliḥ al-Fārisī (Farsy, 1912–82), said that Mazrui "created a tremendous uproar by publishing newspapers and books vilifying forbidden matters and pagan practices" (Farsy 1989: 122). When Farsy became Chief Qāḍī of Kenya in 1968, he attacked scholars associated with the ʿAlawī and Qādirī orders.

ʿAbduh's closest disciple, Muḥammad Rashīd Riḍā (d. 1935), was more focused than his master on the need to defend Islam against Western criticisms. His zeal for Islamic political strength led him to admire the Wahhābīs of Saudi Arabia and the Muslim Brotherhood, founded in Egypt by his friend, Ḥasan al-Bannā, in 1928. Gradually the term Salafī has been co-opted by Muslims of a far sterner persuasion, who would be characterized by outsiders as Wahhābī or fundamentalist, but who reject such labels for themselves.

In recent decades, the political aspirations of Muslims in East Africa have given radical Salafism new strength, as recent Islamic reformism has taken on a political character. Like Islamist groups elsewhere, the leaders of recent reform movements have tended not to be trained as *ʿulamāʾ*, but in secular professions like medicine, engineering, and education, taking the title *ustādh* (teacher or professor) rather than *shaykh*. Unlike the modernist reformers of the late nineteenth and early twentieth centuries, who often took a cautious approach to *ḥadīth*, in recent decades reformers have tended to emphasize the importance of *ḥadīth* and of learning Arabic philology – emphases that are associated with fundamentalist rather than modernist approaches to reform. They also attack Sufism, saint veneration, and Islamic divinatory practices as un-Islamic superstition. Loimeier describes the recent reformists as rejecting all forms of spiritualism, favoring a process of gradual rationalization of religion and society, in which all forms of magic are rejected as superstition (Loimeier 2003: 254–5). Islamic reformism introduces new ideological cleavages and tensions among Muslims, though Loimeier observed that some politically oriented Islamic groups in the 1990s found it prudent to refrain from anti-Ṣūfī polemics in the interest of Muslim unity in the face of authoritarian secular regimes (Loimeier 2003: 255). In Kenya and Zanzibar, Muslim political parties in opposition to the government have emerged, leading to public disturbances and violent clashes with government troops. The formation of Muslim political parties is motivated mainly by Muslims' economic and political deprivation in countries where they are a minority. Nonetheless, the effectiveness of Islamic political movements has been hampered by rifts caused by interpersonal rivalries (Loimeier 2003: 259; Oded 2000: 171).

The rival Islamist governments of Saudi Arabia and Iran have tried to influence Islamic trends in East Africa, particularly in Kenya. While the Saudi government and Al Qaeda are both anti-Shīʿī, Iran promotes Sunnī–Shīʿī rapprochement and its own brand of Islamic activism in East Africa. Many young Kenyan Muslims admire Iran for promoting a politically relevant and modern form of Islamism. There have been a number of conversions of Sunnī Muslims to Shiʿism in Kenya (Oded 2000: 118), and this trend continues (personal communication with Shaykh Hammad Kassim Mazrui, Shaykh Ahmad Msallam, and Kadara Harith Swaleh, May 2007).

Al Qaeda's bombing of the American embassies in Nairobi and Dar Es Salaam in August 1998 sent shock waves throughout the region, especially when some local Muslims were implicated. Somalia in particular was seen as a haven for Al Qaeda. In May to June 2006, a group called the Islamic Courts Union (ICU) captured Mogadishu and much of Somalia with the intention of enforcing the *sharīʿa*. They began prohibiting cinemas, soccer, and the chewing of the narotic leaf *qāt*, leading to fears of a Taliban-style government in Somalia. The UN-recognized Transitional Government, which held out in northern Somalia, invited Ethiopian troops to intervene, and in January 2007 the USA bombed ICU positions. The power of the ICU is limited to a few towns on the Kenyan border.

Conclusion

Islam came first to the Horn of Africa very early in Islamic history, but Islamization nonetheless proceeded over the course of many centuries and is still ongoing. Yemen and the Hadramawt have played a major role in the development of Islam in the region, where the Shāfiʿī school predominates and great importance was traditionally attached to those who claimed descent from the Prophet. Although Omanis ruled parts of the Swahili coast and southern Somalia from the seventeenth century through the nineteenth century, and in Zanzibar until 1964, their sect, Ibadism, made no impact on the broader Swahili and African population. The first Sūfī order, the Qādiriyya, did not enter the region until the fifteenth and sixteenth centuries, and it was not until the nineteenth century that other orders proliferated. Pre-Islamic customs and beliefs pertaining to spirits persist and take on an Islamic guise. Since the mid-twentieth century the religious landscape of the region has changed through the impact of secular education, Islamic reformism, African nationalism, and political upheaval. The enormous prestige once held by the *ʿulamāʾ* and the *ashrāf* is largely a thing of the past.

References and further reading

Alpers, E. A. (2000) "East Central Africa," in N. Levtzion, R. L. Pouwels, eds., *The History of Islam in Africa*, Athens: Ohio University Press, 303–25.

Bang, A. K. (2003) *Sufis and Scholars of the Sea: Family Networks in East Africa, 1860–1925*, London, New York: RoutledgeCurzon.

Esmail, A. (1975) "Towards a History of Islam in East Africa," *Kenya Historical Review*, 3: 147–58.

Farsy, A. S. (1989) *The Shāfiʿī ʿulamāʾ of East Africa, ca. 1830–1970*, trans. R. L. Pouwels, Madison: University of Wisconsin African Studies Program.

Hoffman, V. J. (2006) "In His (Arab) Majesty's Service: The Career of a Somali Scholar and Diplomat in Nineteenth-Century Zanzibar," in R. Loimeier, R. Seesemann, eds., *The Global Worlds of the Swahili: Interfaces of Islam, Identity and Space in 19th and 20th-Century East Africa*, Berlin: LIT Verlag, 251–72.

Hollingsworth, L. W. (1929) *A Short History of the East Coast of Africa*, London: Macmillan.

Jamalilyl, A. B. (1999) "Penetration of Islam in Eastern Africa," *SwahiliOnline*, http://www.swahilionline.com/features/articles/islam/binsumet1.htm.

Kapteijns, L. (2000) "Ethiopia and the Horn of Africa," in N. Levtzion, R. L. Pouwels, eds., *The History of Islam in Africa*, Athens: Ohio University Press, 227–50.

Kassim, M. (1995) "Islam and Swahili Culture on the Banadir Coast," *Northeast African Studies*, 2: 21–37.

Kimyoro, J. L. (2000) "East African Coastal Historical Towns: Asiatic or African?" http://www.urban-research.net/consultants.jkimaryo.2000paper1.html.

Lewis, I. M. (1998) *Saints and Somalis: Popular Islam in a Clan-Based Society*, Lawrenceville, NJ and Asmara, Eritrea: The Red Sea Press.

Loimeier, R. (2003) "Patterns and Peculiarities of Islamic Reform in Africa," *Journal of Religion in Africa*, 33: 237–62.

Loimeier, R. and Seesemann, R., eds. (2006) *The Global Worlds of the Swahili: Interfaces of Islam, Identity and Space in 19th and 20th-Century East Africa*, Berlin: LIT Verlag,

Martin, B. G. (1975) "Arab Migrations to East Africa in Medieval Times," *International Journal of African Historical Studies*, 7: 367–90.

—— (1976) *Muslim Brotherhoods in Nineteenth-Century Africa*, Cambridge: Cambridge University Press.

Mukhtar, M. H. (1995) "Islam in Somali History: Fact and Fiction," in A. J. Ahmed, ed., *The Invention of Somalia*, Lawrenceville, NJ: The Red Sea Press, 1–27.

Nimtz, A. H. (1980) *Islam and Politics in East Africa: The Ṣūfī Order in Tanzania*, Minneapolis: University of Minnesota Press.

Oded, A. (2000) *Islam and Politics in Kenya*, Boulder, CO and London: Lynne Rienner.

Pouwels, R. L. (1978a) "The Medieval Foundations of East African Islam, 1," *The International Journal of African Historical Studies*, 11: 201–26.

—— (1978b) "The Medieval Foundations of East African Islam, 2," *The International Journal of African Historical Studies*, 11: 393–409.

—— (1987) *Horn and Crescent: Cultural Change and Traditional Islam on the East African Coast, 800–1900*, Cambridge: Cambridge University Press.

—— (2000) "The East African Coast, c. 780 to 1900 C.E.," in N. Levtzion, R. L. Pouwels, eds., *The History of Islam in Africa*, Athens: Ohio University Press, 251–71.

—— (2002) "Eastern Africa and the Indian Ocean to 1800: Reviewing Relations in Historical Perspective," *The International Journal of African Historical Studies*, 35: 385–425.

Risso, P. (1986) *Oman and Muscat: An Early Modern History*, London and Sydney: Croom Helm.

Sperling, D. C. (2000) "The Coastal Hinterland and Interior of East Africa," in N. Levtzion, R. L. Pouwels, eds., *The History of Islam in Africa*, Athens: Ohio University Press, 273–302.

Trimingham, J. S. (1952) *Islam in Ethiopia*, London: Oxford University Press.

—— (1964) *Islam in East Africa*, Oxford: Oxford University Press.

4

TURKEY

Markus Dressler

Anyone embarking on writing a history of Turkey with a focus on Islam faces a cluster of methodological challenges. The ambitious task is to write history without succumbing too greatly to the paradigmatic conceptual knowledge of our modern age, which is shaped by categories like nation, state, and religion – categories which do not always do justice to pre-modern realities.

Ottoman Turks have only rather recently – at the turn of the twentieth century – begun to imagine themselves as a Turkish nation. For most of the six centuries of Ottoman rule, Turkish speakers were in a minority position in the large empire. Today, Turkey's official language is Turkish, and it is promoted by the state as a symbol of Turkish identity and unity. The strong symbolic character of knowledge renders it at the same time an issue of contestation, articulated, for example, in the Kurdish minority's demand for recognition of its language and identity.

Anatolia and eastern Thrace historically have been home to a profusion of religious and ethnic groups. The fact that the Republic of Turkey adopted a coercively inclusive nationalism as its state ideology, which was in its own terms relatively successful with regard to safeguarding its territory, should not make us forget the non-Turkish, and non-Muslim voices without which neither pre-modern nor modern Turkish history could be legitimately told. The Ottoman openness to Jewish communities fleeing from Christian persecution is as much part of the Turkish legacy as the Young Turks' genocidal politics against the Armenians, and the Republic's inability to quell the Kurdish nationalist insurgency in the Southeast. On the other side, the ethnic and religious minorities of Turkey should not be reduced to mere victims devoid of agency. Nuanced analysis of the specific and multi-layered contexts of politics of discrimination and subversion, assimilation and separatism, terror from above and from below, ought to be preferred to simplistic black and white schemata. This said, however, the particular hegemonies expressed in an imbalance of power between state and subjects, majority and minorities, has to be taken into account.

Historiography is always shaped by the present from which it is approached, and neither Turkish nor Muslim Turkish history can be convincingly told without taking seriously discursive shifts in time, and without considering the voices from the margins, which are sometimes more telling about the constitutive elements of the mainstream than the voices from the centre. These elements have to be considered when putting the focus on Islam. As with all religious traditions, Islam – while evolving around a core narrative that makes people understand themselves as Muslim – has to be seen as a dynamic plural tradition that defies essentialist renditions. To illustrate

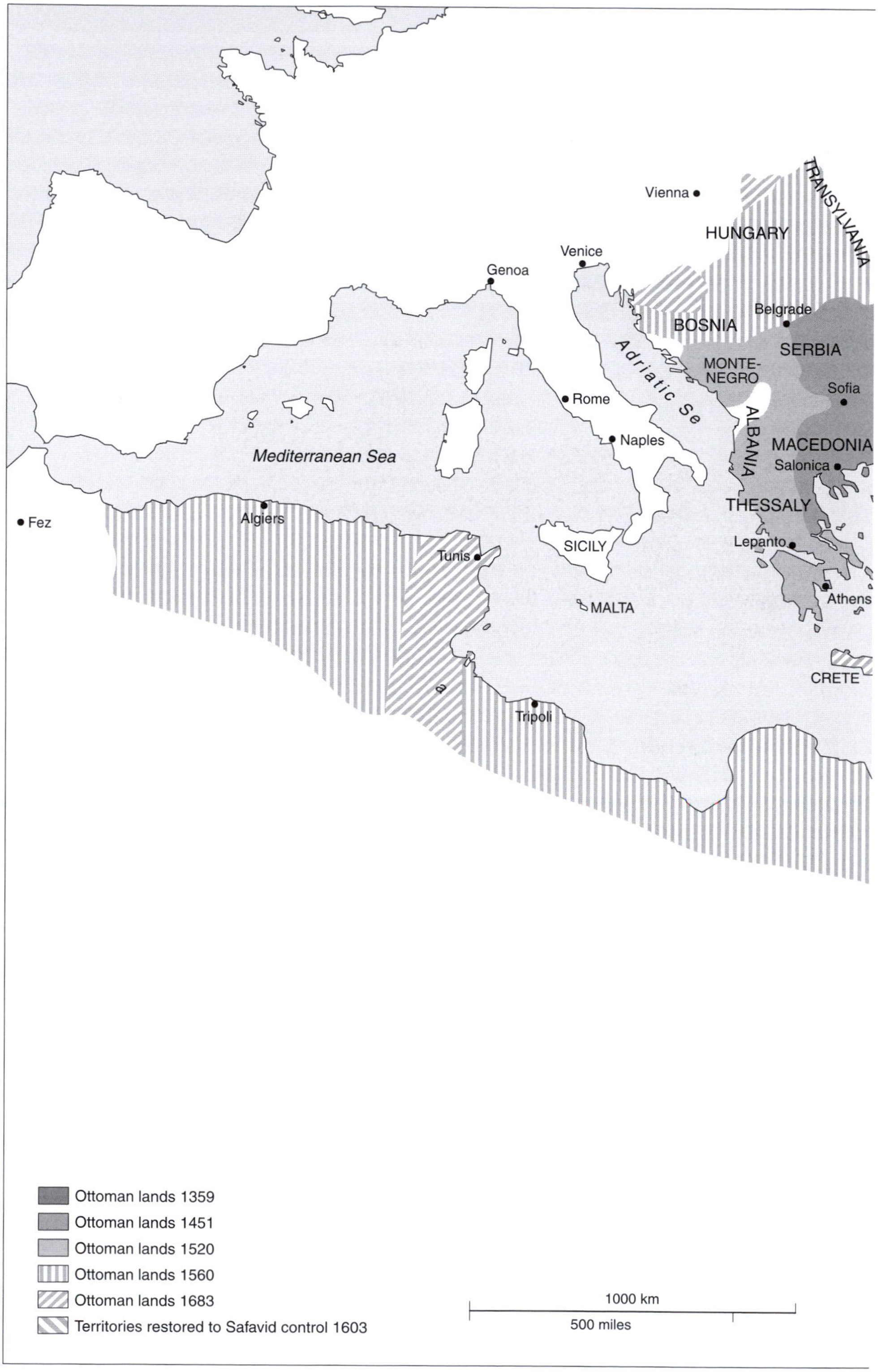

Map 4 Ottoman empire.

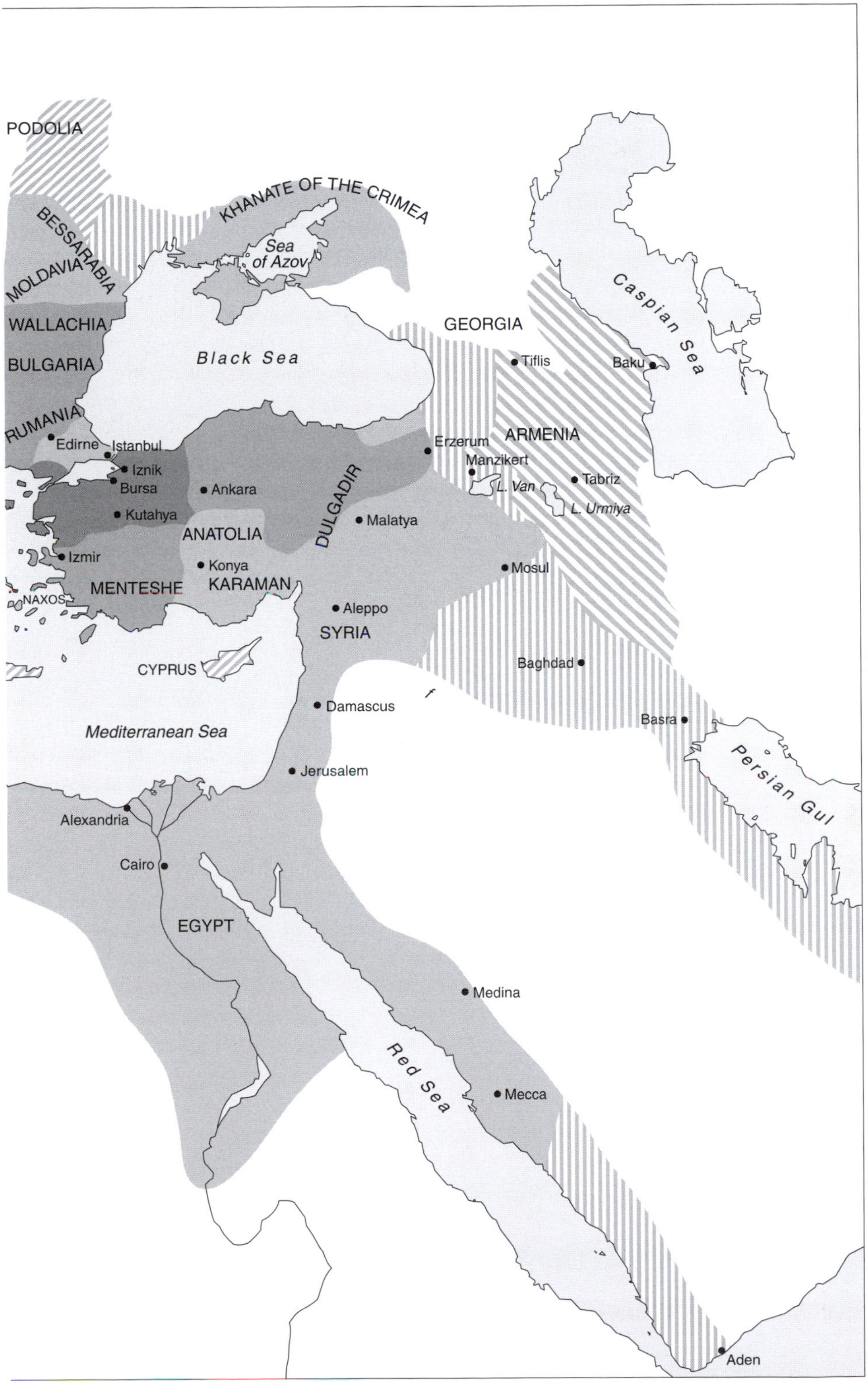

PODOLIA
KHANATE OF THE CRIMEA
BESSARABIA
MOLDAVIA
Sea of Azov
WALLACHIA
BULGARIA
Black Sea
GEORGIA
Tiflis
Baku
Caspian Sea
RUMANIA
Edirne
Istanbul
Iznik
Bursa
Ankara
Kutahya
ANATOLIA
DULGADIR
Erzerum
ARMENIA
Manzikert
Tabriz
L. Van
L. Urmiya
Malatya
Izmir
Konya
KARAMAN
MENTESHE
NAXOS
Mosul
Aleppo
SYRIA
CYPRUS
Baghdad
Damascus
Basra
Mediterranean Sea
Jerusalem
Persian Gul
Alexandria
Cairo
EGYPT
Medina
Red Sea
Mecca
Aden

this point, it is helpful to reflect on the popular forms of Islam espoused by most parts of the rural Anatolian populations of Seljuk and early Ottoman times. This Islam shared in its basic orientation much of the charismatic and mystical worldview and ethos of Turkish Sufism, traces of which survive today. However, since Islamic mainstream in Ottoman and Republican times took a road that aligned the Turkish Muslim world much stronger with Sunnī orthodoxy, more syncretistic and less legalist interpretations of Islam have often been discredited. The Islam espoused by the early Ottomans would be regarded by many mainstream Muslims today as rather heterodox. Religious orthodoxy changes over time.

Another difficulty is to do justice to the internal dynamics of Ottoman-Turkish history without succumbing to Eurocentric views, as characteristic of much of traditional Orientalist scholarship. Too often, Ottoman history has been constructed rather simplistically as a story of a decline that lasted three-and-a-half centuries between a perceived apex in the mid-sixteenth century and the final collapse of the Ottoman empire after World War I, out of which the secular Republic of Turkey emerged in 1923 like a phoenix rising out of the ashes. Such a reading, focusing firstly on military history and secondly on economic and scientific development, takes the Western European experience as its exclusive point of comparison, and, as recent scholarship convincingly shows, does not do justice to the complexities of Turkish history. However, the decline paradigm works well with Turkey's master narrative of the Kemalist Revolution since it legitimates radical reform. The recent development of a moderate Islamic political elite apparently much more committed to Western-style political liberalism than its secularist political rivals challenges such biased views and asks for a readjustment of simplifying dichotomous notions that pit the Secular-Western-Modern against the Islamic-Oriental-Traditional.

Rum-Seljuk empire (1077–1302)

The Seljuks were the first Turks to establish a lasting Turkish political rule and presence in Anatolia. Until the Seljuk invasion, Anatolia had been under Byzantine control and comprised the economically most prosperous parts of the East Roman empire. The Seljuks, an Oghuz Turkish tribal confederation that originated from the steppes of Central Asia and had converted to Islam since the tenth century, had been raiding Byzantine territory ever since the early eleventh century. After a decisive victory over Byzantine forces at Malazgirt (1071), they began to settle in Anatolian lands, which they called *Rūm* ("Roman"). The Seljuk conducted their initial offences and raids through their *ghāzī* warriors, mainly tribally organized bands who specialized in borderland warfare that promised booty in the name of the ideals of *ghazā* (military conquest) and *jihād*, i.e., the virtuous practice of extending the abode of Islam. Only after the initial raids orchestrated by the *ghāzī*s ("raiders") would the regular Seljuk armies follow and secure more permanent dominance if deemed worthwhile. This basic pattern of raiding and subsequent establishment of a more organized order remained a basic characteristic of Turkish conquest until well into Ottoman times. It reflects a social distinction between, on the one hand, a nomadic Turcoman culture led by *ghāzī* chieftains and dervishes – who promote *jihād* and conversion in the name of an ecstatic, charismatic, and inclusive Islam with pre-Islamic elements, well equipped to absorb local traditions – and, on the other hand, an elite close to the dynastic centre of power, increasingly settled, influenced by Persian language and culture and closer to the egalitarian and legalist Sunnī Islam espoused by the *madrasa*s. While this is an ideal typical distinction and the boundaries between the two types certainly are not always clear-cut, the dynamic tension between charismatic *ghazā* ethos and legalist bureaucratic control, which erupted periodically in violent conflict, remained characteristic of the dynamics of Turkish expansion until the late sixteenth century.

With the Seljuk conquest of Nicaea (today Iznik) roughly a decade after Malazgirt and the establishment of Konya as capital of Seljuk rule in Anatolia half a century later, the basis for a Turkish Anatolian civilization was created, and processes of displacement, Turkification as well as Islamization of the majority Greek population began and would continue over the following centuries.

The early thirteenth century was economically and culturally the most prosperous period of the Rum-Seljuk empire. Sultan ʿAlāʾ al-Dīn Kay Qubādh (r. 1220–37) was a promoter of the arts and the religious sciences and established Konya as a major centre of Islamic learning. To this day, architectonic and literary masterpieces remind us of the glory of Seljuk rule. Among the most famous witnesses of this time we find Jalāl al-Dīn Rūmī (d. 1273), the author of an amazing work of mystical poetry (the *Mathnawī* being his masterpiece). The Ṣūfī order of the Mevleviye, known in the West as the order of the "Whirling Dervishes," traces its roots back to him. The life story of scholars such as Rūmī, whose family had moved to Khurasan fleeing the approaching Mongol hords, reflects the political turbulence of the time, which contributed to the blooming of the Rum-Seljuk empire – many Turkish and Persian scholars and artists were among the refugees fleeing from the destruction that had swept over Persia.

The two centuries of Rum-Seljuk dominance in central Anatolia were rather tumultuous. In the twelfth century, military competition with the Byzantines, and occasionally Crusaders, as well as fierce internal rivalry between Seljuk principalities, meant constant challenge to Seljuk authority. In the late twelfth and early thirteenth centuries, Southeast Anatolia witnessed a series of battles first between the Seljuks and the Ayyubids, then between Seljuks and the Khwarazmians, who had fled Khwarazm from the Mongols and were in search of new territories westwards. The consequences of warfare, as well as the constant influx of new Turkish and Persian immigrants, challenged the social and economic order. The rapid increase of the rural population brought Turcoman and Iranian nomads, who needed extensive lands for pasturing, into conflict with the local farmers. Due to the extensive military expenses Konya raised taxes. Internal disquiet broke out in 1240, when the Bābāʾī movement, named after a certain Bābā Ilyās, orchestrated a revolt that spread over Southeast and Central Anatolia and developed into a serious threat to Seljuk authority. Contemporary chroniclers describe the revolt, which appears to have been motivated by the deteriorating socio-economic situation, as extremely ferocious with devastating effects on the involved areas. The Seljuk Sultan Kay Khusraw II (r. 1237–46) was able to quell the uprisings, but the harm done by internal strife further weakened the battered empire. After a severe military defeat at Köşe Dağ (1243), the Rum-Seljuk empire became a client state of the Mongols. The empire was subsequently integrated into Mongol administration, and finally dismantled around the turn of the thirteenth century.

In early thirteenth-century Anatolia, emigration from the East had rendered the country into a medley of diverse cultures, languages, and beliefs. It can be assumed that in rural areas away from scripturalist religious discourse religious boundaries were somewhat fluid. As for the Turcoman immigrants, although already nominally converted to Islam, they still upheld features of pre-Islamic Turkish traditions. Rural, mostly illiterate areas were often only superficially familiar with the urban Muslim culture of a city like Konya, where Persian was the language of the arts and the elite, and Arabic the language of religion. The scripture and law-centered Islam of the *madrasa* as embraced by the Seljuk elite was alien to the majority of the people, many of whom had joined the Islamic tradition only relatively recently. Popular, rural Islamic religiosity of this time period was influenced by *ghazā* ethos and various anti-legalist Ṣūfī traditions, and it had a strong charismatic tone expressed, for example, in its allegiance to the Turkmen holy men venerated as *bābā*s. The Bābā'ī movement is an early Anatolian manifestation of a state-critical rural ethos from which we can track traces to the early Bektaşi milieu and then to the Kızılbaş movement that crystallized in the late fifteenth century.

The demographic, socio-economic, and political turbulences between the Mongol invasion and the formation and consolidation of Ottoman rule, i.e., roughly the time from the mid-thirteenth to the mid-sixteenth centuries, facilitated the formation of powerful Ṣūfī orders, which developed a net of trans-local allegiances and hierarchies. The development of Islamic networks allowed for accumulation of considerable political influence outside the direct control of the central power and carried a potential of resistance that was periodically activated in regional rebellions.

The Ottomans (1300–1923)

Beginnings: Ghazā *ethos and charismatic Sufism*

At the beginning of the fourteenth century, one of the competing semi-nomadic clans and principalities which inherited the post-Seljuk territory of Anatolia began to play a more dominant role. Located at the eastern borderlands of the Byzantines (area of modern Eskişehir), this clan would soon become known under the name of its chieftain Osman (d. 1326).

Hagiographic traditions relate Osman to saintly figures in the vicinity of the Bābā'ī movement and the charismatic milieu of Turkish dervish Islam. In Ottoman chronicles, these dervishes appear under names such as Abdal, Kalender, and Rum Erenleri, currents that would by the sixteenth century merge into the Bektaşi Ṣūfī tradition. *Ghazā* was the raison d'être of the early Ottoman emirate, and the Ottomans relied on the *ghāzī*s and dervishes for support of their military conquest. The dervishes played an important role as cultural mediators to the populations of newly conquered areas, predominantly in the Balkans. It is often argued that their non-formalistic and inclusive faith eased conversion to Islam. The fact that Hacı Bektaş, the namesake of the Bektaşi order, became the patron saint of the Ottoman Janissary army pays tribute to the early connection of the Ottomans with the charismatic Turkish Ṣūfī tradition.

By the end of the fourteenth century the Ottomans had incorporated all Turcoman principalities of Central and Western Anatolia into their domains and made significant gains in the Balkans.

In the early fifteenth century the growth period was interrupted by a new phase of extreme political turmoil and anarchy following yet another Mongol attack and succession wars between competing aspirants to the throne. When Mehmet I (r. 1403–21) emerged as new Ottoman Sultan, his rule would mark the beginning of a gradual shift in the Ottomans' religious self-understanding and their relation to Islam. Mehmet was leaning more towards the scholarly and sober Islam of the Sunnī mainstream than to the ecstatic and charismatic Islam of the *ghāzī*s and nonconformist Ṣūfīs. The final defeat of the Byzantines and the conquest of Constantinople in 1453 as well as further acquisitions in the Balkans, Anatolia, the Levant, Mesopotamia, North Africa, and the Hijaz – including the holy cities Mecca and Medina in 1517 – enhanced the increasingly imperial aspirations of the Ottoman dynasty. This imperial habitus was fuelled not only by the control over Islam's holy sides, which granted them Islamic legitimacy, but also by the Ottomans' self-perception as heirs of the East Roman empire.

For logistical reasons, the breathtaking expansion of the Ottoman empire could not continue endlessly. A more bureaucratic mode of state organization was developed and reached its first apex in the mid-sixteenth century. Although the Ottomans continued to rely on the *ghāzī*s in their borderlands and used them as storm troops for their military operations, the importance of *ghazā* as a legitimation for the empire decreased. Loyalty to the *devlet-i al-i Osman* ("the domains and rule of the House of Osman") was promoted as a major value in itself. In turn it was the responsibility of the Ottomans to secure order in the existing domains. The shift in legitimation reflects changing socio-economic realities, namely the move to a sedentary culture and reliance on a peasant economy focused on farming and trade instead of raiding. At the same time the Ottomans increased their sponsorship of Islamic institutions of learning. Specialists in Islamic jurisprudence became a cornerstone of the Ottoman state organization and assumed crucial positions within the growing bureaucracy of a centralizing state. The beginnings of this rationalization of rule can be traced back to the reign of Murat I (r. 1360–89), who was the first to systematically attract experienced administrators as well as Muslim scholars and judges from neighboring countries with the aim of boosting the Islamic legitimacy of the empire. All of these factors contributed to a gradual reorientation towards legalist Sunnism that was, however, not completed until the second part of the reign of Süleyman I (r. 1520–66).

Military and religious centralization

It is often argued that the key to Ottoman success was the establishment of a centralist state organization that was based on loyal slave elites and the sultan's unmediated sovereignty. The centralized organization of provincial administrative units secured the flow of revenues from the provinces to Istanbul. Murat I established the *devşirme* system, the levy of boys from non-Muslim subjects. As slaves of the sultan, they underwent thorough training in either administrative or military skills and formed the backbone of the ruling elite and the new Janissary army, which was, unlike the *ghāzī* bands, a standing army loyal to the sultan alone. The new system was in part motivated by the need to create a military elite independent of the *ghāzī* warlords, who were outside direct administrative control – a position that enabled them to periodically challenge the sultan's power. The Janissaries were infantry forces complementing the *sipahi*, cavalry officers who were bestowed with the collection of taxes (*timar*s) for an allocated area, which they were in turn obliged to protect. Initially, the Janissaries were not allowed to marry and the *timar*s could not be inherited, a practice that

Figure 2 Süleymaniyye interior, Istanbul, Turkey, 1550–57. Christian and Muslim builders were employed to raise the domes and reinforcing half-domes of the Süleymaniyye mosque that was supported by four massive piers and giant columns.

Source: Reproduced by kind permission of Michael Greenhalgh

prevented division of their loyalty. To the detriment of the *ghāzīs*, the *sipahi* and Janissary became the cornerstones of the military system of the Ottoman empire. The effective centralization of the main military forces proved a strong asset in keeping at bay the political ambitions of the tribal forces of the borderlands.

The reorganization of the Ottomans' military forces went hand in hand with the differentiation of Ottoman society in *askeri* and *reaya*, that is a ruling and a subject class. The *askeri* were mainly slaves who were trained as military and administrative elites. The *ʿulamāʾ* were also part of the *askeri* and virtually the only class of non-slaves among the ruling elite. In time, the *ʿulamāʾ* became more and more centralized and closely incorporated into the state's administrative body. From the sixteenth century onwards they were led by the *shaykh al-Islām*. The position of the *shaykh al-Islām* had originally been created by Murat II (r. 1421–44) as that of a head *muftī* (responsible for issuing legal recommendations, *fatwās*). In the course of the sixteenth century, with the increasingly Sunnī-Islamic character of the empire, the significance of the position increased. The *shaykh al-Islām* acquired the right to appoint *qāḍī*s (judges) and became the overseer of the entire judicial administration. The judicial system was closely linked with the religious educational institutions, the *madrasas*, where the jurists received their training. Both the educational and judicial systems were organized through a top-down hierarchy with the *shaykh al-Islām* at its head. Appointed and dependent on the sultan, the *shaykh al-Islām* was the only authority with the right to depose the sultan. His position, following the sultan, was only rivalled by that of the Grand Vizier.

Political unrest and the consolidation of Sunnī orthodoxy

For the establishment of Sunnī Islam as orthodoxy, reflected in the growth in numbers of *madrasa* students and comparatively less support for Ṣūfī orders, the sixteenth century was decisive. While the Ottomans started out as a semi-nomadic *ghazā* clan, the Sultans of the huge Ottoman empire two centuries later re-imagined themselves as guarantors of stability and lawful rule. This changing ethos and legitimacy of Ottoman rule between the fourteenth and sixteenth centuries is aptly captured in the epithets of the Ottoman Sultans from Bayezit "the Thunderbolt" (r. 1389–1402) and Mehmet "the Conqueror" (r. 1451–81) to Süleyman "the Lawgiver" (r. 1520–66).

Of lasting impact with regard to the future development of Islam in Turkey were the so-called Kızılbaş uprisings in the early sixteenth century. Kızılbaş (lit. redhead) was the name for the lower ranks of the Safawī Ṣūfī order, its mainly Turcoman adherents in Anatolia and Iran who provided the military force of the emerging Safavid empire. The attraction of the Anatolian Kızılbaş to the Safawīs was fuelled by economic frustrations and political resentments against the Ottomans. During a land reform under Mehmet II (r. 1451–81), many Turkmen settlements and pious foundations had been annexed by the central state. Although these reforms where taken back by Bayezit II (r. 1481–1512), strong animosities against the Ottomans remained, especially among the increasingly marginalized dervishes and *ghāzī*s of the Anatolian periphery. The Kızılbaş put their hopes in the Safawī Ismāʿīl, in whom they saw a political and religious redeemer (*mahdī*) with divine qualities. In 1501, Ismāʿīl established the Safavid state in Iran and declared himself Shāh. Inspired by their messianic hopes in Shāh Ismāʿīl, Anatolian Kızılbaş groups initiated a series of local uprisings against Ottoman authority between 1511 and 1529. However, the Ottomans were able to suppress these uprisings and toughened their rule in the respective areas. They defeated the Safavids several times and forced them to the peace treaty of Amasya in 1555, which permanently established the Turkish–Iranian borders.

The religious ethos of the Kızılbaş defied *sharīʿa* law, expecting salvation instead through the guidance of holy men. Shāh Ismāʿīl had been raised among the Turcoman Kızılbaş and shared their values and beliefs. He formerly declared Twelver Shiʿism the official religion of the Safavid state, but his interpretation of Shiʿism was informed by the syncretism of the borderlands, where pre-Islamic Turkish and Islamic elements had undergone a powerful symbiosis. He saw himself as the ultimate authority of the religion, as divine incarnation of ʿAlī. Although the subsequent Shāhs of Persia gradually redirected the course to a more mainstream interpretation of Shiʿism, the Anatolian Kızılbaş, who got, due to the political developments, separated from their Safawī *pīr*s (principals of a Ṣūfī order), maintained their basic understandings of Shīʿī mythology as they had adopted it in this time period. While some of the Kızılbaş over time assimilated into mainstream Sunnism, others upheld their traditions and were never totally integrated into Ottoman society. The contemporary Alevis are their heirs, still upholding the *buyruk* manuals – manuscripts with ritual instructions, Ṣūfī concepts, and mythology revolving around ʿAlī, which the Kızılbaş had received from the Safavids – as important religious texts.

The Kızılbaş uprisings and the later series of regional unrest generally known as Celālī rebellions (1593–1610) reflect a serious alienation of the Ottomans from their roots in the charismatic non-conformist dervish and *ghāzī* milieu. Gradually, the Ottomans distanced themselves from the less conformist Ṣūfī orders and dervish groups of the rural borderlands who had an ambiguous relation to scripturalist and legalist interpretations of Islam and who remained adverse to the centralist authority of a distant and impersonal state bureaucracy. On the other side, the Ottomans maintained their support for the more urbanite and Sunnī Ṣūfī orders like the Mevlevis and from the seventeenth century onwards also the Nakşibendis, whose members began to figure prominently among the *ʿulamāʾ*. The revivalist Kadızādeli movement of the seventeenth century, which agitated against allegedly non-Islamic innovations – many of which associated with popular Sufism – further helped to marginalize practices of Islam held at doubt from a legalist position. Nevertheless, until today many of the popular Turkish Islamic practices survive, though often pejoratively labelled remnants of a superstitious age or referred to in terms of culture rather than religion – an apologetic position reflecting a modernist and essentialist reading of Islam that relegates the plurality of Islamic practices and beliefs to the realm of culture.

The streamlining of the religious discourse of the empire marks a turning point in the legitimization of Ottoman rule. In its early phase, Ottoman authority had been grounded in *ghazā* and dynastic-genealogical claims enriched with features of the Iranian kingship tradition, which situated the sultan cosmologically as the shadow of God on earth. Without totally forsaking these aspects, there was now a strong emphasis on legitimation through rational and religious legalism, which weakened in particular the *ghāzī* component.

Between the late sixteenth and early eighteenth centuries, the foreign policy of the empire shifted further from expansion to maintenance of existing borders, accompanied by an enlargement of the legal system. Contradicting the paradigm of the decline of the Ottoman Empire after the sixteenth century, we observe in this period increased diplomatic and international trade activities as well as a flourishing in cultural and artistic production – for example in the short but influential Tulip Era (1718–30).

Already in the late sixteenth century, a new phase of decentralization and opening of the strict hierarchies led to a gradual breach of the *askeri–reaya* distinction. This had far-reaching consequences. The elites of the empire became free men, and ordinary subjects could now acquire and accumulate property. Military, administrative, and religious offices gradually turned into factual birthrights, and a new class of province notables emerged.

The decentralization of state rule led to a decline in tax revenues and a distribution of economic and political power to the disadvantage of the sultan. It also allowed for the formation of religious, military, and administrative aristocracies, who are generally given the major blame for the state's increasing economic stagnation and the loss of its military superiority vis-à-vis its European foes. Between the seventeenth and eighteenth centuries, military victories and defeats alternated regularly. However, by the late eighteenth century, after major military setbacks against the Russians in the Crimea and Romania, the decreasing military power of the empire was so obvious that voices urging reforms became louder. Reform and transformation became major topics in the eighteenth and increasingly so in the nineteenth century. In the nineteenth century, separatist movements spurred by growing national sentiments emerged first in Greece and in the Balkans, then also in the Arab parts of the empire, most prominently Egypt. These political challenges became ever more difficult to master and further increased the need for reform.

Modernization

Efforts to modernize the Ottoman empire began in the late eighteenth century with first attempts to reform the military. In 1826, Sultan Mahmut II (r. 1808–39) created a new, modern army and crashed the Janissary corps, which were seen as inefficient, corrupt, and a major obstacle to reform. The connection of the Bektaşis with the Janissaries proved fateful for the former, and the Bektaşi order was outlawed. Leading Bektaşis were executed or fled to Albania, and Bektaşi lodges and premises were assigned to state-loyal orders, mostly Nakşibendi sheikhs. However, by the nineteenth century, the Bektaşi order had regained semi-official recognition.

Abdülmecit I (r. 1839–1861) broadened the scope of the modernization project. In the Tanzimat ("Regulations") decrees, the name by which this reform period became known, the people of the Ottoman empire were granted citizen rights, and declared equal by law irrespective of religious affiliation. These important changes were to a strong degree concessions to the rising political demands of non-Muslim minorities and European pressures. Gradually, secular educational and legal institutions were built, challenging the traditional supremacy of their Islamic counterparts.

Figure 3 Dolmabahçe Palace, Istanbul, Turkey, 1853. This building, which is European in appearance but Turkish in plan, was the principal administrative building in the new palace complex of the still vast and vibrant Ottoman empire.

Source: Photographer Özgür Basak Alkan, 2003, Courtesy of the Aga Khan Visual Archive, MIT

The ʿ*ulamāʾ* were unable to prevent the gradual disestablishment of Islam. ʿ*Ulamāʾ* ranks had by the early eighteenth century become more or less hereditary, reflecting the broader changes from a merit-based to an aristocratic political order. Their privileges as a religious class were challenged by the beginning secularization of the Ottoman empire in the nineteenth century, and it is thus not surprising that many of them opposed the reforms. The *madrasa* system itself, where the ʿ*ulamāʾ* were trained, was overpopulated, antiquated in its structures and contents, and politically conservative.

The cooptation of the ʿ*ulamāʾ* by the state had secured their social status, but weakened their credibility and religious authority. Ṣūfī sheikhs, not to the same extent dependent on state appointments and in closer contact with the ordinary people, were often deemed more credible authorities. It would, however, be an undue simplification to present *madrasa* Islam and *ṭarīqa* Islam as antagonistic counter-poles. There always were ʿ*ulamāʾ* with Ṣūfī leanings or affiliations. Although the Ṣūfī orders were relatively more independent from the state than the state-employed ʿ*ulamāʾ*, the Ottomans were still trying to co-opt the Ṣūfī orders by making them dependent on granted foundations (*awqāf*). The integration of the Ṣūfī orders into the state bureaucracy reached a new height in 1866, when a Ṣūfī *shaykh* council (*meclis-i meşayih*), subordinated to the *shaykh al-Islām*'s office, was created aiming at further-reaching control of the orders' activities.

Besides the Ṣūfī orders of the Mevlevi and Bektaşi dervishes, which both emerged from Anatolia, the Nakşibendi Ṣūfī order made inroads into Anatolia in the early fifteenth century, and soon developed good terms with the Ottoman sultans. Since the seventeenth century, the Nakşibendis of the empire were dominated by its Mujaddidī and then Mujaddidī-Khālidī branches, which promote a state and law-centred approach to Islam and which historically showed strong interest in politics. This put them at times in conflict with the Mevlevis, who had since the seventeenth century been the favored order of the Palace, as well as with the Bektaşis. However, one should not imagine impenetrable boundaries between these traditions, and there are plenty of Ṣūfīs with double or triple *ṭarīqa* affiliations deliberately bridging Ṣūfī lineages.

Muslim intellectuals prominently participated in the modernization debate. In the Ottoman empire it was Namik Kemal (1840–88) who introduced ideas of Islamically grounded constitutionalism and republicanism. Iran-born Jamāl al-Dīn al-Afghānī (1838–97) was dedicated to a pan-Islamic nationalism as a response to European imperialism. Such modernist Muslim intellectuals held a mediating position between the traditionalist ʿ*ulamāʾ* and the more radical secular modernizers who were the product of the military schools and European enlightenment thought. The later strata would eventually seize power through the Young Turk coup in 1908, when a group of high-ranking officers, who had been organized in the secretive Committee of Union and Progress, forced Sultan Abdülhamid II (r. 1876–1909) to re-establish the constitution of 1876, which he had shelved in 1878. The Young Turks remained in power until the end of World War I, in which they sided with the Germans in what proved to be a fateful political mistake. They furthered the disestablishment of Islam and curtailed the Sultan's power. Initially they set out to reorient the ideological foundation of the empire from Ottomanism to a republican Turkish nationalism, i.e., from an ideology based on loyalty to the Sultan towards an ideology based on the sovereignty of the people. Above all, the minorities among the Ottoman subjects had placed great hopes in the new regime, expecting an increase in political and religious freedom after the authoritarian reign of Abdülhamid, who had halted the Tanzimat period. However, they were soon to be disappointed. Military setbacks on the Balkans (1912/13) and the masses of Balkan Muslim refugees pouring into Istanbul led to increasing animosities particularly against the Christian minorities, who were more and more suspected of sympathizing with, if not actively supporting, the enemy – and some certainly did so. When the Young Turks established a one-party dictatorship in 1913, the liberal idea of an Ottoman civil society was sacrificed for the Pan-Turkist idea of an ethnically homogeneous Turkish Muslim nation. The defeat against the Russians at Sarıkarmış in January of 1915, supported by Armenians from outside as well as to a lesser extent inside the empire, contributed to the Young Turks' decision to rid itself of the "Armenian problem". The tragic events that followed, the killings and deportations of most of Anatolia's Armenian population arguably constituted the first genocide of the twentieth century, leading to the death of more than a million Armenians and purportedly several hundred thousand Assyrians, who were also affected by the Young Turks' politics of ethno-religious cleansing.

The defeat in the Great War discredited the Young Turk regime, and their leaders fled the country in fear of being held accountable for war crimes. Temporarily, the old regime was able to regain authority, but the Peace Treaty of Sèvres in 1920 greatly reduced the remaining territory of the Ottoman empire and seriously infringed the Sultan's authority in the remaining domains. Leading army generals under the guidance of Mustafa Kemal (1881–1938), the later Atatürk ("Father of the Turks"), defied the Sultan's command and began to organize a National Liberation movement, which organized the War of Independence (1919–22). Led against the will of the Sultan-caliph, it was fought in the name of Muslim–Turkish nationalism. Its goal was to re-establish the sovereignty of the empire and to liberate the caliphate from foreign control. After a decisive military victory against occupying Greek forces in 1922, a sovereign Republic of Turkey could be established in 1923, internationally recognized in the Treaty of Lausanne (1923).

Under the authoritarian leadership of Kemal Atatürk as president from 1923 until his death in 1938, Turkey continued on its modernization path. While the constitution of 1923 still defined Islam as the state religion, Kemal Atatürk continued to push further secularization. Whereas the majority of the Ṣūfī orders, like most province notables and the conservative middle class, had supported the War of Independence, the abolishment of the caliphate in 1924 led to severe criticism and even open revolt. The Sheikh Said rebellion, led by a Kurdish Nakşibendi sheikh, broke out in the spring of 1925 in Southeast Anatolia. It was directed against the dismantling of Islamic institutions, but also asserted the voice of Kurdish nationalism and regional autonomy in the face of the centralist politics of the new regime, which aimed at the Turkification of the Kurds – now the largest ethnic minority. In the state-centred Turkish perspective, the Sheikh Said uprising of 1925 still serves as paradigmatic example of reactionary religious resistance against the new secular republican order.

Faced with increasing opposition, Mustafa Kemal used the Sheikh Said rebellion as a pretext to toughen authoritarian rule, and to criminalize political opposition. Especially the powerful Ṣūfī networks were now seen as a threat to modernization and the new republican order, and in the fall of 1925 the Ṣūfī lodges were closed down and Ṣūfī titles, garment, and practices outlawed. In a time period in which the new course of the Republic was still in the process of formation, the secularization of Turkey had its own dynamic in which resistance encouraged even tougher authoritarian measures. While opposition rose from very different parts of society, allegiance to the caliphate was its common rally cry, at least in the early years of the Republic. The ruling elite, however, was committed to push as hard as necessary for the creation of a secular and modern nation-state that was to be politically independent but envisioned in its social, political, and cultural style as radically "Western". Until 1950, Turkish politics were, notwithstanding brief unsuccessful periods of democratic experiments, defined by the one-party rule of the Republican People's Party, grounded in Kemalism, a set of ideological principles named after Kemal Atatürk. Kemalism aimed at creating a homogeneous nation orchestrated by a centralist, republican, and laicist state. Despite its outwardly secular appearance, the Turkish nation was implicitly understood as Sunnī Muslim. The practical consequence has been a criminalization of identities diverging from the Sunnī-Turkish norm, affecting groups who have strong non-Turkish ethnic identities (such as the Kurds – roughly 20 percent of the population), and/or non-Sunnī Muslim religious identities (as espoused predominantly by the Alevis – approximately 15 to 20 percent of the population).

Turkish nationalism, laicism, and Islam: continuing contestations

Republican Turkey continued and radicalized the secularization process begun in the late Ottoman period. Structural reforms of the legal and educational systems were accompanied by a series of innovations of strong symbolic power. The most significant among these reforms were the "hat reform" that required men to abandon the traditional fez in favour of a brimmed hat (1925), the adaptation of the Gregorian calendar (1926), and the replacement of Arabic by Latin script (1928). Atatürk and his entourage were not only political revolutionaries but cultural entrepreneurs who aimed for the creation of a modern and West-oriented Turkish nation. The Ottoman past now served as the negative other against which the reforms were orchestrated. However, the Kemalist modernization project was an elitist enterprise that provoked a lot of opposition, and it could only be accomplished by a combination of military force and political and cultural re-socialization.

Many of the cultural and political conflicts that shaped the foundational years of the republic carried over into contemporary times. The revolutionary years still serve as a matrix for contemporary conflicts, for example when the military justifies its interference in politics with its role as guardian of the still sacrosanct Kemalist revolution. Repeatedly, the military intervened in politics, most ostensibly in the coups of 1971 and 1980, as well as less physically in 1997 when it forced a religious-conservative government to resign. In all of these interferences the officers justified their actions with their vow to the Kemalist legacy. The coup d'état of 1980, which ended years of political stagnation and the anarchical street violence of the 1970s, had a strong impact on the further political and economic development of the country. In an attempt to de-politicize the public sphere, the generals set in place a considerably more authoritarian constitution that increased the military's political influence. A major motivation for the generals was to weaken the left and pave the ground for a restructuring of the economic order in line with the neo-liberal paradigm. The generals also strengthened Islamic institutions hoping that religion could help contain extreme, primarily leftist, political sentiments. As a consequence, religion went public to an unprecedented extent, facilitated by an extending media sector that was liberalized under Turgut Özal, prime minister between 1983 and 1989. Like the leading generals of the coup, Özal supported the *Turkish-Islamic Synthesis*, an ideology which aims to reconcile a universalist Sunnī Muslim with a particularistic Turkish identity. This ideology redefines the Turkish state ideology of Kemalism in terms of a conservative modernism, understood as Islamic but secular, economically liberal, and committed to stand strong against separatist threats, be they ethnic or religious. Özal was himself a devout Muslim and was associated with an Istanbul Nakşibendi lodge. In the 1970s, the same lodge had encouraged the creation of an Islamic party, which has been repeatedly banned and reopened under new names. The Justice and Development Party (JDP), which gained an absolute majority in the 2002 parliamentary elections, is its latest incarnation.

In the long run, Turkish nationalism has proved successful insofar as it created a strong national identity, although at times with chauvinist undertones. It failed, however to accommodate the needs of its ethnic and religious minorities, especially the Kurds, and the Alevis. The war between the Turkish army and the separatist Kurdish Workers Party (Partiya Karkerên Kurdistan, the PKK) that has been plaguing the country for two decades now is a consequence of the failures of both an assimilationist nationalism and a lopsided modernization. The later privileged the more urban and industrialized Western parts of the country and was unable to create economic prosperity in the Southeast – although there have been more efforts to improve the infrastructure of this part of the country since Özal. Recent years have seen signs of a gradual political liberalization and improvements with respect to human rights issues mainly as a consequence of pressure from the European Union with which Turkey started formal negotiations for full membership in 2005. However, human rights organizations still report cases of grave human rights violations, and the maintenance of authoritarian laws that severely restrict the freedom of speech. The obstacles on the road to further democratization of the Turkish state are still framed by the Turkish birth trauma, which sticks to the dogma of the indivisibility of the country formed during the War of Independence when the future of the Muslim–Turkish nation was challenged by outside foes and separatist movements from within. Kemalist hardliners still perceive outspoken Islamic identity conceptions and demands of religious and ethnic minorities for political recognition as the biggest threat to the unity and indeed very existence of the Turkish state.

The still powerful narrative of the Kemalist revolution's break with the Ottoman past disguises structural continuities without which contemporary Turkish society cannot be properly understood. An example is the Directorate of Religious Affairs (DRA), which had been established in 1924, and had taken over many of the functions that were in Ottoman times assigned to the *shaykh al-Islām*. The DRA, which grew over the years significantly in size, duties assigned to it, and influence, represents state-sponsored official Islam. A huge bureaucratic apparatus within the state administration, the DRA has exclusive responsibility for the organization and supervision of public Islam. This includes mosque construction, education and employment of mosque personnel, religious education at public schools, issuance of *fatwās*, and the organization of the *ḥajj* pilgrimage. In the pursuit of its duties, the DRA is clearly Sunnī and does not provide any comparable services for Alevis. The Alevis thus have accused the DRA of assimilationist politics ever since they entered the public sphere in the late 1980s with a campaign for recognition as being legitimately different from Sunnī Muslims. Recognized Christian and Jewish denominations, on the other hand, are granted considerable autonomy in their internal affairs.

The DRA embodies the authoritarian character of Turkish laicism (Turk. *laiklik*). The aim of Turkish laicism as established under Atatürk's leadership was to secularize the public and the political spheres, and to reduce religion to a matter of private faith. Turkish laicism is practically defined by the two principles of separation of religion and politics and control of religion by the state. While the former justifies the state's repressive actions against religious movements when deemed to be challenging the Kemalist order, the latter explains the absorption of religious services into the state administration.

With the JDP Turkey experiences for the first time a single-rule government by a party with roots in the Islamist movement. Unsurprisingly, the JDP's actions are observed with suspicion by the Kemalist establishment. The JDP presents itself as a conservative but modern political party with an Islamic value basis, but committed to Turkish nationalism and secularism. Tensions with hardcore Kemalists erupt often around certain issues of strong symbolic character, as for example in the headscarf debate. While the JDP supports the unconditional right to wear the headscarf in the name of religious freedom, Kemalists want to keep public spaces – for example schools and universities – free of religious symbols such as the headscarf, particular forms of which they regard as more politically than religiously motivated.

The success of a moderately Islamic party reflects both the electorate's dissatisfaction with the scandal-ridden Kemalist and nationalist political establishment as well as a certain transformation of the political Islamic movement itself. The JDP tries to present itself not that much through Islamic identity politics but rather through a pragmatic politics of services. This enabled it to broaden its electorate, and since it follows the path of economic liberalism embarked on under Özal, the party also gained the support of conservative segments of the middle class and the economic elite. It seems that the daily responsibility of governing contributes to the JDP's espousal of less ideological and more pragmatic politics which combine traditional Islamic values with a neo-liberal economic agenda.

Kemalism and Islamism embody opposing ends of the political spectrum in regards to the public place and role of religion in Turkey. It would, however, be a mistake to regard these two orientations as totally dominating the political discourse. Most Turks are more ambivalent in their political convictions, and do not easily fit into either category. Still, it is the hegemony of Kemalism embodied in the state's institutions that others Islamism as enemy of the laicist model, thus creating a polarization of the political sphere. Nevertheless, in matters of political preferences regarding economy, welfare, security, as well as domestic security and foreign policy, the political sphere cannot as easily be divided into two antagonistic camps, and allegiance often shifts depending on the issue under debate. For example, the JDP joins secular Turkish voices who advocate the strengthening of civil society institutions. Against the Kemalist establishment, these voices perceive the country's democratic deficits as an impediment on the envisioned road to prosperity via membership in the European

Union. More and more argue for an acknowledgment of the religious and cultural diversity of the country and against the criminalization of those who speak in the name of particular identities unprotected by the state. While the EU is pushing in the same direction, the Turkish public is very sensitive towards outside interference. This sensitivity has increased with the recent developments in the Middle East such as the US-led invasion of Iraq, and the Israeli attack on Lebanon, military aggressions that cause instability in the region and make many Turks reconsider the current value of their traditionally strong military and political alliances with the USA, Israel, and the West in general.

References and further reading

Ahmad, F. (1993) *The Making of Modern Turkey*, London: Routledge.

Akçam, T. (2006) *A Shameful Act: The Armenian Genocide and the Question of Turkish Responsibility*, New York: Metropolitan Books.

Andrews, P. A. (1989) *Ethnic Groups in the Republic of Turkey*, Wiesbaden: Reichert; Supplement and Index, Wiesbaden: Reichert, 2002.

Berkes, N. (1998) *The Development of Secularism in Turkey*, London: Routledge.

Birge, J. K. (1982) *The Bektashi Order of Dervishes*, New York: AMS Press (1st edition 1937).

Bozdoğan, S. and Kasaba, R., eds. (1997) *Rethinking Modernity and National Identity in Turkey*, Seattle: University of Washington Press.

Bruinessen, M. v. (1992) *Agha, Shaikh and State: The Social and Political Structures of Kurdistan*, New York: Zed Books.

Çınar, A. (2005) *Modernity, Islam, and Secularism in Turkey. Bodies, Places, and Time*, Minneapolis: University of Minnesota Press.

Deringil, S. (1999) *The Well-Protected Domains: Ideology and the Legitimation of Power in the Ottoman Empire, 1876–1909*, London: I. B. Tauris.

Findley, C. V. (2005) *The Turks in World History*, New York: Oxford University Press.

Finkel, C. (2005) *Osman's Dream: The History of the Ottoman Empire, 1300–1923*, London: John Murray.

Kafadar, C. (1995) *Between Two Worlds: The Construction of the Ottoman State*, Berkeley: University of California Press.

Karateke, H. T. and Reinkowski, M., eds. (2005) *Legitimizing the Order. The Ottoman Rhetoric of State Power*, Leiden: Brill.

Mango, A. (1999) *Atatürk: The Biography of the Founder of Modern Turkey*, London: John Murray.

White, J. (2003) *Islamist Mobilization in Turkey: A Study in Vernacular Politics*, Seattle: University of Washington Press.

White, P. J. and Jongerden, J., eds. (2003) *Turkey's Alevi Enigma. A Comprehensive Overview*, Leiden: Brill.

Yavuz, H. (2003) *Islamic Political Identity in Turkey*, Oxford: Oxford University Press.

Yavuz, H. and Esposito, J. L., eds. (2003) *Turkish Islam and the Secular State: The Gülen Movement*, Syracuse: Syracuse University Press.

Zürcher, J. E. (2004) *Turkey. A Modern History*, London: I. B. Tauris (1st edition 1993).

5

IRAN

Elton L. Daniel

In considering the history of Islam in Iran, three basic but fundamental questions immediately present themselves: First, how and why were the existing religious traditions of that country supplanted so quickly and thoroughly by Islam? Second, why did the making of Iran as a nation-state become so intertwined with one particular sectarian form of Islam, Twelver Shiʿism? Third, how has that affected the country's national identity and political development? At the present state of historical research, these questions cannot be answered as convincingly as one would like, but at least a general outline of the issues may be given.

Origins and development of Islam in Iran

The area that makes up modern Iran was, at the beginning of the Islamic era, part of a much larger empire ruled by a dynasty known as the Sasanians (*c.* 224–651). The founder of this empire, Ardashir (d. 240), was at first the local ruler of the province of Fars (the same area of southwestern Iran from which the celebrated Cyrus, founder of the earlier Achaemenid dynasty, had come). Around 224, he defeated the last of the Parthian kings, united most of the Iranian plateau under his rule, and then, in 226, conquered Mesopotamia. Later kings continued to try to expand the empire both to the west and the east, with varying degrees of success; in general, the borders of the empire reached (at least nominally) from the Euphrates and the Caucasus as far as the Oxus and the Indus valley.

The ethnic make-up of so vast an empire was naturally quite diverse. The ruling dynasty and core population was "Persian" (i.e., spoke the Middle Persian language), but there were many other Iranian and non-Iranian peoples including Aramaeans, Arabs, and other Semites; Armenians; Khwarazmians; Soghdians, Hephthalites; etc. Just as these groups spoke different languages so they tended to follow different religions. Some of the smaller religions, usually confined to discrete ethnic communities, included Judaism, Mandaeism, Gnosticism, and various obscure pagan cults. Major world religions, which cut across ethnic lines, also had their adherents: Manichaeism, Christianity, and Buddhism. For the Persian population and most of the Sasanian rulers, however, the "official," state-supported, religion was a form of Zoroastrianism.

Numerous maxims attributed to Ardashir in later Islamic sources emphasize that kingship and religion should support each other; the Sasanians clearly believed that a king, with a divinely derived mandate to rule and following and promoting correct religion, was essential for the preservation and protection of both the social and the cosmic order. Their early kings eliminated local cults and temples in favor of fire-temples associated with the ruling dynasty, standardized religious practices, and created a hierarchy of priests headed by a high-priest (*mōbadhān-mōbadh*). The first two of these high-priests, Tansar and especially Kartir, vigorously championed the religious policy of the Sasanian kings, promoted religious activities, and persecuted and suppressed Zoroastrian "heresies" and rival religions. Key Zoroastrian religious texts were collected, collated, and put together in a standard canon. A manual of law based on Zoroastrian principles was also codified, and the courts and administration of justice were primarily in the hands of the Zoroastrian clergy.

It is important to note, however, that this grip of what has been called the Zoroastrian "church" on the Sasanian empire was not quite as pervasive or powerful as it might appear. It had two significant vulnerabilities. First of all, Zoroastrianism was literally an Iranian religion, not intended for non-Iranians. As a national religion, rather than a universal one, it was thus somewhat unsatisfactory as a means of unifying a population as culturally diverse as that of the Sasanian empire. Apparently for that reason, some Sasanian rulers at least experimented with patronizing other more inclusive religions: Shapur I (r. 241–72) was for a while interested in Manichaeism, and Yazdgard I (r. 399–421) was partial to Christianity. Second, Zoroastrianism as practiced in the Sasanian empire was closely linked to the upholding of a conservative social order that greatly favored the interests of a privileged aristocracy, the Zoroastrian clergy themselves being among its beneficiaries. As a result, the oppressed, especially the peasantry, might turn not only to other religions but to heterodox forms of Zoroastrianism, which were never fully suppressed. The best-known example is the great popular upheaval led by the renegade priest Mazdak, who espoused a religious ideology grounded in the egalitarian sharing of property and wealth. Mazdak was executed around 527 and his followers ruthlessly suppressed by the new king Khosrow I Anushirvan (r. 531–79), though the movement would persist well into the Islamic period. It can thus be said that the religious situation throughout the Sasanian period was quite volatile and dynamic and had important implications for broader social and political issues.

Two recurrent themes in Sasanian history were warfare on its borders – with Rome and subsequently the Byzantine empire to the west and with various nomadic invaders to the east – and internal social struggles, especially between the monarchy and high-ranking members of the provincial military aristocracy. Both elements were involved in the last great crisis faced by the empire, just before the beginning of the Islamic era. In 589, the general Bahram Chubin, who had carried out a successful campaign against the Turks, rebelled against the king Hormizd IV (r. 579–90), who was deposed and murdered. Bahram attempted to assume the throne himself, but was opposed by other members of the nobility, who backed the candidacy of Khosrow II Parviz (r. 590–628). With their assistance as well as with aid from the Byzantine emperor Maurice, Khosrow was able to defeat Bahram and eventually had him assassinated. After his benefactor Maurice was himself murdered in 602, Khosrow initiated a new round of wars with the Byzantines. He also took direct control of southern Mesopotamia by removing Nuʿmān, the Christian Arab vassal-king of al-Hira, from office. At first the wars went well as the Sasanians took Antioch, Damascus, and Jerusalem and then advanced all the way to Chalcedon, just across the Bosphorus from the Byzantine capital. Then, in a series of campaigns between 622 and 627, the Byzantine emperor Heraclius repeatedly defeated the Sasanians, recovered the lost territory, and penetrated to the environs of the Sasanian capital at Ctesiphon. Khosrow's efforts to shift the blame for this catastrophe to his generals resulted in a rebellion and his eventual execution. This was followed by a period of near anarchy throughout the empire.

Furthermore, by deposing Nuʿmān, Khosrow had alienated the Arab tribes of southern Iraq. They had already mutinied against Sasanian rule at a skirmish known as Dhū Qār around 610. Taking advantage of the Sasanian military defeats and political chaos, they rebelled again in the 620s and were now able to call for assistance from the newly converted Muslim Arabs of the Hijaz (who had already moved against the Sasanian forces occupying Yemen). After a series of battles, the Sasanians were routed at Qadisiyya (probably in 636); their capital was captured shortly thereafter and the provinces west of the Zagros annexed to the Muslim caliphate. A second phase of the war moved onto the Iranian plateau itself and culminated in the decisive defeat of the last Sasanian ruler, Yazdgard III, at the Battle of Nihavand (*c.* 642). The third campaign, in pursuit of the defeated ruler, ended with his death in 652 and the occupation of eastern Iran.

These wars, which destroyed the Sasanian empire, obviously laid the foundations for the Islamization of Iran. However, it is clear that to begin with the wars had simply conquest, not religious conversion, as their goal. In case after case, we are told that peace was established on the basis of payment of taxes and tribute, while the conquered population was allowed, or even pressured, to follow its own religious tradition. The new regime essentially envisaged a relatively small, more or less exclusively Arab, class of Muslim warriors ruling over a vast empire of non-Muslims, in collaboration with the existing non-Muslim administrative elite. This system quickly began to break down since substantial numbers of non-Arabs did in fact wish to convert to Islam and there were some Muslims who believed that as a matter of policy conversion to Islam should be promoted.

On the basis of the limited and mostly anecdotal evidence available, it seems that the process of conversion began quickly and mostly as a result of individual choices and for pragmatic reasons. Even before the battle at Qadisiyya, some Iranian soldiers had chosen to convert and join the Arab armies; later, around 638 or 639, an entire military detachment sent from Isfahan defected to the Arabs and made at least a nominal conversion to their religion; that same year, the Sasanian commander in Khuzistan, Hurmuzān, converted in order to avoid execution. The people of Qazvin, realizing that the city would fall, decided to convert in order to avoid paying the poll-tax. Many Zoroastrians in Sistan are said to have converted because they were impressed by the just administration of the Muslim governor of the province (*c.* 666–7).

In the early stage of the conversion process, there were apparently several impediments for non-Arabs. Converts usually had to become "clients" (*mawālī*) of an Arab tribe and might be subjected to various forms of discrimination in taxation and other matters. By the middle of the Umayyad period, however, many Muslims viewed the conversion of non-Arabs as not just acceptable but desirable and thus sought to facilitate it. This conversion was not to be obtained through coercion but rather by the inducement of the positive advantages to be gained by converting. In the process, the growing number of non-Arab, particularly Iranian, converts, inevitably helped to bring out the egalitarian and universal aspects of Islam as a religion. Eastern Iran, due to the relatively small Arab presence there and the consequent need to work with the local population to defend and expand the frontier with the Turks in Central Asia, was of particular importance in this regard. Qutayba ibn Muslim, appointed governor of Khurasan in 705, founded new mosques and supported missionary activities, tolerated the use of Persian for religious purposes, paid people (presumably mostly new converts) for attending prayer services, and severely punished converts who attempted to go back to their former religion. The caliph ʿUmar II (r. 717–20) invited the Iranian local rulers in Central Asia to convert to Islam (and some did); he also ordered the governor of Khurasan to facilitate conversion and to govern in accordance with Islamic principles.

Not all of the Umayyad elite, however, supported such policies, and the issues of promoting conversion and treating non-Arab Muslims equitably became caught up in the more general spread of religio-political opposition to Umayyad rule. This culminated in a great rebellion in Khurasan in 747 that brought down the Umayyads and led to the establishment of the Abbasid dynasty of caliphs (r. 750–1258). This "Abbasid revolution" swept away whatever barriers to conversion remained and essentially put an end to discrimination against non-Arab Muslims. It also added a powerful incentive for conversion by definitively ending the former system of maintaining a privileged class of non-Muslims as collaborators in the administration of the empire. Many Iranians now served at the highest levels of the Abbasid government, but it was essential for them to be Muslims and a number of them were converts or came from recently converted families. Considerable pressure was also put on the remaining non-Muslim local rulers in peripheral Iranian areas, such as the military governor (*ispabadh*) of Tabaristan, to convert. Once these elites converted, the general population tended to follow their lead.

It is virtually certain that over the first two centuries of the Abbasid period, the great majority – perhaps as much as 90 percent – of the Iranian population converted to Islam. This impacted on the existing religious communities in different ways. Some, such as the Jews and Armenian Christians, were barely affected by conversion at all. Eastern Christianity (mostly in its Melkite and Nestorian forms) had been flourishing in the late Sasanian period, and its status as a church was not really changed by the advent of Muslim rule. Yet, for reasons that are not really clear, a good many of those Christians willingly chose to convert (in a famous letter, the patriarch Ishoyahb of Rev Ardashir complained about how many of the Christians of Marv were becoming Muslims even though they faced no persecution). Manichaeism had been repressed during the Sasanian period and was already in retreat; it continued to be viewed with suspicion. It had always been a highly syncretistic religion, and Manicheans attempting to assimilate the religion with Islam were probably the main targets of the Abbasid persecution of the *zindīq*s, "heretics." Buddhism virtually disappeared after the Abbasid defeat of pro-Chinese forces in Central Asia, though this process is difficult to trace.

Most of the Iranian converts to Islam, however, must have been Zoroastrians, and the reasons for their conversion are numerous and complicated. With the defeat of the Sasanians, Zoroastrianism, unlike the other religions, lost its status as the official cult and was devastated by the loss of political and economic support for its priesthood. Although it was recognized as a revealed religion which entitled its followers to protected (*dhimmī*) status under Muslim rule, this may have been compromised by the fact that the areas which tended to be strongholds of Zoroastrianism also tended to be bastions of resistance to Arab-Muslim rule. Then the increasing Islamization of the administrative apparatus left members of the Zoroastrian elite with the stark choice of converting or losing their privileged status. Since Zoroastrianism was not a missionary religion, every conversion to another religion tended to permanently diminish the size of the community. Still, Zoroastrianism held out tenaciously in a number of areas such as Fars, Tabaristan, and Usrusana. By the tenth century, however, it was a lost cause, and the dismay and despair of the community at this is well-reflected in the apocalyptic Zoroastrian literature of that period.

This massive and relatively rapid conversion of the Iranian population raises two intriguing but difficult questions. What did the converts understand Islam to be? How much from their previous religion did they preserve and bring into Islam? It seems likely that most early converts would have had only a vague notion of what the religion involved (and even less if they did not have a good command of the Arabic language in which the scriptures were written). The anecdotal evidence suggests that such conversions were inspired more by personal connections and practical interests than by purely spiritual concerns. We are told in the sources that some converts, such as those Qutayba won over in Bukhara, attempted to go back to a previous religion and even when they were definitively converted continued to practice elements of their old religion in private. A little later, a governor of Khurasan complained that people in Samarqand were claiming to be converts (to avoid taxation) even though they were uncircumcised, did not know how to perform the rituals, and could not even recite a verse from the Qur'ān. Even Afshin (d. 841), the local ruler of Usrusana and a general in the service of the Abbasids, whose father had accepted Islam in 822, was accused of continuing to venerate idols (perhaps actually Buddhist statues) in secret. Especially in the early Abbasid period, there were a number of movements which attempted to combine aspects of Islam with other Iranian religions; these were typically branded heretical and insurrectionary by the caliphal government and ruthlessly suppressed. Since Islam itself was still evolving and defining itself as a formal religion well into the Abbasid period, it is also possible, even in cases where converts did have a significant understanding of the new religion they were accepting, that there was still room to accommodate some of their former beliefs and practices, so much so that these eventually came to be seen as actually Islamic. It is suggestive, for example, that the concept of five daily prayers, mentioned nowhere in the Qur'ān, was a well-established feature of Zoroastrianism, or that there is a great similarity in the concern of both Islam and Zoroastrianism with matters of ritual purity. This is certainly not to say that Islam was influenced by Iranian religions or that there was some deliberate effort by Iranians to shape Islam to their taste. It does seem likely, however, that Iranians, like other Muslims, played a role in fleshing out a fully formed Islam that reflected to some extent their former religious traditions.

Islam developed in Iran with the same degree of variety as in other places. Certain rugged and remote parts of Iran were particularly attractive to dissident Muslim sects fleeing defeat and persecution by the caliphal authorities. For example, one group of Kharijites, the earliest of the Islamic sects, after having been driven out of Iraq, took control of Fars and Kirman and established their own principality there. When they were again defeated around 699, they fled further east to remote areas of Sistan. Their

Figure 4 Congregational Mosque of Isfahan, Isfahan, Iran, eighth century to seventeenth. Beginning as a mosque with a columned prayer hall, the Isfahan congregational mosque evolved through time as domes, large arched portals (*īwāns*) in the cour tyard, and tiled surfaces were added by various dynasties.

Source: Photographer May Farhat, 1992, Courtesy of the Aga Khan Visual Archive, MIT

disdain for caliphal authorities and tax-collectors was apparently shared by much of the rural population of that area, Muslim and non-Muslim, and Kharijism was a powerful and enduring influence there well into the Abbasid period. Proto-Shiʿites, supporters of the family of ʿAlī, after being defeated in the central Islamic lands, also took refuge in parts of Iran. One well-known group of them, mostly Ashʿarī tribesmen from Kufa, settled in the area of Qom, which became a stronghold of Shiʿism and resistance to Umayyad and Abbasid authority. Around the middle of the ninth century, Zaydī Shiʿism was firmly established in the western parts of the Caspian provinces.

Khurasan and the central Asian provinces also attracted various religio-political dissidents, not least of whom were those who incubated the Abbasid revolution there. On the whole, though, it became a stronghold of the conventional, pious, *sharīʿa*-minded tendency that eventually became known as Sunnī Islam. One measure of this was the remarkable popularity of *ḥadīth* collection and study in this region. Out of the six canonical Sunnī *ḥadīth* collections, four were by scholars from there – al-Bukhārī (d. 870), Muslim (d. 875), al-Tirmidhī (d. 883 or 893), and al-Nasāʾī (d. 915) – and the other two – Ibn Māja (d. 887) and Abū Dāwūd (d. 889) – from adjacent areas. In jurisprudence, the Ḥanafī school of law spread rapidly during the Abbasid period from Balkh to other parts of Khurasan and Transoxiana; this was probably due to its great flexibility in facilitating conversion of non-Arabs (by authorizing the use of vernacular languages such as Persian instead of Arabic for religious purposes and not insisting on a full and formal acceptance of every aspect of the religion) and adapting to local concerns (on matters such as the laws of water rights). Later on, the Shāfiʿī school of law developed strongholds in Nishapur and other cities and became the most important rival to the Ḥanafī school. The sometimes violent disputes between these two schools were reflected to a degree in theology as well. Since Ḥanafīs emphasized the priority of faith over works, that law school was naturally well disposed towards theological inquiry and was closely associated early on with the moderate Murjiʾa movement and later with the Māturīdī school. The Shāfiʿī school was generally suspicious of speculative and rationalist theology, but many looked favorably on the conservative, literalist, and tradition-oriented theology of al-Ashʿarī (d. 935).

One of the ironic consequences of the increasing conversion of the Iranian population to Islam was political decentralization and fragmentation – religion did not serve so much to hold together the caliphal empire as to legitimize the establishment of local Islamic dynasties. The Tahirid governors of Khurasan (r. 820–72) already asserted a high degree of financial and political autonomy, and they were followed by a number of other more or less independent regional principalities that differed quite a bit in their religious policies. The Samanids, who ruled most of eastern Iran from 874 to 999, depicted themselves as warriors for the faith against the heathen Turks; supporters of orthodox, mostly Ḥanafī, Islam; and, usually but not always, as faithful servants of the Abbasid caliphate. Their main successors, the Ghaznavids (r. 962–1186), a line of rulers which arose from the ranks of their Turkish slave soldiers, followed much the same model. The Saffarids of Sistan (r. 867–903 and intermittently thereafter) had no discernible sectarian interests, even welcoming former Kharijites into their army, and were alternately deferential or hostile towards the Abbasid caliphs. The Būyids in Fars and western Iran (r. 932–1055) were Shiʿites, probably Zaydīs to begin with and then Imāmī-Twelver later on. Even though they conquered Baghdad in 945, they left the mostly powerless Abbasid caliphs in place but gave official sanction to Shīʿī rituals and practices.

Around the middle of the tenth century, the Turkish tribes of Central Asia began converting to Islam in significant numbers. One of their confederations, the Qara-Khanids (r. *c.* 932–1165), swept away the last vestiges of the Samanid principality and established their own rule all the way to the Oxus. In terms of religious policy, they were virtually indistinguishable from their Samanid predecessors in respecting the Abbasid caliphate, supporting the Ḥanafī school of law, and endorsing the teachings of Māturīdī theology. Ethnically, however, they were distinctly Turkish and without much of the Persianized veneer of their Ghaznavid counterparts. From this time on, the region north of the Oxus cannot be considered part of Iran in any meaningful sense.

The areas south of the Oxus were invaded by another confederation of Muslim Turks, the Saljuqs. They seized Nishapur in 1040 and pushed the Ghaznavids out of most of Khurasan, confining them to what today would be part of Afghanistan. From there, they were able to take control of Khwarazm and move into southern and western Iran. In 1055, they captured Baghdad, ostensibly to rescue the Abbasid caliphate from its Shīʿī enemies, and brought the Būyid dynasty to an end. The Saljuq leader then ruled as sultan, essentially a military and administrative leader, in tandem with the Abbasid caliph, as the chief religious authority. The last of the great Saljuq sultans, Sanjar, died in 1157.

The Saljuq conquests reunified most of the Iranian plateau and created an empire somewhat similar in extent to that of the Sasanids. The effects of the Saljuq domination as the product of an alien intrusion were mitigated by its reliance on the existing bureaucratic and cultural elite. This fusion of Turkish military power and Persian intelligentsia marked the culminating and classic stage in the development of a distinct Perso–Turkish Islamic civilization that would affect not only Iran but the whole region for many centuries. In terms of religious policy, the Saljuqs and their apologists attempted to project an image of legitimacy based on piety and devotion to Islam. Earlier rulers had often used enthusiasm for *jihād* for this purpose; the Saljuqs emphasized their patronage of Sunnī religious scholars and institutions, their fondness for Sufism, and their determination to uproot and destroy what they considered the dangerous heresy of Ismāʿīlī Shiʿism. Despite the endorsement of this image by a number of influential figures, the best known clearly being al-Ghazālī (d. 1111), the veneer of pious Islam did not do much to disguise what was in reality a rather crude, brutal, hypocritical, and often ineffective military dictatorship that was denounced by other religious leaders such as ʿAyn al-Quḍāt al-Hamadānī (d. 1131). Not only did relations between Sunnīs and the Ismāʿīlīs take a violent turn during this period, hostilities between Ḥanafīs and Shāfiʿīs also reached a new height of intensity. Even the Abbasid caliphs resented the power of the Saljuqs and sought to undermine it. Not surprisingly, it did not take long for the Saljuq principality to fragment and dissipate, setting the stage for a new wave of Turko-Mongol invasions.

Islam and modern Iran

The Mongol invasions of Iran marked an important watershed in the history of the country. The first wave of Mongol attacks, commenced in 1219 under Genghis Khan, were vindictive and destructive in nature, devastating a number of cities in eastern Iran. The second wave, under Hülegü Khān, was more deliberate and comprehensive and led to the establishment of a dynasty known as the Il Khans (r. 1256–1335). A third conquest of Iran took place under Tīmūr (d. 1405). These events, even more than the earlier Saljuq incursions, led to a massive influx of Turko-Mongol tribes into Iran that dramatically altered the ethnic and demographic make-up of the region, especially in the north. This affected not only politics, with one Turko-Mongol dynasty after another dominating the area, but also the development of religion.

Hülegü was a non-Muslim and hostile to any form of Islam perceived as a threat to Mongol authority. He was much more successful than the Saljuqs had been in destroying the strongholds of the Nizārī Ismāʿīlīs and reducing their influence in Iran. At the same time, Hülegü's forces invaded Iraq, sacked Baghdad, and killed the Abbasid caliph; by bringing the institution of the caliphate to an end for all practical purposes, the Mongols weakened the hold of juridical Sunnī Islam on Iran. Although one of the later Il Khans, Ghāzān (r. 1295–1304), converted to Islam, neither he nor his successors had a very clear religious policy and they seem to have vacillated between various forms of Shīʿī and Sunnī allegiance.

The primary religious force to fill the void left by the collapse of Sunnī and Ismāʿīlī influence in Iran was Sufism, which endured and even flourished throughout the whole of the Turko-Mongol period. Of the many Ṣūfī orders established in Iran and patronized by various Turko-Mongol rulers, the most important would prove to be one in Ardabil headed by a spiritual leader (*shaykh* or *pīr*) named Ṣafī 'l-Dīn (d. 1334) and subsequently by his descendants. By most accounts, the early Ṣafawiyya (commonly called Safavid) order had a fairly conventional Ṣūfī–Shāfiʿī religious orientation. It was apparently quite successful in attracting Turkoman disciples (*murīds*) who accepted the Safavid *pīr* as their perfect spiritual guide (*murshid-i kāmil*). As more and more of the Turkomans placed themselves under the religious aegis of the order, however, it became quite militant, and the Safavid *pīrs* began to act as commanders of warriors for the faith (*ghāzīs*) and sought some degree of political power. Like a number of other Ṣūfī orders during this period of religious syncretism and heterodoxy, the Safavids also absorbed ideas of a distinctly Shīʿī character and carried out a religious propaganda campaign (*daʿwa*) on that basis. Some of these ideas were fairly tame, such as veneration for the twelve Imāms (symbolized by wearing a red cap with twelve pleats, hence the name of *qizilbāsh*, "red-heads," applied to their Turkoman followers). At its peak, however, the *daʿwa* was based on an extremist (*ghulāt*) version of Shiʿism. The central idea was that the Safavid *pīr* was an incarnation (or reincarnation) of God; he was not only infallible but made his followers undefeatable in battle. It is by no means clear whether this ideology was part of a calculated strategy to draw in Turkoman tribes as supporters or rather the result of so many Turkomans declaring themselves followers of the Safavids and influencing the doctrine of the order. The notion of a charismatic, reincarnated, god-priest, for example, is one that might be expected to be encountered in Tibet and Central Asia rather than Islam and Iran, and the Turkomans may well have brought such concepts with them. On the other hand, heterodox religious movements based on *ghulāt* Shiʿism did have a long history in Iran going all the way back to the early Abbasid period (albeit again with a Central Asian dimension to them), and the Safavid *daʿwa* could represent a recrudescence of them.

While many Turkomans became disciples of the Safavids, the rulers of the Turkoman dynasties being established in eastern Anatolia and northwestern Iran during this period often viewed the Safavid *daʿwa* with suspicion and alternated between supporting and opposing it. In 1488, Yaʿqūb, the ruler of the Aq Qoyunlu, conspired to kill the Safavid *pīr* Ḥaydar. Ḥaydar's youngest son, Ismāʿīl, was given refuge at Lahijan in Gilan by the local ruler, who was a Shiʿite (probably Zaydī). Ismāʿīl at that time was only seven years old, but an inner cadre of Safavid devotees (the *ahl-i ikhtiṣāṣ*) continued to conduct a semi-clandestine *daʿwa* on his behalf. Ismāʿīl and his small band of followers emerged from Gilan in 1499 and rallied several thousand *qizilbāsh* tribesmen to his cause. Ismāʿīl avenged his father's murder by defeating the Aq Qoyunlu and occupying Tabriz (1501); over the course of the next decade, his forces conquered the whole of Iran, occupied Baghdad, defeated the Ozbeks in Central Asia and killed their *khān*, and launched raids against the Ottomans in Anatolia. In 1514, the Ottomans counter-attacked and, with their superiority in manpower and gunpowder weapons, utterly routed the Safavid army at the battle of Chaldiran.

Chaldiran represented more than a military defeat; it was also a severe blow to the Safavid *ghulāt* ideology and to Ismāʿīl's prestige among the *qizilbāsh*. This accelerated a process that had begun earlier. As soon as Ismāʿīl had captured Tabriz in 1501, he proclaimed Shiʿism the official religion and began a sometimes violent suppression of Sunnī Islam, but this was not really aimed at enforcing *ghulāt* ideas on the general populace. Sunnī religious scholars were replaced by those with a Twelver Shīʿī orientation, Shīʿī forms of ritual were imposed in the mosques, and public condemnation of the first three caliphs after Muḥammad (venerated by Sunnīs) was mandatory. Practically speaking, this served to distinguish very sharply between the new Safavid polity and its Ottoman and Ozbek rivals, to create a common bond between its Turkoman and Persian subjects, and to establish a broader basis of religious legitimacy for Safavid rule. It may also have been intended to increase support for the Safavids in Shīʿī areas they hoped to conquer, such as Iraq, southern Iran, and eastern Anatolia. After Chaldiran, the *ghulāt* elements faded even more into the background; emphasis was rather placed on the Safavid claim to be Ḥusaynids (descended from Imām Mūsā al-Kāẓim), sharing in the charisma of the Imāms and perhaps acting as the deputy of the hidden twelfth Imām.

In the long term, the Safavid religious policy succeeded in creating an enduring Twelver Shīʿī clerical establishment in Iran, but it was much less successful in subordinating that establishment to the notion of Safavid religious authority. The creation of appointive religious offices such as that of *shaykh al-islām* of Isfahan may have been intended to serve as a mechanism for controlling the Shīʿī religious scholars, but it actually tended rather to institutionalize a powerful and independent religious hierarchy. Even the strongest of Safavid rulers, Shāh ʿAbbās the Great (r. 1587–1629), found it expedient to cultivate an image of deferential piety by lavishing attention on the pilgrimage center at Mashhad and providing charitable endowments to support

Figure 5 Chihil Sutun, Isfahan, Iran, 1647, 1705. Located in the royal park and palace precinct west of Isfahan's newly built *maydān*, this palace pavilion was adorned with interior paintings and provided a place of quiet retreat and reflection.

Source: Photographer Khosrow Bozorgi, 1999, Courtesy of the Aga Khan Visual Archive, MIT

the Shīʿī jurists. Weaker rulers, such as Shāh Sulṭān Ḥusayn (r. 1694–1722), were utterly dominated by the jurists. The greatest of these jurists, Muḥammad Bāqir Majlisī (d. 1699), made it clear that he accepted the legitimacy of Safavid kingship and preached deference to the ruler, but he expected in return financial support and adherence to religious law as defined by the jurists.

That said, it also has to be noted that the exact form of Shiʿism to be followed in Safavid Iran remained a matter of contention. The jurists were themselves sharply divided between *akhbārī*s, who placed primary emphasis on following established traditions from Muḥammad and the Imāms, and the *uṣūlī*s, who insisted on the use of continuous scholarly investigation of religious questions (*ijtihād*). Interest in metaphysical philosophy and theology was also surprisingly strong, and the period produced such important figures as Mullā Ṣadrā (d. 1640) and Mīr Dāmād (d. 1630). Numerous Ṣūfī orders, mostly with a Shīʿī orientation, including that of the Safavids themselves, continued to be active, although they were intensely disliked by most clerics and faced frequent periods of harassment and persecution.

Safavid rule came to an abrupt end in 1722, when Afghans led by the Ghilzai chief Mīr Maḥmūd conquered the capital, Isfahan. The Afghan invasion was largely provoked by the aggressive Shiʿism of the Safavids, which the Sunnī Afghans found offensive, and facilitated by the negligence of state affairs by Safavid rulers overly influenced by the demands of the clerical establishment. The Afghans themselves were ousted within a decade by the great general Nādir Khān Afshār, who first ruled as the protector of a puppet Safavid prince and then on his own as Shāh (r. 1736–47). Acutely aware of his own lack of religious legitimacy as compared to the Safavids, and equally anxious to end a potentially disastrous conflict with the Ottomans, Nādir Shāh attempted to dilute the Shīʿī character of the state but without success. Under the other major successor dynasties, the Zand (r. 1750–94) and the Qajars (r. 1779–1925), Twelver Shiʿism remained an indispensable element of Iranian identity.

By the beginning of the Qajar period, the *uṣūlī*s, led by the great scholar Muḥammad Bāqir Bihbahānī (d. *c.* 1792), had decisively defeated their *akhbārī* counterparts. They would face some other challenges, notably from the *shaykhī* school (which emphasized leadership by a charismatic "perfect Shiʿite") and even more from its Bābī offshoot, as well as from certain forms of Sufism tacitly patronized by the Qājārs, but *uṣūlī* thought remained dominant. The most important practical consequence of *uṣūlī* ideology was the tremendous authority and power it vested in *mujtahid*s, the top level of a hierarchy of religious scholars recognized as qualified to practice *ijtihād* and whose interpretation of religious law was to be followed by other Shiʿites. The Qajars, unlike the Safavids, had no credible claims of religious legitimacy of their own to offset this; consequently, their relations with the *mujtahid*s were ambivalent and fraught with tension. Perhaps inevitably, the role of the *mujtahid*s began to expand into areas that had formerly been within the preserve of the ruler. This tendency was encouraged in particular by the intrusion of imperialist powers into Iranian affairs over the course of the nineteenth century and the inability of the Qajars to resist them. Among other things, *mujtahid*s agitated for war with Russia in 1826, instigated an attack on the Russian legation in Tehran in 1829, demanded the dismissal of government ministers they disliked, and helped organize opposition to the granting of economic concessions to foreigners, above all in the popular mass protest and boycott of the tobacco concession in 1891–2. The latter event in particular left no doubt that the

Shīʿī clergy had a unique ability to mobilize the Iranian populace, and it also created the impression that the *mujtahid*s had become by default the main defenders of Iranian national interests in an age of imperialism.

Nonetheless, the clerical establishment was hardly monolithic in its interests or entirely altruistic in its motives. This was brought out quite clearly in the case of clerical involvement in the constitutional revolution (1905–11). The movement was sparked in part by an affront to religious sensibilities by a Belgian national in charge of the Iranian customs office as well as by government abuse of members of one of the cleric's most important social allies, the bazaar merchants. Initially, a broad spectrum of religious leaders promoted demands for a constituent assembly and constitution, but some were consistently pro-monarchical and anti-constitutionalist in their views. Others turned against the constitutional movement when they perceived that the idea of a parliament based on principles of popular sovereignty conflicted with their desire for the supremacy of religious law. One of the first *mujtahid*s to defect for this reason was the conservative Faḍl Allāh Nūrī, who was executed for his opposition to the constitution in 1909. By the end of the constitutional era, even *mujtahid*s who had been staunch constitutionalists and relatively liberal, such as ʿAbd Allāh Bihbahānī (assassinated in 1910) were alarmed by what they saw as the overly secularist, and sometimes certainly anti-clerical, drift of the constitutional revolution.

After years of chaos and hardship following the collapse of the constitutional movement and the effects of World War I on Iran, a measure of stability was restored by the coup of 1921 and the establishment of the Pahlavi monarchy to replace that of the Qajars in 1926. By that time, Iran had acquired the territorial borders that currently define it, and Reza Shah completed the process of giving it the complementary bureaucratic and institutional features of a modern if autocratic nation-state. This inevitably challenged the role the Shīʿī clergy had played in Iranian affairs since the Safavid period. In light of the developments of the constitutionalist era and under the influence of the reforms initiated by Mustafa Kemal in Turkey, Reza Shah's program was quite secularist in tenor. Instead of religion intruding on matters of state, the state now began to intrude on matters of religion, eroding even fundamental areas of *sharīʿa* law such as those pertaining to commerce and the family by introducing new codes based on European models.

Intimidated by Reza Shah, and also somewhat disillusioned by earlier events, the Shīʿī leadership generally reverted to its pre-Safavid preference for shunning political life and concentrated on rebuilding the institutions of religious education in Iran (especially at Qom, which under the guidance of ʿAbd al-Karīm Hāʾirī became a pre-eminent center of Shīʿī scholarship). The fundamental issue of state–clergy relations, however, could not be avoided indefinitely and reasserted itself after World War II. The driving forces, just as in the late nineteenth century, were concerns over foreign influence and economic interests, now further exacerbated by conflicts over secularism and religious law. One of the first notable *mujtahid*s (now usually referred to by a new form of titulature as *āyatullāh*s) to reassert an active role in politics was Abū 'l-Qāsim Kāshānī. He had a long record of anti-British sentiments and enthusiastically supported the efforts of the prime minister Muhammad Musaddiq to nationalize the Anglo–Iranian Oil Company in 1951. He later turned against Musaddiq (at least in part because of a CIA-backed plot that played on Kāshāni's anxieties about the influence of the Tudeh Communist party) and supported the coup that overthrew

Musaddiq in 1953. Kāshāni died in 1962, just as the religious establishment was facing a new challenge in the form of Muhammad-Reza Shah's "White Revolution." There is not much doubt that many Shīʿī leaders were disturbed by this but did not openly oppose it, either because of quietist convictions or reluctance to be seen as reactionary opponents of things like land reform and giving women the right to vote. One relatively junior member of the Shīʿī hierarchy, however, did not hesitate to denounce the government as both un-Islamic and in the thrall of the USA and Israel: Ruhollah Khomeini. In 1963, the Shāh retaliated by having paratroopers attack the school in Qom where he was teaching, arresting him, and eventually sending him into exile. In 1965, Khomeini was allowed to start teaching at Najaf in Iraq, where he continued his criticism of the Pahlavis. He also developed the ideas and gave lectures that evolved into his now famous book, *Islamic Government* (*Ḥukūmat-i islāmī*), with its core notion of *vilāyat-i faqīh* (the desirability of placing the control of government in the hands of a supreme authority on Islamic law). A cadre of loyal former students, many now making their way into the upper echelons of the Shīʿī clerical hierarchy, propagated his views to a much wider audience, especially among expatriate Iranians in Europe and the USA. In Iran itself in the period after 1963, the idea that politics and religion should again be mixed – and using this as a way of implicitly or explicitly denouncing the Pahlavi regime – was most visibly promoted by laymen who were not part of the formal religious leadership. Two rather different but highly influential such figures were ʿAlī Sharīʿatī (d. 1977) and Mehdi Bazargan (d. 1995). Both clearly wanted a society based on what they saw as Islamic values, but neither seems to have wanted to have these values imposed by clerics.

By 1978, disdain for Muhammad-Reza Shah, his despotic and repressive policies, his astonishing cultural insensitivities, and his apparent megalomania was shared by secularists and the religious, on both the right and left of the political spectrum. The Shāh replied in kind to those he denounced as the agents of "black reaction" (the activist clergy) and "red revolution" (the leftists). In January 1978, an article appeared in a newspaper regarded as a mouthpiece for the regime that made a vicious attack on Khomeini and questioned even his personal integrity. This sparked a large protest in Qom that was suppressed by the police forces with some loss of life, creating a spiraling cycle of demonstrations, riots, and uprisings that eventually forced the Shāh to leave the country and brought down the American-backed transition government he attempted to leave in his place (January–February 1979). In the course of this, Khomeini had emerged as the prime leader of the opposition, around whom all the major groups rallied to overthrow the Pahlavis, and he returned triumphantly to Iran.

Any number of people, including some who appeared to be very close to Khomeini, thought that he had been a mostly symbolic leader who would now fade away to resume his religious teaching at Qom. Instead, he and his inner circle of adherents moved steadily, relentlessly, ruthlessly, and effectively to orchestrate a second phase of the revolution in Iran, one that would make the principles of *Ḥukūmat-i islāmī* those of the new Islamic Republic of Iran – especially the key concept of *vilāyat-i faqīh*. This was in fact incorporated into the new constitution, approved by a referendum in December 1979 (against the background of the hostage crisis with the USA, which served to stifle any effective dissent). Ultimate power as *faqīh* was of course immediately and unquestionably vested in Khomeini himself.

Concerning the events since the revolution of 1978–9 suffice it to say that the direct involvement of the clergy in politics runs the risk of the clergy and religion being tainted by political failures, and that has happened to some extent in Iran due to the clerical regime's reputation for violence, repression, and a certain amount of corruption. Thus, the Khomeinist solution to the problem of legitimate government and state–clergy relations in an officially Shīʿī country, an issue that has persisted since Safavid times, has been and still is being contested, but to what end is uncertain. The ideas of *Ḥukūmat-i islāmī* were not accepted by many high-ranking *mujtahid*s; one who was openly critical of them, Muḥammad Kāẓim Sharīʿatmadāri, was defrocked, humiliated, and persecuted for that reason. Some others who once did accept them have since turned against them, notably Ḥusayn ʿAlī Muntaẓirī, an associate of Khomeini since at least 1963 and who was thought to be Khomeini's likely successor until he was pushed out of office in 1989. Perhaps the highest-ranking and most outspoken clerical critic of *vilāyat-i faqīh*, he was essentially placed under house arrest in 1997. Lay figures who had supported Khomeini and the revolution, such as Bazargan, also became disaffected and disillusioned, especially over issues related to human rights and the role of clerics in politics. Currently, one of the most prominent such critics, though he is effectively in exile, is ʿAbd al-Karīm Surūsh (Abdolkarim Soroush), who had earlier been an architect of the "cultural revolution" aimed at Islamizing Iranian universities. Among young people, especially those in urban environments who have come of age in the period since Khomeini's death, there appears to be a growing sentiment of outright secularism and even a certain nostalgia for Pahlavi times.

References and further reading

Abisaab, R. (2004) *Converting Persia: Religion and Power in the Safavid Empire*, London: I. B. Tauris.

Abrahamian, E. (1989) *Radical Islam: The Iranian Mojahedin*, London: I. B. Tauris.

—— (1993) *Khomeinism: Essays on the Islamic Republic*, Berkeley: University of California Press.

Afary, J. (1996) *The Iranian Constitutional Revolution 1906–11*, New York: Columbia University Press.

Akhavi, S. (1980) *Religion and Politics in Contemporary Iran: Clergy–State Relations in the Pahlavi Period*, Albany: State University of New York Press.

Algar, H. (1969) *Religion and State in Iran, 1785–1906: The Role of the ʿUlamā in the Qajar Period*, Berkeley: University of California Press.

—— (1983) *The Roots of the Islamic Revolution*, London: Open Press.

Algar, H., ed. and trans. (1981) *Islam and Revolution: Writings and Declarations of Imam Khomeini*, Berkeley: Mizan Press.

Arberry, A. J., Bailey, H. *et al.*, eds. (1968–91) *The Cambridge History of Iran*, 7 vols, Cambridge: Cambridge University Press.

Arjomand, S. (1984) *The Shadow of God and the Hidden Imam: Religion, Political Order, and Societal Change in Shiʿite Iran from the Beginning to 1890*, Chicago: University of Chicago Press.

Babayan, K. (2002) *Mystics, Monarchs and Messiahs: Cultural Landscapes of Early Modern Iran*, Cambridge: Harvard University Press.

Bakhash, S. (1984) *The Reign of the Ayatollahs: Iran and the Islamic Revolution*, New York: Basic Book.

Bayat, M. (1982) *Mysticism and Dissent: Socio-Religious Thought in Qajar Iran*, Syracuse: Syracuse University Press.
Browne, E. G. (1910) *The Persian Revolution of 1905–1909*, Cambridge: Cambridge University Press.
Bulliet, R. W. (1972) *The Patricians of Nishapur*, Cambridge, MA: Harvard University Press.
Cole, J. (1998) *Modernity and the Millennium: The Genesis of the Bahai Faith in the Nineteenth-century Middle East*, New York: Columbia University Press.
—— (2002) *Sacred Space and Holy War: The Politics, Culture and History of Shiʿite Islam*, London: I. B. Tauris.
Daniel, E. L. (1979) *The Political and Social History of Khurasan under Abbasid Rule*, Minneapolis: Bibliotheca Islamica.
de Groot, J. (2007) *Religion, Culture and Politics in Iran: From the Qajars to Khomeini*, London: I. B. Tauris.
Keddie, N. R. (1981) *Roots of Revolution: An Interpretative History of Modern Iran*, New Haven: Yale University Press.
Khanbaghi, A. (2006) *The Fire, the Star and the Cross: Minority Religions in Medieval and Early Modern Iran*, London: I. B. Tauris.
Lambton, A. K. S. (1987) *Qajar Persia*, London: I. B. Tauris.
Manz, B. (2007) *Power, Politics and Religion in Timurid Iran*, Cambridge: Cambridge University Press.
Martin, V. (2003) *Creating an Islamic State: Khomeini and the Making of a New Iran*, London: I. B. Tauris.
Momen, M. (1985) *An Introduction to Shiʿi Islam: The History and Doctrines of Twelver Shiʿism*, New Haven: Yale University Press.
Morgan, D. (1988) *Medieval Persia 1040–1797*, London: Longman.
Mottahedeh, R. (1986) *The Mantle of the Prophet: Religion and Politics in Iran*, London: Chatto and Windus.
Newman, A. J. (2006) *Safavid Iran: Rebirth of a Persian Empire*, London: I. B. Tauris.
Paidar, P. (1995) *Women and the Political Process in Twentieth-Century Iran*, Cambridge: Cambridge University Press.
Savory, R. (1980) *Iran under the Safavids*, Cambridge: Cambridge University Press.
Stewart, D. (1998) *Islamic Legal Orthodoxy: Twelver Shiite Responses to the Sunni Legal System*, Salt Lake City: University of Utah Press.

6

CENTRAL ASIA

Devin DeWeese

Central Asia played a major role, often overlooked today, in the formation of many of the central religious, political, and cultural features of the Islamic world as a whole. In the initial era of the Arab conquest, it was the scene of important debates over the nature of membership in the Islamic *umma*. From the tenth to the twelfth century, it was a major center of scholarship and learning in the worldly and religious sciences, playing a key role in the development of the classical cultural profile of the Islamic world, and in the same period experienced the impact of the Turks, as they became part of the *umma* and began their millennium-long military and political domination of the central Islamic lands. In the thirteenth century, what has often been portrayed as a pivotal and destructive setback for Islamic civilization, the Mongol conquest, was experienced somewhat differently in Central Asia. The legacy of Mongol rule and the Islamization of the Mongol rulers led to a creative synthesis that shaped the region (with ramifications stretching into Iran, South Asia, and the northern and eastern frontiers of interaction with, and later imperial conquest by, the Russian and Chinese states) down to the twentieth century. And more recently, the experience of colonial rule was shared with much of the Islamic world, though in Central Asia it was shaped in distinctive ways by the specific trajectories of the Russian conquest and the Soviet experiment.

The impact of Soviet times remains strong today, after the political independence of the Central Asian heartland; indeed, the perception of the region nowadays as on the peripheries of the Islamic world, or as the home of Muslims not sure about their status as Muslims or their relationship with the larger Islamic community, is overwhelmingly the product of the region's domination by the Soviet state throughout most of the twentieth century, and its consequent isolation from many of the intellectual and cultural currents affecting the rest of the Islamic world during that period. That isolation, in turn, has led to a disturbingly low level of scholarly study and understanding of the Islamic heritage of Central Asia, and, consequently, of the character of Central Asia's rediscovery, or reformulation, of its Islamic identities today.

Before reviewing the history of Islam in this region, it is important to consider briefly what "Central Asia" means. It is, after all, a thoroughly modern designation (emerging only in the nineteenth century) with geographical referents that cover substantial political, ethnic, and linguistic diversity, both at present and throughout the Islamic era. Today the term "Central Asia" is typically used to refer to the post-Soviet states of Kazakhstan, Uzbekistan, Kyrgyzstan, Turkmenistan, and Tajikistan, but consideration of historical cultural patterns demands that the term refer also to parts of Xinjiang province in the People's Republic of China, of northern Afghanistan, of northeastern Iran, and of the Russian Federation as well. If what most of these regions share in recent times is the experience of outside imperial rule in the shape of the Russian/Soviet or Chinese states, the historical marker of Central Asia's regional coherence has been a distinctive cultural synthesis of the civilization of Inner Asia (itself a synthesis of the oasis civilizations of the Silk Road and the nomadic cultures of the steppe) with that of the Near East and the Islamic world.

What must be stressed is that historically, as today, Central Asia defies any neat definition in purely political, ethnic, linguistic, or economic terms. Definitions from a cultural perspective work better, but, to a greater extent than is often acknowledged – as a result of various modern ideologies and intellectual trends that downplay or misconstrue religious identities – the key element in the cultural synthesis that best defines Central Asia is precisely the role of Islam, and the shifting understandings, among Central Asia's peoples, of what it means to be a Muslim. In referring to a Central Asian synthesis of Inner Asian and Islamic elements, then, it is important not to lose sight of the fact that, outside the Soviet interlude and its lingering effects, the central and defining cultural element for Central Asians from the eighth to the twenty-first century has been an intimate relationship with the Islamic *umma* (and not any particular national element rooted in the pre-Islamic past or in non-Islamic Inner Asia). In short, if the region's history is properly understood, Islam may be seen to have been as crucial to the character of Central Asia as Central Asia was to the development of Islamic civilization.

Geography

In political terms, Central Asia in the Islamic period has only occasionally known unity on a substantial scale, usually when it formed part of a larger (but mostly short-lived) imperial structure based outside Central Asia itself (e.g., the Abbasid Caliphate, the Mongol empire, the USSR). As a result of this tendency toward political decentralization and outright fragmentation, indigenous geographical terms, reflecting historical regions defined both by natural features and by traditional cultural, economic, and political patterns, provide a more convenient and consistent framework for analyzing political history than any of the contemporary political boundaries. This must be stressed precisely because of the tendency, fostered by the nation-building proclivities of current Central Asian regimes (and helped along by the purely contemporary perspective of most scholars interested in Central Asia), to project modern boundaries into the past, and to present, for instance, the medieval history of Kazakhstan or of Uzbekistan, polities whose independence, of course, dates to 1991, but whose very boundaries date only to the 1920s. The historical experience of Islam in Central Asia cannot be understood seriously in terms of contemporary political structures, or in terms of contemporary (i.e., Soviet-shaped) markers of ethnic and national identity.

Among the chief historical regions comprising Central Asia, the traditional heartland was Mawarannahr, often called Transoxiana or Transoxania in Western literature. This term refers to the territories between the Amu Darya and the Syr Darya, above all the rich agricultural region dominated by the cities of Samarqand and Bukhara (anchoring the eastern and western ends, respectively, of the Zarafshan river valley), as well as the towns of the Qashqa Darya basin (Kesh, later called Shahr-i sabz, and Nakhshab, or Nasaf, later Qarshi) and those of the Surkhan Darya valley (including the ancient city of Tirmidh). Northeast of Samarqand lies the mountain-ringed valley known as Farghana, traditionally regarded as part of Mawarannahr, but often closely linked with the towns of the Tarim basin to the east. The latter region, often called Chinese or East Turkistan, and now forming the major part of the province of Xinjiang in the People's Republic of China, consists of two strings of agricultural oases along the northern and southern edges of the Takla Makan desert, irrigated by waters from the Tianshan and the Tibetan plateau.

The middle and lower course of the Syr Darya, downstream from the Farghana valley, marked a frontier zone between Mawarannahr and the vast steppe lands to the north; this region, with towns such as Tashkent, Isfijab/Sayram, Sighnaq, and Jand, came to bear the name Turkistan quite early, well before that label was applied, in nineteenth-century Russian usage, to the whole of Central Asia. The steppe lands themselves were known in indigenous sources from the eleventh to the early twentieth century as the Dasht-i Qïpchaq ("the Qïpchaq steppe," from the name of the nomadic Turkic group that dominated the region for two centuries before the Mongol conquest), and include a special subregion, to the south of Lake Balkhash, known as the "Seven Rivers" (Turkic Yeti-su, or Qazaq Zhetisu, Russian Semirechye); most of this region belongs now to Kazakhstan.

To the south of Mawarannahr, across the Amu Darya, lay the important region of Khurasan (dominated by four major cites, Marv, Balkh, Herat, and Nishapur), typically regarded as the northeasternmost province of Iran, but often more closely linked politically, ethnically, and economically with Mawarannahr; today the northern part of the historical region of Khurasan belongs to Turkmenistan and the easterly regions to Afghanistan (the rest of modern-day Afghanistan, including the regions around such cities as Kabul, Ghazna, and Qandahar, were historically regarded as part of the Indian subcontinent, or "Hind"). In the delta of the Amu Darya, south of the Aral Sea, finally, lies the irrigated oasis of Khwarazm, another rich agricultural region with its own distinct political, economic, and cultural traditions; the region was more often linked politically with part of Khurasan than with Mawarannahr.

The traditional economy of Central Asia throughout the Islamic period reflected its natural regions. In the sedentary areas, land was the primary basis of wealth, and the structures of landholding and of revenue collection keyed to productive land, as well as the management of irrigation works, were the pivotal economic issues affecting all Central Asian polities; the overland caravan trade that linked Central Asia with other parts of the world was also an important source of wealth, and urban craft production was highly developed and specialized. The pastoral nomadic economy of the steppe regions always interacted with the sedentary zones, especially through trade in horses (and slaves) from the steppe for manufactured goods and foodstuffs from the oases. In ethnolinguistic terms, Central Asia in the Islamic period has been dominated by Iranian- and Turkic-speaking peoples, with important roles played by peoples originally from outside the region, such as Arabs, Mongols, Russians, and Chinese. The indigenous population of Central Asia at the time of the Arab conquest included some Turkic elements already, but was dominated by Iranian groups known (as are their languages) by the regions they inhabited (e.g., Sogdian, Khwarazmian, Bactrian, Khotanese); the ethnic history of Central Asia during the Islamic period is one of the gradual supplanting of these Iranian-speaking groups by various Turkic peoples, who came first as a military and political elite.

From the Arab conquest to the Mongol invasion

Islam came to Central Asia during the earliest phases of the phenomenal expansion of Arab power following the career of Muḥammad; it came not through commercial contacts or missionary efforts or gradual cultural penetration, but through military campaigns that resulted in the establishment of Arab rule within the framework of the Umayyad Caliphate. Military conquest, however, was accompanied by a more gradual process of conversion among the indigenous population, facilitated both by specific inducements and, more generally, by the attractive force of the fuller participation in social and political affairs afforded by the adoption of Islam.

Arab forces were conducting raids as far as Balkh and even into Mawarannahr as early as the 650s, and by 667, Marv, in Khurasan, had replaced Basra as the seat of Arab governors responsible for operations in the region. A decisive step in the Arab conquest was marked by the career of Qutayba ibn Muslim, who as governor of Khurasan from 705 until his death in 715 achieved the subjugation of Bukhara, Samarqand, and the region of Khwarazm, as well as the launching of campaigns into the Farghana valley and the Syr Darya basin. Qutayba's rule was important also for several institutional and procedural developments that furthered the entrenchment of Islam as well as of Arab rule: Arab garrisons were quartered in local inhabitants' homes in Bukhara and Samarqand, mosques were built there, troops were levied from the local populace to serve alongside Muslim troops, and various other measures were undertaken to foster conversion to Islam, and more generally to provide an infrastructure of relationships between the local society and the conquerors. Some measures appear to have had immediate effect: when revenues declined because of the growing numbers of new converts, who upon adopting Islam were exempted from the *jizya* or "poll tax," Umayyad governors felt compelled to stiffen the requirements for conversion (and even rescinded the tax remission).

For over 20 years following his death, Qutayba's conquests were undone, as divisions among the Arabs encouraged local rulers to reassert their independence, and as the Türgesh nomadic confederation, based in the steppe, inflicted major defeats on the Arabs. Arab successes resumed in the late 730s, and a new Umayyad governor based in Marv, Naṣr ibn Sayyār, managed to re-establish control in Mawarannahr and to resume the projection of Arab power into the Farghana valley and as far north as Tashkent. The pattern of local rulers seeking outside intervention to avoid Arab control continued until 751, when a Chinese army sent to aid a client in Farghana was defeated near the Talas river; the Tang dynasty was itself rocked by internal rebellion soon thereafter, leaving no serious source of outside support for resistance to Arab rule.

As the Umayyad reconquest of Mawarannahr was underway, however, the Abbasid movement was gaining strength both among Arab troops based in Khurasan and Mawarannahr and among local converts to Islam; the latter were especially resentful of Umayyad policies that privileged Arabs over non-Arab converts, and Khurasan, in particular, played a key role in the success of the Abbasid revolution. Abbasid control was not solidified in Central Asia until the early ninth century, when a serious revolt, led by a grandson of the last Umayyad governor of the region, prompted a major campaign to Khurasan by the Caliph Hārūn al-Rashīd (r. 786-809). The campaign, continued by Hārūn's son al-Ma'mūn (r. 813–33) (who for a time made Marv the center of his Caliphal rule), marked the culmination of the Arab conquest and the end of local rulers' resistance to Abbasid rule.

It was also during this campaign that two prominent families, upon whom actual power in Central Asia would devolve as the Abbasid Caliphs gradually became figureheads rather than rulers, began their rise to military and political prominence. A participant in the campaign, a certain Ṭāhir, was made governor of Khurasan in 821, and the Tahirid dynasty ruled all of Central Asia for half a century, until its destruction by the Saffarid movement based in Sistan. Members of the Samanid family likewise served in the campaign, and governed various regions in Khurasan and Mawarannahr first under the Tahirids, and later with direct Caliphal approval. Ismāʿīl Sāmānī put an end to the Saffarid threat in 900, and established an essentially independent state based in Bukhara that ruled all of Central Asia and projected its power deep into the steppe regions.

The Samanid period (900–999) marked an important formative era in the religious and cultural profile of Central Asia, and also saw the large-scale emergence of three major Turkic dynastic groups that would eventually put an end to the Samanid polity, marking the beginning of the political ascendancy of Turkic peoples in the Muslim world: the Ghaznavids, originating among Turkic military slaves in Samanid service; the Qarakhanids, who converted to Islam in the middle of the tenth century and by 999 seized Bukhara from the Samanids; and the Saljuqs, whose rulers were at first tribal leaders among the Oghuz Turks, or Türkmens, and who destroyed Ghaznavid power in Khurasan before moving west to seize Baghdad in 1055 and inflict a severe defeat on the Byzantines in Anatolia in 1071. In Central Asia, however, Saljuq success was undermined by attacks from other Turkic nomads (their kinsmen the "Ghuzz"), and in 1141 the Saljuq ruler Sanjar, based in Marv, was defeated by the Qarakhitays (the remnants of a people who had ruled in northern China since the early tenth century but had been driven out just over a decade prior to their appearance in Central Asia).

The Qarakhitays were based in the steppes north and east of Mawarannahr, and remained a powerful non-Muslim force in Central Asia nearly down to the Mongol conquest; for the most part they ruled through local elites, however, including members of the Qarakhanid dynasties, and interfered minimally in the affairs of the urban and agricultural population. The blow to the Saljuqs dealt by the Qarakhitays allowed a local dynasty based in Khwarazm to extend its power into Khurasan and the lower Syr Darya valley, and the state thus built by these rulers, known as the Khwarazmshahs, became the most powerful in the eastern Islamic world for a brief time in the late twelfth century and early thirteenth centuries; its last ruler, Muḥammad (r. 1200–18), was ultimately driven from power by the Mongol advance.

The religious history of Central Asia from the Arab conquests to that of the Mongols is marked above all by the process of Islamization, first among the sedentary population of Khurasan and Mawarannahr, and later among the Turkic nomads of the steppe regions. Central Asia was thus both a political and a religious frontier zone, and as such it was a primary venue for practical negotiations about the social and religious prerogatives of Muslims, non-Muslims, and converts; not surprisingly, then, the region was at the forefront of debates about the nature and conditions of membership in the Muslim community. The consensus that emerged there, already during the eighth and ninth centuries, favored an inclusive approach toward membership in the *umma*, and hence toward conversion, that emphasized the affirmation of faith, and of membership in the community, over specific ritual proficiency or even proper moral behavior. Associated at first with a movement known as the Murji'a, popular in Khurasan and Mawarannahr, but later adopted as a hallmark of Ḥanafī juridical thought (which dominated Central Asia down to the twentieth century), this approach had obvious implications for the process of Islamization, and was especially important in the conversion of the steppe nomads; it sanctioned their adoption of Islam as a formal acknowledgment of affiliation with the Muslim community (entailing economic and political benefits), with details of belief and practice not entirely ignored, but certainly deferred. In part as a result of the successive periods of Islamization affecting new groups of nomads, this inclusive Ḥanafi approach helped frame the basis religious profile of Central Asia and much of the eastern Islamic world for centuries.

Whether in spite of its frontier character, or because of it, Central Asia had emerged already before the tenth century as a center of religious scholarship, and, relative to the Islamic world as a whole, played a disproportionately large role in the development of the Islamic religious sciences. Four of the pivotal Sunnī *ḥadīth* collections were compiled by figures who lived under the Tahirids and early Samanids (Muḥammad ibn Ismāʿīl al-Bukhārī, d. 870; Muslim ibn Ḥajjāj of Nishapur, d. 875; Abū ʿAbd Allāh Muḥammad al-Tirmidhī, d. 893; and Abū ʿAbd al-Raḥmān al-Nasā'ī, d. 915). The Samanid era, in particular, was crucial for forging the Sunnī synthesis that became normative in Central Asia and later, through Saljuq patronage, came to dominate parts of the Middle East as well. The fusion of Ḥanafī jurisprudence and exegesis with the credal formulations of Māturīdī theology (itself rooted in Samanid Samarqand, in the person of Abū Manṣūr Muḥammad al-Māturīdī, d. *c.* 944) continued the inclusive emphasis upon the affirmation of faith, and of membership in the salfivic community of Islam, rather than specific doctrinal knowledge or ritual performance, as the marker of Muslim identity.

At the same time, parts of Central Asia remained hospitable to other outlooks. The region of Khwarazm remained a bastion of rationalist Muʿtazilī thought well into the fourteenth century. Ismāʿīlī missionaries found receptive audiences in the first half of the tenth century, even attracting members of the Samanid dynasty; though the violent backlash that ensued substantially weakened the Ismāʿīlī presence in Central Asia, the famous poet and traveler Nāṣir-i Khusraw could still find his way to Ismāʿīlism in eleventh-century Khurasan. Sectarian movements such as the pietistic Karrāmiyya, which briefly enjoyed Ghaznavid patronage, were likewise part of the religious culture of Central Asia in the pre-Mongol period.

Mystical religious currents also emerged early in Central Asia, as Khurasan and Mawarannahr had produced a host of ascetics and pietist preachers already by the late eighth and early ninth centuries. Later celebrated as early Ṣūfīs, these figures (such as Ibrāhīm ibn Adham of Balkh [d. 777–8], Bishr al-Ḥāfī of Marv [d. 840 or 841–2], or Fuḍayl ibn ʿIyāḍ of Samarqand [d. 803]) most likely reflected distinct traditions that were later absorbed, along with local "wisdom" traditions represented by figures such as al-Ḥakīm al-Tirmidhī from the beginning of the tenth century, and specific doctrinal, ritual, or communal profiles of such movements as the Karrāmiyya and Malāmatiyya, into the Ṣūfī synthesis that emerged, with input from currents rooted in Baghdad, by the end of the tenth century. With the eleventh and especially twelfth centuries, new patterns of Ṣūfī disciplinary and organizational activity emerged, with Ṣūfīs from Khurasan such as Abū Saʿīd ibn Abīʾl-Khayr (d. 1049) and Aḥmad-i Jām (d. 1141); the hereditary Ṣūfī transmission linked to the latter was maintained, alongside control of his shrine, at least as late as the seventeenth century. By the time of the Mongol conquest, some Ṣūfī communities were developing into hierarchical corporate entities with substantial followings of lay adherents among the people. This development led to the formation of the *ṭarīqa*s or Ṣūfī orders, and Central Asia played a prominent role in this trend as well, producing the eponyms of several major orders (e.g., the Chishtiyya, the Kubrawiyya, the Yasawiyya, and the Naqshbandiyya) between the twelfth and fourteenth centuries.

It was above all in the field of jurisprudence that pre-Mongol Central Asia produced scholars and works pivotal in defining Islamic civilization; both the Shāfiʿī and Ḥanafī juridical schools were prominent in the region. Several towns of Khurasan as well as Tashkent (Shash), Taraz, and Khwarazm were Shāfiʿī strongholds in pre-Mongol times, and the region produced the prominent tenth-century jurist Abū Bakr al-Qaffāl al-Shāshī (d. 976). The Ḥanafī school was dominant elsewhere, especially in Bukhara, where its establishment was linked with the ninth-century figure of Abū Ḥafṣ al-Bukhārī (d. 832). The literary corpus of Ḥanafī jurisprudence was largely the work of Central Asian jurists from the tenth to the fourteenth century, and the period after the forging of the Ḥanafī–Māturīdī synthesis under the Samanids was particularly fruitful. Prominent Ḥanafī jurists active under the Saljuqs and Khwarazmshahs include Fakhr al-Islām ʿAlī ibn Muḥammad al-Pazdawī (d. 1089), Muḥammad ibn Aḥmad al-Sarakhsī, known as Shams al-Aʾimma (d. *c.* 1096), Najm al-Dīn Abū Ḥafṣ ʿUmar al-Nasafī (d. 1142), and Burhān al-Dīn ʿAlī al-Marghīnānī (d. 1197), whose *Hidāya* was especially influential throughout the Islamic world. In addition to their intellectual legacy, Central Asian jurists played prominent social roles as well; the Shāfiʿī and Ḥanafī *madhhab*s served as focuses of sectarian affiliation in the cities of Khurasan and Mawarannahr, and a family of Ḥanafī jurists based in Bukhara, known as the Āl-i Burhān, emerged as the chief civil authorities in that city under the non-Muslim Qarakhitays.

Mongol and Timurid eras

The Mongols are known in Islamic history above all as the destroyers of the Abbasid Caliphate, with the seizure of Baghdad in 1258; but the Mongol presence in Central Asia predated that event by nearly half a century, and the legacy of Mongol rule likewise persisted far longer in Central Asia than in many other parts of the Muslim world. The Mongol conquest profoundly altered the ethnic and religious profile of Central Asia, bringing substantial new groups of non-Muslim nomads from the Inner Asian steppe (predominantly Turkic-speaking, but organized into "tribes," based on military and administrative assignments, bearing names of both Mongol and Turkic origin) into the sedentary regions of Mawarannahr and Khurasan and thus setting the stage for a crucial new phase in the process of Islamization. The impact of the Mongol conquest on the communal formation and development of the peoples known as Uzbeks and Qazaqs, for instance, persists to this day, as do the consequences of the new lines of contestation regarding the character of Islam adopted by these peoples' ancestors. Islamization of the Mongol elites, moreover, affected Muslim society as well, as various groups vied for patronage and support from the newly converted rulers. At the same time, the new political principles established by the Mongol conquest throughout the Inner Asian world were maintained in Central Asia down to the eighteenth century, and continued to shape political order in the region as late as 1920.

The political principles introduced through the Mongol conquest are of particular importance for understanding the course of Central Asian history from the thirteenth to the twentieth century, and introduced important new variables into longstanding debates within the Islamic community regarding the conditions for membership in the *umma*, and regarding the relationship between religion and politics. According to the Mongol dispensation, ensured by the division of the empire conquered under Chinggis (Genghis) Khān and his sons, sovereign rule was a prerogative reserved solely for blood descendants of Chinggis Khān. This dispensation in turn set the stage for a profound political tension, between Chinggisid descendants who could claim the right to rule (and who could thus serve either as real contenders for power, or as puppets), and the class of tribal chieftains who often held greater practical power, through their direct command over the tribal military forces that were the basis for all military and political power. In theory, only descendants of Chinggis Khān could bear the title *khān*, emblematic of sovereign authority, while the tribal chieftains were known by the Turkic title *bek*.

This division of titulature underwent a further development in Central Asia and other parts of the Mongol-ruled world influenced by Islamic political terminology: Chinggisid princes who did not accede to sovereign power were distinguished from the *khān*s by the title *sulṭān*, while the Arabic term *amīr* came to refer to the tribal chieftains (as did the Arabo–Persian hybrid *amīr-zāda*, meaning "born of an *amīr*," usually abbreviated to *mīrzā*). These adaptations of Islamic terminology were peculiar to Central Asia and adjacent regions, but their significations were respected even when representatives of the tribal elite came to hold de facto power, or advanced claims to political authority on other foundations (e.g., with legitimacy framed in Islamic, rather than Chinggisid, terms); *amīr*id groups (e.g., the Timurids) often held real power, and not a few *khān*s in Central Asia were little more than puppets or fronts for *amīr*id warlords, but not until the eighteenth century do we find members of the tribal aristocracy venturing to adopt the title *khān*.

During the middle of the thirteenth century, the Mongol empire was divided into four major realms, ruled by lineages stemming from the sons of Chinggis Khān; Central Asia was divided among three of these realms. Most of the region, including Mawarannahr and the Tarim basin, as well as parts of Khurasan and the eastern sections of the Dasht-i Qïpchaq, belonged to the *ulus* ("portion" or "realm") of Chinggis Khān's son Chaghatay (which, however, was dominated by outside forces for much of its existence, first by the Great Khāns, based in Mongolia and China, and later by a descendant of Chinggis Khān's son and first successor, Ögedey). Parts of Khwarazm and the lower Syr Darya basin, as well as most of the Dasht-i Qïpchaq belonged to the *ulus* of Chinggis Khān's eldest son, Jochi, centered in the lower Volga valley. Other parts of Khurasan, finally, belonged to the realm of the Ilkhans, centered in Azerbaijan, which was established through the conquests of Chinggis Khān's grandson Hülegü in Iran and the Middle East from 1256–8.

Each of these western Mongol successor states underwent a protracted period of Islamization, as both the ruling elites and ordinary tribal communities adopted Islam; by the second quarter of the fourteenth century, *khāns* from each of the Chinggisid dynasties ruling in those successor states had become Muslims, and the net result of the Mongol conquests was thus a significant expansion of the *dār al-Islām*. It is often assumed that Islamization in the Mongol era was a top-down affair, with a forceful *khān* being convinced of the truth, or the usefulness, of the new religion and imposing it upon his tribal subjects (who are in turn often portrayed as indifferent or even hostile to the new religion). This model becomes less attractive when considering the essential weakness of many Chinggisid *khāns*, and contenders for power, especially in the *ulus* of Chaghatay. The importance of the tribal elements who formed the basis of would-be *khāns*' military power suggests that the *khāns* who became famous as the Islamizers of their realms (Ghāzān in Ilkhanid Iran – whose conversion was in effect challenged by the jurist Ibn Taymiyya [d. 1328], providing a foundation for Islamist critics of insufficiently observant Muslim rulers even today – Berke and Özbek in the *ulus* of Jochi, Tarmashirin and Tughluq Temür in the *ulus* of Chaghatay) may well have followed, rather than led, their subjects into the new religion, deciding that Islam had developed a substantial enough constituency among the nomads to make a declaration of support for the religion politically advantageous.

By the 1330s, real power in much of the *ulus* of Chaghatay was in the hands of the tribal chieftains, who sought compliant Chinggisids to install as *khān* to secure their own interests. About the same time, the Chaghatayid realm split into two parts, one centered in Mawarannahr and the other, which became known as Moghulistan, comprising the Tarim basin and the region of Yeti-su. Though both sections were increasingly dominated by the tribal chieftains in this era, this division of the Chaghatayid realm in the first half of the fourteenth century set the two regions on divergent paths of political history that, with some adjustments, are still reflected in the present political structures of Central Asia (i.e., the division between the western regions, which later came under Russian rule, and the eastern, which remain under Chinese rule).

In Moghulistan, a line of Chaghatayid *khāns* remained in power until the end of the seventeenth century. The major tribe was that of the Dughlats, which dominated the southern part of the Tarim basin, and both Dughlat *amīrs* and Chaghatayid *khāns* defended their interests against a series of threats, whether Timurid and later Uzbek Chinggisid inroads from the west, Qazaq encroachments from the northwest, or attacks from the Mongol Junghars to the north. Beginning in the seventeenth century, rival branches of a family of Naqshbandī *shaykhs*, descended from a Ṣūfī master of the sixteenth century, based near Samarqand, known as Makhdūm-i Aʿẓam, played important roles in the political history of the Tarim basin. The rivalry between these lineages, which took on broader ramifications through the devotion of various Qïrghïz groups to one branch or the other – hence the emergence of the Aqtaghlïq ("White-Mountain") and Qarataghlïq ("Black-Mountain") labels – facilitated the conquest of the region by the Junghars in 1681, but continued rivalries, fuelled by shifting Junghar support, eventually played into the hands of the Manchu empire (the Qing dynasty of China), which destroyed the Junghars and conquered the Tarim basin by 1758. Both the Tarim basin and the old Junghar homeland were incorporated into the Qing state, in which it eventually became known as the "New Province," Xinjiang.

The struggle among tribal chieftains in the western portion of the Chaghatayid realm culminated in the rise to power of Timur, an *amīr* of the Barlas tribe, during the 1360s. After consolidating his power in Mawarannahr and Khurasan, Timur began a series of campaigns through which he destroyed the political unity of the Jochid *ulus*, established his control over Iran and much of the Middle East, and projected his power as far east as Delhi and as far west as Ankara. The Timurid state survived its founder's death in 1405 by a century, but in a steadily diminishing form; during its last 30 years, it was reduced to Mawarannahr and Khurasan alone. The Timurid political legacy continued, after the dynasty's expulsion from Central Asia, in the form of the Moghul state established in India by Bābur; in Central Asia itself it is overwhelmingly the tradition of royal patronage of scholarship, literature (including historiography), art, and architecture that marks the chief legacy of Timurid rule.

The Mongol and Timurid eras were marked not only by the process of Islamization, but by other important religious developments as well. Juridical scholarship was maintained in Central Asia throughout these periods, and indeed down to the Soviet era, but from the thirteenth century, the social, political, and economic roles of Ṣūfī communities expanded dramatically. The Ṣūfī groups active in this period increasingly defined themselves in terms of *silsilas*, "chains" of initiatic transmission, named for prominent shaykhs of the recent past or for particular styles of mystical practice.

Figure 6 Shaykh Aḥmad Yasawī Tomb, near Turkestan City, Kazakhstan, 1394–9. The grave of the Ṣūfī saint Aḥmad Yasawī (d. 1166), who is credited with the conversion of Kazakh Turks to Islam, attracted numerous pilgrims including Tīmūr, who ordered this massive tomb be built.

Source: © Ceylan, Zafer/Aga Khan Trust for Culture

During the fourteenth and fifteenth centuries groups labeled Kubrawī, Yasawī, ʿIshqī, Khalwatī, Zaynī, and Naqshbandī were active in Khurasan and Mawarannahr, and often competed with one another for court patronage and popular followings. Partly overlapping the proliferation of Ṣūfī groups in this era was the increasing importance of shrine traditions, not merely as centers of pilgrimage (*ziyāra*), but also as focuses for royal patronage and political symbolism, and as beneficiaries of substantial pious endowments (*waqf*) whose administrators became important economic forces in Central Asian towns.

The sixteenth to nineteenth centuries

The expulsion of the Timurids was the work of a family of Chinggisids from the Jochid *ulus* and the nomadic peoples they ruled in the Dasht-i Qïpchaq; those nomads had become known, by the late fourteenth century, as Uzbeks (*özbek*), an ethnonym whose origins were linked, in indigenous tradition, with the adoption of Islam by the Jochid ruler Özbek Khān (r. 1313–41). The Chinggisids who led them in the conquest of Mawarannahr and Khurasan from the Timurids belonged to a lineage traced to Shiban, the fifth son of Jochi, and are thus sometimes referred to as the Shïbanids (and, less exactly, as Shaybanids). Chief among them was Muḥammad Shïbānī Khān, who managed to restore at least parts of the first major Uzbek confederation (formed by his grandfather Abū 'l-Khayr Khān, in the middle of the fifteenth century) but whose ambitions were cut short in 1510, when he was killed in battle with the Safavid ruler Shāh Ismāʿīl near Marv. The Uzbek forces soon withdrew from Mawarannahr, but then regrouped under other descendants of Abū 'l-Khayr Khān and expelled the Safavid troops as well as their Timurid supporters. Parts of Khurasan remained a contested zone between the Uzbeks and the Safavids well into the seventeenth century, and this political and military rivalry had important religious overtones as well, with the Safavid sponsorship of Twelver Shiʿism prompting mutual anathematizations, toward the end of the sixteenth century, by the *ʿulamāʾ* of Safavid Khurasan and those of Uzbek Mawarannahr.

As the Uzbeks faced the Safavids to the south, they faced their nomadic kinsmen to the north, in the Dasht-i Qïpchaq; though of the same ethnic stock as the Uzbek nomads who conquered Mawarannahr, they came to be known, beginning in the second half of the fifteenth century, as Qazaqs, a term meaning "freebooter" and first applied pejoratively to the nomadic elements who served other Chinggisids and opposed the rule of Abū 'l-Khayr Khān and later that of Muḥammad Shïbānī Khān. The distinction between Qazaqs and Uzbeks was thus purely political, but nevertheless became reified in separate identities. The Qazaqs remained nomadic, dwelling in the expanses of the Dasht-i Qïpchaq, and were ruled by separate lineages of Chinggisid princes, under whom they came to be divided into three loosely connected groups known as *zhüz*es (and in the west termed "hordes"), while the Uzbeks moved into Mawarannahr and Khurasan, where they adapted to more restricted pastures that favored their eventual sedentarization, and were ruled by Chinggisid *khān*s, first of the Shïbānid lineage. The religious differences between the tribal Uzbeks and the Qazaqs have been overestimated, in part due to the conscious effort by supporters of Muḥammad Shïbānī Khān to depict the Qazaqs as poor Muslims or even apostates and thereby to justify his wars against them on religious grounds. In any case, the middle

Syr Darya valley became a contested region between the Qazaq Chinggisids and the Chinggisid *khāns* of the Uzbeks based in Mawarannahr.

The power of those Chinggisid *khāns* of the Uzbeks, however, should not be overstated. What emerged in Mawarannahr under "Uzbek" rule, rather, was a distinctly decentralized polity consisting of loosely connected appanages assigned to the Chinggisid princes who participated in the conquest, and later, in theory, to their heirs. Separate Chinggisid *sulṭāns* thus ruled from Samarqand, Bukhara, Tashkent, Balkh, and other appanages, with the senior member of the extended ruling clan acknowledged as *khān*, but enjoying thereby no real ability to interfere in the internal affairs of each appanage. This decentralized polity was a factor in religious life as well, fostering heightened competition among Ṣūfī communities. In the first half of the sixteenth century, Naqshbandī, Yasawī, and Kubrawī *shaykhs* vied for popular support and political influence, with different results in the various appanages. By the second half of the sixteenth century, however, Naqshbandī groups were clearly dominating the other orders, and remained a pervasive influence in the political, social, economic, and cultural life of Central Asia well into the eighteenth century.

Toward the middle of the sixteenth century, the rough equilibrium among the various appanages began to break down, resulting in a series of struggles that culminated in the consolidation of power by ʿAbd Allāh Khān (a descendant of Jānī-bek, a grandson of Abū ʾl-Khayr Khān). His ruthless elimination of potential rivals left only his son to contend with him in his last years, and when the son was murdered by a group of *amīrs* shortly after ʿAbd Allāh's death in 1598, the dynasty stemming from Abū ʾl-Khayr was replaced by *khāns* from a different Jochid lineage, invited in by the tribal chieftains and the urban elites of Bukhara. Members of that lineage, recently ousted from their hereditary domains along the lower Volga by the Russian conquest of Astrakhan, had entered the service of ʿAbd Allāh and led campaigns on his behalf in Khurasan. The dynasty they established is referred to as that of the Janids (after one of its members), or the Ashtarkhanids (after the Central Asian form of the name of its hereditary center, Astrakhan), or the Toqay Timurids (after the son of Jochi through whom its Chinggisid descent was traced). The Ashtarkhanid era lasted until 1747, but was marked by the steady erosion of the *khān*'s authority, the rise in power of the tribal chieftains, and the loss of substantial territories. The region of Tashkent, for instance, was lost permanently to the Qazaqs, the Farghana valley became essentially independent in the later seventeenth century, and the old system of multiple appanages was reduced, in the Ashtarkhanid state, to two basic divisions, with the nominal *khān* ruling Mawarannahr from Bukhara, and the heir-apparent ruling parts of Khurasan from Balkh.

Meanwhile, as the Uzbeks retook Mawarannahr early in the sixteenth century, under the leadership of the Abū ʾl-Khayrid family, another Chinggisid dynasty ruling over Uzbek nomads from the Dasht-i Qïpchaq succeeded in driving out the Safavid occupiers of Khwarazm and seized power in that region. The Khwarazmian Uzbek dynasty they established, sometimes referred to as the ʿArabshahids or Yadgarids, managed to extend its control southwards into parts of Khurasan (thereby maintaining pressure against the Safavids), but was often at odds with the Uzbeks of Mawarannahr. (Khwarazm was seized twice during the sixteenth century by rulers based in Bukhara, while in the second half of the seventeenth century Khwarazmian rulers were able to lead campaigns deep into Ashtarkhanid territory.) The Khwarazmian Uzbek dynasty endured down to the early eighteenth century; one of its members was the *khān* Abū 'l-Ghāzī (r. 1643–63), who left two important Chaghatay Turkic historical works, one outlining the history of the Chinggisid dynasties (including original material on his own lineage), and the other presenting a history of the Türkmens, who dwelled on the frontiers of the Khwarazmian oasis and of Khwarazmian domains in Khurasan.

The power of the Chinggisid *khān*s was substantially weakened, both among the Ashtarkhanids and the Khwarazmian Uzbek dynasty, by the beginning of the eighteenth century. In the same era, Central Asia was beset by severe economic stress and military invasions, setting the stage for a substantial restructuring of the region's political and military foundations that was still underway at the time of the Russian conquest. The external invasions came from the north and the south. The Mongol Junghars (known also as Oyrats or, in Central Asia, as Qalmaqs), who had threatened Central Asian polities as early as the mid-fifteenth century, grew strong again in the later seventeenth century, dominating the eastern Dasht-i Qïpchaq and launching repeated raids in the Syr Daryā basin. A series of devastating Junghar attacks on the Qazaqs sent waves of refugees into Mawarannahr during the 1720s, destroying that region's agricultural production for several years, and leading much of its settled population to abandon central Mawarannahr (many fled to the Farghana valley). The Qazaqs managed to regroup and resist further Junghar encroachments by the late 1720s, but the remains of the Ashtarkhanid state were left in disarray, and the region was easily seized by Nādir Shāh – the Afshār warlord who took power in Iran in 1728 – as he invaded from Khurasan in 1740; Nādir Shāh also conquered Khwarazm in the same year, and his own assassination in 1747 set the stage for the transformation of Central Asia's political structure.

In Mawarannahr, power was seized by a chieftain of the Manghït tribe who had served, but dominated, the weak Ashtarkhanid ruler Abū 'l-Fayḍ Khān (r. 1711–47), and who had spent time in Nādir Shāh's army. The Manghït dynasty he thus established – whose rulers, as non-Chinggisids, hesitated for a time to claim the title *khān* but eventually preferred the title *amīr* – endured until 1920, when its last member was ousted by the Soviets. In Khwarazm, a period of near anarchy following Nādir Shāh's conquest culminated in the capture of the region's capital, Khiva, by the Türkmen tribe of the Yomuts, in 1768; the Yomuts were driven out, and order was restored, by a chieftain of the Qonghrat tribe, who had likewise been in the service of the earlier Chinggisid *khān*s of Khwarazm, but now assumed power in his own right. The Qonghrat dynasty (whose members adopted the title *khān* only in the early nineteenth century) also survived as a Russian protectorate until eliminated by the Soviets in 1920. A final direct result of Nādir Shāh's conquests was the emergence of the Afghān state under Aḥmad Shāh Durrānī, who in the face of Manghït weakness, and disarray in Iran, was able to add Herat and Balkh to his domains in Kabul and Qandahar, thus forging the basis for modern Afghanistan and adding yet another non-Chinggisid polity to the map of Central Asia.

The other major non-Chinggisid political newcomer of the eighteenth century was the small realm in the Farghana valley that came under the leadership of chieftains of the Ming tribe. Based eventually in the town of Khoqand, the Ming rulers – at first maintaining the tribal title *biy* but adopting the title *khān* late in the eighteenth century – consolidated their control in the Farghana valley, exploiting its agricultural and commercial wealth to make the khanate of Khoqand the most powerful and dynamic of the Central Asian states during the first half of the nineteenth century. The *khān*s of Khoqand were able to expand the state substantially, seizing Tashkent under ʿĀlim Khān (r. 1798–1809) and the towns of the middle Syr Daryā under his brother ʿUmar Khān (r. 1809–22). Umar Khān's son Muḥammad ʿAlī (Madalī, r. 1822–42) continued the expansion, as he erected a series of forts in the Dasht-i Qïpchaq in order to control the Qazaqs – an effort that would bring the khanate of Khoqand into direct confrontation with the Russian empire, which was expanding into Qazaq territory from the north – extended his authority over the Qïrghïz tribes of the Tien-shan region, and conquered several small principalities in the Pamirs as well. Madalī Khān's campaigning fostered resentments in the Farghana valley, leading some local elements to summon the Manghït *amīr* of Bukhara, Naṣr Allāh (r. 1826–60), to their aid; the Bukharan army eventually seized Khoqand itself, and Madalī was killed. Though the Ming dynasty's rule was soon restored, the khanate was beset by vicious internal strife, between the sedentary population of the Farghana valley and the nomadic Qïpchaq tribe, that weakened the state on the eve of its direct confrontation with the Russians.

The khanate of Khoqand was also heavily involved in the affairs of the Tarim basin, and supported efforts by exiled Aqtaghlïq *khwāja*s to stir up rebellions among the Muslim population of the region. Later, as the Qing dynasty was preoccupied with a major uprising among Chinese Muslims from 1862 to 1876, a former military commander under the khanate of Khoqand, Yaʿqūb Bek, succeeded in carving out his own state, with Aqtaghlïq support, based in Kashghar, and sought diplomatic recognition from the British, until the suppression of the revolt allowed the Qing to reconquer the Tarim basin by 1878. Following the demise of the Manchu dynasty in 1911, the Turkic-speaking Muslim population of the Tarim basin sought occasionally to reassert its independence, adopting the old ethnonym "Uyghur" and creating an "East Turkistan Republic" in the 1930s and 1940s. With the victory of Mao Zedong's communists in 1949, however, the region's incorporation into the People's Republic of China was assured, and its designation as the Xinjiang Uyghur Autonomous Region masked both its political domination by the Chinese majority, and the increasing dilution of its Muslim character through extensive colonization by Han Chinese.

In addition to their Uzbek tribal origins, the rulers of the khanates of Bukhara, Khiva, and Khoqand shared a pattern of military, administrative, and religious reforms aimed at centralizing their power and reducing their dependence on tribal forces for their military strength (a goal that had eluded most of the Chinggisid *khān*s). The religious reforms, which preceded the Western-inspired reform efforts of the Russian era, advocated by the so-called *jadīd*ists, by nearly a century, were in fact aimed at undermining locally entrenched and politically influential Ṣūfī communities, and the local urban elites and tribal forces with which they were often allied, by attacking the traditional devotional practices they cultivated as alien to Islam. In these efforts, the rulers were often supported by Ṣūfī *shaykh*s of the Mujaddidī branch of the Naqshbandiyya, which had emerged in seventeenth-century India and had moved into Central Asia in the early eighteenth century, challenging the indigenous Naqshbandī communities and the popular practices that had come to be associated with them. Local Ṣūfī traditions survived, however, as did the local customs which had been fought against by the reformers, and the real blow to Central Asia's legacy of Sufism came only with the Soviet era.

Russian and Soviet impact

The nineteenth century also saw renewed economic development in the khanates, but in the end the Central Asian states were simply outmatched by the power of the Russian empire. Russian commercial ties with Central Asia dated to the sixteenth century, and Russian expansion eastward to the Pacific, through Siberia, completed by the later seventeenth century, led to encroachments on Qazaq pasture lands that ultimately reduced most of the Qazaqs to vassal status by the end of the eighteenth century; the suppression of Qazaq revolts during the 1830s and 1840s brought Russian armies into the Syr Darya basin, and outposts of the khanate of Khoqand were captured in the 1850s. With the end of the Crimean War, and the suppression of Muslim resistance to Russian rule in the North Caucasus, the way was open for expanded Russian military operations in southern Central Asia; the Syr Darya valley was seized in 1864, Tashkent fell in 1865, Samarqand was captured in 1868, and Khiva was taken in 1873. The khanates of Bukhara and Khiva were left as Russian protectorates, though with their territories reduced, as some lands were put under direct Russian rule; the khanate of Khoqand was accorded the same status at first, but unrest in the Farghana valley prompted Russian officials to dissolve the khanate in 1876. The last military resistance in the region came from the Türkmen tribes dwelling southwards from Khiva; they were subjugated by the early 1880s.

Russian rule initially entailed few direct challenges to traditional social, religious, and cultural patterns; these were ultimately affected more by the disruptions of traditional economic patterns entailed by the Russian conquest than by particular government policies. Among the changes to local society, special attention has long been focused on the emergence of small native circles, largely among the new economic elites fostered by increased commercial ties with Russia, who grew critical of traditional society in Central Asia and called for its revitalization through educational and cultural change. Although it was among these elements, often collectively referred to as *jadīd*ists, that the first nationalists, intent on defining communal identity on an ethnic and linguistic, rather than religious, basis, emerged in the early twentieth century (including some who would be the earliest native allies of Russian revolutionary parties), their impact on their own society is often exaggerated. They were, after all, inspired largely by Western (in this case, Russian) modes of thought and expression, and were largely ignored by the vast majority of Central Asians who maintained their traditional outlook and lifestyle. The extent to which these elements were out of touch with the real concerns of most Central Asians is suggested by the lack of any role played by the *jadīd*ists in the Central Asian revolt of 1916, a genuine popular uprising that took months to suppress and shook the Russian state on the eve of the upheavals of 1917. Nevertheless, elements of their program were eventually implemented (though in ways few of the *jadīd*ists could have expected) by the Soviet state, and the reevaluation of communal identities and mores they pioneered likewise found expression through state policies that created the modern Soviet nations of Central Asia.

The revolutions of 1917 in Russia, and the Bolshevik victory in the ensuing civil war, were instrumental in creating the modern map of Central Asia, through the national delimitation undertaken in 1924–5 by the Soviet government. The aim was to create state structures for people's republics that reflected both ethnically defined communities and the rhetoric of Lenin and Stalin about self-determination on a national basis. Subsequent changes in the status of the units created then continued until 1936, yielding the five Central Asian republics that not only defined the region for the rest of the Soviet era, but also survive today with their Soviet-drawn borders intact. Soviet policy required that national identities be subordinated to the task of building a socialist society. While this entailed the heavy Russification of local culture and language, and the centralization of political control and economic decision-making in Moscow, local Communist Party elites succeeded, beginning from the 1960s, in exercising considerable autonomy within the respective republics, and it was these elites who, after an interlude in which the central government attempted to reassert control in the name of reform and an end to corruption, managed to co-opt the nationalist sentiments that emerged during the late 1980s, and to hold on to power as the Soviet Union was dissolved and the former Soviet republics became independent states.

These local elites succeeded, during the 1990s, in stifling political dissent in all the Central Asian states, though each republic's development has been shaped by specific local factors as well as the shared Soviet legacy. Perhaps the most important aspect of that legacy, broadly speaking, is a commitment on the part of each republic's elite to the ongoing viability of the Soviet-defined nations they now dominate. In effect, administrative and intellectual tools heavily shaped by the Soviet experience have been used in the service of forging and solidifying national identities that were themselves largely products of the Soviet era. In each case, however, they became a fresh synthesis of selected elements of indigenous Central Asian culture – whether rooted in Inner Asian or Islamic or Soviet tradition – regarded as compatible with the outlook and interests of the respective republican elites.

It remains unclear what role Islam, in its various interpretations, will play in these syntheses. What is clear is that Soviet-era policies and approaches toward religious life continue to play an important role in Central Asia, and not merely through the official administrative structures created by the Soviets to manage religious affairs (which survive now, on a republican basis) or through the legal regulations on religious practice that were routinely transferred from the Soviet constitution into the republican constitutions. Rather, the Soviet era shaped religious life in more fundamental ways, and the present elites were decisively shaped, in terms of their attitudes toward religious life, by their Soviet training; yet the Soviet impact on Islam is typically misunderstood, in part because of the Sovietological emphasis on contrasting Islam with nationalism, each (but particularly the former) understood in overly simplistic terms. On the one hand, many aspects of traditional Islamic religious life persisted through the Soviet period, and experienced a revival of sorts as anti-religious pressures abated in the late 1980s. On the other hand, the Soviet government itself, ironically and no doubt unwittingly, took measures that fostered the viability of narrower, "fundamentalist" interpretations of Islamic legality and propriety that were quite foreign to Central Asia's traditional Islamic religious life, but now receive support from abroad, and play on the insecurities of Central Asian Muslims, after 70 years of antireligious pressures, by assuring them that their Islam was spoiled during the Soviet era, and that they thus require instruction and reform from outside.

What is missing, still, from the debates about the role of Islam in Central Asia's future – above all, the debate about what kind of Islam will find support and commitment among the people – is a substantive appreciation of the patterns of traditional Islamic life that marked Central Asia for centuries prior to the Soviet period. These include the crucial role of shrine-centered religious practice, often linked with sacralized kinship groups, in the religious life and lore of Central Asian Muslims (a prime target of Islamist attacks today); the patterns of hereditary prestige and authority invested in families linked with important figures of the past, especially Ṣūfī saints; the impact of Ṣūfī practice and thought in life-cycle rites and communal ceremonies; the integration of economic and religious life through sacralized occupational groups (infusing labor and its products with religious meaning); and the recollection of religious lore linked to saints and sacred sites, and to narratives transmitted for centuries about the establishment of Islam in particular regions, in the communal and personal identities of Central Asian Muslims.

Ironically, the era in which Central Asia was dominated by the Uzbek Chinggisid and tribal dynasties is the most poorly studied, and poorly understood, period in Central Asian history, especially in terms of its religious history; yet it is clearly this period that holds the most promise in terms of understanding the antecedents to the impact of the Soviet experiment and of independence. To be sure, considerable attention has been devoted to the period of Russian rule, from which we have Russian descriptions of religious life in Central Asia, as background to the Soviet and post-Soviet eras; but much of the substance of religious life in Central Asia, certainly from the sixteenth to nineteenth century, and even in the Russian period as well, remains inaccessible to those who will consult only Russian sources (and the same holds true for those who consult only materials in the modern, Soviet-defined national languages of Central Asia). At its best, this approach results in a skewed understanding of the religious landscape of Central Asia before the Soviet impact (distorted above all by the inordinate attention given to the thin layer of reformists); at its worst, this approach yields the sweeping generalizations and baseless characterizations of what "Central Asian Islam" was and is that fill some popular accounts of Central Asia today.

References and further reading

Babadžanov, B. M. (1996) "On the History of the Naqšbandīya Muǧaddidīya in Central Māwarā'annahr in the Late 18th and Early 19th Centuries," in M. Kemper, A. von Kügelgen, D. Yermakov, eds. *Muslim Culture in Russia and Central Asia from the 18th to the Early 20th Centuries*, Berlin: Klaus Schwarz Verlag, 385–413.

Barthold, V. V. (1962) *Four Studies on the History of Central Asia*, trans. V. and T. Minorsky, 3 vols, Leiden: E. J. Brill.

Bartol'd, V. V. (1977) *Turkestan Down to the Mongol Invasion*, trans. V. and T. Minorsky, ed. C. E. Bosworth, 4th edn., London: Luzac & Co.

Bosworth, C. E. (1963) *The Ghaznavids: Their Empire in Afghanistan and Eastern Iran 994–1040*, Edinburgh: Edinburgh University Press.

Bregel, Y. (2003) *An Historical Atlas of Central Asia*, Leiden: Brill.

Burton, A. (1997) *The Bukharans: A Dynastic, Diplomatic and Commercial History, 1550–1702*, New York: St. Martin's Press.

Daniel, E. L. (1979) *The Political and Social History of Khurasan under Abbasid Rule 747–820*, Minneapolis and Chicago: Bibliotheca Islamica.
Dankoff, R. trans. (1983). Yūsuf Khāṣṣ Ḥājib, *Wisdom of Royal Glory (Kutadgu Bilig), A Turko-Islamic Mirror for Princes*, Chicago: University of Chicago Press.
DeWeese, D. (1994) *Islamization and Native Religion in the Golden Horde: Baba Tükles and Conversion to Islam in Historical and Epic Tradition*, University Park, PA: Pennsylvania State University Press.
Fletcher, J. (1995) *Studies on Chinese and Islamic Inner Asia*, ed. B. F. Manz, Aldershot: Variorum.
Frye, R. N. (1997) *Bukhara: The Medieval Achievement*, Costa Mesa, CA: Mazda Publishers; 1st ed., 1965.
Golden, P. B. (1992) *An Introduction to the History of the Turkic Peoples: Ethnogenesis and State-Formation in Medieval and Early Modern Eurasia and the Middle East*, Wiesbaden: Otto Harrassowitz.
Gross, J. and Urunbaev, A. eds. and trans. (2002) *The Letters of Khwāja ʿUbayd Allāh Aḥrār and his Associates*, Leiden: Brill.
Kim, H. (2004) *Holy War in China: The Muslim Rebellion and State in Chinese Central Asia, 1864–1877*, Stanford: Stanford University Press.
Madelung, W. (1971) "The Spread of Maturidism and the Turks," in *Actas do IV Congresso des Estudos Arabes et Islâmicos, Coimbra-Lisboa*, Leiden: E. J. Brill, 109–68.
Manz, B. F. (1989) *The Rise and Rule of Tamerlane*, Cambridge: Cambridge University Press.
McChesney, R. D. (1991) *Waqf in Central Asia: Four Hundred Years in the History of a Muslim Shrine, 1480–1889*, Princeton: Princeton University Press.
—— (1996) *Central Asia: Foundations of Change*. Princeton: Darwin Press.
Privratsky, B. G. (2001) *Muslim Turkistan: Kazak Religion and Collective Memory*, Richmond: Curzon Press.
Saray, M. (1989) *The Turkmens in the Age of Imperialism: A Study of the Turkmen People and their Incorporation into the Russian Empire*, Ankara: Turkish Historical Society Printing House.

7

SOUTHEAST ASIA

Nelly van Doorn-Harder

Living far away from the heartlands of Islam, Muslims in Southeast Asia used to be hardly known and seldom heard of. Their expressions of Islam had the reputation for being moderate, pluralist and less influenced by Arabic culture than was the case in some other Muslim countries outside the Middle East. But after the terrorist attacks of September 11, 2001, the area suddenly became scrutinized as part of the world-wide networks of Islamic terrorism and burst onto the scene with mostly negative news of bombings on the idyllic island of Bali in Indonesia, the application of the *sharīʿa* law in certain Malaysian states, terrorists who were hiding and plotting in Singapore, kidnapped tourists in the Philippines, and an escalation of violence in southern Thailand that remains inexplicable to observers of Thai Islam. These events and the flood of publications analyzing them have not only created negative impressions of the region, but also overshadow the real image and expressions of Islam. These have to be sought in an ongoing struggle to re-establish Islamic religious values and to make Islam a force of change on which to build a just and prosperous society. In fact, a virtual revival is taking place that is expressed in intentional religious observance, in creating new Muslim institutions, in building mosques and schools, and in ever increasing numbers of Southeast Asian pilgrims going on the *ḥajj* to Mecca.

Over 250 million of the world's Muslims live in Southeast Asia, a region that stretches over a 3,000-mile maritime crescent east of India, south of China and north of Australia. Forming a geographical unity, the countries in this area used to be known as "the lands below the winds." The Muslim communities that are living in Malaysia, Thailand, Singapore, Indonesia, Brunei and the Philippines historically shared customs and unique characteristics but were separated by colonial forces. Situated at the crossroad of extensive global trade networks, they were introduced to Islam by Arab, Indian, and incidental Chinese Muslim merchants. Currently the estimated numbers of Muslims in this area are: Malaysia, around 55 percent of 24 million inhabitants; Thailand, of 64 million 5 percent are Muslim, most of whom live in the southern provinces that border Malaysia; Indonesia, 87 percent of 245 million; Brunei, 67 percent of 380,700; and the Philippines where Muslims (5 percent of 84 million) are concentrated in the south on the island of Mindanao and the Sulu Archipelago that lies in the vicinity of north-east Malaysia.

The era of commerce

Tombstones found on the northern coast of Sumatra dating from 1211 and 1297 are silent witnesses to the reality that Islam spread in the area between the thirteenth and sixteenth centuries. Coastal ports and kingdoms thus became part of an expanding Muslim community that linked Arabian, Indian and Chinese Muslims. The most famous early communities under Islamic rule were those of the port city of Melaka (1430s), and the kingdom of Aceh at the northern tip of Sumatra (1515) where the sultans applied Islamic law. The area known as Patani, now in southern Thailand, was another leading center of knowledge and preaching of Islam in Southeast Asia.

With local rulers embracing Islam, the religion spread rapidly and took over political, educational and legal systems. Nominal Muslim communities slowly incorporated orthodox rituals, practices, and texts. For example, they gave up the food staple of pork, stopped cremating the dead, and men were circumcised and adopted Arab-Islamic names. A pluralist version of Islam developed that was mostly tolerant of the Hindu, Buddhist, and indigenous traditions it encountered. Incorporating local trends of mysticism, a vibrant Ṣūfī tradition arose that became informed by the works of the great Islamic scholars from the Middle East such as al-Ghazālī (d. 1111). Islamic learning focused on *fiqh* (jurisprudence), *kalām* (philosophy) and Sufism. Local communities were centered around the village mosque or individual *shaykhs* of Ṣūfī brotherhoods (*ṭarīqa*), while local scholars of Islam (*ʿulamāʾ*) guided the believers in their faith. Malay became the vehicle to transmit Muslim learning while those who had studied Islam deeply knew Arabic, a language the populace considered to be sacred.

Although geographically far removed from the heartlands of Islam in the Middle East, the area nevertheless was part of the cosmopolitan Muslim community. Connections were maintained through the *ʿulamāʾ* who studied in Mecca and Medina and already by the sixteenth century had started to form a distinct community in the Hijaz. They brought back a more *sharīʿa*-oriented Islam and upon return to the homelands, in an ongoing attempt to deepen the understanding of their faith, they wrote and translated *fiqh* manuals according to the *madhhab* of al-Shāfiʿī (d. 820) that until today is predominant in Southeast Asia.

The Islamic faith developed within a cultural and religious melting pot in which Islamic literature was being grafted on to existing stories and pre-Islamic Hindu stories were recast into an Islamic mould. Stories from Arabic and Persian literature about the Prophet Muḥammad, his companions, family, and the prophets of Islam, were retold as *hikayat* in Malay and written in the adapted Arabic script called Jawi. These stories, for example the folkloristic/mystical *Hikāyat Nūr Muḥammad* ("The Story of the Mystic Light of Muḥammad") were recited out loud and circulated in tandem with tales about local Muslim saints, and heroes from Hindu epics. Later on the *sejarah* genre developed. It was modeled on the *Sejarah Melayu* (History of the Malays, written around 1612) and explained how societies became Muslim and how sultanates were founded.

Religious and cultural domination could go several ways. At the same time that in Northeast Sumatra Sultan Malik al-Saleh (d. 1297) founded the Islamic government of Pasai, Sri Maharaja Kertarajasa (1294–1309) founded the Hindu/Buddhist Majapahit empire in East Java. Pasai went on to become a model state for Islam while

Majapahit provided the prototype for Javanese court ceremonies, ceremonial behavior and the arts.

By the end of the sixteenth and during the seventeenth century, intense religious activities developed in the sultanate of Aceh. Pilgrims such as the famous sixteenth-century Malay writer Hamzah Fansuri settled there after studying the mystical schools of thought in Siam (Thailand) and Arabia. Writing about the religious and philosophical debates of his time, Fansuri placed these in his own local environment in Sumatra. Drawing from the idea of the five grades of being of Ibn al-ʿArabī (d. 1240), Fansuri furthermore formulated key theosophical doctrines based on a monistic view of God (Riddell 2001: 104–10). Later on, the scholar Nūr al-Dīn al-Rānirī (d. 1656) who was influenced by Islamic teachings from the Hadhramawt in South Arabia, refuted these mystical works as heretical. Thus he ignited doctrinal disputes and initiated a virtual process of religious reform that eventually affected the entire region. This was a vibrant period of time during which the lands below the winds were connected to a global Muslim community, while, at the same time, developing deeply local expressions of Islam in which sultans were believed to hold extraordinary powers and other possessors of magic prowess were held in high esteem.

Localized Islam

From the coastal communities, Islam spread to the inner lands where local Hindu/Buddhist rulers – *raja*s – accepted Islam and decreed their entire family, staff, and subjects to follow them in the new faith. Under the patronage of the new Muslim rulers *sharīʿa* law was then applied by court-appointed judges and scholars. They furthermore enforced a form of nominal Islam on their vassal states and some even embarked on warfare to convert non-Muslim cities and villages. The earliest coastal Muslim courts of Pasai and Melaka served as important models in the Islamization process: Pasai for its religious scholars, and the court of Melaka because "its style of living, its religious learning, and its literary language became standards for later sultanates" (Gelman Taylor 2003: 75).

According to the legends, the conversion of kings often came suddenly through magical intervention that later on served to impress upon their subjects that they had mystical and supernatural powers. These were necessary as the ruler, for example according to Javanese Muslim beliefs, "was God's 'screen' (*warana*) on earth, the screen through which people must pass to reach God and through which God must pass to reach people" (Owen 2005: 58).

The nine holy men or *walī*s who are credited with introducing Islam to Indonesia went through similar conversion experiences. The stories and traditions about these events and the miraculous powers held by the *walī*s continue to inspire Muslims who retell them in the *wayang* or shadow puppet theater and perform pilgrimages to their holy graves that are scattered throughout Indonesia. The foremost *walī*, Sunan Kalijaga, became a saint after years of meditation near a river. This practice allowed him to speak Arabic without studying the language and to fly through the air. Sunan Kalijaga introduced the method of infusing local customs and practices with Islam, which provided a model of peaceful religious transmission. He used local practices and culture such as the shadow puppet theater (*wayang*) and the *selamatan*, a ceremonial, communal meal of reconciliation, to gradually convert the population to Islam.

Customs and beliefs that later developed in the various Muslim regions started to vary considerably as the numerous Malay states lacked central Islamic authorities while having to accommodate to the colonial powers.

Colonizing powers

While the process of Islamizing continued in the respective countries, European colonial powers began to encroach upon the area. By the sixteenth century, the Spaniards had successfully driven the Muslims (and Jews) out of Spain and, acting in the same spirit of reconquista, took Manila in 1570. At the time Islam had just settled in the south of the Philippines in the newly established Islamic sultanates of Sulu and Mindanao that lie across from north-east Malaysia. The Dutch arrived during the seventeenth century in search of spices and other goods to trade. Their colonizing activities reduced the traffic between the Indonesian islands and the rest of the Muslim world; between 1750 and 1914 they gradually expanded their power over the archipelago.

Through treaties between the Dutch and the British (1824 and 1871), a relatively coherent, interactive region became cut up in dependencies and the Malaysian and Indonesian borders were realigned. European powers also encroached on Brunei that had been ruled by a sultan since the fourteenth century, and became a British protectorate in 1906. In 1819, Singapore was set up by the British as a maritime base and free port. The only country that escaped colonization was Thailand. Through these colonial pressures, commerce gave way to a peasant-based society. Islam became more inward-oriented, loosing some of its original vibrancy of applying and producing Islamic laws and texts. Colonial powers also dealt with their Muslim subjects in a variety of ways.

In Malaysia, the administration of Islam was village-based under the rule of sultans. The British preserved the prevailing system of sultanates and, while taking control in most other areas, left Islam and Malay customs in the hands of the sultans and religious officials. By the nineteenth century, the sultans began to apply Islamic law in an attempt to strengthen Malay society against the British and to enhance their own royal power. Via the Council of Islamic Religion and Malay Customs (*Majlis Agama dan Isti'dat Melayu*) that was set up in 1915 in Kelantan, the sultans forged a close relationship between the state sultan and Islam.

In contrast, the Dutch colonial government in Indonesia tried to curtail the autonomy of the Muslim community. In principle, Muslims could practice the rituals pertaining to the five pillars of faith, and they could marry and be buried according to Islamic law. However, the Dutch controlled Muslim autonomy via special courts called the *Raad Agama* (religious court) and required that all mosques should be under supervision of Dutch-appointed civil servants or *bupati*. In an attempt to diminish the influence of Islamic law, the colonial government gave preference to indigenous or *adat* laws.

Over the course of the nineteenth century, the rural boarding schools called *pesantren* developed into central institutions for transmitting Islamic knowledge and preserving Islamic rituals. Often far removed from the centers of power, these schools largely escaped Dutch interference and grew phenomenally during the nineteenth century when links to international Muslim networks were expanded. The educational system was founded on the classical Middle Eastern mosque-model of a close relationship between teacher (*kiai*) and student (*santri*) who each followed their own curriculum. Today, the student–teacher relationship is still significant and continues even after the death of an influential teacher.

Reformist Islamic movements

By the early nineteenth century the sea routes between India and China became heavily used due to Western commercial activities driven by the industrial revolution. Benefiting from improved means of communications and transportation, Southeast Asian Muslims could travel with greater ease to the Middle East for study and pilgrimage. The opening of the Suez Canal in 1869 was a watershed event and allowed greater volumes of traffic to the Middle East. By the 1880s Southeast Asians formed the largest contingents of pilgrims in Mecca. Many stayed in the holy city for study and returned with new ideas about Islamic reform that could be transmitted via print and telegraph at greater speed than ever before. Muslim traders especially connected with Islamic networks of knowledge and transmitted these throughout the region. A trend of thinking that took hold of several parts of Southeast Asia was radical reformism. In the early nineteenth century, inspired by puritanical Wahhābī ideas, radical reformists called Padri became active in the Minangkabau area of Sumatra, where they tried to eradicate Islamic folk practices. Forming pockets of "correct" Islam in fortified villages, they attacked cockfighting, the use of opium, gambling, drinking, matrilineal marriage practices, and raided neighboring communities to enforce their understanding of Islam.

With the increased modes of transportation, more Arab immigrants moved to Singapore, Malaysia and Indonesia. On the wings of these exchange movements came the ideas about reformation and modernization proposed by the Egyptian scholar Muḥammad ʿAbduh (d. 1905) and his disciple Rashīd Riḍā (d. 1935) who taught that a return to the scriptural sources of Islam and purification of indigenous practices would lead to re-definition and reformulation of Islamic ideas. Via publications distributed via Singapore these modernist ideas influenced Southeast Asian Muslims in various degrees.

Naturally, the reformist movement was at odds with many local practices and beliefs such as Sufism. However, it seldom eradicated these practices by force, but rather convinced Muslims gradually to abandon rituals that it deemed reprehensible and to focus on the purely spiritual aspects of Sufism instead. Reformists furthermore considered practices such as chanting praises for the Prophet and holding *dhikr*s (circles that repeat phrases of the Qur'ān, or the name of God) as un-Islamic. They also condemned the veneration of holy persons and visiting their graves (*ziyāra*). The success of the reformist movement in Indonesia can especially be ascribed to the fact that up to this day it has been replacing indigenous practices slowly with its own puritanical models.

As was the case in the Middle East, reformist Islam greatly influenced society at large since it became a rallying banner against colonialism. Reformists set up schools that democratized education and brought Islam outside what were considered to be dusty *pesantren* (Islamic boarding schools) with "backward" (or un-modern) leaders, the *kiai*. These modern forms of Islamic education led to an intellectual revolution that still yields fruit in contemporary Indonesia and Malaysia today.

In Indonesia the movement gained strength when several organizations came into existence that applied the reformist message to society. The largest and most influential of these was the Muhammadiyah organization that was set up by Muhammad Dahlan in 1912. The schools it built opened wide vistas for Muslims who, up to then, could only follow religious curriculums at the *pesantren* Qur'ān schools as the majority of the Muslim population was denied access to the Dutch school system. Muhammadiyah schools offered a mixed curriculum of religious and academic or "secular" subjects. They trained Indonesia's future leaders, included women in the educational process, and provided venues for upward mobility. Moreover, the reformist movement inspired the *pesantren* to reconsider their role in the Muslim landscape. In fact, Muhammadiyah's presence forced the *pesantren* leaders, the *kiai*, to work together which resulted in the founding of the Nahdlatul Ulama movement (NU) in 1926. Continuing until today, NU espouses the interpretation of Islam that allows the practice of indigenous and Ṣūfī rituals as long as these do not infringe on the teachings of Islam. NU members consider *dhikr*s as prayers of praise, and students in the *pesantren* honor the Prophet weekly by chanting songs in his praise and they visit the graves of their great leaders, insisting that they neither venerate them, nor pray to them, rather, that they "honor them with a visit."

NU-minded Muslims became known as "traditionalist," while "reformist" or "modernist" remained the epithet for Muhammadiyah-minded Muslims. At the time of their establishment, both the organizations of Muhammadiyah and of the NU were part of a larger movement in which Muslims and non-Muslims in the area formed voluntary associations such as literary clubs, labor unions, and educational and religious groups. Via these initiatives local populations could pursue their own agendas while living under colonial rule.

In Malaysia, Islamic reformists spread their views via the Singapore-based journal *al-Imam* in which the Kaum Muda (Young Group) criticized the sultans and their religious bureaucracies. They were equally opposed by the British, by traditional religious authorities and by nationalists, but after World War II their activities resulted in the establishment of several Islamic reform organizations. In 1951 several of these organizations found a home in the PAS Party (The Islamic Party of Malaysia) that won local elections and applied the *sharīʿa* in some of Malaysia's states.

Indonesian reformers furthermore carried the message to Thailand. For example, in 1926, the political refugee Ahmad Wahad sought refuge in Thailand where he started to promote reformist ideas among his followers. Building on the puritanical reformist teachings, by the 1970s, Thai Muslims who had studied in the Middle East launched missionary activities (*dakwah*).

Era of independence: Islam and politics

During World War II the colonial forces had to turn their attention to their homelands with the result that dreams of independence held by many who were active in organizations and voluntary associations in Southeast Asia came within reach. In 1942, Japanese forces moved into the region and encouraged the formation of local militia from which national armies evolved after the war. Japanese rule was vicious and impoverishing but made the birth of independent nation-states in the area possible.

One of the new challenges each state faced was to decide about the impact and role of Islam upon the state and politics.

Indonesia

Indonesia declared independence in 1945, and, guided by the new president Sukarno (1945–66), its leaders designed a model for religious harmony that is still enshrined in the Constitution and in the state philosophy of Pancasila which accepts the religions of Islam, Christianity, Buddhism, Hinduism and Confucianism on equal footing. This model, however, was accepted under great protest from certain Muslim political parties who wanted to include the Jakarta Charter into the Constitution. The Charter consists of seven words that mandate Muslim Indonesians must follow the *sharīʿa* law. The inclusion of the seven words was dropped for fear that Christian regions would break away from the young nation.

In spite of this compromise, certain groups and parties did not give up their dream of exercising political power. Between 1948 and 1962 the so-called Darul Islam movement led several rebellions against the secular state. In 1962 its leader was captured and executed, and the movement broke up; what was left of it went underground. The Masyumi Party, one of the main political parties, was dissolved by Sukarno in 1959 when its leaders participated in a rebellion against his government. The party was heavily populated by members of the Muhammadiyah movement whose goal it was – and still is to this day – to Islamize Indonesia but not by using violence or force.

Although removed from the public stage, former leaders of these political Islamic movements intensified their goal to Islamize Indonesia, among others, by launching an organization for Islamic mission, the Dewan Dakwah Islamiyah Indonesia (DDII, Indonesian Council for Islamic Predication) which, since 1973, has developed close ties with the Islamic World League that was launched by Saudi Arabia. These connections were translated into the organization's journal that remains filled with imagined enemies of Islam: Christians, Zionists, the West, Shiʿites, feminists, and liberal Muslims.

Both Sukarno and his successor Soeharto (1966–98) saw political Islam as a threat to the stability of the nation. Especially after 1978 when the Islamic Revolution in Iran emboldened Muslims worldwide, Soeharto's regime curbed the potential powers of Islam and suppressed the extremist voices that later on re-emerged after circumstances forced him to step down. The Muslim reaction to the government restrictions on Islam was to focus on a spiritual, intellectual and economic renewal of Islam, rather than reaching for political power. In preparation for a Muslim civil society, Muslim leaders and intellectuals such as Abdurrahman Wahid (b. 1940) and Nurcholish Madjid (1939–2005) started to design models for an Islamic-based democracy and civil society. The form of Islam proposed by this movement is often referred to as "cultural Islam."

Around the 1980s the tide turned when the Soeharto regime saw it as expedient to improve relationships with the Islamic organizations. The result was, for example, the lifting of the ban on wearing the veil in state schools. Around the same time, young Indonesians became attracted to stricter forms of Islam. On university campuses the ban on political Muslim activities led students to set up religious study groups through which they also channeled expressions of discontent with the regime. These groups became part of what is now called the *tarbiyah* or education movement. Some of these groups adopted the organizational models of the Egyptian radical Muslim Brotherhood that used small, tightly knit cells or "families" (*usra*) for the formation of "pious, professionally successful young Muslims" who saw Islam as "an all-embracing and self-sufficient system" (Fealy and Hooker 2006: 48). Women affiliated to these groups started to wear the veil; some even opted for covering their face as well.

In spite of these intensified efforts of searching for deeper religious meaning, the call from radical groups to implement Islamic law failed and, with the support of Muhammadiyah and NU, Parliament rejected it in 2003. Application of the Islamic law shifted to the district level where it appeared in the form of bylaws if a majority of the population endorsed it by a vote. So far it has been adopted as state law in the province of Aceh only. There still is a segment of Indonesia's society that has vested its hopes in the *sharīʿa* as the law that can help combat social ills ranging from immorality to corruption. In the 2004 elections, for example, the *sharīʿa*-minded Justice Party (PKS) went from less than 2 percent of the vote in the 1999 national elections to over 7 percent.

In spite of its suppression of radical voices, the Soeharto regime supported the endeavor to establish Islamic values through the legislation of at least five new laws that contain "strong *shariʾa* influences" (Salim and Azra 2003: 5). One of these laws was the 1974 marriage law while the others concern charitable foundations, religious courts, Islamic banking and inheritance. In 1991 the so-called Compilation of Islamic Law was introduced to guide judges in the Islamic courts in the application of the laws. Without referring to the *sharīʿa*, these laws have accommodated the wish of Indonesian Muslims to be governed by rules prescribed by their religion and match the ongoing Islamic revivalism.

Malaysia

Malaysia achieved independence in 1957 when it became the Federation of Malaya which adopted Islam as the nation's official religion. It did not become an Islamic state and its government is obliged to uphold the freedom of religion for non-Muslims who are mostly Indian or Chinese. All Malay and a small number of Indians are Muslim. In states that have a sultan, he is still the head of Islamic affairs.

In 1981 Mahathir became prime minister and appointed Anwar Ibrahim as his deputy. Inspired by Islamist ideologists such as Sayyid Quṭb (d. 1966) and Mawdūdī (d. 1979), Ibrahim had been among the initiators of the Malaysian Islamic Youth Movement (ABIM). Buoyed by the Islamic resurgence in the Middle East, during the 1970s, ABIM and other Islamist revival groups started what is referred to as the *dakwah*, or Muslim propagation movement. They emphasized direct interpretation of the holy texts of the Qurʾān and *ḥadīth* and demanded Islamic education, economics and the application of the *sharīʿa*. At that time ABIM gained great popularity among the emerging middle classes. It stressed the Islamic values of equality, morality and spirituality as antidotes for corruption, consumerism and other excesses of modernity, seeing these Islamic values as the foundations for a redefined moral identity and Muslim community, a new *umma*.

In 1972, the Malaysian state launched a New Economic Policy that not only aimed at securing welfare and productivity, but also at reorganizing Malaysian social life. For this plan to reconstruct Malaysian society to succeed, the state needed to respond to the Islamic initiatives which it did, among others, through the Islamization program it launched in 1982 in conjunction with the leading UMNO Party (United Malays National Organization). This program generated official Islamic institutions such as banks, university education, and Islamic television and propagation programs. Furthermore, gambling, drinking alcohol and illicit sexual relationships became punishable by law. Through its involvement in corporate business, the patronage of the UMNO Party not only helped define and empower Malay Muslim identity vis-à-vis non-Malays, but also strengthened middle-class participation of Muslims. UMNO is in direct competition with the Islamic Party of Malaysia; the PAS party that defines itself as an "Islamic Political party based on the Qur'ān and *ḥadīth* of the Prophet Muḥammad."

The influence of the PAS party has pushed Malaysia in a more conservative Islamic direction, although the call for stronger Islamic structures has had distinct economic overtones. A similar observation may be made for Indonesia. Malay and Indonesian Muslims felt they had to catch up with the lack of participation in business and industry that were overwhelmingly in the hands of non-Muslims, especially the Chinese. The economy of both countries went into severe recession when an economic crisis hit Southeast Asia in 1998. In the midst of the turmoil of that same year Anwar Ibrahim fell out of favor and was sentenced to six years in prison on charges of corruption, abuse of power, and sexual misconduct. Government repression and a decline of civil liberties led to the formation of a coalition of Islamic parties called Barisan Alternatif (Alternative Front) that attracted new votes in predominantly Malay – that is Muslim – regions.

Thailand

Living in the southern provinces, most Thai Muslims share the culture of their neighbors in Malaysia. According to the Constitution (1997), the King is the patron of all religions and the Ministers of Interior and Education – two Buddhist officials – are responsible for the application of the laws regulating the affairs of the Thai Muslim community. From the beginning of the twentieth century Thai Muslims have gone through recurring times of conflict with the national government that wished to impose its "Thaicization" rules on the community. During the 1960s, the government tried to influence the Islamic boarding schools (*pondok*) which caused Muslim students to move to countries such as Malaysia, Pakistan and the Middle East. Supported by money from the Middle East, separatist Muslim groups arose that strove for independence from Thailand during the 1970s. These groups trained in Malaysia and, during the 1980s, in Afghanistan.

In spite of the 90 percent Buddhist majority, during the 1980s and 1990s Muslims began to play key roles in their country's local and national administration. However, violence resumed in December 2001 and has continued until now. In conditions similar to those in Malaysia and Indonesia, the Thai government keeps close tabs on the regulation of Islamic affairs via a centralized Islamic administration. Since the seventeenth century, the highest Muslim authority, who issues *fatwā*s and regulates

Islamic affairs, is the *shaykh al-Islām* (the Chularajamontri) who is chosen by members of the Provincial Councils for Islamic Affairs and appointed for life by the king. The first Chularajamontri was a Shīʿī from Persia. Nowadays Shīʿīs form a strong minority presence in Thailand.

The Philippines

The Muslims in the Philippines, the Moros, live in the only Christian-dominated country in Southeast Asia and do not identify themselves as Filipinos. Projects to assimilate the Muslims into the multi-ethnic Philippines failed and feelings of being marginalized gave rise to armed secession movements such as the Moro National Liberation Front (MNLF). Its actions caused the Filipino government to implement affirmative action programs for the benefit of the Moros such as building religious schools, and scholarships for Moro students. These initiatives were also reactions to a revival in Muslim piety that started in the 1950s.

Brunei

Brunei is the only country in the region that is an Islamic monarchy ruled by a sultan who traces his ancestry back to the fourteenth century. The clashes between reformist and conservative Muslims that changed the religious maps in the other countries have been virtually absent in this tiny sultanate. Observers ascribe its peaceful character to the fact that the sultan promotes religious harmony. Furthermore, a strong Ministry of Religious Affairs regulates a wide range of Islamic matters, including festivities and Qur'ān reading competitions.

Political Islam and the call for *sharīʿa*

Political change and events on the worldwide Muslim scene have fueled proponents of political Islam and, especially in the aftermath of the attacks on September 11, 2001, a radicalization process seems to have accelerated in several Southeast Asian countries. From the outside this seems to be a sudden development that comes out of nowhere. But in most countries there has been a steady move towards a stronger influence of Islam on society in recent decades.

Radical Muslim groups were not entirely new to Indonesia although they had not been visible during the Suharto regime. Some of the extremist leaders had been in exile in Malaysia, others – for example Abu Bakir Ba'asyir, the inspirational source behind the Bali bombers – kept quiet, while running an extremist *pesantren*. A *dakwah* movement (Islamic mission) had operated underground, transmitting radical ideas from the Middle East that expressed a goal of reducing the role of women, propagated anti-Christian ideas and called for the establishment of an Islamic state.

The roots of these extremist groups can be found in a variety of sources. Some relate to the early homegrown reformist movements that had lobbied for the introduction of Islamic law since the independence of Southeast Asian countries; others thrive through their extensive Middle Eastern connections. Police investigation into the bombing in Bali of October 2002 revealed the existence of several Southeast Asian radical networks that work towards the establishment of an Islamic state or caliphate that will include Indonesia, Malaysia, Brunei, Singapore, and the southern Philippines. Of great influence also were students who pursued their Islamic education in the Middle East, or in nearby countries such as Pakistan, and returned home with radical ideas. The radical agendas range from a call to re-instate the caliphate to establishing political parties and institutions to gain access to the centers of political power. The early reformists agitated against the colonial powers while contemporary Islamists see the repressive regimes, state control, and their western supporters as their enemy.

The voices of Islamists attract especially the poor since they present Islam as the antidote to their economic woes that were exacerbated by the economic crisis of 1998. Furthermore, they battle corruption and moral vices such as lotteries, gambling, and prostitution. The core of the struggle then is to apply Islamic law to the entire society. Apart from Brunei, the states in Southeast Asia are secular. However, in all of them, including those with Muslim minorities, following the wish of the Muslim populations, laws have been introduced that are strongly influenced by the *sharīʿa*. For example, the Suharto regime in Indonesia introduced laws governing marriage, regulating the Islamic courts and charitable endowments (*waqf*), and concerning inheritance and Islamic banking. Radicals find these laws a travesty of the Islamic law and demand punishment for acts such as drinking alcohol, gambling, and unlawful proximity between men and women. Currently these offenses are regulated by the secular laws in most countries and enforcing punishment is against the national law.

The discussion about the full application of *sharīʿa* on the national level has been rejected by the majority while the ongoing debate about the role of Islam in the social order was reflected in the development of the so-called *Kompilasi Hukum Islam* (Islamic law codes). In Malaysia and Singapore there was no such debate because following the British colonial practice *sharīʿa* law has always been recognized.

Radical groups in Indonesia now try to circumvent the national laws and the sentiments of the large contingent of Muslim society by pressing their agenda on the autonomous regional levels where local authorities have drafted *sharīʿa*-like bylaws that aim to regulate public behavior. Many of these laws concern women's modesty in dress, for example, by enforcing the veil. By 2008, 72 of the 440 regions had introduced such *sharīʿa*-like rules.

The Indonesian laws are not as draconian as those in Malaysia, where, in their quest to create an Islamic state, proponents of the *sharīʿa* law could connect with the PAS party, even though Muslims are barely the national majority. Similar to the Indonesian process, the Malaysian government introduced new Islamic laws in the 1990s and amended existing laws such as the personal status law, taking away women's protection against unilateral divorce by the husband and against polygamy. In certain provinces (such as Kelantan and Teranggu) where PAS has the majority vote, laws with provisions for punishments such as flogging, death by stoning for adultery, and amputation of limbs for theft have been introduced; the laws have not yet been enforced because of federal government opposition. Both in Indonesia and Malaysia the introduction of such laws has led to great resistance from groups advocating human rights and women's rights.

Expressions of spirituality

In all countries in Southeast Asia, especially since the 1980s, the desire to be more dedicated to religion is growing. Southeast Asian Muslims are searching for ways to apply their beliefs to daily life, for example, in following the fast of Ramaḍān, intensified study of the Qur'ān, and women donning the veil. Surveys in Indonesia show that local non-Islamic rituals and practices are diminishing while more Muslims follow the basic tenets of their faith. Especially among middle-class Muslims Sufism has become popular.

Indonesian Muslims have also developed new appreciations of the Islamic boarding school tradition of Islamic learning, the *pesantren*. Through "study circles" (in Arabic *ḥalqa*) organized under the direction of progressive teachers (*kiai*) young thinkers sought integrated approaches to questions important to the community in everyday life. Beyond these intellectual aspects of Islamic revival, there has also been a tremendous amount of activity in the fields of the arts and culture more broadly. The fruits of these developments have been myriad, ranging from the publication and public recitation of Muslim poetry to significant developments in the fields of painting, calligraphy, music and Qur'ān recitation.

Public schools offer religious lessons as well and, with the increased levels of religious literacy, Qur'ān study sessions have mushroomed all over Indonesia, catering to a variety of groups within society. There are, for example, study groups for women, children, mothers, teachers, students, factory workers and so on. Television programs are crammed with Qur'ān recitation, religious education programs for children, and call-in shows during which scholars and *imāms* answer questions from the believers. Love for God is expressed in musical groups that range from rock bands to children's choirs. These trends have also influenced the discussions of the formative influence of the Muslim family on raising future generations of Muslims with, as a corollary, intense discussions about the role of women. In most countries in Southeast Asia, women play important roles as leaders and teachers of Islam, in both the private and the public spheres.

Women

Traditionally, Southeast Asian women have enjoyed more rights and freedoms than women in other Muslim countries. This observation can even be made in historic contexts. Between 1584 and 1688 in the sultanate of Patani, and between 1641 and 1699 in the sultanate of Aceh, there were four successive sultanas in each. During the time of the female rulers Aceh's royal harem continued to exist because its primary function was political, not sexual. Women had a certain degree of independence and influence on household and other affairs. As early as the seventeenth century, Muslim women could initiate divorce. The "Great" Sultan Agung (1613–46) institutionalized the conditional divorce (*ta'līq al-ṭalāq*) formula during the wedding ceremony by which the husband agreed to certain conditions that would grant the wife valid grounds for a divorce.

Women could have joint property ownership with their husbands and were seldom confined to the household or dependent on men for their income. Customary or *adat* laws in many parts of Southeast Asia allowed sons and daughters to inherit equal land shares. These rules have been challenged by *sharī'a* laws that grant sons a double share compared to daughters.

The legal position of Muslim women in the region varies, however. Unlike other countries, more than 50 percent of Indonesia's *sharīʿa* judges are women. Through the influence of the Muhammadiyah and NU organizations, women are directors of *pesantren* for women, have become active and influential religious leaders, and some are specialists of Islam who teach at the Islamic universities. NU leaders encouraged women to memorize the Qur'ān which resulted in Maria Ulfah (b. 1955) being the first woman to win the international Qur'ān recitation competition in Kuala Lumpur in 1980.

Tradition

Islam as a force in the political and personal life of the millions of Muslims in the region seems to be growing, while local traditions and rituals are waning. Although puritanical Muslim groups have attacked many of these local expressions they continue to provide solace to many in Southeast Asia who do not perceive these rituals as contradicting Islamic practices. In most Southeast Asian countries, Muslims still feel influenced by the supernatural. They respect the ancestors and believe in ghosts and in the power of specialists mediating with ghosts. In order to maintain a balance between this world and the one beyond, ritual meals called *slametan* on Java (and *kenduri* in other parts of Indonesia and Malaysia) are held regularly. Many Muslims still deem it appropriate to guide momentous life events such as pregnancy and birth, circumcision, marriage, life-crises, and death with such a meal during which prayers are said in a mix of Arabic and local languages.

At the onset of the twenty-first century, once again the vibrancy and creativity of scholars and thinkers that have shaped Islam in Southeast Asia are starting to be noticed outside the region. Works by formative scholars such as Nurcholish Madjid have been translated into English and have become noticeable voices in international discussions on Islamic developments. In Indonesia, the ongoing struggle to shape Islam into a force of societal change has given birth to innovative projects, for example, on the re-interpretation of *fiqh*, and on inter-religious dialogue. Scholars and activists from outside now visit Indonesia to draw inspiration from the models and methods that are taking shape in the midst of a changing society. The ideas put forward by Abdurrahman Wahid, the former president of Indonesia, and long-time Chair of the Nahdlatul Ulama, continue to be of note to all those interested in his assessments on the role of Islam in politics and society, and in peacemaking initiatives as evidenced by the website www.gusdur.net.

References and further reading

Andaya, B. W. and Andaya, L. Y. (2001) *A History of Malaysia*, 2nd edition, Honolulu: University of Hawai'i Press.

Azra, A. (2004) "Southeast Asian Islam in the Post-Bali Bombing: Debunking the Myth," in N. Eschborn, S. Hackel, J. H. Richardson, eds., *Indonesia Today. Problems and Perspectives. Politics and Society. Five Years into Reformasi*, Jakarta: Konrad-Adenauer Stiftung, 143–61.

Barton, G. (2004) *Indonesia's Struggle: Jemaah Islamiyah and the Soul of Islam*, Sydney: University of NSW Press.

Barton, G. and Fealy G., eds. (1996) *Traditional Islam, Nahdlatul Ulama and Modernity*, Clayton, NSW: Monash Asia Institute.

Bowen, J. R. (2003) *Islam, Law and Equality in Indonesia*, Cambridge: Cambridge University Press.

Drewes, G. W. J. (1977) *Directions for Travellers on the Mystic Path: Zakariyya' al-Ansari's Kitab Fath al-Rahman and its Indonesian Adaptations*, The Hague: Martinus Nijhoff.

Fealy, G. and Hooker, V., eds. (2006) *Voices of Islam in Southeast Asia. A Contemporary Sourcebook*, Singapore: ISEAS Publications.

Forbes, A., ed. (1989) *The Muslims of Thailand*, 2 vols, Gaya: Center for Southeast Asian Studies.

Gade, A. (2004) *Perfection Makes Practice. Learning, Emotion, and the Recited Qur'an in Indonesia*, Honolulu: University of Hawai'i Press.

Gelman Taylor, J. (2003) *Indonesia. Peoples and Histories*, New Haven: Yale University Press.

Gowing, P. G. (1979) *Muslim Filipinos: Heritage and Horizon*, Quezon City: New Day Publishers.

Hefner, R. W. (2000) *Civil Islam. Muslims and Democratization in Indonesia*, Princeton: Princeton University Press.

Hefner, R. W. and Horvatich, P., eds. (1997) *Islam in an Era of Nation-States. Politics and Religious Renewal in Muslim Southeast Asia*, Honolulu: University of Hawai'i Press.

Hooker, M. B. (2003) *Indonesian Islam. Social Change through Contemporary Fatawa*, Crows Nest, NSW: Allen & Unwin; Honolulu: University of Hawai'i Press.

Ichwan, M. N. (2003) "The Seven Word Controversy," in *IIAS Newsletter* no. 30, March 2003: 23–4; available online at http://www.iias.nl/iiasn/30/IIASNL30_23_Ichwan.pdf.

Laffan, M. F. (2003) *Islamic Nationhood and Colonial Indonesia. The Umma below the Winds*, London: Routledge Curzon.

McKenna, T. M. (1998) *Muslim Rulers and Rebels: Everyday Politics and Armed Separation in the Southern Philippines*, Berkeley: University of California Press.

Muzaffar, C. (1987) *Islamic Resurgence in Malaysia*, Petaling Jaya: Fajar Bakti.

Nagata, J. (1984) *The Reflowering of Malaysian Islam*, Vancouver: University of British Columbia Press.

Nakamura, H. (2006) *Conditional Divorce in Indonesia*, Cambridge, MA: Islamic Legal Studies Program, Harvard Law School.

Noer, D. (1973) *The Modernist Muslim Movement in Indonesia 1900–1942*, Singapore, Kuala Lumpur, London, New York: Oxford University Press.

Ong, A. and Peletz, M. G., eds. (1995) *Bewitching Women, Pious Men. Gender and Body Politics in Southeast Asia*, Berkeley: University of California Press.

Owen, N. G., ed. (2005) *The Emergence of Modern Southeast Asia. A New History*, Singapore: Singapore University Press.

Peletz, M. G. (2002) *Islamic Modern. Religious Courts and Cultural Politics in Malaysia*, Princeton: Princeton University Press.

Reid, A. (1990) *Southeast Asia in the Age of Commerce 1450–1680: The Lands below the Winds*, New Haven: Yale University Press.

—— (1995) *Southeast Asia in the Age of Commerce 1450–1680: Expansion and Crisis*, New Haven: Yale University Press.

Ricklefs, M. C. A. (1993) *History of Modern Indonesia, c. 1300 to the Present*, Bloomington: Indiana University Press.

Riddell, P. (2001) *Islam and the Malay–Indonesian World. Transmissions and Responses*, Honolulu: University of Hawai'i Press.

Roff, W. R. (1998) "Patterns of Islamisation in Malaysia, 1890s–1990s," *Journal of Islamic Studies*, 9: 210–18.

Salim, A. and Azra, A. (2003) *Shari'a and Politics in Modern Indonesia*, Singapore: ISEAS.

Solamo-Antonio, I. (2003) *The Shari'a Courts in the Philippines: Women, Men and Muslim Personal Laws*, Davao City: Pilipina Legal Resources Inc.

Tan, S. K. (2003) *Internationalization of the Bangsamoro Struggle*, 2nd edition, Quezon City: University of the Philippines.
Van Doorn-Harder, N. and de Jong, K. (2001) "Ziarah to Tembayat," *The Muslim World*, 91: 325–54.
Van Doorn-Harder, P. (2006) *Women Shaping Islam. Indonesian Women Reading the Qur'an*, Urbana, Chicago: University of Illinois Press.
Yegar, M. (2002) *Between Integration and Secession: The Muslim Communities of the Southern Philippines, Southern Thailand, and Western Burma/Myanmar*, Lanham, MD: Lexington Books.
Zainah A. (1987) *Islamic Revivalism in Malaysia*, Petaling Jaya: Pelanduk Publications.

8

EUROPE

John R. Bowen

The history and current activities of Muslims in Europe sharply challenge older notions of "Muslim societies." The very idea of "Europe" as a cultural region rests on notions of its Christian roots, and the recent debates about the European Constitution testify to the continued strength of these notions. The medieval Papal efforts to rally Christians to fight Muslims in the Crusades depended on a sense of an infidel enemy opposed to Christendom, and this way of thinking has continued to shape European attitudes toward Muslims. And yet belying this idea is the long presence of Muslims in Europe: in southern Spain, the Balkans, Turkey, and Russia. The expansion of British, Dutch and French empires led European traders and rulers to live in and eventually control many long-standing Muslim societies, and immigration from these societies to all parts of Europe has redefined what it is to be European. Muslims also have begun to question ideas about boundaries between a land of Islam and the lands of non-Muslims as they have settled in large numbers across Europe and begun to build Islamic social and religious institutions.

Muslims become Europeans

Muslim empires left long-lasting legacies in many parts of Europe. The Ottoman expansion into the Balkan Peninsula led to many conversions to Islam, and Islam remains the majority religion in Albania and in Bosnia and Herzegovina (and in Turkey, which for the moment is considered to straddle the border between Europe and Asia). Slightly northward, the majority of peoples in the Volga region of Russia, certainly part of Europe, are Muslim as well. In Andalusia, not only was a particularly rich Islamic heritage developed during Muslim rule (711–1492), but today many in Spain reclaim this Muslim heritage. Muslims ruled Sicily from the seventh to the ninth centuries and had communities elsewhere in today's Italy. These long-standing Muslim-majority parts of Europe have left a two-fold legacy in European thinking. On the one hand, they place into question the prevailing notion that Europe is defined by a Christian heritage. On the other hand, they have long defined the frontiers of Europe, and this sense of boundaries is only strengthened today by the idea that a civilizational divide separates Latin Christendom, on one side, and both Orthodoxy and Islam, on the other.

Turkey's candidacy for the European Union is, if course, the major challenge to this idea of a boundary between Christendom and the "Muslim World." Many do not realize that Turkey already belongs to the Council of Europe, and by this fact comes under the jurisdiction of the European Court of Human Rights. Indeed, many of the recent key cases concerning religious freedom heard by the Court have come from Turkey. Turkey is thus already part of one legal version of "Europe."

Europe's own colonial expansions outwards and the resulting migrations back to the metropole further challenged notions of boundaries between Europe and Muslim lands. Three moments define these broad political, cultural, and demographic shifts: the building of empires, the recruitment of labor, and the settlement of Muslim families in Europe.

Colonization and empire building meant that Muslim-majority societies became in some sense part of Europe, in ways that differed by colonial policies. France tended toward a policy of assimilation; the Netherlands tried to maintain a strict separation of colonizer and native; Britain's policy lay somewhere in between. When in the 1830s France made Algeria into French territory, all its inhabitants became French nationals, not merely subjects, and the dominant lines of French policy aimed to develop Muslims to the point where they could become full French citizens. At the other extreme, Dutch rulers of Indonesia forbade the use of Dutch in courts and offices, trying to preserve the distinction between European and native. British paternalism meant that the colonizers encouraged the spread of English and of British culture in Asia (as in Macauley's reforms of the 1830s), but also preserved a racial dividing line. These distinct policies of colonial governance had profound effects on subsequent Muslim immigration to Europe.

By the end of the nineteenth century, small numbers of Muslims had begun to settle in Europe. France made the earliest and most concerted effort to import male labor onto its European soil to work in its factories. Indeed, France proclaimed itself "a great Muslim power," seeking to develop French territory in Mecca as well as in North and West Africa, and built the Paris Mosque in the 1920s in part to proclaim its new role. South Asians migrated to Britain in the late nineteenth century: sailors came after the 1869 opening of the Suez Canal, and students sought higher education in the cities. The Netherlands governed the largest Muslim colony, the Dutch East Indies, today's Indonesia, and most Muslim immigrants prior to the 1950s were from the Indies or from Suriname. But there were few of them, and the new wave of Muslims moving to the Netherlands in the 1970s and 1980s were from Morocco and Turkey and had no colonial ties with their host country.

Large-scale movement of Muslims to Europe began after the World War II, as the demand for unskilled labor far outstripped the European supply. Shortly after the war's end, Britain gave free entry to Commonwealth residents. As a result, increasing numbers of Muslims, largely from Kashmir and what is today Bangladesh, followed kinsmen to Britain. By the early 1960s Britain was debating new limits on migration; these debates had the effect of speeding up migration and settling of families in Britain's cities. Immigrants settled where they had relatives, producing concentrations of people from one village or lineage in certain neighborhoods of Birmingham, Bradford, or East London. In France, the Algerian War (1954–62) led many French Algerians to settle in the metropolis, and, given the uncertainties produced by the war, to settle with their families rather than engage in circular migration, much as happened in Britain. By the late 1960s, new populations of Muslims from North Africa and Turkey were moving into the Netherlands and the Scandinavian countries.

Figure 7 Alhambra, Granada, Spain, mid-fourteenth century. Comprised of a series of palace and garden courts, the Alhambra palace complex is one of the best preserved examples of medieval Islamic palatial architecture.

Source: Peter Wilson © Dorling Kindersley

In the aftermath of worldwide recession in 1973–4, European countries severely limited labor migration. Ironically, one major result was to increase still further the proportion of people who settled with families. After restrictive laws were put into place in the mid-1970s, the two major ways to gain legal entry to Europe were to join a close family member already enjoying legal residence, or to claim asylum on grounds of conflict or persecution. In those areas of Europe that had experienced relatively little earlier labor immigration, including the Scandinavian countries and Italy, asylum seekers make up a relatively large proportion of the Muslim population.

These distinct migration histories produced widely differing sociological profiles of Muslims across Europe. Muslims coming to France or Britain were much more likely to know something of the host country's language than were Muslims arriving in Denmark or Austria. Non-Muslim French or British residents also were more likely to have had past interactions with Muslims, particularly for French who had spent time in Algeria. Spanish Muslims have come overwhelmingly from neighboring Morocco, and they have maintained close ties with their home country. Turkish Muslims arriving in Germany may have known some German language because of the long history of labor migration from Turkey to Germany. But Moroccans traveling to the Netherlands or Norway, or Senegalese arriving in Italy, were and are unlikely to arrive with more than a smattering of words in their new country of residence, and their hosts are, in turn, unlikely to know much about Morocco or Senegal (see the essays in Hunter 2002 and in *Journal of Ethnic and Migration Studies* 2004).

These differences in turn favored the development of ethnic enclaves in those countries with little prior Muslim presence, and exacerbated difficulties of integration even for Muslims born in their new countries. Today we see the sharpest conflicts on religious grounds precisely in those counties where, either because of multicultural policies or because of an absence of shared cultural knowledge, Muslims live apart from others.

Recognizing Muslims in Europe

The children of the major wave of Muslim immigration came of age in the 1980s and began to demand public recognition of their religion. They did so at the very moment when the rise of what came to be called "political Islam" elsewhere in the world – Khomeini in Iran, new political movements in North Africa and the Middle East – stoked fears about Islam in Europe. Debates about the character of European Islam thus began at about the same time as the rise of a strong anti-immigrant trend in many countries, and the rise of anti-Islamic sentiment.

It is difficult to say how many Muslims live in Europe in the early twenty-first century, because many states do not keep such records and because it is unclear how one would wish to define a "Muslim." The numbers are themselves the objects of controversy: if there are fewer Muslims, then perhaps the government need not overly exert itself on their behalf. Some states produce numbers based on highly debatable methods. Neither France nor Germany, for example, keeps counts of residents by religion. The German government estimates its Muslim population by counting immigrants from Muslim-majority countries, thereby ignoring Muslims who are German citizens or who come from other states (such as Russia), and counting Christians from Lebanon or Syria. French state agencies make estimates in similar ways, but also offer survey data suggesting that few Muslims are regular practitioners of their religion and that the "real" Muslim population is thus quite low.

Organizations

In each country, Muslims have tried to create new religious institutions and to open up space within preexisting institutions to allow Muslim participation. They have sought to create religious schools and asked for recognition of Islamic history and the right to wear Islamic dress in public schools. They have sought to build mosques that would be public reminders of the new, permanent Muslim presence. They also have sought accommodations in a number of other domains, from food preparation to cemeteries, to permit them to follow Islamic norms in their new societies.

Efforts to create Muslim representative organizations to manage these issues have reflected country-specific political traditions and the nature of the Muslim population. French centralizing traditions and the tradition of the "Gallican church" led the state to create a single, national body for Muslims, the French Council for the Muslim religion. This Council suffers from a fundamental ambiguity: does it represent religious authority, or the range of interests of all Muslims? It cannot easily claim the former, as its leaders are not trained in Islamic studies, and it has difficulty claiming the latter, as mosques selected its members, and many Muslims do not attend mosques.

By contrast, Muslims living in Britain first organized locally. They realized that they could become members of local community councils or create their own community organizations and thereby effect changes in schools and neighborhoods. Some British municipal councils welcomed, and indeed subsidized, Islamic community associations. Although Muslims later created a number of national organizations, most notably the Muslim Council of Britain, their success in lobbying for the inclusion of Islamic religious materials and *ḥalāl* meat in local schools has largely been due to local mobilization.

In Germany, most of the issues affecting Muslims are decided at the level of the states (*Länder*). German state governments require that religious communities be constituted as at least private associations, if not public ones, before they can ask for their religion to be taught in the public schools. (Having religious education in school is a right guaranteed by the German Constitution.) However, many German judges and officials, faced with what they find to be a confusing welter of Muslim affiliations – Alevis and Aḥmadī as well as Shīʿīs and Sunnīs – and forgetting how complex Protestant Christian denominational distinctions can be, have required that Muslims agree among themselves about Islamic textbooks before they can enjoy that right. The result has been a stalemate in most parts of Germany.

Efforts to organize national Islamic bodies encounter not only the difficulty of bringing Muslims of diverse backgrounds together but also the fact that many Muslims identify strongly with transnational religious associations. Some of these, such as the various local associations sponsored by the Turkish government, are explicitly linked to a Muslim-majority country, and thus introduce a foreign element to domestic policy issues. Others, such as the Tablīghī Jamāʿat, have no particular country affiliation, but emphasize the primary responsibility of Muslims to the worldwide *umma* (see Masud 1999). The extreme example of what we could call these anti-nationalist Islamic movements is the Hizb ut-Tahrir, which calls for Muslims to refrain from participating in secular politics and to work for the re-establishment of the caliphate.

Throughout Europe, Ṣūfī organizations maintain ties to spiritual leaders residing elsewhere, usually in Muslim-majority countries in Africa or Asia. For example, the Mouride order, founded in the 1880s by Sheykh Amadou Bamba, is centered in Senegal, where its followers consider the mosque to be the Mecca of West Africa. The order maintains close ties among followers living in Europe and North America through local associations and through periodic visits by the current head of the order (the founder's son). Trade and spirituality pass along these networks, although they are open to others from West Africa as well.

An Iranian order, the Shahmaghsoudi, illustrates another geographical possibility: centering an order in the diaspora. Founded in California, the order includes over 75 lodges throughout the world and was created to provide alternative forms of Islam to those promoted by the Iranian Revolution. At the same time, it taps into the centuries-old Oveyssi Ṣūfī tradition. Whereas Senegalese Mourides take their affiliation with them as they move out into other parts of the world, Iranians already in exile came to the Shahmaghsoudi order as a way to recapture something of their Iranian spiritual heritage (see essays in *Journal* 2004, and Werbner 2003).

A third possibility is illustrated by a lodge north of Paris simply called the "Sufi and Cultural Association," who acknowledge as their teacher a Ṣūfī master living in Tunisia and part of the al-ʿAlawiyya order. The active participants are French men of origins in diverse Muslim-majority countries who grew up together and converted to the Sufi path as an alternative to drugs and delinquency.

Alongside these and other religious-based organizations are ethnic ones, such as the various associations of Turks in Germany, of Kashmiris in Britain, or of Senegalese in Italy. In these countries ethnic-based associations can bring together people of differing religious affiliations and at the same time provide a more open route to interaction with members of the host country.

Institutions

Because the large Muslim presence in Europe is of relatively recent date, the institutions Muslims most rely on for religious practice and education – most importantly, mosques, schools, and universities – are only now coming into existence. Other institutions whose services many Muslims find essential, such as banks that offer non-interest-bearing loans and slaughter houses that can supply *ḥalāl* meat in large quantities, are present in uneven fashion. European Muslim institutions are, it is safe to say, in their infancy.

Although mosques often have been flash points for opposition to an Islamic presence in Europe, if we consider only religious obligations special mosque buildings need not exist. Muslims can pray anywhere, and on the special occasions when Muslims should pray as a congregation – most notably Fridays and the two major feast-days – any large place will do. However, having a mosque is never just about prayer. The presence of a mosque – a public, religious-looking place, with the capacity to hold all who wish to worship – creates a Muslim presence in a village, a neighborhood, or a city. In many cities in Europe building a public mosque – a "cathedral mosque" – has been the central focus of controversy. Mosques present city officials with political opportunities, from showing their hostility toward Islam to showing their willingness to work with Muslim residents. On the one hand, public figures in Britain and the Netherlands have labeled mosques as breeding grounds for hatred and terrorism; on the other, municipal leaders in Rotterdam, Marseille, and the Paris region have encouraged local committees to develop mosques that also would serve as cultural centers. Mosques often become signifiers in alternative semiotic frames developed by politicians: as symbols of "French Islam," or of "multicultural Birmingham," or of good neighborhood planning in Rotterdam.

Some European mosques are strongly associated with transnational organizations, such as the Tablīghī Jamāʿat or the mosque networks controlled by the Turkish Directorate of Religious Affairs. The Algerian government exerts control over the Paris mosque. Mosques, of course, are supposed to be open to all Muslims who wish to worship, but some mosques are mainly frequented by Muslims from a particular country. In some cases, inter-community rivalries lead mosque committees to choose as *imām* someone from a third country – I know of several mosques with Moroccan, Tunisian, and Algerian worshippers that are led by men from the Comoro islands

The nature of schooling differs markedly from one European country to the next, of course, but nowhere have Muslims yet developed sufficient sources of education that satisfy their own demands. Britain has produced the highest relative number of Islamic private schools, over 100 by the early 2000s, but only a handful of these receive the state subsidies enjoyed by many Christian and Jewish schools. However, in some districts Muslim families have succeeded in introducing Islam as a subject matter alongside Christianity in the regular school curriculum. Britain's proclaimed policies of promoting multiculturalism within schools has allowed Muslim girls to wear Islamic dress – as long as it matches the official school colors!

Germany emphasizes public education and it is difficult to gain permission for private schools. Because the Islamic associations in Germany have not reached agreement on a curriculum, schools do not provide a full-fledged program of instruction in Islam, as they do for religions of longer standing. The Netherlands emphasizes the rights of parents to choose schools, and subsidizes religious schools, as it had done for 46 Islamic primary schools by 2006.

France presents the most complex case. The long history of combat in France over the role of the Catholic Church in schooling produced sharp cleavages concerning the presence of religion in the public schools. This history predisposed teachers to be hostile toward Muslim girls' wearing of Islamic head scarves. But private religious schools flourish. The twentieth-century compromise between the Republic and Catholics guaranteed state subsidies for private religious schools, and about 40 percent of French families make use of a private religious school at some time. Muslims have not yet (as of 2007) benefited from this possibility, but several schools are part-way toward receiving state subsidies.

Eating

Finally, Muslims have tried to develop ways of obtaining *ḥalāl* meat on an everyday basis and, on a massive scale, on the day of *ʿīd al-aḍḥā*, the "Feast of Sacrifice." It is much more difficult in Europe than in Muslim-majority countries to put meat on the Muslim table, because European rules of hygiene prohibit certain practices, and for the purely logistical reason that sheep are more likely to be far from where Muslims live. These problems have given rise to a near continual experimenting with different ways to certify practices as *ḥalāl* and to distribute meat quickly, and also to suggestions that Muslims reinterpret the rules to lighten the burden.

European law requires that animals be stunned before they are killed, on humanitarian grounds, but allows states to grant exemptions for religious practices. These exemptions were first granted to Jewish organizations; this precedent no doubt paved the way for Muslims. States that do grant these exemptions (which include all the countries of large Muslim minorities and exclude Scandinavia) are thereby obliged to license and regulate the process of ritual sacrifice in slaughter houses. In practice they may subcontract to mosques the right to license sacrificers, who then secure a considerable revenue. The certification of butcher shops and food production companies has itself become a major business line for Muslims.

Muslim legal opinion on the requirements for *ḥalāl* is not uniform. Some authorities argue that stunning is not allowed because it may kill the animal; others that it depends on the method. The famous lecturer Yūsuf al-Qaraḍāwī has argued that Muslims may accept meat from Christians and Jews, and that because Islam facilitates life, eating meat killed with stunning is acceptable.

Ever since Muslims began to arrive in large numbers in Europe after World War II, local authorities have tried to develop acceptable facilities to provide massive amounts of meat on the Feast of Sacrifice. Indeed, the story of the decades of experimentation belies the notion that European governments have ignored the problems surrounding integration of Muslims. In some counties, officials looked the other way when newly arrived Muslims would kill a sheep in the bathtub, or behind their home. It was easier to do so in Belgium, for example, where immigrants were more likely to live in a detached house, or in Britain, where South Asians had settled in ethnic enclaves, than in ethnically mixed apartment buildings in France. Some immigrants sent money back to their home countries instead, where their relatives could sacrifice in their name.

European Muslims faced a second problem as well. Muḥammad had enjoined them to give a portion of the sacrificial meat to the needy, but who are the needy in France? Muslims may be poor, but many find that the households to their right and left also are able to afford to buy a sheep to sacrifice. In any case, in crowded urban settings, many find it difficult to locate people in a position to accept raw meat. This problem has added to the impulse to contribute to the home country, where, most believe, the needy are to be found in greater numbers.

Since the 1970s, mayors throughout Europe have worked with private companies and Islamic associations to find spaces where licensed sacrificers could kill animals en masse, or urged abattoir operators to devote one day to Muslim needs. In 2006, when the Feast of Sacrifice fell around New Year's Eve, Paris officials brokered deals between grocery chains and Muslim sacrificers: the former were able to produce large numbers of animals to a central point of sacrifice and to then prepare them quickly for purchase by Muslims.

Sacrifice's practical difficulties have led some Muslims to ask whether they can abstract from long-standing practices – and even from the Prophet Muḥammad's example – sacrifice's ethical message. Can ethics replace ritual, and should it do so in Europe?

Marrying and divorcing

The vast majority of Muslims follow the laws in place where they live regarding marriage and divorce. However, a small number of cases highlights the question of how Muslims should best articulate Islamic norms and European laws on family matters. Most famously, Muslims in Britain have constructed a kind of "English *sharīʿa*" that adapts religious norms to British laws and is enforced informally. There and elsewhere, Islamic leaders have urged Muslims not to make the mistake of considering an "Islamic marriage" conducted before an *imām* but not registered with the state to be a legal marriage. Some young couples are creatively using both systems, marrying Islamically to satisfy their parents, and as an equivalent to an engagement, which does not exist in Islamic law. They then marry some time later. Yet a sufficiently large number of cases exist where women are abandoned and cannot divorce – because they never were married – for state and religious officials in several countries to actively discourage the practice.

Legally more complex issues arise with respect to marriage and divorce carried out abroad. Although at a very general level European countries recognize the legal validity of marriage and divorces carried out overseas, they may or may not recognize as valid the Islamic procedure of repudiation (*ṭalāq*) of a wife by her husband or a polygamous marriage. Some courts cite considerations of "public order" to deny recognition to some Islamic marriages and divorces carried out in other countries, depending on the substantive conditions. If the wife was present during a divorce hearing, for example, a court may accept a *ṭalāq* divorce.

Can European societies be Muslim?

Life in Europe raises long-standing questions about whether Muslims' obligations to God change when they move to lands not ruled by Muslims. In the early centuries of Islam scholars developed a distinction between two realms, the *dār al-Islām* (abode of Islam), versus the *dār al-ḥarb* (abode of war). The former included the countries ruled under Islamic principles; the latter referred to all other places, where, presumably, Muslims would not be free to worship. Today, many Muslims find discomfort in this way of viewing the world. How is one to define "Muslim societies," the *dār al-Islām*? Does one look to the correctness of the government, the piety of the people, or simply the fact that most people living in the country profess Islam as their religion? Is a majority-Muslim country whose government represses its people, and prevents the free expression of religious ideas to be considered part of *dār al-Islām*? Conversely, why should countries not governed by Islamic laws but where Muslims are free to worship be considered as belonging to an "abode of war"? As many Muslims in Europe began to think about religion in terms of the essentials of worship and spirituality, this category seemed increasingly out of date.

Some Muslims have proposed alternatives. Referring to the protection given to religious minorities by international law, some scholars have proposed *dār al-ʿahd*, "abode of treaty," while others have proposed *dār al-daʿwa*, "abode of predication," or *dār al-shahāda*, "abode of witness," emphasizing the possibilities open to Muslims in these lands. For many Muslims in Europe, the key issues are not labels – Muslim world versus non-Muslims lands – but of the social and cultural conditions for Muslims to live fully satisfying lives as Muslims. Two categories of Muslims would not accept this proposition. Some consider religion a private matter not in need of new institutions, and hence see no particular challenge to living in Europe. Others consider it provisional to live anywhere but an Islamic state, a category that includes neither European nor most Muslim-majority countries.

The practical significance of this question emerged most recently regarding bank interest. One of the more pressing questions for Muslims who are planning to reside permanently in Europe is whether they may take out loans at interest to purchase homes. The Islamic prohibition against lending or borrowing at interest would seem to prevent them from so doing, but in the late 1990s some Muslims living in Europe put the question to the European Council for Fatwa and Research, a collection of jurists of various nationalities who now reside in Europe. The Council is led by the highly influential Egyptian jurist, Shaykh Yūsuf al-Qaraḍāwī, who lives in Qatar. In 1999, the Council responded to the question in the form of a *fatwā*, a non-binding legal opinion issued by a qualified person or group. The jurists stressed that the prohibition on usury does mean that Muslims everywhere should take steps to avoid borrowing from banks that charge interest, and should devise alternative ways of financing homes, such as paying more than the stated price but in installments. However, if Muslims in Europe could not practice such alternatives, then they could take out a mortgage for a first house.

In their argument the jurists cited two considerations. First, the doctrine of extreme necessity (*ḍarūra*) allows Muslims to do what otherwise is forbidden under compulsion or necessity. Why is it a necessity to own a house? Renting keeps the Muslim in a state of uncertainty and financial insecurity, stated the Council. Owning a house allows Muslims to settle in close proximity to a mosque, and to modify their house to accommodate religious needs. Moreover, Muslims living in Europe had reported to the Council that mortgage payments were equal to or lower than rents. Secondly, the jurists argued that while living in non-Muslim countries, Muslims may make contracts that violate Islamic law. Past jurists belonging to two of the traditional schools of Sunnī legal interpretation, the Ḥanafī and the Ḥanbal ī, had made this argument, they said. Muslims cannot change the institutions that dominate life in their host countries, and thus they are not responsible for the existence of an interest-based financial system. If they were forbidden to benefit from banking institutions then Islam would have weakened them, a result that would contradict the principle that Islam should benefit Muslims.

The ruling did not change the traditional prohibition of lending at interest, but exempted Muslims living in Europe from the prohibition because of a combination of empirical circumstances: the importance of owning a house, the high level of rents, and the absence of viable alternatives. These circumstances allow the jurists to apply the principles that necessity allows for exemption, and that Muslims may use otherwise invalid financial instruments when they live in "non-Islamic countries."

As noted earlier, in the late 1980s many Muslims in Europe shifted from seeing themselves, and being seen by others, mainly as immigrants, to taking on identities mainly as Muslims. Some Muslims and non-Muslims began to see religious commitments and practices as distinct from ethnic particularities and immigration histories. This shift has had a number of repercussions that have played themselves out over time and at different rhythms in different countries, but we can best understand these changes as the creation of a number of new possibilities in self-identifications and in treatment by others. These new possibilities do not resolve to one single trend, such as "individualization," but engender new tensions.

For Muslims, the shift has made possible several different ways of thinking about what it means to be a Muslim in Europe. For some, being a Muslim becomes a matter of faith and private religious practice, along the lines of older forms of European Protestantism. For others, it becomes a tradition to which they can refer, but to which they do not feel bound or obligated. Such, for example, is the position taken by self-styled "secular Muslims" in France. The opposite is equally possible; many Muslims have to come to see Islam as a set of norms and constraints that are detached from any one time or place and opposed to the traditions of various home countries. Muslims may see Islam in this last way and become highly involved in European public life, or, to the contrary, they can withdraw from public life on grounds that one can best live as a Muslim if one remains detached. These possibilities are all well represented among European Muslims today.

The "secular Muslim" approach is most present in France because the secularist media find this approach closest to proper French attitudes. Writers such as Malik Chebel promote in their books and through frequent television appearances an "enlightened Islam" that would consist of philosophy and spirituality, but eschew the legal and institutional aspects, which, he writes, do not fit well in Europe. "Self Islam" was the French title of a recent popular book that brings together the notions of religion as mainly and properly individual and internal. Several sociopolitical movements use the phrase "secular Muslims" (*Musulmans laïcs*) and call for keeping Islam out of the public sphere, and eradicating beliefs and practices deemed inimical to the Republic. In this approach, individuality, privacy, *laïcité*, and European values are bundled.

What could be called the "public Muslim" approach argues that this bundle must be untied, and that the public presentation of Islam does not conflict with European values. The Swiss intellectual Tariq Ramadan (1999), for example, argues that at the level of values one can find a convergence between Islamic norms and those of Europe, and that to do this one need not abandon the ideal of a visible, public Islamic presence. (Ramadan also argues for a geopolitical strategy of encouraging this convergence within each distinct cultural or religious tradition.) The "young Muslim" movements once associated with Ramadan seek to change political life as coalitions of Muslims, rather than as coalitions of secular citizens. If the "secular Muslim" approach grows out of French secularism, the "public Islam" accords best with countries supporting a multicultural recognition of ethnic differences such as Britain.

Opposed to both these stances are separatists, either those who simply keep to themselves, such as the Tablīghī Jamāʿat, or those that promote the eventual recreation of an Islamic state, such as the Hizb ut-Tahrir or its more radical offshoots. Muslims who are attracted to one of these movements make the same distinction between "religion" and "tradition" as do those who see themselves as "secularists" or as "publicly Muslim." But whereas a figure such as Tariq Ramadan sees a way to adapt Islamic norms to Europe, on condition that Europe accepts Muslims' public presence, the Hizb ut-Tahrir does not.

For non-Muslims, the shift in frames, from immigrants to Muslims, also can produce diverse effects. By and large, albeit unevenly, European governments have moved toward recognizing Islam as a legitimate faith, deserving of the same recognition and resources as are accorded forms of Christianity and Judaism. At the same time, however, highlighting the religion of a certain segment of the population emphasizes an element that separates them from the majority population, religion, and places into the background cross-cutting elements that form the basis for allegiances and solidarity, such as occupations, political allegiances, or cultural interests.

As a result of these differences in migration histories, Muslims differ markedly across Europe in their own sense of identification. A 2006 Pew Global Attitudes Survey (2006) asked Muslims in different countries around the world to choose between religion and nationality as their primary identity. While 42 percent of French Muslims said they were French first and Muslim second, only 7 percent of British Muslims and 3 percent of Spanish Muslims put nationality first. (Pew reports that American Christians choose between religious and national identities in almost exactly the same proportion as do French Muslims.) These same differences also show up for the population of each country as a whole. When asked if there is a conflict between being a devout Muslim and living in a modern society, 74 percent of all French people said there was none, about twice as high a figure as that for other Europeans or

Americans. Indeed, French people are more positive about modern Islam than are people in Indonesia, Jordan, or Egypt!

The distinctive feature of the French experience within Europe is that there, and there alone, both colonial history and current policies push in the same direction, towards integration. Today's French Muslims, or their parents or grandparents, came from former French territories in North or West Africa, where they learned that they were now part of the grand story of France, albeit in second-class roles. French Muslims today are demanding long-denied equal status and respect, as did African Americans in the USA. Their experience is quite unlike that of, say, Moroccans arriving in Denmark, where no common pasts, languages, or experiences prepare their way, or, for that matter, South Asians in Britain, who never were told that they could become English – and many of whom today demand a distinct mode of governance under *sharīʿa* law.

Nor do French Muslims live in ethnic enclaves. The housing projects around Paris contain people from different parts of Asia, Africa, and Europe, and stand in stark contrast to all-Turkish neighborhoods in Belgium and or all-Pakistani parts of British cities. Young Muslims who emerge from this mixed environment speak only French, demand French-language sermons in their mosques (and increasingly get them), and they flock to French-medium Islamic schools and institutes.

French policies also push toward integration, with a mix of carrots and sticks. Headscarves are out at school, but some enlightened mayors are giving land for mosques. The state gives newly arrived men and women hundreds of free hours of French language lessons, in an effort to make them more competitive for employment. Contrast recent Dutch policies (applied mainly to poorer counties) that require would-be immigrants, even the spouses of Dutch residents, to prove that they already speak good Dutch *before* arrival but provide no help in learning the language.

Whether Muslims living in Europe come to consider their countries of residence as part of the "Muslim World" may depend less on whether Islamic law ever gains official recognition, or Islamic private schools grow and flourish, than on whether they find themselves recognized as equal citizens. Or perhaps they will rephrase the question, and suggest that there are no more Muslim and non-Muslim worlds or countries, but places where one is more or less respected in one's quality as a Muslim man or woman.

References and further reading

Abou El Fadl, K. (1994) "Islamic Law and Muslim Minorities: The Juristic Discourse on Muslim Minorities from the Second/Eighth to the Eleventh/Seventeenth Centuries," *Islamic Law and Society*, 1: 143–87.

Bowen, J. (2007) *Why the French Don't Like Headscarves*, Princeton: Princeton University Press.

Bringa, T. (1995) *Being Muslim the Bosnian Way: Identity and Community in a Central Bosnian Village*, Princeton: Princeton University Press.

Brubaker, R. (1992) *Citizenship and Nationhood in France and Germany*, Cambridge, MA: Harvard University Press.

Caeiro, A. (2004) "The Social Construction of Sharīʿa: Bank Interest, Home Purchase, and Islamic Norms in the West," *Die Welt des Islams*, 44: 351–75.

Cesari, J. (2004) *When Islam and Democracy Meet: Muslims in Europe and in the United States*, New York: Palgrave.
Favell, A. (2001) *Philosophies of Integration: Immigration and the Idea of Citizenship in France and Britain*, 2nd edition, Basingstoke and New York: Palgrave.
Fetzer, J. S. and Soper, C. (2004) *Muslims and the State in Britain, France, and Germany*, Cambridge: Cambridge University Press.
Goody, J. (2004) *Islam in Europe*, Cambridge: Cambridge University Press.
Haddad, Y. Y., ed. (2002) *Muslims in the West: From Sojourners to Citizens*, Oxford, New York: Oxford University Press.
Hunter, S. T., ed. (2002) *Islam, Europe's Second Religion: The New Social, Cultural, and Politcial Landscape*, Westport, CT: Praeger.
Journal of Ethnic and Migration Studies (2004) Special Issue on "Islam, Transnationalism and the Public Sphere in Western Europe," 30 (5).
Kastoryano, R. (2002) *Negotiating Identities: States and Immigrants in France and Germany*, Princeton: Princeton University Press.
Kepel, G. (1997) *Allah in the West: Islamic Movements in America and Europe*, Stanford: Stanford University Press.
Lewis, P. (2002) *Islamic Britain: Religion, Politics, and Identity among British Muslims*, 2nd edition, London: Palgrave.
Masud, M. K., ed. (1999) *Travelers in Faith: Studies of the Tablighi Jamaat as a Transnational Islamic Movement for Faith Renewal*, Leiden: E. J. Brill.
Maussen, M. (2007) "Constructing Mosques, Negotiating Islam and Cultural Diversity in the Netherlands and France (1900–2004)," Ph.D. Thesis, University of Amsterdam.
Nielsen, J. S. (1999) *Towards a European Islam: Migration, Minorities and Citizenship*, London: Palgrave.
Modood, T., Berthoud, R. and Lakey, J. (1997) *Ethnic Minorities in Britain: Diversity and Disadvantage*, London: Policy Studies Institute.
Pearl, D. and Menski, W. (1998) *Muslim Family Law*, 3rd edition, London: Sweet and Maxwell.
Pew Global Attitudes Project (2006) "The Great Divide: How Westerners and Muslims View Each Other," http://pewglobal.org/reports/display.php?ReportID=253, June 26 (accessed January 18, 2007).
Ramadan, T. (1999) *To Be a European Muslim*, Leicester: The Islamic Foundation.
Rath, J., Penninx, R., Groenendijk, K. and Meyer, A. (2001) *Western Europe and its Islam*, Leiden: Brill.
Werbner, P. S. (2003) *Pilgrims of Love: Anthropology of a Global Sufi Cult*, Bloomington: Indiana University Press.

9

THE DIASPORA IN THE WEST

Amir Hussain

> Also, with the dream America everyone carries round in his head, America the Beautiful, Langston Hughes's country that never existed but needed to exist – with that, like everyone else, I was thoroughly in love. But ask the rest of the world what America meant and with one voice the rest of the world answered back, Might, it means Might. A power so great that it shapes our daily lives even though it barely knows we exist, it couldn't point to us on a map.
>
> (Rushdie 1999: 419–20)

The terrorist attacks in the USA on September 11, 2001, in Madrid on March 11, 2004, and in London on July 7, 2005, changed the way Islam was understood in North America and Europe. The attacks also changed the lives of North American and European Muslims, many of whom see themselves in various ways as "Western." The weeks immediately following the first attacks in the USA saw a rise in interest about Islam. Newspapers, magazines, web sites, and radio and television programs all addressed issues of Islam in North America and around the world. American Muslims both as individuals and in organized American Muslim groups condemned the attacks, and argued that the terrorists had twisted interpretations of Islam in order to justify their atrocities.

Many Muslims and experts on Islam were also busy giving presentations on Islam and Muslim communities after the attacks. These presentations were given in schools, places of religious worship, community centers, libraries, and other venues. Unfortunately, the demand for speakers or interpreters of Islam sometimes outstripped the supply of qualified individuals, resulting in the instant appearance of a number of self-styled "expert commentators" on Islam in the West. As a result, many negative stereotypes of Muslims were generated or reinforced.

This chapter will describe some of the realities of Muslim life in North America and Europe. Of course, the situations of Muslims of various backgrounds living in North America (with important differences between Canada and the USA) and Europe are myriad and diverse – all varying considerably upon their respective contexts.

Definitions: "Muslim," "diaspora" and "the West"

Some working definitions for the three key concepts in the title need to be provided: "Muslim," "diaspora" and "the West." By "Muslim," is meant any person (or group) who identifies her or himself as a follower of the religion of Islam. There are of course controversies among Muslims as to who is a "proper" or "true" Muslim. Some of those controversies will be described here, but no judgments will be advanced on who should or should not be referred to as a Muslim.

There are tremendous variations in what it means to be a Muslim. The majority of Muslims in the West are Sunnī, but approximately 30 percent are Shīʿī, double their representation worldwide. Within the Shīʿī traditions, the main split is between the Ithnā-ʿasharīs (or "Twelvers") and the Ismaʿīlīs (or "Seveners"), both of whom have a substantial presence in the West. The two branches of the Aḥmadiyya, a tradition which is proscribed in Pakistan, are represented in the West and have built the largest mosque in Canada. The Nation of Islam is still active in North America. A minority of Muslims are "official" members of Sufi organizations, but many more (as well as an increasing number of non-Muslims) are influenced more generally by Sūfī teachings. Along with these variations in doctrine and sectarian affiliation, Muslims have the same internal differences of gender, sexuality, generation, ethnicity, socio-economic status, etc. that are found in any large community. There is no one way to be Muslim in the West, just as there is no one way to be Catholic, Jewish, or "secular".

The word "diaspora" is understood here as it is frequently defined by scholars of religion, i.e., "members of any religious body living as a minority, whether in or outside their homeland, and maintaining contact with the central authorities of that body" (Suelzer 1979: 1051). Later in this chapter the question of whether Islam in North America and Europe is a collection of diaspora religions will be discussed. While some Muslims (for example, Somalis or Iranians) may see themselves as members of ethnic diaspora communities, many other Muslims in the West are deeply rooted in the countries in which they live, with no other "homeland" to which they wish to return.

As with "Muslim", there is considerable controversy over what is meant by "the West," and whether Islam is a "Western" religion. Many scholars consider the modern Western world – meaning North America and Europe for the purposes of this chapter – to be deeply influenced by Muslim cultures. Whether it be in mathematics, spirituality, science, philosophy, geography, medicine or art, Muslim thinkers throughout history have helped to shape our understanding of the world in the West and vice versa.

Muslims in North America and Europe: history

Islam has long existed in Western societies, first in Europe and later in North America. From the eighth to the fifteenth centuries, much of Spain was Islamicized and al-Andalūs (the Arabic term for Muslim Spain) remains a high point in the history of Islamic civilization. Historically, there was also an Islamic presence in Southern France, Italy, and Sicily, where Arabic was a language of learning and the royal court. And of course, Turkey is geographically located in Europe, even if some people do not think it of as "Western" or "European."

Furthermore, the Arabic language (especially via Spanish and French) has contributed to the vocabulary of English. Common English words such as "coffee," "sofa," and "alcohol," technical words such as "algebra," or "alkaline," and even archaic words such as "lute" and "alchemy" all have their roots in Arabic. More recently, Arabic words such as "Hajj," "jihad," or "hijab" have become commonplace enough so as to often require no accompanying translation.

Muslims had a complex role in the Old World. The ordinary European might come into contact with Muslims as merchants, traders, seafarers or pirates. However, the educated classes read works of Islamic philosophy, as well as classics of Greek philosophy (such as Aristotle) translated into Arabic and then into Latin. Muslim physicians were among the best of their day, and Muslim scientists and mathematicians (in collaboration with non-Muslims) made great advances in the sciences. Anybody familiar with Thomas Aquinas's *Summa Theologica* has felt the hovering presence of medieval Muslim scholars.

Prior to the Crusades (in the eleventh century), Muslims were relatively unknown by the European public. After the Crusades, with the making of enemy images on both sides, there was a great deal of polemic in European texts about Muslims. Norman Daniel has written the classic study of this in his magisterial *Islam and the West: The Making of an Image* (1997).

It was colonization that brought large numbers of Muslims to Europe, particularly Great Britain and France. French colonization of North Africa brought Muslims to France in the late 1800s, with immigrant workers from Algeria and Morocco arriving in greater numbers in the early 1900s. In 1926, the Paris Mosque was established to recognize those Muslims who sided with France during the occupation of Algeria. Muslims began to settle in Great Britain in the late 1800s and early 1900s as a result of British colonialism in India. The first mosque in Britain was founded in the London suburb of Woking in 1889.

The development of Islam in the USA has its roots in the slave trade, particularly the Muslim slaves from West Africa who retained their Islamic beliefs in their captivity. As a result, from the time of the slave trade there has been a consciousness about Islam in African American communities. As will be discussed later in this chapter, African Americans are one of the largest ethnic groups in the USA, and help to make American Islam different from Canadian Islam.

There has been a Muslim presence in Canada since very early in Canadian history, with the first national census for 1871 showing 13 Muslims. These Muslim immigrants quite clearly were diaspora Muslims, who sought to return home when they had made enough money in North America. It was not until the twentieth century that Islamic institutions became established in North America. The first mosque in the USA was built in Cedar Rapids, Iowa, in 1934, with the second being completed in Ross, North Dakota, in 1937. The first mosque in Canada was the al-Rashid Mosque in Edmonton, Alberta, built in 1938. June 28, 1952, saw the first national Muslim conference in Cedar Rapids, Iowa, with four hundred Muslims from Canada and the USA in attendance. In July 1954, the Federation of Islamic Associations of the United States and Canada (FIA) was formed. The first conference of the FIA was held a year later in London, Ontario. These conferences are important because they mark the beginnings of the institutionalization of Islam in America, and signal a shift from diaspora Islam to American Islam.

With the growth of the Muslim community in North America, and the migration of Muslim students from other countries (particularly the Arab world, but also Iran, India, Pakistan, and Turkey) to study in North America, the Muslim Students Association (MSA) was formed in 1963. Today, there are active chapters of the MSA in most major colleges and universities in North America.

Out of the MSA, the Islamic Society of North America (ISNA) was created in 1981.

It is the largest Islamic organization in North America, with its headquarters (including a large new mosque) in Plainfield, Indiana. ISNA has encouraged Muslims in North America to develop more extensive links with their local communities, including full participation in American and Canadian political processes. There are of course many other Muslim communities in North America, representing more restrictively defined groups as the Shīʿī (both Ithnā-ʿasharī and Ismaʿīlī) and Sūfī societies, the Nation of Islam (and all of its splinter groups such as the "Five Percenters," formed in 1963 by Clarence 13X), the Dar ul-Islam (a messianic group centered around the person of Dwight York) and others.

Immigration and ethnicity

In North America, Islam is an "immigrant" phenomenon, with the great majority of Muslims being immigrants, or the children of immigrants. There is also conversion to Islam, most notably in the African American populations. In Canada, the largest Muslim ethnic component is South Asian (Pakistani, Indian, Bangladeshi, Sri Lankan and through somewhat more recent migration, East African), but there are also significant populations from the Middle East and North Africa, and more recently from places like Somalia and the former Soviet Union and Yugoslavia. The Canadian Muslim population is mostly concentrated in the major cities of Toronto, Ottawa, Montréal and Vancouver, with smaller populations in cities like Calgary, Edmonton, Winnipeg, Saskatoon, Windsor and Halifax.

In the USA, one of the largest Muslim groups is comprised of African American converts and their children. There is some dispute as to the size of this community, and African Americans are estimated to comprise some 25 percent of the Muslim population in the USA. There has been a great deal of adult conversion in this community. This process of "conversion" is often self-described as being one of "reversion," with the understanding that people were Muslim when they came as slaves from West Africa, that "Christianity is the religion of the slave-master" imposed on slaves, and so you "revert" to your original religion instead of "converting" to it. The African American populations help to make American Islam distinct from Canadian Islam. After the African American populations (30.2% of American Muslims according to 1980 data), the next largest ethnic groups were Middle Eastern/North African (28.4%), Eastern European (26.6%), and Asian (11.5%) (Stone 1991: 28). A 2001 study of mosques in America (Bagby *et al.* 2001: 3) documented the change in ethnic composition, finding that: "At the average mosque, one-third (33%) of members are South Asian, three-tenths (30%) are African American, and a quarter (25%) are Arab."

In European countries, Muslim immigrants tend to be from one specific geographical area. Thus the majority of immigrant Muslims in Great Britain are from South Asia, while immigrant Muslims in Germany are largely from Turkey, immigrant Muslims in Italy are from Morocco (although with a significant number from Albania), and the majority of Muslims in France are immigrants from North Africa.

Colonialism

France, Italy, England and the Netherlands, through their own respective colonial and economic empires, have a history that is interwoven with that of Muslims in North and East Africa and South and Southeast Asia. The French were a colonial power in North Africa, particularly in Egypt, Algeria, Morocco and Tunisia. Italy was also involved in North Africa, most notably in Libya. The British empire had control of India, which before the partition of 1947 into India and Pakistan was the country with the world's largest Muslim population. The British were also a colonial presence in East Africa, particularly in countries like Kenya, Uganda and Tanzania. The Dutch colonial presence was felt in Indonesia, now the country with the largest Muslim population.

Given the French and British histories of colonialism and colonized peoples, there are similarities to the situation of those Muslims of Algerian descent in France with those Muslims of South Asian descent in Great Britain. One sees the Muslim Parliament in England as an example of the attempt to create separate but parallel institutions for Muslims in Great Britain. While there have been similar calls in North America, they have been unheeded by the majority of American or Canadian Muslims.

With the exception of the Philippines (which has a minority Muslim population), the USA was not officially a colonial power. However, the USA has played a dominant, if "unofficial" role in countries such as Iran and Jordan. Not surprisingly, the largest concentration of Iranians outside of Iran is found in the USA, specifically in Los Angeles. The role of the cultural colonization by the USA of the rest of the world should not be underestimated. As a result of America's different colonial history, there is much more ethnic diversity within its Muslim population than is found in Europe.

Populations

There is no accurate count of the Muslim populations of Canada, the USA or Europe. The Canadian census does ask the question of religious affiliation. The 1981 Census of Canada was the first one to recognize Islam as a separate, distinct religious category. According to the 1981 census, there were 98,165 Muslims in Canada (Rashid 1985: 15), so the Muslim population in Canada almost tripled from the 33,370 recorded in 1970. The overwhelming majority (77%) of Canadian Muslims were foreign-born, with only 23 percent being born in Canada (Rashid 1985: 17). The figures from the 1991 census show 253,260 Muslims in Canada, an increase of over 2.5 times the number from 1981.

The figures from the 2001 census list 579,600 Muslims in Canada, an increase of almost 2.3 times the number from the 1991 census. The estimate of 579,600, however, may be low. The main reason is that most Muslims are recent immigrants, who are reticent to self-identify as members of a minority religious group, for reasons ranging from personal privacy, to a perception of discrimination, to a desire to fit in. This is particularly true with the recent immigration of refugees into Canada from countries such as Somalia, Bosnia and Albania. On the other hand, estimates of population numbers are often linked with self-worth; that is, minorities may tend to prefer higher estimates for their own group and lower estimates for others.

The US census does not ask the question of religious affiliation. However, there has been a move by local governments to count "under-represented" groups in the total American population. Using data from the 1980 census, Carol Stone (1991: 27) estimated a Muslim population in America of some 3.3 million people in 1980, rising to 4 million in 1986. A 2001 study of mosques in America estimates a Muslim population in America between 6 and 7 million (Bagby *et al.* 2001: 3). California is the state with the greatest number of Muslims, including the largest concentration of Iranians. The best estimate of the current Muslim population in the USA is at least 6.5 million in this author's opinion. This would make Islam the third largest religion in North America, behind Christianity and Judaism. With the Jewish population in North America being usually estimated at about 7 million, it will not be long before Muslims outnumber Jews in North America if present demographic trends persist.

One researcher (van Koningsveld 1995: 290) estimates that "In the late twentieth century, there are about 18 million Muslims in Europe, with approximately 9 million each in western and southeastern Europe. In addition, small communities of a few thousand Muslims live in Poland and Finland." Muslims are the largest religious minority group in both Britain and France. In Britain, the Muslim population is estimated at anywhere from 1.5 million to 3 million (Vertovec 2002: 21). The Muslim population of France is estimated at some 4 million, of whom half are French citizens (Cesari 2002: 36). In Germany, there are an estimated 900,000 Turkish Muslims (Stowasser 2002: 56). Italy has an estimated 600,000 Muslims (Roggero 2002: 133). One sees the same upward trends in population evident in Europe as in North America.

European movements

European Muslims have often had to define themselves in the double contexts of racism and colonialism. During 1988–9, Muslims in Europe were often defined by the "Rushdie affair," their reactions to Salman Rushdie's novel, *The Satanic Verses*. Published in September 1988, the book was Rushdie's fourth novel, and dealt with the theme of migration, of being brown in England and the multiple identities that come with being Asian in London.

In Germany, racism and anti-Muslim sentiment has often led to violence against Turkish immigrants. On November 13, 1992, three Turkish immigrant women, aged 51, 14, and 10 were murdered in Mölln after German youths fire-bombed the hostel in which they were living.

One of the largest Muslim groups in Europe is an organization of Turkish immigrants (with headquarters in Cologne, Germany) Avrupa Millî Görüş Teşkilâtleri (AMGT), or Millî Görüş as it is more generally known. Millî Görüş, which is often translated as "The Religious Standpoint," refers to itself officially as "The Union of the New World View in Europe" (Pedersen 1999: 56–7). The organization is most active in Germany and France, with chapters in other countries such as Denmark and Australia. Millî Görüş serves a number of functions for Turkish Muslims, including organizing trips for *ḥajj*, collecting *zakāt*, sponsoring Islamic schools and other opportunities for young people, offering Turkish language education, and organizing sports clubs and athletic instruction. According to Lars Pedersen, Millî Görüş has

> undergone a transformation from being a Turkish Islamist movement in exile, whose interests lay primarily within the Turkish state-political landscape, to being a Turkish–European Islamic movement whose interests now lie to a

> great extent in the area of the organization of Islamic identity among Turkish immigrant minorities in Europe.
>
> (Pedersen 1999: 105)

In France, there are a number of Muslim organizations which serve a similar purpose to the Turkish group described above. Gilles Kepel describes the impact of these organizations in the 1990s:

> a growing number of young French people of North African origin defined themselves in relation to Islam. In most cases, the allegiance is specific to that particular generation and only partly draws on the "traditional" Islam of their parents' generation. Unlike in Britain, where Muslim immigrants from the Indian subcontinent brought with them tight and durable community structures, North African immigrants in France only really started to set up Islamic associations and open mosques in the mid-1970s.
>
> (Kepel 1997: 150)

Kepel points to an important issue, that of generation. While an earlier generation of North African immigrants may have one relationship with France, their children often have a very different relationship. This new generation refers to themselves as *beurs*: "The term '*beur*' is widely used in France to designate children born in France of immigrant (or pre-independence Algerian) parents. They usually have French nationality but many of them claim an identity independent of both their parents' and the dominant French culture" (Kepel 1997: 239).

North American movements: African-American Islam

The Nation of Islam and its offshoots do not have a strong presence in Canada and Europe. In the USA, as mentioned previously, African Americans make up one of the largest ethnic Muslim groups. However, there are disputed claims as to the size of this community. Using data from 1980, Stone (1991: 28) described them as the single largest ethnic Muslim group in the USA, composing 28.2 percent of the population. Jane Smith (1999: xiii) writes that "while it is difficult to determine exact proportions, many scholars of American Islam project that perhaps 40 percent of the Muslim community is African American." From talking with African American Muslims and scholars, and examining census figures, my own estimate is that there are no more than 1.5 million African American Muslims. This would include all who identify themselves as Muslims, whether they be Sunnī Muslims, members of the Nation of Islam, or belong to any one of the many small splinter groups such as the Five Percenters. Using the figure of 6 million American Muslims, this means that African Americans constitute some 25 percent of the Muslim population in America.

From the time of the slave trade, there has been a consciousness about Islam in African American communities. Moreover, beginning with the early Aḥmadī missionary work in the nineteenth century and continuing in the 1920s, there was a specific attempt to introduce and convert African Americans to Islam. Other groups, such as the Moorish Science Temple and the Nation of Islam, exclusively targeted African Americans. When Warith Deen Muhammad took over the leadership of the Nation of

Islam from his father in 1975, he brought the majority of his followers into Sunnī orthodoxy. Today, the majority of African American Muslims are Sunnī Muslims.

In contrast to the situation in the USA, there is not the same consciousness of Islam among Black Canadians as there is among African Americans. To begin, the majority of Black Canadians see their roots as being in the Caribbean rather than in Africa. To be sure, many of them trace their ancestral roots to Africa, but the Caribbean base is "home." For example, the Canadian Census of 1996 lists under the category of "immigrant population by place of birth" 279,405 people with their roots in the "Caribbean and Bermuda" and 229,300 with their roots in "Africa." Of course, this count would also include "White" people who have their roots in these two geographical categories. Moreover, the largest "Black" event in Canada is Toronto's annual Caribana Festival, which attracts over one million people from Canada and the rest of the world. Additionally, Canada does not have the same history of slavery that America does. To be sure, a number of freed slaves found their way into Canada, particularly the Atlantic provinces. However, like many other immigrant groups, the majority of Black Canadian immigrants came after the immigration reforms of the 1960s and are not the descendants of slaves brought over during the slave trade. For those immigrants from countries such as Trinidad or Jamaica, Islam is a known religious tradition, practiced mainly by South Asians. It is not a "new" or a "fresh" religion with which to make a counter-cultural stand as it is for African Americans.

It has been the Sunnī form of Islam that has been active in the conversion of Black Canadians, often spurred by the ministry of dynamic Black *imāms* such as Shaikh ʿAbdullah Hakim Quick or Imam Siraj Wahhaj from New York. The Nation of Islam has not had nearly the same history of conversion activity in Canada that it has had in the USA.

Other than the attention paid to the personal charisma of its current leader, Louis Farrakhan, the Nation of Islam has not played a significant role among the Muslim communities of Canada. Where they have played a role is in their influence on rap and hip-hop music by artists such as Public Enemy or Ice Cube, listened to by Muslims and non-Muslims, Blacks and non-Blacks. Gardell (1996: 295) has written of this influence, concluding that "what reggae was to the expansion of the Rastafarian movement in the 1970s, so hip-hop is to the spread of black Islam in the 1980s and 1990s."

It is interesting to note that it is not only Black recording artists who have been influenced by Islam and spread its message. In 1997, Everlast (born Erik Schrody), the leader of the Irish American rap group, House of Pain, became a convert to Islam. Of that conversion, he has said in an interview (DeRogatis 2001: 46): "Islam made a lot of things make a lot of sense to me. It makes me look at life from a lot of different sides, and it's definitely one of the things that made me be honest enough with myself to sing and write some of the stuff about my life that I never would have let out before." As an example, his *Eat at Whitey's* CD released in 2000, ends with the track "Graves to Dig" that begins with the following lyrics: "They go one for the Prophet/ Two for Islam/Three for the *khuṭba* from the *Imām*." Not only do his lyrics introduce others to Islam, they again demonstrate the "Americanization" of Islam. Islamic themes are being expressed in English by a Muslim using an art form that is indigenous to the USA.

Law

There have been some calls by Muslims in the West to implement Muslim family law in their respective countries. For example, the Canadian Society of Muslims has called for the allowance of Muslim personal law in Canada. Arguing from what they considered to be special treatment given to French-speaking citizens and First Nations in Canada, it wanted the right to be ruled by Muslim personal law. The society was quite clear in arguing not for the implementation of the *sharīʿa* in its entirety but only for "Muslim personal law dealing with family relationships – mainly marriage, divorce and intestate succession" (Ali 1992: 17). Also, it only wanted this for those Muslims who would register to be governed by Muslim personal law: "those Muslims who prefer to be governed by secular Canadian family law may continue that way" (Ali 1992: 17).

The Canadian Society of Muslims has also spoken out against the fact that Muslims, along with members of other religious traditions, are unable to use government funds for religious education: "Thus Muslims – and this is also true of Jewish, Hindu, Buddhist, Sikh, Native peoples and the Protestant Christians – must bear a special burden of paying twice if they want an education that reflects the values and practices of their religious tradition" (Ali and Whitehouse 1992: 165). In the USA, with the official separation of church and state, the situation is of course different. The Canadian Society of Muslims continues with its campaign, having met with some success in getting the Ontario court to recognize the validity of Muslim mediation in some cases. In 2005, however, the Premier of Ontario moved to prohibit any religious tribunals to settle family law disputes.

Education

One of the main concerns of Muslims in the West is the education received by the younger generation. To take the case of Toronto – the city with the largest population of Canada's Muslims – in 2001 there were 18 Islamic schools in the Greater Toronto Area, with another seven in the rest of the Province of Ontario. While the number of Islamic schools is greatly increased from the first school in Toronto, established in the basement of the Jami Mosque in 1981, Islamic schools represent only a small fraction of the some 725 independent schools in Ontario. Estimates of the number of children enrolled in Islamic schools in Ontario in 1999 ranged from 2,240 (from the Ontario Ministry of Education) to 4,000 (from Muslim organizations). Clearly, the issue of Islamic schools in the West is an important one. Both Muslims and non-Muslims are concerned about the quality of the education received by the students. Recently, there have been concerns that the funding of some schools by the government of Saudi Arabia leads to an education where the students are taught Wahhābī doctrines as the only acceptable interpretation of Islam.

It is in colleges and universities that Muslims in the West usually have their first serious opportunities to learn about their own traditions and to articulate their own ways of being Muslim. There is a marked difference here from the experience of Christian or Jewish students. There are any number of Christian or Jewish schools in North America and Europe, in addition to a number of religious institutions of learning. By contrast, only a small percentage of Muslim students are the product of

Islamic schools. They do not have the same opportunities to learn about their religion that are available to Jewish or Christian children. It is also at the university level that many non-Muslims first learn about Islam.

Political activity

There are a number of North American groups that are involved in Muslim political activity. The Muslim Public Affairs Council (MPAC) was founded in 1988 and has offices in Los Angeles and Washington, DC. According to their web site: "The Muslim Public Affairs Council is a public service agency working for the civil rights of American Muslims, for the integration of Islam into American pluralism, and for a positive, constructive relationship between American Muslims and their representatives" (http://www.mpae.org/about). MPAC has sponsored numerous forums on topics ranging from civil rights to hate crimes against Muslims to issues of social justice such as hunger and homelessness.

Another North American group is the Council on American–Islamic Relations (CAIR). According to its web site, CAIR was "established to promote a positive image of Islam and Muslims in America" (http://www.cair.com/AboutUs/VisionMissionCarePrinciples.aspx). CAIR is most involved with media relations, and serves as a "watchdog" for negative stereotypes of Islam and Muslims. CAIR also sponsors numerous conferences and seminars, as well as publications. Perhaps its most important role is in "action alerts," which focus on local community issues that affect Muslims in America. The important work of CAIR since the terrorist attacks on September 11 has been mentioned at the beginning of this chapter.

In addition to MPAC and CAIR, there are two other important political organizations for American Muslims. The American Muslim Alliance was founded in 1989, and the American Muslim Council a year later. These four groups together form the American Muslim Political Coordinating Council.

For many American Muslims, there was a tragic irony following the terrorist attacks on September 11, 2001. In the 2000 presidential elections and with the support of CAIR, many American Muslims voted for George Bush, particularly after he spoke out against the "secret evidence" that had been used against Arabs and Muslims. To see their president then use secret evidence in broader and more insidious ways offended many of the American Muslims who had voted for Bush.

In 1997, ISNA formed the Canadian Muslim Council, a counterpart to the American Muslim Council. This council was designed to involve Muslims in the Canadian political process. It encouraged Muslims to vote and supported a number of Muslim candidates at various levels of government. While none of these candidates were elected, it did formally signal an involvement by ISNA in the Canadian political process. Since 1997, ISNA has encouraged Muslims, as Muslims, to vote in Canadian elections.

Islamization in the public sphere

While the Islam that is lived out by Muslims in the West is affected by their being in the West, it also has an affect on the West. For example, one sees the common use of words such as "jihad" or "hijab" in the popular media without any translation.

Muslims have established themselves in the West, and included themselves in the conversations between Christians and Jews. One rarely reads phrases such as "churches and synagogues" without "mosques" included, or "ministers, priests, and rabbis" without "*imāms*" included. Muslims have become active as chaplains, both in the military and in prisons. A Muslim *imām* has opened the prayers of Congress, and the White House has sponsored an *ifṭār* to mark the end of a day's fast during Ramaḍān. The sight of Muslim women in various forms of *ḥijāb* or Muslim men in various head coverings has become commonplace. Television stations routinely offer Eid and Ramaḍān greetings along with Christmas and Hanukkah greetings. The US Postal Service has issued an Eid stamp, and Muslim athletes such as Muhammad Ali, Kareem Abdul Jabbar, and Hakeem Olajuwon have become fixtures in the sporting life of North America. Many members of the French national soccer team, including its star player, Zinedine Zidane, are Algerian Muslims. Islamic banks and other financial institutions that work without interest are available, as are "Islamically acceptable" investments in the stock market. *Ḥalāl* meat is increasingly to be found in grocery stores, as are other *ḥalāl* products.

However, this is not to say that there has, or ever will be, a total Islamization of the West. No matter how large the populations of Muslims become, they will not equal the populations of Christians in the West. And one can hardly imagine the bias against Muslims (or any other minority group for that matter) ever being totally eliminated. To return to the Rushdie quote with which I began, Muslims are an integral part of the West, even if the West sometimes does not realize this.

Note

This chapter is dedicated to Salman Rushdie who taught me much about essays and literary criticism, and to Pat Nichelson who continues to teach me about scholarly writing. I am indebted to David Horne for his help with the estimate of African American Muslims.

References and further reading

Ali, S. M. (1992) "Complementary Equanimity: A Balancing Principle of Gender Equality," *Newsletter* (Toronto: Canadian Society of Muslims), 2: 2.

Ali, S. M. and Whitehouse, A. (1992) "The Reconstruction of the Constitution and the Case for Muslim Personal Law in Canada," *Journal of the Institute of Muslim Minority Affairs*, 13 (1): 156–71.

Bagby, I., Perl, P. M. and Froehle, B. T. (2001) *The Mosque in America: A National Portrait*, Washington: Council on American–Islamic Relations.

Cesari, J. (2002) "Islam in France: The Shaping of a Religious Minority," in Y. Y. Haddad, ed., *Muslims in the West: From Sojourners to Citizens*, New York: Oxford University Press, 36–51.

Daniel, N. (1997) *Islam and the West: The Making of an Image*, Oxford: Oneworld.

DeRogatis, J. (2001) "Whitey Sings the Blues," in *Penthouse*, 32 (7) March: 46–9.

Gardell, M. (1996) *In the Name of Elijah Muhammad: Louis Farrakhan and the Nation of Islam*, Durham: Duke University Press.

Kepel, G. (1997) *Allah in the West: Islamic Movements in America and Europe*, trans. S. Milner, Stanford: Stanford University Press.

Pedersen, L. (1999) *Newer Islamic Movements in Western Europe*, Aldershot: Ashgate.

Rashid, A. (1985) *The Muslim Canadians: A Profile*, Ottawa: Statistics Canada.
Roggero, M. A. (2002) "Muslims in Italy," in Y. Y. Haddad, ed., *Muslims in the West: From Sojourners to Citizens*, New York: Oxford University Press, 131–43.
Rushdie, S. (1999) *The Ground Beneath Her Feet*, Toronto: Alfred A. Knopf.
Smith, J. I. (1999) *Islam in America*, New York: Columbia University Press.
Stone, C. L. (1991) "Estimates of Muslims Living in America", in Y. Y. Haddad, ed., *The Muslims of America*, New York: Oxford University Press, 25–36.
Stowasser, B. F. (2002) "The Turks in Germany: From Sojourners to Citizens," in Y. Y. Haddad, ed., *Muslims in the West: From Sojourners to Citizens*, New York: Oxford University Press, 52–71.
Suelzer, M. J. (1979) "Diaspora," in P. K. Meagher, T. C. O'Brien and Sister C. M. Aherne, eds., *Encyclopedic Dictionary of Religion*, Washington: Corpus Publications, vol. I: 1051.
van Koningsveld, P. S. (1995) "Islam: Islam in Europe," in J. L. Esposito, ed., *The Oxford Encyclopedia of the Modern Islamic World*, New York: Oxford University Press, vol. II: 290–6.
Vertovec, S. (2002) "Islamophobia and Muslim Recognition in Britain," in Y. Y. Haddad, ed., *Muslims in the West: From Sojourners to Citizens*, New York: Oxford University Press, 19–35.

Part II

THE RELIGIOUS ISLAMIC WORLD

10

THE QUR'ĀN

Gordon Nickel and Andrew Rippin

The Qur'ān is the scripture of the Muslim community, revered by Muslims around the world and given authority to determine both faith and life. Many features of the Qur'ān can be fruitfully explored by the general reader. Other matters related to the Qur'ān, such as claims to its divine provenance and linguistic perfection, are matters of religious conviction rather than objective fact. At a number of points the Qur'ān plays an important role in the development of Muslim identity, both in the contents of the book itself and in the claims which Muslims make for their scripture. The Qur'ān is believed by Muslims to be the revelatory word of God, dictated by the angel Gabriel to the Prophet Muḥammad in segments between the years 610 and 632. Muslims believe that as Muḥammad recited the revelations, the words were memorized by his companions. They believe the recitations were later recorded word for word and are today found in the Arabic text of the Qur'ān in precisely the manner God intended.

General physical description

Consisting of 114 chapters, called *sūra*s, the Qur'ān is arranged approximately in order of length from the longest chapter (some 22 pages of Arabic text for *sūra* 2) through the shortest (only a single line for *sūra* 108). Acting as a short introduction to the text is the first chapter, called "The Opening," *al-Fatiḥa*, which is a prayer-like segment used within the Muslim *ṣalāt* ritual. Each chapter is divided into verses, *āya*s, the total number being reckoned somewhere between 6204 and 6236, differing according to various schemes of counting. These verse divisions do not always correspond to the sense of the text but are generally related to the rhyme structure of the individual *sūra*s. The rhyme is constructed through a vowel plus the final consonant at the end of each verse, although few chapters have a consistent rhyme scheme throughout and in the longer narrative chapters, the rhyme is created by the use of stock phrases such as "God is all-knowing, all-wise."

Twenty-nine chapters are preceded by disconnected letters of the Arabic alphabet, some single letters (Q – *qāf, sūra* 50; N – *nūn, sūra* 68) or up to five different letters together. The significance of these so-called mysterious letters has eluded traditional Muslim and modern scholarship alike. Also prefacing each chapter, with the exception of *sūra* 9, is the *basmala*, the statement, "In the name of God, the Beneficent, the Merciful." This phrase acts as an opening to all Muslim religious statements and is found within the Qur'ān itself as the opening phrase of the letter written by Solomon to the Queen of Sheba (Q 27:30).

The text as it is generally found today indicates both the Arabic consonants and the vowels according to a standard system of notation, along with a variety of other marks connected to recitation practices and verse divisions. Early manuscripts of the Qur'ān dating from the eighth and ninth centuries provide only a skeleton-like primitive written outline of Arabic, however. The standard, fully vocalized text of the Qur'ān was established only in the first half of the tenth century.

Organization

Apart from the mechanical arrangement of the Qur'ān by length of chapter, the organizational principle behind the text is unclear. Despite the best efforts of many scholars from both within and outside the faith perspective, the sense of an apparent random character and seemingly arbitrary sense of organization is hard to overcome. There seem to be no historical, biographical, thematic, aesthetic or poetic criteria by which one can understand the overall structure of the work. To the source critic, the work displays all the tendencies of rushed editing with only the most superficial concern for the content, the editors/compilers apparently engaged only in establishing a fixed text of scripture.

Traditional story of the collection

The Muslim tradition has provided an explanation for why the Qur'ān looks the way it does, although the contradictions created by the multiplicity of versions of the story have raised grave doubts on the part of many scholars as to their plausibility and motivation. Generally, Muḥammad himself is excluded from any role in the collection of the text. Zayd ibn Thābit, a companion of Muḥammad, is generally credited with an early collection of the scripture following the death of Muḥammad. Zayd is said to have worked with pieces of text written "on palm leaves or flat stones or in the hearts of men" (a standard way of expressing the idea, found in collections of *ḥadīth*). The pages of the text were then entrusted to Hafṣa, one of Muḥammad's wives. Under the instructions of ʿUthmān, the third ruler of the empire after the death of Muḥammad, the major editing of the text took place. The complete text (deemed to have survived in full) was then written out in full and distributed to the major centers of the expanding Muslim empire. Thus, within 25 years of the death of Muḥammad, Muslims understand that the Qur'ān existed in at least its skeletal but fixed form; theologically, it is held that the form that the text was in at this point was an image of a heavenly tablet, suggesting that its form and content were precisely that which God desired for it. For some Muslims, the emergence of the written text is moot: they believe that an oral tradition preserved the full text from the time of its revelation, while the written form served only as a mnemonic device for memorization of the text.

The scholarly difficulties with this traditional account relate to both the state of the Muslim sources for the account and the historical evidence for its authenticity. The many accounts in *ḥadīth* collections and other sources from the early centuries contradict each other in the details of formation as well as in the protagonists to whom they give credit for the collection among the first four caliphs. Early Muslim sources also contain reports of the persistent survival of rival codices (*muṣḥaf*s) to the so-called ʿUthmanic *muṣḥaf*. These and other discrepancies have led some scholars to reject the traditional account altogether, opting instead to suggest either a collection during the lifetime of Muḥammad or a longer process of formation and canonization during the first two centuries of Islam.

The earliest sources for the collection accounts are the *ḥadīth* collections of the third Islamic century. Though they claim to report traditions reaching back to Muḥammad himself through a reliable chain of transmission, the *ḥadīth* collections have come under close scrutiny by Western scholars and their historical reliability has been challenged. Added to this is a paucity of manuscript evidence for an early establishment of the Qur'anic text. Some scholars have suggested dating a number of leaves from ancient codices to as far back as the end of the first Islamic century, but paleographical study of the oldest codices has produced no clear and unambiguous results with respect to the dating of ancient Qur'ān manuscripts which are generally acknowledged by scholars. Further, the oldest manuscripts are too fragmentary to allow the conclusion that the earliest Qur'āns were identical in form, size and content to later Qur'āns. Finally, the text of the Qur'ān itself offers few clues – if any – to its authorship, transmission or editing. Scholars who seek to argue that the Qur'ān is the collection of Muḥammad's recitations have been obliged to return to the Islamic tradition to make their case.

The speaker of the Qur'ān

The difficulties in understanding the text are by no means confined to the issue of its organization. One other issue which confronts most readers is the idea of the "speaker" of the Qur'ān. Muslim theology understands that God speaks throughout the Qur'ān. Yet He refers to Himself in both the singular (Q 2:30) and plural (Q 12:2) first person forms, as well as in the third person (Q 5:9) as though we were dealing with an omniscient narrator. Furthermore, statements which a reader might have conceived to be Muḥammad's are frequently preceded by the word "Say," a stylistic device understood to be God giving the authorization for Muḥammad to speak through his own person while reciting the "dictated word" (Q 2:94). The identity of the addressee of the Qur'ān is not always clear: much of the text is in the second person singular, but much also addresses a plural "you" and even a dual "you" (*sūra* 55); and some passages mix singular and plural (Q 2:155). Similarly, the reader encounters passages in which the voice of the text clearly cannot be God (*sūra* 1; 2:286; 6:104, 114), but the Muslim interpretative tradition has always been able to provide a corrective understanding to maintain a consistent presence of the divine voice throughout the text.

The Qur'ān contains a fair number of passages in which the speaker addresses "the messenger" regarding various aspects of a prophetic mission. These aspects include a commission, calls to patience and faithful recitation, words of comfort and encouragement, various directives, and even a rebuke. Along with these personal messages come self-conscious affirmations of the message which include rebuttals of accusations made by the messenger's contemporaries. Throughout the Qur'ān brief statements appear which assert the authenticity or veracity of the recitation, or its function as a reminder. A characteristic expression of this kind is the verse, "We have revealed it, a *qur'ān* in Arabic, that you may understand" (Q 12:2; cf. 20:113; 13:37).

Themes

A reading of the Qur'ān shows that it has a thematic preoccupation with three major topics: law, the previous prophets and the final judgment. The three topics appear to presuppose on the part of their readers some biblical knowledge along with a reference point within some variation of a native Arabian tradition.

Ruling over all of the Qur'ān, and the reference point for all the developments of its major themes, is the figure of God, Allāh in Arabic. The all-mighty, all-powerful and all-merciful God created the world for the benefit of His creatures, has sent messages to them in the past to guide them in the way of living most befitting to them and to Him, has given them the law by which they should live – and which has reached its perfection and completion in Islam, and will bring about the end of the world at a time known only to Him when all shall be judged strictly according to their deeds. The basic message is a familiar one from within the Judaeo–Christian tradition. This emphasis on the uniqueness of God, that Allāh is the only god who exists, is presented both in opposition to the Jewish–Christian tradition and in opposition to the polytheist Arabian idolaters who worshipped spirits (*jinn*, "genies"), offspring of God and various idols.

The reader of the Qur'ān in its canonical progression quickly encounters passages which contain a range of polemical forms and terminology and which seem to reflect polemical encounters. A prominent element in the Qur'ān appears to be polemical responses to resistance to the reciter's claim to prophethood and to the claim that the words he is reciting are from God. The antagonists are sometimes specified as Jews, Christians (*Naṣārā*), "associators," or simply as "disbelievers." *Sūra*s 2 through 7, the long *sūra*s which make up the opening fifth of the Qur'ān, contain a great deal of polemical material. In the midst of these passages, assertions are made for the truth of the recitations being "sent down" in response to the disbelief of the "people of scripture" and the associators.

The polemical passages show signs of being part of a larger process of the development of Islamic identity. On the one hand the recitations of the present messenger are said to "confirm" the scriptures of the Jews and Christians. The messenger is also portrayed as belonging to the same line as biblical messengers and prophets, and "no distinction" is to be made among these prophets (Q 2:136). The recitations of the messenger seem to be characterized in some passages as an Arabic translation of earlier scriptures (Q 26:192–7). On the other hand, Abraham is claimed for Islam while denied to Jews and Christians (Q 3:67–8). Frequently, Islam is put forward as the religion above all others: "You are the best nation ever brought forth to humankind" (Q 3:110); "Whoso desires another religion than Islam, it shall not be accepted of him" (Q 3:85); "Today I have perfected your religion for you, and I have completed my blessing upon you, and I have approved Islam for your religion" (Q 5:3).

The text at times gives the impression of an effort to measure up to the strong religions thriving in the Middle East at the time of the Muslim conquest, along with a simultaneous effort to distinguish the new religion and raise it above the others. The basic components of divinity, prophet/messenger and scripture are repeatedly signaled in the text of the Qur'ān. These are what the Jews and Christians were known to possess. The claim of the Qur'ān is not only that the new religion has achieved these features as well, but also that the Muslim components are purer and more authentic: "It is He who has sent His messenger with the guidance and the religion of truth, that He may render it victorious over every religion" (Q 9:33).

Qur'anic polemic with the Jews centers mainly on Jewish resistance to the religious claims of Islam. Reference is made to the covenants which the "children of Israel" made with God in the past, and to the Torah which is "with them" (Q 2:89). In spite of the prophecies of the present messenger assumed by the Qur'ān to be contained in both their covenants and scripture, the Jews accept neither the messenger's prophethood nor his authority. One sub-theme of the polemical passages is that the Jews are "tampering" with the Torah in a variety of ways. The perceived obduracy of the Jews who are hearing the messenger's present recitations is said to match Jewish misdeeds of the ancient past. Polemical passages relating to the Jews begin with an extended passage taking up nearly one half of the Qur'ān's longest *sūra*.

Qur'anic polemic with Christians is not as abundant as with Jews, but it seems to already occupy a substantial portion of the third *sūra*. Polemic with Christians mainly concerns the identity of Jesus. Christian resistance seems to be related to their reluctance to accept the "true narrative" about Jesus which the messenger asserts. Polemic with a third group, the polytheists, is also reflected in many Qur'anic passages. The resistance of the polytheists seems to include skeptical comparisons of the recitations of the messenger with the orations of poets, *kāhin*s, or those possessed by *jinn*. "The disbelievers say, 'This is nothing but the fairy-tales of the ancient ones' " (Q 6:25). A rumor is circulating that another person is teaching the messenger what to say (Q 16:103). The polytheists also seem to demand a miracle to support the messenger's claims to prophethood. The harshest polemic against this group is for their sin of "associating" (*shirk*) with God that which is not divine. In contrast to the "people of scripture," polytheists in the Qur'ān appear to have no redeeming features. Instead, God's curse is frequently pronounced on them and their destination after the Judgment is consistently said to be hell.

The God of the Qur'ān is the God who communicated to the prophets of the past. Most of the stories of the past prophets as recounted in the Qur'ān are familiar from the Hebrew Bible and the New Testament but are presented shorn of the extensive narrative element. The Qur'ān tends to present summaries of the stories and to get directly to religio–moral points interpreted from them. This feature has led some modern scholars to suggest that the audience of the Qur'ān was assumed to have known the biblical stories, and perhaps much else from the Judeo–Christian tradition.

A number of prophets are named in the Qur'ān as having been commissioned or selected by God to spread the message of the true way of obedience to Him. A limited number of these people were given scriptures to share with their communities: Abraham, Moses, David and Jesus are clearly cited in this regard. Not all of the named prophets are familiar from the biblical tradition (or at least their identification with personages of the past is less than clear): for example, Hūd, Ṣāliḥ, Shu'ayb and Luqmān are generally treated as prophets of the specifically Arabian context prior to Muḥammad.

The stories of these prophets are frequently recounted through a formulaic structure. The prophet is commissioned by God and sent with a message to his people. The people reject the message. The prophet then confronts his people and warns them of the consequences of disobedience. The people begin to manhandle the messenger. At the point of crisis, God destroys the people and saves the prophet and any persons faithful to his message. The story of some of the prophets is told in more expansive form, for example in the case of Joseph which is recounted in *sūra* 12 and is one of the most cohesive narratives found in the Qur'ān. Elaborations within the story indicate that the Qur'ān is not simply retelling stories read from the Bible, but is reflecting their popular form in the Near Eastern milieu of the seventh century.

Of all the biblical figures mentioned in the Qur'ān, Moses garners by far the most attention. His name appears some 136 times. In 36 of the Qur'ān's 114 *sūra*s Moses is mentioned in 50 separate pericopes totaling more than 500 verses. Even more striking than the abundance of material is the special profile which the Qur'ān seems to give to Moses. In the Qur'ān, God speaks directly with Moses (Q 4:164), and says to him, "Moses, I have chosen you above humankind by My messages and My word" (Q 7:144). In five extended versions of the Moses story, the Qur'ān relays different elements of the narrative in different sequences, with differences in the details within the narrative elements. These many Qur'anic versions – described by one scholar as "variant traditions" – contain elements which are familiar from the Hebrew Bible. Other details in the Qur'anic narratives match the details in extra-biblical tellings such as in Midrash and Talmud, while some details are not known from any other recorded source. The frequency of the prophetic stories and the differences between them have led some scholars to speculate on what these phenomena might tell about the provenance of Muslim scripture. Scholars suggest a scenario of differing stories gathered from different sources, perhaps different regions of the Muslim empire, collected and incorporated into scripture without either editing or selection of the "best" version.

The Qur'anic material on Jesus – called ʿĪsā in the Qur'ān – is concentrated in *sūra*s 3, 5 and 19. The greatest amount of attention is given to the circumstances of Jesus' birth, some of which resemble those of the first chapter of the Gospel according to Luke. Jesus is presented as a miracle worker who heals the blind and the lame, and who raises the dead "by leave of Allah" (Q 3:49). The Qur'anic report that Jesus created a bird from clay and blew life into it (Q 5:110) resembles a story in the apocryphal *Gospel of Thomas*. When it approaches the death of Jesus, the Qur'anic material appears ambiguous, ranging from verses which seem to assume his death (Q 3:55, 19:33) to an explicit denial that the Jews killed Jesus (Q 4:157). However, there is little ambivalence in the Qur'anic denial of Jesus' divinity. The Qur'anic Jesus is emphatically not God, not the Son of God, not to be "associated" with God, and not the "third of three." On the other hand, Jesus is given the name "Messiah" (Q 3:45) and is mysteriously called the "word" of God and "a spirit" from God (Q 4:171).

The Qur'anic prophets are generally portrayed as bringing the same message of the coming judgment for those who do not repent and follow the law of God. The message is a simple and familiar one. All people shall die at their appointed time and then, at a point known only to God, the resurrection shall take place at which all people shall be strictly judged according to the deeds they have performed on earth. The image of the weigh scale is brought in to emphasize that not even an "atom's weight" of good or evil (Q 99:7–8) will be neglected in the final reckoning. Pronouncements of judgment, along with the theological theme of the "God of justice," are touched on in approximately every third verse of scripture. Scenes of reward and punishment as a result of God's judgment are frequently painted in graphic style within the Qur'ān.

To be granted eternal existence in heaven, one must believe in the truth and the contents of the scripture and put those contents into action in day-to-day life. It is on the basis of one's intentional adherence to the will of God as expressed through legal requirements indicated in the Qur'ān that one's fate in the hereafter will be determined. The Qur'anic law contains elements familiar from Jewish law, such as the prohibition of pork and the institution of ritual slaughter, some purity regulations (especially as regards women) and the emphasis on the regulation of marriage, divorce and inheritance. In the discussion of law, however, the theme of Muslim identity appears to be a factor. For example, in the midst of a polemical discussion of the direction of prayer which draws in both Jews and Christians comes the expression, "We appointed you a midmost nation" (Q 2:143).

As well, various ritual practices of Islam are mentioned in the Qur'ān, but often only in an unelaborated form. The pilgrimage, the month of fasting, the institution of prayer and the idea of charity are all dealt with to varying degrees. In many cases the directives of the Qur'ān come from both "God and his messenger." Commands to obey, for example, hold God and the messenger together in all but one of 13 such occurrences. Overall, the law is conceived as a gift given by God to humanity to provide guidance in living the proper, fully human life.

Among the repeating imperatives of the Qur'ān are commands to fight and kill, as well as the command to "strive (*jāhada/jihād*) in the way of Allah." These imperatives frequently appear in contexts which seem to reflect a battle situation. In the battle passages, the "believers" are exhorted to participate fully in the conflict: to "go forth" and to "expend" gold and silver in God's way. Those who hold back from the struggle are promised chastisement in this life and punishment in the life to come. God's way in these battle passages appears to be equated with the career of "the messenger," and opposition to this career is characterized as the way of Satan and promised harsh punishment. Not all of the uses of the verb "to strive" (*jāhada*) come in the midst of battle passages, however. The command at Q 22:78, for example, appears to instruct Muslims to perform the religious duties originally prescribed to Abraham.

Symbolic language

Conveying these Qur'anic themes are vast complexes of symbolic language, the ranges of which have not been catalogued through any contemporary literary perspective. The mix of biblical and Arabian motifs renders the task a difficult one. Some scholars have tended to interpret the text as reflecting the contemporary situation of Muḥammad, and thus picturing the symbolism in materialist terms; others have emphasized the biblical (or general ancient near eastern) context and see the Qur'anic language as reflecting the nature of monotheistic language in that milieu. Clues to the latter approach include prophetic themes which are repeatedly signaled in the Qur'ān but seldom developed, such as retribution, sign, exile, and covenant. These materials seem to reflect a traditional stock of monotheistic imagery.

Doctrine of inimitability

The Qur'ān is, and has been from the beginning of the emergence of the religion, the primary source and reference point for Islam. Indeed, the Qur'ān in its function as a source of authority is the defining point of Islamic identity. The emergence of the Muslim community is intimately connected with the emergence of the Qur'ān as an authoritative text in making decisions on matters of law and theology.

Allusions to and direct quotations of the Qur'ān are pervasive in Muslim literature. While imitation of the Qur'ān is considered both impossible and sinful (because it is God's word), the contents of the Qur'ān and its particular form of classical Arabic create the substrata of literary production. The widespread knowledge of the words of the Qur'ān, traditionally instilled in most children through memorization, means that reverberations of the text are guaranteed to be felt by most readers. Direct quotations of the Qur'ān and the use of some of the text's striking metaphors abound in the literature of all Muslim languages.

Beyond deep appreciation for the sounds and contents of the Qur'ān, Muslims share a belief in the linguistic perfection of the Arabic text and advance this as a proof of its divine origin. This "miracle" of language is then brought in as a demonstration of the true prophethood of Muḥammad. The Islamic doctrine of the inimitability of the Qur'ān, in Arabic *iʿjāz*, is also related to Muslim beliefs that the Qur'ān is eternal, uncreated, and kept safe from change or corruption in a heavenly tablet. These doctrines are supported with expressions from within the Qur'ān such as, "It is a glorious *qur'ān* in a guarded tablet" (Q 85:21-2). Muslim scholars also refer to a series of "challenge verses" which begins at Q 2:23: "If you are in doubt concerning what we have sent down on our servant, then bring a *sūra* like it." What may appear to non-Muslim readers as discrepancies or contradictions, or inexplicable changes of subject, voice and mood, are believed by Muslims to be aspects of the precise form which God gave the book. Claims to the status of the Qur'ān were at times matters of great controversy within the Muslim community during the early centuries. By the fourth century, however, an orthodoxy began to set in concerning these and other doctrines which has continued to the present day.

Interpretation

The meaning and applicability of the Qur'ān has not, of course, been immediately obvious in every situation. Interpretation, called *tafsīr* as both a process and a genre of literature which undertakes the task, aims to clarify a text. Starting with the text of the Qur'ān, *tafsīr* pays close attention to the grammatical, lexicographical and theological details of the text itself in order to make the meaning clear. *Tafsīr* is also the process by which the text is adapted to the needs of the present situation, adding a practical aspect to the task, by making the text relevant to individual believers and their faith and way of life. As well, *tafsīr* served the practical purpose of making the text understandable to those for whom Arabic was not their mother tongue. This was especially an issue as the Muslim empire expanded and Islam became the religion of the area. Sometimes this act of interpretation was couched in the form of a translation of the Qur'ān (such texts had no role in ritual activity, however); in other instances, rendering the text of the Qur'ān into simpler Arabic minus the ambiguities

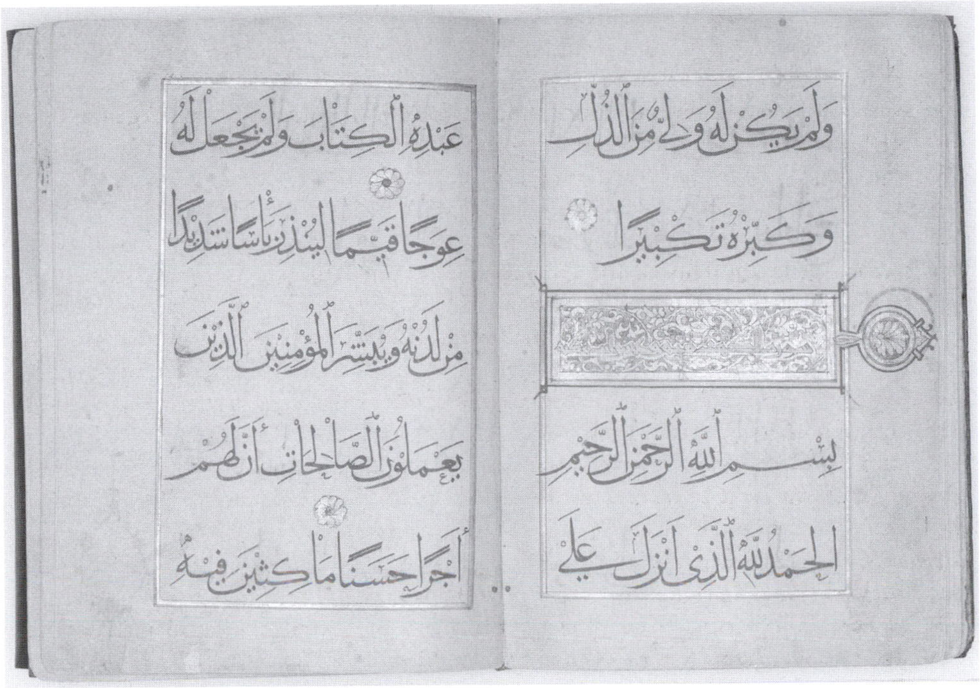

Figure 8 Qur'ān page. Yāqūt al-Mutaʿṣimī, Iraq, 1282–3. Yāqūt's calligraphic style is distinctive for its thin and broad strokes, achieved by cutting the pen nib diagonally.

Source: The Nasser D. Khalili Collection of Islamic Art, London, inv.no. QUR 29. Copyright the Nour Foundation. Courtesy of the Khalili Family Trust

and difficulties of the original scriptural text allowed easier access to the book for new converts.

One of the earliest Muslim methods of interpreting the Qur'ān was to connect particular passages in the text with incidents in the story of Muḥammad. The name Muḥammad is only mentioned four times in the Qur'ān; in all four cases he is referred to in the third person rather than directly addressed. References to the career of Muḥammad in the Qur'ān are not sufficiently frequent to construct a biography of Muḥammad from its materials. However, Muslims have traditionally identified Muḥammad with "the messenger" or "the prophet" ubiquitously addressed in scripture; Muslims conceive of the Qur'ān as having been revealed not only through Muḥammad, but also according to the needs of his prophetic mission. The individual traditions which link Qur'anic verses with events in the career of Muḥammad are called the "occasions of revelation." These traditions are recounted in commentaries, in *ḥadīth* collections and in special works of *asbāb al-nuzūl*. An overarching narrative framework, which incorporated and arranged chronologically the separate traditions, was provided in early works of both *sīra* and *tafsīr*. The most famous of the earlier biographical works is the *Sīrat Rasūl Allāh*, an eighth-century work of Ibn Isḥāq (d. 767) which exists in a ninth-century edition.

Related to this narrative framework was the development of a scheme whereby the *sūra*s of the Qur'ān could be assigned to initial recitation in either Mecca or Medina. Within these two general categories each *sūra* was given a place in a continuous chronology from the first recitation through to the death of Muḥammad. This systemization of the contents allowed Muslim scholars to account for the abrupt changes of topic, voice and mood between *sūra*s – and indeed within a single *sūra* – in the canonical progression of the Qur'ān.

The concept of a Mecca–Medina chronology also allowed Muslim scholars a way to deal with the apparent inconsistencies and contradictions within the Qur'ān. If a specific injunction in a passage considered Meccan disagreed with the instruction in a "Medinan" passage, the discrepancy was explained as between passages revealed earlier and later in the career of Muḥammad. The situation of the Muslim community in Medina was different from that of Mecca, reasoned the scholars, so the words revealed by God in Medina would naturally correspond to the new needs of the community. The later recitation was then considered to abrogate the earlier one.

For example, Muslim scholars speculated on the reasons for the differences among the various approaches to situations of conflict within the Qur'ān. They observed a range of approaches from patient tolerance to open warfare. The basic difference could be accounted for by the different circumstances in Mecca and Medina. In Mecca the Muslim community was small and could not mount a military action against its persecutors even if it wanted to. However, in Medina military action was not only possible, but was approved by explicit permission from God (Q 22:39, according to Ibn Isḥāq's *Sīra*). As for the differences among the postures of fighting, from defensive to aggressive, some Muslim scholars arranged the commands according to the dating of the Medinan *sūra*s in which they are found. Since the so-called "sword verse" (Q 9:5) is found, according to many schemes, in the final *sūra* to be revealed, some Muslim scholars gave it abrogating power over verses in all other *sūra*s which suggest less than total warfare.

Muslims at the start of the third millennium interpret the Qur'ān in a variety of ways according to their basic approaches to Muslim tradition and to the impact of Western civilization. Most Muslims would tend to interpret a text in line with the traditional medieval interpretation as represented for example by the fourteenth-century exegete Ibn Kathīr (d. 1373) and perhaps mediated by local Muslim teachers.

Modernist Muslims may seek to interpret the Qur'ān in line with recent Western sensibilities. The first modernist exegetes attempted to interpret the Qur'ān from the perspective of Enlightenment rationalism. In their commentaries the Qur'ān's miraculous elements, for example, were eliminated. Some modernist interpreters attempt to show the Qur'ān to be compatible with a modern scientific worldview; indeed, according to some authors the Qur'ān contains scientific facts divinely revealed a millennium before they were "discovered" in the West. More recent modernist interpreters will feature Qur'anic materials which they consider to affirm gender equality or democratic institutions. Post-modern Muslims may even look for a reading which is compatible with the philosophy of religious pluralism.

Several recent Muslim interpreters living in the West seek to lay traditional Muslim understandings to one side, return to the Qur'ān and the story of Muḥammad, and interpret scripture through an historical approach. In their view, God adapted the

Qur'ān's narrations to the situation of Muḥammad and those who heard his recitations. Some Muslim authors suggest that the portions of the Qur'ān believed to have been revealed in Mecca provide the basic principles of Islamic faith, while the Medinan *sūra*s are historically specific and therefore not open to universal application. Such interpretations go against the traditionalist scheme of the forward flow of abrogation, and therefore generally have trouble finding a hearing in Muslim-majority societies. However, these interpretations allow modernist and post-modern Muslims to understand that the Qur'anic commands to fight and kill were meant for specific situations in seventh-century Arabia, and that these commands are not to be applied generally to the behavior of Muslims today.

Revivalist Muslims, including Islamists, similarly seek to return to the text of the Qur'ān and the story of Muḥammad, but reject both traditionalism and Western modernity. Islamists take the Qur'ān to be God's message for the establishment of the Islamic system. They tend to prefer the *ḥadīth* materials from the exegetical tradition, because they understand these to be Muḥammad's own commentary. They find in "Medinan" passages the directives for the behavior of the Muslim community today. Such interpretations locate the primal vision of the Muslim community in Medina, and seek to revive the kind of state which Islamists believe to have existed in Medina under Muḥammad. The rule of Islamic law must therefore be established in the whole world by all the means understood by them to have been used by Muḥammad and the earliest Muslims. In seeking to prescribe behavior in situations of conflict, revivalist Muslims may highlight the scriptural commands to fight and kill and urge that believers today put them into practice. Their belief in a golden age in seventh-century Arabia trumps any fears of modern Western disapproval. Such interpretations of the Qur'ān, from famous Islamists like Mawlānā Mawdūdī and Sayyid Quṭb, tend to be the most popular among well-educated Muslim youth today.

As the global Muslim community continues to look to the Qur'ān as the source of truth and authority, many non-Muslims will share a lively interest in the interpretation of the scripture by various groups of Muslims. The Qur'ān promises to be a touchstone of Muslim identity well into the twenty-first century. The claims which Muslims make for their scripture are powerful and inspiring. The results of a more critical approach to the Qur'ān among Muslim scholars remain to be seen.

References and further reading

Ayoub, M. (1984) *The Qur'an and Its Interpreters*, Albany: State University of New York Press, 1992.

Boullata, I. J., ed. (2000) *Literary Structures of Religious Meaning in the Qur'an*, Richmond: Curzon.

Burton, J. (1977) *The Collection of the Qur'ān*, Cambridge: Cambridge University Press.

Cook, M. (2000) *The Koran: A Very Short Introduction*, Oxford: Oxford University Press.

Esack, F. (2005) *The Qur'an: A User's Guide*, Oxford: Oneworld.

Guillaume, A., trans. (1955) *The Life of Muhammad: A Translation of Isḥāq's Sīrat Rasūl Allāh*, Oxford, Karachi: Oxford University Press.

Ibn Warraq, ed. (1998) *The Origins of the Koran*, Amherst, NY: Prometheus Press.

Jeffery, A. (1950) "The Qur'ān as Scripture," *The Muslim World*, 40: 41–55, 106–34, 185–206, 257–75.

Lester, T. (1999) "What is the Koran?" *The Atlantic Monthly*, January: 43–56; http://www.theatlantic.com/doc/199901/koran.

McAuliffe, J. D., ed. (2001–6) *Encyclopaedia of the Qur'ān*, Leiden: Brill, 6 vols.

Motzki, H. (2001) "The Collection of the Qur'an: A Reconsideration of Western Views in Light of Recent Methodological Developments," *Der Islam*, 78: 1–34.

Rahbar, M. D. (1960) *God of Justice: A Study in the Ethical Doctrine of the Qur'an*, Leiden: E. J. Brill.

Rahman, F. (1994) *Major Themes of the Qur'ān*, Minneapolis: Bibliotheca Islamica.

Reeves, J. C., ed. (2003) *Bible and Qur'an: Essays in Scriptural Intertextuality*, Atlanta: Scholars Press.

Rippin, A., ed. (1999) *The Qur'ān: Formative Interpretation*, Aldershot: Ashgate Varorium.

—— (2000) *The Qur'ān: Style and Content*, Aldershot: Ashgate Varorium.

Robinson, N. (2004) *Discovering the Qur'an: A Contemporary Approach to a Veiled Text*, 2nd edition, Washington: Georgetown University Press.

Sells, M. (1999) *Approaching the Qur'ān: The Early Revelations*, Ashland, OR: White Cloud Press.

Stanton, H. U. W. (1919) *The Teaching of the Qur'an: With an Account of its Growth and a Subject Index*, London: Society for Promoting Christian Knowledge.

Wansbrough, J. (1977) *Quranic Studies: Sources and Methods of Scriptural Interpretation*, Oxford: Oxford University Press; 2nd edition, ed. A. Rippin, Amherst, NY: Prometheus Press, 2004.

11

MUḤAMMAD

Michael Lecker

The Prophet of Islam, Muḥammad ibn ʿAbd Allāh, was one of the most influential men of all time. The term "Muḥammadanism" sometimes used as a substitute for the term Islam faithfully reflects his unique position in the edifice that he created and in the hearts of his followers. Before him the Arabs were a marginal factor in world politics, whereas following his brilliant political and military achievements they became the masters of a huge empire.

Muḥammad's veneration by the Arabs and all the other Muslims knows no bounds. Ever since the early days of Islam popular preachers depicted him and the miracles ascribed to him in great detail. Trees bowed before him and a cloud shaded him from the sun. The palm trunk on which he had leaned while delivering his sermons in the mosque moaned when he abandoned it for his new *minbar* or pulpit. His urine, saliva and washing water were filled with *baraka* or charismatic power and had therapeutic qualities. *Nūr Muḥammad* or the Muḥammadan light that predated the creation of Adam stands for Muḥammad's primordial existence. It is identified with the spermatic substance that reached the corporeal Muḥammad from his progenitors through procreation. Muḥammad was in Adam's loins in paradise, in Noah's loins on the Ark and in Abraham's loins when the latter was thrown into the fire. A gleam on the forehead of Muḥammad's father attracted a female soothsayer who wished to obtain it through conception. When Muḥammad's mother Āmina conceived him, she received the gleam and the soothsayer was no longer attracted to him.

Muḥammad was a member of the Quraysh tribe, more precisely the Hāshim family. He was born in Mecca around the year 570 and had an unhappy childhood. In his twenties he married a woman from his tribe, Khadīja, who had previously employed him in her caravan trade. Khadīja who was several years older than Muḥammad bore him both male and female children. However, the male children died in their infancy, while the females survived. The most famous among them, Fāṭima, married Muḥammad's cousin ʿAlī ibn Abī Ṭālib. Shortly before his death Muḥammad had another male offspring, Ibrāhīm, by a Coptic slave girl. But this son too died in his infancy. Muḥammad can be considered a tragic figure in this respect.

The crucial moment in his life came when, at the age of 40, according to tradition, he received his first revelation at the Ḥirāʾ mountain east of Mecca. For 10 or 13 years he attempted, with little success, to win the hearts of his fellow Meccans. The turning point came when Muḥammad concluded an agreement with Arabs from Medina (or Yathrib, as it had been called before Islam) who embraced his religion and secured for him a safe haven for pursuing his mission. Most of these Medinans belonged to one of the two major Arab tribes of Medina, the Aws and Khazraj. Islamic literature refers to them by the honorific appellation al-Anṣār or "the helpers." The link with Medina was not accidental: there was a close network of contacts between Mecca and Medina that has not yet been investigated.

Muḥammad's emigration from Mecca to Medina – or rather his breaking away from his tribe, Quraysh – is called *hijra* and took place in 622. It marks the beginning of Muḥammad's Medinan period and of the Muslim calendar. Muḥammad's activity during his Medinan decade to his death in 632 made Islam a world power.

It is mainly with regard to the Medinan period that a student of Muḥammad's biography finds him/herself on relatively firm ground. The study of Muḥammad's life is still a major scholarly challenge. The huge source material about him has to be scrutinized before some of it is accepted as historical fact. Research into central issues of Muḥammad's biography has not yet gone far beyond the starting point, mainly because the accounts of specific events in Muḥammad's life, their chronology and their sequence are incoherent or contradictory. In addition, the accounts reveal legal and exegetical prejudices, beside political and tribal ones. The famous biography of Muḥammad by Ibn Hishām (d. 833), that is based on the earlier biography written by Ibn Isḥāq (d. 767), and several other early mainstream compilations have always been the mainstay of scholarship regarding Muḥammad. However, in recent decades an increasingly critical attitude to these sources has been adopted by several scholars, and it became obvious that the writing of a modern narrative biography of Muḥammad along the lines of the medieval ones must be ruled out.

Several aspects of Arabian society at the time of Muḥammad deserve special attention. During the golden age of Arabic philology in the eighth century, the philologists, many of whom were non-Arab converts to Islam, collected for their specialized monographs rich evidence on Arabia before Islam. However, the picture of pre-Islamic Arabian society created by their monographs is imbalanced, with some geographical areas and some aspects of life in Arabia receiving more than their due amount of attention.

It is natural that Mecca and Medina are better known to us than other places; after all, they were the scenes of Muḥammad's activity. We do not know much about many other settlements, some of which were probably wealthier and more populous than Mecca or Medina. For example, Hajr (near present-day Riyadh), which was the central settlement of the Ḥanīfa tribe, is described rather sparingly in the sources, and hence hardly figures in scholarly descriptions of pre-Islamic Arabia. As a matter of fact most parts of Arabia are simply absent from the source material and next to nothing is known about their inhabitants.

The imbalance extends to the social and economic spheres. Much of the evidence on pre-Islamic Arabia deals with tribal warfare rather than the more mundane activities of the pre-Islamic Arabs such as trade and agriculture. The detailed accounts of intertribal warfare create the wrong impression that the tribes were only engaged in warfare. Nothing can be farther from the truth. Moreover, the concentration of the sources on wars between nomads creates the impression that Arabian society before Islam was mainly made of nomads. Although Arabian agricultural settlements receive relatively little attention in the sources, the settled population in Arabia probably outnumbered the nomadic and semi-nomadic ones.

Muḥammad's tribe, Quraysh, lived in Mecca which for centuries had been a cultic center for Arabian polytheists before becoming the holy city of Islam. The Arab idol-worshippers were polytheists, but they also believed in a High God, Allāh, whose house was in the Kaʿba and who was supreme to the tribal deities. There was much diversity in the forms of Arabian idol worship, but on the whole it was a common characteristic of pre-Islamic society.

In the centuries preceding the advent of Islam, Christianity and Judaism were struggling with each other in the Yemen to win over its people. Medina had a large and dominant Jewish population, while Yamama (near Riyadh) and settlements in eastern Arabia and in the Gulf had a large Christian one. Christianity and Judaism also penetrated several nomadic tribes. The *ḥanīf*s, or the ascetic seekers of true religion who abandoned idol worship, were probably few in number. Moreover, the identification of some of them as *ḥanīf*s is questionable and probably goes back to false apologetic claims made by their families. Several early converts to Islam from the large tribe of Tamīm had been former Zoroastrians. On the whole, however, idol worship prevailed, with the prominent exception of the Yemen. According to Muslim historians, the Yemen was predominantly Jewish even after the demise of the Jewish king Dhū Nuwās roughly a century before Muḥammad's *hijra*.

Pre-Islamic Arabia was not isolated from the outside world but was infiltrated by the Byzantine and Sasanian empires, with the latter probably playing a more significant role. The Byzantine Emperor, for example, is said to have been instrumental in the takeover of Mecca from the Khuzāʿa tribe by Muḥammad's ancestor Quṣayy. The Byzantines and Sasanians conducted their Arabian politics through their respective Arab buffer kingdoms, Ghassān and Ḥīra. The king of Ḥīra appointed governors to the frontiers extending from Iraq to Oman, each of whom had a bedouin subordinate who was put in charge of the Arab population.

As for Medina, it was controlled roughly to the middle of the sixth century by a *marzubān* (a military but also civil governor) whose seat was on the coast of the Gulf. The main Jewish tribes of Medina, Naḍīr and Qurayẓa, exacted tribute on his behalf from the Aws and Khazraj tribes. In the last quarter of the sixth century the king of Ḥīra, al-Nuʿmān ibn al-Mundhir, declared a member of the Khazraj as the king of Medina. In other words, Sasanian control there continued in the second half of the sixth century.

The Quraysh of Mecca had a high degree of internal stability that was based on the equilibrium between two rival alliances rather than on tribal solidarity. In the accounts of Mecca's pre-Islamic history, for example concerning the establishment of its international caravan trade, Muḥammad's ancestors probably receive more credit than is due to them. In any case, Meccan trade was Mecca's main source of revenue regardless of the items and profits involved. In Arabian terms Mecca was a major trade centre, although it is not known if it was the largest of its kind in Arabia. Trade in Mecca and around it was connected to pilgrimage; every gathering of thousands of people from all over Arabia was bound to include trade. The more so since pilgrimage took place in the holy months of truce that were respected by many Arabian tribes.

Following Mecca's position as a cultic and trade centre, the prominent men of Quraysh were constantly in touch with tribal leaders from all over Arabia. They had comprehensive command of tribal genealogies, internal tribal feuds and inter-tribal politics in general. Mecca absorbed many tribesmen from all over Arabia, among them asylum seekers escaping blood vengeance. These tribal settlers were instrumental in forming links between Mecca and their tribes of origin. Mecca's knowledge of tribal affairs and its network of intertribal relations were put to good use during Mecca's war against Muḥammad that came to an end with Muḥammad's takeover of his hometown.

Muḥammad's wars were but a rehearsal to the *ridda* wars that aimed to suppress the Arab opposition to Muslim control that started shortly before Muḥammad's demise, and the subsequent *futūḥ*, "conquests". These wars were fought under the command of able Qurashī generals.

Muḥammad himself had been a merchant before receiving his first revelation, and trade partnerships were a significant aspect of the economic cooperation between Quraysh and the Thaqīf tribe that controlled Taif southeast of Mecca. However, a significant aspect of Mecca's economy is often overlooked. Since conditions in Mecca itself were uninviting for agriculture, the entrepreneurial Qurashīs invested in agriculture elsewhere. Hence it can be said that Qurashī expansion in Arabia preceded the advent of Islam. The precise details of this expansion still await further investigation.

After the *hijra*, Muḥammad himself was involved in agriculture in the vicinity of Medina and in the date orchards that he had taken from the Jews as booty. Muḥammad's grandfather, ʿAbd al-Muṭṭalib, is said to have owned an estate in Taif, and this was also true of numerous other Meccans. After the *hijra* it was one of Muḥammad's companions, Ṭalḥa, who introduced the sowing of wheat in Medina.

The cluster of towns or villages known before Islam as Yathrib after a town in its northwest became known under Islam as al-Madīna (Medina). Major political and military upheavals that preceded the *hijra* contributed to Muḥammad's success there in ways that are not yet completely clear to us.

Medina's large Jewish population was dispersed in both Lower Medina (*Sāfila*) in the north, and Upper Medina (*ʿĀliya*) in the south. The Naḍīr and Qurayẓa tribes lived in Upper Medina, while a third large tribe, the Qaynuqāʿ, lived in Lower Medina.

The oldest Arab population of Medina was made up of members of the Balī tribe and several other tribes, many of whose members converted to Judaism. The Aws and Khazraj or the Anṣār allegedly settled in Medina after the collapse of the Maʾrib dam in the Yemen. Unlike the older Arab settlers, most of the Aws and Khazraj remained idol worshippers. When the Aws and Khazraj settled in Medina, their position vis-à-vis the Jewish tribes was weak. However, gradually they gained strength through the building of fortresses and the planting of date orchards. In early Islam the Anṣār were ridiculed for their initial subjection by the Jews, particularly with regard to the Arab Jewish king Fiṭyawn who reportedly practiced the *ius primae noctis*. Consequently, Fiṭyawn figures prominently in Anṣārī apologetic historiography. The Anṣār, while admitting their initial inferiority, claimed that it came to an end with the killing of Fiṭyawn by a member of the Khazraj. Allegedly, from that moment onwards the Jews were at the mercy of their former clients. However, Anṣārī historiography should be taken with a grain of salt. The Jews no doubt suffered a setback, or a member of the Khazraj would not have been appointed by the king of Ḥīra as the king of Yathrib in the last quarter of the sixth century. However, by the advent of Islam the Naḍīr and Qurayẓa regained their strength, as is shown by their victory in the Battle of Buʿāth several years before the *hijra*, where they fought with their allies from the Aws against the powerful Khazraj.

On the eve of Islam a member of the Khazraj called Ibn Ubayy was nearly crowned by his tribe. Following the Battle of Buʿāth in which he had not participated Ibn Ubayy became the strongest leader among the Khazraj and managed to reestablish the system of alliances that had been in place before Buʿāth.

At the time of the *hijra* the Naḍīr and Qurayẓa were the main owners of fortresses and weapons in Medina, which made them the dominant power there when Muḥammad arrived.

One would expect the Qur'ān to be the best source for the study of Muḥammad's life. But the Qur'ān hardly offers any concrete evidence and one needs to resort to exegesis in order to relate it to specific events in Muḥammad's life. In any case, it should not be assumed a priori that the Qur'ān is irrelevant to Muḥammad's biography, or that when a detail in the biography conforms to what the Qur'ān says, it must be apocryphal.

Archaeology could fill in some gaps in our knowledge, but its potential remains largely unexplored. It seems that excavations of pre- and early Islamic sites in Mecca and Medina will not take place in the foreseeable future. Moreover, there are indications that Arabian archaeological sites are in danger. It is hoped that they are still there when excavations in the most interesting sites for the history of Islam become possible.

The little amount of concrete evidence that can be drawn from the Qur'ān and the lack of meaningful archaeological excavations in crucial sites leave us with our main source on Muḥammad's life, namely the literary evidence, problematic as it may be. When enough scholarly output accumulates to justify a new critical biography of Muḥammad, it is unlikely to be an adaptation of Muḥammad's medieval biographies, even if the basic outline of these biographies remains intact. A large proportion of the source material included in the medieval biographies may not survive scholarly scrutiny, but enough evidence will remain to support a reliable description of Muḥammad's life and work. Every piece of evidence, no matter how trivial, can throw light on Muḥammad or on the context of the early attempts to record his life.

Muḥammad's biography has always been popular among Muslims, although it never reached the status of Scripture or of the canonical collections of traditions (*ḥadīth*s) that are among the sources of Islamic law. Some scholars who specialized in legal matters even boasted of their ignorance of matters historical. They were suspicious of non-legal literature, including Muḥammad's biography, because compilers of such literature did not observe the standards of the transmission of knowledge adopted in the legal trade.

Muḥammad's biography often focuses on Muḥammad's companions, while he himself remains in the background. The reason is that the thousands of accounts included in the biography were not preserved and transmitted by direct descendants of Muḥammad or by other members of his extended family, but by direct descendants and other relatives of his companions. Keen to preserve for posterity the role of their ancestors during the short and eventful period that changed the world, they gave precedence to the role of these ancestors. Muḥammad is always the cause behind the events, but quite often he is not the protagonist and is taken for granted. The tribal and family informants cannot be blamed for concentrating on "their people" while neglecting the general context; they faced competition from other informants attempting to secure for their own people a better place in history. The informants did not stop short of harming Muḥammad's image, as is shown by the story of his encounter with one of the celebrated *ḥanīf*s, or ascetic seekers of true religion. Zayd ibn ʿAmr ibn Nufayl lived in Mecca several years before Muḥammad's mission (yet some pronounced him a companion of Muḥammad). He is credited with guiding Muḥammad – to be sure, before he received his first revelation – to avoid meat that had been sacrificed to an idol. Zayd declined such meat when it was offered to him by Muḥammad, and following Zayd's example Muḥammad himself abstained from consuming meat slaughtered in connection with idol worship. This unorthodox report goes back to Zayd's son, Saʿīd, through Zayd's grandson and great-grandson. The report probably escaped censorship because it also includes an element of "proofs of Muḥammad's prophethood" (*dalāʾil al-nubuwwa*).

The volume of texts on the life of Muḥammad is immense. However, in actual fact it is much smaller than it seems to be at first sight because repetition was an accepted norm among the compilers. Muḥammad's biographies emerged as a branch of the traditional Islamic sciences. Consequently, they generally adopted the viewpoint of these sciences, particularly with regard to the attachment of a chain of transmitters (*isnād*) to each report. Moreover, many scholars involved in the transmission of Muḥammad's biography also engaged in other Islamic sciences. In the conceptual environment of these sciences the ideal scholar was one who transmitted to his students an exact copy of what he had learned from his teachers.

The evidence on Muḥammad extends far beyond the monographs specifically dedicated to his life. Muḥammad's unique position in Islamic history and the unrestricted wandering of the accounts about him in all genres of Islamic literature mean that evidence relating to him is to be found almost everywhere: general history books, histories of towns such as Mecca and Medina, Qurʾān exegesis and collections of annotated poems, among other genres. Research cannot afford to overlook evidence merely because it is outside the "designated" sources or the mainstream ones. For example, there is rich evidence in the biographical dictionaries of Muḥammad's companions and the dictionaries of traditions going back to them. The criteria for acceptance into non-mainstream sources were generally more lenient than those applied in the mainstream biographies. We often find in the former significant evidence that for whatever reason was relegated to the less prestigious sources.

The quest for source material concerning Muḥammad should not be limited to compilations from the first centuries of Islam, since valuable accounts are found in relatively late sources. Compilers who lived several centuries ago had access to much older books that have meanwhile disappeared. Quotations in the later sources are on the whole trustworthy and we cannot afford to disregard them.

In recent decades several scholars have brilliantly pointed out weaknesses in the evidence on the history of early Islam, including the life of Muḥammad (see Peters 1991). They have challenged the very premises of the accepted story of Muḥammad's life and the environment in which he emerged. Misguided scholars who approached the sources with preconceptions and summed up the medieval biographies instead of studying them critically attracted much of the fire for their vices. While the weaknesses in the literary source material on Muḥammad's life are real, the solutions offered so far are too radical. There is enough reliable evidence to support a trustworthy picture of Arabia at the time of Muḥammad and at least an outline of his biography.

The verdict of these contemporary scholars regarding Muḥammad's biography and its compilers is too harsh. It is doubtful that the biography can be considered a history book in the modern sense of the word, and that its compilers considered themselves as historians. Tribal, factional and political prejudices often take precedence over the recording of the events "as they really occurred." The survival of many versions of Muḥammad's biography compiled by authors down through the centuries attests to its exceptional success among Muslims over the last 13 centuries. Its popularity cannot be ascribed to whatever solid evidence it provides on the life and work of Muḥammad. Regardless of the circumstances in which it came into being and the original goals of its compilers, its didactic, propagandistic, entertaining and edifying features make it a forceful and enjoyable work that addresses the needs of its readers and listeners on various psychological and artistic levels. Had it not been for these merits, it would have been forgotten or at least marginalized.

For a history book Muḥammad's biography is exceptionally poor in solid, factual, evidence and there is a huge contrast between the sheer volume of the source material and the amount of concrete details it contains. For example, one looks in vain for the names of certain fortresses besieged by Muḥammad. Obviously, the names were not deemed significant.

The editorial work in which the compilers of Muḥammad's biography engaged raises serious questions regarding their concept of history. For example, they employed the technique known as "combined report" that was adopted as early as the beginning of the eighth century. It was called for by the existence of accounts of a certain event which agreed on some details but differed on others. The "combined report" no doubt omitted incongruous or inconvenient details found in the earlier, individual, accounts. Moreover, compilers who took a fragment from source X and attached it to a fragment taken from source Y creating a new sequence of events had a singular concept of history. However, this and indeed any other weakness in the evidence must not lead to the conclusion that it is irrelevant for historical research.

Conflicts and contradictions are often quoted as yet another weakness in the source material and they do form a typical feature of Islamic literature from its outset. The improved accessibility of primary sources through the Internet and electronic resources makes the discovery of new conflicts easier than ever before. But one should not expect a unified version of the Islamic past since conflicts and contradictions are a true reflection of divisions in early Islamic society. Above all there was the tribal factor; the pedigrees of Muḥammad himself and of his companions clearly show their tribal affiliations. Genealogy is both a unifying factor and a dividing one, with every splinter of a tribe clinging to its unique place in the tribal system and its own version of the past. The compilers of Muḥammad's biography limited their role to the sifting and editing of the materials received from their informants.

Should we expect Muḥammad's fellow Qurashīs who rejected him and the Anṣār who secured for him a safe haven to have the same view of the *hijra*, that crucial event that marks the beginning of the Medinan period? For Quraysh, it was a resounding failure. For the Anṣār, a glorious event they could go back to when they saw Quraysh reaping the fruits of Muḥammad's achievement. The pro-Anṣārī and anti-Qurashī story of the *hijra* is a permanent reminder of this major turning point in his history.

It is similarly unrealistic to expect the Aws and Khazraj to adopt a unified view of

Figure 9 Fāl-nāma (Book of Divinations): Ascent of the Prophet to Heaven. Angels pour fire on Muḥammad as he ascends to heaven upon the mythical beast Būraq. This commonly reproduced text was typically opened at random to offer clues to divine the future. Tabriz or Qazvin, Iran, *c.* 1550.

Source: Arthur Sackler Gallery, Smithsonian Institution, Washington DC. Purchase – Smithsonian Unrestricted Trust Funds, Smithsonian Collections Acquisition Program, and Dr. Arthur Sackler. Reproduced with permission

the past. Tribes and families competed with each other to get their own stories into the history books; for them, unity was not a sought after goal.

Early Islamic society was also divided along political/dynastic, factional or ideological lines. Umayyads, Shiʿites, Kharijites, Abbasids and others held different versions of the past, not to mention the many regional disputes such as the one between the people of Kufa in Iraq and the people of Damascus in Syria. Precisely because they are so widespread, differences and conflicting versions can be a blessing for research if they are studied systematically for what they are: reflections of a divided society. They reveal a lot about the environment in which Muḥammad's literary biography was created, by pointing out the matters considered worth disputing and the sensitivities of the various elements in the social fabric. Such sensitivities are revealed, for example, by apologetic accounts relating to the opposition to Muḥammad in Mecca and Medina.

Differences and contradictions are yet another challenge awaiting modern scholarship. Many people took part in the preparation of Muḥammad's biography in which several voices speak to us, all at the same time. Despite some attempts to create harmony, a certain cacophony is inevitable.

The Islamic literature on Muḥammad's life is at the same time our only reliable source and a barrier to be crossed by the development of accurate analytical tools. In order to learn the limitations of the literature we need to study in detail widespread phenomena such as apologetic, self-censorship – declared or undeclared – and politically motivated reports. Weaknesses in the evidence should not lead to its total rejection. Even if most of the sources are deemed irrelevant or suspicious for a variety of reasons, enough will be left to support progress in the study of Muḥammad's life.

To begin with, substantial historical studies can be based exclusively or almost exclusively on background information that is unlikely to have been invented. This approach should replace non-analytical research that merely reiterates in Western languages what one finds in the Muslim sources. Resorting to background information means the circumvention for the time being of the main issues involved in Muḥammad's history. Over a period of time enough research of this kind will accumulate for reconstructing various aspects of life in Arabia at the time of Muḥammad. Then we shall be better placed to venture into the heart of Muḥammad's biography.

References and further reading

Guillaume, A., trans. (1955) *The Life of Muhammad: A Translation of Ibn Isḥāq's Sīrat Rasūl Allāh*, Oxford: Oxford University Press.

Horovitz, J. (2002) *The Earliest Biographies of the Prophet and their Authors*, ed. L. I. Conrad, Princeton: The Darwin Press.

Kister, M. J. (1983) "The *Sīrah* Literature," in A. F. L. Beeston *et al.*, eds., *Arabic Literature to the End of the Umayyad Period*, Cambridge: Cambridge University Press, 352–67.

Lecker, M. (1998) *Jews and Arabs in Pre- and Early Islamic Arabia*, Aldershot: Variorum.

Motzki, H., ed. (2000) *The Biography of Muḥammad: The Issue of the Sources*, Leiden: Brill.

Peters, F. E. (1991) "The Quest of the Historical Muhammad," in *International Journal of Middle Eastern Studies*, 23: 291–315; revised version in F. E. Peters, *Muhammad and the Origins of Islam*, Princeton: Princeton University Press, 1994, 257–68; reprinted in Ibn Warraq, ed., *The Quest for the Historical Muhammad*, Amherst, NY: Prometheus Press, 2000, 444–75.

Rodinson, M. (1981) "A Critical Survey of Modern Studies on Muhammad," in M. Swartz, ed., *Studies on Early Islam*, New York, Oxford: Oxford University Press, 2000: 23–85.
Rubin, U. (2003) "Muḥammad," in J. D. McAuliffe, ed., *Encyclopaedia of the Qur'ān*, Leiden: Brill, vol. III: 440–58.
Rubin, U., ed. (1998) *The Life of Muḥammad*, Aldershot: Ashgate.
Ṭabarī, al- (1987) *The History of al-Ṭabarī, VII: The Foundation of the Community*, trans. M. V. McDonald, annotated W. M. Watt, Albany: SUNY Press.
—— (1988) *The History of al-Ṭabarī, VI: Muḥammad at Mecca*, trans. and annotated W. M. Watt, M. V. McDonald, Albany: SUNY Press.
—— (1990) *The History of al-Ṭabarī, IX: The Last Years of the Prophet*, trans. and annotated I. K. Poonawala, Albany: SUNY Press.
Watt, W. M. (1953) *Muhammad at Mecca*, Oxford: Oxford University Press.
—— (1956) *Muhammad at Medina*, Oxford: Oxford University Press.

12

SUNNĪ LAW

Robert Gleave

The Muslim conception of God is of an all-knowing, all-powerful being, who, after creating the world and all that is in it, sent prophets and messengers to humankind. The prophets and messengers were given the responsibility of informing humankind of God's nature, and of demanding humankind's unconditional obedience to God. Obedience to God consists of submitting to his demands, and his demands are to be found in a set of rules and regulations which some (though not all) prophets and messengers have promulgated on God's command. In Muslim discourse, these rules and regulations are collectively known as the *sharīʿa*, and by obeying the *sharīʿa*, Muslims demonstrate their total submission to God, thereby gaining benefits in the next life.

This (rather simplified) account of God's relationship with humanity in classical Islamic theology has dominated Muslim discussions about the regulations they should follow in order to demonstrate their obedience to God. This conception, with perhaps minor variants and qualifications, is presupposed (and hence rarely stated explicitly) by the Muslim authors of a great corpus of legal literature collectively known by the Arabic term *fiqh*. Amongst the earliest extant sources from the incipient Muslim community are documents discussing legal questions (that is, the correct actions Muslims should perform). These texts, if authentic (and there is much debate about the dating of such documents), indicate that correct personal behavior and effective societal organization were topics of dispute and debate from the early period of Islamic history. Whether or not these early documents can be called works of *fiqh* is largely a matter of classification. Later works which are called *fiqh* are often much fuller, expanded accounts of God's law. What is significant is that the early Muslim community was intensely interested in legal questions ranging from the correct system of community organization to the most intimate details of human life. Obedience to God was presumed to be total, and hence there was no human activity, no situation for which God has not produced a ruling. Human beings are called to obey these rulings, and disobedience leads to punishment, in this life, or in the next.

The most pressing concern, once such a conception of law is accepted, is the manner in which the community comes to know the law which God has provided. When prophets are present, this would seem unproblematic. Since prophets are guided by God in micro, they can be asked about the law, and problems can be easily solved. Indeed, for most Muslim writers, there was no need for legal discussions during the Prophet Muḥammad's life. His judgment, as prophet and leader of the community, was the law. Hence, Muslim conceptions of revelation are not limited to the Qur'ān (as is often thought), but for most Muslim theologians (both in the past and in the present), God's revelation (*waḥy*) is found in two forms: recited (or textual – *matlū*) and unrecited (*ghayr matlū*) (Burton 1977: 64–6). The former is a reference to the Qur'ān, and the latter to the words and actions of the Prophet (known in the classical period as *sunna*). When a prophet is absent, however, the process of discovering the law to which God demands obedience becomes more problematic. It is for this reason that Muslim jurists have developed a set of interpretive rules whereby the clues left by God and the Prophet (called "indicators," in Arabic *adilla*) might be assessed, understood and applied to the process of explicating the law of God. Naturally, the activities of assessment, interpretation and application are human activities, and the results of these efforts were, epistemologically speaking, of a lower rank than the knowledge gained directly from the Prophet (when he was alive) or (according to some) directly from the Qur'ān, if its meaning was seen as unequivocal.

The result of this conceptual framework was a theoretical schema in which legal knowledge is attained through the application of interpretive rules to source texts. These texts included the Qur'ān itself (which was not always unambiguous), but also the texts recording the words and actions of the Prophet (known as *ḥadīth*), the texts recording the words and actions of the Prophet's companions (which were seen as indicators of what the Prophet would have said if given the chance, or perhaps what he did say, but was, by accident of history, left unrecorded) and, on occasions, statements which the Muslim community (or the learned stratum thereof) had agreed to be true (known as *ijmāʿ*). Each legal scholar's assessment, interpretation and application was subjective and the result of the scholar's "best effort" (termed *ijtihād*) to reach an opinion about God's rule for a particular circumstance, or set of circumstances. This, at least, was the theory of how knowledge of God's law was accrued by the Muslim jurists (and through them, the Muslim community generally). This theory was described in great detail in works of *uṣūl al-fiqh* (the "principles" or "roots" of *fiqh*). Once a scholar had mastered the rules of assessment, interpretation and application, they might produce an extended work which describes the actions Muslims should (in that scholar's opinion) perform on particular occasions. This type of work, oftentimes called *furūʿ al-fiqh* (the "individual instances" or "branches" of *fiqh*, usually abbreviated to *fiqh*), intended to lay out the author's knowledge of the law in its entirety (which was, after all, only his own opinion). These *furūʿ* books were, inevitably, very long, extremely detailed, and at times involved tortuous and complicated reasoning, as the author attempted to use the limited sources at his disposal to describe God's rules for the whole of human existence. There is then an implicitly understood (and, on occasions, explicitly stated) distinction in Muslim legal scholarly literature between *sharīʿa* and *fiqh*. The former refers to the law which God wishes his human subjects to obey. The latter is best understood as human attempts to discover the *sharīʿa*. There was an instinctive humility in the classical Muslim jurist's intellectual endeavor. He was involved in trying to describe law in his *fiqh*, though the true nature of the *sharīʿa* could only be known to God. A classical jurist (and here they can be distinguished from some modern Muslim legal scholars) would probably be uncomfortable saying that the *sharīʿa* "decrees" a particular ruling. This, in part, explains the frequent use of the phrase *wa-Allāhu aʿlam* ("and God knows best") at the conclusion of legal argumentation in works of *fiqh*. The author is effectively saying "this is my best guess, given the evidence available to me, but I do not condemn those who take a different view" (see Calder 2007).

Apart from works of *uṣūl* and *furūʿ*, other sources for the academic study of Islamic law include documents in which the scholar replies to an individual question concerning some element of the law. They have also survived in large number, and are called *fatwās*. These are much shorter than the *fiqh* works mentioned above. When a scholar gives a *fatwā*, he is acting as a *muftī* ("jurisconsult"); when he writes an extended work of *fiqh*, he is acting as a *faqīh* ("scholar jurist"). Finally, court records (*sijillāt*) and other legal documents have survived from the later classical period (most date from 1500 onwards). In these records, the decisions of a judge (*qāḍī*), who was normally trained in the academic legal sciences, are recorded. They are, then, the most important sources for how the religious law of the Muslims was applied to actual cases in particular periods. These types of literature – namely *uṣūl al-fiqh, fiqh* (or *furūʿ*), *fatwās* and *sijillāt* – constitute the most important sources for anyone wishing to describe the development of religious law amongst the Muslims. Other material related to the study of Sunnī law can be found in biographical dictionaries (where often the life of a judge or a scholar is described and his legal activity outlined) or historical chronicles (where important cases are sometimes recorded, or a ruler's promotion of, or deviation from "the *sharīʿa*" is described).

The above summary, describing how the Muslim community comes to know the rules God commands them to obey, dominated Muslim legal scholarship (whether by Sunnī, Shīʿī or Ibāḍī authors) during the so-called "classical" period (i.e., from *c.* 1000 to *c.* 1800). However, it took some time to develop and reach this expression. It was not fully formed at the inception of Islam in the seventh century, and was still developing at the outset of the eleventh century. The debate lasted until (and to an extent beyond) the point when Sunnī jurists, almost universally, accepted the "orthodoxy" of four schools. It is from this date that the classical period is normally dated, and which, it is often argued, occurred in the late tenth/early eleventh century. The remainder of this chapter will look at how the "classical" account of the legal enterprise came to dominate Sunnī Islam, how the four schools emerged as pre-eminent and how their rivals were eclipsed. This leads on to a discussion of how, once established, the four schools of Sunnī law became entrenched (institutionally and intellectually), providing the only real framework in which legal activity (be it scholarship, advising or judging specific cases) took place. The conclusion will show some of the developments in Sunnī law in the modern period (which, for convenience, one can date from around 1800), and how these have altered the conception of the *sharīʿa* and the nature of legal scholarship amongst Muslims.

The emergence of legal thought and juristic schools in Sunnī Islam

Apart from a limited number of verses in the Qurʾān, the earliest Muslim literature which dealt with legal issues are probably the *ḥadīths* – the accounts of the actions and words of the Prophet Muḥammad, his companions and other luminaries of early Islam. Since the Prophet was an obedient servant of God who implemented God's law perfectly, these reports of his sayings and actions became sources for understanding God's law. The reports are, then, indicators of the Prophet's *sunna* – his example for the Muslims. Collections of these sayings first emerged in the early ninth century, in which are recorded the sayings of individuals from the mid-seventh century onwards, including the Prophet. Each saying is usually accompanied by a chain of transmission, known as an *isnād*. Each *isnād* is an attempt to demonstrate that the report is an accurate account of the events described, and consists of a list of names of transmitters who "heard" (*samiʿa*) or "report" (*ḥaddatha*) from the next person in the list, all the way back to an eye witness to the events. The actual description of the event is called the *matn* ("text") and together the *matn* and the *isnād* are called a *ḥadīth* or a *khabar*. Muslim scholars knew early on that *isnād*s do not guarantee perfect accuracy, and developed a series of tests whereby an *isnād* (and hence the *ḥadīth* as a whole) can be seen as "sound" (*ṣaḥīḥ*) or otherwise. These included the evaluation of the characters of the transmitters (Were they trustworthy and honest?), as well as factual information about them (Did they live and work at the same time as the people they were supposed to have transmitted from?). Even when they declared a *ḥadīth* and its *isnād* "sound," later Muslim scholars recognized that this did not prove that the reports in the *matn* necessarily happened in exactly the way described. A single witness is not enough, they argued, to prove a case beyond doubt; similarly, a single *ḥadīth* does not mean one irresistibly trusts the *matn*. However, if one has a large number of *ḥadīth*s, all transmitted by different people, all saying the same thing, then one's trust of the *matn* grows. Eventually it becomes insuperable. It becomes, for Muslim jurists, inconceivable that so many people would be involved in a deception. This sort of "well-attested" report they called *mutawātir* ("frequently transmitted"). For later Muslim legal scholars, however, there are very few *ḥadīth*s which reach this level. The more *isnād*s attached to a report, the more likely it is to record the event accurately. Hence when later Muslim scholars used reports to prove a particular legal point, they built in caveats to their reasoning, always being sure to let the reader know that, for example, although a *ḥadīth* can be doubted, it is more likely to be true than false. The scholar takes that into account when describing the law he derives from the report. This is, once again, evidence of the humility built into the medieval system of Sunnī law – the jurists accepted that the sources themselves were not always certain, and therefore any laws derived from them were also going to be provisional.

Scholars outside of the Sunnī Muslim tradition also have their doubts about the *isnād* system as a means of ensuring authenticity (Berg 2000: 8–64). However, these doubts do not arise from any assessment of the transmitters' reliability. Rather, their criticisms emerge from an evaluation of the concept of *sunna*. In classical Muslim jurisprudence – that is, from around 1000 onwards – the idea of *sunna* is clearly marked as the example of the Prophet Muḥammad. However, earlier texts (such as the reports of the opinions of Prophetic companions and early Muslims) contain the word "*sunna*," but there it seems to indicate not specifically the Prophet's *sunna* but the tradition of legal practice in a particular location. This was most famously argued by Joseph Schacht (1950), a German scholar, who proposed the view that in these early texts *sunna* did not mean the example of the Prophet, but rather the "living tradition" of a particular locality. This *sunna* was sometimes made up of maxims which were used to justify legal opinions, or rules which are applied to particular legal cases. It was these maxims, the "living tradition," which was, Schacht argued, eventually put in the mouth of the Prophet. Crucial to this transfer from legal practice to Prophetic precedent was the work of Ibn Idrīs al-Shāfiʿī (d. 820). Al-Shāfiʿī argued in his various works, but particularly in his *Risāla* (or "Treatise"), that all law must be justified either by the Qurʾān or by the *sunna* of the Prophet. Al-Shāfiʿī's argument was so persuasive that Muslims elsewhere, trying to preserve their local legal tradition, began to attribute popular legal maxims to the Prophet. Hence the *ḥadīth*s we have in the collections of the ninth and tenth centuries are, Schacht argued, "back-projections" of local practice appearing as Prophetic *sunna*. Their *isnād*s, Schacht maintained, "grew backwards" over time as the same maxim was attributed to earlier and earlier Muslim figures until eventually they were attributed to the Prophet himself. It is important to note that Schacht did not accuse the Muslims of simply fabricating the *isnād*s, but rather he argued that this was a natural development as local custom had to be reconciled with al-Shāfiʿī's new doctrine. This insight has dominated Western scholarship on early Islamic law – and has been subjected to criticism not only by Muslim scholars (such as al-Azmi 1985) but also non-Muslim scholars (most recently Motzki 2002).

All the historical evidence points towards the establishment of local schools of law both before al-Shāfiʿī's work, but with increased structure afterwards. These local schools were often based around particular great jurists who each (allegedly) proposed a distinct set of legal doctrines. So, for example, a school emerged around the great scholar ʿAbd al-Raḥmān al-Awzāʿī (d. 744) in Syria; a school in Kufa following the teachings of Abū Ḥanīfa Muḥammad al-Nuʿmān (d. 767); one in Medina was based around the Mālik ibn Anas (d. 796). Eventually al-Shāfiʿī's disciples began their own school, promoting his legal ideas. Similarly schools developed later around Aḥmad ibn Ḥanbal (d. 855), Dāwūd al-Iṣfahānī (d. 883), and Muḥammad ibn Jarīr al-Ṭabarī (d. 923). These scholars not only composed works (or had works attributed to them) but often promoted a particular legal methodology. This is perhaps best understood through an example.

Muslims should abstain from food, drink and sexual intercourse during the daylight hours throughout the month of Ramaḍān. For each day they fail to fast, they should pay a penance and fast an extra day after Ramaḍān. However, what if the Muslim temporarily forgets it is Ramaḍān and accidentally eats or drinks or has sexual intercourse? He did not intend to break the fast, but did so by mistake. Should he still pay a penance and fast an extra day? There does not seem to have been one rule from the Prophet – in some *ḥadīth*s he said the forgetful person should pay penance and perform extra fasts, and in others the Prophet says that he should not. Furthermore, the scholars differed over which of the *ḥadīth*s were more likely to be accurate, since they had different views on the reliability of the people who transmitted the reports (that is, the names in the *isnād*). The difference of opinion (*ikhtilāf*) was as follows: al-Shāfiʿī and al-Awzāʿī (and their followers) said that the forgetful Muslim has not broken his fast and need not pay penance or fast an extra day. They argued this on the basis of a report which they considered reliable in which the Prophet said, "Whoever is fasting and then forgets and eats and drinks, then his fasting is still complete and he need not fast an extra day." This, for them, was the end of the matter. The Prophet had spoken and the issue was settled. However, Abū Ḥanīfa (and his followers, the Ḥanafīs) did not think this was a reliable *ḥadīth*, so for the Ḥanafīs, it did not count as proof. However, they still agreed with al-Shāfiʿī and al-Awzāʿī that there should be no penance and no extra fast. The Ḥanafīs argued that strictly speaking there should be penance and extra fasting in these circumstances, just as there is if one forgets to pray on a normal day. However, through his own legal reasoning, Abū Ḥanīfa came to the conclusion that fasting is not like prayer. Fasting requires you to continually remember that you are fasting. Prayer requires you only to remember that you should pray at particular times. Continually remembering something is harder than remembering something every now and again. One could dispute this, but Abū Ḥanīfa argued that it is obvious that continually doing something (like fasting) is always going to be harder than doing it intermittently (like prayer). Since it is harder work, the penalty for failing to do this should be less strict. For this reason, he argued that even though it would appear logical that forgetfully eating during Ramaḍān would break a fast, fasting was, in fact, different from other religious duties and the fast is not broken. A number of jurists were not convinced by this view. The followers of Mālik (the Mālikīs) said that it was obvious that forgetting the fast and accidentally eating something constitutes a breaking of the fast. However, Mālikīs did concede one point to the Ḥanafīs, namely that this was quite different from an intentional breaking of the fast. For the Mālikīs, intentionally eating something means both paying a penance and fasting extra days. Forgetfully eating something only needs one to fast the extra days. One does not perform a penance because one did not intend to break the fast – one just forgot.

From this example, one can see that different early jurists had not only different opinions, but different methods of proving their opinions. Al-Awzāʿī, al-Shāfiʿī and their followers, on this occasion, took the saying of the Prophet as authoritative (on other occasions they might have taken a different view). Mālik, Abū Ḥanīfa and their followers did not, presumably because they thought the report unreliable. (It is not easy to distinguish the opinions of the jurists from those of their followers because their followers were, in the main, responsible for recording their masters' opinions.) In any case, all the major jurists of the late eighth and early ninth centuries argued that legal reasoning, such as that used by Abū Ḥanīfa and Mālik in the above example, was acceptable in certain circumstances. Jurists could use it and come to their own opinion (in Arabic, *ra'y*) about a case.

Sometime in the ninth century, there emerged a rejection of the use of personal reasoning. Some scholars felt that both the true meaning of the Qur'ān and the reports of the Prophet were being cast aside without due care and attention by scholars being too eager to follow their own opinions and not the texts. Foremost amongst those who rejected *ra'y* was Aḥmad ibn Ḥanbal. He argued against the use of personal opinion in legal matters; he also argued against metaphorical interpretation of, for example, the verses in the Qur'ān which talk of God sitting on a throne and such like. This movement, sometimes called "the people of tradition" (*ahl al-ḥadīth*) took al-Shāfiʿī's argument to its logical conclusion. If the Qur'ān and the Prophetic *sunna* were the supreme legal authorities, then they had to be taken seriously. The personal opinion of one jurist or another was as nothing compared with the unassailable authority of the sources. Ibn Ḥanbal and his followers embarked on an attempt to defend the idea that the law should be based squarely on the Qur'ān and *sunna*, and the different opinions of the jurists (called *ikhtilāf* in Arabic) were damaging to the unity of the Muslim community and its obedience to God's will. A similar worry about *ikhtilāf* was expressed by Dāwūd al-Iṣfahānī, supposedly a pupil of al-Shāfiʿī. Dāwūd argued that the jurists of his time had erred by over-interpreting the texts of Qur'ān and *sunna*. So, for example, the Qur'ān said that those who are traveling can shorten their prayer, but what sort of journey counts as "traveling"? How long must it be before one can shorten one's prayer? Al-Awzāʿī argued that a journey consists of one *marḥala* (which was around 24 miles). Al-Shāfiʿī, Mālik and Ibn Ḥanbal said you should be travelling two *marḥala*. Abū Ḥanīfa said it should be three *marḥala*. Dāwūd said that the Qur'ān does not say how long the journey has to be – it simply says "traveling" (Qur'ān 4:101, "when you go on a journey, there is no harm if you shorten your prayer"). Therefore, any travel – however short or long – qualifies as "a journey," and consequently the Muslim can shorten his or her prayer. For Dāwūd (and the Ẓāhirī school), the other jurists had indulged in over-interpretation by attempting to specify how long the journey must be. Crucially, they brought in ideas about "travelling" which have nothing to do with the meaning of the word. The followers of Dāwūd al-Iṣfahānī were supposedly only concerned with a verse's "literal" meaning (or, more specifically, its "apparent" meaning, in Arabic *ẓāhir*). They rejected any attempt to interpret the Qur'ān and *sunna* which might lead one away from what the sources actually said. For this reason, they are often called "the literalists" (in Arabic, *al-Ẓāhiriyya*).

The four schools of Sunnī law and their elaboration

Out of these various schools of law, with competing opinions and methods of legal reasoning, emerged an acceptance amongst the Sunnī jurists that there were four "orthodox" schools, and all others were to be rejected. How did this come about? Why four schools (and why these four and not others)? What implications did this have for the acceptance of *ikhtilāf*? These questions have been much debated in Western academic literature. Even the date as to when the four schools became pre-eminent is debated. Medieval Muslim accounts tend to portray the founders of the schools (Mālik ibn Anas, Abū Ḥanīfa, al-Shāfiʿī and Ibn Ḥanbal) as responsible for establishing the schools. Schacht considered the accounts unreliable, seeing them as an *ex post facto* justification for a school's existence. Following him, Christopher Melchert (1997) has argued that it was not the founder who was really responsible for the establishment of the "school" (*madhhab*) named after him. Instead, it was probably one of his pupils, or his pupils' pupils, who established the basic elements of a *madhhab*. The basic elements of a *madhhab*, he argued, are the establishment of a predominant teacher, an educational system whereby the teachings of the *madhhab* might be transmitted from generation to generation and the composition of summaries (called *mukhtaṣar*s, along with commentaries, *taʿliqāt*). Melchert argues that all these criteria of a *madhhab* were in place in the early tenth century, and three of the *madhhab*s (Ḥanafīs, Shāfiʿīs and Ḥanbalīs) can be dated from then. Geographically, they can be located in Baghdad. The Mālikī school predominated in the Muslim West (North Africa and Spain), and the establishment of the Mālikī *madhhab* in the West can be dated to roughly the same time, perhaps a little earlier. Over the next century or so, other potential schools emerged, but failed to establish themselves. They failed, Melchert argues, because they never instituted the basic elements of a *madhhab*. They did not establish a system of knowledge transmission from one generation to the next, nor did they compose useable legal summaries to be used as subjects for later commentaries. Amongst the schools which did not survive were the Awzāʿī, Ẓāhirī and the Jarīrī *madhhabs*. The Awzāʿī school has already been mentioned, and was swallowed up in the general traditionalist movement and the shift of the empire's political centre to Iraq and Baghdad. The Jarīrī school was based around the teachings of Muḥammad ibn Jarīr al-Ṭabarī, and whilst there were jurists who clearly continued to support his opinions, neither he nor his followers established a stable system for the transmission of legal knowledge. He was also vilified by the followers of Ibn Ḥanbal, and hence became unpopular. The Ẓāhirī School, supposedly founded by Dāwūd al-Iṣfahānī promoted the "literal" or "apparent" meaning of the legal source texts (the Qur'ān and *sunna*). Such a method was seen as too rigid to be practical by other scholars; perhaps this is the reason why the Ẓāhirīs following Dāwūd failed to get positions of patronage in Abbasid Baghdad, whilst jurists from the other schools did. The ability of a school based around an individual scholar to transform itself into a full-blown teaching institution was crucial in securing its long-term survival. Those schools which could effect this transformation survived. Those that could not, just disappeared. These are amongst the possible explanations for the failure of some schools to gain sufficient popularity to be included in the final four.

The acceptance that there were four schools of Sunnī law, and that no new schools could be established, happened gradually. Exactly when a consensus was reached is the matter of some debate amongst historians of Islamic law, but it is better to see it as a process rather than a single event (i.e., there was no meeting at which jurists agreed there were four schools and no others). It happened in tandem with the emergence of a theological orthodoxy – namely the increased popularity of the theological ideas of Abū 'l-Ḥasan al-Ashʿarī (d. 935) and Muḥammad al-Māturīdī (d. 944) and the reduction in the popularity of Muʿtazilī doctrines. One can probably say that it was in the late eleventh century at the latest, that the vast majority of Sunnī jurists decided to affiliate themselves to one of the four schools (Makdisi 1981: 10–32). There were, of course, schools of jurisprudence emerging outside of Sunnī "orthodoxy" – including the Shīʿī schools of the Zaydīs and Ithnā ʿAsharīs, and the Ibāḍiyya – in what is likely to have been a parallel process.

Concomitant with the establishment of a set number of schools was the writing of works of *uṣūl al-fiqh*. Within the purview of *uṣūl al-fiqh* was the selection and proof of the sources of the *sharīʿa* – that is, an examination of which sources can act as the objects of exegesis in the first place. Once Muslim scholars started writing works of *uṣūl al-fiqh*, the sources of law were listed as four. The earliest surviving examples of full works of *uṣūl al-fiqh* are from the late tenth century, though it was clear that these theoretical issues had been discussed well before the earliest full text of *uṣūl al-fiqh* (*al-Fuṣūl* by Aḥmad al-Jaṣṣāṣ (d.981)) was written. The *Risāla*, supposedly authored by al-Shāfiʿī, has also survived, and is, of course, much earlier than al-Jaṣṣāṣ's *al-Fuṣūl*. However, the *Risāla* is much less developed than *al-Fuṣūl* and is, at best, a prototype work of *uṣūl al-fiqh*. Whilst we have no texts between the *Risāla* and *al-Fuṣūl*, it is clear that works of legal theory were being written, which may be lost now, but which established the genre for al-Jaṣṣāṣ's work. The *uṣūlīs* (as the authors of *uṣūl al-fiqh* became known) listed four sources of law:

1 *kitāb* (the "book" – meaning the Qur'ān)
2 *sunna* (the "example" – meaning the actions and deeds of the Prophet)
3 *ijmāʿ* (the "consensus" – meaning the consensus of the Muslim community, normally meaning the community of scholars)

4 *qiyās* (sometimes translated as "analogy," but in truth meaning any means of extending the message of the text to circumstances not mentioned in the text).

For each of these sources, the *uṣūlīs* supplied proofs of their role as a source. Establishing them as a source though does not necessarily establish what they might mean. Rather, the legal rulings within these sources are potentially part of the *sharīʿa*. The *uṣūlīs* argued that these four were the sources of law because, first, the Qur'ān is the revelation of God, and we know its contents because it has been transmitted perfectly by generations of Muslims. The example of the Prophet is a source because the Qur'ān established that the Prophet is a guide for the believers. The consensus of the Muslims is a source because the Prophet said that when his community agrees on something, then it is a rule ("My community shall not agree upon an error" and many other similar sayings). The community (in particular the scholars within the community) have agreed that if one can discover the reason why God or the Prophet made a ruling in one case, one can transfer that ruling to other cases, unmentioned by God or the Prophet. By following these sources, the individual jurist could reach a decision. Most importantly, he could identify within these sources "indicators" (*adilla*) from which the jurist can assess an action. In these works, jurists attempted to describe the method whereby a particular rule might be developed. So, for example, works of *uṣūl al-fiqh* discussed questions like "When God gives us a command in the Qur'ān, or through the Prophet Muḥammad, can we be certain that he is making the thing he is ordering obligatory?" It would seem obvious, at first blush, that an order to perform an action creates an obligation to perform that action in the recipient. Hence when God says, "O Believers! Uphold the prayer!," he has made prayer obligatory for the believers (i.e., the Muslims) to perform prayer and to persuade others to do so. However, there are a number of examples in the Qur'ān and elsewhere when God orders something, but it is not obligatory. For example, when God says, "Marry as many women that seem good to you" (Qur'ān 4:3), is he saying that everyone must marry (i.e., it is an obligation, and if one does not marry one is disobeying God), or is he merely giving us a recommendation to marry? Similarly, when God says, "when the pilgrimage is over, then go hunting" (Qur'ān 5:2) is he saying that when the pilgrimage is over everyone must go hunting (or even that it is recommended to go hunting), or is he saying that hunting, which was forbidden during the pilgrimage, is permitted once it is over? Is he in fact saying, "Once the pilgrimage is over, you are permitted to hunt"? This sort of question concerns the manner in which sources might be interpreted, and though one finds these theoretical questions discussed in other genres of literature (in some *ḥadīth*s, and in works of *fiqh* more generally), the genre of *uṣūl al-fiqh* became popular amongst jurists because it concentrated on these issues of exegetical theory.

Whether an action was permitted (*ḥalāl*) or forbidden (*ḥarām*) was central to the methodology found in works of *uṣūl al-fiqh*. Within the category of *ḥalāl*, a jurist could also decide whether the indicators pointed towards the action being reprehensible (*makrūh*, that is allowed, but discouraged), neutral (*mubāḥ*), recommended (*mustaḥabb*), and obligatory (*wājib*). For example, consider the four sources of law:

1 and 2 The Qur'ān and the *sunna* of the Prophet establish that the consumption of wine is forbidden (e.g., Qur'ān 5:90 "Wine and gambling (games of chance) and

sacrificing to stones and (divination) by arrows are a disgrace, the works of Satan").

3 The *ijmāʿ* (consensus of jurists) was that all the evidence points towards there being a reason for this prohibition (i.e., it is not simply a demand from God without a reason). The reason was, they all agreed, wine's intoxicating properties.

4 Therefore by *qiyās* (extension), if wine is intoxicating, all things with this property are also forbidden.

Each jurist when searching through the sources for a ruling on a particular issue would go through a reasoning process similar to the one just outlined. God, it was believed, required jurists to carry out this search to the best of their ability and with maximum effort. The process was called in Arabic *ijtihād* ("to try one's hardest") and the one who did it was called a *mujtahid*. Each *mujtahid* needs to be qualified in the religious sciences to search the sources and to interpret them correctly, and *mujtahid*s are very likely to disagree. For example, on the question of wine, some jurists (particularly some of those who followed Abū Ḥanīfa) argued that the rules concerning wine were designed to stop people getting drunk. Therefore, if someone could consume a substance and not be affected by it at all, then surely (they argued) consuming this substance was not forbidden. The classic case is that of date-wine (*nabīdh*, which is usually made to be much weaker than grape wine). Consuming intoxicating substances such as *nabīdh* until one was drunk may be forbidden, but consuming them without any intoxication (in small quantities and with low alcohol content) was surely permitted (though it might be discouraged). Nearly all other jurists disagreed, and maintained a total prohibition on the consumption of alcoholic substances. However, there remained both amongst and within the four schools a difference of opinion (*ikhtilāf*). Works of *uṣūl al-fiqh* generally explained this *ikhtilāf* by reference to the individual *ijtihād* of great *mujtahid*s which, because of the limited nature of the sources, was bound to lead to different opinions.

An examination of the works of *fiqh* of the various Sunnī schools shows that on nearly every area of law, the jurists differed. They all agree that one should pay alms (*zakāt*), but they differ on how much, to whom and for what it might be spent. They all agree that an adult woman must consent to any marriage arranged by her guardian, but they differed over how consent might be known to have been given. For every area of law, personal morality and religious ritual practice, the jurists differed amongst themselves. They were not embarrassed by this *ikhitlāf*, but instead they saw it as a "mercy" from God (indeed the Prophet Muḥammad is supposed to have made this point himself). The longer works of *fiqh* recorded the *ikhtilāf* on every issue, beginning with ritual purity (*ṭahāra*) running through the "pillars" (*arkān*, prayer, fasting, almsgiving, pilgrimage), and moving onto societal matters such as marriage and divorce, trade contracts, rental agreements, judicial organization, criminal law, tort law and state organization and warfare. *Fiqh* works, then, reflected the fact that the *sharīʿa* covers every possible area of human activity from the individual and ritual acts (known as *ʿibādāt*) to societal organization and relations (known as *muʿāmalāt*).

Scholars drew on these works of *fiqh* when asked for their opinion on individual matters (and they gave *fatwā*s in response to such questions). Judges drew on the *fiqh* (though they also used many other sources such as local custom) when they had to make decisions in the cases heard before them (described in court records or *sijilāt*).

However, despite the *fiqh* being enormously important and influential in the operation of the law in Muslim society, any work of *fiqh* was always considered to be an individual scholar's opinion about the content of the *sharīʿa*. This scholar may be learned, and respected, but his opinion as to the content of the *sharīʿa* is not the same as God's law. There was always a difference between what scholars put forward as their best attempt at finding God's rule on any issue (*ijtihād*), and God's own opinion. God has given us indicators (in the texts) of his opinion, but interpreting them was a human activity.

Modern developments in Sunnī legal thought

The above account describes the overwhelming emphasis of the Sunnī Muslim juristic tradition from the eleventh to the late-eighteenth century. This is not to say that there were not advancements within this period or that the law remained static. Because of the approval of *ikhtilāf* and independent inquiry, there were always novel opinions emerging. There were scholars who presented novel re-workings of the law in this period, and there were certainly innovative applications of the law by judges in the many dynasties which ruled the Muslim world during this period. However, the basic structure of the intellectual investigation of the law – that is *fiqh* and *uṣūl al-fiqh* – remained remarkably stable. Some scholars, both Muslim and non-Muslim, have argued that this stability implied a lack of innovation, and that the Muslims were merely following (*taqlīd*) previous scholarship. This led to atrophy or ankylosis within the study of the law; some even said that after the tenth century the "gate of *ijtihād*" was closed. Certainly some later Muslim scholars were so much in awe of the great achievements of the early generations of jurists, in particular the founders of the Four Schools, that they did proudly proclaim themselves as mere "followers" (*muqallidūn*) of past legal authorities. Much of this so-called classical and post-classical legal scholarship was not geared towards discovering the *sharīʿa* through an examination of the sources. Rather later scholars aimed to discover (from the available sources) the *madhhab* founder's opinion of the *sharīʿa*. It was the founder's opinion that became important, because God's actual ruling (i.e., the *sharīʿa*) was seen as too difficult to attain. One would have to work through the sources to understand God's intended meaning, and that was beyond scholars so removed from the circumstances of revelation.

In the eighteenth and nineteenth centuries, movements appeared in the Muslim world which were unhappy with merely following established school traditions (*taqlīd*, see Vikor 2005: 222–54). Some of these movements can be seen as internal Muslim developments. For example, in Arabia, the scholar Muḥammad ibn ʿAbd al-Wahhāb (d. 1792, and the founder of the Wahhābī trend) argued that much of previous Muslim scholarship and practice – both legal and theological – had been infected by "un-Islamic" ideas, and scholars were slavishly following the ideas of their predecessors. What was needed, he argued, was a renewed emphasis on the sources of the law (the Qur'ān and the *sunna*) and the interpretation of the first generations after the Prophet.

Other movements are better viewed as Muslim reactions to Western colonialism (particularly Britain and France) and the ideas that they brought. For example, the Egyptian jurist Muḥammad ʿAbduh (d. 1905) spent time in Paris, and he developed a distinctly modern approach to legal questions. He argued that Islamic law had to adapt in the light of reason. After returning to Egypt (and eventually becoming Grand Mufti of Egypt in 1899), he promoted novel re-interpretations of Islamic law in the light of Western science and rationality. For example, he allowed meat slaughtered by Christians and Jews to be eaten by Muslims whereas most schools previously had viewed this as at least reprehensible (*makrūh*), and perhaps even forbidden (*ḥarām*).

Scholars such as these, and the movements they inspired, have led in the last two centuries to a reduction in the importance of the school tradition (*madhhab*) across the Sunnī world. With this, there has been a concomitant increase in legal ideas which are not tied to a particular school, but aim to reform (*iṣlāḥ*) the law so that it fits in with the modern world. Islamic legal scholarship, for the foreseeable future, will not be restricted to the structures and ideas of the classical period and the Four Schools. Instead, novel and challenging questions are emerging which, in the opinion of most modern Muslim intellectuals, cannot be answered by loyalty to a school system that was formed over a thousand years ago.

References and further reading

Al-Azami, M. (1985) *On Schacht's Origins of Muhammadan Jurisprudence*, New York: Wiley; Riyadh: King Saud University.

Bearman, P., Peters, R. and Vogel, F. E., eds. (2006) *The Islamic School of Law: Evolution, Devolution, and Progress*, Cambridge, MA: Harvard University Press.

Berg, H. (2000) *The Development of Exegesis in Early Islam: The Debate over the Authenticity of Muslim Literature from the Formative Period*, Richmond: Curzon Press.

Burton, J. (1977) *The Collection of the Qur'ān*, Cambridge: Cambridge University Press.

Calder, N. (2004a) "*Sharīa*," *Encyclopaedia of Islam Second Edition*, CD-Rom version, Leiden: Brill.

—— (2004b) "*Uṣūl al-fiḳh*," *Encyclopaedia of Islam Second Edition*, CD-Rom version, Leiden: Brill.

—— (2007) "Feqh," *Encyclopaedia Iranica*, online at http://www.iranica.com/newsite (accessed September 10, 2007)

Goldziher, I. (1971) *The Ẓāhirīs: their Doctrine and their History: a Contribution to the History of Islamic Theology*, Leiden: E. J. Brill.

Hallaq, W. (1997) *A History of Islamic Legal Theories: an Introduction to Sunnī uṣūl al-fiqh*, Cambridge: Cambridge University Press.

—— (2001) *Authority, Continuity and Change in Islamic Law*, Cambridge: Cambridge University Press.

Hurvitz, N. (2002) *The Formation of Ḥanbalism: Piety into Power*, London: RoutledgeCurzon.

Makdisi, G. (1981) *The Rise of the Colleges: Institutions of Learning in Islam and the West*, Edinburgh: Edinburgh University Press.

Masud, M. K., Messick, B. and Powers, D., eds. (1996) *Islamic Legal Interpretation: Muftis and their Fatwas*, Cambridge: Harvard University Press.

Masud, M. K., Peters, R. and Powers, D., eds. (2006) *Dispensing Justice in Islam: Qadis and their Judgements*, Leiden: Brill.

Melchert, C. (1997) *The Formation of the Sunnī Schools of Law, 9th–10th Centuries C.E.*, Leiden: Brill.

Motzki, H. (2002) *The Origins of Islamic Jurisprudence: Meccan Fiqh before the Classical Schools*, Leiden: Brill.

Schacht, J. (1950) *The Origins of Muhammadan Jurisprudence*, Oxford: Clarendon Press.

Vikor, K. (2005) *Between God and the Sultan: a History of Islamic Law*, London: Hurst.

13

THEOLOGY: FREEWILL AND PREDESTINATION

Suleiman Ali Mourad

The debate over freewill and predestination represents one of the earliest theological schisms in Islamic history. It began in the Umayyad period (661–750), though its roots actually go back to the troubled second half of the caliphate of ʿUthmān ibn ʿAffān, whose assassination in 656 led to the first intra-Muslim civil war, which included the Battle of the Camel in 656 and the Battle of Ṣiffīn in 657. During his reign, ʿUthmān made a number of appointments of governors and officials that were seen by his opponents as favoring the members of his extended family – the Umayyad clan of Quraysh – and their supporters. ʿUthmān was thus accused of making wrong decisions, and dissatisfaction with his rule increased. The rebels besieged his house, and because he refused to honor their demands, they killed him. From that point onward, there was no caliph in Islam whose authority and legitimacy went unchallenged by some Muslim groups.

ʿUthmān's successor, ʿAlī, could not establish his legitimacy either, and following the Battle of Ṣiffīn in 657, a group of his supporters, who came to be known as al-Khawārij ("the Dissenters"), denounced him because he agreed to make peace with his opponent Muʿāwiya. In their view, ʿAlī had violated God's commandments and committed a grave sin, and they assassinated him in 661.

How did the question of a caliph's authority come to be associated with the predestination/freewill controversy? The answer is that Muslim scholars and politicians began to debate whether or not the caliph is to be held accountable for his decisions. Those who favored accountability were therefore legitimizing military opposition and assassination as a way to punish a caliph, whereas the other side would insist on unconditional acceptance or at most pacifism. But opposition leads to intra-Muslim civil war, which Muslims had just experienced. Therefore, the larger question was whether the bloodshed was something for which the Muslims were responsible or part of a divine plan, which led to the theological inquiry into human behavior, ability and responsibility.

The first group to articulate a position in this controversy were the Umayyads, the dynasty that ruled the Muslim world from the time of the assassination of ʿAlī until 750. The Umayyads, starting in 661 with caliph Muʿāwiya, recognized the problems that would ensue if their authority was not accepted. Their solution was to redefine the concept of the caliph as not simply a successor of the Prophet Muḥammad, as the term was previously understood, but as God's caliph, in the sense of God's deputy.

The caliph is simply the agent who executes God's will; he does not determine it himself, and thus he cannot be held accountable.

The customary method of investigating questions of Islamic doctrine is to begin by examining pre-Islamic Arab society, Qur'ān, and *ḥadīth* for evidence about whether the Arabs in pre-Islamic times upheld a particular doctrine, and whether it was endorsed by the prophet Muḥammad and his new religion. In the case of the predestination/freewill controversy, however, this traditional exercise does not provide satisfactory answers as to why Muslims uphold one doctrine or the other, in part because the roots of the debate are primarily political, and it was shaped over a number of decades. Moreover, most of the theologians who elaborated the doctrines of predestination and freewill were not Arabs, nor did they live in Arabia. Thus the supporters of each position were not necessarily adhering to an already established doctrine, and they did not approach the religious sources with an open mind, in order to determine what they said and follow it. Rather, they went back to the religious sources (Qur'ān and *ḥadīth*) – and only after these were established as the most important religious sources for Islam – in order to find legitimization and support for their already formulated ideologies, and refutations of their opponents' views. Invariably, when they came across verses or *ḥadīth*s that disagreed with their position, they either simply ignored them or reinterpreted them to mean something else. When we look at pre-Islamic customs, Qur'ān, and *ḥadīth*, we must keep in mind that they did not necessarily predetermine the controversy, but rather they were sources for the ammunition that each camp used against the other.

Pre-Islamic Arabs

Medieval Muslim sources tend to stress that pre-Islamic Arabs were predestinarians, though the evidence at hand is not conclusive. Our clearest window into the pre-Islamic Arab belief system is pre-Islamic poetry, which contains many references to time (*dahr*), death (*manāyā*), and other terms as agents that determine people's fate. But these references are often associated with one's life span (*ajal*). For example, the pre-Islamic poet Zuhayr ibn Abī Sulmā (d. before 625) included in his famous ode the line "Death, I believe, is like a sightless, aimless camel: whom it strikes it kills, and whom it misses lives and grows old." Another well-known pre-Islamic poet, Ṭarafa ibn al-ʿAbd, chanted: "If you cannot stop death from reaching me, let me, at least, face it with what I have." The Qur'ān seems to confirm this pre-Islamic belief, as in verse 63.11: "God does not save a person's life when his/her *ajal* comes." Yet the issue of one's responsibility for his or her actions is rarely discussed in the poetry, and the historical record, as slim and unreliable as it is, tends to support an ideology of freewill mixed with a belief in fate. It is said that when the notable poet Imru' al-Qays (d. *c.* 550) received the news of the slaying of his father, he was feasting with a group of companions. He said to them: "Today we drink wine, and tomorrow we attend to this matter" (*al-yawm khamr wa-ghadan amr*), "this matter" being the seeking of revenge on those who killed his father. He did not say "This has been predestined and I have to accept it." It is also said that the grandfather of prophet Muḥammad made an oath to sacrifice his son ʿAbdallāh, the Prophet's father, for God, the Lord of the Kaʿba. But he had a change of heart and decided to cast lots before God to see if it would be acceptable to substitute a number of camels for his son. He received a negative result, but did not give up and accept the decision as God's predestined plan. He kept repeating the casting of lots and raising the number of camels, until it came out to his liking, and his son was saved. What this tells us, if these stories are authentic, is that some pre-Islamic Arabs did not simply accept fate as an inevitable thing, but rather made every attempt to manipulate it.

Qur'ān

In the Qur'ān we find a rather conflicting position on the doctrines of freewill and predestination. On the one hand, it contains verses like the two below that assert God's control of everything.

> We have created for Hell many of the Jinns and humans. They have hearts but no awareness, have eyes but no vision, and have ears but no perception. They are like beasts of burden, even worse. They are the heedless ones.
>
> (Qur'ān 7:179)

> Every single thing we have created with divine portion.
>
> (Qur'ān 54:49)

Qur'ān 7:179 declares that God has created a group of people whose end is known to be in Hell and who are incapable of avoiding that fate; it is inescapably ordained. Qur'ān 54:49 says that behind everything is a divine plan. Nothing escapes God.

On the other hand, there are Qur'anic verses that seem to say the exact opposite. For instance, in matters of belief, one verse in the Qur'ān instructs the prophet Muḥammad: "Say: Here is the truth from your Lord, it is to you to believe [it] or disbelieve [it]" (Qur'ān 18:29). The prophet is to offer the revelation to his audience, and it is up to them to accept or reject it; that is, their freewill determines their acceptance or rejection of God's message. Another verse suggests that God interferes only after the act has been committed: "He leads astray none but the wrongdoers" (Qur'ān 2:26). Here the Qur'ān speaks "wrongdoers," people who have already chosen to do wrong. God's leading them astray refers to the punishment they have earned by their choice of actions.

This inconsistency caused immense anxiety for later theologians who struggled with the verses of the Qur'ān in order to streamline them in support of their respective theologies. A predestinarian theologian would dismiss the verses that endorse freewill as requiring further inspection. Similarly, a freewill theologian would dismiss the predestination verses as requiring further scrutiny. This led to the development of a genre of Qur'anic exegesis called *Mutashābih al-Qur'ān* (the "ambiguous verses" of the Qur'ān), where the *ambiguous* verses, the verses that contradict one's beliefs, are listed and then are interpreted to mean the exact opposite of what they appear to say.

Ḥadīth

The *ḥadīth*, which was collected long after Muḥammad's death, is not as confusing, although it has its own problems. The prophet Muḥammad is reported to have said, "He [i.e., any Muslim] who denies *qadar* has reneged his faith," and "Those who believe in *qadar* are the heathens of my community." The problem with these two *ḥadīth*s lies in the term *qadar*, which means either freewill (humans' power to determine their actions) or predestination (divine decree). Obviously, Muḥammad could not have uttered both *ḥadīth*s, for in the first he makes the belief in *qadar* a basis of faith, whereas in the second, it becomes a basis of disbelief. Moreover, there is no way to determine in what sense the Prophet and his audience understood the term *qadar*. Later Muslim scholars from both the predestinarian and freewill camps quoted these *ḥadīth*s to refer to the opponents of their camp. Hence, the believers in freewill, originally named Qadarites (*al-Qadariyya*), and their successors consistently used the two *ḥadīth*s cited above to denounce the predestinarians, whom they also called Qadarites or Compulsionists (*al-mujbira*); the latter term reflects the belief that God compels the individual to a certain behavior and the individual has no power to change it. Similarly, the predestinarians would cite the same *ḥadīth*s as denouncing the believers in freewill.

The majority of *ḥadīth* material tends to endorse predestination, but that does not necessarily mean that the prophet Muḥammad promoted this doctrine. Rather, it is a reflection of the fact that most *ḥadīth* scholars, especially those who collected the authoritative books of *ḥadīth*, were predestinarians, and thus often fabricated sayings that endorse their beliefs and attributed them to the prophet of Islam and his companions. The few traditions that uphold freewill they intentionally ignored, and did not include them in their *ḥadīth* collections. But at the same time, those *ḥadīth*s that endorse freewill are not necessarily authentic either. They might equally well have been fabricated by the proponents of the freewill doctrine in order to legitimize their belief and at the same time answer the predestinarian *ḥadīth*s.

Two of the *ḥadīth*s that endorse predestination read:

> The Prophet said: "God, almighty, took a handful of mud and said: 'These are in Paradise and I do not care.' He took another handful and said: 'These are in Hell and I do not care'."
>
> (Ibn Ḥanbal 1954–8: V, 68)

> The Messenger of God said: "A human is conceived in his mother's womb for forty days, for another forty days he becomes a clot, and for another forty days he becomes an embryo. Then God sends an angel to establish four things: its allotment, its life-span, and whether damned or blessed. Then he blows into it the soul. By God, a person would do the work that leads to Hell until he is an arm away from it, but what has been predestined [for him] gears him to do the work that leads to Paradise, and so he enters it. Similarly, a person would do the work that leads to Paradise until he is an arm away from it, but what has been predestined [for him] gears him to do the work that leads to Hell, and so he enters it."
>
> (al-Bukhārī 1984: *Kitāb al-Qadar*, 1)

*Ḥadīth*s like these clearly state that God predestined everything at the time of creation: the people of hell as well as the people of heaven. Each human receives his lot while in the womb. He will do exactly what had been predestined for him – no more, no less.

An example of a *ḥadīth* that endorses freewill reads:

> The Messenger of God said: "At the end of time, there emerges in this [Muslim] community a group who commit sins and blame them on God's decree. He who refutes them is like one who unsheathes his sword (to fight) in the path of God."
>
> (Mu'ayyadī 1993: I, 250)

This particular *ḥadīth* is quoted in a Zaydī text, which considers fighting in the path of God (*jihād*) a binding duty on Muslims. Thus equating the act of standing up to refute the claims of the predestinarians is as noble as fighting *jihād* in the path of God.

The Umayyads

Now, to return to the Umayyads, they championed and promoted an ideology that rested primarily on predestination. Concerned with the challenges to their legitimacy as a ruling dynasty, they and their supporters maintained that the caliphs were God's deputies, who simply execute God's will. Thus any criticism of them is a criticism of God, and any revolt against them is a revolt against God. In order to disseminate this ideology, the Umayyads enlisted in their service a number of religious scholars and poets whose task was to provide a religious defense of the predestination doctrine. It was these religious scholars who furnished a number of *ḥadīth*s that depict the prophet Muḥammad and his companions defending predestination and condemning freewill.

Caliph ʿAbd al-Malik ibn Marwān (r. 685–705) is probably the most important political figure in early Islam who sponsored the dissemination of Umayyad predestination theology. When he was named caliph, there were several contenders who challenged him, most notably Ibn al-Zubayr in Mecca. Even after Ibn al-Zubayr was killed in 692, it took ʿAbd al-Malik seven more years to subdue other contenders, especially in Iraq. ʿAbd al-Malik emerged from these encounters victorious, and that success helped cement the ideology that he promoted among the large majority of Muslims. Indeed, according to the Umayyad propagandists, if he had not had God's backing, he would not have been able, against all odds, to defeat his many enemies. The poets of his court composed verses that praised ʿAbd al-Malik as "the Caliph of God." For example, the renowned Christian poet al-Akhṭal (d. before 710), wrote in an 84-line ode: "To a man whose gifts do not elude us, whom God has made victorious. . . . The Caliph of God, through whom men pray for rain." It is God who made ʿAbd al-Malik victorious, and as God's deputy, people should seek his intercession with God for such divine favors as rain. Another renowned poet, al-Farazdaq (d. 728), wrote: "You are to this religion like the direction of prayer, by which people are guided from going astray." Again, ʿAbd al-Malik is the compass that keeps Muslims on the right path to God, and prevents their going astray. Such poetry was not simply meant to praise and please ʿAbd al-Malik. It was intended to rally the general Muslim public around the doctrine of predestination, and in doing so the court poets were primarily promoting the official Umayyad ideology.

Besides poetry and *ḥadīth*s, ʿAbd al-Malik took other measures that help us understand how he wanted his subjects to perceive him and his rule. The construction of the Dome of the Rock in Jerusalem and the widespread Islamicization process were also indicative of an Umayyad predestinarian ideology. One of ʿAbd al-Malik's objectives in ordering the construction of the Dome of the Rock was to provide the Muslims under his rule, those in Syria and Egypt, with a holy place to which they could go on pilgrimage, especially since Mecca was then under the control of his rival Ibn al-Zubayr. Obviously the Dome of the Rock was not meant to replace Mecca, but rather to provide a temporary alternative. Moreover, ʿAbd al-Malik also intended to send a message to the other two monotheistic religions – Judaism and Christianity – that Islam had triumphed by God's decree. Other aspects of the Islamicization process include the move to a new system of coinage that did not have images of rulers on either side. That ʿAbd al-Malik was able to enact and enforce these changes tells us a great deal about the fact that he believed, or at least wanted his subjects to believe, that God was guiding his way.

The Qadarites

That the Umayyads and their supporters rallied around the ideology of predestination meant that some, but not all, of their rivals chose the freewill doctrine. They came to be known as Qadarites, because they believed in humans' ability (*qudra*) to determine their own actions. The extremists among the Qadarites promoted a complete freewill theology: everything that happens in this world is the result of human behavior, and God has no power to change it. Among the early theologians of freewill were Maʿbad al-Juhanī (d. *c.* 700) of Baṣra and Ghaylān (d. *c.* 743) of Damascus, both of whom were executed by Umayyad rulers because of their religious opposition, but more importantly their involvement in anti-Umayyad political factions.

The moderate Qadarites, who represented the majority of the movement, upheld a more balanced theology: good deeds result from God's guidance, but sins are the sole responsibility of those who act them out. It is important to note here that the only thing that united these Qadarites was the belief in freewill. They did not share political goals, nor were they united on other religious views. Their only political success occurred in 744, when a group of Qadarites in Syria staged a revolt and declared as caliph a member of their movement named Yazīd ibn al-Walīd, who was the son of an Umayyad caliph. Yazīd died six months into his term in office, and the Qadarites again were subjected to Umayyad persecution. When the Umayyads were ousted from power by the Abbasids in 750, the views of the Qadarites became less popular, since their main appeal had been that they challenged the Umayyads.

One major figure to promote the moderate Qadarite view in the Umayyad period was al-Ḥasan al-Baṣrī (d. 728). He was from the town of Baṣra in southern Iraq; Baṣra at that time was an anti-Umayyad stronghold, and in a span of 40 years, several major rebellions against Umayyad rule took place there. Al-Ḥasan seems to have been involved in anti-Umayyad activities, and had to hide from the ruthless Umayyad ruler of Iraq al-Ḥajjāj (d. 714). His main specialty as a scholar was in Qurʾānic studies, as both a reciter and an interpreter of Islam's holy book. He also made a living by preaching, especially on moral issues. Al-Ḥasan gathered around him a large group of disciples, most of whom were Qadarites, who passed down some of his teachings. But some of his students became predestinarians, and they claimed that he was never a believer in freewill, or that he had been at one time but changed his mind toward the end of his life and became a predestinarian. Both groups generated sayings and short letters that they attributed to him in order to back their claims. One such text is an epistle, allegedly written by al-Ḥasan to ʿAbd al-Malik, which contains a sophisticated, highly developed, and comprehensive refutation of predestination theology that accepts only the authority of the Qur'ān and ignores entirely *ḥadīth*.

The Muʿtazilites

The Epistle to Caliph ʿAbd al-Malik, which could not have been written by al-Ḥasan al-Baṣrī, provides the general theology of freewill that was upheld and defended by the groups that elaborated the freewill doctrine and made it a sound theological system in the eighth and ninth centuries: the Muʿtazilites. An excerpt from the *Epistle* shows how the Muʿtazilites refuted their opponents and argued the case in support of freewill:

> Among the issues they also contest is [God]'s, almighty, saying: *We have created for Hell many of the Jinns and humans. They have hearts but no awareness, have eyes but no vision, and have ears but no perception. They are like beasts of burden, even worse. They are the heedless ones* (Qur'ān 7:179). They have interpreted this to mean that God has predisposed his creation. He made one group for Hell; they are unable to [show] the obedience he demanded from them. He made another group for Heaven; they are unable to [show] the disobedience he forbade them from. This is similar to creating the short unable to become tall, and the black unable to become white, and then torturing them for not obeying Him. They have indeed described God with the most repulsive descriptions. But God [in Qur'ān 7:179] has foretold that they shall end in Hell because of their malicious acts. He described them when He said: *They have hearts but no awareness, have eyes but no vision*, [till the end of] the verse. He, almighty, similarly said: *Then he was picked up by the family of Pharaoh to be their enemy and a cause for regret* (Qur'ān 28:8). But they picked him (Moses) up to be a comfort for them, similar to His, almighty, saying: *We give them respite that they sink deeper into sin* (Qur'ān 3:178). He foretold that they increase in sins by His decree because they abandon obedience. For God has spoken to the Arabs in the way they know their language. One of the sages of the Arabs said in poetry:
>
> > For death mothers feed their babies,
> > just as for the destruction of time houses are built.
>
> [God] has informed that children will ultimately die and houses will ultimately become ruins. But the young are fed to grow and live, not to die, and houses are constructed to provide a shelter, not to be destroyed. After all, the Qur'ān, O Commander of the Faithful, is in Arabic. God has revealed it to an Arab people. He spoke to them in their own language, which they mastered very well.
>
> (Mourad 2006: 221–2)

The quote starts by stating the predestinarians' belief that God creates a group of people predisposed to a particular type of behavior and then tortures them for engaging in that behavior. This claim is then refuted, the main argument being that in Qur'ān 7:179, God is actually foretelling that the end of those people will be in Hell because of their disbelief and malicious acts. God did not create those people to be destined for Hell. What shows the veracity of the argument is that in another verse (Qur'ān 28:8), God says that the Pharaoh and his wife picked up Moses to be their enemy, and clearly what is meant is that they picked him up from the Nile river to be comfort and joy to them, as an adopted son, but that he ended up being their enemy.

This style of dialectical diatribe was originally championed by the Muʿtazilites, and because of its effectiveness was later adopted by most Muslim theologians. It was originally borrowed from Hellenistic philosophical and Christian theological disputations. Moreover, as we can see in the quote above, the proponents of freewill argued that an excellent command of Arabic semantics and poetry were required for the proper interpretation of the verses of the Qur'ān. In other words, when one goes to the Qur'ān to determine its position on a particular issue, one must be well equipped with the necessary tools to decipher its true meanings. Otherwise, one risks being misguided by the apparent, but incorrect, meanings.

This theology was first introduced by Abū 'l-Hudhayl al-ʿAllāf (d. *c.* 842), and was further developed by later Muʿtazilites, including Abū ʿAlī al-Jubbā'ī (d. 915) and his students. Abū 'l-Hudhayl was born in Baṣra to Persian parents. At that time, Baṣra was the most powerful base for the Muʿtazilites; the movement had started there in the early eighth century. Abū 'l-Hudhayl was the first Muʿtazilite theologian to conceptualize some of what later became known as the five principles (*al-uṣūl al-khamsa*) of the Muʿtazilites; the belief in these five principles became the defining factor that determined who is/was and who is/was not a Muʿtazilite. One of these principles is the belief in God's justice. According to Abū 'l-Hudhayl, God does not do wrong. When he punishes and rewards a person, he does so because of the obligation (*taklīf*) under which he placed that individual. *Taklīf* means that God established the laws and gave humanity the choice of abiding by them or violating them. He warned humanity that those who violate the laws will be punished and those who abide by them will be rewarded. (The belief in punishment and reward is another of the Muʿtazilite five principles.) Hence, for God to impose a punishment or grant a reward and at the same time be just, people have to have the choice to obey or disobey, which means that they have to have the freedom as well as the capability to choose.

The Muʿtazilite movement, which comprised scholars who championed the use of dialectical disputations to argue theological questions, was initially divided over the question of freewill. The point that had to be settled was not only whether or not God predetermines everything, for there are other theological convictions that could be compromised by accepting one position or the other. For instance, if one accepts predestination, then humans have no power over their actions, and subsequently an individual cannot be held accountable for his or her sins. But since these sins lead to Hell, that would mean that God destines a person for a particular sinful behavior and then punishes him or her for acting those sins out. This makes God unjust. But God is just (*ʿādil*). Therefore, the belief in the justness of God requires the rejection of predestination.

The belief in freewill, however, has its own theological challenges. If humans are responsible for their actions, then the question that poses itself is whether or not God knows of human action prior, during, or after the act. If God does not know of the action until it is happening or just happened, then he is not all-knowing (*ʿalīm*), for the latter requires that he knows everything before it occurs. And because some theologians would not accept a compromise in the belief that God is all-knowing, they would reject freewill as a plausible doctrine. These challenges to both sides of the freewill question were no secret to the theologians of medieval Islam.

One theologian who did not accept either position was Ḍirār ibn ʿAmr (d. *c.* 815). He asserted on equal par the justness and all-knowing-ness of God, and therefore, to settle the problems in each doctrine, he proposed the notion of *kasb* (acquisition), which was later elaborated by other theologians, such as al-Ashʿarī (d. 935) and his school. What this notion of *kasb* means is that at the time of action, God creates in the individual the ability to act independently of His knowledge. Thus the individual acquires this power and acts, and God judges him or her on the basis of the choices the individual makes and the result of his or her action. Ḍirār was a member of the Muʿtazilites, but because his views were rejected by all subsequent Muʿtazilte theologians, he was posthumously ostracized from the movement.

Another example that demonstrates the interdependence of theological doctrines relates to the doctrines of God's justness, freewill, and the createdness of the Qur'ān. Again, if one were to start from the assertion that God is just, then God could not condemn an individual to Hell without giving that individual the chance to save himself or herself. For example, Qur'ān 111:1–5 reads:

> May the hands of Abū Lahab perish, and may he himself perish. Neither his wealth nor gains will avail him. He will burn in a flaming fire. His wife will carry the firewood that will burn her, with a rope of fiber round her neck.

Here, if the Qur'ān is not created, that is, if it is co-eternal with God, then God condemned Abū Lahab and his wife to Hell before they were even born and therefore they had no chance whatsoever to save themselves from that fate. This makes God unjust. But, again, God is just. Therefore, these verses must have been created by God after Abū Lahab, who was Muḥammad's uncle, and his wife persisted in their rejection of God's message and their persecution of Muḥammad's followers. Therefore, the Qur'ān is created (the belief in the createdness of the Qur'ān is one of the five principles of Muʿtazilite theology).

Sunnīs

When Sunnī Islam started to form itself into an independent sect in the ninth century, Sunnī theologians were initially divided over the issue of freewill and predestination. Some adopted the Muʿtazilite position, but most Sunnī scholars favored predestination. Gradually, the Muʿtazilite movement fell from favor with Sunnī political rulers, and by the thirteenth century it had lost its appeal and it became nonexistent.

The downfall of the Muʿtazilites meant the success of the dominant theological school in Sunnī Islam: the Ashʿarite school. Al-Ashʿarī, whose name was given to this school by later followers, borrowed Ḍirār ibn ʿAmr's concept of acquisition (*kasb*) and made it the central point of his predestination theology. Al-Ashʿarī began his career as a Muʿtazilite theologian, one of the students of the notable Muʿtazilite scholar Abū ʿAlī al-Jubbā'ī. Following the death of his mentor, al-Ashʿarī established his own teaching circle and gradually distanced himself from some of al-Jubbāʾī's views. The concept of *kasb* was meant to introduce a compromise that both predestinarians and believers in freewill would accept.

The Ashʿarites' articulation of their position is that at the time of action, God creates in the individual the ability to do the act on his or her own, but that ability cannot overpower God's predestination. In other words, even though God has already determined what the individual will or will not do, the actions will be acted out on the basis of the individual's decision. But this decision is not an open choice. The Ashʿarite school maintained that the ability created in the individual only allows him or her to perform the act; it does not allow him or her to do its opposite. This view challenges the Muʿtazilite position, which asserted that this ability is created long before the act is about to be committed, and the individual has a free choice to perform either the act or its opposite.

The Ashʿarite position in support of predestination was primarily promoted on the basis of an "accept it as is" approach. It was not, therefore, a satisfactory option for theologians, who would naturally want to pursue the issue and revisit it in light of the religious and socio-political developments in the Muslim world. For example, another popular theological movement among Sunnīs, the Maturidite school, named after the theologian al-Māturīdī (d. 944), who came from Samarqand in Central Asia, was not satisfied with the rather unconvincing assertions of the Ashʿarites, especially the question of when people receive the power to commit the act. The Maturidites maintained that humans possess the ability to act long before the acts are committed. Another Sunnī position is represented by the Ḥanbalites, one of the four schools of Sunnī law and the only one that developed its own theology. They asserted that God is the creator of everything and His sovereign will governs human acts, yet humans have the capability to choose between good and evil. However, it was precisely out of fear that the fierce theological debate within Islam might be ignited again that later Sunnī scholars became more and more alienated from the field of theology and did not encourage specializing in it. The most prolific scholar of medieval Islam, Jalāl al-Dīn al-Suyūṭī (d. 1505), wrote that the study and teaching of theology leads to losing one's coherence, common-sense, and above all faith. This position contributed to the transformation of Sunnī Islam into primarily an orthopraxy rather than an orthodoxy; in other words, the religion's main emphasis became proper behavior rather than proper belief. It also enhanced the popularity of mysticism as an alternate theology among Sunnī scholars.

The Shiʿites

The success of the Muʿtazilites can only be measured in Shiʿite Islam, for it made a lasting impact on Zaydite and Twelver theologies; the other major Shiʿite sect, the Ismāʿīlites, adopted a neoplatonic system of theology. The Shiʿites, who call their leaders *Imāms*, believe that the leadership of the Muslims belongs to the descendants of Muḥammad through his daughter Fāṭima and her husband ʿAlī. Like the Umayyads, the Shiʿites initially adopted a predestination theology: their right as leaders of the Muslims is a divine ordinance, and it is not for the Muslims to decide or debate the matter. One early Shiʿite theologian who endorsed predestination was Hishām ibn al-Ḥakam (d. 795), who lived in Kūfa, Iraq, and was a close disciple of the fifth Shiʿite

Imām Jaʿfar al-Ṣādiq (d. 765) and his son Mūsā al-Kāẓim (d. 799). Hishām believed that the acts of humans were created by God, and that there is an element of compulsion that determines the outcome of human behavior. But God does not know of or determine the acts of a given human being until he or she is born.

In time, predestination became unpopular among Shiʿite theologians. The Zaydites elaborated a leadership system emphasizing that an Imām's legitimacy has to be demonstrated on the battlefield, by standing up to challenge injustice. Thus their theologians realized that predestination would not work for them, because it requires accepting things as they are. By the end of the ninth century, the Zaydites had adopted Muʿtazilite theology, including the freewill doctrine.

Similarly, the Twelver theologians, especially after the occultation (*ghayba*) of the twelfth Imām in 874, started too to realize that predestination was becoming a dissuasive rather than persuasive theology. In other words, if God preordained that leadership belongs to the direct family of the prophet Muḥammad, then the Imāms should be in power; but many of the Imāms died in prison or as a result of poisoning. The fact that they were not in power means that there is no such thing as complete predestination.

The Twelver theologian who made the most compelling case for the freewill creed was al-Sharīf al-Murtaḍā (d. 1044). He was heavily influenced by the teachings of the Muʿtazilites, and borrowed some of his views from them. Al-Murtaḍā asserted that good behavior is by God's decree, but evil behavior is the result of the choices humans make. He refused to accept that calamities (natural disasters, sickness, etc.) are included in the category of evil, for there is a divine wisdom for them to occur. Only the acts of humans fall under evil or good, and they are produced on the basis of freewill.

Once the freewill doctrine became popular among Shiʿite theologians and scholars, they began to invent sayings and anecdotes that endorse it and back-projected them to their Imāms in order to demonstrate that the freewill belief had always been the hallmark of Shiʿism.

Modernity

In modern times, the two dominant sects in Islam, Sunnīs and Shiʿites, maintain their respective positions. The Sunnī theologians for the most part adhere to Ashʿarite theology that endorses predestination along with the notion of acquisition; the Maturidites still have a following in Turkey and Central Asia, and the Ḥanbalites in Saudi Arabia. On the other hand, the Shiʿite theologians (Twelvers in Iran, Iraq, Lebanon, and some other Muslim countries, and Zaydites in Yemen) assert the moderate freewill belief. Yet, within Sunnī Islam there can be detected a growing trend, though it remains a minority movement, that pushes for the re-adoption of the Muʿtazilite position concerning freewill. This has been especially the case given the socio-political conditions of the modern Muslim world.

At the popular level, however, the situation is much more complex. One often hears the words "what is written cannot be avoided" (*al-maktūb mā minhu mahrūb*). What this means is that what God has predestined for a person or a community cannot be changed. Thus people must accept what comes to them of good or bad fortune. This rather passive approach is reminiscent of those medieval groups labeled as Compulsionists. Yet, again, the situation is much more complicated than that. Many of the same people who repeat "what is written cannot be avoided" would also say "the individual should seek in order for God to help him or her" (*isʿā yāʿabdī la-isʿā maʿak*), which asserts a moderate freewill belief: the individual has to take the initiative, and God's blessing follows. Thus, after some 13 centuries of debate, the difficult issues of freewill and predestination remain essentially unresolved in the minds of many Muslim believers.

References and further reading

Abrahamov, B. (1998) *Islamic Theology: Traditionalism and Rationalism*, Edinburgh: Edinburgh University Press.

Bukhārī, al- (1984) *Jāmiʿ al-ṣaḥīḥ*, ed. I. al-Anbārī, Beirut: Dār al-Kitāb al-ʿArabī.

Crone, P. and Hinds, M. (1986) *God's Caliph: Religious Authority in the First Centuries of Islam*, Cambridge: Cambridge University Press.

Elad, A. (1995) *Medieval Jerusalem and Islamic Worship: Holy Places, Ceremonies, Pilgrimage*, Leiden: E. J. Brill.

Ess, J. van (1991–7) *Theologie und Gesellschaft im 2. und 3. Jahrhundert Hidschra*, Berlin: Walter de Gruyter.

—— (2006) *The Flowering of Muslim Theology*, trans. J. M. Todd, Cambridge: Harvard University Press.

Frank, R. M. (1994) *Al-Ghazālī and the Ashʿarite School*, Durham: Duke University Press.

—— (2005) "Remarks on the Early Development of the Kalām," in D. Gutas, ed., *Philosophy, Theology and Mysticism in Medieval Islam: Texts and Studies on the Development and History of Kalām, Vol. I*, Aldershot: Ashgate Publishing, Chapter VI.

Ibn Ḥanbal, A. (1954–8) *Musnad*, ed. A. M. Shākir, Cairo: Dār al-Maʿārif.

Judd, S. C. (1999) "Ghaylan al-Dimashqi: The Isolation of a Heretic in Islamic Historiography," *International Journal of Middle East Studies*, 31: 161–84.

Khan, S. (2003) *Muslim Reformist Political Thought: Revivalists, Modernists, and Free Will*, London: Routledge.

Martin, R. C., Woodward, M. R. and Atmaja, D. S. (1997) *Defenders of Reason in Islam: Muʿtazilism from Medieval School to Modern Symbol*, Oxford: Oneworld.

Mourad, S. A. (2006) *Early Islam between Myth and History: al-Ḥasan al-Baṣrī (d. 110H/728CE) and the Formation of His Legacy in Classical Islamic Scholarship*, Leiden: Brill.

Mu'ayyadī, al- (1993) *Lawāmiʿ al-anwār fī jawāmiʿ al-ʿulūm wal-āthār wa-tarājim awliyāʾ al-ʿilm wal-anẓār*, Ṣaʿda: Maktabat al-Turāth al-Islāmī.

Nagel, T. (2000) *The History of Islamic Theology: From Muhammad to the Present*, trans. T. Thornton, Princeton: Markus Wiener.

Robinson, C. F. (2005) *ʿAbd al-Malik*, Oxford: Oneworld.

Salisbury, E. E. (1866) "Materials for the History of the Muhammadan Doctrine of Predestination and Free Will: Compiled from Original Sources," *Journal of the American Oriental Society*, 8: 105–82.

Watt, W. M. (1948) *Free Will and Predestination in Early Islam*, London: Luzac.

—— (1985) *The Formative Period of Islamic Thought*, Edinburgh: Edinburgh University Press.

Wolfson, H. A. (1976) *The Philosophy of the Kalam*, Cambridge: Harvard University Press.

14

RITUAL LIFE

Zayn Kassam

At every moment of the day, somewhere in the world, a Muslim is reciting the Qur'ān in prayer. Thus, an observant Muslim is connected to another observant Muslim regardless of where in the world she or he goes, since the formal ritual prayer, the *ṣalāt*, is recited in Arabic and follows a similar format of recitation of verses from the Qur'ān. Rituals punctuate a Muslim's day, and the Islamic lunar calendar year is filled with ritual observances. Considered to be following a faith that inculcates a high degree of discipline in its required ritual observances, Muslims worldwide are infused with a sense of Qur'anically inspired ethics, values, modes of behavior, and attitudes to life and its purpose. This chapter describes the obligatory rituals of Muslims (the *arkān*), some commemorative occasions observed by Muslims.

Muslim law books generally identify the *arkān*, or pillars, as obligatory practices for Muslims. Sunnī Muslims delineate five such *arkān*, whereas Shīʿī Muslims add a sixth pillar. The *arkān* are: the witnessing (*shahāda*), prayer (*ṣalāt*), the payment of obligatory alms or charity (*zakāt*), fasting (*ṣawm*), and pilgrimage (*ḥajj*), and struggle in the path of God (*jihād fī sabīl Allāh*). Sunnīs adhere to the first five of these, whereas Shīʿīs will add the additional sixth in their list of required Muslim ritual practices. In addition to these *arkān*, there are also rituals that mark festive or commemorative occasions, such as the two ʿĪd celebrations, the days marking the Prophet's ascension into the divine presence (*miʿrāj*), the deaths of the Prophet (*mīlād al-nabī*), significant members of his family, especially among the Shīʿa, the death of Ḥusayn, the grandson of the Prophet (*ʿāshūrāʾ*) and men and women deemed to have attained the status of holiness through their nearness to the divine (*mīlād*), and in some locales, the spring equinox that coincides with the Persian New Year (*Nawrūz*). Muslims also engage in ritual activity pertinent to the major life passages, such as birth, the attainment of puberty, marriage, and death. Finally, there are ritual activities associated with groups such as the Ṣūfīs, discussed elsewhere in this volume, and the myriad ritual activities that recur as often or as infrequently as the Muslim wishes, associated with emulating the Prophet, engaging in supplicatory and propitiary prayer (*munājat, duʿāʾ*), repetitions of one of the many names of God or phrases (*dhikr*), the composition and singing or recitation of poetry in honor of the divine or the Prophet (*naʿt*) or a saint, or as expressions of devotion or of the human relationship with the divine (in the poetic forms known as *ghazal, qaṣīda*, for instance). Among these may also be counted acts of charity (*ṣadaqa*).

The *arkān*

Shahāda, *witnessing*

One becomes a Muslim by uttering the *shahāda*, "There is no god but God, and Muḥammad is (God's) messenger" to which Shīʿīs will add, "and ʿAlī is the Master/Lord of the believers." Thus, the *shahāda* is whispered into a newborn's ears at birth. It is heard daily by Muslims during the call to prayer, and recited at each prayer. The phrase *Lā ilāha illa Allāh* ("There is no god but God") is recited at the time of death and during burial ceremonies. The phrase is often found inscribed on coins, on tile utilized for public buildings and mosques, and on pottery. As an article of faith, the *shahāda* is a subject of much meditation and discourse by mystics, theologians, and philosophers as well as by artists and poets.

Ṣalāt, *prayer*

The Qur'ān exhorts Muslims to pray: "And be steadfast in prayer" (Q 2:43, 83, 110, 153). Sunnī Muslims pray five times a day at specified times: early morning (*al-fajr*), noon (*al-ẓuhr*), mid-afternoon (*al-ʿaṣr*), sunset (*al-maghrib*), and evening (*al-ʿishāʾ*), while Shīʿīs, who combine the noon and mid-afternoon prayers, and the sunset and evening prayers, pray three times a day. With the exception of the Friday noon prayer, Muslims are not required but are recommended to be in congregation for daily prayers. The Friday noon (*jumʿa*) congregational *ṣalāt* is accompanied by a sermon (*khuṭba*). Other obligatory *ṣalāts* are those performed at funerals, at the eclipses of the sun and the moon, while the *ṣalāts* performed during the two ʿĪd celebrations are recommended but not required.

In preparation for the *ṣalāt*, a believer must perform ablutions called *wuḍūʾ*, through which minor impurities may be removed. Impurities are of two kinds: major and minor. A person enters a state of major impurity through seminal emissions, or other bodily emissions such as menstruation and postpartum bleeding. In such cases, ritual purity is restored through taking a bath, and every Muslim is recommended to bathe before attending the Friday congregational prayer. Minor impurities are brought about by sleeping, bodily functions such as urinating, or defecating, passing wind, touching the genitals, or sexual contact short of engaging in sex. These may be removed by performing *wuḍūʾ*, which entails, according to Qur'anic prescription (Q 5:6), washing the face, hands up to the elbows, wiping the head and the feet up to the ankles, all of which must be done with water, with the right side being washed first, following the Prophet's custom. If water is unavailable, as in the case of travelers, then sand or dust may be used instead. It is not unusual to find in many mosque compounds areas where the faithful may perform *wuḍūʾ*. Short prayers or *duʿāʾ* are often recited as each bodily part is washed; for example, while the feet are being washed, one might say, "God, Make my feet firm on the path, on the day when the feet easily slip away from the path!" (Denny 1994: 117). Along with purification, the believer must take care to be appropriately dressed, and to approach the prayer with proper intention, or *niyya*, at which the believer's intention to pray is articulated and the number of cycles of prostration the believer intends to perform are specified. The believer then faces Mecca, having been purified, dressed appropriately, possessing a mental and emotional frame of mind that is appropriate to the performance of prayer.

At the approach of the time for *ṣalāt*, the call to prayer (*adhān*) is sounded, usually by the *mu'adhdhin* (one who calls to prayer). Travelers to Muslim countries often awaken to the sonorous recitation of the call to prayer as it is broadcast using modern technology through loudspeakers; often several calls to prayer may be heard seconds apart emanating from different mosques in the city. The call to prayer, recited in Arabic, consists of the following statements:

> God is the Most Great (4 times)
> I testify that there is no god but God (twice)
> I testify that Muḥammad is the Messenger of God (twice)
> Hasten to prayer! (twice)
> Hasten to salvation! (twice)
> Prayer is better than sleep (only before the dawn prayer; not recited by Shī'īs)
> Hasten to the best of actions (said twice by Shī'īs only)
> God is the Most Great (twice)
> There is no god but God (Sunnīs once, Shī'īs twice)

Those who so wish will proceed to the mosque (*masjid*, "place of prostration"), line up in rows facing Mecca, usually with men in the front and women and children either behind them, or in a separate room or balcony. In some contemporary mosques in North America, men and women can now be found standing in rows side by side, separated by a curtain or a space, although the more usual arrangement of women and children sectioned off behind the men, or off on a separate balcony, prevails. In a mosque, the direction (*qibla*) of Mecca is usually marked by a *miḥrāb*, traditionally a recession in the wall, and it is before the *miḥrāb* that the *imām* or leader of the prayer stands, the rows of the congregation falling in place behind him. Each person silently whispers his or her intention (*niyya*) to pray, and the *ṣalāt* proper begins.

The basic unit of the *ṣalāt* consists of a cycle, called *rak'a*, and each *ṣalāt* has a specified number of cycles. The morning *ṣalāt* requires two cycles, the noon, afternoon, and evening *ṣalāts* each require four cycles, and the evening *ṣalāt* requires three cycles. While these are obligatory, the worshipper may, if he or she wishes, increase them. A cycle of prayer begins with the worshipper standing erect, facing the *qibla* with the hands raised to the side of the head. The *takbīr* is recited (*Allāhu akbar*, "God is most great"), either by the *imām* if in congregational prayer, or by the worshipper if praying alone. The hands are then placed at the side of the body or folded loosely upon the chest, at which point the opening chapter of the Qur'ān, the *Sūrat al-fāṭiha*, is recited, followed by the recitation of a few more verses of the Qur'ān. After another *takbīr* with its accompanying hand movement, the worshipper bows, saying "Glory be to God" (*subḥān Allāh*), returns to the standing position with a *takbīr*, and then prostrates on the floor with toes, knees, and forehead touching the floor, with palms on either side of the head. Another *takbīr* is recited as the worshipper comes to a sitting position, before another prostration is performed, ending also in a *takbīr*. The standing position is then resumed, marking the end of one *rak'a* or cycle. When the specified cycles of the *ṣalāt* are completed, the worshipper, in a sitting position, pronounces the *shahāda*,

Figure 10 Cosmic mountain (Gunungan) of *minbar* (pulpit). This traditional Malay mountain motif and Qur'anic calligraphy was incorporated into a mosque pulpit used for delivering Friday sermons.

Source: © Photo: Spirit of Wood – The Art of Malay Woodcarving, by Farish Noor & Eddin Khoo, photograph David Lok. Reproduced by kind permission of Kandis Resource Centre

followed by calling down blessings on Muḥammad and in the case of the Shīʿīs, his family. The worshipper then turns to the worshipper on either side and utters the *taslīm*, "Peace be upon you and the mercy and blessings of God." Thus ends the *ṣalāt*.

Zakāt, *almsgiving*

The payment of *zakāt* is a legal obligation upon all Muslims, introduced by Muḥammad in Medina, based upon various Qur'anic passages that identify the giving of alms as a virtue (Q 23:4), as a sign of righteousness (Q 76:8), as sharing the benevolence bestowed upon humans by God (Q 35:29). The term is used almost synonymously with *ṣadaqa*, which also means giving in charity and was known to pre-Islamic Arabs through the Jewish practice of giving in charity called by the same name. The key difference between *zakāt* and *ṣadaqa* is that in later Islamic law, *zakāt* is made a legal obligation whereas *ṣadaqa* remains a voluntary gift. In the Qur'ān the terms are used interchangeably, as for example in Q 9:60 where the recipients of *ṣadaqa* are named variously as the poor, the needy, those who care for them, travelers, and the like. Such a verse along with Q 2:215, which names parents, relatives, orphans, travelers, slaves, and the poor and needy as among those meriting *zakāt* became the basis for later laws governing the disbursement of funds collected through obligatory donations. *Zakāt* expresses the vertical relationship with God in the form of giving thanks for all the bounties that God has made available to one, and is properly considered an extension of *ʿibāda* or worship, as well as the horizontal relationship with one's community, acting to redistribute wealth in manners that materialize the values of care and compassion for others. The notion of purity is imbedded in *zakāt*: by giving *zakāt*, a Muslim thereby purifies that which remains and renders it lawful wealth in the sense that it is hoped that the remainder will cause one no harm but rather, will benefit self and others. Wealth that has not been thus purified is considered unclean.

Most legal schools also made obligatory upon all who could afford it a special category of *zakāt* payable at the end of the fasting period in Ramaḍān, *zakāt at-fiṭr*, entailing the provision of one day's food for a needy person. Both *zakāt*, obligatory giving, and *ṣadaqa*, voluntary giving, are considered extremely meritorious by Muslims, and are considered to be a source of purification, which is the basis of spiritual development. By and large the payment of *zakāt* today is a matter of individual conscience. Almsgiving in its many forms is considered part and parcel of the Muslim ethic of social justice, echoed throughout the Qur'ān, as in 2:261–3

> Those who spend their wealth in God's way are like a grain that grows seven ears, in every ear a hundred grains. . . . Those who spend their wealth for the cause of God and afterward make not reproach and injury to follow what they have spent, their reward is with their Lord. No fear shall come upon them, nor shall they grieve. . . . A kind word with forgiveness is better than almsgiving followed by injury.

Ṣawm, *fasting*

Fasting occurs during the month of Ramaḍān. The Arabic term for fasting, *ṣawm*, meaning "to be at rest" is connected also to silence, according to Qur'ān 19:26, in which Mary is told to say: "I have made a vow of *ṣawm* to the Merciful, wherefore I speak to no one this day." Qur'ān 2:183–5 prescribes fasting for Muslims, just as it was prescribed "for those before you" (that is, the Jews and the Christians) during the month of Ramaḍān, "in which the Qur'ān was sent down, a clear guidance for humankind" along with exceptions made for the ill and for travelers, for God "desires not hardship for you." Qur'ān 2:187 specifies that eating, drinking, and sexual relations are permitted until "the white thread becomes distinct to you from the black thread of the dawn" at which time the fast must be observed until nightfall. During the period of fasting, sexual activity is not permitted; rather, God exhorts those fasting to "be at your devotions in the mosques." Technically, the fasting period ought to begin as soon as the new moon has been sighted heralding the month of Ramaḍān; often this occurs on the last days (29th or 30th) of the previous month, Shaʿbān.

Muslim legal scholars devised criteria for those who qualified to undertake the fast; thus, a person had to be a physically fit Muslim over ten years of age and in full possession of his or her senses; a fasting woman must not be menstruating or just have given birth. A person wishing to fast must declare their intention (*niyya*) to do so in their prayers. The fast was considered invalid if food or drink were ingested during the fast, or if the person fasting engaged in sexual activity. Legal scholars also considered deliberate vomiting, inhaling tobacco smoke, deliberate sexual emission, menstruation, intoxication, and evidence of an unsound mind as invalidating the fast. If days of fasting were missed due to travel or illness they could be made up at a later time.

Ending the fast (*ifṭār*) should be a conscious act, not one that occurs by accident. The fast ends as soon as the sun sets, and Muslim tradition holds that the Prophet typically ended his fast with two dates and water, before the evening prayers were recited, after which a full meal is eaten. Muslims will often celebrate the end of the fast with gatherings of family and friends during which poetry or other entertainments are enjoyed.

While fasting is obligatory during the month of Ramaḍān, it may also be undertaken for other reasons, such as during a period of drought, or if one has taken a vow entailing fasting. Voluntary fasting is recommended on the day of ʿĀshūrāʾ on the tenth day of the month of Muḥarram, and if possible, on the day preceding as well as the day following it; on the day of ʿArafat (discussed below under *ḥajj*); for six days from the 2nd to 7th of the Muslim calendar month Shawwāl; for ten days in the Muslim calendar month of Dhū ʾl-Ḥijja; and on the day of the *miʿrāj*. Additional days historically recommended include every Monday and Thursday; the first, middle, and last day of each Muslim calendar month; the days of the "white" nights of each lunar month (12th, 13th, 14th, and 15th) and the days of the "black" nights (28th, 29th, 30th, and sometimes the 1st). The *ḥadīth* literature further reports that the Prophet recommended the practice of a person who fasted every other day. A well-known *ḥadīth* reported by the legal scholar and theologian Aḥmad ibn Ḥanbal (d. 855) declares, "The scent of the breath of a fasting man is more pleasant than the scent of musk" to God. Fasting is forbidden during the two ʿId celebrations, *ʿīd al-aḍḥā*, and *ʿīd al-fiṭr*.

Fasting at any time, whether obligatory or voluntary, is considered a time for atonement of past transgressions and the renewing of a commitment to be more mindful of one's ethical behavior towards God, self, and others. Many view fasting as a time in which to reflect with gratitude on the bounties provided by God, and a time during which awareness of the need for compassion for those who go hungry or suffer is strengthened for the whole year.

Ḥajj, *pilgrimage*

The *ḥajj*, or pilgrimage to Mecca, ʿArafat, and Mina, is considered to be a duty incumbent on all adult Muslims who are able-bodied and financially able to undertake the pilgrimage at least once in their lifetimes, or to appoint someone to make the pilgrimage on their behalf especially if the Muslim is elderly or infirm. The pilgrimage proper is traditionally performed during the month of pilgrimage – Dhū ʾl-Ḥijja, from the eighth to the twelfth days, although a Muslim may make the *ḥajj* at any time of the year, especially during the Muslim calendar month Rajab. The pilgrimage consists of various parts including the many rites that make up the *ʿumra* or smaller pilgrimage, a visit to the plain of ʿArafat to observe standing or *wuqūf*, stone-throwing at

(a)

(b)

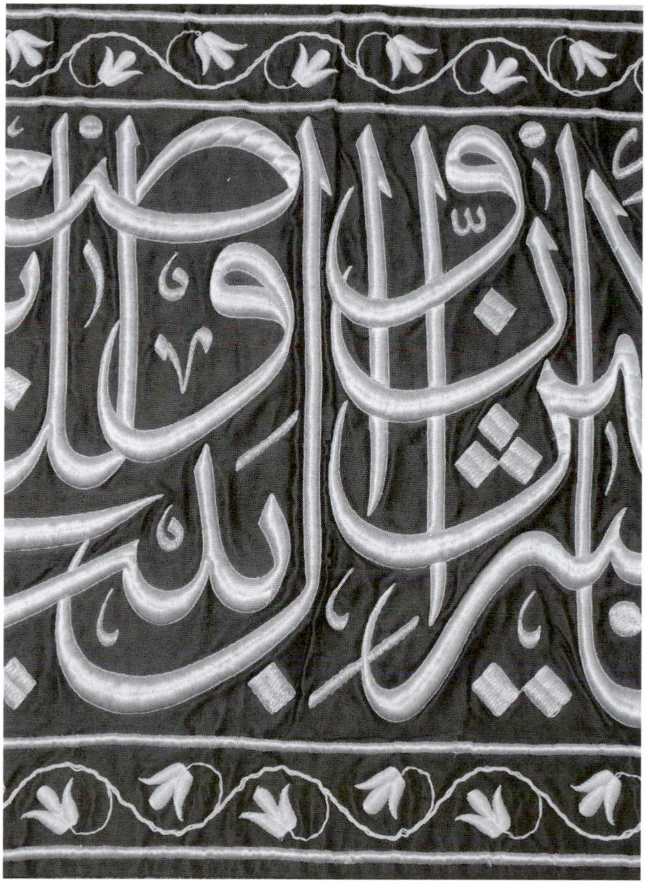

Figure 11a and b The inscription on this costly shroud for the Kaʿba begins with the *basmala* (In the name of God, most benevolent, ever-merciful) followed by Qurʾān 3:95–7 which refers to Abraham and the first house of worship for the one God, the Kaʿba.

Source: Nasser D. Khalili Collection of Islamic Art, inv.no. TXT 39a. Copyright the Nour Foundation. Courtesy of the Khalili Family Trust

the plain of Muzdalifa, a ritual sacrifice in observance of the *ʿīd al-aḍḥā* (Festival of Sacrifice), and the concluding rite of *taqṣīr* or haircutting that signals the commencement of the end of the *ḥajj* proper. The pilgrimage over, those Muslims who wish to do so may continue with a visit to Medina to sites such as the Prophet's tomb before returning to Mecca and leaving for home. The *ḥajj* season lasts three months: Shawwāl, Ramaḍān, and Dhū 'l-Ḥijja. Many pilgrims arrive during the month of Shawwāl, observe the fasts of Ramaḍān while in Mecca, and remain for the *ḥajj* in Dhū 'l-Ḥijja, celebrating *ʿīd al-aḍḥā* before returning home. A pilgrim is henceforth accorded the title *Ḥājjī*, meaning one who has performed the *ḥajj*.

While there are pre-Islamic antecedents to the ceremonies performed during the pilgrimage, rites to be performed at the Kaʿba in Mecca were introduced by Muḥammad seven years after the Muslim emigration from Mecca, which occurred in the year 622. Muḥammad himself was unable to undertake the pilgrimage to Mecca until the year he died, 632. The annual performance of the pilgrimage dates from this time. Due to the lunar Muslim calendar, the dates of the pilgrimage cycle through different seasons, falling 10 to 11 days earlier than the previous year, and completing the entire cycle of seasons every three decades or so.

In preparation for the annual pilgrimage, the Kaʿba is draped in a gold-embroidered black brocade covering known as the *kiswa*, prepared in Egypt each year. The *shahāda* or testament to faith, is woven into this covering, as are Qur'anic verses in a band about two-thirds of the way down the cloth in gold embroidery, in fine calligraphy. The garment is taken down each year in the Muslim calendar month Dhū 'l-Qaʿda, and pieces are sold off as relics, and the new garment is placed on the Kaʿba at the end of the pilgrimage rites.

In pre-modern times, pilgrims traveled to Mecca by land in caravans or by sea; the journey was long and difficult, and punctuated by stops on the way for supplies and to rest. Contemporary air, rail and motorized forms of transport have made traveling to Mecca for the annual *ḥajj* much easier, resulting in between 2 and 3 million pilgrims each year, in contrast to the figure of approximately 200,000 pilgrims noted during the turn of the twentieth century. Pilgrims are responsible for settling all debts as well as their affairs before embarking upon the pilgrimage, and for having drawn up a will in case they die before returning from the pilgrimage. A person who passes away while on pilgrimage is considered to be an extremely fortunate martyr who was guaranteed entrance into paradise. Advances in health care have significantly reduced the number of pilgrims who die each year on the pilgrimage; however, accidents do happen such as a stampede that occurred at the symbolic stoning ritual during the *ḥajj* pilgrimage in January 2006, at which 600 people were either killed or injured.

Before arriving in Mecca, the pilgrim puts on garments called *iḥrām* to mark entering a state of holiness and readiness for the pilgrimage. For men, the *iḥrām* consists of a white, seamless, two-piece garment that erases all traces of class and status differentiating male pilgrims from each other, thereby rendering the pilgrims equal before God. While women may wear an *iḥrām*-type garment that ensures full bodily coverage, most tend to dress according to their regional customs, thereby attesting to the diversity of cultures espoused by Muslims. Pilgrims enter Mecca through a number of checkpoints beyond which non-Muslims may not progress. If they have not already done so, pilgrims must don the *iḥrām* at this point. Each pilgrim will now renew his or her intention (*niyya*) to perform the pilgrimage and its rites; henceforth, until the end of the pilgrimage, the pilgrim is forbidden to engage in sexual intercourse, nail clipping, hunting, wearing perfume or jewelry, cutting hair, arguing, and so forth. As they approach Mecca, and throughout the *ḥajj*, pilgrims recite the *talbiya*:

> Here I am, O our God, here I am! (*labbayka allāhumma labbayk*)
> You who are without any associate, here I am!
> To You are praise, blessing and power.

Pilgrims then proceed into Mecca through the "Gate of Peace" (*bāb al-salām*) to recitations of verses from the Qur'ān, and continue onwards to circumambulate the Kaʿba in an anti-clockwise direction seven times, in a rite known as the *ṭawāf*. This rite is performed three times: once upon entering Mecca, once after the ritual haircutting after the sacrifice, and once before leaving Mecca. Pilgrims will extend their arms towards the Black Stone embedded five feet above the ground in the eastern corner of the Kaʿba if they are not close enough to touch it; the Black Stone is considered a sign of God's covenant with Abraham and Ishmael. After the *ṭawāf*, pilgrims perform two *rakʿas*, cycles of prostration and prayer, at the *maqām Ibrāhīm*, the place of Abraham, believed to be the place where Abraham worshipped while building the Kaʿba. The pilgrims then perform the rite of *sa'y*, running or walking seven times between the two hills Ṣafā and Marwa, in emulation of Hagar's panic-stricken search for water for Ismāʿīl (Ishmael), Abraham's son by Hagar. Legend has it that Ishmael's heel struck water where he had been left, and the wellspring is named Zamzam, from which pilgrims bring back a vial of water on their return from Mecca. The total distance covered amounts to a little less than 10,000 feet. At this point, pilgrims symbolically mark the end of the *ʿumra* (smaller pilgrimage) rites. Now begin the rites related to the *ḥajj* proper, beginning with a sermon on 7 Dhū 'l-Ḥijja at the Grand Mosque of Mecca reminding pilgrims of their duties during the pilgrimage.

On 8 Dhū 'l-Ḥijja, pilgrims will move eastward towards Mina, where they will stop for the night, or to ʿArafat. The 9th of Dhū 'l-Ḥijja is spent standing in the valley or plain of ʿArafat; pilgrims are expected to stand at least for an hour between noon and sunset. The act of standing or *wuqūf* is considered the central and obligatory rite of the *ḥajj*, for during it pilgrims contemplate, each in his or her aloneness with God, the test to which Abraham was put when asked by God to sacrifice his son. ʿArafat also derives its significance as having been the place where the Qur'ān "descended" or was revealed to the Prophet, and it was here that the Prophet stopped to deliver a sermon to those who had accompanied him on his final and only pilgrimage to the Kaʿba in Mecca, during the year of his death. For those on *ḥajj*, this is a time for solitary prayer, repentance, renewal of commitment, and the giving of praise and thanks to God. At sunset, the pilgrims move to the plain of Muzdalifa and communal prayers combining the evening and night prayers are recited, after which 49 pebbles are collected for stone-throwing rites. The next day, directly after the morning prayers, pilgrims leave Muzdalifa for Mina where seven pebbles are flung at the devil for having attempted to dissuade Ismāʿīl from cooperating with his father's decision to comply with God's command to sacrifice him. On this day, if the pilgrim wishes, a goat or a sheep may be ritually slaughtered. In contemporary times, the Saudi government has much of the meat packaged for later use and distribution. The *ʿīd al-aḍḥā* is celebrated; pilgrims may now proceed with the ritual shaving of the head or *taqṣīr* (sometimes a token piece of hair is cut off), and return to Mecca for another *ṭawāf* around the newly adorned Kaʿba. The pilgrims will spend the next three days in Mina, congregating and visiting in a festive spirit, with the obligation of casting seven stones at each of the three pillars within Mina, ending finally with stoning the three pillars, each symbolizing

Satan. Pilgrims usually leave Mina on the 12th or 13th, stopping one last time at Mecca to perform a final *ṭawāf* around the Kaʿba, before proceeding homewards or visiting sites connected to the early days of Islam such as the Prophet's tomb and mosque in Medina.

Through the centuries, Muslims have reflected extensively on the spiritual significance of the *ḥajj*. According to the *ḥadīth*, performing the pilgrimage results in the forgiveness of all sins. Here Muslims become cognizant of the vastness and international nature of the worldwide Muslim *umma*, a community of fellowship and surrender to God. Muslims re-enact their connection to Ibrāhīm (Abraham), mentioned in the Qur'ān as the first to have surrendered to God's will, that is, the first *muslim*. They reflect on the difficult ethical choices made by Abraham regarding whether or not to obey God; by Ismāʿīl regarding whether or not to succumb to the devil's entreaty that Ismāʿīl not comply with his father's wishes; by Hagar regarding whether or not to trust in God's compassion and benevolence as she hungered in the desert fearful for herself and her son; and they see a sign of God's bounty and grace as Ismāʿīl's heel strikes the ground to reveal the flowing waters of the well known as Zamzam. The many linkages to Abraham and his family are brought to consciousness as Muslims remember that Abraham is thought to have built the Kaʿba (according to legend, at the place where Adam and Eve fell to earth) with Ismāʿīl; close to the Kaʿba there is a dome in which is preserved a tablet bearing the imprint of Abraham's feet; there is also a trough that is remembered as the place where Abraham and Ismāʿīl mixed the mortar for the Kaʿba; at the northwest corner of the Kaʿba is a circular wall about six feet away at which Ismāʿīl and his mother Hagar are said to be buried.

Muslims reflect on the Qur'ān as a source of guidance revealed as a sign of God's compassion and mercy for humankind as they stand at ʿArafat. They reflect upon the difficulties encountered by the Prophet as he introduced monotheism in a polytheistic environment and bore hardship while preaching the revelation, for ʿArafat points at both the beginning and the end of the Prophet's career. It is not surprising to find that meditations on the *ḥajj* and what it signifies for the interior development of the soul continue long after the pilgrim has returned.

Commemorative occasions

Such occasions include the birth of the Prophet (*mīlād al-nabī*), the night of revelation (literally night of power, *laylat al-qadr*), his night journey (*isrā'*) and ascension (*miʿrāj*), the two festival days (*ʿīd al-aḍḥā*, *ʿīd al-fiṭr*), the commemoration of the death of the Prophet's grandson Ḥusayn and members of his entourage, and the Persian New Year (*Nawrūz*). Other commemorative occasions include the *mīlāds* (also termed *moulid* or *mawlid*) of various personages considered sacred or of major importance, held at the shrines or burial places of the many saints associated with the Ṣūfī tradition, and other important personages. Shrine visitations (*ziyārāt*) are found in many Muslim countries, notably Egypt, India, Morocco, Iran, and others where mosques built around the cemeteries of noted personages become sites of festivals held in their honor, usually to commemorate a birthday (*mawlid*) or death (*ʿurs*, lit. "wedding") anniversary. For instance, in Iran the mausoleums of Rūmī (d. 1273), Ḥāfiẓ (d. 1390), and Khomeini (d. 1989) command large numbers of pilgrims who come to pay homage as well as to make supplications for help with difficulties. Similarly in Egypt, shrines of Sayyida Nafīsa (d. 824) and Zaynab (d. 629; she was the daughter of Muḥammad by Khadīja) are visited during festivals in their name, and Moroccan saints are also honored for their piety and exemplary behavior in festivals held throughout the year. In recent years, the Moroccan government has instituted a Festival of Sacred Music that honors the devotional musical traditions of Moroccan and North African Muslims, and the success of the festival has led to its inclusion of other sacred musical traditions.

Mīlād al-Nabī, the birthday of the Prophet

The Prophet's birthday celebrations are held on the Muslim calendar date of 12th Rabīʿ al-Awwal, which some have considered to be also the date of his death. The birthday of the Prophet is generally referred to as his *mawlid*, and the alternative term, *mīlād*, is also used. The Egyptian historian Maqrīzī (d. 1442) describes a *mīlād* celebration from Fatimid records dating from the tenth to twelfth centuries, during which scholars delivered lectures and sermons, sweets were distributed, and alms were given to the poor. A thirteenth-century eye-witness account describes *mīlād* celebrations entailing elaborate food preparation for guests, prayer meetings and sermons, *samāʿ* or mystical dance performances, and processions with candles as well as shadow plays. In Turkey, mosques are festooned with candles or lights. Many *mawlid* celebrations are conducted through the recitation of poetry in honor of the Prophet, often expressing the deep love felt by the poet for the blessing received by humankind in the person of the Prophet. Tapes of such recitations may be found in bazaars or marketplaces throughout Muslim countries. In some parts such as South Asia, the 12 days leading up to the birthday of the Prophet were commemorated through the sounding of drums, special prayers for the Prophet, exhibitions of paintings, lectures, dance, acrobatics, the performance of heart-stirring *ghazal*s or love-poems. Such popular manifestations of love for the Prophet were often denounced by theologians who deemed only recitations of the Qur'ān and sermons to be appropriate modes of celebration of the Prophet's birth. In contemporary times, it is not unusual to find cities with large Muslim populations decorated with flags and other festoonery, with special programs featured on radio and television and print media, and gatherings at which poetry, music, and sermons and lectures are featured for the enjoyment and edification of the populace. During these gatherings, attention is often drawn to the miraculous events surrounding the Prophet's birth.

Such miracle stories relate that the angels and *jinn* congratulated themselves on the Prophet's birth, that gardens blossomed, the sky came close to the earth as his birth took place, and so forth. Muḥammad's associations with light metaphors are also found, as for example, his mother's womb is thought to emanate a light at his birth, and poets have drawn upon the Qur'anic epithet for Muḥammad, "a shining lamp," to tell of how the whole world was illuminated at his birth. Some stories relate how a light shone from his father's forehead on the night that Muḥammad was conceived. The Turkish poet Suleymān Čelebi (d. 1422) celebrated such details in verse and versions of this poem are still recited during *mīlād* celebrations in Turkey, the opening of which is reproduced here:

> Amina Khatun, Muhammad's mother dear:
> From this oyster came that lustrous pearl.
> After she conceived from ʿAbdullah

Came the time of birth with days and weeks.
As Muhammad's birth was drawing near
Many signs appeared before he came!
. . .
Amina said: "When the time was ripe
That the Best of Mankind should appear,
I became so thirsty from that heat
That they gave me sherbet in a glass.
Drinking it, I was immersed in light
And could not discern myself from light.
Then a white swan came with soft great wings
And he touched my back with gentle strength."
(Schimmel 1985: 153–4)

Laylat al-Qadr, the night of power

Laylat al-Qadr which falls on the 27th night of the month of Ramaḍān, is described in *sūra* 97 of the Qur'ān as a night which is better than a thousand months, during which the angels descend with blessings. It is the night during which the Qur'ān was first revealed to Muḥammad. Muslim communities around the world commemorate this occasion often by staying up all night for prayer and sermons and recitations of the names of God and hymns of praise. The night of power culminates the days of fasting undertaken during the month of Ramaḍān and is considered to be the night when the human and divine are at their closest proximity.

*Isrā*ʾ (night journey) and *Miʿrāj* (ascension)

Qur'ān 17:1 alludes to an event that graphically portrays for Muslims Muḥammad's ability to traverse the distance between the physical world and the spiritual world, from the plane of humanity to the realm of divinity: "Praise Him, who traveled in one night with His servant from the *masjid al-ḥarām* to the *masjid al-aqṣā*, whose surroundings We blessed, in order to show him Our signs." Muslim tradition considers the one to be praised to mean the angel Gabriel, the servant to refer to Muḥammad, the Prophet, the *masjid al-ḥarām* to be the Kaʿba in Mecca, and the *masjid al-aqṣā* to be a reference to Jerusalem, whether in its earthly or in its heavenly form. The term *miʿrāj*, understood as Muḥammad's ascension to God's presence, means a ladder, and there are several Qur'anic references to a ladder connecting heaven and earth.

The *ḥadīth* literature reports that angels came upon Muḥammad while he was sleeping, opened his heart, and washed away all doubt, idolatry, and error with water drawn from the well of Zamzam, and filled him instead with wisdom and belief. Thus purified, Muḥammad was then taken on his nocturnal journey (*isrā*ʾ) from Mecca to Jerusalem and then on the ascent (*miʿrāj*) to the heavens.

The earliest biography of Muḥammad related that the angel Gabriel came to him while he was asleep and led him to a white animal, half mule, half donkey, with wings on its sides, named Burāq (popular Pakistani artisan depictions of Burāq give the flying animal a woman's head and face). Gabriel and the Prophet rode on Burāq to Jerusalem, seeing all the marvels of heaven and earth on the way. In Jerusalem, they found

Abraham, Moses, and Jesus among a company of the prophets. There, the Prophet led them in prayer, and then was offered various drinks: water, wine, and milk, of which he chose the milk, understood as "the middle path." Upon drinking it, he was told by Gabriel that in so choosing, he would be rightly guided, as would his people. Thereafter it is reported that Muḥammad was brought a ladder "finer than any I have seen. It was that to which the dying man looks when death approaches." Here begins the ascent to the lowest heaven, under the command of Ismāʿīl, who oversaw 12,000 angels, each with 12,000 angels under its command (Qurʾān 74:34: "And none knows the armies of God but God"). The angel Mālik, the keeper of Hell, showed him its flames. Muḥammad then continued his ascent to the second heaven, where he met Jesus and John, and then to the third, where he met Jacob, and to the fourth, where he met Idrīs (Enoch), and the fifth, where he met Aaron, and the sixth, where he met Moses, and finally to the seventh, where he met Abraham, and finally to paradise, where he saw a beautiful red-lipped woman before proceeding to the immortal mansion. There he saw "the lote-tree of the furthest boundary," the divine throne, a house called the *bayt al-maʾmūr*, considered the celestial counterpart to the Kaʿba, and entered the divine presence where he was given the prayers ordained for his community. The narrative goes on to relate that it was there that the duty of 50 prayers was laid upon Muslims, but when Muḥammad began his descent, Moses sent him back repeatedly until he had reduced the number of prayers to five (Ibn Ishaq 1955: 181–7). It is said that when Muḥammad returned to his bed after the journey, a tumbler of water that had been spilt when he arose from his bed had not yet completed running out, suggesting that the entire journey and its momentous experiences took place in the twinkle of an eye, in a time not of this time.

Muslims commemorate the occasion of Muḥammad's ascent through various ritual observances. Usually celebrated on 27 Rajab, ritual observances, which vary from region to region and from community to community, may entail fasting, recitations of the Qurʾān, readings from texts detailing the journey, lectures on its importance and meanings, poetry performances, and prayer, silent or communal. The *miʿrāj* legend inspired poets, artists, and thinkers through the ages, resulting in a significant amount of literature and art depicting, elaborating upon, and exploring the significance of the *miʿrāj*. Theologians, for instance, argued over whether Muḥammad's night journey was undertaken in spirit or entailed the body, since a *ḥadīth* reports ʿĀʾisha as commenting that Muḥammad's body was not missed during the night on which he experienced the ascent. Evidence of Muḥammad's high stature among all the prophets was found in the Qurʾanic verse stating that during the divine encounter, Muḥammad's eye did not rove (Q 53:17), suggesting that none other was able to behold the divine presence without flinching. The question has also been raised as to why Muḥammad did not remain in the divine presence, but rather chose to return to earth in order to communicate the divine message, thereby staking a claim to his mission to improve the lot of creation. The word *ʿabduhu* (God's servant) applied to Muḥammad in the Qurʾanic account of the *miʿrāj* has suggested to Muslims that despite his access to the divine, Muḥammad remained a created being. Thus, the story of the *miʿrāj* serves to reinforce the possibility for a human being to be graced with proximity to the divine, with Muḥammad serving as a model for this possibility. The circular dance of the Mevlevi tradition in Sufism has been described by its founder, the celebrated mystic poet Rūmī, as "a ladder that leads higher than the seventh sphere," since the whirling dervish's aim is to attain proximity to the divine being with Muḥammad as a spiritual model par excellence. Scholars have suggested that the *miʿrāj* legend was circulated in the Mediterranean lands during the middle ages and may have contributed to Dante's descriptions of heaven and hell (Schimmel 1985: ch. 9).

ʿĪd al-aḍḥā

ʿĪd al-aḍḥā, also called *ʿīd al-qurbān, ʿīd al-naḥr* (sacrificial feast) or *ʿīd al-kabīr* (major feast) or *bakrīʿīd* in South Asia, or *kurbān-bayram* in Central Asia, marks the ending of the rite of pilgrimage to Mecca and commemorates the Abrahamic sacrifice commanded by God. Abraham's difficult decision to comply with God's wishes and to sacrifice his son as a token of his unswerving loyalty, devotion, and obedience to God, is remembered during this *ʿīd* or celebration, during which an animal is slaughtered of which at least two-thirds is to be shared with the community, in remembrance of the goat or lamb that replaced Abraham's son on the sacrificial altar. The day occurs on 10 Dhū 'l-Ḥijja. One does not have to be a pilgrim in order to observe this commemorative celebration, and it is observed throughout the world where Muslims live. Pilgrims who have participated in the *ḥajj* or pilgrimage to Mecca will make their sacrifice in the valley of Mina. The festival lasts two or three days, and for this *ʿīd* as well as the one following, special *ʿīd* prayers are recited in lieu of one of the regular prayers at the commencement of the *ʿīd*. For both festivals, the *ʿīd al-aḍḥā* and the *ʿīd al-fiṭr*, Muslims will put on their best clothes, visit friends and family, exchange or give gifts, and celebrate the occasion in myriad ways.

ʿĪd al-fiṭr

ʿĪd al-fiṭr, the festival marking the ending of the period of fasting during the month of Ramaḍān, is also called the minor festival, *ʿīd al-saghīr*, even though it is celebrated with intense joyousness at having borne the hardship with equanimity of fasting for the entire duration of the month of Ramaḍān. It is celebrated on 1 Shawwāl and lasts two to three days. Muslims are enjoined to have paid their *zakāt* or religious dues by the time of its commencement, and the *ʿīd* begins with special prayers, as with *ʿīd al-aḍḥā*.

Muḥarram rites: ʿĀshūrāʾ and the tragedy at Karbala

Muḥarram is the first month of the Muslim lunar calendar; also the first month of the Jewish calendar. This month is significant for various reasons. The early Muslim community considered Muḥarram to be one of the four sacred months, hence its name, "that which is sacred," during which no blood could be shed. The first of the month is the New Year, not to be confused with the Persian New Year (*Nawrūz*), but rather, the first day of the new year according to the Muslim lunar calendar. The 10th of Muḥarram is significant to Sunnīs and the Shīʿa for entirely different reasons, although as a mark of respect to Jewish tradition due to its connection to Abraham, and as a mark of respect to the family of the Prophet, both communities remain mindful of the multiple reasons for which the day is commemorated.

For many pious Muslims regardless of whether they are Sunnī or Shīʿī, the 10th of Muḥarram is a day spent in fasting according to the Prophet's decision to adopt the Jewish day of atonement observed on 10th Tishri (the Jewish month), as a practice for Muslims, for whom this day is called ʿĀshūrāʾ. In Muḥammad's time, the Jewish practice of fasting from sunset to sunset was observed; however, the practice was made voluntary rather than obligatory when Muḥammad's relations with the Medinan Jews deteriorated. Since that time, fasting on the day itself, rather than from the sunset of the previous day to the sunset of the following day, is highly recommended rather than obligatory, and on this day the Kaʿba's doors are opened to visitors.

For Shīʿī Muslims, this day has additional significance as the day on which the Prophet's grandson Ḥusayn was martyred in the year 680 on the battlefield by Yazīd (r. 680–3), the son of Muʾāwiya, founder of the Umayyad dynasty, as he attempted to restore his claims to the caliphate. Ḥusayn, the son of the Prophet's daughter Fāṭima and his cousin ʿAlī, is held in great reverence by the Shīʿa as the holder of the Imāmate. This is a day of intense mourning for Shīʿīs, and pilgrimages are made to Karbala in Iraq, the town closest to the battlefield, especially to the shrine of Imām Ḥusayn, the place at which it is believed he was killed and where his decapitated bodily remains are buried.

The rites surrounding mourning for Ḥusayn are observed during the first 10 days of Muḥarram. During this time, the sufferings of Imām Ḥusayn and his entourage are recited in passion plays called *taʿziya* (offering condolences) or *rawḍa-khwānī*, which include elegiac chants called *nawḥa* or *marthiya*. These 10-day performances culminate in the story of Ḥusayn's martyrdom in a retelling that invokes expressions of profound sorrow among those present. Acts of mourning or *mātam* are performed, usually by men's guilds (*guruhan*), at religious assemblies (*majālis*) held at shrines called Ḥusayniyya in Iran or *ʿāshūrkhānas* or *imāmbāra* in India and Pakistan, many of which are located in either public spaces or in private homes. In such *majālis, marthiyas* or funeral laments are recited, followed by a sermon reflecting on the fateful events at Karbala and how the virtues displayed by those killed there may serve as guideposts for the faithful present at such gatherings. Ritual lamentation, termed *ʿazādī*, follows, with participants weeping as they remember the suffering of those at Karbala, culminating with ritual prayers.

Traditionally, sermons delivered, usually by a *dhākir* ("one who remembers"), detail the events leading up to the death of Ḥusayn. Although the following order is not always kept to and varies by location and the preference of the lamenter retelling the fateful events, often the first to third of Muḥarram will focus on the arrival of Ḥusayn at Karbala and his refusal to acquiesce to Yazīd. The fourth day is devoted to Hurr, the commander of the Umayyad army, who repented his opposition to the family of the Prophet and joined Ḥusayn. The fifth day celebrates the lives of Ḥusayn's nephews, his sister Zaynab's sons, Awn and Muḥammad, also martyred at Karbala. The sixth commemorates Ḥusayn's infant son ʿAlī Aṣghar, and also his 18-year-old son ʿAlī Akbar killed in battle. On the seventh day, the wedding of Ḥusayn's daughter Fāṭima Kubrā to his brother Ḥasan's son Qāsim is detailed in its poignancy, for Qāsim died soon thereafter on the battlefield, and the eighth day remembers the bravery of the water-carrier, ʿAbbās in his frantic search for water for the warriors and the holy family. On the ninth and tenth days, Ḥusayn's grisly martyrdom on Yazīd's orders at the hands of his commander Shimr is recalled amidst much lamentation. Aside from the sermons delivered during this period, the battle standards (singular: *ʿalam*, plural: *aʿlām*) of Ḥusayn and his fellow martyrs, and replicas of Ḥusayn's tomb are brought out from storage, and passion plays known as *taʿziya* depicting the tragic events at Karbala are performed over several days, moving the faithful to tears and cries of lamentation. The *ʿalams* often bear the shape of a hand or *panje*, with the names of the five holy persons (Muḥammad, ʿAlī, Fāṭima, Ḥasan and Ḥusayn) comprising the family of the Prophet or the *ahl al-bayt* ("people of the house") inscribed on the standard. Some standards also bear depictions of ʿAlī's sword, *Dhū ʾl-faqār*. Mourning ceremonies take the form of street processions, at which ritual performers will engage in acts of *mātam*, most often expressed through a stylized beating of the chest (*sīna-zan*) or through repetitive motions during which chains, sometimes fastened to razor blades or small knives, are struck on the ritual performer's back, drawing blood (*zanjīr-zan*), although such displays of devotion are increasingly being discouraged. Acts of *mātam* are performed to the rhythmic beats of chants.

Nawrūz, New Year

The festival of *Nawrūz* (literally "new day") is observed primarily by Shīʿī Muslims within the Iranian sphere of influence. Coinciding with the spring or vernal equinox, that is, the time when the sun enters the zodiacal sign of Aries, crosses the equator and the length of the day and night is equal in all parts of the earth, the date of *Nawrūz*, March 21 has been celebrated from ancient times to the present in Persian spheres of influence. The Achaemenid (559–330 BCE) and Sasanian (226–652 CE) kings celebrated the festival with public feasts and the giving of gifts, while the populace lit fires and sprinkled water on each other. Among the customs observed by the Sasanids the number seven figured prominently; for instance, seven kinds of seeds were sown in small containers; seven kinds of grain, along with seven kinds of twigs and seven silver coins were submitted to the king. This ancient memory is still preserved in modern-day Iran in the *haft-sīn*, where seven items beginning with the letter *sīn*, or s, are gathered together in the household, comprising apples, vinegar, garlic, sumac, sorbapple, silver coins, and fresh grass.

Under the Muslims, who vanquished the last of Sassanid rulers in 651, *Nawrūz* soon became invested with Islamic and specifically Shīʿī symbolic importance. The Shīʿī Imām Jaʿfar al-Ṣādiq (d. 765) established its importance to the Shīʿa with his statement: "And there is no *nawrūz* but that we have ordained that some divine felicity takes place therein because it is one of our days and the days of our Shīʿa." According to him, this day is associated with primordial time as the day of the primordial covenant recorded in Qurʾān 7:172 where God asked humanity collectively: "Am I not your Lord?" to which humanity replied in affirmation. It is the day on which the sun first rose at the dawn of creation, and in prophetic time, the day on which Noah's ark came to rest on Mount Judi, an event referred to in Qurʾān 11:44. The *Biḥār al-anwār*, an encyclopedic collection of Shīʿī *ḥadīth* prepared in the seventeenth century by Muḥammad Bāqir Majlisī (d. 1699), further reports on the authority of Imām Jaʿfar al-Ṣādiq that *nawrūz* was the day on which the Prophet designated his cousin and son-in-law, ʿAlī ibn Abī Ṭālib, as his successor and *amīr al-muʾminīn* (commander of the faithful). It is also the day on which the Prophet along with ʿAlī destroyed the idols in the Kaʿba, just as Abraham had destroyed idols on that same day many generations ago. Finally, *nawrūz* is recorded as the day on which the Qā'im or messiah will appear at the end of time and destroy the archenemy of justice, al-Dajjāl, at Kufa.

In commemorating the first day of spring and the religiously significant events associated with it, *Nawrūz* holds importance in both the natural seasonal order and the religious order, both of which are necessary to sustain the human being. In including that which is necessary for human physical well-being (spring makes possible the fruition of the harvest in the summer) and that which is necessary for spiritual growth and self-realization (revelation is a benefit to humankind and the guidance of the Imāms, according to the Shīʿa, is essential in understanding the meaning of revelation so as to attain a state of inner enlightenment), *nawrūz* marks the significance of new beginnings in both the outer (physical) and the inner (spiritual) worlds. The philosopher and poet Nāṣir-i Khusraw (d. *c.* 1074) made the analogy of the soul of a human being in this world as being like a tree in winter; if living, like the healthy tree, it has an "eye" watching for the advent of spring, or *nawrūz*.

In keeping with the theme of springtime – in the natural as well as in the spiritual order – preparations for *nawrūz* typically include the planting of grains in small containers. The resulting grass (*sabzī*) is a symbolic decoration gracing tables of offerings. Decorated eggs, along with fresh fruit, sweet baked goods and other offerings are all part of the elements of observing *nawrūz*, along with new clothing for members of the family. Visiting friends and relatives form part of the activities surrounding the celebration of the new year, as do the offering of special prayers. In Iran, the *Nawrūz* table of offerings in the household will likely include *sabzī, haft-sīn*, a mirror, a copy of the scripture observed by the household (not all Iranians are Muslims; there are Zoroastrian, Jewish, Christian and Bahá'í faithful as well), a bowl of water in which leaves and flowers are set afloat, along with the usual delectable sweet goods. The new year "season" lasts about 12 days, and on the 13th day, the *sabzī* is cast into running water, which, it is hoped, will remove the tribulations of the previous year.

Ritual as grounding

Cultural variations in the manner in which rites and rituals are performed serve to ground a Muslim within his or her larger geographical location and culture, even as the rituals and celebrations observed simultaneously create a common lexicon of beliefs and practices that is shared by Muslims worldwide. As beliefs, sacred narratives, and historical events are re-enacted and retold and commemorated in ritual action, celebration, dirge, and food, a sense of community organized around belief, values, and practices is passed down from generation to generation and is carried across borders and oceans through migration. In this a religious tradition finds both its anchor to the past and its continuance into the future, while negotiating the present.

References and further reading

Berg, C. C. (2004) "Sawm," *Encyclopaedia of Islam*, CD-ROM edition, Leiden: Brill.
Denny, F. M. (1994) *An Introduction to Islam*, New York: MacMillan.

Hodgson, M. G. S. (1974) *The Venture of Islam, Conscience and History in a World Civilization*, vol. 2, Chicago: University of Chicago Press.
Ibn Ishaq (1955) *The Life of Muhammad: A Translation of Ibn Isḥāq's Sīrat Rasūl Allāh*, A. Guillaume, trans., London: Oxford University Press.
Ivanow, W., trans. (1949) *Six Chapters or Shish Fasl by Nasir-i Khusraw*, Bombay: The Ismaili Society.
Lawson, B. T. (1995) "Nawruz" in J. L. Esposito, ed., *The Oxford Encyclopedia of the Modern Islamic World*, New York: Oxford University Press, vol. 3: 243–4.
Momen, M. (1985) *An Introduction to Shīʿī Islam*, New Haven, London: Yale University Press.
Pinault, D. (1992) *The Shiites: Ritual and Popular Piety in a Muslim Community*, New York: St. Martin's Press.
Schimmel, A. (1985) *And Muhammad is His Messenger*, Chapel Hill: University of North Carolina Press.
Schubel, V. J. (1993) *Religious Performance in Contemporary Islam: Shīʿī Devotional Rituals in South Asia*, Columbia: University of South Carolina Press.
Yarshater, E. (1993) "Nawruz" in M. Eliade, ed., *The Encyclopaedia of Religion*, New York: MacMillan Publishing Company, vol. 10: 341–2.

RITES OF PASSAGE

Zayn Kassam

The first words a Muslim newborn is likely to hear at birth are the *shahāda*, whispered into its ear by a proud parent, followed by the call to prayer. The opening verses of the Qur'ān (*sūrat al-fātiḥa*) are then recited. An infant's palate is sweetened with a date, harking back to an account in which the Prophet is said to have done so with a newborn presented to him, a practice known as *taḥnik*. On the seventh day, the child is named, and sometimes the child's head is shaved and a sheep or ram sacrificed on behalf of the newborn, a practice known as *ʿaqīqa* and thought to date back to the days of the Prophet. After 40 days, the mother is considered to be able to resume her ritual duties once again, from which she was exempted during pregnancy, birth, and recovery.

At puberty, male children are circumcised (although in many parts, especially North America, Muslims will circumcise their male children at birth, utilizing hospital procedures, or seven days after birth alongside the naming and other ceremonies). Although circumcision (called *khitān* for males, and *khafḍ* for females; also dubbed *ṭahār* or purification) is not mentioned in the Qur'ān for either males or females, the practice entered Muslim legal ritual codes by the time of the jurist al-Shāfiʿī (d. 820), and appears to be a pre-Islamic practice from evidence found in pre-Islamic poetry. In the *ḥadīth* literature, there are references to Abraham's circumcision, suggesting that Muslim observation is in emulation of Abraham. With the exception of al-Shāfiʿī, who considers both male and female circumcision obligatory, the other legal schools consider male circumcision *sunna* (that is, in accordance with the practice of the Prophet), while female circumcision is considered honorable (but not obligatory). There are wide regional differences in how and when male circumcision is performed: often, the ceremony is conducted on the seventh day after birth alongside the *ʿaqīqa*, or on the 40th day after birth, or between the age of 3 and 5 in North Africa, or at puberty in Mecca and Egypt. Often the child is dressed as a bridegroom (in Southeast Asia, especially Java) or as a girl (Egypt); on the day of circumcision, the male child is sometimes placed on horseback in a procession replete with musicians, making it a ceremonial affair (as in Mecca). In parts of North Africa, communal circumcision ceremonies may be held every two years, leading to a range in the ages of the boys being circumcised.

Although female circumcision is considered recommendable but not obligatory in Islamic law, the earliest legal documents suggest a small removal of the skin in the highest part of the genitalia, far removed from the rather extreme lengths of circumcision found practiced along the Nilotic region. Both male and female circumcision practices predate Islam; however, they appear to have been incorporated into Islamic practice due to local custom. The religious antecedents for female circumcision are attributed to a *ḥadīth* in which Abraham asked Hagar to circumcise herself in order to appease Sarah's desire to have Abraham shed Hagar's blood, as part of the rivalry between mistress and slave. Regardless, it appears that Muslim appropriation of pre-existent North and East African practices in this regard are now being addressed through recommendations that there are no religious bases for the custom, in an attempt to curtail the more extreme forms of the practice that have deleterious effects on the health of women.

Regarding marriage, the Qur'ān recommends abstinence until a male has the means to marry: "Marry the spouseless among you, and your slaves and handmaidens that are righteous; if they are poor, God will enrich them of His bounty. . . . And let those who find not the means to marry be abstinent till God enriches them of His bounty" (Q. 24: 32, 33). Marriage is recommended in the *ḥadīth* literature, in which Muḥammad is reported as saying, "Marriage is half the religion." Celibacy was not encouraged, and the mystics or Sūfīs, even while they practiced austerities to discipline the body, were known to marry and have children. In the Qur'ān, while marriage is encouraged, it is considered a legal contract and not a sacral act. Thus, many of the verses in the Qur'ān pertaining to marriage were regulatory in nature and became the basis of the Islamic legal regimes governing family law. As a result, Muslims observe the marital regimes in their countries of residence, and these regimes differ in the extent to which they incorporate Islamic law. Depending on where they live in the world, Muslims may or may not engage in polygamy; a wife may or may not have the right to initiate divorce, and child custody laws will vary according to the legal regime of the country in which the Muslim lives. In Muḥammad's own time, the Qur'anic regulations pertaining to marriage were aimed at improving women's position, although today activists pursuing legal reform in Muslim countries have identified the marital regime as an area deserving attention, all the more so since the *sharīʿa* family laws are no longer as beneficial to women and children in society in the manner they once were. Thus, family legal codes are undergoing revision spearheaded by Muslim activists in many Muslim nations including Tunisia, Morocco, Egypt, Indonesia, Pakistan, and Iran. Muslims in Europe, North America, and Australia follow the legal regimes of their adopted lands, in all of which polygamy is forbidden.

Whether a marriage is something agreed upon by the families or whether the bridge and the groom happened to meet and fall in love and decide to marry, the protocol that is followed is that the details of the marriage are arranged between the families of the bride (usually her *walī*, or guardian) and the groom. Preparations for the marriage may include an exchange of gifts between the two families, ceremonies in which the marriage is agreed upon between the two parties, bridal parties at which a trousseau for the bride is gaily packaged and the bride is hennaed, with ceremonies in which the groom is given a bachelor's party and often also similarly prepared for the wedding. The marriage ceremony proper entails the enunciation and signing of the *nikāḥ* (or marriage contract), often accompanied by a recitation of verses from the Qur'ān, to be followed by local customary observances such as an *ʿurs* or wedding celebration replete with musicians, dancers, and food to be shared by all, followed by traditional rites marking the bride's joining the groom's family as one of their own. Some regions ritually mark whether the bride is a virgin or not by displaying the bloody sheet from the wedding night as proof, while others consider the bride's virginity a matter of privacy between the bride and the groom, depending on local custom or region. A key feature of Muslim marriages is the bridal gift, known as *mahr*, a gift given to the bride by the groom's family that is hers to keep, even after divorce. Practice regarding the *mahr* varies widely depending on the locale and the culture; as with other practices, it may be abused and revert to the groom's family, and often is gifted as a promissory note which is not honored should the marriage dissolve. However, it is often given in the form of gold jewelry or other assets that become the bride's to keep. The marriage also extends the wife's *maḥram*, or list of relatives to include in-laws with whom it is appropriate to maintain social relations (and without whose presence a woman may not entertain or otherwise socially interact with non-related males). Again, this is a feature of Muslim social life that is observed in relative degrees depending on the culture and location of the Muslim; in some societies it is observed with far greater force than in others.

At the time of death, if possible, a Muslim is positioned facing Mecca, and the prayers recited around the deathbed will include the chapter titled *Yā Sīn* (*sūra* 36) from the Qur'ān. A popular *ḥadīth* recommends the recitation of this chapter to have one's past sins forgiven. A meditation on punishment for evil deeds done and rewards rendered for good deeds, the chapter contains verses such as 36:82: "Therefore glory be to Him in Whose hand is the dominion over all things!" Upon death, a ritual washing called *ghusl* is performed three times, using soap and water, to which scent is added for the final washing. The parts that are normally washed in preparation for prayer are cleansed first, followed by the remainder of the body. The body is not embalmed, and once cleaned, is wrapped in a white shroud. A special prayer *ṣalāt* (*ṣalāt al-janāza*) is recited over the body before it is buried, preferably not in a coffin, often placed on its right side with the head facing Mecca. Family members and friends will gather either at the home of the deceased or in a mosque to recite prayers between the time of the death and the burial ceremony; thereafter, prayers will be recited for 40 days, after which special prayers are recited every month until the end of the first year, and thereafter, yearly on the anniversary of the death.

15

SUFISM

Art Buehler

> The human family is one body with many parts – creations arising from one unseen essence. Any harm to any part summons an awakening – a disease and a healing response from all parts. You who fail to feel the pain of others cannot be called truly human.
>
> Saʿdī (Shiraz, Iran, thirteenth century), quote found on the entrance to the Hall of Nations of the United Nations building in New York)

Historically the word *ṣūfī* was first used in an eighth-century Islamic context for ascetics wearing woolen cloaks – like their Christian counterparts – in the deserts of the Near East. Eventually by the tenth century this activity developed into a branch of the Islamic religious sciences which has become known in the West as Sufism. In the Sunnī world (the mainstream Muslim community) "the process of becoming a Ṣūfī" (*taṣawwuf*) and in the Iranian Shīʿī world "theoretical mysticism" (*ʿirfān*) are conflated by the English term Sufism. The activities of Ṣūfīs are generally acknowledged by historians to be responsible for the spread of Islam in the eastern Islamic world, including present-day Turkey, India, Indonesia, and Africa. Investigations into the historical processes of Islamization, still going on today, indicate that the Ṣūfī message is more expansive yet inclusive of the doctrinal, orthopraxic religion known as Islam. That is, although Sufism historically has been practiced almost exclusively by Muslims, it has also gone beyond the human-created boundaries of the religion of Islam to include anyone who seeks to submit to God, the technical meaning of *muslim* in Arabic.

The practice of Sufism involves the inner aspect of *islām* (the submission to God/ultimate reality), including mysticism/spiritual transformation and ethics/character development. To the extent that Ṣūfīs desire closeness or intimacy with God, Sufism can be roughly translated as Islamic mysticism. Insofar as these interior experiences and transformations are not apparent to others (in contrast to woolen clothing) Sufism can be said to be the esoteric aspect of Islam. From the mystical perspective, Sufism is the study and cultivation of one's actual experience with God. In a more poetic fashion, one could say that Sufism is the intentional act of plunging into a wave from the Infinite Ocean and being drawn back with it toward the Eternal Source.

The goal for Ṣūfīs is to become a complete, perfected human being. To be whole or complete means to realize the fullness of our own nature, physically, emotionally, mentally, psychically, and spiritually. Sufism is about cultivating unconditional love and becoming truly human. From a Ṣūfī perspective this comes about by realizing who one is ultimately, which is the total reflection and image of God's names and attributes. Ṣūfīs would assert that this wholeness is a human being's natural state and that an experience of fragmented selves is an indication of separateness from God. To embark upon the path of Sufism one usually finds a teacher or *shaykh*, formally makes a commitment through an initiation ritual, and then proceeds to incorporate a contemplative discipline into one's life.

Another oft-mentioned triad associated with explicating Sufism is Islamic law (*sharīʿa*), the Ṣūfī path (*ṭarīqa*), and reality (*ḥaqīqa*). For Muslims, Islamic law represents the wide path outlining (what are perceived to be) the timeless God-given rules that govern everyday life for all humans. It is the path leading to salvation. The Ṣūfī path is a narrower path leading to reality, the experience of the Ultimate. These three interrelated aspects of Islam have been depicted as the one circle of Islamic law with a multiplicity of radii or Ṣūfī paths leading to the reality at the center. In transformative terms, Islamic law is medical science, the Ṣūfī path is preventing disease and taking medicine, and experiencing reality is eternally perfect health. The latter metaphor implies a necessary doctor or guide who has eternally perfect health. These triads clearly show the role of Islamic ritual practices in Sufism.

A Ṣūfī's experience-based religious authority has often been contested by jurists focusing on Islamic law whose knowledge is based upon book learning (though one can be both a Ṣūfī and a jurist). Jurists are interested in the external symbols and outward behavior that are associated with maintaining and outwardly legitimizing Islamic social structures through a system of law, schools, and mosques. For this reason their activities and interests overlap considerably with those of the rulers who have the power to enforce such concerns and who need such legitimacy to keep their power. It is the jurists (often called *ʿulamāʾ*) who justify war in the name of *jihād* and who provide the basis of salvation to give meaning for performing such endeavors (martyrs go immediately to heaven). This outer level supplies soteriological formulae, important psychologically, to enforce the dictates of society (if you do these things you go to heaven, otherwise you go to hell). This is the "stick approach" to human psychology (versus the "carrot approach" of Sufism). The jurist's expression of religion integrates and stabilizes society. Islamic law is the "kernel" that protects, legitimizes, and tempers the precious "seed" of spiritual practice.

This spiritual practice is required for the integration and stabilization of the outer social structure and presumes movement, change, and transformation within the individual. Instead of *jihād* as war, Ṣūfīs stress the inner struggling (*jihād*) in the path of God, controlling the desires and ignorance of one's lower carnal nature (*nafs*). The transformation process implies an unfolding, a transcending of prior states and perceptions. Often this transformation in the Ṣūfī environment is associated with the spiritual experiences in conjunction with performance of Ṣūfī contemplative practices.

One who had certainty through direct intuitive knowledge of God overshadowed ordinary jurists whose book knowledge had to rely on long chains of transmitters, some of whom might not have been reliable. In the words of Abū Saʿīd-i Abū ʾl-Khayr (d. 1049), "Having seen, who needs reports?" Speaking from the depths of spiritual experience, Abū Yazīd Bisṭāmī (d. *c.* 874) proclaims, "You have had your knowledge from a dead man who had it from a dead man while we had our knowledge from the living one who never dies." As jurists maintain the legitimacy of social structure, Ṣūfīs are involved in a complementary process of transformation and anti-structure, which is required for a dynamic integration and stabilization of the outer social structure.

Practicing Ṣūfīs work and live in the everyday world with an emphasis on ritual purity, the segregation of sexes, and a plethora of utterly mundane details. Yet, it is precisely the genius of Sufism that enables the life of the ordinary householder to be imbued with spirituality. Although Sufism is the mystical dimension of Islam, this aspect is only a minuscule slice of what Sufism means to contemporary Muslims who visit Ṣūfīs, both dead and alive. A tour of Ṣūfī lodges in the Islamic world demonstrates that the primary activities of Ṣūfīs are assisting believers in their worldly affairs, counseling them in mental and physical health problems, and making amulets to protect them. Most likely only a minority of those going to Ṣūfī *shaykh*s have ever yearned for mystical experience (even though those relatively few had importance beyond their numbers). Few contemporary *shaykh*s outside the West have emphasized a contemplative discipline and guided others along the Ṣūfī path. The scholarly and popular Western notion that simply equates Ṣūfīs with mystics is only a partial story of Ṣūfī activity.

How is Sufism central to the practice of Islam? The easiest way to answer this is to quote the famous *ḥadīth* of Muḥammad known as Gabriel's *ḥadīth*. It is so famous that it is the first *ḥadīth* in some *ḥadīth* collections. In shortened form, it tells about a man with very white clothing and very black hair coming up to the Prophet and his companions. No mark of travel was visible on him, and no one recognized him. Sitting down before the Prophet he said,

> "Tell me Muḥammad about submission to God (*islām*)." He replied, "Submission means that you should bear witness that there is no god but God and that Muḥammad is God's messenger, that you should perform the ritual prayer, pay alms, fast during Ramadan, and make the pilgrimage to the House if you are able to go there." The man said, "You have spoken the truth." Then he said, "Now tell me about faith (*īmān*)." Muḥammad replied, "Faith means that you have faith in God, his angels, his books, his messengers, and the last day and that you have faith in the measuring out, both its good and its evil." Remarking that the Prophet had spoken the truth, he then said, "Now tell me about doing what is beautiful (*iḥsān*)." Muḥammad replied, "Doing what is beautiful means that you should worship God as if you see him, for even if you do not see him, he sees you." When the man left, Muḥammad informed his astonished companions that the angel Gabriel had come to teach them about their religion.
>
> (Tabrīzī 1965: I, 5)

Here was religion in a nutshell: what one does – *islām* – what one thinks – *īmān* – and what one intends in one's heart – *iḥsān*. The point here is that each of these three religious dimensions is interconnected with each other dimension like a tree's roots, branches, and fruit. Being a perfected or complete human being involves an integration of these three dimensions. Sufism is that third dimension, the fruit of action and faith. Those who deny Sufism, for example, the Wahhābīs of Arabia, do not recognize this integral heart dimension in Islam.

Such a three-dimensional conception of Islam assumes that different persons have varying potential and ability for spiritual accomplishment. The vast majority of Muslims seek salvation through their daily practices, informed by a faith commitment. Sufism, on the other hand, encompasses these activities working toward the field of consciousness and experience represented by acting in a beautiful manner. Such an enterprise assumes a firm foundation in faith and in the practice of submitting to God before achieving an extraordinary degree of proximity to God. Surely not all who call themselves Ṣūfīs are able to achieve this advanced goal and not all of the few who reach this stage are necessarily Ṣūfīs.

Several books could be written on Ṣūfī activity in the contemporary world. Political leaders in the Middle East have Ṣūfī advisors – some are even Ṣūfīs themselves, for example, Turgut Özal, a former Turkish Prime Minister. University professors teach required literature classes using Ṣūfī materials that do not have the outward appearance of Sufism, for example Asad ʿAlī at Damascus University. Ṣūfī musicians have shared their music and feelings with other musicians from around the world, as in the collaboration between Mickey Hart and Hamza al-Din, for the benefit of millions of listeners who have no idea that there are underlying Ṣūfī connections. Ṣūfīs seldom attract attention to themselves, quietly working to make the world a better place in whatever walk of life they happen to be. Historically Ṣūfīs have been involved with resistance to colonial incursions, for example, the Sanūsī lineage in Libya and the Naqshbandī and Qādirī lineages in Chechnya. Ṣūfīs can be found in all walks of life in all spheres of human activity.

Outer rituals in the public domain are what people usually see and associate with Sufism, for example, *qawwālī* music from Pakistan, video clips of the "Whirling Dervishes," or visiting shrines of deceased Ṣūfīs. If one goes to visit a prominent Ṣūfī in an Islamic country one can expect to witness healing rituals, psychological counseling, and the dispensing of amulets. For those in harmony with the local culture and who express good intentions, the doors of a Ṣūfī lodge are usually wide open. An insider is defined usually as someone who has cultivated a formal relationship with a Ṣūfī, having gone through some kind of an initiation ritual and making a commitment to that Ṣūfī *shaykh* and his (sometimes her) contemplative practices of the lineage. Usually for Ṣūfīs the intention is to get closer to God – to experience a personal transformation. The practice of Sufism is learning by imitating the personal model of the *shaykh* first and foremost. Though books can be involved (and there are thousands to choose from), the primary focus is on experience instead of another set of mental constructs.

Historical snapshots of Sufism

Even during Muḥammad's lifetime some of his followers desired to enter into a more intimate relationship with God beyond performing required ritual practices. Over the next three centuries a discipline of pious self-examination and refined religious psychology came into existence. The specialized technical vocabulary of this discipline, now known as Sufism, came directly from the Qur'ān. Muslims who engaged in these pious activities, in addition to the required religious practices of the wider Muslim community, became known as Ṣūfīs. In short, Sufism can be both an Islamic religious science and the collective spiritual practices of a person who desires to have a more encompassing experience of submitting to God. Ṣūfī practice began in the Arab-speaking world and is coterminous with the worldwide spread of Islam itself. Indeed, there is considerable evidence that Ṣūfīs were directly involved in the spread of Islam in the eastern Islamic world, a dynamic that will be discussed later.

Lineage is important to understand the construction of Sufism since the tenth century. Creating spiritual lineages, continuous chains of pious Ṣūfīs leading back to the Prophet, Ṣūfīs legitimized their authority and met juristic challenges to their authority. For jurists the lineage of transmitting authorities (*isnād*) defines the legitimacy of a sound *ḥadīth* (the recorded saying of Muḥammad). Thus, by the eleventh century a number of international pan-Islamic Ṣūfī lineages named after their founder figures came into existence, including the Kāzarūniyya or Murshidiyya from Abū Isḥāq Kāzarūnī (d. 1033 in Shiraz) and the Qadiriyya lineage from ʿAbd al-Qādir al-Jīlānī (d. 1166 in Baghdad) the most widely spread lineage in the Islamic world. Other major lineages include the Suhrawardī lineage from Abū Ḥafṣ Suhrawardī (d. 1234 in Baghdad); the Chishtī lineage in India from Muʿīn al-Dīn Chishtī (d. 1236 in Ajmer, Rajasthan, India); the Naqshbandī lineage from Bahāʾ al-Dīn Naqshband (d. 1389 Bukhara, Uzbekistan); and the Mevlevī lineage from Jalāl al-Dīn Rūmī (d. 1273 in Konya, Turkey), so named because Mevlānā (*mawlānā*) is the honorific title given to Rūmī in Turkish.

These lineages prospered through the institutionalization of subsidized Ṣūfī lodges throughout the Islamic world where Ṣūfīs endeavored to replicate the model community of the Prophet and his companions. A set of rituals governed life in this new institution, including initiation, special contemplative exercises, the bestowal of Ṣūfī robes, and a set of elaborate ritual injunctions governing every aspect of life – justified on the basis of the prophetic *sunna*, what the Prophet allegedly did. The development of the Ṣūfī lodge began in Nishapur, Iran, where the local elites could channel resources into religious schools, *madrasa*s, and Ṣūfī lodges. In this way they could recruit and train new members and continue to stay in control by maintaining their elite power and prestige.

One crucial function of the Ṣūfī *shaykh* was his being a mediator between God and human beings, and as such he needed to appear aloof from any particular worldly faction, making a lodge outside the city an ideal location. Since he was a spiritual mentor to people from all strata of society, including the influential and powerful, the initiatory bond set him up to have mediating powers throughout society. Add to this relationship a perceived ability to manifest supernatural powers and each Ṣūfī initiation becomes a serious bond indeed. Because Ṣūfīs embodied the figure of the Prophet, they could command even more obedience and compliance. By the tenth century the combination of the Ṣūfī manipulation of supernatural power and the ability to intercede with God on behalf of others motivated sultans and other wealthy figures to establish pious trusts for the Ṣūfī lodges. In return the donors stipulated that Ṣūfīs regularly offer prayers on the benefactor's behalf. This scenario was often repeated in the settled agrarian areas throughout the pre-modern Islamic world – but resisted by nomadic tribes, e.g., in Central Asia. As Ṣūfīs patterned their micro-communities on the sacred community of Muḥammad and his companions, they succeeded beyond their wildest dreams. Ṣūfī lodges, often in combination with tomb-shrines, spread from Iran to North Africa, Turkey, Central Asia, India, and Indonesia.

This special community, or *communitas* in Victor Turner's words, made Ṣūfīs prime agents in the Islamization of society. On one hand, the veneration of Muḥammad and his central place in the hearts of Muslims created an environment parallel to the early charismatic community in Arabia. On the other hand, the Ṣūfī lodge became a mediating place to incorporate popular local culture into an increasingly Islamic society. The legend of the prophetic Golden Age and the "enchanted universe" of local culture met in the Ṣūfī lodge. Whether a literate practicing Muslim or a non-Muslim peasant passing through the tomb-shrine, the lodge managed to accommodate divergent religious tendencies by exposing visitors to an intensified Islamic ritual environment where the Ṣūfī master harnessed supernatural power for the benefit of all. In the process entirely new elements were added to the Islamic mystical repertoire, for example, the practice of visualizing the *shaykh*, listening to ecstasy-producing music, extended periods of seclusion (even upside down), and holding the breath while meditating.

An example of the complex conversion process is the role that Bābā Farīd's (d. 1265) shrine, located in the present-day town of Pakpattan, Pakistan, had in slowly Islamizing the Panjab region from its prior Hindu orientation. When he arrived in Pakpattan early in the thirteenth century there was already a communal mosque and a judge to rule according to Islamic law, appointed by the Muslim governor in a neighboring town. In addition to his small circle of initiates, Bābā Farīd daily attracted huge crowds coming to get amulets, small pieces of paper with Qur'anic verses believed to be additionally blessed by him in his role as one of "God's friends." (This continues today at most shrines in the Panjab and requires teams of people writing these amulets just like it did then.) In return, the devotees gave gifts to the shrine, which then would be distributed among those living at the shrine and other needy devotees. When Bābā Farīd died his son presided over a huge complex – believed to be especially blessed by Bābā Farīd's burial there and by his blood relatives living there. Hundreds of thousands of people each year still visit Bābā Farīd's grave for blessings and intercession with God. Although Bābā Farīd avoided contact with rulers, in less than a century after his death the reigning Tughluq rulers in Delhi were given turbans by Bābā Farīd's grandson and in turn generously patronized the shrine. In the next generation Bābā Farīd's descendants were appointed to high government offices and the shrine became more dependent on court patronage.

Subsequently villagers using their own resources began to build subsidiary shrines in the central Panjab, establishing Bābā Farīd's spiritual authority throughout the countryside. Over a period of four centuries the nomadic Jat tribes in the Panjab had become successful peasant farmers claiming that Bābā Farīd (that is, his spirit) had been responsible for their conversion. The shrine rituals and celebrations gave the neighboring Jat leaders and their followers access to Islam in a sacred ritual package of imperial Mughal glory, without needing to submit directly to the leaders in Delhi. From the fourttenth century the clans regularly gave brides to the male descendants of Bābā Farīd. Over a period of 400 years the combination of political, economic, kinship, and religious ties with Bābā Farīd's shrine integrated the Jat clans into a larger Islamic culture while preserving their local identities, until eventually members of the Jat clans identified themselves in Muslim terms. Conversion happened slowly and sporadically over a long period as in other parts of the (now) Islamic world.

The diversity of Sufism can be seen in a snapshot of Ottoman Sufism. First there are the wandering dervishes of the fourteenth century who appealed to the nomadic Turcomens (emigrating from the present-day Turkmenistan) who, like the Jats in the Panjab, were becoming assimilated into a sedentary peasant lifestyle in eastern

Anatolia. Baraq Bābā Tokatī (d. 1307–8) wore only a red loincloth and a turban with two buffalo horns stuck in it while blowing a horn or playing a drum and dancing in the street with his entourage of disciples. It appears that he performed the Islamic ritual prayers but did not fast during Ramaḍān. His antinomian belief in reincarnation did not fit into any Islamic paradigm. Other Ṣūfīs, wandering Qalandars, some with all the hair on their body shaved and others with matted long braids, ranged all the way from Central Asia through India to present-day Turkey and apparently regularly behaved in a scandalous and deviant manner wherever they went, including the consumption of wine and hashish in public. These are some examples of Ṣūfī fringe elements, but elements that nonetheless contributed to the long-term Islamization of Anatolia.

Ṣūfīs also were involved with protest politics and rebellions. As Shī'ī Ṣūfī lineages grew popular in sixteenth-century Anatolia there were clear political overtones. What made these Shī'ī lineages different from the mainstream Sunni Ṣūfī lineages mentioned above was the glorification, even deification, of 'Alī, the fourth caliph after Muḥammad died in 632. 'Alī is often the focus of devotional piety for Shī'īs, who believe that he should have been the primary successor to Muḥammad. This politico-religious disagreement in the seventh century continued (and to this day continues) to have political ramifications. This is one reason why the Ottomans had conflicts with the neighboring Safavid empire (who had violently enforced Shi'ism on Iran in the sixteenth century). Many Shī'ī Ṣūfī groups in Anatolia (some actively supported by the Safavids) rebelled against the Ottomans, who quickly saw any group with Shī'ī tendencies as a political threat.

An interesting twist to this saga is the Bektāshī Ṣūfī lineage (whose members sometimes also rebelled against the Ottoman government), named after the founder figure, Ḥajjī Bektāsh (d. 1271 in Hacibektas), whose teacher was a wandering Qalandar. It is still a very popular Turkish lineage with many Shī'ī and Christian devotional elements. For example, in the Bektāshī initiation ceremony known as *aynicem*, wine and bread is used to remember Ḥusayn's martyrdom. Ḥusayn, the Prophet Muḥammad's grandson, was brutally killed on the plains of Karbala in 680 and commemorating his martyrdom is a central event for Iranian Shī'īs. Parallels with Christian practices include ablution to cleanse sins before the *aynicem*, similar to Christian baptism, celibate priests, and Bektāshī versions of confession and penitence. Like the Christian Trinity, the Bektāshīs have God, Muḥammad, and 'Alī. Bektāshī Ṣūfī practices have accommodated Christian ideas and practices just as 1,000 years earlier Christians had adapted pagan practices. By the fifteenth century the Janissaries, an elite core of Ottoman soldiers, all had Bektāshī affiliations. This lasted until 1826 when the Janissaries were disbanded and the Bektāshī lineage was temporarily outlawed. It continues to flourish today in Turkey.

Many major Sunnī Ṣūfī lineages in the Ottoman empire became an integral part of Otttoman culture, for example the Naqshbandiyya who remain politically influential to this day. The Qādiriyya are also well represented. One special Turkish sub-lineage of the Qādiriyya, the Bayrāmiyya named after Ḥajjī Bayrām Walī (d. 1430 in Ankara), has been popular in Turkey. The Halvetiyye (Khalwatiyya) *tarikat*, founded in Tabriz, Iran, by 'Umar Khalwatī (d. 1397 in Tabriz), spread to Anatolia. The founder figure of one of its sub-lineages, the Sha'bāniyya, is Sha'bān Walī (d. 1568 in Kastamonu) who is celebrated, along with Jalāl al-Dīn Rūmī, Ḥajjī Bektāsh, and Ḥajjī Bayrām, as one of the "four poles" of Anatolian Sufism. They, like Bābā Farīd's perceived role in the Panjab, are attributed with Islamicizing Anatolia. These "four poles" parallel the *Wali Sanga*, the Nine Holy Men of Java, who are attributed with the Islamicization of Indonesia during the same period.

In the Indonesian case, the Islam taught to the first people on the Indonesian archipelago was very likely in the package of Ṣūfī ideas and practices – some have suggested that these Ṣūfīs came with the Indian Muslim merchants as early as the thirteenth century. By the seventeenth century there are full legendary accounts of the *Wali Sanga*, whose graves have continued to be places of pilgrimage. These are accounts of Ṣūfīs (like similar accounts in India) overcoming the magic of Hindus and Buddhists and miracle stories of kings becoming Muslims through a vision, a dream, or the visit of a wandering Ṣūfī. The most famous of these nine holy men is Sunan Kalijaga who is said to have been responsible for the conquering of the Hindu kingdom of Majapahit and who is said to have founded the Muslim kingdom of Demak, acting as a spiritual guide. An entire 200-year process of Islamization in Java is attributed to Sunan Kalijaga, who is the founder-figure for Javanese Islamic culture. Thus Javanese puppet theatre (*wayang*) and the ritual meal (*salametan*) are attributed to him. Although scholars lack the kind of historical records extant in India and Turkey to piece together the Indonesian Islamization process, Indonesia has the largest Muslim population of any nation in the world today. Ṣūfīs clearly facilitated the process of Islamization.

Deniers of Sufism

Like in other religions, mystical perspectives and experiences can often threaten the dogmatic and political status quo. In mainstream Islam and in the Qur'ān, God is usually conceived as transcendent. Ṣūfī experience, however, includes what Ṣūfīs interpret as the immanent experience of God, which jurists often interpret as idolatry. Second, if God is beyond good and evil as conceived by many Muslim theologians then it is a small step for the Perfected Human, who has the attributes of God in human form, to claim he or she has transcended good and evil. Historically, persons with such ideas were punished severely even if they publicly insinuated a possibility of going beyond Islamic law since these ideas threatened social stability. Another point of contention is between the rank of prophets and holy people like Ṣūfīs. In Sunnī dogma prophets are ontologically superior to other human beings. As a result, jurists strongly denounced any Ṣūfīs who affirmed that anyone could be superior to Muḥammad. In the context of the master – disciple relationship it is natural to respect and even venerate one's spiritual mentor. Veneration of the Ṣūfī master, whether dead or alive, has always been suspect to certain segments of the Muslim community since it runs the risk of becoming a quasi-divinization of another human being. Like Protestant Christians, many Muslims, jurists or not, reject the Ṣūfī notion that there can be mediation between God and humanity. These tensions continue to the present day.

In the past century this difference of perspective has gone beyond tensions, unfortunately, to all-out war in some cases. The rivalry revolves around the control of religious symbols and authority. Ṣūfīs have controlled much property (as they still do in Pakistan and Senegal) and have had a large mass following – putting them into positions of political power like the descendants of Bābā Farīd. When another group wants to take power their anti-Ṣūfī stance makes political sense. The Ibn Saʿūd tribe with its Wahhābī ideology had been seeking to dominate the Arabian Peninsula since the eighteenth century. They finally had their chance with the dismemberment of the Ottoman empire after World War I. Hundreds of thousands of Muslims were killed in this military–ideological alliance. They successfully (with the exception of the Kaʿba and Muḥammad's tomb) obliterated almost all tombs in Arabia – particularly those of Ṣūfīs or Shīʿī *Imāms*. Ṣūfīs who did not flee were among the primary targets. In 1925 Mustafa Kemal Atatürk, the new leader of the secular republic of Turkey, banned Ṣūfī activity and public performance of their rituals. Ṣūfī lodges were taken over by the Republican government. Sufism is still de facto illegal in both these countries.

Sufism in the West

In the West Ṣūfī activity is flourishing and Ṣūfī teachers are seen first and foremost as spiritual teachers. Even though non-Western teachers still teach, Western Ṣūfīs are fulfilling all the roles of spiritual teachers who are in the process of adapting Ṣūfī teachings to the needs of modern Europeans and Americans. As a frame of reference, a genuinely Western version of Sufism is emerging throughout the Western world. This is true for other spiritual teachings also. There is a greater variety of spiritual teachers in the West than has ever existed before and more pioneering spiritual work being done in the San Francisco Bay area than in any other comparable region in the world. Sufism has its niche along with all the other mystical traditions that used to be located predominantly in the "East."

This new, modern configuration of cross-fertilization affects Ṣūfī teaching and means that notions of Sufism have to be expanded even more. The first such notion is that of the relationship between Islam and Sufism. Historically the vast majority of Ṣūfīs – 95 percent at least – have been practicing Muslims. In India, Africa, and Indonesia there continue to be non-Muslims initiated into Ṣūfī lineages, who are being taught the full range of Ṣūfī practices. This even includes the Indian Naqshbandiyya, who place high importance on the assiduous performance of Sunnī religious ritual – as evidenced in Irena Tweedie's experiences with her Hindu Naqshbandī teacher in Kanpur, India, and her subsequent book, *Daughter of Fire* (1986). As already discussed, Sufism encompasses a large spectrum of perspectives and practices as varied as the Islamic world itself.

There is a tendency in the West not to require those practicing Sufism to be formal Muslims in belief or ritual action. Many who do participate in these groups *are* formal Muslims and the teachings are in accordance with Ṣūfī teachings, which in turn are harmonious with a universal Islamic message based upon the Qur'ān and *ḥadīth*. This approach was pioneered by one of the first Ṣūfīs to come to the West, ʿInāyat Khān. He came from Hyderabad, Deccan, in southern India to the USA in 1910, following the command of his teacher, Saʿīd Abū Hāshim Madanī, to harmonize the East and the West with the harmony of his music and spread the wisdom of Sufism abroad.

ʿInāyat Khān's brand of Sufism is very different from Indian Chishtī Ṣūfī practice, or any other type of Sufism. He did not technically require one to become a formal Muslim, for example, and he gave a central place to women in the leadership of his groups. The only people to receive the highest initiation from him, the rank of *murshida*, were four women. Yet, he required his senior disciples to become familiar with Islamic ritual practices, including ritual prayer, evidenced in the unpublished materials circulated among his disciples. The Muslim identity of his teaching was not too far beneath the surface.

One of the most popular and accessible Ṣūfī activities in the world, pioneered by Sam Lewis (d. 1971), is the "Dances of Universal Peace." Sufi Sam, as he has been affectionately called since the 1960s, was a teacher who transcended the rule-book. After ʿInāyat Khān, his teachers included the Hindu teacher Ramdas in 1954, Ṣūfīs ʿAbd al-Ghafūr Chishtī in Bangladesh and Barakat ʿAlī in Pakistan, and a formal Zen dharma transmission in 1964. Yet, 30 years after his initiation with ʿInāyat Khān, he said, "I have not met any non-Muslim superior to my own teacher [ʿInāyat Khān]" (Rawlinson 1997: 397). In 1968 he began receiving inspirations for various dances as a means of spiritual transformation, and these dances became known as the Dances of Universal Peace. Although they outwardly appear to be simply folk dances incorporating symbols from the Native American, Hindu, Christian, Jewish, and Islamic traditions with songs and music from around the world, the intent is to involve meditation and inner attunement through the sounds and symbols expressed in the dances.

Presently the Dances of Universal Peace are led by Shabda Khān, the current head of the Ṣūfī Ruhāniyyat Society (see Table 15.1). Many members of the Ṣūfī order also practice these dances since Sufi Sam recognized Vilāyat Khān's spiritual leadership and encouraged his disciples to affiliate with Vilāyat Khān's group. Both the Ṣūfī order (based in the USA) and the International Sufi Movement (based in Holland and active in Canada) continue to have quite similar organizations and teachings as they endeavor to bring ʿInāyat Khān's message to the world.

There are still numerous Islamically oriented Ṣūfī groups in the West, one of the most popular and entrepreneurial being the Naqshbandī-Ḥaqqānī lineage led by Shaykh Nazim of Cyprus. Men in this group often dress in robes and wear large turbans, the

Table 15.1 ʿInāyat Khān's selected sub-lineages (leadership dates are indicated).

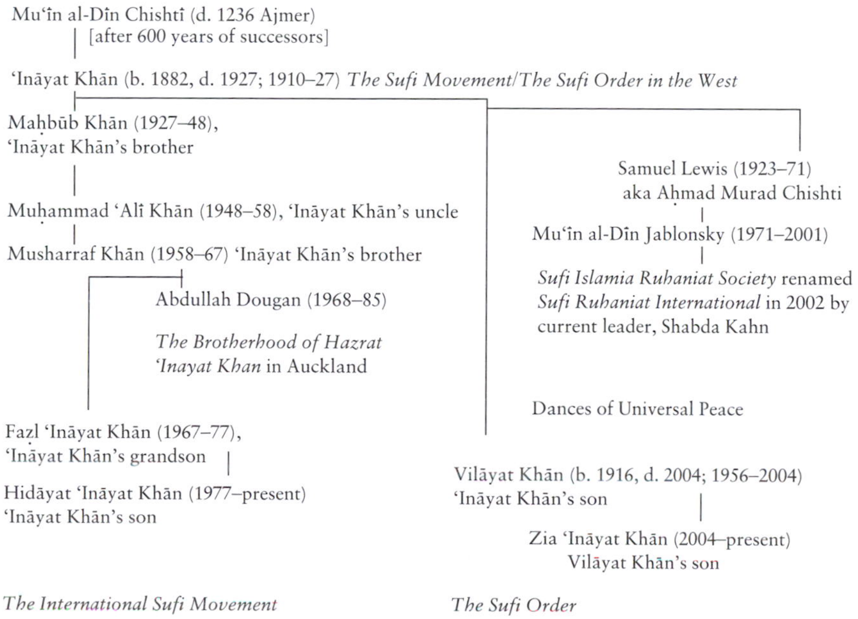
Mu'în al-Dîn Chishtî (d. 1236 Ajmer)
[after 600 years of successors]
'Ināyat Khān (b. 1882, d. 1927; 1910–27) The Sufi Movement/The Sufi Order in the West
Maḥbūb Khān (1927–48),
'Ināyat Khān's brother
Muḥammad 'Alî Khān (1948–58), 'Ināyat Khān's uncle
Musharraf Khān (1958–67) 'Ināyat Khān's brother
Abdullah Dougan (1968–85)
The Brotherhood of Hazrat 'Inayat Khan in Auckland
Fazl 'Ināyat Khān (1967–77),
'Ināyat Khān's grandson
Hidāyat 'Ināyat Khān (1977–present)
'Ināyat Khān's son
The International Sufi Movement
Samuel Lewis (1923–71)
aka Aḥmad Murad Chishti
Mu'în al-Dîn Jablonsky (1971–2001)
Sufi Islamia Ruhaniat Society renamed
Sufi Ruhaniat International in 2002 by
current leader, Shabda Kahn
Dances of Universal Peace
Vilāyat Khān (b. 1916, d. 2004; 1956–2004)
'Ināyat Khān's son
Zia 'Ināyat Khān (2004–present)
Vilāyat Khān's son
The Sufi Order

color of which identifies their ethnicity, for example, red for Afro-American or gold for Latinos. In addition, one finds a plethora of small Ṣūfī groups from around the world mostly catering to specific immigrant Muslim communities with their leaders usually coming from the Islamic country of origin.

Another Ṣūfī flavor in the West is the increasingly popular poetry of Mawlānā Jalāl al-Dīn Rūmī – and it is no surprise since it is some of the most sublime and heart-opening poetry in any language. Much of the popularity of Rūmī in the English-speaking world is due to the poetic accomplishments of Coleman Barks' renditions. This combination has made Rūmī's poetry the best-selling poetry in the USA for the last decade. Why is Rūmī so popular? Through the beautiful poetry, the reader is constantly reminded of Rūmī's message of love and opening one's heart. In times of fear, fuelled by the media, this Ṣūfī message of love is a life-giving elixir to heal and reorient oneself. Emphasis is on the heart and cultivation of the heart and opening one's heart to love – for Ṣūfīs, love is a way of being. Indeed, Sufism is an aspect of Islam which, suitably shared, could do much to make the world a better place.

One should not expect to find Ṣūfīs or Sufism discussed in mainstream media – Ṣūfīs work behind the scenes. One example is Bawa Muhaiyaddeen (d. 1986) a Ṣūfī from Sri Lanka invited to the USA, who deeply influenced many people, one of whom was Coleman Barks. Bawa is buried in a shrine outside of Philadelphia that has become a place of pilgrimage for devotees around the world. Note may be taken of Bawa's words:

> If each of you will open your heart, your actions, your wisdom, and your conduct and look within, you will see that every face is your face, every nerve is your nerve, each drop of blood is your blood, all hunger is your hunger, all sorrow is your sorrow, and all lives are your life. You will experience all this in your body and what you see and that is God's love. If that love develops you will not hurt any living thing, you will not cause pain, and you will not torture any other life because if you hurt anyone it will hurt you.
>
> (Muhaiyyaddeen 1981: 22–3)

Sufism has had an impact over the past 50 years on Western literature, as seen for example in Doris Lessing, music, and philosophy, especially that of Ibn al-ʿArabī (d. 1240). As more Islamic literature becomes translated into English and Ṣūfī activity continues to increase, one can expect Sufism to continue to grow in the West without any connection with Islamic ritual practices. Ironically, if the Salafi or Wahhābī perspectives on Islam continue as the mainstream mode for Muslims in the West, there might be even less Ṣūfī activity over time in the Western Muslim community.

References and further reading

Addas, C. (1993) *Quest for the Red Sulphur: The Life of Ibn ʿArabi*, Cambridge: Islamic Texts Society.

ʿAṭṭār, Farīd al-Dīn (2001) *The Speech of the Birds: Concerning Migration to the Real, the Mantiquʾt-tair*, Cambridge: Islamic Texts Society.

Barks, C. (1995) *The Essential Rumi*, San Francisco: HarperSanFrancisco.

Buehler, A. (1998) *Sufi Heirs of the Prophet: The Indian Naqshbandiyya and the Rise of the Mediating Sufi Shaykh*, Columbia: University of South Carolina Press.

Chittick, W. (1989) *The Sufi Path of Knowledge*, Albany: State University of New York Press.
Chodkiewicz, M. (1993) *Seal of the Saints: Prophethood and Sainthood in the Doctrine of Ibn ʿArabi*, Cambridge: Islamic Texts Society.
Ernst, C. (1997) *Shambhala Guide to Sufism*, Boston: Shambhala.
Ghazālī, al- (1999) *Deliverance from Error: an Annotated Translation of al-Munqidh min al Dalal*, Louisville, KY: Fons Vitae.
Helminski, K. (1999) *The Knowing Heart*, Boston: Shambhala Press.
Hoffman, V. J. (1995) *Sufism, Mystics and Saints in Modern Egypt*, Columbia: University of South Carolina Press.
Legall, D. (2004) *A Culture of Sufism: Naqshbandis in the Ottoman World, 1450–1700*, Albany: State University of New York Press.
Lings, M. (1971) *A Sufi Saint of the Twentieth Century: Shaik Ahmad al-ʿAlawī: His Spiritual Heritage and Legacy*, 2nd edition, London: Allen and Unwin.
Merton, T. (1999) *Merton and Sufism: The Untold Story: A Complete Compendium*, Louisville, KY: Fons Vitae.
Muhaiyyaddeen, B. (1981) *A Book of God's Love*, Philadelphia: Bawa Muhaiyyadeen Fellowship.
Rawlinson, A. (1997) *Enlightened Masters*, Chicago: Open Court.
Renard, J. (2004) *Knowledge of God in Classical Sufism: Foundations of Islamic Mystical Theology*, New York: Paulist Press.
Schimmel, A. (1975) *Mystical Dimensions of Islam*, Chapel Hill: University of North Carolina Press.
Sells, M. (1996) *Early Islamic Mysticism: Sufi, Qurʾan, Miraj, Poetic and Theological Writings*, New York: Paulist Press.
Sulami, M. b. al-H. (1999) *Early Sufi Women*, Louisville, KY: Fons Vitae.
Tabrīzī (1965) *Mishkāt al-masābīh*, trans., J. Robson, 4 vols, Lahore: Shaykh Muhammad Ashraf.
Tweedie, I. (1986) *Daughter of Fire: A Diary of a Spiritual Training with a Sufi Master*, Inverness, CA: Golden Sufi Center.

16

Shiʿism

William Shepard

Shiʿism is one of the two major denominational divisions among Muslims, the other being the Sunnīs. The adherents of Shiʿism are referred to as Shīʿīs or Shiʿites, and Shīʿa may be used as a collective term. The original name in Arabic is *shīʿat ʿAlī*, the partisans of ʿAlī. The Shīʿa constitute approximately 15 percent of the world Muslim population today. They are divided into several sub-groups, particularly the "Twelvers," "Seveners" or Ismāʿīlīs, and the "Fivers" or Zaydīs. This chapter will give primary attention to the Twelvers, who recognize twelve Imāms (authoritative leaders) and who form the vast majority of Shīʿīs today. They predominate in Iran and form significant minorities elsewhere, most prominently in Iraq and Lebanon. Brief attention will be given the Zaydīs and Ismāʿīlīs at the end.

Early history

The accounts on which our knowledge of the first three centuries of Shīʿī history is based are often obscure and conflicting. In the view of many modern secular historians Twelver Shiʿism comes clearly to light only at the end of this period. The following account derives largely but not exclusively from traditional Shīʿī sources.

During his lifetime the prophet Muḥammad was the political leader of the Muslim community (*umma*) as he was its guide in other areas of its life. With his death the issue immediately arose as to who should succeed to his political role. Many believed that Muḥammad had not designated any particular successor and, in a rather disorganized meeting, one of his earliest converts and closest lieutenants, Abū Bakr, was chosen as his successor or *khalīfa* (caliph). Others, however, believed that Muḥammad had in fact chosen a successor, his cousin and son-in-law, ʿAlī, the son of Abū Ṭālib, at a place called Ghadīr Khumm, a few months before his death. Moreover, ʿAlī was Muḥammad's closest male relative and a man of sincerity and courage. After initial protests, however, ʿAlī and his followers, in the interests of communal peace, refrained from pushing his claims against the caliphate of Abū Bakr and his successors, ʿUmar and ʿUthmān.

Increasing dissatisfaction during ʿUthmān's rule led to his assassination, and in this context ʿAlī was chosen as caliph by the people of Medina in 656. Powerful elements, however, opposed him. In the Battle of the Camel (656) his army defeated two powerful Meccan leaders. More serious was the opposition of Muʿāwiya, the governor of Syria and scion of the prominent Umayyad family, whose father had opposed Muḥammad until almost the end. He alleged that ʿAlī had been implicated in the death of ʿUthmān, a kinsman of his, and that revenge should be exacted. Their armies met at Ṣiffīn (657), but when the battle was going ʿAlī's way the followers of Muʿāwiya successfully called for arbitration. This arbitration went against ʿAlī, and he refused to accept it, but Muʿāwiya, a shrewd and pragmatic politician, was soon gaining the upper hand against him. Meanwhile, a group of ʿAlī's supporters who opposed the arbitration defected and campaigned against both sides. These were known as the Khawārij (singular: Khārijī or Kharijite, seceder or rebel) and gave rise to several related sectarian movements in the years to come. ʿAlī defeated the Khawārij in battle but in 661 one of them assassinated him, and Muʿāwiya went on to establish the Umayyad (or Umawī) dynasty, which continued until 750. It is worth noting that two of the leading women of early Islam played important roles on opposite sides of this conflict. ʿĀʾisha, the youngest and favorite wife of Muḥammad and daughter of Abū Bakr, disliked ʿAlī and was involved against him in the Battle of the Camel. Fāṭima, the daughter of Muḥammad, was the wife of ʿAlī, and considered that she was wronged by Abū Bakr, who denied her an inheritance from Muḥammad.

According to the Shīʿa, ʿAlī had designated his son, Ḥasan, as his successor. Ḥasan, however, was in a very weak position, and so abdicated in favor of Muʿāwiya in order to avoid useless bloodshed. He retired to a quiet life until his death in 669 but in the Shīʿī view he continued to be the legitimate ruler or Imām. After his death his younger brother, Ḥusayn, became Imām. He too remained quiet until Muʿāwiya was succeeded by his son, Yazīd, who is pictured, especially by Shīʿīs, as exceedingly corrupt and immoral. In 680, responding to calls for help from the people of Kufa, in Iraq, Ḥusayn set forth from Mecca, where he had been living, with a small band of some 72 loyal followers. They were met by an Umayyad army of several thousand at Karbalāʾ, on the way to Kufa, and in the ensuing battle Ḥusayn and his men were all savagely slaughtered, while the women and children were taken prisoners to Damascus, the Umayyad capital. This defeat was to play a major and distinctive role in Shīʿī religious consciousness and its anniversary is commemorated on ʿĀshūrā, the 10th day of Muḥarram, the first month of the Muslim year.

Among the prisoners was Ḥusayn's young son, ʿAlī, who is known as Zayn al-ʿĀbidīn ("Ornament of the Worshippers") and recognized by Shīʿīs as the fourth Imām. He led a life of pious seclusion and had contact with only a few followers. He avoided involvement in the political movements of his time from which Fiver Shiʿism emerged. He died in 712 or 713. His son, Muḥammad al-Bāqir, is recognized as the fifth Imām. He, too, remained politically quiescent but was active as a teacher and began the dissemination of Shīʿī scholarship. He died between 732 and 743. His son, who became the sixth Imām, known as Jaʿfar al-Ṣādiq, was an even greater scholar and teacher than his father and is credited with being the founder of the Twelver Shīʿī school of *fiqh*, known as Jaʿfarī *fiqh*. During his time the Umayyad dynasty was replaced by the Abbasids, under whom he suffered more persecution than before, although they claimed connection with the Prophet's family and had initially appealed to Shīʿī sentiment. He died in 765.

The death of Jaʿfar occasioned a dispute over the succession. He had designated his son, Ismāʿīl, as his successor but Ismāʿīl died during his father's lifetime. Some claimed that the succession should continue through Ismāʿīl's descendants and these became the Ismāʿīlīs. The group we know as Twelvers, however, hold that after Ismaʿil's death Jaʿfar designated another son, Mūsā al-Kāẓim, who became the seventh Imām. He suffered considerable persecution at the hands of the Abbasids and, died, it is said, by poisoning, in 799. The eighth Imām was ʿAlī al-Riḍā, whom the then ruling Abbasid caliph appointed to be his successor, for reasons debated by historians. ʿAlī al-Riḍā died, however, in 818 before al-Maʾmūn (r. 813–33), and Shīʿī historians accuse al-Maʾmūn of changing his mind and poisoning him. ʿAlī al-Riḍā's sister, Fāṭima Maʿṣūma, was revered in her own right and her shrine in Qum is the most important one in that city, which has been and is a major center of Shīʿī learning. The ninth Imām, Muḥammad al-Taqī, succeeded his father while still a child and died while still in his twenties, in 835. There are reports of his precocious knowledge. The tenth Imām, ʿAlī ibn Muḥammad al-Hādī, or al-Naqī, also succeeded to the imamate as a child. He died in 868. During his time the Abbasid rulers began to persecute Shīʿīs again after a period of relative tolerance.

The eleventh Imām, Ḥasan al-ʿAskarī, was under detention or in hiding during the whole of his six-year imamate, and was accessible to only a few of his followers. When he died, in 873 or 874, there was considerable disagreement about whether he had left an heir and what should be done. According to the Twelver view, Ḥasan al-ʿAskarī designated his young son, Muḥammad, who upon his father's death went into occultation (*ghayba*, absence) and communicated with the world only through a chosen deputy (*nāʾib*). This was the "Minor Occultation" (*ghayba sughrā*), during which there were four successive deputies. In 941 even this communication ended and the Imām entered the "Greater Occultation" (*ghayba kubrā*), which will end only when he reappears as the *mahdī* and "will fill the earth with equity and justice as it has been filled with oppression and tyranny" (Ṭabāṭabāʾī 1975: 211, translation modified).

Although he is in occultation, he is still the true and legitimate ruler of the world, and is given titles such as *imām al-ʿaṣr* ("Leader of the age") and *ṣāḥib al-zamān* ("Master of the time").

Later history

The Greater Occultation represents a major watershed in the history of Twelver Shiʿism, since the community was now deprived of the kind of guidance on which its claims to authority and its distinctiveness were based. It is also the point where the community begins to appear more clearly in the historical sources and from which the earliest surviving writings attributed to the Twelvers date.

In most places and at most times during their later history, as during the earlier period, the Twelvers have been a politically quiescent and oft-suffering minority, but there have been significant exceptions. Very soon after the Greater Occultation, the Shīʿī Būyid (also spelled Buwayhid) family came to power as viziers of the Abbasid caliphs in Iraq (945–1055) and, even after them, Shīʿīs sometimes had influence at court. Another Shīʿī family, the Hamdānids, took control in Syria (944–1003) and there were other Shīʿī dynasties in parts of Syria and Iraq until about 1150. While it is not totally clear whether the Shiʿism of all of these was of the Twelver form, life under them was congenial for Twelvers, and this period witnessed a flourishing of their scholarship, under figures such as Ibn Bābūya (*c.* 918–91) (also spelled Ibn Bābawayh), Shaykh al-Mufīd (*c.* 948–1022) and Shaykh al-Ṭāʾifa (955–1067), who set the main lines their doctrine would take in the future. Before them, al-Kulaynī (d. *c.* 939) had written the earliest authoritative collection of Shīʿī tradition (*ḥadīth*).

Under the Mongols, who conquered Baghdad in 1258 and ended the Abbasid Caliphate, the Twelvers suffered less than did the Sunnīs as many of the Mongol rulers and their successors were sympathetic to Shiʿism. One, Öljeitü (also spelled Ūljāytū; r. 1304–16), converted to Shiʿism. The great Shīʿī scholar and philosopher, Khwāja Naṣīr al-Dīn al-Ṭūsī (1201–74), was an advisor to the Mongol conqueror, Hülegü Khān, and his student, ʿAllāma al-Ḥillī (d. 1325), was a key figure in the development of *fiqh*.

Ismāʿīl (d. 1524), the leader of the Ṣafawī Ṣūfī order, invaded Iran in 1500 and became Shah (king), and declared Twelver Shiʿism the state religion. He claimed descent from the seventh Imān and also the status of "perfect master" and divine manifestation, claims inconsistent with Twelver thinking. These claims were dropped by his successors, who ruled as (fallible) deputies of the Hidden Imām. Twelver Shiʿism was so weak in Iran at the time that it was necessary to bring in scholars from Arab areas to instruct the people. This work was done so well, however, that Iran became the major bastion of Shiʿism that it still is today. If one seeks evidence that religion can be imposed by force of authority, Safavid Iran provides it. The scholars (*ʿulamāʾ*, sing. *ʿālim*) also claim to be deputies of the Hidden Imām and the interplay between this claim and that of the Shahs has been a major feature of Iranian religion and politics since then, although in the Safavid period the Shahs held the upper hand. This period witnessed the greatest cultural flowering of Twelver Shiʿism, as can be seen in the impressive mosques and palaces of the capital, Isfahan. It also represented the height of Twelver political power, especially under Shāh ʿAbbās I (r. 1587–1629). Scholarship prospered as a system of *madrasa*s (schools) was established. Probably the most influential scholar of the Safavid period was Muḥammad Bāqir Majlisī (1628–99), a scholar of *ḥadīth*, a popularizer of strict Shīʿī doctrine, an opponent of Sufism, and a major political force.

The Safavid dynasty ended in 1736 and an effort by the following ruler to impose Sunnī Islam failed. In 1796 the first Shah of the Qajar dynasty came to the throne. The dynasty was to last until 1925 but was never as strong as the Safavids had been and had to struggle against the growing power of European imperialism and the increasing influence of the *ʿulamāʾ*. This situation was dramatically illustrated by the controversy over a tobacco monopoly granted by the Shah to an Englishman. A *fatwā* against the monopoly in 1891 by the leading *ʿālim* of the day forced the Shah to retract it. The *ʿulamāʾ* also participated in the Constitutional Revolution that began in 1906, but they were divided in their attitudes toward the constitution. In 1925 Reza Khan ended the Qajar dynasty and made himself the first Shah of the Pahlavi dynasty. While proclaiming his loyalty to Shiʿism and initially courting the *ʿulamāʾ*, he shortly introduced secularizing reforms that curtailed their prerogatives and influence as much as possible. His ideology was Iranian nationalism, but Shiʿism was important as part of this, since it had come to distinguish Iran from other Muslim nations. When Reza was replaced in 1941 by his son, Muhammad Reza Pahlavi, there was a decade of lively political activity in which explicitly religious approaches were represented by the politician and *ʿālim*, Ayatollah Kashani, and by the extremist Fedayan-i Islam, who were responsible for several assassinations. Prime Minister Muhammad Mossadegh, under whom oil was nationalized in 1951, was personally pious but secular and nationalist in his politics. The Shah was briefly forced out but then returned to rule with a firm authoritarian hand.

In the following years the Shah destroyed or co-opted his secular opposition but also lost the confidence of the people, leaving the field open to several diverse religious ideologies, among both *ʿulamāʾ* and laypeople. Among these one may discern three main tendencies. One, illustrated by Mehdi Bazargan, who was briefly prime minister after the Islamic Revolution, may be called liberal or modernist and interprets Islam largely in terms of Western liberal democracy. The second, prominently illustrated by ʿAlī Sharīʿatī (1933–77), who greatly influenced the students, interprets Shiʿism in terms of contemporary Third World revolutionary ideologies. The last, successfully articulated by Ayatollah Khomeini, who had earlier been exiled for his opposition to the Shah, combines a radically conservative Shīʿī vision with a call for social justice and opposition to imperialism. These tendencies and others stimulated the broad popular movement that toppled the Shah in 1979 under Khomeini's leadership and continue to contend with each other under the Islamic Republic that he founded. The popular designation of Khomeini as Imām, a title given to some leading *ʿulamāʾ* in the Arab world but not previously in Iran, indicates the status he came to have. His main slogan and doctrine was *vilayat-i faqih* ("the governance of the jurisprudent"), effectively that the *ʿulamāʾ* should take charge of government, something that had never happened before among Twelver Shīʿīs or Sunnīs. This doctrine was enshrined in the 1979 constitution of the Islamic Republic of Iran, though its interpretation has changed somewhat, and the *ʿulamāʾ* have played a major role in the government of the Republic. While the Republic has faced enormous economic and political problems, and there has been no lack of factionalism, so far this has been contained with the framework of the constitution and its ideology.

There are also significant Shīʿī populations in Arab countries, especially Iraq and Lebanon. The city of Kufa in Iraq was the early stronghold of Shiʿism and Iraq has had a significant Twelver population since then, constituting more than half the population of modern Iraq. Also, the most important shrines and many of the most important centers of learning are there, such as those at Karbala and Najaf. For most of the time, and certainly since the beginning of Ottoman rule there (sixteenth century), Sunnīs have ruled the country and Shīʿīs have been more or less disadvantaged politically and economically. In the last century they have become more active politically. They played an important role in the rebellion against British rule following World War I and, encouraged by the Islamic revolution in Iran, they developed their own revolutionary movement, but this was brutally repressed by Saddam Hussein's government, which was Sunnī though secular. After his removal in 2003 Sunnī–Shīʿī tension developed into a virtual civil war in Iraq as Shīʿīs demanded greater rights and effective representation in government.

There has also long been a significant Twelver population in Lebanon, which has also tended to be politically and economically disadvantaged. They have played their role in the confessional politics of the post-Ottoman period and they markedly increased their political strength under the leadership of Imām Mūsā al-Ṣadr from 1959 until his disappearance in Libya in 1978. During the civil war that began in 1975 the Amal party, founded by al-Ṣadr developed in a secularist direction and the radically Islamist and Iranian-influenced Hizbullah split off from it to become more popular and to mount effective guerrilla and suicide operations against American and Israeli military presences.

There are also significant Shīʿī populations in Bahrain and Eastern Saudi Arabia, usually under Sunnī rule and, in the latter case, that of strongly anti-Shīʿī Wahhābīs, who, at the beginning of the nineteenth century, had sacked the Shīʿī shrine centers in Iraq. Shīʿīs have had a significant presence in India since at least the fourteenth century and have sometimes had political influence or power. Over the last century there have been a number of clashes between Sunnīs and Shīʿīs there, and since the partition of India and the creation of Pakistan, tension between Shīʿīs and an increasingly Sunnī-oriented Pakistan government. Important Twelver populations are also found in Azerbaijan, among particular tribes in Afghanistan, in parts of East Africa and among Lebanese in West Africa, as well as in the diasporas of Europe, America and Australasia.

Main Twelver doctrines

Twelvers recognize five basic principles of religion (*uṣūl al-dīn*): belief in divine unity (*tawḥīd*), prophecy (*nubuwwa*), resurrection (*maʿād*), imamate (*imāma*) and justice (*ʿadl*). On the principles of prophecy and resurrection they agree essentially with the Sunnīs. On the others they have generally held to the views associated with the Muʿtazilīs, the early rationalist school of Islamic theology, whose influence peaked in the ninth century. In particular they have held that God's justice demands that humans must have free will if they are to be recompensed for their deeds. Along with this belief in God's justice goes a strong sense of His demand for justice in human affairs and a belief that human reason can recognize the difference between justice and tyranny, in contrast to the view that whatever happens is God's will and must therefore be accepted as right.

The primary point of difference, however, is their doctrine of imamate, or leadership of the community. The Imām must be one of or descended from the *ahl al-bayt*, the immediate members of Muḥammad's family, and must be explicitly designated (*naṣṣ*) by his predecessor. This is necessary because the Imām is not just a capable and righteous political leader, but also a spiritual guide and doctrinal teacher. For this purpose he is *maʿṣūm*, divinely protected from error, as was Muḥammad himself. Shīʿīs argue that God would not send an infallible prophet with an infallible scripture and then fail to provide an infallible leader to interpret and implement His revelation. There is, moreover in their view, a very important esoteric side to the Qur'ān that only the Imām can know and transmit. He is understood, moreover, to have a cosmic and mystical function, enshrining the primordial divine light and pre-existing the created universe. It is sometimes said that Shiʿism arose from the purely political struggles over the succession after Muḥammad, but, in fact, what was at issue was the divine guidance of the community (*umma*), both its nature and who would exercise it. It follows from this that one cannot be a true believer unless one recognizes and follows the Imām of his time. Others, as Jaʿfar al-Ṣādiq stated, might be called Muslims but not believers.

Given these views, Shīʿīs have a darker and more tragic view of history than Sunnīs. For Sunnīs, the early history of the *umma* is one of both spiritual and worldly success, though not without significant blemishes, especially after the period of the four "rightly guided" (*rāshidūn*) caliphs. For Shīʿīs it is greatness gone disastrously wrong almost from the start. No sooner had Muḥammad died than his followers perversely rejected the rightful leader and chose a usurper, and then another and then a third.

The resulting corruption was such that when ʿAlī finally did come to power and tried to reform the situation, he was unable to do so and was soon killed. From this point on the Imāms were sidelined politically although they were able to carry out their teaching role for their followers and sometimes influence the larger community through their moral example and intellectual prowess. According to many Shīʿī accounts all of the Imāms except the twelfth were murdered, usually by Sunnī rulers. Finally the corruption reached such a depth that the Imām could no longer function in the world, and entered into occultation. The result is a marked tension between a high standard of piety and righteousness for the leaders and a dismal sense of the world as a place where such piety and righteousness is persecuted, as well as a desire for doctrinal certainty and absence of the only one who can provide it. This tension often develops into a lively eschatological expectation, as happened during the Islamic Revolution in Iran, which many saw, and still see, as a preparation for the return of the Twelfth Imām.

The beliefs about the third Imām, Ḥusayn, and the rituals connected with him exemplify the intensity of this feeling. By his suffering and death at Karbala Ḥusayn is seen as having gained the merit to intercede for his followers with God, although in more recent decades a new interpretation has come to the fore with thinkers such as ʿAlī Sharīʿatī: he is the great revolutionary who, by fighting for the right in a hopeless situation, de-legitimated tyranny for all time and inspired the desperate struggles of future revolutionaries. It was this interpretation, which undoubtedly owes something to Marxism, that has inspired the revolutionary and the reform movements of recent decades. Shīʿīs show their devotion to Ḥusayn in extremely emotional rituals, which include dramatic recitations of the events of his life, self-flagellation, and a "passion play" during the month of Muḥarram (*taʿziya*) which re-enacts the events of Karbala.

Not only Ḥusayn, however, but all of the Imāms, as well as Muḥammad and Fāṭima, are highly revered and events in their lives commemorated. They are all models for believers, as only Muḥammad is for Sunnīs. On the other hand, it has been common practice, at least until recently, to ritually curse the first three Sunnī caliphs as usurpers. Such cursing when done publicly, as well as the emotional Muharram rituals, have often occasioned clashes with Sunnīs. In line with their view of the world and in response to persecution suffered, Shīʿīs have practiced *taqiyya* (prudent dissimulation), disguising their views and even their identity in order to protect their community. This is viewed not only as permissible but sometimes obligatory. This has, unfortunately, tended to make Sunnīs suspicious of their real intentions in any attempted rapprochement.

Twelver law

Twelver legal practice (*fiqh*) is often referred to as Jaʿfarī, after the sixth Imām who first developed it in a major way and also influenced some of the early Sunnī scholars of *fiqh*. Over the last four centuries there have been two major schools of Twelver *fiqh*, the Akhbārīs and the Uṣūlīs, with the Uṣūlīs predominant for the last two centuries. Shīʿīs, like Sunnīs, accept the Qur'ān and the prophetic *sunna* as the sources of authority, but the Shīʿīs include in the *sunna* not only the *ḥadīth* of Muḥammad but also the *akhbār* (reports) of the Imāms. The Akhbārīs limit themselves to these two sources. The Uṣūlīs also accept *ijmāʿ* (consensus, though in a somewhat different way from Sunnīs) and reason, and they stress the activity of *ijtihād* (interpretive effort) by the most qualified of the *ʿulamāʾ*. The results are not infallible but are authoritative and in theory every believer who is not himself a *mujtahid* (one qualified to do *ijtihād*) must follow (*taqlīd*) someone who is. As a result a small number of scholars gather a following and become *marjaʿal-taqlīd*, "source of emulation" (*marjaʿ-i taqlīd* in Persian) and are given the title Grand Ayatollah (*āyat Allāh ʿuẓmā*). The term *āyat Allāh* (Ayatollah) means "sign of God" and at present is generally given to any *mujtahid*. It was hardly used before the twentieth century and, at first, only for *marjaʿ*s, but has become progressively more common. *Marjaʿs* also receive a religious tax, *khums*, from their followers and this has enabled them in the twentieth century to build sizeable educational and social service institutions. Usually there have been several *marjaʿs* at any one time, but on at least three occasions this authority has been concentrated in one person, including Ayatollah Shīrāzī at the time of the Tobacco Protest (1891–2) and Ayatollah Burūjirdī in the 1940s and 1950s. Ayatollah Khomeini was a *marjaʿ* but never a sole *marjaʿ*. The *marjaʿs* exercised varying degrees of political influence, but only with the Islamic revolution in Iran and Khomeini's leadership of it did they either claim or exercise direct political power. Khomeini's doctrine of *vilāyat-i faqīh* explicitly extended their authority to this area. Khomeini's successor as leader, Ali Khamenei was not a *marjaʿ* at the time he took over though he has since been recognized as such. He does not have the same kind of personal following as Khomeini did. Increased involvement in politics has made the role and identification of the *marjaʿ* more complex and less clear than it was.

In its content, Twelver *fiqh* does not radically differ from Sunnī *fiqh* at most points, though there is a greater concern for ritual purity. Distinctive to Shiʿism is the *khums*, a tax of one-fifth of one's income, one-half of which goes to the *sayyids*, the descendants of Muḥammad and the other half to the *ʿulamāʾ* as the representatives of the Hidden *Imām*, and *mutʿa* (temporary marriage).

Philosophy, mysticism, Sufism

The Greek philosophical tradition, much of which was translated into Arabic and then Islamicized and further developed by philosophers such as al-Fārābī (d. 950) and Ibn Sīnā (Avicenna) (980–1037), died out as a separate discipline in the Sunnī world after the twelfth century. It continued and developed in the Iranian Shīʿī world in a more mystical direction in the form of *ʿirfān* or *ḥikmat-i ilāhī* (divine wisdom), building on the writings and insights of "theosophists" such as al-Suhrawardī (d. 1191) and Ibn ʿArabī (d. 1240). Its greatest representative was Ṣadr al-Dīn Shīrāzī, known as Mullā Ṣadrā (d. 1640), whose teachings have been influential down to the present time. Being an intellectual mysticism it has been popular among many of the *ʿulamāʾ* although it is looked on with suspicion by others. Khomeini was one of its practitioners and also taught it for a time, and this undoubtedly contributed to his charisma.

The early Ṣūfī movement, though having high regard for ʿAlī, was generally Sunnī and in general Sufism has fitted better into the Sunnī than the Shīʿī order. Some general considerations may partly account for this. The cosmic role and authority of the *quṭb* ("axis" of the universe, highest of the Ṣūfī *walī*s or "saints") in much Ṣūfī thinking seems to conflict with that of the Imām in Shiʿism. Also the type of authority claimed by

Ṣūfī *shaykhs* generally complements that claimed by the Sunnī *ʿulamāʾ*, but it tends to compete with the greater personal authority claimed by *uṣūlī mujtahids*. Nevertheless, there has been and still is a significant Shīʿī Sufism. Beginning in about the fourteenth century, several initially Sunnī Ṣūfī orders evolved in a Shīʿī direction, such as some lines of the Kubrawiyya including the Dhahabīs and the Niʿmatullāhīs. The Safavids, who made Iran Shīʿī, also began as a Sunnī order. Although suffering suppression in the late Safavid period and generally opposed by the *ʿuṣūlī ʿulamāʾ*, several orders have continued to be active and even to have some following in ruling circles. The line of the Niʿmatullāhīs led by Dr. Javad Nurbakhsh has also expanded into the Western world.

Zaydīs

The Fiver Shīʿīs or Zaydīs developed in the context of several Shīʿī oriented rebellions in the late Umayyad period. As fifth Imām they recognize Zayd, a different son of Zayn al-ʿĀbidīn from the one recognized by the Twelvers. Zayd was killed in an unsuccessful revolt against the Umayyads in 740 and several later revolts against the Abbasids were considered to be Zaydī. There was a Zaydī state south of the Caspian Sea in northern Iran from about 913 until about 1032 and another Zaydī state was established in Yemen in 901 or earlier and continued until 1962. The Zaydīs accept the caliphates of Abū Bakr and ʿUmar on the grounds of expediency. Their Imām must be a descendant of ʿAlī and Fāṭima but beyond that no specific lineage or designation is required. He must be knowledgeable in religious matters and able to lead a successful revolt against unjust authorities. In *fiqh* they generally follow the (Sunnī) Ḥanafī school.

Ismāʿīlīs

According to the Ismāʿīlīs, or Seveners, the designation of Ismāʿīl by his father, Jaʿfar al-Ṣādiq, remained valid even though Ismāʿīl died before his father, and the line of Imāms is believed to continue in Ismāʿīl's descendants down to the present time, with some uncertainty and dispute about the succession at certain points. These Imāms have sometimes been in concealment (*satr*) and sometimes visible, but when concealed they have had a visible spokesman, often called *ḥujja* (proof), and under him *dāʿīs* (propagators, missionaries), who led the movement in particular areas. Muḥammad the son of Ismāʿīl and the next few successors were in concealment (non-Ismāʿīlī historians have doubts about them).

Around 900 an Ismāʿīlī-led rebellion, known as Qarmaṭī (or Carmatian), took place in Syria and Iraq and lasted for some decades. Another movement by the same name in Bahrain and eastern Arabia adopted the Ismāʿīlī cause and established a republic that lasted until 1078. At one point they carried off the Black Stone from the Kaʿba in Mecca (they viewed the devotion given to it as idolatrous).

In 909 a claimant to the Ismāʿīlī succession took power in Tunis and proclaimed himself *mahdī* and caliph of all Muslims. This movement, known as Fatimid, extended its power over North Africa and took Egypt in 969, building Cairo as its capital. Strong militarily, economically and culturally, the Fatimids posed a major material and spiritual challenge to the Abbasid caliphate in Baghdad. It was under them that the Azhar mosque/university was built. The Qarmaṭīs did not recognize them but *dāʿīs* in Syria and Iraq did until 1094, when they recognized a claimant to the succession, al-Nizār, not recognized in Egypt. There, the Fatimid dynasty followed his brother al-Mustaʿlī (r. 1094–1101) and the dynasty continued until 1171, when it was replaced by the Sunnī rule of Ṣalāḥ al-Dīn (Saladin). Its later Imāms gave rise to two groups, the Mustaʿlīs and the Ṭayyibīs, due to a succession crisis in 1130. Meanwhile, Syrian followers of the Fatimid Imām al-Ḥākim (r. 996–1021), who had disappeared but was viewed as a manifestation of deity, became the Druze sect.

The Nizārīs, even before breaking with the Fatimids, had established themselves at Alamut in the Daylam mountains under the leadership of Ḥasan-i Ṣabbāḥ (r. 1090–1124), who claimed to be the *ḥujja* of the Imām. Under him they mounted a decentralized revolutionary effort against the Abbasid rule whose main tactic was the public assassination of key leaders, a tactic which eventually made them feared and hated. The West knows them as "the Assassins," a name deriving from their alleged use of hashish. By about 1120 the revolution had reached a stalemate. In later years their leaders claimed to be Imāms and they went through several striking doctrinal transformations before the material basis of their power was destroyed when the Mongols captured Alamut in 1256. For some centuries afterwards they survived taking the form of a Ṣūfī *ṭarīqa*, appearing openly again in the nineteenth century when their leader shifted to Bombay, which has been their center since then. Today they are a generally prosperous and peaceful community spread throughout the world, linked by their allegiance to the Aga Khan, as their leader is known.

In general, Ismāʿīlī thinking and practice has been strongly hierarchical and esoteric, carrying the idea of *taqiyya* much further than others do. It has also stimulated and encouraged intellectual speculation. Ismāʿīlīs developed distinctive and complex doctrines considerably influenced by Hellenistic philosophy as well as by other pre-Islamic traditions. In turn it contributed, sometimes by provoking reaction, to the larger Islamic intellectual tradition. For example, Ḥasan-i Ṣabbāḥ developed an impressive defense of the Imāms which the Sunnī thinker, al-Ghazālī (d. 1111), undertook to refute, but in so doing his own thinking was influenced.

Sunnī–Shīʿī "ecumenicism"?

Although recent political events have underscored and exacerbated tensions between Sunnīs and Shīʿīs, there has also been a significant rapprochement under the conditions of modernity and in the face of Western presence. The prominent nineteenth-century reformer, Jamāl al-Dīn Afghānī Asadābādī (1838/9–1897), was an Iranian Shīʿī who was active in both Sunnī and Shīʿī worlds. The Indian Muslim leaders, Syed Ameer Ali (1849–1926), Abdullah Yusuf Ali (d. 1953), the translator of the Qurʾān, and Muhammad Ali Jinnah (1876–1948), the leader of the movement for Pakistan, all had Shīʿī family backgrounds (Ismāʿīlī in the latter two cases). Among the examples of official rapprochement, in 1951 the *ʿulamāʾ* of the Azhar declared Jaʿfarī *fiqh* to be a valid school of *fiqh* alongside the four Sunnī schools. In 2005 an International Islamic Conference held in Jordan, basing itself on *fatwās* by several prominent *ʿulamāʾ*, declared that Sunnīs, Twelvers, Zaydīs and Ibāḍīs (a branch of the Khawārij) are to be considered true Muslims.

An interestingly ambivalent case is that of the Iranian Revolution. The rhetoric of the revolutionary leaders often spoke of Sunnīs and Shīʿīs as brothers and Khomeini had positive things to say about Abū Bakr and ʿUmar (Khomeni 1981: 57). Yet the revolution was distinctively Shīʿī, relying as it did on the distinctive authority of the Shīʿī *ʿulamāʾ* and the distinctive passions aroused by Ḥusayn. It has attempted to influence Sunnīs but, in fact, has directly influenced mainly Shīʿī populations. Equally ambivalent is the Iraqi situation, where there is a virtual civil war between Shīʿī and Sunnī elements but significantly a degree of cooperation also. A grim but probably apt symbol of the current situation is the journalist, Atwar Bahjat, daughter of Sunnī and Shīʿī parents, murdered by a death squad whose sectarian identity has never been discovered.

References and further reading

Ajami, F. (1986) *The Vanished Imām: Musa al-Sadr and the Shiʾa of Lebanon*, Ithaca: Cornell University Press.

Ayoub, M. M. (1978) *Redemptive Suffering in Islam: A Study of the Devotional Aspects of Ashura in Shiʿism*, The Hague: Mouton.

—— (2003) *The Crisis of Muslim History. Religion and Politics in Early Islam*, Oxford: Oneworld.

Dabashi, H. (1993) *Theology of Discontent: Ideological Foundations of the Islamic Revolution in Iran*, New York and London: New York University Press. (Chapters on the main thinkers in the movement leading to the Islamic revolution in Iran.)

Enayat, H. (1982) *Modern Islamic Political Thought*, London: Macmillan. (Includes useful information on Shīʿī–Sunnī contrasts and a good chapter on Shīʿī modernism.)

Fischer, M. J. (1980) *Iran, from Religious Dispute to Revolution*, Cambridge: Harvard University Press. (Very informative anthropological study of the Iranian *ʿulamāʾ* just before and during the revolution.)

Fuller, G. E. and Francke, R. R. (1999) *The Arab Shiʾa: The Forgotten Muslims*, New York: St. Martin's Press.

Hodgson, M. G. S. (1974) *The Venture of Islam*, 3 vols., Chicago, London: University of Chicago Press. (A magisterial study of Islamic civilization. Hodgson did important work on the Ismāʿīlīs, the substance of which is found here.)

Khomeini, R. M. (1981) *Islam and Revolution, Writings and Declarations of Imām Khomeini*, trans. H. Algar, Berkeley: Mizan Press. (Khomeini's lectures, declarations, and interviews from 1941 to 1980.)

Milani, M. M. (1988) *The Making of Iran's Islamic Revolution: From Monarchy to Islamic Republic*, Boulder: Westview Press. (Covers developments from about 1900 to 1990.)

Momen, M. (1985) *An Introduction to Shiʿi Islam: The History and Doctrines of Twelver Shiʿism*, New Haven and London: Yale University Press. (A thorough study of history, doctrines and practices.)

Mottahedeh, R. (1986) *The Mantle of the Prophet: Politics and Religion in Iran*, London: Chatto & Windus. (Excellent introduction to the varied aspects of Iranian religion and culture and the events leading up to the revolution, using the life-story of a contemporary *ʿālim* as a framework.)

Richard, Y. (1995) *Shiʿite Islam: Polity, Ideology and Creed*, trans. Antonia Nevill, Oxford: Blackwell. (Deals with Shiʿism generally.)

Shariati, A. (1979) *On the Sociology of Islam*, trans. H. Algar, Berkeley: Mizan Press. (One of a number of sources for Sharīʿatī's lectures and writings.)

Ṭabāṭabāʾī, M. H. al- (1975) *Shiʿite Islam*, trans. S. H. Nasr, London: Allen & Unwin. (Statement of Shīʿī doctrine by a leading traditional scholar.)

17

THE IBĀḌĪS

Valerie J. Hoffman

The Ibāḍī form is a distinct sect of Islam which nonetheless shares with the other major groups of Islam, the Sunnī and Shīʿī branches, the same basic doctrines and practices. Ibāḍī Islam's distinctions lie mainly in its doctrine of the necessity of overthrowing unjust rulers, if feasible, and in its definition of who is considered a Muslim. Ibāḍī Islam also preserves doctrines popular in the early Muʿtazilī theological school that have been discarded in Sunnī Islam, though preserved in some Shīʿī sects, regarding God's essence and attributes and the createdness of the Qur'ān. Ibāḍī Islam is a small sect found today only in Oman, in small pockets of Algeria, Tunisia and Libya, and among Omanis living in east Africa.

The Ibāḍīs are an offshoot of the first sectarian movement in Islam, the Khawārij or Kharijites ("those who went out"), which formed at the battle of Ṣiffīn in June 657 CE when a group of several thousand in the army of the Caliph, ʿAlī ibn Abī Ṭālib, seceded from his camp over their disagreement with the Caliph's consent to subject to arbitration his dispute with Muʿāwiya ibn Abī Sufyān. Muʿāwiya was the son of Abū Sufyān, the former ruler of Mecca who had resisted Islam for so long during the lifetime of the prophet Muḥammad. Muʿāwiya was also a cousin of the former Caliph, ʿUthmān ibn ʿAffān (r. 644–56) and had served as ʿUthmān's governor in Syria. In selecting governors for the provinces, ʿUthmān favored his own relatives from the clan of Umayya, who had been the most resistant to Islam, though ʿUthmān himself was an early convert. This selection was somewhat understandable, given the Umayyad clan's experience of leadership, but ʿUthmān's nepotism and unequal distribution of the wealth derived from the Muslim conquests aroused widespread discontent that led to a conspiracy in the army and ultimately to his assassination.

ʿUthmān's assassination revealed deep divisions within the Muslim community regarding what was required of a Muslim and what was to be expected from the ruler of the Muslims. The Khawārij believed that faith must be proven by works, and that any Muslim who commits a grave sin, or who persists in a minor sin without repentance, should no longer be considered a Muslim, but rather an apostate deserving of death. From the Khārijī perspective, ʿUthmān's failure to repent when confronted by his soldiers' demands justified his assassination. Some other Muslims, however, felt that those who profess faith in Islam should be recognized as Muslims, regardless of their deeds. A group known as the Murji'a ("Postponers") held that faith does not increase or decrease according to one's deeds, and that judgment should be "postponed," i.e. left to God. Although this position is now deemed heretical because the notion that faith is unaffected by works gives the impression that acts of faith and morality are meaningless, it is actually very close to standard Sunnī teaching, which accepts as Muslims all who profess faith in Islam, regardless of their sins. Such Muslims were shocked by the killing of the ruler of the Muslims, whose offenses were deemed quite minor.

Those who supported ʿUthmān's assassination were among the supporters of his successor, ʿAlī ibn Abī Ṭālib, who felt Muslims were too divided over the justice of ʿUthmān's killing to make it prudent or feasible to punish the assassins. His failure to punish ʿUthmān's killers led Muʿāwiya to claim the right of blood vengeance and declare ʿAlī unfit to be Caliph. When their two armies met at Ṣiffīn, however, Muʿāwiya's soldiers tied copies of the Qur'ān to the end of their lances and called for the matter to be settled by arbitration. When ʿAlī agreed, the Khawārij seceded from his camp, saying "no judgment but God's," meaning that the matter had already been settled by the Qur'ān, from which it was clear that ʿUthmān and Muʿāwiya were both sinners worthy of death, and that by agreeing to submit the matter to human arbitration ʿAlī was making an agreement with unbelievers, in violation of the Qur'ān's injunctions, and so likewise had become an apostate. The Khawārij declared the necessity of a new *hijra* or withdrawal from the society of such "unbelievers" and the necessity of founding a new Islamic society. Anyone who did not join them in this belonged to the "Abode of War." By declaring war against the majority of Muslims, the Khawārij sealed their own fate and, after two hundred years of assassinations, rebellions and general harassment of the imperial government, they died out as a sect.

Ibāḍīs are often called "moderate Khawārij" and are the only surviving Kharijite sect. However, while Ibāḍīs recognize their derivation from the Khawārij, they do not like to be called Khawārij, as the Khawārij have been universally denounced by all Muslims as deviant. Rather, the Ibāḍīs refer to themselves as "the people of straightness" (*ahl al-istiqāma*) and the only true Muslims. Their perspective on the Caliphates of ʿUthmān and ʿAlī is similar to that of the Khawārij, and they share with the Khawārij the perspective that grave sin or persistence in minor sins causes infidelity (*kufr*) and that sinners should not be considered Muslims but are infidels (*kuffār*) subject to dissociation (*barā'a*) and are not included in the bond of spiritual friendship (*walāya*) that true Muslims share. However, whereas other Muslims equate infidelity (*kufr*) with unbelief, Ibāḍīs distinguish between two types of infidelity: the infidelity of ingratitude for God's blessings (*kufr niʿma*) and the infidelity of polytheism (*kufr shirk*). Ibāḍīs feel the Khawārij were wrong to castigate sinners as polytheists and apostates; they classify both sinning Ibāḍīs and Muslims of other sects as *kuffār niʿma* who are not really "Muslims" but who are nonetheless monotheists (*muwaḥḥidūn*) who face the same direction in prayer as true Muslims – they are *ahl al-qibla*, and they are members of the community (*umma*) of Muḥammad, and therefore deserve the courtesies extended to all who belong to the *umma*. Ibāḍīs do not deem it permissible to kill monotheists; the only ones who may legitimately be killed (aside from the perpetrators of capital crimes) are an unjust ruler who refuses to repent or step down, and those who support the unjust ruler and resist calls for justice.

History

The Ibāḍīs derived from the "quietist" (*qaʿada*) Khawārij of the town of Basra in southern Iraq. Kharijite rebellions posed a serious threat during the civil wars that plagued much of the Umayyad period after the death of Muʿāwiya's son and successor, Yazīd I, in 683. The earliest and most violent Khawārij were the Azāriqa or Azraqīs, followers of Nāfiʿ ibn al-Azraq, who conquered Basra in 684, opening the doors of the prisons there and assassinating the governor. Outraged Basrans of the Azd tribe, of Omani origin, expelled the Azraqīs, and Nāfiʿ was killed in battle the following year. ʿAbd al-Malik ibn Marwān (r. 685–705), one of the most capable of the Umayyad caliphs, was able to regain control of all the provinces of the Islamic empire.

The Ibāḍī sect is named after ʿAbd Allāh ibn Ibāḍ (or Abāḍ), who broke with the Azraqī Khawārij after ʿAbd al-Malik ibn Marwān's accession to the throne. Jābir ibn Zayd, a well-known transmitter of *ḥadīth*, is generally seen as the true organizer of Ibāḍī Islam, though this has also been questioned (Wilkinson 1982: 133–6). He hailed originally from Oman and belonged to the Azd tribe, which had many important representatives among the moderate Khawārij of Basra. For many years Jābir had friendly relations with the powerful Umayyad governor of Iraq, al-Ḥajjāj ibn Yūsuf, who apparently saw the Ibāḍīs as a bulwark against the growth of Kharijite extremism.

When ʿAbd al-Malik ibn Marwān died in 705 and was succeeded by the pious ʿUmar ibn ʿAbd al-ʿAzīz, many Ibāḍīs hoped for the realization of their dreams of a righteous Islamic Imamate. They were disappointed, and many of the new Ibāḍī leaders wanted to embrace a more activist stance toward *jihād*. Jābir himself felt compelled to take action, and instigated the assassination of one of al-Ḥajjāj's spies. This led to a complete rupture in the friendly relations the Ibāḍīs had enjoyed with the Umayyad regime. Al-Ḥajjāj imprisoned many Ibāḍīs, and others were exiled to Oman.

Among those imprisoned in Iraq was Abū ʿUbayda Muslim ibn Abī Karīma al-Tamīmī, one of Jābir's students. Released after the death of al-Ḥajjāj in 714, he was appointed leader of the Ibāḍīs of Baṣra. Inclined at first to come to terms with the Umayyads, his fear of schism among the Ibāḍīs led him to embrace a different strategy. He established missionary teams called *ḥamalat al-ʿilm*, "bearers of knowledge," to propagate Ibāḍī teachings and promote anti-Umayyad insurrections in provinces that were less susceptible to immediate Umayyad control, like Khurasan (in northeast Persia), Oman, Yemen, the Ḥaḍramawt region (in the southeast of the contemporary republic of Yemen), and the Maghrib (the north coast of Africa west of Egypt). The Ibāḍīs of Baṣra embraced a strategy of *kitmān*, living in a state of "concealment" – that is, not openly espousing political rebellion, though they were well connected with the rebellions occurring in the provinces. Abū ʿUbayda's successor as leader of the Ibāḍīs in Basra, al-Rabīʿ ibn Ḥabīb, author of the authoritative compilation of Ibāḍī *ḥadīth*, migrated to Oman. Increasingly, in response to persecution, Ibāḍīs were pushed to the margins of the Islamic empire.

The first Ibāḍī state was established in the Hadramawt in 745 under the leadership of ʿAbd Allāh ibn Yaḥyā al-Kindī, known by the nickname Ṭālib al-Ḥaqq (seeker of truth). He was able to conquer the northern Yemeni city of Sanaa in late 746, and from there moved on to capture Mecca and Medina. This Imamate ended when Ṭālib al-Ḥaqq was killed in battle at the end of the Umayyad period in 749. One of his followers, an Omani named al-Julandā ibn Masʿūd, fled to Oman, where he was elected Imām of a new Ibāḍī state – a short-lived effort that lasted only two years (750–2), ending in an Abbasid military expedition in which the Imām was killed. However, the next Omani Imamate, established in 793, lasted a century.

Abū'l-Khaṭṭāb al-Maʿārifī, one of the *ḥamalat al-ʿilm* sent out by Abū ʿUbayda to the

Maghrib, was elected as Imām in North Africa in 757. He seized Tripoli, in present-day northwestern Libya, and in 758 he captured Qayrawan (Kairouan), in present-day Tunisia, the chief Muslim city of the Maghrib at the time. He entrusted its government to ʿAbd al-Raḥmān ibn Rustam. Although the Abbasids recaptured Qayrawan in 761, Ibn Rustam was able to found an Ibāḍī state at Tahart, in present-day Algeria. The Rustamid Imamate, as it is known, lasted – though not without schisms and political crises – until it was overthrown by the Shiʿite Fatimids in 909. Although Ibāḍī communities remain in small pockets in the Jabal Nafūsa mountain range of northwestern Libya, the island of Jirba (Djerba) off the east coast of Tunisia, and the Mīzāb (Mzab) valley of Algeria, an Ibāḍī Imamate ceased to exist in North Africa.

In Oman, however, aspirations to establish a righteous Imamate became a recurring theme in its tumultuous political history, riven by conflicting religious and tribal aspirations. The Imamate of al-Ṣalt ibn Mālik (845–79) ended with his deposition, the correctness of which was contested by rival theological schools associated with the towns of Nizwa and Rustaq. The Imamate of al-Khalīl ibn Shādhān ibn Ṣalt ibn Mālik (1016–34) inaugurated a period of important scholarly reflection and exchanges between the Ibāḍīs of Oman and the Hadramawt, although the dispute between the theological schools of Nizwa and Rustaq continued. In the middle of the twelfth century the Imamate collapsed when the Nabhānī family came to power in Oman, a period seen by Ibāḍī historians as tainted by tyranny and bloodshed, though Wilkinson sees little difference between it and the more idealized periods of the Imamates (Wilkinson 1987: 12). New Imamates arose in the early fifteenth century, but Oman was united only with the establishment of the Yaʿrubī dynasty in 1624, which lasted until the founding of the Bū Saʿīdī dynasty in 1753.

The founder of the Bū Saʿīdī dynasty, Aḥmad ibn Saʿīd (r. 1753–83), was the last ruler in the dynastic succession recognized as Imām, though his son, Saʿīd, claimed the title. Subsequent rulers were called by the honorific title *Sayyid* ("master"), or *sulṭān*, a title that carries no religious signification. Sayyid Saʿīd ibn Sulṭān (ruled 1806–56), a grandson of Aḥmad ibn Saʿīd, commanded an empire that extended over Oman and the East African coast, and in 1832 he transferred his capital from Muscat to Zanzibar. After his death, his son Thuwaynī ibn Saʿīd ruled over Oman, while East Africa, with its capital at Zanzibar, was ruled by another son, Mājid ibn Saʿīd. The Bū Saʿīdī family continued to rule in Zanzibar until the anti-Arab revolution of 1964; they continue to rule in Oman, where the sultan since 1970 has been Qābūs ibn Saʿīd ibn Taymūr.

The impulse to establish a righteous Ibāḍī Imamate did not die out, however. In 1868 a very successful revolt, led by the scholar and mystic, Saʿīd ibn Khalfān al-Khalīlī, overthrew Sayyid Sālim and installed another member of the Bū Saʿīdī family, ʿAzzān ibn Qays, as Imām. This Imamate was overthrown in late 1870 through a combination of British and Omani forces. In 1913 another revolt, led by the influential scholar, Nūr al-Dīn ʿAbd Allāh ibn Ḥumayd al-Sālimī (1864–1914), established the Imamate of Sālim ibn Rāshid al-Kharūṣī in the Jabal Akhḍar ("Green Mountain") region of the interior that has always been the heart of the Ibāḍī impulse in Oman. But this Imamate was not able to command the coast, and Oman was effectively divided between the Sultanate in Muscat and the Imamate in the Jabal Akhḍar region. This division was formalized by the British-officiated Treaty of Sib in 1920, and remained in effect until 1953, when Sultan Saʿīd ibn Taymūr reunited Oman under his rule.

Ibāḍī doctrine

What follows is a summary of the ways in which Ibāḍī teachings are distinct from those of other Muslim sects.

The status of sinning Muslims

As explained above, Ibāḍīs reject the Sunnī position that faith is unaffected by works, and do not believe, as the Muʿtazila did, that there is an intermediary status between faith (*īmān*) and infidelity (*kufr*), but neither do they castigate grave sinners as unbelievers or "polytheists" (*mushrikūn*) deserving death, as the Khawārij did. Rather, they distinguish between two types of infidelity: (1) *kufr shirk*, the "infidelity of polytheism," and (2) *kufr nifāq*, "the infidelity of hypocrisy," or *kufr niʿma*, "ingratitude for one of God's blessings." Only righteous Ibāḍīs are worthy of being called "Muslims" or "the people of straightness" (*ahl al-istiqāma*); non-Ibāḍī Muslims are *ahl al-khilāf*, "the people of opposition," who are nonetheless included among the "monotheists" (*ahl al-tawḥīd* or *muwaḥḥidūn*), the "people of the *qibla*" who face the Kaʿba in prayer, and the *umma*, the religious community of Muḥammad.

*Religious friendship (*walāya*) and dissociation (*barāʾa*)*

Although the concepts of *walāya* and *barāʾa* are derived from the Qurʾān, Ibāḍīs are unique in their insistence on their priority. Religious friendship (*walāya*) is reserved for Ibāḍīs living in obedience to God; sinning Ibāḍīs and non-Ibāḍī Muslims are subject to "dissociation" (*barāʾa*). However, this does not necessarily mean severance of all contact or cordiality. Rather, as one early twentieth-century Ibāḍī author explained it (Hoffman: forthcoming), *barāʾa* is a matter of internal dissociation from spiritual fellowship, but this does not imply social avoidance or discourtesy, nor does it disallow genuine affection; it is simply an inner awareness that the person is not a true co-religionist. These days "dissociation" is more cognitive than actual. In fact, some British observers of the Ibāḍīs in Oman and Zanzibar came to the conclusion that Ibāḍīs are the most tolerant of all Muslims, living in harmony with all religious and ethnic groups. Furthermore, all "monotheists" are to be treated as "Muslims" under the law, with whom one can enjoy intermarriage, mutual inheritance one from the other, the Muslim greeting of peace, and other courtesies.

Reward and punishment in the afterlife

Although one must treat non-Ibāḍī Muslims with the courtesy all monotheists deserve, Ibāḍīs believe nonetheless that neither they nor sinning Ibāḍīs will be allowed into paradise. Unlike most Sunnī Muslims, Ibāḍīs deny that the Prophet will intercede for sinning Muslims to rescue them from hellfire. Ibāḍīs believe, in keeping with the strict teaching of the Qurʾān, that punishment in hellfire is eternal and that it is impossible for one to pass from hellfire into the garden of paradise.

Freewill versus predestination

On this controversial theological question, which in early Islam pitted the upholders of freewill (the Qadariyya and Muʿtazila) against the "People of *ḥadīth*," who upheld predestination, Ibāḍīs embrace the solution proposed by Abū ʾl-Ḥasan al-Ashʿarī (d. 935), which has been accepted by many Sunnī Muslims (though many Ḥanafī Sunnīs subscribe to the Māturīdī theological school, with an analogous doctrine of the "acquisition" of human acts, and Ḥanbalīs reject theology altogether). This position holds that God creates human acts and humans acquire them. People are given a choice between two opposite acts (e.g., to do or not to do something, to believe or not to believe), but that choice does not in itself cause the act; it is simply God's custom to create an act according to human choice, though He is under no obligation to do so. This solution was intended to preserve God's power over all things and place Him above human categories of right or wrong, while at the same time accounting for God's justice in punishing and rewarding people for the acts they choose to do.

Anthropomorphic descriptions of God and the vision of God

Like the Muʿtazila, who were the first Muslims to apply Greek-style philosophical logic to Islamic theology, Ibāḍīs reject a literal interpretation of the anthropomorphic descriptions of God found in the Qurʾān: God does not have a body, so descriptions of Him that seem to imply that He does have one must be interpreted as metaphors – for example, His sitting on a throne means that He has dominion over all creation, and His hand means His power. Sunnī Muslims, on the other hand, accept the anthropomorphic descriptions of God as literally true, although they do not say that God has a body; they simply affirm that these descriptions must be accepted "without asking how" (*bi-lā kayf*).

As a consequence of their rejection of anthropomorphic descriptions of God, the Ibāḍīs also agree with the Muʿtazila that God cannot be seen, either in this world or the next. The word "gazing" (*nāẓira*) in the Qurʾanic verse "On that day faces will be radiant, gazing at their Lord" (Qurʾān 75:23) must be interpreted to mean "expecting" God's reward; this is permissible because *nāẓira* can mean "expecting," though "expecting" is more typically rendered as *muntaẓira*, a word from the same root as *nāẓira*. Ibāḍīs say that *ḥadīths* that say that the best reward God will give to believers in the afterlife is the vision of His self cannot be accepted as authentic. Ibāḍīs also agree with the Muʿtazila in seeing such eschatological symbols as the scale in which deeds will be weighed on the Day of Judgment as mere metaphors, because deeds are accidents, not bodies, and cannot literally be weighed.

Reason and revelation

Ibāḍīs agree with the Muʿtazila that the truths of Islam can be discerned by the intellect without the need for prophetic revelation. Prophets are a grace from God, sent to remind people of what they already know, or to force upon them the evidence of the truth that they can perceive with their senses and their intellect. Prophets are needed only to reveal specific laws. It is therefore entirely impermissible to adopt religious belief through *taqlīd*, blindly following the opinions of others. The revelation of the prophets is entirely compatible with reason; if a verse's literal interpretation is incompatible with reason, it must be subjected to an alternative interpretation. Ibāḍīs believe that humans have an innate knowledge of God from childhood, whereas Sunnī Muslims believe knowledge of God comes through education and occurs at the age of legal accountability.

The unity of God, His essence and attributes

Early Muslim theological discussions revolved around the question of whether or not God's attributes are real things distinct from His essence. For every one of the 99 beautiful names of God given in the Qur'ān, such as "the all-Merciful," "the Living," "the all-Powerful," "the all-Knowing," and "the Creator," there was said to exist a corresponding attribute, which for the above-mentioned names would be mercy, life, power, knowledge, and creation; many Muslims held these attributes to be real, though incorporeal, things that exist in God. Like the Muʿtazila, Ibāḍīs believe that the unity of God is compromised if one posits the existence of the attributes as real things distinct from His essence; God's unity implies that He cannot be composed of parts (essence and attributes), but must, in Aristotelian terms, be "simple," not composite. Sunnī Muslims, on the other hand, accept the reality of God's attributes as inhering in His essence from all eternity, and do not believe that this compromises His transcendent unity. On the contrary, they accuse the Muʿtazila of "stripping" (*taʿṭīl*) God of all meaning.

The creation of the Qur'ān

The question of whether the Qur'ān is created or eternal was the topic of heated discussions in the ninth century. It is connected with the controversy over God's attributes as well as the belief in the existence of the Qur'ān before its revelation, even before the creation of the world: the Qur'ān speaks of itself as being on a tablet preserved in heaven (Qur'ān 85:22). Sunnī Muslims believe the Qur'ān is uncreated or eternal, because it is associated with God's attributes of word, speech, and knowledge, which are eternal. The Muʿtazila, on the other hand, denied the reality of God's eternal attributes, and said that belief in the eternity of the Qur'ān was tantamount to polytheism. They were supported in this view by the three Abbasid caliphs between 833 and 847, who, in the *miḥna* ("Inquisition"), persecuted religious scholars like Aḥmad ibn Ḥanbal who insisted that the Qur'ān was uncreated. Aḥmad ibn Ḥanbal held that the Qur'ān is knowledge from God, and since God's knowledge is uncreated, the Qur'ān must be uncreated. Despite – or perhaps because of – the *miḥna*, the doctrine of the eternity of the Qur'ān came to be embraced by the majority of Muslims. Nonetheless, some distinguished between the Qur'ān that has an eternal existence in God and its temporal revelation, utterance and writing.

Ibāḍīs distinguish between God's essential speech (*kalām nafsī*), which is an attribute of His eternal essence, and the Qur'ān and other revealed scriptures, which are created indicators (*madlūlāt*) of His knowledge and consist of letters and words. The Ashʿarites also hold that *al-kalām al-nafsī* does not mean that letters, sounds, sentences or words subsist in His essence; God's knowledge of the revealed scriptures as letters, sounds and words is eternal, as all His knowledge is eternal and unchanging, including His knowledge of all His creatures, but that does not mean that the objects of His knowledge are eternal or unchanging. However, Ibāḍīs point out that there is no evidence in the Qur'ān or *ḥadīth* to indicate that the Qur'ān is identical with God's essential speech; hence, their affirmation that the Qur'ān is created does not mean that God's essential speech is created. Most Ibāḍīs affirm that God has an eternal attribute of speech (although none of God's attributes are real things subsisting in God's essence, as the Sunnīs would say) in order to deny that He is mute. Nonetheless, it is unnecessary to affirm specifically the attribute of speech as an eternal characteristic of His essence, as this is subsumed under the affirmation of omnipotence as an eternal characteristic of God's essence. The affirmation of an attribute is only necessary to deny its opposite, but the opposite of speech is silence, not muteness. The affirmation of God's eternal omnipotence is enough to guarantee that He is eternally capable of speech; it is not necessary to affirm that He is eternally speaking.

Political theory

Like the Khawārij, Ibāḍīs say that the Imām, or legitimate ruler of the Muslims, should be a man selected on the basis of his piety alone, without regard to race or lineage. Nonetheless, historically the Ibāḍīs have tended to select Imāms from particular families who have ruled in dynastic succession. It is not necessary for the Imām to be a scholar – though some Ibāḍī Imāms have been – as long as he submits to the religious authority of the *ʿulamāʾ*.

Ibāḍīs categorize the Imamate into a number of different types: (1) the hidden Imamate (*imāmat al-kitmān*), which exists in a situation of political oppression and weakness; (2) the activist Imamate (*imāmat al-shirāʾ*), which becomes possible when at least 40 men pledge to die in order to establish a righteous Imamate; (3) the Imamate of defense (*imāmat al-difāʿ*), an emergency appointment of someone as Imām in order to repel an invading enemy; and (4) the declared Imamate (*imāmat al-ẓuhūr*), which is established after enemies have been defeated and there is stability.

Ritual observances

There are minor differences between the prayer observances of Ibāḍīs and Sunnīs. Ibāḍīs, like the Shīʿa and the Mālikīs, pray with their arms down at their sides. They do not say *Āmīn* after the *Fātiḥa*, and they do not say the *qunūt* invocation in the *fajr* prayer. Until recently, most Ibāḍī scholars taught that Friday prayer should be held only in major cities in which justice prevails – meaning that for centuries Ibāḍīs did not observe congregational prayer because of the lack of a just Imām – and they reject the blessing of tyrannical rulers in the *khuṭba*.

Place of theology and mysticism

Unlike modern Sunnī and Shīʿī Muslims, who focus in their writings almost entirely on issues of legal, social and political importance, Ibāḍīs continue to write about purely theological issues, especially those that separate them from Sunnī Islam. Their continued interest in these matters probably derives from the fact that they are a very small minority who need to defend their very existence against attacks from scholars in places like Saudi Arabia.

There are no Ṣūfī orders (*ṭuruq*) in Ibāḍī Islam, but the teachings and practices of Sufism, including the writings of al-Ghazālī and Ibn al-Fāriḍ, were part of standard life for many serious Ibāḍīs until the mid-twentieth century. Some of the most prominent Ibāḍī scholars of nineteenth- and early twentieth-century Oman were true mystics to whom miracles are attributed, and who taught Sufism to their close students in a manner not dissimilar to the Ṣūfī *shaykh*s of Sunnī Islām. A number of them also practiced the occult arts known as "the divine sciences" (*al-ʿulūm al-rabbāniyya*), including the writing of talismans and manipulation of Qurʾanic verses to powerful effect, if we are to believe the stories told in Nūr al-Dīn al-Sālimī's important history of Oman, *Tuḥfat al-aʿyān bi-sīrat ahl ʿUmān*.

One might also note that whereas theology, *fiqh* (jurisprudence), and mysticism are usually entirely separate domains in Sunnī Islam (though one may well be competent in all three), the separation between them is not so neat in Ibāḍī literature. A nineteenth-century encyclopedia of Ibāḍī teachings is entitled *Qāmūs al-Sharīʿa*, which would lead one to think that it deals entirely with law, when in fact it is a compendium of all types of religious knowledge – theological, legal, ethical, and mystical.

Ibāḍī Islam in the modern world

In the late eighteenth century Ibāḍī scholarship experienced a revival in both Oman and the Maghrib. The nineteenth century saw a number of outstanding scholars who wrote commentaries on early Ibāḍī works as well as explanations of Ibāḍī Islam aimed at non-Ibāḍī Muslims. The most celebrated scholar of the Ibāḍī renaissance was an Algerian, Muḥammad ibn Yūsuf Aṭfayyish (or Aṭṭafayyish, or Iṭfayyish, or Aṭfiyyāsh – there does not seem to be any agreement on how to render his name), whose long life, from 1820–1914, overlapped the careers of three of the most important scholars of Oman, with whom he was in contact. Aṭfayyish visited Zanzibar, and his works were first published there, where the ruler, Sayyid Barghash ibn Saʿīd (1870–88), was an avid promoter of Ibāḍī scholarship and had established a printing press. In the early twentieth century the works of Aṭfayyish and other Ibāḍī scholars were published in Cairo, at al-Maṭbaʿat al-Salafiyya, a printing press established by the Libyan Ibāḍī, Sulaymān Pasha ibn ʿAbd Allāh al-Bārūnī (1870–1940), who was a strong supporter of the ideas of Muḥammad ʿAbduh. Both Aṭfayyish and al-Bārūnī emphasized Ibāḍī Islam's commonalities with Sunnism, and concurred with the Salafī notion that sectarianism was one of the causes of Muslim weakness that allowed for European dominance of the Muslim world. Aṭfayyish was so highly respected in the world of Ibāḍī scholarship that he is universally referred to as *quṭb al-aʾimma* (Pole of the Imams), or *al-Quṭb* (the Pole) for short. Nonetheless, in many respects he was untraditional, ready to reconsider issues that had long been decided in Ibāḍī tradition. In Oman, outstanding Ibāḍī scholars include Abū Nabhān Jāʿid ibn Khamīs (1734–1822), his son Nāṣir ibn Abī Nabhān (1778–1847), Saʿīd ibn Khalfān al-Khalīlī (1811–70), and the most influential and prolific of them all, "Nūr al-Dīn" ʿAbd Allāh ibn Ḥumayd al-Sālimī (1869–1914). Like the Salafī scholars of the Sunnī Muslim world, some Ibāḍī scholars exhibited reformist tendencies, insisting on examining the Qurʾān and *ḥadīth* as the basis for all Islamic teachings and promoting the idea of pan-Islamism – though insisting all the while that Ibāḍī Islam is the earliest form of Islam and the true Salafī faith. Despite Wilkinson's characterization (1987: 244–5) of at least some of these scholars as "fundamentalists," the Omani scholars also exhibited very strong mystical tendencies: Saʿīd ibn Khalfān al-Khalīlī, leader of the successful revolt that installed ʿAzzān ibn Qays as Imām from 1868–71, was profoundly Ṣūfī in his orientation, and wrote mystical poetry and guides to the Ṣūfī path for his students. The greatest poet of Oman and Zanzibar, "Abū Muslim" Nāṣir ibn ʿUdayyim al-Bahlānī al-Rawāḥī (1860–1920), whom Muḥammad ibn Yūsuf nicknamed "the poet of the Arabs," was earnestly interested in promoting both pan-Islamism and the Ibāḍī Imamate movement of 1913, but many of his poems are intensely Ṣūfī. In spite of common notions in the West of the alleged incompatibility of mysticism with political activism, these mystical scholars were profoundly involved in political affairs. The scholar whom Wilkinson (1987: 231) calls the "father" of the modern Ibāḍī renaissance, Abū Nabhān, strongly opposed Sayyid Saʿīd's policies, but Sayyid Saʿīd feared his popularity as well as his power in the esoteric arts, and waited until Abū Nabhān's death before attacking his family. Sayyid Saʿīd soon discovered, however, that Abū Nabhān's son Nāṣir was similarly powerful in the making of talismans, and decided that it was prudent to make Nāṣir a close ally and take him with him to Zanzibar; when Nāṣir died in 1847, his head was on Sayyid Saʿīd's lap. We have already mentioned the key role of the mystical scholar, Saʿīd ibn Khalfān al-Khalīlī, in the overthrow of Sultan Sālim ibn Thuwaynī in 1868 and the installation of ʿAzzān ibn Qays as Imām, and Nūr al-Dīn al-Sālimī's leadership of a second successful rebellion in 1913, leading to the Imamate of Sālim ibn Rāshid al-Kharūṣī (1913–20).

Abū Isḥāq Ibrāhīm Aṭfayyish (1886–1965), a nephew of Muḥammad ibn Yūsuf Aṭfayyish, went even further than his uncle in minimizing the differences between Ibāḍī Islam and Sunnism, even to the point of denying any historical link between Ibāḍī Islam and Kharijism (Ghazal 2005: 131–5). In 1917 he joined the faculty at al-Zaytūna University in Tunis, where he and other Ibāḍīs became involved in the Tunisian Constitutional Party founded by the Sunnī reformer, ʿAbd al-ʿAzīz al-Thaʿālibī (1876–1944). He and al-Thaʿālibī were both exiled from Tunisia in 1923, and both moved to Cairo, where Aṭfayyish established *al-Minhāj*, a journal published from 1925 to 1930 that received much support from Sunnī reformers. He was a founding member of the Islamic Guidance Society and the Society of Muslim Brothers and was a close friend of Rashīd Riḍā, Ḥasan al-Bannā and Sayyid Quṭb. Nonetheless, Ibrāhīm Aṭfayyish clearly preserved his distinctive Ibāḍī identity, and had a significant impact on his generation of Ibāḍī activists and intellectuals; he edited a number of important Ibāḍī works and represented the Omani Imām at the Arab League and the United Nations.

The main spokesman for Ibāḍī Islam today is the Grand Muftī of Oman, Shaykh Aḥmad ibn Ḥamad al-Khalīlī. Like Ibrāhīm Aṭfayyish, al-Khalīlī feels that the differences between Sunnī Islam and Ibāḍī Islam are insignificant, and strongly promotes the unity of all Muslims, though he feels that there are significant differences between Ibāḍīs and the Shīʿa. In contrast, the nineteenth-century scholar, Nāṣir ibn Abī Nabhān, felt that the differences between Ibāḍī Islam and Shiʿism were less significant than the differences between Ibāḍī and Sunnī Islam, because the latter are theological, whereas the former concern secondary matters mainly of a political nature. Although al-Khalīlī is well aware of the classical Ibāḍī doctrine of dissociation from non-Ibāḍīs, he denies the relevance of that doctrine today. Nonetheless, when a prominent Saudi scholar attacked Ibāḍī Islam in 1986, al-Khalīlī did not hesitate to defend Ibāḍī doctrines, and his book, *al-Ḥaqq al-Dāmigh* ("The Irrefutable Truth"), is devoted to the articulation and defense of the theological doctrines in which Ibāḍīs differ from Sunnīs. Ibāḍī students who wish to pursue higher theological education beyond a bachelor's degree must study at Sunnī institutions, like al-Azhar University in Cairo or King ʿAbd al-ʿAzīz University in Medina, but al-Khalīlī is not afraid that this will lead to a decline in allegiance to Ibāḍī Islam, and hopes that eventually higher theological institutes specializing in Ibāḍī Islam will be founded in Oman.

References and further reading

Eickelman, D. F. (1989) "National Identity and Religious Discourse in Contemporary Oman," *International Journal of Islamic and Arabic Studies*, 6 (1): 1–20.

Ennami, A. K. (1971) *Studies in Ibadhism: Al-Ibadhiyah* (n.p.), a printing of his Ph.D. dissertation, Cambridge University. Also available online at http://www.islamfact.com/books-htm/amribadhism/amribadhismstudies.htm (accessed October 2006).

Ghazal, A. (2005) "Seeking Common Ground: Salafism and Islamic Reform in Modern Ibāḍī Thought," *Bulletin of the Royal Institute for Inter-Faith Studies*, 7 (1): 119–141.

Hoffman, V. J. (2004) "The Articulation of *Ibāḍī* Identity in Modern Oman and Zanzibar," *Muslim World*, 14: 201–16.

—— (2005) "Ibāḍī Muslim Scholars and the Confrontation with Sunnī Islam in Nineteenth- and Early Twentieth-Century Zanzibar," *Bulletin of the Royal Institute of Inter-Faith Studies*, 7 (1): 91–118.

—— (forthcoming) *The Essentials of Ibāḍī Islam*, Syracuse: Syracuse University Press.

Lewicki, T. (2004) "Al-Ibāḍiyya," *Encyclopaedia of Islam Second Edition*, CD-ROM version, Leiden: Brill.

Rawas, I. al- (2000) *Oman in Early Islamic History*, Reading, England: Ithaca Press.

Savage, E. (1997) *A Gateway to Hell, A Gateway to Paradise: The North African Response to the Arab Conquest*, Princeton: Darwin Press.

Talbi, M. (2004) "Rustamids," *Encyclopaedia of Islam Second Edition*, CD-ROM version, Leiden: Brill.

Wilkinson, J. C. (1982) "The Early Development of the Ibāḍī Movement in Basra," in G. H. A. Juynboll, ed., *Studies in the First Century of Islamic Society*, Carbondale and Edwardsville: Southern Illinois University Press, 125–44.

—— (1985) "Ibāḍī Ḥadīth: An Essay on Normalization," *Der Islam*, 62: 231–59.

—— (1987) *The Imamate Tradition of Oman*, Cambridge: Cambridge University Press.

—— (1990) "Ibāḍī Theological Literature," in M. J. L. Young, J. D. Latham, and R. B. Serjeant, eds., *Religion, Learning, and Science in the Abbasid Period*, Cambridge and New York: Cambridge University Press, 33–9.

18

RELATIONS WITH OTHER RELIGIONS

David Thomas

Islam originated in a world of major religious rivalries. The warfare that was waged around the turn of the sixth and seventh centuries between the Byzantine and Sasanian empires was characterized as competition between Christian monotheism and Persian dualism (Arab merchants in the new Islamic era would have grown used to new Byzantine coins bearing the sign of the True Cross which the emperor Heraclius seized back from Sasanian possession in 628). Within the Byzantine empire, and wherever else they met, there was endemic rivalry between Jews and Christians over God's relationship with the created world, and among Christians themselves there was unremitting debate over the precise manner in which the divine and human natures had united in the person of Jesus Christ. In its home environment of Mecca the nascent faith was confronted with the ancestral polytheism of Arabia, and its first martyrs were victims of staunch followers of the old ways.

The Qur'ān addresses many of these diverse matters, and on the basis of its teachings Muslim theologians and legal experts in the first centuries of the new era developed elaborate understandings of the relationship between Islam and other religions that have served as precedents to the present day. This relationship has been both constructively fertile and fiercely arid, contributing ideas and influences to Islamic thought, but also hampering growth away from faith-based inequality to full recognition of non-Muslims in Muslim society. It comprises surprisingly liberal and open forms of acceptance, but also the myopic incomprehension that is the normal currency of interfaith relations.

The Qur'ān and other faiths

The Qur'ān perceives itself as the definitive statement of God's guidance to humankind. As the last in a series of revealed messages, it comes to confirm what has been given before and also to correct errors it detects among the communities that have been blessed with messages from God. So its tone towards those who do not follow Islam is both confirmatory and critical.

There are verses which suggest the variety of faiths is intentionally ordained by God (Qur'ān 5:48; 11:118; 22:67), and that their followers have a sort of equality with Muslims as long as they observe their own teachings (Qur'ān 2:62; cf. 22:17). These are refreshingly open in their unqualified acceptance of a plurality of faiths with different ways, echoing the great imperative of Qur'ān 2:256, "There is no compulsion in religion," that sanctions freedom of choice in believing. In such verses the Qur'ān accepts that followers of the great religions all agree on fundamentals of belief, and acknowledge the lordship of God. In this respect they differ from the pagan Arabs among whom the revelation came into historical form, for these latter neglect the true God and worship a diversity of beings (Qur'ān 39:3; 53:19–22). The Qur'ān seeks to bring its listeners back into line with the great revealed teachings of old (Qur'ān 2:136), and it sees itself as coming to confirm and safeguard previous scriptures (Qur'ān 3:3–4). Therefore, it respects the Jews and Christians as possessors of revealed scriptures, calling them the "People of the Book," *ahl al-kitāb*, and expanding upon the stories of Moses and Jesus, the prophetic messengers who were sent to them. And it sanctions the marriage of Muslim men to women from the People of the Book (Qur'ān 5:5).

However, while it signals acceptance for other believers in such verses as these, elsewhere it criticizes the faiths for falling away from their original undiluted monotheism. It complains that the Jews and Christians are intolerant towards the teachings brought by the Prophet Muḥammad and refuse to acknowledge his authenticity (Qur'ān 5:15; 5:68). And it accuses them of the same sin of associating other beings with God as the pagan Arabs, the Jews of taking ʿUzayr (usually understood to be Ezra) as God's son, and the Christians of taking Jesus (Qur'ān 9:30).

The Christians are particularly mistaken. For not only do they wrongly say that Jesus was God and Son of God, they also imply that there are three gods (Qur'ān 4:171; 5:73), and that the Virgin Mary is divine in addition to her son (Qur'ān 5:116). Jesus may have been a word and spirit from God (Qur'ān 3:45; 4:171), performed spectacular miracles of making clay bird shapes fly and raising the dead (Qur'ān 3:49; 5:110), and was saved from crucifixion by the Jews through God's direct intervention (Qur'ān 4:157–8), but he was no more than a creature (Qur'ān 3:59), and he readily admitted this (Qur'ān 5:116–17).

The People of the Book compound their errors of doctrine by tampering with their scriptures. The Qur'ān accuses them of concealing the teachings within them (Qur'ān 2:140, 146, 159; 3:187, etc.), distorting their pronunciation when reciting them (Qur'ān 3:78; 4:46), replacing words (Qur'ān 2:59) and making alterations (Qur'ān 2:75; 4:46; 5:13, 41), though it does not elaborate on this activity and leaves the extent to which it was perpetrated an open question.

These depictions of other religions in the Qur'ān build to a picture of original acceptance of non-Muslim traditions as essentially consistent with the teaching that it itself proclaims, and also anticipating it. (In Qur'ān 61:6 Jesus, in fact, openly exclaims that he brings "good news of a messenger to follow me whose name is Aḥmad," which is tantamount to predicting Muḥammad and his message.) But this acceptance is severely qualified by the errors in scriptural and doctrinal teachings that have entered over time, and the stubborn refusal of these elect communities to accept the last messenger whom God chose for all humanity. These acknowledgments and criticisms formed the basis of Muslim attitudes to other faiths in the formative centuries of Islam, and they have more or less continued to the present.

Non-Muslims in the Islamic empires

With the rapid expansion of Islam in the decades following the Prophet's death, vast populations of Jews, Christians, Zoroastrians and allied dualists, and probably some Buddhists came under Muslim rule. During the Prophet's lifetime meetings with such non-Muslims were relatively infrequent, apart from a remembered meeting with a Christian monk that gave rise to the Baḥīrā legend which has come down in contrasting Muslim and Christian forms, the possible arrival at his house-mosque in Medina of a deputation from the south Arabian Christian town of Najrān, and the stubborn rejection of both his person and his message by the Jewish tribes in Medina that led to their expulsion and the massacre of one of them. But with the capture of populous cities in former Byzantine and Sasanian territory, meeting became a daily matter, with immediate consequences for communication, mutual influence and tolerance.

Whether there was any large-scale conversion to Islam in the early centuries is very difficult to say. Given the tax burden imposed on non-Muslims and the gradual Islamization of society, there were clear inducements to abandon former faiths and become Muslim. These may have proved particularly attractive at times: the Umayyad Caliph ʿUmar ibn ʿAbd al-ʿAzīz (r. 717–20) is recorded as discouraging his governors from preventing conversions, a case of a particularly pious ruler who desired new Muslims expressing disapproval of his pragmatic officials who coveted tax revenues. Richard Bulliet (1979) has argued on the basis of name changes over time that conversion did not gather pace for at least four centuries after the coming of Islam, which suggests that in the first centuries of the Islamic empire the ruled did not in general feel discrimination to any intolerably excessive degree.

In early times relations between Muslim rulers and their non-Muslim subjects were in principle governed by the provisions set out in pacts that were thought to have been agreed by Muslim generals and captured cities at the time of the second Caliph ʿUmar ibn al-Khaṭṭāb (r. 634–44). While it is unlikely that in the detailed form in which they are known from classical Muslim authors these actually derive from the seventh century, some key elements are almost certainly early, and most appear to have been widely known by the early ninth century. The overriding relationship between the ruler and those communities which could be identified as People of the Book (usually Jews, Christians and Zoroastrians) was that of the *dhimma*, the covenant of protection that the Prophet himself was remembered to have extended to some Jewish tribes and the Christians of Najrān. According to this, one side offered to protect the other in return for some concession. In the Muslim legal agreements extended to non-Muslims, the latter came under the protection of the former in return for paying the poll tax, *jizya*, and other taxes, not bearing arms, acknowledging Muslims in public by dismounting or stepping aside, not retaliating when struck by Muslims, distinguishing themselves by wearing yellow sashes and other forms of dress, not using Muslim names, not building new churches or repairing existing ones, and a number of other observances. The "People of Protection," *ahl al-dhimma* or *dhimmīs*, were thus in principle marked out from wider Muslim society, and while they had a definite status in law they could not ignore the secondary social position they were required by law to occupy.

It seems clear that from the ninth century at least these regulations were in existence in some form in Muslim society. But it is very unlikely that they were enforced in any systematic manner. For one thing, Muslim historians apparently considered it a significant event worthy of recording that they were applied on a number of occasions, particularly by the Abbasid caliphs al-Mutawakkil (r. 847–61) and al-Qādir

(r. 991–1031), and the Fatimid caliph al-Ḥākim (r. 996–1021), suggesting strongly that for the rest of the time there was no systematic implementation. And for another thing, certain non-Muslim individuals feature prominently in the society of early times in positions of seniority and some influence, suggesting that they at least did not feel constrained by overburdening legislation. It is indicative that for many years in early Abbasid times the caliph's personal physician was a Christian from the Bakhtishūʿ family that preserved this position in a succession from father to son. Furthermore, many of the officials in the caliphal bureaucracy were non-Muslims, often Zoroastrians, or in the case of the medical expert and philosopher ʿAlī al-Ṭabarī (d. *c.* 864), a Nestorian Christian who maintained his faith under a series of caliphs until he finally converted at the advanced age of 70 in the time of the caliph al-Mutawakkil (r. 847–61).

Some measure of the standing of religious leaders in these relatively enlightened times is afforded by the understandably keen interest taken by caliphs in the election of the Nestorian patriarch, who was recognized as the leader of all Christians in the empire, and the caliphs' tendency on occasion to sway the outcome through bribes in favor of a man whom they might find amenable. The best known of these patriarchs was Timothy I (d. *c.* 823), under whom the church engaged in extensive missionary activities (though outside the boundaries of the empire in deference to the *dhimmī* regulations), and who himself enjoyed personal access to the caliph. On one notable occasion in 781, he took part in a debate about matters of faith over two entire days with the caliph al-Mahdī (r. 775–85), and according to his own account acquitted himself with honor and dignity.

It was the fashion at this time for noblemen and the caliph himself to arrange debates on matters of religion or ethics in which they would bring together representatives of Muslim groups, sometimes Shīʿīs or rationalist Muʿtazilīs, Jews, Christians, Zoroastrians and others, to present their different views and attempt to outdo one another in argument. The surviving accounts of some of these debates suggest they were highly ritualized and civilized affairs, and intended more for edification and entertainment than for promoting the superiority of Islam or any other faith over all others. It was also a recognized pastime for Baghdad society, and the caliph himself, to visit monasteries in and around the capital to enjoy the comparative calm of their gardens and also to sample the produce of their vineyards. The caliph al-Ma'mūn (r. 813–33) was known for his acquaintance with the liturgy of the church, and according to some Christian traditions even converted to Christianity.

A valuable insight into the tolerant, open world of interfaith respect is afforded by remarks in a letter written by the rationalist theologian and stylist Abū ʿUthmān al-Jāḥiẓ (d. 868). Attempting to explain why Christians were so successful in Abbasid Muslim society, he resentfully refers to the way in which they appear to flout all the regulations of the *dhimmī* legislation and are applauded for doing so by Muslims themselves:

> We know that they ride highly bred horses, and dromedary camels, play polo . . ., wear fashionable silk garments, and have attendants to serve them. They call themselves Ḥasan, Ḥusayn, ʿAbbās, Faḍl and ʿAlī, and employ also their forenames. There remains only for them to call themselves Muḥammad, and employ the forename Abū 'l-Qāsim [the Prophet's own forename]. For this

> very fact they are liked by the Muslims! Moreover, many of the Christians fail to wear their belts, while others hide their girdles beneath their outer garments. Many of their nobles refrain out of sheer pride from paying tribute. They return to Muslims insult for insult and blow for blow. Why indeed should the Christians not do so and even more, when our judges, or at least the majority of them, consider the blood of a patriarch or bishop as equivalent to the blood of Jaʿfar, ʿAlī, ʿAbbās and Ḥamza [Muslim martyrs of the first generation]?
>
> (Finkel 1927: 328–9)

While there may well be a considerable degree of exaggeration here for literary and polemical purposes – it is suspicious that these Christians appear systematically to disregard one by one the provisions in the pact of ʿUmar – these comments point to a group that enjoyed prestige and influence in a society where they moved with freedom and even acclaim.

However, this same complaint reveals a group that was identifiably distinct from its wider context, and either sought to integrate by using Muslim dress and names, or pointedly ignored instructions to distinguish themselves in open defiance. Christians and others cannot have felt entirely at ease in Muslim society, no matter how keenly they were courted for their professional expertise and technical skills. The difference of faith and to some extent cultural background remained, and the *dhimmī*

Figure 12 Vank Cathedral, Isfahan (New Julfa), Iran, 1606, 1658–63. The Safavids resettled a Christian Armenian community from Azerbaijan in their own quarter in Isfahan, resulting in the construction of this church built in the Safavid style.

Source: Photographer Saif Ul-Haq, 1991, Courtesy of the Aga Khan Visual Archive, MIT

regulations could always be enforced without warning or appealed to in a legal wrangle.

A disturbing practice among Christians in al-Andalūs at this time expresses the dilemma presented to non-Muslims who lived in Islamic society of whether to integrate or maintain some distance. While it was not typical, it is indicative of the problem. By the mid-ninth century the society of the southern parts of the Iberian peninsula, captured more than a hundred years earlier by Umayyad armies from North Africa, was achieving distinctly Muslim characteristics. The fashionable language of culture was Arabic, the modish dress was Arab, things Arabic were sought by everyone who wanted to get on in society. Then suddenly, over a period of ten or so years, a steady succession of about 50 Christians made public insults against the Prophet Muḥammad. When they refused to retract their statements there was no legal alternative to execution, and one by one they suffered the penalty. The reasons why they deliberately sought this end have not been finally agreed, though it has been plausibly suggested that many of the martyrs were seeking in this dramatic way to draw their fellow Christians' attention to the differences between themselves and their Muslim rulers in order to prevent them from losing their identity entirely.

This extreme example, which is mirrored by martyr stories elsewhere in the Islamic world, though never in such concentrated numbers, shows what was at stake between Muslim rulers and non-Muslim subjects. On the one hand, society was open and welcoming with the possibility of employing sought-after skills and gaining advancement, but on the other, religious differences always threatened to erect impenetrable barriers between the faith of the rulers and others. The martyrs graphically demonstrated that integration could never succeed as long as religious differences persisted.

The doctrinal challenge of non-Muslim religions

The comments in the Qur'ān on Judaism, Christianity and other religions constitute elements of a debate between the principles being proclaimed in the scripture and those being held by the other communities. On the basis of what the Qur'ān says, this debate was continued and expanded in the interreligious milieu of the early imperial centuries of Islam. And here again both cooperation and judgmental hostility are evident.

As Muslim thinkers reflected on the teachings of their revelation, they were given new direction by what they learnt from Christians and others living under their rule. For example, some of the major questions within Muslim theological debates, such as the relationship between divine omnipotence and human responsibility, the status of the divine attributes as formally identical with God's essence or distinct, and the eternity or createdness of the Qur'ān, may have been introduced in this form through discussions with Christian theologians. The extent of any possible influence remains an open matter, though whether such discussions provided material for borrowing or questions to challenge and stimulate, it is hard to avoid concluding that contact with exponents of Christian theology provided some stimulus. On the other hand, Christians were the direct channel through which the repository of knowledge from the classical Mediterranean world was introduced into the world of Islam. Translations of works from Greek into Arabic were commissioned as early as late Umayyad times, within a century of the death of the Prophet. And in the first Abbasid centuries a whole literature was made available to Arabic-speaking readers, either directly from Greek or through Syriac. The Caliph al-Ma'mūn sponsored what is known as the *bayt al-ḥikma*, the "House of Wisdom," which was probably a cluster of Christian translators responsible for turning works of philosophy, astronomy, mathematics, medicine and so on into Arabic. The best known of these translators were Ḥunayn ibn Isḥāq (d. 873), his son and their colleagues, whose translations of Plato, Aristotle and Galen were prized for their consistent representation of a given term in the original by one translation, and they could command huge sums for their output. Whether the service they performed endeared them to their sponsors, who paid them in gold, is by no means certain, and the debates over religious differences that are recorded between them and their Muslim contemporaries serve to indicate that they felt no attraction to the faith of their readers.

A sign of the ambivalent attitude of Christians towards the teachings of Islam in the open atmosphere of early Abbasid Iraq is the use they made of the argumentative logic that was being developed by Muslim theologians. At this time, a major problem of controversy in Islamic theology was the issue of the attributes of God. The more traditional thinkers held that if human descriptions of God, that He is knowing, living, powerful and the like, have any meaningful sense, they must imply the existence of real attributes of knowledge, life and power as part of His being, unless such descriptions were only human approximations that had no correspondence in the being of God Himself. Their rationalist Muʿtazilī opponents, however, resisted this implication because in their eyes the existence of such attributes would turn the strict unity of God into a relative unity through the addition of a range of formally existent entities to His divine essence. Thus, they interpreted the descriptive statements as human safeguards against God being ignorant, lifeless, powerless and so on. They refused to presume any positive knowledge about the being of God in itself.

It is fascinating to see what Christian theologians who lived in the Islamic world made of this divisive debate. From the early ninth century the first known Christian theological works written in Arabic began to appear and they show that their authors were fully cognizant with Muslim theological principles, as though they not only wrote in Arabic but had also been trained according to the rules of Muslim theological procedure. One of them, a little-known Nestorian named ʿAmmār al-Baṣrī (fl. ninth century), whose views were probably familiar to the leading Muʿtazilī of the day, Abū 'l-Hudhayl al-ʿAllāf (d. *c.* 840), argued in the same way as Muslim traditionalists and against Muʿtazilīs that unless we can say that God has life and knowledge we turn Him into a lifeless, ignorant non-entity. He went further, and argued that these two attributes were integral to the very essence of God and gave rise to other attributes such as power, hearing and seeing. What this meant is that for God to be God He must himself exist and in addition have life, identifiable as the Holy Spirit, and knowledge (or word), identifiable as the Son, and must therefore have a trinitarian nature. This Nestorian borrowed into the debate among Muslims in an expert and enterprising way to demonstrate the truth of his own doctrines.

Muslim theological reaction to Christianity and other religions

Such measures of integration in theological thought did nothing, of course, to make Christian doctrines more acceptable to Muslim theologians. It served only to make their errors comprehensible in new ways and open to new criticisms. For example, with regard to this particular explanation, Muslim opponents pointed out that the two attributes of life and knowledge could not be convincingly prioritized in the way proposed, and so, following the reasoning applied by ʿAmmār, since God must also have attributes of power, will and so on, the number of divine persons in this Godhead must far exceed three. The Christian was defeated by his own borrowed logic.

In these important formative centuries when Muslim scholars were working out the implications of the terse injunctions of revelation, and formulating their faith in a systematic manner, there was intense theological debate between exponents of Islam and other religions. This is attested by the inclusion, among the works of nearly all the leading Muslim theologians active at this time, of books written about or against Jews, Christians, dualists and others, and sometimes books about all religions together. Sadly, the vast majority of these are lost, but their titles give clear indications that their authors were intensely concerned with the claims of non-Muslim religions.

This concern was in all probability largely polemical, though there is evidence to suggest that at least some individuals had an interest in the beliefs and practices of the followers of the religions in their own right. One ninth-century work of this kind, the *Kitāb maqālāt al-nās waʾkhtilāfihim* ("The Book of People's Teachings and the Differences between Them"), of the free-thinking rationalist Abū ʿĪsā al-Warrāq (d. *c.* 864) proved so useful to later scholars that enough information about its contents has survived to allow an outline reconstruction. This shows that the book was very probably descriptive in form and brought together the beliefs of the Jews, Christians, Zoroastrians and other dualists, pre-Islamic Arabs and at least some Muslim groups. It went into intricate detail about such matters as calendar differences between Jewish sects, and it portrayed the teachings of the dualist sects with such impartiality and even sympathy that afterwards its author was often accused of being a dualist himself. This intriguing description of what appear to be the beliefs of all the main religious groups known in the Islamic world (there is no apparent mention of Indian religions although these were mentioned by other authors at the time) is, if it really was descriptive and no more, one witness among many of what can be called a detached, dispassionate interest in the beliefs and practices of non-Muslims conducted simply out of curiosity. In this it anticipates later descriptive studies of religion, such as that found in the work of Abū Rayḥān al-Bīrūnī (d. *c.* 1050), *Āthār al-bāqiya ʿan al-qurūn al-khāliya* ("The Chronology of Ancient Nations"), and that of Abū ʾl-Fatḥ al-Shahrastānī (d. 1153), *Kitāb al-milal wal-niḥal* ("The Book of Religions and Sects").

Both these authors appear to have attempted to describe non-Muslim religions without denouncing their beliefs. But in the case of al-Shahrastānī at least, the approach was by no means neutral, because he was following a precedent that by his time had become the accepted attitude towards the relationship between the different branches of faith. It is based on a saying of the Prophet, that the Jews would be divided into 71 sects, the Christians into 72 sects, and the Muslims into 73 sects, and only one would be saved. This led authors of the great heresiographical works that appeared from the tenth century onwards to place the various groups and religions in a hierarchical order with the predicted number of sects set out (often these bear little resemblance to reality), and the relationship between other faiths and Islam, and the various sects within Islam itself, represented in the order of their appearance according to how their teachings met such key criteria as the strict unity of God, prophethood and adherence to revelation. Inevitably, the non-Muslim faiths and the Muslim sects other than the author's own failed in one way or another, and it is thus possible to see how these authors estimated the different faith traditions according to the degree by which they met the established base criteria.

The same attitude is even more apparent in works of refutation. Here, a negative approach to non-Muslim faiths is to be expected, but what is typically found is not so much attacks on the beliefs of a faith as such, as attacks on selected beliefs only. This characteristic of works from the early Abbasid period onwards provides an eloquent testimony to the way in which Muslim theologians thought of the religions they encountered.

Debates between Muslims and others date from the earliest times of Islam. But it is only in the ninth century that works containing systematic arguments can first be seen. If works written against Christianity are taken as an example, they bear strikingly similar characteristics to one another, in that while their authors frequently show they know details of all the major Christian teachings in some depth (for example, the Baghdad Muʿtazilī al-Nāshiʾ al-Akbar, who died in 906, was able to list more than 20 different Christological doctrines that had been held over the centuries up to his own time), they routinely ignore these in favor of discussing only the two doctrines of the Trinity and Incarnation.

This tendency is repeated in so many works that it clearly cannot be fortuitous. As time goes on Muslim polemicists often appear less and less interested in the historical circumstances in which differences of doctrine evolved, and even the names of the main denominations that held them (Melkites, Nestorians and Jacobites are clearly distinguished in earlier refutations, but their distinctive differences often become blurred later on), suggesting increasing distance from active debates with Christians and greater focus on the doctrines as theoretical propositions divested of their historical or religious contexts.

Of course, the Trinity challenges the Muslim doctrine of divine unity, *tawḥīd*, by claiming that the Godhead is not a solid, undifferentiated unity but a relationship of three divine entities. And the Incarnation challenges this doctrine by claiming that God came into intimate relationship with a creature and even mingled his being with it – the Jacobites likened the Incarnation to a red-hot bar in which the iron and fire could each be perceived but were intimately blended with each other. The two Christian doctrines can be said to bring into question the internal and external aspects of the Muslim doctrine, and so threaten the very basis of Islam.

The reason why Muslim polemicists chose only these two doctrines to attack becomes clear. They were interested in them because of their relationship to this fundamental doctrine of *tawḥīd*, for by attacking them they were defending it. Thus, authors such as al-Qāsim ibn Ibrāhīm (d. 860), Abū ʿĪsā al-Warrāq and al-Nāshiʾ al-Akbar who have been encountered already, and Abū ʿAlī al-Jubbāʾī (d. 915), the leader of the Baṣra Muʿtazilīs in his time, all wrote works in which these two doctrines were submitted to intense scrutiny and found to be incoherent or inconsistent in various ways. What they were all doing was expressing in the form of refutation the by now generally accepted view of what the Qurʾān taught about the relationship between Islam and other religions, that they were all originally in agreement because at their beginnings they were teachings revealed from the one divine source, but through casual attitudes, oversight and maliciousness they had all become distorted and corrupted. Thus, to prove the erroneousness of their doctrines was to show that they had fallen away from the rational perfection of their original state and also that the one remaining religion that promoted *tawḥīd* was right. The polemicists did not see these doctrines as part of religious systems that perhaps possessed internal integrity (in their eyes they were not religions in the modern sense of the term) but as aspects of forms of the one faith that had decayed into caricatures. In this respect, refutations of these doctrines were only partly attacks on other religions, because they were as much defenses of Islam and its central truth.

In this attitude there is some lack of seriousness towards believers in non-Muslim religions, who in effect are portrayed as inferior or misguided Muslims. It is repeated to its logical limit in the later theological works that build upon the writings of the first Abbasid century and bring together the topics they often debated in isolation into integrated wholes to form the first theological compendia of Islam. From the tenth century a number of impressive examples survive, and these exhibit this striking relationship between Muslim and non-Muslim doctrines in a way that makes the inherent lack of seriousness unmistakable. An excellent example is the *Kitāb al-tamhīd* ("The Book of Introduction") that was written by Abū Bakr al-Bāqillānī (d. 1013), the leading representative of the Ashʿarī theological school in his day, for a prince of the ruling house.

Like other works of its kind, the *Tamhīd* seeks to give no less than a total account of the elements of faith in a logical and rationally sound way. So, it begins with the foundations of knowledge, progresses to proofs for the existence of God, and goes on to show the character of God, his relationship with the world through prophetic messengers, the doctrinal and ethical teachings contained in the revelations they brought and how these inform personal and communal conduct, and lastly the legitimate leadership of society. It is an ambitious and comprehensive account of the religiously inspired nature of the world, and right behavior within it.

A notable and at first curious feature of this work is the appearance of a whole series of refutations of groups and religions who oppose the author's views on the teachings he expounds. These are both Muslim and non-Muslim, and they crop up at frequent intervals throughout the work. Careful examination shows why al-Bāqillānī has included them, and why he has placed his refutations of them where he has. They represent, as it were, the reverse position to the one he is setting out at that point in the work, and hence constitute a direct challenge to it. It follows that for him, like his predecessors in the previous century and contemporary writers on theological compendia like his own, defeat of these opponents buttresses the arguments he has presented in favor of his own position. By demonstrating the irrationality and confusion of what they try to prove, he is able to show persuasively that any alternative to the teaching he presents is logically unviable.

In this process of showing his readers that only the way of Islam, and within that way only the form of faith he advocates, is safe, al-Bāqillānī turns the non-Muslim religions he treats into representations of single doctrines, to be inserted at the appropriate turn in the discussion as effectively no more than warnings of what lies in store if any reader should veer from the path of truth. Thus, Christianity and Persian dualist religions come to embody denial of strict monotheism in favor of two or more divinities, and al-Bāqillānī's refutation of them is placed as a warning after his treatment of the Islamic doctrine of *tawḥīd*; the *Barāhima*, "Brahmins," or Hindus, embody denial of prophethood, and the Jews denial of the Prophet Muḥammad, and the fallacy of their position is shown as part of the treatment of the prophet as key channel of instruction from God to the creation. Each of these groups (and also the Muslim groups whose teachings al-Bāqillānī considers wrong) is simplified down to one main religious alternative to al-Bāqillānī's own, and their function is to provide a cautionary example to any loose-thinking orthodox Muslims.

In this work, and theological compendia like it, the attitude towards the beliefs and doctrines of non-Muslim religions appears to lack not only seriousness but also respect. These religions are often over-simplified to the point where recognition becomes difficult, and the doctrinal safeguards by which their own representatives seek to avert the very errors which they are made to represent are completely ignored. (This occurs in the case of Christianity, for example, where the unity of the triune God is preserved through the divine substance, or the distinction of the divine nature in some Christologies is safeguarded through differentiation of the hypostases within the one person of Christ.) Here again, as in the earlier works against non-Muslim faiths, refutation serves to enhance and build up Islamic doctrine, and the integrity of the faiths treated is apparently forgotten.

This feature of Muslim theological works from the formative centuries of Islam suggests strongly that at this time theologians were employing their perceptions of non-Muslim religions to help construct their formulations of Islam itself. It would be too much to say that they constructed Islamic orthodoxy in reaction to the errors and deviations they detected elsewhere, but it certainly seems to be the case that they used these doctrines as representatives of unacceptable beliefs, onto which true Muslims should not stray.

The basis of Muslim attitudes to other religions

Muslim theologians' approaches towards other faiths is frequently linked to and constructed upon rejection of the scriptures held by non-Muslim communities. The hints given in the Qur'ān of People of the Book making or allowing changes to their scriptures were soon systematized into accusations that they either misinterpreted what they read or, more dramatically, possessed forms of textually altered books.

As early as the first half of the ninth century, the convert from Christianity ʿAlī al-Ṭabarī graphically attested to the assumption that Christians misinterpreted their scripture when he complained that while the New Testament contained "twenty thousand" mentions of the humanity of Jesus and no more than about a dozen ambiguous mentions of his divinity, the Christians use these dozen to interpret the twenty thousand rather than vice versa. At the same time, al-Jāḥiẓ hinted that the four evangelists were not all direct witnesses of the life of Christ, and may have been inclined to conspire together to lie in what they wrote.

Such insinuations became widespread as time went on, culminating in the widely held assumption that the original *Injīl* (the Gospel) had been lost and that the four canonical Gospels were the best reconstructions available. Some authors went as far as implicating the Apostle Paul or the Emperor Constantine in plots to produce deliberately distorted Gospels for their own ends. For example, in the early fourteenth century Muḥammad ibn Abī Ṭālib al-Dimashqī (d. 1327) explained how at the Council of Nicaea Constantine was presented with 11 testimonies from the disciples of Jesus (excluding Judas), but thought these too many and chose four, having the rest burnt. This author also refers to the (by this time) routine explanation of the corruption of the Torah, suggesting that the original revealed text was lost before or during the destruction of Jerusalem by Nebuchadnezzar and was rewritten by the scribe Ezra.

By the time of al-Dimashqī in the later era of the Crusades the corrupt status of the Jewish and Christian scriptures was taken for granted and few Muslim authors appear to have read these works. However, the eleventh-century Andalūsī polemicist Abū Muḥammad ibn Ḥazm (d. 1064) and the Baghdad theologian Abū 'l-Ma'ālī al-Juwaynī (d. 1095) were notable exceptions. The former compares accounts of the same incidents in Jesus' life as these are recounted in the Synoptic Gospels and points out discrepancies that indicate error and deception, and the latter shows from both internal and external evidence that neither the Torah nor the Gospel can be considered authentic beyond doubt. Their exposures of disagreements and deficiencies in Jewish and Christian scripture give point to the general judgment that the texts suffered corruption and cannot any longer be regarded as reliable.

This being the case, since doctrine and belief must originate in scripture and constantly refer to it, as in Islam, it inevitably follows that these latter must be distorted, and require the corrective arguments from Qur'ān-based teachings to restore them to their original monotheistic purity. Hence the educative stance of Muslim theologians towards Christians, Jews and others, intent upon exposing the confusion they purvey, and at the same time upon using their mistakenness to show fellow Muslims that there can be no logical alternative to Islamic doctrines.

The relationship between these theological positions and the popular attitudes of Muslims towards people of other religions is hard to plot. It is undeniable that while non-Muslims, and particularly People of the Book, did not often suffer active persecution at the hands of Muslims, their numbers inevitably declined within Islamic society through conversion and, later, migration. Structural discriminatory pressure must be held responsible, and attempted reforms – for example, the Tanẓīmāt ("regulations") which were decrees issued at various points by the Ottoman Sultan 'Abd al-Majīd I (1839–61) and which, among other things, instituted equality for all of his subjects irrespective of creed – proved dramatically ineffective because attitudes had become immovably fixed.

Even today, traces of the *dhimmī* measures enacted according to the precedent of the Caliph 'Umar are to be found in many Islamic constitutions and law codes (it is, for example, often difficult in many countries to gain permission to erect a new church, or to carry out repairs to existing buildings). The typical Muslim religious attitude towards other believers, that they have lapsed from the knowledge and beliefs that they received through the prophetic messenger who, according to the dogmatic interpretation of the Qur'ān, was originally sent to them, has for the most part changed little. There are exciting attempts to rethink these age-old attitudes, but as yet this is in a small minority with little influence. One wonders what might happen if some of the radically pluralistic verses to be found in the Qur'ān were taken as the basis for new thinking, and what creative theologies were then promoted in the name of Islam.

References and further reading

Armour, R. Sr. (2002) *Islam, Christianity, and the West*, New York: Orbis Books.

Bulliet, R. W. (1979) *Conversion to Islam in the Medieval Period: an Essay in Quantitative History*, Cambridge: Harvard University Press.

Coope, J. (1995) *The Martyrs of Cordoba, Community and Family Conflict in an Age of Mass Conversion*, London: University of Nebraska Press.

Ebied R. and Thomas, D., eds. (2005) *Muslim–Christian Polemic during the Crusades, the Letter from the People of Cyprus and Ibn Abī Ṭālib al-Dimashqī's Response*, Leiden: Brill.

Finkel, J. (1927) "A Risāla of al-Jāḥiẓ," *Journal of the American Oriental Society*, 47: 311–34.

Fletcher, R. (2003) *The Cross and the Crescent*, London: Penguin.

Gaudeul, J.-M. (1984) *Encounters and Clashes, Islam and Christianity in History*, Rome: PISAI.

Goddard, H. (2000) *A History of Christian–Muslim Relations*, Edinburgh: Edinburgh University Press.

Gutas, D. (1998) *Greek Thought, Arabic Culture: the Graeco-Arabic Translation Movement in Baghdad and Early Abbāsid Society (2nd–4th/8th–10th Centuries)*, London: Routledge.

Ridgeon, L., ed. (2001) *Islamic Interpretations of Christianity*, Richmond: Curzon Press.

Thomas, D. (1996) "Abū ʿĪsā al-Warrāq and the History of Religions," *Journal of Semitic Studies*, 41: 275–90.

Thomas, D, ed. (2003) *Christians at the Heart of Islamic Rule, Church Life and Scholarship in ʿAbbasid Iraq*, Leiden: Brill.

Tritton, A. S. (1930) *The Caliphs and their Non-Muslim Subjects*, London: Oxford University Press.

Waardenburg, J. (1999) *Muslim Perceptions of Other Religions*, Oxford: Oxford University Press.

Watt, W. M. (1991) *Muslim–Christian Encounters, Perceptions and Misperceptions*, London: Routledge.

Wheatcroft, A. (2004) *Infidels, a History of the Conflict between Christendom and Islam*, London: Penguin Books.

Young, W. G. (1974) *Patriarch, Shah and Caliph*, Rawalpindi: Christian Study Centre.

Part III

THE INTELLECTUAL ISLAMIC WORLD

19

THE ARABIC LANGUAGE

Mustafa Shah

The Arabic language today is the mother tongue of over 250 million people across the Middle East and North Africa. Its modern standard representation, whose form is ultimately derived from the Classical Arabic idiom, is officially adopted as the primary language of administration, education, and discourse in countries as diverse as Oman, Yemen, Saudi Arabia, Kuwait, the United Arab Emirates, Bahrain, Qatar, Iraq, Syria, Lebanon, Jordan, the Palestinian territories, Egypt, the Sudan, Libya, Tunisia, Algeria, and Morocco, notwithstanding the significance of the language's official status in neighboring states such as Mauritania, Chad, Djibouti, and Somalia. There are marked variations among the varieties of spoken Arabic: distinctions between the colloquial vernaculars and modern standard Arabic remain obvious. These clusters of vernaculars are said to have originally existed alongside the esteemed classical idiom and were disseminated as the result of the resettlement of Arab tribes following the Islamic conquests of the seventh century; a continuum of affinity therefore defines their Arabic status. Nonetheless, the Arabic language does not serve solely as an integral symbol of Arab national identity; it also functions as the revered language of the religion of Islam, occupying a sacrosanct place in the religious psyche of Muslims. The sacred book of Islam, the Qur'ān, was revealed in the Arabic language and everyday ritual observances are likewise articulated in its diction. Given that adherents of the faith number around one-fifth of the world's population, the symbolic compass of the Arabic language remains altogether pervasive. It must also be borne in mind that for many Christians in the Middle East, Arabic too has liturgical importance, serving as the language of religious ceremonies and services. The widespread migration of Arab and Muslim peoples into all parts of the Western world has further brought the Arabic language into focus as a unifying symbol of cultural and religious identity. A corollary to this is that varying levels of interaction with the language take place in social, cultural, and religious contexts; Arabic is taught in religious seminaries, mosques, and schools. Moreover, the study of Arabic has long been on the curriculum of academic institutions in the West. Chairs for the study of Arabic were established in reputable centers of learning such as the Collège de France in 1539 and the University of Leiden in the Netherlands in 1613. Oxford and Cambridge both had Chairs of Arabic created in the 1630s; and academic interest in the language and religion continues to thrive. Yet, the place of Arabic in the world of Islam is defined by a lengthy and intricate historical odyssey which begins with its position among the Semitic languages.

Semitic nexus

Arabic belongs to the family of languages traditionally identified as being Semitic, a term coined in the late eighteenth century CE and inspired by the Book of Genesis's account of the physical dispersal of the descendants of Noah together with the "tongues" they spoke. Semitic languages are members of the Afro–Asiatic (Hamito–Semitic) phylum of languages. Emphasizing the geographical bearing of this label, Semiticists use it to map out a typological classification of the syntactic, morphological, phonological, and lexical features which are collectively defined to be characteristic of these languages. These traits include triliterality (many of the morphemes of Arabic are traced to a triliteral root), parataxis (the omission of conjunctions in clauses), the appendage of conjugational markers, and resemblances in the lexical repertoire of the languages in question. The suggestion is that these languages branched out from a common root, namely a proto-Semitic archetype, although the schema was inspired by earlier efforts to postulate the proto-type of the family of Indo-European languages. In the attempts to reconstruct the proto-Semitic language, great significance was attached to the language of Arabic: it was the most prolific of the surviving Semitic languages and preserved a profusion of linguistic sources germane to its early development and history.

Despite the differences in opinions regarding the classification of the branches of the Semitic languages and their identification, a tripartite division of Eastern, North West and South Semitic languages is presented by Semiticists to provide some perspective to the linguistic features and affinities shared by languages of the same branch along with their overall relationship with one another. Eastern Semitic comprises the extinct language of Akkadian, which is divided into Old Akkadian, Babylonian, and Assyrian dialects. It employed a cuneiform script which was based on the intricate arrangement and characterization of wedge-shaped imprints on clay and is attested as early as 2400 BCE. North West Semitic (or Western Semitic) principally comprises Ugaritic; Canaanite, a general label covering the Phoenician, Punic, Edomite, Moabite, Ammonite, and Hebrew languages. It also includes Aramaic, which was used in Syria from around 900 BCE. Aramaic became the *lingua franca* of the Near and Middle East, dominating the linguistic landscape of the region until the Islamic conquests of the seventh century when Arabic assumed that role. Aramaic is classed as having Imperial, Standard, and Middle designations. It is further separated into Western and Eastern branches: the Western branch comprises Nabataean, Palmyrene, and a number of dialects spoken in biblical Palestine such as Samaritan and Jewish Aramaic, including the language associated with Christ. Eastern Aramaic includes Syriac and Mandaean among its dialects. The former is significant as the liturgical language of the early Christian church, flourishing at Edessa; while the latter is associated with a Gnostic sect based in Upper Mesopotamia. The South Semitic (or South West Semitic) group brings together the ancient dialects of South Arabia: Sabaean, Minaean, and Qatabanian; the Pre-Islamic Northern Arabian languages of Thamudic, Lihyanite, Safaitic, and Hasaean, which is associated with central eastern parts of the Arabian peninsula; and the Ethiopian languages of Ge'ez, Amharic, Tigrina, and Tigre. Although Arabic used to be enumerated among the South Semitic group of languages, there has been a recent tendency to place it among the North West Semitic languages on the basis that it shares greater grammatical affinities with them (see fig. 13). The

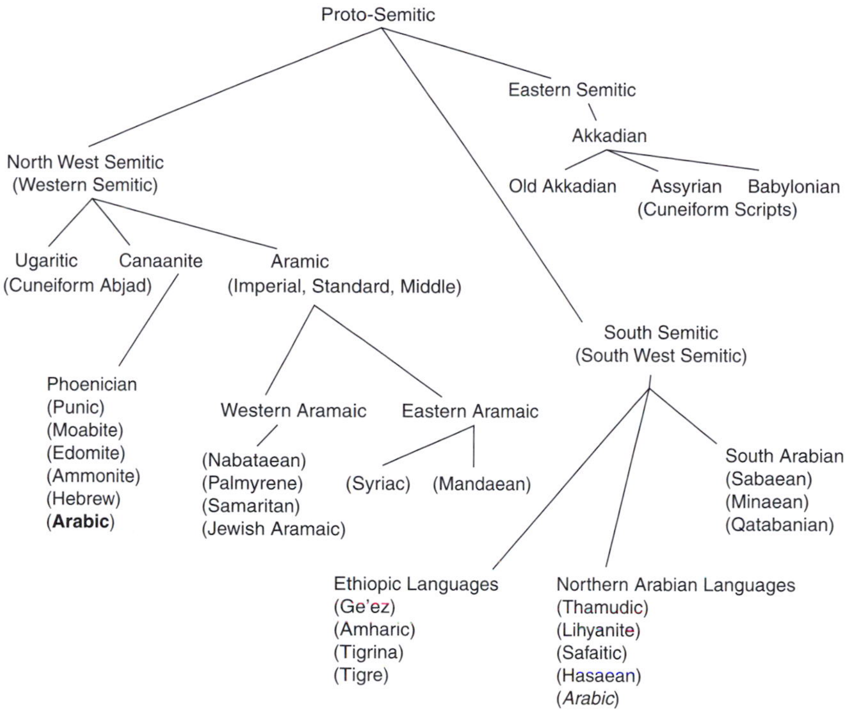

Figure 13 Semitic languages.

historical homeland of the proto-Semitic peoples has been a subject of debate: one view is that the Syrian plains once served as their original abode. Groups of migrants are said to have left the sedentary settlements of Syria and moved southwards, adopting a living as desert-dwelling nomads; the progressive migratory waves are said to have continued over a period of time, resulting in the physical distribution of the proto-Semitic language. In addition, there are also separate opinions which respectively identify North Africa and the Arabian Peninsula as original homelands of the proto-Semitic peoples. The shared affinities among the Semitic languages are supposedly an intricate result of gradual but decisive geographical diffusion, although the fact that each of the languages in question undergoes complex stages of development and is subject to a range of substrate influences renders such theories as being speculative. Furthermore, Semiticists generally favor playing down the hypothetical nature of the genetic link among the languages in question, choosing to focus instead on the typological similarities among these languages.

Towards the emergence of the classical Arabic language and script

Traditional Islamic sources divide the Arabian Peninsula into three broad geographical regions: Tihama, Hijaz, and Najd. Tihāma comprises the vast tracts of territory which run along the Red Sea coast reaching as far south as Yemen. Its northern edges are contiguous with the southern Mesopotamian desert plains. The central coastal plains of Tihāma blend into the region of Ḥijāz, which includes the towns of Mecca and Medina, extending eastwards, where it is bounded by the central plateau of the area known as Najd and its surrounding terrain. Arabic in the form of its many dialects was spoken in these regions alongside an elevated diction (Classical Arabic) which was retained for very formal contexts. The Arabs are mentioned in a range of sources from antiquity: Biblical, Greek, and Persian materials all refer to their presence in the geographical area designated as the Arabian Peninsula. Assyrian and Babylonian cuneiform inscriptions dated to the ninth century BCE provide a number of references telling of dealings with Arabs from the northern desert regions of the peninsula bordering the Fertile Crescent. These so-called ʿAribi were known for their nomadic way of life, although many of them sought a sedentary existence in oasis settlements. Many settled in northern and central regions of the peninsula and were ancestors of those Arabs who were historical witnesses to the birth of Islam. During the second millennium BCE, the southwest region of the peninsula was home to a high-level material culture: archaeological finds such as temples, dams, and elaborate watercourses confirm its cultural sophistication in the world of antiquity. The southern Arabian states organized the ancient trade routes which traversed the western coast of the Arabian Peninsula and the eastern expanses. These routes connected the Mediterranean countries with the Far and Near East. Mecca and Medina were both settlements situated near the ancient trade routes, although in the case of the former town it was also the home of a pre-eminent religious shrine, the Kaʿba, to which pilgrims flocked. Bedouin Arabs had played a key role in the movement of commodities and goods: they settled in oases and stations along the ancient routes. The language of the south was sharply distinguished from the Classical Arabic idiom employed by the Arabs at the dawn of Islam. It had also developed an elegant script, which is referred to as epigraphic South Arabian, due to its being preserved on durable materials such as stone, ceramics, coins, and metals. It was apparently derived from a proto-Canaanite archetype. The South Arabian script, which originally comprised 29 consonants, adopted a right to left format, although there do exist inscriptions in which a boustrophedon convention is followed with lines being written alternately in a right to left, left to right direction. Some South Arabian inscriptions clearly adhere to a left to right convention. The Ethiopic scripts of Ge'ez, Amharic, and Tigre were developed from this South Arabian archetype and actually adopted a left to right convention.

Numerous monumental inscriptions and graffito found along the ancient trade routes and in northern and eastern areas of the Arabian peninsula utilized the South Arabian script. These include inscriptions associated with the Northern Arabian languages of Thamudic, Lihyanite, Hasaean, and lastly Safaitic, of which there exist some 15,000 inscriptions. Certain correspondences existed between the vocabulary of the northern Arabic languages and Classical Arabic of the late pre-Islamic period. The pre-Islamic Northern languages, which are often designated as Proto-Arabic, are theoretically considered somewhat distant ancestors of Classical Arabic. Some of the Thamudic inscriptions, which are rather short, can be dated as early as the sixth century BCE, while even the Lihyanite inscriptions have an early provenance, dating to around the fifth century BCE. The definite article in these scripts followed a convention established in Southern Arabian languages, namely the use of (*h*) and (*hn*). Later inscriptions dated to the second and third centuries CE reveal that (*al*) was used to represent the definite article. Proper names and loanwords from inscriptions found within the pagan kingdoms of the Nabataeans and the Palmyrenes, who had their respective capitals at Petra (in modern-day Jordan) and Palmyra (in modern-day Syria) use (*al*) as the definite article. The Nabataeans and the Palmyrenes are identified as Arabs who developed a highly sophisticated culture. Petra was annexed by the Byzantines in 106 CE, while Palmyra was destroyed in 274 CE. The decline of these kingdoms, which was coupled with the steady economical and political demise of the Southern Arabian entities, ushered in a prolonged period of rivalry between the Persian and Byzantine empires. This culminated in several wars which were fought between the fourth and sixth centuries CE. A number of Arab tribes had served as vassals for the warring empires: the Lakhmids served the Persians at Hira, an important center for the dissemination of Christianity, while the Ghassanids performed a similar function for the Byzantines in Syria. In the case of the Nabataeans, they spoke a variety of Arabic which was a precursor of Classical Arabic, despite employing the Aramaic script and language as their formal *lingua franca*. This is noteworthy as the Arabic script which appears in later inscriptions was apparently based on a Nabataean–Aramaic model. This earlier model had developed both monumental and cursive forms. Cursive and linear scripts were evolved to facilitate writing, breaking away from the rigid physical strictures imposed by monumental characters; ligatures were devised to join the separate consonants, giving them, where appropriate, initial, medial, and terminal forms. The Arabic script was to make vital use of these qualities.

One inscription which is considered important for gauging the historical crystallization of Classical Arabic and its script is the funerary epitaph found at Namara 120 km southeast of Damascus. Devoted to a Lakhmid king by the name of Imru 'l-Qays, it is preserved in a script which scholars view as being one of the earliest forms of the developing Arabic orthography. Moreover, its language significantly reveals distinct affinities with the Classical Arabic idiom which defined the literary tradition of the post-Islamic epoch, although Aramaic loanwords do feature in this epitaph. However, the Raqūsh tombstone from Madā'in Ṣāliḥ in the northwest region of the Arabian peninsula, which is dated to 267 CE, has been cited by some scholars in terms of its furnishing early evidence of the development of Classical Arabic and its script (Healey and Smith 1989: 77). A first-century inscription discovered in ʿEn ʿAvdat in the Negev and dated to the first century CE has even led some researchers to countenance a much earlier historical stage in the emergence of language and script. Additional pre-Islamic inscriptions examined in this context include a tombstone from Umm al-Jimal (250 CE), which lies south west of Bosra in Syria; the Jabal Ramm (300–350 CE) inscription from a Nabataean temple near the sea port of al-ʿAqaba in Jordan; the trilingual inscription found on a lintel at Zabad (512 CE) near Aleppo; an inscription located in a church at Umm al-Jimal (520 CE) in Jordan; a reference to a military expedition of a Ghassanid king found at Jabal Usas (528 CE) south east of Damascus; and an inscription referring to the erection of a martyrium in Harran (568 CE).

One has to concede that the early inscriptions provide only fleeting glimpses of the historical emergence of the Arabic language in the pre-Islamic period and the evolution of its script, although one scholar concludes that among the Arabs from the first century CE onwards, a language closely related to Classical Arabic was in use (Versteegh 2001: 35). The paucity of surviving epigraphic and paleographical evidence has led to suggestions that writing was not widespread among the Arabs of the late pre-Islamic period; and, that the literary tradition must have remained essentially oral in character, although the sophistication and maturity of the Classical Arabic idiom are not in dispute. Many scholars argue that the rudimentary nature of available writing materials was not conducive to the spread of writing. These materials included parchment, papyrus, the ribs and shoulder-blades of animals, the stalks of palms, ostraca (fragments of pottery), linen, thin pieces of limestone, and vellum, which was rather expensive. Nevertheless, it is striking that the symbols of literacy are freely accentuated in the Qur'ān, which pre-eminently serves as one of the earliest written sources in Arabic. Indeed, references to scribes, scrolls, scripts, parchment, writing, books, ink, recitation, and indeed the (reed) pen permeate the sacred text. Historical treatments of the biography of the Prophet also refer to the transcription of pacts, transactions, and the dispatch of correspondences; and this is similarly true in chronologies of the post-prophetic periods. Modern scholarship is of the view that at the time of Islam's appearance the Arabic language possessed a highly elevated diction. The rhetorical flair imposingly displayed in the composition of the Qur'ān serves as testimony to that fact. Classical Islamic scholarship argued that proof of the text's divine origin rested in its matchless linguistic style. Poetry had been an important vehicle for literary expression among the Arabs. In the late pre-Islamic period, its composition had reached significant levels of sophistication; odes were composed in intricately rhymed verse and there existed an impressive range of poetic metres and thematic formats from which poets could select. All of which imply that a perceptive appreciation of literary refinement existed among the Arabs at the time of the Qur'ān's revelation. The Qur'ān deliberately dissociates its style and arrangment from that of classical poetry, declaring that it was not the "word of a poet." The emphasis on rhetorical eminence appears as an imposing motif in the literature which recounts the life of the Prophet, who is said to have remarked that he was the most eloquent of Arabs, referring to his being reared among Bedouin Arabs. In their empirical quest to define the perfect Arabic diction, early grammarians and philologists sought out the modes of parlance and linguistic predilections of Bedouin Arabs. They were used as one of the sources for the codification of Arabic grammar.

Linguistic impact of the Islamic conquests

In the seventh century, the advent of Islam and the rapid Muslim conquests of vast swathes of territory across the Near and Middle East, North Africa, and Central Asia, consequently followed by their assimilation, settlement, and administration placed the Arabs along with their language and faith onto a much broader religious, social, political, and geographical stage. The conquests ultimately brought together a miscellany of peoples, faiths, traditions, and cultures all of which intermingled to facilitate the conditions for the materialization of a civilization shaped by the overarching constructs of a monotheistic creed. This civilization, which had centers in locations as culturally and ethnically diverse as Cordoba and Seville in Andalusia, the Island of Sicily in the Mediterranean, Damascus in Syria, Baghdad in Iraq, Cairo in Egypt, Nishapur in Persia, and Samarqand and Bukhara beyond the Oxus, was receptive to a wide gamut of influences, although the language of Arabic remained the defining feature of its political, cultural, and religious identity. Much of this civilization's literary achievements were articulated, refined, and preserved through the language of Arabic. During the rule of the Umayyad caliph, ʿAbd al-Malik ibn Marwān (r. 685–705), Arabic was made the official language of administration (700). It was employed throughout Muslim controlled territory, achieving a status akin to that enjoyed by Aramaic in the pre-Islamic periods. New converts, and more crucially, their offspring adopted the Arabic language as their mother tongue. The language became a unifying symbol of religious identity and in many instances, indigenous languages were eclipsed by Arabic's prominence due to its being the language of state and religion. Even with the fragmentation of the Islamic polity (the Abbasids, who ruled from 749–1258, had become a nominal authority giving way to independent dynasties and principalities), Arabic retained, at the very least, the status of being the language of faith. For example, in the tenth century the dynasty of the Samanids, who ruled in the eastern parts of Persia, replaced Arabic with Persian as their language of culture and administration; and, the renaissance of the symbols of Persian identity was also promoted by the Safavids in the sixteenth century. They elevated Shiʿism as the official religion of state. Yet, even within these confines, Arabic preserved it role as the language of the faith.

The Islamic tradition, with its monotheistic message and proselytizing ethic, did not distinguish between spiritual and secular spheres of human activity. Throughout the first three centuries of the Islamic tradition, Muslim scholarship produced a detailed system of law and ritual practice which auspiciously engendered rich literary traditions of learning. These were initially formulated to explicate the religious sources: exegesis, law, theology, history, linguistic thought and philosophy, developed as separate fields of learning, while disciplines of a more secular flavor such as astronomy, geometry, alchemy, medicine, mathematics, geography, and logic all flourished. During the rule of the Umayyads (661–749) and their successors the Abbasids, attention was turned towards translating into Arabic much of the medical, scientific, and philosophical heritage of the classical traditions of antiquity. The Abbasid caliph al-Maʾmūn (r. 813–33), established the famous *Bayt al-ḥikma* ("House of Wisdom") in Baghdad during 830 for this very purpose. Texts were often retranslated in the pursuit of precision and subsequently furnished with elaborate commentaries. Thus for example, Ptolemy's *Almagest* and Euclid's *Elements* were the subject of several translations all aimed at improving the quality of earlier works. In due course, many of these materials entered the sphere of Europe via Islamic Spain: treatises and tracts which had been previously translated into Arabic from Greek and Syriac were rendered into Latin before being studied in Western medieval institutions. Access to these resources was therefore aided via the study of Arabic. It is interesting to note that Peter the Venerable commissioned the first Latin translation of the Qurʾān in 1143; he was behind a project for the translation of Islamic sources. Despite the fact that polemical motives were often behind such enterprises, the ground was laid for scholarly interaction with Arabic in the Western world.

Traditions of Arabic linguistic thought

The Arabic tradition recognized two classical traditions of linguistic thought. These two traditions were respectively associated with the settlements of Kufa and Basra in Iraq. Much of what is studied in the fields of Arabic grammar, philology, lexicography, and prosody has its roots in the traditions of learning cultivated in these two cities, although the Kūfans were eventually based in Baghdad. Scholarship connected with the Qur'ān appears to have provided the impetus for the developing linguistic sciences. Lexical paraphrase, the collating of variant readings of the Qur'ān, phonological conventions regarding the recitation of the Qur'ān, and even the enumeration of the verses of scripture in codices lay at the heart of these endeavors. A rational schema of thought which formulated rudimentary syntactic constructs designed to elucidate the linguistic configuration and constitution of the sacred text enhanced activities in these interconnected areas. The patterns of speech in the language of the Arabs and their ancient poetry were adduced by these pioneering grammarians to provide the Qur'anic diction with theoretical context and definition. The integration of all these approaches and methods gave birth to the first systematic attempt to present a theory of the language of the Arabs; and it was a Basran individual by the name of Sībawayhi (d. 796), the son of a Persian convert, who achieved this distinction. His book was named *al-Kitāb* and, over successive centuries, it served as the foundation for the theoretical analysis of Arabic linguistic thought. Attempts to locate an external influence upon the development of Arabic linguistic thought in the form of Greek, Syriac, Pahlavi, and Indian antecedents have never been adequately substantiated. The Kufan and Basran traditions ultimately developed unique methodologies and approaches to the study of the phenomenon of language, although there was a later tendency to accentuate the conceptual and methodological differences between the traditions. However, this should not disguise the swiftness with which the traditions of linguistic thought developed. The literary legacy of these two traditions was promulgated in the different regions of the Islamic world. Many of the traditions' luminaries were the sons of converts who had espoused the new faith. Their contribution was keenly felt in all fields of scholarship. It has been argued that the grammarians had operated on the assumption that there was only one proto-classical idiom – the diction derived from selected Bedouin Arabs – and, given that their informants were principally Arabs from the tribes of Najd in the central eastern heartlands of the Arabian Peninsula, a rather restricted model of the formal idiom emerged. This has led to the view that the purpose of grammar was simply to preserve and emulate this ancient idiom; however, grammatical thought was initially rather descriptive in countenance and concerned with Arabic as a living language, hence the countless references to Bedouin usage in grammatical and philological treatises as a means of giving bearing to morpho-syntactic, phonetic, and phonological axioms. The language of the Qur'ān and poetry critically assisted in the fleshing out of precepts and constructs. It is the case, however, that once a standard of the classical language was defined, it became the yardstick for later grammarians. Medieval biographical literature implies that mistakes by native speakers of Arabic and a failure on the part of converts to attain proficient levels of usage of the language initially prompted scholars to devise simple grammatical models which aimed to assist the learning of Arabic. Linguists did produce texts devoted to the phenomenon of solecisms (*laḥn*), which developed as a rich genre of writing. Nevertheless, the earliest literary works in the field of grammatical thought are not strictly pedagogical writings, but decidedly more abstract treatments of language. Over subsequent centuries, the grammatical tradition as a whole took the literary writings and achievements made by scholars during the first four centuries of Arabic linguistic thought and used these as the critical basis for their own endeavors. Such was the profusion of the corpus of sources furnished by the early grammatical tradition that later scholarship could devote voluminous treatises to defining Classical Arabic, while also offering contrasting as well as complementary paradigms of its features. The originality, creativity, and precision of the early tradition were never quite matched, but its legacy was preserved.

Classical Arabic idiom and the Qur'ān

Traditional Islamic scholarship held that the Qur'ān was revealed in the Meccan dialect of Quraysh, the tribe to which the Prophet Muḥammad belonged, notionally reflecting western Arabian dialectal influences. The dialect had seemingly assimilated and integrated all that was refined among the various vernaculars of the Arabs. It had supposedly developed into the distinguished *lingua franca*, serving as an elevated diction and the common medium of literary expression. During the early pre-Islamic periods, poetry and the formal discourse of the Arabs were said to have employed this elevated literary *koine*. The impression was that the prominence of Quraysh as the custodians of the Meccan sanctuary gave their native diction a unique seal of authority; that Quraysh were also influential merchants purportedly assisted the linguistic ascendancy of their dialect. However, recent scholarship has questioned the traditional emphasis placed on the significance of Quraysh's dialect, reckoning that although western dialects were represented in the classical idiom, the eastern Arabian dialects associated with the tribes of Najd (Qays, Tamīm, and Asad) practically shaped the definitive form of the Arabs' literary *koine*. Scholars remarked that pre-Islamic poetry dated to the sixth century, which was transmitted orally and codified by philologists much later, had actually been written in this elevated *koine*. The Qur'ān is viewed as being composed in a dialect which encapsulates this *koine*, although idiosyncratic phonological features associated with the Ḥijāzī dialects are likewise retained in its composition. Western Arabian dialects favored the omission (*tasḥīl*) of glottal stops (*hamza*). The Prophet is reported to have praised the fact that glottal stops did not feature in the phonemic repertoire of the dialect of Quraysh. In

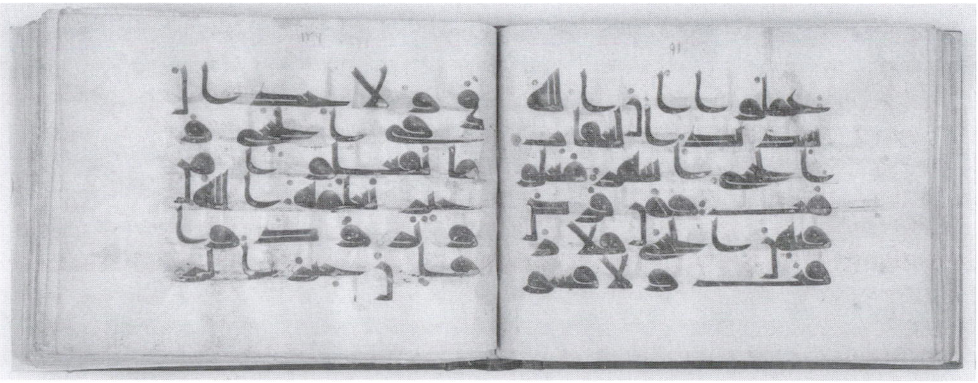

Figure 14 Qur'ān, late ninth century, Iraq. Modern writers have termed this bold script "Kufic," implying it originated solely in Kufa, Iraq, though this is not certain.

Source: Nasser D. Khalili Collection of Islamic Art, inv.no. QUR 372. Copyright the Nour Foundation. Courtesy of the Khalili Family Trust

contradistinction, the eastern dialects favored their inclusion (*taḥqīq*), irrespective of where they occurred in the articulation of a word or expression. The term "believer" would be pronounced by the Ḥijāzīs as *mūmin*; whereas, the eastern tribes would articulate the same term as *mu'min*. The feature of assimilation (*idghām*), in which geminated consonants of a close phonological proximity are vigorously integrated, is identified as an eastern Arabian dialectal predilection; the western dialects favored separating such geminated consonants (*fakk al-idghām*); both phonological traits are found in the Qur'an. A phonological quality referred to as *imāla* ("inclining or fronting of the vowel") was a typical characteristic of the Najdī dialects, whereas, the western dialects preferred the converse quality of *fatḥ* ("opening the vowel"). There are even different conventions adopted by these tribes regarding the gender of selected nouns and further phonological, morphological and syntactic variances which are documented in classical grammatical and philological literature.

Nonetheless, accentuating the predominance of these dialectal traits and their eastern provenance in the literary *koine* should not be allowed to obscure the more imposing question of the compositional features of the Qur'anic text. The Qur'ān consistently asserts the supreme and matchless nature of its literary arrangement. This rests not simply on subsidiary phonological and phonetic qualities but rather on the stylistic and rhetorical conventions of its linguistic configuration. The doctrine of the Qur'ān's linguistic inimitability (*i'jāz*) inevitably proceeds from a compositional substratum. Qur'anic allusions to the religion's Meccan opponents report that they believed the text resembled the poetry of the Arabs; so one might assume that the Meccans recognized that the Qur'ān's literary arrangement was similar in format to their valued poetic *koine*. The Qur'ān states that the Meccan opponents of the Prophet characterized its early contents as being comprised of "ancient fables," "handed down sorcery," and that the text was essentially "the words of a mortal." Reference is also made to its being comparable to the rhymed utterances of a soothsayer or a man possessed by demons or spirits. Against this background of rejection, the Qur'ān issued a challenge to its Meccan critics. It was based on the premise that the ancient Arabs believed themselves to be paragons of linguistic eloquence and rhetoric. Accordingly, if the contents of the Qur'ān represented the mere words of a mortal, then the Arabs should have been able to match and surpass its linguistic splendor. The Qur'ān states the Arabs were unable to rise to the challenge, demonstrating not only the text's inimitable quality as reflected in its composition and style, but also its divine status as a book of revelation.

Arguments that the Prophet was apparently illiterate are also adduced in classical discourse on the Qur'an's inimitability. There exists an anecdote in which the Prophet remarked of the Arabs "We are an illiterate people; we can neither read nor enumerate." The Qur'ān refers to the Prophet as being *al-nabī al-ummī* (often translated as the "illiterate prophet"). Recently, discussions have persisted concerning the etymology of this term and whether it actually connotes a gentile. Classical scholarship imported the issue of the illiteracy of the Prophet into the equation of the Qur'ān's inimitability. The irony was all too apparent: the Arabs were paragons of linguistic eloquence and claimed the Qur'ān was the composition of an unlettered individual yet they were unable to match it. This led medieval scholars to argue that the Qur'ān's miraculous nature resided in the composition of the text (*naẓm*); its style had broken previous literary conventions with which the Arabs were familiar. One figure who helped refine the subtleties of the doctrine of *iʿjāz* was the theologian and jurist Abū Bakr al-Bāqillānī (d. 1013), although enterprising discussions on this subject had been broached much earlier among theologians. Indeed, a figure by the name of al-Naẓẓām (d. 836) claimed that the miracle (*iʿjāz*) was not the linguistic inimitability of the text per se but rather the fact that the Arabs had been prevented from producing a text to match it; they had the capacity to do that but God had prevented them from doing so! The doctrine was called (*ṣarfa*), namely deflection or prevention. Bāqillānī and others argued that the gist of this concept made the act of "prevention" the miracle and not the unique literary composition of the text. Over ensuing centuries later scholarship refined an astute synthesis of all these various arguments when formalizing the doctrine of *iʿjāz*.

Simple linguistic constructs often played a profound role in the fleshing out of theological dogma. An excellent case in point is the infamous episode of the inquisition (*miḥna*). A group of theologians known as the Muʿtazilites, who were renowned for having refined rational approaches to the interpretation of religious doctrines, employing modes of thought and argumentation derived from Greek philosophical thought, had promoted the belief that the Qur'ān was in essence a created document. Orthodoxy had championed the view that God was a speaker in the literal sense of the word, advocating that the Qur'ān encapsulated His veridical expression in the language of Arabic. They further postulated that speech (*kalām*), as manifested in the Qur'ān, was one of His eternal attributes. According to Muʿtazilite reasoning, such a view predicated that God had a physical organ with which to articulate words and thereby conceptually compromised the nature of His transcendent status. It led them to formulate an abstract proposition which posited that God was not a speaker in the literal sense of the word, but rather he created speech temporally. They persuaded the Abbasid caliph al-Ma'mūn (r. 813–33) to adopt this doctrine as an official creed, having those who refused to accept it imprisoned. There are also instances in which theological considerations foreshadowed linguistic discussions. The issue of whether foreign loanwords could be found in the Qur'ān's Arabic vocabulary is one such example. Some medieval scholars did subscribe to the view that this was a plausible thesis which did not impinge upon the Arabic character of the text; conversely, others were concerned such an admission might be used in an insidious way to undermine the linguistic integrity of the Qur'ān's Arabic status. The contentiousness of the issue was lessened by the suggestion that lexical parallels between Arabic and other languages could be explained through the phenomenon of correspondence (*tawāfuq*), although issues such as this one did not arrest the inventiveness with which such subjects were tackled. Classical Islamic discourse on the origin of language was another theologically charged question. Orthodoxy initially espoused the belief that language was a divinely inspired phenomenon (*tawqīf*) with its primary elements being imparted to Adam by God, who taught him the names of all things created; Muʿtazilite theologians elaborated an opposing theory which identified human agency (*iṣtilāḥ*) in the genesis of the conventions of language. The philological concepts of metaphor, synonyms, antonyms, homonyms, and etymology were incorporated into the various deliberations. One even finds a number of scholars countenancing the view that there existed a natural affinity (onomatopoeia) between meanings and sounds. A prominent medieval philologist by the name of Ibn Fāris (d. 1004–5), who was an avid supporter of the thesis of *tawqīf*, claimed that Arabic grammar, orthography, and prosody were not invented by the Arabs, but rather rediscovered by them; they too had their origin in the divine imposition of language. Again, at stake were underlying theoretical principles about the nature of God. In general, however, such discourse reveals the subtle arcing of theological and linguistic concepts in the medieval Islamic tradition.

Declension and the Qurʾān

One of the defining characteristics of Classical Arabic is that it possesses a fully operational system of declension (*iʿrāb*): for instance, nominative, accusative, and genitive case endings, along with a range of grammatical moods and tenses, are indicated by specific vocalic values, which serve as tangible features of this intricate system of *iʿrāb*. Some recent scholars have proposed the thesis that the Qur'ān's diction, as it was preserved in the Meccan dialect, did not originally exhibit the declensional features associated with the Arabs' esteemed poetic *koine*. The fact that the early written script was without *matres lectionis* (the notation of vowel markings) seemingly added weight to this theory. The inference is that grammarians and philologists of the developed traditions of linguistic thought, which were established in eighth-century Iraq, superimposed such features onto the Qur'anic diction. These traditions primarily based their study of language on eastern Arabian sources whose dialectal conventions were deemed linguistically superior. The claim was made that the elevated literary form of the Arabs' literary *koine*, which employed the full operational declension, was mastered only by skilled poets and their informants, while the colloquial modes of speech, which dispensed with declension, were mostly in usage among the indigenous Arabs. It was argued that even the Bedouin Arabs had not retained declension in their everyday forms of communication. Interestingly, the linguistic variety which defines the many modern dialects of Arabic is outwardly traced to this state of affairs. The implication is that following the Islamic conquests, and the movements of population accompanying them, the Arab settlers simply preserved their characteristic dialectal distinctions, disseminating them in the places they settled; such dialects were naturally exposed to substrate influences.

Ultimately, reference is made to the fact that neither the pre-Islamic Arabic inscriptions nor the early Ḥijāzī Qur'anic manuscripts exhibited the syntactic inflection associated with the classical idiom. Nevertheless, it must be remembered that writing systems are essentially devised to facilitate the accurate recovery of a text without the assistance of an actual speaker (Daniels and Bright 1996: 3). The Arabic script had inherited the Aramaic–Nabataean abecedaries (*abjad*s) which had not fully developed an advanced system for the notation of short vowels and indeed certain long vowels. The orthographical deficiencies inherent in the Aramaic–Nabataean model were replicated in the early Arabic script (Diem 1976: 56). Yet, these relate to issues of "recovery" and are hardly an indication that declension was not a distinctive feature of Qur'anic Arabic. Given the status of the Qur'ān as a devotional and recited text, great emphasis was placed on its oral preservation and transmission, a fact which appears to be overlooked in the arguments about the poetic *koine* and the use of declension in Arabic. The Qur'anic codices initially served as mnemonic devices. Their design was to perfect the precise physical recovery of the oral expression.

Developments in this respect show the increasing importance of the written tradition. The declensional features of Arabic would have been principally preserved through the oral transmission of the text. Orthographical improvements in the shape of vowel markings, diacritical dots, and verse markers were later innovations refined by pioneers of Arabic linguistic thought.

The sharp distinction between the elevated form of Classical Arabic, which was the esteemed literary idiom, and the colloquial vernaculars in common usage among the early Arabs has been hypothetically defined as a form of diglossia; moreover, it has led to the contention that this state of affairs permeated certain forms of literary prose. Hypocorrections and hypercorrections (the former relates to partial grammatical corrections found in early manuscripts, while the latter defines the affected grammatical emendation of texts) in early Islamic papyri and materials from later periods are highlighted to demonstrate this point. It has led to the designation of a type of literary idiom referred to as Middle Arabic and a number of further complex sub-divisions of Classical Arabic. One scholar has argued that this tells us little about the actual state of the vernacular: accordingly, Middle Arabic texts may reflect only the levels of proficiency of the individuals who transcribed these texts (Versteegh 1997: 114). Although Middle Arabic constitutes deviations from the norms of standard grammar, the Classical Arabic idiom always served as the definitive model and yardstick of such derived styles and the intended literary paradigm of aspiring authors. Besides, Classical Arabic was the unquestionable object of attention and target language as far as the Arabic grammarians were concerned.

Development of the script after the rise of Islam

The issue of whether the Arabic script evolved from either a Nabataean or Syriac archetype has been the subject of much debate among paleographers. There is a tendency to accept that while the cursive used by the Nabataeans served as the principal model for the Arabic script, Syriac influences also had an impact upon the script's development. It should be noted that the Nabataean and Syriac scripts both had an Aramaic derivation. Arabic required a total of 28 characters which it derived from the 15 available graphemes (characters). In a number of instances, the same grapheme was used to represent dissimilar phonemic values. Diacritical dots and markings were eventually devised to distinguish these graphemes, allowing the script to accommodate the phonemic range of the Arabic language. There existed precedents regarding the use of diacritical dots: they were actually used in the Nabataean cursive script for the purpose of differentiating certain characters; furthermore, Syriac employed a strategically placed dot to distinguish the homograph used to denote the characters *d* and *r*. One of the earliest Islamic papyri which display diacritical markings is dated to the year 642, although the use of diacritical markings in the Arabic script appears to have a pre-Islamic provenance. The addition of diacritics is technically called *iʿjām*, which, through a quaint etymological rule, literally connotes making clear. The official (*textus receptus*) of the Qur'ān, which was compiled under the aegis of the third caliph ʿUthmān (r. 644–56), is said to have been deliberately stripped of diacritical dots to accommodate occasional consonantal variants in the recitation of the text. Most paleographers accept that the use of diacritical markings in the early Ḥijāzī scripts was somewhat irregular. This is true of their incidence in papyri, inscriptions, and coins. The argument is that they originally appeared in the form of "dashes" in older Qur'anic manuscripts; and initially there was even religious opposition to their usage. However, arguments were advanced for their utility, and diacritical dots gradually permeated manuscripts and folios of the Qur'ān, becoming a ubiquitous feature in later codices. In the same way the numbering of individual verses was a later introduction based on conventions preserved through oral transmission among reciters of the Qur'ān. A system of vowel notation pioneered by the early Arabic grammarians also made use of dots.

Arabic models of vowel notation were conceived for the intention of aiding the recitation of the sacred text. Their inception is linked with the Basran Abū 'l-Aswad al-Du'alī (d. 688), who is hailed as the architect of Arabic grammar. The suggestion is that there was awareness among those pioneers of Arabic, and indeed Hebrew orthography, of the developments relating to vowel notation in Syriac. It had developed three unique scripts with the earliest of these being the Estrangelo cursive. One such text in this script, which is dated to 411 CE, reveals the use of diacritical and vowel markings in the form of strategically placed dots (Healey 1990: 245). Eastern and western models of vowel notation in Syriac were in use. The former was formulated in the fourth and fifth centuries CE; while the latter system is associated with Jacob of Edessa (d. 708). In the Basran scheme, a single red dot was placed above, below, and in front of a given consonant to indicate the short vowels of *fatḥa, kasra*, and *ḍamma* correspondingly. Doubled red dots were used for instances of *tanwīn* (nunation), while blue, yellow, and green dots were employed to indicate pauses, glottal stops, and a range of phonological traits. The process of vowel marking was formerly referred to as *naqṭ* (literally adding dots), although later on the term *tashkīl* was applied. Reference is also made to the fact that the Meccans previously adhered to an ancient system of dot placement which was not in concord with the Basran scheme: a dot placed above a consonant was used to represent the short vowel of *ḍamma*, while a dot situated in front of, or adjacent to, a consonant denoted the *fatḥa*. The system was eventually discarded for the Basran model. Sets of fine strokes, dots, and circles were used to mark off separate verses of the Qur'ān with further markers being devised to indicate batches of five and ten Qur'anic verses. Gradually, these were improved through the use of decorated bands and rosettes. A Basran individual renowned for his creative brilliance in the fields of grammar, lexicography, and prosody, Khalīl ibn Aḥmad (d. 791–2), eventually devised a format which allowed the use of dots to be replaced. His scheme of supra-linear and sub-linear notation was based on graphic proto-types of the three Arabic vowels: *alif, wāw*, and *yā'*. They were used to represent the vocalic values of *fatḥa, ḍamma*, and *kasra*. Khalīl proposed further orthographical improvements to denote geminated consonants and other phonological properties.

Classical Arabic biographies do speak of the pre-Islamic Meccans being taught the art of writing by the people of Anbār, which is situated close to Ḥīra in Iraq, where Syriac was formally dominant. It was said that the script was brought back to Mecca by itinerant merchants and that it influenced indigenous scripts of the Ḥijāz. Nevertheless, this view does tend to deflect attention from the fact that Arabic scripts were already in use in the Ḥijāz and that, steadily, a range of individual techniques and styles had developed in the conventions of writing. Paleographic and epigraphic evidence appears to support this judgment. The term Kufic was used to designate the

Figure 15 Al-Ghad font, Al-Ghad newspaper – Jordan. A special font was designed for this Jordan newspaper that desired a distinct visual identity.

Source: Tarek Atrissi Design, the Netherlands, www.atrissi.com, 2002

calligraphic style of early Qur'anic codices, although its links with the city of Kūfa, which was established in the year 639, remain vague. However, it is the case that such was the predominance of this Iraqi script that most early specimens of Qur'anic manuscripts were actually designated as being Kufic. This tended to overshadow the variety of styles which had existed and led to the proposal of an alternative system of classifying early Arabic scripts (Déroche 1992: 16), particularly as far as Qur'anic codices were concerned. Additionally, the so-called Kufic script was used for monumental purposes and for non-Qur'anic transcription. Paper was introduced into the Islamic world around 733 and this had a dramatic impact upon the further development of the script. The so-called *naskh* style which was employed for copying was given meticulous definition first by Ibn Muqla (d. 940) and then by Ibn al-Bawwāb (d. 1022). The prohibition of representational art in the Islamic tradition meant that calligraphy became an important medium for artistic expression furthering the aesthetic development of the script.

The Arabic script was adopted in those parts of the world where Muslim rule and influence was in the ascendancy. The basic model of the Arabic script was used for the transcription of the Iranian languages of Persian, Kurdish, and Pashto; it served the Indic languages of Urdu, Sindhi, and Kashmiri; and the Berber languages of North Africa. Diacritical markings were devised to enable the phonemic range of these various languages to be accommodated. The Malay languages of Southeast Asia had originally adopted the Arabic script, but it was replaced by the Latin script. African languages such as Swahili, Hausa, and Somali had until recently all employed Arabic scripts, a legacy of the close relationship between language and faith. The Ottoman empire, whose rule stretched over six centuries, used the script for the intricate language of Ottoman Turkish until its use was banned in the 1920s with the abolishment of the caliphate. A new Latin-based script was developed. The Arabic script was even used by the Balto-Slavic languages of Polish and Ukrainian. Despite being relinquished in a number of these Muslim countries, the script of Arabic retains its devotional importance as it continues to be taught for the recitation of Islam's sacred scripture, the Qur'ān.

References and further reading

Abbott, N. (1939) *The Rise of the North Arabic Script and its Kur'anic Development*, Chicago: University of Chicago Press. (Provides a detailed survey of the factors which shaped the emergence of the Arabic script as reflected in its Qur'anic usage.)

Baalbaki, R. (1983) "Early Arab Lexicographers and the Use of Semitic Languages," *Berytus*, 31: 117–27.

—— (ed.) (2007) *The Early Islamic Grammatical Tradition* (The Formation of the Classical Islamic World Series), Aldershot: Ashgate.

Beeston, A. F. L. (1970) *The Arabic Language Today*, London: Hutchinson.

—— (1981) "Languages of Pre-Islamic Arabia," *Arabica*, 28: 178–86.

Bellamy, J. (1985) "A New Reading of the Namārah Inscription," *Journal of the American Oriental Society*, 105: 31–48.

—— (1990) "Arabic Verses from the First/Second Century: the Inscription of ʿEn ʿAvdat," *Journal of Semitic Studies*, 57: 73–9.

Bloom, J. (2001) *Paper before Print: the History and Impact of Paper in the Islamic World*, New Haven: Yale University Press.

Bohas, G., Guillaume, J. P. and Kouloughli, D. E. (1990) *The Arabic Linguistic Tradition*, London: Routledge. (This text offers a clear overview of the theoretical issues explored in medieval linguistic thought.)

Carter, M. (1981) *Arab Linguistics: An Introductory Classical Text with Notes*, Amsterdam and Philadelphia: John Benjamins. (A valuable translation of an influential medieval grammatical treatise.)

—— (1984) "Linguistic Science and Orthodoxy in Conflict: the Case of al-Rummānī," *Zeitschrift für Geschichte der Arabisch–Islamischen Wissenschaften*, 1: 212–32.

—— (1990) "Arabic Lexicography" and "Arabic Grammar," in M. Young, J. D. Latham, R. B. Serjeant, eds., *Cambridge History of Arabic Literature. Religion, Learning, and Science in the ʿAbbasid Period*, Cambridge: Cambridge University Press, 106–17, 118–38.

—— (2004) *Sībawayhi*, London: I. B. Taurus. (An analysis of the theoretical features of the first systematic work of Arabic grammar.)

Daniels, P. and Bright, W., eds. (1996) *The World's Writing Systems*, Oxford and New York: Oxford University Press. (Several articles on the historical development of the Arabic script.)

Déroche, F. (1992) *The Abbasid Tradition: Qur'ans of the 8th to 10th Centuries*, London: Nour Foundation in association with Azimuth Editions and Oxford University Press. (A superb collection of illustrative plates of early Qur'anic manuscripts.)

—— (2006) *Islamic Codicology: an Introduction to the Study of Manuscripts in Arabic Script*, London: Al-Furqan Islamic Heritage Foundation.

Diem, W. (1976) "Some Glimpses at the Rise and Early Development of the Arabic Orthography," *Orientalia*, 45: 251–61.

Gruendler, B. (1993) *The Development of the Arabic Scripts. From the Nabatean Era to the First Islamic Century According to Dated Texts*, Atlanta: Scholars Press.

Gutas, D. (1998) *Greek Thought, Arabic Culture: The Graeco–Arabic Translation Movement in Baghdad and Early ʿAbbasid Society (2nd–4th/8th–10th Centuries)*, London and New York: Routledge. (Deals with the conceptual thrust of the translation movement and its achievements.)

Healey, J. (1990) "The Early Alphabet," in J. T. Hooker, ed., *Reading the Past: Ancient Writing from Cuneiform to the Alphabet*, London: Guild Publishing, 197–257.

Healey, J. and Smith, R. (1989) "Jaussen-Savignac 17: the Earliest Dated Arabic Document," *Aṭlāl*, 12: 77–84.

Heinrichs, W. (1995) "The Classification of the Sciences and the Consolidation of Philology in

Classical Islam," in J. W. Drijvers, A. A. MacDonald, eds., *Centres of Learning: Learning and Location in Pre-Modern Europe and the Near East*, Leiden: E. J. Brill, 119–39.

Hetzron, R., ed. (1997) *The Semitic Languages*, London: Routledge. (A superb range of authoritative articles on the Arabic script, standard forms of the language, and grammatical theory can be consulted in this reference work.)

Holes, C. (2004) *Modern Arabic: Structures, Functions, and Varieties*, Washington, DC: Georgetown University Press. (An up-to-date critical survey of the state of Modern Arabic.)

—— (2005) *Dialect, Culture, and Society in Eastern Arabia*, Leiden: Brill.

Hopkins, S. (1987) *Studies in the Grammar of Early Arabic, Based on Papyri datable to Before A.H. 300/912 A.D.*, London: Oxford University Press. (Deals with the theoretical nuances and conventions in early grammar.)

Ingham, B. (1994) "The Arabic Language in Iran," *Indian Journal of Applied Linguistics*, 20: 103–16.

Kopf, L. (1956) "Religious Influences on Mediaeval Arabic Philology," *Studia Islamica*, 5: 33–59.

Lipinski, E. (1997) *Semitic Languages: Outline of a Comparative Grammar*, Louvain: Peeters.

Mahdi, M. (1970) "Language and Logic in Classical Islam," in G. E. von Grunebaum, ed., *Logic in Classical Islamic Culture*, Wiesbaden: Otto Harrassowitz, 51–83.

Meuleman, J. (1994) "Arabic in Indonesia," *Indian Journal of Applied Linguistics*, 20: 11–34.

Rabin, C. (1951) *Ancient West Arabian*, London: Taylor's Foreign Press. (This remains the standard text for the historical analysis of Classical Arabic and its dialects.)

Rippin, A. (2003) "The Designation of 'Foreign' Languages in the Exegesis of the Qur'ān," in J. D. McAuliffe, B. D. Walfish, J. W. Goering, eds., *With Reverence for the Word: Medieval Scriptural Exegesis in Judaism, Christianity, and Islam*, Oxford and New York: Oxford University Press, 437–43.

Semaan, K. (1968) *Linguistics in the Middle Ages, Phonetic Studies in Early Islam*, Leiden: E. J. Brill. (A traditional survey of developments in medieval linguistic thought based on classical sources.)

Shah, M. (2003) "Exploring the Genesis of Early Arabic Linguistic Thought: Qur'anic Readers and Grammarians of the Basran Tradition (Part II)," *Journal of Qur'anic Studies*, 5: 1–48.

Stetkevych, J. (1970) *The Modern Arabic Literary Language: Lexical and Stylistic Developments*, Chicago and, London: University of Chicago Press. (Focuses on the aesthetic dimensions of the literary diction.)

Suleiman, Y. (2002) *The Arabic Language and National Identity: a Study in Ideology*, Edinburgh: Edinburgh University Press.

Ullendorff, E. (1958) "What is a Semitic Language?" *Orientalia* 27: 66–75.

Versteegh, K. (1997) *Landmarks in Linguistic Thought III: the Arabic Linguistic Tradition*, London and New York: Routledge. (A selection of translated classical texts on linguistic thought.)

—— (2001) *The Arabic Language*, Edinburgh: Edinburgh University Press. (Provides an authoritative survey of the Arabic language, encompassing the history, development, and structure of all aspects of Arabic in its classical, standard, and dialectal forms.)

Watson, J. (2002) *The Phonology and Morphology of Arabic*, Oxford: Oxford University Press.

Zaborski, A. (1991) "The Position of Arabic within the Semitic Dialect Continuum," *Arabist: Budapest Studies in Arabic*, 3–4: 365–75.

20

PHILOSOPHY

Oliver Leaman

It is futile to try to date precisely the start of philosophy in the Islamic world. Philosophy in its technical sense certainly did not arise for a long time, but the sorts of issues which philosophy raises were themselves often part of the new religion itself. Theoretical questions were raised in the initial phases of Islam, questions which were generally addressed to specifically Islamic texts such as the Qur'ān, the practices of the community (*sunna*) and the traditional sayings of the Prophet and his companions (*ḥadīth*). For the Shīʿī community one has to add the teachings of the Imāms. Added to this canonical foundation a whole range of what came to be known as the Islamic sciences were produced, and these consisted largely of religious law, the study of the language in which God transmitted the Qur'ān (Arabic), and the various schools of theology which represented differing understandings of Islam. Some of the early issues were dealt with by the theological schools but are clearly philosophical, such as the problem of free will, the nature of human and divine knowledge, issues about what counts as evidence, the relationship between our actions and divine will. These and many other debates came to be seen as the main controversies that served to distinguish the basic intellectual groups in the Islamic world.

The early conquests of the Muslims brought them into close contact with centers of civilization heavily influenced by Christianity and Judaism, and also by Greek culture. Some Muslims rejected the use of Greek concepts, arguing that the Islamic sciences were sufficient themselves to resolve any theoretical problems that might arise. The Islamic sciences also had the advantage of being Islamic, and so were based on the last revelation of God, something that the works of the Greeks could not hope to emulate. On the other hand, many Muslims were interested in using knowledge wherever it came from, and were intrigued by the high level of intellectual work in the contemporary world that used techniques and ideas based on ancient Greek thought. A political decision was taken from quite early on to use Greek forms of knowledge, in particular Greek science, mathematics and medicine. The caliph al-Ma'mūn (r. 813–33) was a strong advocate of Greek thought, and founded an institution with the main purpose of collecting, translating and disseminating important Greek texts into Arabic. He may have had in mind the practical benefits to be derived from Greek thought, since Greek culture seemed to go along with material benefits, but along with the practical science came theory, and in particular philosophy. The philosophy in fashion then was not Greek philosophy from the Peripatetic or Socratic periods, which had both finished a long time previously. The leading school of philosophy during the early centuries of Islam was Neoplatonism; this was what was translated into Arabic, sometimes via Syriac by Christian translators, and the Neoplatonic school of philosophy really established the philosophical curriculum in the Islamic world. The early translations included works of Aristotle, commentaries on him, summaries of many of Plato's dialogues, and later Greek commentaries of their work, often stressing what is taken to be a basic agreement between Plato and Aristotle and going far beyond them in approach. In addition, several important Neoplatonic works by Plotinus, Porphyry, Themistius and Alexander of Aphrodisias were used alongside Aristotle, and some works were misattributed to him, further confusing the exact understanding of the ideas of Aristotle and Plato themselves. A good example of the eclectic form of philosophy is to be seen in the thought of the Ikhwān al-Ṣafā', the Brethren of Purity, a tenth-century group who argued that philosophical perfection is the route to spiritual liberation. They used a wide variety of Neoplatonic ideas in their work, in particular in their notion of how the world is constructed and works. They pursued a number of intellectual disciplines in their work along with philosophy, very much a characteristic of the times that encouraged thinkers to link their study of philosophy to a range of disciplines. Philosophy was usually only one of the intellectual interests of the early Islamic philosophers.

Al-Kindī (d. 867) is often called the first philosopher of the Arabs, and he took a Neoplatonic path. He is often criticized for having changed his mind on a number of important issues, in the sense that in some of his books he argues for theses that he rejects in others. However, it needs to be acknowledged that he worked right at the start of philosophy in the Arabic language and had to establish a whole new vocabulary and working methodology, something that he got off the ground and which was to become much more complex and sophisticated later on. Of added significance to the development of the discipline were the Christian Yaḥyā ibn ʿAdī (d. 974) and his Muslim teacher al-Fārābī (d. 950), the latter being decisive in the construction of Islamic philosophy over the next few centuries. Al-Fārābī took al-Kindī's fluid philosophical vocabulary and made it much more stable, far better able to represent complex theoretical work. He discussed the issue of the origination of the universe, stimulated by the discussions he found in Aristotle and the subsequent debate in the Islamic world. Aristotle argues that the world is eternal, and this seems to contradict the normal interpretation of creation in the Qur'ān, which suggests that the world was created out of nothing at a particular time as a result of the will of God. Al-Fārābī tried to resolve this issue by identifying creation with the process of emanation, the notion that reality continually flows out of the source of perfect unity, easily identified with God, so that the world is not created at a particular time but God creates it all the time and it has been in existence all the time. This became a heated debate in Islamic philosophy, as was the debate over the relative significance of language and logic. Al-Fārābī argued that logic is the deep structure of language, which attributes the leading role to logic in understanding language. The point of this argument was to give philosophy a major role in the analysis of language, as against those who argued that Greek logic had nothing to contribute to the study of the Arabic language, which was a position attractive to many theologians and grammarians suspicious of the claims of logic to be so important. What lay behind this controversy was a demarcation dispute between the claims of the traditional Islamic sciences, and the "new" Greek-based forms of knowledge such as philosophy. Those who specialized in the study of Arabic grammar thought they were the leading authorities on how to interpret language, especially language that contained theoretical difficulties. The criticisms of them by the philosophers was really about who had the right to decide what texts mean, the theologians, grammarians and legal thinkers on the one hand, or the philosophers and logicians on the other.

A particularly creative thinker called Ibn Sīnā (d. 1037), known in the West as Avicenna, developed al-Fārābī's views further, using the notion of emanation to argue that everything which happens in the universe is necessitated by what brings it into existence. Only God who is the ultimate cause is free of this system of causes and effects, but al-Ghazālī (d. 1111) points out that this still does not leave God with anything to do. If everything that happens has to happen, because of what brought it about, and if God has to act in the most perfect sort of way since He is after all a perfect being, then the world has to be the way it is. For example, God has to choose certain people to be prophets, since it is their nature to prophesy, and He is limited in His knowledge of the ordinary world, since He only has perfect knowledge of eternal principles and things, not of the contingent events of the world of generation and corruption. Al-Ghazālī provided a powerful attack on the whole philosophical project, arguing that it was both contrary to the principles of Islam and did not work even given the principles that the philosophers themselves accepted. He is sometimes credited with having brought to an end that whole way of doing philosophy in the Arabic world, and there is some plausibility in this idea. On a more positive note, he defended logic as an intellectual discipline, arguing that it was a tool independent of philosophy and so uncontaminated by the latter's problematic features.

The study of philosophy in the peripatetic tradition reached considerable heights in Andalusia, the Islamic part of the Iberian peninsula, and in North Africa. Many of the thinkers in this region, like most Islamic philosophers in the *falsafa* (philosophy) tradition, had a strong commitment to mysticism, which they regarded as a deeper route to the same sort of truth that could be acquired using either religion or philosophy. Ibn Sīnā really typified this dual strategy in apparently being both enthusiastic about a rational approach to knowledge and yet regarding mysticism as representing another, and deeper, form of access to reality. An exception here is the most outstanding thinker in the peripatetic tradition, Ibn Rushd (d. 1198), known in the West as Averroes, who tried to cleanse what passed at his time as Aristotelianism of its Neoplatonic accretions. Ibn Rushd wrote an extensive body of commentaries on Aristotle that came to be influential for many subsequent centuries when translated into Latin and Hebrew, and some of his work became highly controversial and significant in Christian Europe. In particular, his theory that there are different routes to the truth, and that the religious and the philosophical routes are distinct, was often interpreted as suggesting that the philosophers know the real truth by contrast with ordinary people who have to be content with the version of truth offered by faith in the form of religion. The religious authorities were, hardly surprisingly, not enthusiastic about this view, and Averroism came to be regarded as a radical attack on religion in the medieval Christian world. It did for the first time perhaps place religion and reason in clear contrast with each other, something that is often held to have played a part in an earlier and more subdued version of the Enlightenment in Europe. Ibn Rushd presented a lively response to al-Ghazālī's attack on philosophy, a response that sought to examine that attack point by point. Even several centuries after the arrival of philosophy in the Islamic world it had not lost its capacity to shock and challenge the parameters of traditional thought.

Mysticism in Islamic philosophy

Mysticism was a topic of interest to almost all Islamic philosophers. Some like Ibn Sabʿīn (d. *c.* 1269–71) had such a strong commitment to mysticism that he argued that Aristotelian philosophy and logic were of no use in understanding the way things really are. Logical thought works by dividing a concept into its parts, analysis, and philosophy organizes arguments into their constituents, this being part of the process of the syllogism as a form of reasoning. Yet such a process fails to represent accurately the basic unity of everything, a unity which mirrors the unity of God, and any system of thought which is capable of representing reality will have to be based on unity, not division, on putting things together, not taking them apart. The outstanding mystical thinker Ibn ʿArabī (d. 1240) represented himself as dispatching the old peripatetic form of thought when he transported the bones of Ibn Rushd back to al-Andalūs. Mysticism was thereby symbolically replacing and burying philosophy. The main objection that mystics had to philosophy was that it presented a very limited form of knowledge when understood as the apex of what human beings can attain. Philosophers thought in general that the active intellect, the repository of abstract ideas that could be applied in our thinking about the world, was the nearest we could get to understanding God, that is, through understanding His thinking. Mystics argued by contrast that working with a teacher one could reach much higher and gain far closer contact with divine reality. Many philosophers tried to combine mysticism with peripatetic philosophy, arguing that these were just different ways of working, and that mysticism went deeper into the nature of reality. It is important to distinguish the sort of mysticism that the philosophers defended from a subjective and untrained approach to mystical knowledge. The philosophers argued that there is a science of mysticism, and adopted a systematic attitude to Sufism, according to which it represented an alternative and just as rational a way of understanding the nature of reality as analytical thought. The main difference is that Sufism goes further; it allows the skilled individual to acquire valuable experiences as well as valid ideas. Al-Ghazālī did a good deal to make Sufism intellectually respectable by excluding it from his attack on philosophy.

The contemporary thinker Seyyed Hossein Nasr is an important interpreter of the mystical tradition in Islam. He is critical of any form of thought, whether philosophical or scientific, that does not refer to spirituality. Science without spirituality is without limits, he argues, since it holds nothing sacred, and bases itself entirely on quantity not quality. A more spiritual and integrated approach is required, and mysticism provides the rationale for it. He sees Islamic philosophy as just one aspect of what he calls perennial philosophy, which he takes to be a tradition of spiritual thought in both Eastern and Western philosophy. Nasr criticizes recent developments in philosophy for ignoring this aspect of its history and argues that philosophy will only regain its authenticity when it re-establishes links with this traditional form of thought.

Illuminationist philosophy

Illuminationist (*ishrāqī*) thought comes from the term *ishrāq*, which indicates the east, the source of light. Illuminationism attacks some of the central principles of *falsafa* or peripatetic thought, in particular the notion of definition which lies at the heart of the peripatetic way of working philosophically. The peripatetic view is that reasoning and valid knowledge starts with definition in terms of genus and differentia, which means explaining what something is by linking it with other things and examining the parts that make it the thing it is. Illuminationist thinkers such as al-Suhrawardī (d. 1191) argue that this is to explain the unknown in terms of something even less known than itself, which is pointless. After all, how do you know what the parts of a definition are unless you can define them, and so on ad infinitum. The *ishrāqī*s thus see deductive knowledge, which starts with definitions, as unsatisfactory and they replace it with knowledge by presence, which they describe as knowledge that is so immediate that it cannot be doubted. This has the advantage of not requiring a process of reasoning to justify it, since it can be justified merely by considering it, given its immediacy. The notion of light comes in usefully here, since the idea is that the possessor of such knowledge is lit up in a way which makes it impossible to doubt, and this is a result of the way in which light flows through the universe and brings to existence and awareness different levels of being. Light plays in *ishrāqī* thought the role of emanation in *falsafa*; it is everywhere in the universe and operates apparently automatically to affect particular things and events. The differences between beings depend on degrees of luminosity or light, not on their essences, another departure from *falsafa*. God is often identified with the Light of Lights, the light that is the source of all other light and that does not itself receive or require light.

Iluminationism certainly resembles a mystical theory, but in fact was developed in a way that would make it rather similar to *falsafa*, based as it is on objective argument and reasoning. It is often associated with the notion of a subjective route to knowledge of deep spiritual truths, like Sufism, but it also adopts a technical vocabulary like peripatetic thought and presents an objective analysis of reality. It replaces the language of object and properties with the language of light and what is lit up, with gradations of light resembling the properties of objects.

All three main varieties of Islamic philosophy – illuminationist, Ṣūfī, and peripatetic – flourished in the past and still flourish today in the Persian-speaking world. Most of the important Islamic philosophers were themselves Persians, although they generally wrote in Arabic, and Persia has for a long time been very open to philosophical ideas from a range of different cultural traditions. A highly creative thinker who has had a great impact on subsequent Persian thought is Mullā Ṣadrā (d. 1640) whose thought has dominated the Persian philosophical curriculum since his day. He argued that the most significant ontological category is existence, and our view of the nature of reality should be firmly based on that notion. Existence is equivalent to God and so when we talk of ordinary things existing, we are really describing in an inexact way a relationship that they have with God. This is problematic in the sense that ordinary language is based on a form of existence that it itself cannot explain. What is required for us to understand existence is first of all to grasp all the different ways in which things exist, how those different forms of existence are interrelated, and the nature of the intermediaries between the different levels of existence. This concern for grasping the unity of being links Mullā Ṣadrā with the mysticism of Ibn ʿArabī, while the desire to understand the nature of the different levels of existence involves the sort of analysis found in the Illuminationist tradition. His thought achieved a complexity and yet also a profundity that led to its leading role in Persian thought, as evidenced by the huge number of commentaries based on his work and on that of his followers.

Islamic philosophy and religion

The use of philosophy within a religious context always produces problems. There is a tendency to think that if the philosophy is serious then it cannot be religious, since that might involve rejecting ideas and conclusions just because they appear to differ from those arrived at by religion. In any case, why would religious believers require philosophy at all, since their religious books and their teachers should be capable of telling them what they ought to know and how they should behave? Could religion be replaced by reason as a source of knowledge, and is this not what philosophy suggests, given the leading role it gives to reason? These issues did figure throughout the history of Islamic philosophy, and were of course answered in a range of ways. A popular approach was to suggest that philosophy and religion were two different approaches to the truth, and neither invalidated the other. Philosophy is available to a relatively limited constituency, given its academic nature, while religion is open to everyone; the latter raises issues that require philosophical resolution at least for those who are inclined to tackle such issues.

For example, a religious believer might find in the Qur'ān advice on how to live and on the difference between right and wrong. But they would not find an answer to the question of whether these rules are objective or subjective. That is, do these rules depend on God or would they be the same were God not to speak on the subject? Is what is right right because it is right, or is what is right right because God says it is right? Another controversy lies in the reconciliation of the social virtues that arise through living with other people and the intellectual virtues that tend to involve a more solitary and independent lifestyle. What need is there for the philosopher who can understand how he or she is to act though the use of reason to be a part of the social and religious activities of the community? The philosophers tended to argue that social and religious activity was necessary for intellectual activity to be possible, but sometimes it seems that the only link here is based on what is in the philosophers' own interests rather than on anything more substantial. As one might imagine, this made their lives often rather hazardous within communities that placed religion in an important position. The philosophers looked like they were setting themselves above the religion of the ordinary believer, and a price was often paid when rulers needed to gain the support of the religious community as a whole.

Political philosophy in the peripatetic tradition often used Greek philosophy to discuss the nature of the state, yet also combined Platonic ideas with Qur'anic notions, ending up with the argument that the state ought to represent both the material and the spiritual interests of the individual members of the community. Rulers are expected to display advanced theoretical and spiritual skills, while those ruled should be content to be directed, and everyone in the best sort of state has the possibility of achieving the degree of perfection, which is appropriate to him or her. The philosopher is the best ruler because he can dispassionately understand what is in the general interest, and religion is often the means by which each individual can be taught how to behave and how to fit in with the whole while at the same time perhaps not understanding precisely the rational basis for how society ought to be organized.

A particular source of controversy was the debate over the nature of the soul, the thinking part of human beings. Many peripatetic thinkers followed Aristotle in regarding the soul as the form of a person, so that once the body or matter dies, the soul or form of the matter disappears also. Even on the Platonic view of the afterlife, which is very much in terms of an immaterial soul, the notion of the afterlife is very different from that specified by Islam. Islam has a well-developed notion of an afterlife, and the individual is described as continuing in the next world very much as he is in this world, as both a soul and a body. Some philosophers argued that this religious notion is only allegorical, and so our actions in this life have consequences which extend farther than this life, and a good way of illustrating that is through talking about us as having eternal souls. They tended to argue that the religious account places emphasis on the physical because for most people that is what is important. It is a way of making vivid to them why it is important for us to behave well, since the more spiritual understanding of the links between this world and the afterlife is comprehensible only to a limited number of intellectuals and should not be forced onto everyone. If it is, it will result in widespread confusion and hostility to philosophers due to their apparent lack of belief in the evident meaning of scripture. Philosophers defended their unusual understanding of this doctrine by arguing that the Qur'ān requires interpretation and it is their role to interpret it using reason. Since they are the experts in the use of reason, Ibn Rushd argued that they are the very best people to resolve longstanding theological debates, since they can produce a demonstrative argument that will settle the issue once and for all. It is hardly surprising that the theological community was not persuaded of this view, which would of course imply the subordination of theology to philosophy, a position which was commonly upheld by Islamic philosophers.

One of the ways in which Ibn Rushd extended his notion of philosophy as lying at the peak of intellectual life was by elevating logic. He came to argue that logic represents a set of techniques that lies behind what we think and what we do. Even poetry and drama are taken to have a logical structure, although with only limited scope, however the rules of poetry are seen as linked with logical rules. There is a range of logical approaches that are appropriate for different people for different purposes on different occasions, and there are times when one wants to evoke an emotional response and then poetry is appropriate. The construction of the poem will be based on all these factors and will deliver a message in the form of an emotion based on a reasoning process which makes that message the appropriate conclusion. For the theologian and the lawyer, though, dialectic is the right logical technique, since dialectic operates logically from generally accepted propositions (coming from religion and law) to conclusions that are valid, but only within the limitations set by the premises. Within the context of Islam, then, if we accept the premises of the Qur'ān, certain conclusions quite rationally follow, but their validity is limited by the fact that they depend on premises which not everyone accepts and which cannot necessarily themselves be proved to be true. Philosophers work at the highest level of logic; they are the only people who use completely certain and general premises, and so their conclusions are universally valid. A similar point can be made about knowledge. Ordinary people are limited in their knowledge to what they can find out through their experience and through their understanding of what they are told. This basically means they are limited to the range of their senses and the images and allegories of religion. Religion is so effective because it is based on imaginative language, language that appeals to those who require material examples before they can really understand an idea and be moved by it. By contrast, philosophers can reach much higher levels of knowledge through their use of logic and their ability to perfect their understanding of the very general logical principles which underlie the whole of reality.

It is worth saying something about the influence of logic on theology, since this gives us an example of how philosophical discussions moved into the wider cultural sphere of the Islamic world. Some theologians like Ibn Taymiyya (d. 1328) rejected the use of logic and so their theology is ostensibly logic-free. Other thinkers such as al-Ghazālī argued that while philosophy was objectionable, logic was acceptable since it is only an instrument and not part of philosophy itself. His position here did a lot to naturalize logic within the Islamic world even while philosophy itself was in disgrace. Al-Ghazālī goes so far as to argue that one can create a logic out of an examination of the Qur'ān itself since the work demonstrates how reasoning is supposed to operate. This brings out a difficulty in the Ibn Taymiyya position that will have been obvious, and that is how can one argue to a conclusion that logic ought to be excluded, since any such argument is either valid or otherwise, and how would one know without employing logic of some kind?

A slightly different attack on the use of logic in theology is provided by Ibn Khaldūn (d. 1406), best known as a social historian and philosopher of history. Logical techniques are, he suggests, important if we are to be clear on the nature of any issue, but it does not follow that we must have confidence in the capacity of reason to reveal to us the ultimate truths which are accessible to us only through religion. Often called an anti-rationalist position, this view is in fact quite different. It is a rational position based on concerns about the limits of reason to reveal the truth. Arguing that there are limits to reason is not to attack reason but is rather to suggest that it be restricted by being used with some other technique, perhaps religious knowledge, and that we remain aware of our limited grasp of how far we can operate with it. Both these views seek to restrict the scope of logic to deal with theological issues, although in Islamic theology as it developed a great deal of reliance on logic did become common, especially after al-Ghazālī's argument in favor of its acceptability. The real object of concern was an argument such as that of Ibn Rushd in his *Faṣl al-maqāl* where he suggests that the ultimate authority on theological issues is not the theologian but the philosopher, since only the philosopher has the skill to understand the appropriate syllogistic principles that lie behind interpretive issues in religion, and only he can resolve such issues once and for all. This would place logic ahead of theology in terms of who has the right to claim an understanding of religion, and the idea that they are basically redundant did not seem to impress the theologians. Logic is necessary for everyone who wants to reach true knowledge, according to Ibn Sīnā, and if this is accepted then the balance of power between theologians and logicians will be radically changed.

Islamic philosophy today

Within modern times a number of themes in Islamic philosophy have become much discussed. One topic is how distinct Islamic philosophy ought to be from philosophy in general, and in particular from systems of thought not based on religion. Another, and related, issue is what relationship Islamic philosophy should have with Western thought. Further, some thinkers in the Islamic world have used general philosophical ideas from outside their specific discipline and have applied them to what they see as the leading issues of the day within the Islamic world. Finally, traditional ways of doing Islamic philosophy have continued, especially in the Persian world, and the three main categories of Islamic philosophy all find their adherents and promoters.

An issue which philosophers have dealt with at some length is the relationship that the Islamic world should have with the West. This issue is, of course, one that has existed for some time, but it arose with particular force from the nineteenth century onwards with the success of colonialism, imperialism and Zionism in apparently gaining supremacy over the Islamic world. In earlier periods the Islamic world had represented a superior cultural and material force in the world, but over the last few centuries it had radically declined, and the reasons for this apparent decadence were and continue to be much discussed by philosophers.

Of great significance was the *nahḍa* or Islamic renaissance which started in the nineteenth century and really took root first in Egypt. The point of the movement was to maintain a distinctive Islamic identity and yet at the same time incorporate modern scientific and cultural values, where these are compatible with Islam. The two leading thinkers were Jamāl al-Dīn al-Afghānī (d. 1897) and Muḥammad ʿAbduh (d. 1905) who argued that Islam is just as rational as any other system of thought and in no way opposed to Western scientific and cultural ideas. The Egyptian philosopher Muṣṭafā ʿAbd al-Rāziq (d. 1947) extended their argument to include all the main Islamic schools of thought, even the mystical schools of Sufism which were much suspected by the *nahḍa* thinkers. They are all inherently rational and quite compatible with Western science and rationality. Some Arab thinkers have been more skeptical of this point. The contemporary philosopher Muḥammad ʿĀbid al-Jabrī is critical of much traditional Islamic thought, arguing that we need to analyze clearly the reasons for the decline of the Arab world and the role that traditional Islam has played. He calls for a deconstruction of the clash between those who emphasize the glory of the Islamic past and those who praise Western modernity. What is required is a liberation of the Arab consciousness from its traditional ties with its Islamic heritage, and yet also a cautious attitude to the ideas which have come from the West and are aspects of foreign domination.

Fouad Zakariyya agrees that Arab failure is linked with the failure to criticize tradition, while Fazlur Rahman (d. 1988) stresses the links between Islam and social progress. Islamic traditionalism is opposed to Islam itself, Rahman argues, since the religion is in favor of economic and social development and change. The attempt to fix a rigid and stultified version of Islam as the ideal is to fail to grasp the ways in which science and technology can improve the lifestyle and moral welfare of the mass of the community. That sort of narrow attitude does not do justice to the flexibility of the Qur'anic message and its openness to interpretation. Ḥasan Ḥanafī is one of the many contemporary Arab philosophers who uses a novel philosophical technique, in his case phenomenology, to develop a traditional Islamic concept, that of *tawḥīd* or unity. He suggests that Islam is dynamic enough to broaden this notion so that it can provide a generally acceptable principle of unity and equality. He is also critical of the idea of Western progress, suggesting that the West itself is now entering into a period of decadence that will require an infusion of ideas from elsewhere and in particular the East. Like Rahman, he takes the idea that Islam is based on fixed rules to be unacceptable and based on a revelation appropriate at a former time and place, but now other interpretations of the message should be adopted to fit present conditions and represent more accurately the dynamism of Islam.

It is often said that philosophy declined in the Islamic world after the death of Ibn Rushd in the twelfth century, but this is far from the truth. Today there is a lively philosophical presence in most of the Islamic world, often with the incorporation into Islamic philosophy of ideas like logical positivism, hermeneutics, pragmatism, Hegelianism and so on. Philosophy continued very vigorously in the Persian cultural world, especially the philosophy of Ibn Sīnā and the *ishrāqī* (illuminationist) thinkers, and the whole range of commentatorial work on the thought of al-Suhrawardī and Mullā Ṣadrā. In Iran philosophy has now moved away from the theological school, the *madrasa*, into the university, and a good example is provided by the thought of Mahdī Ḥa'īrī Yazdī. He develops a sophisticated theory of knowledge by presence, a form of knowledge which is incorrigible and which grounds our other knowledge claims. He bases his approach on material from both *ishrāqī* thinkers like al-Suhrawardī and the modern philosopher Wittgenstein. ʿAlī Shariʿātī uses the *ishrāqī* school's intermediary position between mysticism and peripateticism to develop a view of the human being as having God at its essence while maintaining the scope to determine its own form of existence. The notion of unity (*tawḥīd*) is seen as therapeutic; it is designed to establish both personal and political justice and harmony. He interprets the main figures of Shīʿī Islam as models for us not only personally but also to bring about progressive social ideals. He sees them as satisfying models of behavior which have always been regarded as desirable. Over time the archetypes themselves have not changed essentially, but they have changed in appearance, to make them more effective at relating to local times and conditions. Philosophy is a particularly vibrant cultural force in Iran and most varieties of philosophy that are practiced elsewhere have their adherents in the country.

References and further reading

Fakhry, M. (1987) *A History of Islamic Philosophy*, 2nd edition, New York: Columbia University Press.

—— (1997) *A Short Introduction to Islamic Philosophy, Theology, and Mysticism*, Oxford: Oneworld.

Hahn, L., Auxier, R. and Stone, L., eds. (2001) *The Philosophy of Seyyed Hossein Nasr*, La Salle: Open Court.

Hallaq, W. (1993) *Ibn Taymiyya against the Greek Logicians*, Oxford: Clarendon Press.

Hourani, G. (1976) "Faṣl al-maqāl," in *Averroes on the Harmony of Religion and Philosophy*, trans. G. Hourani, London: Luzac.

—— (1985) *Reason and Tradition in Islamic Ethics*, Cambridge: Cambridge University Press.

Kennedy-Day, K. (2003) *Books of Definition in Islamic Philosophy. The Limits of Words*, London: RoutledgeCurzon.

Kurzman, C. (2002) *Modernist Islam: A Source Book*, New York: Oxford University Press.

Leaman, O. (1997a) "Logic and Language in Islamic Philosophy," in B. Carr, I. Mahalingam, eds., *Companion Encyclopedia of Asian Philosophy*, London: Routledge, 950–94.

—— (1997b) *Averroes and his Philosophy*, Richmond: Curzon.

—— (1999) *Brief Introduction to Islamic Philosophy*, Oxford: Polity.

—— (2000) "Islamic Philosophy and the Attack on Logic," *Topoi*, 19: 17–24.

—— (2002) *Introduction to Classical Islamic Philosophy*, Cambridge: Cambridge University Press.

Leaman, O., ed. (2006) *Biographical Encyclopedia of Islamic Philosophy*, London: Continuum.

Nasr, S. H. and Leaman, O., eds. (1996) *History of Islamic Philosophy*, London: Routledge.
Rahman, F. (1982) *Islam and Modernity: Transformation of an Intellectual Tradition*, Chicago: Chicago University Press.
Yazdi, M. H. (1992) *The Principles of Epistemology in Islamic Philosophy: Knowledge by Presence*, Albany: State University of New York Press.

21

THE SCIENTIFIC TRADITION

George Saliba

From its beginnings, in the seventh century, Islamic science should be understood in the context of the political and religious experience of Islamic civilization. With the rapid rise of the Islamic political order, which came to encompass the largest land mass any empire had ever controlled, it was natural that the exigencies of the developing empire would require solutions to problems that had never been encountered before. The mere vastness of the empire, even as early as the times of the early Umayyads, required that someone like the caliph ʿAbd al-Malik ibn Marwān (r. 685–705) would make an attempt to streamline its various administrative departments that were up until that time still run in the same languages and styles of the previous Sasanian and Byzantine empires that the Islamic empire came to replace.

That streamlining act itself, which is commonly singled out in the historical sources under the phenomenon of the Arabization of the *dīwān*, entailed the translations of some elementary sciences, particularly those relating to government revenues such as land surveying, tax assessment, public health, and the like, that were all needed for the proper functioning of any empire. Once translated, the new sciences that came to be used by the new Arabized bureaucracy brought to an end the bureaucratic careers of various classes of people who had functioned up till that time in the same manner they always did under the previous empires. Deprived of their livelihood, those same bureaucrats must have then felt that they needed to change their tactics. They had to urge their children and associates to seek and translate the higher sciences so that they could deploy those sciences in their bureaucratic competition. That would have been the only way for them to return once more to their fathers' jobs and to the new ones that the flourishing and expanding administration was continuously creating.

It is in these administrative and bureaucratic needs that one must seek the competitiveness and the motivation for the vast translation movement of the more advanced sciences that was started under the Umayyads but came to bear more fecund fruits about half a century later when the Abbasids came to power around 750. The sciences of the earlier empires, which were the target of this conscious acquisition drive, were mainly to be found in the vast Hellenistic domains that were either replaced by the expanding Islamic empire or overlapped with it, and in the domain of the Sasanian empire which was completely uprooted by the advancing Islamic civilization. In one fell swoop, and starting towards the middle of the eighth century, the historical sources speak of direct acquisitions from such varied fields and languages as Sanskrit and Pahlevi to the east and southeast, and Syriac and Greek to the west. And although the earliest scientific translations that we know of mostly favored the Sanskrit and Pahlevi domains, as is evidenced by the early translations of Sanskrit astronomical works during the reign of the second Abbasid caliph al-Mansur (r. 754–75), and the Pahlevi or Syriac logical works that were translated by Ibn al-Muqaffaʿ (d. 760) and others, the Greek scientific sources very quickly came to replace the eastern sciences and to maintain their supremacy for the generations and centuries that followed. This may have something to do with the perceived unity of the Greek sciences as elaborated within the overarching Aristotelian philosophy, while the eastern sciences were perceived as disconnected individual sciences of particular authors solving particular problems. It is not surprising then to find in the early part of the ninth century an abundance of Greek philosophical and scientific works that were being rendered into Arabic, either as direct translations or as sources of inspiration for original works freshly composed in Arabic.

Religion in need of science: "foreign" versus "religious" sciences

It was at this time that the two major world views, sometimes expressed as religious versus rational, began to take shape. Those who depended for their government jobs on the sciences that were being translated from the various languages of the earlier civilizations naturally became the proponents of the rational, or more properly "foreign," sciences that they hoped to traffic with in the new civilization. While those who appointed themselves as guardians of the moral, legal, and spiritual domains of that civilization, and who were the natural critics and opponents of political authority, saw their access to power as channeled through the advanced elaboration of the legal and religious sciences that were all expressed in Arabic, the very language through which the Qur'ān itself was revealed. This dual epistemology had clear implications for the following generations and in more than one juncture determined the shape and scope of the very intellectual institutions that permeated the long history of the Islamic civilization. As an expression of this dichotomy one could point to the institution of the *madrasa* on the one hand which embodied the propagation of the religious and legal sciences, while the foreign rational sciences were left to fend for themselves. The latter were mainly promoted in the private circles of working scientists, who in turn worked mostly in the service of the political power by constantly updating its administrative machinery with the importation of new translations and the creation of new sciences to respond to the ever-changing needs.

In some instances, the two world views could at times cross paths. Serious legal and religious scholars could not pursue their work in shaping the popular practice of Islam, as a religion, without being able to determine in some "rational" way the basic tenants of that religion such as determining the intricate regulations for inheritance laws, or elaborating the rituals of prayers, the direction of those prayers, and such mundane practical affairs. In as much as they could avoid using the results of the new sciences that were being translated from the foreign languages or freshly created under their inspiration, religious scholars attempted to do so, and mostly resorted to the very basic sciences that were already mastered by the pre-Islamic people who now populated the massive Islamic empire and were being converted to Islam at a steady pace. For instance, some knowledge of basic astronomy, as expressed in such works as the *anwāʾ* literature, dealing with the movement of heavenly bodies as a way of measuring time, could answer most of the questions the new religion required. So naturally that literature was especially favored by religious scholars, because it had no philosophical underpinnings that could interfere with the religious dogma, and the *anwā'* system was originally developed for the safe purposes of attending to basic agricultural calendars that depended on the risings and settings of specific stars and the like. However, it was not possible to avoid the introduction of more sophisticated techniques in order to determine the more elaborate inheritance system that was clearly stipulated in the Qur'ān. For the latter, some use of what was later called algebra, had to be relied upon, and authors like the polymath Muḥammad ibn Mūsā al-Khwārizmī (d. *c.* 850) had to develop the discipline expressly for those who needed to determine those religious obligations.

That particular inheritance legislation, and the particular Algebra that applied to it, eventually gave birth to the discipline of *ʿilm al-farā'iḍ* (science of inheritance obligations), which became an acknowledged discipline in its own right in the later centuries. In those centuries as well, the new discipline of algebra was also merged with other more general astronomical and mathematical geographical sciences in order to create the more elaborate discipline of *ʿilm al-mīqāt* (science of timekeeping). This particular discipline was also developed in response to religious needs and was clearly designed to answer the more vexing religious questions of determining the times and direction of prayers. The prayers themselves were all defined by such astronomical phenomena as dawn, twilight, and shadow lengths that varied for different days of the year and for different latitudes, where the ever-expanding Muslim community was taking root.

Mathematical sciences at the crossroads

Another domain at which both world views intersected was the domain of mathematics and arithmetic in particular, or at least that part of it which dealt with regular transactions of daily commercial activities. In that area, Islamic civilization rendered a real service to the rest of humanity by adopting the Indian numerical decimal system and popularizing it to become the universally used system it now is. The actual numerals themselves, commonly called Arabic numerals in the West, were first encountered outside the Indian domain in a Syriac treatise written during the early years of Umayyad times, in upper Mesopotamia, in which the author bragged about the Indians' ability to write any number they pleased by just using nine symbols. The treatise said nothing of the essential number zero, whose concept and symbol is at times falsely credited to mathematicians of the Islamic civilization. In fact both the concept of the number zero as well as a symbol for it were both known in ancient Mesopotamian times either in the form of an empty space or using a separation sign formed with two marks. From there the concept seems to have migrated to India, where it was later encountered in the shape of a small circle, which is still in use today, and was fully integrated within the remaining familiar numerical symbols that are now in universal use. Those numerals finally returned to Mesopotamia and were fully adopted by the early mathematicians of the Islamic civilization.

The innovations that were brought about by those mathematicians were more in the generalization of the Indian numerical system to include concepts and numbers that were not previously known from Greek or Sanskrit. In particular, a mid-tenth

basic changes in the fundamental astronomical theories, but also raised the question of the reasons that led the earlier Greek astronomers to commit such grave errors. The same ninth-century sources preserve for us a detailed discussion of this question and the final determination that the mistakes were indeed due to the inadequacy of the observational methodology that was followed by Ptolemy. It was concluded that Ptolemy had made a strategic error in observing the position of the sun at the times of the equinoxes and the solstices, where the changes in the declination of the sun from day to day in the case of the solstices would be close to zero, and thus practically impossible to determine accurately. In lay language, at the time of the solstices the sun would seem to rise and set at the same points of the local horizon for several days, and this phenomenon would make it very difficult to determine the exact time when the sun would indeed reach the solstices.

Instead, the ninth-century astronomers, who seemed to have worked in the circle of Banū Mūsā, the three brothers who flourished during the reign of al-Ma'mūn and al-Mutawakkil (r. 847–61), thought of a better observational strategy and decided to observe the variations in the declination of the sun when the sun was passing through the points of the mid seasons, that is when the sun was at the 15th degree of Taurus, 15th degree of Leo, and so on. The new method was then dubbed as the *fuṣūl* (seasons) method on account of its reliance on points of the mid seasons, and when applied did indeed determine much more precisely the amounts of such values as the solar eccentricity, solar apogee, and the ensuing solar equation. These of course necessitated the construction of mathematical models that would predict the position of the sun at any time of the year. Needless to say, those models were different from the Ptolemaic ones.

These results also had other more important consequences, chief among them was the loss of confidence in Greek astronomical theory in general and the realization of the urgent need to critique and reconstruct that astronomy on much firmer grounds that were to be determined with fresh observations. One could simply characterize the whole history of Islamic astronomy as a continuous attempt to achieve just that goal in particular.

Once the Greek observational mistakes were dispensed with, those same astronomers who established the new results felt much more empowered to raise more fundamental objections of a cosmological and theoretical nature, at times touching the very foundations of Greek astronomy. And since Ptolemaic astronomy was itself founded on the all-encompassing Aristotelian cosmology, the discussion was then moved to a debate with Aristotle himself. In one instance, and at a much later date, someone like Ibn al-Shāṭir of Damascus (d. 1375) would go as far as questioning whether the Aristotelian celestial fifth element ether was indeed as simple as Aristotle had stipulated.

There were other more obvious observational mistakes that also needed to be attended to. In the case of the motion of the moon, for example, Ptolemy had to explain, in one mathematical model, all the variations in the observed behavior of the moon. After conducting several observations, and after trying out two or three mathematical models, Ptolemy finally settled on a model that could predict reasonably well the longitudinal positions of the moon. But the model also incorporated an odd phenomenon of which he said nothing, namely that the moon should look twice as big when it was one week old, as it would be when it was full. In the words of the same Damascene Ibn al-Shāṭir the moon was never seen like that (*lam yurā kadhālika*).

The Ptolemaic lunar model had yet another problem with it which was cosmological in nature. The Aristotelian spheres that were supposed to account for the behavior of the celestial planets around us could not explain how a sphere could possibly move, in place, at uniform speed – both Aristotelian notions of celestial motion – about an axis that did not pass through the center of that sphere. Not only the moon, but every wandering planet for which Ptolemy had constructed a mathematically predictive model, contained such a sphere, which was by itself a physical impossibility. No wonder then that such a major theoretical failing would on its own eventually give rise to a whole tradition of doubts (*shukūk*) that kept recurring throughout Islamic history.

The doubts at times led to the construction of new alternative models. And there were many astronomers who participated in that endeavor. Most notable amongst them was also the Damascene astronomer Ibn al-Shāṭir who managed to construct a whole series of new models that could supplant the whole works of Ptolemy. In the case of the moon, for example, he designed a new model that solved, in one fell swoop, both of the Ptolemaic problems just mentioned. As it turned out, and maybe because of its success, the very same model was later adopted, as is, by Copernicus (d. 1543) during the European Renaissance (see fig. 16). Although modern historians of science cannot yet determine, with any certainty, the manner in which this model of Ibn al-Shāṭir could have reached Copernicus, there are, however, enough such intersection points between the works of the two astronomers to allay any doubts that the transmission from Ibn al-Shāṭir to Copernicus had indeed taken place.

Another astronomer by the name of Naṣīr al-Dīn al-Ṭūsī (d. 1274) also tried to cleanse Greek astronomy of its contradictions. In the process, he had to introduce a new mathematical theorem, now known as the Ṭūsī Couple. It stipulated the addition of two new spheres, one twice the size of the other, and if the smaller sphere were placed inside the larger one in such a way that it was internally tangent to it at one point, and if one assumed that the larger sphere moved, in place, at a specific speed, in any direction, and assumed the smaller sphere to move, also in place, at twice that speed, in the opposite direction, then the original point of tangency would oscillate back and forth along the diameter of the larger sphere.

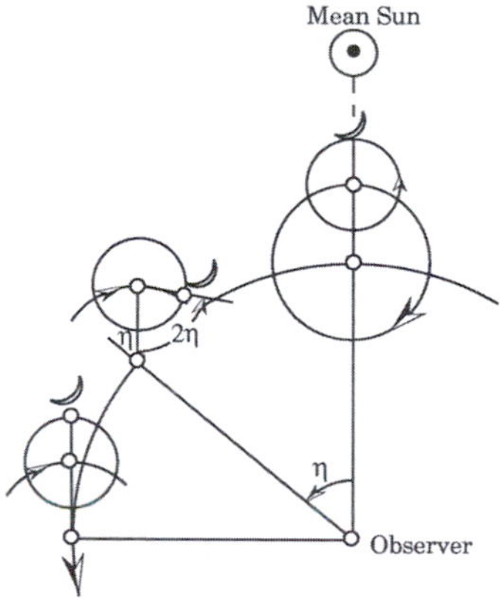

Figure 16 Ibn al-Shāṭir's (d. 1375) model for the moon which was adopted fully by Copernicus (d. 1543).

In essence the new theorem allowed for the production of linear motion as a result of two circular motions. Al-Ṭūsī's Couple seems to have reached Copernicus as well who, for reasons of his own, also needed to produce linear motion out of a combination of two circular motions. In his latest astronomical work, *De Revolutionibus*, he devoted a whole chapter [Book III, chap. 4] to the proof of the same theorem. As it turned out, he even used the same alphabetical symbols to designate the same geometric points in the diagram that were already used by al-Ṭūsī some 300 years earlier.

Yet another astronomer, who was also a colleague of al-Ṭūsī, by the name of Mu'ayyad al-Dīn al-'Urḍī of Damascus (d. 1266), had his own cleansing to perform of the Greek astronomical tradition. In the process, he too had to propose a new theorem, in which if one were to take two lines, of equal length, and assume that those two lines made equal angles with a base line, either internally or externally, then the line that joined the extremities of those two equal line would be parallel to the base line. This new theorem that is now dubbed as the 'Urḍī Lemma was also used by every astronomer to have come after 'Urḍī, up to and including Copernicus himself. Here again, although the route of the transmission of ideas from the Islamic world to Renaissance astronomers, and to Copernicus in particular, cannot be determined with certainty, the abundance of similarities between the results established in the two places leaves no doubt about the likelihood of such a transmission.

In one telling case, we also find Copernicus using the same model for the motion of the planet Mercury that was already devised by Ibn al-Shāṭir some two centuries earlier. But this time the editor of the earliest Copernican astronomical work, the *Commentariolus*, reached the conclusion that Copernicus did not fully understand the functioning of this model, and thus the case for his indebtedness to Ibn al-Shāṭir would even become much stronger. What seems to have happened was that Copernicus was willing to use the same model of Ibn al-Shāṭir before having digested its technical implications. A similar thing occurred in the chapter of *De Revolutionibus* in which Copernicus adopted and proved the Ṭūsī Couple. In it, he speculated about the significance and implications of the theorem in an additional paragraph that he first appended to this chapter, but later decided to cut out. This must mean that he was incorporating material that he had not yet fully understood, and that can only strengthen the argument of indebtedness as opposed to independent discovery.

With this kind of evidence, which is now rather well established and only surveyed here in the briefest of statements and examples, one can safely surmise that the main character of Islamic astronomy was that it was a fundamental rebellion against Greek astronomy, both observationally and theoretically. Muslim astronomers corrected the Greek observations and critiqued their observational strategies, and made observation itself more systematic on the theoretical level. For that reason the received Greek astronomy had to be completely overhauled. And when one looks at the multitude of similarities between the works of Copernicus and the works of his Islamic predecessors, one can only confirm that the Islamic astronomy that passed on to Europe during the Renaissance was first and foremost written in that spirit of rebellion against Greek astronomy. In that context, Copernicus's reliance on his Islamic predecessors was a reliance on the latest ideas in astronomy.

In that context, the Islamic *hay'a* texts, which contained the alternative planetary theories were not only distancing Islamic astronomy from astrology, but through their adoption by the Renaissance scientists were also laying the foundations of the modern science of astronomy.

Medical sciences

Unlike the other "foreign" sciences that were usually received critically by the Islamic religious community, medicine had a special status. Although it owed a great deal to Greek medical theory, it was mostly welcome and well used even by people in religious circles. So much so, that this receptive environment gave rise to the famous dictum, at times attributed to al-Imām al-Shāfiʿī (d. 820), "science is of two kinds: science of religion and science of medicine" (*al-ʿilm ʿilmān: ʿilm al-adyān wa-ʿilm al-abdān*). That environment certainly encouraged the practice of medicine even when the practitioners were not themselves Muslims as was frequently the case in most of Islamic history.

Like the *anwāʾ* literature mentioned earlier, much of the pre-Islamic folk medical knowledge also survived well into Islamic times and sometimes co-mingled with sayings of the Prophet that had some medical import, thus forming a separate branch of medicine called prophetic medicine, before it was juxtaposed with the incoming more analytical and philosophical Greek medical tradition.

Once Greek medical theory was acclimatized into the Islamic environment, there too it tended to reflect similar tendencies that it had experienced in classical Greek works. Physicians like Abū Bakr al-Rāzī (Latin Rhazes d. 924), who had favored clinical observations more, were perceived as pursuing a line of medicine similar to that of Hippocrates. While others like Abū ʿAlī Ibn Sīnā (Latin Avicenna d. 1037) followed lines very similar to those of Galen, and in fact championed the introduction of the latter into the Islamic environment. Despite the usefulness of this two-prong characterization to understand the state of the medical sciences in Islamic civilization, that characterization should not mean that either side was incapable of practicing medicine in the style of the other. After all, it was al-Rāzī's combined analytical and observational talents that allowed him to make a distinction between the two diseases of smallpox and measles that were not noted by anyone before, and certainly not in the Greek tradition.

Al-Rāzī's more important work though should be sought in his deliberate and scientifically based critique of the Greek medical tradition as evidenced in his *al-Shukūk ʿalā Jālīnus* ("Doubts Regarding Galen"). It was this work and the later work of Ibn al-Haytham (d. *c.* 1038) *al-Shukūk ʿalā Baṭlamyūs* ("Doubts Regarding Ptolemy") that constituted the backbone of the critical doubts (*shukūk*) tradition that was mentioned earlier. Others like ʿAbd al-Laṭīf al-Baghdādī (d. 1231), who also criticized the work of Galen on the matter of the jaw bone, followed suit, although they did not compose their own *shukūk* books.

The major work of Ibn Sīnā, *al-Qānūn fīʾl-ṭibb* ("Canon of Medicine"), which managed to synthesize the Greek Galenic tradition and to propagate it in Arabic, giving rise to various commentaries, became very influential not only because it contained an elegant and parsimonious version of the verbose and widely scattered Galenic ideas but because it also became influential in the Latin west where it was used as the standard medical textbook for centuries. This book also represented the best of the Islamic medical tradition, in the sense that although it did not contain some critical medical observation that no one else had noticed before, as was the case with Rāzī, it managed to digest the whole extensive corpus of Galenic medicine and to reproduce it in a smartly edited format ideal for medical students. In that sense Avicenna's *Canon* became an ideal textbook. The fact that it was appreciated as such is clearly noted by the Renaissance scientist Guillaume Postel (d. 1581) who thought that Avicenna "says more on one or two pages than does Galen in five or six large volumes" (Dannenfeldt 1955: 111). No wonder that a few years after Postel's death, even the Arabic text of the *Canon* was printed by the Florentine Medici Oriental Press in 1593.

Avicenna's impact on the Latin west, both in his medical and in his philosophical writings, could only be compared to the impact of his co-religionist Ibn Rushd (Latin Averroes d. 1198). They were both diligently studied for centuries in their Latin translations. More importantly, between the two of them, they barely left a single Aristotelian or Galenic work that was not fully digested and made accessible to the much wider reading public of the Latin Middle Ages and the Renaissance.

It was also Avicenna's commentator, Ibn al-Nafīs (d. 1288) of Damascus and Cairo, who again used the text of Avicenna to get back at Galen, in his own critique of Galen's theory of the heart and of the circulation of the blood, setting thereby the first analytical argument for the pulmonary circulation of the blood. The works of this commentator were translated and studied by the Venetian physician Andreas Alpagus (d. 1522) who became a professor of medicine at Padua in 1505 after having spent close to 20 years in Damascus studying Arabic and translating Arabic medical and philosophical works into Latin. After all it was at Padua, a century later, that Harvey (d. 1657) came to obtain his final degree, and to rearticulate the rediscovery of the small circulation of the blood in 1627.

The related field of pharmacology also took a similar trajectory in combining pre-Islamic knowledge of medical plants and the more elaborate formal translations of the Greek herbal treatise of Dioscorides of Anazarbus (d. first century) as well as the relevant pharmacological works of Galen. With the intertwining of the two traditions, here too Islamic pharmacology managed to transform the Greek pharmacological chest from some 700–800 drugs described by Dioscorides to a chest of more than twice that many elaborated by Ibn al-Bayṭār (d. 1248) in his encyclopedic work on *Simple Drugs*.

Technology and the representation of nature

Observations in general are as good as the observational strategies they follow or the instruments they employ. For purposes of achieving the higher precision that was required to critique the faults of the Greek authors, scientists of the Islamic world had to develop their own new instruments and strategies. Some of those instruments, such as time-measuring instruments, also served civilian purposes, as was the case with water clocks whose archeological remains are still in view.

As far as astronomical instruments were concerned, the two most popular that were used in early Islamic culture were the planispheric astrolabe and the quadrant. Both were based on the single mathematical theorem of stereographic projection, which was already known from Greek times, with the quadrant being mostly a theoretical folding of an astrolabe along two of its axes. The more serious observational instruments were usually much larger in size and were mostly quadrants that included mural constructions that were tens of feet high.

Like all instruments, once developed, their application could be extended to cover a variety of fields. For example, astrolabes that could be used to perform astronomical observations could also be used for religious purposes to determine times and directions of prayers, or used to solve land surveying problems. In fact some astrolabes also included graphic representations of trigonometric tables and graphic solutions of mathematical functions, and were distinctively Islamic because those added features, that were nowhere found in the Greek or any other tradition, were simply developed to respond to specific needs of the *mīqāt* requirements of Islamic religion. Projections of world maps, centered around Mecca, also served similar purposes. Because of the appeal and educational value of astrolabes, Arabic treatises describing their constructions and use were either translated into Latin or composed afresh in that language, as was done by Chaucer for example. Or take the sixteenth-century Florentine architect Antonio de Sangallo the Younger (d. *c.* 1525), who even drafted copies of Islamic astrolabes that were made some 700 years earlier in Baghdad so meticulously that, in one instance, he inadvertently copied the name of the astrolabe maker which was engraved on the back and had no scientific value by itself. Others still, like the sixteenth-century Arsenius family of astrolabe makers, made extensive use of Islamic astrolabes, either by re-using some of their parts, or by imitating their designs.

As for instruments that served such varied civilian purposes as agriculture, commerce, industry, or even entertainment they found their adepts and skilled artisans and theorists to supply them. People like Banū Mūsā, already mentioned, and Abū 'l-ʿIzz al-Jazarī (lived *c.* 1206) both excelled not only in supplying new instruments for social needs, but broke new ground in their conscious effort to produce instruments that incorporated technical innovations or were themselves representations of sophisticated natural physical principles. In the work of the formidable theoretician al-Jazarī, which was titled *al-Jāmiʿ bayna 'l-ʿilm waʾl-ʿamal al-nāfiʿ fī ṣināʿat al-ḥiyal* ("A Compendium of Theory and Useful Practice in the Art of Mechanical Devices"), al-Jazarī states explicitly that his book described devices that demonstrated how the hidden principles of nature worked. With those devices he was only enabling principles that existed in potential to materialize in actuality. This theoretical bent did not stop those devices from being useful in real life, or at times even entertaining. But the most awe-inspiring function those devices could fulfill was their deployment in political circumstances to impress upon a visiting ambassador the richness and awesome knowledge of the potentate, all in a political game of brinksmanship that was and probably still is usually played among rulers.

Artisans who produced those instruments, and who at times also doubled as alchemists, whose own discipline was called "art" (*ṣanʿa*) par excellence, also possessed advanced knowledge about metals which was also socially useful. But when they lacked the theoretical scientific information that was required for their instruments they always found mathematicians and astronomers, like Abū 'l-Wafāʾ al-Būzajānī (d. 998), who would write special books for their education. Artisans who produced industrial products such as steel, sugar, ceramics and so on, did not usually leave a record of their crafts. And although we may assume that they learned their profession by apprenticeship we also know that their knowledge was somehow passed on to Europe as happened in the case of sugar making. The geographic span of the Islamic civilization itself, from the borders of China and India to Spain, also allowed the transfer of similar techniques from east to west through the lands of Islam. Indian numerals, known as "Arabic numerals" in the West, paper making, and the use of the magnetic compass, are well-known examples of this trend.

References and selected reading

Ali, J. (1967) *The Determination of the Coordinates of Positions for the Correction of Distances Between Cities*, Beirut: American University of Beirut. (On al-Bīrūnī.)

Dannenfeldt, H. (1955) "The Renaissance Humanists and the Knowledge of Arabic," *Studies in the Renaissance*, 2: 96–117.

Kennedy, E. S. (1970) "The Arabic Heritage in the Exact Sciences," *al-Abḥāth*, 23: 327–44.

Kennedy, E. S., Kunitzsch, P. and Lorch, R. P., eds. (1999) *The Melon-Shaped Astrolabe in Arabic Astronomy*, Stuttgart: F. Steiner.

King, D. (1999) *World-Maps for Finding the Direction and Distance to Mecca: Innovation and Tradition in Islamic Science*, Leiden: Brill.

—— (2004) *In Synchrony with the Heavens: Studies in Astronomical Timkeeping and Instrumentation in Medieval Islamic Civilization*, Volume I: *The Call of the Muezzin*, Leiden: Brill.

Makdisi, G. (1970) "Madrasa and University in the Middle Ages," *Studia Islamica*, 32: 255–64.

—— (1981) *The Rise of Colleges*, Edinburgh: Edinburgh University Press.

Neugebauer, O. (1962) "Thābit Ben Qurra 'On the Solar Year' and 'On the Motion of the Eighth Sphere,' translation and commentary," *Proceedings of the American Philosophical Society*, 106: 64–299.

Rashed, R. (1994) *The Development of Arabic Mathematics: Between Arithmetic and Algebra*, Dordrecht: Kluwer.

Rashed, R. and Morelon, R., eds. (1996) *Encyclopedia of the History of Arabic Science*, London: Routledge.

Rhazes, Abū Bakr Muḥammad ibn Zakarīya al-Rāzī (1848) *A Treatise on the Small-Pox and Measles*, W. A. Greenhill, trans., London: Sydenham Society.

Rosen, F. (1831) *The Algebra of Mohammed ben Musa*, London: J. Murray for the Oriental Translation Fund.

Rosenfeld, B. A. (1988) *A History of Non-Euclidian Geometry: Evolution of the Concept of a Geometric Space*, New York: Springer.

Saidan, A. S. (1978) *The Arithmetic of al-Uqlīdisī. The Story of Hindu-Arabic Arithmetic as Told in "Kitab al-fusul fial-hisab al-Hindi" Damascus, ad 952/3*, Dordrecht: Reidel.

Saliba, G. (1973) "The Meaning of *al-jabr wa-l-muqābalah*," *Centaurus*, 17: 189–204.

—— (2007) *Islamic Science and the Making of the European Renaissance*, Cambridge, MA: MIT Press.

22

EDUCATION

Jeffrey C. Burke

According to the Islamic tradition, the Prophet Muḥammad received revelations, the Qur'ān, in seventh-century Arabia. Initially, this text was taught to learners through processes of oral recitation and memory recall. Students committed to memory written accounts of how Muḥammad received this sacred revelation and used it to guide the nascent community of Muslims. Therefore, the origins of education in Islam involved proper recitation and writing of scripture in order to more fully understand the actions of the Prophet. Islamic education, at its heart, was intertwined with Qur'anic revelations. These revelations themselves endorsed education for believers.

With the expansion of their territories in the decades after Muḥammad's death in 632, Muslims encountered other educational systems, such as rabbinic schools in southern Iraq and the academies of Alexandria. As *dhimmīs* ("protected minorities"), Jews, Christians, and Zoroastrians had felicitous relations with their Muslim overseers. Reciprocal curiosity among these communities eventually resulted in the widespread translation of various works into the Arabic language. A principal proponent of this movement was the ninth-century caliph al-Ma'mūn (r. 813–33) who promoted the translation of Greek philosophic works. Through this effort, al-Ma'mūn sought to encourage Muslim scholars to combine knowledge based on revelation (*naql*) with knowledge based on reason (*ʿaql*).

Early Islamic civilization was enriched by such exchanges of ideas and information. Muslims sought to preserve and transmit not only their sacred corpus of writings, but also the works of Plato, Aristotle, and others. However, the Prophet Muḥammad remained the exemplar of the faith in terms of etiquette and custom. Pursuant to his example, the Qur'ān formed the first didactic book for learners of all ages.

Islam's earliest educators spread Qur'anic knowledge through lessons conducted at home and in mosques. The gateway to wisdom involved precise memorization of sacred scripture. All other academic disciplines such as philosophy, *ta'rīkh* (history), and theology were seen as subordinate to and understood through the Qur'ān. The Rabbinic and Socratic methods of questioning were secondary to successful memorization. Muslim scholars taught that too much time spent on investigating Qur'anic textual meanings would detract from internalizing God's word.

Muḥammad imparted his knowledge to believers through *ḥalqa* (small circle) instruction, elaborating on Qur'anic revelations and explaining how Muslims should apply the teachings of their faith. This time-honored tradition continued in Islam based on the Prophet's example. Most often, worship and education occurred in the same sacred space. Gathering at a mosque, students would sit cross-legged in explanatory circles with the *shaykh* (teacher) in front of the group. The *shaykh* would use a cushion or chair and wall or pillar support for ease of comfort. Typically, the most advanced or favored students sat closest to the teacher. These informal study circles were the precursors to the earliest formal mosque schools. This style of learning became widespread in the Islamic empire. By the tenth century, approximately 3,000 mosque schools existed in Baghdad alone.

Baghdad, at this time, also featured palace and bookshop schools, the latter of which were the forerunners of Islamic libraries. As these alternative forms of Islamic learning became more popular, a key concern was how to preserve the mosque-like aura in other educational venues. Mosque training gave students the rudimentary lessons in Qur'anic verse to dovetail with the fostering of religious piety. The next step of education engaged students in higher critical thinking. Newly developing centers of higher education in Islam were referred to as *madrasa*s, meaning "places for giving lessons."

Mosque and *madrasa* educational developments in Islam reflected attempts to educate Muslim pupils in textual and higher critical studies built around a base of Qur'anic moral and ethical ideals. Like other monotheistic faiths such as Judaism and Christianity, the Islamic religious tradition emerged from a vibrant intellectual heritage in pre-Islamic Arabia. *ʿIlm* (knowledge) always formed a central component of the faith as evidenced by abundant references to this term in the Qur'ān and *ḥadīth*. Although Qur'anic knowledge was instilled through recitation and memory check, the overall pursuit of *ʿilm* was not meant to be a static enterprise. Believers were expected to exemplify Qur'anic ethical ideals and teachings through their daily actions. To do so required proper guidance and teaching from the religious scholars (*ʿulamāʾ*), who not only passed on the "correct" sacred texts but also were actively involved in the lives of their students in regard to whether these ethical teachings were put into practice. During the early Islamic centuries, *madrasa*s were conjoined with mosque structures sponsored by wealthy female and male patrons who sought to support such learning and inquiry.

Local involvement and private benefactors enabled these institutions to flourish. Unlike numerous modern school systems, the first mosques and *madrasa*s were not publicly funded and often lacked significant organizational structure or governmental control. As a result, the Islamic faith remained the epistemological nucleus of the education they provided.

In tenth-century Iraq and the Eastern provinces of the Islamic world, hostelries (sing. *khān*) cropped up next to mosques that offered serious Qur'anic training. This convenient arrangement afforded students and professors alike the chance to gather for lessons over an extended period of time. The Baghdadi *khān*s served as magnets to those who yearned for this type of learning but lived in more remote areas.

The distinguished scholar George Makdisi (1981) has written extensively on the origins of the *madrasa* in the early Islamic centuries and its growth in eleventh- and twelfth-century Syria and Iraq. Although some of Makdisi's conclusions remain points of contention in modern scholarship, a review of his thoughts on the curriculum and structure of *madrasa*s is worthwhile. According to Makdisi, *madrasa*s were thought to involve the study of Islamic law or jurisprudence in one of four Sunnī rites or law divisions: the Ḥanafī, Shāfiʿī, Ḥanbalī, or Mālikī. Other principal subjects included Qur'anic *tafsīr* (commentary), the sayings and actions of Muḥammad (*ḥadīth*), and linguistics. *Madrasa* education involved a mastery of the Arabic language in order to facilitate interpreting and understanding commentaries and other books assembled by Islamic scholars throughout the centuries. In preparation for entering a *madrasa*, students acquired basic Arabic skills through private tutoring at home or at a *kuttāb* (Qur'ān school). *Madrasa* education flourished to no small degree because of private donors who supplied monies for student scholarships or stipends and endowed funds for the professoriate. In addition, students and teachers were often provided with accommodations on school grounds.

Other means of support for *madrasa*s were found in medieval Cairo. *Waqfiyya*s (deeds of endowments, some of which are extant today) were set up by individuals to provide financial arrangements for the establishment and ongoing support of selected schools. Benefactors, in turn, oversaw the governance of these institutions and often wanted them modeled after other successful Cairene *madrasa*s. The quality and the size of *madrasa*s varied, subject to the wealth of patrons that came from the ranks of government bureaucrats, *amīr*s, scholars, sultans, and the wives and daughters of these leaders. Despite the strings attached to endowed *madrasa* centers of learning, the process of education remained fluid and focused on the magnetism of individuals instead of institutions.

As referred to earlier, students of Islam sought out individual *shaykh*s to imbibe knowledge as part of an unbroken *isnād* (chain of transmission). This model of learning predated mosque and *madrasa* instruction and continued long after education became more regulated in *madrasa*s. Through oral recitation, dictation, and reading passages aloud, students reinforced the idea of receiving sacred knowledge from *shaykh*s who were seen as authoritative figures. Students would come from near and far to sit with the most prominent *shaykh*s in order to acquire knowledge. The personalities and reputations of individual *shaykh*s attracted many students to choose a particular course of training rather than to select a *madrasa* based on its curricular offerings. As transmitters of the texts of the Qur'ān and *ḥadīth*, these religious leaders were expected to be models of piety and learning. They also were responsible for ascertaining student progress in the thorough mastery of selected traditions or texts. Once these requirements were met, a *shaykh* had the authority to issue a certificate (*ijāza*) granting permission to his student to depart and teach particular texts to his own pupils.

The *shaykh* was the key ingredient in this religious learning ritual. The members of his *ḥalqa* (devotional circle) were connected to him as the focal point. Some of them would form deep friendships and lifelong relationships. The vital linkages between master and pupil were cemented by strong bonds of loyalty and obedience. All other social bonds and attachments were subordinate to the *shaykh*–student relationship. A premium was placed on this social arrangement because of its singular importance. It represented the ongoing transmission of sacred texts dating back to the Prophet and his companions, as accurately passed on from one generation to the next.

In addition to oral memory, a student was expected to write down individual teachings of his esteemed *shaykh*. The teacher would then read his version aloud so the student could correct the mistakes before an *ijāza* was issued. The *shaykh*'s commentaries on texts were placed in the text and margins. These oral and written exchanges between a *shaykh* and his followers served to reinforce bonds of felicity and trust. After the death of a *shaykh* a number of possible scenarios played out.

His study circle might be disbanded. Typically, some students would migrate to another teacher, while others would rekindle the study circle. His most capable and brilliant students were often tapped to succeed the late *shaykh* or assume professorships in other mosques.

Following the death of Muḥammad, Friday mosque gatherings became a customary time to memorize the Qur'ān. In addition, pious literature such as the *ḥadīth* (traditions) of the Prophet and the *sīra* (biographical accounts) increasingly became the focus of learning. Pursuant to this pattern, *shaykh*s relied upon this collection of canonical materials as the most authoritative and legitimate knowledge for students to learn in mosque and *madrasa* settings. During the ninth to twelfth centuries, *madrasa*s became the principal learning centers with curricula based on core Islamic teachings.

The five daily prayers (*ṣalāt*) were an integral part of the rhythm of activities in *madrasa*s. Makdisi (1981: 93) notes that prayers were also offered at the beginning and conclusion of individual classes. Unlike most schools of today, these *madrasa*s did not have set lengths of study for various disciplines. The time it would take for a student to receive an *ijāza* for a particular subject varied considerably. There were no specific age requirements for students advancing from primary training at home and in private Qur'anic schools to *madrasa* education. *Madrasa*s were not uniform in which rite or rites they emphasized and were also uneven in endowment totals, intellectual rigor, and the overall quality of education that was offered.

Individuals with the most exemplary memories were prized in medieval Islamic education. Recall of information would often include the recitation of a full lineage of former sages and *shaykh*s dating back to the lifetime of Muḥammad and/or his companions. It was not uncommon to be blind and illiterate but revered as a sage who possessed an "ocean" of knowledge about Muḥammad and his teachings. In the eleventh century, newly appointed *madrasa* professors often gave inaugural lectures (followed by lively *ḥalqa* disputation sessions) that were attended by dignitaries and open to the public. Formerly, students paid fees to help support *madrasa* professors. However, al-Ghazālī (d. 1111) refers to a controversy over whether professors should actively seek money from their pupils by citing the example of the Prophet who openly shared his religious knowledge and didactic teachings as the exemplar of the faith. Monthly salaries, pension arrangements and tenure considerations were instituted for selected *madrasa* teaching faculty. Some scholars engaged in political machinations to secure funds for their impoverished students. Others chose to decline caliphal-sponsored pensions in order to remain autonomous in their issuance of legal opinions.

This sense of independence was perhaps natural for many *shaykh*s. The earlier style of learning had involved students journeying from teacher to teacher as they decided where to linger or take up residence and join study circles. *Awqāf* (sing. *waqf*) from the eleventh century enabled benefactors to establish a more fluid system of funding for teachers and their students, most of whom were boarders. *Madrasa*s were not expected to focus on rudimentary education in literacy training and introductory Qur'anic lessons or other literary pursuits. This first level of education was conducted by private tutoring or enrollment in Qur'anic schools. To reiterate, *madrasa*s were set up for the express purpose of educating students about the specifics of Islamic religious law. Also, students were taught how to apply and interpret Islamic law proceedings via proper use of the Qur'ān and *ḥadīth*. Intensive study of grammar, rhetoric, and logic (to analyze Muḥammad's words and Qur'anic teachings) were the tools by which students could gain more in-depth analysis and understanding of the interrelatedness of jurisprudence coupled with understanding the complexities of the sacred texts.

*Madrasa*s resembled fortresses in the sense that they occupied a prominent place in an Islamic city much like the caliphal palace, bazaars, or mosque complex. The caliph himself had a vested interest in these scholastic enterprises because they produced newly minted graduates who could fill government posts and interpret law under auspices of state authority. At times they were used to buttress caliphal authority and the reigning theological orthodoxy of the period. In addition, local *ʿulamāʾ* were pressed to have their congregants pay heed to this particular brand of state orthodoxy as the "true" faith.

Madrasa construction in late-eleventh and early-twelfth-century Baghdad occurred at an accelerated pace. More than 20 *madrasa*s were built at this time, in affiliation with the area's most influential schools of jurisprudence: Ḥanafī, Ḥanbalī, and Shāfiʿī. Some of the schools were placed in close proximity to the Tigris River. The well-known Niẓāmiyya *madrasa*, the initial scholastic edifice to be constructed during this era, was the teaching venue of al-Ghazālī before he left the school at the height of his popularity due to a serious illness.

Members of the royal family along with the leading *ʿulamāʾ* supported these educational efforts. Women had equal footing with men in this regard because Islamic law permitted both genders not only to own, but to cede private land for charitable or religious purposes. Thus, women were also able to enter the public space as donors to help construct and endow *madrasa*s.

Travel narratives reflect the continued expansion of *madrasa*s in thirteenth-century Baghdad to a total of over 30. Transient *ʿulamāʾ* who were trained at these schools returned to their homes or other locations to share their wealth of knowledge. The success of this interwoven system was short-lived, coming to an end with the Mongol destruction of Baghdad in 1258. However, by the time Baghdad had passed its zenith, the educational elite had succeeded in spreading their institutionalized form of religious learning to other parts of the Islamic world. Numerous Shāfiʿī and Ḥanafī *madrasa*s flourished in fourteenth-century Delhi. In the 1300s, Mansa Musa constructed a university in Mali at Timbuktu and mosques in the larger urban areas. The Muslim quarter of Hezhou is still known as China's "Little Mecca" in part due to its rich collection of mosques and *madrasa*s.

Learning styles in the *madrasa* system

Indigenous students and scholars as well as those from far reaches of the Islamic world were drawn to medieval *madrasa*s for their instructional facilities and burgeoning collections of books. Scholars and travelers from around the globe copied books and selected library materials to help promote the written form of knowledge (*ʿilm*) on return trips to places such as Syria, North Africa, and other Muslim lands. Of key concern to scholars and religious authorities was how this transmission of knowledge should best take place. An ongoing tension existed between those who preferred oral recitation of complete texts verified by distinguished *shaykh*s versus other teachers who encouraged their students to master texts aurally through memory but also to seek and acquire printed books for further knowledge. The traditional oral transference of information between *shaykh* and pupil gradually gave way to a system of physical, hand-copied manuscripts to spread information, although such documents were scant in number during the middle period of the Islamic empire (750–1000). *Madrasa*s also served to help leaders such as Niẓām al-Mulk (vizier 1063–92) crystallize Sunnī identity, and, contrary to previous scholarly assessments of this movement, were not principally a response to counter the influence of Shiʿism.

Religious knowledge and Muslim piety were fostered in a variety of ways within diverse social groups that were not limited to men. Muslim women seeking spiritual blessing or power (*baraka*) also sought out *ʿilm* at the feet of master teachers who bestowed *ijāzas* upon them to go and become teachers of selected texts themselves. Although few in number, some Muslim women were active partners in this medieval transmission of knowledge. *Madrasa* life principally benefited the teachers and students who were supported by endowments. However, these schools were open to the public for prayer and were an integral part of the religious milieu in urban settings such as Cairo and Damascus, in addition to Baghdad. Lines between mosque and *madrasa* became blurred as the former also began to provide funds and other material support for *shaykh*s and students. The process of developing a "learned" person had evolved from basic memorization of Qur'ān and *ḥadīth* to a complex web of socialization and modes of learning overseen by the *ʿulamāʾ* in medieval religious institutions of learning.

The noted theologian, mystic, and philosopher al-Ghazālī had a profound impact on a lasting model of education in Islam. His view of learning involved the fostering of a deep sense of piety combined with a reliance upon human reason. Al-Ghazālī had an abiding concern for children, whom he thought were all capable of learning. After embracing the mystical path of Sufism, al-Ghazālī asserted that human reason had its limits. In fact, children were in need of spiritual direction for precisely this reason. In his spiritual autobiography *Deliverance from Error*, al-Ghazālī concluded that curricula should be designed to impart knowledge of the faith and spiritual development. Knowledge is to be received in humility which leads to good manners – a sign of a devout person. Inward spiritual growth is reflected in how well a person treats others and whether her actions reveal the light of *ḥikma* (wisdom) and prudent decision making pertaining to matters of *ʿadl* (justice). These human reflections of divine attributes are cultivated in the context of *sharīʿa* (divine law).

Al-Ghazālī's heartfelt desire involved having communities of students engaged in the study of Islamic law enriched by Ṣūfī practices and beliefs. According to his ideal, nurturance of the soul should begin at a tender age as children learned Islamic teachings to aid in character development. This instillation of religious knowledge would give them greater discernment between good and evil as they came of age.

At this stage of learning (Sunnī and Shīʿī Muslims had separate mosque and school programs), children memorized Qur'anic and *ḥadīth* passages, a process which remains the modus operandi in *kuttāb*s throughout the Islamic world today. The *ʿulamāʾ* concentrated on the rational study and examination of sacred scripture in connection with jurisprudence. Ṣūfī circles emphasized that true learning starts from the heart under the ongoing guidance of a *murshid* (spiritual master). In some instances, the roles of religious scholars overlapped as selected members of the *ʿulamāʾ* were also active in Ṣūfī *ṭarīqa*s (orders). Other *ʿulamāʾ* remained at odds with Ṣūfī masters over religious rituals, doctrinal beliefs, and other concerns. After subsequent training, students experienced mosques as places where they could raise questions about religious knowledge, have debates with their *shaykh*s, and engage in discussions on a wide range of topics.

Competing forms of education

Curricula, teachers, and students form the backbone of an educational enterprise. These three elements are tied together through the methods used to impart knowledge to students. Selected teaching methods employed in mosque and *madrasa* settings are often reflective of particular indigenous cultural norms regarding how students should be learning. In the Islamic world, it is not unusual for pious young Muslims to have memorized the Qurʾān by the age of eight or nine. To understand how education works in Islam, one must carefully examine traditional Islamic and Western models of education. Aspects of these two systems often have blended together in many countries. Complete memorization and subsequent recitation of the Qurʾān were thought of as the ideal during the formative period of education in Islam. However, students were expected to wrestle with variant meanings of Qurʾanic exegesis at the *madrasa* stage and during their professional careers. The introduction of new ideas and beliefs into the somewhat static system of Islamic learning was often untenable.

In the nineteenth century, schools in Europe and the USA were also characterized by exacting discipline and rote learning of subject materials. For example, during Lord Cromer's governance of Egypt, the English statesman opposed expanding schools for Egyptians that would enhance their critical thinking skills or elevate the status of Egyptian women. The former concern reflected his desire to "control the masses," so to speak, and his nonchalance about gender inequity was characteristic of attitudes toward women in England, where they were viewed and treated as second-class citizens. Western forms of education gradually made inroads into Middle Eastern cultures with European teachers who were hired to teach in some of the reformist schools.

Traditional European styles of formal lectures void of questions with a focus on memorization were the predominant teaching methods which paralleled how students were taught in Islamic schools. However, a key difference between the European and Islamic ways of educating youth lay in curricular content. European educators brought their own literatures and cultures with them into Islamic classrooms. These new forms of knowledge fostered curiosity in the students to learn more about a wide array of subjects outside the confines of a classic Islamic education. They also sparked indignation and protests from those responsible for maintaining the status quo of perpetuating centuries-old lessons on Qurʾān and *ḥadīth*.

Al-Azhar, the most distinguished mosque-university in the world, was founded in the centrally located city of Cairo in 972. *Shaykh*s would gather their pupils near pillars in the mosque setting. Pillar education at the feet of the school's teachers was typical fare as students learned to memorize and master voluminous amounts of sacred texts and commentary. Students from many different countries traveled to Azhar to sit with their *shaykh*s of choice. Religious endowments supported the cost of living arrangements, bread supplies, libraries, and other fiscal matters. Initially,

Western-style schools were established in countries such as Egypt and Lebanon alongside traditional Islamic schools. In 1872, state reformers attempted to push for a significant revision of the Azhar curricula in order to more effectively train future graduates to assume government posts. Muṣṭafā al Marāghī, the leading *shaykh* of al-Azhar during the 1930s, sent Azharites to Europe for further studies.

By the late nineteenth century, the composition of al-Azhar's student body had begun to change. Previously, poor, illiterate students from the country had mixed with those from the urban elite classes. Toward the turn of the century, students from the latter category began to opt for state and private school slots that would help them secure better positions in government and industry.

Today, al-Azhar is seen as the educational centerpiece of higher learning in Sunnī Islam and Arabic language studies. Students come from over 75 countries. Women are now educated at al-Azhar although housed in a separate college. Both genders are required to take a Western language and can enroll in commerce and engineering courses, evocative of the reforms hailed long ago by Muḥammad ʿAbduh (1849–1905) and his feminist compatriot Qāsim Amīn, whose *Taḥrīr al-Marʾa* ("The Liberation of Woman") was published in 1899. ʿAbduh helped to institute the teaching of geography, mathematics, literature, and other contemporary subjects at al-Azhar. Al-Azhar remains a conservative institution, still not far removed from the 1920s condemnation of Egyptian luminary Ṭāhā Ḥusayn (1889–1973) for his controversial book *On Pre-Islamic Poetry*. In more recent decades, Azharite leaders roundly condemned Salman Rushdie's *The Satanic Verses* and certain novels by the Egyptian Naguib Mahfouz, the first Arab to win the Nobel Prize for Literature (1988). Perhaps there was a grain of truth in Ṭāhā Ḥusayn's *The Stream of Days: A Student at the Azhar*, when he refers to young Azharīs who were critical of teaching methods used by their *shaykh*s and wondered if books on literature disdained by their elders had even been read!

An Islamic traditionalist movement led to the founding of the Deoband *madrasa* in India in 1867. This school was established in the Delhi region of northern India in the late nineteenth century while the subcontinent was occupied by British colonialists. Urdu was the language of choice for this school founded by *ʿulamāʾ* who were specialists in *ḥadīth*. Deobandi scholars relished stories about the Ṣūfī mystics of Islam. Their students were expected to exemplify the prophet Muḥammad in all manners of speech and action. Characteristic of this era, the Deobandis employed the post office, railroads, and printing presses to seek popular funding for their nascent educational institution. Although Arabic was used at the school, Urdu remained the principal language of instruction with the goal of producing *ʿulamāʾ* who would be not only well-versed in Islamic scriptures but also attuned to India's predominantly Urdu-speaking Muslims.

English and French colonial systems had a significant impact on traditional Islamic venues and modes of instruction. The former educational system of intensive oral learning and instruction from a small number of *shaykh*s or guides in an open, hall-like setting gradually gave way to students being grouped together in classrooms to cover a wide range of subjects on a daily basis. Competition from missionary and state-sponsored schools increased pressure on Islamic schools to institute European and Western Christian didactic methods of learning. The Islamic emphasis on teacher-centered character development through the careful learning of Qurʾān and *ḥadīth* contrasted with the mastery of multiple subjects along with specific skills needed to acquire gainful employment.

Contrasting and evolving approaches to learning

The two competing systems of education resulted in what Suleman Dangor describes as the "bifurcation of education" (2005: 520). Newly minted graduates were being produced with expertise in modern science while others were being trained in traditional Islamic subjects. How could Islamic values and teachings be retained in public and private schools without being overshadowed by Western pedagogical practices and views of the world? Furthermore, would it be possible to successfully blend the teaching of Islamic sciences with secular curricula? In the formation of a classic Islamic education, these educational forays were not viewed as being mutually exclusive. In fact, to even consider them as separate entities would have evoked astonishment in early Islamic societies. For devout Muslims, the study of natural sciences and Islamic materials alike centered around the linchpins of the Qur'ān as the source of knowledge and Muḥammad as the exemplar of the faith. Therefore, many Muslims would argue that contemporary education worth its salt would continue to reflect Islamic ethico-religious teachings in conjunction with newer subject matter.

Western missionary and secular approaches to education were perceived as a threat to *madrasa* and *kuttāb* forms of education. The style of schooling that developed in nineteenth-century Europe featured standard textbook instruction, teachers with vastly different instructional styles and knowledge compared to the *'ulamā'*, and a grouping of students by age and subject to aid in school decorum and order. In the 1800s, foreign mission and other private schools and colonial government-supported institutions in the Islamic world emulated a Western model of education in order to train citizens to promote economic prosperity, scientific advancements, and military might.

A pivotal figure in this new educational thrust was the viceroy of Egypt, Muḥammad 'Alī Pasha (r. 1805–49), who took the initiative to sponsor selected Egyptian students on educational missions to Europe, sought the advice of foreign experts to help with the revivification of national educational curricula, and established military schools to dovetail with his central goal of military reform. The *'ulamā'* were suspicious of these curricular reforms because they served to import the teaching of Western languages, thoughts, and ideals. In particular, they felt the need to be guardians of Islamic culture in regard to Muslim girls and women. They worried as well about the attempts of Western missionaries to convert people to Christianity. Traditional religious instruction was being supplanted by educational instruction tailored to meet the political and economic needs of the Egyptian state. Also, the country's educational system was gradually moving away from being under the total control of religious leaders.

Increasingly, this development left marginalized and impoverished citizens in schools characterized by increasingly static forms of Islamic learning. The education of girls and those of the urban and rural poor continued to be neglected. English and French became the preferred classroom languages in elite schools. It was not until the 1950s and 1960s that Arabic, Farsi, and Urdu assumed their proper place as principal languages of modern instruction in the Arab world, Persia, and the Indian subcontinent. Thus, a social stratification arose between the elites who could afford a Western-style education and students of lesser means who studied traditional Islamic sciences. This development, in effect, reduced the prominent role played by authorities in charge of religious instruction.

The *ʿulamāʾ* and other religious leaders were concerned that European and American-style schools would lack the essence of Qurʾanic ethics and moral teachings. At the same time, a number of governments in the Islamic world began to implement national exams to help streamline the educational system and sift out students not headed for higher education. Many school administrators continue to face the learning challenges caused by classroom overcrowding and the lure of extremist groups. Gregory Starrett (1998) notes that in the decade after the 1952 Egyptian revolution, Egypt's total school population doubled in size while a dearth of qualified educators became a serious issue.

Comprehensive educational reforms require flexibility and long-range planning on the part of educational experts, government officials, and their constituents. Today, illiteracy continues to remain at high levels in many parts of the Islamic world.

Education of girls and women

Traditional gender barriers faced by Muslim females in education were somewhat malleable in regard to *ḥadīth* compilation. Some women competed favorably with men despite their gender, having been excluded from the formal educational structure in the early centuries of Islam. These scholars acquired knowledge from a learned *shaykh* and distinguished themselves as skilled *ḥadīth* transmitters. The exemplar in this vein of thought was ʿĀʾisha, the third wife of Muḥammad, who made significant contributions to the *ḥadīth* corpus during her lifetime. ʿĀʾisha learned about the teachings of Islam through her husband Muḥammad, her father Abū Bakr, and other leading members of the nascent Islamic community. Approximately 100 years later, "The city of Mecca offered opportunities, even for a slave girl, to sit at the feet of some of the day's most learned or prominent theologians" (Abbott 1986: 40–1).

In the modern era, girls were also part of an informal educational structure in nineteenth-century Central Asia, where *maktabs* (schools) often featured both genders in classes together prior to the onset of puberty. These mixed classes were educated by female family members of the religious elite who had a following of their own. Meanwhile, elite-level women in Syria were directing Arabist schools, in part to fight the pervasive influences of French colonialism. Likewise, women's associations in Lebanon and Egypt founded schools that were autonomous from foreign government and missionary control. In the 1920s, women's associations began to press for the state to assume a greater role in educating females. Nevertheless, public education for girls did not become widespread in the Middle East until after World War II.

Islamization of knowledge

Muslim thinkers responded to Westernization and colonial educational practices in a variety of ways. Egypt's distinguished literary figure Ṭāhā Ḥusayn sought to revise education along the lines of Western European secular reforms. His seminal work, *The Future of Culture in Egypt* (1938), outlined this plan influenced by his training as a student at al-Azhar and at Cairo University, as well as by his years of study in France. Another path was taken by Egyptian figures such as Ḥasan al-Bannā' (d. 1949; founder of the Muslim Brotherhood in 1928) and his disciple Sayyid Quṭb (d. 1966), along with the Pakistani Abū 'l-A'lā Mawdūdī (d. 1979). The writings of these early Islamists have had a mixed legacy. On the one hand, they have fueled the ideologies of Al Qaeda and other extremist groups. On the other hand, they have also inspired moderate Islamic factions.

Islamist groups proliferate in Saudi Arabia, where Wahhābī Islam was instrumental in founding an elaborate system of *madrasas* throughout the nation as well as in Afghanistan and Pakistan. The majority of these *madrasas* offer classical training in Islamic subjects. A sliver of these institutions have functioned to spread an intolerant interpretation of Sunnī Islam that promotes a violent, jihadist form of Islam. This virulent form of militancy blossoms in parts of the Muslim world that are mired in high unemployment, poverty, illiteracy, and a lack of hope.

The Crimean Muslim intellectual Ismail Gasprinskii (d. 1914) was effective in expressing the potentials for modernity within Islamic society. He established *uṣūl-i jadīd* (new method) schools, which retained Islamic subjects but stressed other topics, including literacy, history, geography, mathematics, applied science, and Arabic language. Perhaps the most strikingly modern of his undertakings were his advocacy of women's education and roles, and his creation of new means to serve the underprivileged (namely, mutual aid societies).

Syed Muhammad Naguib al-Attas was a proponent of integrating Islamic thought with education in Malaysia. He sought to Islamize the hard sciences as well as the social sciences. For example, the Malaysian Islamic Academy of Sciences was founded in 1977 to encourage the study of science from an Islamic perspective. The late Professor Isma'il Raji al Faruqi (d. 1987) sought to address the pervasive influence of Western sciences by promoting what he termed "the Islamization of knowledge." Faruqi advocated Islamizing the social sciences by upholding the Qur'anic concept of *tawḥīd* (unity), which he felt should permeate all forms of human knowledge. He called for Muslims to reexamine Islamic epistemology and design a plan to Islamize education in its various forms. To accomplish this task, Faruqi founded the International Institute of Islamic Thought in 1981 in Herndon, Virginia, USA. In tandem with this development, World Conferences on Muslim Education have been held in Islamabad (1980), Dhaka (1981), Jakarta (1982), Cairo (1987), and Cape Town (1996). In Faruqi's *Islamization of Knowledge: General Principles and Workplan* (1982), he explained that the *sharī'a* should be the guidepost tethered to the process of *ijtihād* (independent legal reasoning). Scholars such as Fazlur Rahman (d. 1988) critiqued the skeletal methodology of *tawḥīd* and the overall strategy of Islamization of all knowledge, arguing that it seemed untenable.

Modern educational issues for Muslim children

In Indonesia, many private Islamic schools (*pesantrens*) now offer secular as well as religious courses of study. At the same time, a number of *pesantrens* provide opportunities for students in secular public schools to receive religious training through extracurricular classes.

In the USA, the majority of Muslim children receive their instruction in public schools. The public educational network has experienced growing pains as educators work to address the needs of student populations with diverse religious backgrounds. Immigrant Muslim parents often have contrasting views of how they think children should be educated. School districts and local school boards are wrestling with issues such as inaccurate textbooks on Islam, dietary limitations in cafeterias, and the need to provide Muslim students with both time slots and suitable locations for prayers. Shabbir Mansuri founded the Council on Islamic Education (CIE) in California after his daughter discovered misinformation about Islam in one of her textbooks. Today, the CIE advises editors of textbooks prior to publication.

Other points of dispute have included attire for Muslim girls in gym classes, whether school calendars should include the Muslim holidays of *ʿīd al-fiṭr* (festive meal and celebration at the end of Ramaḍān) and *ʿīd al-aḍḥā* (feast of sacrifice at the conclusion of *ḥajj* rituals), and co-education after puberty. Muslim parents often want their children to receive instruction in the Arabic language and the Islamic sciences. Some Muslim families choose to enroll their children in private Islamic institutions. Muslim schools blend traditional Islamic education with Western knowledge and pedagogy. These institutions face a host of challenges as part of the changing American religious landscape. Matters of governance and educational goals often are points of contention. In the wake of the attacks on September 11, 2001, monitoring of Islamic schools by the US government is ongoing.

Conclusion

Educational institutions in the USA and across the Islamic world face challenges of modernization in devising pluralistic education systems that often clash with traditional forms of Islamic learning. Will governments choose to allot more money to provide well-trained teachers and schools that enable their graduates to successfully enter the global market? In ancient Arabia, education and religion went hand-in-hand. Muḥammad encouraged his followers to seek knowledge as devout Muslims. He also wanted believers to use education to develop more compassion for the plight of the downtrodden and illiterate. His educational and religious ideals continue to be sought after in the twenty-first century.

Note

I would like to thank Salima Burke for her important contribution to this essay.

References and further reading

Abbott, N. (1986) *Two Queens of Baghdad*, London: Al Saqi Books.

Berkey, J. P. (1992) *The Transmission of Knowledge in Medieval Cairo: A Social History of Islamic Education*, Princeton: Princeton University Press.

Choudhury, M. A. (1993) "A Critical Examination of the Concept of Islamization of Knowledge in Contemporary Times," *Muslim Education Quarterly*, 10: 3–34.

—— (2001) "Perspectives on the Islamization of Knowledge and their Implications for Organization of the Occupational Composition: The Case of the Canadian Muslims in the Labour Market," *Journal of Muslim Minority Affairs*, 21: 93–107.

Cook, B. J. (2000) "Egypt's National Education Debate," *Comparative Education*, 36: 477–90.

Dalrymple, W. (2005) "Inside Islam's 'Terror Schools'," *New Statesman*, 28 March: 14–18.
Dangor, S. (2005) "Islamization of Disciplines: Towards an Indigenous Educational System," *Educational Philosophy and Theory*, 37: 519–31.
Eickelman, D. F. (1985) *Knowledge and Power in Morocco: The Education of a Twentieth-Century Notable*, Princeton: Princeton University Press.
Ephrat, D. (2000) *A Learned Society in a Period of Transition: The Sunni ʿUlamaʾ of Eleventh-Century Baghdad*, Albany: State University of New York Press.
Fleischmann, E. L. (1999) " 'The Other 'Awakening': The Emergence of Women's Movements in the Modern Middle East, 1900–1940," in M. Meriwether, J. Tucker, eds., *Social History of Women and Gender in the Modern Middle East*, Boulder, CO: Westview Press, 89–139.
Halstead, J. M. (2004) "An Islamic Concept of Education," *Comparative Education*, 40: 517–29.
Herrera, L. (2004) "Education, Islam, and Modernity: Beyond Westernization and Centralization (Book Review)," *Comparative Education Review*, 48: 318–26.
Hilgendorf, E. (2003) "Islamic Education: History and Tendency," *Peabody Journal of Education*, 78: 63–75.
Hussein, T. (1948) *The Stream of Days: A Student at the Azhar*, trans. H. Wayment, London: Longmans, Green and Company.
—— (1959) *The Future of Culture in Egypt*, Washington: ACLS.
Lovat, T. J. (2005) "Educating about Islam and Learning about Self: An Approach for Our Times," *Religious Education*, 100/Winter: 38–51.
Makdisi, G. (1981) *The Rise of Colleges: Institutions of Learning in Islam and the West*, Edinburgh: Edinburgh University Press.
Rahman, F. (1982) *Islam and Modernity: Transformation of an Intellectual Tradition*, Chicago: University of Chicago Press.
—— (1988) "Islamization of Knowledge: A Response," *The American Journal of Islamic Social Science*, 5: 3–28.
Ramadan, T. (2004) *Western Muslims and the Future of Islam*, New York: Oxford University Press.
Ringer, M. M. (2001) *Education, Religion, and the Discourse of Cultural Reform in Qajar Iran*, Costa Mesa, CA: Mazda Publishers.
Saeed, A. (2003) "The Official Ulema and Religious Legitimacy of the Modern Nation State," in S. Akbarzadeh, A. Saeed, eds., *Islam and Political Legitimacy*, London: RoutledgeCurzon, 14–28.
Sirozi, M. (2005) "The Intellectual Roots of Islamic Radicalism in Indonesia: Jaʿfar Umar Thalib of Laskar Jihad (Jihad Fighters) and His Educational Background," *The Muslim World*, 95: 81–120.
Starrett, G. (1998) *Putting Islam to Work: Education, Politics, and Religious Transformation in Egypt*, Berkeley: University of California Press.
Talbani, A. (1996) "Pedagogy, Power, and Discourse: Transformation of Islamic Education," *Comparative Education Review*, 40: 66–82.

23

THE TRANSMISSION OF KNOWLEDGE

Paul L. Heck

Muslims have traditionally understood knowledge to exist for the sake of moral guidance – of individuals, communities, and societies. Knowledge thus holds the key to human prosperity in this world and eternal salvation in the next. This, however, does not make knowledge a simple phenomenon for Muslims. It is divided into the secular and the religious. Secular knowledge, ethics and sciences as attained by human inquiry and effort and verified by rational and experimental analysis, has constituted an important source of guidance for Muslim life in this world. Of great interest to Muslims through the centuries, its worth has been evaluated in terms of its ability to stand up to human examination, developing in relation to human discovery of the world and its ways. In contrast, religious knowledge, both revealed and prophetic, has a supra-human character to it, putting it above ratiocination and experimentation. Its worth thus stands apart from human analysis of its content, verifiable only by determining its accurate transmission from the source of the religion, generally understood in Islam as twofold: revealed source, the speech of God as the Qurʾān; and prophetic source – reports (*ḥadīth* in the singular) of the sayings, actions, and decisions of the Prophet Muḥammad, referred to collectively as the *sunna*. To be sure, religious knowledge was never static, but did develop in response to changing realities; moreover, the importance of religious knowledge in Islam did occasionally lead to treatment of secular knowledge (for example, geography and optics) in terms of its accurate transmission. Still, it was the venture of religion, indeed its foundation, for which the transmission of knowledge became, at least in traditional Islam, paramount concern.

Religious knowledge defines the beliefs and actions held to be pleasing to God, thus making salvation in the next world possible. Therefore, even if Muslims have recognized the value of secular knowledge for effective living in this world, religious knowledge (doctrines, rituals, morals) acts as primary reference point for Muslim life in this world, for this world is understood as a bridge to the next, one's life here determinative of one's final standing there. Traditionally, then, Muslim society was to be shaped by *sharīʿa*, the body of knowledge – flexible, diverse, but in the main known with more or less certainty – that contained the commands and prohibitions of God: religious rulings delineating correctness in life's varied domains – prayer, pilgrimage, diet, clothing, distribution of inheritance, conduct in war, contracts for commerce and marriage, financial practices, punishment of crimes transgressing boundaries set by religion, and so on.

These rulings are understood to have been given by God – generally in the Qur'ān, more specifically in the *sunna*, as discovered and formalized by those learned in the religion (*ʿulamāʾ*). It was thus an educated class, not political power, that was to supervise the knowledge given by God to guide Muslims along the right path. As the domain of a select group, religious knowledge brought social prestige to those who could claim possession of it, and supervision of its transmission became a means for prominent families to exert a measure of influence, even control, over social institutions, both educational and political, making transmission of knowledge a mechanism for ensuring elite status in Muslim society. While the patrimonial state – varied dynastic houses and their administrative servitors – did play a significant role in the production and patronage, not to mention definition, of knowledge and its various divisions, religious knowledge – embodied as *sharīʿa* – was considered the preserve of religious scholars, not state officials; moral identity was a matter of religion, not the state.

The rise of the national state during the last century in traditional Muslim lands, with its claim to define knowledge, a national curriculum, to make it available to all through a national educational system, and to define moral identity through national legislation, has thus not only undermined the importance of religious knowledge, in preference for technical expertise, in shaping the moral life of Muslim society. It has also eroded the authority and corresponding prestige of those who dominated the networks of personal relations through which religious knowledge was transmitted and the traditional educational institutions that facilitated that process, the *madrasa* above all. The *madrasa* is, to be sure, alive and well but has had to reshape its role in Muslim life, now a place where Muslims at large go for the sake of a moral and cultural formation – in the face of or alongside of secular education as defined by the state – and not the site where a scholarly elite engage in the authorized transmission of religious knowledge per se.

In short, modernity's elevation of the secular as guide to life has resulted in the marginalization of religious knowledge for the functioning of society and has downplayed the religious scholar in favor of the national state as final arbiter of knowledge. To be sure, religious knowledge remains at play in society, as a way to contest governance, mediate concerns of society not adequately represented by the state, and shape the values of the nation. The reassertion of religion as of public concern in recent years, in the Muslim world and elsewhere, has not, however, translated into any rekindled interest in the epistemological significance of the transmission of knowledge apart from analysis of its contents. Today, an alternative, more comprehensive and more ideological process has emerged for determining the religious character of knowledge: the Islamization of knowledge, by which all knowledge, including the secular, is read through the lens of – if not made to conform to – the beliefs of Islam. Religious knowledge is now not transmitted so much as it is publicized through cassettes, pamphlets, and the internet, and is applied to all subjects, both secular and religious. Religious authority, as a result, is not based so much on the authority to transmit religious knowledge but, increasingly, the ability to communicate it skillfully through public media – whether or not one has received a traditional training in religious knowledge.

It is worth dwelling for a moment on concepts of knowledge in traditional Islam. A passage from *The Letters of the Brethren of Purity*, although the work of a minor group, illustrates the religious significance given to knowledge by Muslims in general.

The underlying concern was certainty, certainty of living a life in sufficient conformity to religious knowledge as guide to both the good in this world and salvation in the next. Religious knowledge in Islam has not been first and foremost theological reflection, that is, a reasoned defense of the existence, essence, and attributes of God, the purpose of creation, nature of prophecy, and so on. Rather, it has presented itself more as moral details that comprise a way of life identified with the commands and prohibitions of God. Moreover, since human intellect can and does err, only knowledge determined to have originated in the other world can enjoy the status of certainty. Certainty that one's beliefs and actions are correct – and thus merit a favorable place in the next world – depends on determining the source of the knowledge informing beliefs and actions. The consequences of living a life according to purportedly prophetic knowledge that a pernicious scholar had invented and circulated as authentic would be disastrous. Indeed, since the good of society, associated with the divine will, depended on accurate knowledge of that will, then those who fabricated prophetic knowledge put at risk not only the authenticity of the religion but the welfare of the community as a whole.

It was therefore not enough to summarize prophetic knowledge in a book. Considerable scholarly energy had to be continuously devoted to verifying the transmission of knowledge claiming to be religious in origin, especially knowledge attributed to Muḥammad. This knowledge, after all, was not a matter of general ethical principles – justice, honesty, fidelity to one's obligations – that human intellect alone could affirm as true, but detailed norms specific to a communal way of life, a set of traditions and customs – what was permissible to eat and drink, how to marry and divorce, penalties for infractions against communal norms, and so on – that differed from one people to another, the product of particular traditions, not universal principles that all peoples acknowledged. What made these particulars of Muslim life any more or less true than those of another way of life? The possibility of moral relativism made it doubly important to demonstrate a sound connection between the Muslim way of life and the prophetic source from which it allegedly originated. Other religions had their books recording norms and a way of life, but without chains of transmission. It was a source of pride among Muslims that their records of prophetic knowledge were accompanied by chains of transmission, a mechanism claimed to be exclusive to Islam (although also known in rabbinical Judaism). How else could one be certain that a book actually contained the commands and prohibitions of God and not mere human customs interpolated into the corpus of religious knowledge? The very truth of religion was at stake.

Controversy over the transmission of religious knowledge arose with the death of the Prophet Muḥammad, until then sole authoritative conveyor of religious knowledge. Verses of the Qur'ān, as he had conveyed them via oral recitation, had been recorded, but in no organized fashion, etched into animal bones, written on palm leaves, or recorded on paper as notes of a sort; no order had been given to collect them in a single book. Promulgation of the Qur'ān fell to those with expertise in oral recitation (*qurrā'*), whose role in narrating the Qur'ān recalled that of the oral transmitters of early Arabic poetry (*ruwāt*). Oral narration, to be sure, did not imply illiteracy. Verse, scriptural or poetic, was set down as notes (i.e., writing as aide-mémoire), but not compiled in the form of a book proper. The transmitter, narrating the verse of another, might add or alter a word here and there to improve it, a practice acceptable in the case of poetry as record of tribal prestige, but not so in the case of scripture as the force binding together a nascent community based on ties not of tribe but of faith. Diversity in oral recitation therefore challenged the prospects of maintaining communal unity under a single leader, especially when the success of the early conquests (*futūḥāt*) led to Arab dispersion to and settlement in places distant from the Arabian Peninsula.

The tradition holds that it was the death in battle of a considerable number of *qurrā'* that lead to the decision to reduce the variant forms of Qur'ān recitation to a single recension, that is, a text fixed in writing, under the supervision of the caliphal center, a process finalized in the time of 'Uthmān (r. 644–56), third of the four "rightly-guided" successors to the Prophet. This official recension was distributed to the various Muslim camps as an edict of communal policy, and other versions were repressed. By such a process, writing, initially ancillary to the transmission of the Qur'ān, became essential – a book in fixed form as authoritative source of the revealed message and thus independent of the persons transmitting it, the *qurrā'*, who, as one might imagine, were not at all pleased with the caliphal decision to "control" the oral recitation of the Qur'ān, viewing it as a sacrilegious reduction of revelation to textual constraints. Still, since God was the authorial promulgator of the Qur'ān, it was held that He would see to its sound transmission. Moreover, given the importance of the Qur'ān to the community, knowledge of it – it was held – was so widespread (*mutawātir*), in all generations and certainly in the first, as to preclude the possibility of error in transmission or interpolation; some prophetic reports fell into this category of widespread knowledge, but far from all, making verification of prophetic reports much more problematic than the Qur'ān.

The issue at stake in the codification of the Qur'ān, however, was not simply the prestige of a group of people whose work of promulgating the Qur'ān in oral form had been usurped by a written publication of the text. The efficacy of divine speech was at stake. Could it be formulated as a written edict issued by the leaders of the newly established Muslim polity? Was it not more properly the domain of religious specialists who mediated a liturgical space for the believing community by reciting – and thus re-presenting the experience of – revelation? Is divine speech more properly transmitted through writing or reciting? Both came to be acknowledged. The Qur'ān was indeed a book, even if unlike any other, but it operated first and foremost at the oral level – memorization and recitation – as mark of its liturgical purpose. Partiality for the oral transmission of the Qur'ān, even once codified as a fixed text, was linked to a deeper recognition of its divine origin and authority. To this end, the illiteracy of Muḥammad became important evidence for the claim that what he had conveyed as the speech of God could not have come from any human source, that is to say a book that he might have read somewhere. In confirmation of the primarily oral nature of scripture, variant readings of the Qur'ān – seven, ten, or fourteen – were preserved and continue to be studied until today as an important religious science, that is, the domain of religious specialists and not political authorities.

Other forms of religious knowledge posed more complex challenges: 1) reports about the first Muslims in general and the Prophet in particular; 2) statements attributed to God but falling outside the final recension of the Qur'ān; and 3) a mysterious document known as "the scroll" (*al-ṣaḥīfa*). The first two came to be combined in one category, the *sunna* of the Muslim community as set by the Prophet and those who witnessed his life, combined with extra-Qur'anic instances of divine speech that were defined as *ḥadīth*, narrated by Muḥammad, but distinguished with the label "sacred." The so-called scroll was seen by Shīʿī partisans to contain additional knowledge of godly provenance given to the Imāms as rightful successors to the Prophet as leaders of the Muslim community, but was viewed by proto-Sunnī circles as a threat to the purity of the Qur'ān, possessing the potential to destroy the community in the fashion of previous communities which had perished as a result of straying from the path of God – the result of their conflating human knowledge with revealed scriptures. There was a tangible fear of awarding scriptural status to non-scriptural material, since it would result in ignorance of the true message of God that made salvation possible. This was, at least initially, no less true in the case of *ḥadīth*, the writing down of which posed a dilemma to the first generations of Muslims. As prophetic, they were a kind of knowledge distinct from the merely human, and yet, if set in writing, were they not likely to be confused with revealed scripture? Moreover, similarly to the scroll (written knowledge of a religious kind and yet not speech of God), the promulgation of *ḥadīth* in writing ran the risk of associating what was not the speech of God with the speech of God. How, then, to ensure that prophetic knowledge was not confused with revealed knowledge and, even more importantly, with human knowledge parading as religious knowledge?

Preservation of the purity of the *sunna* thus depended on knowledge of its chain of transmission. The fabrication of reports attributed to Muḥammad led scholars to compile vast collections of reports according to the evaluation of their chain of transmission – weak or sound. Very early on, the question of writing down prophetic reports arose, with much controversy. It was increasingly difficult to find Muslims with memories capacious enough to hold the vast corpus of prophetic reports along with knowledge of their chains of transmission. Moreover, books were being effectively used for the transmission of secular knowledge – literary, geographical, medical, administrative, and so on – apart from the documentation of those transmitting it. Writing in book form and not simply as notes to aid the memory had come to be seen as an authoritative source of knowledge. Could the promulgation of religious knowledge ignore these emerging cultural standards that worked to define the worth of knowledge in terms of intellectual content or rhetorical eloquence apart from its chain of transmission? Littérateurs expressed enthusiasm for books as companions and confidantes, conveying wisdom of the ancients. Poets presented their verses as books to rulers in the hope of patronage. Secretaries composed official letters as edicts of those holding political power, obviating the need to trace them to an authoritative source. Philosophy and medicine, the works of Plato, Aristotle, and Galen, had been translated and set down in book form for human examination. Administrators of the realm – governors, magistrates, scribes of varied rank – depended on a succinct presentation of knowledge; even when it came to prophetic knowledge, if of interest to governance (e.g. as related to tax matters), the need for easy access required its presentation in an "abbreviated" (*mukhtaṣar*) form shorn of chains of transmission.

This "culture of the book" did not sit well with the religiously learned, even if religious knowledge did appear in book form in the first Islamic centuries. Some objected to the use of writing in any form for the transmission of prophetic knowledge (or any knowledge derived from it). Others permitted writing, but only as an aide-mémoire – notes which once memorized were to be erased. Even if one were endowed with a weak memory, requiring life-long reliance on notebooks, one should still make sure to destroy them prior to death, lest they fall into the hands of the ignorant or ill-willed, who might insert into them self-serving material, garnering for it the status of religious knowledge. Since such knowledge could act as communal, even legal, precedent, it was imperative that what was passing as precedent was actually traceable to the Prophet as final touchstone of Islam. There were still others, however, who permitted the circulation of prophetic reports and other religious material in book form with the condition that those transmitting the material, the teachers, issued an authorization to those to whom they had transmitted the material, the students, when it was felt that they were worthy and competent of doing so responsibly and accurately. The chain of transmission, the authoritative base of religious knowledge, an inherently oral phenomenon as signified by the word used to indicate its transmission from teacher to student, "audition" (*samāʿ*), was thus recast as an "authorization" (*ijāza*) in written form. In that way, the chain of transmission, guarantor of the reliability of religious knowledge, was maintained, even if as written conveyance, permitting scholars to continue to refer to the transmission of such material as "audition," even material they had received from a book without ever having met its "authorial" transmitter. For religious scholars to maintain lines of authority *and* live within a cultural reality in which the preservation and distribution of knowledge via books had become routine, it was necessary to define the book in a particular way – as alternative to memory, but not an independent source of knowledge, and one still in need of being bound by a chain of transmission.

The reality remained problematic. Could one simply copy prophetic material from a book without authorization if the book were widely recognized to be sound in content? Or was one obliged to find the authorial transmitter of the material contained in the book and recite back to him or her what one had copied from it, to ensure that what one had in writing was the same as what the transmitter had narrated? A book was itself not free of suspicion, and even the practice of reciting back (*ʿard*) a book's contents to its transmitter was suspect, since the authorial transmitter, that is the teacher, might not have full mastery of his own received knowledge as now recorded in a book. A story has it that Ibn Masʿūd, towering figure of the first century of Islam, was challenged by his son, Masrūq, who said that his father's oral narration of a prophetic report was at variance with his, Masrūq's, written record of it (al-Baghdādī 1949: 39). Ibn Masʿūd ordered his son to come forward and proceeded to erase his notes. How was the authorial and thus authorizing source of knowledge to be defined – in terms of written record or the person who had received it by a sound transmission, ultimately from its prophetic source? Failure of memory was no less plausible than inaccurate recording of a narration. More significantly, a written record, whether accurate or not, was still cut off from the chain of transmission, an oral phenomenon by nature, in which persons, not books, carried and conveyed the tradition. The knowledge retained in memory by scholars enjoyed an authority even over the contents of their own books! How was a scholarly relation to be understood, as a dynamic between students and teachers or as one between scholar and his or her books? The gravity of this question was particularly clear in the case of a book that one happened to come across (*wijāda*). Who had authored it? Was one entitled to narrate its contents to others if its authorial transmitter was unknown? If the identity of the authorial transmitter was established, was it necessary, before narrating its contents to others, to travel to him or her to determine whether or not what was "found" in the book represented the transmitter's narration? In short, could one make use of what one found in a book without obtaining authorization from the scholar whose knowledge it purportedly represented?

Knowledge here was strikingly defined in terms of a personal relation, even networks of personal relations, through which religious knowledge flowed and was kept alive, animating in turn the community for which it was meant, as its primary point of reference, guide, and educator. Those with expertise in this knowledge thus played a significant role in mediating the identity of Muslim society, a role maintained by careful differentiation between secular and religious knowledge, specifically the respective standards by which each was to be judged. It was this defense of epistemological "turf" that underlay the unique role of religious scholars in the shaping of traditional Muslim society, giving them – even apart from "secular" rulers – control of considerable social capital. Amazingly, it all depended on the chain of transmission, without mastery of which anyone could claim to speak with religious authority (as is the case today when custodianship of religious knowledge is increasingly claimed by those with no training in its transmission, often with a corresponding attack on traditional religious authority).

For religious scholars, then, only those with expertise in the transmission of religious knowledge could speak authoritatively about it. For example, in a manual on the rules for transmitting religious knowledge, *The Comprehensive Treatment of the Qualities of the Narrator and the Norms of the Auditor*, al-Khaṭīb al-Baghdādī (d. 1071), a towering figure in the science of *ḥadith*, makes the following statement (al-Baghdādī 1996: 370–2 for all following quotes): "The authoritative basis (*isnād*) of [human] wisdom is its existence." In other words, its worth can be evaluated apart from its transmission. He bases this conclusion on a response given by Ibn al-Mubārak (d. 797), celebrated scholar and ascetic warrior of early Islam, when asked whether any benefit could be had from moral wisdom found in books: "It is alright. If you find such moral wisdom [inscribed] on a wall, consider it and be exhorted." When, however, asked about religious knowledge (*fiqh*), he responded: "It has no worth [if received] without audition (*samāʿ*)." Thus, by delineating the space where the chain of transmission was indispensable criterion of truth, religious scholars guarded their place in Muslim society.

This line of argument, however significant societally, never squared with the reality. Religious knowledge did become fixed in book form; one no longer had to travel in pursuit of knowledge or even learn it at the foot of eminent masters, but rather simply open the two covers of a book. The book did permit a wider dissemination of religious material, but the silent reading of a book, absent magisterial authority supervising the process, stood at odds with the very notion of religious tradition. This is epitomized in another statement attributed to Ibn al-Mubārak in the abovementioned work: "The chain of transmission is for me a part of the religion. If it were not for the chain, whoever wanted could say whatever he wanted [i.e., make any claim for religious knowledge]." This attitude was widespread, confirmed, for example, by ʿAbd al-Wahhāb al-Shaʿrānī (d. 1565), renowned Egyptian religious scholar and spiritual master, who in his famous ethical treatise (al-Shaʿrānī 1975: I, 129), rails against anyone who would read a book of prophetic knowledge in the absence of a master, comparing such a person to a student of medicine who reads books but has no experience of illnesses and their cures.

In fact, at least in one area, a genre of literature arose to censure those who spoke of religious matters without adherence to traditional teaching as soundly transmitted. This censure of theology (*dhamm al-kalām*) was an attack against disputation on religious matters, a practice which had arisen out of the need for a rational defense of the creed, especially in a cosmopolitan milieu, but which often descended into rhetorical competition, sophistry, generating theological division among the scholarly elite and sowing confusion among the people at large. Theology was thus excoriated in traditional religious circles as pursuit of knowledge in religious matters that did not respect the very criterion by which certainty in religion was determined – the chain of transmission: "Whoever seeks religion through theology commits heresy." Such words, attributed by al-Sulamī (d. 1021) in his *Book on the Censure of Theology* to Abū Yūsuf (d. 798), legal scholar in the service of the Abbasid caliph Harūn al-Rashīd (r. 786–809), epitomizes a situation in which efforts to preserve the boundaries of religious knowledge were repeatedly challenged by efforts to articulate and comprehend it in human – that is, rationally comprehensible and communicable – terms.

Such an "uncontrolled" pursuit of religious knowledge was, however, never far from traditional circles themselves, since the book as vehicle of transmission held the potential to "democratize" religious knowledge, making it available to anyone who could read, irrespective of traditional authorization. Indeed, the widely accepted use of books for the study and promulgation of religious knowledge had led to the neglect of the chain of transmission, accustoming people to cite religious knowledge without checking its authoritative basis (*isnād*); this, as noted, ran the risk of breaking down the barrier between secular and religious knowledge. The great scholar of the prophetic tradition, Ibn Ṣalāḥ (d. 1245), sought to end the dilemma, once and for all. His solution was to canonize certain collections of prophetic material, the so-called six books (*al-kutub al-sitta*), which had come to be widely recognized as authoritative; his move finalized the process by which these collections came to enjoy the status of scripture, i.e. religious knowledge independent of traditional authorization. This meant, of course, that all other works of religious content were reduced to ambiguous status. As he says (Ibn Ṣalāḥ 1990: 159–60): "Thus, the long and short of it . . . is reliance on what the masters of *ḥadīth* composed in their reliable and universally recognized compilations that are considered – on account of their reputation – above change and distortion."

This reservation of canonical status to a limited group of texts, meant to end confusion as to what was and what was not religious knowledge, went a long way to resolve the epistemological – and social – conundrums involved in the transmission of religious knowledge via books, enabling recognition of what had been a long-standing reality. Indeed, traditional religious education in Islam has been synonymous with the study and mastery of books as repositories of religious knowledge, books which, although associated with individual teachers, came to epitomize the course of instruction in the various branches of knowledge studied in the *madrasa* as institutional center of traditional religious education in Islam. The transmission of knowledge – although necessarily embodied in the personal relation of teacher to student, in view of the epistemological concerns discussed above – was institutionalized in the *madrasa*, arena of educational life in all its forms: not only the transmission of knowledge, but disputes about it, commentaries on it, and, in the final analysis, extension of it in ways responsive to the circumstances of the age.

It is difficult, but not impossible, to speak of a set and prescribed curriculum that would lead to what we understand today as a degree, granted not by individual teacher, but a university corporation. There were recognized stages of education, and the terms of the endowment may have mentioned specifics about the instruction to be given, but the *madrasa* on the whole should be viewed as an institution facilitating, rather than defining, the pedagogical relation between teacher and student. The *madrasa* did not offer clear guidelines for becoming a teacher, a status one achieved through a long-term scholarly companionship with one's own teacher. The *madrasa* was more a place of residence and source of financial support, for both students and teachers – thus ancillary, but still integral, to the transmission of knowledge from teacher to student. The *madrasa* came to symbolize education in religious knowledge no less than the books transmitting it and the teachers authorizing it. Life in the *madrasa* varied in time and place, but its educational life coalesced around the study and mastery of books and the teachers transmitting the religious knowledge they contained. As such, instruction in the *madrasa* was a religious no less than scholarly event, requiring an atmosphere of reverence and purity – ritual and spiritual. In certain contexts, such as pre-Ottoman Egypt, the *madrasa* also served as the site of judicial hearings, in lieu of a centralized court system. Since the pursuit of knowledge was also intimately linked to social status, there were recognized, even regularized, stages of advancement, establishing institutional expectations: a system of posts and positions, fixed rules of admissions, behavior, scholarly ranks, a known curriculum and process for granting/receiving authorization to transmit the knowledge of books and to teach law and issue legal opinions. Teaching in a *madrasa* could be linked to a certain legal or theological school or, conversely, include multiple schools.

It can be said that the *madrasa* formed a major thread in the fabric of Muslim life, connecting scholars across vast regions and serving as logical stopping point for itinerant scholars in search of religious knowledge, such as the celebrated Ibn Baṭṭūṭa (d. 1368–9 or 1377). The costs for the construction and upkeep of the *madrasa* necessitated financing via endowment, donations of the elite class which also acted to ensure a close relation between religious knowledge and social influence. Such benefaction, it should be noted, was at times initiated by female members of prominent families. This richly woven tapestry of educational life in Islam underwent radical transformation with the rise of the national state in traditional Muslim homelands in the wake of European colonial domination. It was increasingly state authorities that administered education, not religious ones. The promulgation of religious knowledge in traditional institutions came to be monitored by supervisory boards appointed by states, exposing the personal character of traditional education to increasing bureaucratization, rationalization, and thus modernization – the beginnings of a "hybrid" discourse about knowledge in Islam. Degree requirements came to be set by the state, and progress to teaching, preaching, and other posts defined by state-sanctioned curricula and exams. Eventually, schools of an entirely secular orientation, under the direction of national authority, were established, including a religious curriculum. By dislodging the authority over religious knowledge from traditional figures and institutions, the national state made of it a more academic, even secular, affair, fully subject to human analysis and state oversight, a process that undermined the value of the chain of transmission and the traditional religious authority it represented.

Only rarely today does one come across a scholar fully devoted to the authoritative transmission of religious knowledge. Such figures are still to be found, having memorized and being capable of reciting not only entire corpuses of prophetic material but also the chains of transmission by which they themselves personally received such material, apart from books and apart from state inspection. And there are still institutional expressions of *isnād*-based knowledge, such as the Dār al-Ḥadīth al-Nabawī al-Sharīf in Damascus, where canonical *ḥadīth* collections are read orally by a recognized *ḥadīth* master. Auditors do not write down what they hear, since the book form is at hand, but can still claim to have been "authorized" with the transmission of a particular body of religious knowledge. Still, this traditional mechanism of connecting the Muslim community today to the source of the religion, through personal relations across history, has largely disappeared. Networks of personal relations do remain important, but the chain of transmission as epistemological mark of religious knowledge has given way to the "religionization" (Islamization) of knowledge, all knowledge, even of a secular kind (e.g. sociology and economics).

The neglect into which the chain of transmission has fallen has brought about a markedly different understanding of religious knowledge, even of religion itself. Notwithstanding the staying power of traditional religion, a new concept of religion has emerged within Islam, unmoored from the transmission of traditional knowledge and thus hostile to traditional religious authority no less than to secular educational authorities and their attempts to secularize knowledge, i.e. bring it under the control of secular states and define it within a secular framework of knowledge. The "new" Islam that has emerged has ironically assumed the modernizing point of view that all knowledge can be defined within a single framework, but, of course, has conceived that framework in religious, not secular, terms. Whether or not this is a viable project, it has greatly disrupted, if not closed, traditional reflection on the classification of knowledge into that which is defined by chain of transmission (religious knowledge) and that which is not (secular knowledge). The many treatises written on the divisions of knowledge, for example Ibn Ḥazm's (d. 1064) *Ranks of Knowledge*, clearly distinguished the purpose of religious and secular kinds of knowledge: even if religious knowledge was to impact belief and action in this world, its primary goal was to achieve salvation in the hereafter and a blissful existence in paradise, since, after all, religious knowledge was religious because it came from the source of religion, as guaranteed by chain of transmission, not human examination of the world. A significant tendency today, however, is to define knowledge as religious not in terms of its source, but to the extent to which it has been religionized, irrespective of source. In short, the decline of the chain of transmission not only implies significant diminishment of traditional religious authority, but also tangibly new conceptions of religious knowledge itself.

References and further reading

Abū Ḥātim al-Rāzī (1977) *A'lām al-Nubuwwa*, ed. Ṣ. al-Ṣāvī, Tehran: Anjuman-i Shānanshāhī-i Falsafah-'i Īrān.

Baghdādī, al- (1949) *Taqyīd al-'Ilm*, ed. Y. Eche, Damascus: n. p.

—— (1996) *al-Jāmiʿ li-Akhlāq al-Rāwī wa-Ādāb al-Sāmiʿ*, ed. ʿAbd al-Raḥmān Ṣalāḥ b. Muḥammad b. ʿUwayza, Beirut: Dār al-Kutub al-ʿIlmiyya.
Berkey, J. (1992) *The Transmission of Knowledge in Medieval Cairo. A Social History of Islamic Education*, Princeton: Princeton University Press.
Bulliet, R. W. (1994) *Islam. The View from the Edge*, New York: Columbia University Press.
Chamberlain, M. (1994) *Knowledge and Social Practice in Medieval Damascus, 1190–1350*, Cambridge, New York: Cambridge University Press.
Cook, M. (1997) "The Opponents of the Writing of Tradition in Early Islam," *Arabica*, 44: 437–530.
Eccel, A. C. (1984) *Egypt, Islam and Social Change. Al-Azhar in Conflict and Accommodation*, Berlin: K. Schwarz.
Heck, P. L. (2002) "The Epistemological Problem of Writing in Islamic Civilization," *Studia Islamica*, 94: 85–114.
Grandin, N. and Gaborieau, M., eds. (1997) *Madrasa. La transmission du savoir dans le monde musulman*, Paris: Arguments.
Hefner, R. W. and Zaman, M. Q., eds. (2007) *Schooling Islam: The Culture and Politics of Modern Muslim Education*, Princeton: Princeton University Press.
Ibn Ṣalāḥ (1990) *al-Muqaddima fī ʿUlūm al-Ḥadīth*, ed. ʿĀʾisha ʿAbd al-Raḥmān, Cairo: Dār al-Maʿārif.
Ikhwān al-Ṣafāʾ (1928) *Rasāʾil Ikhwān al-Ṣafāʾ wa-Khullān al-Wafāʾ*, ed. Khayr al-Dīn al-Ziriklī, 4 vols in 2, Cairo: Maṭbaʿat al-ʿArabiyya.
Kadi, W. and Billeh, V., eds. (2006) "Special Issue on Islam and Education – Myths and Truths," *Comparative Education Review*, 50/3.
Madigan, D.A. (2001) *The Qurʾân's Self-Image. Writing and Authority in Islam's Scripture*, Princeton: Princeton University Press.
Makdisi, G. (1981) *The Rise of Colleges. Institutions of Learning in Islam and the West*, Edinburgh: Edinburgh University Press.
Melchert, C. (2000) "Ibn Mujāhid and the Establishment of Seven Qurʾānic Readings," *Studia Islamica*, 91: 5–22.
Messick, B. (1993) *The Calligraphic State. Textual Domination and History in a Muslim Society*, Berkeley, Los Angeles, London: University of California Press.
Rosenthal, F. (1970) *Knowledge Triumphant. The Concept of Knowledge in Medieval Islam*, Leiden: E. J. Brill.
Roy, O. (1994) *The Failure of Political Islam*, Cambridge: Harvard University Press.
Schoeler, G. (2006) *The Oral and the Written in Early Islam*, London: Routledge; translation of *Écrire et transmettre dans les débuts de l'Islam*, Paris: Presses universitaires de France, 2002.
Shaʿrānī, al- (1975) *al-Akhlāq al-Matbūliyya*, ed. Manīʿ ʿAbd al-Halīm, 3 vols., Cairo: Maṭbaʿa Ḥassān.
Stewart, D. J. (2004) "The Doctorate of Islamic Law in Mamluk Egypt and Syria," in J. E. Lowry, D. J. Stewart, S. M. Toorawa, eds., *Law and Education in Medieval Islam: Studies in Memory of George Makdisi*, Cambridge: Gibb Memorial Trust, 45–90.

24

TRAVEL

David Waines

The medieval world was a world in motion. People traveled in groups, small or large – rarely alone – from a variety of motives. Merchants transported goods of many kinds over short or long distances. Recent research even proposes that diseases like the plague travel along with people and by plotting the path of a pandemic manifold "corridors of communication" are thereby revealed crisscrossing the medieval landscape. This last approach, however, is not the object of the present chapter. Rather, the aim is more modest, to examine who traveled and why, the means employed for the journey, distances and routes covered and difficulties encountered. Two examples drawn at random from quite different medieval Arabic sources will serve to formulate some initial questions concerning the nature of travel in a world distant from the present day dominated by the airplane and the periodic venture of the spaceship.

In the introduction to a tale found among the famous *Arabian Nights' Entertainments* a dyer by trade and his neighbor, a barber, discuss the benefits of journeying to a distant country to start a new life and, hopefully, achieve a less precarious existence than their present one. The dyer recites some verses to his companion in which the advantages of travel are noted. First, it dispels one's present anxiety, clearly the immediate relief sought by the two unfortunates. Travel also, the poem adds, allows gaining one's subsistence, acquiring knowledge, good manners and the opportunity even to come into contact with noble society. From their home in Alexandria they set sail on a galleon (*ghalyūn*). The barber successfully plied his trade among the passengers to earn the fare and food for both men. After many days on the open sea they arrived at the harbor of a large city where they secured lodgings in a *khān*. Their new life of adventure and misadventure now commences, occupying the major part of the story. A tale of the imagination to be sure, although the anonymous narrator begins it with plausible circumstances that listeners, or readers, would easily recognize.

Quite different is the personal account of a journey told by a Syrian prince, Abū 'l-Fidā (1273–1331), ruler of the principality of Hamah, located between Damascus and Aleppo. His official title was al-Malik al-Mu'ayyad Ismāʿīl and he owed allegiance to the famous Mamluk Sultan of Egypt, al-Nāṣir Muḥammad. Abū 'l-Fidā was also a scholar and poet, the author of a well-known geographical work and a chronicle entitled *A Short History of Mankind*. The last section of the chronicle contains a brief memoir of his life and times. At the beginning of February, 1314, he set out on his second pilgrimage (*ḥajj*) to the holy cites of Mecca and Medina, a religious duty performed by all Muslims at least once in a lifetime, financial and physical conditions permitting. Abū 'l-Fidā's already comfortable finances had been supplemented by a

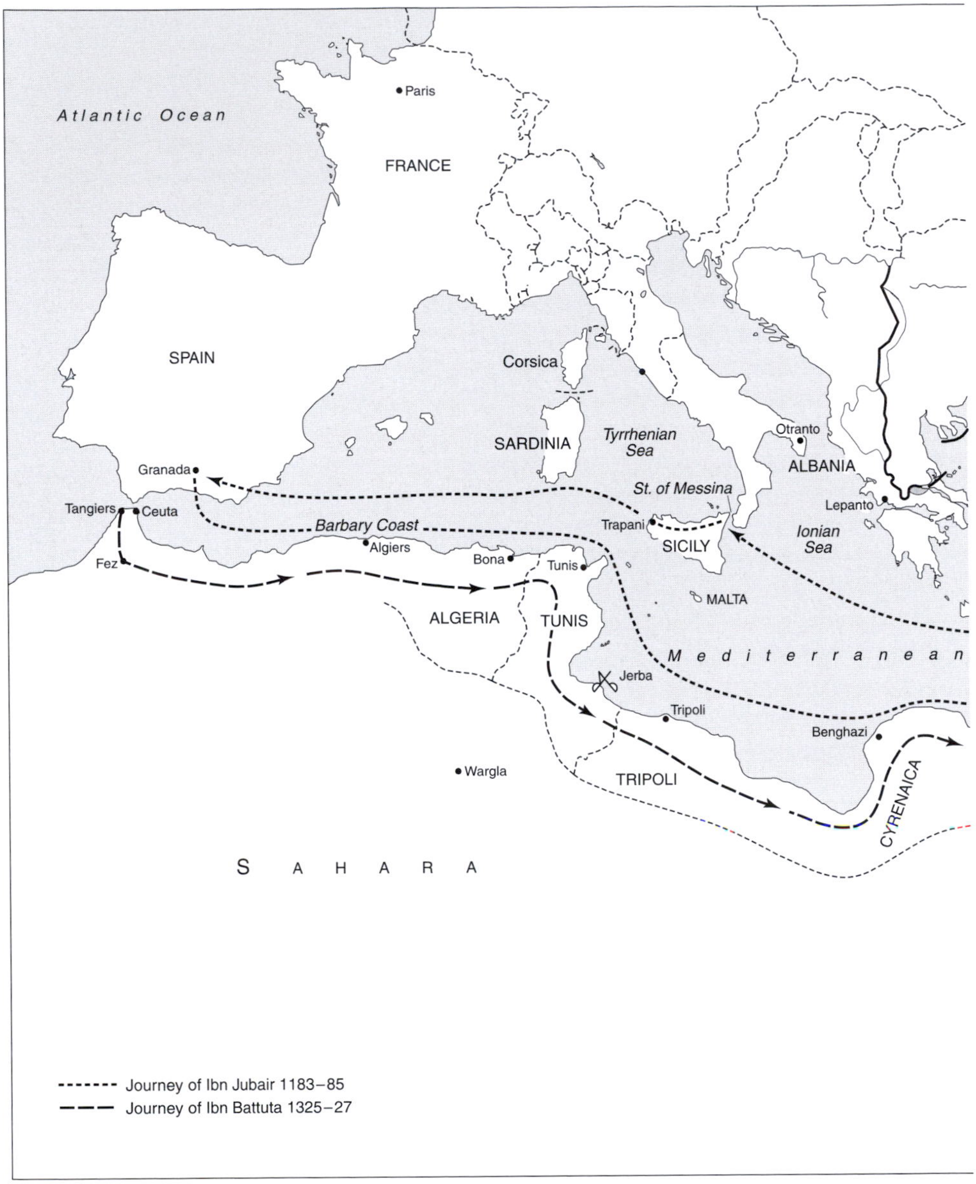

Map 5 Route of Medieval Travellers.

cash gift from the Mamluk Sultan of one thousand *dīnār*s for expenses. Dromedaries were dispatched on ahead to the great castle of al-Karak in southern Palestine to which Abū 'l-Fidā himself set out on horseback. Heavy baggage had been sent to join the main pilgrim caravan leaving from Damascus. From al-Karak Abū 'l-Fidā proceeded by dromedary, accompanied by six led horses and a number of Mamluk guards armed with bows and arrows. Traveling light in this fashion he reached Medina and visited the Prophet's tomb by himself while awaiting the arrival of the

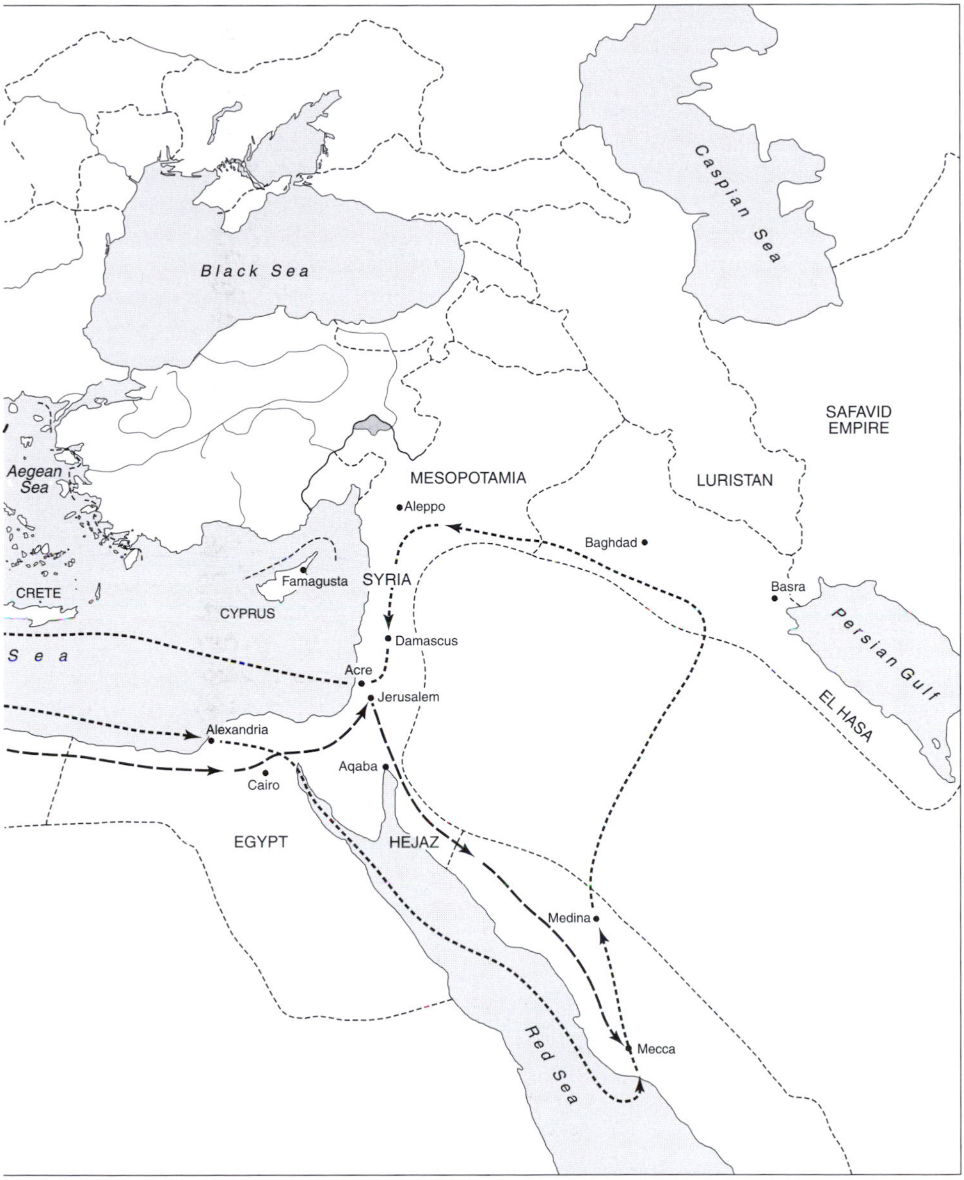

caravan. Again proceeding in front of the main pilgrimage body, he reached Mecca in late March, seven weeks after his departure from Hamah. The return trip took only 22 days for, as Abū 'l-Fidā explains, "I traveled by dromedary, taking a horse and a mule with me, and stopped for nothing."

First, then, both the rich and the restless traveled. The dyer and barber were poor folk if not reduced to abject circumstances. The only details of the journey the narrator provides is that they traveled in the company of 120 male passengers apart from the captain and crew and that the journey lasted 20 days; this was probably intended to suggest a long voyage which apparently passed without mishap. We are left to imagine whether the time excluded stopover in ports along the way and we are not informed of either the ship's route or destination. Indeed, the very term used for the ship, galleon, is problematic for it is known to have been applied to various types of vessel of differing function. We are reminded that this is a fictional tale and the narrator perhaps only wished to convey the sense of a very large, rapid sailing vessel of the most modern kind. The prince's story, by contrast, is autobiographical. He was wealthy and enjoyed good relations with Mamluk power in Cairo. His journey was a religious obligation. Organization was complex, the means of transport varied. Given his rank he traveled with armed protection. A stopover in Damascus to arrange his baggage, again a stop at al-Karak and elsewhere along the way accounted for the lengthy outward trip. He did not join the main caravan of perhaps several thousand pilgrims which proceeded at a slower pace. The return trip was swift although the prince was likely still accompanied by guards as pilgrim routes were favored territory of brigands.

Suggestive as these episodes may appear, they are not travel narratives, accounts of travelers' experiences over a greater span of time and space. Yet, given the numbers that must have traveled throughout medieval times, few actually left tales of their journeys, and the accounts of unknown others would simply have been lost. More striking, perhaps, is the fact that many narratives may never have been written had they not been dictated to or recorded by others than the travelers themselves. Take a couple of examples from the literature of European Christian pilgrims to Jerusalem shortly after the rise of Islam. Adomnan, the Abbot of Iona between 679 and 704, received an unexpected visit from a bishop of Gaul named Arculf who, on his return by ship from the holy places in Palestine, was driven by a fierce storm onto the shores of Britain. Delighted to hear of Arculf's first-hand adventures, Adomnan introduces them in his *De Locis Sanctis* ("Concerning the Sacred Places") for the benefit of posterity saying, "I first took down his trustworthy and reliable account on tablets; this I have now written on parchment in the form of a short essay." A second example is that of the English pilgrim Willibald who traveled to Syria and the Holy Land between 724 and 730. Upon his return to Europe he eventually became a bishop in Germany and dictated his lively experiences to a nun named Hugeburc. It was not until a half century later, however, that she wrote the life of – now Saint – Willibald based on his own account. It is by such means, a violent storm or a nun's lasting devotion to her bishop, that some travel narratives were written at all. On the other hand the monk Bernard the Wise, writing about 870, did compose his own account but which provides few details of the hardships of travel on land and sea.

In the medieval Islamic tradition, travel molded the lives of many of the literate class of scholars. Certainly Europe knew its own wandering scholars but much of Christian scholarship was more closely associated with the sedentary life of the monasteries. The acquisition of knowledge (cited in the poem mentioned above) was one object of travel; this meant primarily gathering religious knowledge from other learned persons although travel alone opened much broader horizons, an experience that was often put to other ends. The historian al-Masʿūdī (d. 957) for example, alludes to the extent of his travels in his surviving works, but he left no separate account of them. Born in Baghdad, he ventured as far afield as India, various parts of Arabia including the holy cities, and to islands off the east African coast. The geographer, Ibn Ḥawqal, who also lived in the tenth century, undertook major journeys from his birthplace in Nisibis, Upper Mesopotamia. His major work on the geography of Muslim lands was written from notes compiled on these travels, but he left no travel account as such. He journeyed to the west across North Africa from Egypt to al-Andalus covering also the southern edge of the Sahara. He traveled east as far as Transoxania and we lose sight of him with his mention of a sojourn in Sicily.

There are extant, however, three travel (*riḥla*) narratives that relate to the eleventh, twelfth and fourteenth centuries. The first was written in Persian by Nāṣir-i Khusraw whose absence from home took up the seven years between 1046 and 1053. Of the other two, both written in Arabic, Ibn Jubayr's account covers just over two years between 1183 to 1185, while Ibn Baṭṭūṭa's travelogue remarkably occupies over a quarter century between 1325 and 1354. A common strand found in each of the narratives is the pilgrimage to the Muslim holy cities of Medina and Mecca. There are important differences, too, not least the route followed by each traveler to the holy places and that taken on the return journey home. The focus of the present chapter is not, therefore, on the religious ritual of pilgrimage but rather on what experiences these pilgrims relate as travelers.

This is not without its problems either. Modern scholars of the genre often express concern over the degree of trustworthiness of travelers' accounts. Some of the difficulties noted are an author's "shameless" plagiarism from earlier writers, or his display of a "multitude of prejudices," or a fascination with "myth, miracle and magic." A traveler might elaborate some myth, for example, to suggest he had visited somewhere he had not in fact been. On the other hand, tales of miracles and other wonders witnessed or claimed to have been witnessed may be used by the scholar to judge a traveler's "gullibility" or "credibility." And certain details in an account which one scholar treats as having a "ring of truth" about them, another scholar would dismiss with the caution that the author had included them only to provide a ring of truth to an otherwise preposterous account. It may seem that the modern scholarly use of medieval travelers' narratives is about as hazardous as the journeys undertaken by the travelers themselves. An extreme case is the widely popular European account by one John Mandeville who, in the prologue, offers his book as a pilgrims' guide to Jerusalem and a description of lands further east both claimed to be based upon recollections of his own journeys. His travels were contemporaneous with the adventures of Ibn Baṭṭūṭa. Modern scholarship, however, while unable to determine Mandeville's actual identity, has concluded that the book is an entirely imaginary compilation drawn from the real travels of others supplemented by a wide variety of other identifiable sources. It is interesting to note that Mandeville's relentless plagiarism is not decried as "shameless" by today's leading authority but assessed as an essentially accurate rendering of the sources plagiarized.

To return then to our three intrepid Muslim travelers. First, none belongs within the "Mandeville" paradigm. Of the concerns noted above, most have been directed at the *riḥla* of Ibn Baṭṭūṭa, while it is nonetheless accepted as invaluable in many parts. The other two have received general commendation. Second, if the accounts are approached for insights into the medieval travel experience, then descriptions of encounters with the forces of nature, the vagaries of fortune and of human behavior may be accepted as reflecting the traveler's actual experience because they could be shared within a broader common-sense understanding of travel. Even descriptions of uneventful stages of a journey are useful in recovering aspects of medieval travel realities. Or, to express it in a rather different way, the medieval belief in divine intervention and rescue from grave danger or threatening encounter does not mean the danger was any less real to the traveler. Taking now our three accounts one by one but always with an eye to comparing them where this may clarify or illuminate an episode, we may commence with the earliest narrative of Nāṣir-i Khusraw.

Nāṣir-i Khusraw

Nāṣir's travel book is also the shortest of the three. In 1046, he left his job as a government official and set out from Marv in eastern Iran, intent on pursuing a dream vision which urged him to seek his spiritual health in Mecca. While the undertaking appeared urgent, its fulfillment was less so. With his brother and a Hindu servant for company throughout, their leisurely route to the west took them across the upper reaches of the Tigris-Euphrates valleys and then south along the Mediterranean coast. They arrived in Jerusalem exactly one solar year after their departure from Marv. According to his own estimate they had covered 3,066 miles (4,934 kilometers) but, he adds, without stopping anywhere long enough to become completely rested. Two months after his arrival, in 1047, Nāṣir made the first of his four pilgrimages. Accompanied by a small group of people and a guide, they set out on foot. Given their overall journey time of 49 days to Mecca and back, including performing the pilgrimage rites, they must have acquired another more rapid mode of transport soon after departure. However, they had not been able to join any official pilgrimage caravan as that year there were none issuing either from Cairo, Damascus or Baghdad. The problem was shortage of foodstuffs and water in the holy cities together with the threat from marauding bands of bedouin. He would face similar difficulties again.

Along the eastern Mediterranean Nāṣir had noted shipping and ship-building facilities. All the main coastal towns had harbors which he aptly describes as "stables for ships," protected by a heavy chain across the entrance which could be raised and lowered to let friendly craft in and keep hostile ones out. In Haifa large seagoing vessels called *jūdī* were being built.

Nāṣir, however, had no experience of the Mediterranean. When he left Jerusalem, he had hoped to travel to Cairo from Ascalon on the Syrian coast but owing to adverse winds boats could not set sail. Venturing overland he reached an eastern branch of the Nile and caught a boat going upstream towards the Egyptian capital. He nevertheless leaves a sense of the awe with which the great sea was regarded. A piece of sea lore related to him by "many reliable persons" claimed that one of its branches led to the Darkness as the head of that inlet was permanently frozen because the sun never reached it. Actual experiences of sea travel will be treated below.

Nāṣir's next two pilgrimages, in the years 1048 and 1049, proceeded from Cairo. By this time he was almost certainly in the employ of the Fatimid caliph whose Ismāʿīlī doctrines he had embraced, whether in Cairo itself or much earlier is debated. In both years the Sultan had publicly declared that owing to continuing drought and the resulting scarcity of food that had caused many deaths in the Hijaz, pilgrims were excused from their religious obligation. The Sultan still dispatched the annual covering for the Kaʿba, a robe of honor and the bi-annual stipend for the Amir of Mecca so

Nāṣir, on both occasions, attached himself to the official in charge as the much reduced but well-guarded party set off. Their route took them first to Qulzum near modern-day Suez at the head of the Red Sea. From there, the caravan route normally traversed the Sinai and down the western flank of Arabia. Nāṣir, however, was taken each year by boat south to al-Jar, a port on the Red Sea coast four days distant from Medina. Mecca was a further eight days travel south, 36 days in all having elapsed since their departure. Nāṣir mentions neither disturbance nor danger on route, but conditions in Mecca and Medina were distressing. Many pilgrim sojourners in Mecca had chosen to leave and no new pilgrims had come from anywhere. Some 35,000 people fled the Hijaz to Egypt to escape the hunger and misery and to be cared for by the Sultan. In Medina a reported 2,000 North African pilgrims were killed in a battle with Arabs demanding protection money. Nāṣir's privileged position, however, had spared him any unpleasant consequences of these troubled times.

Following the feast of sacrifice (*ʿīd al-aḍḥā*) in 1050, Nāṣir departed Cairo for the last time traveling by boat upstream along the Nile. He stopped at Qus, a town lying on a large bow in the river where it runs closest to the Red Sea. Here he seems to have contemplated heading for the coast and taking a boat to the Arabian side of the Red Sea and thence to Medina. Finally, he ventured to Aswan where pilgrims returned from Mecca made camels available for hire. Before him lay a 15-day desert ride to the Red Sea port of ʿAydhab situated more or less opposite Mecca's own port of Jedda. Nāṣir's brief description highlights the crucial importance of the noble one-humped "ship of the desert." The camels were rested during the heat of the day until the afternoon prayer, and then traveled the rest of the day and night. Stopping places were all known, since camel dung was essential as fuel for cooking. The camels themselves seemed aware they would die of thirst if they tarried along the way and, as if by their own initiative, they pursued their goal unerringly through trackless wastes.

ʿAydhab, according to Nāṣir, had a population of 500, a Friday mosque and little else to recommend it. Funds, moreover, were exhausted and they had to wait three months for favorable southerly winds to take them to Jedda. Nāṣir acted as preacher for the community and was fortunate to be able to secure money from a friend's agent in ʿAydhab who apparently expected no repayment. Essential purchases were flour and water. Their eventual arrival in Mecca was in time for the rituals of the months of Rajab and Ramaḍān both of which preceded the pilgrimage season still six months away. The conditions of previous years continued. Nāṣir notes empty rain reservoirs and that hospices for travelers from distant regions had fallen into ruin.

Having completed the pilgrimage of 1051, they embarked upon the most tortuous part of their travels to date – due east across Arabia towards Bahrain in the Persian/Arab Gulf rather than adopting the more usual, shorter, northerly route via Medina to Kufa. Hazards included securing safe passage from one rival tribe to the next. Nāṣir notes he could not share the tribesman's diet of lizard and camel milk and perforce subsisted on berries. Ten weeks out of Mecca they reached a desert settlement of fortresses inhabited by a "bunch of filthy, ignorant bandits" who were also destitute. In return for nourishment of dates, Nāṣir painted the prayer niche of the mosque which still left them without a single *dīnār* to hire a camel. Four months later they managed to join a caravan on a credit loan of 30 *dīnār*s to be repaid in Basra which, with great relief, they finally saw eight full months after their departure from Mecca. Nāṣir assures his reader of the accuracy of his account based on harsh experience and not false rumor. Ten months later Nāṣir and his party returned to Khurasan having covered, by his own calculation without counting numerous side trips to visit shrines, nearly 8,000 miles.

Ibn Jubayr

Like Nāṣir, Ibn Jubayr was a well-educated man. He also held a government post, but in the far western Muslim domains of Andalusia where he served the governor of Granada. The widely accepted story of the motive for his pilgrimage is that it was as penance for having consumed alcohol even though he had been forced to this sinful act by his master, the governor. Ibn Jubayr, however, was a very devout Muslim, a feature clearly expressed in the style of his travel composition with its constant references to the power, generosity, wisdom, mercy and so on of God. His desire to pursue the pious life had been kindled by his study of the very popular work exalting the Prophet's merits written by the famous Qāḍī ʿIyāḍ ibn Mūsā (d. 1149). The decision to visit the holy places of the Prophet's birth and death was then understandably swiftly prompted by the wine-drinking episode.

Be that as it may, Ibn Jubayr's travel account is centrally dedicated to minute descriptions of Mecca and Medina and the pilgrimage rites. Almost in passing, it also contains some of the most vivid and perspicuous passages on sea travel found anywhere in the medieval literature. The focus of this section, therefore, will be upon the Mediterranean portions of his outward and return journeys and his single experience of crossing the Red Sea. While the narrative of the land portion of his return journey from Mecca to Baghdad, Mosul and Damascus does contain interesting reflections on travel, limits of space oblige us to pass over them.

The opening pages of his travels recount the sea journey aboard a Christian Genoese owned ship sailing westward from Ceuta (in modern Morocco) to Alexandria in Egypt. He departed with a companion toward the end of February, 1183, commencing his travelogue the same day. The type of vessel was a *markab*, a vague, unhelpful term. Given the confusion of medieval maritime terminology, Ibn Jubayr's account nonetheless suggests it was a sail powered vessel only (without oarsmen), perhaps one of the variety known as a "round ship." The journey lasted 30 days in all. Paraphrasing the pilgrim's account, during the first 12 days they covered about 1,200 miles (1,930 kilometers) from Ceuta to the coast of Sardinia; a crossing, he notes, of remarkable speed. Sailing conditions westward during the winter months of February and March were strongly assisted by the prevailing winds and sea currents. The ship arrived at the well-known anchorage of Cape St. Mark on the west coast of Sardinia allowing for the essential supplies of water, food and wood to be renewed. A week after their first sighting of the island, they set sail again on a favorable wind traveling about 200 miles along the Sardinian coast. Then one evening and for more than 24 hours the ship was engulfed in a violent storm. Through the night the wind drove the rain with such force it resembled a shower of arrows. Daytime brought no relief. The main sails had to be lowered, the ship now running on only the small top sails. One of these, torn by the tumult, caused a spar to snap. As the wind abated somewhat by nightfall, they proceeded under bare masts at great speed and by morning the ship had almost passed the southern coast of Sicily. Ibn Jubayr notes that experienced sea captains and travelers present all agreed they had never in their lives seen such a tempest, the description of which only diminished its reality. Heading now into the open sea and navigating by estimation they reckoned they were off the coast of Crete although it was not visible, leaving them still some 600 miles from Alexandria. Their first sighting of the city was of the famous lighthouse protecting the approach to the harbor.

From Cairo, following the route of Nāṣir-i Khusraw's last trip, Ibn Jubayr took the Nile route upstream. He bitterly lamented the treatment of pilgrims, travelers and merchants by rapacious tax collectors who prodded and probed their persons and belongings in search of money or goods upon which illegal "alms" were assessed. After 18 days on the Nile he reached Qus from where, unlike Nāṣir, he and a companion joined the caravan traffic into the desert and followed the crucial watering places towards ʿAydhab. He observes that the finest camel litter, accommodating two persons side by side and protected by a canopy, allowed travelers the comfort of eating, reading or even playing chess while on the move.

Ibn Jubayr's experience of ʿAydhab confirmed it to be the abomination experienced by Nāṣir-i Khusraw. Spending less than a month there, also during the summer season, he said it was like living between air that melted the body and water that killed the appetite. He describes the type of boat, the *jilāba*, used to take pilgrims to and from Jedda. Its wooden planks were sewn together with thread made of coconut fiber and caulked with wooden shavings of palm trees; the hull was then smeared with grease or oil to make it supple against encounter with the many reefs off shore. The sails were woven from palm leaves. The pilgrim's first hazard was the extreme overcrowding of these craft prompted by the owners' greed. A second hazard was the crossing itself and the perversity of the winds. The Jedda-ʿAydhab crossing could be even more dangerous as winds often drove boats far to the south of ʿAydhab leaving pilgrims stranded in hostile barren mountainous terrain. Ibn Jubayr's trip to Jedda took a week during which he witnessed one of the Red Sea's famous tempests. In early August, 1183, he entered Mecca, the pilgrimage season still eight months away.

By October, 1184, a year and seven months after leaving Granada, Ibn Jubayr was set for his homeward journey from the port of Acre on the Syrian coast. The first stage of the trip, his second on a Genoese ship, was bound for Messina on the eastern tip of Sicily. Although probably traveling aboard one of the largest and most advanced vessels of its day, the voyage was fraught with troubles. Ibn Jubayr's wry comment told its own tale, "What think you of a voyage of two months on board a ship over a distance we had thought to cross in 10 or 15 days at most. The prudent was he who brought victuals for 30 days, but the rest brought only enough for 20 or 15." The sailing season was drawing to a close for commercial shipping rarely ventured out between November and March. The ship's departure had initially been delayed nearly two weeks, becalmed and awaiting a favorable east wind. Ibn Jubayr and his companion passed the nights ashore and were caught unawares when the captain set out one morning at daybreak. They hired a large boat powered by oarsmen and set out in pursuit, overtaking the ship by late afternoon. For five days wind conditions were propitious until the ship was ambushed by a west wind forcing the captain to tack back and forth in order to make even modest progress. Next, a sudden westerly squall broke the foremast spar and much labor was required to retrieve it and the attached sail from the sea. Between being buffeted about and becalmed, with individual's rations becoming scarce, the death of several pilgrims, both Christian and Muslim, the captain succeeded in finding an island harbor where travelers purchased bread and meat from the inhabitants. A further westerly tempest that tossed the great ship like a tender twig forced another island anchorage and provisions were again renewed. Then, with Sicily in sight, storm force winds drove the ship back and forth until finally it came to anchor opposite the Italian mainland. There yet lay ahead the treacherous Messina Straits where the sea pours through the gap between Sicily and the mainland like "the bursting of a dam" (Qur'ān 34:16). On this occasion, within a half mile of Messina itself, wind and wave drove the ship against the shore, grounding it and snapping a rudder. Rescue operations to save the passengers were successful but the following day the ship was found shattered to pieces on the shore.

Ibn Jubayr relates these events with the keen awareness of a seasoned voyager together with the solid protective shield of faith; moments of crisis are expressed in religious terms of his fear and hope, yet always in firm trust of divine delivery, whether in this world or the next. The end of the story can be briefly told. The shipwreck occurred on December 9, 1184. He found another Genoese ship in Trapani harbor (Sicily) waiting to sail to Andalusia. Not until March 13, 1185, was he able to board the vessel which was then delayed for lack of wind until the 25th. The journey began smoothly as the ships were carried by an easy wind although, writes Ibn Jubayr, "our longings for Andalusia almost took the place of the wind, for their excitement and commotion." Despite being blown off course towards the North African coast, the ship landed safely at Cartegena on April 15. Ten days later Ibn Jubayr reached Granada, and home. The return had taken exactly six months.

Ibn Baṭṭūṭa

Ibn Baṭṭūṭa left his hometown, Tangiers, on June 12, 1325. Aged only 21, he was half the age of the other two travelers when they set out for distant parts. Upon his return many years later and on the orders of the Sultan of Fez, he dictated his travelogue to the secretary Ibn Juzayy (d. *c.* 1355–7) completing the task in 1357. His account, therefore, is an act of *recollection* supplemented by passages drawn from other travel works, including that of Ibn Jubayr whom he uses with and without attribution; recollection, too, in the sense that he had lost his notes on at least one occasion and had to re-write them from memory. In the book's opening passage, he says he wished to fulfill a long-cherished desire to visit the holy cities. Recalling his departure, he expresses the anguish of separation from friends and parents, coping also with having neither fellow wayfarer nor caravan for company. The major asset he took with him was a basic jurist's education according to the Mālikī legal school, a tradition in his own family.

Ibn Baṭṭūṭa's is the longest travel narrative of the three, the English translation now complete in four volumes. He was an experienced traveler but suffered mishaps on both land and sea. His journeys were the most extensive as well covering the Near and Middle East, Afghanistan, India, Ceylon, Bengal and Sumatra thence to the Chinese port of Zaytun. He also visited trading ports in East Africa, and in the final stage of his travels crossed the Sahara to the country of the Niger returning at last to Morocco and settling there where he died in either 1368 or 1377, aged 64 or 73 years. His wanderings included sojourns of three years in Arabia, nearly nine years in Delhi, India, and a year and a half in the Maldive Islands. Altogether he performed six pilgrimages.

Consonant with the theme of the present chapter only Ibn Baṭṭūṭa's first journey to the holy cities can be examined here. His eastward course, unlike that of Ibn Jubayr, was overland along the North African coast to Alexandria. He set out on foot with a pack animal, probably a donkey, laden with necessities for the journey. The first major town he mentions is Tlemcen. Land travel presents choices to pilgrims not available to those at sea where the elements and the ship's master will determine them. Ibn Baṭṭūṭa had been advised to join the company of two official envoys who had just left the city heading east. Therefore, he consulted God. He prayed for guidance of alternatives, intending to follow the one he judged "opened his heart with joy." So, spending three nights in Tlemcen to procure things he needed, he chased after the envoys catching up with them at the town of Milyana. These were the dog-days of the year and the oppressive heat struck down the two envoys causing a delay of two weeks. The condition of one seriously worsened and he died and was quickly buried in Milyana.

Ibn Baṭṭūṭa then joined a party of merchants from Tunis. They camped several days outside the town of Algiers where they were rejoined by members of the original party of envoys. Then they passed on to Bougie where Ibn Baṭṭūṭa was himself attacked by strong fever. He refused advice to rest saying that if his time had come he would wish it to be on the road with his face set towards the holy cities. The surviving envoy, a pious *shaykh* called al-Zubaydī, suggested Ibn Baṭṭūṭa sell his donkey and heavy baggage so as to travel swiftly on another animal and lightly carrying only a tent both of which al-Zubaydī would loan him. This was to avoid possible encounter with Arab bandits on the way. This, Ibn Baṭṭūṭa notes, was the first divine mercy shown him on the pilgrim path. On the outskirts of Constantine, torrential rain forced them to abandon their tents and seek shelter inside town buildings. The next day, noting Ibn Baṭṭūṭa's disheveled attire, the town governor ordered his clothes washed at his house and he replaced his torn mantle with a fine new one into which he had tied two gold *dīnār*s. This was the first alms received on his pilgrim venture.

They remained a few days in Bone then headed in great haste towards Tunis, 150 miles away. Dangers reportedly lurked along the way. Fever struck Ibn Baṭṭūṭa once again and he was forced to tie himself into the saddle in fear of tumbling to the ground from weakness. Approaching Tunis a wave of loneliness swept over him and he wept. A fellow pilgrim comforted and accompanied him to his lodgings in a *madrasa*. At a few points in the narrative, Ibn Baṭṭūṭa exposes his vulnerability in this way. It is, perhaps, an uncommon characteristic in the literature but one that readily engages the reader with the traveler.

The journey from Tunis to Alexandria was even more eventful. Ibn Baṭṭūṭa had celebrated the feast of Ramaḍān in Tunis and was appointed *qāḍī* of the outgoing caravan; a troop of archers was assigned to it to ward off possible attack from brigands. On the road, before reaching the city of Tripoli, the Feast of Sacrifice was celebrated marking the end of the pilgrimage rites in Mecca. Incessant rains and cold had pursued the caravan and it remained in Tripoli for some time. Then, in a matter of weeks, Ibn Baṭṭūṭa contracted marriage with the daughter of a guild master from Tunis, separated from her owing to a quarrel with her father, married a second time and threw a wedding feast for the whole caravan. Presumably with new spouse in tow, Ibn Baṭṭūṭa arrived in Alexandria in April, 1326, almost ten months to the day after departing Tangiers. Recall that by sea, Ibn Jubayr had reached Alexandria from Ceuta in one month.

Whatever the relative dangers and discomforts between land and sea travel, undeniably each had its hardships to cope with and overcome. Conditions on board ship were cramped and confined, the monotony broken only by anchorage in a new port, while land travel had the advantage of variety, not only of scenery – with the exception of severe desert conditions – but the availability of lodging, rest and changing company. Ibn Baṭṭūṭa's journey illustrates the point. Passing through the seasons, he had slept under the stars, in a tent, likely in a mosque or two and lodged in a *madrasa*, an institution of religious learning, widespread at the time, with rooms to accommodate teachers, students and guests. On his landward journey from Cairo up the Nile towards ʿAydhab and the Red Sea crossing to Mecca, he stayed in *ribāṭ*s and *zawīyas*, religious institutions that also provided food and shelter for wayfarers and with pious *shaykh*s or *qāḍī*s who offered their pilgrim colleague hospitality. On his journey from Cairo to Syria across the northern Sinai he mentions way stations with hostelries called *funduq*s or *khān*s where travelers could stop to water their animals and purchase goods required for both themselves and their beasts. He does not mention the most common, early features of this pre-Islamic institution, as lodging for travelers and storage for merchants' goods. It is possible that by his day these *funduq*s tended to store goods rather than shelter people. Or, as is perhaps more likely, Ibn Baṭṭūṭa preferred while traveling through Egypt and Syria what was offered by religious institutions, particularly the *zawīya*, or the hospitality of local *qāḍī*s. He notes that outside Latakiya there was a large Christian monastery that provided lodging and simple fare such as bread, cheese, olives, vinegar and capers for all wayfarers, including Muslims.

Returning briefly to his trip to ʿAydhab, Ibn Baṭṭūṭa, like Ibn Jubayr before him, faced a 15-day desert crossing by camel from the Nile to the port, a trip he declared to be quite safe; the only incident he reports was of a band of hyenas that one night had to be continually driven off to prevent them robbing the baggage. The site of their stopover was where the tomb of the famous Ṣūfī, Abū ʾl-Ḥasan al-Shādhilī (d. 1258), was located. A litany of the sea, attributed to him, is cited by Ibn Baṭṭūṭa. It was an appeal to the Almighty to deliver pilgrims safely on the dangerous Red Sea crossing to Jedda. Ironically, Ibn Baṭṭūṭa was unable to use the litany for his own crossing as all the boats in ʿAydhab had been sunk during hostilities between local forces and the Egyptian authorities. Perforce, he sold all his provisions, returned across the desert to Qus and down the Nile, which was then in flood, to Cairo. He set off immediately for Syria finally reaching Damascus, via a brief tour of many coastal towns, in early August, 1326, where he resided in the Mālikī *madrasa*.

On the first of September, 1326, the large pilgrim caravan for the Hijaz set out from Damascus. Normally, counting stopovers and the visit to Medina along the way, it could take between 45 and 50 days for a caravan to reach Mecca. Ibn Baṭṭūṭa gives no date of his arrival in either holy city. However, his own journey this year was uneventful. Still he warns of the desert's dangers. Water supplies were crucial for survival especially between Tabuk and al-ʿUla, passing through the so-called valley of Hell where pilgrims were known to have perished from the dry, suffocating sand-wind or simoom that shrivels all in its wake. Ibn Baṭṭūṭa quotes a saying referring to this region, "Whoever enters it is lost; whoever exits it is born." A maxim which, when applied more broadly to travel experience on both land and sea, serves as a fitting close to this survey of the trials and triumphs of the medieval wayfarer. Ibn Baṭṭūṭa had years of adventures still ahead of him but that, as they say, is another story.

References and further reading

Benjamin, S. (1995) *The World of Benjamin of Tudela: A Medieval Mediterranean Travelogue*, London: Associated University Presses.

Broadhurst, R. J. C., trans. (1952) *The Travels of Ibn Jubayr*, London: Jonathon Cape.

Bulliet, R. (1975) *The Camel and the Wheel*, Cambridge, MA: Harvard University Press.

Constable, O. R. (2003) *Housing the Stranger in the Mediterranean World: Lodging, Trade and Travel in Late Antiquity and the Middle Ages*, Cambridge: Cambridge University Press.

Dunn, R. E. (1989) *The Adventures of Ibn Batutta: A Muslim Traveller of the Fourteenth Century*, Berkeley: University of California Press.

Eickelman, D. and Piscatori, J. (1990) *Muslim Travellers: Pilgrimage, Migration, and the Religious Imagination*, London: Routledge.

Friedman, J. B. and Figg, K. M. (2000) *Trade, Travel and Exploration in the Middle Ages*, London: Garland Publishing.

Gibb, H. A. R., trans. (1958–2000) *The Travels of Ibn Battuta AD 1325–1354*, 4 vols., Cambridge: Cambridge University Press [for the Hakluyt Society, London].

Labarge, M. (1982) *Medieval Travellers*, London: Hamish Hamilton.

Macrides, R., ed. (2002) *Travel in the Byzantine World*, Aldershot: Ashgate.

Netton, I. R., ed. (1993) *Golden Roads: Migration, Pilgrimage and Travel in Medieval and Modern Islam*, Richmond: Curzon Press.

—— (1996) *Seek Knowledge: Thought and Travel in the House of Islam*, Richmond: Curzon Press.

Peters, F. E. (1994) *The Hajj: The Muslim Pilgrimage to Mecca and the Holy Places*, Princeton: Princeton University Press.

Pryor, J. (1988) *Geography, Technology and War: Studies in the Maritime History of the Mediterranean, 649–1571*, Cambridge: Cambridge University Press.

Thackston, W. M., trans. (1986) *Naser-e Khosraw's Book of Travels (Safarnama)*, New York: Bibliotheca Persica.

Verdon, J. (2003) *Travel in the Middle Ages*, G. Holoch, trans., Notre Dame: University of Notre Dame.

Waddell, H. (1949) *The Wandering Scholars*, London: Constable (1st edition 1927).

Wilkinson, J. (1977) *Jerusalem Pilgrims before the Crusades*, Warminster: Aris & Phillips.

25

ʿABD AL-JABBĀR

Gabriel Said Reynolds

Al-Qāḍī Abū ʾl-Ḥasan ʿAbd al-Jabbār ibn Aḥmad al-Hamadhānī al-Asadābādī (d. 1025) a prominent judge in Rayy, Iran (now a southern suburb of Tehran) during the Būyid period, is today remembered above all as an eminent theologian of the Muʿtazilī school. His writings record otherwise lost excerpts of the early Muʿtazila and reflect his original contributions on a wide range of topics, not only theological but also jurisprudential, exegetical and apologetical. The last term in his name represents his place of birth (probably in the mid-930s): Asadābād, a small town (also the birthplace of Jamāl al-Dīn al-Afghānī) known for its honey production in a mountain valley in western Iran, to the southwest of Hamadhān. The first term represents his profession later in life, when he worked as a judge under the vizier al-Ṣāḥib ibn ʿAbbād (d. 995), during the reigns of the Būyid princes Muʾayyid al-Dawla (r. 977–84) and Fakhr al-Dawla (r. 984–97) in Rayy.

Muslim observers are conflicted over the personality of ʿAbd al-Jabbār, a conflict emerging from the Qāḍī's political and sectarian allegiances. The poet and satirist Abū Ḥayyān al-Tawḥīdī (d. 1023) knew ʿAbd al-Jabbār from Ibn ʿAbbād's court and, having been dismissed from that court, held a grudge against all of those associated with the vizier. He describes ʿAbd al-Jabbār as a hypocrite and quotes a speech in which Ibn ʿAbbād publicly humiliates the Qāḍī with insinuations of sexual immorality. The theme of ʿAbd al-Jabbār's hypocrisy is continued by later authors, including Yāqūt (d. 1229), who notes the great fortune that ʿAbd al-Jabbār had amassed (despite his reputation for severity in ethical matters), and comments, "He claimed that a Muslim would go to eternal hellfire over a quarter *dīnār*, but all of this money came from his corrupt judgeship. He is the true unbeliever." Similarly, Ibn Ḥajar al-ʿAsqalānī (d. 1449), who disdained the theological science with which ʿAbd al-Jabbār became closely associated, remarks that the Qāḍī was like "Croesus in the extent of his riches, but was corrupt on the inside, espoused hateful doctrine and understood little" (Reynolds 2004: 51–2).

On the other hand, in two official letters attributed to Ibn ʿAbbād, the vizier praises ʿAbd al-Jabbār and his Muʿtazilī writings. According to the Muʿtazilī hagiographer al-Jishumī (or al-Jushamī, killed in 1101), Ibn ʿAbbād considered ʿAbd al-Jabbār "one of the best and most knowledgeable people of the land" (Reynolds 2004: 50). Other reports (see below) suggest that ʿAbd al-Jabbār and Ibn ʿAbbād's relationship eventually soured, yet ʿAbd al-Jabbār's standing among the Muʿtazila, and subsequently among the Zaydī/Fiver Shīʿa (and to a lesser degree among the Imāmī/Twelver Shīʿa), did not. To al-Jishumī ʿAbd al-Jabbār was a scholar "whose fame has no need of an exaggerated description." Even a scholar from the opposing Māturīdī school, Maymūn al-Nasafī (d. 1114), noted that the Muʿtazila considered ʿAbd al-Jabbār without equal.

Yet it was not only ʿAbd al-Jabbār's theological views that had an impact on the intellectual life of the Islamic World. Over three centuries after his death ʿAbd al-Jabbār's controversial work *Tathbīt dalāʾil al-nubuwwa* ("Confirmation of the Proofs of Prophecy") was influential in the Damascene circle of Ibn Taymiyya (d. 1328), who found in it a resource for their polemics. Ibn Qayyim al-Jawziyya (d. 1350) quotes extensively from the *Tathbīt*, while Ibn Kathīr (d. 1373) describes it as the greatest of ʿAbd al-Jabbār's works.

Modern scholars, on the other hand, have been most interested in the *Mughnī fī abwāb al-tawḥīd wa-l-ʿadl* ("Summa on Monotheism and Divine Justice"), ʿAbd al-Jabbār's *magnum opus* of *kalām* (five chapters of which are dedicated to monotheism and 15 to divine justice), the great part of which was discovered and filmed in the 1950s by an Egyptian project in Yemen, where it had been preserved due to the continued Zaydī interest in Muʿtazilī theology (additional excerpts have more recently been uncovered; see Hamdan and Schmidtke 2007). Thereafter ʿAbd al-Jabbār gained a reputation as the Muʿtazilī *par excellence*, who faithfully recorded and transmitted the views of his Muʿtazilī intellectual ancestors, especially those of the Basran school: Abū ʾl-Hudhayl (d. *c.* 841), Abū Yaʿqūb al-Shaḥḥām (d. *c.* 881), Abū ʿAlī al-Jubbāʾī (d. 915), his son Abū Hāshim al-Jubbāʾī (d. 933), Abū ʿAlī ibn Khallād (d. 961) and ʿAbd al-Jabbār's teacher, Abū ʿAbd Allāh al-Baṣrī (d. 980). J. R. Peters describes ʿAbd al-Jabbār as "a true and good Muʿtazili: he knew the history of his school and its ideas and became the great 'compiler' of the Muʿtazilī ideas as developed in former centuries by his great predecessors" (Peters 1976: 14). Among Muslim scholars as well the discovery of the *Mughnī* inspired renewed interest in the Qāḍī's theological doctrine.

Life

ʿAbd al-Jabbār's biography is itself worthy of attention, as it illuminates an important era of Islamic history, in which intellectual life flourished even in the midst of great political and sectarian tension. The most reliable source of this biography is al-Khaṭīb al-Baghdādī (d. 1071), who passed through Rayy just after the Qāḍī's death in 1025. Yet al-Baghdādī, other than reporting ʿAbd al-Jabbār's opinion on a variant reading of Qurʾān 48:9, relates only that the Qāḍī aligned himself with the Shāfiʿiyya in law, the Muʿtazila in theology and was Qāḍī al-Quḍāt ("Chief Judge") in Rayy. However, from diverse later biographical writings – not least of which are al-Samʿānī (d. 1166), ʿAbd al-Karīm al-Rāfiʿī (d. 1226), Ibn al-Athīr (d. 1233), al-Ṣafadī (d. 1363) and Aḥmad ibn Saʿd al-Dīn al-Miṣwarī (d. 1668) – the outline of ʿAbd al-Jabbār's life can be sketched.

ʿAbd al-Jabbār, born into a peasant family, nevertheless found the means as a young man to travel to regional Iranian centers, including Qazwin, Hamadhan and Isfahan, to study *ḥadīth* and Islamic jurisprudence (*fiqh*). When he moved to the Iraqi city of Baṣra in 948, ʿAbd al-Jabbār, who heretofore is said to have followed al-Ashʿarī (d. 935) in *kalām*, now embraced the teachings of the Muʿtazila. He thus took the opposite path of al-Ashʿarī, who began as a Muʿtazilī but later adopted the literalism and determinism of Ibn Ḥanbal (d. 855). More generally, ʿAbd al-Jabbār became convinced of the virtue of theological reflection. He later commented: "Those who study jurisprudence seek the things of the world. But theology has no goal other than God most high" (Reynolds 2004: 46). From Basra ʿAbd al-Jabbār moved to Baghdad where, under the mentorship of Abū ʿAbd Allāh al-Baṣrī, ʿAbd al-Jabbār became an influential figure in the Muʿtazila. Because of this, the philo-Muʿtazilī vizier, Ibn ʿAbbād, called on him to work as a judge in Rayy in 977.

As ʿAbd al-Jabbār's social position increased his academic reputation spread. In Rayy ʿAbd al-Jabbār was the leader of the Bahshamiyya (a name derived from the aforementioned Abū Hāshim al-Jubbāʾī) movement of the Muʿtazila, a movement with which Ibn ʿAbbād himself was closely involved. In this capacity ʿAbd al-Jabbār wrote treatises in response to questions put to him from as far away as Egypt in the West and Khwārazm in the East. Yet his rising status seems to have caused some friction with Ibn ʿAbbād. Al-Ṣafadī quotes the vizier publicly declaring that ʿAbd al-Jabbār's insolence has grown to the point that he no longer signs his books ʿAbd al-Jabbār ("Servant of the Mighty") but simply al-Jabbār ("The Mighty," one of the divine names).

According to al-Ṣafadī, this public rebuke led ʿAbd al-Jabbār to withhold the funeral blessing for Ibn ʿAbbād when the vizier died in 995. This refusal, in turn, was cited by Fakhr al-Dawla as a pretext to dismiss and fine ʿAbd al-Jabbār exorbitantly. There are reasons to doubt this pretext. More likely is that Fakhr al-Dawla turned against ʿAbd al-Jabbār since the Qāḍī had been closely associated with Muʾayyid al-Dawla, his brother, predecessor and rival. Moreover, Fakhr al-Dawla was badly in need of funds, having recently paid an exorbitant ransom to the Ghaznavid forces of Sebüktigin (d. 997) to save the city from invasion.

The damage to ʿAbd al-Jabbār's reputation was nevertheless significant. He continued to teach thereafter in Rayy, Iṣfahān and Qazwīn, but he did not regain his social or political position. Among his disciples, however, ʿAbd al-Jabbār remained a respected figure. When ʿAbd al-Jabbār suffered gout in his old age, it is said, his supporters carried him from place to place. Furthermore, al-Miṣwarī relates that when ʿAbd al-Jabbār died in Rayy in 1025 eight descendants of the Prophet prayed over his body. In this regard it should also be noted that much of ʿAbd al-Jabbār's teaching has reached us only through his students' compilations thereof, such as the *Taʿlīq sharḥ al-uṣūl al-khamsa* ("Report on the Commentary on the Five Principles [of the Muʿtazila]") of Shashdīw Mānkdīm (d. 1034) and *al-Majmūʿ fī l-muḥīṭ bi-l-taklīf* ("The Composition on the Comprehensive Work on Obligation") of Ibn Mattawayh (d. 1076), two works that have been mistakenly attributed to ʿAbd al-Jabbār himself. Later Muʿtazilī authors, meanwhile, refer to ʿAbd al-Jabbār simply as the Chief Judge, now in an honorary sense.

Thought

Among modern scholars ʿAbd al-Jabbār has largely been cast as the prototypical Muʿtazilī scholar, the defender of the doctrines that the Qurʾān is created and humans have free will. Thus Peters (1976) titled his book on ʿAbd al-Jabbār *God's Created Speech: A Study in the Speculative Theology of the Muʿtazilī Qâdî l-qudât*, while George Hourani (1971) called his book *Islamic Rationalism: the Ethics of ʿAbd al-Jabbār*. Indeed ʿAbd al-Jabbār might profitably been seen in light of the larger Muʿtazilī enterprise, and his career measured by that of his Ashʿarī contemporary al-Bāqillānī (d. 1013). Yet in his day ʿAbd al-Jabbār was an authority not only in theology, but in a number of Islamic sciences. According to al-Jishumī, ʿAbd al-Jabbār wrote four separate treatises on jurisprudence. He also wrote against the philosophers (attacking especially their belief in celestial bodies) and thereby attracted the attention of Avicenna (d. 1037), who also worked in Rayy under the Būyids (see Dhanani 2003, who suggests that the two might have met). He also composed four commentaries on the Qurʾān, two of which are extant.

Even in these two commentaries, however, ʿAbd al-Jabbār focuses on the fundamental theological principles of the Muʿtazila, namely God's transcendence and justice. In *Tanzīh al-Qurʾān ʿan al-maṭāʿin* ("Exaltation of the Qurʾān above Abuses"), ʿAbd al-Jabbār argues against opposing interpretations of the Qurʾān, especially those involving anthropomorphism (although ʿAbd al-Jabbār tends to interpret literally the Qurʾān's eschatological imagery). In *Mutashābih al-Qurʾān* ("The Ambiguous in the Qurʾān"), ʿAbd al-Jabbār explains how Qurʾanic passages that seem to suggest divine predetermination are in fact consistent with the Muʿtazilī doctrine of free will. In this regard it is worth mentioning the report of the Shāfiʿī al-Zarkashī (d. 1392), that when ʿAbd al-Jabbār thus explained the meaning of Qurʾān 76:3 ("We have guided [humanity] to a path, either of gratitude or unbelief") in front of Ibn ʿAbbād's court, the Muʿtazilī vizier's face lit up with joy.

ʿAbd al-Jabbār's belief in free will is based on the theological position that God, being just, would not reward or punish humans in the afterlife unless they are free to choose obedience or disobedience in this life. He argues, then, that moral objects in this life are, *a fortiori*, capable of being properly evaluated by human reason and engaged with the human will. This process of evaluation and engagement is the fundamental human task, God's assignment (*taklīf*) to humanity. Yet God assists the moral life with grace (*luṭf*), a topic to which ʿAbd al-Jabbār dedicates an entire volume of the *Mughnī*. This grace, a concept that helps ʿAbd al-Jabbār negotiate the passages in the Qurʾān that suggest predetermination, can take the form of wisdom, health or even pain (which may act as a warning of the greater suffering of hell). However, it is most evident in the ministry of prophets and their revelation. If God has imposed a moral obligation on man, He has also, according to His mercy and justice, sent a ministry of prophets to help man meet that obligation.

On the other hand, ʿAbd al-Jabbār's doctrine of justice leads him to take a conservative position on the possibility of the prophetic intercession on Judgment Day. The Prophet will not intercede for grave sinners, since humans must be judged according to their moral life.

ʿAbd al-Jabbār's view on divine justice is ultimately informed by the Muʿtazilī conviction that God's attributes can be understood by humans. Their opponents, the Ashʿariyya, rejected this premise. They held that whatever God commands is good, even that which does not seem good in human terms. Yet ʿAbd al-Jabbār counters that goodness must have meaning independent of God's command. If the only good is that which is commanded, then God himself, never being commanded, could not be good. From ʿAbd al-Jabbār's Muʿtazilī perspective, then, humans have the ability, if not the duty, to study and to understand the logic and meaning of God's attributes and actions.

This conclusion means that ʿAbd al-Jabbār is in a need of a theodicy, a way to explain the coexistence of evil and a good God. He fulfills this need by arguing that evil in this world always serves a positive purpose, often as a trial or a lesson. In any case, God will duly compensate extraordinary suffering, either in this life or the afterlife. This compensation extends even to animals whose slaughter is divinely sanctioned.

Thus ʿAbd al-Jabbār has a high estimation of human comprehension. The ways of God are not unfamiliar to the ways of man. This position is evident also in regard to ʿAbd al-Jabbār's views of the createdness of the Qurʾān. He argues that God's speech should be understood in a manner cognate to human speech (although this might seem, contrary to ʿAbd al-Jabbār's intentions, to compromise God's transcendence). Since human speech is produced, and is an accident of time, so too is divine speech (speech is thus a temporal attribute of God).

By now it will be clear that ʿAbd al-Jabbār believed a well-reasoned argument, no less than a reasonable interpretation of revelation, can lead to reliable theological doctrine. The validity of this method, he contends, is confirmed by the tranquility and certainty (*sukūn al-nafs*) that accompanies a well-reasoned argument. ʿAbd al-Jabbār applied this belief to jurisprudence, as well. He argues that matters which fall outside of the revealed law might still be evaluated, according to the principle that whatever does not harm the agent of the act or someone else should be considered licit.

ʿAbd al-Jabbār's rational method is typical of the Muʿtazila, but his political doctrine is less so. Ibn Taymiyya describes ʿAbd al-Jabbār as a philo-Shīʿī Muʿtazilī, attributing to him the view that ʿAlī is superior to the first caliph, Abū Bakr. In fact, ʿAbd al-Jabbār's ʿAlid sympathies go still further. He argues that not only ʿAlī but also his two sons, Ḥasan and Ḥusayn, were valid leaders, or Imāms, of the Islamic community. (Of course, it should be kept in mind that he worked under the Shīʿī Būyid regime.) On the other hand, he disagrees with his Shīʿī contemporaries such as al-Shaykh al-Mufīd (d. 1022), whom he knew personally and with whom he shared many theological views, on the doctrines that the Imām was infallible, capable of miracles and, most importantly, that the twelfth Imām had gone into occultation in 874, later to return as the apocalyptic ruler, the Mahdī.

In his *Tathbīt*, in fact, ʿAbd al-Jabbār develops a detailed polemic against Shīʿī apocalyptic views. Yet his polemics in the *Tathbīt* do not stop there. ʿAbd al-Jabbār joins historical and social observations to rational arguments to refute the teachings of philosophers, astronomers, and various Muslim and non-Muslim sects (extending his treatment even to Zoroastrians and Hindus). Yet he is most concerned with the Sevener/Ismāʿīlī Shīʿa of the Qarmaṭī movement (in light of their strength in his native Rayy and their revolutionary tenth-century state in the Bahrain) and with Christians. His treatment of this latter group, in fact, is extraordinary.

In the *Mughnī* ʿAbd al-Jabbār refutes Judaism (primarily the doctrine of the Torah's eternal nature) and Christianity through the theological "questions and answers" dialectical method. His theological critique of Christianity therein is informed by his position on the createdness of Qurʾān. In His transcendence God does not reveal His Being or His Word, not in a book and not in a person. He only gives verbal commands. In the *Tathbīt*, however, ʿAbd al-Jabbār's approach is historical and sociological, as he engages the history of Christianity and the practices of the Christians in his day. While earlier Muslim scholars developed the doctrine of *taḥrīf*, that Christians falsified the true Islamic religion and scripture of Jesus, ʿAbd al-Jabbār develops a theory of *how* the Christians accomplished this. He argues that the powerless political position of the first disciples of Christ (unlike that of the first Muslims) led them to compromise their religion. In return for the political support of the Romans certain disciples abandoned the Islamic religion of the prophet Jesus and embraced the antinomian, philosophical teachings of their pagan overlords, calling it Christianity. Thus ʿAbd al-Jabbār reverses a traditional Christian apologetical argument, that the truth of Christianity (and, by extension, the falsehood of Islam) is shown by its emergence from the humble political circumstances of its first generation.

Importance today

Ultimately ʿAbd al-Jabbār must be appreciated in light of the larger tradition of the Muʿtazila with which he consistently identifies himself. His writings are full of references to "our *shaykh*s" or "the forbearers" (*salaf*). Part of his importance for the Islamic world, then, is as the primary exemplar of classical Muʿtazilī theology. This theology had a significant impact on the development of Shīʿī (especially Zaydī) theology. It also impacted the Sunnī Qur'ān commentary of al-Zamakhsharī (d. 1144). Recently it has even been suggested that Avicenna's philosophy was in some ways affected by the challenge of ʿAbd al-Jabbār's theology.

Yet it is perhaps especially important to note the manner in which the Muʿtazila's emphasis on reason has attracted many twentieth and twenty-first century Muslim intellectuals, especially those who critique the imitation of tradition (*taqlīd*) and seek a revival of Islamic rationalism. ʿAbd al-Jabbār wholly rejected *taqlīd*, arguing that the use of the intellect is a duty imposed by God. To him intellectual reasoning is ultimately reflection on God-given knowledge, and thus is not fully distinct from reflection on revelation. In other words, with ʿAbd al-Jabbār, reason and faith are united.

At the same time, and in line with his Muʿtazilī predecessors, ʿAbd al-Jabbār was devoted to religious apology. Thus he accepts against the apparent meaning of the Qur'ān and against his larger rational principles that Muḥammad performed miracles (while denying that either the Imāms or al-Dajjāl, the anti-Christ, could perform miracles), even those contrary to nature (e.g., moving a tree back and forth by his command). He also argues that the Qur'ān is inimitable, not because God prevented the Arabs of Muḥammad's time from matching his proclamations, but because its style and message are beyond human capabilities. In these arguments ʿAbd al-Jabbār anticipates a trend among later medieval and modern Islamic authors, who, motivated by a sectarian environment, adopt doctrinal positions according to their apologetical usefulness.

Moreover, inspired by these apologetical motives, ʿAbd al-Jabbār takes a position towards other religions that is no less hostile than it is rational. As Guy Monnot puts it (1974: 143ff.), if ʿAbd al-Jabbār represents the height of Muʿtazilī heresiography, this is despite the fact that he makes no effort to find the value of foreign beliefs. Instead, ʿAbd al-Jabbār's writing on competing religions is devoted to *theologumena*, individual theological arguments for the invalidity of other religious systems. It is due to this strategy, apparently, that ʿAbd al-Jabbār's *Tathbīt* attracted the attention of Ibn Taymiyya's circle. The thought of that circle, in turn, helped inspire the Sunnī Islamist movement of the present day.

References and further reading

Bouman, J. (1964) "The Doctrine of ʿAbd al-Jabbār on the Qur'ān as the Created Word of Allāh," in H. Obbink, ed., *Verbum: Essays on Some Aspects of the Religious Functions of Words*, Utrecht: Kemink, 67–86.

Dhanani, A. (2003) "Rocks in the Heavens?! The Encounter Between ʿAbd al-Ǧabbār and Ibn Sīnā," in D. Reisman, ed., *Before and after Avicenna: Proceedings of the First Conference of the Avicenna Study Group*, Leiden: Brill, 127–44.

Hamdan, O. and Schmidtke, S. (2006) "Qadi ʿAbd al-Jabbar al-Hamadhani (d. 415/1025) on the Promise and Threat. An Edition of a Fragment of his *Kitab al-Mughni fi abwab al-tawhid wa l-ʿadl* preserved in the Firkovitch-Collection, St. Petersburg (II Firk. Arab. 105, ff. 14–92)," *Mélanges de l'Institut dominicain des études Orientale*, 27: 45–138.

Heemskerk, M. (2000) *Suffering in the Muʿtazilite Theology, ʿAbd al-Jabbār's Teaching on Pain and Divine Justice*, Leiden: Brill.

—— (2005) "A Muʿtazilite Refutation of Christianity and Judaism: Two Fragments from ʿAbd al-Jabbār's *al-Mughnī fī abwāb al-tawḥīd wa-'l-ʿadl*," in B. Roggema, M. Poorthuis, P. Valkenberg, eds., *The Three Rings: Textual Studies in the Historical Trialogue of Judaism, Christianity and Islam*, Leuven: Peeters, 183–201.

Hourani, G. (1971) *Islamic Rationalism: the Ethics of ʿAbd al-Jabbār*, Oxford: Clarendon.

Martin, R. C., Woodward, M. R. and Atmaja, D. S. (1997) *Defenders of Reason in Islam, Muʿtazilism from Medieval School to Modern Symbol*, Oxford: Oneworld.

McDermott, M. (1986) *The Theology of al-Shaikh al-Mufīd*, Beirut: Dār el-Machreq.

Mohammed, A. (1984) "The Notion of Good and Evil in the Ethics of ʿAbd al-Jabbār," Ph.D. dissertation, Temple University.

Monnot, G. (1974) *Penseurs musulmans et religions iraniennes: ʿAbd al-Jabbār et ses devanciers*, Paris: J. Vrin.

Peters, J. R. (1976) *God's Created Speech: a Study in the Speculative Theology of the Muʿtazilî Qâdî l-qudât*, Leiden: E. J. Brill.

Reynolds, G. S. (2004) *A Muslim Theologian in the Sectarian Milieu: ʿAbd al-Jabbār and the Critique of Christian Origins*, Leiden: Brill.

26

NIẒĀM AL-MULK

Neguin Yavari

Ḥasan the son of ʿAlī, known as Niẓām al-Mulk, was a celebrated Persian vizier and administrator, born on a Friday in 1018 in Tus, near the city of Mashhad in the province of Khurasan. He was stabbed to death in a village outside Isfahan on another Friday in 1092, a couple of months after he had been removed from the vizierate by the Turkic ruler, Malikshāh (r. 1073–92), of the Saljuq dynasty (r. 1040–1194). In the course of those 74 years, he rose from the relatively humble status of a bureaucrat in the service of the provincial governor of Balkh in Afghanistan to become the de facto ruler of a vast empire stretching east to Central Asia and Afghanistan and west to Syria and Anatolia, with a final apotheosis as the archetypal good vizier in Islamic history. As his honorifics – Niẓām al-Mulk ("Pivot of the State"), Ghiyāth al-Dawla ("Mainstay of Government"), Qiwām al-Dīn ("Pillar of Religion"), and Raḍī Amīr al-Mu'minīn ("Favored One of the Commander of the Faithful") – indicate, he was extolled in his own time and by posterity as the most able politician of the era, and upheld as an exemplar of justice, political astuteness and overall good governance in the medieval Islamic sources. His was a long-lived administration, a remarkable achievement in itself in the Islamic empire in the eleventh century. Moreover, he was the progenitor of a dynasty of viziers and high officials, with several of his sons and grandsons serving as councilors to the Saljuqs.

About his life we know very few details. There are many accounts of him in medieval chronicles and biographical dictionaries, but the structure and form of these entries are determined to a large extent by their well-established framework and conventions. Individual traits and idiosyncrasies are passed over in silence. Consequently, there is little in the way of personal detail on Niẓām al-Mulk that sets him apart from other heroes of the medieval world. The purpose of biographical writing was to present the subject as a model of moral excellence, an exemplar whose correct social and political values the reader should strive to emulate. Moreover, the idealized template of a hero, coupled with a generous sprinkling of anecdotes, the staple narrative form of these historical accounts, created an often inextricable fusion of legend and history, making it difficult to unravel what did happen or could have happened from threads borrowed from popular tales or accounts of other famous lives.

What detail we know about Niẓām al-Mulk's life can be summed up briefly. We are told that Ḥasan was born into a family of hereditary administrators (*dihqāns*), thereby signifying that he came from a locally eminent lineage. The sources, especially the *Tārīkh-i Bayhaq* of Ibn Funduq (d. 1170), elaborate on the prominence of Niẓām al-Mulk's family, since noble birth is among the prerequisites for men destined for high office, but they give few details. His father ʿAlī served, according to Ibn Funduq, as provincial governor of Tus. Treated unfairly by his superiors and accused of corruption, ʿAlī was ultimately vindicated and went to Bayhaq with his sons. Ibn Funduq tells us that his grandfather had been alive then, and remembered vividly the day when *Khwāja* (person of high social standing) ʿAlī, the father of Ḥasan, arrived with his son, and how the latter, though of a tender age, had impressed him with his precocious sagacity.

According to the sources, Ḥasan made his way to Nishapur, to pursue his studies. We have only a very general picture of what Niẓām al-Mulk studied. He received a mainstream Sunnī education in the Qur'ān, prophetic traditions (*ḥadīth*), and Islamic history. As a Sunnī and a Shāfiʿī (the law school of choice for elite Iranian families in Khurasan in that period), Niẓām al-Mulk studied with Imām al-Muwaffaq al-Shīrāzī (d. 1048), leader of the Shāfiʿī faction in Nishapur, the provincial capital of Khurasan. Like almost all Iranian Shāfiʿīs of the eleventh and twelfth centuries, Imām al-Muwaffaq was a follower of Ashʿarī theology, known for a more expansive human interpretation of knowledge about God and His commands compared to other contemporaneous schools of Islamic theology.

Ḥasan proved an excellent student of religious sciences and the Qur'ān, and was therefore recommended to the newly established Saljuq chancellery for an administrative job. One spurious source (Anonymous n.d.) records that it was Abū ʿAlī al-Shādhān, the governor of Balkh, who introduced him to the Saljuqs. Other sources say that it was Imām al-Muwaffaq who recommended him. Ḥasan was 20 years old when the Saljuqs conquered Khurasan. The historian Bayhaqī (d. 1077) was an eyewitness to the arrival of the Saljuqs in Nishapur in 1038. The population of Nishapur was mostly Sunnī, either Ḥanafī or Shāfiʿī, with a Shīʿī community large enough to have its own leadership. As is often the case, competition was fiercest between the Sunnī coreligionists. Bayhaqī tells us that the Ḥanafī leadership remained skeptical of Saljuq victory. It was Niẓām al-Mulk's teacher and leader of the Shāfiʿī camp, Imām al-Muwaffaq, who greeted the Saljuq sovereign at the city gates.

Boosted by his early support for the Saljuqs, Imām al-Muwaffaq was quick to place his students and disciples in the administration. Besides Ḥasan, Imām al-Muwaffaq taught another star student, later known as ʿAmīd al-Mulk al-Kundurī (d. 1064), who was chosen as vizier by Ṭughril (r. 1040–63), the first Saljuq sultan of eastern Iran. As for Ḥasan, he gained a prominent position in the court of Chaghrī Beg (r. 1040–60), Ṭughril's brother and governor of Khurasan. Little is known about the next 20 years of Niẓām al-Mulk's career in the Saljuq bureaucracy. He was inherited by Ṭughril's nephew and crown prince, Ālp Arslān ibn Chaghrī Beg (r. 1063–72), who succeeded his father as governor of Khurasan. It is when Ālp Arslān succeeds Ṭughril on the throne, and retains al-Kundurī as vizier, while Niẓām al-Mulk is kept as his personal secretary, that events take a dramatic turn and the medieval accounts become more expansive.

The ensuing rivalry between Niẓām al-Mulk and al-Kundurī is used as a context in the medieval sources to express both disdain for partisan politics and to commend Niẓām al-Mulk for his subsequent attempts to transcend sectarianism. Niẓām al-Mulk is blamed for the murder of al-Kundurī, driven by his desire to replace al-Kundurī as vizier. The sources are also adamant about Ālp Arslān's foreknowledge of and acquiescence in the murder. Al-Kundurī's last words before his execution became enshrined in later chronicles. He sent a message to Ālp Arslān and his vizier:

> I praise the Lord for all the blessings I have received at the hands of the Saljuqs. Your uncle gave me happiness in this life, and you have insured my happiness in the next. Tell Niẓām al-Mulk that he has established a dire precedence, and promoted the innovation of murdering viziers; and that he has not pondered the ramifications of his action: I fear the cursed repercussions of what he has initiated will ultimately afflict his own descendants.

Ẓahīr al-Dīn al-Nīshāpūrī (d. sometime between 1176 and 1186), who recorded this account in his *Saljūqnāma* (2004: 21–2), also observed that not one vizier of the Saljuq dynasty died a natural death. Other sources claim that al-Kundurī also added, "For you have taught the Turks the custom of killing their viziers." Niẓām al-Mulk and at least three of his sons were murdered under mysterious circumstances while serving under one or another Saljuq sultan. It is no wonder that both versions of Niẓām al-Mulk's fictitious last will warn his sons to stay away from the vizierate (Anonymous n.d.; Anonymous 1993). Niẓām al-Mulk had nine (or according to some sources 12) sons. Of his sons, Jamāl al-Mulk was killed at Malikshāh's order in 1082. ʿImād al-Mulk (d. 1095) was killed by Malikshāh's brother, Arslān Arghūn (d. 1097); Muʾayyad al-Mulk was murdered by Birkyāruq ibn Malikshāh in 1101; Fakhr al-Mulk (d. 1106) served as vizier to Malikshāh's son, Sanjar (r. 1097–1157), and was beheaded by one of Sanjar's slaves and lover in 1106. Another son, Ḍiyāʾ al-Mulk was deposed and imprisoned for 12 years by Muḥammad Tapar ibn Malikshāh who reigned briefly in 1105. Malikshāh's grandson, Maḥmūd ibn Muḥammad Tapar, took arms against Shams al-Mulk, another of Niẓām al-Mulk's sons, and had him murdered in 1123. Niẓām al-Mulk had four daughters; one was married to the Shīʿī leader of Rayy, another to ʿAmīd al-Dawla, the Abbasid vizier. When she died in 1078 while giving birth to a stillborn child, she was buried in the caliphal palace, an exceptional honor and a token of respect in memory of her father (Ibn al-Athīr 2002: 195).

Ālp Arslān was succeeded by his son Malikshāh, who inherited both the empire and the vizier. Niẓām al-Mulk had been entrusted with raising the young prince; he had been given the title *ātābeg*, or father-tutor. By the time of Malikshāh's accession, Niẓām al-Mulk had already assumed full charge of the affairs of state. One of his first moves as vizier was to reverse the public cursing of Ashʿarīs from the pulpits in Khurasan, a policy championed by al-Kundurī and allowed by Ṭughril. The unpopular act had exacerbated the rift between the Shāfiʿīs – most of whom were Ashʿarī – and the Ḥanafīs of Khurasan, increasing the already existing factionalism and simmering unrest.

Medieval historical narratives do not offer direct, detailed and descriptive accounts of the administrative, economic and political organization of the period in the manner of modern textbooks. The magnitude of Niẓām al-Mulk's dominion over the Saljuq state is implied obliquely through the portrayal of Malikshāh, who is characterized as more interested in hunting than in governance, a sovereign in name alone, as far as the daily affairs of the realm were concerned. The vizier had a free rein, and he spent his 20 years with Malikshāh endowing schools, financing construction projects, quelling internal dissent, countering the ploys of the Fatimid Shīʿī dynasty in Egypt, composing the *Siyar al-mulūk*, marrying his daughters to prominent figures, and bestowing governorships on his sons and sons-in-law. In the meantime, he associated with the *ʿulamāʾ*, administered justice, and maintained a strong army of Turkic slaves. Of all the stories told about Niẓām al-Mulk, the most popular one repeated in medieval and modern histories, including al-Rāwandī's *Rāḥat al-ṣudūr wa āyat al-surūr* written in the early thirteenth century, points not just to the vast expanse of his dominion but also to its moral temper. The empire administered by the vizier was prosperous, stable, and secure from willful usurpation and exploitation. When the armies of Malikshāh passed the Oxus River, Niẓām al-Mulk paid the sailors there with draft notes drawn on the treasury in the faraway Antioch. On the day when the sultan was holding a public audience to address his subjects' grievances, the sailors presented their complaint that they could ill afford to travel all the way to Antioch to collect their pay. Malikshāh turned to Niẓām al-Mulk for an explanation. The vizier responded that the sailors need not go to Antioch, for they could exchange the draft notes drawn on the royal treasury for gold anywhere in the empire. "I paid them in this manner," Niẓām al-Mulk added, "for I wanted the world to know the extent of your domain, and to extol your rule. So that it will be recorded in the histories, that in such and such year, the empire enjoyed such stability" (al-Rāwandī 1985: 128–9). The sultan was delighted. In this anecdote and numerous others, the vizier is not just impeccable in virtue but also always one step ahead of his master, and his potential qualms.

The relationship between Niẓām al-Mulk and Malikshāh is also often likened in the sources to that between a father and his son, but this should be taken with a grain of salt. In 1082, Malikshāh arranged for the murder of Jamāl al-Mulk, Niẓām al-Mulk's impetuous son who had offended him. When news of his death reached the sultan, he went to Niẓām al-Mulk, and informed him of his son's demise and offered him his condolences. He said, "I am your son, and you of all men are the fittest to show resignation and win merit in heaven" (Ibn al-Athīr 2002: 206). To extend the simile, finally there was patricide: Malikshāh arranged for the assassination of his trusted vizier in a plot that included numerous players in the Saljuq court, and which signaled the downfall of Saljuq central power.

The death of Niẓām al-Mulk is considered a watershed in most historical accounts of the twelfth century and later. The Saljuq state was beset with short-lived reigns and frequent rotations in the highest echelons, and its enemies, including the Ismāʿīlīs, took full advantage of the instability in the kingdom to pursue their political objectives. The Saljuq state blamed the murder on an assassin dispatched by the Ismāʿīlī propaganda movement (*daʿwa*). Among the medieval historians, the Shāfiʿī jurist, al-Subkī (d. 1369), had his own explanation for Malikshāh's part in the plot against Niẓām al-Mulk. Malikshāh, he maintained, was determined to put an end to the Abbasid caliphate by transferring it to his own progeny through his grandson Jaʿfar, the offspring of the marriage of his daughter, Māhmalik Khātūn – or sister according to al-Rāwandī and others – in 1087 to the Abbasid caliph al-Muqtadī (r. 1075–94). Only Niẓām al-Mulk stood in his way (al-Subkī 1964–70: IV, 322). Niẓām al-Mulk's support of the Abbasids as a check on Saljuq power and ambition is corroborated by several anecdotes in the *Siyar al-mulūk*, one of which tells the tale of an unnamed Turkic general who roamed the streets of Baghdad at night, and whose travesties against the people were finally checked by the vigilant and pious caliph who took to heart his duty to safeguard Muslims.

Most modern historians of Niẓām al-Mulk have praised his policies while in office mainly on the basis of his support for the Sunnī creed, ideological and institutional. His championing of the *madrasas*, for example, was long considered by scholars to represent his Sunnī impositions. Known as the Niẓāmiyya, the schools were scattered all over the empire – in Baghdad (1066), Nishapur, Mosul, Herat, Balkh, Basra, Marv, Isfahan, and elsewhere. The endowment deeds stipulated that each professorship had to be occupied by a prominent jurist of the Shāfiʿī faction. Not much is known about the fate of the schools after the passing of Niẓām al-Mulk and the Mongol invasions of the mid-thirteenth century. Paralleling the inordinate emphasis placed by the medieval scholars on Niẓām al-Mulk's exemplarity rather than his actual administration and policies, the sources record the establishment of the *madrasas* with great fanfare, but say very little about the fate of these institutions after the demise of their founder. The preoccupation of the medieval Islamic intellectuals was to embellish, as much as possible, the greatness and prescience of Niẓām al-Mulk, rather than the uniqueness of the institutions or their academic quality. In tangible terms, the Niẓāmiyyas were the least consequential instrument of Niẓām al-Mulk's policies, although they were the most visible reminders of his greatness. Financed by private endowment, they were functional only in times of peace, stability, and political continuity, scarce commodities in the twelfth and thirteenth centuries. ʿAṭāʾ al-Mulk al-Juwaynī (d. 1283), a Persian historian made governor of Baghdad by the Mongols, lamented their dilapidated condition and embarked on reconstructing them.

Much of the modern elaboration of Niẓām al-Mulk's partisanship and religious policies is derived from passages in his *Siyar al-mulūk*, where he warns the sultan of the dangers of heresy, unorthodox religions, and heeding bad advice. The primary sources, however, reveal a prudent politician who tried to quell partisanship at every turn. This apparent discrepancy is resolved by a critical reading of the text. Every narrative source of the medieval period represents a political position, and offers a rhetorical arsenal for its explication. Niẓām al-Mulk's *Siyar al-mulūk* is no exception. As an illustration, we should remember that Niẓām al-Mulk was a Shāfiʿi vizier serving Ḥanafī Turks. In a text presumably written to educate and please his master, why would he include anti-Turkic slurs, and why would he tell Malikshāh that in the reign of Ālp Arslān, the acme of Saljuq might, the sultan repeatedly informed his vizier that he wished he had not been a Shāfiʿī? Taking such passages in the *Siyar al-mulūk* at face value is only possible if we, as modern readers, disregard the historical context of the text and its plausibility and appeal for its own contemporary audience.

On the face of it, the many negative references to Shīʿīs and other peoples of "bad religion" scattered throughout the *Siyar al-mulūk* would stand to contradict a claim for Niẓām al-Mulk's non-partisanship. But his anti-Shīʿī rhetoric in the *Siyar al-mulūk* and his anti-Ismāʿīlī policies recorded in the medieval sources jar with the appraisal of his term in office as preserved in contemporary Shīʿī sources, as well as with his policies toward non-Ismāʿīlī Shīʿīs. For example, the account written in Rayy in the late 1160s by ʿAbd al-Jalīl al-Qazwīnī al-Rāzī, enumerates various deeds attributed to Niẓām al-Mulk and Malikshāh to refute the allegation that they held the Shīʿa in disdain or discriminated against them. Al-Rāzī argues that Niẓām al-Mulk, the most important Sunnī of all and the jewel in the crown of Sunnism, had given his daughter to Sayyid Murtaḍā al-Qummī, a prominent eleventh-century Shīʿī, and asked for the hand of the daughter of another Shīʿī, Amīr Sharaf Shāh Jaʿfarī, for his son ʿUmar. In addition, al-Rāzī points out, although the vizier had built many *madrasas* dedicated to the Shāfi'ī creed, he did not prevent Shī'ī notables from dedicating mosques or schools to the Shī'ī rite in Qazvin and other Shī'ī strongholds. Finally, the Sunnī historian, Ibn al-Athīr, informs us that on their first trip to Baghdad in 1086, Niẓām al-Mulk and Malikshāh visited the tombs of several Sunnī *imāms* including Aḥmad ibn Ḥanbal (d. 855) and Abū Ḥanīfa (d. 767), but also made a point of paying their respect at the shrines of ʿAlī ibn Abī Ṭālib (d. 661), the fourth caliph and the first Shī'ī Imām, and his son, al-Ḥusayn (d. 680), the Prophet's grandson and the third Shī'ī Imām (Ibn al-Athīr 2002: 228).

A cursory glance at the few instances in the primary sources where specific policies or acts adopted by Niẓām al-Mulk are discussed further demonstrates the pitfalls of taking the ideological content of medieval narratives at face value. Niẓām al-Mulk's disdain for partisanship was best reflected in his unusual proximity to various Ṣūfī dignitaries of his time. As a buffer against the widespread and increasing popular support for Ismā'īlī ideology, the more spiritualist, experiential, and mystical tendencies of Ṣūfī groups were particularly effective. Their insistence on non-sectarian politics, tolerance and the unity of the community also resonated with Niẓām al-Mulk's desire to quell internecine warfare and maintain social stability. His decidedly non-sectarian policies and preoccupation with the political as opposed to the partisan were documented in a letter he sent in 1077 to Abū Isḥāq al-Shīrāzī (d. 1083), the Shāfi'ī teacher he had appointed to the Niẓāmiyya in Baghdad. Interestingly, the letter is preserved not in a Shāfi'ī source, but in the universal history of Ibn al-Jawzī (d. 1200), an ardent Ḥanbalī in Baghdad. News had reached the vizier that the strong Ḥanbalī community in Baghdad had taken offense at the teachings of al-Shīrāzī and that there had been riots. He advised the Shaykh Abū Isḥāq to be cautious in his teaching there, as the majority of the population were Ḥanbalīs and Aḥmad ibn Ḥanbal, the progenitor of the creed, was among the most venerated of early Muslim dignitaries. The schools were founded to propagate learning and to protect the learned, he wrote, and should they fall short of this objective, he would have no alternative but to shut them down.

Niẓām al-Mulk's association with prominent Ṣūfīs who were recognized not only as exemplars of piety and Islamic propriety but were also at the forefront of social and political debates further confirms his ability to project an aura of even-handed authority and political legitimacy. Prominent eleventh-century Ṣūfīs, including the Ḥanbalī ʿAbd Allāh Anṣārī (d. 1089), and the prominent Shāfi'īs Imām al-Ḥaramayn al-Juwaynī (d. 1085), and Abū Qāsim al-Qushayrī (d. 1072) all applauded him in one way or another, and this in spite of their many ideological and political differences. In a treatise ascribed to the vizier, al-Juwaynī (1979) went as far as suggesting that, of all the politicians in the Islamic world, Niẓām al-Mulk was best suited for leadership and he should replace both the Abbasid caliph and the Saljuq sultan.

The mutual admiration of Niẓām al-Mulk and the Ṣūfīs points to paradigms of rulership and religiosity that prevailed in later centuries. Niẓām al-Mulk patronized their religious establishments and the Ṣūfī *shaykhs* found in the vizier a powerful supporter, able to formulate a religio-political vision and enforce it. The alliance with the Ṣūfī *shaykhs* afforded the vizier a chance to undermine sectarianism and factionalism. It also obviated the possibility of religious challenges to his rule, for the vizier's credentials in that area were validated by the most outstanding clerics of the time. A strong and powerful ruler, who associates with learned men and heeds their advice, not only ensures successful rule but also domesticates religious zeal and extremism. The twinning of religion and politics is one of the precepts propagated by Muslim political thinkers of the medieval period, an aphorism with a pre-Islamic Iranian lineage. A king who is an effective ruler but also capable of religious guidance and intervention and can hold his own in a debate, will succeed in robbing his opponents of the mantle of piety and rectitude. It is by gaining legitimacy in both realms that effective rule is secured, and in that, Niẓām al-Mulk stood alone in medieval Islamic memory and came to define, posthumously, the paradigm of the just, effective ruler.

By the fourteenth century, the legend of Niẓām al-Mulk was fully articulated, so much so that in the twentieth century and after the establishment of the Shīʿī Islamic republic in Iran in 1979, a treatise was published in Qum – allegedly recorded by a contemporary scholar – based on an eleventh-century debate among several Shīʿī and Sunnī scholars, organized by the vizier and the Saljuq sultan. As a result of the Shīʿīs' overwhelmingly persuasive arguments, those alleged restorers of Sunnī glory, Malikshāh and his vizier, both embrace Shiʿism and renounce Sunnī beliefs. This, too, is a testament to the non-sectarian ideals espoused by Islamic thinkers of all stripes. This brings into question the study of Islamic history as a continuous chain of variegated partisanships. More often than not, the blurred boundaries of religion and politics are no more than a trope, an articulation of concrete political and secular concerns couched in the language of religious metaphors and ethical precepts.

References and further reading

Anonymous (1993) *Khiradnāma*, ed. M. Minovī and M. Thirvat, Tehran: Amīrkabīr. (From the early thirteenth century Niẓām al-Mulk was considered to have authored, in addition to his book of advice to princes, a testament, extant in at least two versions. The second is preserved in a recently discovered twelfth-century manuscript, a collection of ethical treatises and pseudo-Aristotelian tidbits in Persian that contains two letters by Niẓām al-Mulk, one being his will addressed to one son, and the other being a series of counsels addressed to another son.)

Anonymous (n.d.) *Waṣāyā'-i Khwāja Niẓām al-Mulk*, Tehran: n.p. (The printed edition of this text has adopted the uniform title of "The Testament of Niẓām al-Mulk", although clearly, the vizier's last will is appended to the anonymous biography. Although unknown to most Arab historians of the twelfth century and beyond, the "Testament of Niẓām al-Mulk" was referred to in the chronicle of Mīrkhwānd (d. 1498), a Persian historian, that of his grandson Khwāndmīr (d. 1535), and in another and earlier Persian source, Sadīd al-Dīn ʿAwfī's (fl. *c.* 1200) massive compendium of tales and anecdotes. See Sadīd al-Dīn al-ʿAwfī, *Jawāmiʿ al-ḥikāyāt wa lawāmiʿ al-riwāyāt*, Section II of Part II, ed. A. Muṣafā', M. Muṣafā', Tehran: Mu'assissa-yi Muṭāliʿāt va Taḥqīqāt-i Farhangī, 1983, 442; Muḥammad ibn Khwānshah Mīrkhwānd, *Rawḍat al-ṣafā' fī sīrat al-anbiyā' wa al-khulafā'*, vol. IV, Tehran: Khayyām, 1960 295; and Ghiyāth al-Dīn ibn Humam al-Dīn Khwāndmīr, *Dastūr al-wuzarā'*, ed. S. Nafisī, Tehran: Iqbāl, 1938/168, 175.)

Bayhaqī, Abū 'l-Faḍl Muḥammad ibn Ḥusayn (1971) *Tārīkh-i Bayhaqī*, ed. ʿA. A. Fayyāḍ, Mashhad: Mashhad University Press.

Bulliet, R. (1972) *The Patricians of Nishapur*, Cambridge: Harvard University Press.

Al-Bundārī al-Iṣfahānī, al-Fatḥ ibn ʿAlī ibn Muḥammad (1980) *Ta'rīkh dawla Āl-i Saljūq (Zubdat al-nuṣra wa nukhbat al-ʿuṣra)*, Beirut: Dār al-Āfāq al-Jadīda. (The memoirs of Anūshīrwān ibn Khālid (d. 1137–8 or 1138–9), who served as vizier to the Abbasid caliph al-Mustarshid

(r. 1118–35), is a first-hand intricate account of political factions and machinations in Baghdad and Saljuq provincial capitals. Anūshīrwān's history was expanded by 'Imād al-Dīn Kātib al-Iṣfahānī (d. 1201), who changed its title to *Nuṣrat al-futra*. 'Imād al-Dīn's expanded version survives only in the abridgment of al-Bundārī (d. 1235), completed in 1226, and entitled *Zubdat al-nuṣra*. It was published in Beirut as *Ta'rīkh dawla Āl-i Saljūq*.)

Ephrat, D. (2000) *A Learned Society in a Period of Transition: The Sunni 'Ulama' of Eleventh-Century Baghdad*, Albany: State University of New York Press.

Ibn al-Athīr (2002) *The Annals of the Saljuq Turks: Selections from al-Kamil fi'l ta'rikh of 'Izz al-Din Ibn al-Athir*, trans. D. S. Richards, London: RoutledgeCurzon.

Ibn 'Aṭiyya al-Bakrī al-Ḥanafī, Abū 'l-Hijā' Shibl al-Dawla Muqātil [Pseudo] (1979) *Kitāb mu'tamir 'ulamā' Baghdad*, introduction by Ayatollah Sayyid Shihāb al-Dīn al-Ḥusaynī al-Mar'ashī al-Najafī, Qum: n.p. (Published by a private citizen, Hāj Sayyid Hidāyat Allāh al-Mustarḥamī al-Iṣfahānī, and not widely distributed, the unedited text is a transcript of the debate among several Sunnī and Shī'ī scholars organized by the vizier and the Saljuq sultan. The introduction by Ayatollah Mar'ashī states that the manuscript, in the author's hand, was found in the Rājā Library in Mahmudabad in 1882–3. The *Zubda al-tawārīkh* of Ṣadr al-Dīn Abū 'l-Ḥasan 'Alī ibn Nāṣir ibn 'Ali al-Ḥusaynī (d. after 1225) mentions a poem by Abū 'l-Hijā' Shibl al-Dawla al-Bakrī (d. 1111–12) in praise of Niẓām al-Mulk, to whom he was related by marriage. The poem is also found in Ibn al-Athīr's history; see Ibn al-Athīr 2002: 255.)

Ibn Funduq, Abū 'l-Ḥasan 'Alī ibn Zayd al-Bayhaqī (1938) *Tārīkh-i Bayhaq*, ed. A. Bahmanyār, Tehran: Forūghī.

Ibn al-Jawzī (1940) *Al-Muntaẓam fī ta'rīkh al-mulūk wa'l-'umam*, Hyderabad: Osmania, vol. VIII.

Al-Juwaynī, al-Imām al-Ḥaramayn Abū 'l-Ma'ālī (1979) *Qiyāth al-'Umam fī iltiyāth al-ẓulam*, ed. F.'A. Aḥmad, M. Ḥilmī, Alexandria: Dār al-Da'wa.

Khwāndmīr, Qiyāth al-Dīn Humām al-Dīn (1977) *Dastūr al-wuzarā'*, ed. S. Nafisī, Tehran: Eqbāl, 2nd edition.

Niẓām al-Mulk (1960) *The Book of Government or Rules for Kings*, trans. H. Darke, London: Routledge and Kegan Paul.

Al-Rāwandī, Muḥammad ibn 'Alī ibn Sulaymān al-Rāwandī (1985) *Rāḥat al-ṣudūr wa āyat al-surūr dar tārīkh Āl-i Saljuq*, ed. M. Iqbāl, Tehran: Amīr Kabīr.

Al-Rāzī, Nāṣir al-Dīn Abū Rashīd 'Abd al-Jalīl al-Qazvīnī (1980) [*Kitāb al-naqḍ*] *Ba'ḍ mathālib al-nawāṣib fī naqḍ "Ba'ḍ faḍā'iḥ al-rawāfiḍ,"* ed. J. Muḥaddith, vols. I–III, Tehran: Intishārāt Anjuman Āthār Millī.

Al-Subkī, Tāj al-Dīn Abū Naṣr 'Abd al-Wahhāb ibn 'Alī (1964–70) *Ṭabaqāt al-Shāfi'iyya al-kubrā'*, ed. M. M. Ṭanāḥī, 'A. M. al-Ḥulw, Cairo: 'Isā al-Bābī al-Ḥalabī, vol. IV.

Talas, A. (1939) *La Madrasa Nizamiyya et son histoire*, Bordeaux: Université de Bordeaux.

Yavari, N. (2004) "Polysemous Texts and Reductionist Readings: Women and Heresy in the *Siyar al-mulūk*," in *Views from the Edge: Essays in Honor of Richard W. Bulliet*, ed. N. Yavari, L. Potter, J.-M. Oppenheim, New York: Columbia University Press, 322–46.

—— (2008) "Mirrors for Princes or a Hall of Mirrors: Niẓām al-Mulk's *Siyar al-mulūk* Reconsidered," *Al-Masaq: Islam and the Medieval Mediterranean*, 20: 1.

Zahīr al-Dīn Nīshāpūrī (2004) *Saljuqnāma*, ed. A. H. Morton, Chippenham: The E. J. W. Gibb Memorial Trust.

27

AL-GHAZĀLĪ

Frank Griffel

Abū Ḥāmid Muḥammad ibn Muḥammad al-Ghazālī was one of the most prominent theologians, jurists, and mystics of Sunnī Islam. Later Arabic medieval historians say he was born in 1058 or 1059 in Tabaran-Tus (15 miles/25 kilometers north of modern Meshed, northeast Iran), yet notes about his age in his letters and his autobiography indicate that he was born in 1055 or 1056. Al-Ghazālī received his early education in his hometown of Tus together with his brother Aḥmad (d. 1123 or 1126–7) who later became a famous preacher and Ṣūfī scholar. Muḥammad went on to study with the influential Ashʿarite theologian al-Juwaynī (d. 1085) at the Niẓāmiyya *madrasa* in nearby Nishapur. This brought him in close contact with the court of the Grand-Seljuq sultan Malikshāh (r. 1071–92) and his grand-vizier Niẓām al-Mulk (d. 1092). In 1091 Niẓām al-Mulk appointed al-Ghazālī to the prestigious Niẓāmiyya *madrasa* in Baghdad. In addition to being a confidante of the Seljuq sultan and his court in Isfahan, he now became closely connected to the caliphal court in Baghdad. He was undoubtedly the most influential intellectual of his time, when in 1095 he suddenly gave up his posts in Baghdad and left the city. Under the influence of Ṣūfī literature al-Ghazālī had begun to change his lifestyle two years before his departure. He realized that the high ethical standards of a virtuous religious life are not compatible with being in the service of sultans, viziers, and caliphs. Benefiting from the riches of the military and political elite implies complicity in their corrupt and oppressive rule and will jeopardize one's prospect of redemption in the afterlife. When al-Ghazālī left Baghdad in 1095 he went to Damascus and Jerusalem and vowed at the tomb of Abraham in Hebron never again to serve the political authorities or teach at state-sponsored schools. He continued to teach, however, at small schools (singular *zāwiya*) that were financed by private donations. After performing the pilgrimage in 1096, al-Ghazālī returned via Baghdad to his hometown Tus, where he founded a small private school and a Ṣūfī convent (*khānqāh*). In 1106, at the beginning of the sixth century in the Muslim calendar, al-Ghazālī broke his vow and returned to teaching at the Niẓāmiyya *madrasa* in Nishapur, where he himself had been a student. To his followers he justified this step with the great amount of theological confusion among the general public and the pressure from authorities at the Seljuq court. Al-Ghazālī regarded himself as one of the renewers (singular *muḥyī*) of religion, who, according to a *ḥadīth*, will come every new century. He continued to teach at his *zāwiya* in Tus where he died in 1111.

Al-Ghazālī is a towering figure in Sunnī Islam, active at a time when Sunnī theology had just passed through its consolidation and entered a period of intense challenges from Shīʿī Ismāʿīlī theology and the Arabic tradition of Aristotelian philosophy (*falsafa*). Al-Ghazālī understood the significance of the confrontation with these two movements and after having made his name as a competent author of legal works, devoted much of his efforts to addressing the challenges posed by these two schools of thought. He closely studied the works of the Aristotelian philosophers Ibn Sīnā (Avicenna, d. 1037), al-Fārābī (d. *c.* 950), and of others within the movement of *falsafa* and wrote *Tahāfut al-falāsifa* (*The Incoherence of the Philosophers*). Al-Ghazālī describes this book as a "refutation" (*radd*) of the philosophical movement, which has contributed to the erroneous assumption that he opposed Aristotelianism and rejected its teachings. His response to *falsafa* was far more complex and allowed him to adopt many of its teachings. The philosophers are convinced, al-Ghazālī complains, that their way of knowing by "demonstrative proof" (Greek: *apodeixis*, Arabic: *burhān*) is superior to theological knowledge drawn from revelation and its rational interpretation. In his *Incoherence* al-Ghazālī discusses 20 teachings of the *falāsifa* and rejects the claim that these teachings are demonstratively proven. In a detailed and intricate philosophical discussion al-Ghazālī aims to show that none of the arguments in favor of these 20 teachings fulfills the high epistemological standard of demonstration (*burhān*). Rather, the arguments supporting these 20 positions rely upon unproven premises that are accepted only among the *falāsifa*, but are not established by reason. Only after achieving this first step does al-Ghazālī ask whether or not these teachings are true: some may be true, others are wrong, yet pose no problem in terms of religion. A third group of positions is considered wrong as well as religiously problematic. These are three teachings from Ibn Sīnā's philosophy, namely (1) that the world has no beginning in the past and is not created in time, (2) that God's knowledge includes only classes of beings and does not extend to individual beings and their circumstances, and (3) that after death the souls of humans will never again return into bodies. In these three cases the teachings of Islam, which are based on revelation, suggest the opposite and thus overrule the unfounded claims of the *falāsifa*. What is more, these three teachings may mislead the public into disregarding the religious law (*sharīʿa*) and, therefore, are dangerous for society. In his function as a Muslim jurisprudent al-Ghazālī adds a *fatwā* at the end of his *Incoherence* and declares that everybody who teaches these three positions publicly is an unbeliever (*kāfir*) and an apostate from Islam, who can be killed.

Al-Ghazālī's efforts in dealing with the philosophical movement amount to defining the boundaries of religious tolerance in Islam. Soon after the *Incoherence*, he wrote a similar refutation about the movement of the Ismāʿīlī Shīʿa, known as the Bāṭiniyya ("those who arbitrarily follow an inner meaning in the Qur'ān"). He looks closely at their teachings and discusses which of them are merely erroneous and which are unbelief. He assumes – not entirely correctly – that the Ismāʿīlī preachers teach the existence of two gods. This dualism and the Ismāʿīlī denial of bodily resurrection in the afterlife leads to their condemnation by al-Ghazālī as unbelievers and apostates.

In his attempt to define the boundaries of Islam al-Ghazālī singles out a limited number of teachings that in his opinion overstep the borders. In a separate book al-Ghazālī clarifies that only teachings that violate certain "fundamental doctrines" (*usūl al-ʿaqāʾid*) should be deemed unbelief and apostasy. These doctrines are limited to three: monotheism, Muḥammad's prophecy, and the Qur'anic descriptions of life after death. He stresses that all other teachings, including those that are erroneous or even regarded as "religious innovation" (*bidʿa*), should be tolerated. Again other teachings may be correct, al-Ghazālī adds, and despite their philosophical background, for instance, should be accepted by the Muslim community. Each teaching must be judged by itself, and if found sound and in accordance with revelation, should be adopted. This attitude leads to a widespread application of Aristotelian teachings in al-Ghazālī's works on Muslim theology and ethics.

Al-Ghazālī's refutations of the *falāsifa* and the Ismāʿīlīs have a distinctly political component. In both cases he fears that the followers of these movements or people with only a cursory understanding of them might believe that they can disregard the religious law (*sharīʿa*). In the case of the Ismāʿīlīs there was an additional theological motive. In their religious propaganda the Ismāʿīlīs openly challenged the authority of Sunnī theology, claiming its religious speculation and its interpretation of scripture is arbitrary. The Sunnī theologians submit God's word to judgments that appear to be reasonable, the Ismāʿīlīs said, yet they are purely capricious, a fact evident from the many disputes among Sunnī theologians. No rational argument is more convincing than any of its opposing rational argument, the Ismāʿīlīs claimed, since there is equivalence among rational proofs (*takāfuʾ al-adilla*). Only the divinely guided word of the Shīʿī Imām conveys certainty. In response to this criticism al-Ghazālī points to the Aristotelian notion of demonstration (*burhān*). Sunnī theologians argue among each other, he says, because they are largely unfamiliar with the technique of demonstration. For al-Ghazālī, reason (*ʿaql*) was executed most purely and precisely by formulating arguments that are demonstrative and reach a level where their conclusions are beyond doubt. The results of true demonstrations cannot conflict with revelation, al-Ghazālī says, since neither reason nor revelation can be considered false (*khādhib*). If demonstration proves something that violates the literal meaning of revelation, the scholar must apply interpretation (*taʾwīl*) to the outward text and read it as a symbol of a deeper truth. There are, for instance, valid demonstrative arguments proving that God cannot have a "hand" or sit on a "throne." These prompt the Muslim scholar to interpret the Qurʾanic passages where these words appear as symbols. The interpretation of passages in revelation, however, whose literal meaning is not disproved by valid demonstrations, is not allowed.

In his critique of the Ismāʿīlīs and Aristotelian philosophy al-Ghazālī focuses on the epistemological question of what we truly know through demonstration (*ʿan burhān*). Against the *falāsifa*, for instance, he argues that the world's eternity in the past cannot be demonstratively proven. His critique of philosophical metaphysics aims to make room for the truth-claims of revelation. The *Incoherence of the Philosophers* is a significant milestone in the history of philosophy as it advances the nominalist critique of Aristotelian science we find later in medieval Europe, and the development of modern sciences. On the Muslim side al-Ghazālī's acceptance of demonstration led to a much more refined and precise discourse on epistemology and a flowering of Aristotelian logics. While al-Ghazālī's approach to resolving apparent contradictions between reason and revelation was accepted by almost all later Muslim theologians, not all agreed with his findings on demonstration. The philosopher Ibn Rushd (Averroes, d. 1198), for instance, composed a refutation of al-Ghazālī's *Incoherence*, which he called *Tahāfut al-tahāfut* ("The Incoherence of the Incoherence"). While accepting the principle that only a valid demonstration allows interpretation of the Qurʾān symbolically, he maintained, for instance, that the past eternity of the world can indeed be demonstrated. On the traditionalist side Ibn Taymiyya (d. 1328) criticized al-Ghazālī's argument denying the possibility that God sits on a "throne" (e.g., Qur'ān 2:255), which would allow the understanding that the throne is just a symbol for God's lordship. Since al-Ghazālī's argument fails to be demonstrative, Ibn Taymiyya said, we must conclude that God truly sits on a throne, even if we cannot say how.

Soon after al-Ghazālī had published his two refutations of *falsafa* and the Ismāʿīlīs, he left his position at the Niẓāmiyya *madrasa* in Baghdad. During this period he began writing what most Muslim scholars regard as his major work, *Iḥyāʾ ʿulūm al-dīn* (*The Revival of the Religious Sciences*). The voluminous *Revival* is a comprehensive guide to ethical behavior in the everyday life of Muslims. It is divided into four sections, each containing ten books. The first section deals with ritual practices (*ʿibādāt*), the second with social customs (*ʿādāt*), the third with those things that lead to perdition (*muhlikāt*) and hence should be avoided, and the fourth with those that lead to salvation (*munjiyāt*) and should be sought. In the 40 books of the *Revival* al-Ghazālī severely criticizes the coveting of worldly matters and reminds his readers that human life is a path towards judgment day and the reward or punishment gained through it. Compared with the eternity of the next life, this life is almost insignificant, yet it seals our fate in the world to come. In his autobiography al-Ghazālī writes that reading Ṣūfī literature made him realize that our theological convictions are by themselves irrelevant for gaining redemption in the afterlife. Not our good beliefs or intentions count. Only our good and virtuous actions will determine our life in the world to come. This insight prompted al-Ghazālī to change his lifestyle and adopt the Ṣūfī path. In the *Revival* he composed a book about human actions (*muʿāmalāt*) that wishes to steer clear of any deeper discussion of theological insights (*mukāshafāt*). Rather, it aims at guiding people towards ethical behavior that God will reward in this world and the next.

In the *Revival* al-Ghazālī attacks his colleagues in Muslim scholarship, questioning their intellectual capacities and independence as well as their commitment to gaining reward in the world to come. This increased moral consciousness brings al-Ghazālī closer to Ṣūfī attitudes, which have a profound influence on his subsequent works, such as *Mishkāt al-anwār* (*The Niche of Lights*). These later works also reveal a significant philosophical influence on al-Ghazālī. In the *Revival* he teaches an ethic that is based on the development of character traits (singular *khulq*, plural *akhlāq*). He criticizes the more traditional concept of Sunnī ethics that is limited to compliance with the ordinances of the religious law (*sharīʿa*) and following the example of the Prophet Muḥammad. Traditional Sunnī ethical thinking is closely linked to jurisprudence (*fiqh*) and limits itself, according to al-Ghazālī, to determining and teaching the rules of *sharīʿa*. Traditional Sunnī jurisprudents are mere "scholars of this world" (*ʿulamāʾ al-dunyā*) who cannot guide Muslims on the best way to gain the afterlife.

In his own ethics al-Ghazālī stresses that the Prophet – and no other teacher – should be the only person a Muslim emulates. He supplements this key Sunnī notion with the concept of "disciplining the soul" (*riyāḍat al-nafs*). At birth the essence of the human is deficient and ignoble and only strict efforts and patient treatment can lead it towards developing virtuous character traits. The human soul's temperament, for instance, becomes imbalanced through the influence of other people and needs to undergo constant disciplining (*riyāḍa*) and training (*tarbiya*) in order to keep these character traits at equilibrium. Behind this kind of ethic stands the Aristotelian notion of *entelechy*: humans have a natural potential to develop rationality and through it acquire virtuous character. Education, literature, religion, and politics should help in realizing this potential. Through the books of Muslim *falāsifa* like Miskawayh (d. 1030) and Muslim scholars like al-Rāghib al-Iṣfahānī (d. *c.* 1025), who strove to make philosophical notions compatible with Muslim religious scholarship, al-Ghazālī became acquainted with an ethics that focuses on the development of virtuous character traits. As a result he rejects the notion, for instance, that one should try to give up potentially harmful affections like anger or sexual desire. These character traits are part of human nature, al-Ghazālī teaches, and cannot be given up. Rather, disciplining the soul means controlling these potentially harmful traits through one's rationality (*ʿaql*). The human soul has to undergo constant training and needs to be disciplined similarly to a young horse that needs to be broken in, schooled, and treated well. At no point does al-Ghazālī reveal the philosophical origins of his ethics. He himself saw a close connection between the ethics of the *falāsifa* and Ṣūfī notions of an ascetic and virtuous lifestyle. In his *Revival* he merges these two ethical traditions to a successful and influential fusion. In his autobiography al-Ghazālī says that the ethics of the *falāsifa* and that of the Ṣūfīs are one and the same. In an attempt to counter accusations of having followed the *falāsifa* all too closely he adds that the philosophers have taken their ethics from the Ṣūfīs.

Despite his declared reluctance to enter into theological discussions, al-Ghazālī addresses important philosophical problems related to human actions in his *Revival*. In the 35th section called *Kitāb al-tawḥīd wa-l-tawakkul* ("Belief in Divine Unity and Trust in God") he discusses the relationship between human actions and God's omnipotence as the creator of the world. Al-Ghazālī teaches a strictly determinist position with regard to human actions. God creates and determines all events in the universe including the actions of humans. Every event in creation follows a predetermined plan that is eternally present in God's knowledge. For humans this predetermination of events manifests itself as causal connections. We witness in nature causal processes that add up to longer causal chains. God creates and controls each element in these chains. He leaves open whether God controls each element in these chains directly in an occasionalist way or whether God mediates his control through each preceding element of the causal chain. In the latter model of so-called "secondary causality" God would be the first element of all causal chains and He would control the other elements through the laws of nature that He creates. The metaphysical dispute between an occasionalist explanation of God's creative activity, or one that is based on secondary causality cannot be decided, al-Ghazālī implies, as God has not given us knowledge about the way He creates and controls His universe.

For all practical purposes it befits humans to assume that God controls everything through chains of secondary causes. Every human action, for instance, is caused by a person's volition, which is caused by a certain motive (*dāʿiya*). The person's volition and motive are, in turn, caused by the person's convictions and his or her knowledge (*ʿilm*). Human knowledge is caused by various factors, like one's experience of the world, one's knowledge of revelation, or the books one has read. It is clear, however, that there is no single event in this world that is not determined by God's will. While humans are under the impression that they have a free will, their actions are in reality pre-determined like the movements of a large water-clock. Al-Ghazālī viewed the world as a conglomerate of connections that are all pre-determined and meticulously planned in God's timeless knowledge. Nature is a process in which all elements harmoniously dovetail with one another. Celestial movements, natural processes, human actions, even redemption in the afterlife are "causally" determined. Whether we will be rewarded or punished in the afterlife can be understood, according to al-Ghazālī, as the mere causal effect of our actions in this world. All these are teachings that are very similar to those of Ibn Sīnā. Al-Ghazālī also followed Ibn Sīnā in his conviction that this universe is the best of all possible worlds and that "there is in possibility nothing more wondrous than what is" (*laysa fī l-imkān abdaʿ mimmā kān*). This led to a long-lasting debate among later Muslim theologians about what is meant by this sentence and whether al-Ghazālī is, in fact, right. It must be stressed, however, that contrary to Ibn Sīnā and other *falāsifa*, al-Ghazālī held that when God creates, He exercises a free will and chooses between alternatives. God's will is not in any way determined by God's nature. God's will is the undetermined determiner of everything in this world.

In Islamic law al-Ghazālī maintained the traditional Ashʿarite position that human rationality is mute with regard to normative judgments about human actions and cannot decide whether an action is "good" or "bad." When humans think they know, for instance, that lying is bad, their judgment is determined by a consideration of their benefits. With regard to ethical judgments on our actions we have a tendency to confuse moral value with benefit. We generally tend to assume that whatever benefits our collective interest is morally good, while whatever harms us collectively is bad. These judgments, however, are ultimately fallacious and cannot be the basis of jurisprudence (*fiqh*). "Good" actions are those that are rewarded in the afterlife and "bad" actions are those that are punished. The kind of connection between human actions and reward or punishment in the afterlife can only be learned from revelation. Muslim jurisprudence is the science that extracts general rules from revelation. Like most religious sciences it aims at advancing humans' prospect of redemption in the world to come. Therefore it must be based on the Qurʾān and the *sunna* of the Prophet while it uses logic and other rational means to extract general rules.

Al-Ghazālī was one of the first jurists who introduced the consideration of a "public benefit" (*maṣlaḥa*) into Muslim jurisprudence. In addition to developing clear guidance of how to gain redemption in the afterlife, religious law (*sharīʿa*) also aims at creating an environment that allows each individual well-being and the pursuit of a virtuous and pious lifestyle. Al-Ghazālī argues that when God revealed divine law (*sharīʿa*) He did so with the purpose (*maqṣad*) of advancing human benefits in this world *and* the next. Al-Ghazālī identifies five essential components for well-being in this world: religion, life, intellect, offspring, and property. Whatever protects these "five necessities" (*al-ḍarūriyyāt al-khamsa*) is considered public benefit (*maṣlaḥa*) and should be advanced, while whatever harms them should be avoided. The jurisprudent (*faqīh*) should aim at safeguarding these five necessities in his legal judgments. In recommending this, al-Ghazālī practically implies that a *maṣlaḥa mursala*, a public benefit that is not mentioned in the revealed text, is considered a valid source of legislation.

References and further reading

Frank, R. M. (1994) *Al-Ghazali and the Ashʿarite School*, Durham: Duke University Press.

Ghazālī, al- (1997) *The Incoherence of the Philosophers/Tahāfut al-falāsifa, a Parallel English–Arabic Text*, ed. and trans. M. E. Marmura, Provo: Brigham Young University Press.

—— (1998) *The Niche of Lights: A Parallel English–Arabic Text*, trans. D. Buchman, Provo: Brigham Young University Press.

—— (2000) *Deliverance from Error. Five Key Texts Including His Spiritual Autobiography al-Munqidh min al-Dalal*, trans. R. McCarthy, Louisville: Fons Vitae.

—— (2001) *Faith in Divine Unity and Trust in Divine Providence*, [Book 35 of *The Revival of Religious Sciences*], trans. D. Burrell, Louisville: Fons Vitae.

—— (2002) *On the Boundaries of Theological Tolerance in Islam: Abū Hāmid al-Ghāzalī's* Fayṣal al-Tafriqa bayna al-Islām wa al-Zandaqa, trans. S. A. Jackson, Karachi: Oxford University Press.

Griffel, F. (2005) "Taqlīd of the Philosophers. Al-Ghazālī's Initial Accusation In the *Tahāfut*," in S. Günther, ed., *Ideas, Images, and Methods of Portrayal. Insights into Arabic Literature and Islam*, Leiden: Brill, 253–73.

—— (forthcoming) *Al-Ghazālī's Philosophical Theology*, New York: Oxford University Press.

Hourani, G. F. (1976) "Ghazālī on the Ethics of Action," *Journal of the American Oriental Society*, 96: 69–88; reprinted in *Reason and Tradition in Islamic Ethics*, Cambridge: Cambridge University Press, 1985: 135–66.

—— (1985) *Reason and Tradition in Islamic Ethics*, Cambridge: Cambridge University Press.

Marmura, M. E. (1965) "Ghazālī and Demonstrative Science," *Journal of the History of Philosophy*, 3: 183–204; reprinted in *Probing in Islamic Philosophy*, Binghampton, NY: Global Academic Publishing, 2005: 231–60.

—— (1968–9) "Ghazālī on Ethical Premises," *The Philosophical Forum*, 4: 393–403; reprinted in *Probing in Islamic Philosophy*, Binghampton, NY: Global Academic Publishing, 2005: 261–5.

—— (2005) *Probing in Islamic Philosophy*, Binghampton, NY: Global Academic Publishing.

Opwis, F. (2007) "Islamic Law and Legal Change: The Concept of *Maṣlaḥa* in Classical and Contemporary Legal Theory," in A. Amanat, F. Griffel, eds., *Sharīʾa: Islamic Law in the Contemporary Context*, Palo Alto: Stanford University Press, 62–82, 203–7.

Ormsby, E. L. (1984) *Theodicy in Islamic Thought. The Dispute over al-Ghazâlî's "Best of All Possible Worlds"*, Princeton: Princeton University Press.

28

IBN ʿARABĪ

Sajjad H. Rizvi

Muḥyī ʾl-Dīn Muḥammad ibn ʿAlī al-ʿArabī is perhaps the most influential Ṣūfī of the medieval period and continues to inspire Ṣūfī movements in the contemporary world as well as institutions devoted to him such as the Muhyiddin Ibn ʿArabi Society in Oxford. Popularly known as Ibn ʿArabī, he is often also given the honorific of *al-Shaykh al-Akbar* (The Greatest Ṣūfī Master) because of his influence, his writings and spiritual authority for Ṣūfīs throughout the ages. His impact on Islamic intellectual history has been such that one might appropriately paraphrase A. N. Whitehead's famous saying about Plato and argue that the subsequent history of thought, metaphysics, and self-realization in Islam is a series of footnotes to Ibn ʿArabī.

Life

An Arab of the tribe of al-Ṭayy, he was born in Murcia in southern Spain in 1165 during the rule of the Almohads. His father may have been a significant courtier of the local ruler Ibn Mardanīsh (d. 1172) and, after his fall, entered the service of the Almohad sultan Abū Yaʿqūb Yūsuf (d. 1224) in Seville. He later claimed to have experienced visions as an adolescent that inspired him to the Ṣūfī path. In the hagiographical account of his meeting with the philosopher Ibn Rushd (Averroes, d. 1198), an acquaintance of his father, in 1180 in Cordoba, he is already presented as a spiritually precocious young man. The philosopher, impressed by his knowledge, embraced him and said, "Yes." The young man replied, "Yes," but seeing the resultant joy on the face of Averroes, said, "No." The philosopher's colour changed and he asked, "What kind of solution have you found through illumination and divine inspiration? Is it just the same as we receive from speculative thought?" Ibn ʿArabī replied, "Yes and no. Between the yes and the no spirits take flight from their matter and necks break away from their bodies." This highly stylized account is designed to assert the superior insight of the Ṣūfī in comparison to the philosopher at a time when Ibn ʿArabī had not yet taken a Ṣūfī guide. It also reveals his ambivalence towards philosophy: he always claimed to have mastered philosophy and in his works displayed knowledge of philosophical terms and arguments, but remained critical of the inability of rational speculation to arrive at the truth and reality of existence. Alongside his studies in jurisprudence and theology, he studied the works of Ṣūfīs such as Ibn al-ʿArīf (d. 1141) and Ibn Qaṣī (d. 1151), and began to frequent Ṣūfī masters in Seville, especially Abū ʾl-ʿAbbās al-ʿUraybī, his first master. He claimed a connection with the famous Maghribi Ṣūfī Abū Madyan (d. 1198), both through a spiritual initiation (as he never met him) and through that Ṣūfī's disciple ʿAbd al-ʿAzīz al-Mahdawī in Tunis. In his work *Rūḥ al-Quds*, he gives an account of his contacts with Ṣūfīs including two female spiritual guides, Shams of Marchena and Fāṭima of Cordoba. In the 1190s, he left Andalusia for the first time to study with Ṣūfī masters in Tunis. He continued his travels in search of knowledge and had further visions of famous Ṣūfīs and prophets. He acquired a companion ʿAbd Allāh al-Ḥabashī who would remain a disciple and scribe.

By 1200, he left Andalusia for good, partly due to the political upheavals and headed East. By this time, his fame had spread and he was met in cities like Cairo by Ṣūfīs and scholars. He may also have believed in his superior spiritual authority following a vision in 1198, when he realized that he was the seal of Muḥammadan sainthood, a rank that would place him at the head of the spiritual hierarchy in the totality of sacred space and time after the Prophet. He set out for the pilgrimage to Mecca in 1200 and spent a few years there, pivotal years that inspired his magnum opus *al-Futūḥāt al-Makkiyya* ("The Meccan Revelations"), a vast treasury of knowledge, and *Tarjumān al-ashwāq* ("Interpreter of Desires"), a set of allegorical love poems addressed to Niẓām, the daughter of his friend Abū Shujāʿ. His travels took him to Konya in 1210, which established a link later to flourish in the Mevlevī Ṣūfī order that drew upon his teachings. Finally, in 1223 on the invitation of the Ayyubid ruler al-Malik al-ʿĀdil, he settled in Damascus, where he died in 1240 and was buried in the cemetery of the Banū Zakī.

Works

Ibn ʿArabī affected the apophatic style of many Ṣūfīs and often claimed that his experiences were ineffable. Yet, perhaps as a corollary of this claim, he was extremely prolific. He wrote short treatises recounting his views, his "ascensions," and his understanding of certain key Ṣūfī texts and doctrines. However, the majority of his tradition and scholarship has focused on two texts. The first is his vast compendium *al-Futūḥāt al-Makkiyya* inspired during his first pilgrimage in 1202, the first draft of which was completed in 1231 in Damascus; the second draft was later completed and rehearsed with his disciples in the last two years of his life. An autograph copy that was preserved by his disciple Ṣadr al-Dīn Qūnawī (d. 1274) survives and is known as the "Konya manuscript" because of its provenance. The text is divided into 560 chapters hugely variant in length, arranged in six sections. The work is prefaced by an introduction that introduces the reader to the epistemological method of Ibn ʿArabī and provides insights into his hierarchy of knowledge. The first section on inspired knowledge (*maʿārif*) includes a chapter on his key notion of *al-insān al-kāmil* ("the perfect man"), chapters on the spiritual reality of Islamic worship, and a key chapter (73) on the spiritual hierarchy and sainthood (*walāya*). The second section on agency and transactions (*muʿāmalāt*) includes discussions of law, spiritual rank and station. The following section focuses on spiritual states (*aḥwāl*) and includes an ontological and spiritual commentary on the vast literature of Ṣūfī works preceding him. The fourth section describes "points of ascent" (*manāzil*) along the Ṣūfī path and includes his discussion of eschatology. The fifth section on "mutual points of encounter" (*munāzalāt*) draws on insights upon Qur'anic and other scriptural texts. The final section on spiritual stations (*maqāmāt*) includes his commentary on the

99 names of God, the return to God and a recapitulation of the whole work. The text has been studied since the thirteenth century; it does not have an extensive commentary tradition although his sixteenth-century Egyptian devotee ʿAbd al-Wahhāb al-Shaʿrānī (d. 1565) did write an influential summary entitled *al-Yawāqīt waʾl-jawāhir fī bayān ʿāqāʾid al-akābir* ("Rubies and Gems Explaining the Doctrines of the Elders").

Ibn ʿArabī's other main text has spawned a vast commentary culture. In 627/1230, he claims to have encountered the Prophet Muḥammad in Damascus who gave him a book to disseminate. This is *Fuṣūṣ al-ḥikam* ("The Ring-Settings of Wisdom"), a work divided into 27 chapters, each one on the particular wisdom associated with one of the prophets mentioned in the Qur'ān. As such it can be seen as a metaphysical commentary upon the prophetology of the Qur'ān, and even as a mystical exegesis of the Qur'ān itself.

Ideas

Reading Ibn ʿArabī can be quite taxing. He is not a systematic theologian like al-Ghazālī (d. 1111), nor a philosopher like Ibn Sīnā (Avicenna, d. 1037). Rather, writings, for him, are aids to spiritual guidance and tokens to facilitate the development of the soul towards perfection. Reading and the pursuit of knowledge thus exist within the context of the spiritually examined life seeking what is found.

Consistent with many gnostic thinkers and Neoplatonists, Ibn ʿArabī espouses a metaphysics and cosmology of the revelation of God or the One through the process of the cosmos' becoming and the desire from the cosmos to return and revert to its origins in the One. He propounds the Ṣūfī myth of creation based on the famous divine *ḥadīth*: "I was a hidden treasure and wished to be known so I created that I might be known." God was hidden but became manifest through love and desire. That creation which was an effect of that original *eros* then seeks to know itself (expressing the *ḥadīth*: "Whosoever knows his self, knows his Lord") and return to its origins through love for that hidden treasure. The function of religion, of spiritual practice and of gnosis is to facilitate the path of self-knowledge and love that reveals for the seeker the truth. The study of Ṣūfī texts and meditation upon scriptures, therefore, is the quest for grace and provides spiritual "switches" through the striking of words on the heart of the initiate to transform the self into a mirror that can truly reflect the truth. This quest must further be guided by an appropriate spiritual master. Thus, the process of seeking and finding God requires the confluence of gnosis, love and discipline.

According to Ibn ʿArabī, all that is sought and indeed found is God. The term *wujūd* that was used in the philosophical tradition to render the metaphysical notion of existence became the name for God, the Truth insofar as only He is found. In one's phenomenal experience, everything that one encounters is the face and manifestation of God; only He is found in these myriad of forms. God brings everything into existence so that He can be manifest; but nothing exists in itself, only possessing a rather annexed and derivative "image" of existence.

This is Ibn ʿArabī's famous concept of the unity of existence (*waḥdat al-wujūd*), although he himself never used the term. Modifying the Islamic declaration of faith, nothing exists except Existence/God. Consonant with Neoplatonic thinkers, he held that God is utterly transcendent, inaccessible to a communicable experience, a pure being (*al-wujūd al-muṭlaq* or *al-Ḥaqq*) that was devoid of properties. The cosmos, in contrast as a locus of attributes, multiplicities and accidents, is impoverished and completely dependent on that pure being. Only God exists really and all that we perceive as existing does so by virtue of being a self-disclosure (*tajallī*) or manifestation (*maẓhar*) of the hidden existence of God. His monism and skepticism about the reality of phenomenal experience did not entail an other-worldly rejection of life in this world, but entailed an ethics of community and moral agency of equivalence across different beings, an idea taken up by his Indian disciples later on and given the name *sulḥ-i kull* (peace to all). While the universalist intention of this doctrine is clear (since everything one experiences is ultimately the "face of God"), it does not mean that Ibn ʿArabī was a moral relativist who did not believe in the superiority of the application of the Law of Islam.

A concomitant of this doctrine is Ibn ʿArabī's influential notion of the Perfect Man (*al-insān al-kāmil*) as an ontological presence and comprehensive microcosmic reality that acts as an isthmus (*barzakh*) between God and the cosmos, since he reflects the perfection of the divine, and in his humanity is the face and hopes of all humans oriented towards God. An alternative name for this notion is the Muḥammadan Reality (*al-ḥaqīqa al-Muḥammadiyya*) since this mesocosmic property existed in the nature of the Prophet and his spiritual successors. This notion of sainthood (*walāya*) plays a pivotal role in Ibn ʿArabī's metaphysics. The quest for finding the One is mediated by the Perfect Man and by saints and reflects the manifestation of the One through grades of presence. God is manifest in the cosmos through grades of presence, in the higher intelligible world of forms (or the mind of God), at the level of the celestial beings such as angels, in the celestial spheres, and on this earth and its people. The most intense divine presence that manifests God is the Perfect Man, exemplified in the person of the Prophet Muḥammad and his spiritual successors, the saints. This hierarchy of sainthood has the role of spiritual guidance and perfection, facilitating the process by which people can realize their humanity and move towards the perfection of the Perfect Man. Ibn ʿArabī states that like prophethood, of which it is a mirror image and continuation, sainthood has a seal, indeed two seals. Just as Muḥammad was the seal of the prophets, so too are there two seals of sainthood: one is the seal of absolute sainthood encompassing all space and time and all religious dispensations, and for Ibn ʿArabī this is Jesus; and the other is the seal of Muḥammadan sainthood, of the religious dispensation of Islam, and according to his own words, that seal is Ibn ʿArabī himself. Saints guide seekers towards finding the One, lead their spiritual development through the prescription of litanies, formulae of remembrance and invocations. They intercede and mediate and even after the death of the body continue to possess spiritual authority.

The doctrine of Ibn ʿArabī may also be categorized as a metaphysics and hermeneutics of mercy. In the *Ring-Settings* in particular, he stresses the relationship between divine mercy as an essential attribute and the property of existence, and the recognition of the self in and as the other through compassion. The first act of mercy is the provision of existence through God's self-disclosure. Mercy encompasses everything (a Qur'anic maxim) even mercy itself and is the most essential of the divine attributes. As such, it is a unitary and unifying entity. It represents God's goodness, grace and favor towards all creation and especially to humans. The Qur'ān as the word of God, as an act of mercy, as a revelation of the divine speaks directly to the seeker, each particle of which is uniquely disclosing God. Just as God's mercy is all-encompassing, the gaze of the seeker turned towards Him requires a compassionate approach to His manifestations in this world. God provides mercy within each human in the formation of their primordial nature (*fiṭra*) that inclines towards perfection, towards mercy (its origin) and recognizes the token of its similitude in other human beings and ultimately in God Himself. An important implication of this is that religious and social diversities among humans are also manifestations of divine mercy, and that while the promise and threat of paradise and hellfire are acts of mercy to encourage one to seek the love of God, God in His infinite mercy cannot permit any of His creatures to languish forever in hellfire. Thus, Ibn ʿArabī argued that even figures infamous for their evil such as Pharaoh will be redeemed, and hellfire extinguished, a position for which he was severely condemned in later medieval polemics.

The school of Ibn ʿArabī

The increasingly philosophical sophistication of Ibn ʿArabī's ideas already began in the work of his disciple and stepson Ṣadr al-Dīn al-Qūnawī, who entered into a correspondence with the scientist and philosopher Naṣīr al-Dīn al-Ṭūsī (d. 1274). The legacy of Ibn ʿArabī centered on the teachings of his major works and commentaries upon them. Al-Qūnawī wrote the first commentary on the *Ring-Settings*, but it was ʿAbd al-Razzāq Kāshānī's work that began the shift to a more philosophically intuitive understanding of his teachings. This convergence of Ṣūfī metaphysics, philosophical theology and philosophy is a central feature of the later intellectual history of Islamic societies and reveals the imprint of Ibn ʿArabī on the course of Islamic thought beyond the circles of Ṣūfīs. Through the work of the Shīʿī Ṣūfī Sayyid Ḥaydar Āmulī (d. after 1385), these teachings entered and influenced Shīʿī thought and were profoundly transformed and naturalized. But perhaps the most important medieval conduit for the school was the famous Persian poet ʿAbd al-Raḥmān Jāmī (d. 1498). The poetic dissemination of the ideas of Ibn ʿArabī was especially significant in the work of the Persian poets of the Mughal–Safavid period, most notably Mīrzā Bedil (d. 1762) and Mīr Dard (d. 1785).

There was also an experiential, Ṣūfī initiatic inheritance through developing Ṣūfī orders both in the Maghrib and the Islamic East. Some Ṣūfī orders such as the Shādhiliyya in North Africa, Kubrawiyya in Iran and the Chishtiyya in India adopted whole-scale the metaphysics of Ibn ʿArabī. Because the focal idea that they preached was *waḥdat al-wujūd*, the monistic unity of existence, they became known as the *wujūdiyya*, a term used pejoratively by detractors and as a badge of honor by like-minded individuals. As the school spread, so did the polemics and attacks upon monism and the spiritual hermeneutics of the school. The metaphysics and spiritual legacy of Ibn ʿArabī was dominant in Muslim India and famous Ṣūfīs and commentators on his works, such as Shaykh Muḥammad Ghawth (d. 1563), ʿAbd al-Quddūs Gangohī (d. 1537), ʿAbd al-Raḥmān Chishtī (d. 1683) and Muḥibb Allāh Ilāhābādī (d. 1641), spread his doctrines. From Western India, and especially mediated by the works of the Persian ʿAbd al-Raḥmān Jāmī and Ibn Fażl Allāh Burhānpūrī (d. 1619), the doctrine of Ibn ʿArabī spread to the Malay world where important thinkers such as Ḥamza Fansūrī (d. 1590) and Shams al-Dīn Sumatrānī (d. 1629) were at the forefront of the *wujūdiyya*. Major commentaries continued into the nineteenth century, when Amīr ʿAbd al-Qādir, who led Algerian resistance to the French, wrote *al-Mawāqif* ("The Stops") having settled in Damascus, and arranged for the publication of the *Meccan Revelations*. The Shādhilī-Darqawī-ʿAlawī order in Algeria through the leadership of Shaykh al-ʿAlawī (d. 1934) influenced a number of Ṣūfī and perennialist groups espousing the doctrine of Ibn ʿArabī in Europe and North America, most notably the group following Frithjof Schuon (d. 1998). Even well into the late twentieth century, the Syrian Shādhilī Shaykh ʿAbd al-Raḥmān Shāghūrī (d. 2004) was teaching classes on the works of Ibn ʿArabī and transmitting his initatic *khirqa* (mantle). Similarly, the leader of the Iranian Revolution, Ayatollah Khomeini (d. 1989), wrote commentaries on the works of Ibn ʿArabī and in his famous letter to the then Soviet president, Mikael Gorbachov, urged the study of the work of the famous Andalusian. The works of Ibn ʿArabī are still being studied in the Shīʿi seminaries of Qum.

References and further reading

Works of Ibn ʿArabī

Anqa Publishing specializes in producing editions and translations of his works. See http://www.ibn-arabi.com.

Austin, R. W. J., trans. (1971) *Sufis of Andalusia: The Rūḥ al-quds and al-Durrah al-Fākhirah*, London: George, Allen & Unwin.

——, trans. (1981) *The Bezels of Wisdom [Fuṣūṣ al-Ḥikam]*, New York: Paulist Press. (Another recent translation is *Ringstones of Wisdom*, trans. C. Dagli, Chicago: Kazi Publications, 2004. An older, partial translation is T. Burckhardt, *Ibn ʿArabī: The Wisdom of the Prophets*, trans. A. Culme-Seymour, Gloucester: Beshara Publications, 1975. Another translation based on the Ottoman translation and commentary of ʿAbd Allāh Bosnevī (d. 1644) is Bulent Rauf, trans., *Fusus al-Hikam*, 4 vols., Oxford: Muhyiddin Ibn ʿArabi Society, 1986.)

Beneito, P., Twinch, C., trans. (2001) *Contemplation of the Holy Mysteries [Mashāhid al-asrār al-qudsiyya]*, Oxford: Anqa Publishing.

Chodkiewicz, M., Chittick, W. and Morris, J. W., trans. (2002–4) *Ibn al-ʿArabī: The Meccan Revelations*, 2 vols., New York: Pir Press. (These two volumes contain selections from *al-Futūḥāt al-Makkiyya*.)

Nicholson, R., trans. (1978) *The Turjuman al-ashwaq: A Collection of Mystical Odes by Muhyi'ddin ibn al-ʿArabi*, London: Theosophical Publishing House.

Sells, M. A., trans. (2000) *Stations of Desire: Love Elegies from Ibn ʿArabī*, Jerusalem: Ibis. (Translations of sections are also available on the website of the Muhyiddin Ibn ʿArabi Society http://www.ibnarabisociety.org.)

Winkel, E., trans. (1995) *Mysteries of Purity=Asrār al-ṭahārah*, Notre Dame: Cross Cultural Publications.

Studies on Ibn ʿArabī and his school

Al-Attas, S. N. (1970) *The Mysticism of Hamzah Fansuri*, Kuala Lumpur: University of Malaya Press. (A pioneering study of the *wujūdiyya* in the Malay world.)

Addas, C. (1993) *The Quest for the Red Sulphur*, trans. P. Kingsley, Cambridge: The Islamic Texts Society. (The definitive biography.)

—— (2001) *Ibn ʿArabī: The Voyage of No Return*, Cambridge: The Islamic Texts Society. (A brief, selective but excellent introduction.)

Almond, I. (2004) *Sufism and Deconstruction: A Comparative Analysis of Derrida and Ibn ʿArabi*, London: Routledge. (A creative attempt to bring Ibn ʿArabī to the attention of postmodernism akin to John Caputo's studies of Meister Eckhart.)
Bashier, S. (2004) *Ibn ʿArabī's Barzakh: the Concept of the Limit and the Relationship between God and the World*, Albany: State University of New York Press. (An interesting study of a key doctrine that locates the doctrine within the history of Platonic philosophy.)
Chittick, W. C. (1989) *The Sufi Path of Knowledge: Ibn al-ʿArabī's Metaphysics of Imagination*, Albany: State University of New York Press. (A magisterial study based on extensive translations from *al-Futūḥāt al-Makkiyya*.)
—— (1994) *Imaginal Worlds: Ibn al-ʿArabī and the Problem of Religious Diversity*, Albany: State University of New York Press. (An effective and perennialist deployment of Ibn ʿArabī to argue for religious pluralism.)
—— (1998) *The Self-disclosure of God: Principles of Ibn al-ʿArabī's Cosmology*, Albany: State University of New York Press. (The second volume in his study of *al-Fuṭūḥāt al-Makkiyya*.)
—— (2005) *Ibn ʿArabi*, Makers of the Muslim World, Oxford: Oneworld. (An authoritative yet brief introduction.)
Chodkiewicz, M. (1993a) *An Ocean without Shore: Ibn ʿArabī, the Book, and the Law*, trans. D. Streight, Albany: State University of New York Press. (An important assessment of Ibn ʿArabī's relation to traditional and jurisprudential learning in Islam.)
—— (1993b) *The Seal of Saints: Prophethood and Sainthood in the Doctrine of Ibn ʿArabī*, trans. L. Sherrard, Cambridge: The Islamic Texts Society. (Perhaps the best introduction to this key part of Ibn ʿArabī's metaphysics.)
—— (1995) *The Spiritual Writings of Amir ʿAbd al-Kader*, Albany: State University of New York Press. (An introduction and selection of *al-Mawāqif*.)
Corbin, H. (1969) *Creative Imagination in the Ṣūfism of Ibn ʿArabī*, trans. R. Manheim, Princeton: Princeton University Press. (A pioneering and controversial study of the role of the "imaginal.")
Cornell, V. J. (1996) *The Way of Abū Madyan*, Cambridge: The Islamic Texts Society. (Edition, study and translation of the works of this famous Ṣūfī who influenced Ibn ʿArabī.)
Elmore, G. T. (2000) *Islamic Sainthood in the Fullness of Time: Ibn al-ʿArabī's "Book of the Fabulous Gryphon"*, Leiden: Brill. (An excellent study of sainthood which includes an annotated translation of *ʿAnqāʾ mughrib*.)
Hirtenstein, S. (1999) *The Unlimited Mercifier*, Oxford: Anqa Publishing. (An accessible introduction that is aimed at Ṣūfīs and those seeking spiritual guidance.)
Izutsu, T. (1983) *Sufism and Taoism*, Berkeley: University of California Press. (A philosophically sophisticated, comparative study that reads Ibn ʿArabī through the prism of his commentators.)
Knysh, A. (1992) "ʿIrfan Revisited: Khomeini and the Legacy of Islamic Mystical Philosophy," *Middle East Journal*, 46: 631–53.
—— (1999) *Ibn ʿArabī in the Later Islamic Tradition: The Making of a Polemical Image*, Albany: State University of New York Press. (An important study of the polemics around the image, life and ideas of Ibn ʿArabī.)
Morris, J. W. (1981) *The Wisdom of the Throne*, Princeton: Princeton University Press. (An important work that demonstrates the relationship between Ibn ʿArabī and Mullā Ṣadrā (d. *c.* 1640) and includes a translation of the latter's *al-Ḥikma al-ʿArshiyya*.)
Murata, S. (1992) *The Tao of Islam: A Sourcebook on Gender Relationships in Islamic Thought*, Albany: State University of New York Press. (Deploying the school of Ibn ʿArabī for a creative approach to the question of gender in Islam.)
Nettler, R. (2003) *Sufi Metaphysics and Qurʾanic Prophets: Ibn ʿArabī's Thought and Method in Fuṣūṣ al-Ḥikam*, Cambridge: The Islamic Texts Society. (Stresses the Qur'anic nature of Ibn ʿArabī's thought.)

Rizvi, S. H. (2005) "Mysticism and Philosophy: Ibn ʿArabī and Mullā Ṣadrā," in R. Taylor, P. Adamson, eds., *The Cambridge Companion to Arabic Philosophy*, Cambridge: Cambridge University Press, 224–46.

Sells, M. A. (1994) *Mystical Languages of Unsaying*, Chicago: University of Chicago Press. (A study of apophatic mystical theology comparing Plotinus, Eriugena, Ibn ʿArabī, Marguerite Porete and Meister Eckhart.)

Shah-Kazemi, R. (2006) *Paths to Transcendence: According to Shankara, Ibn ʿArabī, and Meister Eckhart*, Bloomington: World Wisdom.

Takeshita, M. (1987) *Ibn al-Arabī's Theory of the Perfect Man and its Place in the History of Islamic Thought*, Tokyo: Institute for the Study of the Languages and Cultures of Asia and Africa.

Winkel, E. (1997) *Islam and the Living Law: the Ibn al-ʿArabī Approach*, Karachi: Oxford University Press. (Another work that examines Ibn ʿArabī's relationship to Islamic law.)

29

IBN TAYMIYYA

David Waines

Taqī al-Dīn Aḥmad ibn Taymiyya was born on January 22, 1263 (10 Rabīʿ I 661 AH) and lived in troubled times. The Mongol invasions of the eastern Islamic world beginning in 1220 left in their wake widespread devastation and the destruction of numerous cities. Among them, Baghdad was destroyed in 1258 sweeping away the vestiges of 500 years' rule of the Sunnī Abbasid Caliphate. Mongol incursions into Syria forced Ibn Taymiyya, aged six, to leave with his family from their home in Harran to Damascus. Syria together with Egypt had, from 1250, come under the control of a military oligarchy of Turks known as the Baḥrī Mamluks. They were of slave origin (*mamlūk*), converted to Islam and trained in the military arts. Although a Mongol threat remained until the end of the century – Damascus and Jerusalem were briefly occupied in 1300 – Mamluk power checked any decisive Mongol advance further westward. The well-known Muslim historian, Ibn al-Athīr (d. 1233) recorded his thoughts on this catastrophe in the final volume of his universal history. No greater calamity, he says, had befallen the world since God created Adam, not even Nebuchadnezzar's sacking of Jerusalem and his slaying of the Jews; nor had the great Alexander conquered the world so swiftly. Possibly, he concludes, its like will not be witnessed again until the end of time when the destructive forces of Gog and Magog are unleashed upon the world. In addition to his concern for Mongol matters, Ibn al-Athīr frequently mentions events in Syria, Palestine and Egypt during the Muslims' long struggle against the Crusader states founded by Christian invaders from northern Europe. While neither Damascus nor Cairo ever passed into Crusader hands the "sacred house," Jerusalem, fell to them in 1099 and was only recovered by the famous Muslim military leader Ṣalāḥ al-Dīn (Saladin) in 1187. Later, for a brief decade and a half, Jerusalem was again under Crusader control until 1244. It was not until 1291 that the final Frankish stronghold of Acre on the Syrian coast was recovered by Mamluk forces. The Crusader state of Cyprus, however, survived for many decades as a potential base for launching attacks along the Egyptian and Syrian coasts.

Christian Crusader armies and animist Mongol warrior nomads on Damascus's doorstep were constant factors well into Ibn Taymiyya's middle years. The very Mongol mission that appeared bent upon world domination had itself left Christian Europe in shock by extending its sway over large parts of Russia into Hungary and Poland. Then, the moment of danger diminished. In European eyes the Mongol menace turned gradually into the prospect of becoming Europe's ally against the common enemy, Islam. Embassies were exchanged between Mongol leaders and Christian kings and Popes proposing an alliance of arms. Plans for new crusades were drawn up amidst widespread Christian expectation that, despite recent experience, Islam was nearing extinction. While Christian hopes remained alive even when plans or predictions failed to materialize, the dual Christian–Mongol threat never entirely receded from the thoughts of the early fourteenth-century inhabitants of Damascus.

Ibn Taymiyya had a conventional upbringing and education in Damascus befitting one belonging to a family of religious scholars. An uncle and grandfather had both been well-known adherents of the Ḥanbalī school of law, while a cousin had written a celebrated collection of sermons. Two brothers also became scholars. His father, with whom the young Aḥmad studied religious law, was head of a college, a position to which, upon his father's death, Ibn Taymiyya succeeded at the age of 21 in 1284. A year later his training also as a theologian led him to conduct classes in Qur'anic exegesis at the famous Umayyad mosque. In 1296 he joined as a teacher the oldest Ḥanbalī institution in the city. By this time he had written two works. One dealt with a number of ritual acts, not sanctioned by religious tradition, which he witnessed while performing the pilgrimage to Mecca and censured in his subsequent book. Next, an involvement in a public controversy in 1294 was the prelude to another work. A native Syrian Christian had been accused of insulting the Prophet Muḥammad, a capital offence in Islamic law. Ibn Taymiyya led a protest and brought the incident to the Mamluk governor's attention. Following a serious affray caused by the crowd accompanying Ibn Taymiyya, the governor ordered him seized and kept under close guard. Eventually, both the Christian and Ibn Taymiyya were released. His study dealt with the gravity of reviling God's messenger, not only for Christians and Jews but for imprudent Muslims as well.

The latter episode illustrates that Ibn Taymiyya was no mere ivory tower scholar. The subjects he wrote about frequently issued from his active engagement in what he perceived were major socio-political, religious concerns of his day, whether the problems originated from within the Muslim community, or from some external danger. Between 1300 and 1303, as Damascus was threatened again by Mongols, Ibn Taymiyya helped rally the city's resistance. He exhorted the people to undertake *jihād* against the infidel, and was present on one occasion of a Mamluk victory over them. He met with a Mongol general and successfully secured the release of prisoners, Muslim and Christian. Also in 1300, he joined a Mamluk expedition against Shī'ī Muslims in the mountains of Lebanon who were accused of assisting both Crusaders and Mongols; he set out on another campaign against them in 1305. In this same period, together with some followers, Ibn Taymiyya entered the wine market and smashed the jars, empty or full, and applied the punishment allowed by the religious law. He also attacked members of a Ṣūfī order in Damascus whose head was suspected of Mongol sympathies and whose ritual practices he declared breached the norms of the religious law. Again with armed companions he set upon followers of the Muslim philosopher-mystic, Ibn ʿArabī, who had died in the city in 1240.

Activism and forthright denunciation of "un-Islamic" practices and beliefs that Ibn Taymiyya witnessed around him ultimately came at a price. Apart from the incident of 1294 already mentioned, he spent six years in prison on separate occasions, the last of which ended in his death in 1328 at the age of 65. At the first of these trials, a council of religious judges and scholars was convoked in 1306 on the Sultan's orders in Cairo issued to the Mamluk authorities in Damascus. Ibn Taymiyya was questioned particularly on his theological doctrines rather than upon any specific activities. Several of the council were unsympathetic to his traditionalist approach to theology. Ibn Taymiyya based his views firmly upon a literal understanding of both the Qur'ān and the exemplary life of the Prophet Muḥammad (*sunna*) together with the teachings of the community's early notables known as the *salaf* or pious ancestors. Instead, his opponents supported rational speculation in theology arguing especially for allegorical interpretation of the sacred sources of the Qur'ān and *sunna*. Thus, for example, Ibn Taymiyya held that God's description of himself in the Qur'ān such as his possessing hands (Qur'ān 3:73) or eyes (Qur'ān 20:39) is to be accepted "without asking how" this could be so. Opponents, on the other hand, interpreted these same attributes figuratively to mean God's omnipotence and omniscience. They also argued that unless allegory was employed to explain such terms, literalism almost invariably led to a dangerous anthropomorphism, as the Qur'ān itself says of God (Qur'ān 42:11) "There is nothing like him" in the created world, including humans. Ibn Taymiyya accepted this description but without subscribing to a crude literalism. "Without asking how" of the divine attributes, he rejoined, simply did not commit him to any of his opponent's views. Moreover, he was able to address the thorny problem of God's immanence or transcendence, steering a position mid-way between his opponents' support of one or the other position. Ibn Taymiyya argued that God was transcendent in the sense that no likeness to him existed in his own creation; but God was also immanent in the sense that believers could conjure associations *in their minds* between the attributes (hands, face, eyes) of created humans and the same attributes claimed for an uncreated God even though the corresponding abstractions, humanity and divinity, do not concretely exist in the real world. An illustration might be that we can directly experience animals like a rabbit or horse but the abstract concept "animal" exists only in the mind. The trial hearings ended in vindication of Ibn Taymiyya's theological views, the council members in general being impressed by his knowledge and defense skills, if not fully accepting his theology in detail. A contemporary historian likened Ibn Taymiyya and his antagonists to "an ocean beside a tiny stream."

The trial, however, did not end Ibn Taymiyya's troubles with the state. The governor of Damascus had tried to prevent his discussing theological issues on pain of confiscation of his property and goods. Then the Sultan summoned to Cairo both Ibn Taymiyya and his main opponent the chief judge of Damascus, Ibn Ṣaṣarī, to hear their respective arguments. A new council of hearings condemned Ibn Taymiyya's views and he was imprisoned along with his two brothers who had accompanied him. Ibn Ṣaṣarī returned to Damascus and tried to force Ibn Taymiyya's followers to repudiate their master's views while similar actions were taken against Ḥanbalīs in Cairo. Following several vain attempts to get Ibn Taymiyya to renounce his own views, he was released after more than a year in prison but restrained from returning to Damascus. Brief periods of freedom and detention followed until he was "exiled" to Alexandria where he was lodged in a tower of the Sultan's palace overlooking the sea. The eight months of his stay were intellectually productive as he could write, receive visitors and teach. Recalled to Cairo in 1310, he remained there until his return to Damascus four years later in 1313 where he remained until his death.

The relations between the Mamluk authorities and Ibn Taymiyya and his Ḥanbalī followers remained as ambivalent and uneasy as ever. The state welcomed his support in the face of Mongol and Crusader threats. But Ibn Taymiyya saw these crises as divine punishment for Muslims' weak faith, low morals and neglect of the religious law (*sharīʿa*). This produced suspicion towards "old" Muslims judged corrupt in belief and practice that may have cast doubt, too, upon the legitimacy of the Mamluk elite, who were themselves of recent non-Muslim origin. True, the Mamluks were great patrons of religious institutions such as mosques and colleges, guardians of the holy cities of Mecca, Medina, including Jerusalem, protectors of the revived caliphate in Cairo, sponsors of the four Sunnī legal schools, and champions of the struggle against the enemies of Islam. Ibn Taymiyya's style of reformism, however, held those in power responsible in their sphere of influence just as he – a scholar – was in his own. In a work on the relation between religion and the state, he characteristically cited a Qur'anic verse as guidance for the state's mission: "God commands you to judge between people with justice . . . O you who believe, obey God and his Messenger and those in authority among you; if you are in dispute over any matter, refer it to God and the Messenger if you truly believe" (Qur'ān 4:58–9). His own role as an independent religious scholar and critic was the same as the state's, "to command the good and prohibit evil." Hence in "advice" offered to the Mamluk authorities, he felt bound to criticize groups and individuals in the Sultan's entourage who, he judged, adhered to false beliefs and practices, chiefly certain Ṣūfīs known for their bizarre rituals or philosophical mystical beliefs.

The last 15 years of Ibn Taymiyya's life in Damascus were very productive. He wrote lengthy polemics against "heretical" Shīʿī Muslims and Christians as well as the above cited short work on religion and the state. He continued also to teach and deliver legal opinions (*fatāwā*, singular, *fatwā*) on issues he felt should be of public interest. It was these issues rather than the more arcane theological debates confined to religious scholars that now disturbed the Mamluk authorities. On two matters in particular, the manner of a husband's repudiation of his wife and the intention behind visitation to the graves of prophets or holy men, Ibn Taymiyya's legal views clashed with those of the state authorities. Ibn Taymiyya was twice imprisoned over these concerns, for five months in 1320–1, and then for just over two years prior to his death in 1328. His funeral procession, like that of his pious mother known as Sitt al-Munʿim who had died in 1316, was a major public event.

Ibn Taymiyya's reform program and activism had been constant features throughout his life and thought. Various sectors of the religious establishment had endured, at one time or another, the sting of his criticism. In general terms, he charged many with a lack of moral leadership and self-serving arrogance. With the specific works of mystical philosophers or speculative theologians in mind, however, Ibn Taymiyya was at pains to note that inasmuch as their systems of thought contained error, they also contained elements of truth and this entailed that their views be taken seriously. The standard by which all opponents were judged was the view of God as Creator of the entire cosmos and therefore existentially distinct from it, and as Commander of the moral code believers must adhere to, following what God loved and avoiding what he hated. The code was known from the Qur'ān, the Prophet's *sunna* and the pious ancestors (*salaf*).

Among Ibn Taymiyya's chief adversaries were the followers of Ibn ʿArabī's mystical philosophy. His position was judged dangerous because it blurred the distinction between the existence of the Creator and creation, and led to the view that absolute divine existence is inherent in all empirical things; the view, described as monism, denied both God's self sufficiency and independence over against the cosmos and the crucial distinction between deity and man. Thus, Ibn Taymiyya charged, God "assumes the attributes of deficiency and imperfection" shared by all creatures however lowly. Conversely, these Ṣūfīs claim to attain the status of equality with or even superiority to the prophets, leading such persons, in their implied rejection of the teachings of God's earlier messengers, to declare the irrelevance of the *sharīʿa* for themselves. In Ibn Taymiyya's view, this led eventually to the corruption of society. On the other hand, he conceded that Ibn ʿArabī himself had instructed many how to acquire high morals and devotional acts along the path and from whose teachings they had greatly benefited even if they failed to grasp its dangerous subtleties. Recognizing that mystical experience is by its nature ambiguous, inspired either by God or the devil, Ibn Taymiyya called true Ṣūfīs "the people of uprightness" because they lived according to the religious law and fulfilled its ethical challenge embodied in the Qur'ān and *sunna*. Nonetheless, Ibn Taymiyya was appalled at many popular Ṣūfī practices not sanctioned by the law. He campaigned and wrote against them as innovations of the devil. These included pilgrimage to tombs of holy persons or even prophets that demeans the uniqueness of the annual pilgrimage to Mecca; seeking intercession of the dead that contravenes the Qur'anic declaration that only the Prophet Muḥammad may intercede between God and believer, and then only on judgment day. Stories of miracles attributed to holy persons are fraudulent as a true miracle is wrought only by God through a prophet.

Ibn Taymiyya's other major targets were "heretical" Shīʿī Muslims and Christians. Against each community he wrote several pieces but also a single substantial treatise in response to existing works, one by the prominent contemporary Shīʿī scholar, Ibn al-Muṭahhar al-ʿAllāma al-Hillī (d. 1325) and another by the twelfth-century Christian Bishop, Paul of Antioch. The Shīʿa share many of the criticisms that Ibn Taymiyya levels against Christians. Indeed, he sees them as collaborators of the Christian Crusaders and Mongol pagans. But at the heart of his objection to the Shīʿa is their dismissal of the early Muslim leadership, with the exception of ʿAlī, the Prophet's cousin and son-in-law, as apostates and therefore worse than Jews or Christians in their unbelief. ʿAlī, however, is held to be the first in a line of religious leaders or Imāms who guided the so-called "party of ʿAlī," or *Shīʿat ʿAlī* owing to their infallible access to the true meaning of the Qur'ān. From Ibn Taymiyya's viewpoint, the Shīʿa had, in effect, declared the pious ancestors (*salaf*) as unbelievers. The claim to the Imāms' infallibility and their freedom from sin elevated their status above that of the prophets; moreover, this seemed to admit a kind of divine incarnation, a parallel error committed in the Christian doctrine of Jesus. In both cases, the error is the gravest: the idolatrous worship of a lord other than the unique God. Another Christian error was belief in the trinity as their understanding of a triune god had been traditionally understood by Muslim scholars, including Ibn Taymiyya, as a doctrine of tri-theism. Popular Christian practices or festivals like the celebration of Jesus' birth were enjoyed or imitated by Muslims and condemned by Ibn Taymiyya as innovations not sanctioned in the *sharīʿa*. Finally, Ibn Taymiyya reiterates a longstanding Muslim charge against Christians (and by implication Jews as well) that passages in their scriptures foretelling the coming of the Prophet Muḥammad had been misinterpreted, distorted or removed altogether by their scholars.

Contemporary sources agree that Ibn Taymiyya was one of the most accomplished jurists and theologians of his generation; his influence is evident not only among Ḥanbalī but also Shāfiʿī scholars well into the fourteen century. His influence is claimed to have even reached ruling Muslim circles in India. The precise nature of his later impact upon the eighteenth-century Arab reformer Muḥammad ibn ʿAbd al-Wahhāb (d. 1792) remains to be determined. However, the thesis that Ibn Taymiyya (as proposed by some modern Western scholars) is the twentieth-century's "father of the Islamic revolution," is greatly exaggerated. The argument proposes a seamless transition from the medieval to modern periods without close examination of major discontinuities brought about by Muslims' encounter with modernity; moreover, it buttresses the view that the Islamic tradition from its origins has been inherently violent. What is more clearly the case is that Ibn Taymiyya would have been at a loss to understand many claims of modern political Islamists, whether expressed in his name or not.

References and further reading

Al-Matroudi, A. H. (2006) *The Hanbali School of Law and Ibn Taymiyyah: Conflict or Conciliation*, London: Routledge.

Farrukh, O., trans. (1966) *Ibn Taimiyah on Public and Private Law in Islam or Public Policy in Islamic Jurisprudence*, Beirut: Khayats.

Hallaq, W., trans. (1993) *Ibn Taymiyyah against the Greek Logicians*, Oxford: Oxford University Press.

Holland, M., trans. (1985) *Ibn Taymiya, Public Duties in Islam: The Institution of the Hisba*, Leicester: The Islamic Foundation.

Jackson, S. (1994) "Ibn Taymiyyah on Trial in Damascus," *Journal of Semitic Studies*, 39: 41–85.

Khan, Q. (1973) *The Political Thought of Ibn Taymiyah*, Islamabad: Islamic Research Institute.

Little, D. (1975) "Did Ibn Taymiyya have a Screw Loose?" *Studia Islamica*, 41: 93–111.

Makari, V. E. (1983) *Ibn Taymiyyah's Ethics: the Social Factor*, Chico, CA: Scholars Press.

Michel, T., trans. (1984) *A Muslim Theologian's Response to Christianity: Ibn Taymiyya's al-Jawab al-Sahih*, New York: Caravan Books.

Swartz, M. (1973) "A Seventh Century (A.H.) Sunni creed: The Aqida Wasita of Ibn Taymiya," *Humaniora Islamica*, 1: 91–131.

30

NĀṢIR AL-DĪN AL-ṬŪSĪ

Zayn Kassam

Abū Jaʿfar Muḥammad Nāṣir al-Dīn al-Ṭūsī, mathematician, astronomer, philosopher, theologian, honored with titles such as *al-Muʿallim al-thālith* (the "third teacher" after Aristotle and al-Fārābī), *Khwāja* ("distinguished" or "learned" scholar), *Ustādh al-bashar* ("teacher of humankind"), was born on February 17, 1201, in Tus near Mashhad in present-day Iran, and died in Baghdad, Iraq, on June 25, 1274. A prolific scholar, he is rightly reckoned to have been one of the most important thinkers of the thirteenth century. His early education comprised of studies in Arabic, the Qurʾān, *ḥadīth*, and in jurisprudence according to the Twelver Shīʿī school. His father, a well-respected jurist, encouraged al-Ṭūsī to educate himself more broadly in the sciences, philosophy, and other doctrinal positions, and so he journeyed to Nishapur, where he studied mathematics, the natural sciences, and the medical and philosophical works of Ibn Sīnā (Avicenna, d. 1037) under teachers who themselves had studied with the celebrated scholar Fakhr al-Dīn al-Rāzī (d. 1209). Al-Ṭūsī went on to study jurisprudence in Iraq, and proceeded thence to Mawsil to study with the mathematician and astronomer, Kamāl al-Dīn ibn Yūnus (d. 1242).

After completing his studies in 1233, al-Ṭūsī moved to Quhistan, where it is reported he became an Ismāʿīlī Shīʿī Muslim after studying the writings of an Ismāʿīlī Imām, Ḥasan ʿAlā Dhikrihi al-Salām (d. 1166). Scholars debate whether he became an Ismāʿīlī by persuasion or for reasons of patronage. It was here that he penned his works on ethics; for instance, one titled *Akhlāq-i Muḥtashamī*, based on the notes of his Ismāʿīlī patron, the governor of Quhistan, Muḥtasham Nāṣir al-Dīn ʿAbd al-Raḥīm, and a more well-known work, *Akhlāq-i Nāṣirī* (*The Nasirean Ethics*), also named after his patron. The *Akhlāq-i Muḥtashamī* is a work of practical ethics, and consists of 40 chapters that deal with virtues worthy of cultivation and emulation. The work draws upon the Qurʾān, *ḥadīth*, and the writings and sayings of poets, mystics, philosophers and Ismāʿīlī thinkers for its lessons. It is considered to be a work intended as a guide for teachers, and espouses an Ismāʿīlī ethos, with chapters devoted to the Imamate. *The Nasirean Ethics*, a work on political philosophy, is much more philosophical in tenor and for its first part draws upon the work of Miskawayh (d. 1030) on ethics, *Tahdhīb al-akhlāq*, which itself relied on Aristotle's *Nicomachean Ethics* and includes Platonic and Neoplatonic ideas. In addition, for the second part, which deals with domestic economy and political economy, al-Ṭūsī relied on works by al-Fārābī (d. 950) and Ibn Sīnā in addition to *al-Ḥikma al-khālida* of Miskawayh. *The Nasirean Ethics* was completed in 1245. Al-Ṭūsī reissued this work 20 years later, excising the dedication to his patron and also rewriting portions to remove the Ismāʿīlī cast of the work. This latter version has been translated, with an introduction, by G. M. Wickens (1964).

In 1246, after the completion of the original version of *The Nasirean Ethics*, al-Ṭūsī wrote an autobiography titled *Sayr wa sulūk* describing his spiritual journey. In this work, he describes his birth and education among "people who were believers in, and followers of, the exoteric aspects of the religious law (*sharīʿa*)" (al-Ṭūsī 1998: 26). However, an uncle who was a student of Ismāʿīlī thought and doctrine encouraged him to study all the branches of knowledge and hear the opinions of all the sects and branches of Islam. His teacher of mathematics similarly exhorted him to seek the truth, leading him to take up the study of theology (*kalām*) and philosophy (*ḥikma*). The former led him to make a distinction between those who believed truth can be found through human reasoning (*naẓar*) and those who saw the need for a wise and truthful instructor (*muʿallim-i ṣādiq*), that is, the need for instruction (*taʿlīm*). He was much more appreciative of the study of philosophy, but there, too, felt that the intellect (*ʿaql*) alone was incapable of encompassing the giver of intellect (*wāhib-i ʿaql*). Drawing upon the Aristotelian dictum that something cannot change from the state of potentiality to an actualized state without being affected by something that is itself actualized, he was led to conclude that the instruction (*taʿlīm*) of an already perfected (*mukammil*) teacher (*muʿallim*) was necessary in order to attain perfection and true knowledge. Journeying to Khurasan, he came across a copy of the *Fuṣūl-i muqaddas* of the Ismāʿīlī Imām ʿAlā Dhikrihi al-Salām (d. 1166). Al-Ṭūsī reports in his autobiography that reading and studying this work led to the unveiling of his inner sight, and he was then set on a course to enter the Ismāʿīlī *jamāʿa* (mosque) and receive instruction. In the rest of the autobiography, he works out the philosophical underpinnings of the Ismāʿīlī theory of Imamate, found in greater detail in a work he penned several years later at Alamut, titled *Rawḍat al-taslīm*. Although scholars have debated whether al-Ṭūsī became an Ismāʿīlī through persuasion or in search of a patron, the autobiography seems to attest to a genuine search for truth and wisdom, and seems indeed to be a request for direct instruction from the Ismāʿīlī Imām, then located at Alamut. It is no wonder, then, that later in 1246 al-Ṭūsī is to be found at Alamut, one of the key fortresses of the Ismāʿīlīs, where he remained in addition to another Ismāʿīlī fortress, Maymūn Dizh, for the next ten years.

Utilizing the rich resources of the libraries there, al-Ṭūsī was able to develop both his scientific and philosophical leanings. At Alamut he wrote his most important Ismāʿīlī philosophical work *Rawḍat al-taslīm yā taṣawwurāt* ("The Paradise of Submission"). In this work, the Ismāʿīlī conception of the role of the Prophet and the Imām in educating the human soul through revelation and interpretation is conceptualized in Greek philosophical terms drawn in part from Aristotelian and Neoplatonic cosmology. Comprising 28 chapters, the work proceeds from a discussion of the creation of the cosmos to the role of the Prophet and the Imām within it as agents of perfection and beatitude. Falling within the category of Muslim philosophical works that continue the tradition of harmonizing Greek philosophical ideas with revelation, this work contains several interpretations of Muslim ritual and ethical practices for the followers of the Imām cast within their larger ontological and epistemological significance. In addition to this work, S. J. Badakhchani (1989) identifies four other works that he considers Ismāʿīlī in character: *Āghāz wa anjam* ("The

Beginning and the End"), also known as *Tadhkira*, a work that deals with eschatology; *Tawallā wa tabarrā* ("Solidarity and Dissociation"), an ethical work which deals with the path to spiritual perfection; *Maṭlūb al-mu'minīn* ("Provisions for the Faithful"), a short work of four chapters dealing with eschatology, the marks of the faithful, the doctrine of love for the Imām, and the proper interpretation of religious rites; other works noted by Badakhchani appear not to have survived in their Ismāʿīlī form or to have been misattributed to others.

In 1255 al-Ṭūsī was sent as an emissary to the Mongol Khan Hülegü who was about to begin his conquest of Iran; upon his return, al-Ṭūsī advised the Ismāʿīlī Imām Rukn al-Dīn Khurshāh to submit to the Mongols. The advice was to no avail as the Mongols conquered Alamut in 1256, and proceeded to conquer Baghdad in 1258, vanquishing the Abbasid caliphate. It remains unclear whether al-Ṭūsī was a traitor to the Ismāʿīlī cause or whether, thanks to him, he was able to save some volumes of the library at Alamut before it was destroyed by the Mongols, and play a role in the Mongol sparing of many Shīʿī holy places. In any case, he was taken into Hülegü's confidence as his astrologer and astronomer, made responsible for overseeing religious endowments and given several key financial responsibilities.

In 1259, al-Ṭūsī convinced Hülegü to endow the construction of an observatory and its instruments at Maragha, in Azerbaijan, where a rich library was established from the spoils collected by Hülegü. Al-Ṭūsi was able to establish a scientific school there, drawing together scholars of note including scholars from as far away as China, and making it a prestigious institution for scientific learning. As its leading scholar, among al-Ṭūsī's many accomplishments was the preparation of the astronomical tables for which he is known and which remained in use for several centuries, *al-Zīj al-Īlkhānī*, which he completed at the age of 70, shortly before his death. He invented several instruments including astrolabes and others in use at the observatory.

Al-Ṭūsi was clearly one of the most important and prolific scholars of his time. An author of over 150 works, he wrote in both Arabic and Persian, on astronomy, mathematics, philosophy, theology, and mysticism. He re-edited and wrote illuminating commentaries on several Greek and early Muslim scientific works, including those by Euclid, Ptolemy, Theodosius, Aristarchus, Archimedes, Menelaus, Thābit ibn Qurra, among others. These commentaries along with his recensions entered the curriculum of books to be studied for those seeking to master the Greek sciences. As a mathematician, his work titled *al-Shakl al-qaṭṭāʿ* set trigonometry as a discipline apart from astronomy, and is credited with pioneering spherical trigonometry, showing how to solve any kind of spherical triangle. He also wrote on binomial coefficients, later introduced by Pascal. His attempt at his own proof of Euclid's fifth postulate (in a work whose title may be translated as *Discussion Which Removes Doubt about Parallel Lines*) laid the groundwork for his son Ṣadr al-Dīn's work, which, after it was published in Europe in 1594, ultimately became the starting point in Europe for the discovery of non-Euclidean geometry. Famed for his astronomical works, al-Ṭūsī wrote treatises on practical astronomy, instruments, cosmography, and planetary theory, and identified problems with Ptolemy's models on mechanical principles. Dissatisfied with the Ptolemaic planetary model, al-Ṭūsī began work on a new model that was completed by his student Quṭb al-Dīn al-Shīrāzī. The device, named the "al-Ṭūsī couple" by E. S. Kennedy, the American historian of Islamic mathematics, which consists of two spheres rotating at different speeds and in opposite directions, was created by al-Ṭūsī in an attempt to resolve inconsistencies with Ptolemy's conceptions of planetary motion. Al-Ṭūsi's work was further developed by Ibn al-Shāṭir in the fourteenth century with respect to lunar movement, and it has been suggested that Copernicus, who proposed a similar model two centuries later, may have been influenced by the work of al-Ṭūsi and Ibn al-Shāṭir (d. 1375).

Among al-Ṭūsī's religious works is the Ṣūfī treatise, *Awṣāf al-ashrāf*, a guide for the soul. Another work treats the correspondence between himself and Ṣadr al-Dīn Qūnawī (d. 1274) on the philosophical and mystical knowledge of God, centered on the question of how although many, ultimately all things can be derived back to one source. Al-Ṭūsī also composed a commentary titled *Ḥall mushkilāt al-ishārāt* defending the magisterial philosopher Ibn Sīnā's work titled *al-Ishārāt wa'l-tanbīhāt* against the attacks of al-Ghazālī (d. 1111) and Fakhr al-Dīn al-Rāzī, thereby re-establishing the importance of Ibn Sīnā's ideas. Al-Ṭūsi also wrote summaries of Porphyry's *Isagoge* and Aristotle's logic, and evidence of both as well as that of Plato can be seen in his writings. The influence of Ibn Sīnā's metaphysics can also be clearly discerned in his writings, certainly in the post-Alamut period.

Al-Ṭūsī thenceforth wrote theological works such as *Qawā'id al-ʿaqā'id* and *Tajrīd al-iʿtiqād* in support of the Twelver Shīʿī position, without entirely abandoning his Ismāʿīlī sympathies. For instance, in his *Talkhīṣ al-muḥaṣṣal*, a commentary on Fakhr al-Dīn al-Rāzī's *Muḥaṣṣal*, al-Ṭūsī continues to defend the Ismāʿīlī doctrine of *ta'līm* (instruction) and *naṣṣ* (designation).

Al-Ṭūsī spent most of the latter part of his life in Maragha, moving to Kazimayn near Baghdad only at the end of his life, where he died. He is buried next to the tomb of Mūsā al-Kāẓim, the seventh Twelver Shīʿī Imām. His importance in the annals of Islamic learning can be surmised by the 700-year commemoration postage stamp issued in his honor in Iran, as well as by the number of institutions that have been named after him in the Republic of Azerbaijan.

References and further reading

Badakhchani, S. J. H. (1989) "The Paradise of Submission: A Critical Edition and Study of *Rawzeh-i Taslīm* commonly known as *Taṣawwurat* by Khwājeh Naṣir al-Dīn Ṭūsī, 1201–1275," Ph.D. Dissertation, Oxford University.

Dabashi, H. (1996) "The Philosopher/Vizier: Khwāja Naṣīr al-Dīn al-Ṭūsī and the Ismaʿilis," in F. Daftary, ed., *Medieval Ismāʿili History and Thought*, Cambridge: Cambridge University Press, 231–45.

Daiber, H. and Ragep, F. J. (2004) "al-Ṭūsī, Naṣīr al-Dīn, Abū Djaʿfar Muḥammad," *Encyclopaedia of Islam*, CD-Rom Edition, Leiden: Brill.

Madelung, W. (1985) "Naṣīr al-Dīn's Ethics Between Philosophy, Shiʿism and Sufism," in R. G. Hovannisian, ed., *Ethics in Islam*, Malibu: Undena Publications, 85–101.

Nasr, S. H. (1968) *Science and Civilization in Islam*, Cambridge, MA: Harvard University Press.

Ragep, F. J. (1993) *Naṣīr al-Dīn al-Ṭūsī's* Memoir on Astronomy *(al-Tadhkira fi ʿilm al-hay'a)*, 2 vols., New York: Springer-Verlag.

Ṭūsī, Naṣīr al-Dīn (1998) *Contemplation and Action: The Spiritual Autobiography of a Muslim Scholar*, ed., trans. S. J. Badakhchani, London: I. B. Tauris.

Wickens, G. M. (1964) *The Nasirean Ethics by Naṣīr al-Dīn Ṭūsī*, London: George Allen & Unwin.

31

AL-SUYŪṬĪ

Suleiman Ali Mourad

Al-Suyūṭī is one of the most celebrated religious scholars of pre-modern Islam, and definitely the most prolific of them all. He wrote on every conceivable topic, except for philosophy and science – it is said that he authored close to 1,000 works ranging from short pamphlets to multi-volume encyclopedias – thus making a fundamental contribution to the dissemination and solidification of Sunnī religious thought and worldview.

Al-Suyūṭī was born in Cairo on October 3, 1445 (1 Rajab 849 AH). His full name was Jalāl al-Dīn Abū 'l-Faḍl ʿAbd al-Raḥmān ibn Abī Bakr ibn Muḥammad al-Suyūṭī. Jalāl al-Dīn is an honorific title that means "the glory of religion." His nickname is Abū 'l-Faḍl, "father of al-Faḍl," which indicates that his first son was named al-Faḍl (itself an abbreviation of Faḍl Allāh). His first name is ʿAbd al-Rahmān, his father's name is Abū Bakr, and his grandfather's is Muḥammad. As for al-Suyūṭī, it is his *nisba*, which indicates the place from which his family came, and it refers to the town of Asyut, south of Cairo.

Al-Suyūṭī belonged to a family of learned religious scholars and bureaucrats. In his biography, he says that he does not really know anything about the origin of his family except that they were probably Persian and that before coming to Asyūṭ, his ancestors resided for some time in Baghdad. His father, Abū Bakr, moved to Cairo to complete his education, and specialized in Islamic law, particularly Shāfiʿī law. He became an adjunct judge and professor of Shāfiʿī law at the Shaykhū mosque in Cairo. He also occupied the position of preacher at the prestigious Ibn Ṭūlūn mosque. He died in 1451, when al-Suyūṭī was five and a half years old. But because of the father's contacts, al-Suyūṭī was taken care of by a number of guardians, some of whom were his father's former students.

A story circulated about al-Suyūṭī's birth makes it seem that he was destined for greatness in learning. It says that his mother, who was a Circassian slave, gave birth to him in his father's library, so that he literally opened his eyes to books. He was nicknamed "son of books," but this is possibly because of his later addiction-like attachment to learning and composition. Al-Suyūṭī began his education at the very early age of three. His father brought him to the seminars of some of the notable religious scholars of Cairo in order to arrange for him to receive a license (*ijāza*) from them, so that later al-Suyūṭī could teach their books as well as the subjects in which they specialized. One of them was Ibn Ḥajar al-ʿAsqalānī (d. 1448), who was during his lifetime the most renowned scholar of *ḥadīth* in the Muslim world. Needless to say, at such a young age, the child al-Suyūṭī did not really learn anything. But it was a widespread practice at the time, because fathers often feared that by the time the son was intellectually ready to start his education, some notable scholars would have died, and his son would have a disadvantage vis-à-vis his peers. Originally the license was not issued unless the student actually studied with a given teacher, but starting in the eleventh century, teachers agreed to grant open licenses, especially to children whose parents were close friends or colleagues, or had the means to handsomely reward the teacher.

Al-Suyūṭī began his actual education with the customary memorization of the Qur'ān, which he accomplished at the age of eight. Then he attended seminars on Arabic language, grammar, and literature, as well as on a variety of religious topics – law, *ḥadīth*, Qur'anic exegesis, theology, and so forth – with some of the well-known scholars of his time, among them chief-judge ʿAlam al-Dīn al-Bulqīnī (d. 1464), judge Sharaf al-Dīn al-Munāwī (d. 1467), the dean of the Shaykhūniyya school Muḥyī al-Dīn al-Kāfiyājī (d. 1474), and Ibn Quṭlūbughā al-Ḥanafī (d. 1477), who replaced al-Kāfiyājī as dean of the Shaykhūniyya. They would welcome al-Suyūṭī to their highly sought-after seminars primarily because of his father's reputation, but also because of the great promise he was showing. He became a specialist in four areas: *ḥadīth*, law, Qur'anic exegesis (*tafsīr*), and grammar. In 1464 and 1468, al-Suyūṭī embarked on two trips to Mecca to perform the pilgrimage and to benefit from the presence there of several distinguished scholars. After 1468, he never left Egypt. But his passion for learning did not stop, and through reading and research he acquired a great deal of education and knowledge on a variety of religious and literary topics.

Al-Suyūṭī also studied Sufism. He received the initiation in 1465, during his first visit to Mecca, from Shams al-Dīn ibn al-Kamāl (d. 1472), who lived for some time in Mecca and after his return to Cairo became the dean of the prestigious Kāmiliyya school. At the time, mysticism had become so influential that almost every scholar had to have a mystical affiliation. Al-Suyūṭī's preferred mystical tradition was the Shādhiliyya *ṭarīqa*, which was and still is the most popular mystical tradition in Egypt. Al-Suyūṭī never became a teacher of mysticism, however, despite the fact that he authored a number of short pamphlets on the topic, and wrote in defense of the authenticity of the mystical tradition as going back all the way to the Prophet Muḥammad. His involvement was primarily in the administration of mystical retreats. He was appointed dean of two prestigious and well-endowed mystical centers, the Mausoleum of Barqūq and the Baybarsiyya, but lost both jobs because of his unyielding personality and his ineffectiveness in running their affairs.

Al-Suyūṭī started his teaching career when he was only 18, a very early age. In 1463, he was appointed to his deceased father's post as professor of Shāfiʿite law at the same Shaykhū mosque in Cairo. In 1472, he was also entrusted with teaching *ḥadīth* at the prestigious Shaykhūnīyya school, which is adjacent to the Shaykhū mosque. As his fame grew, he received other notable tenures in some of the major *madrasa*s of Cairo. Al-Suyūṭī also made a name for himself by issuing legal opinions (*fatwā*s) in response to queries presented to him.

As mentioned earlier, al-Suyūṭī was a very prolific writer, and it is no exaggeration to say that there is no subject that relates to history, religion, or language that he did not write something about. This vast literary output made him a great celebrity in the Muslim world, during his lifetime and even until today. His books and pamphlets became very popular, not only in Egypt but also in North and West Africa, Syria,

Arabia, and as far east as India. The demand for al-Suyūṭī's books also generated a steady income that, when added to his many stipends from teaching and other related activities, made him very well off.

Al-Suyūṭī's first works were on grammar, and these are for the most part commentaries on important grammar books. He also wrote *al-Itqān fī ʿulūm al-qurʾān* ("The Perfection of the Sciences of Qurʾān"), which deals with the language and grammar of the Qurʾān. Besides the *Itqān*, his specialty in Qurʾanic exegesis is displayed in two other works: *al-Durr al-manthūr fī ʾl-tafsīr bil-maʾthūr* ("The Scattered Jewels of Interpreting the Qurʾān According to the Well-Established Traditions"), which provides a commentary on the Qurʾān according to the well-established traditions that were passed down from the Prophet Muḥammad, his Companions, and the major scholars of exegesis in early Islam; and his continuation of the short exegesis of his teacher and guardian Jalāl al-Dīn al-Maḥallī (d. 1459). This latter work was titled *Tafsīr al-Jalālayn* – that is, the exegesis of the two Jalāls, Jalāl al-Dīn al-Maḥallī and Jalāl al-Dīn al-Suyūṭī. Because of its relative conciseness, especially in comparison to most Qurʾān exegeses which comprise several volumes, it became the most popular exegesis among average educated Muslims.

Equally impressive and of lasting impact on Islamic religious learning are the works of al-Suyūṭī that deal with law and *ḥadīth*. His *al-Ḥāwī lil-fatāwī* ("The Container of Legal Opinions") is a collection of legal opinions that he issued, some as a result of requests by officials, colleagues, or students, and others written to defend his attitude regarding a particular case. Towards the end of his life, he embarked on a project to collect all known *ḥadīth*s and provide an assessment of the authenticity of each one of them. Unfortunately, he died before finishing the project, but had collected close to 100,000 *ḥadīth*s, an achievement unmatched by any Muslim scholar.

Al-Suyūṭī also liked history, and produced several historical works, including a very popular survey of caliphs who ruled in the Muslim world, entitled *Taʾrīkh al-khulafāʾ* ("History of Caliphs"), as well as a history of Egypt entitled *Ḥusn al-Muḥāḍara fī akhbār Miṣr wal-Qāhira* ("The Eloquent Exposition on the History of Egypt and Cairo"). He also produced a study on historiography entitled *al-Shamārīkh fī ʿilm al-tawārīkh* ("The Apogees of the Science of Historiography"). But he had a special dislike for philosophy, theology, and above all logic, which he considered would weaken a person's faith and distance him or her from God. He wrote two works on the prohibition to study and teach these topics: *al-Qawl al-mushriq fī taḥrīm al-ishtighāl bil-manṭiq* ("The Uncontestable Verdict on the Prohibition of having a Preoccupation in Logic") and *Ṣawn al-manṭiq wal-kalām ʿan fann al-manṭiq wal-kalām* ("Protecting Common-sense and Fluency from the Disciplines of Logic and Theology").

It was probably al-Suyūṭī's ability to produce concise yet extremely authoritative works that made his books highly desirable. Many medieval scholars produced multi-volume works that provided an exhaustive treatment of a particular subject. But the problem of such extensive works, for many scholars and even specialists, was the inconvenience of having to read hundreds and thousands of pages; the concept of general indexing was not yet known, so one had to read volume after volume in order to form an idea about a given subject. A short work that gathers the most relevant and important material about a subject was the thing in which al-Suyūṭī excelled. Even his multi-volume works do not really compare in length to similar books by other scholars.

Yet al-Suyūṭī's rapid rise to fame seems to have turned him into an arrogant individual, or at least this is how many of his contemporaries perceived him. He had a confrontational personality, especially with colleagues whose knowledge of the Islamic sciences he considered inferior to his and whom he described as ignorant and corrupt. Al-Suyūṭī's negative relationship with a large number of the scholars of his day was not entirely his fault, however; many of them no doubt were jealous of him because of his vast knowledge, which he lost no opportunity to demonstrate in public, either through debates or publications intended to prove himself right and his opponents wrong. His colleagues often complained and made accusations against him to key political and official figures in Cairo, which gradually discredited him to the extent that he lost much of the support and many of the privileges that these figures bestowed upon the scholarly community.

One anecdote gives us some ideas about al-Suyūṭī's behavior towards scholars, officials, and even sultans. He once paid a visit to sultan Qayit Bay (r. 1468–96) wearing a *ṭaylasān* (a shawl that covers the head and shoulders), which was a very uncommon practice at the time. The sultan criticized him and accused him of arrogance; he had already been told of the scholar's haughtiness. Al-Suyūṭī answered that wearing a *ṭaylasān* is an established prophetic tradition. The sultan's advisor said that there is no such prophetic tradition. Al-Suyūṭī went home and composed a pamphlet that he entitled *al-Aḥādīth al-ḥisān fī faḍl al-ṭaylasān* ("The Sound Traditions on the Virtue of Wearing a *Ṭaylasān*"), in which he listed a number of traditions attributed to the Prophet Muḥammad and his Companions in support of the wearing of *ṭaylasān*. This incident led to a feud between al-Suyūṭī on the one hand and sultan Qayit Bay and his advisor on the other hand. He vowed never to attend the sultan's court, even though his friends and colleagues advised him against that decision. Al-Suyūṭī then wrote another pamphlet, entitled *Mā rawāhu al-asāṭīn fī ʿadam al-majīʾ ilā ʾl-salāṭīn* ("The Traditions Related by the Great Authorities of Islam against Visiting the Sultans"), in which he provided a large number of anecdotes that recommend the practice of avoiding visiting of people in power and ridicule those scholars who make themselves part of a court's retinue. In this short work, al-Suyūṭī also presented the case that all distinguished early Muslim scholars refused to visit the rulers of their time. The decision of al-Suyūṭī not to partake in the customary once-a-month visit to the Qayit Bay's court might have also resulted from the fact that it took time away from his writing, which he was not willing to tolerate. Attending the court would also oblige him to acknowledge the scholars who advise the sultan, whom he of course despised. Al-Suyūṭī's decision deprived him of the stipend for serving as dean of the Mausoleum of Barqūq, which was dispensed by sultan Qayit Bay, and led to his resignation from that position.

Throughout his confrontations with a number of his peers, politicians, and officials, al-Suyūṭī firmly believed that he was supported and protected by God and the Prophet. He claimed that he had several visions, all while he was awake, in which he saw the prophet Muḥammad, and he even wrote a small book (*Tanwīr al-ḥalak fī imkān ruʾyat al-nabī wal-malāk*) to defend the reality of seeing the Prophet and the angels in visions.

Al-Suyūṭī's resentment of both the intellectual and political communities in Cairo grew even worse with age, and their criticism of him did not abate either. But it was often his own actions that damaged him the most. At 50 years of age, al-Suyūṭī declared himself a *mujtahid muṭalq*, that is, someone who can both introduce new legal opinions and adjudicate legal matters without the need to abide by any of the four Sunnī schools of Islamic law. He also declared himself a *mujaddid al-dīn*, that is, the revivifier of the religion of Islam. This second claim came shortly before the advent of the tenth century of the *hijra*. It is linked to a *ḥadīth* attributed to the prophet Muḥammad in which he says that at the beginning of every century, a revivifier will appear to renew the faith of Islam. Al-Suyūṭī was tapping into this particular prophetic tradition when he claimed himself the revivifier of the tenth Islamic century. He also managed in 1496 to convince the puppet-caliph al-Mutawakkil ʿalā Allāh (d. 1497) to declare him supreme judge of the Muslim world, with powers to appoint and dismiss judges as he saw fit. Such a decision was unprecedented in Islamic history, and al-Mutawakkil had neither the authority nor the power to enforce it.

Needless to say, no scholar of that time, irrespective of his command and expertise in the religious sciences, would dare bestow upon himself such titles or be nominated for them by his peers. The reasons why al-Suyūṭī did so are unclear, but it is certain that these claims did not fare at all well with his contemporaries, who now found themselves with more ammunition than they could dream of to further defame and discredit him. It is no exaggeration to say that the claims made it look as if al-Suyūṭī were unrestrainable, that he had crossed all boundaries. In 1501 he was forced to resign his prestigious tenure as professor of *ḥadīth* at the Shaykhūniyya school, and was dismissed from the deanship of the Baybarsiyya mystical center. He also gave up issuing legal opinions (*fatwā*s), and resigned from other positions he had held. He completely retreated to his house on the island of Rawda, in Cairo, and embarked on writing and composition, refusing to teach or answer requests for legal opinions until he died on October 18, 1505 (19 Jumādā ʾl-Ūlā 911 AH), at the age of 60. One short book that he wrote at this time was again against his critics, and reflects his bitterness and sense of desperation. The work is entitled *Taʾkhīr al-ẓulāma ilā yawm al-qiyāma* ("Delaying Seeking Justice until Judgment Day"), and in it al-Suyūṭī presents the case that justice will be served even if it is delayed for a time. He realized that in his lifetime he did not have a powerful ally to bring him the justice that he deserved from his critics. He expresses throughout his belief that they have done him an injustice by spreading rumors and lies about him, and that God is definitely on his side and will exact revenge for him on the Day of Judgment.

That Day of Judgment seemed not too distant to al-Suyūṭī. His claim as revivifier of Islam reflects his conviction that the end of time is near, especially in light of the fact that the tenth century was about to begin, and the conclusion of a millennium is an apocalyptic benchmark in Near Eastern mythology, shared by both Judaism and Christianity. He wrote a short book (*al-Kashf ʿan mujāwazat hadhih al-umma al-alf*) describing what would happen when the Muslim calendar reached 1,000. He argued that the duration of this world is 7,000 years, and that the prophet Muḥammad was sent at the very end of the sixth millennium. So the tenth Muslim century (sixteenth century CE) would bring the end of the last millennium. Moreover, one of the signs of the nearing of the end of time is the corruption of scholars and officials, which al-Suyūṭī believed to be the case throughout his life. He also wrote several works on apocalyptic themes, including a short book (*Nuzūl ʿĪsā ibn Maryam ākhir al-zamān*) on the second coming of Jesus, and another (*al-ʿUrf al-wardī fī akhbār al-mahdī*) on the coming of the *Mahdī*, the apocalyptic figure often confused with Jesus. Taking all of this into consideration, it seems that al-Suyūṭī believed that the world was indeed about to end, and that therefore he had an especially crucial role to play as a revivifier of Islam.

The recognition that al-Suyūṭī was desperately seeking from his peers, which most denied him during his lifetime, was lavishly bestowed upon him after his death. Fortunately for his posthumous reputation, the scholars of Egypt and the rest of the Muslim world came to know him through the many long and short books that he authored, rather than through his obstreperous personality. These books reflect only a scholar of immense knowledge and ability to articulate a case in support of any topic he chose, and they have always been in great demand, from al-Suyūṭī's lifetime to the present day. They contributed immensely to the dissemination of Sunnī religious thought and worldview in the pre-modern Muslim world, especially in parts where Islam had not yet developed fully, such as India and sub-Saharan western Africa. Among ordinary people, al-Suyūṭī was transformed into a saint after his death. His mother had arranged to have a mausoleum built to house his tomb, and the mausoleum became a popular attraction, especially for the poor seeking all kinds of saintly intercession and blessings.

Al-Suyūṭī was married, probably to more than one wife, and had also several concubines. He had a number of children, but none of them seems to have survived him.

References and further reading

Berkey, J. P. (1992) *The Transmission of Knowledge in Medieval Cairo: A Social History of Islamic Education*, Princeton: Princeton University Press.

—— (2001) *Popular Preaching and Religious Authority in the Medieval Islamic Near East*, Seattle: University of Washington Press.

Geoffroy, E. (2004) "al-Suyūṭī," *Encyclopaedia of Islam*, CD-Rom Edition, Leiden: Brill.

Jarrett, H. S., trans. (1970) *Jalálu'ddín a's Suyúti. History of the Caliphs*, Amsterdam: Oriental Press (original: Calcutta 1881).

Kaptein, N. J. G. (1993) *Muhammad's Birthday Festival: Early History in the Central Muslim Lands and Development in the Muslim West until the 10th/16th Century*, Leiden: E. J. Brill.

Sartain, E. M. (1971) "Jalāl al-Dīn as-Suyūṭī's Relations with the People of Takrūr," *Journal of Semitic Studies*, 16: 193–8.

—— (1975) *Jalāl al-Dīn al-Suyūṭī. Volume 1: Biography and Background*, Cambridge: Cambridge University Press.

Winter, M. and Levanoni, A., eds. (2004) *The Mamluks in Egyptian and Syrian Politics and Society*, Leiden: Brill.

32

SHĀH WALĪ ALLĀH

Marcia K. Hermansen

Shāh Walī Allāh (1703–62) was a major intellectual figure of eighteenth-century Islam in India and a prolific writer in Arabic and Persian. He may be considered a precursor to certain trends in critical Islamic studies such as understanding the development of religious interpretation in historical and thematic perspective. At the same time he exemplifies the late medieval synthesis combining Islamic learning of revealed knowledge (Qur'ān and *ḥadīth* studies), logical and rational analysis, and mystical illumination as sources of truth. His life and thought exemplify the pattern of scholars from the far reaches of the Islamic world coming to the pilgrimage centers of Mecca and Medina where they exchanged ideas and experiences. This in turn inspired the diffusion of intellectual trends such as an eighteenth-century revival in *ḥadīth* studies and, it has been suggested, facilitated the development of global trends of Islamic activism.

Biographical material and anecdotes concerning Shāh Walī Allāh's life and family may be found in his brief autobiography, *Al-Juz' al-laṭīf fī tarjamat al-ʿAbd al-Ḍaʿīf* ("The Blessed Portion in the Life of the Weak Servant"), and in his work *Anfas al-ʿārifīn* ("The Souls of the Gnostics"). He was born in Northern India in 1703 in a learned family descended from the Prophet Muḥammad. His father, Shāh ʿAbd al-Raḥīm, was a noted legal scholar who was also a teacher in his own school, the *Madrasa Raḥīmiyya*, in Delhi and a Ṣūfī guide in the Naqshbandiyya order. The honorific title Shāh ("king") in both of their names refers to a Ṣūfī concept of rank in spiritual attainment.

Young Walī Allāh studied *ḥadīth* works such as *Mishkāt al-Maṣābiḥ* and *Ṣaḥīḥ al-Bukhārī*, as well as works on Qur'ān interpretation, Islamic jurisprudence, and theology with his father. In addition, he was exposed to Ṣūfī writings of such masters as Ibn ʿArabī (d. 1240) and ʿAbd al-Raḥmān Jāmi (d. 1492). In fact, when his father died in 1719 and Walī Allāh was about 17 years of age, he was already recognized as an accomplished scholar and teacher and therefore was able to assume his father's position teaching in the *madrasa* and functioning as a Ṣūfī guide.

In about April 1731 Walī Allāh departed India to perform the pilgrimage to Mecca and Medina where he remained for some 14 months. This stay in the Hijaz was an important formative influence on his thought and subsequent life. While in Arabia he studied *ḥadīth*, *fiqh*, and Sufism with various eminent teachers whom he mentions in his book *Anfas al-ʿārifīn*, the most important being Shaykh Abū Ṭāhir al-Kurdī al-Madanī (d. 1733), Shaykh Wafd Allāh al-Makkī, and Shaykh Tāj al-Dīn al-Qalaʿī (d. 1734). Al-Kurdī was the son of Ibrāhīm al-Kurānī (d. 1690), a Ṣūfī guide as well as a very important figure in the revival of *ḥadīth* studies.

These teachers in Mecca exposed Shāh Walī Allāh to the trend of increased cosmopolitanism in *ḥadīth* scholarship which began to emerge there in the eighteenth century due to a blending of the North African, Arabian, and Indian traditions of study and evaluation. While in the holy cities, Shāh Walī Allāh developed a particular respect for the *Muwaṭṭa*' of Mālik ibn Anas (d. 795), on which later he was to write two commentaries, called *Musawwā* ("The Rectified") and *Muṣaffā* ("The Purified"). In these commentaries Shāh Walī Allāh specialized in reconciling divergent applications and interpretations of *ḥadīth* reports.

Shāh Walī Allāh's writing career began in earnest on his return to India in 1732 and the *Ḥujjat Allāh al-bāligha* ("The Conclusive Argument from God"), which is considered his prime achievement, was composed sometime during the decade after his return. This work attempts a revitalization of *ḥadīth* studies as a discipline, a project that has been associated by some scholars with the rise of eighteenth- and nineteenth-century reform movements in the Muslim world enjoining social and moral reconstruction. For the rest of his career Shāh Walī Allāh served primarily as a teacher and writer, composing numerous works in Arabic and Persian, the common scholarly languages of Indian Muslim intellectuals that allowed their works to be appreciated throughout the Muslim World.

One of Shāh Walī Allāh's most famous achievements was an early Persian translation of the Qur'ān and we can take this as an example of what might be termed progressive or populist trends in his outlook. Many religious scholars had considered such translations to be undesirable in terms of injecting human words into the sanctity of the Arabic revelation. Shāh Walī Allāh, however, recognized the need for non-Arabic speakers to read the text, indicating to us that in his time the level of literacy in the Islamic world was increasing and an increasing transfer of sources into vernacular languages was taking place. His son and grandson later collaborated on the first Urdu translation of the Qur'ān and all of these translations are still being used by South Asian Muslims today. Shāh Walī Allāh pioneered in his book *al-Fawz al-kabīr fī uṣūl al-tafsīr* ("The Great Victory Concerning the Sciences of Interpretation") a rhetorical approach in the field of Qur'anic commentary (*tafsīr*) by understanding the holy book thematically rather than using the usual atomistic method of considering a single verse or word in isolation.

Shāh Walī Allāh lived in turbulent times impacted by the decline of Mughal power after the death of the Emperor Aurangzeb in 1707, attacks by the Hindu Marathas, and the sack of Delhi by the Persian ruler, Nādir Shāh, in 1738. Despite that, or perhaps as a result of that, he composed in total some 50 works in various fields of Islamic learning.

Legacy

After Shāh Walī Allāh's death in 1762, his teachings were carried on by his descendants, in particular by his sons, Shāh ʿAbd al-ʿAzīz (d. 1824) and Shāh Rafīʿ al-Dīn (d. 1818), and his grandson Shāh Ismāʿīl Shahīd (d. 1831). The influence of this notable family has been termed a "Walī Allāhī movement." While the works of his descendants show some influence of Shāh Walī Allāh's thinking, they do not appear to have the same grasp of universal principles as the original.

It is interesting that today the most important Islamic religious movements in South

Asia each construe Shāh Walī Allāh as an intellectual precursor. These divergent interpretive possibilities implicit in his thought are also reflected in the variegated careers of his descendants. His son, Shāh ʿAbd al-ʿAzīz, also a *ḥadīth* expert and teacher, whose life reached into the early period of British colonialism in India, sought a way for Muslims to live under colonial rule and taught the founders of the famous Deoband *madrasa*. In the Indian subcontinent the Deobandi school of thought has perhaps the most direct link to the Walī Allāhī heritage. This *madrasa* was founded by Shāh ʿAbd al-ʿAzīz's students and combines traditional learning in *ḥadīth* and legal studies with Ṣūfī traditions of spiritual formation.

Shāh Walī Allāh's grandson, Shāh Ismāʿīl Shahīd seems to have abandoned an early interest in abstract Ṣūfī metaphysics and adopted a puritanical critique of contemporary Muslim practices reflected in his treatise, *Taqwiyat al-īmān* ("The Strengthening of Faith"). He met his death in a Jihadist battle against the Sikhs while participating in a movement that was sometimes known by the British, due to its perceived threat as part of a pan-Islamic movement, as the Indian Wahhābī uprising. Today's South Asian Muslims having a more reformist and puritanical outlook, such as the Ahl al-Ḥadīth who reject Sufism as an innovation and prefer going directly back to the Qur'ān and *ḥadīth* for legal rulings, see Walī Allāh's project primarily in this light. Even the followers of Mawlānā Mawdūdī's (d. 1978) Islamist group, the Jamāʿat-i Islāmī, find an anticipation of their movement's goals in Shāh Walī Allāh's efforts to revive and rationalize the study of *ḥadīth* and Islamic law, and his call for social and political reforms inspired by Islamic norms.

The third major inclination in contemporary South Asia Islam is that of the group known as Barelvis or Ahl-i Sunna wa'l-Jamāʿa ("The people of the *sunna* and the community"). These Muslims, who are the majority in South Asia, are more devotionally oriented towards veneration of Muḥmmad and the practices of popular Sufism such as shrine visitation and honoring the great Ṣūfīs of the past. Certain of Shāh Walī Allāh's successors, for example his closest disciple and cousin, Muḥammad ʿĀshiq (d. 1773), supported practices and beliefs that are closest to these contemporary Ahl-i Sunna positions. Shāh Walī Allāh himself wrote extensively on Ṣūfī theory and practice, and there are indications that he attempted to establish his own eclectic Ṣūfī order and repertoire of spiritual practices. In addition, since Barelvis support the Ḥanafī legal school and have a particular reverence for its founder, Abū Ḥanīfa (d. 855), they would find Walī Allāh's statements in support of maintaining Ḥanafī practice among the Muslims of the Indian sub-continent appealing.

During the twentieth century, Islamic modernists from South Asia such as Muhammad Iqbal (d. 1938) and Fazlur Rahman (d. 1988) drew on Shāh Walī Allāh as a thinker. They appreciated the fact that he responded to the intellectual crisis of his time with an attitude of moderation and a search for the spirit behind the specific injunctions of the tradition, and felt that this was the approach that Muslims needed to apply in the modern age. His method of reconciling divergent positions among Muslim schools of thought through studying the history of how tradition developed in the hands of human interpreters also appealed to liberal reformers.

Outside of the Indian sub-continent, the most readily available of Shāh Walī Allāh's writings in the Islamic world today are *Ḥujjat Allāh al-bāligha* and his treatises on legal theory (*fiqh*), *al-Inṣāf fī-bayān sabab al-ikhtilāf* ("Doing Justice in Explaining the Causes of Juristic Divergence") and ʿ*Iqd al-jīd fī aḥkam al-ijtihād wa'l-taqlīd* ("A Chaplet for the Neck Concerning following Legal Schools"). These books were composed in Arabic and thus were able to reach a wider audience. *Ḥujjat Allāh al-bāligha* remains a source to be consulted among the present generation of liberal reformers as well as among Islamists in the Middle East, South and South East Asia.

His works

Shāh Walī Allāh wrote a large number of works in various fields including biography, legal methodology, and mystical speculation, as well as two comprehensive books, the previously mentioned *Ḥujjat Allāh al-bāligha* and *Al-Budūr al-bāzigha* ("Full Moons Rising on the Horizons"). In general, his Ṣūfī works belong to the earlier part of his career, although establishing the precise enumeration and dating of his works is a lengthy and complex process (see Baljon1986: 8–14; Rizvi 1980: 220–8). The major ones among these are: *Hamaʿāt* ("Outpourings"), *Saṭaʿāt* ("Brilliances"), *Fuyūḍ al-Ḥaramayn* ("Visions of the Two Holy Cities"), *al-Qawl al-jamīl* ("The Beautiful Speech"), *Lamaḥāt* ("Flashes"), *Alṭaf al-Quds* ("The Finest of the Sacred") and *al-Khayr al-kathīr* ("The Great Good"). Among his later works composed after 1756 are the legal works *Musawwā* and *Muṣaffā*, which are commentaries on Mālik's *Muwaṭṭaʾ*, his treatises on law *ʿIqd al-jīd* ("The Adornment of the Neck") and *al-Inṣāf fī bayān sabab al-ikhtilāf* ("Fairness in the Explanation of the Cause of Difference of Opinon"). The subject of juristic disagreement or *ikhtilāf* was often treated by the Muslim jurists once legal schools (*madhāhib*) began to form. Shāh Walī Allāh's position on following the legal schools seems to have been modified over the course of his lifetime. The Pakistani scholar, Maẓhar Baqāʾ, categorizes these developmental stages chronologically as 1) inherited tendencies, 2) the youthful outcome of his own reflections, 3) influences of his stay in the Hijaz, and 4) the effects of the practical environment in which he later taught in India (Baqāʾ 1979: 24–31).

Before performing the pilgrimage in 1731 Shāh Walī Allāh seems to have independently arrived at a rejection of *taqlīd*, the need for an individual to accept the rulings of only one among the four main legal schools. His own research into the early works, specifically the *Muwaṭṭaʾ* of Mālik, led him to examine the earliest sources and original texts in search of a solution. In other words, he undertook his own process of *ijtihād*, or independent investigation, rather than following any one of the schools absolutely. These factors led him to modify his anti-*taqlīd* position so as to allow following one particular legal school in the case of the lay person. At the same time he tried to mitigate antagonism and controversy among followers of various schools by tracing the original rational and historical circumstances behind their apparent disagreement on specific cases. Later in his life Shāh Walī Allāh came to see his mission in the Indian context as one of performing *taṭbīq* or the accommodation of the Ḥanafī and Shāfiʿī schools.

Shāh Walī Allāh's two-volume work, *al-Tafhīmāt al-Ilāhiyya* ("Divine Interpretations") is a compilation of brief passages in Arabic and Persian that are largely mystical in content but also address questions of law and theology. Two of Shāh Walī Allāh's works, the *Izālat al-khafāʾ* ("Removing Rancor in Issues of the Political Succession [i.e., the Caliphate]") and the *Qurrat al-ʿaynayn fī tafḍīl al-shaykhayn* ("Reasons for the Precedence of the First Two Caliphs") were composed in the latter part of the author's life. The fact that they address Shīʿī claims concerning the nature of the caliphate and the superiority of ʿAlī indicates the urgency of Sunnī–Shīʿī tensions in North India at this time.

Significance

Shāh Walī Allāh was primarily a religious thinker and spiritual philosopher rather than a political reformer or activist. Much has been made of the fact that he also turned his attention to the social and political problems faced by Indian Muslims of that time, primarily by using the resources of classical Islamic thought to formulate systems of ideal social and political structures. Many of his economic and political suggestions are idealized and theoretical in the traditions of philosophers such as al-Fārābī (d. 950) and ethicists such as al-Dawwānī (d. 1501). A famous element of his social analysis is a concept of progressive stages of social and institutional development, termed the *irtifāqāt*. There are four of these stages according to Shāh Walī Allāh: nomadism, urbanization, the establishment of political orders, and finally a transnational caliphate that would unite the entire Muslim World as one polity.

Like al-Ghazālī (d. 1111) in his work *Iḥyāʾ ʿulūm al-dīn* ("The Revival of Religious Sciences"), Shāh Walī Allāh in his *Ḥujjat Allāh al-bāligha* attempts to address the religious significance of all areas of life through explaining the moral and spiritual purposes behind the external injunctions of the *sharīʿa*. In addition, the second volume of this work treats each of the topics of the Islamic legal injunctions through the analysis of specific *ḥadīth* that relate to it, in many cases developing original insights and interpretations.

Shāh Walī Allāh's style of explanation, through considering both the material and ideational elements that interact in history to shape human institutions and symbolic understandings, could be said to anticipate some major twentieth-century Western social theories. His thought also speaks to contemporary debates in the Muslim world about the relationship of local cultures to a normative or legal interpretation and religious practice. By setting social and religious development within an ongoing and intertwined process, Shāh Walī Allāh enabled adaptations to local culture and reinterpretation of the Islamic law in the light of historical change. It is for this reason that his true heirs are Muslim thinkers who reject radical *ijtihād* in following their own interpretations of religion and law, especially when such interpretations do not take into account the systematical development of previous intellectual heritage, since, in this case, adjudication of the sources will be made from the position of modernity. Such literalism is also overly simplistic when viewed in the light of Shāh Walī Allāh's method, which takes into account differing interpretative perspectives and the contexts in which these arose. Therefore, in the contemporary Muslim world, either Muslim "traditionalist" readings or Muslim modernist/liberal readings of Shāh Walī Allāh's project would be those most faithful to his methodology and positions.

References and further reading

Baljon, J. M. S. (1986) *Religion and Thought of Shāh Walī Allāh*, Leiden: E. J. Brill. (A comprehensive study and summary of Shāh Walī Allāh's thought based on many of his writings.)

Baqāʾ, M. (1979) *Uṣūl-i-Fiqh aur Shāh Walī Allāh*, Islamabad: Idāra Taḥqīqāt Islāmī. (A study in Urdu of Shāh Walī Allāh's contribution to Islamic legal theory.)

Ghazali, M. al- (2001) *The Socio-Political Thought of Shāh Walī Allāh*, Islamabad: Islamic Research Institute. (A discussion of these aspects of Shāh Walī Allāh's ideas with selected translations from the *Ḥujjat Allāh al-bāligha*.)
Ghazi, M. A. (2004) *Islamic Renaissance in South Asia (1707–1867): The Role of Shah Wali Allah and His Successors*, New Delhi: Adam Publishers.
Metcalf, B. D. (1982) *Islamic Revival in British India: Deoband, 1860–1900*, Princeton: Princeton University Press. (Traces an important intellectual movement after the time of Shāh Walī Allāh that was to an extent influenced by his ideas.)
Rizvi, S. A. A. (1980) *Shāh Walī Allāh and His Times*, Canberra: Maʿarifat. (A detailed discussion of the historical context and major writings of Shāh Walī Allāh. This work contains an extensive bibliography on the Arabic, Persian, and Urdu sources.)
Walī Allāh, Shāh (1985) *al-Budūr al-bāzigha*, English trans. G. H. Jalbani, *The Rising Moons*, Islamabad: National Hijra Council.
—— (1985) *al-Fawz al-kabīr fī uṣūl al-tafsīr*, English trans. G. N. Jalbani, *The Principles of Qurʾān Commentary*, Islamabad: National Hijra Council.
—— (1988) *al-Budūr al-bāzigha*, English trans. J. M. S. Baljon, *Full Moons Rising on the Horizons*, Lahore: Ashraf.
—— (1996) *Ḥujjat Allāh al-bāligha*, English trans. M. K. Hermansen, *The Conclusive Argument from God*, Leiden: E. J. Brill. (A scholarly translation of the first volume of the author's major work.)

33

BEDIÜZZAMAN SAID NURSI

Zeki Saritoprak

Bediüzzaman Said Nursi was born in 1876 in the small village of Nurs in the province of Bitlis in Eastern Anatolia (modern-day Turkey). Although we are not sure of the exact day of his birth, he died on March 23, 1960, in the city of Urfa in Southeastern Turkey, a city believed to be the birthplace of Abraham. His life, particularly since the days of his adolescence, is very well known and recorded. He himself divided his life into two periods: Old Said (*Eski Said*), from 1876 to 1920; and New Said (*Yeni Said*), from 1920 to 1949. Some of his biographers consider the period of 1949 until his death as a third period in his life, due to his limited involvement in politics, at least at the level of voting.

Nursi lived through three remarkable periods during the last two centuries. He lived in the era of the Ottoman empire and witnessed its collapse. He also witnessed the era of constitutionalism, a reform in the Ottoman empire which gave more space to democracy and the parliamentary system. Finally, he lived in the era of republicanism, and observed the establishment of the modern Turkish secular state. His lifetime spanned an era of immense reform in the Islamic world.

From his youth, Nursi manifested an extraordinary talent and questioned everything around him. In his early life he was called Molla Said (*Master Said*). Sometimes he was called Said-i Kurdi in reference to his ethnicity. It was not unusual in the Ottoman era to name people by their regions, of which Nursi's was mainly Kurdish. Later, he used as his last name "Nursi" in reference to his village to avoid being associated with Kurdish nationalism, although his opponents insisted on calling him by the more divisive term "Kurdi."

He received his education in local Ottoman institutions called *madrasa*s, or religious seminaries. After learning the Qur'ān and some basic Islamic knowledge in his family environment, Nursi went to the local *madrasa* in pursuit of knowledge. He studied for only three months in the *madrasa* system. He attended several of these institutions and met with the teachers there asking them to teach him the summaries of their syllabi. These three months of learning became the basis of his future scholarship. As a self-taught scholar, Nursi would later say that, "in thirty years of learning in my life, I learned only four phrases. One is, 'I am not the owner of myself.' Second, 'Death is real.' Third, 'My Lord is One.' And, fourth, 'the self (*ana*) is a criterion to understand the attributes of God' " (Nursi 1996b: II, 1297, *Mesnevi-Nuriye*).

During this period, Nursi spent time in some Naqshabandī Ṣūfī lodges. One of these Ṣūfī masters, Abdurrahman Tağī, found great capacity in young Said, hinting at Nursi's importance and asking elder students to take care of him. Despite his

Naqshabandī environment, he felt more intimacy with the great Ṣūfī master Shaykh ʿAbd al-Qādir al-Jīlānī (d. 1166), after whom the Qādirī order is named.

Nursi was blessed with a photographic memory. On one occasion, Nursi read an entire page of a book from his memory after only a glance. Upon witnessing this, his teacher was amazed to find such a memory as well as capacity for analysis in the same person. It was from episodes like this that Nursi gained his name, Bediüzzaman, which means the "wonder of the age."

In this early period of his life, in 1892, Nursi met with various personalities including some students of Jamāl al-Dīn al-Afghānī (d. 1897), who prompted the pan-Islamic policy of the Ottoman Sultan Abdul Hamid II; and a member of *Sanusi Tariqah* who struggled against colonization in Africa. Later, he would say that he was awakened politically after these meetings. Also, he became aware of some Turkish intellectuals, such as Namik Kemal, whose idea of freedom stirred a passion in Nursi which resulted in his famous statement: "I can live without bread, but I cannot live without freedom." Nursi named Ali Suavi (d. 1878), Hoca Tahsin (d. 1881), Namik Kemal (d. 1888), Jamāl al-Dīn al-Afghānī and Muḥammad ʿAbduh (d. 1905) as his predecessors in the idea of the unity of Muslims.

Nursi was not satisfied with the situation of the *madrasa* system. He found it very old and incompatible with the requirements of the modern age. In one of his analyses of this system, he said, "It has replaced *Ulum-i ʿaliya* [high sciences] with *ulum-i ʾaliya* [basic grammar rules]" (Nursi 1996b: II, 2000, *Muhakemat*). He sought educational reform and re-organization of the *madrasa* system, but was also very aware of the positive general public opinion of these institutions. Therefore, he wanted to establish a university under the name of *Medreset'uz-zehra* (*c.* 1902), with locations in Eastern and Southeastern Turkey. This was to be a full university which would serve the world of Islam. He considered this project the most important endeavor of his life. As al-Azhar University in Cairo, Egypt, met the educational needs of the African continent, he envisioned a similar, but larger, university to meet those needs of Muslims on the Asian continent. Nursi believed that modern science did not contradict Islam. He attempted to reconcile religion and science. He said, "The light of conscience is [the result of] the sciences of religion, and the light of the mind is [the result of] the natural sciences. By bringing these together, the truth will come out as a result. The lack of the modern sciences causes fanaticism, while the lack of religious sciences causes skepticism" (Nursi 1996a: 127)

He found three main enemies in the Islamic world: ignorance, poverty, and division. He believed that these enemies could be defeated by the "weapons" of knowledge, art, and unity. He envisioned that this university would play an important role in combating these enemies. To establish this university, he went to the capital of the Ottoman empire, Istanbul, and met with Sultan Abdülhamid II (d. 1909) to propose his idea. The Sultan was interested in this project, but his associates did not see it as important. Nursi, however, did not give up. He proposed the idea to the next Sultan, Sultan Reşad (d. 1918), who accepted his proposal and financially supported the project. However, the project ultimately failed because of World War I, in which Nursi himself needed to participate to protect his homeland from the Russian invasion.

Before participating in the war as a volunteer lieutenant colonel, he spent some time between 1893 and 1907 in the palaces of the governors of Bitlis and Van. The palaces housed libraries with numerous volumes of Islamic references and Western classics, and also contemporary printed media. While staying with the governors, Nursi memorized more than 80 of these works, which later became essential references for him in exile where he had no books whatsoever. He also came across a newspaper article that quoted William Gladstone (d. 1898), the British colonial secretary at the time, as saying, "So long as the Muslims have the Qur'ān we shall be unable to dominate them. We must either take it from them or make them lose their love of it." In response to this, Nursi said, "I shall prove and demonstrate to the world that the Qur'ān is an undying and inextinguishable sun" (Nursi 1996b: II, 2131, *Bediuzzaman Said Nursi* [*Biography*]).

Also prior to the World War, in 1912, Nursi visited Damascus and gave a remarkable sermon in Arabic to a large group of people, including hundreds of scholars, at the Umayyad Mosque, in which he talked about the problems of the Islamic world and the importance of Muslim–Christian dialogue. The sermon was later revised and translated into Turkish by Nursi.

After the outbreak of the war, Nursi fought and was wounded. He was taken to the Russian city Kostroma as a prisoner of war, where he spent two years and three months. After his successful escape at the end of the war from a Russian camp in the Spring of 1918, Nursi overcame all obstacles and made his way across Europe back to Istanbul. After arriving in the capital, Nursi was appointed as a member of the *Dār al-Ḥikma al-Islāmiyya* (Islamic House of Wisdom). This was the highest religious institution in the Ottoman empire. In this institution Nursi's specific duty was to answer questions posed by foreigners.

Nursi's homeland in this era was undergoing an interesting development. The Ottoman empire came to an end and a new modern state was established with the formation of a new parliament in 1920. While the new government was working to establish a new Turkish Republic, the largest city in the country, Istanbul, was occupied by British forces. Nursi, living in this city, defended it by distributing his anti-occupation writings. The new government of Ankara invited Nursi to come there several times to show their appreciation for his actions against the British occupation. Nursi finally accepted the invitation to go to Ankara. Here, he gave his famous speech to the parliament in which Nursi disagreed with the founder of modern Turkey, Mustafa Kemal Atatürk (d. 1938) on the role of religion in Turkish society. In this speech, Nursi spoke about the importance of prayer and one's relationship with God. He wanted the administrators to be respectful of the religious rights of people. Nursi's speech did not please the leaders of the new government. In exchange for his co-operation with the new government, Nursi was offered a good salary, a palace, and a seat in parliament. However, Nursi rejected all of these preferring to lead an ascetic lifestyle in Eastern Anatolia.

In 1925, the Shaykh Said Piran (d. 1925) uprising occurred in the Eastern part of Turkey against the Ankara government. Although Nursi was not involved in this uprising and rejected the invitation of Shaykh Said to join it, as a precaution the government sent Nursi into exile in Western Anatolia. Nursi spent the next 35 years of his life in exile, writing his works. In order to have purity of mind and body, he abandoned the reading of newspapers (of which he used to read eight daily), as well as smoking cigarettes.

Nursi's writings, like his life, can be divided into two eras, the Old Said and New

Said. In the Old Said era, Nursi wrote several books, most of which are still available in many languages, including Turkish, Arabic, and English.

One of these books is called *Muhakamat* ("Analyses"), which was intended to be an introduction to Nursi's *tafsīr* (commentary on the Qur'ān), which he planned to be 60 volumes. He wrote the only part of this *tafsīr* while at the front in World War I and it is called *Işaratu'l-I'caz* ("The Signs of Miraculousness"). This is the interpretation of the first chapter of the Qur'ān as well as the first 16 verses of the second chapter.

Another small book Nursi wrote is called *Münāzarāt* ("Dialogues"). It details questions and answers given during his visits to tribal leaders in Eastern Anatolia. It was written as an attempt to convince them of the importance of democracy and freedom and that these ideas were compatible with Islam. Another of these early writings is called the *Mesnevi-i Nuriye* ("The Couplets of Light"), which was originally written in Arabic. Although it is not poetry, it is still very beautifully written. On many occasions, Nursi compared his *Mesnevi* to that of Mawlānā Jalāl al-Dīn Rūmī (d. 1273) and believed that as Rūmī's *Mesnevi-i Şerif* served many people throughout history, so his *Mesnevi* would also serve people in their faith in the future. The book was later translated into Turkish by Nursi's brother, Abdulmecid (d. 1967).

In the introduction of the *Mesnevi*, Nursi mentions that he was very interested in logic and philosophy and therefore wanted to search for a way to reach the reality of realities. One can see in Nursi's writings that he considers important figures such as Imām ʿAlī (d. 661), al-Jīlānī, al-Ghazālī (d. 1111), Rūmī, and Sirhindī (d. 1624) as his spiritual masters. Unlike many Ṣūfīs, he was not satisfied with walking the path to God only with the heart since his mind and his thought were "branded" by philosophy. After reading Sirhindī's book, *Maktūbāt* ("The Letters"), Nursi believed that Sirhindī instructed him to "take one direction," that is to follow only one teacher, and Nursi thought this teacher must be the Qur'ān and said, "The real master is the Qur'ān. And, therefore taking one direction would be possible through the masterhood of the Qur'ān" (Nursi 1996b: II, 1277–8, *Mesnevi-i Nuriye*). Then he walked in this special spiritual path with "open eyes" to find the reality beyond realities. The New Said's writings are the result of this journey.

The writings of the New Said era are collectively called *Risale-i Nur* ("The Treatises of Light"). These can be roughly divided into three parts. The first and major part is the *Hakaik-i Imaniyye* ("The Truths of Faith"). The second part is called *Mudāfa'alar* ("Court Defenses"). The third is called *Lahikalar* ("Appendices"), which consists of correspondence with his students. These three parts are presented in his four major books: *Sözler* ("The Words"), *Mektubat* ("The Letters"), *Lem'alar* ("The Flashes"), and *Şualar* ("The Rays"). Many of these books have been translated into various languages, but there are still some that are only in Turkish. In his writings, Nursi answered hundreds of questions and elaborated on themes such as theology, Sufism, reconciliation between science and religion, Islamic law, questions about his personal life (e.g., why did he not marry, why did he not grow a beard, etc.), and social issues. Some of these treatises are very well known, such as *Ayetu'l-Kubra* ("The Greatest Sign"), the seventh "ray" in the book *The Rays*. This treatise, as Nursi himself put it, is "the experience of a traveler who asks the universe about his Creator." Another is *Haşir Risalesi* ("The Treatise of Resurrection"), which is the tenth "word" in his book *The Words*. It is an interpretation of the Qur'anic verse: "Look at the evidences of the mercy of God, how He revives the earth after it was dead. Surely, He will revive the dead and He is All Powerful" (Qur'ān 30:50).

With regard to the style of his writings, one can see a semi-uniform approach that starts with a Qur'anic verse or a question, either from a student or from his own soul (*nafs*), on which Nursi would elaborate. He used a great deal of analogy, especially when he spoke of the invisible world, and was a champion of parables. In his writings Nursi avoided detailing the views of his opponents because he thought that by thoroughly explaining a negative idea he might negatively affect the pure minds of people. Also, he did not preach, but always addressed his own soul and hoped others who shared his spirituality would benefit from his writings.

All of these writings were written in exile, and some of them while in prison. It is worth noting that one cannot find the negative influences of Nursi's prison environment in his writings. In fact, Nursi called prison the *Medrese-i Yusufiyye* ("School of Joseph"), in reference to the Qur'anic and Biblical figure who was unjustly imprisoned by the King of Egypt.

To give an example of one of his writings, one can look at his *Tabiat Risalesi* ("Treatise on Nature"), which is the twenty-third "flash," in his famous collection *The Flashes*. Nursi gives an account of the situation of his time. He explains why he wrote the treatise: "the reason for the writing of this book is the attack against the Qur'ān by using nature against religion and anything that they did not understand they call it 'superstition.' Through this they wanted to weaken the truth of faith of Islam." He says:

> I went to Ankara in 1338 [1922] and the people of faith were enjoying the victory against the Greek army, but among their views I found the very deceiving idea of atheism entering the minds and poisoning the hearts and I was afraid that this "monster" would attack the main principles of faith. Then, this verse of the Qur'ān helped me to write against the idea of irreligiosity: "Their messengers said, 'Is there a doubt about God, the Creator of the Heavens and Earth?' (Qur'ān 14:10)."
>
> (Nursi 1996b: I, 682, *Lem'alar*)

It is highly possible that when Nursi refers to the idea of irreligiosity he is referring to Ludwig Büchner (d. 1899), who mentioned these ideas in his book *Force and Matter: Empirico-philosophical Studies* (1870). The translation of this book was already available in Turkish and influenced many Turkish intellectuals. In his treatise on nature Nursi responds to Büchner's claim of the imperishability of matter. He wanted to show the divine power in nature and that God had created nature, and that nature was not the Creator. Nursi said, "Nature is only an art and cannot be the Artist . . . it is the law, but not the Lawmaker" (Nursi 1996b: I, 682, *Lem'alar*).

Despite his strong responses to European materialistic philosophy, Nursi carefully distinguished between two Europes: the Europe inclined towards materialism and the Europe which benefited from the divine references and helped humanity with sciences and technology. Nursi was very positive about the second Europe. For this reason, he did not hesitate to praise some European philosophers, scholars, and writers. For example, he praised the German chancellor Otto von Bismarck (d. 1898), the Scottish philosopher, Thomas Carlyle (d. 1881), and the influential British historian Edward Gibbon (d. 1794).

Today, Nursi still is considered one of the most influential figures in modern Turkey, despite being dead for nearly 50 years. The readers of his writings come from various segments of society, from lay people to college students to members of parliament. There are many aspects of Nursi and his writings that attract millions of people. First, one has to remember that he was a very well-known scholar in the era of the Ottoman empire. Secondly, he was imprisoned by the government of his time and oppressed. Despite this, however, he never acted violently and never allowed his students to respond with violence. He created a strong, but non-violent, movement. The strong opposition of the government to religion as opposed to Nursi's firm stand against any irreligiosity certainly made him a symbol of religious sentiment in Turkey.

Nursi's community grew to become a powerful and widespread force in Turkey, although it always remained loose-knit and non-political. Because it did not affiliate itself with any political party, it attracted members of all parties. In fact, he and his students always avoided political involvement. Nursi coined a very famous statement in this regard which became a principle for his students: "I take refuge in God from Satan and politics." Nursi believed that one should focus on faith, rather than politics, since faith is essential for the afterlife.

His books still carry very powerful and eloquent messages regarding faith and religion. Therefore, they have successfully attracted younger generations. After the Qur'ān and *ḥadīth*, Nursi's writings are the most read books in Turkey. It is worth noting that Nursi's writings were hand-copied because the government of the time did not allow his students to use printing machines. By the time the government allowed them to print Nursi's works in 1958, over 700,000 copies of his writings had already been copied by hand. Nursi called his *Risale-i Nur* "a collective miracle of the Qur'ān in this century" (1996b: I, 522, *Mektubat*).

Today, his writings are universally esteemed. Academic meetings are often held to discuss his life, views, and writings. In recent decades, Islamic scholars such as Fethullah Gülen (b. 1941) have broadened the horizon of Nursi's thought and successfully managed to lead the establishment of hundreds of schools in Turkey and around the world, as well as media institutions and publications.

References and further reading

Abu-Rabiʿ, I. M., ed. (2003) *Islam at the Crossroads: On the Life and Thought of Bediuzzaman Said Nursi*, Albany: SUNY Press.

Bonner, A. (2004) "An Islamic Reformation in Turkey," *Middle East Policy*, 11: 84–97.

Mardin, Ş. (1990) *Religion and Social Change in Modern Turkey: The Case of Bediüzzaman Said Nursi*. Albany: SUNY Press.

Markham, I. Ozdemir I., eds. (2005) *Globalization, Ethics and Islam: The Case of Bediuzzaman Said Nursi*, Burlington, VT: Ashgate Publishers.

Nursi, Bediüzzaman Said (1996a) *Münāzarāt*, Istanbul: Yeni Asya Nesriyat.

—— (1996b) *Risale-i Nur Kulliyat*, Itanbul: Nesil Yayinlari.

Saritoprak, Z. (1997) "The Mahdi Question According to Bediuzzaman Said Nursi," in *Third International Symposium on Bediuzzaman Said Nursi: The Reconstruction of Islamic Thought in the Twentieth Century and Bediuzzaman Said Nursi*, Istanbul: Sözler, 483–96.

—— (2000) "Said Nursi's Teachings on the People of the Book: A Case Study of Islamic Social Policy in the Early Twentieth Century," *Islam and Christian–Muslim Relations*, 11: 321–32.

—— (2005) "An Islamic Approach to Peace and Nonviolence: A Turkish Experience," *The Muslim World*, 95: 413–27.

Vahide, Ş. (1992) *The Author of the Risale-i Nur: Bediuzzaman Said Nursi*, Istanbul: Sözler.

34

SAYYID QUṬB

William Shepard

Sayyid Quṭb (1906–66) has been one of the leading figures in the Islamist movements that have been so prominent in the Muslim world in recent decades. These involve a reaction against the dominant secularist ideologies that have adopted and adapted Western models of government and law, treating Islam largely as a matter of personal piety and communal heritage or, where Islamic sources are recognized, interpreting them to be consistent with the secularists' goals. By contrast, Islamists insist that Islam has laws and norms for all areas of life, in particular government and law, and these must be seriously and faithfully applied. They usually present a strongly anti-Western stance, although they happily make use of Western technology and, perhaps less consciously, accept other Western ideas and institutions, not least the modern state. They commonly call for an "Islamic Order" or an "Islamic State." They also continue the reform tendency that seeks to purge traditional practices of un-Islamic "innovations." Islamist movements vary considerably, from pragmatic to purist and from gradualist to violent or revolutionary, as well as in other ways.

The first Islamist movement was the Muslim Brothers (*al-Ikhwān al-Muslimūn*), founded in Egypt in 1928. This was followed by the Jamāʿat-i Islāmī in India/Pakistan and the Fadāʾiyān-i Islām in Iran. These reached a peak of influence in the 1940s and 1950s and then retreated in the face of more secular forces. A second and stronger wave of Islamism appeared as part of the broader religious resurgence that began about 1970, partly as a reaction to the perceived inadequacy or even failure of secularism. While there are as yet few Islamist governments, Islamist movements pose a challenge to many regimes and influence their actions.

Sayyid Quṭb was one of the main players in the first wave of Islamism and a major influence on the second. He came to his Islamism, however, only after many years as a member of the secular intellectual and literary elite that flourished in Egypt during the period of the monarchy (1922–52) and included such figures as Ṭāhā Ḥusayn (1889–1973).

Quṭb was born in September 1906 in a village named Musha in Upper Egypt, some 200 miles south of Cairo. At this time the Western-inspired modernization that had begun a century earlier among the elite in Egypt was just beginning to affect visibly the lives of other classes. This included the beginning of Western-style journalism and political parties, calls for the liberation of women and other reforms, and the spread of state schools. Also at this time vocal opposition to British occupation, which had begun in 1882, was beginning to be heard. In fact, the year of Quṭb's birth was the year of the Dinshaway incident, which galvanized opposition to the occupation when several peasants were executed after a quarrel with British soldiers.

Sayyid Quṭb's family was of the sort that could participate in and profit from these developments. His father and mother both came from established and respected families in their village. Although their financial position had weakened, his father was still very much respected as a pious and educated man. He subscribed to a daily newspaper and was a member of the local committee of the Nationalist Party, which opposed the British occupation. In 1912 Quṭb was sent to the recently opened state elementary school after his mother convinced the family that it would give him better prospects than the old-style *kuttāb* (Qur'anic school). In *A Child from the Village*, an account of his childhood experiences, Quṭb makes it clear how much he valued his school experience at the time, even referring to it as the "sacred school." With the outbreak of the revolution of 1919, which led to the incomplete withdrawal of the British three years later, he became an active and enthusiastic partisan of the revolution's leader, Saʿd Zaghlūl, and its party, the Wafd.

He was sent to Cairo to attend secondary school in 1921, a move that had been delayed by the disruptions connected with the revolution. In Cairo he lived with an uncle who was a journalist and through whom he met the prominent man of letters, ʿAbbās Maḥmūd al-ʿAqqād, whose disciple he became. He also worked as a copy editor and began to publish articles and poems.

After completing his secondary education he attended *Dār al-ʿ ulūm*, a teacher training institute, and graduated in 1933. The program here might be described as a half-way house between a traditional Islamic education and a modern university one. He then joined the Ministry of Education, working as a teacher for six years, first in the provinces and then in Helwan, near Cairo, where his mother, brother and two sisters joined him. His brother, Muḥammad Quṭb, was to become a prominent Islamist in his own right. From 1940 until 1952 Sayyid Quṭb worked as an official in the Ministry. It is reported that his strong views and later political writings often got him in trouble with his superiors and that he made many suggestions for educational reform that were not accepted. He was a member of the Wafd party for many years, and then the Saadist Party, but in 1945 resigned from it apparently out of disgust with all party politics.

His primary interest for some 30 years was his literary activity, especially poetry and literary criticism, as well as social criticism and writing on education. During this time he published more than 130 poems and nearly 500 articles in various journals. These included a combative series in the 1930s defending al-ʿ Aqqād, whose disciple he remained until the mid-1940s, and a long article in 1939 critiquing Ṭāhā Ḥusayn's book, *The Future of Culture in Egypt*, a well-known defense of Westernization. He agreed with many of Ḥusayn's specific proposals for education but rejected his contention that the Egyptian mentality is close to that of the West, asserting, rather, the importance of retaining and renewing Egyptian and Arab culture. In the early 1940s he wrote regularly on social issues for a journal published by the Ministry of Social Affairs. In these he showed concern for the moral problems of society and for the unequal distribution of wealth, but he was far from revolutionary and often found positive models in Western institutions and experience.

Up to 1947 he published some nine books, including a book on the task of poetry in the present generation, a volume of his poetry, a collection of some of his articles about current writers, a more theoretical book on literary criticism and two short novels. One of the novels, *Thorns*, tells the story of a failed romance and is almost certainly autobiographical. It may shed light on why he never married. In 1939 he wrote a long article dealing with the literary characteristics of the Qur'ān and then expanded this into two books, published in 1947 and 1948. He was later to describe himself as irreligious during this period, but these studies of the Qur'ān do not seem to be the work of an unbeliever even though they intentionally avoid propagating religious views.

After the end of World War II, Quṭb and others began to speak out forcefully and passionately for full national independence and social justice against the continuing European imperialism and the political corruption and economic inequality that afflicted the country. At first he wrote from a secular and nationalist point of view, but quite abruptly in 1948 he adopted an Islamist approach. He wrote several Islamist articles in a journal that he edited and he wrote the first of his Islamist books, *Social Justice in Islam* (published the following year). This change of orientation may have actually occurred the previous year, but little is known about how or why it took place.

In November 1948 Quṭb was sent by the government on a study tour to the USA returning in August 1950. It is variously claimed that this was arranged to save him from being arrested for his opinions or in the hopes that he would moderate his anti-Western views. The latter definitely did not happen. Quṭb was impressed by American technology but appalled at what he considered the low moral and cultural state of the American people, which he described in several letters and articles.

Quṭb returned to Egypt, all the more set in an Islamist direction. He began to cooperate with the Muslim Brothers, who had become a major force by then. He seems, however, not to have actually joined them until 1953. He wrote Islamist articles for periodicals connected with the Brothers as well as articles for secular journals, some but not all explicitly Islamist. He revised *Social Justice* more than once and wrote at least two more Islamist books, *Islam's Battle with Capitalism* (1951) and *Islam and World Peace* (1951). In these writings he makes many of the same demands for social justice and opposition to imperialism that he had made earlier but they were now given an Islamic foundation. He called for a society governed by Islamic norms though he was still prepared to cooperate with secularists, even Communists, for common goals. He also hailed an "Islamic bloc" of nations that would counterbalance capitalism and communism. In 1952 he began his commentary on the Qur'ān, *In the Shade of the Qur'ān*, which he was to continue working on for the rest of his life. He virtually ceased publishing poetry after 1950. When he did join the Brothers he became one of its leading ideologues and edited its journal for a time in 1954. In the internal struggles of the Brothers he supported the Supreme Guide, Ḥasan al-Ḥudaybī, against his critics. An important influence on him was his meeting with the Indian Muslim leader Abū'l-Ḥasan Nadwī in 1951. He wrote an introduction to Nadwī's book, *What Has the World Lost by the Decline of the Muslims?*, which adumbrates some of his later thinking. About this time he also became familiar with the writings of Abū'l-Aʿlā' Mawdūdī, the leader of the Jamāʿat-i Islāmī, and these influenced his thinking.

When, in July 1952, the Free Officers under Gamal Abdel Nasser took power, Quṭb initially supported them, as did the Brothers. He appears, in fact, to have sat in their inner councils for a few months. He and the Brothers distanced themselves, however, when they realized that the Free Officers were not prepared to institute an Islamist program. He also resigned from the Ministry of Education in October 1952 and criticized its policies. The Brothers increasingly fell out with the regime and, finally, after an attempt on the life of Abdel Nasser in October 1954, their organization was banned. Some of its leaders were executed and many of them were imprisoned, including Quṭb, who was sentenced to 25 years' hard labor in July 1955. He suffered harsh treatment at first but, because of poor health, was soon shifted to the prison hospital, where he spent the rest of his time of incarceration. There he was allowed to continue his writing and was also able to maintain contact with his fellow Brothers in prison.

Quṭb's views became more and more radically Islamist as time went on and it is generally assumed that the harsh treatment that he and others suffered contributed in a major way to this, particularly an incident in June of 1957 in which more than 20 of the Brothers in prison were killed and a larger number injured. He completed *In the Shade of the Qur'ān* in 1959 and then began to rewrite it in a more radical form, completing slightly more than 13 of the 30 parts of the Qur'ān before his death. A significantly revised edition of *Social Justice in Islam* was published in 1958. Other books during this period include *This Religion of Islam*, (1961), *Islam, the Religion of the Future* (1962?), *Islam and the Problems of Civilization* (1962) and *Characteristics of the Islamic Conception* (1962).

After the intervention of the then-president of Iraq ʿAbd al-Salām ʿĀrif, Quṭb was released from prison in May 1964. In November of that year his best-known book, *Milestones*, was published. This book has been considered a blueprint for Islamic revolution. Parts of it draws on his Qur'ān commentary and parts had apparently been circulated in prison. It was reprinted several times before it was banned. The latest and most radical version of *Social Justice* was also published this year. After his release he took over the guidance of a secret organization of young Brothers and in August of 1965 he was rearrested, accused of plotting against the government and convicted. The main evidence against him appears to have been *Milestones*. He was executed on August 29, 1966, thus becoming a martyr in the eyes of many, including many who did not and do not share his most radical views.

Since his death several collections of his articles have been published in book form, including *Toward an Islamic Society* and *Our Battle with the Jews*, as well as his critique of *The Future of Culture in Egypt*, a purported statement of his to his interrogators, *Why They Executed Me*, and the partially completed book, *Components of the Islamic Conception* (a sequel to *Characteristics of the Islamic Conception*).

Quṭb's later Islamist writings are both more radical and more abstract than his earlier ones. This abstractness partly reflects the condition of censorship under which he was writing. It is clear enough, for example, that a major target of his writing is the regime of Abdel Nasser, but he could not say this too openly. This approach, however, also reflects the content of his thinking. He no longer focused on specific problems, such as disparities of wealth, but on something that lies at the root of all of them, *shirk*, the failure to recognize the absolute sovereignty (he uses the term *ḥākimiyya*, a neologism) of God in all areas of life. Islam, in fact, came to "liberate" (*taḥrīr*) humans from service to anything other than God. Any effort to govern by human laws rather than the laws of God or to "interpret" God's laws according to human desires, however attractive it may seem, is anathema. This applies not only to government but also to culture and education. The social sciences should be completely reworked in Islamic terms. The physical sciences are more neutral but should, if possible, be taught by Muslim teachers.

Probably by the early 1960s Quṭb had come to the conclusion that the whole world, including the so-called Muslim world, is in a state of *jāhiliyya*, a term usually referring to the period of "ignorance" before Muḥammad but here meaning active rebellion against God by a society at any time. No longer does he talk of an "Islamic bloc" as he did in his earlier writings. In his thinking now, the contrast between good and evil, belief and unbelief, Islam and *jāhiliyya* is stark. There is no mid-term. (By contrast, Mawdūdī, for example, allowed for societies that are part-Islam and part-*jāhiliyya*.)

The present *jāhiliyya* is too strong for immediate political action to have any chance of success, according to Quṭb. Instead, a small group of believers must be formed and trained over a long period of time in the true meaning of the phrase "No god but God." Only then will the group be able to confront *jāhiliyya* and this confrontation will be violent because *jāhiliyya* will respond violently. Even at this point there is no guarantee of success. God determines the outcome as He wills. But for Quṭb, by this time, the concern was for doing the will of God and reaping an eternal reward, not worldly results.

Consistent with these views, Quṭb holds that Islamic laws and injunctions on specific matters can be determined only in the context of an existing and functioning Islamic society. At present it is counterproductive to speculate about details that cannot yet be put into practice. *Fiqh* (Islamic jurisprudence) must be *ḥarakī* (active, dynamic), not arising in a void but created by an Islamic society as it deals with its needs.

Most of Quṭb's earlier writings are still in print, but it is the later writings that have been widely translated and disseminated. These ideas divided the Muslim Brothers in the 1960s, with the majority rejecting them but smaller and often violent groups such as the so-called *Takfīr wa-Hijra*, *Jihād* and *Jamāʿa Islāmiyya* in Egypt continuing his legacy with variations, as in some respects Hamas does in Palestine. The makers of the Islamic revolution in Iran had a favorable view of Quṭb, but it is hard to say how much influence he had on them. Quṭb has recently received some notoriety as a kind of spiritual godfather of Al Qaeda but we cannot know what Quṭb would have thought of their tactics. Quṭb's heirs follow him often selectively and with varied interpretations.

References and further reading

Calvert, J. (2000) " 'The World Is an Undutiful Boy': Sayyid Qutb's American Experience," *Islam and Christian Muslim Relations*, 11: 87–103.

Carré, O. (2003) *Mysticism and Politics: A Critical Reading of* Fi Zilal al-Qur'an *by Sayyid Qutb (1906–1966)*, trans. C. Artigues, Leiden: Brill. (Study of *In the Shade*, including a selection of passages.)

Euben, R. (1999) *Enemy in the Mirror: Islamic Fundamentalism and the Limits of Modern Rationalism*, Princeton: Princeton University Press. (One chapter focuses on Quṭb but he is central to the whole book.)

Haddad, Y. Y. (1983) "The Qur'anic Justification for an Islamic Revolution: The View of Sayyid Qutb," *Middle East Journal*, 37: 14–29.
Musallam, A. (2005) *From Secularism to Jihad: Sayyid Quṭb and the Foundations of Radical Islamism*, Westport, CT: Praeger.
Quṭb, S. (1990) *Milestones*, revised trans. A. Z. Hamad Indianapolis: American Trust Publications.
—— (1999–2008) *In the Shade of the Qur'an*, vols. 1–14 (*Sūras* 1–39), trans. M. A. Salahi and A. A. Shamis, Leicester: Islamic Foundation.
—— (2004) *A Child from the Village*, trans. J. Calvert and W. Shepard, Syracuse: Syracuse University Press.
Shepard, W. (1996) *Sayyid Qutb and Islamic Activism*, Leiden: Brill. (Translates the last edition of *Social Justice in Islam* and compares it with earlier ones.)
Tripp, C. (1994) "Sayyid Qutb: The Political Vision," in Ali Rahmena, ed., *Pioneers of Islamic Revival*, London: Zed, 154–83.

35

FAZLUR RAHMAN

Earle H. Waugh

Muslim interactions with the West, and subsequent internal movements within Islam are major themes in contemporary history. Indeed, so much has been written on these topics that it is quite beyond easy summary. It is helpful, then, to review the life and work of an individual whose intelligence and character is held in high esteem, even by his detractors, for he expresses so many of the directions and traits loosely gathered under the term "Muslim modernist." Furthermore, because he used his knowledge directly to effect change within the Muslim community, and to shape a new country, he straddles both the academy and the activist government office, something that few academicians in any culture are able to claim. Such an individual was Fazlur Rahman Malik (1919–88). Almost always referred to in the literature as Fazlur Rahman (both names are used in all instances), he was trained to be an academic at Oxford, but early in his career was invited to Pakistan, where he headed a government think-tank on implementing Islamic law (*sharīʿa*) in a modern Muslim state. His fate is instructive in understanding the difficult terrain that Islam has had to travel over the past two to three hundred years.

In order to explore the many dimensions of this trek, we will first examine his life. Then we will delineate some of the crucial aspects of his thought, followed by a summary of some of the most important themes of his work. In that way we can gain some insights into the movement that has had a major impact on Muslims in many lands, and whose issues are part of what Muslims have been wrestling with ever since the incursion of the West into the Islamic heartlands in the post-industrial period.

Life

Born into the Punjabi family of the traditional Muslim scholar Mawlānā Shihāb al-Dīn on September 21, 1919, Fazlur Rahman lived his early life in the Hazara region of what is now Pakistan. He studied the traditional Islamic corpus of Qur'anic exegesis, traditions (*ḥadīth*) of the Prophet, Islamic law and philosophy with his father. Despite his father's conservatism, he was encouraged to apply modern approaches to traditional topics, a feature of modernist ideology until quite recently.

After finishing an MA at Punjab University in 1943, Fazlur Rahman moved to Oxford where he engaged in the study of modern Western thought. His Ph.D. in Islamic philosophy was completed in 1949. Durham University offered him a position in Persian and Islamic philosophy and he taught there for nine years, following which he moved to McGill University's Institute of Islamic Studies in Montreal, Canada. In the meantime, his researches on Islam and modernity garnered him an international reputation, and in 1961 he was invited to become director of the Central Institute of Research in Pakistan. The president of Pakistan, Muhammad Ayyub Khan, installed him as head of a new government think-tank, The Advisory Council of Islamic Ideology, and charged him with the chore of planning the development of governmental policy for a modern Islamic state.

In that position, Fazlur Rahman applied modern techniques and analyses to Islamic sources and to its law, attempting to sketch a modernized Islamic law without divorcing it from its traditional roots. As his productivity grew so did opposition. His views were roundly opposed by conservative politicians and traditional *ʿulamāʾ*, with the latter condemning him to death for his radical ideas. As opposition gelled, he found it more and more difficult to continue his activity, and the government withdrew its support for his ideas. Unable to continue, he moved in 1968 to the University of California, Los Angeles, in the USA and then the following year to the University of Chicago where he was installed as professor of Islamic Studies. Over the next nine years he helped shape a tradition of scholarship in Islamic Studies that impacted both within and beyond the borders of the university. During the same time, he was advisor to the US State Department, the White House and the government of Indonesia. By the time he died on July 26, 1988, he was regarded as one of the world's most important Muslim scholars and intellectuals from the twentieth century.

Corpus

The shifts in Fazlur Rahman's major writings generally tracked his career changes. His earliest work focused on philosophy because he viewed that as foundational to the way that Islamic society had matured. He was concerned to determine how an Islamically modified Greek rational tradition had shaped Islam's early cultural and political successes. His *Avicenna's Psychology: An English Translation of* Kitāb al-Najāt, *Book II, Chapter VI* (1952) and his *Avicenna's* De Anima (1959), both arising out of his early work at Oxford, were informed by the view that philosophy was one of the pillars upon which human society was constructed. This general conception of philosophy in society was articulated most forcefully in *Prophecy in Islam: Philosophy and Orthodoxy* (1958). This might be termed his "foundational" period.

Once he moved to Pakistan, however, he was immediately presented with the hard reality of implementing that view. He was faced with trying to articulate what a religiously oriented state in the modern world would look like, and particularly one in which religion and state were so closely intertwined as they had been in Islamic history. He approached the problem by examining how Islam had, in fact, shaped the state from the time of the Prophet to the moment when the West took over Muslim lands, that is, he tried to extract the basic principles operative in successive Islamic states. Hence his writings gravitated to the problematic of developing a functional methodology for Islam within a modern state, such as is found in *Islamic Methodology in History* (1965). This work embraced a crucial notion: that the Islamic state today had to determine what was decisively Islamic in the political history of Muslim culture. This challenge might be designated as his "Islamic state" period.

Following his immigration to America, he was faced with an academy that knew little of Islam or its history, and whose scholarship was rooted in a Euro-centric and perhaps even Imperialist mode. He took up the chore of re-orienting Western scholarship on Islam. In both *Islam* (1979) and *Major Themes in the Qur'ān* (1980) he not only wrestled head-on with the Orientalist tradition in the West, but tried to show how it could understand Islam in a more adequate manner. At the same time (perhaps chastened by his aborted experience in Pakistan), he responded to changes underway throughout the Muslim world; he addressed his Muslim colleagues with *Islam and Modernity: Transformation of an Intellectual Tradition* (1982) in which he laid out his schema for Islamic adaptation to the currents of the day. This "American" period saw his influence spread rapidly within the academy and even throughout the modernist wing of Islam throughout the world.

Finally, realizing that Islam had to respond to many of the new and powerful currents in contemporary society or be left hopelessly behind, he demonstrated the relevance of Islamic solutions for critical issues in the contemporary world by examining one area of broad concern: health. His *Health and Medicine in Islamic Tradition* (1989) although published posthumously, was a work that applied his analytic technique to an international social issue that crossed cultural and religious boundaries, thus showing the way for future generations of scholars to utilize Islamic principles for the tough decisions ahead. Among other things, his "global issues" period was marked by his response to Islamism and the rise of radicalism within Islamic society, movements that he felt re-directed Islam against the very currents that had shaped its contemporary experience. He could see little of lasting benefit for the community (*umma*) from those movements, despite their short-term power, as we shall discover in the next section.

Major themes

Fazlur Rahman, like many intellectuals throughout the Muslim world, thought one of the primary issues that Islam had to deal with was reform. He was also convinced that Islam had the crucial intellectual and cultural tools to reform itself in the contemporary world. Hence one of the major over-arching themes of his scholarship was Islamic reform – what it was, how it could be effected, what tools to use. In this, he had much in common with reformers both liberal and conservative within Islam. He accepted that Islam had deteriorated considerably from its once stellar position in the world. In order to regain that position, it had to be reformed in a comprehensive way. With liberals, he contended that Islam had to interact with the West; Islam had to integrate itself into modern life. With fundamentalists and conservatives, he held that the only legitimate protocol was to look backward into Islamic history to find the tools to effect current change.

Yet he disagreed with both liberals and conservatives. He resisted the liberal attempt to use the various frameworks of the West and to adapt Islam to them. He thought that gave up too much of Islamic identity. On the other hand, he rejected the fundamentalist call for a return to the time of the Prophet, arguing that that normative moment was unique because of the person and work of Muḥammad: it could not be replicated. Moreover, that moment, however important it was for the development of Islamic religion, had not been the time of Islamic political and cultural greatness, so therefore could not be a blueprint for contemporary Muslim life. Reform, therefore, had to be based upon the foundational elements that had made Islam the power of the world of its time. Thus he looked to the classical period, and the subtexts that had undergirded Islamic consciousness at its zenith, to determine what tools Islam offered for the process. These would then be utilized for Islamic reform.

In constructing the reform project this way, he was responding to various intellectual and theoretical currents present in the Indian subcontinent of his youth. First, of course, was the mystical impetus towards the end of the nineteenth century in India; it was a religious reformism in the person of Ramakrishna Paramahamsa and his pupil Swami Vivekananda, both of whom insisted that religious pluralism was but many ways to the same end. They looked to the universal principles that would bring new perspectives. Second was the influence of Western and secular ideas on Hinduism, in the form of utilitarian and empiricist notions derived from Western thinkers like John Stuart Mill, Herbert Spencer and Jeremy Bentham that took root in India. These influenced Hinduism to such an extent that the Brahmo Samaj movement swept through the intelligentsia and helped shape a rational ideology. The success of these Western ideas stimulated advanced studies in Western philosophy, with the result that the third major impetus came in the form of a Western idealism: Hegelianism. Early in the twentieth century, ancient Vedantic learning was reinterpreted through the Absolute of Hegel, especially in the work of the learned Hindu scholar Hiralal Haldar. On its heels came the works of Immanuel Kant. All of these influences tended to promote the view that human intellectual ability could harness the wisdom of the past for a new and dynamic society. Fazlur Rahman had been a diligent student of these influences in the country of his youth.

Faced with what he saw as concrete evidence of Islamic decline, Fazlur Rahman searched for similar philosophical foundations within his own tradition. Like his Hindu colleagues, he searched for the means for an all-embracing vision of reform. He found three primary catalysts for Muslim greatness, each of which comprised a constellation of ingredients necessary for affecting a reformed Islam. Briefly they can be expressed as Qur'anic normativeness, cultural openness and philosophical acumen. He grounded his analysis on a specific understanding of the Qur'ān and its purpose. It was a text that essentially challenged its readers to situate themselves in relation to its claims, and to apply the resulting stances in their lives. Its norms were based upon a transcendent dimension, an ethical imperative rooted in God's historical concern to guide humans in the right path. Despite being a revelation, it was, nevertheless, a historical text. This meant that time and its changes were part of the medium through which the revelation was spoken. Fazlur Rahman was convinced that one could determine the historical situations at the time the revelation was given, which would then set the occasion for understanding what meaning was being conveyed in the text. With Husserl, he argued for a phenomenological hermeneutic of the text that would reach the basic meaning without reducing that meaning to a particular moment or to his own subjectivity; with Gadamer he attempted to address the narrative of the text as embodying meaning, but he refused to acknowledge (as Gadamer had held) that what one encountered was only one's own constructing mind. Rather he insisted that the writer's message was not just enshrined in the specific words themselves but was comprised of a deeper meaning available beyond the time and place of the utterance itself. In short, a writer's ideas could be directly engaged within the mind of the reader.

Furthermore, the text of the Qur'ān embodied an ethical imperative that required the response of everyone who read the text. One could not assume, then, as many Western scholars did, that the text was a neutral collection of words whose power was bequeathed to it by those who accepted it (i.e., Muslims). In his view, the text was shaped in a historical and religious consciousness that required all people with an historical awareness to engage what it said, for the message could not be abstracted from its religio-historical framework. He was therefore particularly critical of those who argued that the text of the Qur'ān was but a narrative implying several background subtexts, which, when deciphered, would supply the precise details (and thus the meaning) of the text. Such a view disregarded the strong historical position that the Qur'ān took about its own words.

Of course, one could reject history as the medium of knowledge, but by doing so, one removed any hope of communicating with the past in any meaningful manner. The Qur'ān, he insisted, was shaped by a historical consciousness, and its message presumed adherence to that awareness. In addition, he saw the Qur'ān advocating a vision for humans that suggested abiding norms for behavior. For example, Qur'anic discourse was suffused with an egalitarianism that required Muslims to eradicate any social and religious inferiority in their perception of God's plan for the world. It was a norm that required all who read the text to address and respond to. The interpretations of equality obviously changed with time, but the impetus unleashed in the Qur'ān could not be buried as a historical statement of the past – it had to be acknowledged and confronted by all who read the text honestly. In this way, the Qur'ān's challenge was always fresh, inspiring its readers to apply its ethical perspective to the minutiae of everyday living at all periods and in all places. The result was that a Qur'anic worldview was the primary model by which the truths of Islam should be applied today. Thus, he preserved a dynamic role for the Qur'ān even while acknowledging the historical situation of the text itself.

The second catalyst was cultural openness. Fazlur Rahman extended the learning parameters of Islam to the whole world of ideas. In his view, Islam had the tools and the grounding to address modern life in whatever form it came, whether secular or religious. The most creative period of Islam was also a period when it utilized the legacy of learning from many civilizations and put it to work in framing Islam. This is a position he espoused in his earliest work. There, he articulated an Islam that embraced the learning of the Greek philosophical tradition in its earliest development and he saw thinkers like Avicenna constructing a sophisticated model of human life in relation to divine revelation. In consonance with that direction, he insisted that Islamic civilization at its greatest had rational thinking as an essential component. In his view, Islamic history opened many doors for Muslim scholars who wished to plumb the achievements of the past for their application today. He objected vigorously to the Islamist trend to isolate Islam from forces later than the time of the Prophet and particularly to reject the intellectual currents of the twentieth century, which he believed, were necessary to forge a new international Islamic society.

The third catalyst was Islamic philosophy. This catalyst was formulated on the basis of a thorough-going understanding of four basic dimensions of Islamic consciousness: Qur'ān, *sunna*, *ijtihād* and *ijmāʿ* and how they functioned in Islamic life. He objected to the simplistic understanding of these pillars of Islamic life in much modern Islamic scholarship. He pointed out that modernists were selective in their application of Islamic norms to their re-constructions of Islamic society today, a procedure that has no roots in the way Islam developed in history, and which ended up casting aside original insights, like economic equality, which he says, the Qur'ān insists upon.

He particularly disdained the fundamentalist wing for its cursory ability to articulate traditional Islamic fields of knowledge, seeing them as very selective in what they took from the tradition and then treating it only insofar as it met their needs. At the same time, he also challenged Western scholarship on the Qur'ān because it assumed it could disregard its religious message while analyzing it as a literary expression. He argued that Western studies of the *sunna* were correct in holding that it was not historically structured, but he did not then reject it as a source of Islamic development. Rather he saw it as a product of community self-definition and affirmation. It was therefore a child of a burgeoning Muslim identity. As for *ijtihād*, this was the tool by which new interpretations and issues were incorporated into Muslim life, and it had to be extended and provided with proper philosophical underpinnings. Similarly, *ijmā'*, consensus, was a process that brought integrative pressures to bear on disparate understandings, and it had to be shaped by a system that provided it with the position to continue to function properly in a new Islamic order.

Critical positions

A few of the most important perspectives he avowed provide an entrée into Islamic modernism. That was a term he did not feel comfortable being applied to his work. However, it was a term applied to him by both international scholarship and Muslim believers. We can then summarize some key positions of modernism by exploring some of the debates he engaged in.

New methodologies

Insofar as modernists are to be defined by accepting history as an ultimate constraint on intellectual understanding, he accepted the designation "modernist" to that extent. This places him firmly in the modernist camp. However, there was more to it than just accepting history. Fazlur Rahman actually belongs in a distinctive group of Islamic modernists, that is, those who call for a new hermeneutical stance to be taken to the whole Islamic corpus; he and his fellow modernists want a re-vamping of the foundations of Islamic understanding. The modernists include some of the leading lights of the last half century, such as Mohammed Arkoun of Algeria, Muhammad al-Jabiri of Morocco, and Abdullah Laroui of Morocco. They all consciously embrace a revisionist stance of the means by which the Islamic corpus is to be configured today. They uniformly contend that the system of traditional interpretation has to be reconfigured if Islam is to be intellectually viable in the contemporary world.

The difficulty is that these scholars were not opposed just by those conservatives who regarded any methodological change as *shirk* (innovation) and hence anathema for Islam, but by most ordinary Muslims. The very idea of applying ideas not generated from within Islam to interpret things like the Qur'ān or the Prophet's *sunna* was and is almost universally regarded by believers as "against Islam." For most Muslims, the modernists had the cart before the horse: modernity should conform to Islamic jurisdictions, not the other way around.

The true Islamic state

Fazlur Rahman held that the absolutely basic premise of Islam was the construction of an egalitarian, ethical social order. Right from the beginning, then, Islam had been a "state" religion. For him, any attempt to build a true social order is an interpretive activity, since the meanings of "ethical" and "egalitarian" are historically defined. It is "the effort to understand the meaning of a relevant text or precedent in the past, containing a rule, and to alter that rule by extending or restricting or otherwise modifying it in such a manner that a new situation can be subsumed under it by a new solution" (Rahman 1982: 7–8). Modernists point to the position that international Islam had slipped to in terms of the world's power politics as proof that something had gone seriously wrong with the Islamic state. Fazlur Rahman blames the stagnation that has characterized the Islamic world since the Middle Ages, in fact, on the eventual diminution of intellectual vigor, most noticeably in the application of new ideas and perceptions to the Islamic state. He particularly saw the traditional mechanism of legal development, that is, the activity of *ijtihād*, as in decline:

> Most modern Muslim thinkers have laid the blame . . . on the destruction of the caliphate in the mid-thirteenth century and the political disintegration of the Muslim world. But . . . the spirit of Islam had become essentially static long before that; indeed, this stagnation was inherent in the bases on which Islamic law was founded. The development of theology displays the same characteristics even more dramatically than does legal thought.
>
> (Rahman 1982: 26)

The view that the current state of Islam reflects one of serious decline is a hallmark of modernist thinking, and the means by which Islam will regain power is through reform of its institutions, like that of *ijtihād*. It assumes that expressing and maintaining political power in the contemporary political world is a feature of true greatness – a greatness in keeping with the historical position of Islam throughout much of the first several centuries of its existence. Unfortunately for the modernists, both traditionalists and radicals rejected the basis of comparison upon which such an assertion is made. Furthermore, radicals like Osama bin Laden are dedicated to returning Islam to political dominance. Hence the modernist assumptions are rejected by both conservative and radical scholars today.

Debate with fundamentalism

Modernism has had to fight a rearguard battle from within Islamic society itself. Fazlur Rahman reflects another trait of modernism by opposing the fundamentalist and neo-fundamentalist movement. In an article entitled "Roots of Islamic Neo-Fundamentalism" (1981) he notes that Islam is fragmented into four ideological factions: traditionalist-conservatives "interested in preserving Islam's religious and cultural heritage"; "neo-fundamentalists who absolutize Islamic laws contained in the Qur'ān"; modernists "who believe that the Qur'ān produced certain solutions for certain problems in a certain place but say the responsibility of the contemporary Muslim is to get behind the letter of these laws to the spirit that animated them"; and secularists "who make no appeal to religion at all" (Rahman 1981: 25). The later faction he thought irrelevant for Muslims. Traditionalist-conservatives, on the other hand, were well-intentioned but ineffective because they were out of touch with the needs of the modern world. He contrasted them to the neo-fundamentalists because they regarded Islamic history and tradition as "their" purvey, and thus took a proprietary role over its jurisdiction. They could not, however, move beyond what traditionally has been affirmed and thus were doomed to be inflexible because they were too literalist. As for the neo-fundamentalists, he thought them quite out of touch with the contemporary world, since they were post-modernist in thrust, that is, they operated as if the sophisticated history of Islam made no difference to Islam today. Moreover, neo-fundamentalists needed the post-modernist world in order to define their beliefs. He thus defined neo-fundamentalism as:

> An Islamic bid to discover the original meaning of the Islamic message without historic deviations and distortions and without being encumbered by the intervening tradition, this bid being meant not only for the benefit of the Islamic community but as a challenge to the world and to the West in particular.
>
> (Rahman 1981: 33)

For Fazlur Rahman, this movement was a dangerous hiding one's head in the sand.

As events have testified since his death, the conservative renaissance in Islam has continued apace, regardless of the warnings of the modernists, with Islamist groups now well established in all facets of Islamic society all over the Muslim world. Of course, the conservative movement has also fed into the growth of radicalism, especially with the export of a vigorous branch of Wahhabism throughout the Islamic world.

Women in Islam

The role of women in Islam has been fraught with conflict from the time that the West first began its occupation of Islamic lands, when the position of women in such Muslim institutions as the harem prompted widespread criticism and scorn by Western detractors. Fazlur Rahman knew this, but still he pointed to controversies about women as a good example of how far Muslims had strayed from the simplicity and grandeur of the Qur'ān's teachings. He often argued the Qur'ān might be the "official" source of notions about women, but that the real source was social convention (Rahman 1983). He insisted that when the basic principles of the Qur'ān were taken as the foundation of social policy, then verses about women could be fully understood. Otherwise, some verses would be difficult to interpret, precisely because they were particular revelations for a particular circumstance. He distanced himself from any piece by piece interpretation of such verses, and held that all social legislation in the Qur'ān had to be understood through the essential principles of equality and justice (Rahman 1980: 38). These notions, he believed, would progressively change as the community evolved. On the *ḥijāb*, he could not see how an injunction specifically addressed to the Prophet's wives could possibly apply in a general way today, unless one wanted to regard the norms of primitive Muslim community as applying to all time, thus negating even the Qur'ān's own sense of development. On polygyny, or multiple wives, Fazlur Rahman admitted that the Qur'ān allowed this social form, but he held that the norm of monogamy was clearly present in the Qur'anic message and was the intended position of an Islam that gradually grew beyond the critical deaths of its men in Islam's early history. He did not accept that the Qur'ān's norms were influenced by patriarchal assumptions as some feminist scholars have argued. He did insist, however, that each Muslim woman had the right to interpret the rules that apply to her today.

Influence

It is usually thought that Islamic modernism has been offset by the conservative trends within Islamic society, especially in the Islamist and radical movements that appeared in the twentieth century. However, that view is much too simplistic. Islamic liberalism is a movement sparked in Indonesia by his influence, particularly under the guidance of his student Nurcholic Majid (Cak Nur). Much of the Fazlur Rahman agenda is contained in his teachings. In addition, Fazlur Rahman has influenced a sizable population of scholars in the USA through his work at the University of Chicago, and his views cannot be ignored by those in the field who want to deal with Islam in its current configuration in the world. As the Progressive Muslims movement develops, it is quite possible that some of Fazlur Rahman's ideas will continue to affect the world of Islam.

References and further reading

Rahman, F. (1952) *Avicenna's Psychology: An English Translation of* Kitāb al-Najāt, *Book II, Chapter VI*, New York: Oxford University Press.

—— (1958) *Prophecy in Islam: Philosophy and Orthodoxy*, London: George Allen & Unwin.

—— (1959) *Avicenna's* de Anima, New York: Oxford University Press.

—— (1965) *Islamic Methodology in History*, Karachi: Iqbal Academy.

—— (1976) *Philosophy of Mullā Sadrā Shīrāzī*, Albany: State University of New York Press.

—— (1979) *Islam*, 2nd edition, Chicago: University of Chicago Press.

—— (1980) *Major Themes of the Qur'ān*, Chicago: Bibliotheca Islamica.

—— (1981) "Roots of Islamic Neo-fundamentalism," in P. H. Stoddard, D. C. Cuthell, M. W. Sullivan, eds., *Change and the Muslim World*, Syracuse: Syracuse University Press, 23–35.

—— (1982) *Islam and Modernity: Transformations of an Intellectual Tradition*, Chicago: University of Chicago Press.

—— (1983) "Status of Women in the Qur'an," in G. Nashat, ed., *Women and Revolution in Iran*, Boulder: Westview Press, 37–54.

—— (1989) *Health and Medicine in the Islamic Tradition*, New York: The Crossroad Publishing Company.

Waugh, E. H. and Denny, F. M., eds. (1998) *The Shaping of an American Islamic Discourse: A Memorial to Fazlur Rahman*, Atlanta: Scholars Press.

of the sacred text might be bound in multiple volumes and stored in chests. After the ninth century, Chinese paper-making grew more common in the Islamic world spurring on the arts of the book and the sacred text was more often produced as a single volume using paper and a vertical page format instead. These types of Qur'āns also tended to incorporate a new cursive style of calligraphy that emerged in ninth-century Iraq during the Abbasid caliphate.

Figure 17 Portrait of Georg Gisze by Hans Holbein the Younger, London, 1532 (Oil on wood, 96.3 × 85.7 cm Gemäldegalerie). Gisze was a German merchant in London and the painting affirms both the vibrancy of Mediterranean textile trade and that knotted geometric motifs were used in sixteenth-century Anatolian textiles.

Source: Courtesy of bpk/Gemäldegalerie, SMB/Jörg P. Anders

A revolutionary approach to Arabic calligraphy was introduced by an Abbasid official employed in the imperial chancellery named Ibn Muqla (d. 940). Using a circle template and the dot a nibbed pen makes, he standardized the proportions of an unremarkable but compact, cursive Arabic script commonly used in bureaucratic documents. The results were harmoniously composed letters that maintained their grace regardless of the scale at which they were traced out. Unfortunately for Ibn Muqla, his life was marked by tragic irony. As punishment for being on the wrong side of political intrigue, the hand that gave the Islamic world these elegantly formed letters was cruelly chopped off. Proportioned, cursive calligraphy enjoyed extraordinary success throughout the Islamic world and Ibn Muqla's artistic successors, among them Ibn al-Bawwāb (d. 1022) and Yāqūt al-Mutaʿṣimī (d. 1298), introduced several careful refinements by expanding the number of scripts and experimenting with the design of reed pens (see fig. 8). Proficient at proportioned script, Chinese Arabic calligraphers experimented even more boldly, likely inspired by the rich Chinese calligraphic tradition (see fig. 18).

Less common than calligraphy was the art of miniature painting on paper, which was commonly used to illustrate literature, histories, practical manuals and scientific works. The Qur'ān was never illustrated but poetic retellings of Qur'anic stories in Persian could be provided with appropriate illustration. Engaging examples of

Figure 18 Signboard on mosque at Niu Chieh. The mosque dates to the tenth century but was rebuilt in the seventeenth; the date of the calligraphy (the *basmala*) boldly unconstrained by conventional proportions is uncertain.

Source: From the photograph album *Islam in China*, p. [34]. Harvard-Yenching Library, CP03.34.01, Record Identifier: olvwork173761. Rev. Claude L. Pickens Jr. Collection, Harvard-Yenching Library. Copyright President and Fellows of Harvard College

illustrated Arabic literature come from thirteenth-century Iraq and Spain, inspired by the Byzantine traditions of manuscript painting. Among the most popular tales were those of *Kalīla wa Dimna*, a series of ancient moral fables named after two jackals who were the principal characters (see fig. 19). The tales originated in India but were translated from Sanskrit into Persian, Syriac, and then Arabic. The *Maqāmāt* of al-Ḥarīrī (d. 1122) was another popular Arabic literary work and comprised a series of episodes involving a subversive, sometimes lewd anti-hero named Abū Zayd, who was not shy about ridiculing or deceiving members of medieval Muslim society.

Illustrated Persian literature and histories differed considerably in style from Arabic miniatures and were far more common. They owed much to the patronage of the Il-Khanids, Muslim rulers of Iran descended from the Great Mongols and they owed even more to the fourteenth- and fifteenth-century Central Asian dynasty, the Timurids, who traced their roots to Timur (Tamerlane) and Genghis Khan, and who established their own twin legacies of violence and artistic excellence. In the Timurid courts, particularly Herat, teams of artists were employed to produce fine books and their works were a wellspring of deeply influential techniques and ideas. The painter Bihzād (d. 1535) was later celebrated as a master of miniature paintings rendered with opaque watercolors laid over delicate drawings and distinguished by their high horizon lines and highly individualized figures.

By the sixteenth century, painters in the courts of the Safavid, Ottoman, Uzbek, and Mughal empires, immersed in a common Persian literary culture, enthusiastically embraced the medium and were inspired by Bihzād's example for over two centuries. Both fine books and painters traveled from the Safavid court to those of the Ottomans and Mughals, transferring their expertise. Illustrated copies of the masterpiece of Persian literature, the *Shāhnāma*, a verse history of the great kings and heroes of ancient Iran, composed by the poet Firdawsī (d. 1020) between 980 and 1020, was most popular with rulers. The *Shāhnāma's* 60,000 couplets provided rich inspiration for painters, who re-imagined the mythological Persian past in the image of their Islamic present.

One of the greatest illustrated versions ever made was the two volume edition produced in the royal scriptorium of the Safavid ruler Shāh Ismāʿīl (r. 1487–1524) and his son Ṭahmāsp (r. 1524–76). Among the finest illustrated pages is a scene of Guyumarz, the mythical first king of Iran, holding court with all of humanity and the animal kingdom paying him homage. It was painted by Niẓām al-Dīn Sulṭān Muḥammad, whose contemporaries were greatly impressed with the painting and likely observed the Chinese influence in his rocks, trees and clouds, imagery that was easily encountered in imported textiles and ceramics. Sadly, Shāh Ṭahmāsp grew disenchanted with representational art probably due to religious concerns, prompting him to give this extraordinary *Shāhnāma* away to the Ottoman sultan in Anatolia.

Ignored for four centuries, the volumes of the Shāh Ṭahmāsp *Shāhnāma* eventually found their way into the hands of a twentieth-century American collector, Arthur Houghton, who disassembled the volumes and sold the pages one by one for maximum profit. The pages of this were masterpieces of illustrated literature scattered around the world like leaves blowing on a windy day, although the majority of the paintings are now back in Iran. The Houghton *Shāhnāma* serves as a poignant reminder that significant portions of the artistic heritage of the Islamic world, for

Figure 19 In this earliest Mamluk copy of Kalīla and Dimna, the conniving jackal Dimna causes the powerful ox and lion to first befriend each other then fight to the death, a parable about political intrigue.

Source: Dimna with the Lion and the Ox. Syria?, 1354 © Bodleian Library, Oxford, 2001, MS Pococke 400, fol. 45r, reproduced with permission.

better or worse, now reside in private European and American collections and public museums, commodities in a murky international arts and antiquities market. Within the Islamic world important collections have survived in certain cities – Cairo, Istanbul and Tehran for example – and new collections are being amassed in new museums in Doha, Kuwait and Kuala Lampur.

Idealized historical or literary figures were common in Central Asian and Iranian painting, but Ottoman and Mughal imperial patrons also encouraged artists to glorify the lives and histories of emperors and their obedient subjects in illustrated books. This emphasis combined with the influx of European art displaying refined techniques in realistic, three-dimensional portraiture and perspective led to furhter explorations in realism, a feature that characterizes much of Mughal drawing and painting, as a sober drawing of the opium-addicted nobleman ʿInāyat Khān on his deathbed shows (see fig. 20). Images inspired neither from literature nor royal history also gained appreciation and were collected in albums often along with prized pieces of poetry rendered with exquisite calligraphy.

Figure 20 Dying ʿInāyat Khān. Govardhan, North India, 1618 (Brush and ink with colour on paper, 9.5 × 13.3 cm). Astonished at his alcoholic and opium addicted friend's emaciated appearance, the Mughal emperor Jahāngīr ordered court artists to portray his dying friend with unflinching realism.

Source: Museum of Fine Arts, Boston, Francis Bartlett Donation of 1912 and Picture Fund, 14.679. Photograph © 2008 Museum of Fine Arts Boston. Reproduced with permission

One fascinating yet minor current in the Persian painting tradition is the portrayal of the Prophet Muḥammad to accompany narratives of his life, which can occasionally be found in Ilkhanid, Timurid, Safavid and Ottoman painting. Early examples boldly portray the Prophet's face, while later ones surround his head with a flaming halo – also used for other religious personages – but cover the face with a white veil, signaling his sanctity but forestalling criticism by religious authorities (see fig. 9). Such imagery served narrative rather than devotional purposes unlike late Ottoman prayer books or some tiles which could employ symbolic imagery such as the feet of the Prophet, or diagrams with descriptions of the Prophet to focus meditative and devotional activity (see fig. 42).

It is often said that human figural representation is contrary to Islam or words to that effect. In truth, significant portions of the Islamic world, some more than others, abounded in figural imagery that adorned textiles, books, metalware, ceramics and fabrics to name a few important media. To be sure there are certain lines of religious scholarly thinking (Sunnī and Shīʿī) dating to the days of Abbasids in the ninth century that were hostile to figural imagery. For example, the thirteenth-century Shāfiʿī scholar al-Nawawī wrote:

> The learned authorities of our school and others hold that the painting of a picture of any living thing is strictly forbidden and is one of the great sins. . . . So the making of it is forbidden under every circumstance, because it implies a likeness to the creative activity of God, whether it is on a robe, or a carpet, or a coin, gold, silver or copper, or a vessel or on a wall.
>
> (Arnold 1965: 9, quoting al-Nawawī)

Creating figural imagery was perceived by religious scholars not only as an usurpation of God's creative role but as an activity that could lead the weak away from worshipping only one God and they succeeded in ensuring figural imagery had no role in Islamic worship. In some ways, this aversion was simply a revival of a sentiment that had percolated in various Ancient Near Eastern religious traditions including Judaism, Christianity and Zoroastrianism for centuries before the rise of Islam. In any event, Muslim religious scholars by no means succeeded in imposing a ban on all figural imagery in all corners of life; that would have been impossible. But they did manage to create a pervasive discomfort around the practice and discourage the use of figural imagery for religious purposes.

Ceramics

Despite their fragility, luxury ceramics were among the most popular art forms of the Islamic world. Diverse traditions were inherited and innovated upon, but two particular developments should be emphasized. In the ninth and tenth centuries, Iraqi and Egyptian potters grew particularly adept at producing lusterware, named for the lustrous metallic sheen of its designs, which often incorporated figural imagery, geometric patterns and calligraphy. To achieve the distinctive sheen, a metallic mixture was painted onto already fired ceramics and then re-fired. Only if the delicate balance between the composition of metallic paint, firing temperature and air quality was maintained would the shimmering effect be achieved. One of the great achievements in this art was a twelfth century plate now held in the Smithsonian in Washington; a circular band of angular calligraphy circles the plate's rim and filling the center is a young falconer mounted on his splendidly attired horse.

Patrons and artisans from the age of the Abbasids onwards cherished Chinese ceramics, especially porcelains (see fig. 21). It was a passion fueled by trade and diplomatic gift exchanges with China that grew more pronounced during the rise of the Mongol empire. During the rule of the Timurid dynasty in Central Asia, and the Yuan and Ming dynasties in China, Jingdezhen was a major production centre for ceramics designed specially for export to Muslim markets in Central Asia, Iran and

Figure 21 Jug. China, *c.* 1426–35 (Ming dynasty). The shape derives from Timurid metal jugs, further demonstrating the extensive cross-fertilization of Chinese and Islamic art in Central Asia.

Source: The Trustees of the British Museum, OA 1950.3–3.1 (57). Courtesy of The British Museum/ Heritage-Images

Iraq. While contemporary Chinese tastes favored undecorated vessels and focused on shape over surface, ornamented ceramics were the rage among Muslim elites. To meet this demand Chinese producers imported from Iraq cobalt ore, a rare mineral in China, and used it to render striking blue patterns on milky white porcelain surfaces, giving birth to the well-known genre of blue-and-white ceramics which were emulated by potters in the Islamic world. Gradually, Chinese tastes shifted and blue-and-white ware grew popular in China too during the Yuan and Ming dynasties. Though an icon of Chinese civilization, blue-and-white ware is a testament to the vitality of international commerce between Chinese and Muslim lands.

Metalware

The plates, basins, ewers, candle holders, and containers which pervaded the elite domestic environments of a number of Muslim societies were not only crafted as ceramics but as metalware too. Metal production and metalwork (casting, pounding and turning) in Iraq, Iran, Syria and India dated back to antiquity (see fig. 22). Fine works in Muslim societies were typically ornamented with figural and animal imagery, calligraphy, and organic and geometric patterning. Mamluk Iraq and Syria, for example, produced striking works notable for their use of gold and silver delicately inlaid into brass works. The figural imagery employed closely resembles the kind found in contemporary illustrated manuscripts and the patterns used recall those

Figure 22 Decorated Bowl. Ibn al-Zayn *c.* 1290–1310. Eighteen figures with Central Asian, Turkish, Mediterranean features and engaged in hunting, enjoying music and holding court adorn this multicultural bowl.

Source: Musée du Louvre, Paris, MAO 331. Photo RMN © Hervé Lewandowski

incorporated into contemporary textiles as well, testifying to the visual interplay between different media.

The preferred medium for small-scale sculpture in the Middle East and India was metal. Metal figurines of birds, cocks, griffins were often incorporated into functional objects such as incense burners, ewers, or sword hilts, dating as far back as the Umayyad period. One unusual example from seventeenth or eighteenth century Hyderabad, India, rendered a dragon's head with pious calligraphy (see fig. 23). In sub-Saharan African and Southeast Asian societies with significant Muslim presence, pre-Islamic sculptural traditions also appear to have survived, likely coexisting with Islamic practice.

The metal artisan's principal value lay not with his ability to provide shimmering domestic and ceremonial metalware but with his skill in providing leading edge weaponry and armor for the military that also exhibited fearsome beauty and elegance (see fig. 41). Mamluk, Ottoman and Mughal weaponry – ceremonial and functional – typically featured Qur'anic calligraphy, that functioned as talismans for protection in warfare.

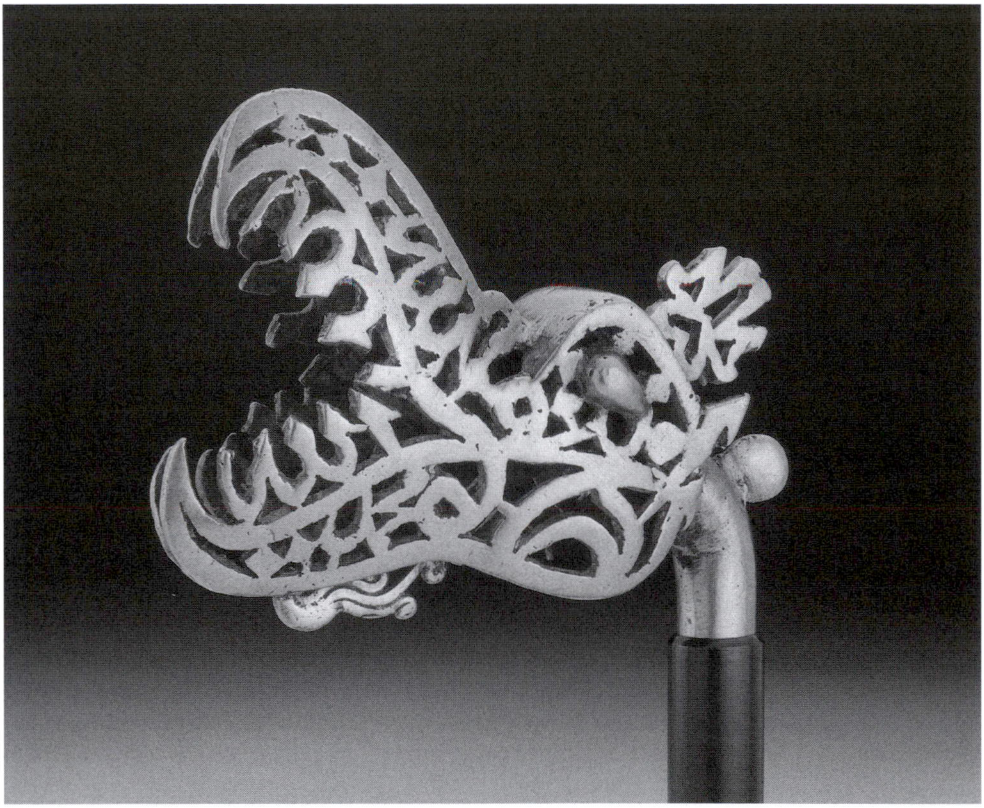

Figure 23 Dragon head. Hyderabad, Deccan, seventeenth or eighteenth century. The word Allāh forms the teeth of this calligraphic dragon which likely adorned a ceremonial standard.

Source: Ashmolean Museum, Oxford, inv. no. 1994.45.

As with textiles, some religious scholarly thinking frowned upon the use of precious metals in association with religious ritual, seeing them as signs of worldly attachment and distractions from the divine. The Syrian Ḥanbalī legist Ibn Qudāma (d. 1223) for instance wrote in his *Kitāb al-ʿUmda*, "Vessels: It is forbidden to use vessels of gold or silver for ablutions or any other thing . . . the same is true of plated articles, unless it be a silver plating of low value" (translated in Williams 1962: 96).

In addition to textiles, books, ceramic and metalwork, artisans of the Islamic world excelled at a number of other media. The most dazzling include carved wood, carved ivory, glassware, carved rock crystal, and jewelry made of gold and precious stones (see fig. 10). Though diminutive in scale and utilitarian by nature the portable arts of the Islamic world never failed to demonstrate excellence in artistry and infuse everyday life with beauty.

Recurring motifs

Across the portable and architectural arts, certain visual motifs recur that often owe their origins to the pre-Islamic past yet find their way into the visual culture of Muslim societies. The most common consisted of floral and organic imagery often fused with geometric devices, the most common being the spiral (arabesque), the rotated square and triangle, medallions, and interlaced knots. A variety of Qurʾanic and benedictory calligraphic inscriptions adorned the portable arts but occasionally emblematic words or phrases appeared, though this was more common in the architectural arts. They commonly included the names Allāh and Muḥammad (sometimes the rightly guided caliphs – Abū Bakr, ʿUmar, ʿUthmān, and ʿAlī), the *shahāda* – a profession of Islamic belief ("There is no god but God, Muḥammad is the messenger of God"), and the *basmala* – the introductory phrase to each chapter in the Qurʾān, which may be translated as "In the name of God, most benevolent, ever-merciful."

In figural imagery, notions of royalty and masculinity were often expressed using images of a seated dignitary usually with drink in hand, a lion devouring a gazelle, dancing girls, musical entertainment, a throne supported on the backs of lions and the archer hunting on horseback to name some common ones. Standard abstract animal imagery (camels, peacocks, dogs, doves, lions) signaling tribal affiliations permeated the rug making traditions of Turkic nomadic peoples. Standardized scenes and compositions were developed for illustrated Arabic and especially Persian literature. In works illustrating the life of Muḥammad his ascent to heaven, the *miʿrāj*, upon the mythical beast of Burāq was a popular subject as well. Circular haloes were used without sacred reference in Arabic miniatures but prophets and sacred individuals in Persian miniatures were generally depicted with a halo of flames alluding to their divine inspiration, though white veils were also used, as seen in Safavid and Ottoman painting. Less common but especially interesting were wondrous beasts like the double-headed eagles, the simurgh (a mythical phoenix) or hybrids like the winged beast Burāq. Zodiac imagery was also commonly found in the portable arts.

Various objects and imagery with strong allusions to the Prophet and his family surfaced sporadically as well. The veneration of the image of the Prophet's feet (and his sandals) has an obscure history in the Middle East, India and North Africa. The hand is a preferred talismanic image in the Middle East and North Africa with an unclear history as well sometimes referring to Fāṭima – the Prophet's most famous daughter – or sometimes referring to the five holy persons in the Prophet's family (Muḥammad, ʿAlī, Fāṭima, Ḥasan, Ḥusayn). Mamluk and Ottoman military and pilgrimage banners, and sometimes manuscript paintings, often bore images of the legendary double-tipped sword of Zulfikar (*Dhū ʾl-fiqār* in Arabic), belonging to Muḥammad and passed on to his son-in law and cousin ʿAlī – the fourth caliph and first Imām of the Shīʿa. In late and post Safavid Iran as well as late Mughal India, the annual Twelver Shīʿī processions and rituals commemorating the martyrdom of Ḥusayn at Karbala, Iraq, include sacred metal standards (*ʿalam*) and fantastical models of Ḥusayn's tomb.

One of the most iconic images of the Islamic world, has little to do with the Prophet. On *miḥrāb*s in mosques and on prayer carpets, a lamp suspended within an arch is often found and likely alludes to the "Chapter of light" (*sūra* 24) in the Qurʾān, in which a lamp figures prominently within a elaborate metaphor of divine light.

Impact of colonial and contemporary European and American art

The portable arts and architectural artistic traditions of the Islamic world were based upon the accumulated understandings of art, tastes and supporting economic relations built up between patron and artist groups. This paradigm survived into the nineteenth century but began to collapse unevenly across the Islamic belt. Undoubtedly, this change was tied to the increasing military and economic dominance of Western Europe and Russia, which dramatically enlarged the presence of European art, aesthetics, mass produced goods and mechanized techniques. The historic paradigm of Islamic art, for urban Muslim elites especially, was soon overshadowed by a globalized European one. The reasons were rooted not only in geopolitics and economics but also in the propagation of the deeply racialist ideology of European cultural superiority in which European forms of art and aesthetics were presented as indisputable beacons of modernity and civilization.

As in Europe and America, the mechanized production of artistic goods fundamentally disrupted the historic manual arts. New technologies, like photography, would also have an impact. The increasingly Europhilic tastes of patrons among the indigenous ruling and economic elites shifted attention away from historic Islamic arts as well. European-made chandeliers and clocks were popular items, for instance, but oil painting portraiture of male rulers was even more popular in the courts of late Mughal India, Ottoman Turkey, Qajar Iran and Egypt.

At the same time, museums, private collectors and scholars in Europe grew increasingly interested in acquiring, trading and studying the finest of historic Islamic arts, whose availability was facilitated by the exercise of European colonial power and the migrations of Christian and Jewish communities away from the fractious Ottoman empire. This interest culminated in a series of international and regionally focused exhibitions that included Islamic art in major cities like London, Paris and Munich during the late nineteenth and early twentieth centuries and that influenced various artists prominent and otherwise. The Islamic Orient imagined in fanciful, romanticized and sexual ways grew to be a popular subject, often painted by those who never traveled there and by some like Eugene Delacroix (1798–1863) who visited Morocco in 1832 (see fig. 49).

Traditional artists, artisans and their skills were rapidly displaced by an entirely new type of artist, primarily males from privileged families and trained largely in the old-fashioned academic tradition of Europe. In the colonized and Westernized Islamic cities the historic Islamic arts experienced a sharp decline in quality and artistic concepts and skills ceased to be passed through families, guilds, or state factories. The arts of textiles, calligraphy, and perhaps jewelry appear to have fared better than most.

European artistic norms were spread by European artists – French, British, German, Italian and Dutch – working in the Islamic belt, local artist societies, and indigenous artists trained either in Europe or in new arts institutions modeled on European precedents. The French established in Algiers the Musée d'Alger in 1900 and the École des Beaux Arts in 1920; the British founded the School of Industrial Art in Calcutta in 1854; the Academy of Fine Arts in Istanbul opened in 1883 and Prince Yusuf Kamal established the Cairo School of Fine Arts in 1908. Inspired by European art, the new artists were initially preoccupied with demonstrating competence with European conventions. As the twentieth century progressed, more emphasis was placed on expressing ethno-national identities by drawing on images of revolutionary heroes, antiquity, and village and peasant life that helped reinforce the re-imagination of the diverse multicultural Islamic world as a group of pre-existing ethnic nation states. Surprisingly, monumental figural sculpture became a popular art form – in Egypt and Iraq at least – reflecting various combinations of secularist, nationalist and authoritarian ambitions.

By the mid-twentieth century, many regions of the Islamic belt, now deeply immersed in the artistic paradigms of the Soviet Union, Europe and America, experienced a belated and often overlooked rise in modern art movements. Two tendencies – abstraction and the employment of visual art for social commentary and critique – took root, but a recurring problem has been how to localize modern art using local folk and Islamic visual traditions. Exploring the abstract potential of calligraphy has been a common strategy. For some – not all – this has meant engaging with or alluding to Islamic faith using the medium of modern art. More significantly, women have become important participants in artistic practice and discourse and the social strata artists come from have broadened (see figs 24 and 25). In the late twentieth and early twenty-first centuries, artists of the Islamic belt, those living transnational lives and those coming from diaspora communities in Europe and North America have actively participated in the global contemporary art world and all its diverse notions of art.

Since the mid-twentieth century, mass media visuals – found in print media, television, film, advertising, the internet and so forth – have saturated the Muslim world as they have the rest of the world. In countries exposed to Euro-American corporate influence, advertising art has flourished but heroic, socialist revolutionary art has also thrived especially under totalitarian regimes. A highly visible symbol of mass media's transformative impact on the arts is the overshadowing of proportioned Arabic script by Arabic typography, for printing presses and the computer (see fig. 15). Still cherished, handwritten and finely proportioned calligraphy has survived even in Turkey where in 1928 Atatürk decreed that Turkish should be written in Latin rather than Arabic script. However, calligraphy survives more as a touchstone for religious and cultural identity and less as an anchor for the arts of the Islamic world it once was.

Figure 24 Target, 1992 (silkscreen on canvas) by Laila Shawa (Contemporary Artist). Walls of Gaza (four works). A young Palestinian boy against a graffiti backdrop is framed within a rifle's crosshairs, a sharp critique of Israeli military action in Palestinian territories.

Source: Private Collection/The Bridgeman Art Library. Nationality/copyright status: Palestinian/in copyright. Reproduced with permission.

Mass consumer products are also an important medium of visual exchange. One innovative trend has been the rise of commercialized religious imagery in which a set of iconic architectural images, the Kaʿba in Mecca, Muḥammad's mosque in Medina, the Dome of the Rock and sometimes prominent Ṣūfī shrines predominate. Though late gunpowder era pilgrimage manuals and memorabilia often focus on the image of the Kaʿba the emphasis these architectural images receive in the contemporary visual lexicon of Muslim identity is new and finds few echoes in the past.

A number of innovative Islamic reformist movements arose in the Islamic belt during the nineteenth and twentieth centuries, some combining intense hostility to European and more recently American influence with a purist, normative notion of Islam that included fierce criticism of figural arts. Inspired by medieval juristic opinion, Ibn ʿAbd al-Wahhāb's views (d. 1792), which deemed art as a dangerous distraction from true religion, were endorsed and propagated internationally due to the oil wealth of a number of Arabian kingdom states, Saudi Arabia being the most prominent. Public figural sculpture is strongly disapproved of in Saudi Arabia, for instance, though political portraiture of the ruling family seems to be permissible. An extreme example of this contemporary hostility towards figural imagery in the name of Islamic purism was the 2001 destruction of the famous monumental rock carving Buddhas of Bamiyan, Afghanistan, by the Taliban regime, who deemed them idolatrous. Despite the publicity such views and actions receive, they do not define the majority of the

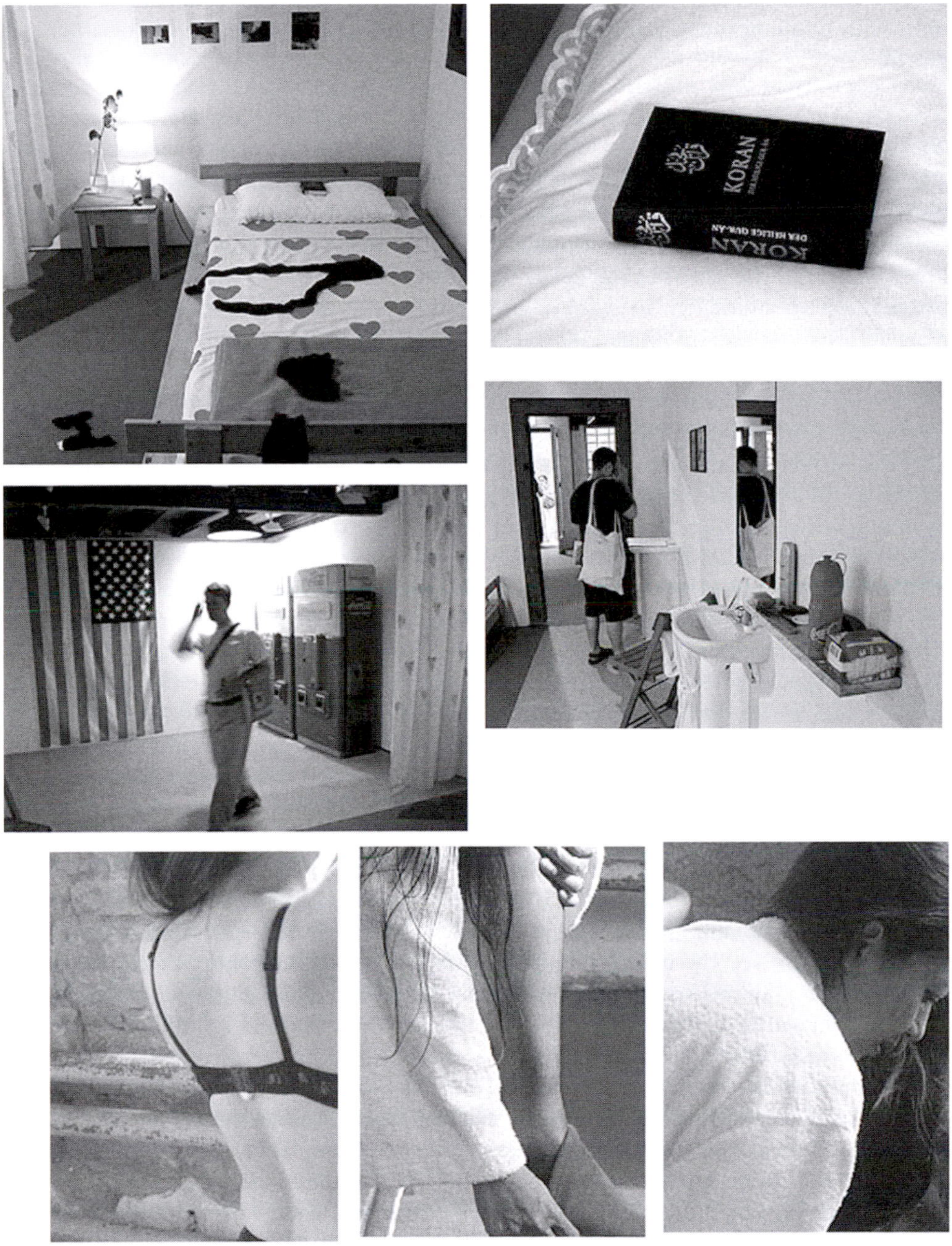

Figure 25 The Indonesian artist Arahmaiani based this performance piece on her experience of being unjustly detained and questioned by US Immigration in the Los Angeles airport because she was a Muslim.

Source: 11 June 2002, 2003. Performance piece at the Indonesian Pavilion at the 50th Venice Biennial 2003 Installation by Arahmaiani. © Photos: Prüss & Ochs Gallery. Reproduced by kind permission of the artist.

37

ARCHITECTURE

Hussein Keshani

The skylines of many of the Islamic world's cities are adorned with the profiles of monumental prayer complexes and to a lesser extent funerary buildings. Unlike pre-colonial Islamic art, in which religious concepts arguably play a subdued role, Islamic architecture seems to rely more deeply on Islam's ever-evolving body of religious beliefs and practices. The quest to accommodate Muslim prayer rituals and funerary practices combined with the aspirations of Muslim elites, who strove to project their power and status in visible ways, drove the development of monumental prayer and funerary monuments that mark the historic cityscapes of the Islamic world.

That being said, pre-modern monumental Islamic architecture, like Islamic art, also blended together common ideas with regional traditions. Urban design and architecture, whether it was religious, residential, palatial, commercial or civic in nature, was often shaped by the diverse pre-Islamic heritage that each region had to offer. These legacies combined with the religious concepts, new patterns of exchange, and technological innovations cultivated by the Islamic world generated a cohesive architectural tradition marked by continuity and innovation. Islamic architecture then is a term that is not typically used to refer only to works of a religious nature. It is broader in scope, alluding to buildings that range widely in nature, purpose and heritage. These works are what brought to life the ambitions and beliefs of Muslim societies as they spread across the Middle East, Africa and Asia after the seventh century.

One way to think about Muslim societies and their urbanization is to see them as following one or more of the following three approaches to urban development: adaptive, aggregative and planned. The building of Jerusalem's Dome of the Rock in 691 at the orders of Umayyad caliph ʿAbd al-Malik (r. 685–705) is a good example of an adaptive strategy at work. A symbol of Muslim authority, the building was deliberately located for all to see on a prominent platform where the city's Jewish temple once stood and had burned down centuries before. The Ghurid dynasty's adaptive strategy in twelfth-century Delhi as their Central Asian empire incorporated northern India went further, resulting in the demolition of the area's Jain and Hindu temple-landscape and the building of the iconic Quwwat al-Islām ("Might of Islam") Friday mosque in its place (see fig. 26). Sometimes adaptive development meant reusing significant monuments, as was the case when the fabled church of Hagia Sophia, Constantinople's symbol of imperial Christianity, was transformed into a Friday

Figure 26 Quwwat al-Islam congregational mosque minaret (phase 1), Delhi, India, 1193–9. Originally 73 m high and later extended, this minaret has large bands of Qur'anic inscriptions and is among the tallest ever built in the pre-modern Islamic world.

Source: Reproduced by kind permission of Michael Greenhalgh

mosque in 1453 after the city's fall to the Ottomans by whitewashing the building interior's beautiful glass mosaic Christian icons and adding minarets to the exterior. In all three cities – Jerusalem, Delhi and Istanbul – existing settlements were adapted and transformed by symbolically charged architectural interventions.

Muslim societies also settled in relatively unpopulated areas that developed gradually over time. A good example of this aggregative style of development is the city of Fez which is said to have been founded in the eighth century by the Idrisid dynasty. Never an imperial centre of power, Fez nevertheless became one of the major metropolitan centers of North Africa especially after the twelfth century.

In addition to following adaptive and aggregative forms of development, Muslim rulers experimented with large pre-planned urban designs that catered to military and elite society. Given the extensive military campaigns of the early caliphs it is not surprising that the earliest planned settlements were garrison cities that evolved from military encampments. The Abbasids were avid builders of new cities, which included the vast palace complexes and military cantonments of the Samarra region in Iraq. They also built the earlier, more unusual, circular city of Madīnat al-Salām ("City of Peace") now known as Baghdad, which bore traces of ancient Iranian urban planning.

The Abbasids' Shīʿī rivals in Egypt, the Fatimids, established al-Qāhira ("the Victorious"), modern day Cairo, near the old garrison city of Fustat. Located adjacent to a canal drawn from the river Nile, the walled city was organized around a long north–south avenue. The urban gem of the Spanish Umayyads was Madīnat al-Zahrāʾ ("The City of the Radiant") near Cordoba, a series of interconnected courts now in ruins. Also in ruins is the imposing fortified city of Tughluqabad in the Delhi region, one among several South Asian Tughluq cities. Tughluqabad consisted of three fortified cities in one and was built next to a large man-made lake. Mughal India offers grandiose examples like the sixteenth-century Fatehpur Sikri (City of Victory, which innovatively combined Indian and Central Asian design elements (see fig. 27), and seventeenth-century Shahjahanabad, named after the builder of the Taj Mahal Shāh Jahān (r. 1628–57) and now engulfed by modern New Delhi. In seventeenth-century Safavid Iran magnificent urban additions were made by Shāh ʿAbbās (r. 1587–1629) to Isfahan. These were partly oriented along a vast, enclosed, rectangular urban plaza called the *maydān*, the largest ever built in the historic

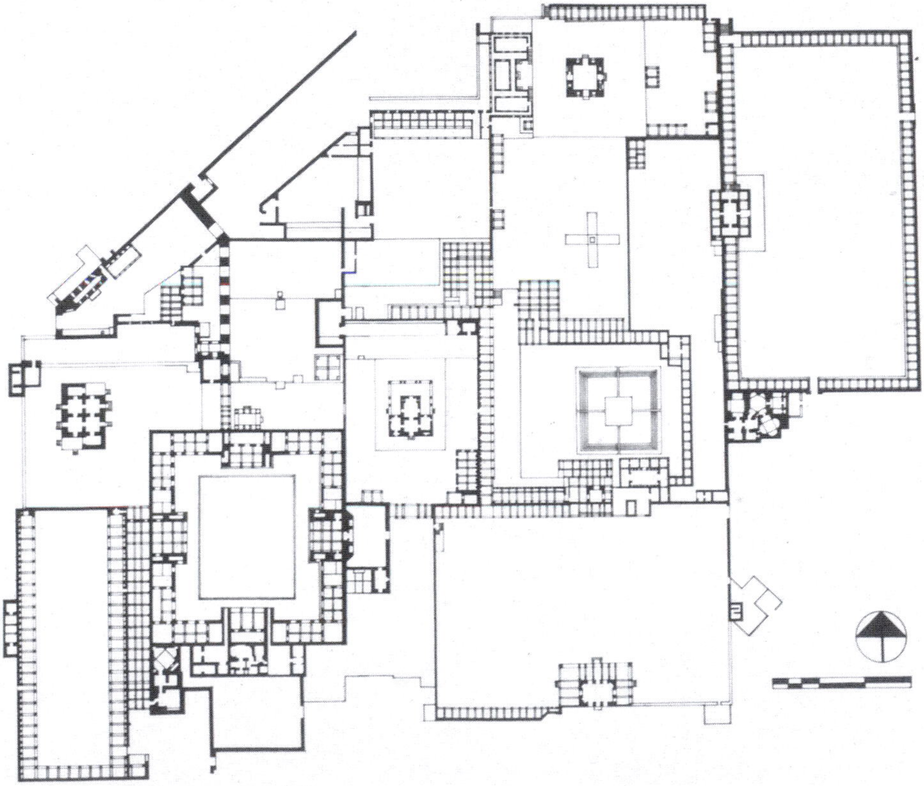

Figure 27 Plan of palace complex of Fatehpur Sikri, Fatehpur Sikri, India, 1571–79. Blessed by Shaykh Salīm Chistī, Maryam al-Zamānī, the Rajput wife of the Mughal emperor Akbar delivered their son in the town of Sikri, which was transformed by Akbar into a palace city following his conquest of Gujarat. It was abandoned before two decades had even passed.

Islamic world measuring about 500 meters by 130 meters (1,500 by 400 feet). All of these cities rank among the premier examples of planned urban development in the Islamic world.

Many cities of the masonry-building Islamic world were extensively fortified with imposing bastioned walls and monumental gateways that restricted access. Both the royal and administrative precincts and the surrounding urban fabric dense with the property of nobles and merchants were typically fortified. A dramatic example of urban fortification from the eighth century is the horseshoe shaped wall of the Abbasid city al-Rafiqa, which adjoined the earlier Syrian city of al-Raqqa and is now in ruins. Around the Islamic Mediterranean, ancient Roman fortifications loomed large, inspiring rulers and builders such as those who built the stunning citadel of Aleppo in Syria, with its steep ramparts and limestone walls (see fig. 1). Just as impressive are the four concentric rings of fortifications in the fourteenth-century South Asian city Daulatabad, which was located around a large granite outcrop and serves as a testament to Sultan Muḥammad Tughluq's (r. 1325–51) failed attempt to control southern India. Such efforts inspired the Mughals and their allies, who were also prolific builders of fortifications.

Masonry fortification appears to be less common in sub-Saharan Africa, though examples exist. Nevertheless, earthen ramparts could be just as imposing as demonstrated by the walled city Birni N'gazargamo. Built in 1470 with walls 7 meters high and spanning 2 kilometers, it was the capital of the Saifawa dynasty of Kanem/Borno in modern Nigeria. The widespread use of urban and palace fortifications across the Islamic world are strong reminders that security against rivals and invading forces were a constant concern for patrons and builders of pre-modern Islamic architecture.

Spaces for living

Warfare and a semi-nomadic lifestyle meant that rulers and military elites were often on the move but when they slowed down, ordinary life unfolded in palaces and pleasure gardens that were located within cities, on their suburbs or in the countryside. The largest palaces tended to be cities within cities, which combined administrative headquarters for government officials and courtiers with a ruler's household, where women, children and servants dwelled. It goes without saying that for more ordinary folks, life was lived on a smaller scale and in more humble dwellings.

Royal palaces and pleasure gardens

Four paradigms of palace architecture have been proposed for the primarily masonry building regions of the Islamic world. Drawing on Byzantine, Roman, Mesopotamian and Sasanian examples, the Umayyads and Abbasids experimented with agricultural villas in the greater Syrian and Iraqi countrysides and the Abbasids tried out urban palace-mosque complexes as well. The Abbasids also refined the concept of a luxurious sprawling multi-court suburban garden palace which inspired many later dynasties to come. The vast scale of the palace complex of Caliph al-Muʿtaṣim (r. 833–42) at Samarra, which spans across 145 hectares, evokes the spectacular concentrations of wealth and power achieved by the Abbasid caliphs.

The Turkic migrations and the spread of Turkic dynasties were accompanied by the rise of the fortified urban citadel from the eleventh century on, such as one built at Aleppo. The concept can even be observed on the East African coast in southern Tanzania, where the Husuni Kubwa palace complex, a collection of courts built of stone overlooking the Indian Ocean, once stood. Its materials and designs shared more in common with the Arabian gulf than sub-Saharan and Eastern Africa, highlighting the exchange of ideas that Indian Ocean merchants fostered. After the Mongol invasions, the urban citadel and multi-court palace were synthesized in unique ways and exploited to their full potential in the capitals of the gunpowder age empires, the Safavids, the Ottomans and the Mughals.

In contrast, the palace complexes of the primarily wood-building Southeast Asian sultanates generally lacked fortifications and looked more to Indian, Chinese and indigenous traditions for inspiration. Courts emanated symmetrically from the centrally located ruler's residence and the axial alignment with local mountains was considered auspicious.

The multi-court palace concept often included a variety of enclosed garden courts with palatial pavilions on the perimeter that could be used for both functional and recreational purposes. The elegant garden courts of the Alhambra palace complex in Granada Spain (fig. 7), though heavily restored, give a glimpse into not only how Roman gardens were adapted in Islamic architecture but more significantly the westward diffusion of Persian garden design concepts such as the *chahār bāgh*, a four-quartered garden subdivided by water channels. Reflecting pools were also used in the garden courts of the Alhambra and in the east, as found in the court of the Chihil Sutun (40 pillars), one of two surviving pavilions from the multi-court Safavid palace precinct that adjoined Isfahan's *maydān* to the west (see figs 5 and 28).

The walled *chahār bāgh* was an extremely popular concept in Central Asia, Iran and South Asia, especially after the fourteenth century. The spread of the concept from Central Asia to India was encouraged by the founder of the Mughal dynasty Bābur (r. 1526–30), who disliked the gardens of earlier North Indian Muslim rulers. The walled *chahār bāgh* would become the preferred setting for Mughal tomb architecture. The *chahār bāgh* concept even served as the underlying planning principle for new urban development such as Shāh ʿAbbās's redevelopment of Safavid Isfahan and Mughal Shahjahanabad, which both had long axial avenues with a continuous water channel. Enclosed gardens were not confined to palace precincts and sometimes they stood alone in urban and suburban areas. The many permutations of the *chahār bāgh* included parterres of flowers, trickling fountains, reflecting pools, and water channels running down steps. Their uses included agriculture, staging encampments, holding court, the performance of religious rites and the hosting of wine parties.

Islamic gardens are frequently said to be mirrors of paradise, attempts to recreate the pleasures of heaven mentioned in the Qur'ān here on earth. This may be, but it would be a mistake to lose sight of the more worldly aspects of Islamic gardens as agricultural sites and spaces where the elites of Muslim societies sought pleasure and recreation.

Figure 28 Mural painting in main hall of Chihil Sutun, Isfahan, Iran, late 1660s. This painting, which combines European and Persian styles, commemorates a famous episode in Mughal–Safavid relations when the Safavid Shah in Iran provided the Mughal emperor Humāyūn, Bābur's son, refuge while his empire was in danger of falling to rivals.

Source: Photographer Khosrow Bozorgi, 1999, Courtesy of the Aga Khan Visual Archive, MIT

Residential architecture

Throughout the historic Islamic world, many forms of more common housing evolved depending on factors like region, social class and environmental context. For example, excavations in the sub-Saharan African kingdom of Mali reveal homes that were circular in plan, mud brick in construction and likely roofed with thatch, but in the southern Arabian peninsula dramatic tower houses were built. A common form of housing in the urbanized Islamic Mediterranean was the courtyard house (figs 38 and 39) but detailed studies of the city of Cairo have revealed a range of housing forms that includes one-room dwellings, multi-room two-storey apartments, and residential caravanserais. This says nothing about the types to be found elsewhere such as the lands of Central, West, South and Southeast Asia. It has been suggested that one strand of continuity between many of these diverse forms of housing is the ability to keep men and women separate in keeping with the customs of gender segregation that permeated Muslim societies shaped by Near Eastern values. Beyond that, continuity in the domestic environments of the Islamic world is difficult to observe.

Prayer spaces

More than the palace complexes and residential quarters, it was the spaces for collective prayer that came to dominate the skylines of historic Islamic cities. Due to the centrality of collective Islamic ritual prayer in Muslim societies, prayer spaces of varying scales spread throughout the urban landscapes of the Islamic world. According to the Qur'ān, Muslims were obliged to remember the one God through daily prayer, however, the sacred text was remarkably vague about what type of prayer should be offered, when, how often, with whom and where this should take place. In theory, any place could become a place of prayer. Prayer was not confined to designated sites and the Qur'ān's most specific directive was to change the direction of prayer from Jerusalem, to which the Jews turned, to Mecca, where Abraham's first shrine devoted to worshipping one God, the Kaʿba, was said to stand.

The Kaʿba

The enigmatic Kaʿba in Mecca stands 13 meters (43 feet) high, 11 meters (35 feet) wide, and 12.5 meters (40 feet) long, a structure that has been rebuilt several times in its history. Once a temple surrounded by sculptures of Meccan deities, it is also a bridge between the world that Muḥammad grew up in and the one he would create in the name of Islam. The entry door sits 2 meters (7 feet) above ground and is accessed through a movable wooden staircase. When Muḥammad brought Islam to Mecca, he is said to have sanctioned the destruction of the religious imagery that adorned the interior with the exception of images of Jesus and Mary. Muḥammad is also said to have arbitrated the embedding of a mysterious black stone, possibly a meteorite fragment, into the east corner of the Kaʿba's outer walls. Under Islam, the Kaʿba was seen as the house of prayer that Abraham built, the focal point of Islam's pilgrimage ritual, the *ḥajj*, and the place to which Muslims around the world should orient themselves in prayer. Throughout the centuries, a vision of the Kaʿba is often described as a spiritual experience and prayers offered there were thought to be multiplied considerably. Yet the Kaʿba never became the model for later centers of communal prayer and it remains unique in Islamic architecture.

Jamāʿa masjid (congregational mosque)

The earliest and more influential example of the development of Muslim prayer spaces was likely the Prophet's residential compound at Medina, whose layout was obscured by later rebuildings though textual descriptions of its original appearance were made. It was a rudimentary residence and multi-purpose facility that seemed to have been a walled quadrangle with a large open space, rooms for the Prophet and his family off to one side and a shady covered area along one wall for regular prayer. It was the first congregational space for Muslims and likely served as a model for the earliest Islamic prayer spaces that also functioned as military camp, administrative center, and treasury, as well as court of justice, learning centre, place of social gathering, banquet hall, inn, and marketplace.

Congregational prayer for men at noon on Fridays was one social norm for ritual prayer that was developed and firmly set in place by the ninth century, reinforced by literature remembering the Prophet's example. The social norm had a considerable impact on the urban environments of Muslim administered cities, giving rise to monumental congregational prayer spaces that would ideally accommodate all of a city's Muslims. Such buildings were known as *jamāʿa masjid*s, which gradually shed their more worldly functions and became mainly religious centers with prayer as the primary activity. The term "mosque" is a European transformation of the Arabic term *masjid*. In theory, women had equal access to the *jamāʿa masjid* but as male juridicial views contributed to the entrenchment of gender segregation and raised questions about women's ritual purity during menstruation, this access was often limited and their presence within the *jamāʿa masjid* was increasingly segregated and marginalized.

Monumental *jamāʿa masjid*s had clear political overtones, informed to a large extent by the example set during the Umayyad and Abbasid caliphates. Umayyad and Abbasid caliphs often conspicuously demonstrated Muslim control over non-Muslim environments while fulfilling expectations to uphold the faith by using the monumental architectural vocabulary at hand. The early caliphs initially led the congregational prayers and a pronouncement (*khuṭba*) of the caliph's authority was introduced into the rituals, making the *jamāʿa masjid* a principal site for the assertion of caliphal authority. Ideally, there was only one official *jamāʿa masjid* per city but as Muslim populations grew this was hard to sustain. Sometimes, the construction of a *jamāʿa masjid* meant pre-Islamic sacred sites were appropriated, legitimately and illegitimately, to emphasize authoritatively the universalistic and abrogative nature of the Islamic vision.

Although regionally distinct conventions for *jamāʿa masjid* architecture did develop, an underlying criteria was formed. This included orientation towards Mecca; a centrally placed arched niche area known as the *miḥrab* signaling the direction of prayer and the place of the prayer leader; large covered lateral spaces to shelter the long parallel lines of believers in prayer; open courtyard spaces for the overflow of people; the supply of water for obligatory cleansing rituals; and towers (minarets) to serve as both landmarks, surveillance tools and possibly as sites to issue the call to prayer. In opposition to the Romano–Byzantine, Turkic or Hindu–Buddhist traditions, figural sculpture and imagery was noticeably absent from *jamāʿa masjid* interiors. In the major cities of the Islamic world, the *jamāʿa masjid* shared in common a tendency to appropriate the monumental conventions of indigenous religious and palatial architecture. Once the major *jamāʿa masjid*s of the Islamic heartland were developed, builders and patrons would look to them as well as antiquity for inspiration.

Perhaps the most famous among the iconic *jamāʿa masjid*s of the masonry building Islamic world is the eighth-century Umayyad *jamāʿa masjid* of Damascus, Syria, Islam's oldest intact congregational mosque. It combined monumental church basilica design with the use of a columned prayer hall, a concept that would prove popular. The old brick *jamāʿa masjid* of Isfahan, the cumulative work of multiple dynasties from the eighth century to the seventeenth, is a classic example of the genre of four- *īwān* mosques (see fig. 4). The four-*īwān* scheme was inserted into the *jamāʿ a masjid* in the eleventh century and included the use of four large arched openings in the courtyard, known as *īwān*s that were likely derived from Sasanian architecture. The *īwān*s were typically placed opposite to each other and the concept was employed widely and in different types of buildings such as religious colleges (*madrasas*) and caravanserais. Both the *jamāʿa masjids* of Damascus and Isfahan incorporated large columned prayer halls. Another iconic *jamāʿa masjid* is the Süleymaniyye Mosque built of stone in sixteenth-century Ottoman Istanbul as part of a large complex (see fig. 2). The *masjid*'s prayer hall was unencumbered by columns since it was covered with a monumental dome revealing the Ottoman's unique preoccupation with domed prayer halls inspired no doubt by the city's fabled Byzantine church, the Hagia Sophia.

Other materials besides brick and stone could be used for erecting monumental *jamāʿa masjids*. For example, the supple Sankore *masjid* in Timbuktu, Mali, an important centre of sub-Saharan African Islamic juristic learning, dates back to the fourteenth century and was built of mud brick and wood, requiring constant renewal and maintenance. In wood building regions like Southeast Asia, *jamāʿa masjids* in the cities of Demak and Yogyakarta employed tiers of pyramidal roofs, inspired by local palaces. In interior China, the fourteenth-century *jamāʿa masjid* of Xian (Changan) cleverly refashioned elements of indigenous temple and palace architecture to create a Muslim space (see figs 29 and 30). These iconic buildings show the many ways that the concept of a *jamāʿa masjid* could be interpreted by different Muslim societies steeped in distinctive local building traditions.

Figure 29 Mosque of Xian, Xian, China, 1392, 1413, 1662–1772. Original construction of this timber mosque, one of China's best preserved examples, began with the onset of the Ming empire and it was located within a series of four courtyards.

Source: Photographers Anuradha Joshi and Samia Rab, 1989, Courtesy of the Aga Khan Visual Archive, MIT

Figure 30 Xian Mosque tower, Xian, China, 1392, 1413, 1662–1772. The distinctive tower/minaret with its brick structure and wooden balcony was appropriately named the Pavilion for Introspection.

Source: Photographers Cherie Wendelken and You-Huan Zhu, 1984, Courtesy of the Aga Khan Visual Archive, MIT

*Muṣallā*s and *ʿIdgāh*s

While routine prayers were performed daily and on Fridays at neighborhood and *jamāʿa masjid*s, special prayers dating back to Muḥammad were offered during the two annual religious festivals of *ʿīd al-aḍḥā*, the commemoration of the sacrifice of Abraham's son and *ʿīd al-fiṭr*, the end of the month of obligatory fasting, Ramaḍān. These were commonly performed en masse outside the city in vast areas usually called *muṣallā*s in Arabic and *ʿidgāh*s in Persian. Festival prayers and their designated suburban space were opportunities for Muslim communities to sustain the ideal of performing prayer collectively in a way which *jamāʿa masjid*s could only approximate (see fig. 31). When not being used for festival prayer, *muṣallā*s served as spaces for recreation and trade among other activities. In some regions such as the Indian subcontinent, *ʿidgāh*s were distinguished by long linear structures that are best described as wall mosques.

While *jamāʿa masjids* were preferred for Friday prayers and *muṣallās* for festival prayers, daily prayers more often took place in the home or in smaller *masjid*s that were loosely organized by a variety of affiliations that could include patrimonial, tribal, ethnic, neighborhood, occupational and religious ties. One example from sixteenth-century India shows how smaller buildings were often executed with the

Figure 31 Painting of *ʿidgāh* at Amroha India, Thomas Daniell, 1810. With the rise of British rule in India in the nineteenth century, British painters traveled to India and captured images of the urban and rural landscape, as this image of a secluded *ʿidgāh*, a site for the performance of annual Muslim festival prayers, shows.

Source: Photograph copyright © Tate, London 2007

same if not greater finesse as larger monuments. Thought to be commissioned by senior officials descended from African slaves, the Sidi Saiyid Mosque in Ahmedabad (see fig. 32) was remarkable for its delicate stonework.

In general, building commissions were driven by varying mixtures of pious intent and cravings for prestige. Such commissions were seen as acts of religious devotion, conspicuous displays of wealth and financial investments. As Islamic legal traditions matured, a common way to finance the operations of *masjid*s, and other institutions too, was to allocate funds or revenue from commercial interests in perpetuity in the form of an endowment known as *waqf* (plural *awqāf*). The *waqf* financing system was integral to maintaining the built landscape which offered not only spaces for living and prayer but also spaces for the deceased.

Spaces for the deceased

Islamic proscriptions to bury the dead led in part to the rise of tomb building and the development of cemetery suburbs. In Islamic practice, those who had passed on to the

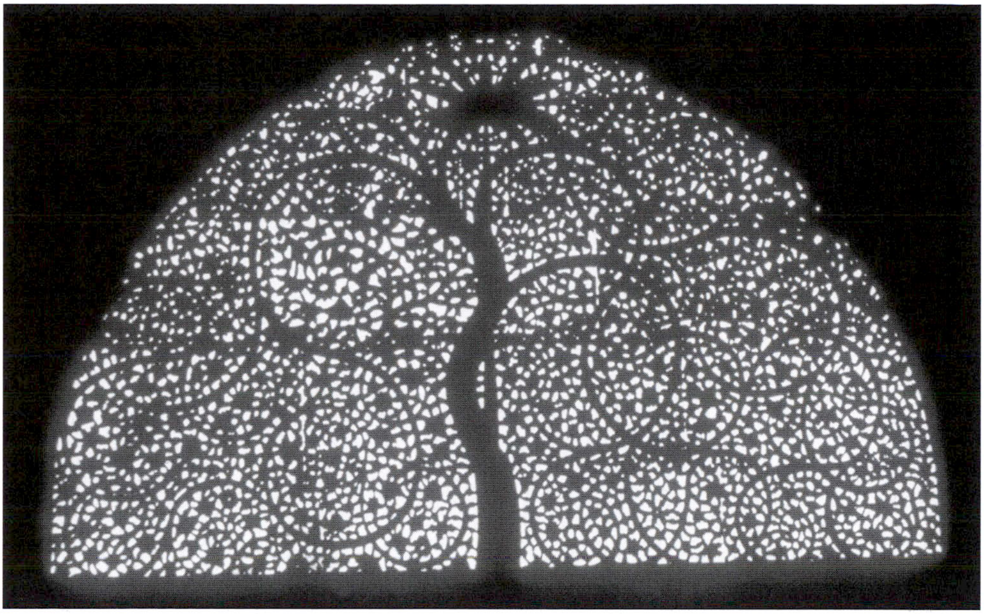

Figure 32 Pierced Screen at Sidi Saiyid mosque, Ahmedabad, India, 1572. This iconic image of Gujarat belongs to the Mecca-facing wall of the Sidi Saiyid mosque and depicts a palm tree being engulfed by a parasitic plant with circular tendrils.

Source: Photographer David H. Wells/Saudi Aramco/PADIA. Reproduced with permission

hereafter were typically laid in the ground perpendicular to the direction of Mecca so that their faces could be turned towards the Ka'ba in final prayer. It was appropriate to bury the deceased in a family dwelling, a suburban cemetery, or later near or within a religious institution such as a *masjid* or religious college. Rural and village landscape were punctuated by graves and tombs as well.

Initially, graves of the deceased were likely no more than unmarked mounds but these gave way to the use of grave markers of many varieties, which were commonly laid out along the length of the body, although in some regions like Ottoman Turkey vertical grave markers were used. Grave markers became an object of artistic endeavor. Niche imagery and Qur'anic calligraphy were often employed to distinguish the grave markers of the nobility, the affluent and charismatic religious figures. Cotton and silk tomb shrouds lent grandeur to grave markers too but after the ninth century tomb construction seems to have also risen in popularity. This may have been tied to the growing religious authority of saintly individuals and the venerative practices their personas attracted.

Building tombs over graves is an old practice in the Islamic world, perhaps dating to the time of Muḥammad and likely influenced by Byzantine Syrian shrines for saints and relics. No tomb was built for the Prophet who was said to have been buried in his home which was also the Medina *masjid*. Centuries later, rebuildings of the Medina *masjid* by the Mamluks and Ottomans led to architectural embellishment of the Prophet's gravesite with a large dome, which was integrated into the *masjid*. The *masjid* and tomb, which were extensively expanded in the late twentieth century, form the second most important pilgrimage destination for pious Muslims after the Kaʿba.

Tomb building stems in part from the urge to commemorate exceptional saintly souls. Earlier on it was the companions of the Prophet, the Shīʿī Imāms and Old and New Testament figures, whose graves – real or otherwise – were distinguished by tombs. Later on, the graves of celebrated Muslim mystics, religious scholars, and frontier soldiers credited with expanding Islam's reach attracted tomb development. The belief that blessings could be derived from visiting the graves of saintly souls was an important impetus for building tombs and the formation of pilgrimage networks that – along with trade networks – helped tie together disparate regions of the Islamic world. Two important groups of early tombs in Fatimid Fustat and Aswan dating from the tenth century suggest small-scale tombs were typical early on, but following the Turkic and Mongol conquests, tomb building took on more monumental proportions and became more closely tied with ruling figures and elites. Two highpoints in this love affair with monumental tombs were the powerful Central Asian ruler Tīmūr's (r. 1370–1405) large rebuilding of the small shrine of twelfth-century Shaykh Aḥmad Yasawī (d. 1166), (see fig. 6), a mystic credited with bringing Islam to Kazakhstan and the famous Taj Mahal in Agra, India. Set within a vast garden enclosure, the marble-clad domed edifice was built by Tīmūr's descendant the Mughal emperor Shāh Jahān, not for himself – though he is buried there – but for his favorite wife, who died in 1631.

Tombs were not lifeless monuments. Graves and tombs attracted ritual prayer activity for a variety of reasons. Their explicit orientation towards Mecca, the use of *miḥrab* imagery, the belief in the sacred aura of the gravesites of charismatic religious individuals, the custom of visiting graves annually, and the practice of employing Qur'ān readers at grave sites are among the diverse forms of beliefs and practices that brought people to grave sites and made them vibrant centers of activity. Religious scholars sometimes took exception to tomb commissions and ritual practices, fearing they resembled idol worship and encouraged vanity instead of humility in the face of death.

The most common form of tomb was the domed cube but this varied. For example, Anatolia and Iran are also known for their distinctive tomb towers with their conical roofs which grew in popularity from the late tenth to the thirteenth centuries. One impressive example is the Gunbad-i Qabus completed with baked brick in 1006 (see fig. 33). Another interesting variation found in Damascus and Baghdad is the *muqarnas* tomb, in which the roof is made up of a series of arched niches, *muqarnas*, that created stunning optical effects.

Tombs were not always independent structures. The case of fourteenth- and fifteenth-century Mamluk Cairo and environs shows that tombs could be integrated into religious institutions such as a *masjid* or a religious college (*madrasa*), securing perpetual prayers for the souls of the deceased (see fig. 34). Such hybrid structures still incorporated prominent funerary domes and roofs that served as an eternal marker of one's spirit on the cityscape.

Figure 33 Gunbad-i Qabus, near Gurgan, Iran, 1006. The patron of this 52m high brick tomb tower was from a family that recently converted from Zoroastrianism to Islam. One text claims that the patron's coffin was suspended by chains hanging from the dome.

Source: Photographer Melanie Michailidis, 2003, Courtesy of the Aga Khan Visual Archive, MIT

Civic spaces

In addition to establishing spaces for living, prayer and the deceased, cities of Muslim societies included a variety of civic spaces offering useful social services. These included religious colleges (*madrasas*), small hospitals (*bīmāristāns*), and bathhouses (*hammāms*).

Early on, *jamā*ʿ*a masjids* and the homes of scholars nourished the minds of intellectuals. However, as Muslim empires grew more complex, institutional buildings dedicated to teaching and learning were developed. These did not emerge first in the Abbasid empire as might be expected but roughly around the tenth century in eastern Iran. They were favored by the westward expanding Turkic dynasty, the Saljuqs,

Figure 34 Dome detail of Sultan Qā'it Bāy *madrasa* and tomb, Cairo, Egypt, 1472–4. Both geometric and floral motifs are used in the masterful stone carvings on the exterior of this dome.

Source: Photographers Vivek Agrawal and Sonit Bafna, 1984, Courtesy of the Aga Khan Visual Archive, MIT

who likely used them to disseminate and institutionalize their doctrinal convictions to subdue a heterodox environment. The concept spread widely and such monuments to learning were often called *madrasa*s, which could stand alone or be joined to *jamāʿa masjid*s or tombs.

*Madrasa*s were primarily devoted to the Islamic religious sciences – Qur'ān interpretation, *ḥadīth* scholarship, and legal studies – but mathematics and science had their place in these institutions that also helped train young men to administer religious institutions and governmental affairs. For the most part these buildings stood one or two stories high and consisted of small chambers surrounding a central rectangular court that was most often open to the sky but was sometimes covered with a dome depending on the region. *Masjid* halls for students and teachers to perform their daily prayers were typically incorporated as well.

In the late twelfth century and early thirteenth century, prior to the extinction of the Abbasid caliphate by the Mongols, several *madrasa*s were built in Baghdad, the most impressive being the al-Mustanṣiriyya named after the Caliph of that name (r. 1226–42). Mamluk Cairo was also a hotbed of *madrasa* construction. Domed tombs for rulers and elites frequently adjoined these lavishly ornamented buildings. The funerary *madrasa* of Mamluk Sultan Qā'it Bāy (r. 1468–96) is a good example of this intriguing marriage between death and learning. Among the grandest *madrasa*s ever built are those found in the Timurid Central Asian capital Samarqand, famed for its religious scholars. The city's Registan Square consists of a group of not one but three monumental *madrasa*s – the Ulugh Beg Madrasa (1418–22), the Shīr Dār Madrasa (1619–36), and the Tilla Kari Madrasa and Mosque (fifteenth to sixteenth centuries) – built between the fifteenth and seventeenth centuries to form a pleasing urban ensemble. The Ottomans were great builders of *madrasa*s as well. Sulaymān (r. 1520–66), one of the most powerful Ottoman sultans and a generous patron of monumental architecture, included at least four *madrasa*s to surround his grand *jamāʿa masjid* in Istanbul.

Muslim societies inherited a long tradition of medical science from the Greeks, the Persians and the Indians so it is not surprising then that hospitals (*bīmāristān*s or *māristān*s) could be found in many of the historic cities of the Islamic world. The Abbasid caliphs and nobility were active patrons of hospitals but surviving examples are scarce. However, later examples dating after the Turkic migrations began to survive in good condition. One well-preserved structure is Mamluk Aleppo's premier hospital the *māristān* of Arghun al-Kamili, which was built in 1354. With its open court and reflecting pool it was a tranquil place to be treated for one's ailments. Equally pleasing is the hospital of Ottoman Sultan Bāyazīd II (r. 1481–1512) in Edirne, Turkey, where music was purportedly one form of treatment prescribed for the mentally ill.

In addition to educational facilities and hospitals, public bathhouses were a common feature in many cities of the Islamic world, in part a legacy of Romano–Byzantine architecture. Bathhouses could be important generators of revenue, a fact not lost upon the Il Khanid ruler Ghāzān Khān (r. 1295–1304) who ordered a *hammām* be built with every *masjid* in the villages of Iran to help finance *masjid* operations. The Yalbugha Hammām in Aleppo (fig. 35), Syria, rebuilt by a Mamluk governor in the fifteenth century and creatively restored in the twentieth century, preserves the subterranean atmosphere of domed bathhouses lit with star-like openings. The charming twin baths commissioned by the famous Hurrem Sultan (Roxelana) in Ottoman Istanbul cleverly separate men and women while using the same heating facilities. These public baths were not intended for rulers and elites, who could afford to build their own private baths in their homes, but for members of the broader society.

In general, commissioning religious and civic buildings was considered pious work, the kind rulers and elites were expected to undertake on behalf of Muslim societies. This responsibility extended to public works such as waterworks, public water facilities, and bridge building, basic infrastructure that breathed life into cities and agricultural districts. Safavid Iran offers the eighteenth-century Khawju Bridge and weir as an example of how such public works could on occasion combine architectural ingenuity with beauty (see fig. 36). Beyond public works, rulers and elites also took it upon themselves to encourage interregional trade by creating spaces for commerce.

Spaces for commerce

Dotted along the Islamic world's vast trade networks were commercial buildings, several of which were built upon an existing infrastructure of military outposts. Most follow a courtyard plan, varying in details and quality depending on the region. In

Figure 35 Yalbugha Ḥammām, Aleppo, Syria, mid-fifteenth century, 1985. Restored in 1985, this Mamluk era *ḥammām* or bath house included typical features like cold, medium and hot chambers, as well as pierced domes with glass plugs.

Source: Photograph courtesy of Architect, © Architect/Aga Khan Trust for Culture

coastal cities, urban bazaars and along various land routes, commercial buildings – the airports of their day – flourished, accommodating merchants and their animals laden with goods. Known by many names which include *funduq, khān a*nd caravanserai they served many functions. Remote hinterland facilities provided fortified overnight accommodations and animal stables while urban facilities focused more on warehousing and shops.

Numerous examples survive after the rise of the Saljuqs, especially in Iran. The Khan Mirjan of Baghdad, remarkable for its elaborate vaulting, is an especially grand example built by a successor dynasty to the Il-Khanids and whose revenue was

Figure 36 Khwaju Bridge, Isfahan, Iran, 1650. Traffic on this bridge was cleverly divided with animals and wheeled carts occupying the central path, which was flanked by vaulted pedestrian paths. The bridge also acted as a weir, regulating the waters of the Zayandeh river.

Source: Courtesy of the Aga Khan Visual Archive, MIT

intended to finance a neighboring *madrasa*'s operations. The dawn of the affluent Gunpowder Age empires was also a golden age for commercial buildings, one example being the elegant sixteenth-century Rüstem Pasha urban caravanserai in Edirne, Turkey, which stood on one of the major trade routes linking Asia with Europe (see fig. 40). Originally commissioned by Rüstem Pasha, the Ottoman emperor Sulaymān's trusted vizier, it was built by the emperor's architect Sinān (1490–1588). Modern restorers have attempted to give this building a new lease of life by converting it into a hotel.

One recurring pattern of commercial development across West Asia and the Islamic Mediterranean that is difficult to date is the development of commercial districts commonly known as bazaars, which included covered streets called *sūq*s. In bazaars, long tracts of single-room shops lined narrow streets that were sometimes arranged in multiple rows. More established areas would cover the streets with materials like cloth, reeds, brick and stone. One of the most elaborate examples of this style of commercial development taken to its logical extreme is the Grand Bazaar of Istanbul, which includes two large fifteenth-century commercial storage buildings (known as a *bedestān*) surrounded by a maze of covered streets forming one large superstructure.

Spaces for minorities

The religious communities of the Islamic world were not uniformly Muslim and at times various groups – Christians, Jews, Hindus and others – found themselves living as tolerated minorities and sometimes as majorities under Muslim rule. Consequently, there are traces of non-Muslim monumental architecture built using the architectural vocabulary of Muslim societies that can be explored. For example, in seventeenth-century Isfahan, the Safavid Shāh ʿAbbās relocated an Armenian Christian community to the Isfahan suburb of New Julfa, where an intriguing church known as the Vank Cathedral was built using the Safavid architectural idiom (see fig. 12). Another interesting example is the restored nineteenth-century Ben Ezra synagogue in Old Cairo (Fustat) that was a reconstruction of a historic eleventh-century synagogue that the famous medieval Jewish philosopher Maimonides (d. 1204) attended.

At times Muslim societies were conquered by outsiders and became minorities themselves, subject to non-Muslim rule as was the case in sixteenth-century Christian Spain, twelfth-century Sicily under the Norman Crusaders, or thirteenth-century Iran under the Mongols. In such cases, the building traditions nurtured by Muslim societies continued to be employed.

Dividing the historic cities of Muslim societies into spaces for living, prayer, the deceased, civic purposes, commerce or minorities is a useful exercise but it is worth remembering that there was no universal archetype of the Islamic city and in actuality these spaces were not always separate. At various times and locations, different combinations of spaces and building types with common affinities occurred. These combinations included palaces and *jamāʿa masjid*s, the *madrasa*s and tombs, commercial and residential spaces, *masjid*s and bathhouses, *masjid*s and tombs, and hospitals and *madrasa*s. Not only were spaces with different functions amalgamated together but individual spaces tended to have only loosely assigned purposes to begin with, making them multifunctional in the truest sense.

Patrons and master builders

In the social imagination, patrons overshadowed builders and architectural personalities were rare. For the most part monumental architecture was commissioned by rulers and their families, military and administrative elites and merchants. Building was expected of cultivated elites and was a means of amassing social prestige.

Women's rights to own property and amass independent wealth in Muslim societies meant that elite women were often important patrons of monumental architecture as a study of any number of dynasties – the Ayyubid, the Timurid, the Safavids, the Mughals or the Ottomans – would reveal. For example, one study of twelfth-century Ayyubid Damascus estimates women patrons accounted for 14 percent of the major religious commissions over an 85 year period. While women were involved as patrons and many buildings were commissioned for them, they were far less directly involved when it came to the actual design and construction.

Despite the vast volume of building that took place in Islamic cities, fairly little is known about the identities and working methods of the builders which depended on regional traditions and materials. In general, construction was rapid, taking years not decades or centuries. Islamic architecture evolved largely through practice, and treatises on the subject were uncommon.

There are some dynasties like the Ottomans that reveal more about master builders than others. For example, biographical information is available for Sinān, the builder of the great Süleymaniyye *masjid* in Istanbul. He was an Anatolian Christian recruited and educated by the Ottoman army, who later professed Islam and came to lead the empire's central building department of around 40 to 50 people responsible for designing military and religious architecture across Ottoman territories. One Ottoman text, the *Risāle-i mi'māriyye*, describes in wonderful detail the life of Ottoman architect Mehmet Aga and his approach to architecture. Imperial financial records allow reconstructions of how building projects were managed. Plans of *masjid*s and bathhouses have even surfaced. The library of the Topkapi palace complex in Istanbul, a treasury of Ottoman records, even boasts a rare surviving set of Iranian or Central Asia drawings for architectural ornaments called *muqarnas* that show how two-dimensional patterns were projected into three dimensions. Models built of wood, ivory, paper and other materials also appear to have been used on occasion to visualize projects.

Laying out building plans on grids traced on paper or slate was likely a technique used in other regions and periods as evidence from Central Asian and South Asian contexts suggest. The use of mathematical proportions to determine the dimensions of spaces was also most likely a common approach shared by builders from various regions. A certain degree of mathematical knowledge would also have been useful for calculating surface areas and the quantities of materials required, an important task performed by builders who were expected to be competent with finances. All of this is still vague and the best way to become better acquainted with builders of the historic Islamic world is to study their works directly and examine their ideas about space and form.

Spatial concepts

Builders in historic Muslim societies tended to choose from and combine remarkably few spatial concepts. These included gendered space, enclosed courtyards and gates, pillared halls, monumental towers and roofs, *īwān*s, and the arch.

Gendered space

Building upon Byzantine and Middle Eastern cultural precedents and creative interpretations of the Qur'ān, the practice of gender segregation entrenched itself in much of the Islamic world from the ninth century on, particularly for the elites. Not all Muslim societies nor all segments practiced gender segregation to the same extent. Nevertheless, it was a recurring feature that had important implications for how men and women used and moved through urban space. In palatial and residential design, the practice translated into the development of special zones for female living which were forbidden to male outsiders (*ḥaram*). In some regions, the practice led to the outright exclusion of women from *masjid*s, while in others they were relegated to separate compartments or balconies a feature commonly found in contemporary *masjid* design.

Literate women were usually educated at home, often by their fathers, uncles, brothers, or male cousins. If their mothers or other female relatives were educated, they often studied with them as well. Women who worked for a wage, generally labored at home doing piecework as seamstresses, weavers, or making other handicrafts.

In addition to serving as a refuge from the outside world, the courtyard was a common area shared by the whole family (or families) who lived around it. Among rural and nomadic populations the courtyard might also serve as a corral for livestock. Women tended to prepare hot meals over a fire in such courtyards or in common neighborhood cooking areas. In the residences of the wealthy and the palaces of the ruling classes, courtyards were often quite elaborate. Many were equipped with fountains, gardens, and sophisticated canopies and trellises that allowed in light, but also provided a cooling shade from the often blistering sun.

The courtyard also served as the public space of the home where guests were welcomed and entertained. In addition to the courtyard there was often a salon that served the same purpose. In either case when male guests were involved, the courtyard or the salon became extensions of the outside world in that such gatherings generally were male-only affairs, especially among the wealthy classes. Since hospitality and generosity were notable virtues throughout the Islamic world, food and beverages were served in such instances. In the medieval Islamic world, few things could ruin one's reputation more than being known as stingy or inhospitable.

Because of the strict rules pertaining to sexual segregation every dwelling had an inviolable space (harem) that was separate from the rest of the house where the women retreated when male guests were present. In palaces and the homes of the wealthy this took the form of well-appointed women's quarters or harems which only women, children, male kin, and eunuchs were allowed to enter. The women of less well-to-do families retreated to a room or an area separated from the rest of the dwelling by a curtain or some sort of partition that served as a harem only when guests were present, but was generally used for other purposes such as cooking, sewing, making handicrafts, study, or sleeping.

Whether one lived in a courtyard house or in a multistorey tenement, a frequent concern was how best to encourage air exchange and cooling breezes in the often stifling summer heat and at the same time preserve the sanctity and privacy of the home's interior space. One common means of achieving both ventilation and privacy is what is known as *mashrabiyya* – a wooden grill or grate that was used to cover windows or balconies. The grills or lattice work were usually made of turned wood that was joined together with carved blocks or spheres of wood to create intricate patterns. (In the homes of the very wealthy or for use in public buildings, the screen was occasionally made of metalwork.) Another means of ventilation was the wind catcher, or *malqaf*. A wind catcher functioned as a kind of reverse chimney in that it was composed of a shaft that rose above the building's roof. The opening of the shaft was positioned to catch the prevailing winds of the region and force them down into the building, often flowing over pools of water or screens that were dampened with wet fabrics.

Domestic life in the medieval Islamic world was generally conducted rather close to the ground. Families did not sit in chairs around a dining room table at mealtime. Nor did they eat from individual plates. Rather, meals were served on large serving trays that were set on the floor or on a low stand. Guests then sat on a carpet, pillow, or very low seat around the serving tray and ate directly from it. They generally ate many dishes with their hands and flat breads; however, utensils (especially knives and spoons) were used for cutting meats and for eating soups.

While furnishings in the medieval Islamic world did include chairs with legs, and beds with frames, it was far more common that homes were furnished with pillows, mattresses, and sofas. Woodworkers and smiths did construct benches and chairs that were comparable in height to modern chairs and benches, but these were generally for use outside the home and generally were used to indicate the higher rank and status of the person (ruler, scholar, family patriarch, or other person of high status) who sat on them in relation to those who were seated below him. Sitting on sofas, large pillows, pillows stacked on one another, or anything that might elevate a person over others could just as easily serve the same purpose of reflecting the hierarchy of status and rank.

The heights and kinds of beds people slept on as well as the kinds of material used to make beds, pillows, and sofas were indications of status and wealth also. Beds with legs and frames were a sign of high status. Beds without them were a step down, sleeping on a mat or carpet a step further, and sleeping on the bare floor was for the poorest as well as for the mendicant Ṣūfīs, who considered themselves as God's poor ones (*fuqarāʾ Allāh*).

Food and water

The diet of even the lowliest peasant in the medieval Islamic world was generally varied and quite healthy. The staple grains in most areas were wheat and in areas with more saline soil, barley. Sorghum was grown widely as well, but it appears that only the lower classes used it as a food crop for both themselves and their animals. Rice could only be cultivated in those areas where there was an abundance of water, such as the southern shores of the Caspian Sea, in parts of Spain, in the Nile Delta and along the Nile in Egypt, along the lower Euphrates in southern Iraq, even along the Jordan River near Beit Shean. In such areas it competed with wheat and sorghum as a staple. However, in many other areas it was an imported luxury that only the wealthier could afford.

Along the Mediterranean coastlands, olive orchards were as thick on the ground as they had been in antiquity. Vineyards were cultivated as well; however, after the Islamic conquests, they gradually became less important to the local diet than they had been in late antiquity as more and more of the population converted to Islam and adopted the Islamic prohibition against the consumption of wine. Nevertheless, grapes continued to be used in Syria to produce raisins and molasses, which were staples of the local diet, especially in the winter months. Baʿlabekk was famous for its molasses and Darayya (southeast of Damascus) for its grapes and raisins.

Some of the oasis settlements of Arabia as well as some of the settlements along the rivers in Iraq and Egypt cultivated vast date palm groves. A wide array of fruits and vegetables native to the region were cultivated along with others such as bananas, citrus, sugarcane, eggplants, watermelons, and mango trees that entered the Middle East from India and Africa in late antiquity or during the early Islamic period. Precisely how these foods spread westward across the Mediterranean to Spain is difficult

complex siege engine used in the period was the simple swing-beam trebuchet, and it was not until the end of the seventh century that Muslim trebuchets were sufficiently developed to enable them to be used against buildings as well as personnel.

The success the Muslims enjoyed derived from a number of factors. The Muslim armies were highly motivated, in contrast to their opponents, who were often divided by internal squabbles; the Muslims fought for their faith, their personal honor, to support their companions and of course for the prospect of plunder. Soldiers were not paid salaries, so their income came from the revenues of conquered lands and the booty taken in combat; indeed, this was such an important concern that the caliph ʿUmar ibn al-Khaṭṭāb (r. 634–44) is credited with setting up a register of Muslims (*dīwān*) to ensure that the booty was shared out fairly. ʿUmar is also credited with ordering the creation of the first *amṣār* (sing. *miṣr*), garrison towns that enabled the Muslims to settle in and control conquered territories while avoiding mingling with the local populations and risking losing their cultural and religious identity. Muslim armies were also highly mobile, traveling long distances on horses and camels, and as a result of the ability of the camel to store large quantities of water in its stomach, they may have been able to take short-cuts and outflanking routes across the deserts, slaughtering their camels and drinking the water from their stomachs along the way! In addition, the Muslims had other advantages over their enemies; the Muslim chain of command was very simple, with army commanders being drawn from important members of the community and answering directly to the caliph, enabling fast and efficient direction of the armies; they made effective use of Roman-style ditch and rampart fortifications (*khandaq*) to protect their armies, a technique pioneered by the Prophet at Medina in 627; and some have suggested that the fact that the Byzantines and Persians had just emerged from a mutually devastating civil war may also have played a role in the Muslims' success.

The first civil war, *fitna*, signaled a number of changes in the Muslim armies. As a result of the divisions that appeared in the Muslim community, most particularly between the troops of Iraq and Syria, tribal loyalties, while important, began to be superseded by regional ones, a development that would prove to be highly influential in the Abbasid takeover of 750. In addition, in the wake of the *fitna* during the reign of the caliph Muʿāwiya ibn Abī Sufyān (r. 661–80), two units, the *shurṭa* (police) and *ḥaras* (guard) became permanent institutions, forming standing units of troops for the caliph. Each local governor also had his own *shurṭa*, used to keep peace in his territories.

Armies of the Marwanid and early Abbasid caliphs

The early Muslim armies consisted primarily of volunteer soldiers, non-professionals who answered the summons issued each time an army was being assembled for a campaign and fighting for the promise of payment and booty at the end of the campaigning season. However, a change occurred during the reign of the caliph ʿAbd al-Malik (r. 685–705). ʿAbd al-Malik created a professional army, largely drawn from Syria, that was paid a regular salary and acted as the instrument of the caliph's authority in the caliphate. Indeed, as long as this army remained united, Umayyad rule was assured; it was only during the last decade of Umayyad rule, when divisions within the caliphal family enabled inter-tribal tensions in the army to come to the fore, that it no longer proved effective as the guarantor of Umayyad rule. In the meantime, the armies of Iraq, the main source of ongoing resistance to Umayyad rule, were defeated and largely demobilized, though many of the troops who served in the ongoing Muslim conquests in Khurasan were of Iraqi origin. Payment was primarily in cash, but soldiers were also sometimes paid in food supplies or given plots of land to settle, either in place of or more commonly in addition to their cash income.

In battle, the formation of a center and two wings was retained, though we also have reports of both a vanguard and a rearguard being used to support the main body of the army. In later years this formation would also be subdivided, with smaller units of various types forming part of each section of the army. The most common tactic, which the Umayyad armies mastered, was the use of the infantry spear-wall, which was highly effective against infantry and cavalry alike, though it required a great deal of discipline. The troops would kneel, pointing their spears against the advancing enemy. When the enemy was almost upon them, they would stand, thrusting their spears at their opponents, and would then advance steadily in a line, aiming to drive their enemies before them. This tactic enabled the Umayyad armies to defeat their opponents again and again. It is ironic that this same tactic was used by troops loyal to the Abbasids to break the Umayyad cavalry at the Battle of the Upper Zab in 750, after the Umayyad caliph Marwān II (r. 744–50) had enacted reforms intended to give a greater role to heavily armored cavalry in the Umayyad forces. The Umayyad armies also mastered the use of the *khandaq*, which now ranged in form from a simple ditch and rampart to a full-blown marching camp with multiple gates and maybe towers as well. Thorns or caltrops were also strewn outside them to protect them, especially during construction.

The Muslim chain of command remained relatively simple, with leaders of armies often drawn from the *ashrāf*, though the government periodically intervened in the choice of tribal leaders. Additional officers were appointed to supervise recruitment, but they served no special battlefield roles. Commanders would appoint leaders of each wing of the army, but these would only be temporary appointments, lasting no longer than the battle being fought.

The early Abbasid caliphs, like the Umayyads, owed their military support first and foremost to a regional salaried army, this time consisting mainly of soldiers from Khurasan (the Khurāsāniyya) and their descendents who came west and settled in Baghdad (the Abnā'), although other elements, including irregular volunteers, were also found in the Abbasid armies. The Syrian troops, meanwhile, found themselves largely demobilized much as the Iraqis had before them. The early period of Abbasid rule also witnesses the widespread emergence of a class of professional salaried military officers (*quwwād*, sing. *qā'id*) who came to replace the tribal leaders as the commanders of the Abbasid armies. These *quwwād* were often early supporters of the Abbasid movement, and they frequently were responsible for recruiting as well as leading their armies, though they and their troops were still paid by the state.

Up to this point the military technology used by Muslim troops remained largely the same as that used earlier. However, there were some important changes that took place. We have evidence of more widespread use of mail armor in Muslim armies, including armor that now protected the legs and arms as well as the body, providing greater protection for the wearer. Horse armor was also used by some cavalrymen to protect their mounts, although it is not clear what this armor was made of. Marwān II sought to make greater use of units of heavily armored shock cavalry to defeat his opponents through repeated charges, though as mentioned above this did not prevent his defeat by the Abbasid troops, using the traditional Umayyad-style spear wall, in 750. Muslim troops also used oil, shot at the enemy (exactly how is not clear) to set fire to their buildings. Meanwhile, Muslim rulers were making wider use of fortifications, primarily in the form of palaces and administrative compounds, usually built of stone with defensive features including both square and round towers, arrow slits, machicolations and crenellations. Such structures were built for their impressiveness as well as for their defensive value, to emphasize the power of rulers through their grandeur. Some cities were also fortified, though there was also reluctance on the part of some rulers to build walls around cities for fear of encouraging revolts by giving their potential opponents defensive structures with which to resist them. Finally, mention should also be made of the adoption of the iron stirrup by Muslim horsemen, which seems to have first taken place in Khurasan at the end of the seventh century. While by now leather and wood stirrups had become known and were used by some, they had a tendency to break. However, iron stirrups did not suffer from this problem, and they thus gave a rider reliable stability and support. This was to have an important impact on later developments in the Muslim military, as will be demonstrated later.

The rise of the Turks

In the wake of the civil war that ended with the accession of the caliph al-Ma'mūn (r. 813–33), the victor and his successor, al-Muʿtaṣim (r. 833–42), sought to establish a new army that was directly loyal to the caliph himself. This army was recruited primarily on the eastern fringes of the Muslim world and consisted of a number of groups, of which the most important were Turks recruited from Transoxania and the Central Asian steppes. The troops recruited by al-Muʿtaṣim in particular were possibly purchased as slaves, since they are referred to using the Arabic term *ghilmān* (sing. *ghulām*), which can mean either a slave or a young boy, though if they were slaves then it seems that they were subsequently freed. Either way, they clearly became regular salaried troops and were expected to be loyal to the caliph. Al-Muʿtaṣim built a new capital for his troops at Samarra in Iraq, which enabled him to give grants of land to his troops and neutralize tensions that had arisen between the new troops and the inhabitants of Baghdad. Unfortunately, the isolation of the caliph with his private army eventually led to these troops dominating the caliphs while also expecting to be paid well and regularly, something that became increasingly difficult as the caliphal finances began to fail. When the caliph al-Mutawakkil (r. 847–61) sought to reduce his dependence on the Turks by removing some of their leaders and recruiting more non-Turkish troops, the Turks reacted with violence, murdering the caliph and installing their own candidate in his place. Thus began a period of conflict, with periodic battles between various factions both within the army of Samarra and between the troops of Samarra and Baghdad. Meanwhile, most of the caliphs were installed or removed by whichever faction of the army happened to be dominant at the time. The conflict placed an additional strain on the caliphal finances that only got worse as the provinces ceased sending in their tax revenues. The chaos only came to an end in 870 with the accession of the caliph al-Muʿtamid (r. 870–92). His brother and deputy, the experienced politician al-Muwaffaq (d. 891), worked out an agreement with the Turks whereby they became dependent on him personally for their salaries, ensuring their loyalty but also taking responsibility for ensuring that they got paid. It is likely that they were also promised that they alone would constitute the elite of the caliphal army. Al-Muʿtamid was succeeded by al-Muwaffaq's son al-Muʿtaḍid (r. 892–902), who restored Baghdad as the caliphal capital and brought the army firmly under his own control. However, the decades that followed saw the army decline with the caliphal finances, and the first half of the tenth century saw the subsequent caliphs lose control of their troops to their deputies.

So why were the Turkish troops so important? The Turks brought into the Muslim world a new and deadly technique of fighting: mounted archery. The Turks were expert horsemen, and were equally skilled at shooting from the saddle, something that was assisted by their use of the iron stirrups mentioned above. They also probably imported shorter composite bows that were usable from horseback, and they are described as carrying two or three of these and a lasso, which they used to pull enemy riders from the saddle. In addition to these weapons they would be equipped with hand weapons; mail, lamellar, leather or felt armor for both themselves and their horses; shields; helmets; and lances. Unlike conventional armies, they maintained a loose formation on the battlefield, with multiple units alternately advancing on their opponents to unleash volleys of arrows against them, then retreating before the enemy could respond, thus maintaining almost constant fire on their enemies. Once the enemy army was on the point of collapse, the Turkish armies would close into close combat to finish it off. These Turkish horse-archers soon came to constitute the elite backbone of the caliphal armies, with most of the infantry being of non-Turkish origin. Unfortunately, the Turkish cavalry were expensive to maintain, which contributed to the strain on the caliph's treasury, and they were also likely to react aggressively if they felt that their elite status was threatened.

The collapse of Abbasid authority and the Būyid takeover of Baghdad witnessed the establishment of numerous independent dynasties in the provinces. This was accompanied by a diversification in the ethnicities, equipment and tactics of troops found in Muslim armies. However, it was only a century before the Turks again established their pre-eminence as the Seljuks swept across the Muslim world. Despite this, in the eleventh to thirteenth centuries Muslim armies retained and even expanded the diversity in their composition, probably in recognition of the dangers of placing one's trust too much in troops of only one ethnicity. Thus troops used against the crusaders by Nūr al-Dīn (d. 1174) and Ṣalāḥ al-Dīn (Saladin) (d. 1193), for example, included a mixture of Turkish heavy cavalry archers, Kurdish and Arab mercenary cavalry fighting with lances (using both the two-handed and the classic "couched" hold) and swords, and infantry drawn from local militias and volunteers, equipped for close and missile combat. It is worth noting that by now both composite and crossbows were being used, though the general preference of mounted archers was for composite bows, which were much more practical to use from horseback. The centuries following the Seljuk conquest also saw the popularization of Turkish-style curved sabers, especially in the twelfth and thirteenth centuries, whereas Muslim swords up until this point had been predominantly straight. By this time it is also clearer that the cavalry archers in these armies incorporated a core of elite troops of genuinely slave origins, *mamālīk* (sing. *mamlūk*), who had been purchased at a young age in the lands on the fringes of the Muslim world (principally Central Asia), educated in both Islam and the arts of war, then freed upon reaching adulthood, though they generally preserved their loyalty to their former owners. On the battlefield, these mixed armies were usually arranged, broadly speaking, in the same way as in earlier centuries, with a center and two wings, though greater flexibility was employed in assigning additional contingents like vanguards and flanking units to support the main body of the army.

While many of the troops in Muslim armies were paid in cash, the Būyids, the Seljuks and their successors also made widespread use of *iqṭāʿāt* (sing. *iqṭāʿ*). These were assignments of the revenues of estates that were made by a ruler to his followers in return for military support or other services. They were revocable and theoretically non-hereditary, though it was not uncommon for the son of an *iqṭāʿ*-holder to be granted or seize his father's lands upon his death. The lands themselves remained the property of their previous tenants, but they now paid their taxes to the assignee rather than the ruler. In this way, as in Europe, many members of the nobility came to be supported by the land, but only through the permission of their rulers.

During this period the Muslims continued to build fortifications, though for the most part these were used in cities, rather than to build independent strongholds akin to the castles built by Europeans in both the west and the crusader states. There were castles built by the Muslims, but these were generally fairly simple in form with few of the elaborate defensive devices used in western castles. Instead, the Muslims preferred to strengthen the defenses of cities by building both walls around the cities and, most importantly, fortified citadels within them, to which the inhabitants could withdraw if their city was taken, and from which the rulers could assert control over their subjects. Meanwhile, the Muslims made advances in the technology of their siege weapons. In particular, by now the swing beam trebuchet had given way to the counter-weight trebuchet, and large mechanical crossbows were also being used by both the attackers and defenders of fortifications.

The Mamluks

In May 1250, the Ayyubid sultan of Egypt, Tūrān-Shāh, was murdered by some of the senior Mamluks in the army. He was replaced initially by his mother, Shajar al-Durr, a Turkish freed slave who had been a wife of the previous Ayyubid sultan, who reigned for nearly three months before being replaced by a senior Mamluk officer. Over the following decades the Mamluks both extended their hold over Syria and instituted a carefully centralized state that included a rigidly stratified military hierarchy and supervision of the non-military spheres of society by senior military officers. In the military sphere, the supreme commander was the sultan himself, defended by a royal guard of highly trained Mamluks. Below the sultan was an advisory council of 24 *amīrs*, each of whom held senior positions at court and commanded 100 Mamluk troops and 1,000 *ḥalqa* troops. These held the title of *amīr miʾa wa-muqaddam alf* (commander of 100 and leader of 1,000). Below these *amīrs* were commanders of 40 Mamluks (each with the title *amīr arbaʿīn*, "commander of 40"), then the commanders of 10 Mamluks (each with the title *amīr ʿashara*, "commander of 10"). These officers were supported by *iqṭāʿāt* of values corresponding to their statuses.

Figure 41 Helmet. Ottoman, sixteenth century. The *shahāda*, the Muslim profession of faith in God and Muḥammad, ornaments the tear dropped standard on this ceremonial, jewel encrusted, soldier's helmet.

Source: Topkapı Palace Museum, 2/1192. Reproduced with permission.

The non-Mamluks in the army were recruited into the *ḥalqa*, which was composed of free-born non-Mamluk cavalry of various origins, including both Kurdish, Turkish and Mongol horsemen and, in particular, the sons of Mamluks (known as *awlād al-nās* ["sons of the people"]). It was not usually possible for a son of a Mamluk to rise to the senior ranks in the Mamluk army, which were reserved only for Mamluks; instead, *awlād al-nās* enjoyed social privileges but were restricted to the lower ranks of the army. The exception were the sons of the sultans, in as far as the sultans often attempted to institute a hereditary succession to the Mamluk sultanate, with varying degrees of success. The *ḥalqa* was usually commanded by both Mamluk officers and leaders from among their own ranks. In addition to the *ḥalqa*, the Mamluks also employed a number of types of auxiliaries, both cavalry and infantry.

The Mamluk troops were highly trained, expert horsemen and proficient with a number of weapons. In particular, they were trained to fight with two swords, and their skill with these was said to be so great that they were able to control precisely the locations and depths of any cuts they made. They were also equally skilled at horse-archery, able to shoot both rapidly and accurately while on a swiftly moving horse. On the battlefield a Mamluk would usually be mounted on a large Arabian horse, clad in mail or lamellar armor (the fifteenth century saw the start of use of a mixture of mail and plate) with a turban or helmet, and would carry one or two swords, a dagger, a lance, a mace or axe, a shield and a composite bow and arrows. Naturally, the level of training and equipment any given Mamluk possessed varied, with the sultan's personal Mamluks receiving the most thorough training and the highest quality equipment. Against less mobile foes, the Mamluks would take advantage of their greater mobility to weaken their foes with hit-and-run arrow volleys before delivering a heavy charge to finish the enemy off. Against more mobile foes, they would seek to repel the enemy's own hit-and-run shooting attacks with volleys of arrows delivered from stationary, disciplined ranks, only making hit-and-run arrow volleys if appropriate, and they would seek to break their enemies with one or more heavy cavalry charges.

The Mamluk armies reached their height, in terms of quality and power, in the thirteenth and fourteenth centuries. This enabled the Mamluks both to sweep the Crusaders from the Levantine coast and to repel repeated attacks by the Mongols, essentially bringing the Mongol expansion to the west to an end. However, in the later centuries of Mamluk rule the quality of the army declined and the training facilities, in which the earlier sultans had invested heavily, fell into disrepair. In the meantime, a new military power was entering onto the world stage.

Gunpowder and the rise of the Ottomans

Incendiary and explosive weapons had continued to evolve over the centuries. It is known that in the thirteenth and fourteenth centuries the Mamluks were making use of Greek fire, shot in casings of various types from bows and siege engines and also used in flamethrowers. In this period they also made use of a number of gunpowder weapons, including grenades and simple rockets and torpedoes. Beginning in the early fourteenth century, various states in both the eastern and western Muslim world began to adopt both cannons and handguns. The most successful of these states was the Ottoman sultanate, founded in about 1300. In the late fourteenth century the Ottoman rulers began recruiting young slaves and training them in the arts of war, forming them into a personal infantry unit known as the janissaries. It is not known whether this form of recruitment was inspired by the slave-soldier systems used by earlier dynasties. These janissaries were originally archers, but in the fourteenth and fifteenth centuries they were equipped with arquebuses, and other Ottoman infantry troops also came to be equipped with similar weapons. In the meantime, the janissaries came to be an elite core of the Ottoman armies, which remained a mixture of infantry and cavalry. In time they also came to be an influential force in Ottoman society and politics.

Until recently much was made in scholarship of the Ottomans' use of firearms and artillery, with the prevailing view being that the Ottomans' greater willingness in adopting such weapons was what enabled them to expand their hold over most of the Muslim world. However, lately scholars have questioned this view, suggesting that while in some instances a greater openness to gunpowder weapons may have been influential, a number of other factors may well have contributed to their success, including greater adeptness in using such weapons, easier access to supplies of gunpowder and firearms, a high level of discipline and training, use of armies outnumbering those of their opponents and an understanding that victory did not derive from gunpowder alone. In fact, early gunpowder weapons were cumbersome to transport and slow to fire. In the sixteenth century the re-curved bow was still, overall, a superior weapon to the handgun; in the hands of a skilled wielder, it had a greater range and rate of fire, was more accurate, and could be used both on foot and on horseback, unlike the arquebus that had to be fired on foot. Thus it was only gradually that the arquebus replaced the bow.

Europeanization of the Ottoman army

Scholars are divided as to exactly when and to what extent the technology of Ottoman armies declined in comparison to that of their Western counterparts. However, it is clear that starting in the early nineteenth century, in response to both internal decadence and military defeats by European powers, the Ottoman sultans and their provincial governors sought to reform their armies radically. The janissaries, the major opponents of reform, were disbanded in 1826, and the Ottoman rulers recruited new armies and had them trained by European instructors in Western fighting techniques and military technology. However, these reforms, while helping to extend the lifetime of the Ottoman empire, proved insufficient to prolong the Ottoman sultans' rule beyond their defeat in World War I.

Conclusion

As already stated, this chapter can only provide a brief survey of the most important military developments that have taken place in the Muslim world. It must be emphasized that the broad points made here are subject to regional influences and customs; the armaments used by a soldier in medieval Muslim Spain, for example, differed greatly in their composition and design from those used by his counterpart in Iraq, which themselves differed greatly from those used by a warrior in Muslim India. Indeed, in terms of mutual influences on military developments, the borders of the Muslim world were highly porous, with technology and tactics passing into the Muslim world from a variety of cultures. Thus it is very difficult to describe a particular type of warfare as being distinctively "Islamic." It is only when we come to discussions of *jihād* that we can begin even to approach a concept of "Islamic" warfare, and here the distinctiveness remains in the details, for Islam is not the only religion with a holy war doctrine.

References and further reading

The Osprey (Oxford) *Men at Arms* series provides concise illustrated introductions to armies and their armaments from various periods in history; particularly pertinent to this topic are

Vol. 125 (*The Armies of Islam, 7th–11th Centuries*), Vol. 140 (*Armies of the Ottoman Turks 1300–1774*), Vol. 171 (*Saladin and the Saracens*), Vol. 222 (*The Age of Tamerlane*), Vol. 259 (*The Mamluks 1250–1517*), and Vol. 314 (*Armies of the Ottoman Empire 1775–1820*), all by David Nicolle and Angus McBride, and Vol. 269 (*The Ottoman Army 1914–1918*), by David Nicolle and Raffaele Ruggeri. The Osprey Elite series focuses on particularly distinguished contingents of armies through history; of particular interest is Vol. 58 (*The Janissaries*), by David Nicolle and Christa Hook.

Amitai-Preiss, R. (1995) *Mongols and Mamluks: The Mamluk-Ilkhānid War, 1260–1281*, Cambridge: Cambridge University Press.

Ayalon, D. (1978) *Gunpowder and Firearms in the Mamluk Kingdom: A Challenge to a Medieval Society*, 2nd edition, London: Frank Cass.

—— (1994) *Islam and the Abode of War: Military Slaves and Islamic Adversaries*, Aldershot: Variorum.

Crone, P. (1980) *Slaves on Horses: The Evolution of the Islamic Polity*, Cambridge: Cambridge University Press.

Elgood, R., ed. (1979) *Islamic Arms and Armour*, London: Scolar Press.

Firestone, R. (1999) *Jihād: The Origin of Holy War in Islam*, New York: Oxford University Press.

Goodwin, G. (1994) *The Janissaries*, London: Saqi Books.

Gordon, M. S. (2001) *The Breaking of a Thousand Swords: A History of the Turkish Military of Samarra (A.H. 200–275/815–889 C.E.)*, Albany: State University of New York Press.

Hillenbrand, C. (1999) *The Crusades: Islamic Perspectives*, Edinburgh: Edinburgh University Press.

Imber, C. (2002) *The Ottoman Empire, 1300–1650*, Basingstoke: Palgrave Macmillan.

Irwin, R. (2004) "Gunpowder and Firearms in the Mamluk Sultanate Reconsidered," in M. Winter, A. Levanoni, eds., *The Mamluks in Egyptian and Syrian Politics and Society*, Leiden: Brill, 117–39.

Kennedy, H. (2001) *The Armies of the Caliphs: Military and Society in the Early Islamic State*, London: Routledge.

—— (2002) *Mongols, Huns and Vikings: Nomads at War*, London: Cassell and Co.

—— (2006) "The Military Revolution and the Early Islamic State," in N. Christie, M. Yazigi, eds., *Noble Ideals and Bloody Realities: Warfare in the Middle Ages*, Leiden: Brill, 197–208.

Khan, I. A. (2004) *Gunpowder and Firearms: Warfare in Medieval India*, New Delhi: Oxford University Press.

Lev, Y., ed. (1997) *War and Society in the Eastern Mediterranean, 7th–15th Centuries*, Leiden: E. J. Brill.

Matthee, R. (1996) "Unwalled Cities and Restless Nomads: Firearms and Artillery in Safavid Iran," in C. Melville, ed., *Safavid Persia*, London: I. B. Tauris, 389–46.

Murphey, R. (1999) *Ottoman Warfare, 1500–1700, Warfare and History*, London: UCL Press.

Nicolle, D. (1999) *Arms and Armour of the Crusading Era, 1050–1350: Islam: Eastern Europe and Asia*, London: Greenhill Books.

Sandhu, G. S. (2003) *A Military History of Medieval India*, New Delhi: Vision Books.

Savory, R. (1980) *Iran under the Safavids*, Cambridge: Cambridge University Press.

40

POPULAR PIETY AND CULTURAL PRACTICES

Earle H. Waugh

Popular religious practices and pious activities of Muslims have always been matters of debate from the very early days of Islam precisely because Islam was born into Mecca – Mecca was a pagan pilgrimage centre that commanded the allegiance of people throughout the region. Consequently, early Islam had to define itself over against other religious practices of the time, and in its first days the fledgling community was in contention with various pagan rites. Conflicts with Jews and Christians gradually developed a little later. Indeed, the Qur'ān itself critiques various types of spiritual and religious activities, indicating that Muslim rules for relating to such practices had to be established. Hence we can assume that during Muḥammad's time, jostling about normative religious practice was a common, perhaps almost constant occurrence. The important feature to note for our purposes is that both the Qur'ān and the developing Islamic religion affirmed that culture was not a neutral force in religious life, and that it had to be transformed to conform to true religious standards.

The Qur'ān did, however, add a new theoretical framework to the general debate with its pejorative attitude toward all pre-Islamic cultures. Out of this grew a general resistance to and critique of all cultural features of paganism, along with the development of an infrastructure of code-words to go with it. Thus there evolved various theories about the notion of *jāhiliyya*. As Islam expanded, *jāhiliyya* changed from being the time period before the coming of Islam to a complex term carrying significant theological freight. In one of its most advanced forms, *jāhiliyya* was applied negatively to all aspects of any society that existed outside of the influence of Islamic culture and religion. Such a designation demonstrates that the term had picked up several theological and perhaps even legal nuances in its development.

For example, the Qur'ān accepts that many prophets brought God's message to their lands and communities over the history of the world's peoples, and concludes that these messengers have sometimes been successful. Hence the Qur'ān also recognizes the various religious cultures surrounding these messengers. In its view, the messages brought by these chosen people had become distorted, so that what existed today had to be challenged by the true word of God brought by Muḥammad. Presumably, however, some form of Islam continued to exist in truncated ways throughout the whole earth, so the world was not without testimony to Islamic presence.

All this indicates how religious cultures differing from Islam had a continuing place in traditional Muslim theory. The Qur'ān makes quite clear that all People of the

Book (that is, the Jews and Christians) were to be free to practice their religions. Hence early Muslim expansion frowned on the destruction of churches and synagogues by military forces. Rather, as was the case in Damascus, a large central church would be taken over and converted to a mosque but all others were left to their original believers. In addition, special taxes were levied upon these religious communities as their contribution to public good (they were not subject to military call-up as were Muslims). In such a multi-religious environment, constructing religious markers was an important aspect of the way identity was forged. Thus, designating practices as normative was one way of marking religious identity over against other traditions. When Muslims were challenged, their practices were tested against principles drawn from the Qur'ān or the Prophet's *sunna*. If there was no authorized source found advocating some practice, then authorities deemed such practices non-Islamic. The net result was that all practices within the Muslim religious environment had to be rooted either in the Qur'ān or the *ḥadīth*, since practices arising from somewhere else were viewed as foreign to true Islam. Practices that were not spelled out by these authoritative texts had to resort to some kind of theological argument based on the sources for justification. Sometimes this process took place over a considerable length of time, so that issues were left up in the air until Muslim opinion had solidified about their legitimacy. Where no clear-cut designations existed on whether a practice was non-canonical or not, there was much room for differences of opinion; a good example of this is seen in the current debate over female circumcision. Thus it was that the Islamic legal system came to be the mediator on matters of practice, and the decision of the court formed the basis for one component of what we may call the "Muslim marker" system.

Finally, because Islamic society developed with state and religion so closely intertwined, several technical issues not directly related to practice played important roles. For example, classical Islamic state theory distinguished those lands under Islamic influence from those outside and in conflict with it. In its starkest form this was known as the division between *dār al-Islām* (the world of Islam) and the *dār al-ḥarb* (the world of war). This theory assumed that there was an Islamic cultural environment that was opposed by other non-Islamic systems. Even when there were no hostilities with non-believing neighbors, the belief was that an Islamic cultural milieu was best. Obviously the theory had other repercussions, such as involvement in the development of *sharīʿa* or Islamic law, for relationships with non-Muslims were adjudicated by Muslim legal systems. The result was that the state itself was critical in shaping what a true Islamic culture was to be. This had implications for local practices, since the trend was to eliminate local practice in favor of a "universal" Islamic practice. Yet this could never be by fiat alone, or even by legal directive, for cultural influences cannot be manipulated so easily. Thus, we can see that elements of a tribal and popular sort continue to have an impact on Muslims even to our own day, regardless of what the authorities say.

All of these factors suggest a continuing influence of popular ideas and practices in Muslim cultures throughout history, and the relationship between canonical and non-canonical is a dynamic one. As in all great religious cultures, then, Islamic culture is a rich tapestry, and there is a continuing place for non-canonical practices, which we will now briefly survey.

Piety around the Qur'ān.

Muslim piety concerning the Qur'ān is particularly rich and we can do little more than indicate some main lines. First is that the Qur'ān itself sets some of the protocols about its treatment; for example *sūrat al-wāqi'a* (Qur'ān 56: 77–9) states, "That this is indeed a Qur'ān most honorable, in a book well-guarded, which none shall touch, but those who are clean." These verses have been interpreted to mean that one should not read the Qur'ān unless the ceremonial washing, *wudū*, has been performed, with the Qur'ān having set itself above all other texts through revelation. Many other protocols have followed from this sacred designation.

The Qur'ān has been subject to a number of special practices that may not be canonical in the sense of protocols within the sacred text itself but which appear to derive from its position. These range from the special rules about its use, as well as to how it is to be handled in the ordinary affairs of life. For example, there are various stories of popular usage of the text: of Qur'ans being fixed to spears as a claim to cease hostilities between Muslims, or of the authority of some text as the means to bring about compromise in a protracted dispute, or of the reading of the Qur'ān in its entirety during the month of Ramaḍān as a mark of piety. Since there can be no higher authority in Islamic culture and tradition than the Qur'ān, popular practices have been built up around its place in Islamic culture.

In addition, there are some important practices related to how the Qur'ān is to be treated in everyday life, such as when one is carrying it, the scripture should not be placed underneath other books in one's arms, nor should it be placed on a table under other books. It should not be left open when not in use, and it should not be placed on the ground or in an unkempt and dirty area. A Qur'ān should not be torn or frayed, and when, through use, it falls apart, it should not be separated into sheets and left around. An old or dismembered Qur'ān should be burned or buried with appropriate ceremony. Accordingly, there are some places one should not take a Qur'ān, such as the toilet, and it should not be placed in one's bed. When reading it, it is best to place it in a reading stand, and one should not hold one's place in the text with a vulgar marker.

There are a plethora of rules regarding recitation of the Qur'ān that have come to be known as the science of *tajwīd*. Many of these have grown up because of the place of Qur'ān reciting in public piety: one should not recite a partial *āya*, in effect taking part of the verse from its context, or emphasizing some aspect of the verse at the expense of the whole. Nor should one vary the text through lack of breath: most published Qur'ans contain indications where one should take a breath – how much one must recite until the next breath is clearly marked. All of these complex rules are based upon the perception of the Qur'ān as the ultimate symbol in Muslim piety.

Then there are practices built upon special kinds of piety. For example, it is commonplace that official religious meetings begin with Qur'ān reciting; meetings that lack such recitations risk being regarded as unofficial and not Islamic. Likewise, one will have the Qur'ān recited at the wake of a beloved who has passed into eternity. Families who are pleased at the birth of a child may well hire a Qur'ān reciter as a way of expressing appreciation to God. Individuals may also recite certain *āyāt* for their perceived power to assist them in difficulties, such as selected verses for help in an examination. It was also well known in medieval Islam, and to some extent still today among some classes of believers, for verses to be written out on paper, dissolved in water and ingested as a way of invoking the Qur'ān's curative powers. Verses may also be used as protection from adversity, and the practice of carrying *āyāt* on oneself when going into battle is seen as a claim to divine assistance and protection. Finally, verses may be inscribed and carried as amulets by some believers.

There are special sections of the Qur'ān that have received extra attention in the history of the text. *Sūrat al-fātihḥa*, while the opening chapter of the Qur'ān, has assumed the place of final benediction and blessing in Muslim piety. Mystically oriented believers have taken sustenance in *Sūrat al-nūr* (Qur'ān 24), and have intoned its vivid passages for the special meanings seen there. During Ramaḍān, some believers place a great deal of emphasis on the night when the Qur'ān was believed to have been first delivered to Muḥammad, *laylat al-qadr* (see Qur'ān 97) and remain awake in vigilance all night hoping to see a re-enactment of this event which portents a good year for the observer. Furthermore, there are some verses that are regarded as powerful in certain circumstances, such as in the face of a drought, and the community may gather to collectively recite these to bring rain. Of course, there have also been sections that have played key roles in Islamic law and culture, such as marriage and divorce (as in *Sūrat nisā'*, Qur'ān 4), thus shaping Muslim practices in very meaningful ways in the ongoing history of Islam.

Piety around Muḥammad and the earlier prophets

In myriad ways, the pious have tried to emulate the practices of Muḥammad. One relates to his views of the icon. The Prophet had strong views about the ease with which an image becomes an object of worship. In deference to the Qur'ān's sensitivity about the human propensity to worship religious figures, the community has steadfastly refused to create images of Muḥammad. Even when figures of the Prophet appear in pious material, such as pictorial representations of his life created by artisans for the personal use of the powerful, the faces may be veiled or appear without visage; thus there is no "official" portrait of the Prophet, nor any attempt to establish a canonically acceptable representation. Severe penalties are meted out to those who would attempt such a thing. One result has been the transference of emphasis in Islam from pictorial representation to the written report. The net result has been the authority granted to the *ḥadīth*, the collections of written statements about Muḥammad which represent the community's collective understanding of his role and effectiveness within the *umma*.

In textual media one can find elaborate descriptions of both the appearance of the Prophet and his character. Indeed, stories and poetry eulogizing his character are greatly prized. These became crucial in education where they provided justification for various kinds of normative behavior. The actions of the Prophet, retained in the *sunna*, are held to reflect both his specifically endowed life and his superior qualities as leader. His actions became a normative vehicle for conveying a divinely sanctioned lifestyle. Scholars devoted lifetimes to recording these activities, and then set about determining just what had been the context for such actions. The most authoritative of these reports passed into the great *ḥadīth* collections, and became grist for the courts and for theologians, with direct ramifications for Muslim society.

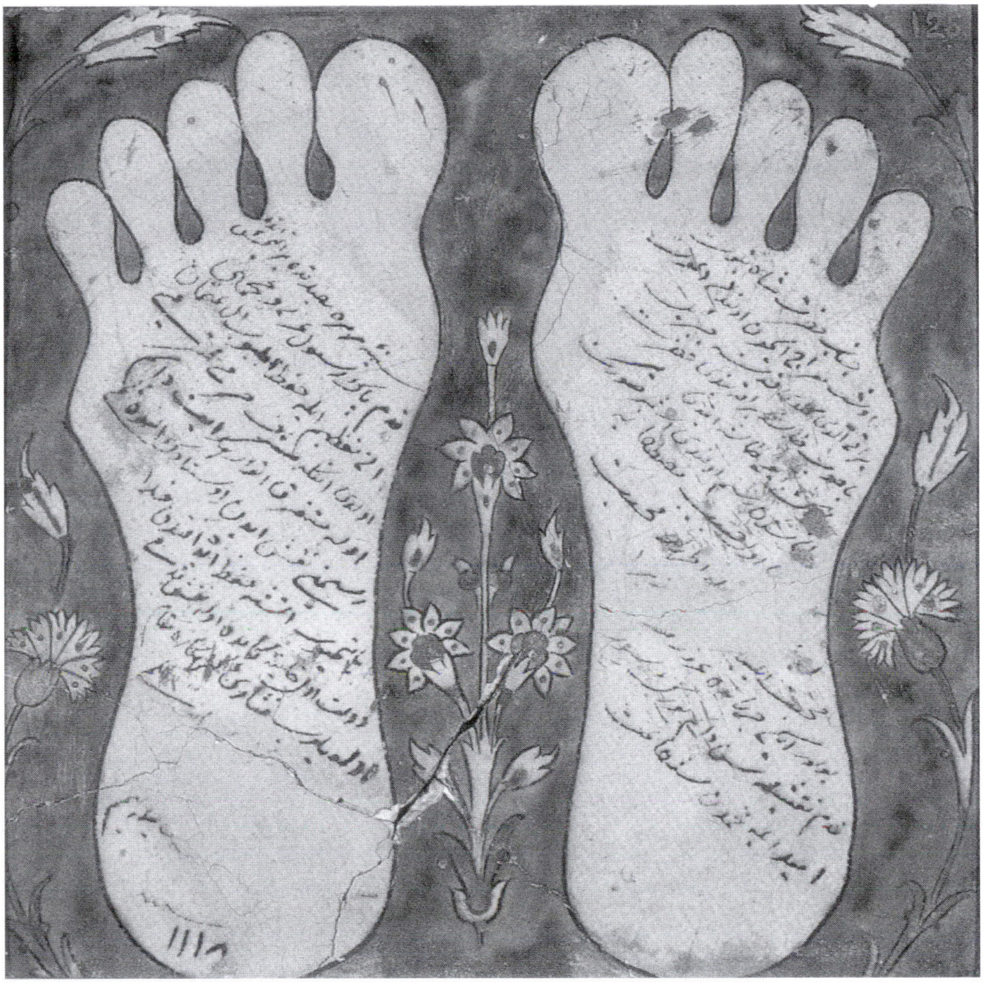

Figure 42 Footprints of the Prophet. Ottoman Empire, 1706. Legends say the Prophet's footprints were imprinted in stone, when he embarked on his journey to heaven, giving rise to venerative shrines and images of the Prophet's feet in Anatolia and India especially.

Source: Benaki Museum, Athens, inv. no. 125. Photograph © 2006 Benaki Museum. Reproduced with permission

Popular stories about the Prophet are often joined by tales about all the prophets. This genre of writing is well known in Islam. It is the *Qiṣaṣ al-anbiyā*ʾ or "Stories of the Prophets." These are adaptations of stories referred to in the Qurʾān which are expanded by popular lore or other religious sources. The justification for doing so was not just pious happenstance; the commitment of Abraham (Ibrāhīm in the Qurʾān) to serving God even to the point of sacrificing his firstborn son Ismāʿīl, is a key ingredient in the rites of the pilgrimage. Both his temptation by Iblīs (Satan) and his wife Hagar's frantic search for water are crucial elements, the former commemorated by the throwing of the stones at the three stone Satans, and the latter by the seven running treks between the hills Ṣafā and Marwa, indicative of her traumatic experience in seeking water for her son on the verge of his dying from thirst. These details indicate that Muslim piety expanded its religious horizons very early to accommodate the need for more detail about how Muslims should understand their Islamic religious practices, thus opening the door to many sources for help in understanding Muslim religious commitments.

We may conclude this section by indicating that the very pious were not satisfied with the physical reportage of the Prophet's actions, because they saw in him the very model of spirituality. Hence over the centuries, Muḥammad more and more was idealized with special gifts as a spiritual person. Following the Prophet became the dedicated means to a deeper life in Islam, and meditations on his life and work constituted an important practice that grew out of early asceticism. Eventually this piety flowered into a full-fledged mystical orientation called Sufism with significant ramifications for religion, art and culture.

Recitations of special sacred writings

Muslim piety also reflects a sophisticated network of recitations. In addition to piety associated with the Qur'ān and Muḥammad, there are also specialized practices arising out of Islamic religious culture, and expressed at certain times and by particular groups of Muslims. Most notable among this class of activities are those associated with Shīʿī Islam, and gathered under the collective title of Muḥarram rites, carried out by Twelver Shīʿīs (best known as represented in Iran) but also throughout the world wherever Twelver Shīʿīs have settled. The rites constitute a public *majlis* or lamentation assembly at which the martyrdom of Ḥusayn is commemorated by ritual acts and recitations. The rites begin on the first day of the month of Muḥarram, and they last for ten days. They feature community-wide activities, complete with black and somber decor and dress, along with *ma'tam* (rhythmic beating of the breast) and flagellation rites during processionals. The recitations are performed by a *zakir* (*dhākir*), a *majlis* reader, who reads from time-worn religious documents about the events that led to the horrific deaths of Ḥusayn and his closest relatives and associates at Karbala in the early days of Islam. These stories place the five principle figures of Shīʿī Islam in a prominent position: Muḥammad, Fāṭima, ʿAlī, Ḥasan and Ḥusayn, all of them woven into a religious text replete with allusions to the spiritual and physical costs of following God's true path. Of a similar tenor, but of more specialized piety are texts like the *Secret Words of Fāṭima* which reflect a sensitivity to Shīʿī values, and are recited in pious gatherings for the edification of the believers.

Other texts of spiritual edification are associated with another branch of Shiʿism, that of the Ismāʿīlīs. During their rituals, special *ginān*s are performed. These *ginān*s evolved in India, pre-modern Pakistan and Afghanistan, and have much in common with Hindu pious writings. Poetic in form, they contain allusions not only to special events of history but to the role of the Imāms in leading the community aright. They are particularly influenced by Ṣūfī conceptions and language, yet they rest within a Shīʿī worldview of persecution. They often feature strategies for maintaining the truth despite a culture hostile to them, such as the well-known *taqiyya* dissimulation.

Within the same genre, we should mention the chanting of the sacred texts of *shaykhs* of Sufism. This is a mystical practice enlivened by sacred poetic forms and carrying a particularly potent spiritual message – a personal encounter with spiritual realities. The *shaykhs* are formidable figures who fashioned an Islam of the heart and created organizations that spread throughout the Muslim world. These texts usually carry the signature beliefs of the *shaykh* and constitute a kind of creedal declaration to the spiritual life as perceived by the founder and his followers. Often the texts are the principle ingredients of meditations called *dhikr*, remembrance, which usually proceeds with stylized movements. Sometimes the meditations are verses from the Qur'ān knitted together into pious figurations. In all occurrences, *dhikr* indicates a spiritual language deemed to bring one closer to God or to the Prophet, or to the spiritual founder of the order.

Finally, throughout Islamic history, a variety of pious forms have developed for giving voice to the inner longings of the heart. The rhythmic recitation of the Qur'ān, the call of the muezzin, the chants of the faithful while on pilgrimage to Mecca, the Ṣūfī meditators and chanters who use song and incantation as vehicles for the heart's spiritual longings, all indicate a wider range of expression than the normal spoken word. These pious expressions have a musical content and shape, yet they deliberately follow musical traditions that have been specifically adopted for spiritual purposes. In all of them the goal is to carry the deeper messages of the heart in a medium that will appeal to the ordinary believer.

Visitations to sacred places and people

Rites of journey for spiritual purposes are enshrined in Islam in the *ḥajj* or pilgrimage to Mecca and Islam's attending places. This canonical rite is mandatory upon every Muslim as long as health and finances permit. But the significance of rites of journeyings grew beyond this exemplary event to include other quasi-canonical acts. Such acts were signaled in the Qur'ān by the diversifying of the *ḥajj* to include the *ʿumra*, which is a less formal pilgrimage that stresses a visit to the holy places of Islam, a rite that could be completed at any time during the year and is less rigidly structured. Visiting the sacred sites of early Islam continues to be regarded by Muslims as having special provenance, and increasingly groups travel throughout the Muslim world visiting such sacred places every year.

The most dramatic example of the piety of journeying takes place each year at the celebration of the birthday of the founding *shaykhs* of the Ṣūfī orders. Believers travel to the shrines where they are buried, to beseech them to help them with their difficulties and to refresh themselves spiritually. Believers go to these shrines because of the belief that these people had *baraka*, a special spiritual power bequeathed only to them from a divine source. A good example of the power of such traveling is the *mawlid* of Shaykh Aḥmad al-Dasūqī in Tanta, Egypt; here hundreds of thousands of followers come every year to petition the *shaykh*'s assistance. The practice is not restricted to one country, however, and the rite is carried out in all countries where important spiritual figures of Islam are buried, including North Africa, Pakistan and Iran. In India and Pakistan, this festival is called *urs*.

The veneration accorded to these exemplary figures constitutes one of the great expressions of popular Islam and consequently is often the focal point for conservative criticism. The *karamāt*, or spiritual gifts and miracles associated with the saints inspire great devotion and intense religious petitioning. Often these practices include seeking out the current representative of the founders to request their benediction or assistance, which conservative Muslim groups regard as deviation from Islamic norms. Requests are made at shrines for healing, for children and for prosperity, among other things. Sometimes the journey is made to thank the *shaykh* for some benefit deemed to have been received through a past request, and it is usually accompanied by a gift given as appreciation to the order. When one has received some result of this spiritual beneficence, it signals a permanent relationship with a sacred dimension of life that often empowers the believer to live a better Islamic life. Hence the practice is connected to both the spiritual and esoteric side of Islamic tradition.

Gendered piety

Another group of practices can be best regarded as specifically gendered. The focus of these practices is overwhelmingly female. These activities are sometimes loosely regarded as canonical, such as prayer in the mosque on Friday. Others are regarded as marginally canonical, such as wearing the veil, while some, like attending a *zār* (spirit healing ritual) are distinctively local and non-canonical. All of them have had to deal with debates about canonical expression. It is the case that few women attend Friday prayers, the official gathering of all believers for corporate prayer at mid-day on Friday. While attendance by women was never forbidden outright, nevertheless, in the growth of Islamic society, women's attendance was frowned upon and customarily not encouraged. Muslim males, as representative of their families, prayed this "official" prayer. Time and reformist movements have had an impact on these restrictions. Under the influence of modern Islamism, women in Muslim countries have been insisting that male resistance to women's attendance at Friday prayers is canonically forbidden. Hence the issue is a matter of fervent debate in recent Islamic culture.

The case is similar with the wearing of the veil. To Western observers, the veil has long been a symbol of the oppression of Muslim women by a patriarchal social system. To Muslim women it has been either a practical matter or an expression of pious choice. In any case, it is a complex issue. The veil arose in medieval Islam where it originated as a feature of upper-class values. Since women were imbued with maintaining and assuring family integrity, the veil offered a public modicum of protection and personal freedom for those ends. It built upon verses of the Qur'ān addressed to the Prophet's wives, the context of which was to set them apart from other women and society at large through specific dress codes. How wide the application of these codes should be has been a point of contention. In modern Islam, it has become a matter of Islamic identity. In point of fact though, both style and functionality have additionally played roles in the history of this practice.

Another class of rites associated with females whose connection to canonical sources is challenged today is that of female circumcision. While not universal by any means, it is practiced in some Arab and African Muslim communities, and has been translated to other venues via migration. The rite is not necessarily an identity marker the way circumcision is for a Muslim male; rather, it is a practice that loosely relates to the perceived sexual appetites of women and the need to bring them under Islamic discipline. There are various types of rites, ranging from a pinprick on the genitals to full clitoridectomy and vaginal modification. Normally the rite is carried out by a local Muslim woman, although in some settings, physicians may carry out the procedure. For traditional believers, the rite is considered to be a religious ceremony signaling the submission of the girl's entire being to religious behaviors. For others, under the pressure of modern knowledge, it is a savage practice from the *jāhiliyya* that should have been long ago banned in Islam.

Finally, there are a group of practices that can be summarized by pointing to the example of the *zār*. This rite of trance and chant is known throughout Egypt and Africa, and normally is perceived of as a healing rite based upon religious trance. During these rites, chanting assists the ill to connect with supernatural powers and to receive various kinds of blessings. Ceremonies are conducted by women officials who understand the spiritual needs of the participants and who lead them through chanting into trance. There are considerable regional differences in these practices, but they all utilize Muslim language and ideas in the service of practices that are usually regarded as non-canonical (and thus suspect) by both the conservative and modernist factions in contemporary Muslim societies.

Amulets and sacred items

One further area of popular piety is associated with the use of amulets and symbols of a religious nature. There are official symbols of Islamic identity that may be associated with this, such as the writing of pious verses around doorways and in shrines and mausoleums of the pious. These serve equally as Islamic markers as well as pious expressions. But there are other, more potent practices associated with negative powers. This may be illustrated by the position of the so-called "evil eye" in Muslim Egypt. At birth, a child does not just come into a family, but into a culture. The evil eye is a belief that the culture into which a child comes has negative powers inherent in it. These forces are potentially destructive to the child's well-being. Steps must be taken to protect that child. Those steps are the subject of local lore: boys may be dressed as girls to throw evil portents off their tracks, girls may be protected by the hanging of verses from the Qur'ān in tiny containers around their necks, and so forth. Furthermore representations of the eye of Horus from ancient Egypt may be placed on the walls as an effective means to protect the child, especially until the child is old enough for its parents not to fear its early death.

These kinds of amuletic practices may be expanded greatly depending upon local customs and traditions. For example, students may recite the Qur'ān before crucial tests, or visit a local shrine for help, and mothers of girls may seek out a *shaykh* known to be effective in the production of boys for their next pregnancy. A vast array of acts related to health, well-being, prosperity and accomplishment can be found within the multi-layered tapestry of Islamic belief which, technically speaking, do not arise from the canon, but nevertheless give hope and sustenance in times of difficulty and thus find a place within Muslim piety. Many of these are found in practices related to so-called "Prophetic medicine," a loose conglomerate of activities and popular perceptions about health and well-being. These ideas grew up outside the more official health practices espoused by the caliph's court, whose more "scientific" model was passed on to medieval European medical schools. Rather, popular conceptions and techniques continued to serve the public because either official medicine was not available or it was too expensive. This type of medical assistance still exists throughout the Islamic world.

Coming to terms with Islamic pious complexity

What this brief survey indicates is that Islamic piety is far more complex than popular slogans about "the five pillars" would have us believe. Islam can, in fact, be regarded in simplified terms as a tradition of the starkest of legal regulations, but that is to reduce its richness. In reality, it is far more. Because of the long and fruitful interaction of Islam with its cultural surroundings, the real life that Muslims live is far more rich and vigorous, with much local color informing its tradition.

Hence the issue of canonicity is a lively Islamic topic. As we have seen, popular piety intersects with contemporary issues of Muslim identity in almost every example cited above. This is not just a matter of the West becoming more aware of Islamic variety. Debates about the application of canonicity within the Islamic community continue from its origins down to our time, especially as significant portions of the *umma* moves towards traditionalist or neo-conservative stances. The centre of Islam itself is shifting.

Moreover, as we indicated at the beginning of this chapter, Islamic theory accepted several types of cultural framework that interacted with each other in the ongoing development of the Islamic world. What this demonstrates is that no singular model of how all Muslims relate to their tradition is adequate. Indeed, popular piety indicates that Muslims interact with both "the tradition" and their own local expression of Islam in several ways, such that Muslims attach different meanings to their religion depending upon the context within which they are engaged. Hence, to affirm what is canonical and what not seems to be much too reductionistic in the face of the texture of the Islamic fabric. For some Muslims, magical trends may be peripheral to normative practice, but they nevertheless connect some believers to the reality that they associate with the great tradition to which they belong, and all Islamic societies have some evidence of such practices. Thus, popular piety has carved out its own influential trajectory in Islamic culture, and such spiritual and religious practices form a living part of Islamic tradition today.

References and further reading

Abu-Lughod, L. (2005) "Modesty Discourses: An Overview," *Encyclopedia of Women and Islamic Cultures*, Leiden: Brill, vol. 2: 494–8. (A beginning article of a whole series of important articles in this encyclopedia on the pieties of veiling, modesty and so forth.)

Andrae, T. (1956) *Mohammed: The Man and His Faith*, trans. T. Menzel from 1936 edition, London: Allen and Unwin. (Emphasis on the religious dimension of Muḥammad and its impact on Islam.)

Boddy, J. (1989) *Wombs and Alien Spirits. Women, Men and the* Zār *Cult in North Sudan*, Madison: University of Wisconsin Press. (In-depth study of the *zār* cult and its intersections with local popular piety and Islamic tradition.)

Budge, E. A. W. (1970) *Amulets and Talismans*, New York, Collier Books. (General overview of the diversity of this kind of piety in the world along with illustrations.)

Cragg, K. (1971) *The Event of the Koran*, London: Allen and Unwin. (Analysis of the Qur'ān within the framework of its religious meaning for Muslims.)

Esmail, A. (2002) *A Scent of Sandalwood: Indo-Ismaili Religious Lyrics (Ginans)*, Richmond, Curzon. (Helpful source on an important Ismāʿīlī practice.)

Hoffman, V. J. (1995) *Sufism, Mystics and Saints in Modern Egypt*, Columbia: University of South Carolina Press. (Competent contemporary survey of Sufism in a crucial Islamic state.)

Kassamali, N. (2005) "Genital Cutting," *Encyclopedia of Women and Islamic Cultures*, Leiden: Brill, vol. 3: 129–32. (Competent overview of the issue with foundational bibliography.)

Macdonald, D. B. (1970) *The Religious Attitude and Life in Islam*, New York: AMS Press, reprint of 1909 edition. (Insightful description of a Sunnī religious lifestyle.)

Massignon, L. (1982) *The Passion of al-Hallāj: Mystic and Martyr of Islam*, 3 vols., trans. H. Mason, Princeton: Princeton University Press. (Classical study of a spiritual genius in early Islam, reflecting many of the characteristics associated with Ṣūfī saints.)

Nelson, F. H. (2000) *Talismans and Amulets of the World*, New York: Sterling Publishers. (Cross-cultural survey of the role, type and meaning of talismanic traditions.)

Padwick, C. E. (1961) *Muslims Devotions*, London: SCM Press. (Examines the devotional life of Sunnī Muslims, and the role of the Qur'ān in that life.)

Pinault, D. (1992) *The Shiites: Ritual and Popular Piety in a Muslim Community*, New York: St. Martin's Press. (Exploration of popular forms of Shīʿī devotionalism.)

Qut el-Qulub (1954) *La Nuit de la destinée*, Paris: Gallimard. (Egyptian novel expressing many popular Muslim practices in Cairo with profound feeling for the power of local traditions.)

Schimmel, A. (1975) *Mystical Dimensions of Islam*, Chapel Hill: University of North Carolina Press. (Standard reference work on Sufism, with emphasis on the role of conceptions and ideas upon Islamic tradition.)

Schubel, V. J. (1993) *Religious Performance in Contemporary Islam: Shiʿi Devotional Rituals in South Asia*, Columbia: University of South Carolina Press. (A now-standard study on Shīʿī devotionalism.)

Sengers, G. (2002) *Women and Demons: Cultic Healing in Islamic Egypt*, Leiden: Brill. (Anthropological study of *zār* and other trance-states in popular Muslim environment.)

Watt, W. M. (1961) *Muḥammad: Prophet and Statesman*, Oxford: Oxford University Press. (Standard work outlining the many dimensions of Muḥammad's life and work.)

Waugh, E. H. (1974) "Following the Beloved: Muhammad as Model in the Sufi Tradition," in D. Capps, F. Reynolds, eds., *The Biographical Process*, The Hague: Mouton, 63–85. (Exploration of the role of Muḥammad as a spiritual figure in Islamic piety.)

—— (1989) *The Munshidin of Egypt: Their World and Their Song*, Columbia: University of South Carolina Press. (Examines the role of the chanting of spiritual texts within the religious life of Egyptian Ṣūfīs.)

41

MUSIC

Michael Frishkopf

What is "music of the Islamic world"? Indeed, what is "the Islamic world"? The "world" metaphor implies coherence, at least relative to other "worlds," and for a particular observer. Musing freely about the "Islamic world," one might arrive at any one of the following four definitions:

1 The socio-cultural world of Islamic religious practice and discourse, over time and space. Though diverse, significant internal linkages lend coherence; this world is viewed – from within and without – as "Islamic."
2 The elite socio-cultural world of literate, urban Muslim-majority communities that arose and flourished as a consequence of Islamic political expansion which outside observers have associated with Islam, what Marshall Hodgson called "Islamicate."
3 The socio-cultural world of Muslim communities everywhere. This enormous "world" – reified mainly from an outsider perspective that views religion as providing the overriding cultural identity for all Muslims – is diverse to the point of incoherence.
4 The cosmos, as viewed from an Islamic perspective, i.e., the Islamic world-view, through which the universe, a temporal creation of the unitary uncreated Divine Reality (Allāh), is full of signs (*āyāt*) pointing to its Divine source.

Using the above definitions, "music of the Islamic world" may be defined, respectively, as the following categories: (1) religious music, used in Islamic practices; (2) Islamicate music: music of the elite culture associated with Muslim rule; (3) Muslim music: all music consumed or produced by Muslims; and (4) music symbolically encoding the traditional Islamic world-view, what might be termed "spiritual" (rather than overtly religious) music.

However in proposing such definitions, one encounters at least four problems. First is one of objectivity: how to define the category precisely in order to assure agreement? What is the "litmus" test determining whether or not a particular thing is in fact an instance of the category? Second, does the category really cohere? From whose perspective? Outsider and insider (i.e., non-Muslim and Muslim) perspectives may not accord, yet neither can be privileged *a priori*; the former, experience-thin, risks discursive reproduction (e.g., Orientalism), while the latter, experience-rich, risks parochialism. Third, even if the music category is coherent, it may no longer exist, in which case contemporary music must be ignored, decreasing the category's social

Table 41.1 Four ways of defining "music of the Islamic world" and four criteria for evaluating them

World of . . .	*Music category*	*Criteria* a. Coherence	b. Objectivity	c. Present extension	d. Local knowledge?
1. Islamic practices	Islamic religious music	high	high	high	yes
2. Islamicate culture	Islamicate music	medium	medium	low	somewhat
3. Muslims	Muslim music	low	medium	high	no
4. Islamic cosmos	Islamic spiritual music	high	low	low	somewhat

relevance. On the other hand, as music has left few durable traces prior to the twentieth century (even the Islamicate tradition rarely included music notation), studying anything earlier tends to be conjectural. Finally, the "Islamic world" derives from a colonial (even medieval) European perspective. The continued privileging of outsider perspectives of Muslims constitutes an intellectual colonialism. Many Muslims reject the assumption that Islamic identity is always primary; why should a singer who happens to be a Muslim be known as a "Muslim singer"?

If one is prepared to accept the concept "music of the Islamic world," what sort of music should be presented under that heading? Islamicate music is coherent only during periods of unified Islamic cultural ascendancy, primarily from early Islam to the peak of Abbasid and Umayyad Andalusian culture. From about the tenth century onwards, it becomes increasingly difficult to speak of a single Islamicate musical tradition. Subsequently, European cultural hegemony, followed by the rise of mass media and globalization, caused its eclipse.

The category of "Muslim musics" is far less acceptable. By definition it must contain such a diverse musical range, which is furthermore so closely tied to "non-Muslim" musics, that merely to consider it is already to fall into error. Another possible stance is that "music of the Islamic world" is that which expresses and instills Islamic spirituality. "To grasp fully the significance of Islamic art is to become aware that it is an aspect of the Islamic revelation" (Nasr 1987: 13). However, such a metaphysical stance does not provide an objective criterion for distinguishing what is, or is not, "Islamic music." Of the four possibilities, then, only "Islamic religious music" exhibits high coherence, high objectivity, high extension, and appears as a category of local knowledge. Therefore, it is this category which will be elaborated in the remainder of this essay.

Music in the world of Islamic practices

To some degree, a practice must be considered "Islamic" if its practitioner deems it so, though that degree is proportional to the number who actually practice it. By this definition, the world of Islamic practices – though broad – is well defined according to intentions of participants. The sound of Islamic practice almost invariably derives from the oral performance of sacred texts in group settings. Such performance is required for intragroup communication, and as an act of devotion. Yet it also displays tonal-temporal organization far beyond the requirements of communicative or devotional functions, pointing towards an aesthetic-emotional function as well. Even the sound of public canonical prayer (*ṣalāt*) is typically melodic. Furthermore, non-linguistic sound – often produced by instruments – not infrequently appears. Melodic recitations – often ornated, sometimes metric – developed in order to beautify and extol texts, to draw the listener's attention, to facilitate retention, to clarify meaning, to coordinate performance, and to develop appropriate emotional responses. Furthermore, because the purely sonic aspect of Islamic practice is only loosely regulated by Islamic discourse, melodic styles tend to elaborate, and also to develop local variants.

However, the word "music" and its cognates among languages commonly spoken by Muslims (e.g., Arabic *musīqā*) are typically not applied to the sounds of Islamic practices. Distinctions are conceptual (classificatory), semantic (due to differences in text, context, intention), and sonic. With respect to the latter, it should be noted that "music" typically implies use of melodic instruments; singing and even percussion are usually not considered "music." Throughout Islamic history there has been disagreement over the legitimacy of public musical practice – as entertainment, or even (sometimes, especially) as devotion. Suspicion towards music resulted from its association with two prohibitions: mixed gender gatherings, and alcohol. Due to their mystical orientation, Ṣūfī *ṭuruq* ("orders"; singular *ṭarīqa*) have frequently (though not always) been more tolerant of "spiritual audition" (*samāʿ*), yet even here caution prevails.

Genres and contexts

Across the Islamic world, three categories of recurring performance contexts may be discerned, characterized by three degrees of sonic genre variation within each context. The least variable category comprises core ritual contexts, prescribed by Islamic law, and centering on vocalized text. Musical instruments are absent, and the sacred liturgical language (Arabic) is used. While discursive aspects of performance are prescriptively fixed, sonic and social aspects of performance may participate in the local ramification of style which is a natural consesquence of any oral tradition.

More variable than the core are festival contexts, occurring in connection with Islamic holidays. Such contexts feature looser, less explicit constraints, sometimes carried by oral more than written tradition, because performance in these contexts, though regarded as devotional, is not required or closely regulated by Islamic law. The result is greater localization in language, poetic genre, and musical tradition, though common themes (e.g. *madīḥ*, praise for the Prophet) emerge everywhere.

Still less constrained are life-cycle contexts in Muslim societies, such as birth, circumcision, marriage, and death. As such contexts are not exclusive to Muslim communities, they are frequently linked to ceremonies in historically or socially proximate non- or pre-Islamic traditions. Such ceremonies vary greatly from one culture to another. As a result, the genres performed within these contexts – even while carrying Islamic meanings within universal contexts – are highly localized.

Arabic terms are widely used to denote Islamic musical genres, sometimes acquiring specifically religious meaning outside Arabic areas. Thus the *qaṣīda*, a word whose generic Arabic meaning is simply "poem," comes to mean "Arab Islamic song" in southeast Asia (see Rasmussen 2001: 55, n. 16).

Generally, Islamization (and Arabization) of traditional music was an effective means by which those dedicated to propagating Islam could lead a broad following to the faith. Conversely, this strategy might entail localization of global Islamic expressive forms via absorption of vernacular literary and musical styles. Outside overtly religious contexts, in the broader realm of live musical entertainment, Islamic themes frequently emerge in Muslim areas; less constrained by context and more driven by market factors, these genres are even more multifarious, drawing more heavily on local musical tradition. With the rise of context-free broadcast and product media (e.g., radio, phonograms), Islamic music is commodified and embedded in a media space. Most of this output is distributed through local music media, while some is absorbed into a pan-Islamic media system, or into the global music media system (under the guise of "world music"), distributed via international festivals and recordings.

In recent times, however, such diversity – along with the use of "music" in word or deed – has been inhibited by globalization, which, through rapid mass dissemination of both pan-Islamic reformism and high-status sonic models has tended to contract the formerly broad range of practices to a great extent, either by condemning them as *bidʿa* ("heretical innovation") or *ḥarām* ("forbidden") or, less confrontationally, by providing more attractive, mass-mediated musical alternatives. Whether or not these alternatives are religious in character, they tend to crowd out more traditional practices through media prestige, and their greater compatibility with contemporary television-centered life, in which traditional live performance plays a smaller role than before.

Recurrent genres: ritual core

The ritual core is most tightly defined by standard Islamic discourse, and thus most universal; performance centers on standardized sacred Arabic texts clearly differentiated from poetry. Local traditions may be absorbed to a limited degree in the sonic and social aspect only. The word "music" is least likely to be applied here; musical instruments are almost never deployed, and regular meter is avoided in favor of a free, contemplative style.

The call to prayer: adhān

The *adhān* has Sunnī and Shīʿī variants. The Sunnī format shown in the following table is widespread and is based in *ḥadīth*. According to *fiqh* it must be audible to other than the caller (*mu'adhdhin*), that time should be taken with it, including pauses between phrases, and that the caller should possess a strong and pleasant voice (Ibn al-Naqib 1999: 114–6).

Each phrase is performed in a single breath, repeated twice, except the final two which occur once only. The repetitive structure of the *adhān* is evidently designed for melodic recitation; whereas the first repetition is typically presented unadorned (thus ensuring communication), the second repetition is embellished with elaborate

Table 41.2 The Sunnī *adhān* as performed before the dawn prayer (other prayers omit line 6)

	Phrase	*Meaning*
1	Allāhu akbar Allāhu akbar	God is greater
2	Ashhadu an lā ilāha **illā** Allāh	I testify that there is no deity but God
3	Ashhadu a**nn**a Muḥa**mm**ad ras**ū**l Allāh	I testify that Muḥammad is the messenger of God
4	Hayya ʿalā ʾl-ṣa**lāh**	Come to prayer!
5	Hayya ʿalā ʾl-falāh	Come to salvation!
6	al-ṣalātu khayrun min al-nawm	Prayer is better than sleep
7	Allāhu akbar Allāhu akbar	God is greater
8	lā ilāha illā Allāh	There is no deity but God.

melisma (thus ensuring feeling). Long melismas occur primarily on the letters in boldface.

Sonic aspects of the *adhān* are carried by oral tradition, yet certain features are nearly universal. The usual ideal is a highly melismatic, ornamented, ametric vocal solo. An Arabic *maqām* (melodic mode), most commonly Hijaz or Rast, is typically used (see fig. 43). Melodies outline the *maqām*, developing the lower registers, then the upper, particularly during the second repetition of each phrase. Phrase contours are standardized. More complex presentations utilizing multiple *maqāmāt* (see Shannon 2006: 190–1) or *muʾadhdhin* also occur. The Egyptian style predominates throughout the Sunnī world, due to the influence of al-Azhar University, and Egypt's long-standing media power. In modern times, amplification creates a striking aleatoric polyphony in urban areas, due to extensive overlap of *muʾadhdhin*s' vastly expanded sound-spheres.

Localizations occur as well. In Turkey, the *adhān* sounds Turkish; in Iran, Persian modes (*dastgah*) and ornaments (e.g., *taḥrīr*) are employed. The surging *adhān* of the *masjid al-ḥarām*, the vast mosque enclosing the Kaʿba in Mecca, is instantly recognizable. Certain religious movements proscribe the melodically elaborate styles on ideological grounds. In southeast Asia a drum (*bedug*) has also been used to call to prayer.

Qurʾanic recitation: tilāwa

All observant Muslims practice Qur'anic recitation (*tilāwa*), at least in prayer (*ṣalāt*), while the specialist (*qarīʾ*, *ḥāfiẓ*) dominates public recitation. Recitation includes fixed and variable parameters. The underlying written text, the *muṣḥaf*, is fixed, as are recitational rules (*aḥkām al-tajwīd*) governing phonetics, phrasing, syllable length, and tempo. However, the authoritative *muṣḥaf* (codified under Caliph ʿUthmān) lacks diacritical marks specifying vowels and differentiating many letters. Variant readings (*qirāʾāt*) developed through oral tradition, supposed by Muslims to be grounded in the seven dialectical versions (*aḥruf*) revealed to the Prophet.

Other free parameters allow the same passage to be recited in many ways. In par-

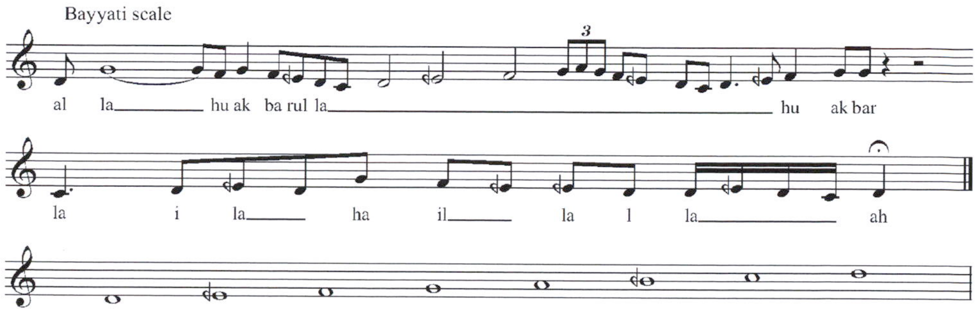

Figure 43(a) A simplified notation of the last two phrases of the *adhān* in *maqām* Bayyati, performed by Shaykh Muḥammad al-Hilbāwī. The symbol 'd' indicates a half-flat (quarter tone flat).

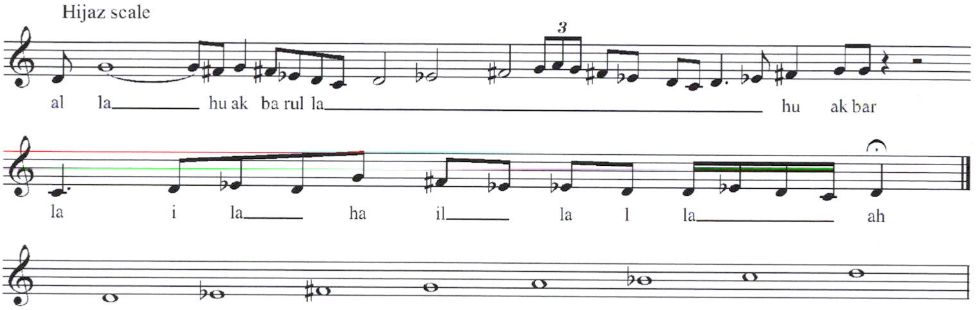

Figure 43(b) A simplified notation of the last two phrases of the *adhān* in *maqām Hijāz*, performed by Shaykh Muḥammad al-Hilbāwī. Note that the phrases are nearly identical; only the pitch set is different.

Figure 43(c) A simplified notation of the last two phrases of the *adhān* in *maqām Rast*, performed by Shaykh Muḥammad al-Hilbāwī.

ticular, timbral and melodic aspects are highly variable. Carried by oral tradition, they have allowed distinctive styles to emerge reflecting contextual factors, as well as regional, or ideological traditions. Many *ḥadīth*s suggest the permissibility and desirability of beautiful recitations, and this beauty is generally interpreted to include melodiousness. The Prophet himself said, "He who does not recite the Qur'ān tunefully is not one of us" (Nawawi 1989: 187), but the *ḥadīth* does not elaborate the nature of this "tunefulness."

Normatively, Qur'anic recitation must be ametric (lacking periodic rhythm), strictly vocal, and improvised; human melody beautifies Divine text without any fixed association with it. Attempts to set Qur'anic verses to fixed music have been roundly condemned by religious authorities. However, recordings have effected such associations, enabling memorization of fixed melodies. Around the world, reciters can replicate famous recordings by Shaykh ʿAbd al-Bāsiṭ. The rise of mass media has also tended to contract the variety of oral tradition.

The two primary contextual styles are the elaborate *mujawwad* and the faster, simpler *murattal*. The former has evolved as the preferred style for listening, while the latter is used primarily in prayer and study. Both styles are melodic, but conservatives sometimes criticize *mujawwad* as overly musical. *Mujawwad* features ornate melody, lengthy melismas, full development of the *maqām*, modulations to related *maqāmāt*, frequent repetition of passages in new melodic settings, and long pauses between breath-phrases, culminating in a powerful cadence (*qafla*), elicting listeners' verbal and gestural feedback, and helping to build emotion in dialog with the reciter.

Egyptian reciters have exerted the greatest worldwide influence. There are several reasons for this: (1) al-Azhar University, where students from throughout the Sunnī world study recitation; (2) the wide travels of Egyptian reciters; and (3) early development of audio mass media, including *tilāwa* broadcasts and recordings. Since the 1990s, a Saudi recitational style has gained worldwide influence. Both Egyptian and Saudi reciters use Arab *maqāmāt*, but differ stylistically.

Formerly local traditions arose, and some persist. For instance in Central Asia an "international" *tilāwa* style is contrasted with local ones resembling folk melodies; Bukharan styles have been considered exemplary and widely disseminated in the region. In West Africa one may find entirely different melodic patterns. A solo ametric voice is most common in performance, but metered or corporate chanting occurs too, for instance in the distinctive Berber *tolba* of Morocco.

Adʿiyya

Supplications to God, *adʿiyya* (singular *duʿāʾ*), indicating and promoting faith, are an essential form of Islamic worship (Qur'ān 2:186, 40:60). Standard *adʿiyya* are provided by *ḥadīth*, the Qur'ān, and traditional usage. Two especially common themes are the *istighfār* (request for forgiveness), and *ṣalawāt* (requests that God bless the Prophet, his family and companions). Free-form supplications allow a wide range of topics, including political *adʿiyya* calling for liberation of occupied Muslim territories (e.g., Chechnya, Palestine). *Duʿāʾ* recited by a prayer leader before a group is responsorial. An expressive melodic intonation is often employed; the leader's *duʿāʾ* is assumed vicariously by the group, who answer each supplicatory phrase with *āmīn* (cf. "amen").

In the Arab world the highest level of melodic elaboration occurs in *ibtihālāt*, a genre of *inshād* combining prose prayer with poetry. But other public performances feature melodic elaboration as well, especially the congregational *qunūt* (performed in the second dawn *raqʿa*, and after night prayers, during *witr*). During Ramaḍān the *qunūt*, full of fear and hope, can be extended to nearly an hour, becoming highly expressive and often eliciting mass weeping.

Ritual periphery: poetic texts – *inshād*

Intoned recitation of poetry as a religious act is termed *inshād dīnī* (or *nashīd*; pl. *anāshīd*) in Arabic; around the Islamic world a wide range of terms (e.g. *ilāhī* in Turkey, *nasyid* in Southeast Asia, *qawwālī* in South Asia, *zikir* in parts of Southeast Asia) are used for semantically equivalent or subordinate categories. *Inshād dīnī* is a form of supererogatory worship (*nāfila*), also serving pedagogical and affective functions. Lying outside the ritual core, drawing upon poetic texts, and often performed outside the mosque, it enjoys greater aesthetic flexibility, and interacts more freely with local music. *Inshād* is always performed tonally, and musical style varies.

Inshād is especially important in Ṣūfī orders, where poetry is generally regarded as the ideal vehicle for expressing spiritual knowledge and feeling. Spiritual guides often compose poetry, and performance of one's *shaykh*'s poetry affirms devotion to him, regardless of content. While classical Arabic is widely distributed, poetry often appears in other languages, including Arabic vernaculars, Islamicate languages of the core (Persian, Turkish, Urdu), and periphery (e.g., Hausa, Malay). Unlike *tilāwa, inshād* derives spiritual, emotional, and pedagogical force from lingustic intimacy.

Despite localizations of musical style and language, forms – such as *qaṣīda* (monorhyme poem) and *rubāʿī* (quatrain) – cross language boundaries, and themes recur everywhere: praise for God (*ḥamd, takbīr, tasbīḥ, tamjīd*) or the Prophet (*madīḥ, madḥ, naʿt, durūd*), supplication to God (*ibtihāl*) or the Prophet (*tawassul, istighātha, madad*), and love for God (*al-ḥubb al-ilāhī*), or the Prophet (*madīḥ, ghazal*). Ṣūfīs compose similar poems for their spiritual guides (*shaykh*s, *pīr*s, saints), the Shīʿa for their Imāms, and both for the Prophet's family, the *ahl al-Bayt*.

Other poetic genres are narrative (e.g., *mawlid*, a panegyric biography of the Prophet), theological (*tawḥīd*), legal (*fiqh*), or exhortative (*waʿẓ, ḥikma*). Ṣūfī poems express the mystical experience: gnosis (*maʿrifa*), love and longing (*ghazal*), or spiritual intoxication (*khamriyya*); many of these are thought to have been composed while in a state of mystical love (*ʿishq*), trance (*ḥāl*), or even Divine union (*ittiḥād, wisāl*), states also invoked by performed poetry.

Particular poems and poets renowned throughout the Muslim world deserve mention. These include two *mawlid* poems – *al-Burda* and *al-Hamziyya* – in praise of the Prophet by an Egyptian, Sharaf al-Dīn al-Būsīrī (d. 1212), the *mawlid* of Jaʿfar ibn Ḥasan al-Barzanjī (d. 1765), and the mystical poetry of Jalāl al-Dīn Rūmī (d. 1273).

Traditionally *inshād* is performed at the periphery of core rituals (e.g., before or after prayer), at festivals, and to accompany mystical practices. Each region of the Islamic world boasts its distinctive genres and styles. However, localizations have recently been attenuated by the impact of mass media, especially religious programming on satellite television, radio and Internet, together with reformist ideologies condemning traditional *inshād* practices as *bidʿa*. New music media tend to popularize fewer, more widely disseminated styles carrying high cultural capital, at the expense of local, live performance.

Prose texts: prayers

Prayers substantially consisting of prose have often been developed, mainly by Ṣūfīs, to serve supererogatory rituals. These texts, often recited melodically, include *ṣalawāt, istighfār* ("penitential prayers") and *ḥizb* ("office"). A few such texts have transcended Ṣūfī boundaries, to be widely recited throughout the Islamic world. The most famous of these are probably the *ṣalawāt* entitled *Dalā'il al-khayrāt* ("The Waymarks of Benefits") by the Moroccan Muḥammad Sulayman al-Jazūlī (d. 1465), and the *Ḥizb al-baḥr* ("Sea Office") of Abū 'l-Ḥasan al-Shādhilī (d. 1258), both widely recited for their spiritual benefits.

The following (translated by the author) is one of the shortest of 40 *ṣalawāt* composed by Shaykh Ṣāliḥ al-Jaʿfarī (1910–78) of Egypt, in rhyming Arabic prose (*saj'*), recited melodically during the evening *ḥaḍra*.

Oh God, bless our master Muḥammad, pure of hearts
Full of love for the Lord of Worshippers
Possessor of comprehensive words, beneficial knowledge, and radiant lights
Your bringer of glad tidings
Your warner
Your illuminating lamp
Most successful of the fortunate
Best of those who call to piety
And upon his family, and give them peace.

Islamic music in context: ritual core

If genres are the morphemes of Islamic music, contexts generate the utterances. Certain genres are distributed throughout most contexts, while others are more specialized. Congregational prayer features a sequences of genres. *Mujawwad tilāwa* often comes first. The *mu'adhdhin* may precede *adhān* with solo ametric *inshād* supplications (*ibtihālāt*), especially at dawn, and follow it with *ṣalawāt*. Before Friday prayer (*ṣalāt al-jumʿa*) there may be more *mujawwad*, followed by a second *adhān*. *Ṣalāt* proper comprises a series of *raqʿāt* ("bowings"), including *murattal* Qur'anic recitation performed aloud during the first two (except for noon and afternoon prayer), and other formulae (*takbīr, tasmīʿ, taslīm*) pronounced melodically by the *imām* ("prayer leader"). A *muballigh*, if present, repeats these formulae more ornately. A melodic *duʿā'* may be inserted in the final *raqʿa*. The *imām* often follows prayer with a melodic recitation of formulae (*khitam al-ṣalāt*), after which *mujawwad* recitation may resume. *ʿĪd* prayers are preceded by a melodic chant called *takbīr*, which glorifies God.

Ritual periphery: Ṣūfī performance

Following al-Ghazālī (d. 1111), Sufism is generally tolerant of certain kinds of music carrying spiritual messages, if used by the spiritually mature under the proper conditions. Music performance transforms through poetry, sound, breathing techniques, and associated physical movement. Within Ṣūfī *ṭuruq*, formal rituals – generally called *ḥaḍra* ("presence") – are used to promote spiritual development, and to ensure the viability of the *ṭarīqa* as a social community. Each *ṭarīqa* typically performs one or two *ḥaḍras* per week. Melodic language performance is central to such rituals.

Ḥaḍra usually features solo, responsorial, or corporate *inshād*, as well as a number of non-poetic genres including *tilāwa, adʿiyya, ḥizb*, and *ṣalawāt*, performed in a melodic style. Such performance is sometimes called *samāʿ* (listening). Another fixture is *dhikr*: regular rhythmic chanting of divine names, often accompanied by movement, and sometimes leading to ecstatic trance (*wajd, ḥāl*). *Inshād* and *dhikr* may be performed together, or separately. Instrumental accompaniment may occur. Though frame drums (sometimes with reed flutes) are often preferred, and some *ṭarīqa* reject instruments altogether, others absorb local instruments into the mix, particularly when performing outside the mosque. The quantity of public music, movement and ecstatic behavior is an index of *ṭarīqa* doctrine, and of its strategies for self-presentation.

Despite common purposes, meanings, and genres, *ḥaḍras* may contrast sharply, resulting from the absorption of local culture, and variant approaches towards the twin problems of spiritual development, and social continuity (see fig. 45). Two contrastive *ḥaḍra* liturgies are shown below. The first is from the contemporary Egyptian *ṭarīqa*, the *Jaʿfariyya Aḥmadiyya Muḥammadiyya*, founded in 1979. Linked to the reformer Aḥmad ibn Idrīs (d. 1837), the *ṭarīqa* is outwardly conservative, yet musical. The founder, Shaykh Ṣāliḥ al-Jaʿfarī, composed 12 volumes of poetry, used in *ḥaḍra*. One or two soloists sing a poem, with choral refrain from the congregation; all remain seated and no instruments are employed. Occasional pentatonic singing indicates Sudanese influence.

Figure 44 The weekly *ḥaḍra* of the Jaʿfariyya *ṭarīqa*, Darasa, Cairo, in February 1998. (Photo by M. Frishkopf)

1 Non-poetic recitations (~1 hour)

 a Collective recitation of *al-Fātiḥa* (Qur'ān 1)
 b Recitation of *ṣalawāt, duʿāʾ*.
 c Recitation of prayer by Aḥmad ibn Idrīs
 d Recitation of *adʿiyya* composed by Shaykh Ṣāliḥ

2 Night prayer (*al-ʿishāʾ*) (~30 minutes)
3 *Inshād* recitations (~2.5 hours)
 Around 15 long *qasīdas* (poems) by Shaykh Ṣāliḥ.
4 Conclusion (15 minutes)

 a *Adʿiyya*
 b Closing prayers
 c Final *qaṣīda*

The following is the form of ritual liturgy (*samāʿ, ayin* or *mukabele*) in a Turkish *ṭarīqa*, the Mevlevi. Firmly established by Jalāl al-Dīn Rūmī's son, Sultan Veled (d. 1312), it eventually rose to great prominence at the Ottoman court, diffusing throughout the Ottoman world. The Mevlevi *ayin* comprises a variety of instrumental and vocal compositions. Most poetry is Persian, often by Rūmī himself. Mevlevi composers would set the four *salams* ("greetings") as a suite. A rich ensemble may include *ney* (reed flute), *kudüm* (kettle drums), *bendir* (frame drums), *tanbur* (plucked lute), *rebab* (bowed lute), and *halile* (cymbals). In Turkey, Mevlevi rituals were halted by Kemal Mustafa Atatürk in 1925, but recently have begun to revive.

1 *Naʿat-i serif*, an ametric solo *madīḥ* for the Prophet. The poem is by Rūmī; the melody (in *makām Rast*) by Buhuriz Itri (d. 1712)
2 *Taksim* (improvisation) on *ney* (reed flute)
3 *Pesrev* (instrumental piece, using 56/4 meter), while dervishes circle and salute
4 *Salam-i Evvel* (first greeting; poetry by Rūmī sung by chorus in 14/8 meter)
5 *Salam-i Sani* (second greeting; poetry by Rūmī; in 9/8)
6 *Salam-i Salis* (third greeting; Mevlevi poetry; several meters, increasing tempo)
7 *Selam-Rabiʿ* (fourth greeting; Mevlevi poetry; in 9/8)
8 *Son pesrev* (instrumental piece, in 4/4)
9 *Son yuruk semaʿi* (instrumental piece, in 6/8)
10 *Taksim* (instrumental improvisation)
11 *Tilawa* (dancing stops)

Ṣūfī music often draws upon local culture. Thus music of Sudanese Qādirīs sounds Sudanese; in East Africa, the same *ṭarīqa* spread among the non-literate population via colloquial devotional poetry. South Asian *ṭarīqas*, such as the Chishtiyya, draw upon Hindustani musical materials.

Some Ṣūfī musicians are professionals, performing Ṣūfī musical traditions outside the *ṭarīqa ḥaḍra* at festival occasions. Freed from the constraints of the ṭarīqa and its *shaykh*, such performances become musically richer, bordering on secular music, and feature more ecstatic behavior. Examples include professional Ṣūfī *inshād* of Egypt (e.g., Shaykh Yāsīn al-Tuhāmī), and professional *qawwālī* of Pakistan and India (e.g., Nusrat Fatih Ali Khan), most closely associated with the Chishtiyya *ṭarīqa* but drawing on Hindustani *khiyal*. Since the early twentieth century such popular Ṣūfī performances have been mediated and commodified.

Festivals: holidays

Performance during Islamic holidays, more informal than the ritual core, and often occurring outside the mosque, exhibits a wider range of genres, drawing more heavily on local music cultures, synthesized with distinctive Islamicate instruments and styles. Increasingly, Arab Islamic culture is held up as the ideal. Combined effects of reformism and mass media have greatly shrunk the sphere of live performance, which however is maintained by Ṣūfīs.

Ramaḍān

At sunset, percussion, such as the Javanese *bedug* (bass drum) or Uzbek *naghara* (kettledrums), has been used to mark the fast's conclusion. Evenings, professional reciters perform *tilāwa; inshād* celebrates Ramaḍān, the Qur'ān, and the Prophet, and supplicates God. In Kano, royal Hausa musicians perform *Gaisuwar barka da shan ruwa* during the final ten nights. At dawn, street music rouses the devout for their pre-dawn meal (*sahūr*). In Marrakech, *ghaita* (oboe) and *nfir* (trumpet) play melodies based on religious chants from mosque minarets. In Egypt, the *masahharātī* awakens the faithful by calling names and chanting religious formulae, accompanied by a small drum (*baza*). In the Philippines a drum marks the fast's onset. Among the Dagbamba (Northern Ghana), a *jenjili* (musical bow) player circulates at dawn, playing and singing.

ʿĪd

Ḥadīth indicate that the Prophet permitted musical celebrations during *ʿĪd*. Consequently, *ʿĪd al-Fitr* and *ʿĪd al-Aḍḥā* are traditionally full of music. *Inshād* style varies widely. Thus monophonic *ʿĪd* songs in Egypt contrast with polyphony of the Rasha'ida, an Arab tribe of Eritrea. In Java a gong orchestra is used. Hausa beat the kettle-drum to signal the *ʿĪd*, and elaborate *ʿĪd* festival music continues to be performed there by court musicians (*maroka*). Spectacular all-night drum history narrations, involving a lead singer-drummer supported by a chorus of up to a hundred others, and climaxing in a dance (*bangumanga*), are performed among the Dagbamba of Ghana.

Ḥajj

The embarkation and return of pilgrims to Mecca is a joyous annual celebration. *Inshād* called *zikir* is performed in peninsular Malaysia, with frame drum (*rebana*) accompaniment. In Sumatra *diki Mauluk*, remembering the Prophet, is performed. Yoruba women used to welcome returning Muslims with *waka* songs (from Hausa *wak'a*, "song"), evincing Arab influence (melismatic, nasal, embellished), accompanied by metallic idiophones (*seli*). Returning pilgrims from the Khatmiyya *ṭarīqa* in

Sudan are expected to sponsor a special collective ritual (*karama*) in their honor. Today, mediated music is also recycled for folk use. Thus, in Egypt, families might sing a film song popularized by actress Layla Murad "*Yā Rayihin lil-Nabī al-Ghālī.*"

Mawlid al-Nabī

Despite criticism from reformers, the day and month of the Prophet's birthday (12 *Rabīʿ al-awwal*) is celebrated throughout the Islamic world via musical performances of biographical panegyric texts (also called *mawlid*), as well as *madīḥ* and other *inshād*. Often the *mawlid* (Arabic "birth"; elsewhere known as *milad, mawlud, mevlut, mulud*, etc.) is performed for life-cycle occasions too, or even as a weekly devotion. The *Mawlids* of al-Busīrī and al-Barzanjī are performed throughout the Islamic world. Many Ṣūfī *shaykhs* compose *mawlids* for use in their orders.

Local languages and poetic forms, as well as socio-musical resources, are also expressed during *mawlid*. The Turkish *Mevlid* of Suleymān Čelebī (d. 1422) became part of the official Ottoman *mawlid* celebration, and is still widely performed in Turkey today. In northern Ghana, the week-long Damba festival includes traditional singing, drumming, and dancing honoring the Prophet, and the chief. In Java a sacred *gamelan* (gong-chime ensemble) called Sekaten (probably from "*shahādatayn*," the Muslim confession of faith) is played for the *mulud*, to call people to the mosque. Some of the most elaborate *mawlid* performances are found in coastal East Africa.

Saint festivals

Muslim saints (*awliyāʾ, pīr*) are celebrated in annual festivals called *mawlid* ("birth"), *ʿurs* ("wedding"), or *mawsim* ("season"), centered on the shrine (*maqām*). Ṣūfī orders celebrate their founder-saints with expanded versions of musical *ṭarīqa* traditions. Most festivals are public occasions, inviting general community participation, socially and sonically open; instruments and ecstatic behaviors are common. The music of saint festivals includes *ṭarīqa* traditions of *inshād* and *dhikr*, along with professional Ṣūfī musical traditions. As always, *madīḥ* is central.

Saint festivals may also draw upon the wider range of local music, which develops religious meanings in context. Spectacular processions, including music, often mark celebratory commencements or conclusions. Enormous *mawlids* in Egypt incorporate musical diversity, from Ṣūfī *inshād*, to secular folk traditions. Music praises Moulay Idris at his Moroccan festival, while Amadou Bamba enjoys musical pride of place during the Grand Maggal, an annual Mouride pilgrimage to his birthplace, Touba in Senegal.

Since Muḥammad ibn ʿAbd al-Wahhāb (d. 1792), Islamic reformism has taken a particularly strong stand against saint veneration (considered *shirk*, "polytheism"), and therefore these celebrations are on the decline in many areas (most notably in Saudi Arabia itself), though they still enjoy mass popularity.

ʿAshurāʾ

Among the Shīʿa, *ʿAshurāʾ* commemorates the martyrdom of the Imām Ḥusayn and his family at Karbala. In the period leading up to this occasion, the Ithnā-ʿasharī ("Twelver") Shīʿa convene for the *majlis* (mourning assembly) held in a *Ḥusayniyya* or *Imāmbāra*, as well as outdoor processions and gatherings. Various genres of hymns are performed, including elegy (*marsiya*), eulogy (*salām*), lament (*nawha, soz*), dirge (*nawha, matam*). The passion play (*taʿziyya*), dramatizing events of Karbala, symbolizes the struggle of good and evil, accompanied by programmatic music from singers, drum, trumpet, flute, and cymbals. In Iran, the *rowzekhan* (preacher) narrates the story of the martydom, triggering mass weeping. In South Asia assembly hymns as well as evocative outdoor drumming is performed.

Festivals: life-cycle

Unlike holidays, most life-cycle contexts – births, circumcisions, weddings, and funerals – are not unique to Muslims. Here, then, one finds accumulation and retention of a greater variety of non-religious and pre-Islamic genres and musical features, resulting in complex convergences, synergies, and syncretisms between Islamic styles (as marked by text and sound) and popular ones. One generally observes greater liberality in use of musical instruments, musical sounds, dance, and mixing of the sexes, and participation of ordinary professional musicians.

Inshād, especially *madīḥ*, is widely performed for all life-cycle events. Often a Ṣūfī *ḥaḍra* or *mawlid* (e.g., of al-Barzanjī) is performed; the latter is common in Arab Gulf countries. Malaysian *Rodat*, in praise of the Prophet, was also performed at weddings. In Sumatra, *salawat dulang*, using metal trays for percussion, contains sung sermons, which may be set to popular songs and performed at weddings. In Egypt, *inshād* performed for circumcisions, weddings, or memorials may incorporate popular Arabic songs and instruments. Hausa Bandiri music transforms Hindi film songs into *madīḥ nabawī*. In Kenya, a birth may be celebrated with *mawlid* performance. The Songhoi (Niger) circumcision ritual (prayers, songs, *tilawa*, dancing and drumming) fuses Islamic and pre-Islamic performance elements, illustrating how functional homology creates pathways for continuity and syncretism.

Spirit ritual contexts

Though many Muslims denounce spirit possession rituals as "pagan" (*wathnī*), in Islamic regions such rituals evince Islamic features, typically by associating spirits with elements of Islamic cosmology (*jinn* or saints), recognizing a class of "Muslim spirits," or assimilating with Sufism. While women are peripheral in most *ṭarīqa*s, they often play a principal role here. Spirit rituals often draw upon sub-Saharan African musical structures (polyrhythmic percussion, and pentatonicism), center on spiritual therapy (via exorcism or propitiation), and frequently feature ecstasy, self-mortification, and possession. Particular melodic or rhythmic patterns may placate particular spirits. Yet Islamic *madīḥ* are sung as well.

Examples of this include the Moroccan *derdeba* or *lila* and Algerian *dīwān* performed by *Gnawas* (claiming descent from the Prophet's Ethiopian muezzin, Bilāl);

the parallel *stambeli* of Tunisia; and the *ḥaḍra* of the Moroccan *Hamādsha*. In Egypt, Sudan, and Ethiopia, *zār* performances include Muslim spirits, and feature *madīḥ*.

Mediated Islamic music

With the rise of mass music media – beginning with early twentieth-century phonograms – new modes of commodified production and consumption were enabled, transforming the sound and meaning of Islamic music. Mass media tend both to replace traditional performance, and to standardize it, according to high-value models. While cassettes (in the 1970s) greatly extended the musical influence of mass media, until recently most distribution was regional.

Since the 1990s, a studio-produced style called *nashīd* or *anāshīd*, has been globally disseminated via satellite television and Internet, carrying the ethos of Islamic reformism. While traditional themes of praise and supplication remain, new ones – political or social – are also taken up, in keeping with reformism's more socially engaged worldview.

Conservative performers avoid instruments, though often admitting all percussion as a rule. Such *inshād* is restrained, with little improvisation or elaborate melisma, yet modernized through digital processing, harmonization, and music videos. One of the most media-savvy voices is that of the Kuwaiti Mashārī Rashīd al-ʿAfasī (b. 1976), who also recites Qurʾān and *adʿiyya*, serves as *imām* of Kuwait's Grand Mosque, and even owns his own religious television station (al-ʿAfasī TV).

The work of others is closer to popular music, often incorporating melodic instruments, and featuring contemporary arrangements, inflected by pop style, regional and international. Such performers include the British–Azeri Sami Yusuf, Zain Bhikha from South Africa, Mesut Kurtis from Macedonia, the Indonesian Haddad Alwi and the phenomenal Malaysian boy band, Raihan.

Islamic versions of Western popular music genres, usually created by Muslims living in the West, maintain musical style, while inserting Islamic texts and intentions. Examples include Islamic hip hop (Amir Sulayman), Islamic punk rock (Taqwacore), Islamic folk-rock (Dawud Wharnsby Ali), even Islamic country (Karim Salama). These musics tend to engage social issues afflicting diasporic Muslim communities such as discrimination and drug use, while addressing non-Muslims as well.

A different category of mediated Islamic music is that which is marketed for a non-Muslim audience, as a form of "world music." A number of "ethnographic" recordings of traditional Islamic music are available. Other "world Islamic music" is more market-driven. The bulk of world Islamic music emphasizes exoticism and spirituality, prioritizing music over text, while avoiding Islamic puritanism. Such attitudes are most plentiful in Ṣūfī music and spirit rituals – precisely what the new *nashīd* rejects. Examples include Hassan Hakmoun (Gnawa fusion), Hamza ʿAla al-Din (Nubian Ṣūfī), Nusrat Fateh Ali Khan's *qawwālī* fusions, and Mercan Dede, inspired by Mevlevi music.

Interactions

Conceptual boundaries notwithstanding, it is clear that interactions between Islamic music and the broader music field have always been extensive. Islamic music and themes have influenced music generally. Throughout the world, singers-to-be first studied *tilāwa* in a Qur'ān school (*kuttāb*), or performed in Ṣūfī orders. The high status of religious music also tended to set aesthetic norms and establish legitimacy. Groups of composers and performers affiliated with Ṣūfī religious organizations (e.g., the Mevlevi, the ʿĪsāwiyya) functioned as virtual music conservatories for art music. *Adhān, tilāwa* and *duʿā'* have infused Arab vocal style throughout Muslim Africa. American hip hop incorporates a wide range of Islamic messages, as does popular music in Senegal. In the reverse direction, core recitations absorbed local music, in its timbral, tonal, and temporal aspects. Outside the core ritual contexts, traditional religious music often assimilated local instruments and non-religious music genres and styles.

A contemporary decrease in interactions is due to several factors. Secular education means that Qur'anic training is less common, while Islamic reformism discourages music. The mass media have played a dual role, encouraging Islamic reform and disseminating the new mediated Islamic music on specialized channels, while underlying the emergence of a system of music commodification in which Islamic music – far less marketable than female-centered dance hits – is relatively marginalized. Thus the broad social role Islamic music once enjoyed has contracted considerably, even as diversity has diminished. However core ritual and Ṣūfī *ḥaḍra*, together with the new Islamic mass media, ensure its continued presence throughout the Islamic world.

References and further reading

Abdul Khabeer, S. (2007) "Rep that Islam: The Rhyme and Reason of American Islamic Hip Hop," *The Muslim World*, 97: 125–41.

Al Faruqi, L. I. (1985) "Music, Musicians and Muslim Law," *Asian Music*, 17: 3–36.

Ames, D. W. (1973) "Igbo and Hausa Musicians: A Comparative Examination," *Ethnomusicology*, 17: 250–78.

Chernoff, J. M. (1979) *African Rhythm and African Sensibility: Aesthetics and Social Action in African Musical Idioms*, Chicago: University of Chicago Press.

Danielson, V. (1991) " '*Min al-Mashāyikh*': A View of Egyptian Musical Tradition," *Asian Music*, 22: 113–27.

Frishkopf, M. (2000) "*Inshād Dini* and *Aghani Diniyya* in Twentieth Century Egypt: A Review of Styles, Genres, and Available Recordings," *Middle East Studies Association Bulletin*, 34: 167–83.

—— (2008) "Mediated Qur'anic Recitation and the Contestation of Islam in Contemporary Egypt", in L. Nooshin, ed., *Music and the Play of Power: Music, Politics and Ideology in the Middle East*, North Africa and Central Asia, London, Ashgate Press.

Gribetz, A. (1991) "The Samaʿ Controversy: Sufi vs. Legalist," *Studia Islamica*, 74: 43–62.

Hood, M. (1985) "Javanese Gamelan Sekati. Its Sanctity and Age," *Acta Musicologica*, 57: 33–7.

Ibn al-Naqib, A. (1999) *Reliance of the Traveller: The Classic Manual of Islamic Sacred Law ʿUmdat al-salik*, Beltsville, MD: Amana Publications.

Kinney, S. (1970) "Drummers in Dagbon: the Role of the Drummer in the Damba Festival," *Ethnomusicology*, 14: 258–65.

Larkin, B. (2002) "Bandiri Music, Globalization and Urban Experience in Nigeria," *Cahiers d'études africaines*, 168: 739–62.

Matusky, P. (1985) "An Introduction to the Major Instruments and Forms of Traditional Malay Music," *Asian Music*, 16: 121–82.

in Tunis in 1897. The first reported African film, *Ain el Ghezal/The Girl of Carthage* (1924) was made by Tunisian filmmaker Chemama Chikly. Although they have not benefited from the same local popularity as the Egyptian films, Maghreb films are better known in European art houses.

After liberation, Algerian cinema tried to come to terms with the recent trauma and explored the notion of an Algerian identity (Mohammed Lakhdar-Hamina, *Le Vent de Aurés/The Wind from the Aurés*, 1967). By the mid 1970s, focus shifted to the post-war difficulties (Mohamed Boumari, *Le Charbonnier/The Charcoal Burner*, 1972), which gradually gave way to themes of neo-colonialism, urban alienation, bureaucracy, emigration to France, emancipation of women and Islamic fundamentalism. Issues of youth and marginals gained focus (Merzak Allouache, *Omar Gatlato*, 1977; Mohammed Chouikh, *The Citadelle*, 1988; *Youcef ou la légende du septiéme dormant/The Legend of the Seventh Sleeper*, 1993). The free market economy and the closure of all audiovisual institutions by the government were a drawback. However, with the *Millénaire d'Alger* project, several films received public funding in 2005 and the Algerian cinematèque was restored to its original vocation, transforming into a modern cinema museum with the necessary technology for the conservation of film.

Production of truly Moroccan films only started in 1968 with *Vaincre pour vivre/Conquer to Live* by Mohamed Abderrahmane Tazi and Ahmed Mesnaoui and *Quand murissent les dates/When the Dates Ripen* by Larbi Bennani and Abdelaziz Ramdani. International fame arrived with *Le Mille et une mains/One Thousand and One Hands* (1972) by Souheil Ben Barka.

Morocco does not produce many films but it has good production facilities and a large number of theatres. Social themes such as delinquency and polygamy are popular. In the 1970s, a more ethnographic approach was developed, and in the 1980s, the place of women in Islamic society became one of the core subjects. Farida Benlyazid, a prominent woman filmmaker, reflects on emancipation of women in *Bab al-sama Maftouh/A Door to the Sky*, (1988). Whereas Tunisian women filmmakers Moufida Tlatli (*Samt al Qusur/Les Silences du palais/Silences of the Palace*, 1994) and Raja Amar (*Satin Rouge*, 2002) rebel against the constraints of a society based on patriarchal religious practices, Benlyazid sees emancipation in religion.

A golden year for Moroccan film was 2005. Several films were screened at prestigious international film festivals; both the Ministry of Communication and Moroccan television announced increased funding; co-productions with France, Spain, Italy and Norway increased with possibilities of South/South co-productions with Sub-Saharan Africa; several film festivals, among them the 5th Marrakech International Film Festival, presented ambitious programs; and King Mohammed VI inaugurated the Dino de Laurentis' CLA studios in Ouarzazate which opened in partnership with Cinecittà Roma.

In Tunisia, the number of film clubs in 1949 was the highest in the continent. With the launching of the Carthage International Film Days in 1966, the atmosphere was favorable to establishing quality filmmaking. In 1986, *Rih Al-Sid* (*The Man of Ashes*, 1986) by Nouri Bouzid broke box-office records outdoing Hollywood and Egyptian films. From the same generation, Férid Boughedir (*Halfaouine – l'enfant des terasses*, 1990), Nacer Khmir (*Les Baliseurs du desert*, 1985) and Moufida Tlatli have carved a niche for an *auteur* cinema that does not favor populist films and grand epics. But the proliferation of cheap television satellite dishes and piracy has been detrimental to the development of a national cinema and production has been reduced.

The films made by filmmakers of North African origin living and working in France (most of whom are born after Independence and several belong to mixed races) show new styles and new aesthetics. They explore African social reality as well as the experiences of Africans in the West.

Arab Middle East

Egypt

Egyptian cinema has been the source of inspiration (and imitation) for the Arab world and beyond. In the years after World War II, Egyptian cinema was a "dream factory," churning out farce or melodrama spiced with ample belly dancing to lure viewers away from the mundane realities – very similar to Bollywood that has established itself in India. The star-led industry quickly established its hegemony over the Arab world, particularly due to its accessible language; from the post-war period into the 1990s, Egypt was the major exporter of films throughout the African continent.

Kemal Selim, Youssef Chahine, Salah Abu-Sayf and others began to make realistic films during a period when locally produced Indian imitations were saturating the market and American box-office hits were a big success. "New Realism" used the melodrama aspects of the commercial genre in exposing the new social evils such as the encroaching materialism and its product, the nouveau riche.

From *Cairo Station* (1958), considered as one of his masterpieces, to *The Emigrant* (1994), which brought him accusations of blasphemy by the Islamic fundamentalists, Youssef Chahine has successfully created works that are both popular and intellectual. In *Destiny* (1997), Chahine examines the historic battle between Islamic fundamentalists and liberals through the story of the enlightened twelfth-century Andalusian philosopher and Qur'anic scholar Ibn Rushd (Averroes) (d. 1198), the supreme judge of the caliph of Muslim Spain battling the Christians to the north. The fundamentalists struggle for power and want Averroes' writings burned. The film is an apt exposé of the historical religious tensions within the Islamic world and the position of the Islamic moderates on fanaticism.

A handful of young talents today try to continue the artistic tradition but censors, commercialism, inflation, video piracy, lack of government sponsorship and lack of originality have had detrimental effects. Today, Bollywood musical melodramas and Chinese kung-fu films have replaced the strong position that Egyptian films held in export markets.

Syria

Arab cinema outside Egypt has generally developed as a resistance to colonialism. In 1972, the alternative cinema in Syria openly opposed the commercial cinema of Egypt and focused on pan-Arab nationalism and social justice with the Palestinian question at the core, but the Arab defeat in the Six Day War in 1967 altered the official ideologies and political discourse. Oussama Mohammad, one of the most prominent Syrian filmmakers (*Nujūm al-naḥār/Stars of the Day*, 1988), has succeeded in following an independent stance in an industry entirely run by the state since 1963. However, *Stars of the Day*, which has received international accolades, was never released in its own country. Nationalization of the cinema sector resulted in a drainage of resources that benefited television production. Since the 1970s, Syria produces one feature film per year but, after Egypt, it is the second producer of soap operas in the Middle East.

Palestine

Palestinian cinema worked as a cultural arm of the Palestinian resistance after the Zionist occupation, using cinema as a weapon to publicize their plight but during the 1980s, when Lebanon was invaded by Israel, Palestinian filmmaking stopped. Several talented filmmakers, including Michel Khleifi, left for the West. Feature films are now made with sources outside Palestine and by filmmakers living elsewhere.

One of the most prominent filmmakers today is Elia Sulieman, (*Segell Ikhtifa/ Chronicle of a Disappearance*, 1996). Hany Abu-Hassad has won the Golden Globe for Best Foreign Film and was nominated for an Academy Award with *Paradise Now* (2005), a controversial film about two suicide bombers at a time when to give a human face to terrorism is almost a sacrilege.

Lebanon

In Lebanon, the civil war and the subsequent Israeli occupation of southern Lebanon were detrimental to the film industry. Many Lebanese movie theatres were converted to boutiques or local shopping centers. Several filmmakers, including Jocelyn Saab, (*Once Upon a Time in Beirut*, 1994) emigrated. Feature films can only be made with foreign funds. Randa Chahal Sabbag, a woman filmmaker, received the jury award at the Venice International Film Festival in 2003 with *Le Cerf-volant/Tayyara men wara/ The Kite*, a border-crossing love story.

Iraq

In Iraq, the British started the first cinema before 1920 when they occupied the country. The industry was built by private firms in the early 1940s with the help of the French and the Egyptians, who had already emerged as pioneers in the Arab world. Together they produced pastoral romances spiced up with singing and dancing.

After the 1958 military coup, which ousted the British-installed King Faisal, cinema industry became part of the new government's ambitious program of social reform with Arab nationalist ideals. When the Baath Party seized power in another coup in 1968, state control intensified. The 1970s were the golden period with several Iraqi films winning awards abroad although the melodramas of the earlier years were gradually replaced by state-sanctioned "historical" pieces or reflections on the revolution. Saddam Hussein even ordered the production of a propagandistic account of his own life, *The Long Days* featuring his cousin, Saddam Kamel, who resembled him. Military propaganda became prominent during the Iran-Iraq war.

In the 1970s and 1980s, going to the cinema with the family was a social event, but that culture gradually disappeared under Saddam's Baath regime, which curbed events that required gathering of people; people were also afraid to sit in dark public places as there were assassinations and disappearances.

After Saddam invaded Kuwait, the United Nations imposed sanctions on Iraq in August 1990 and the cinema industry came to a halt. New equipment, film and chemicals for film laboratories were forbidden under the new import rules designed to curb Saddam's chemical, biological and nuclear weapons program. During the US led invasion in 2003, the cinema inside the Baghdad University film school burned down in a bombing and looters took the remaining equipment.

Very few cinemas are in operation in Baghdad under invasion. The audience is only male and to cater to them, these cinemas show "sexy" films, which are actually 1970s soft pornography from Turkey and Italy. But at the Academy of Fine Arts in Baghdad University, students continue to study degree courses in filmmaking, relying on video rather than celluloid. In September 2005, Baghdad had its first film festival since the invasion showcasing films made by Iraqis focusing on the themes of terrorism, violence, the Baath era and the current state of society underlining the long suffering of the Iraqi people.

The first feature film to be shot in post-war Iraq was *Underexposure* by Oday Rasheed, which looks at American-occupied Baghdad through the eyes of six different characters. Rasheed is a founding member of *al-Najeen* (The Survivors), established in 1992 by a group of writers, poets, directors and artists from different ethnic backgrounds and faiths. Semi-autobiographical, *Underexposure* was shot around insurgent mortars and American patrols with film stock from 1952. The title refers to both the film stock and the current generation of Iraqi artists whose lives were underexposed under Saddam Hussein, which almost destroyed Iraq's artistic culture.

Iranian Kurdish filmmaker Bahman Ghobadi's *Turtles Can Fly*, also shot right after the invasion, explores the bleak life of refugee children in Iraqi Kurdistan on the eve of the 2003 American invasion. Both Ghobadi's and Rasheed's films expose the reality of daily life for millions of Iraqis, destroying not only the personal myth Saddam Hussein built by abusing Iraqi cinema during his dictatorship but also the "liberation" myth created by the USA and other invading powers.

For the other Arab nations in the Middle East, establishing a film industry is a distant dream mainly because of the constraints of religion. Kuwait and Bahrain have already had their taste of cinema and Dubai has started an international film festival that aims to compete with Cannes in France. Concerted efforts have started in Saudi Arabia to break down barriers in a situation in which Muslim scholars have pointed out that cinema can even be used to promote Islam.

Turkey

Cinema arrived in Turkey in 1896 through a Frenchman named Bertrand. His private show at the palace of the last Ottoman Emperor, Sultan Abdülhamid II, was followed by public screenings in the European part of Istanbul (Pera) by a local agent of the French company Pathé Brothers who, in 1908, opened the first movie theater in the same district and called it Cinema Pathé. The district eventually changed its name to Beyoğlu but remained as the center of the film industry and a particular street called Yeşilçam (The Green Pine) gave its name to Turkish commercial cinema that was the dominant form of entertainment until the arrival of television in the 1970s.

Figure 45 Zahra Bahrami, in *Baran* (2001), courtesy of Fouad Nahas/Majid Majidi/The Kobal Collection

During the time of the Ottoman empire, the Macedonian Manaki brothers made documentaries starting in 1907. However, the first national film, a long documentary called *Aya Stefanos'taki Rus Abidesinin Yıkılısı/The Demolition of the Russian Monument at St. Stephan*, was made in 1914 by Fuat Uzkınay, an officer in the Turkish army. The first feature film, *Himmet Ağanın İzdivacı/The Marriage of Himmet Aga*, a free adaptation from Molière, was begun by Sigmund Weinberg in 1918 but was suspended due to war and completed two years later by Uzkınay.

As in several other Muslim countries, cinema began as entertainment for men by men. At the beginning of the twentieth century, armed fundamentalists were occupying theatres threatening to knife any woman who dared to enter. Special screenings had to be arranged for women on certain days or divide the cinema halls in the middle with a wooden board to seat women on one side and men on the other until Kemal Atatürk, the founder of modern Turkey, decreed an end to such segregation. Women had to wait even longer to become actors. All female roles were played by non-Muslims until the foundation of the secular Turkish Republic in 1923.

Early Turkish cinema often depicted women (perhaps as an excuse to show the female body provocatively) as "fallen" – prostitutes disguised under the euphemism of dancing girls and cabaret singers. Village maidens lost their virginity through weakness or rape or were left without protection by the death of the husband or the desertion of the lover and became a threat to the family and a disgrace to Muslim society. Even when they were not responsible for the fall, this did not change the stigma attached to their condition.

Figure 46 *Umut* (1970), courtesy of Güney Filmcilik/The Kobal Collection.

Umut/Hope (1970) by Yılmaz Güney marks the beginning of New Turkish Cinema. The story of a phaeton driver (a trade which became obsolete with the arrival of the taxi system), *Hope* is a realistic portrayal of Turkey in a period of transition to capitalism. The film was banned for propagating class differences, alluding to American imperialism, degrading religion, and provoking workers to resist authority.

The international reputation of Yılmaz Güney is built around two important films, which he scripted while in prison, trusting his assistants to direct: Zeki Ökten for *Sürü/The Herd* (1979) and Şerif Gören for *Yol* (1982). *The Herd* focuses on the disintegration of nomadic life and the patriarchal structure with changes in the economic structure. When placed in liminal positions, women are at a double disadvantage, although feudal oppression destroys men and women alike. Women and honor are the main themes of *Yol/The Way*, one of the masterpieces of Turkish cinema, a film that is constructed around the stories of five prisoners on leave. A society where women are not free cannot be free, asserts Güney.

The number of women filmmakers in the history of Turkish cinema is negligible. The most important one, Bilge Olgaç, started her career within the confines of Yeşilçam, but moved on to several exceptional works (*Kaşik Düşmanı/Spoon Enemy*, 1984) that exposed men's oppression by the established customs and traditions and the patriarchal bias of Muslim religion as the driving force behind the oppression of women.

Figure 47 *Umut* (1970), courtesy of Güney Filmcilik/The Kobal Collection.

In the 1970s, when migration from the country to the city intensified, a cinema with a strong religious ideology and morals appeared as a reaction to trashy commercial cinema and the *engagé* films of the left. A small group around Yücel Çakmaklı tried to win back the alienated conservative audience with so called *milli* (national) cinema.

The movement re-surfaced in the 1990s under the banner of *beyaz cinema* (*white cinema*) and Çakmaklı's *Minyeli Abdullah/Abdullah of Minye* (1990) was a big box-office success. Mesut Uçakan's *Yalnız Değilsiniz/You Are Not Alone* (1990), blatant religious propaganda about the headscarf issue, was also very popular. However, its sequels did not receive the same response. *White cinema* claimed that since the foundation of the Turkish Republic, cinema in general has served negative aims instead of directing the youth to positive channels and women were treated in a manner similar to the period of *cahiliyye (jāhiliyya* in Arabic), pre-Islamic Arabia (as the lowest of all creatures, even below animals according to Qur'ān). However, far from trying to find a solution to the problems of women, *white cinema* only showed them as stereotypes.

By the end of the 1990s, new vitality was experienced with the arrival of a young generation of filmmakers such as Derviş Zaim, Nuri Bilge Ceylan, Zeki Demirkubuz and Yeşim Ustaoğlu. Their works display a diversity of genres, styles and subject matter, although the issue of social, political, ethnic and sexual identity in a rapidly changing world is the overriding theme. Turkey's strategic position and recent political developments towards a more conservative lifestyle dictated by Islamic ideology and Muslim identity, on the one hand, and capitalist modernity, embracing Western cultural, political and economic hegemony, culminating in a strong desire to join the European Union, on the other, are contributing factors to this urgency felt by artists to investigate a society in transition. There is also a trend to counteract the hegemony of Hollywood by imitating it. Such films have gained back the audience alienated by the "art films" of recent years by catering to tastes that have been formed by American blockbusters.

Iran

Iranian cinema has had its roots in a popular art form called *pardeh-khāni* – akin to *Benshi* of Japanese silent cinema – which involves a narrator to interpret a painting. A similar art form, *nagali*, was performed in the *ghahve-khānes* (coffeehouses), which were the main venues for cultural interaction.

The first Iranian non-fiction film was shot in Ostend, Belgium on August 18, 1900, by the official court photographer to immortalize the welcoming of the visiting Shah. The first public screenings were held in 1900 in Tabriz at the Cinema Soleil by Roman Catholic missionaries. Commercial viewings were started first in the back of an antique shop and later, in 1904, in a cinema in Tehran.

The first Iranian film, *Abi va rabi/Abi and Rabi* (1930), a silent black-and-white film, was directed by Ovanes Ohanian. However, it took almost a quarter of a century for ordinary women to experience cinema and even then, only in segregated sections. Abdolhossein Sepanta's very popular *Dokhtar-e Lor/The Lor Girl* (1933), which he shot in India, was the first sound film and the first film featuring a Muslim woman on screen. For many years, Iranian cinema was inundated with cheap imitations of Indian films, which showed women as gullible creatures. What came to be labeled as *film farsī* (Persian film) alienated families.

The credit for establishing the foundations of Iranian "new wave" (*Moj-e No*), a movement that flourished in the 1960s and 1970s, goes to Forugh Farrokhzad, a rebel poet. Her *Khaneh Siyah Ast/The House is Black* (1962), a 22 minute documentary about a leper colony (an apt metaphor for the socio-political atmosphere of the period) is acknowledged as the most important film to affect contemporary Iranian cinema. The film's delicate fusion of poetry with actuality and the way it makes use of non-professionals are precursors of the work of Iran's most celebrated filmmaker, Abbas Kiarostami, among others.

In 1970, Dariush Mehrjui's first film, *Gav/The Cow*, about a peasant who goes mad after losing his cow and identifies with the animal, was heralded as the harbinger of *cinéma verité*. One of the most influential filmmakers of the "new wave" was Sohrab Shahid Saless. Distinguished Iranian filmmaker Mohsen Makhmalbaf has called him the father of realism in Iranian cinema mainly for the two feature films, *Yek Ettefaghe Sadeh/A Simple Event* (1973) and *Tabiate Bijan/Still Life* (1974) that he completed before he emigrated to Germany.

The Islamist revolution (1979) was the death knell of Iranian cinema. Ayatollah Khomeini condemned cinema as prostitution although later he praised its power to influence the masses in a positive manner. In revolutionary fervor, many theaters were burned, many people were killed and film footage was destroyed. Prominent film-makers went into exile. Women were erased from the screen unless they served the purpose of raw models of dutiful and obedient wives, mothers and daughters. Innovative filmmakers began to avoid urban adult stories, using children as actors and/or restructuring their scripts.

With the founding of the Farabi Cinema Foundation in 1983, steps were taken to liberate arts and promote national cinema and Iranian films began to win awards abroad with Abbas Kiarostami, Bahram Beyza'i, Dariush Mehrjui and Mohsen Makhmalbaf leading the way, along with several younger talents including Abolfazl Jalili, Majid Majidi and Jafar Panahi. Women moved behind the camera and Rakhshan Bani-Etemad and Tahmineh Milani, among others, have established their fame in the international arena. Iranian cinema today is the most vibrant and challenging cinema of the Middle East.

Afghanistan

Afghanistan is connected to cinema in the Western mind not with indigenous films but rather foreign productions, particularly made by Iranians: Majid Majidi's *Baran/The Rain* (2001), Mohsen Makhmalbaf's *Kandahar* (2001), and Samira Makhmalbaf's *Five In the Afternoon* (2003). The first post-Taliban Afghan film to reach the West is *Osama* (2003) by Siddik Barmak and even that was made with foreign collaboration.

Amir Habibullah is credited for having introduced cinema to Afghanistan at the beginning of the twentieth century, but in the royal court only. Ordinary people had to wait until the dynasty of Amir Amanullah Khan. In 1923–4, the first projector showed a silent film to the public. Mostly European films were also shown in Kabul.

Figure 48 Hossein Abedini, in *Baran* (2001), courtesy of Fouad Nahas/Majid Majidi/The Kobal Collection.

In 1929, the bandit Bacha-e Saqaow took over, but was ousted by Nadir Khan, a former general under Amir Amanullah. Muhammad Nadir crowned himself king, aligning himself with the clergy and followed a very strict religious policy. All theatres were closed and remained so until his assassination in 1933. Muhammad Zahir, Nadir's son, became king in 1934 and films – mostly Indian – began to be shown in theatres.

Although some claim that cinema in Afghanistan began with the *Hafte Sawr* (the first *mujāhidīn*'s revolution), historians point to *Ishq wa Dosti/Love and Friendship* (1946) by Rashid Latifi as the first Afghan film. In 1965, Afghan Film, founded by Muhammad Zahir was established in the capital Kabul and started producing documentaries and newsreels highlighting the official meetings and conferences of the government. By 1972, when the well-equipped building of the Afghan Film Organization was completed, film culture spread throughout the country. Private industries started producing feature films, among which *Rabia e Balkhi* (1974), a joint project of Davoud Farani, Toryalay Shafaq and Khalek A'lil, was very popular.

The political instability of the country has always had its repercussions on cinema. After the 1978 revolution, the government used the medium to propagate its political views and beliefs. Despite difficulties, outstanding films depicting the issues of everyday life were made – *Shekast Mahasera/Halted Failure* (1987) by Faqir Nabi, *Safar/The Voyage* (1988) by Saeed Orokzai, *Faraar/Escape* (1984), and *Sabur-e-sarbaz/A Patient Soldier* (1985) by (Engineer) Latif Ahmadi – and won both national and international acclaim.

The civil wars of the 1990s were not conducive to creative work and many people working in the film industry escaped to Iran or Pakistan. After the fall of Kabul in 1996, the Taliban destroyed an irreplaceable archive of film. In 2001, the staff of Afghan Film were ordered to burn their entire stock of 3,000 films. They managed to save around 1,000 by hiding tapes, among which was the first Afghan film, *Love and Friendship*.

Siddiq Barmak, the former Director of Afghan Film, made international fame with *Osama* (2003), about a young girl who lives in a household without men, cuts her hair and pretends to be a boy so she can take a job in a local bakery. When her identity is discovered, she is prosecuted by a religious court and forced to marry an elderly Mulla. Mohsen Makhmalbaf who shot *Kandahar* on the borders of Afghanistan was behind a large part of the funding. In 2004, *Osama* received the Golden Globe for best foreign-language film.

Numerous production companies have opened their doors recently in Kabul. One important movement is the appearance of women behind the camera. Roya Sadat, a 24-year-old autodidact from Herat, made her debut with *Se noughta/Three Dots* (2005) about a single mother of three; she has won international acclaim. Political issues are now treated with relative liberality, but controversy over the prevalent interpretation of Islam and its tradition in Afghanistan is still sensitive.

Indian sub-continent

India produces nearly 1,000 films per year. Mainstream cinema aspires to present Indian society as one uniform culture, the Hindu. Muslim stars dominated the formative years of Bollywood, Mumbai-based commercial Indian cinema, although many

avoid hostility from a faction of Hindus who threatened to burn the theatre where his *Dukhey Jader Jibon Gora/Misery is their Lot* (1946) was to premiere. Bangladeshi historians have now reached a consensus that the first film production of Bangladesh is *Mukh-o-Mukhosh/The Face and the Mask* (1956).

In the 1960s, the social realist tradition of Bengali cinema was prevalent but, following the war of liberation in 1971, formula melodramas with cliché morals began to invade the screens. The murder in 1975 of Sheikh Mujibur Rahman, the founder of Bangladesh, and the subsequent political upheavals that pushed the country to right-wing reactionalism and Islamic conservatism had their repercussions on the film industry. Tanvir Mokammel is one of the most important contemporary filmmakers from Bangladesh. He explores faith and deception in the countryside in *Lalsalu/A Tree Without Roots* (2001) about a charlatan who willfully misinterprets the ideals of Islam and exploits the villagers.

Southeast Asia

In Indonesia, the most populous Muslim nation, the history of cinema runs parallel to the history of the country: the Dutch colonial period to 1942, the Japanese occupation to 1945, and the struggle for Independence, lasting from 1950 to the present, highlighted by the 1965–7 transition from the Sukarno period to the New Order of Suharto.

The first public cinema opened in Batavia (Jakarta) in 1900. The first feature, *Loetoeng Kasaroeng/Enchanted Monkey* by Heuveldorp, a Dutchman, and Kruger, a German, based on a Sundanese (West Java) folktale about a supernatural monkey, is said to have been released in 1926. The films of this period, made mainly by Europeans and Chinese, revolved around traditional plots.

During the Japanese invasion, cinema was used for propaganda purposes; however, some of the changes the invader imposed, such as replacing the Europeans and the Shanghai Chinese who owned the industry along with Indonesians, and stressing the use of the Indonesian language on screen were beneficial to the national industry. The Central Art Office, established in Jakarta in 1943, was instrumental for the formation of talents such as Usmar Ismail, considered the father of Indonesian cinema. Ismail established the National Film Corporation (PERFINI) after the formalization of Independence (1949). Unfortunately, out of the 23 films produced in 1950, only *Darah Dan Doa/The Long March* by Usmar Ismail, recounting the Indonesian war of independence, is preserved.

Ideological controversy around cinema and national culture reached its peak in 1964 and many cinemas were closed or burned down. Film personnel were persecuted both before and after the abortive communist coup of 1965 and the film industry was paralyzed. In the 1970s, several socially engaged films were made; however, dedicated filmmakers often resorted to formula pieces to raise the funds. Sex and violence thrived.

Unlike Hollywood films in which conflict arises from the clash of discordant elements of good and evil, Indonesian films put the emphasis on order and disorder. At the center is a character whose act has negative consequences for others. The main plot deals with the attempts of the others to solve the problem and restore order. This is the essence of *wayang*, the shadow puppet play of Central Java. Many well-known Indonesian filmmakers such as Usmar Ismail, D. Djajakusuma, Teguh Karya and Slamet Rahardjo are from the theater and carry on such traditions in their works.

Film industry in Indonesia is national, not regional. Generalized Indonesian behavior patterns are displayed without regional ethnic characteristics. Regional settings are used for local color. Almost all films are made in Jakarta in *Bahasa Indonesia*, the Indonesian language, despite the fact that the first language of most Indonesians is still their regional language. Eros Djarot's *Tjoet Nja Dhien* (1988) was revolutionary in the sense that much of the dialogue was in Acehnese (spoken by the Muslim population of Aceh in the north).

Garin Nugroho is one of the most celebrated Indonesian filmmakers today. Controversial in style and ideas, he broke away from the tradition right away and has made all his films in the different languages of the country, defending his view of cultural pluralism. Despite accolades abroad with such films as *Bulan tertusuk ilalang/ . . . and the Moon Dances* (1995), he has had difficulties releasing his films in Indonesia.

Women filmmakers traditionally have been scarce, and they have followed the male point of view. But with the new millennium, a new generation has emerged with a different vision. Of the five producers actively working, four are women. Their efforts are supported by Christian Hakim, celebrated star and producer.

In Malaysia, traditionally, films have focused on the Malays and Malay culture although the industry was founded on Chinese investments and the creative contribution of the Indian population. In recent years, a trend has emerged to create a cinema that reflects the multi-cultural aspect of the society. The most important influences on Malaysian cinema are

> the native popular musical theater form known as *bangsawan*; Indian cinema (especially Tamil language films); transplanted Chinese culture; Japanese cinema of the Occupation (especially the films of such directors as Kurosawa, Ozu, Naruse, and Mizoguchi), as well as the films of popular Japanese film genres such as the *shomin-geki* (comedies about the lower-middle class), and *nonsensu-mono* ("nonsense" comedies); Islam; and, perhaps most important, Hollywood films of the 1930s and 1940s (especially comedies, film noir, and monster movies)
>
> (White 1996)

The controversial U-Wei bin Hajisaari was the first Malay director to have had a screening at the Cannes film festival with his *Kaki Bakar/The Arsonist* (1995). *Perumpuan, isteri dan Jalang/Woman, Wife, Whore* (1993) was cut in 36 places and the word "whore" in the title replaced by three dots before it could have public screenings. In his films, U-Wei Hajisaari delves into the psyche of the Malay man and woman and tries to understand why they are what they are, without moralizing. Shuhaimi Baba and Erma Fatima are two women filmmakers with a feminist point of view. Shuhaimi Baba's *Selubung/Veil of Life* (1992) deals with young, educated people's misunderstanding of Islam. In *Perempuan Melayu Terakhir/The Last Malay Woman* (1999) and in *Embun/Dewdrops* (2002) Erma Fatima explores the search for Malay identity and the identity of women in Malay society.

Muslim states of the former USSR

In Azerbaijan in the Caucasus, a Muslim state of the former USSR, projections began three years after they began in Paris. The first film, *V Tzarstve Nefti I Millionov/In the Kingdom of Oil and Millions* by Boris Svetlov, was made in 1916. Popular folk operas were adapted into film and Svetlov's *Archin Mal Alan/The Cloth Peddler* (1917) became a favorite. *Mavi Danizin Sahilinde/On the Shores of the Blue Sea* (1935), the first Azeri talkie, was shot in the silent film style by Boris Barnet and Samed Mardanov. In the 1920s and 1930s, with the fervor of revolution, collaborations with the Russians or filmmakers from the other Caucasian states were very common and these collaborations were beneficial in the formation of young Azeri filmmakers.

Political jargon became blatant in the 1950s, but in the 1960s the focus shifted to dramatic films such as Edgar Guliev's *Bir Djanoub Saharinda/In a Southern City* (1969) about the clash of old and new values. With the emergence of good script-writers such as Rustam Ibrahimbekov, themes of identity crisis, the conflict between the old and new order, and social evils such as the mafia and corruption entered cinema.

With independence and the seven-year-war with Armenia, almost all film production came to a halt. Cinema is not on the priority list of the government. Barely one full-feature film a year is produced there and the quality is usually very poor. Most of the cinemas of the republic show American films. For the majority of the population, television is the best entertainment.

In Central Asia, cinema began early with the newsreels and documentaries. The first known screening was in Tashkent in 1897, the capital of Uzbekistan. Under the restrictions of the Communist regime, however, cinema did not have much chance to flourish. From the time of its nationalization by a Lenin decree in 1919, film production and distribution were regulated by a government institution, the State Committee for Cinematography (Goskino), which gradually gained control, only to be dismantled with the arrival of *perestroika*.

The first Kazakh documentary was shot in 1925 and released in 1929 under the historical title *Pribytie Pervovo Poezda v Alma Atu/The Arrival of the First Train in Alma Ata*. Five years later a documentary film studio was founded where newsreels, documentaries and a few feature films were made. During World War II, Mosfilm and Lenfilm were evacuated to the capital Alma Ata, and Sergei Eisenstein shot two parts of *Ivan Grozyj/Ivan, the Terrible* there between 1943 and 1945. For the Kazakhs, however, national cinema began in 1954 with the first Kazakh fiction film, *A Love Poem*, by Shaken Aimanov.

After the fall of the Soviet Union, a new vitality was evidenced in Kazakhstan, which was perhaps the only Central Asian state not seriously affected by the social, economic and ethnic turmoil that swept the former republics. Under the liberal policies of President Nursultan Nazarbayev, the country easily moved to a free market economy. However, when investments on the film industry did not show profit, the private sector withdrew and film production fell considerably. Rachid Nugmanov, Darejan Omirbaev, Serik Aprimov, Ardak Amirkulov, Yermek Shinarbaev, Amir Karakulov, and Talgat Temenov are important representatives of the Kazakh "new wave." However, very few are able to make films today unless financially supported by foreign producers.

Bolakbet Shamshiev and Tolomush Okeev are considered the founders of the national cinema in Kyrgyzstan. Following independence, 35mm films became an impossibility. Aktan Abdykalykov, who makes his films with foreign funds, has been very successful internationally with his trilogy, *Selkinc hek/The Swing* (1993), *Beshkempir/The Adopted Son* (1998) and *Maimyl/The Chimp* (2001).

Davlat Khudonazarov, a political activist, is an important representative of the *new wave* (1960–70) in Tajikistan, marked by a diversity of styles and themes. The civil war that followed independence resulted in many filmmakers moving to Moscow or to western countries and making films with foreign financing. The most successful two are from the younger generation: Bakhtiyar Khudoynazarov, who has shown his talents starting with his first film *Bratan/Brothers* (1992), a black-and-white road movie that crosses the Pamirs with a steam engine; and Djamshed Usmanov, whose latest film *Bihisht Faqat Barqi Murdagon/To Get To Heaven First You Have To Die* (2006) received favorable reviews after its screening at the Cannes Film Festival.

Some of the most prominent filmmakers from Turkmenistan are Khodzakuli Narliev, Biul-Biul Mamedov, Usman Saparov and Halmammet Kakabayev. After independence, the country now has the most limited production of the Central Asian states. Shooting 35mm films is no longer possible. The government controls the media, and many talented filmmakers have found themselves in conflict with the regime.

Nabi Ganiev and Kamil Yarmatov are the founders of modern Uzbek cinema. During the 1960s, following the "thaw" of Khrushchev, Uzbek "new wave" was born with Ali Khamraev as one of the important representatives. With *perestroika*, talented young filmmakers such as Jahangir Faiziev, Zulfikar Mussakov and Yusuf Razikov entered the industry. One of the most prominent filmmakers of Uzbekistan is Kamara Kamalova, a woman.

The capital Tashkent with a population of two million people is the home of a modern, popular narrative cinema with strong social themes in a variety of genres and styles, from irony and farce to science-fiction and period pieces. However, just as in Kyrgyzstan and Turkmenistan, among recent productions, political films dealing with the issue of coming to terms with the Soviet period or an analysis of the present situation are absent.

Conclusion

Territorial disputes, civil wars, attempts at ethnic cleansing, foreign invasions, colonial ambitions and the heavy hand of censorship have had repercussions on cinema in the Islamic world. Film archives were either never kept, or kept in deplorable conditions subject to forces of nature, or looted and burned by extremists who viewed cinema as the propaganda tool of the non-Muslim devil.

The film industries of the former Republics of the Soviet Union faced the cruel reality of the price of freedom when they lost the support of the Soviet Union after its demise. In comparison to the Soviet regime, when the industry was under the tight control of Moscow, there is a certain amount of freedom. However, controversial political subjects are still met with automatic censorship, if not state intervention. Hollywood films are the most popular. The biggest drawback to the development of the national cinemas is the lack of money.

In the Indian subcontinent, the partition of India caused lasting damage to the film industry. Most of Lahore's Hindu film producers migrated to India and a number of talented Muslim film workers moved from Bombay film studios to Pakistan. The prevailing animosity between India and Pakistan has kept cooperation between the filmmakers under the scrutiny of their respective governments. In Afghanistan, the number of coups or government changes seems to be higher than the number of films made. With the arrival of the Taliban, the industry was erased from Afghan history. Long years under Saddam Hussein did not give Iraq much chance to create a viable film industry.

Faced with production obstacles, lack of structure, funding and distribution, censorship, satellite television and piracy, national film industries have been relying on foreign monetary backing. A majority of the North African films are fully financed by former colonial powers, mainly France. It would be naïve to think that such dependence does not determine the direction and destination of the end-product. The number of festivals, which has increased beyond proportion, also plays a certain part in the proliferation of films from the so-called "third world" or "the South" that are supposed to be for a universal audience, but are in fact made for festival audiences with little to offer to their home audience.

The exotic quality of such films appeals to Western audiences, and hence they attract foreign finance. Some are, no doubt, of exceptional quality, whereas others try to bank on a tried-and-true formula and inadvertently reinforce the Orientalist point of view that assumes the East as the "other" of the West – an "othering" that reduces whole cultures to one dimension. A case in point is the post-Islamist revolution Iranian cinema, which, under the severe restrictions of a fanatical regime has shifted to the countryside where the mandates of *ḥijāb*, the Islamic code of dress, are less severe. Iranian "village films," some of which display remarkable qualities in the hands of master craftsmen, have begun winning international awards with their "humanistic" stories. Since such films position their narrative outside history and outside time, they imply that humanity is the same everywhere, which is an attractive notion in an age of globalization.

Following the events of September 11, 2001, the relations of the Western world with Muslims in general and Arabs in particular have acquired a new dimension. Hollywood, which has never presented a favorable image of the Muslim world (*Midnight Express, Not Without My Daughter* easily come to mind, not to mention the endless sheiks and their harems yarns), has taken the opportunity to exploit public sensitivity by presenting Muslims as more villainous than they already have been. Unfortunately, such films find their way to Muslim markets as well. Although negotiations have started to establish a counter cinema that would offer a viable alternative to Hollywood in the Muslim world, such a project seems to be utopian considering the diversity of cultures, cultural styles, and languages, as well as the different forms of Islam practiced.

Cinema and its evolution in the world of Islam carry transnational elements in several aspects – its assimilation as a Western non-Muslim invention, its adoption or rejection, the forms of censorship imposed that arise from religious beliefs. However, several other aspects are universal and related to socio-political and economic circumstances and not necessarily religion.

What does Senegalese Ousmane Sembène have in common with Turkish Yılmaz Güney? Four years apart, each made a film on a similar subject, a man going mad after losing his livelihood. Both films depict dilemmas of progress and survival, expose different forms of oppression, criticize easy adoption of Western values and point to religion and the traditional belief in past glories (embodied by the *griot* in *Cart-Owner* and *hodja* in *Hope*) as a paralyzing force. Did Güney see Sembène's *Cart-Owner*? I doubt it.

While Güney was shooting *Hope*, Iranian Dariush Mehrjui completed *Gav/The Cow*, about a poor man who also goes mad after losing his livelihood. The binding element of these three films, apart from the essential narrative, is the neo-realist aspect and the minimalist language. All three in essence question the system and are excellent examples of "third cinema," the principal characteristic of which, as Gabriel points out, "is really not so much where it is made, or even who makes it, but, rather, the ideology it espouses and the consciousness it displays. The Third Cinema is that cinema of the Third World which stands opposed to imperialism and class oppression in all their ramifications and manifestations" (Gabriel 1982: 2).

References and further reading

Amilcar, C. (1973) *Return to the Source*, New York: Monthly Review Press/Africa Information Service.

Arasoughly, A., ed. and trans. (1998) *Screens of Life: Critical Film Writing from the Arab World*, St. Hyacinthe: World Heritage Press.

Armbrust, W. (1995) "New Cinema, Commercial Cinema, and the Modernist Tradition in Egypt," *Alif: Journal of Comparative Poetics*, 15: 81–129.

—— (1996) *Mass Culture and Modernism in Egypt*, Cambridge: Cambridge University Press.

—— (2002) "The Rise and Fall of Nationalism in the Egyptian Cinema," in F. M. Gocek, ed., *Social Constructions of Nationalism in the Middle East*, Albany: State University of New York Press, 217–50.

Armbrust, W., ed. (2000) *Mass Mediations: New Approaches to Popular Culture in the Middle East and Beyond*, Berkeley: University of California Press.

Armes, R. (1987) *Third World Film Making and the West*, Berkeley: University of California Press.

—— (1996) *Dictionary of North African Film Makers/Dictionnaire des cinéastes du Maghreb*, Paris: Éditions ATM.

—— (2005) *Post-Colonial Images: Studies in North African Film*, Bloomington: Indiana University Press.

Bakari, I. and Cham, M., eds. (1996) *African Experiences of Cinema*, London: BFI.

Barlet, O. (1996) *Les Cinémas d'Afrique noire: Le regard en question*, Paris: Harmattan.

Bayo, O. (1985) "Ritual Archetypes: Ousmane's Aesthetic Medium in *Xala*," *Ufahamu* 14(3): 128–38.

Benali, A. (1998) *Le Cinéma colonial au Maghreb*, Paris: Cerf.

Berstein, M. and Studlar, G., eds. (1997) *Visions of the East: Orientalism in Film*, London and New York: I. B. Taurus.

Boughedir, F. (1987) *Le Cinéma africain de A à Z*, Brussels: Éditions OCIC.

Bouzid, N. (1995) "New Realism in Arab Cinema: The Defeat-Conscious Cinema," *Alif: Journal of Comparative Poetics*, 15: 242–50.

Cham, M. B. (1984) "Art and Ideology in the Work of Ousmane Sembène and Haile Gerima," *Présence Africaine* 129(1): 79–91.

Cheah, P. "Garih Nugroho, (1996) 'No Son on his Own Soil'," *Cinemaya*, 34: 20–2.

Dabashi, H. (2001) *Close Up: Iranian Cinema, Past, Present, and Future*, London and New York: Verso.
Diawara, M. (1992) *African Cinema: Politics and Culture*, Bloomington: Indiana University Press.
Dönmez-Colin, G. (1993) "Contre l'héritage de Kemal Atatürk: Cinema et morale Islamiste," *Le Monde Diplomatique* (Paris) October, 15.
—— (1994) "Reflections of a Culture in Conflict – Turkish Cinema of the Nineties," *Blimp*, 27/28: 15–19.
—— (1999) "Malayalam Cinema: Aesthetics with a Social Vision," *Blimp*, 41: 25–32.
—— (2000) "A Brief Look at Indonesian Cinema," *Blimp*, 43: 79–83.
—— (2004) *Women, Islam and Cinema*, London: Reaktion Books,
—— (2006) *Cinemas of the Other: A Personal Journey with Filmmakers from the Middle East and Central Asia*, Bristol: Intellect Books.
Feuser, W. F. (1986) "Richard Wright's Native Son and Ousmane Sembene's *Le docker noir*," *Komparatistische-Hefte*, 14: 103–16.
Gabriel, T. H. (1982) *Third Cinema in the Third World*, Ann Arbor: UMI Research Press.
Hanan, D. (1997) "Five Classic Indonesian Masters," *Cinemaya*, 35: 58–61.
Heider, K. G. (1991) *Indonesian Cinema: National Culture on Screen*, Honolulu: University of Hawai'i Press.
Leaman, O., ed. (2001) *The Companion Encyclopedia of Middle Eastern and North African Film*, London, New York: Routledge.
Nwachukwu, F. U. (1994) *Black African Cinema*, Berkeley: University of California Press.
Said, E. (1981) *Covering Islam: How the Media and the Experts Determine How We See the Rest of the World*, New York: Pantheon Books.
Said, S. and McGlynn, J. H., eds. (1991) *Cinema of Indonesia*, New York: Festival of Indonesia Foundation.
Sen, K. (1994) *Indonesian Cinema: Framing the New Order*, London: Zen Books.
Solanas, F. and Getino, O. (1976) "Towards a Third Cinema," in B. Nichols, ed., *Movies and Methods. An Anthology*, Berkeley: University of California Press, 44–64.
Spaas, L. (2000) *The Francophone Film: A Struggle for Identity*, Manchester and New York: Manchester University Press.
Thackway, M. (2003) *Africa Shoots Back: Alternative Perspectives in Sub-Saharan Francophone African Film*, Bloomington: Indiana University Press.
White, T. (1996) "Historical Poetics, Malaysian Cinema, and the Japanese Occupation," *Kinema*, Fall: 5–11; available online at http//www.kinema.uwaterloo.ca/white962.htm.

Part V

SOCIAL ISSUES AND THE ISLAMIC WORLD

43

CIVILIZATION

Akbar Ahmed

Unfortunately, the names of Muslim scholars are not as well known in the West today as I believe they should be. When I talk of Ibn Khaldūn (d. 1406), people usually ask: Who is he? Another terrorist? Any links to Osama bin Ladin? Or is he an oil sheik or an Arab minister? Even the scholars who have heard of Ibn Khaldūn may well ask: How is Ibn Khaldūn, the Arab in question, relevant to our problems in the twentieth-first century?

Not only is Ibn Khaldūn generally recognized as the "father, or one of the fathers, of modern cultural history and social science" (Mahdi 1968: VII, 56) influencing and shaping these disciplines into our time, but his work also provides the intellectual point at which other world scholars connect in genuine appreciation (see, e.g., Gellner 1981; Rosen 1984; Lings 1995; Mahdi 1957). Ibn Khaldūn's ideas foreshadow those of our own time. "Some of the central formulae of the modern age," I noted with an element of awe while attempting to discover the relationship of Muslim history to society over a decade ago,

> are reflected in Ibn Khaldūn's theories: Karl Marx's stages of human history which provide the dynamics for the dialectics of conflict between groups; Max Weber's typology of leadership; Vilfredo Pareto's circulation of elites; and Ernest Gellner's pendulum swing theory of Islam, oscillating from an urban, formal literal tradition to a rural, informal and mystical one.
>
> (Ahmed 1988: 101)

Indeed, Emile Durkheim's concept of "mechanical" and "organic solidarity" reflects Ibn Khaldūn's notion of *ʿaṣabiyya* or "social cohesion." It is *ʿaṣabiyya* that is at the core of the Khaldunian understanding of society. Durkheim, himself one of the founding fathers of modern social science, showed us how the collapse of solidarity led to abnormal behavior. He called this anomie. It will be argued below that a kind of global anomie is what Muslim society is experiencing as a result of the breakdown of *ʿaṣabiyya*.

There is a fundamental difference however between the modern Western sociologists and Ibn Khaldūn. For all his "scientific" objectivity – and for many Muslims it is excessive – Ibn Khaldūn still writes as a believer. There is a moral imperative in his interpretation of *ʿaṣabiyya* as the organizing principle of society. Muslims see human beings as having been created to implement the vision of God on earth through their behavior and organization of society. The human being is a vice-regent of God according to the Qur'ān 2:30. So *ʿaṣabiyya* as an organizing principle is not "value free."

"Social organization," Ibn Khaldūn (1969: 46) wrote, "is necessary to the human species. Without it, the existence of human beings would be incomplete. God's desire to settle the world with human beings and to leave them as His representatives on earth would not materialize. This is the meaning of civilization, the object of the science under discussion." The social order thus reflects the moral order; the former cannot be in a state of collapse without suggesting a moral crisis.

Ibn Khaldūn's methodological approach demonstrates intellectual confidence. Although based in sociology, Ibn Khaldūn discussed in his analysis the impact of Greek philosophy on society (1969: 373–5), the interpretation of dreams (1969: 70–8), the influence of climate and food (1969: 58–69), and the effect of the personality of the leader in the rise and fall of dynasties (1969: 238–61). In using cross-cultural comparison, Arab, Berber, Turk and Mongol groups would provide him with the data for his theories. Besides, he was not writing as an isolated scholar in an ivory tower but from the vantage point of a political actor in the history of his time. The rich material he gathered was the basis for his *ʿilm al-ʿumrān* or "the science of culture or society."

Ibn Khaldūn's life

> forms a bridge, a transition, between the distinct phases of Muslim history which we are examining: the Arab dynasties in the tail-end of which – as in Umayyad Spain – he lived, and the great Muslim empires which would develop by the end of the century in which he died. His life also teaches us many things, confirming them for us in our own period: the uncertainty of politics; the fickleness of rulers; the abrupt changes of fortune, in jail one day, honored the next; and finally, the supremacy of the ideal in the constant, unceasing, search for *ʿilm*, knowledge, and therefore the ultimate triumph of the human will and intellect against all odds.
>
> (Ahmed 1988: 106)

All of us in the twentieth-first century need to be grateful to Ibn Khaldūn for reminding us of the lesson of "the human will and intellect." The American University in Washington DC has kept the memory of Ibn Khaldūn alive by naming a Chair after him. I held the Fellowship (Chair) named in honor of Allama Muhammad Iqbal at Cambridge University for five years. For me now to write as the Ibn Khaldūn Chair at another Western University is a singular honor because I believe that though the two, Iqbal the poet-philosopher and Ibn Khaldūn the sociologist, represent different zones, different disciplines and different approaches, together they provide a rich mine for contemporary scholarship and an authentic basis for the dialogue of civilizations. Let us examine some current global theories about society.

Global theories

We must not consider this discussion as merely an academic exercise or one motivated by a woolly if well-intentioned effort at interfaith dialogue. The events of September 11, 2001, have made it clear how urgent it is to understand Islam in our world. Just the span and scale of Muslim society warrant understanding. There are 57 Muslim states – of which at least one is a nuclear power – and Islam has over one billion followers with abundant vitality and passion whose spread is now truly global. The urgency demands a two-way process: for Muslims to explain Islam to non-Muslims and for non-Muslims to be responsive and make an effort to understand.

Yet Muslims appear to be reluctant to participate in dialogue. They appear to be challenged by certain cultural and intellectual aspects of globalization because many appear to equate globalization with Westernization. In this, they echo many Western analysts who also equate the two. Indeed Anthony Giddens (1990: 174) argues modernity itself, the very engine driving globalization, is a "Western project." Thomas Friedman (2000: xix) narrows globalization down further to "Americanization."

Although Muslims appear to be uncomfortable with globalization, the idea and practice of globalization are familiar to Muslim history. Islam's vision of the world is by definition global. There is neither East nor West for God (Qur'ān 2: 115). Islamic history has had long periods in which we recognize elements from what we today call globalization: societies living within different ethnic, geographic and political boundaries, but speaking a language understood throughout, enjoying a common cultural sensibility and recognizing the same over-arching ethos in the world-view (see Hourani 1991 and Hodgson 1974 for just how much globalization there once was in Islamic civilization). A man could travel from Granada in Europe to the Maghreb in North Africa, on to Cairo, then to the Arabian peninsula and from there to Baghdad across three continents, and still be in one familiar culture. Ibn Khaldūn in the fourteenth century is just one such example.

Another aspect of that time can provide inspiration for those of us searching the past for examples of the dialogue of civilizations. The Jews, Christians and Muslims living in Spain until late in the fifteenth century created a rich cultural synthesis, each culture enriching the other, which resulted in literature, art and architecture of high quality. The library in Cordoba in Spain (al-Andalūs) had more books than all the other libraries of Europe put together. There were long periods of religious and cultural harmony. The influence of Muslim ideas, culture, art and architecture on Europe was wide and deep. Key figures like Thomas Aquinas were influenced by Islamic thought. The Greeks were introduced to Europe via Muslim Spain and through the filter of Arabic.

Most people in the West are unaware of Europe's cultural and intellectual debt to Islam. Muslims take this indifference as a deliberate slight. It provides the background to why they view with suspicion developments in our time. It allows them to simplify global issues and interpret a series of recent developments, on the surface unconnected, as a well-laid plan by the West to humiliate and even subjugate them: Salman Rushdie's *The Satanic Verses* controversy, the collapse of the Bank of Commerce and Credit International (BCCI), the Gulf War, the rape and death camps of Bosnia, Kosova and Chechnya, the wars in Afghanistan and Iraq, and the continuing plight of the Palestinians and Kashmiris. In turn, critics accuse Muslims of human rights abuse in many countries including Sudan, Afghanistan and Pakistan. In Pakistan, in an extreme act of desperation, a bishop shot himself in protest at the treatment of his community.

In this milieu of suspicion even scholarly exercises such as the essay by Samuel Huntington (1993), "The Clash of Civilizations?", and his later book (Huntington

1996), Francis Fukuyama's *The End of History and the Last Man* (1998), and Felipe Fernandez Armesto's *Millennium* (1995) are seen by Muslims as part of a global conspiracy against Islam, part of a bludgeon-Islam-out-of-existence school of thought.

However, what cannot be denied is that these theorists made an unexpected contribution to the discussion of Islam by underlining the role of religion in contemporary global society. It is no longer possible to talk of globalization in terms of world trade and high finance only. However, these theories have allowed deeply rooted historical prejudices to resurface in discussion, and at times, lamentably, even giving them a degree of respectability.

In his influential essay "The Clash of Civilizations?" Huntington argues that future conflicts will be based on religious culture, not on ideology or economic interests. Islam is singled out as a potential enemy civilization in an argument that is as deterministic as it was simplistic. "Islam has bloody borders," concludes Huntington (1993: 35). But if the Bosnians and Chechens, the Palestinians and the Kashmiris are asked about their borders they would say the same of, respectively, Christianity, Judaism, and Hinduism. This dangerously deterministic argument takes us directly to a clash of civilizations. It carries the danger of becoming a self-fulfilling prophecy. Yet we will see below the real clash, the cause of the turmoil, is to be located *within* Islam.

The global strategic and security interests of the West are directly related to Muslim lands and many Muslim nations are seen as important allies: of the nine "pivotal states" identified in a recent article by Western experts (Chase *et al.* 1996) around which America forms its foreign policy five were Muslim: Algeria, Turkey, Egypt, Pakistan and Indonesia. In addition over 20 million Muslims are permanently settled in the West and ignored by the "Clash" writers like Huntington. The events of September 11, 2001, underlined their role as a bridge between the two civilizations. They carried the potential to challenge the "Islam versus the West" dichotomy.

Then there are the serious efforts, at a global level, perhaps for the first time on this scale and frequency, of influential individuals advocating mutual understanding. The late Pope John Paul II's statements in his *Crossing the Threshold of Hope* are one example. The Prince of Wales' initiative to bring better understanding between Islam and Western civilization, which began with his celebrated lecture at Oxford in 1993 on "Islam and the West," is another example. The speech was widely reported in the Muslim world and struck a chord. The King of Saudi Arabia, one of the most powerful and inaccessible monarchs on earth, broke all protocol and drove to the Prince's hotel late at night to congratulate him when the Prince visited his country shortly after the lecture.

Although provocative and widely discussed, theories like Huntington's are inadequate. Let us look elsewhere for explanations as to what is happening in the Muslim world.

Breakdown of Ibn Khaldūn's cycle

Ibn Khaldūn highlighted the importance of the ruler and his duties to the ruled in this world so that both might aspire to and secure the next. The leader embodies both political and moral authority. Ibn Khaldūn's science of culture ultimately functions to illuminate the science of good governance. In our time, one of the major crises that faces Muslim society is that of leadership. Yet even influential contemporary Western thinkers commenting on Islam, like Huntington and Fukuyama, have failed to discuss the importance of Muslim leadership. On the surface there is a bewildering range of Muslim leadership: kings, military dictators, democrats and, as in Afghanistan at least until recently, young and inexperienced tribal men or religious scholars (the meaning of *Taliban*) running a country. The Taliban and their guest from Saudi Arabia, Osama bin Ladin, who is accused of masterminding the attacks on America on September 11, 2001, and before that the bombing of the American embassies in Africa in 1998 and the USS *Cole* in Aden harbor in his war against "Jews and Crusaders," symbolize a certain Muslim response to our time. In other countries such as Algeria, Egypt, Pakistan and Indonesia, Muslim leaders akin to the Taliban in thought and behavior actively challenge government. The Iranians, themselves considered fanatics by some in the West, complain that the Taliban are so extreme that they are giving Islam a bad name. Clearly, ideas and styles of Muslim leadership are varied and hotly contested.

What then is going on in Muslim society? Who are the emerging leaders? Defining these leaders is no longer a simple question of taxonomy but of examining what factors are responsible for their emergence and the changes taking place in society. The collapse of leadership is thus a symptom of the breakdown of society and is also a cause of the breakdown.

It is time to turn for assistance to Ibn Khaldūn's most widely known theory, that of *ʿaṣabiyya* or social cohesion, which is at the core of social organization. *ʿAṣabiyya* binds groups together through a common language, culture, and code of behavior and when there is conscious approximation of behavior to an idea of the ideal, at different levels, family, clan, tribe, and kingdom or nation, society is whole. With *ʿaṣabiyya*, society fulfills its primary purpose to function with integrity and transmits its values and ideas to the next generation. *ʿAṣabiyya* is what traditional societies possess (the Arabic root has to do with the cohesiveness of the tribe), but which is broken down in urbanized society over a period of time. Of course, Ibn Khaldūn pointed out that certain civilized societies based in cities with developed social organization, arts and crafts may take a long time to break down.

Ibn Khaldūn (1969: 123–42) famously suggested that rural and tribal peoples come down from the mountains to urban areas and dominate them, and four generations on, as they absorb the manners and values of urban life, they lose their special quality of social cohesion and become effete and therefore vulnerable to fresher invasions from the hills. This cyclical, if over-simplified, pattern of rise and fall held for centuries and up to the advent of European colonialism. Even the disruptive force of European imperialism over the nineteenth and twentieth centuries did not fully break the cycle.

Paradoxically, it is only after independence from the European colonial powers in the middle of the twentieth century, when Muslim societies should have become stronger and more cohesive, that Ibn Khaldūn's cycle began to be seriously affected. It is now drying up at the source. Tribal and rural groups can no longer provide *ʿaṣabiyya*; urban areas in any case are inimical to it: the result is loss of vigor and cohesion. Muslims everywhere will voice their alarm at the breakdown of society. They know that something is going fundamentally wrong but they are not sure why.

Some Americans thought they had the answer. It came in response to the question Americans asked after the events of September 11, 2001, "Why do they hate us?"

And, because psychiatrists play such an important role in interpreting behavior in American society, the answers were couched in terms of "envy," "jealousy," and "hatred." We will look elsewhere for the answers. We will examine the reasons why *ʿaṣabiyya* is collapsing and the consequences of the collapse.

ʿAṣabiyya is breaking down in the Muslim world because of the following reasons: massive urbanization, dramatic demographic changes, a population explosion, large-scale migrations to the West, the gap between rich and poor which is growing ominously wide, the widespread corruption and mismanagement of rulers, the rampant materialism coupled with the low premium on scholarship, the crisis of identity and, perhaps most significantly, new and often alien ideas and images, at once seductive and repellent, instantly communicated from the West, which challenge traditional values and customs. This process of breakdown is taking place when a large percentage of the population in the Muslim world is young, dangerously illiterate, mostly jobless and therefore easily mobilized for radical change.

Globalization is the easy target when looking around for something to blame for the problems of our world. But *ʿaṣabiyya* was damaged from the mid-twentieth century onwards as a direct result of political developments: the creation of Pakistan and Israel, the full-blown revolution in Iran, the civil war situation in Algeria, Afghanistan and parts of Central Asia displaced and killed millions, split communities and shattered families.

Jahannum (Hell) or jail: the dilemma of the Muslim scholar

Following Khaldunian logic, with *ʿaṣabiyya* breaking down, society can no longer implement God's vision for human civilization. The crisis is compounded as the scholars of Islam who can offer balanced advice and guidance are in disarray. Muslims believe that those who possess *ʿilm*, or knowledge, best explain the idea of what God desires from us on earth. So central is *ʿilm* to understanding Islam that it is the second most used word in the Qurʾān. A *ḥadīth* from Muḥammad, "The death of a scholar is the death of knowledge" (al-Bukhārī 1979: IX, Book 92, no. 410) emphasizes the importance of scholarship. Unfortunately, the reality in the Muslim world is that scholars are silenced, humiliated or chased out of their homes. The implications for society are enormous. In the place of scholars advising, guiding, and criticizing the rulers of the day, we have the sycophants and the secret services. The wisdom, compassion and learning of the former risk the danger of being replaced by the paranoia and neurosis of the latter. And where do the scholars escape? To America or Europe. Yet it is popular to blame the West, to blame others, for conspiracies.

With the scholars driven out or under pressure to remain silent it is not surprising that the Muslim world's statistics in education are among the lowest in the world. The literacy figures are far from satisfactory, and for women they are alarming. As a result women in the Muslim world are deprived of their inheritance and their rights, and the men in their families tell them that this is Islam.

With those scholars silenced who can provide objectivity within the Islamic tradition and resilience in times of change, other kinds of religious scholars – like the Taliban – working in a different tradition interpret Islam narrowly. Islam for them has become a tool of repression. Its brunt is felt by women and the minorities. Political tyranny also grows unchecked, as the scholars are not at hand to comment and criticize.

Professor Abdul Hamid Abu Sulayman, the President of the International Institute for Islamic Thought and based in America, summed up the crisis to me in personal conversation: "The Muslim scholar is either caught between the ignorant Mullahs threatening him with *Jahannum* (hell) or the corrupt rulers threatening him with jail." *Jahannum* or jail was the choice. This was the direct consequence of the collapse of *ʿaṣabiyya*.

Challenge to identity

The scale of the collapse of *ʿaṣabiyya* and the power and speed of globalization – and the two appear to be related – have challenged ideas of identity which define and shape Muslim society. Primary identities in society are based in blood, place or religion. Language is sometimes shared as reinforcing identity in all three categories. In Iran, the Persian language is a source of pride for each and every category. In other countries, language expresses the barriers between the categories. In Pakistan, Urdu is the declared national language, Punjabi the language of the ethnic majority, and Arabic the language of religion. Invariably linguistic tensions translate into ethnic and political clashes. Sometimes the divisions within religion into sects result in conflict and violence. The clashes between Shīʿīs and Sunnīs in Islam have formed a major historical theme in the Middle East. In South Asia the annual clashes still cost lives.

In the last century, of the three main sources of identity which defined an individual, race or ethnicity, nationalism and religion, it was nationalism which was the dominant source of identity. The two world wars were fought on the basis of nationalism. With the emergence of Communism as a world force in the middle of the last century and its aggressive hostility to religion, it appeared that religion, as a source of identity, would soon be irrelevant to most people.

With the processes of globalization accelerating at the end of the last century, the situation has changed. Ethnicity fused with religion, as in the Balkans. In other places ethnicity re-emerged with virulence, as in the war between Hutus and Tutsis in central Africa. Nationalism changed too, as national borders have melted for business people, specialists and experts who cross the globe pursuing their economic, cultural or political interests. Hundreds of thousands of Asian workers in information technology, for example, have recently been welcomed by the USA and Europe. The poor, however, find borders as impenetrable as ever; even the border between Mexico and the USA is no exception.

With migration, nationalism and ethnicity are weakened, despite usually being associated with a particular region. Religion on the other hand can be transported and can flourish anywhere in the world given the right circumstances. We have the example of Islam, which began to make an impact in America at the turn of this century. Muslim political commentators feel that, although the Muslim vote is still small in terms of voter strength, it made a contribution to the election in 2000 by supporting George Bush against Al Gore in their tightly contested election battle.

Muslim leaders confirm these trends. The leaders of the first part of the twentieth century would be cast in nationalist terms leading "national" movements – for examples, Mustafa Kemal Atatürk in Turkey, Mohammad Ali Jinnah in Pakistan, Sukarno of Indonesia and Gamal Abdel Nasser in Egypt. Later in the century, other kinds of leaders would be at the head of movements with a religious message not restricted to national borders; Ayatollah Khomeini is an example for one tradition in Islam; the Taliban are another. The opponents of the former would be national opponents – the Greeks for the Turks and the Indians for the Pakistanis. The opponents of the latter would be moral opponents – the Great Satan or America for Iran and Afghanistan.

The tidal wave of religion which engulfed national and ethnic identities, has yet to crest in the Muslim world. It has translated into political power in countries such as Iran and Afghanistan. The tensions between the three sources of identity are acute. In some countries the old-fashioned nationalism left over from the past means a ruthless suppression of other forms of identity. Iraq and Syria provide us examples of this. Countries like Pakistan exhibit severe tension between an emerging religious identity and a battered nationalist one. Ethnicity also remains an unresolved factor in Pakistan. The tensions are expressed through the violence and political instability in the country.

With the inherited colonial structures of administration, politics and education disintegrating and new ones yet to supplant or even consolidate them, with old identities being challenged, Muslim society is in flux. *ʿAṣabiyya* is at its weakest in these societies. Central and South Asian states provide us with examples.

Paradoxically, it is in those parts of the Muslim world where there is the unifying factor of dynastic rule or language, as, for example, in the states on the Arabian peninsula, that there is comparative stability; we say "paradoxically" because these states are seen as reactionary by Muslims who want genuine democracy and stagnant by those who want an Islamic state based on the pristine principles of the early egalitarian Islamic order. Nonetheless the unifying factors of dynasty and language sustain *ʿaṣabiyya*, which ensures continuity and stability in times of global change. Let us examine a case study involving Muslim responses to the challenges of our world.

Case study: the scholarship of exclusion

Because so little is known of the Taliban in Afghanistan, re-emerging along the border of Pakistan, several false assumptions are made about them: that they are a political party; that they are defined and contained by Afghanistan; that they are a passing phenomenon and quite marginal to the Muslim world and that by ignoring them or bombing them they will fade into oblivion.

While commentators saw the Taliban as an "Islamic" body, few knew that as much as by Islamic fervor the Taliban were driven by *Pukhtunwali* or the code of the Pukhtuns also known in the Afghan context as Pashtun. The Taliban in Afghanistan were Pukhtun/Pashtun. Their treatment of women and minorities has more to do with Pukhtunwali than Islam. The laws of hospitality and revenge dominate the code. Pukhtunwali explains why the Taliban would not surrender their guest Osama bin Ladin even though they faced death and destruction. It also suggests that the laws of revenge will be activated and individuals or groups will extract vengeance for what they have suffered as a result of the war in 2001. The Americans, the British and their allies the Pakistanis would be the likely targets. It is well to remember that their victims have included a Viceroy of India killed at the high noon of empire (Lord Mayo, killed in 1872) and a popular prime minister of Pakistan (Liaqat ʿAli Khan in

1951). There is no limitation of space or time in the implementation of Pukhtunwali: "I took revenge after a hundred years and I took it quickly" is a well-known Pukhtun proverb.

The tribal interpretation of Islam explains why there is a sympathy for the Taliban in those parts of Muslim society where tribalism is strong, as in some parts of Saudi Arabia; it also explains the aversion to them where it is not, as in the middle-class sections of society in Cairo or Karachi. The Taliban also have some sympathy among Muslims who look for alternative answers to Western modernity.

To make matters worse the social and political factors that explain the emergence of the *madrasas* (usually *madrasa* in Pakistan) or religious schools, which produced the Taliban, remain largely unstudied. The emergence of the prototype *madrasas* of Pakistan needs to be viewed in the context of the decline of Western-style education and administration and their loss of credibility for ordinary people. *Madrasas* stand for a system, which is the cheaper, more accessible and more "Islamic" alternative.

The syllabus of a typical *madrasa* is exclusively Islamic in content. Its basis is the Qur'ān and the *sharīʿa*. That is how it should be for an Islamic school. But the Qur'ān – and the *sunna* of the Prophet (together, the *sharīʿa*) – repeatedly ask Muslims to acquire knowledge. One proverbial instance is "Seek knowledge, even unto China." China then, in the seventh century, symbolized the farthest non-Muslim civilization. It was a challenge to the imagination to even think of the journey.

Yet after numerous discussions with teachers and an examination of *madrasa* syllabi one notes that there are no non-Muslim philosophers or historians on those syllabi – not even modern ones like Karl Marx or Max Weber. Worse: even the Muslim ones, like Ibn Khaldūn, who are thought to be too "scientific" are missing. The philosophy of the typical syllabus is reduced to what commentators call "political Islam": Islam as a vehicle for all-encompassing change; Islam as a challenge not only to the corrupt local elite but also to the world order.

While the often Westernized nationalist leaders of the post-independence period sought to hold on to the state and consolidate it, the new leaders hope to destroy it as a legacy of the West and then re-create it in an Islamic mold. The former sought survival in a transitional world; the latter demand purity in an impure one.

After an initial period after independence when prestige was attached to Westernized schools, *madrasas* began to flourish from the 1970s onwards, most notably in South Asia (there are estimated to be 50,000 in Pakistan alone). Remittances from the Middle East provided funding and allowed central government channels to be bypassed. The war in Afghanistan against the Soviet occupation in the 1980s provided a global stage and a global cause to the young and the zealous.

These *madrasas* laid the foundations for the populist and militant Islamic leadership that would emerge in the 1990s. Mostly from poor, rural backgrounds, speaking only the local language, dressed traditionally with beards that assert their Islamic identity, these students would become the warriors who formed the Taliban and go on to conquer Afghanistan. The word Taliban – from *ṭālib* or student, the product of the *madrasa* – entered the global vocabulary.

The battle of Afghanistan against the Soviets was won not on the playing fields of the Etons of the Muslim world but in the humble classrooms and courtyards of the *madrasa*. Its outcome challenged and changed the already shaky educational and political structures in the entire region and not just in Afghanistan. The impact of the Taliban kind of thinking, the frame of mind, the style of behavior, and logic of argument, can be seen in different measure in Muslim groups from Los Angeles to Lahore. Living in the West is no guarantee of freedom from Taliban thinking.

The war in late 2001 against the Taliban may have hammered them in Afghanistan but did little to counter the influence of the Taliban kind of thinking elsewhere in the Muslim world. On the contrary, the sympathy helped to throw a blanket over their misdeeds in the cry of anger that spread throughout the Muslim world.

Wherever they live, Muslims are aware of the injustices of their rulers and the fact that some enjoy support in the West, the cultural invasion from the West, and the stereotypes of Muslims in the Western media including the Hollywood films in which Muslims are shown as terrorists and fanatics. These are not marginal or art films but big star, big budget, mainstream "blockbusters" seen by millions. They influence public opinion. Such negative propaganda coupled with what is seen as the indifference of the West to the outstanding political problems in the Muslim world combine to create a focus on the West as the root cause of Muslim problems. We have lost our honor, the honor of our faith and traditions and have no power to correct the wrongs of our own world, Muslims lament, blaming the West for this loss. From this perception to actively opposing the West as a form of *jihād*, or religious war, is one short step for groups like the Taliban.

The bitter anti-Western edge to the Taliban comes partly from their feeling that while they sacrificed their lives and land in fighting the Soviets as allies of the Americans, when it was over the Americans left them and their devastated land in the lurch. They will remind you that those being called "crazies" and "extremists" were once hailed as "freedom fighters" by the West. Their actions, such as the destruction of the priceless Buddhist statues, are partly motivated by a psychological compulsion to enrage and defy their critics.

Although the Taliban-style leadership is "new" in the sense that it emerged in opposition to the more Westernized leaders in power after World War II, in fact the division in Muslim leadership goes back to the nineteenth century. In 1857, after the great uprisings in India against British rule ("the Indian Mutiny"), two rival models of leadership began to emerge. Sir Sayyid Ahmad Khan, who created the Aligarh University on the model of Oxbridge, was a loyal servant of the Raj and wished to synthesize Islam and modernity. Iqbal, Jinnah, and the leaders of the Pakistan movement would be inspired by Sir Sayyid. In contrast, the founders of the *madrasa* at Deoband near Delhi fought the British during the uprisings, and their influential schools created networks throughout India and now influence groups like the Taliban. The schism in Muslim leadership, Osama at one end and Jinnah at the other of the spectrum, is thus rooted in the indigenous response to modernity and the threatening presence of Western imperialism.

We saw the interconnectedness of our world even before September 11, 2001. In the aftermath of the attack on the *USS Cole* in Aden in October, 2000, President Bill Clinton in Washington threatened Osama; the head of the Islamic party, the JUI (Jamīat ʿUlamāʾ-i-Islām), in Pakistan in turn threatened all Americans in Pakistan, including the Ambassador, if Osama were harmed; Afghanistan was on high alert and Americans throughout the world were warned to be on guard. Once again Islam had been pushed in a certain direction by those of its leaders wanting confrontation with the West.

Clinton and his Secretary of State, Madeleine Albright, had correctly predicted that such events were a foretaste of things to come; that this is the way that the wars of the future will be fought. They may be right. But the response of the Muslim world will depend on the nature of Muslim leadership; whether the Osama model prevails, or that of Jinnah. The relationship between Islam and the West will play a major part in influencing the course of events in the twenty-first century.

We have established through the case study above that there is an ongoing, sometimes simmering, sometimes explosive, conflict of civilizations; but we have also illustrated earlier that there is a serious and committed movement towards dialogue. Let us now explore possible directions for the future.

Searching for a post-Khaldunian paradigm: global society in the twenty-first century

With Ibn Khaldūn's cycle broken down – with the interpenetration of global religious cultures, with the emergence of the audio-visual media penetrating even the most remote areas, with the mounting clamor of those who see the signs of the apocalyptic end of time, with the scholars marginalized, with the growing sense of despair at the poverty and inequality in many parts of the world that challenges the notion of a just God in heaven who maintains a balance in human society based on justice and order we need to develop a post-Khaldunian paradigm; a new theoretical and methodological framework to study global society in the twenty-first century; to discover a general theory.

The unexpected and unpredictable expressions of religious revivalism today would have surprised the philosophers and sociologists of the modern age. Certainly Nietzsche, who declared God dead, and even Max Weber who saw the Protestant ethic as laying the foundations for a stable, safe, capitalist, and bureaucratic world, would have been surprised. For the former, God was back and it seemed with a vengeance; for the latter He was busy challenging and upsetting the very order that He was supposed to champion. Perhaps Marx would be the most surprised. Religion is no longer an "opiate" numbing people into docility; if one needs a drug metaphor, it is more like "speed."

Studying the main global religions in interplay, sometimes clashing, sometimes in alliance, can provide a clue. Of these, Islam remains the most misunderstood. All the religions are in need of understanding, as they are usually viewed through the lens of stereotype and caricature, perhaps none more so than Islam. Islam continues to get a bad press and evoke hostility globally.

The thesis about the clash of civilizations, which remains influential in some circles, rests on the assumption that the wars of this new century will be fought along religious lines. It is therefore logical and urgent to understand what factors are responsible for the emergence of religion, and how religion will be playing a role in deciding political developments in this century. However, we need to penetrate beneath the sensationalist nature of these theories and discover alternative ways of understanding society. We do not suggest that we accept each other's, or all, religions uncritically but that we understand them in order to make sense of what is happening in global society.

In this connection certain important questions need to be asked which are of immediate and urgent relevance to the world civilizations. Different civilizations look differently at the idea of the divine. Muslims are often attacked in the media for what is called revivalism or the resurgence of Islam, but religious revivalism is taking place globally, in Judaism, Christianity, in Hindu, and in Buddhist societies. The "rediscovery" of the divine is noted even in Western scientific and intellectual circles once dismissive of religion. We need to know how the different world civilizations view themselves and each other; we need to know what they see as their vision of the coming time; we need to view their ideas of "the end of time."

This raises our first set of questions: Why is there a revival of religions, and how are people negotiating the idea of God or the divine? Is the revival a consequence of the processes of and transformations resulting from globalization? Is the explanation to be found in the weakening of traditional structures – like the family and the nation-state – as individuals look to religion to provide certainty in an uncertain world, continuity in a changing one. Is it an attempt to (re)create *ʿaṣabiyya* in order to (re)build human civilization? But can we apply Khaldunian theories to non-Muslim civilizations? Indeed, can they be applied to Muslim societies when there are no significant cyclical – or even linear – movements of tribal or rural people taking place anymore in the way Ibn Khaldūn described them?

A second set of questions to raise, which has a global resonance after September 11, 2001, is: Why is the understanding of the divine often distorted through the prism of violence? Why are people killing and raping in the name of the divine? No religion encourages violence of this kind, and yet we see examples throughout the world today on our television sets and read about them in the news. Why are people not able to focus on the compassion and goodness in the idea of the divine? This failure has global implications for the so-called "clash of civilizations."

Third, we need to ask: What is to be done about it? Can there be genuine dialogue across religions and national boundaries that negates the idea of a clash of civilizations? How can this be implemented in a practical way, which will affect the thinking and behavior of people?

These are questions which would not have occurred naturally to Ibn Khaldūn. His was a Muslim world, admittedly disintegrating in one part but strong in other parts, and there was nothing but Islam on the horizon. For us, the dialogue of civilization is a necessary pre-condition to global harmony. But dialogue by itself is no solution. There has to be dialogue that leads to the understanding of other civilizations. For this, we have to move beyond, for example, Islam and understand the religions it interacts with: Judaism, Christianity, Hinduism and Buddhism. Muslims are living as neighbors with these other civilizations, and are often isolated and do not understand them. The same is true of other faiths looking at Islam. Too many non-Muslims see Islam as caricature and as distorted images from press reporting. With understanding comes sympathy and compassion towards those who do not belong to our group or community or religion. This is where scholars and thinkers who can transcend religious and national positions and reach out become crucial to the global debate that is taking place.

Conclusion

In conclusion: What can be done to encourage dialogue? The first steps are to try to understand the world we live in and the way it is forming. In the short term the prospects for a harmonious relationship between Islam and the West look uncertain, even pessimistic. In the longer term a great deal will depend on whether those who encourage dialogue and understanding will succeed or not.

The common problems – which affect everyone regardless of race, nationality or religion – in this shrinking world need to be identified to strengthen the idea of dialogue: drug and alcohol abuse, divorce, teenage violence and crime, ethnic and racist prejudice, the problems of the aged and the poor; the challenge of the growing sense of anarchy and rampant materialism; the sexual debasement of women and children; the depletion of our natural resources and ecological concerns. On all these issues many Muslims find support for taking a strong, enlightened position in Islam. This is the real Islamic *jihād* and, if it is properly harnessed and understood, it can provide fresh, sorely needed strength to these most crucial of global issues.

Muslims face an internal challenge. Reducing a sophisticated civilization to simple rituals encourages simple answers: reaching for guns and explosives, for instance. For Muslims to confront the world with poise and confidence is to re-discover and even begin to repair the mainsprings of Islamic civilization. They need to re-build an idea of Islam which includes justice, integrity, tolerance and the quest for knowledge – the classic Islamic civilization – not just the insistence on the rituals; not just the five pillars of Islam but the entire building. The West must put pressure on Muslim governments – and it interacts with most of them overtly or covertly – to "get their act together," to ensure justice and provide clean administration. It must send serious signals to the ordinary Muslim people – through its media, through seminars, conferences, meetings – that it does not consider Islam as the enemy, however much it may disagree with certain aspects of behavior carried out by Muslims.

This discussion is merely exploratory suggesting directions for research. Serious and urgent re-thinking is required by the scholars, policy planners and policy makers in the corridors of power – not only in Washington, London, Moscow and Paris, but also in Cairo, Kabul, and Tehran.

We need to be thinking in terms of what Ibn Khaldūn called "human civilization" or, to use the contemporary term, globally. We may not like words such as post-modernism and globalization, but only with the compassionate understanding of other civilizations, through the development of the scholarship of inclusion, can we resolve some of the deleterious consequences of globalization such as the increasing gap between the rich and the poor and the growing sense of despair especially amongst the latter. The tragic confrontation among the great faiths taking place in the Balkans, the Middle East, and South Asia, the mindless cycle of violence, must be checked in this century through the dialogue of civilizations.

The events of September 11, 2001, appeared to push the world towards the idea of the clash of civilizations, but they also conveyed the urgency of the call for dialogue. The creative participation in the dialogue of civilizations, to find an internal balance between tradition and the world increasingly dominated by technological changes, the committed search for global solutions to the global problems confronting human society, and the quest for a just and peaceful order will be the challenge human civilization faces in the twenty-first century.

Note

This essay is adapted from the author's "Ibn Khaldun's Understanding of Civilizations and the Dilemmas of Islam and the West Today," *Middle East Journal*, 56/1 (Winter 2002): 20–45.

References and further reading

Ahmed, A. S. (1980) *Pukhtun Economy and Society: Traditional Structure and Economic Development in a Tribal Society*, London: Routledge & Kegan Paul.

—— (1988) *Discovering Islam: Making Sense of Muslim History and Society*, London: Routledge.

—— (1991) *Resistance and Control in Pakistan*, London: Routledge.

—— (1997a) *The Quaid: Jinnah and the Story of Pakistan*, Karachi: Oxford University Press.

—— (1997b) *Jinnah, Pakistan and Islamic Identity: The Search for Saladin*, London: Routledge.

Armesto, F. F. (1995) *Millennium: A History of the Last Thousand Years*, New York: Scribner.

Bukhārī, al- (1979) *Sahih al-Bukhari*, 4th edition, trans. M. Muhsin Khan, Chicago: Kazi Publications.

Chase, R., *et al.* (1996) "Pivotal States and US Strategy," *Foreign Affairs* 75/1, January/February.

Friedman, T. (2000) *The Lexus and the Olive Tree: Understanding Globalization*, New York: Straus and Giroux.

Fukuyama, F. (1998) *The End of History and the Last Man*, New York: Bard.

Gellner, E. (1981) *Muslim Society*, Cambridge: Cambridge University Press.

Giddens, A. (1990) *The Consequences of Modernity*, Cambridge: Polity Press.

Hodgson, M. G. S. (1974) *The Venture of Islam*, Chicago: The University of Chicago Press.

Hourani, A. (1991) *A History of the Arab Peoples*, London: Faber and Faber.

Huntington, S. P. (1993) "The Clash of Civilizations?" *Foreign Affairs* 72/3, Summer.

—— (1996) *The Clash of Civilizations and the Remaking of World Order*, New York: Simon and Schuster.

Ibn Khaldūn (1969) *The Muqaddimah: An Introduction to History*, trans. F. Rosenthal, abridged N. J. Dawood, Princeton: Princeton University Press.

Lings, M. (1995) *What is Sufism?* Cambridge: The Islamic Texts Society.

Mahdi, M. (1957) *Ibn Khaldūn's Philosophy of History: A Study in the Foundation of the Science of Culture*, Chicago: University of Chicago Press.

—— (1968) "Ibn Khaldūn," in D. L. Sills, ed., *International Encyclopedia of the Social Sciences*, New York: MacMillan Co., 7: 53–6.

Najjar, A. M. al- (2000) *The Viceregency of Man: Between Revelation and Reason*, Herndon, VI: International Institute of Islamic Thought.

Rosen, L. (1984) *Bargaining for Reality: The Construction of Social Relations in a Muslim Community*, Chicago: University of Chicago Press.

44

SOCIAL CHANGE

Ebrahim Moosa

The Muslim part of the modern world has seen numerous experiments in social change, some more successful than others. The overall balance sheet beginning with anti-colonial struggles, to experiments with nationalism, socialism, liberal capitalism and Islamism reveal mixed outcomes and a chary prognosis. Religious fervor, often utilized as means to mobilize the multitudes, has proven to be as productive as well as destructive. It will be helpful to keep this background in mind when trying to grasp twenty-first century Muslim concerns about social change. What we encounter is the vertiginous intersection of culture, politics, economic power or its absence, with historical memory producing different configurations that coalesce in ethics.

Militant forces claiming to rid post-colonial Muslim societies from catastrophic misrule in the shape of coup d'états and despotisms, grinding poverty, and economic underdevelopment are also responsible for silencing sober voices of integrity, reconstruction and progress. It takes extraordinary courage to confront menacing forces, especially when entire nations and their peoples have become the expendable playgrounds for neo-imperialist occupation and exploitation, amply aided by compradores or indigenous elites. Social change faces both insurmountable internal and external challenges.

Some might view such a judgment to be unnecessarily alarmist. Yet, revitalization and renewal of Muslim societies can only be realized through a radical improvement in people's material conditions. While it remains uncertain whether optimal economic conditions inspire large social visions or vice versa, what we do know is that societies need both vision and growth. Yet, we also know that communities in crisis often find opportunities for creative solutions within the very maelstrom of chaos. Thus it was no surprise that energetic social movements emerged in the twentieth century in both Muslim majority as well as minority contexts from Egypt to Indonesia, and from India to South Africa. In the latter half of the twentieth century, mass global migrations also opened up new spaces and possibilities for the practice and renewal of Muslim thought. Muslim communities in the New World – the USA, Canada and South America, as well as Europe and Australia – offer opportunities but also challenges to imagine Islam as a tradition of practice in very creative ways.

Identity without culture

Throughout much of the twentieth century several major to medium-sized Muslim social movements evolved in an effort to reinvigorate Muslim religious thought. They all labored under the idealist vision that something deep within the human soul can create something new irrespective of material challenges. Influential among these were the Muslim Brotherhood in Egypt, the Jamāʿat-i Islāmī in Pakistan and the Muḥammadiyya in Indonesia. There were also intellectuals like Bediüzzaman Said Nursi in Turkey, from Iran ʿAlī Sharīʿatī and the Ayatollah Khomeni, the latter as architect of the Islamic revolution, Sayyid Quṭb in Egypt, Malik Bennabi in Algeria/France and many others also made significant contributions. And towards the close of the twentieth century the Afghan Mujāhidūn in Afghanistan were succeeded by the militant Taliban/Al Qaeda alliance that had all the trappings of a global movement located within a nation-state.

For several generations of Muslims, a cacophony of voices inspired both young and old to reassert their Muslim identity within a strict religious ethos yet they were culturally as rootless as dandelion spores. While commitment to these religiously austere social movements fueled the passion to attain political success, in practice success was often less apparent than failures. Excessive religious zeal was often mistaken for commitment. Whether in Egypt or Pakistan, Iran or Indonesia the results were disturbingly similar: fellow Muslims upbraided their co-religionists in "show-trials" targeting academics, bringing blasphemy charges against dissenting individuals, launching witch-hunts, fostering violence against political foes, perpetrating intimidation and communal conflict with neighbors irrespective of whether they were Christian, Jewish or Hindu in a variety of Muslim majority as well as minority contexts. Cumulatively, these scenes paint a dismal picture of Muslims worldwide: images that are as confusing as they are demoralizing to a broad spectrum of adherents. The result is that Westerners as well as Muslims living in non-Western and Western contexts are petrified as the gradations of violence and counter-violence flourish, too often at the expense of innocent civilians.

Simultaneously, Muslim middle classes serve as a weathervane of the poisoned mood. They are increasingly aware of the grotesque injustice that their co-religionists experience at the hands of intrusive Western powers, and in particular at the hands of American and European military powers. Aside from the physical assault on Muslims resulting in countless deaths, even secular-minded Muslims are outraged by the ghastly media misrepresentations of Islam demonizing their culture, history and achievements. Now even elite Muslims have lost perspective and balance. The result is the rapid consumption of conspiracy theories that feature Muslim victimhood and innocence. Victimhood replaces sound strategy and the fury of the multitude is directed not only at Westerners but also at Muslim leaders, institutions and individuals who do not acquiesce to this distorted mindset are not spared. Such fears and paranoia have been validated by the invasion of Iraq and Western double standards regarding nuclear weapons policies that punish Iran but reward Israel. While angry Muslims manage to contain their unhappiness to the level of peaceful protest, a sizeable minority have also opted for destructive remedies such as violence.

To trace the emerging realities of the Muslim world to cataclysmic events such as the attacks on the World Trade Center in New York on September 11, 2001, is analytically unsound. To reduce the roots of the conflict to a simplistic contest between Muslim civilization pitted against Western Christian civilization is lazy analysis. The Western stand-off against some Muslim states as well as non-state actors remains shrouded in complexity: history and power lurk behind these developments. One would have to take into account the consequences of the historical record of relations between various power blocs over the past three centuries that play out today. It is crucial to recall that during the nineteenth and twentieth centuries, the map of the Muslim world underwent massive changes physically and psychically. The rise of Western powers through imperialism and colonial conquest irreversibly transformed the Muslim world, often in unanticipated ways.

Traditions in the making

Whether the decline of Muslim political fortunes was due to internal or external factors pales in significance to the fact that for nearly two centuries, new narratives and ways of life have been grafted onto the Muslim world through developments brought about by Western power. The juggernaut of modernity and industrialization followed by the information age have accelerated the ambitions of liberal capitalism and democracy with a transformative impact on the traditional Muslim world. If the thumb-nail sketch offered here is contested, few could argue that for the better part of two centuries a host of Muslim societies have been trying to come to grips with the outcomes of modernity in its various guises and shapes.

Since then, many Muslim societies have since been in search of a psychic space in which they could harmonize their inherited traditions with the flood of modern ones arriving on their shores. The operative words have been reform and renewal. Imagine the Islamic tradition to be a piece of cloth that contains many different strands and fibers given the multiple manifestations of Islam. Over time, the fabric of tradition that held together patterns of existence, practices, beliefs and rituals was worn and torn in many places. In trying to repair the fabric of tradition by way of invisible mending modern reformers hoped to suture new fibers into the tradition.

In the aftermath of decolonization some Muslims believed that the solution to their problems was to capture political power and to establish an Islamic state. Power, they hoped could transform their own societies as well as others. A different option was proposed by pietist groups such as the Tablīghī Jamāʿat, a global intra-Muslim evangelizing group: if one pursued a pious lifestyle with total reliance on divine providence, then, and only then, could human affairs and the material conditions of the Muslims would change dramatically (see Masud 2000). Another perspective claimed that the recovery of Muslim self-respect in the global community could occur only if education became a priority and when skilled cadres could address all the needs of Muslim society from economics to religion, as suggested by Sir Sayyid Aḥmad Khān (d. 1898) in India, Muḥammad ʿAbduh (d. 1905) in Egypt and many others. Ultra radical groups, like Al Qaeda and their antecedents, maintained that it was only through the annihilation and defeat of the Western "Christian"enemy that Muslims could ever gain peace and self-respect. Each one of these manifestations is observable in the contemporary Muslim world.

Imagined history

A prominent school of thought linked to the puritan Salafīs, but also an attitude prevalent among modernists, revivalists and even traditionalists of different stripes, promises to reconnect contemporary Muslim societies with their glorious past. They have one precondition: our understanding of Islam must be completely stripped of all its historical and cultural accretions; all past interpretations and elaborations are to be eschewed. The credo of this group is to return to the Qur'ān, and for some, to engage with a sliver of the authentic prophetic tradition, that will incredulously lead to the recovery of a "true" Islam. Devoid, as it is, of a sense of history and culture, it might be preferable to say that these reformers have their own restrictive view of both. Failing to view Islam as a religious tradition that forcefully expressed itself within the context of history produces insuppressible phantoms and harmful distortions. If the Muslim historical tradition teaches one thing, it is that over the centuries many Muslim thinkers were realists who rarely disowned history but assessed the Muslim intellectual tradition with the constraints of history.

In the very first revelation, Muslims are told to observe and understand the universe around them. The first message that the Prophet Muḥammad received involved the word *iqra'*, "Recite," and Muḥammad asks the angel, "What must I recite?" to which the angel responds again with "Recite." One interpretation of "recite" is that Muḥammad must tell and retell the story of humanity. He must re-examine life around him and with a particular urgency call for the renewal of humanity. Gabriel by implication instructs all Muslims to "re-cite" the stories of human experiences from the past, not as a series of random arbitrary events, but as a search for ultimate reality in the warp and woof of life in Arabia and beyond.

The Prophet Muḥammad was not only instructed to "recite" in the name of his Lord who created everything and who created all human beings from a lump of congealed blood (Qur'ān 96). In fact, he was instantly reminded that he was being addressed by the God of knowledge and history. God teaches and speaks to humanity within the rhythms of human history, not outside history. History is an important part of the knowledge of the Muslim revelation. For that reason the calls of those who invite one to disavow history sound discordant to the ears of informed Muslims.

From the very beginning, Islam as a practice and imaginary was ensconced in an Arabic-speaking culture. Within the context of this culture and language, Muslim discourses drew on the practices prevalent in Mecca and Medina and later, beyond their confines. The Arabian crucible in itself offers incontrovertible proof that as a religious phenomenon Islam was inextricably intertwined with the cultures it contacted. The founding experience of the first Muslim communities is inconceivable without the concreteness of its Arabicity: cultural habitat, geography, language, practices, stereotypes and rhythms. Muḥammad never advocated the dissolution of Arabian culture, rather he attempted to raise the moral bar of his native culture. Side by side with the egalitarian message that there was no superiority of Arab over non-Arab, he also advocated affection for his people as Arabs and esteem for the prestige of their tongue as the language of paradise. One can speculate that were Islam revealed in North America, it would take shape within the rhythms of North American culture and the English language, and if it were revealed in Africa, it would take the shape of African culture with Swahili or other African rhythms.

Unable to come to grips with the historical nature of religious practice, its uncertainties, differences and changes, many Muslim apologists are in the habit of disowning culture. Their aggrieved parody calls on observers to make a distinction between "Islam" in its absolute perfection as against "Muslims" as the epitome of imperfection. This rhetorical move is intended to suggest that the actions of Muslims are not necessarily representative of "Islam" as if "Islam" can be perceived outside human experience. It sounds benign were the goal to show the gap between normative prescription and everyday practice. But often the rhetoric is invoked to deny the discursive and constructed nature and diversity of practices and prescriptions. Of course this rhetoric is invoked when Muslims in good conscience cannot justify the acts perpetrated by their fellow religionists, whether it be the treatment of women or acts of terror. When pressed, apologists will point to texts as representatives of "pure" Islam, unsullied by history and human interpretation but not to a "thing" called Islam. They forget that the philosopher Immanuel Kant too was unable to convincingly show the "thing" to exist in conditions unlimited by time and space. The phenomenon known as "Islam" is always embodied within specific historical and cultural realities. The Qur'ān and the prophetic tradition in their fullness, save for allegories, are always anchored in very concrete spaces and times.

Interpretation

One example will suffice. When Muslims are instructed in the Qur'ān to perform ablutions involving washing their faces and hands "up to" the elbows, wiping their heads, they differ among themselves whether the next step in the ritual involved *wiping* the feet that was more grammatically sound, or whether they should *wash* their feet. A seemingly straightforward instruction is tied up to human understandings of grammar, language and history. So, followers of the Ja'farī Shī'ī creed understand the commandment to mean wiping the feet, drawing on Qur'anic and prophetic authority. Most of the schools affiliated to the Sunnī creed claim the commandment is to wash the feet, drawing on other *ḥadīth* sources as authority and invoking consensus as the grounds for their practice. Another animated interpretative controversy centers around the fine grammatical point whether the elbow is inclusive in the instruction to wash the hands "up to" the elbows. Thus, even the most literal statements of the Qur'ān are mediated by human experience, which we call interpretation.

Muslims not only do what they perceive "Islam" instructs them but they are also compelled by a range of factors that confirm their variant modes of being. Islam can be defined largely by what Muslims make of it, attribute to it, and call it, the Canadian scholar, W. C. Smith (1959) suggested some time ago. The flawed sundering between "Islam" and "Muslims" does carry echoes of the culture of responsibility rooted in Muslim teachings. This makes the ornery split even less attractive, since it serves as a rhetorical escape route from responsibility by blaming "Muslims" for all wrongs, and cynically saving an abstract "Islam" for everything that goes right. "Islam" is at best a discursive tradition; in other words it is largely about debates as to what is knowledge or its opposite, what is valid or invalid or authoritative or optional. Knowledge, too, is not abstract but a practice. Consequently, there can be as many "islams" with a small "i," and many Muslims with differences in terms of their practices and their understandings, since each person or Muslim community appropriates the discursive tradition differently. "Islam" is embodied in the lives of "Muslims" and despite their differences, one can point to Islam in the pulsating bodies of Muslims and their footprints on the past. And as fallible humans, they do good things just as they are susceptible to doing ugly things: even when they perpetrate the latter, they remain Muslims, albeit "bad" Muslims if one feels obliged to classify people and their acts.

Sharīʿa and time

The God of the Qurʾān often speaks concretely drawing on local cultures and local experiences while eschewing abstract thinking. "We do not send a messenger unless he speaks in the language of his people," observes Qurʾān 14:4. There are many ways that people express their commitment to the Creator in the form of an amalgam of normative practices and values which Muslims call *sharīʿa*. Literally *sharīʿa* means "the trodden path." Muslims understand that Moses had a *sharīʿa*, just as Jesus and countless other prophets had an equivalent of the *sharīʿa* as moral point of reference.

The questions of law and values are as troubling for modern-day Muslims as they were for believers in the past. It is agreed that people express their loyalty and commitment to God through certain communitarian and individual practices, by way of habits, beliefs, norms and values that were advanced by the respective messengers and prophets. That is what Muslims understand as a *sharīʿa*. In fact, when a community consecrates specific practices these become normative and part of the community's tradition. The Indian thinker Shāh Walī Allāh (d. 1763) felt obliged to share with his readers what appeared to be his struggles with changing times and inherited moral and legal practices. Walī Allāh, who is held in high esteem by traditionalists and modernists alike, in his widely acclaimed book *The Conclusive Proof of God* courageously grapples with the question of cultural specificity, origins of the law and the evolution of the community with respect to *sharīʿa*.

Pondering the sociology of law and government Walī Allāh argues that one of the challenges that a prophet faces is to share his teachings with communities that differ greatly in their practices and predispositions. If the prophet's message reaches a range of communities, then ideally the *sharīʿa* should include the practices that are common to all of them. But the realist in Walī Allāh makes him recognize that prophets and their missions are not orderly and regulated processes: they cannot like bureaucrats regulate the unfolding of their communities for they start off with a nucleus of followers which increases over generations. Hence, prophets, in order to give coherence to their nascent community, use the law of their own community or ethnic group as the reference point for their normative values. Over time these norms become the hegemonic law, *sharīʿa*, for all subsequent people who join his community of faith and practice.

Showing awareness that the culturally specific practices of peoples who later join the community of faith may be at odds with the habits and legal culture of the founding community that served as a template for the *sharīʿa*, Walī Allāh issues a crucial but highly subtle caution. Followers of the prophetic teachings at the inception followed the law, he explains, for two chief reasons: first, they witnessed and attested to the original tradition, and secondly, because they were organically attached to these practices in their daily lives. In other words, these founding customs, practices and norms optimally worked for the early communities because of the natural fit these customs had with their environment. Later followers of this prophet adhered to the law and some of the normative practices of the founding community out of sheer loyalty to the early founders of the tradition and to demonstrate that they belonged to the original community. They did so, even though the law may have been at odds with their own practices and values. At this point Walī Allāh observes:

> There is nothing more perfect and convenient than the prophet giving consideration to the custom of his people to whom he had been dispatched in matters related to religious symbols, penalties and matters related to the civilizing process. Neither should later followers be coerced, instead they should receive overall compassionate consideration. For the early followers adhere to those norms (*shirʿa*) by virtue of the testimony of their hearts since it accords with their customs, while the later followers adhere to it due to a desire to follow the example of the leaders of the community and rulers: this is a natural phenomenon for every nation in every age, ancient or modern.
>
> (2005: I, 338)

Of course this eighteenth-century Indian thinker is provocative and suggestive. He does not advocate the radical position of abandoning those practices of the law that conflict with contemporary culture and temporality but he does advocate contextual flexibility. At the same time, Walī Allāh also said that the duty of the leader was to enforce the law the way it was given. As a true reformer, and thanks to his candid musings, he does leave us a great deal to think about.

Some of the difficult issues that modern Muslims confront include questions of political order, justice, human rights, gender equality, the treatment of the "other," and questions of economic justice and the environment. Modern Muslims have inherited an ethical and juridical legacy that was construed in a world very different from the one that they experience today. A thoroughgoing engagement of Islamic teachings from the vantage point of modern knowledge, traditions and practices is still at its very nascent stage. Muslim scholars and communities have a primary responsibility to begin to reinterpret and understand the inherited tradition in the light of new realities, an invitation made by the poet-philosopher Muḥammad Iqbāl in the early part of the twentieth century. Iqbāl (1960: 97) was blunt in his assessment stating that "concepts of theological systems, draped in the terminology of practically dead metaphysics" will be of little help to those who espouse a "different intellectual background." "Equipped with penetrative thought and fresh experience," Iqbāl (1960: 179) continued, "the world of Islam should courageously proceed to the work of reconstruction." In addition to the intellectual and social reconstruction that Iqbāl envisaged, he also fostered a worldview in which the ultimate reality was spiritual.

Muslim jurists in the past had labored hard to adapt norms that were formulated in the crucible of the Arabian context to meet the needs of the new societies to which Islam had spread. An examination of Muslim laws and their ethical practices reveal how later jurists interpreted the culturally specific Qur'anic and prophetic provisions and transplanted these to new Persian, Indian, east Asian and African contexts. In each of these applications, there was continuity with the original tradition as well as a great deal of discontinuity and mutation, both necessitated by geographic and temporal changes. The history of Muslim law and ethics offers a rich archive of insights on how Muslims realigned history and revelation to find the norm of God in new cultural contexts.

Note that in a major departure from how the intellectual tradition functioned previously, modern Muslims rely on the Qur'ān almost exclusively, ignoring insights derived from prophetic reports and almost devoid of discursive reasoning and history. Take for example the attitude of lay as well as educated Muslims who believe it to be obligatory to follow the Qur'anic prescription regarding women, notions of female modesty, marriage and repudiation practices, rules of inheritance and testimony because these have been revealed. Few recognize that these time-sensitive directives were aimed at seventh-century Arabian society in very specific historical and geographic realities. Many modern Muslims feel wracked by guilt if they do not adhere to these commandments, and would find it incredulous if they were told that medieval Muslim jurists never followed the Qur'anic dicta exclusively: they always blended it with *ḥadīth* reports, general social practices and customs in order to generate a realistic and socially viable teaching.

As the Algerian thinker Malik Bennabi (1991:10) observed several decades ago, the modern Muslim social and religious imaginary has not yet come to terms with the new bio-historical synthesis that modern humans have experienced. This is the world of science and empirical rationality that transforms our notions of self, history, nature and the cosmos. This also alters our understanding of what it is to be human. The presumption encoded in the modern social imaginary differs in significant ways with the social imaginary of past epochs, especially the social imaginary construed by select narratives of the Qur'ān and the prophetic practices of seventh-century Arabia. Islam's intervention in the seventh century on behalf of women's role and status was, by all accounts, a liberatory perspective. The same recipe might not have the same impact in the twentieth-first century.

The teaching that women use their ornamental neck scarves to cover their bosoms (Qur'ān 24:31) should be viewed as one attempt in an Arabian milieu to inculcate a new social imaginary about the body and public decorum. Under different conditions prescriptions might vary. Thus, instead of pursuing the fruitless question as to whether rules derived from a different social horizon are still applicable today or offer apologetic rationalizations in order to buffer certain anachronistic practices, one might do well by exploring the viability, affinity and fit of such practices to a modern social imaginary. So classical Muslim juridical ethics designate men as the economic provider for women. But in an economic and social system where women's participation in the workforce is unrestricted, women themselves become autonomous economic agents rendering the teaching to be redundant.

One way of addressing the dilemma that many practicing Muslims experience regarding the rules affecting women would be to compare it to the practice of slavery. By most modern Muslim accounts slavery is excised from the modern Muslim imaginary because it clashes with a new sensibility of freedom while bearing in mind that it was perfectly acceptable in another epoch. The Qur'ān never advocated the abolition of slavery as an institution nor did the Prophet obligate it. However, there were strong hints that slavery was not the best of human conditions. The Qur'ān advocated the freeing of slaves as an act of expiation for various violations in rituals while the Prophet Muḥammad also proclaimed that it was better to free a slave than keep someone in bondage. Muslim political leaders like the caliph ʿUmar (r. 634–44) and later Muslim thinkers gradually narrowed down the prospects of slavery. ʿUmar held that if a slave woman had borne a child from a slave master, she could no longer be sold in slavery. Even though the momentum to abolish slavery in modern times came from the West, very few Muslims would wish to install slavery again as a provision sanctioned by the Qurʾān as an option. Similarly, Islamic teachings advocating differential treatment of women in the law can follow the reasoning of abrogation and change advanced in the example of slavery: in other words, a practice sanctioned by the tradition does not foreclose the possibilities of abrogating it or seeking other remedies that fulfill a higher principle or value.

There are also examples of differences between modern and traditional interpretations in the area of criminal law. Muslim criminal law sets out a hierarchical order in the case of murder with guidelines to deal with an offender (see Qurʾān 2:187–8). In the case of injury or murder, the offender can either be executed, or be forgiven, or the offender's family may be required to pay compensation to the victim's family. In the medieval interpretation of the law there was also a hierarchical order that determined the kind of punishment for murder. For example, if a free man killed a slave, he could not be executed for the murder. Instead, he only had to compensate the victim's family. If a believer killed an unbeliever, then the unbeliever's family could not demand the execution of the believer but had to accept monetary compensation, according to most Sunnī schools of law, except for the Ḥanafī school. This differential method of determining punishment offends a twentieth-first century Muslims' sense of justice. A modern sense of justice does not tolerate discrimination between male and female, slave and freeman, and believer and unbeliever.

At least two motifs in the Qurʾān encourage one to pursue different attitudes to interpretation, moving away from literalism and towards an approach that is sensitive to changes in time and space as well as in reaching for higher values. For example, in Chapter 39, known as *sūrat al-zumar*, verses 17–18, say: "Give good tidings to those of my servants who listen to the word and follow the best part of it. Those are the people whom God had guided and those are the people of insight." This verse empowers the reader or listener of the Qurʾān. One is urged to discriminate between the different registers of meaning in the message: to choose the most beautiful (*aḥsan*) or intellectually more perfect message in any given situation. The interpreter of the revealed message must be able to separate between what is historically contingent and what is eternal, and decide what is meaningful and what is just. For individuals who can put their discretion to its best use and who are able to understand the nuances of the revelation, there is a promise of further divine guidance. Whether Muslims recite the book of God or the book of nature, they have a responsibility to interpret what they recite. There is also the burden to understand the cumulative meaning of the message rather than grasp piecemeal instructions. A Muslim sentiment is "Show understanding in your learning; do not parrot learning." Ibn ʿAsākir, the historian, wrote: "The learned endeavor to understand; the foolish endeavor to quote only" (Al-Muttaqī al-Hindī 1986).

In a chapter of the Qurʾān known as "The Bee" one passage (16:68–9) invites the listener or the reader to reflect on the allegory that stirs imaginative interpretation. The Lord of humankind, the Qurʾān says, inspired the bee to make a habitat in every mountain, tree, and terrace. Then the Lord instructed the bee to walk humbly in His path, taking whatever it needs from all the fruits and all the flowers. Then out of the belly of the bee comes a liquid that we know as honey. But the Qur'ān describes it as a "beverage of many hues," claiming that it contains a "remedy for humanity." In the allegory the bee is not only remembered for its industriousness but also for taking nectar from a variety of sources to produce something new. The bee becomes an allegory for a toiling humanity that finds remedy in newness and creativity. Here humans are encouraged to take learning from multiple sources and produce a whole new edifice that is unparalleled. No wonder the Messenger of Islam noted that knowledge was the lost treasure of the believer and that wherever he or she found it, believers were the most deserving of it. In one fell swoop the allegory of the bee renders redundant the age-old debate about Muslim antipathy for "foreign sciences" and for being obsessed with only "insider knowledge" namely knowledge discovered and produced by people adhering to Islam. While Muslims in later centuries might have developed allergies to outsider knowledge as a valid source of learning, early Muslim intellectuals harbored no such compunctions. Knowledge of Indian, Chinese and Arabian provenance was healthily integrated into Muslim life and practice.

In order for Islam to flourish as a civilizational project it requires labor and energy. The Qur'ān (9:20) promises: "Those who strive in Our path, We will open up for them multiple ways." Clearly, intellectual effort (*ijtihād*) that produces new knowledge must of necessity result in fresh inspiration and diversity, an approach that was once vibrant in Muslim societies but seems to have run shipwreck in the twentieth century. Muslims, both laypersons and religious authorities, seem perplexed and resistant to new changes and are also estranged by the dynamism evident in the past.

For example, in his novel *The Satanic Verses*, Salman Rushdie re-tells the poignant story of the struggle of the Prophet Muḥammad in his attempts to convince and negotiate with a Meccan elite hostile to his prophetic call. Rushdie's unfortunate way of telling the story perhaps offended more people than the moral of the story itself. However, we know that for centuries the Muslim tradition endorsed the satanic verses incident as a true occurrence. It was only after the fourteenth century when some Muslim commentators began to argue that that story was concocted (see Ahmad 1998).

The story centers on the recitation of the Prophet Muḥammad of a portion of revelation that gave his Meccan interlocutors the impression that he was endorsing their idols. "Those were the high flying cranes whose intercession is sought," he chanted. On hearing this, his Meccan foes understood the innuendo as his endorsement of their idols. Some time later the Prophet announced that the revelation was not an angelic inspiration, but a satanic one. The story is poignant. It revealed the Prophet's struggle with the different impulses within his soul – his unyielding care and enthusiasm for the Meccan clans to accept Islam. Should he like a good trader yield to the impulse to negotiate with the Meccans by considering a portion of their beliefs and gradually integrate them into Islam? Or, must he act decisively like a prophet in this instance and cherish the uncompromising monotheism of his message over a gradualist strategy? The satanic verses incident suggests that in a moment of human weakness he succumbed to the trader instinct but his subjectivity was quickly straightened by divine intervention. The event only enhanced the Prophet in the eyes of his opponents and hardly anyone assailed his credibility because of it.

By contrast, for many modern Muslims unaccustomed to a complex understanding of revelation, the very acknowledgment of the event was sacrilege. It is the lack of complexity that renders modern Muslim thought so sterile. In fact, Iqbāl (1960: 154) insightfully wrote that an act inspired by the infinite complexity of life becomes spiritual; when it is bereft of this complexity, it is profane. Railing against God about the state of Muslims in his *Complaint and Answer*, Iqbāl ends his poem with an answer from God, who invites Muslims to commit themselves to the way of Muḥammad. Muḥammad's way, in Iqbāl's view (1960: 126), allows one to achieve full self-consciousness, come to terms with complexity and to rely on human resources. Creativity inspired by human experience, nature and history were the ingredients for a vibrant civilization. Iqbāl's hope was that if Muslims realized their commitment they could be in charge of their own destiny. He wrote:

> With reason as your shield and the sword of love in your hand.
> Servant of God! The leadership of the world is at your command.
> The cry "Allah-u-Akbar", destroys all except God, it is a fire.
> If you are true Muslims, your destiny is to grasp what you aspire.
> If you break not faith with Muḥammad, we shall always be with you;
> What is this miserable world? To write the world's history, pen and tablet we offer you.
>
> (Iqbāl 1981: 96)

Note

I would like to thank Bruce Lawrence for his gracious feedback. Youshaa Patel, Ali Mian and Mashal Saif also provided comment. Any remaining errors are mine. A version of this chapter was published as an occasional paper by the Centre for Studies in Religion and Society, University of Victoria, under the title "Islam and Cultural Issues: Talk Given at the Milad Celebrations, University of Victoria, Victoria, BC, June 3, 2001."

References and further reading

Ahmad, S. (1998) "Ibn Taymiyyah and the Satanic Verses," *Studia Islamica*, 87(2): 67–124.

Bennabi, M. (1991) *Islam in History and Society*, trans. A. Rashid, Kuala Lumpur: Berita/Islamic Research Institute.

Iqbāl, M. (1960) *The Reconstruction of Religious Thought in Islam*, Lahore: Javid Iqbal/Shaikh Muhammad Ashraf.

—— (1981) *Shikwa and Jawab-i-Shikwa – Complaint and Answer: Iqbal's Dialogue with Allah*, trans. K. Singh, New Delhi: Oxford University Press.

Masud, M. K. (2000) *Travellers in Faith: Studies of the Tablīghī Jamāʿat as a Transnational Islamic Movement for Faith Renewal*, Leiden: Brill.

al-Muttaqī al-Hindī (1986) *Kanz al-ʿummāl fī sunan al-aqwāl waʾl-afʿāl*, Hyderabad: Maṭbaʿ Majlis Dāʾirat al-Maʿārif al-ʿUthmāniyya.

Smith, W. C. (1959) "Comparative Religion: Whither-and Why?" in M. Eliade, J. M. Kitagawa, eds., *The History of Religions: Essays in Methodology*, Chicago: University of Chicago Press, 31–58.

Walī Allāh, Shāh (1996) *The Conclusive Argument from God (Ḥujjat Allāh al-Bāligha)*, trans. M. K. Hermansen, Leiden: E. J. Brill.

—— (2005) *Ḥujjat Allāh al-bāligha*, Deoband: Maktaba Ḥijāz.

45

SECULARISM

Amila Buturovic

Secularism, in its contemporary connotations, may refer to a philosophical position, a discourse, as well as to a system of governance. Although all deriving from the notion of the *saeculum* – a condition pertaining to this day and age – they are not to be completely equated: the former two may be confined to a particular philosophy of morality that removes God from the affairs of life, while the third seeks to establish a system through which such morality is implemented – not necessarily at the complete exclusion of God – as a political and social norm. Insofar as secularism, in all senses, prioritizes this-worldly forces, its ambivalent – at times antagonistic and at others reconciliatory – relationship to the religious and the sacred is contingent on the context through which this relationship is created and sustained. Just as the religious/sacred possesses many different and changing meanings, even within the same system, so does the secular, in reaction to these mutations, lend itself to a set of variants that speak of a need for caution in approaching different case studies and experiences. Nowadays, wherever implemented and practiced, secularism generates constant challenges, so much so that some analysts warn that the struggle between religion and state is one of the most persisting problems in international relations nowadays (Juergensmayer 1993: 5–10). Indeed, one need not look too far to encounter such problems: from France to the USA, from India to Russia, from Iran to Great Britain, the struggle between secular values and political theologies take on many different shapes and forms.

Whose secularism? A question of perspective

Historically, it is generally understood that secularism emerged out of the struggle between church and state in pre-modern Europe, setting it on a rapid transformative course that eventually spread through the rest of the world, so much so that secularism is the overwhelming principle of political governance nowadays. In that regard, secularism as a political platform was born out of a specific relationship between church and state. In the commonly accepted historical narrative, the Reformation, launched in reaction to the papacy and certain practices of the Catholic church, brought about the transfer of church matters to the authority of the princes. As Peter Berger (1973: 118) observes, "Protestantism cut the umbilical cord between heaven and earth." In that sense, secularism is to be understood as a post-Reformation shift from the medieval Christian understanding of the church and state relationship as regards the spiritual and temporal loci of authority. Such secularism is not inherently anti-religious but anti-theocratic. It negates not the religion but the political power of the church in its medieval normative self-definition as the one true state. The Reformation disrupted that norm by splitting this coercive power into two – the religious and the temporal – whereby the state was imbued with the authority to regulate, or even banish, the role of the church in public life. As a consequence, the term secular/temporal entered the vocabulary as the antonym to the religious/spiritual, while the equivalent term laicism/laïcité in the Catholic context set off to differentiate lay and clerical spheres of action and influence (Berkes 1964: 3). From this angle, secularism indeed is both historically and doctrinally tied with the relationship between state and church in post-Reformation Europe.

Despite this intimate relationship between European Christianity and secularism, the process is neither to be associated with Europe at large nor Christianity as a whole. In fact, Eastern Orthodoxy and other forms of eastern Christianity point to the historical specificity of the Catholic/Protestant experience as regards this tension between theocratic and anti-theocractic models. Since early medieval times Eastern Orthodox and Catholic polemics paved the way for a markedly different role of the church in public life. In contrast to the Catholic worldview which occasioned the ascendance of the Pope's supremacy in the West, the Eastern Orthodox doctrine, based on the ecumenical councils, had from the beginning divided its spiritual authority over five patriarchates so much so that the Emperor was in many ways closer in function to the Islamic caliph than the Catholic Pope. Moreover, medieval Orthodoxy that spread through missionary activities among the Slavs with the help of vernacular translations of the Bible saw a growth of ethnocultural Orthodoxy and a gradual decentralization of spirituality in favor of a stronger association between the "national" church and the state. This is especially true of Eastern Orthodoxy in the Balkans, where, later on, the Ottoman *millet* system of religious grouping reinforced deep associations between religion and identity, and, in modern times, the church and the nation, so that the church maintained itself as a central agency in kindling group sentiments. In that sense, at least as far as southeast Europe is concerned, modernity propelled the Orthodox church into the forefront of political self-determination, not into its background as was the case with the Catholic or Protestant Church. In fact, the French scholar François Thual, asserting that in the Eastern Orthodox world the religion consecrates the nation and the nation protects the religion, concludes that, "in its historical practice, Caucasian, Balkan, Greek and Slav Orthodox Christianity has never known secularism/laïcité in its French sense, based on the separation of the Church and state" (Thual 1998: 4–5, also see Buturovic 2007: 284–7).

Thus, historical experience as well as current political trends suggest that the application of Western Protestant/Catholic style secularism in and on other societies has been neither linear nor simple. At the same time, many of these societies have been shown to generate and process autochthonous forms of secularity in accordance with their own understanding and negotiation of the sacred, religious authority, and morality. This is especially the case with religiously plural societies which, even in the case of a close association between the government and one particular religion, have required the creation of adequate mechanisms of accommodation, negotiation, toleration, and acculturation in order to prevent the disintegration of the political and cultural fabric of the society.

One seldom explored example of a proto-secular state in pre-Reformation times in which the ruler distanced himself from the administration of religious life, for example, is medieval Bosnia in which different forms of Christianity – Orthodoxy, Catholicism, dualist Bogomilism, and the local Bosnian Church – coexisted in the course of several centuries, disallowing any denomination to hold either political or theological grip over the entire population. Despite the Papal pressure to eradicate non-Catholic religious practices and belief, no Bosnian king, and despite repeated crusade expeditions, imposed his religion over his subjects. Not only was the confessional pluralism preserved over many centuries, but this profile continued being sufficiently relaxed so as to occasion conversions in different directions, the most important of which were to occur to Islam under the Ottomans in the course of the sixteenth and seventeenth centuries. The Ottomans preserved this religious pluralism and even enriched it by virtue of settling many Sephardic Jews into the territory after their expulsion from Spain. As the Ottoman records show, cross-religious conversion and pollination continued throughout the Ottoman times. Even if the vicissitude in religious loyalty was motivated by complex political and other factors (including religious persecution), such flux nevertheless alludes to the fact that interconfessional boundaries in pre-modern Bosnia were both flexible and porous, and thus generative of a shared set of values that transgressed and challenged any confessional or theocratic exclusivity. While this example does not necessarily bespeak a separation of church and religion characteristic of modern secular societies, it nevertheless allows for a rethinking of the trajectories through which such separation could, and has evolved, in different confessional and political contexts. Essentializing secularism as a singularly Protestant Christian phenomenon often precludes the possibility of a cross-cultural examination of these differentiated formations of the secular within non-Western societies, including Islamic ones. In that sense, it seems neither useful nor helpful to mimic and validate the historical experience of north-western Europe as the only workable and acceptable development of secularism.

The secular in Islamic history and experience

In the wake of the attacks on the USA of September 11, 2001, and in the midst of the subsequent "war on terror," the question of whether Islam is compatible with secularism or is inherently alien to it has become a commonplace question. The predominant presence of secular models across the Islamic world, from Turkey to Indonesia, Bosnia to Algeria, former Soviet republics to Syria, has been eclipsed by questions of their stability and authenticity as secular societies. Internal struggles and challenges to sustain secular principles have certainly been onerous, but this can be said about most countries in both the developed and the underdeveloped world in which the technologies of religious and spiritual interconnection have enabled the rise and presence of movements with new public face and force. Yet it is certainly true that Muslims around the world struggle to reconcile their religious tradition as expressed historically, scripturally, and ritually, with secular principles which dissociate human rights, civil rights and liberties from the grips of theocratic governance.

Given the putative correlation between secularism and the notions of progress and modernization, the question of such reconciliation has often been cast in form of an urgent appeal to moderate Muslims, especially those living in Western countries, to launch an Islamic Reformation and thus put an end to their overtly theocratic and literalist attachment to religion: authors and analysts like Daniel Pipes, Irshad Manji, Salman Rushdie, Robyn Wright, and many others, have all animated such discussions. Among the most vocal has been Salman Rushdie, a voice from within, who in 2005 gave this appeal a new impetus, ushering Muslims in the West in particular to think in terms of freedom from theological incarceration to which Islamic history and tradition seem to hold them hostage. He writes:

> The traditionalists' refusal of history plays right into the hands of the literalist Islamofascists, allowing them to imprison Islam in their iron certainties and unchanging absolutes. If, however, the Koran were seen as a historical document, then it would be legitimate to reinterpret it to suit the new conditions of successive new ages. Laws made in the 7th century could finally give way to the needs of the 21st. The Islamic Reformation has to begin here, with an acceptance of the concept that all ideas, even sacred ones, must adapt to altered realities.
>
> (Rushdie 2005: B07)

While resonating with all the necessary moral imperatives of our post-modern condition – rejection of absolutes, alterity, openness to re-interpretation – Rushdie's appeal appears problematic on several levels. To begin with, the traditionalists he evokes hardly refuse history; rather, they read it as a history of regress, not a history of progress. As Cantwell Smith aptly observes:

> The fundamental malaise of modern Islam is a sense that something has gone wrong with Islamic history. The fundamental problem of modern Muslims is how to rehabilitate that history: to set it going again in full vigour, so that Islamic society may once again flourish as a divinely-guided society should and must.
>
> (Smith 1957: 41)

In other words, the traditionalists' views are deeply nostalgic for the so-called golden age of Islam associated with the nascent Muslim *umma* which, they believe, has been eclipsed in later history through internal disunity, colonial humiliation, and a continuous internal and external attack on the fundamental ethics of Islam. Secondly, contrary to Rushdie's assertion, the Qur'ān has always been treated, at least in part, as a historical document, in the sense that the tradition of *tafsīr* is based in the acceptance that Muḥammad's prophetic career was deeply embedded in history, that most Qur'ān passages respond directly to the challenges of history, and that the *ḥadīth* and the "occasion of revelation" (*asbāb al-nuzūl*) supply important background material for contextualizing specific revelations. It is, however, their imperative to extract and sustain a transcendental lesson of that history and ensure that the Qur'ān has timeless value. Furthermore, even the most extreme of Islamists and traditionists hardly claim that the laws of Islam were made in the seventh century. While among most traditionalists the seventh century represents a time to emulate, authenticity is captured in their rejection of later scholastic developments in favor of the pristine custom. It is not the search for authenticity that prevents Rushdie's much needed reinterpretation of Islam; rather, it is the assumption that authenticity can be found outside of the human agency that engenders exclusivist and purist posture, as it does in all claims to authenticity. For the most part, such claims are often ethnocentric in the sense that they accentuate a particular aesthetic born in a specific place at a specific time (in this case, Arabia of the seventh century) and elevate it out of space and time in order to make it into the universal Muslim identity. And often, as many scholars have observed, the promotion of local knowledge is done in antipathetic reaction to Western modernity. Consequently, as Mona Abaza remarks (2002: 21–40), most of such movements are too defensive and insular to be effective in terms of global (and global Islamic) values which they try to promote (although, one should emphasize, locality is not by definition a counterproductive framework for action).

Finally, Rushdie's assumption that an Islamic Reformation would resolve the malaise of Muslims' proclivity for theocracy posits Western European history as the only compelling trajectory to achieve a functioning secular society. In so doing, Rushdie negates important moments in Islamic history when the negotiation between the secular and the religious came out of home-grown concerns about spiritual authority, religious rights, and institutional tensions and compromises. These concerns grew in both intensity and depth, changed radically through time and place, and challenged the blind theocracy that seems to be sweepingly associated with Islam. In fact, twentieth-century Egyptian scholar ʿAlī ʿAbd al-Rāziq, rejecting the notion that Islam is by definition at once a spiritual and political system, has argued, albeit controversially, that a separation of secular and religious matters on both Qurʾanic and legal grounds has been, and ought to be, the imperative of a true Islamic society. He says:

> Once again we warn the reader not to confuse the two kinds of governments, and not to conflate the two kinds of trusteeships – the trusteeship of the Messenger, on account of his being a messenger, and the trusteeship of powerful kings. The Messenger's trusteeship over his people is a spiritual one whose origin is faith from the heart, and the heart's true submission is followed by the submission of the body. On the other hand, the trusteeship of the ruler is a material one. . . . While the former is trusteeship leading to God, the latter is one for managing life's concerns and populating the earth. While the former is religion, the latter is the world. The former is divine, the latter is human. The former is a religious leadership, the latter a political one – and there is much distance between politics and religion.
>
> (Kurzman 1998: 31)

In rather detailed, though inevitably contentious sets of arguments, ʿAbd al-Rāziq questions the establishment of theocracy on the grounds that neither the Qurʾān nor the *sharīʿa* stipulate the nature of political leadership. Instead, he says, they open up to the idea of different governmental possibilities, including those relevant for secular democracies. While he acknowledges the necessity of establishing unity of the *umma*, he challenges the view that political unity must go hand in hand with religious unity since the management of worldly (and perhaps thus secular) matters is a human, not divine, concern:

> It is reasonable to say that the world could adopt one religion and that all human beings could be organized into one religious union. However, for the

> entire world to adopt one government and to be grouped in a shared political union would be foreign to human nature and have nothing to do with God's will.
>
> (Kurzman 1998: 35)

ʿAbd al-Rāziq's views, highly controversial as they were at the time of their publication (though shared by some other contemporary thinkers), point to the fact that, within the Islamic tradition itself, the understanding of what constitutes political leadership does not automatically imply an endorsement of theocracy. In fact, the objection raised to ʿAbd al-Rāziq's argument was often phrased around his view of the *sharīʿa* rather than his anti-theocratic claims, and especially his view that the *sharīʿa* does not hold all answers to the human condition and instead compels different societies to choreograph their own political system. Charles Kurzman (1998: 18–25) refers to this stance as the "silent *sharīʿa*," and lists it as one of three principal modes in which liberal Muslim thinkers have positioned themselves towards divine law. In Kurzman's assessment, because ʿAbd al-Rāziq, much like Saʿīd al-Ashmawī, born in 1923 in Egypt as well, views the *sharīʿa* as silent on some matters, he leaves it open to historical intervention. The objection to this mode is that it treats God's revelation as incomplete and, by extension, imperfect. In contrast, the other two modes, "liberal *sharīʿa*" and "interpreted *sharīʿa*," do not take away from the authenticity or completeness of revelation but posit human agency as central for the implementation of the revelation, and as such prone to historical change, even deviation and error. Yet in all three modalities, the issue of theocracy is problematized in reference to historical experience, rather than against it. This is perhaps where the most fruitful discussions on the place of the secular in Muslim (or any other) society can be achieved, namely, within the tradition rather than outside of it, so that the secular is not tied with Western-style modernization but, quite to the contrary, evoked through the historical experience of the *umma* in its multifaceted and complex manifestations. Whether that can be achieved through a synthetic effort of bringing together different strands in Islamic humanist and political tradition – which not only showed agility but also adaptability to specific contexts – or through cross-cultural outreach to non-Islamic models, seems to be a task that Muslims across the world must take on in order to rescue their history from the perils of any totalizing discourse, from within and without.

Needless to say, the assumption that the history of Islam has witnessed or favored secular (or proto-secular) sensibilities in any sustained and straightforward manner cannot be easily defended. In fact, the modern history of Islam, and especially current experiences, bespeak a discouraging appeal to theocracy among many Muslim groups around the world and a lack of radical repositioning towards those normative elements within Islam that stand in the way of the modern notions of human rights, gender equality, respect for other religions, and the accommodation of civil codes of behavior. However, one of the key issues that can be brought into consideration is that Islamic history may offer answers which Islamic doctrines, when essentialized and treated in a temporal vacuum, may not. In a variety of secular experiences around the world, only some may claim to have successfully implemented the values of secular tolerance by which divinely sanctioned hierarchies and exclusions are regulated, uprooted, or even discarded. For the most part, it is the matter of revisiting old experiences with new articulations and more latitude that can allow the historical experience to serve as a basis for home-grown secularism in modern times. More importantly, the regulation of the secular and religious need not be found through mutual exclusivity but at a level of amalgamation and accommodation, and it seems that the most successful examples of secular societies are precisely those that are able to amalgamate and accommodate rather than reject and negate. The separation of state and religion can be thus posed in a number of historically and culturally specific ways and the articulations of the secular can be expressed accordingly. In the case of Islamic societies, the issues of the power and agency of religious institutions, the loci of spiritual authority, and inter- and intra-religious relations, have been worked out in a variety of dynamic ways throughout the history of the *umma*. Moreover, as Talal Asad (2003: 9–12, 23–6) persuasively argues, the secular should hardly be treated as a successor to religion, or be seen as in its opposition as on the side of the rational. Rather, the secular relates to major premises of modernity, democracy, and the concept of human rights in more complex ways than as a simple opposition to religion, and there it is mainly intertwined with the question of authority rather than institutional frameworks. A glimpse at some cases drawn out of Islamic history may be helpful to understand the genealogy of secular (and anti-secular) sensibilities and practices in Islam, which do not necessarily lie on the opposite sides of the spectrum but in each other's relative, if contentious, proximity.

History as illustration

Taking a cue from ʿAbd al-Rāziq, it can and has been argued that the tension between political and religious loci of power lies at the core of the *umma* since its birth, and especially since the subsequent evolution of the caliphate. With the establishment of the first Muslim polity in Medina, the Prophet served as both the spiritual and political leader of the proto-theocratic state enunciated by the "Constitution of Medina." Charted in the aftermath of the 622 migration (*hijra*), the document specifies the rights and obligations of the members of the new polity and binds them contractually to the new leadership. Although most of the regulatory parameters of the document derive from the existing tribal customs, its framing as a new Islamic era garbs these new parameters into a new cloak and posits Muḥammad as a theocratic leader: "This is a document from Muḥammad the Prophet (governing the relations) between the believers and Muslims of Quraysh and Yathrib, and those who followed them and joined them and labored with them. They are one community (*umma*) to the exclusion of all men" (Guillaume 1955: 231). The bringing together of the worldly and the sacred in the public realm ensured the implementation of divine laws through the exegetical mediation of the messenger of God. He epitomized God's laws as well as the communal aspirations for a just and functioning society that, from its inception, wove into its fabric, albeit in a hierarchical way, religious plurality. In that sense, while the messenger established the message as the legal principle of the Muslim polity, the recognition that some members within it have their own laws to follow and that everyone is contractually bound into a new political framework, introduced an element of legal complexity and distance that would be addressed by all subsequent rulers of the *umma* with varying degrees of success and toleration. The theocratic society that Muḥammad laid out contained a theocracy based on a one-state–many-religions model, as well as the amalgamation of the existing customary laws under the Islamic umbrella.

After the Prophet's death, however, the cessation of divine intervention, at least in the belief of those who were to call themselves Sunnī Muslims, enunciated a need to differentiate the nature of authority, spiritual and political, and to configure institutional and other frameworks that would ascertain the continuation of the Prophet's message in his absence yet not endow his successors with comparable spiritual powers. This process was to be framed around what some scholars refer to as the exoteric, contractualist model of political legitimacy whereby the establishment of a trust or contract (*bayʿa*) between the caliph and the people divested the caliph of the possibility to hold a spiritual sway over the members of the *umma*. Inspired by the Qur'anic injunction that the caliph is the Prophet's vicegerent on Earth, and as such the figure who oversees the correct implementation of the principles on which the *umma* is established, the question of whether he could possess authority, obligation, and capacity to manage or oversee the spiritual life of individual Muslims in addition to ensuring the well-being of the *umma in toto* remained unresolved. Theoretically, the caliph regulated the matters of the here-and-now, not those of holy relevance. But the early caliphs never stayed out of religious matters altogether and some sought absolute control: in fact, in the period between 661 and 750, the Umayyad caliphs tried to ensure absolute authority over the *umma* and dealt with the opposition in particularly cruel ways which, both politically and theologically, occasioned much divergence and dissent as regards the nature of governance. The rise of different factions – Kharijites, Murji'ites, Shiʿites – that debated and discredited Umayyad absolutism indicated acute vigilance in the *umma* on what and who constituted authority, under what conditions, and in what spheres of influence. The contractual nature of the caliph's responsibility thus carried in itself a level of accountability that, to varying degrees, legitimized a plurality of theological opinions and political positions. In and of itself, this form of plurality did not give rise to secular values, but it did create a framework in which theocracy was scrutinized from within by virtue of dissociating political allegiance from religious duties, leaving the latter prone to expansion and growth while the former was increasingly envisioned as necessary primarily for effective but uncorrupted centralized governance.

In that sense, the process of defining the political authority went hand-in-hand with the *umma*'s self-actualization as a culturally plural, polyglot empire that necessitated the accommodation of its different constituencies under the same legal and ethical principles. This process was neither linear nor simple. Once the Umayyads were deposed, the rise and decline of the Abbasid caliphate in the mid-eighth century was predicated on the negotiation of multiple sources of authority and power. In the course of time, the emergence of independent or semi-dependent polities within the empire, the expansion of theological and legal debates on what constituted Islamic norms, and the formation of alternative spiritual models, especially through Ṣūfī praxis and teachings, lent itself increasingly to the shifting lines of demarcation between the sacred and profane sources of power and authority. Most significantly, the idea of religious unity rested on local contexts within which one could and did strive for religious fulfillment and identity, even identities, outside the realm of political authority, and even more so, without having to answer to the central political authority. The disenchantment with the potentially despotic and totalitarian government of the *umma* gave rise to a new *modus vivendi* that fragmented religious authority along theological, legal, devotional, regional, and other lines.

In his article on the separation between state and religion in early Islamic societies, Ira Lapidus (1975) argues that, contrary to the prevailing Islamist view in modern times that the Islamic worldview does not bifurcate between religious and political spheres of life, medieval Islamic governments were effectively secular regimes – Sultanates – that possessed no intrinsic religious character despite their principled allegiance to Islamic teachings. Lapidus argues that the historical developments, associated with the breakdown of the unity of the *umma* through internal strife and the Umayyad despotism, led to an ostensibly un-Islamic disposition of the government and increasingly differentiated political and religious developments in the life of the *umma*. The Sunnī establishment could neither uphold nor strive for the unity of state and religion in the face of an increasingly autonomous religious life in the *umma* and the rise of independent legal schools:

> Though they headed the community, the religion, and the state, the caliphs did not inherit Muhammad's prophethood, nor were they a source of religious doctrine and law. At the core of their executive and symbolic primacy there was a void, for neither the office nor the caliph himself held the authority from which Muslim religious conceptions and practice were derived. The Qur'ān, the revealed book, stood apart from the authority of the caliph, and was available to every believer.
>
> (Lapidus 1975: 369)

Lapidus builds his argument around historical rather than scriptural sources, highlighting the realities of the Islamic experience rather than the ideals that may have been upheld. He emphasizes that, in contrast to the Sunnīs, the Shī'a maintained a political theology that continued to tie politics and religion. Indeed, the Shi'ite conceptualization of the leader – the Imām – prioritized the designated rather than elected characteristics of his office. While both Sunnīs and Shī'īs agree on the necessity of maintaining the Prophet's family lineage for the leadership of the *umma*, in the Shī'ī teaching, the authority of each Imām is divinely sanctioned and as such could neither be challenged nor overturned on temporal grounds. The spiritual/inward and the political/outward were seen as embodied in the person of the Imām and therefore inseparable:

> [The members of the Prophet's family are] the locus of divine mystery: they are where His commandments are guarded. They are repositories of His knowledge, refuges for His wisdom, sanctuaries for His books, and mountain strongholds for His religion. Through them He straightened Religion's bending back and through them He ended the trembling of its flesh.
>
> (Sharīf al-Raḍī 2007: sermon 2, translation modified)

The historical realities that occasioned a growing rift between the state and religious authorities in Sunnī Islam were seemingly absent in the Shī'ī context, which is why Lapidus (1975: 368) suggests that the integration of the political and the spiritual as maintained by the Shī'īs was an essentially anachronistic and conservative condition.

Such characterizations may be too stringent: after all, Shīʿī teachings were not frozen in an era gone by but rather firmly grounded in the context in which several mechanisms and platforms of opposition to political absolutism and religious dogma were at play. Reacting to the precarious condition on the nature of rule and its effects on the increasingly diverse and poly-centered *umma*, Shīʿī teachings reflected yet another direction in which the mainstream political theory and practice were evolving, and their own conceptualizations were put to test and modified in the course of time.

More than the Shīʿī alternative that held a relatively marginal political sway despite their initial involvement in the Abbasid revolution, it was the intra-Sunnī theological debates that occasioned the main rift between the political establishment and the scholastic elite. The *miḥna* authorized by caliph al-Ma'mūn (r. 813–33) in the mid-ninth century against Aḥmad ibn Ḥanbal and his followers who contested a number of the Muʿtazilite rationalist views on creation and on the Qur'ān, led to a social and political upheaval which effectively removed the caliph from interfering in the religious affairs, leaving the theologians, as the intellectual elite, triumphant in the face of political pressure. The relatively short-lived intermeshing of political and religious powers was now seriously jeopardized and the new era of relative independence of theological and legal elite – the *ʿulamāʾ* – from the political establishment was ensured. In the period to come, as the *ʿulamāʾ* and the legal schools were crystallized and the doctrinal differences among different factions became more pronounced, the quest for intellectual and spiritual advancements became more enriched through Shīʿī, Ṣūfī and other teachings, while the political authority became better demarcated and the spheres of political powers more fragmented. Most, if not all, subsequent Islamic governments were compelled to present themselves as the relevant loci of religious authority with a sufficient degree of political transparency in order to ensure not only their legitimacy but also their survival.

By the time of al-Māwardī (d. 1058), the famous political theorist of the (Shīʿī) Būyid era, the empire had evolved in ways that necessitated a rethinking of the grounds on which the *umma* functioned as a political and social whole. Needless to say, the relevance of that period for the conditions which Muslims around the world face nowadays is hardly there; however, the relevance of the fact that the Muslims at the time faced changing conditions and processed them in theoretical, intellectual, and cultural terms is what makes that history relevant today. Witnessing the political fragmentation of the caliphate into competing sultanates and dynasties, al-Māwardī wrote a groundbreaking work which demarcated the nature of Islamic political authority by carefully weaving in different aspects of legal theory, views on sovereigns, state officials, judges and military leaders:

> The imamate, or supreme leadership, is intended as vicarate of the prophecy in upholding the faith and managing the affairs of the world. Its establishment is unanimously considered to be obligatory on the Community. There is disagreement, however, as to whether the obligation is derived on rational grounds or imposed by heavenly law.
>
> (al-Māwardī 2000: 3)

While in al-Māwardī's view the caliphate/imamate is sanctioned by revelation and therefore not a matter of historical choice, he was all too aware of the historical experience in which the caliphs (used synonymously with Imāms in his work) could not uphold political stability and a sense of authority, and could therefore be deposed and replaced by an *amīr*. The dissociation of the politics and religion through such empirical analyses tells a story of a society which, while concerned about legitimacy of the rulers, was all too aware of its limitations, and accepted *real politik* and the necessity to treat governments in a historical rather than extra-temporal manner.

At the level of political deliberations, al-Māwardī set the grounds for a series of theoretical positions on the interference of the rulers into the affairs of religion as well as the nature of religious authority that could facilitate the strengthening of individual and/or collective spiritual life. While all subsequent Islamic governments never fully excluded themselves from the sphere of religion, they negotiated in a variety of inventive ways the bounds of their power vis-à-vis these multiple religious structures of influence and hardly ever exercised it on individual believers. On the political front, the emergence of sultans as supreme temporal rulers who had no entitlement to religious knowledge and authority (though some attempted to gain them) occasioned a shift in the increasingly utopian understanding of what constituted a true Islamic polity. The Ḥanbalī jurist Ibn Taymiyya (d. 1328) argued that the only true Islamic government was in the period of the first four caliphs, before the advent of the Umayyad dynasty. After this golden period, the only acceptable ruler was the one who ensured the proper functioning of the religious elite – the *ʿulamāʾ* – and not the one who imposed his will on religious matters and the spiritual life of the *umma*. While indisputably obedient to divine edicts, the *umma* as organized in Ibn Taymiyya's social scheme possessed the power to steer its political destiny by prioritizing its allegiance to God over the ruler. Ibn Taymiyya's theocracy was more populist than autocratic.

In contrast, a century later another social theorist and a Mālikī judge at the Mamluk court, Ibn Khaldūn (d. 1406), offered a highly anthropological analysis of Islamic history, arguing for a cyclical rise and fall of great civilizations in accordance with their socio-economic conditions of life. Animated by customary laws of different tribal peoples who had ruled over the Islamic empire, Ibn Khaldūn's *ʿilm al-umrān* (science of culture of society) rested on the assumption that it is tribal solidarity – the *ʿaṣabiyya* – that ensured social stability and successful governance, rather than divine law. Solidarity that was most pronounced in migratory nomadic conditions yields to sedentarization, the breakdown of power structures and, ultimately, the demise of stability and authority. In this cycle of rise and fall Ibn Khaldūn perceived the basic mechanism of social and political interaction and thus put the onus on an anthropological rather than cosmic teleology. In the view of some scholars at least (e.g., Schmidt 1967), Ibn Khaldūn's analysis is fundamentally secular, as it excludes divine purpose from any political history. However, although God may be removed from the intervention in the political processes, He is not completely absent from Ibn Khaldūn's cosmology. Ibn Khaldūn is not a non-theist. His argument is so much more interesting precisely for its ability to accommodate human agency in the context of divine hierarchy of creation. God frames the universe, designs it in a layered way and creates spheres of knowledge that are bound by the limits of intellect and intuitive thinking.

Like many of his predecessors and contemporaries, Ibn Khaldūn wore many hats that interwove devotional/mystical, legal, theological and other epistemologies. The recognition that the realities, the visible and the invisible, continuously intermesh is what was rarely, if ever, lost to medieval Islamic thinkers – especially after al-Ghazālī's (d. 1111) famous synthetic gesture to explore reconciliation rather than mutual exclusion of intellectual and spiritual epistemologies – and so frequently to those who argue for black-and-white realities nowadays. The polarization of views, so typical in much of both secularist and anti-secularist discourse today, was lessened in the environment in which spiritual edification and self-actualization could be channeled in differentiated ways, and political rulers had rarely, if ever, direct business in it. They stood apart, and while that distance may have often been both tenuous and tentative, it nevertheless signaled that one's religious choice rested on a variety of possibilities associated with Ṣūfī schools, public endowments, private tutelage, guilds, and other modes of group identification.

Two cases may be briefly cited to exemplify such political distancing albeit in markedly different ways: the Mamluks and the Ottomans, both of whom exhibited a variety of political models regarding religious matters as they rose to power and sought to cement legitimacy as restorers of (Sunnī) religious unity and power.

In the case of the Mamluks, once they seized power over Egypt and Syria (1250–1517), the quest for political success rested on appeasing local Arab *ʿulamāʾ* who regarded the Mamluks primarily as soldiers with no skill in matters of religion and culture. "*ʿUlamāʾ* continued to write about *ʿulamāʾ* and for *ʿulamāʾ*, paying little or no attention in their works to all those who stood outside their own circles" (Haarman 1988: 84). Despite this attitude of cultural stereotyping, the ties of the religious and cultural élite with Mamluk aristocracy were eminent. Because – as it was usually the case – the *ʿulamāʾ* did not pertain to one class or group but permeated the entire economic and social structure of the state, a partial integration of the *ʿulamāʾ* into the political apparatus was an important process carried through the appointment of the chief judges, army officials, market inspectors, preachers, administrators of schools and hospitals, and so forth. In many respects, religion was exploited for political gains, as can be inferred from specific policies towards both the subjects of different confessions and the dominant religious élite. The most interesting of the policies of negotiating the distance between politics and religion was the gesture by the Sultan Baybars (r. 1260–77) to install four chief judges of all four Sunnī legal schools rather than elevate one over the others as was often the case with political leadership. On the one hand, the breach was closed among the legal schools and the plurality of religious opinions assured while, on the other hand, religious and political stability for the regime was secure. At the same time, the Jews and Christians were given important positions in bureaucratic apparatus, mainly as scribes and tax collectors, although appeasing Sunnī majority inevitably led to discrimination of other religious minorities, including non-Sunnī Muslims. The precarious bonds in inter- and intra-religious relations were a historical reality which the Mamluks had to warily sustain in order to gain legitimacy and stay in power, as opposed to imposing a theocracy that eliminated social layers. Although in a truly secular society all religious values, regardless of their genesis, would acquire the same status rather than be placed in a hierarchy of importance in relation to the state, the fact that the Mamluks, despite their military proclivities, labored hard to find an equilibrium with the major sources of religious/legal authority rather than ally themselves with one speaks to the fact that such authority was contained in more than one significant locus and that its repositioning was only partly the matter of governmental maneuvering. Moreover, the existence of other factors, such as class, ethnicity, culture, and so on, affected the ways in which the distance between religion and state was played out, shortened, or increased. Theocracy here was not the matter of a blind application of divine laws but a consideration of effective social stability that had to take into the account the fact that by the thirteenth century, much of the *umma*'s spiritual well-being had already been anchored in different sources of power, and hardly political ones at that.

The Ottoman case, more complex given the scope and duration of the imperial rule, reveals a different but comparably complex trajectory. While modern Turkey's surgical removal of the religious laws of the empire is usually interpreted as a radical shift from the past towards Western-style secularism, many scholars have argued that the genesis of Turkish secularization was embedded in its very structure. To that end, the Young Ottomans movement of the mid-nineteenth century that sought to modernize and democratize the political system is argued to have been embedded not only in Western ideas but in the reflections on Islamic legal reasoning in an attempt to reconcile Western liberal philosophy with Islamic religious and intellectual tradition. The Ottoman administrative system was believed to contain a sufficiently strong basis to support such democratic changes and carry on appropriate reforms. Sunnīs of Ḥanafī legal orientation, the Ottomans began to rely quite regularly after the mid-fifteenth century on a dual system whereby Islamic legal system was supplemented by local tribunals and the *kānūn* (canonical) edicts that were meant to legitimate many aspects of customary code of life and matters otherwise not covered by, but also not superior to, the *sharīʿa*. Fortified under the reign of Sulaymān the Lawgiver (r. 1520–66) – better known in the West as "the Magnificent" – the effectively parallel legal system on the one hand delineated the scope of judicial power of the chief Islamic cleric, Şeyhülislam, and on the other enabled the expansion of non-religious legal matters into the hands of administrative officers, especially in the aftermath of the 1839 Tanzimat Reforms. Within such a system, the decentralization, and in some ways the diluting, of religious power in the imperial context allowed for the distancing of politics and religion despite the theocratic nature of the empire.

Furthermore, the creation of the *millet* system whereby the religious communities answered to their governmentally appointed clerics reinforced the religious heterogeneity of the empire while allowing for the formation of semi-autonomous religious communities that followed their own laws and preserved their own identities. While scholarly opinions differ as to the origins, span, and institutional makeup of the *millet* system, it is widely held that – as far as the imperial court was concerned – the *millets* gradually became the main sources of group identity for the subjects of the Ottoman empire. The heads of the *millet*s were state functionaries appointed by the sultan and given significant ecclesiastical, fiscal, and legal control over their populations. In that sense, despite the administrative centralization and hierarchy, religious life of the empire was markedly decentralized and differentiated. While it is certainly true that Islam was the privileged and preferred religion of the empire, it is also true that within such a system, non-Muslim subjects had a recourse to at least two loci of religious authority – their own and the Islamic ones – since the law required that unresolved communal matters in non-Muslim *millet*s find solutions in the Muslim court. The Muslims, on the other hand, had recourse to different legal schools in matters of religious practice (even if the Ottoman state adopted Ḥanafī law), or Ṣūfī *ṭarīqa*s in spiritual matters, so they too enjoyed a certain level of religious flexibility and liberty outside the state. Within such a system, as Stanford Shaw (1962: 618) points out, in which the *millet*s functioned separately as concerns religious and communal matters, they were significantly brought together by the guilds, which were not influenced by religious divisions, and which functioned as modes of "social fusion in a society which otherwise might easily have split entirely apart."

Secular sensibilities

The examples cited above do not provide a basis to argue that Islamic history reveals secular sensibilities in any consistent or persuasive way. However, they do indicate that the question of the separation of religion and state – *dīn wa dawla* – in Islam, which is so often answered in the negative by both Islamists and Western critics, does in fact lend itself to complex and distinctive ideas about the manifestations of the secular in non-Western societies. The secular cannot be treated as a conceptual or historical privilege only of those who have separated church and state in a straightforward, mutually exclusive way. Islamic tradition and history – especially in the Sunnī context – have evolved not around a single religious or spiritual establishment that took control over everyday life in union with the political establishment, as is the case with mainstream European history, but in reference to several sources of religious and spiritual authority, which varied in power and influence depending on multifaceted factors and players. In light of such circumstances, the religious versus secular dichotomy, which informs the discussions about the current state of affairs in Islam, appears painfully simplistic and inadequate. For as long as Muslims nowadays are supposed to either mimic or reject the Western experience, depending on which side of the spectrum they are asked to align themselves, their own history of secular and humanist compromises will be ignored or deemed irrelevant by both Muslims and non-Muslims. To learn something from this experience means not only drawing attention to the ways religious liberties can be and have been conducted, sustained, and disregarded in Islam, but also prompting Muslims themselves to reach into their own past to contribute to the discussions on what constitutes secular values in the modern world. Finally, it means recognizing the many daring engagements that Muslims have embarked upon in the course of their history as a way of dealing with the pressures of political and ideological absolutism, from within and without.

References and further reading

Abaza, M. (2002) *Debates on Islam and Knowledge in Malaysia and Egypt: Shifting Worlds*, London: Routledge.

Asad, T. (2003) *Formations of the Secular: Christianity, Islam, Modernity*, Stanford: Stanford University Press.

Berger, P. (1973) *The Social Reality of Religion*, Harmondsworth: Penguin.

Berkes, N. (1964) *The Development of Secularism in Turkey*, Montreal: McGill-Queens University Press.

Findley, C. V. (1980) "The Advent of Ideology in the Islamic Middle East," *Studia Islamica*, 56: 147–80.

Fine, J. (1975) *The Bosnian Church: A New Interpretation*, Boulder, CO: East European Quarterly.
Glidewell-Nadolski, D. (1977) "Ottoman and Secular Civil Law," *International Journal of Middle Eastern Studies*, 8: 517–43.
Guillaume, A. (1955) *The Life of Muhammad: A Translation of [Ibn] Ishaq's* Sirat Rasul Allah, Karachi: Oxford University Press.
Haarmann, U. (1988) "Arabic in Speech, Turkish in Lineage: Mamluks and their Sons in the Intellectual Life of Fourteenth-century Egypt and Syria," *Journal of Semitic Studies*, 33: 81–114.
Juergensmayer, M. (1993) *The New Cold War: Religious Nationalism Confronts the Secular State*, Berkeley: University of California Press.
Kurzman, C. (1998) *Liberal Islam: a Sourcebook*, New York: Oxford University Press.
Lapidus, I. (1975) "The Separation of State and Religion in the Development of Early Islamic Society," *International Journal of Middle East Studies*, 6: 363–85.
Lybyer, A. (1913) *The Government of the Ottoman Empire in the Time of Suleiman the Magnificent*, Cambridge, MA: Harvard University Press.
Māwardī, al- (2000) *The Ordinances of Government*, trans. W. H. Wahba, Reading: Garnet Publishing.
Rushdie, S. (2005) "The Right Time for an Islamic Reformation," *Washington Post*, Sunday, August 7, page B07.
Schmidt, N. (1967) *Ibn Khaldun: Historian, Sociologist, and Philosopher*, New York: AMS Press.
Sharīf al-Raḍī (2007) *Nahj al-Balāgha*, English translation at http://www.al-islam.org/nahj/.
Shaw, S. (1962) "The Aims and Achievements of Ottoman Rule I the Balkans," *Slavic Review*, 21: 617–22.
Smith, W. C. (1957) *Islam in Modern History*, Princeton: Princeton University Press.
Thual, F. (1998) "Dans le monde orthodoxe, la religion sacralise la nation, et la nation protége la religion," *Le Monde* January 20, online at http://www.fsa.ulaval.ca/ personnel/vernag /EH/F/cause/lectures/orthodoxie2.html.

46

PUBLIC ETHICS

Amyn B. Sajoo

The central role for Muslim ethics of the Qur'ān and the body of prophetic guidance and conduct, the *sunna*, is accompanied by a key principle, one that underlies the oft-repeated assertion about Islam being "a way of life." It is the idea of the historical locus of the life of Muḥammad, with its series of well-documented struggles to fulfill a prophetic mission in which the pursuit of ethical ideals is not an abstraction but a practical matter. This is reflected in the sensibility of the founding Shīʿī and Sunnī ethical discourses of Miskawayh (d. 1030), al-Ghazālī (d. 1111) and Naṣīr al-Dīn al-Ṭūsī (d. 1274), among others.

There have always been among us Muslims and non-Muslims who prefer to treat religious texts as bearing singular and fixed meanings, the life of Muḥammadas closed to the creative interpretation that it richly merits, and the diverse histories of Muslims as a unitary history of "Islam." This perspective yields, predictably enough, an ethos that is readily identified as a body of sacred rules, some finding their way into law or *fiqh*, and the rest into the wider *sharīʿa* as a normative expression of Islam. Applying this ethos to the daily challenges that confront a Muslim is, then, an act of *will*, albeit with discernment as far as identifying the relevant principles is concerned.

It is not only those of a "fundamentalist" persuasion – better referred to as political Islamists – who adopt that view, in which human agency and reason are reduced to acts of compliance. Ironically, this ideological posture is shared by numerous commentators on Islam who, like the Islamists that they tend to be obsessed with, would rather not grapple with the intricacies of pluralist Muslim worlds, historical and contemporary, textual and social, orthodox and heterodox, and all the shades in between such binaries. The reductive tendency has rarely been as conspicuous as it is today, in the aftermath of the events of September 11, 2001. Vexing issues of political violence, tolerance, the nexus of individual and community, even the fresh challenges of biotechnology, are too loudly treated as if the ethical problems at hand have ready-made solutions that only need uncovering in scripture. Alas, the decibel level at which ideological Islam is proclaimed by a militant minority is echoed by observers – scholarly and journalistic – eager to explain the conduct of political Islamists at face value, which is precisely how commentators with any degree of sophistication are *not* supposed to commentate.

Among the principal burdens of this chapter is the claim that it is the element of motivation that makes religious ethics in general, and Muslim ethics in particular, an especially rewarding field of study. This is not about an exploration of how one attributes motive and responsibility to an actor in ethics (as compared with law, for example), and least of all about the psychology of motive-formation in its interface with social and private ethical action. Those are vast and relevant fields that merit attention in their own right. Rather, the concern here is with a fundamental problem in approaches to modern ethical conduct that straddles easy divides between the "secular" and "religious," and not only among Muslims. It has to do with the question, "*Why* act ethically ?"

Responding coherently to that query requires one to consider various conceptions of the "good" in settings that are private and public, socio-political and scientific, past and present. Asking whether an act is "inherently" right or wrong as the primary question, and building an approach thereon in terms of secular or religious perspectives, is to miss the real question. When wedded to an adamantly secular framework, this gives short shrift to the discourses and praxis that religious affinities bring to the ethical choices that individuals actually make. The deficit is surely fatal when it comes to the Muslim world, where the prevalence of the secular has played itself out so differently than in Europe and North America. At the same time, an absolutist frame of reference, secular or religious, gives short shrift to the complexities of human motivation that attend such judgments in the real world. It reduces the interplay of reason and faith or commitment to nothing more than passive compliance within an impoverished, *deus ex machina* view of the world. Both frameworks exist for some, of course; but they can hardly tell the whole story. One is also mindful in all this that there is more to scripture than scripture itself. I have sought to range beyond sources and contexts that usually receive attention in discussions of ethics – such as references to cultural expressions – in which conceptions of the ethical are embedded. They evoke the supple nature of the questing in which Muslims and others seek to bridge the complex truths of normative texts and empirical reality.

In seeking to do justice to contending and plural realities, this chapter ventures first to consider an array of public settings in which Muslim conceptions of the good have developed and are today unfolding, including biotechnology and ecology. Asking how and why those conceptions are to be taken seriously is the underlying thread that connects the settings, yielding continuities and remakings of tradition and reason. Next, the chapter addresses successively three distinct yet overlapping domains – of civility, humanism and governance – that engage such basic notions as social order and individual liberty in which conceptions of the good, whether as ethos or specific moral judgments, are vitally entwined. In conclusion, the chapter will reflect on how the "unity in diversity" of Muslim public ethics reinforces distinctive social imaginaries – the maps of moral order that underlie how ordinary individuals see others and themselves, within and beyond the Islamic world.

Taking ethics seriously

In asserting that an act was authentically moral only in terms of the intention that accompanies it – unsullied by self-interest or mock virtues – Naṣīr al-Dīn al-Ṭūsī anticipated Kant by over five centuries. The harmony of outward and inner disposition and character was of the essence, both for the quality of the act itself and, ultimately, for the health of the soul. Muḥammad had, after all, proclaimed the primacy of moral intent over all else, including legal obligation. It is true that this perspective is shared among the major traditions of faith-based ethics. Yet in the merging of sacred and secular that became the leitmotif of normative Islam, the congruence of external and internal universes of meaning also bridged the moral choices of the individual and the community (*umma*). As al-Ṭūsī and a host of Muslim thinkers saw it, often in an Aristotelian vein, individual happiness and virtue were premised on a life of association. A reasoned account of the good and why it should be pursued must, then, repose on the quality of interaction of the personal and societal. "Let there be among you," proclaimed the Qur'ān 3: 104, "a community that calls to the good (*al-khayr*), bidding virtue (*maʿrūf*) and forbidding vice (*munkar*)." Rooted in *ʿarafa*, to know or recognize, *maʿrūf* signified the social transparency of the idea of virtue.

The ethos that emerges from scripture, whether through narratives or injunctions, is of necessity about the practical unfolding of moral principles: ideals and their implications are set forth within the bounds of the relationship among the individual, society and the divine. Layers of meaning attach themselves through the course of history to those ideals, and to the nature of the threefold relationship within which they are to be realized. In Islam, the primary ethical corpus derived from Qur'anic and prophetic direction and, for the Shīʿa, the guidance of designated Imāms, is interwoven with literary and social mores (*adab*), as well as a robust intellectual tradition of which al-Ṭūsī, Miskawayh, al-Ghazālī, Ibn Rushd (d. 1189) and Fakhr al-Dīn al-Rāzī (d. 1209) are exemplars. Even the *sharīʿa*, often thought of as a body of law, is foremost an encompassing ethics derived from the primary sources – of which legal norms (*fiqh*) drawn out over time are only a part. Then there is the hallowed tradition of resolving grievances (*maẓālim*) outside the scope of the *sharīʿa*, through sovereigns and their tribunals righting wrongs under principles of equity beyond any formal codes. Thus the ethical tradition finds rich expression in the plenitude of virtually a millennium-and-a-half of historical experience.

Yet this picture is incomplete, for it does not convey the sense of the quotidian, the ordinary encounter of community and individual with moral choices, large and small. This is not merely about the relationship between ideals and realities, which after all is integral to human frailty and pervades all normative systems. Rather, it is about recognizing that the tenets or ideals themselves are framed in the crucible of human experience, amid the congruence and tension of the demands of intellect, faith and tradition. After all, that is why scriptures find compelling expression in narratives that echo across the boundaries of culture, time and space. Creation, death, sacrifice and love are staples of narrative and norm in the Bhagavad Gita and the Upanishads, the Hebrew and Christian Testaments, the Qur'ān, as well as cultural epics such as those of Gilgamesh, Manas and Homer. Their parables generate and impart human context to the norms which they proclaim, weaving sacred and secular into lived experience. The same is true of the spaces – physical and psychological – in which that experience unfolds.

Less majestically, oral as well as written narratives of daily experience that are part of our shared heritages capture the detail of lifeworlds in which religio-ethical principles are mediated by the mundane exigencies of moral choice by individuals, families and communities. Thus the Qur'ān's normative universe is given specificity by Muḥammad's pragmatic engagement with vexing moral problems as captured in the *ḥadīth* tradition. *Adab* often captures this sense of the empirical, not only in popular tales like *Kalīla wa Dimna*, the *Maqāmāt* of al-Ḥarīrī (d. 1122) and *Ḥayy ibn*

Yaqẓān of Ibn Ṭufayl (d. 1185), but also in the behavioral codes of artisans, calligraphers, musicians and painters. One is mindful too of the informal – even unlettered – codes that were a conspicuous part of early Islam, like the *sharīʿa ummiyya*. There are hymnal narratives of mystical or devotional bent, always bearing an ethos and sometimes affirming a specific set of ethical norms; examples in Arabic, Persian and a host of Indic languages include *qaṣīda, qawwālī* and *ginān*s. Modern secular chronicles can convey and influence the ethical sensibilities of the Muslim public square, as in the novels of Naguib Mahfouz, Orhan Pamuk, Tayib Salih, Ahdaf Soueif and M. G. Vassanji. Their characters are as familiar as the difficult choices that they encounter in settings or states of mind where Islam is at the epicenter, lending credence to the notion that the deepest truths are located in fiction. To this can be added the impact of contemporary cinematic culture, as purveyor of common and elite values alike as they reflect as well as mould social identities. Post-revolutionary Iranian cinema is a prime instance, with the forthright yet subtle handling of the most serious philosophical issues by *auteurs* who have endured first-hand the vicissitudes of radical social and political change.

Taking ethics seriously implies coming to terms with the variegated social canvas on which reasoned accounts of right and wrong are played out; it cannot be about the abstractions of moral theory or divine commands alone. The latter approach would amount to a retreat into what the contemporary Iranian thinker Abdolkarim Soroush calls "the ethics of the Gods," where the palpable sense of the mundane that humans must inhabit is altogether lacking. This is not to gainsay the rewards of delving into the primary sources for renewed inspiration, in this as in earlier epochs. Thinkers such as Soroush, Mohammed Arkoun, Ebrahim Moosa and others have been at the forefront of such endeavor – to recall the late Fazlur Rahman – as an exercise in *rational* historical retrieval that aims to grasp an ethical unity beyond isolated commands and injunctions. This effort, in contrast to what is commonly referred to as fundamentalist or Islamist revivalism, is firmly anchored in historicity and context: the past is not for imitation (*taqlīd*) but part of a continuum in which texts, narratives and experience are shared by a diverse *umma*. Moreover, it is worth recalling that the *umma* was conceived not as an abstract ideal but a real entity with all the ambiguity and complexity of actual communities, religious or not. As such, it was enjoined by the Qur'ān 3:110 to be more than a nominal *umma muslima* and to merit the status of the "best community" by affirming right conduct.

The intertwining of the individual and communal selves is firmly grounded in the way that ethical life is actually constructed. For the narrative of an individual's life is tied invariably to an interlocking set of narratives that involve others. The atomized, much less the disembodied, self is hardly a meaningful subject on which to build an edifice of right and wrong that has practical relevance. This is implicitly recognized by religious traditions, where the individual is embedded in a larger whole: *re-ligare*, to bind together, is the font for "religion." Islam has made it pivotal to its scriptural as well as civilizational thrust. In the merging of secular and sacred, as well as the interlocking lives of the individual and the *umma*, Muslims recognize intuitively that faith traditions are the primary models for a lived ethics.

What this points to is a key divergence in the approach to the subject between much of modern philosophy and religion. The former offers elaborate theories – stressing consequences, a social contract, social justice, human nature, and the like – that purport to be grounded in ideas either of what we ought to do as a moral duty (deontology) or what we should do to maximize social happiness (teleology). These theories purport to give us coherent responses to Socrates' observation that the unexamined life is not worth living. Aristotle, like an array of eastern sages before him, sought to give both deontological and teleological answers to Socrates' question, for in their cultural universes the unity of the individual and the community was not yet sundered. Their rationalist humanism was to profoundly shape early Muslim thought, which in the hands of Ibn Rushd attained fresh heights in the nexus of faith and reason, and which in turn influenced the rebirth of European philosophy. Yet if that rationalist thrust came to be muted in Muslim religious discourse amid the rise of conservative theology (*kalām*), the opposite was to occur in Occidental thought. Reflection on what one was to do was less about the examined life as a whole than about the preoccupations of the secular citizen or collective, usually in the abstract. The stress in utilitarian philosophy on social consequences may give the impression of tying the individual to the whole, but it treats the former as an impersonal agent in the process of maximizing collective benefit. Again, the notion of a social contract to maximize justice for all treats the contracting parties as anonymous actors in a formula for shared existence, without asking who the actors are in imparting content and context to what they ought to do.

Critical ethical themes

Moral choices have to do with a deliberative priority that is accorded to specific courses of action, and this priority in turn relates to a whole range of possible motivations, of which obligation is only one. Ethically outstanding choices may not be a matter of obligation at all, in that they cannot be demanded or the actor subjected to blame for not doing them; instead, they may be done because the actor feels there is no alternative for him or her personally, while recognizing that this could not be demanded of others. This brings us to shades of difference that often characterize contemporary usage of the terms "ethics" and "morals." Sharing as they do Greco–Latin roots (*ethikos, mores*, relating to custom), they are often used interchangeably. In formal discourse, however, ethical perspectives are about what guides an individual or a community in choices that concern the "good," relating closely to perceptions of who one is and how best to live in one's universe. Morals, on the other hand, are more specifically about rules that concern what is right or wrong, whether for the individual or society. Certainly the concepts overlap substantially in theory and practice; but it is well to bear in mind the more encompassing sense of reality that typifies ethics.

Whether a particular outlook on ethics corresponds to the standard of a pluralist ethos with a commitment to deliberative morality is not about its religious or secular identity as such, but a matter of actual as well as normative orientation. Just as there are secular ideologies, including mainstream variants of Liberalism, that eschew claims to the "good" against what they perceive as "just," so there are religious outlooks that resist any departures from their orthodox conceptions of the good against fresh claims to justice. In positing that a *bona fide* commitment to ethical conduct must involve the harmony of external action and moral motivation, Naṣīr al-Dīn al-Ṭūsī and Kant in their different ways staked out an approach to mediating the rational and the good. Both espoused reason as central to their moral venture, and nourished variant streams of humanist thought and praxis, whether in religious or secular vein. Kant's "categorical imperative" and "transcendental self" with a "reverence for the law" may seem at a considerable remove from al-Ṭūsī's intellect as the seat of the soul in a moral search for "the perfection of defective faculties," until one recalls Kant's espousal of the ideal Church as an ethical republic rejecting dogma in favour of rational faith. Still, Kant has been assailed for his excessively abstract deontology, and its heritage in Western philosophy, against which al-Ṭūsī epitomizes the notion of a lived ethics.

The perspectives offered here explore critical ethical themes in Muslim contexts, mindful of scriptural, intellectual and cultural heritages and influences. Non-Islamic currents run through those historic and contemporary elements, for reasons that have to do with the quintessentially shared nature of lived ethics. Indeed, the Qur'anic ethos itself embodies a plurality of cultural and confessional elements that Muslims made their own, a synthesis that in turn was to impact the metamorphosis of secular and religious frameworks far beyond the Muslim world. One often sees the characterization of modern Muslim discourse as involving conversations with authoritative scholars who lived long ago, alongside the need to return to primary sources, in understanding novel situations in the light of traditional values. This is true enough if it is not taken to imply that the ethical venture is effectively about applying traditional norms to new problems. As already suggested, the understanding of those traditions as well as their content are themselves in constant flux, or should be in the name of a pluralist and rational stance that partakes fully of the modern. An ethical critique of civic conduct, including that of rigid, traditionalist applications of the *sharīʿa*, remains characteristic of Muslim contexts because it is supple in looking forward. It entails conversations not only with interlocutors of the past, Muslim and otherwise, but also of the present. Among the most acute tests of its relevance as well as fidelity today are the emergent challenges posed by biomedical, ecological and development issues, in a techno-secular age with its peculiar theology and ethos.

As evidence of a practical turn in Muslim ethico-philosophical discourse, one is inclined to cite the early derivation of juridical principles (*fiqh*) by communities whose rapid geo-cultural expansion beyond the original Arabian domain (*dār al-Islām*) mandated a rule of law that enjoyed the imprimatur of the new faith. Indeed, one may lament the overly legalistic guise that the *sharīʿa* and *fiqh* conferred from the eighth to the tenth centuries upon a discourse still in the early stages of metamorphosis as moral reasoning. However, as the threads of this reasoning were picked up and woven into a full-fledged philosophical discourse by Miskawayh, al-Ghazālī and al-Ṭūsī, among others, it found rich application and maturation within the emergent sciences of Islam in the early medieval period. Medicine, in particular, as institutional-clinical practice and as a field of advanced learning, extended the normative morals, *akhlāq*, into the quotidian, building on a Hellenistic (as well as a significant Indian) legacy of pathology and its appropriate social locus. In founding the world's earliest hospitals (*bimaristān*) in Baghdad, Damascus and Cairo, while deploying the empirical method in a discipline hitherto dominated by theoretical modes of reasoning, Muslims and their Judeo-Christian collaborators developed a humanistic ethos that prized the rational. It flourished across the urban centers of the Middle East not only as part of Islam's civilizational impetus but also as a social institution.

Issues of professional conduct by health practitioners, open access to hospitals, and sensible attitudes among patients, physicians and pharmacologists were of vital importance. In these matters, Hippocratic and Galenic writings were certainly influential. Yet here, as in the determination of those like ʿAbd al-Laṭīf al-Baghdādī (d. 1231) and Ibn al-Nafīs (d. 1288) to test canonical claims by rigorous anatomical samplings and examination, Muslims made science and its universal outlook very much their own. A new medical ethics grew from the writings of ʿAlī ibn al-ʿAbbās al-Majūsī (d. between 982 and 995), Ibn al-Bayṭār (d. 1248), the Damascus medical school founder and teacher Ibn al-Dakhwār (d. 1231), and his illustrious pupils Ibn Abī Uṣaybiʿa (d. 1270) and Ibn al-Nafīs himself, also a fine *ḥadīth* scholar. In their writings, the practice of medicine – as art and science – acquired what might be described as a rational teleology: it demanded the fullest commitment to pursuing scientific accuracy and truth, coupled with a recognition of the purposive nature of that pursuit as an extension of man's relationship with God. Virtually all the luminaries were trained not only in medicine but also in law and theology; sundered universes of secular science and religious morals did not exist. When Ibn al-Nafīs was confronted with the *akhlāq* tenet that required the integrity of human organs to be preserved after death, he nonetheless found it justifiable to conduct cadaver dissections to establish vital facts (like the heart's ventricular structure) that made for effective treatment. Time and again, such rationales were found on behalf of therapeutic action and sound health.

While this may be interpreted as evincing the cognitive and value autonomy of science from "Islam," it is more cogently seen in terms of an integrated ethos in which normative fidelities were balanced by a sense of the larger good. It was here that the *akhlaq* values of compassion, charity, wisdom and solidarity found some of their most creative and conscious expression, beginning with the physician's oath that put the welfare of the patient and the avoidance of harm at the forefront. Nor is this in the least surprising: the encounters with birth, death and the elements that challenge them are, after all, the métier from which ethical narratives are derived and given meaning. The capacity of science in general, and medicine in particular, to account for – and control – key aspects of these fundamental encounters has long been obvious. Where that capacity is part of a broader canvas of shared meaning such as that provided by religion or other metaphysical sources, the ethical compass for action finally sits *outside* the scientific universe. One cannot offer a purely biological, chemical, or other physical rationale in response to questions about the morality of an innovation or intervention. Ibn al-Nafīs could ground his defense of dissection and anatomical knowledge in *maṣlaḥa*, the public good; he could not assert an absolute or unqualified right to pursue anatomical curiosity irrespective of the results. With the advent of the techno-secular age, science often purports to provide its own ethical compass, rejecting social values that are deemed irrational; yet motives of profit and publicity are part of the scientific warp and woof.

When the innovative and intervening prowess of medical science touches on the very foundations of birth, death and all that connects them, the relocation of the ethical compass matters all the more to society at large. When Francis Crick and James Watson established in 1953 the three-dimensional structure of DNA that is the basis of cellular life, their discovery made possible the Human Genome Project, which a half century later has decoded the sequence of the three billion DNA units in the human genome. The ability to fight through prevention and treatment a spectrum of disorders such as Alzheimer's and Parkinson's, cardiovascular disease and various forms of cancer would on its face seem a profoundly welcome outcome. But can those ends warrant the means involved in the process, such as gene intervention and manipulation whose effects we only dimly grasp, and which may radically alter the foundations of "human nature"? Is there a stable human nature whose alteration ought to raise moral concern? Where the ends include not simply preventing or treating disease but "enhancing" the human body, biologically and aesthetically, where do we draw the line ?

Plural ethical approaches

The answers to these questions can scarcely be sought within the confines of biotechnology itself, least of all for Muslim and other societies where techno-secular values do not have a putative primacy. Certainly, there is an overlap between secular and religiously based ethics of maximizing public benefit from biomedical interventions – in Islam, on the basis of *maṣlaḥa* and *istiḥsān* (discretion, equity). But such claims must also be tested against prior moral as well as human rights constraints. Nor can one ignore commercial factors that have ramifications for how seriously we take claims to serving the public good or pursuing pure science. The stakes at hand make the exercise of nuanced moral reasoning more intricate than ever, between the application of given norms on the one hand and of professional standards on the other. If the former runs the hazard of retreating into a traditionalism that is divorced from modern imperatives, then the secular extreme can spur reliance on "situational" reasoning where an *ad hoc* approach prevails, or on regulatory schemes that are impelled by ideological or corporate concerns. The problem is illuminated when one considers the standard bioethical guidelines that have come to be widely adopted by clinicians, namely the tenets of beneficence, non-maleficence, autonomy and justice. "Do no harm" (non-maleficence or *ḍarar* in Islam) as a rule of professional conduct may be well grounded universally as a starting point for the clinician. Determining what constitutes harm and how to resolve conflicts between the principles themselves (such as when the wishes of the patient clash with the obligations of the clinician), however, requires a degree of specificity that takes us outside biomedicine itself.

For Muslims, the public policy dilemma in balancing secular and faith-based perspectives in this regard involves steering an accountable course on issues ranging from cloning and organ transplants to abortion and euthanasia within an ethos that integrates *dīn* (religious) and *dunyā* (secular), while recognizing their separate institutional domains. That ethos is pluralist in keeping not only with varying doctrinal views but also the flux of historical and cultural context, and the emergence of human rights norms. Here are some examples that illuminate the specific dilemmas that stem from today's biomedical and social realities.

Regarding abortion – differentiated from the involuntary termination of pregnancy (*ijhād* or *siqṭ*), which is deemed natural – a broad range of stances has emerged historically on doctrine and public policy. On the basis of Qur'anic verses that refer to the development of the foetus from zygote and embryo to "another creature" (Qur'ān 22:5, 23:14), the ensoulment of the foetus is generally thought to occur 120 days from conception; a minority regards the operative period to be 40 days. This is distinct from the question "When does life begin?" The ensoulment phase is widely thought to be the pertinent boundary for a voluntary abortion on approved grounds, which primarily turn on safeguarding the mother's health. As contraceptive devices gained approval across the Muslim world from the 1950s onward, drawing in part on the traditional acceptance of *coitus interruptus* (*ʿazl*), modern opinion has often treated abortion within the 120-day phase as legitimate birth control. The Shīʿī tradition in general is especially permissive in this respect. However, some scholars have argued that *ʿazl* is not a proper analogy because an embryo/foetus is an "existing presence" (*mawjūd ḥāṣil*), a perspective that dates back to al-Ghazālī.

Hence we have plural ethical approaches rather than merely competing doctrinal views. One approach stresses the pragmatic results that are considered desirable, notably family planning and protecting the mother; these are considered to outweigh the undesirability of ending a potential life. Another approach deems abortion to be inherently disapproved, subject only to protecting the mother; the social context is not considered relevant. The choice of approach in legal regulation and ethics, public and private, does not occur in a vacuum. There is increasingly ready access to non-surgical forms of abortion like the "morning-after" and RU486 pills, as well as to clinical sites of varying degrees of safety for abortion, often beyond the ambit of local or national frontiers. New medical understandings of foetal development, changing demographic and economic climates in a society, together with the impact of media portrayals of alternative lifeworlds (whether negative or positive), provide the practical canvas against which both public and individual interpretations of ethico-legal norms take place. Between a woman's human right to basic autonomy on the one hand, and the protection of a fetal claim to life on the other, coercive legal regulation may be of limited effect or efficacy. The dominant personal and societal moral reality becomes one of difficult choices.

Again, in such areas as genetic intervention and cloning, same-sex marriage, organ donation and transplant, surrogate motherhood, and euthanasia, a plurality of ethical approaches prevails amid the unfolding of new perspectives in the biomedical and social sciences. In the rapidly developing field of genetic technology, for instance, a qualified acceptance of therapeutic cloning of stem cells has emerged in the Muslim world, with its comparatively open stance on early embryonic status. A new stem cell research centre in Saudi Arabia has the endorsement of *fatwā*s that emphasize the public welfare element (*maṣlaḥa*) in allowing the use of cells taken from miscarried or aborted foetuses, subject to the 120-day norm. Nevertheless, there are grounds for concern about therapeutic cloning, which in practice straddles "therapy" and "enhancement." Stem cells developed for muscle tissue may assist therapy for cardiac damage or muscular dystrophy, yet the same process could lend itself for commercial use in boosting muscular or cardiac tissue for elite participants in sports. It is doubtful that *maṣlaḥa* could justify the second choice as a rationale for cloning. A related issue is that of equitable access to biomedical resources within and among societies, if there is not to be a "biotech divide" in favor of the privileged few. Then there is the prospect that embryos created by the same process of fusion for therapeutic cloning may end up being implanted for reproductive purposes, either by accident or design to circumvent legal constraints. At a more fundamental level, one must ask whether genetic manipulation and control may impact the autonomous basis of the identity of humans as responsible for their fate, and as ends in themselves rather than as instruments for ends chosen by others. Could we in the process put at risk the gamut of human responses that allows us to connect with other human beings as individuals and communities? As Muslim health professionals and scholars reflect on these very questions, the rush of developments in the laboratory and biotechnological market only elevates the ante.

A professional *Islamic Code of Medical Ethics* affirms broadly the principle that a physician "shall not take away life even when motivated by mercy," based upon the guidance of the Prophet against suicide, and the dignity of the human person (the text may be found at www.islamset.com/ethics/code/index.html). But where a medical condition reduces the body to a vegetative state or medical intervention is otherwise deemed futile, treatment may cease and life be allowed to lapse. Or, as the Islamic Code casts it, the physician must then recognize his limits as upholder of life, and desist from "heroic measures" or other passive preservation of the patient. However, active euthanasia – such as by lethal injection – is prohibited. Still, the physician's obligation under the Islamic Code to safeguard "freedom from pain and misery" is acquiring a greater profile, as Western medical practices become universalized. Not surprisingly, there is strong resistance to some of the implications in Muslim societies, as in non-Muslim quarters, including to the prospect of physician-assisted suicide.

This is no less true of organ donation and transplants, despite the professional invocation of the traditional principle of *farḍ kifāya*, an obligation upon those capable of fulfilling it to do so on behalf of the *umma* at large. It is bolstered by the norm that the saving of life warrants all essential measures, including transgressions of standard prohibitions – even if it entails transplants from the dead. Yet in the face of shortages in supplies of blood and human organs, the hallowed notion of bodily integrity raises for some the problem of desecrating the body by severing its parts, which has caused resistance to post-mortem examinations. Likewise, the tenet that the body is a custodial charge rather than individual property might be read to imply that organ donations, in life or death, are violations of a sacred trust; this claim is more persuasive when it is directed at prohibiting the sale of human organs. Recent developments relating to the use of animal organs (xenotransplants), and their genetic modification for this purpose (transgenic breeding), raise fresh concerns. Pigs and other animals that are farmed for humans are commonly confined in highly oppressive conditions to preserve them from infections. Further, in order to mute human rejection of alien organs (especially in xenotransplants), the genomes of source animals are modified, often by inserting human genes. These practices have already resulted in a decline in public trust over biotechnologies, including more benign ones.

Suffice it to observe that bioethical evaluation – whether consequentialist or essentialist – ultimately engages the acuity of our intuitions, as well as that of our rationality. Neither is dispensable for a lived ethics. Moreover, doing right and doing good are not necessarily the same thing. Matters of affection and personal commitment are not marginal but key facets of the telos, or whole life, in which moral choices find meaning. There is more to these choices than obligations, and more to the telos than choices. In the domain of character, intuitions are rife in shaping views and conduct in the real world. Religions stake their claim on the human conscience not just where one encounters a difficult choice, but in the continuum of mind and habit. Islam is wedded quintessentially to character-in-action wherein the *umma* serves as the vehicle for practical ethics. The decree of the caliph ʿUmar (r. 634–44) that a community shared the burden of the fate of its poorer members expressed a civic ethos, while a plurality of *ṭarīqa*s came to embody solidarities of the spirit in personal as well as institutional action. The telos framing the acts or virtues of the individual and the community gives a central place to the notion of custodianship at several levels: the community as caretaker for its members, especially the disadvantaged (those disabled or indigent, orphaned or widowed); the individual as fiduciary for those in his/her charge; the human body itself as a charge on behalf of the Maker.

Underlying these is the Qur'anic bestowal of trust (*amāna*) and vicegerency (*khilāfa*) upon humankind with regard to the earth (Qur'ān 33:72; 35:39), for which the "inheritors" have the fullest accountability. This is no fall from grace into nature, as in Aquinas, but a quest that links our telos to ecological ethics in a context of justice. An extensive body of socio-economic and legal literature as well as practice has built on this foundation, touching on issues such as fair access to water, the husbanding of flora, fauna and soils, the proper treatment of animal life, and the aesthetics of public gardens. The notion of *ḥimā* (protected space) evolved from scripture and *ḥadīth* into an instrument of policy to create sanctuaries for forests, grazing and related environmental purposes in the public interest, parallel to the *ḥarām* (sacred space), which extended beyond places of worship to natural springs and wells, vulnerable plants and wastelands. Privileged status is accorded to gardens (*bustān, bagh*) as appendages to mosques, tombs and palaces as well as independent public refuges, celebrated from Moorish Spain to Mughal India as earthly reflections of paradise. These are not only symbolic or functional elements but entail recognition of intrinsic merit within the schema of natural balance and its counterpart in social justice. Hence the solemn rituals that must attend the licit slaughter of animals (*dhabḥ*) – and the injunctions that abound on their humane treatment. "Do not treat the back of your animals as pulpits, for God the most high has made them subject to you only to convey you to a place which you could not otherwise reach without much difficulty" (Haq 2001: 170–1) is exemplary; cats, sparrows, dogs and livestock feature in innumerable exhortations, leading to the *fiqh* rule making animal-owners liable for their well-being. Muḥammad's acute distress at seeing the branding of an animal's face and at the idea of blood sports finds its way into the normative corpus.

Stewardship today pervades the discourse on the environment and sustainable development, against the wider background of globalization and its mixed blessings. Secular and religious ways of approaching stewardship differ particularly when it comes to normative views of dominion over nature in Judeo-Christian traditions; but the emphasis on accountable trust in Muslim ethics narrows the discrepancy considerably. Commitments to ecological stewardship – and their parallels with respect to biomedical, corporate and other public practices – call attention to the nexus between ethical and legal orientation. Since tangible sanctions usually attach to the law as compared with the more voluntary nature of ethical codes, the willingness to legalize or otherwise make enforceable such commitments often becomes the criterion of "seriousness." This seems especially reasonable in the regulatory realm where effective protection of the public interest has primacy; equally, an appeal to that interest at the moral level is of obvious import for the law itself. Legislation to foster urban green spaces, or to ensure thresholds in the treatment of captive animals or the use of embryonic stem cells, relies on shared values beyond deference to the rule of law. Hence the assumption that the law reflects a society's ethos, signalling the obligations deemed most fundamental. Yet the profuse legalization of the public sphere can obscure the vitality of ethical life in its own right. For Muslims, the overlap of individual and public interest – indeed, of the individual as an extension not only of the *umma* but also a cosmic telos – is part of the principle of *ẓulm al-nafs*, of wrong to the other as injury to the self. As such, it lends a poignancy all its own to a commitment to particulars in taking ethics seriously.

Civility, humanism and governance

There is rich irony in today having to negotiate the nexus between ethics and civic culture past the currents and eddies of "secularism" and "religion," and not only in the Cartesian context of Western societies where this dualism has long prevailed amid the ascendancy of the secular. In the *Weltanschauung* of Islam, where the sacred and secular (*dīn* and *dunyā*) are merged – and in which some are inclined to subsume the state (*dawla*) – there is a different challenge. There is a tendency to conflate the *Weltanschauung* with the institutional arrangements of the polity, claiming that church and state are not "separable" in Islam. This would imply that civic life cannot accommodate a deep regard for the sacred amid such legal/political separation. The real problem has to do with the continuing pervasiveness in Muslim discourses of what Arkoun (1996: 117) calls a "moral totality validated entirely by divine teaching," which is given further public momentum by an attentive media.

In the classical age of Islam when the leading ethical texts were authored, drawing inspiration both from scripture and the philosophical heritage of the Mediterranean world at large, a moral critique of politics was not seen as a profaning of sacred norms. The pragmatic rationale for the "virtuous city" of al-Fārābī (d. 950) is the interdependence of human beings in pursuit of self-sufficiency and fulfillment, a voluntary quest that ultimately requires the social and spiritual aid of Islamic tenets. Moral traits (*akhlāq*) and habits (*adab*) were individual acquisitions with a social purpose, transcending the public–private divide. *Adab* as a code of dignity and social refinement had ancient roots in the Near and Middle East, into which Islam infused a conscious moral purpose. Miskawayh's *The Cultivation of Morals* (*Tahdhīb al-Akhlāq*), and its Persian-Shīʿī counterpart, *The Nasirean Ethics* (*Akhlāq-i Naṣīrī*) of al-Ṭūsī, drew conspicuously on Aristotle and neo-Platonist sources. Indeed, writings on ethics caught fire after the translation by Ibn Ḥunayn (d. 911) of the *Nicomachean Ethics*, on which Farabi was the first scholarly commentator in Arabic. The ethos of the Greek *polis* was subsumed into a new universe where integrity, courage, temperance, charity, justice and reason were virtues that made for individual happiness and the ideal *umma*. For al-Ghazālī in the *Criterion of Moral Action* (*Mīzān al-ʿamal*) the virtues found expression in the very process of moral reasoning.

That aspect of ethics, as furnishing a critique of political and individual conduct, was in contestation with the role of the enacted *sharīʿa*, itself derived from the moral framework of the Qur'ān and the *ḥadīth*. While al-Ghazālī was able to bring his considerable authority to bear in casting a skeptical eye on what he perceived as the ethical deficits of those wielding the enacted *sharīʿa*, the overarching historical trend was of the latter's dominion. The reasons ranged from the need for an authoritative corpus of law over a rapidly expanding Muslim empire, to the political conservatism of Arabia from around the eleventh century that led many jurists to affirm the "closure of the gate of *ijtihād* (independent legal reasoning)." The decline of *ijtihād* was accompanied by a pattern of compartmentalizing law and politics, so that the latter – *siyāsa* – became the domain of the caliph or sultan, as an exercise in kingship. The law, in all its potent civic and religious if not intellectual authority, was the domain of the *ʿulamāʾ* or religio-jurists.

Hence, the die was cast for the ruler to seek the collaboration of the *ʿulamāʾ* in an expedient arrangement: the former in pursuit of "religious" legitimacy, the latter for enhanced political influence. Although this did not preclude *ad hoc* ethical judgments by communities and individuals about the conduct of civic affairs through to the modern era, the sacralization of the law inevitably curtailed the scope, potency and systematization of such a critique. The potential of ethico-legal principles as *rationes legis* – generalized tenets that lent themselves to application in particular cases – was overshadowed by the spirit of *taqlīd*, an imitative compliance with a set of specific rules extracted from the manuals of various legal schools.

Since the sacralization of law enhances the legitimacy of political establishments that can invoke it for the exercise of their authority, the tension with those seeking civic accountability is obvious. The hallowed phrase *siyāsa sharīʿa* refers formally to the political and administrative facets of the law; but it also signals attempts at sacralizing political power. In post-revolutionary Iran, for example, the constitutional tenet of *Velāyat-e-Faqīh* (rule of the juriconsult) confers supra-democratic authority on the un-elected supreme religious leader and renders the clergy and their courts as guardians of the political process, including control over the media. On an even more pervasive level, civic life in Saudi Arabia has been stifled by conservative, intertwining princely and clerical institutions that claim religious legitimacy – and, ironically, face a still more conservative challenge on those very grounds of legitimacy. Elsewhere, the primacy of the *sharīʿa*, as interpreted by traditionalist establishments, operates to trump secular law and effectively circumscribe civic discourse, as witness recent developments in societies as diverse as Egypt and Pakistan, with regard to strictures on blasphemy, apostasy and gender equality.

All of this underscores the need to separate the institutions of state, religion and society, as a shared modern democratic and ethical imperative. That proposition was famously advanced in the 1920s by the Egyptian ʿAlī ʿAbd al-Rāziq (d. 1966), only to run into a wall of orthodox opposition. Yet far from violating Islam's *Weltanschauung*, this institutional separation is a means of advancing its civic spirit in practice, and builds on historical realities long manifest in Muslim experience. Secular culture in this respect is an ally rather than an antagonist of religious well-being, with social ethics serving as a bridge between the two in the public sphere. It is in this sense that Abdolkarim Soroush (see Sadri and Sadri 2000) advocates the secularization of ethics en route to modernity, abjuring the "ethics of the Gods" for "concrete and accessible rules" that admit of human frailty. Judging by the results of successive Iranian elections since the mid-1990s, in which ordinary citizens have repeatedly and overwhelmingly endorsed the most anti-clerical choices available, it is obvious that Soroush (a key supporter of the 1979 revolution) speaks to a deep disenchantment with theocratic claims over the public sphere. "Having freed themselves from the cordon of previously luminous ideologies," notes Mehrzad Boroujerdi (2001: 24), "many of Iran's intellectuals are now busy articulating serious and sophisticated criticisms of . . . authoritarianism, censorship, clientilism, cult of personality, etatism, fanaticism, influence peddling, partisanship, and violence."

Moreover, sacralizing the law provides no guarantee of the primacy of the rule of law as an institution, identified earlier as a vital element of civil society. Indeed, the argument can be made that sacralization actually undermines the rule of law, since both the content and the implementing institutions *ipso facto* operate outside the framework of democratic/civic accountability in all its contemporary pluralist complexity. It is tantamount to a foundationalist approach of the type explicitly rejected in the preceding segment. The more general problem of the weakness of the rule of law shared by emerging democracies – especially those in post-civil conflict transitions (like Afghanistan, Algeria, Bosnia, Indonesia, Iraq, Lebanon, Somalia, Sudan and Tajikistan) – only reinforces the ethical imperative. That is, public respect for social ethics acquires the burden not merely of supporting the rule of law, but of actively filling a normative as well as practical gap in the latter's absence or enfeebled condition.

Sociological data on citizen perceptions of civic life in Muslim-majority contexts are revealing on that score. Surveys indicate that on attitudes toward democratic ideals and disapproval of political strongmen, there is minimal difference between the Muslim world and the West (see Norris and Inglehart 2004). However, religious authorities receive stronger support in Muslim societies than in Western ones, though other types of society also support an active role for religious leaders in public life. On gender equality and sexual liberalization, there is a significant cleavage between conservative attitudes in the Muslim world and those in the West generally, including among younger generations. Even in relatively secular Turkey, according to another recent survey, where majorities of 78 to 85 percent oppose amending the civil code to accommodate *sharīʿa* norms concerning women, robust majorities favor prohibiting the sale of alcohol during Ramaḍān, allowing exclusively religious marriages, and modest public dressing by women (Carkoglu 2001: 29). There and elsewhere in the Muslim world, support for secular culture and religiously based social ethics is generally perceived as compatible and also desirable.

More broadly, a symbiotic nexus between law and social ethics is integral to the evolution of modern legal systems, and a seminal principle of Muslim ethics is respect for the rule of law. If transitional societies often draw upon their ethical heritage to compensate for the weakness of the rule of law, they may also need to do so in terms of solidarity and self-organization – the social capital of civic culture – especially necessary when state institutions are weak. Social capital is customarily seen as stemming from engaged citizenship, an elusive expectation in pre-democratic states. Legacies of authoritarian or communist regimes tend to vitiate citizen trust in public organizations and curtail associational life, at least among those who recall the experience of that past. On the other hand, social traditions relating to charitable endowments (*waqf*s), direct and institutional aid through religious tithes (*zakāt*) for the disadvantaged, and community-based schools (*madrasas*) have deep roots in Muslim praxis. Regional variants of these include the *maḥalla*s (neighborhood organizations) and *gap* (consultative groupings that include interest-free loan associations among women), as well as other indigenous networks whose critical role in post-Soviet Central Asia has been well documented.

What is discomfiting about religiously inspired ethical critiques from a statist perspective, of course, is their capacity to appeal to sources of legitimacy beyond the democratic framework of the modern polity, especially in transitional contexts when the state's democratic credentials have yet to be fully established. Freedom of the media, judicial independence, clean elections and the probity of public finances, along with secessionist movements and the role of the military, are issues that can profoundly undercut claims to democratic legitimacy. In these circumstances, political accountability may be elicited through appeals to the *sharīʿa*, as has occurred in Afghanistan, Algeria, Iran, Sudan and, to a lesser degree, in Nigeria. The results for individual liberty and civil society have often been disastrous, because of the sundering of the *sharīʿa* from its ethical roots.

Still, secular citizenries are cognizant of the civic value of Muslim ethical precepts, including normative expectations of financial probity and consultative policy-making. To the value of social ethics as a compensatory buffer against the frailty of the rule of law and of formal citizenship in transitional states can be added its prospective role in fostering public accountability and participatory politics. In states where the primacy of the *sharīʿa* curtails democratic avenues of accountability and participation, an ethical critique may effectively be the only available means to challenge the clerical establishment. This has typically been the case at various stages in post-revolutionary Iran, notably with regard to the contest between reformists and conservatives on the status of women. By grounding challenges to male-dominated readings of the *sharīʿa* in wider Muslim notions of social equity and solidarity, Iranian intellectuals and activists have acquired a platform with a competing claim to legitimacy. Thence, such platforms can bridge appeals to more universal norms of human rights and pluralism that would not otherwise get a hearing in such theocratic contexts. Iranian women, for instance, have been actively engaged in United Nations conferences on gender equality – and not merely to influence the latter in favor of conservative interpretations of international human rights law. Rather, progressive global agendas can find expression in otherwise hostile territory through legitimate indigenous actors.

Maps of moral order

If social ethics have an empowering role to play for assorted Muslim publics, they can offer crucial restraints, not only as proto-rule-of-law but also as a compass for appropriate means to respond to and foster change. The very notion of a civil society is grounded in opposition to uncivil conduct, involving not only disrespect for the rule of law but also the absence of comity and nonviolence. Indeed, democratic orders alone offer no assurance of civility, as instanced by the violent twentieth-century histories of both eastern and western European states. Taming the impulses of incivility is a precondition for civil society that enjoys a distinct ethical status. Within a Muslim ethos, this expectation is not merely a pragmatic or functional one but also, in the Kantian sense, moral.

Applied in the context of transitions to democracy, amidst the pressures of new global economic and political forces, change rather than continuity is the norm. The pace and radical quality of that change may be perceived as a deliberate assault on indigenous values. On occasion, the assault is physical, when politico-economic establishments use the security apparatus of the state to stifle dissent and protest, or to deny the exercise of the right to collective self-determination. The responses by citizens and groups are often also violent, with the rationales drawing on a religious vocabulary. "Islam" is readily harnessed as a legitimating discourse and ideology that privileges opposition to social, political and economic injustice, while its clear proscriptions against violent reaction are simply discarded. In self-reinforcing cycles of militancy – epitomized by the tragic recent histories of Algeria, Afghanistan and Palestine – the result is to profoundly debilitate the public sphere.

The events of September 11, 2001, and their fallout serve to underscore graphically those patterns of civic subversion. In this political climate, normative frameworks like those of international human rights that outlaw the use of violence to advance claims of justice can be resisted (if not dismissed) *qua* ideologies emanating from the same Western establishments that collaborate with oppressive governments in the Muslim world. This also applies *a fortiori* with regard to transnational criminal law directed at terrorism. Hence, invoking ethical injunctions against violence becomes imperative. I am not, of course, suggesting that such injunctions are a substitute for the rule of law as *cordon sanitaire* for civic culture. Rather, the latter must be an integral part of the revival of dialogical, nonviolent politics as the prevailing ethos.

There is no dearth of Islamic tradition and authority in this regard. "Whoever slays an innocent soul . . . it is as though he slays all of humanity," is an oft-quoted Qur'anic verse (5:32). Muslims are forbidden from initiating hostilities, and warned when taking up arms in self-defense to "not transgress limits" (Qur'ān 2:190). The rationale for *jihād* was to limit the legitimacy of warfare to preserving the loftiest moral values (Qur'ān 4:75; 22:40), not to provide an alibi for the discontented. Those moral values could never, for example, include forced conversion: "There must be no coercion in matters of faith!" (Qur'ān 2: 256). Ideologues who claim that Muslims are enjoined to "slay [enemies] wherever you find them!" (Qur'ān 4:89) tend to overlook not only the defensive context, but also the fact that the same verses insist that if the enemy ceases hostilities, "God does not allow you to harm them" (Qur'ān 4:90). Repeatedly, Muslims are urged to abjure revenge (Qur'ān 5:45; 2:192, 193), and to iterate "Peace" in response to provocation from the ignorant (25:63). The *ḥadīth* cherish an even disposition, as in the sentiment: "The most worthy of you is one who controls himself in anger" (cited in Donaldson 1953: 70).

A key underlying principle, noted earlier, is that an act that violates "the bounds" amounts, in the final analysis, to an injury against the self (*ẓulm al-nafs*). The individual is made inseparable from the other, the natural and social context in which he is entwined with community and cosmic home alike. This finds concrete expression in the ethos of inclusiveness, compassion and reason conveyed by *ḥilm* (derived from *al-Ḥalīm*, one of God's scriptural names and attributes), that even non-Muslim scholars have seen as definitive of Islam. Izutsu sees it thus:

> In a certain sense the Koran as a whole is dominated by the very spirit of *ḥilm*. The constant exhortation to kindness (*iḥsān*) in human relations, the emphasis laid on justice (*ʿadl*), the forbidding of wrongful violence (*ẓulm*), the bidding of abstinence and control of passions, the criticism of groundless pride and arrogance – all are concrete manifestations of this spirit of *ḥilm*.
>
> (Izutsu 1964: 216)

In this vein, there ensues a convergence of individual and communal, private and public notions of rectitude. The idea of the *umma* becomes the embodiment of ethical affinity, bridging the sacred and the secular. The ethos at hand is one of principled embrace of civility (as befits a religiously motivated outlook), which is to be distinguished from a mere tactical adoption of nonviolence (guided by expedient judgment that an adversary can be more effectively dealt with by such means). Recourse to self-serving, decontextualized quotation from scripture and prophetic tradition in support of political agendas whose legitimacy beggars the sanction of reason, revelation or civility, is not peculiar to the Muslim world. That such claims appeal to the socially and politically disenchanted is testimony to their ability to integrate themselves into the social imaginaries that undergird identities. This is endemic to an approach that focuses on a notion of "origins" that subsumes multiple affinities to a single dominant identity under an imagined unity. Such frameworks of identity can only be meaningful if they are integrative, capable of absorbing new ideas and evolving along the way. This brings us full circle to the need to conceive of ethics as moral reasoning, rather than normative rule-making and compliance, or the slave of an instrumental reason that denies the sacred on the basis of an ideological construction of rationality. The burden of such a revival must fall ultimately on the intelligentsia, whose need for spaces of freedom underscores, in turn, the primacy of a civil society.

The world's 1.5 billion Muslims are diverse in their cultures and understandings of Islam. But they share a *Weltanschauung* in which *dīn* and *dunyā* (but not the modern *dawla*) are merged, so that both secular and sacred resonate in the public domain. Far from precluding the institutional separation of mosque and state, this perspective takes no ideological position in that regard: the *umma* can thrive in a plurality of political arrangements. In other words, the occidental liberal conception of civil society is not inimical to Muslim traditions simply because it is wedded to secular space. On the contrary, the primacy of the rule of law, participatory politics, and the integrity of individual membership in a pluralist community are values cherished by both traditions. However, a radical secularity that banishes social ethics from the public sphere is patently inimical to Muslim society, for the moral orientation of individual and *umma* alike are privileged as public as well as private goals. Such a banishment also amounts to squandering potential social capital in the form of citizen-public trust, which enables associational life and civic culture to flourish. Yet there is more than instrumental value in espousing social ethics that have a religious grounding: there is also the critical dimension of moral capital, for all its seeming dissonance in the secular liberal mind. Therein arguably lies the scope to enhance motivation in taking civility seriously – amounting to a deeper regard for the other that individual rights and civic identity alone cannot furnish.

Pluralism – of life-goals and culture – as well as the capacity of modern states to abuse power, suggest that ethical frameworks should be bounded by principles of democratic and civic commitment, including human rights. For all the cultural anomie that is said to afflict Muslim elites in this age of anxiety, it is true that civic life is unlikely to be enhanced by theologically led invocations of political or social authority. As well, the rigidities of traditionalism that can reduce ethics to the minutiae of law call for resistance.

If Muslim ethics are to occupy a salient position in the civitas, the veins of moral reasoning need to be tapped beyond turning scripture into ideology. This resonates deeply with the idea of discourse ethics as the ideal of the public religion of civil society, where citizens engage in reasoned deliberation on quotidian moral issues. On this basis, the issue of political violence would be confronted in the public square, setting the limits of what is acceptable even in response to injustice, when the result is a rupturing of civility and social order in which the *umma* has its being. Certainly, the interdependence of individuals and societies demands an ethos whose frontiers are global and require integrative quests in the civitas. But ecumenicalism cannot dispense with the need to draw upon and evolve indigenous cultural-religious traditions. For the latter impart incision and substance to the ever-thinning identities and ethical frames of reference of our postmodern age.

References and further reading

Abou El Fadl, K. (2002) *The Place of Tolerance in Islam*, J. Cohen, I. Lague, eds., Boston: Beacon Press.

An-Na'im, A. (1990) *Toward an Islamic Reformation: Civil Liberties, Human Rights and International Law*, Syracuse: Syracuse University Press.

—— (2001) "The Synergy and Interdependence of Human Rights, Religion and Secularism," *Polylog* (Online) 2:1; available online at http://www.polylog.org/them/2.1/fcs7-en.htm.

Arkoun, M. (1996) "Ethics and Politics," in M. Arkoun, *Rethinking Islam*, Boulder, CO: Westview Press, 114–20.

Asad, T. (2003) *Formations of the Secular: Christianity, Islam, Modernity*, Stanford: Stanford University Press.

Boroujerdi, M. (2001) "The Paradoxes of Politics in Postrevolutionary Iran," in J. L. Esposito, R. K. Ramadani, eds., *Iran at the Crossroads*, New York: Palgrave, 13–27.

Brockopp, J., ed. (2003) *Islamic Ethics of Life: Abortion, War, and Euthanasia*, Columbia: University of South Carolina Press.

Carkoglu, A. (2001) "Religion and Public Policy in Turkey" (Report on Political Islam in Turkey Project), *Institute for the Study of Islam in the Modern World (ISIM) Newsletter* 8: 29.

Clarfield, A. M., Gordon, M., Markwell, H. and Alibhai, S. (2003) "Ethical Issues in End-of-Life Geriatric Care: The Approach of Three Monotheistic Religions – Judaism, Catholicism, and Islam," *Journal of the American Geriatric Society*, 51: 1149–54.

Cook, M. (2001) *Commanding Right and Forbidding Wrong in Islamic Thought*, Cambridge: Cambridge University Press.

Cornell, V. (1999) "From Shariah to Taqwa," in J. L. Esposito, ed., *The Oxford History of Islam*, Oxford: Oxford University Press, 95–105.

Daar, A. S. (1994) "Xenotransplantation and Religion: The Major Monotheistic Religions," *Xeno*, 2: 61–4.

Daar, A. S. and Khitamy, A. (2001) "Islamic Bioethics" (Bioethics for Clinicians Series), *Canadian Medical Association Journal*, 164 (1): 60–3; available online at www.cmaj.ca/cgi/reprint/164/1/60.

Dallal, A. (1999) "Science, Medicine and Technology," in J. L. Esposito, ed., *The Oxford History of Islam*, Oxford: Oxford University Press, 155–213.

Deen, M. Y. I. (1990) "Islamic Environmental Ethics," in J. R. Engel, J. G. Engel, eds., *Ethics of Environment and Development: Global Challenge, International Response*, Tucson: University of Arizona Press, 189–98.

Donaldson, D. M. (1953) *Studies in Muslim Ethics*, London: Luzac.

Draz, M. A. (2002) *The Moral World of the Qur'an*, London: I. B. Tauris.

Esmail, A. (2002) "Self, Society, Civility and Islam," in A. B. Sajoo, ed., *Civil Society in the Muslim World*, London: I. B. Tauris, 61–94.

Fakhry, M. (1994) *Ethical Theories in Islam*, Leiden: E. J. Brill.

Haq, S. N. (2001) "Islam and Ecology: Toward Retrieval and Reconstruction," *Daedalus*, 130 (4): 141–78.

Hashmi, S. H., ed. (2002) *Islamic Political Ethics: Civil Society, Pluralism and Conflict*, Princeton: Princeton University Press.

Hourani, G. (1985) *Reason and Tradition in Islamic Ethics*, Cambridge: Cambridge University Press.

Hovannisian, R. G., ed. (1985) *Ethics in Islam*, Malibu, CA: Undena Publications.

Izutsu, T. (1964) *God and Man in the Koran: Semantics of the Koranic Weltanschauung*, Tokyo: The Keio Institute of Cultural and Linguistic Studies.

—— (2002) *Ethico-Religious Concepts in the Qur'ān*, Montreal: McGill-Queens University Press.

Johansen, B. (1999) *Contingency in a Sacred Law: Legal and Ethical Norms in the Muslim Fiqh*, Leiden: Brill.

Kamali, M. H. (1999) "Law and Society: The Interplay of Revelation and Reason in the Shariah," in J. L. Esposito, ed., *The Oxford History of Islam*, Oxford: Oxford University Press, 107–53.

Keddie, N. (2003) "Secularization and its Discontents," *Daedalus*, 132 (3): 14–30.

Kelsay, J. (1993) *Islam and War: A Study in Comparative Ethics*, Louisville, KY: Westminster John Knox Press.

Maguire, D. C. (2001) *Sacred Choices: The Right to Contraception and Abortion in Ten World Religions*, Minneapolis, MN: Augsburg Fortress Publishers.

Masud, M. K. (1995) *Shatibi's Philosophy of Islamic Law*, Islamabad: Islamic Research Institute.

Mayer, A. E. (1995) *Islam and Human Rights: Tradition and Politics*, 2nd edition, Boulder, CO: Westview Press.

Metcalf, B., ed. (1984) *Moral Conduct and Authority: The Place of Adab in South Asian Islam*, Berkeley: University of California Press.

Nanji, A. (1996) "The Ethical Tradition in Islam," in A. Nanji, ed., *The Muslim Almanac*, New York: Thomson Gale, 205–11.

Nasr, S. H. (1992) "Islam and the Environmental Crisis," in S. Rockefeller, J. Elder, eds., *Spirit and Nature: Why the Environment is a Religious Issue*, Boston: Beacon Press, 83–108.

Norris, P. and Inglehart, R. (2004) "Religion and Politics in the Muslim World," in P. Norris, R. Inglehart, *Sacred and Secular: Religion and Politics Worldwide*, Cambridge: Cambridge University Press, 133–58.

Ozdalga, E. and Persson, S., eds. (1997) *Civil Society, Democracy and the Muslim World*, Istanbul: Swedish Research Institute in Istanbul.

Rahman, F. (1982) *Islam and Modernity: Transformation of an Intellectual Tradition*, Chicago: University of Chicago Press.

Rispler-Chaim, V. (1993) *Islamic Medical Ethics in the Twentieth Century*, Leiden: E. J. Brill.

Runzo, J. and Martin, N. M., eds. (2001) *Ethics in the World Religions*, Oxford: Oneworld.

Sachedina, A. (2000) "Islamic Perspectives on Research with Human Embryonic Stem Cells," in *Ethical Issues in Human Stem Cell Research, Religious Perspectives*, Rockville, MA: National Bioethics Advisory Commission, 3, G1-G6.

Sadri, M. and Sadri, A., eds. (2000) *Reason, Freedom and Democracy in Islam: Essential Writings of Abdolkarim Soroush*, Oxford: Oxford University Press.

Sajoo, A. B. (1994) *Pluralism in Old Societies and New States*, Singapore: Institute of Southeast Asian Studies.

—— (2002) *Muslim Ethics: Emerging Vistas*, London: I. B. Tauris.

Tamimi, A. and Esposito, J. L., eds. (2000) *Islam and Secularism in the Middle East*, New York: New York University Press.
Tibi, B. (2001) *Islam between Culture and Politics*, New York: Palgrave Macmillan.
Ṭūsī, Naṣīr al-Dīn al- (1964) *Akhlāq-i-Naṣīrī* (Nasirean Ethics), trans. G. M. Wickens, London: Allen and Unwin.
United Nations Development Program (2002) "Liberating Human Capabilities: Governance, Human Development and the Arab World," *Arab Human Development Report 2002: Creating Opportunities for Future Generations*, New York: United Nations Development Program, 105–20.
Walzer, R. (1985) *Al-Farabi on the Perfect State*, Oxford: Oxford University Press.
Zubaida, S. (2003) *Law and Power in the Islamic World*, London: I. B. Tauris.

47

MARRIAGE, FAMILY, AND SEXUAL ETHICS

Kecia Ali

Despite the seemingly inexhaustible appetite among Muslim and non-Muslim audiences for information about "Islam and women," "Muslim women's status," and "the woman question in Islam," it is very difficult to generalize about the hundreds of millions of Muslim women living at the turn of the twenty-first century. Muslim women's life circumstances tend to closely parallel those of non-Muslims with similar backgrounds; a poor Indian Muslim villager has more in common with her rural Hindu counterpart than with a career woman in Mumbai who happens to be her co-religionist. Put simply, economic, geographic, and social factors do more to shape the circumstances of Muslim women's lives than religion.

Yet despite an undeniable diversity of life patterns among Muslim women, the proper gendered organization of social, familial, and sexual life is a central topic of debate for Muslim thinkers, policy-makers, and ordinary individuals across the Islamic world and among Muslims living as minorities elsewhere. Matters such as sex-segregation, female appearance in public space, and family law are at the forefront of public consciousness, and religion takes pride of place in discussions of these topics. In the contemporary Islamic world, debates over sexual ethics are both inseparable from broader debates over women's appropriate social roles and also deeply intertwined with concerns over Western influence and Islamic authenticity. The preoccupation with women and sex derives in part from a shared defensive response to negative Western stereotypes of Islam that have come to center on Muslim gender norms. Concern with "women's status" appears at the core of both reformist and conservative discourses in contemporary Muslim societies, and has become a proxy for other measures of social health, vitality, and progress.

The complex and multifaceted relationship between Islam and modernity is embedded in postcolonial political and social contexts throughout the Islamic world. The struggle over what constitutes an appropriate configuration of sexual ethics manifests itself in rhetoric about morality and debauchery, often presented as Western afflictions that Muslims must avoid, and in campaigns to implement or reform Islamic family law (An-Na'im 2002). Islamist activists portray *sharīʿa* as the last bulwark of Muslim life and society against threatened decadence from the West; ordinary Muslims, particularly those living in economically highly stratified and politically repressive societies, understand *sharīʿa* to embody justice without necessarily linking it to specific policy objectives. The parties in these debates often appeal to (supposedly) traditional gender roles and the timeless essence of "real" or "true" Islam, although the ways in which matters of family and sexual ethics are discussed today depart from the foundational texts of Qur'ān and *sunna* and the medieval scholarly heritage in significant ways (Ali 2003; Stowasser 1993). Despite these shifts, everyone from Muslim feminists to neo-traditionalist pundits to members of the *ʿulamāʾ* continues to grapple with canonical texts as they attempt to shape the ideals and realities governing Muslims' intimate lives.

Classical texts and contexts: history, scripture, and law

Before turning to modern legal reform and public discourses on matters of sexual ethics, it is important to briefly survey the treatment of marriage and sexual ethics in the classical textual tradition and in pre-modern legal thought. The Qur'ān speaks eloquently of marriage and its cosmic, emotional, and legal dimensions. Marriage and procreation organize the created world; kinship ties create mutual bonds of obligation and affection. Within the marital relationship, where spouses are described as like "garments" for one another (Qur'ān 2:187), God has "placed love and mercy" between spouses, who are to "dwell together" or find "rest" or "tranquility" in one another (30:21); they are in fact created for one another (4:1; 7:189). Marriage is both a "solemn covenant" (Qur'ān 4:21) and also a contract with mundane interpersonal consequences. Husbands and wives have rights and obligations, differentiated by gender, although husbands are given a privileged role of both authority and responsibility (Qur'ān 2:228; 4:34, 128).

One crucial element of male responsibility is the obligation of support; men support women (Qur'ān 4:34) and owe them "compensation" or "reward" (*ajr*) for what they "enjoy from them" (4:24). Some of the Shīʿa take this to be a reference to compensation provided in *mutʿa*, a marriage contracted for a fixed time period (and which Sunnīs have rejected), but Sunnīs usually understand it as dower (*mahr* or *ṣadāq*), which Qur'ān 4:4 declares "a free gift" and which has been an important source of wealth for women in many pre-modern societies. The dower, which is the wife's exclusive property, likely modifies pre-Islamic Arab patterns of property exchange at marriage, perhaps replacing compensation paid to a bride's father or tribe. Little can be known for certain of pre-Islamic marriage patterns because the later Muslim sources are generally polemical. One must be wary of claims that the coming of Islam drastically improved women's status; it is likely that it did in some ways, for some women, while restricting the options available to others (Ahmed 1992).

Marriage in the seventh century and thereafter was very much a family affair; kin were involved in most marital arrangements, particularly those of children of either sex – such marriages were usually consummated around puberty – or adult females. A number of Qur'anic verses, for example Qur'ān 2:221, have women "married off" rather than "marrying" and this practice is confirmed in the *ḥadīth* sources; the majority of legal schools – the Shīʿa and the Ḥanafī being exceptions – required a woman's marriage guardian (*walī*), usually her father or brother, to contract marriage on her behalf. Both the Qur'ān and early Muslims were ambivalent about the importance of lineage and status, assuming certain hierarchies such as free over enslaved while at the same time denying them any value for assessing the true worth of a human being (Qur'ān 49:13). Some jurists viewed social parity (*kafāʾa*) as an important criterion for valid marriage, while others largely disregarded it. In any case, parity required only that the man be the woman's equal in terms of descent, wealth, occupation (as measured against her father), and/or piety; a male was free to marry beneath himself.

Other marriage prohibitions could arise due to kinship (of blood, affinity, or "milk," the latter meaning a foster relationship created by wet-nursing, Qur'ān 4:22–4) or marital status: a married woman cannot be a lawful spouse for another man (4:24), and a man is limited in his number of wives to four (4:3). As for marriage across religious boundaries, Qur'ān 2:221 forbids marriage to idolators (*mushrikūn*) for both male and female Muslims. Qur'ān 60:10 declares that the unbelieving (*kuffār*) husbands of refugee converted women are not lawful spouses for them. Qur'ān 5:5 makes both the food of the People of the Book and marriage to their women permissible, although Sunnī jurists have historically viewed such unions as undesirable at best and Shīʿī doctrine generally rejects them outright. Muslim women's marriage to Jewish or Christian men has been nearly universally forbidden. Children born of any mixed union are considered Muslim.

One of the critical functions of marriage is to make progeny legitimate. It shares this trait with concubinage, the right of a male owner to have sex with his own female slaves, whom the Qur'ān refers to as "what their right hands possess" (Qur'ān 23:5–6; 70:29–30). The Qur'ān is vague about many details of slave ownership but subsequent generations of legal authorities elaborated on the rules for acquiring slaves and especially slave concubines both through capture in war and by commerce. Eventually, authorities agreed that a slave who bore a child to her master would become an *umm walad* (literally "mother of a child"), meaning she could not be sold and would be manumitted at his death; if not disavowed by the father, the child would be free from birth and of equal status as an heir to children born to a free wife. Later thinkers cited Muḥammad's precedent in freeing his Coptic slave Māriya, a gift from the governor of Egypt, after she gave birth to a son, Ibrāhīm, who died in infancy. In royal courts of the Abbasid times, concubinage developed into a finely honed institution, with female slaves, as well as some male ones, serving as entertainers as well as sexual partners. Paradoxically, enslaved women could become influential figures. In the Ottoman royal household, generations of rulers were born not to wives but to the sultans' "favorites" (Peirce 1993). Concubinage was not limited to royalty but existed in elite households as well. Hudā Shaʿrāwī (1879–1947), co-founder and first president of the Egyptian Feminist Union, was the daughter of a Circassian concubine. Concubinage became illegal throughout the Muslim world with the abolition of slavery from the late nineteenth century through the mid-twentieth century.

Like dower and concubinage, divorce by repudiation (*ṭalāq*) was a pre-Islamic Arab custom that was modified, first by the Qur'ān and then by the legal tradition. As with dower, the scriptural changes are thought to have improved women's standing, by restricting the number of times a husband could repudiate and reclaim his wife. And as with concubinage, *ṭalāq* reflected male privilege, giving a man greater say in dissolving or maintaining his marriage; a wife had to compensate her husband through *khulʿ* if she wanted to end her marriage. The jurists regarded *khulʿ* as impermissible without the husband's agreement, but allowed for judicial dissolution at the wife's behest on various grounds, which could range from fairly broad (abandonment, non-support, serious communicable illness, abuse) to quite narrow (total impotence preventing consummation of the marriage). A couple of Qur'anic verses recommend reconciliation mechanisms for spousal conflict (arbiters in Qur'ān 4:35 or settlement in 4:129) and a few famous *ḥadīth* discourage divorce of all types: "Of all things permitted, *ṭalāq* is the most repugnant to God" stands with traditions invoking curses on women who seek divorce for compensation, *khulʿ*, without legitimate reason. Nonetheless, no real stigma attached to divorce among early Muslims and remarriage for divorced (and widowed) men and women has been common in most Muslim societies. Although studies of dower amounts in marriage contracts for diverse historical locations reveal a virginity premium, a bride's social status generally meant more in determining dower amount than whether it was her first marriage.

The jurists' discussions of mutually interdependent spousal claims assumed a husband's dominance over his wife in a number of respects beyond what was clearly articulated in the Qur'ān: he had the right to control her movements outside the household, expect her sexual availability, and limit her social interactions. Yet the assumption of wifely subordination was tempered even within the legal treatises by the acknowledgment that a woman's duty to obey God always took precedence over her duty to obey her husband. Moreover, discussion of strategies to restrict male prerogatives of polygamy or to guarantee a wife the right to remain in her hometown, visit her family, or have the right to opt for divorce herself under certain circumstances attest to the ways that gendered obligations were negotiated. Notably, opinion about including conditions to secure these rights in marriage contracts varied widely; the moralistic scholar Ibn Ḥanbal (d. 855) presents them as praiseworthy insofar as they sought to protect women, while the roughly contemporaneous *Kitāb al-ḥujja*, a Ḥanafī text, at times seems to advise men how to wriggle out of improperly constructed stipulations.

Court practice and modern legal change

The law as conceived and enforced was unabashedly patriarchal in numerous respects, assuming men's greater rights as fathers and husbands in relation to mothers and wives. Yet archival research, especially for the Ottoman period where sources are plentiful, shows that Muslim women often maneuvered around doctrinal constraints. They put stipulations in marriage contracts and enforced them, obtained divorces against the odds, and maintained custody of their children when dominant legal views dictated otherwise (Sonbol 1996). For instance, the official Ottoman Ḥanafī school allowed virtually no grounds for women to obtain judicial divorce after consummation. Yet in seventeenth-century Syria and Palestine, women who sought judicial divorce on grounds of non-support usually received it. Although the Ḥanafī judges could not pronounce a divorce in case of poverty or abandonment, they could arrange for the appointment of a deputy judge from another *madhhab* – in Judith Tucker's terms, a "pinch hitter" – to oversee the case, and in Ottoman Nablus, Damascus, and Jerusalem, often did so (Tucker 1998: 84). More generally, court records, including some papyrus documents from eighth to tenth-century Egypt, show that female-initiated divorce was relatively commonplace (though undoubtedly overrepresented in the sources, as *ṭalāq* was extrajudicial and would only require judicial intervention if there were issues with property settlements or custody) (Rapoport 2005). Not surprisingly, women in all eras were more likely to initiate divorce when they were financially self-sufficient. Independent property ownership – married women continued to have separate legal personalities, and elite women could transact business through agents even if they remained secluded – was one determining element of Muslim women's lives. Maya Shatzmiller's observation about fifteenth-century Granada applies more broadly: women's "property rights" were "central to the conjugal relationship" and "mitigated the negative effects of patriarchy" (Shatzmiller 2007: 197).

In the waning years of colonialism, Islamic law in its various forms was largely displaced by secular legislation. Though ultimately the least affected area, laws governing family life also underwent significant shifts, both codification and modification. Beginning with the Ottoman Majalla in the late nineteenth century, legal codes modeled on European laws were put into place in numerous nations. Although some notions of women's rights were circulating in the post-Enlightenment West, these European laws took for granted key principles of male dominance within the family, such as the role of husband/father as head of household. These codes did not simply document existing rulings but also restructured, altered, and eventually reformed laws on matters from inheritance to polygamy. Legislative change relied on two main methods: "selection" (*takhayyur*) and "patching together" (*talfīq*). Selection refers to adopting a legal rule from a school other than the one on which a country's laws were based. Patching together refers to a more extensive reconfiguration process where elements from various schools, or from minority opinions within the schools, were put together, creating a new doctrine. Using these strategies, Ḥanafī jurisdictions such as Egypt and India adopted elements of the more extensive Mālikī grounds for judicial divorce (Esposito with DeLong-Bas 2001).

Codification went along with increased control by the nation-state and modernizing reforms, both substantive and procedural, which were not necessarily grounded in classical legal doctrine. Common reforms included the imposition of minimum marriage ages for girls and the requirement – often flouted in practice – of registration for all marriages and divorces. Restricting male prerogatives in divorce and polygamy has proved challenging, but increased female access to divorce has been more easily obtained. The codes themselves, ironically, had diminished the judicial flexibility which had in the past provided women avenues to obtain divorces that were theoretically not permitted. Struggles to pass further reforms, usually in more egalitarian directions, continue; transnational coalitions such as "Women Living under Muslim Laws" and local organizations such as the Malaysian group "Sisters in Islam" have tried to both enact further reforms, such as allowing for mothers to exercise guardianship as well as custody of children, and stem a rising tide of demands for Islamization of the law.

The implementation of *sharīʿa* – often functionally reduced to *ḥadd* punishments, marriage and divorce, and inheritance – has become the key demand of Islamist movements but it has also been used strategically by governments seeking to shore up their popular support and demonstrate their religious credentials. In the colonial and post-colonial era, the role of Islamic law in society has become central to larger debates about political structure and governance in many countries with Muslim majority populations, particularly in the Middle East and North Africa. At the same time women's status has come to be seen as an index of civilization. The merging of the two areas of concern in Islamic family law has made it an irresistible focus for identity politics. Parties with contradictory aims each try to lay claim to *sharīʿa*, defining justice in their own terms. Lama Abu-Odeh (2004) has argued that attempts by liberal feminists to reform family laws in Egypt to grant women greater equality were hampered by the unwillingness of many to relinquish the remaining religiously informed law in favor of complete secularization; perhaps paradoxically, she argues that the acceptance of a broader Islamization project for the Egyptian legal system allows for liberal feminist goals to be reframed and potentially accepted. Likewise, the Moroccan Moudawwana reform of 2003 – which among other changes removed the requirement that women be represented by a male marriage guardian, made headship of the family equal, and further restricted polygamy – used religious language to argue for new rules as manifestations of Islamic principles of justice and equality. One other shift in language is also noteworthy: the Moroccan activists campaigned for the law in Arabic rather than French, a tactical move that contributed in some measure to the victory.

Prior to this successful campaign, there was in Morocco, as elsewhere in the Islamic world, a conflict of both ideals and strategy among women's rights activists. Through much of the second half of the twentieth century, liberal feminists committed to secular legal norms and universal human rights standards argued that Islam was incompatible with equal rights for women in the family and society. Other activists argued for the need to couch arguments for reform in religious language, either to make them acceptable to a broader segment of the population or because they identified gender justice as best achieved through a religious framework. Polarizing rhetoric occasionally paints this as an irreconcilable conflict between the Qurʾān and the United Nations "Convention on the Elimination of all Forms of Discrimination against Women" (CEDAW). Still, most participants in these debates offer some attempt at reconciling the two, just as most Muslim nations, including Saudi Arabia, have passed CEDAW, albeit with reservations.

The cases of India and Iran illustrate the variety of dynamics involved in legal codification, reform, Islamization, and more significant reconceptualization of what Islamic law means. In Iran, the clerical government that took power after the 1979 revolution overturned the 1967 Family Protection Act which had made divorce judicial and raised the age of marriage for females; Jaʿfarī jurisprudence became again the basis for judicial practice, lowering the age for girls' marriage to nine years (with paternal consent), allowing free rein to unilateral male repudiation (*ṭalāq*), and reinstituting unequal compensation for male and female injury. These actions provoked harsh criticism from Iranian women, who were harshly suppressed, and international women's rights activists, who were largely ignored. Eventually, Ziba Mir-Hosseini (1999) has argued, the injustice of these rules – which claimed to be Islamic and therefore just – generated widespread popular opposition as well as reasoned dissent from within the religious establishment in Iran. In the second and third decades of Islamic rule, legislation has been passed that removes some of these discriminations. *Ṭalāq* remains possible but has been hedged in with certain restrictions, and the law upholds the right of women repudiated without cause to be compensated for household services provided during the course of a marriage.

Issues of religiously legitimate law arise as well in countries that do not purport to be Islamic. An Indian case from the mid-1980s illustrates the tensions between religious and civil law in one pluralist society. Shah Bano was an elderly woman, divorced by her long-time husband. According to India's Muslim personal law, based on modified Ḥanafī jurisprudence, she was entitled only to her deferred dower, worth nearly nothing after decades of inflation, and three months of post-marital support. Supported by some non-Muslim women's rights activists, in 1985 she petitioned for the alimony she would be due under India's civil code, igniting long-simmering tensions over a uniform civil law. In the ensuing debates, Islamic family law was upheld by many Muslim activists as inherently superior to secular laws, uniquely suited to protect and provide for women, notwithstanding the obvious injustice of Shah Bano's predicament; opponents used the opportunity to denigrate Islam. The Protection of Muslim Women's Rights on Divorce Act (1986) that was eventually passed limited the husband's liability to the post-marital waiting period, with the exception of an unspecified "provision" he must make for her. It stressed the right of Muslim females to be provided for by male relations but, affirming again the religious separateness of Muslims, placed the notoriously inefficient charity-trust (*waqf*) system in the role of guarantor for otherwise indigent women.

Modern discourses: neo-traditionalism and Muslim feminisms

Shah Bano's case clearly illustrates the way Islamic law functions as a key terrain on which issues of identity are contested, reinforcing the role of women and gender as the essential locus for contests over religious authenticity. In India, the debate was between a religious and a secular law. In Iran, the combination of an almost exclusively Muslim populace and an avowedly religious legal system meant, as Mir-Hosseini (1999) has pointed out, that a purely civil law has not been an option. Iranian reformists and conservatives framed their arguments in religious terms, advocating particular positions as most in keeping with specific provisions of jurisprudence or general principles of Islam. In both societies, however, the rhetoric used by even those claiming the mantle of traditionalism is profoundly affected by modern assumptions about the family and women's place within it.

The nuclear family lies at the core of neo-traditionalist discourses. The notion that the family unit is the basis of the wholesome Muslim social structure echoes Qur'anic statements about the role of lineage and procreation in creating ties of interdependence among kin. Yet Victorian domestic imagery, portraying women as emotional and fragile as well as uniquely suited for childcare and homemaking, inflects much modern Muslim thought on marriage, sex, and women. These features are pervasive in contemporary Muslim discourses despite their absence from classical Muslim texts (Abugideiri 2004; Ali 2003). In modern texts, men and women are described in terms of complementarity rather than superiority and inferiority (Stowasser 1993). Nonetheless, complementarity for many Muslim thinkers is compatible with hierarchy. Modern conservatives, unlike their medieval counterparts, often deem it necessary to defend their views of women's rights and roles; they do so by asserting that gender difference means that men and women can have different rights and roles without inequality or injustice. Often, the resulting claims respond to real or imagined critics; in a clear rejoinder to Western claims of Muslim women's oppression, apologists adopt the terminology of liberation to argue that the protected statuses of wife, mother, and homemaker constitute the true expression of women's nature and God's plan. In this view, the valuing of male, public-oriented achievement and wanting women to have the same public rights and recognition constitutes a capitulation to a worldly, male-dominated value system alien to Islam; a similar argument is made by some Western feminist thinkers, though to quite different effect.

The debate over whether equality or equity is necessary for justice – and whether equality requires sameness or permits gender-division of roles – lies at the heart of current debates over women's place in family and society. Many activists for gender justice reject the term feminism due to its Western connotations, but even scholars who have used the term feminism more broadly note that there is great variety as to both methods and ultimate aims. Some have suggested a distinction between Islamic feminism and Muslim feminism, with the latter using religious language but not ruling out a secular state. The assumption of religious language by women's rights activists is one of the most dramatic shifts in the late twentieth century. At a 2007 workshop of Muslim scholars discussing Islamic feminism, one participant referred to Islamic feminism as the unwanted child of political Islam. Another participant jumped in with a clarification: unwanted, perhaps, but nonetheless legitimate. The adoption of religious language to express political aims and make claims for gender equality or gender justice is a remarkable facet of late twentieth- and twenty-first century women's activism within the Middle East and elsewhere.

Shifting norms: public space and polygamy

The remainder of this chapter will consider aspects of two issues that have played out through Muslim history and that illustrate both major and subtle shifts in both ideal and practice: sex-segregation in public space and polygamy. Concern over women's appearance – both where they appear and what they wear – in public space is a recurrent feature of Muslim discourses, touched on by the Qurʾān (e.g., 24:31; 33:59) as well as certain *ḥadīth*. Marketplace regulations for medieval Andalusia insist on certain standards of segregation to ensure propriety, even as they take for granted the presence of some women in public streets. The fourteenth-century Egyptian jurist Ibn al-Ḥajj rails against women who do not observe proper standards of seclusion, inadvertently confirming that reality diverged from his ideal vision. However, these issues take on a new resonance in contemporary societies where obvious shifts in work and living patterns mean that women from a variety of social classes are more publicly visible than they have been in the past.

Since the early twentieth century, broad transformations have occurred within the Islamic world in female education and women's presence in the paid workforce. What were once key topics of debate, such as whether girls should attend primary school, are now uncontroversial, with Taliban-era Afghanistan standing as a significant exception. There remains a puberty-gap in some South Asian, Middle Eastern, and African contexts, with poorer and rural girls especially leaving education at a higher rate than boys. This is sometimes due to concern with honor and more often to a perception that there is no valid reason for these girls to pursue education, as it will not aid them in their expected lives as wives and mothers. Yet among other classes, female education has become both desirable and necessary for social and economic success. Among the urban middle classes in places such as Cairo, women's education is largely accepted even by Islamists, provided that proper standards of dress and segregation – and there is a range of views as to how total either must be – are

Figure 50 Les Femmes d'Alger dans leur appartement. INV3824. Delacroix Eugène (1798–1863) Paris, Musée du Louvre. Photo RMN © Thierry Le Mage. Many European painters like Delacroix, who accompanied the French ambassador to Morocco in 1832 following the French invasion of Algiers, based their scenes of the harem more on their imaginations than their experiences.

observed. (This can, however, have the effect of limiting female opportunities to pursue particular courses of study when there are insufficient resources to sustain parallel programs in segregated or separate facilities.)

As for women's workforce participation, the shift in many places to a monetized wage economy makes women's labor noticeable in ways that it may not have been in the past. Non-elite rural women have always done agricultural as well as household work and poorer urban women have worked in a variety of occupations including peddler, laundress, and midwife; elite women managed property, though they might conduct business through an agent rather than appear in court. Today, when many middle-class women are employed in the civil service and the professions, there are contradictory notions about how to understand female work. It may be dismissed as supplementary to women's responsibilities of wifehood and motherhood, but it is nonetheless a fact of life in most economic strata. Among the wealthier classes, women's educational and professional accomplishments may be attractive to potential marriage partners, and the prestige of marrying a doctor or lawyer may override or render irrelevant the concerns about a woman's integration into the public world of work.

While it has become generally accepted that women's work outside the home does not automatically lead to debauchery, sexual (im)morality remains the central criterion on which the moral health of a society is measured. As female education and employment have become more broadly acceptable, other indicators have arisen to affirm Islamic sexual standards; hence, the increased prominence of the headscarf and other forms of Islamic dress in the late twentieth century is partially due to their function as markers of personal chastity as well as religious identity. The *ḥijāb* debates are not reproductions of medieval discourses about sexual temptation or female seclusion but rather are deeply intertwined with modern Muslim engagement with the West. Leila Ahmed (1992: 145, 161) has suggested that the link between "women and culture" was forged in large part by Egyptian Qāsim Amīn's *The Liberation of Women* (1899). In it, women's liberation was linked to Western models and, significantly, unveiling, which Amīn advocated as part of a broader transformation of Egyptian society. (The veil in question was not the headscarf, but rather the face veil then commonly worn by upper-class Cairene women.) Although Amīn has been often credited with providing the watershed moment for the development of Egyptian feminism, issues such as marriage, female education, and the role of the mother were already under discussion in the nineteenth-century Egyptian women's press (Baron 1994), in ways that owed more to women's experience and less to a vision of the West as the pinnacle of civilization.

Like veiling, Muslim polygamy is fascinating to outside observers, who view it as both exotic and oppressive. In another similarity to veiling, it is in part polygamy's salience for Western audiences that accounts for its prominence in Muslim debates. As more than one scholar and activist has pointed out, polygamy has always been the purview of a demographic minority; divorce is of far more importance as a practical matter for the majority of Muslim women. In keeping with the general rule that Muslims are mostly like others of their areas, classes, and backgrounds in their life patterns, even across religious boundaries, polygamy is more common in Africa, where it is also practiced by non-Muslims, than in Asia or the Middle East, where it is uncommon though certainly not unknown. Among Muslim immigrant populations in North America and Europe, where civil laws prohibit polygamy, a tiny percentage of Muslims practice it. It is more widely accepted though still rare among African-American Muslims, the group in the USA most likely to engage in solely religious marriages without civil registration. Variation in the frequency with which polygamy has been practiced illustrates diversity among Muslims both across and within societies and throughout history.

Polygamy also provides an excellent case study for the wide variety of ways in which scriptural texts have been understood and interpreted. That polygamy (more properly, polygyny, or marriage to more than one woman) is permissible was taken for granted by Muslim thinkers until the modern era. Some modern thinkers justify it in tones ranging from defiant (Pakistan's Abū 'l-Aʿlā Mawdūdī saw polygamy as a man's privilege, divinely granted, and objected to any seeming capitulations to Western norms) to polemical (polygamy represents a better solution to the problem of men's naturally greater sexual appetites and demand for variety than extramarital affairs or serial divorce which have wreaked such havoc upon Western societies) to paternalistic (women need protection and therefore polygamy protects and benefits women by giving all women the chance to have a husband and family). Muslim modernist scholar Muḥammad ʿAbduh (d. 1905), who enjoyed an important role as *shaykh* of al-Azhar, the venerable Egyptian institution of Islamic learning in Cairo, argued for making polygamy forbidden on the basis of the general harm it did in modern circumstances; he is thought to have influenced Amīn's reasoning on the topic. Still, neither ʿAbduh's disciple Rashīd Riḍā nor the later rector of al-Azhar Maḥmūd Shaltūt shared his view that polygamy should be abolished.

In the debate on polygamy that has waxed and waned since the late nineteenth century in forums ranging from the Egyptian women's press to the Internet, the Qurʾān plays a key role. Two verses treat the subject of polygamy directly. Qurʾān 4:3, which does not create the institution of plural marriage but regulates already existing pre-Islamic marriage practices, declares: "If you fear you will not deal justly with the orphans, marry such as seem good to you from the women, two or three or four; but if you are afraid you will not be fair, then only one or what your right hands own." Qurʾān 4:129 provides further guidance for the polygamist: "You are never able to be just between women, even if you ardently desire to be, but do not incline completely away from one, leaving her suspended." (Qurʾān 4:23, which states that two sisters cannot be married to the same man simultaneously, tacitly assumes that polygamy is permitted.) Some have suggested a logical clash between the requirement for justice set forth in Qurʾān 4:3 and the impossibility of that justice as defined in 4:129; in this view, the Qurʾanic text has long forbidden polygamy since justice is impossible. But classical exegetes and jurists resolved this seeming contradiction by limiting justice as a man's treatment of his wives in measurable ways such as the amount of time spent, housing provided, or funds allocated for support. Affection and sex were explicitly exempted from the requirement of equality.

A number of twentieth-century scholars have argued against polygamy with both exegetical and social rationales. Fazlur Rahman, the Pakistani modernist, argued that the Qurʾān sought to abolish polygamy gradually, as it had done with slavery. Rahman's work has been influential for Muslim feminist exegetes, who have noted the historical conditions under which the Qurʾān was revealed. Gender-sensitive commentators such as Amina Wadud have emphasized the role of the *pair* of spouses in Qurʾanic depictions of creation (Qurʾān 4:1), marriage, and society, suggesting that Qurʾanic polygamy is exceptional and ought to be considered at the very least disliked. Polygamy serves as an exemplary case for investigating whether scriptural provisions must be always literally applied or whether strategies of historical contextualization can demonstrate other ways to treat Qurʾanic guidance.

In any case, legal campaigning to abolish or, more often, restrict polygamy has been generally promoted not with a rereading of the Qurʾanic text but practical legal strategies. Some countries have instituted a requirement for judicial permission in advance of a second marriage and may take a first wife's permission into account. In the face of the unwillingness of most governments (Turkey and Tunisia are the exceptions) to ban polygamy outright, some activists have begun arguing for the inclusion of stipulations against polygamy as a standard condition in marriage contract; a 1995 initiative to include a condition to this effect, along with several others guaranteeing a wife other rights, provoked extensive debate in Egypt but failed to become law. Nonetheless, if this condition is added by the parties to an Egyptian marriage contract, it will be enforceable. In other instances, where the legal code allows for a wife to seek divorce on the basis of harm, some reforms have affirmed that a husband's second marriage in itself constitutes harm to the first wife and entitles her to seek divorce; this is the case with the Moroccan reform. Like family law more broadly, polygamy serves as a battleground in ongoing contests about whether Islamic law can ever be fair to women.

Future developments

Muslims living in the Islamic world and as minorities outside it are in the throes of complex attempts to negotiate the relationship between tradition and modernity. Matters of marriage, family, and sexual ethics stand at the center of vital debates. Economic changes and related social shifts have altered internal family dynamics in many places but have had even greater impact on patterns of gender integration in the workplace and public sphere. Religious discourses remain influential within the arena of the family as well as the broader society, but cannot be simplistically treated as "traditional" as opposed to modern, secular norms. Rather, although a minority continues to insist that fully secular laws are the only responsible path for attaining women's full legal and social rights, thinkers and activists increasingly use religious language to press claims about ideal gender norms.

Two considerations seem important for future developments in marriage and sexual ethics in the Islamic world. First, there is likely to be more explicit negotiation of sexual norms with the recognition of non-marital sexual activity of various types. Despite persistent patterns of same-sex sexual activity (Dunne 1998), the possibility of religiously licit, mutually committed same-sex relationships remains largely taboo, but debate is emerging on the margins of other progressive, feminist, and reformist Muslim discourses (Ali 2006; Kugle 2006). Between men and women, several types of less formal marriage including *mutʿa* have become more common, not only in Iran but also among some Shīʿī and even Sunnī minorities in the West. Others choose to contract standard religious marriages (*nikaḥ*), but avoid state registration for these marriages; *zawāj ʿurfī* or customary marriage has received a great deal of attention in Egypt, particularly after a juicy paternity scandal, but the pattern is more widespread. How these institutions will develop – as prosecution of illicit sex remains a key demand of Islamist movements and cultural double standards surrounding virginity persist in many majority-Muslim societies and Muslim immigrant communities in the West – remains to be seen. Second, in addressing these issues and others, women's increasing participation as authorities will be vital. Whether as religious officials (the *murshidāt* in Morocco or the female *muftī*s in India), as academics or "scholar-activists" in the West (Webb 2000), or schooled in innovative forms of traditional learning through the Indonesian *pesantran* system, women's participation in these debates will undoubtedly shape their contours in myriad ways.

References and further reading

Abu-Odeh, L. (2004) "Egyptian Feminism: Trapped in the Identity Debate," in Y. Y. Haddad, B. F. Stowasser, eds., *Islamic Law and the Challenges of Modernity*, Walnut Creek, CA: Altamira Press, 183–211.

Abugideiri, H. (2004) "On Gender and the Family," in S. Taji-Farouki, B. M. Nafi, eds., *Islamic Thought in the Twentieth Century*, New York: I. B. Tauris, 223–59.

Ahmed, L. (1992) *Women and Gender in Islam: Historical Roots of a Modern Debate*, New Haven: Yale University Press.

Ali, K. (2003) "Progressive Muslims and Islamic Jurisprudence: The Necessity for Critical Engagement with Marriage and Divorce Law," in O. Safi, ed., *Progressive Muslims: On Justice, Gender, and Pluralism*, Oxford: Oneworld Publications, 163–89.
—— (2006) *Sexual Ethics and Islam: Feminist Reflections on Qur'*an, Hadith, and Jurisprudence, Oxford: Oneworld Publications.
An-Na'im, A., ed. (2002) *Islamic Family Law in a Changing World*, London: Zed Books.
Dunne, B. (1998) "Power and Sexuality in the Middle East," *Middle East Report* 206 (Spring): 8–11, 37.
Esposito, J. L. with DeLong-Bas, N. J. (2001) *Women in Muslim Family Law*, 2nd edition, Syracuse: Syracuse University Press.
Ghazali, Abu Hamid, al- (1984) *Marriage and Sexuality in Islam: A Translation of Al-Ghazali's Book on the Etiquette of Marriage from the Ihya'*, ed. and trans. M. Farah, Salt Lake City: University of Utah Press.
Kugle, S. S. H. (2006) "Sexual Diversity in Islam," in O. Safi, ed., *Voices of Islam, vol. 5: Voices of Change* (gen. ed. V. Cornell), Westport, CT: Praeger, 131–68.
McDonough, S. (1984) *Muslim Ethics and Modernity: A Comparative Study of the Ethical Thought of Sayyid Ahmad Khan and Mawlana Mawdudi*, Waterloo: Canadian Corporation for Studies in Religion, Wilfred Laurier Press.
Meriwether, M. L. and Tucker, J. E., eds. (1999) *Social History of Women and Gender in the Modern Middle East*, Boulder, CO: Westview.
Mir-Hosseini, Z. (1999) *Islam and Gender: The Religious Debate in Contemporary Iran*, Princeton: Princeton University Press.
—— (2003) "The Construction of Gender in Islamic Legal Thought: Strategies for Reform," *Hawwa: Journal of Women in the Middle East and the Islamic World*, 1: 1–28.
Peirce, L. P. (1993) *The Imperial Harem: Women and Sovereignty in the Ottoman Empire*, New York: Oxford University Press.
Rapoport, Y. (2005) *Marriage, Money, and Divorce in Medieval Islamic Society*, Cambridge: Cambridge University Press.
Shaheed, F. (1994) "Controlled or Autonomous: Identity and the Experience of the Network, Women Living Under Muslim Laws," *Signs*, 19: 997–1019.
Shatzmiller, M. (2007) *Her Day in Court: Women's Property Rights in Fifteenth-Century Granada*, Cambridge: Harvard University Press.
Sonbol, A. E. A., ed. (1996) *Women, the Family, and Divorce Laws in Islamic History*, Syracuse: Syracuse University Press.
Stowasser, B. (1993) "Women's Issues in Modern Islamic Thought," in J. Tucker, ed., *Arab Women: Old Boundaries, New Frontiers*, Bloomington: Indiana University Press, 3–28.
Tucker, J. E. (1998) *In the House of the Law: Gender and Islamic Law in Ottoman Syria and Palestine*, Berkeley: University of California Press.
Webb, G., ed. (2000) *Windows of Faith: Muslim Women Scholar-Activists in North America*, Syracuse: Syracuse University Press.

48

WOMEN, GENDER AND HUMAN RIGHTS

Simonetta Calderini

This chapter aims to discuss some issues relevant to women in Islam and will focus on two perspectives: gender studies and human rights. Though these are closely interrelated, with some identifiable developments from one to the other – for example gender studies scholars raising topics which are then addressed by human rights scholars – they have been kept separate here as I believe that neither gender studies nor human rights are necessarily inclusive of one another. Both are, however, critical to understanding issues revolving around women in the modern Muslim context.

The discussion on gender is here limited to women, with no reference to theories of masculinity or transgender. After two overviews of theoretical and scholarly developments and discussions, the chapter will focus on three case studies, two pertaining to women in the public arena, "the veil and authority," and one to family law, "marriage and divorce." The issues of the veil and authority are analyzed from a textual-historical gender studies perspective, while "marriage and divorce" are analyzed from a textual and human rights approach. One underlying theme of this chapter is the interface between religion and culture, which is particularly visible in the discussion on the veil and on forced marriages.

Both gender and human rights issues with reference to the Islamic world, when discussed from either an outsider's or an insider's perspective, are rarely straightforward academic or intellectual topics; rather, they often turn out to be discourses filled with political, ideological, national or other agendas.

Gender studies and Islam

As the sociologist Leila Ahmed (1992: 149) has argued, the issue of gender, with special reference to the veil and women's education, has long been part of "the Western narrative of the quintessential otherness and inferiority of Islam." Moreover, since the late nineteenth century, it has informed both Western colonial discourse and, especially since the work of Egyptian modernist scholar Qassim Amin (1863–1908), reformist and feminist Arab discourse.

Agendas of diverse nature are not absent from the academic study of gender and Islam either. The first studies on women in Islam by Western as well as by Muslim scholars were influenced to different degrees by the debate on women's rights, which pervaded not only European and American but also Egyptian and Turkish intellectual circles. As succinctly pointed out by contemporary scholar Ruth Roded (1999: 11), the first five well-known academic works by Orientalist writers on women spanned a period which coincided with "the high-point of the Western women's rights movement." The groundbreaking works by Nabia Abbott (1897–1981) which were published during the early 1940s are a telling example of Roded's statement. By studying the historical context of early Islam, using textual analysis of the Qur'ān and sifting through the *ḥadīth* material relevant to women's issues, Abbott acknowledged an original intent in the Qur'anic message to end practices such as female infanticide and to legislate on women's rights and religious equality, while at the same time identifying inherent statements which she saw as limiting women's freedom. She attributed such limitations to internal debates and developments in Mecca but also to the influence of Sasanian and Byzantine practices along with local traditions and customs (Abbott 1942: 115). Despite its limitations, with its emphasis on source criticism and the study of pre-Islamic women's status, Abbott's pioneering work paved the way for much deeper and insightful research, including that carried out by twenty-first-century scholars as varied in backgrounds, approaches and arguments as Fatima Mernissi, Barbara Stowasser and Amina Wadud. They too re-read the original sources, contextualized them historically and socially and identified a number of misogynistic interpretations, which they believe had accrued over the centuries.

During the late 1970s several socio-anthropological works on women in specific Islamic countries appeared in print. They reflected efforts on the part of the "outsider" researcher not to impose Western paradigms and let the "informants" speak for themselves. However, they were still shaped through the lenses of paradox, such as that between the "word of God" and the "word of men" which seem a rather simplistic interpretative tool. Since the 1980s and 1990s, the fundamental works by two Muslim female scholars have greatly influenced debates on gender and Islam. Feminist scholar Leila Ahmed (1992: 1–7) convincingly shows that no single or unique meaning of, and approach to, gender issues can be identified in early Islam, not even during the Prophet's life-time. In fact, earlier and neighboring societies, combined with local, social and political circumstances, all contributed to the elaboration of varying discourses on gender. What has been transmitted by the majority of Muslim sources down to the present time, she argues, is only one of these discourses: that which became the dominant expression of "establishment Islam" through its hierarchical formulation of society whereby women are seen as one degree below men. Ahmed contrasts this trend with "ethical Islam," which, in her view, emphasizes the moral and spiritual equality of all human beings. She resolves that these two trends informed, to different degrees, specific periods of Muslim history and have been upheld by different religious groups within Islam. From a strong textual and historical base, Moroccan feminist and sociologist Fatima Mernissi (1991) (one of the founding members of the Moroccan Organization for Human Rights) also argues against a monolithic approach to gender and Islam: while witnessing levels of "institutional/establishment" Islam which confine women to a domestic, submissive role, she restores Muslim women's confidence in original Islam with its egalitarian and "democratic" message, the message conveyed by the Prophet in seventh-century Medina. More recent works continue the textual criticism approach (e.g., Barlas 2002) but also include sociological studies focusing on the status and identity of Muslim women within and beyond Middle Eastern contexts (Moghissi 2006; Roald 2001).

Gender studies: women as equal to men, as equal but different, or as subordinate to them?

When analyzing the relation between the status of women and men in Islam, depending on the approach of study and the selection of textual material, three broad arguments can be sustained. The first argument is that women are in all respects equal to men; this is a minority view held by the so-called liberal, "secular" feminists such as the early Egyptian feminist Doria Shafik (d. 1976), the contemporary Egyptian activist Nawal el-Saadawi, and, to an extent, by some feminist theologians such as the above mentioned Fatima Mernissi and Pakistani scholar Riffat Hassan. Equality is seen as ontological but in need of activism for it to be translated into social, political, economic, legal and other domains. It is a position based on ideological assumptions, and is corroborated by textual evidence from the Qur'ān only in specific areas such as the equality between men and women in faith, spiritual achievements and their equal worth for equal labor.

By far the most commonly held position among Muslim scholars, whether traditionalists or modernists, as well as scholars in Islamic studies, is that in Islam women and men are considered as equal but different. God created them equal, stemming from the same origin (*nafs*), endowing them with the same spiritual worth: "Verily, for all men and women who surrendered unto God, all truly devout men and women, . . . for them God has readied forgiveness of sins and a mighty reward" (Qur'ān 33:35), enjoying the same rights (Qur'ān 2:229), and rewarding them equally for their labor (Qur'ān 3:195; 4:32). Scholars arguing in favor of this view use evidence mainly from the Qur'ān and emphasize the pre-eminence of its divine revelation over the *ḥadīth*. Some of the latter, which contain statements against such equality, are interpreted as historically bound and hence as limited interpretations of divine revelation. While in some cases the Qur'ān specifically addresses women (as in *Sūra*s 33 and 4), its overall language is accordingly to be taken as inclusive, meant for both men and women (Wadud 1999).

Mainly on the basis of *ḥadīth* reports, their use in legal rulings, local practices, as well some traditional interpretations of selected Qur'anic verses, the argument can also be supported for women being presented as subordinate to men. One Qur'anic verse (Qur'ān 4:34) is especially adduced to back this view and is variously translated: "Men are in charge of (*qawwamūn ʿalā*) women because Allah has made the one of them to excel the other" (Pickthall translation); "Men shall take full care of women with the bounties which Allah has bestowed more abundantly on the former than on the latter" (Asad translation). It is on the interpretation of the Arabic expression *qawwamūn ʿalā* and on the context of the *sūra* that scholars differ in their interpretation. Some scholars also add to the above Qur'ān 4:5 "and do not entrust to those who are weak of judgment" (i.e., understood to be minors and women) as well as verses dealing with legal rulings such as inheritance (Qur'ān 4:11–3) or witness (Qur'ān 2:282) which apply differently to women and men.

Muslims believe that, being the direct word of God, the Qur'ān cannot be modified; however, the interpretations of its words and message do vary according to the period, background and approach of its interpreters. As for the *ḥadīth* reports, many can indeed be pointed out as supporting or validating the view of female subordination. Linked to the Qur'anic verse on inheritance mentioned above, one such *ḥadīth*, allegedly on the authority of Muḥammad, explains that the difference in worth of a woman's witness as half that of a man is "because of the deficiency of the woman's mind" (Bukhārī 1973: III, 502).

Some scholars resolve the rift between the intended egalitarian Qur'anic message and the hierarchical "misogynistic" view expressed in some *ḥadīth* reports by uncovering the latter's weak chains of transmitters and pointing out the secondary status of the *ḥadīth* compared to the Qur'anic revelation, arguing that, being the result of human composition, *ḥadīth* reports are time and society-bound. In other words, as the modernist scholar Fazlur Rahman conceded, they reflect the opinions of the first generations of Muslims.

The varying formulations over the centuries of *sharīʿa* rulings have mainly been based on interpretations of Qur'anic verses as substantiated by a fitting selection of *ḥadīth*s. This fluidity has made it possible for reforms to be introduced on most legal fields, including, even though with some delay, family law. Accordingly, the practice of unilateral divorce (i.e., oral repudiation pronounced and repeated by the husband three times) was abolished in 1926 in Turkey. Polygamy has been regulated now in most Islamic countries from Egypt and Iran to the Yemen and Pakistan, with a novel interpretation of Qur'ān 4:3: "Marry from among women such as are lawful to you: two, or three, or four: but if you have reason to fear that you might not be able to treat them with equal fairness, then [only] one" to the extent that, on the basis of the last section of the verse above, polygamy could be abolished in 1924 in Turkey and outlawed in 1956 in Tunisia.

All in all, such fluidity in interpreting and adapting Qur'anic precepts has characterized Islamic civilization over the centuries, as the local legal variations in Islamic countries attest to this day. Minority tendencies to absolutism and uniformity in interpretation have occasionally expressed themselves through literalist and "fundamentalist" claims to a "return" to one a-historical ideal model.

Human rights and Islam: an overview

Even though all Islamic countries, with the exception of Saudi Arabia, did support in 1948 the passing by the United Nations General Assembly of the Universal Declaration of Human Rights (UDHR), some voiced criticism of aspects of it, which eventually led to partial ratifications of the ensuing Human Rights Conventions. The exceptions, which some Muslim representatives raised and which have been more clearly voiced since the 1980s, involve the identification of a Judeo-Christian or a Western bias to the formulation of the Declaration, which was seen as potentially conflicting with some principles of Islamic law. Areas of possible conflict between Islamic and the UDHR principles included freedom of religion (of conversion, of religious minorities) and the equality of the rights of the person regardless of religion and gender. The issue of the universality versus the relativity of the human rights concept is one which is debated to this day by Muslim and non-Muslim scholars alike, with some of them advocating a distinction between the universality of the concept of human rights on the one hand and the specific human rights laws and declarations on the other.

When in 1981 representatives from a number of Islamic countries issued the Universal Islamic Declaration of Human Rights (UIDHR), the very term chosen in Arabic to express "rights" (*ḥuqūq*) highlighted some of the difficulties about the comparability of concepts expressed by the two Declarations. Etymologically, *ḥaqq* means "truth, that which is right, that which is true" and can also be used to mean "obligation" or "limit." Even though the term *ḥaqq* with the meaning of "right" or "claim," as applied to a person, has indeed been traditionally used in Islamic jurisprudence (*fiqh*), it usually did not refer to an inalienable right of the individual but rather to specific legal cases allowing discretionary prosecution as contrasted to cases of *ḥaqq Allāh* "the right of God" with mandatory prosecution. However, not all scholars would agree with the distinction between the rights of God and human rights (see for instance the twentieth-century Egyptian reformist Shaykh Maḥmūd Shaltūt's [1893–1963] identification of the rights of God with the human rights of society). The issue of language is not purely academic. Legal scholar Ann E. Mayer in her seminal 1999 work *Islam and Human Rights* has identified and analyzed a number of significant discrepancies between the English and Arabic versions of the UIDHR which point to the importance of establishing which text is to be considered as the most authoritative.

In 1990 the Organization of Islamic Conference (OIC) issued the Cairo Declaration of Human Rights in Islam, which countries as politically and denominationally varied as Iran, Saudi Arabia and Iraq, strived to present as an Islamic alternative to the Universal Declaration of Human Rights. The link between national and international politics on the one hand, and the desire to represent an "Islamic" formulation of human rights on the other, can be detected in the Cairo Declaration and others which followed it such as the Arab Charter of Human Rights (1994), the Casablanca Declaration (1999) and the Doha Declaration (2001) .

It is especially in the areas of personal status and family law that the debate on human rights and gender intersect. Issues such as the legal equality of women in marriage and divorce (UDHR, article 16), in custody and in witness, are of foremost importance in the efforts to remove those disabilities based on custom and justified on the basis of selected interpretations of scripture. Accordingly, some traditionalist Muslims reject specific articles of the UDHR, such as the abovementioned article 16, as being irreconcilable with *sharīʿa*; however, while the UIDHR devotes a whole section to the rights of married women (article 20), it leaves no specific provisions for the unmarried, divorced or widowed women. On the other hand, alternative voices emerge from the Islamic world, such as that of Iranian Noble Prize lawyer Shirin Ebadi, who affirm both the universality of human rights and their compatibility with Islamic principles.

The discourse of human rights in Islam, and specifically of women's rights, has become entangled with the political polarization within Islamic societies between the "Islamist" and the "secular" perspectives. As the Sudanese scholar in international law and human rights, Abdullahi Ahmed An-Na'im (1995: 55), argues, such polarization has resulted in the Islamist group successfully seizing the definition of the frame of reference of such a discourse, a trend which "is detrimental to the protection and promotion of the human rights of women in Islamic societies."

While the earliest human rights organizations in the Islamic world date back to the 1930s, it is since the 1980s that they have multiplied and established themselves more decisively in the legal and political arenas. Among them are international organizations or networks such as the Arab Organization for Human Rights or Women Living Under Muslim Law, as well as national and more localized groups such as

Afghan Women Welfare Department, the Palestinian Federation of Women's Action Committees and the National Centre for Human Rights, Jordan.

The veil: textual references, interpretations, uses and meanings

Newspapers and magazines often feature the on-going debate in Western Europe, as well as in many other countries throughout the world, about the extent to which Muslim girls and women at school, in the workplace, on television and so forth, should wear partial veil (*ḥijāb*), full head and body-covering (*niqāb*) or none at all. Particularly in France (*Affair du foulard* of 1992, 1994 and on-going) and in the United Kingdom, the contents of such a debate have expanded to include issues of legislation (for example the principle of *laïcité* as a means to prevent discrimination based on religion in French constitutional laws and the Declaration of the Rights of Man and of Citizens (1881, 1905, article 2 of 1946 Constitution)), of educational provisions (state schools, private schools, faith schools), as well as the communal and individual identity of religious, cultural or ethnic minority groups. At the same time, in Turkey, a constitutionally secular country with a Muslim majority population, women in public positions and in state ceremonies are not (to date) allowed to wear the *ḥijāb* (1998 case of Kurdish MP Merve Kavakci; 2003, during the anniversary celebrations of the Republic) while in Tunisia there have been restrictions on the wearing of *ḥijāb* in public since 1981. These are but some facets of "the discourse of the veil" which, as argued by Leila Ahmed (1992), has long implied a connection between the issues of women's status and of culture, that is, to improve the one (status) means to abandon or overcome the other (veil as local custom).

Especially since the age of Western colonialism and the era of legal reforms in Islamic countries, the *ḥijāb* has become a symbol of either male domination (consider Hudā Sha'rāwī's public unveiling in 1923 as a feminist declaration), a statement against colonial oppression, a means of empowerment of young professional women, an expression of resistance to despotic regimes or of conformity to social and cultural customs. Moreover, for several Muslim women living in the West, to wear the veil implies a statement of identity and of opposition to the materialistic and consumerist aspects of Western societies.

There are very few Islamic countries in which a form of veiling is legally enforced on women; one is the Islamic Republic of Iran, where the veil (*chādor*: a long flowing black overcoat, covering the hair but not the face) has been compulsory for all women to wear in public spaces since 1983; another is Saudi Arabia. In Afghanistan, wearing the *burka* (an azure coarse overcoat covering the whole body, including the eyes) was mandatory under the Taliban, and still remains to this day widely in use in rural areas. Conversely, during the 1930s, leaders of modernist and secularist regimes such as Mustafa Kemal Atatürk (d. 1938) in Turkey and Reza Shah (d. 1944) in Iran, as part of their economic and cultural reformist policies, prohibited women from wearing the veil (respectively in 1935 and 1936), which they perceived to be an expression of the backward nature of their societies.

With reference to women, the term *ḥijāb* is only found in the Qur'ān with the meaning of partition, screen or curtain. In Qur'ān 33:53, it is mentioned in connection with Muḥammad's wives within a context of delimitation of the private from the public domain of the Prophet's life: "And whenever you ask them for anything that you need, ask them from behind a *ḥijāb* (screen): this will but deepen the purity of your hearts and theirs."

Two Qur'anic references, specific to a female item of clothing to be worn by the Prophet's wives and by all Muslim women, make use of terms, the exact interpretation of which is subject to debate. Qur'ān 33:59 states, "O prophet, tell thy wives and thy daughters, as well as all believing women that they should draw over themselves some of their *jalābīb*" (outer garments, mantles, cloaks); the main emphasis here rests on identity, so that such women do not suffer sexual harassment. In Qur'ān 24:31, the underlying message is that of modesty of dress and of behavior: "Tell the believing women to lower their gaze and to be mindful in their chastity . . .; hence let them draw their *khumur* (kerchiefs, head coverings) over their bosoms." Fatima Mernissi (1985) has studied the context of the above passages and interpreted them as measures for a specific period of time, when the military defeats of Muḥammad's supporters and the siege of the city of Medina had resulted in community unrest and insecurity.

Unlike the Qur'ān, some *ḥadīth* reports are very specific about what such items of clothing should cover:

> ʿĀ'isha said that when Asmā', daughter of Abū Bakr, came to visit God's Messenger wearing thin clothes, he turned away from her and said, "When a woman is old enough to menstruate, Asmā', it is not right that any part of her should be seen but this and this," pointing to his face and hands.
>
> (Tibrīzī 1975: II, 920–1)

Even though the reliability of the above *ḥadīth* has been repeatedly questioned, the injunction has nevertheless been used in support of the wearing of the *ḥijāb*. With this in mind and considering that the use of the full *niqāb* (veil covering the whole body including face and hands) does not seem to be based on sound *ḥadīth* reports either, the question needs to be raised of the extent to which the use of the veil is linked to cultural, geographical and other factors, which have influenced the interpretation and application of general Qur'anic statements on modesty of dress. It seems likely that from a custom which developed in urban pre-Islamic Near and Middle Eastern settings, most probably to emulate the ruling elites which practiced female seclusion as an expression of wealth and distinction, veiling was adopted by Islam and interpreted to express the values of modesty and piety which were represented by the female members of the Prophet's family.

Muslim leaders have resorted to the "politics" of veiling and unveiling to express and implement their political, social and cultural agendas. Modern stereotypical Western perceptions inform the understanding of donning the *ḥijāb* as a unifying factor characterizing Muslim women, with no differences linked to culture, geography, circumstances, age and so forth. Accordingly, the *ḥijāb* has been perceived in the West as a uniform expression of the status of un-modern, un-emancipated and suppressed women, with no choice on whether to wear it or not. While it is undeniable that there are instances of oppression and pressure by some states, some societies and some families, the media coverage of the *Affair du foulard* in France and similar episodes in Western and non-Western countries, has highlighted the need for a more varied understanding of the numerous uses of the *ḥijāb* (or the *niqāb*) in modern societies as marking difference, stating social and cultural inequalities, as well as representing religious, ideological, cultural and other loyalties.

Women, authority and power

A *ḥadīth* transmitted on the witness of Abū Bakra, a companion of Muḥammad, and included in the authoritative *ḥadīth* collection *al-Ṣaḥīḥ* of al-Bukhārī (d. 870) (1973: IV, 226), states: "Those who entrust their affairs to a woman will never know prosperity." The subject of much study by some contemporary scholars such as Fatima Mernissi (1993), this well-known and often invoked *ḥadīth* has nevertheless not prevented a number of Muslim women, over the centuries and across Islamic countries, from holding temporal authority. They include eleventh-century queen regents such as Sitt al-Mulk (d. 1023) in Fatimid Egypt and outright queens such as the late eleventh-century Yemeni Ṣulayḥid queen Arwā, seventeenth-century Indonesian queens, not to mention sultanas like the twelfth-century Ayyubid Shajar al-Durr (r. 1250) and, up until the nineteenth century, the numerous Ottoman *wālide sulṭān* (Sultan's mother).

In the contemporary Islamic world there have been women Prime Ministers, such as Tansu Çiller in Turkey (1995, 1996), in Bangladesh Khaleda Zia (1991–6) and Sheikh Hasina Wajad (1996–2001) and Benazir Bhutto in Pakistan (1988–90, 1993–6). In the 2006 general elections in Iraq, thanks to the approval of a female quota system, the percentage of women elected in the Iraqi Parliament (25.5%) was higher than that in the United Kingdom Parliament (19.5%) or United States Congress (15.2%). It goes without saying that caution should be used when analyzing the circumstances of women's coming to power, above all their family and tribal connections, or, in the more contemporary case, political cosmetic decisions. Their cases also raise the question of whether having a woman in a position of authority makes any difference to the status of women in her country.

Scholars and men in power who have argued, and continue to argue, against female political involvement on the basis of it being irreconcilable with the preservation of female modesty, usually had recognizable sectarian or other specific agendas addressed against specific females and their families. Two examples of political agendas underlying the opposition to female leadership can suffice here: for the distant past Niẓām al-Mulk (d. 1092), the minister of the Saljuq sultan Malik Shāh, whose vehement criticism of female influence in politics was in fact specifically addressed to Malik Shāh's wife, queen Terken Khātūn, in order to undermine support for her son Maḥmūd's claims to the succession. For the more recent past, a comparable case is that of the arguments against female leadership voiced by the supporters of the Islamic Democratic Alliance of Pakistan to oppose the 1988 election victory of Benazir Bhutto as Prime Minister of Pakistan.

As far as religious authority is concerned, the recorded (male) voices are almost unanimous in stating that a female can never be invested with spiritual leadership, meaning that she can never be a caliph (for Sunnīs) or an Imām (for Shīʿīs). As for leadership in prayer, many authoritative men would concede that a woman can be an *imām* for a congregation of women and children, but not for one of men. Of the main five schools of law, only the Mālikī school is opposed to female *imāms* for an all-female congregation. In Islamic history eminent examples of women *imāms* for other women were ʿĀʾisha and Umm Salama. The contemporary media-renowned Egyptian Muslim preacher and scholar Yūsuf al-Qaraḍāwī (b. 1926) states in this regard, "it is established that leadership in prayer in Islam is to be for men" (Qaraḍāwī 2006) but reports of a few scholars who allow women who are old and well versed in the Qurʾān to lead their family members in prayer. There is indeed the historical precedent of Umm Waraqa, a woman appointed by Muḥammad to act as *imām* for her household of men and women (reported, among others, by Ibn Saʿd [d. 845] 1995: 295).

Voices of Muslim women are emerging from unusual corners of the world as proving the need for tackling the issue of training female *imām*s, be it for a mixed or for an all-female congregation (see the cases of training for female *imām*s in northwest China's Ningxia Hui Autonomous Region or in Indonesia, the inspiring statements by Halima Krauzen [2005] in Hamburg, Germany, and Amina Wadud's 2005 controversial leading the Friday prayer for a mixed congregation in New York City, USA).

Female spiritual authority is not uncommon in Sufism where, in addition to the oft-quoted cases of ninth-century women mystics like Rābiʿa of Basra and Fāṭima of Nishapur, more recent examples can be found of female circle leaders (*muqaddamāt*) or leaders at main spiritual centers (*shaykhāt*) as in nineteenth-century North African Tijāniyya or Raḥmāniyya Ṣūfī orders. Among some Shīʿī traditions, instances can be found of high positioned women in the religious hierarchy (Queen Arwā, possibly a *ḥujja* in the Ismāʿīlī hierarchy and high-ranking women among the Druzes).

All in all, a comprehensive study of gender in Islam reveals in several instances an unmistakable use of gender discourse by men in authority or scholars aimed at stating specific political or other agendas, which they disguise by resorting to selected scriptural passages (and their partial interpretations). It goes without saying that such use may result in real cases of widespread discrimination and limitation for women, and such cases are the prime concern for the actions and legislation of human rights organizations worldwide. However, as in the case of gender, human rights discourses can also become entrenched in political, cultural and other uses.

Women and family law: marriage and divorce

Article 1 of the Cairo Declaration of Human Rights spells out the equality of all human beings in terms of human dignity, duties and responsibilities (but not of rights!) irrespective of race, gender and religion. As is the case with a number of legal or any type of documents, it is not only what is included that is significant for its full understanding, but also what is omitted.

Article 5 of the Cairo Declaration of Human Rights states: "Men and women have the right to marriage, and no restrictions stemming from race, colour or nationality shall prevent them from enjoying this right." One significant omission here, with regard to discrimination, is religion, which can be explained on the basis of the *sharīʿa* ruling that while a Muslim man may marry women of the People of the Book (i.e., Jews and Christians, based on Qurʾān 5:5), a Muslim woman can only marry a Muslim man. The Shīʿī conservative commentator S. Tabandeh (1970: 41) did not fail to notice that the comparable article in the UDHR about the equality of rights for men and women in matters of marriage and divorce (article 16) does contradict in some points the teachings of Islam and ought to be rejected by the representatives of

Islamic countries. Indeed, in most Islamic countries, marriages of Muslim women to non-Muslim men are not legally recognized nor valid, with predictable consequences for the children in terms, for example, of inheritance rights.

The inequality of rights in marriage between husband and wife is also expressed through the reference in some legal rulings to the wife's obligation to obey her husband, loosely based on a Qur'anic verse which in fact does not command women to be obedient but states that righteous women are obedient – that is, to God (Qur'ān 4:34 *qānitāt*).

However, the clearest example of different treatment on account of gender, is in the case of divorce. Prior to the twentieth-century reforms in personal status codes, the interpretation of *sharīʿa* in most Islamic countries differed little with regards to divorce: it was a unilateral right of the husband, with some limited cases of divorce initiated by the wife but requiring the husband's agreement. The 1926 adoption of the Turkish Civil Code marked a clear step away from traditional *sharīʿa*-based legislation and, while outlawing polygamy, it also gave both spouses equal right to divorce. Other Islamic countries were less radical and gradually reformed their family laws, limiting the husband's right to divorce and increasingly giving power to the courts to handle divorce cases. Alimony and maintenance were to be granted, even though for a limited period of time, to the wife by law (Egypt 1979/1985; Jordan 1951; Syria 1953/1975).

Despite legal reforms, divorce in common law and in practice can still be a male prerogative while alimony becomes only a temporary measure. Moreover, politically motivated Islamization programs by governments such as those of post-1979 Iran or Pakistan have resulted in the restriction of some of the rights gained by women in previous decades. This applies also in India, where Muslims are a minority community, and where the tension is felt between the provisions for divorce and maintenance rights according to state laws and those given by the Muslim Divorce Bill.

Forced marriages: culture or religion?

Arranged marriages, defined as occurring between adults with the consent of both spouses, are a long established practice in many countries (Islamic as well as non-Islamic) in the Middle East and the Indian subcontinent; they are tolerated by the laws of the land and by human rights organizations as long as the element of choice is clearly discernible. On the contrary, forced marriages, which by definition lack that element of choice, and, in a number of cases, involve minors, are the object of human rights campaigns aimed at outlawing and eradicating them. While all contemporary Muslim scholars would insist that consent is one of the required elements for a marriage to be deemed valid according to Islamic law, in practice forced marriages are still contracted in countries claiming to adhere to *sharīʿa*.

A fundamental question to be raised is the extent to which forced marriages are a cultural, social, or religious phenomenon. A number of verses from the Qur'ān can be referred to, which indirectly touch upon the importance of consent in marriage and divorce. For instance, in Qur'ān 4:19 it is stated that "it is unlawful for you to inherit the women [of your deceased kinsmen] against their will" (Arabic *karhān*: unwillingly, reluctantly, under compulsion, forcedly) and similarly in Qur'ān 2:232, divorce can be attained if there is mutual agreement. There are also references to slave girls, who can be married only with the permission of their masters (Qur'ān 4:25), implying that they do not have full legal capacity in the matter. The legal role of a guardian (*walī*) in marriage is much discussed in *sharī'a* rulings past and present.

The practice of marrying minor girls is sometimes said to be implied in Qur'ān 65:4, and is further sustained in the *ḥadīth*s where reference is given to Muḥammad marrying 'Ā'isha when she was six years old (Bukhārī 1973: VII, reports 64 and 65). Some modern Muslim writers have dismissed the age given for 'Ā'isha's marriage to the Prophet as incorrect (see Maqsood 1994). Reference remains, however, to the precedent in the Prophetic *sunna* of an arranged marriage contracted with a minor. Whether with or without a guardian, a marriage without consent is indeed deemed not valid in Islamic jurisprudence and can be rescinded (Bukhārī 1973: VII, 69), but for a young, inexperienced girl, consent can simply be indicated by her silence (Bukhārī 1973: VII, 67, 68).

Both the age of consent and the role of a guardian are hotly debated topics in human rights circles. A number of Islamic countries, though signatories of the UDHR, have opted out of the clause of the age of maturity to marry on the basis of culture and tradition. In a number of cases the age of maturity differs between the sexes; for instance since 1923 in Egypt it has been 18 for a boy but 16 for a girl, the same as in pre-1979 Iran (the age of maturity was lowered after the revolution to 15 for a boy, 13 for a girl, in the new Civil Law, clause 1041) with the extreme case of the Sudan where a boy is deemed mature to marry at 10 while a girl is mature at 9.

Notwithstanding extreme cases, the minimum age for marriage was one of the first issues raised by Ottoman reformers as early as the nineteenth century (for example, in the instance of Malak Ḥifnī Nāṣif, (1886–1918)). Without engaging in theological debates on the validity of the *sunna* reports on the age of 'Ā'isha, modern Islamic legislators have attempted to put an end to marriages of minors by refusing to register all those contracted by one or more spouses who are under the legal age of consent.

Similarly, the role of the guardian is under scrutiny. Traditionally the father or a male relative of the bride, the guardian was seen as instrumental in protecting a young woman's interests and the one legally entitled to contract a marriage for her. While, according to most *sharī'a* legal schools, the figure of a guardian is considered necessary for minor or young spouses only, who, once having reached maturity, could legally ask for the marriage to be rescinded by appealing to the "option of puberty," in some Islamic countries such as the Sudan or some states in Malaysia, the figure of the guardian is required to sign a marriage contract irrespective of the bride's age.

Other legal rulings

Many more areas of legal (state enforced or common law) discrimination against women are being identified by human rights organizations operating throughout the Islamic world; among them are the so-called "honor crimes," the punishment for which may either result in a diminished sentence for the perpetrators (Kuwait, Pakistan) or overall lack of punishment (Syria, Personal Status Law number 34, article 548). Other areas include the lack of legal recognition of cases of rape, whereby the victim is persecuted for committing adultery or fornication (see the case of Nigerian Amina Lawal in 2002, 2003) or nationality laws according to which only fathers can pass their nationality on to their children. Areas of undeniable discrimination should not, however, overshadow gains in the field of women's rights which have occurred in a number of Islamic countries, notably Tunisia, Turkey and Indonesia. The 2006 elections in Kuwait marked a significant step in female participation (yet not representation) in the political debate, leaving Saudi Arabia as the only Islamic country where women cannot exercise their right to vote.

Conclusion

The full financial, legal, political and economic equality of women, though recognized in principle by all Western states, is not, for the most part, reflected in practice. In respect of Islamic countries, the rift is not only between specific legal provisions and the practice, but also within the theological and legal interpretations of what constitutes "equality." According to some Muslim scholars, full equality, especially legal and financial equality, is not textually supported, and so it is not encompassed in their interpretation of Islam. It would be naïve not to acknowledge that the work of Western governments and human rights organizations to expose and condemn human rights abuses in some Islamic countries may at times serve political and other uses. However, the gains most likely to succeed towards the protection of women's rights in Islamic countries will arise from those local groups and organizations willing to challenge some of the centuries-old discriminations, which seem to be justified by, and continued in the name of, out-of-context or partial interpretations of scriptural passages.

Other discriminatory rulings towards women, perceived to be deeply embedded in scripture, may need more than a challenge. They may prompt justifiable questions as to the extent to which the human rights concept is indeed a universal one and whether universality can ever apply to specific formulations of such a concept. One of the pivotal issues that will require clear positioning by scholars and leaders who argue for an Islamic concept of human rights, is whether or not human rights are fundamental and inherent to all human beings. If they are, then the human rights concept could indeed be translated into specific formulations and applied in practice within the framework of both the message and the context of Islamic revelation.

Note

Unless otherwise specified, the English translation used for the Qur'ān is that by Muhammad Asad, *The Message of the Qur'ān*, Gibraltar: Dar al-Andalus, 1980. Other translations used are by Marmaduke Pickthall, *The Meaning of the Glorious Qur'ān*, Beltsville, Maryland: Amana, 1996

References and further reading

Abbott, N. (1942) "Women and the State in Early Islam," *Journal of Near Eastern Studies*, 1: 106–26, 341–68.

Afary, J. (2004) "The Human Rights of Middle Eastern and Muslim Women," *Human Rights Quarterly*, 26: 106–25.

Ahmed, L. (1992) *Women and Gender in Islam: Historical Roots of a Modern Debate*, New Haven and London: Yale University Press.

An-Na'im, A. A. (1995) "The Dichotomy between Religious and Secular Discourse in Islamic Societies," in M. Afkhami, ed., *Faith and Freedom: Women's Human Rights in the Muslim World*, London: I. B. Tauris 51–77.

Barlas, A. (2002) *Believing Women in Islam: Unreading Patriarchal Interpretations of the Qur'ān*, Austin: University of Texas Press.

Bukhārī, al- (1973–) *al-Ṣaḥīḥ*, M. M. Khān trans., Beirut: Dār al-Fikr.

Cortese D. and Calderini, S. (2006) *Women and the Fatimids in the World of Islam*, Edinburgh: Edinburgh University Press.

Dalacoura, K. (1998) *Islam, Liberalism and Human Rights: Implications for International Relations*, London: I. B. Tauris.

Esposito, J. (1982) *Women in Muslim Family Law*, Syracuse: Syracuse University Press.

Fernea, E., ed. (1985) *Women and the Family in the Middle East*, Austin: University of Texas Press.

Fernea, E. W. and Bezirgan B. Q., eds. (1977) *Middle Eastern Muslim Women Speak*, Austin: University of Texas Press.

Haddad, Y. Y. and Esposito, J. L., eds. (1998) *Islam, Gender and Social Change*, Oxford: Oxford University Press.

Hunter, S. and Malik, H., eds. (2005) *Islam and Human Rights: Advancing a US-Muslim Dialogue*, Washington: Center for Strategic and International Studies.

Ibn Saʿd, M. (1995) *The Women of Madina*, A. Bewley trans., London: Ta Ha Publishers.

Kandiyoti, D. (1991) *Women, Islam and the State*, London: Macmillan.

Keddie, N. (1979) "Problems in the Study of Middle Eastern Women," *International Journal of Middle Eastern Studies*, 19: 225–40.

Krauzen, H. (2005) "Can Women Be Imams?" Qantara.de: Dialogue with the Islamic World, posted June 3, 2005, http://www.quantara.org/webcom/show_article.php/_c-307/_nr-24/_p-1/i.html.

Mayer, A. E. (1999) *Islam and Human Rights*, Boulder, Co: Westview Press.

Maqsood, R. W. (1994) *Hazrat A'ishah: A Study of Her Age at the Time of her Marriage*, Birmingham: IPCI.

Mernissi, F. (1985) *Beyond the Veil: Male–Female Dynamics in Muslim Society*, London: al Saqi (1st edition 1975).

—— (1991) *Women and Islam: an Historical and Theological Enquiry*, Oxford: Blackwell (French original 1987).

—— (1993) *The Forgotten Queens of Islam*, London: Polity (French original 1990).

Moghadam, V. M. (1999) "Revolution, Religion, and Gender Politics: Iran and Afghanistan Compared," *Journal of Women's History*, 10(4): 172–95.

Moghissi, H. (1999) *Feminism and Islamic Fundamentalism*, London: Zed.

—— (2006) *Muslim Diaspora: Gender, Culture and Identity*, London: Routledge.

Mokbel-Wensley, S. (1996) "Statutory Discrimination in Lebanon: a Lawyer's View," in Yamani, M., ed., *Feminism and Islam*, London: Ithaca, 321–9.

Multi-Douglas, Fedwa (1991) *Woman's Body, Woman's Word: Gender and Discourse in Arabo-Islamic Writing*, Princeton: Princeton University Press.

Qaraḍāwī, Y. al- (2006) "Female Imam: The Fatwa of Sheikh Yusuf Qardawi on the Issue of Women Leading Men in Prayer," Islamic Information Office of Hawaii, posted April 17, 2005, http://www.iio.org/article.php/20050417005930119.

Rahman, F. (1965) "The Concept of *ḥadd* in Islamic Law," *Islamic Studies* 4: 237–51. (See especially 243–7 on the rights of God and human rights with reference to punishment for their violation.)

Roald, A. S. (2001) *Women in Islam: the Western Experience*, London: Routledge.

Roded, R. ed. (1999) *Women in Islam and the Middle East: A Reader*, London: I. B. Tauris.

Saadawi, N. el- (1980) *The Hidden Face of Eve*, London: I. B. Tauris.

Soueif, A. (2001) "The Language of the Veil," *The Guardian Weekend* October 8: 29–32. (Egyptian veils and identity.)
Tabandeh, S. (1970) *A Muslim Commentary on the Universal Declaration of Human Rights*, F. J. Goulding trans., Guilford: F. J. Goulding.
Tibrīzī, Khātib, Muḥammad ibn ʿAbd Allāh (1975) *Mishkat al-Masabih*, J. Robson trans., Lahore: M. Ashraf.
Tjomsland, M. and Karin Ask, K., eds. (1998) *Women and Islamization: Contemporary Dimensions of Discourse on Gender Relations*, Oxford: Berg.
Wadud, A. (1999) *Qurʾān and Woman: Rereading the Sacred Text from a Woman's Perspective*, New York: Oxford University Press.

49

RELIGIOUS MINORITY RIGHTS

Christopher Buck

Islam is experiencing an identity crisis that has precipitated a world crisis. Radical Islamists are in the news almost every day, yet Westerners are taught that radical Islamism is not "true Islam." Islam, we are told, means peace, yet that public identity is typically not reflected in the social mirror of the popular press. Every time a suicide bomb is detonated, the image of a peaceful Islam is exploded along with it. In the popular mind, Islam is as Islam does. Another yardstick by which Islamic claims to a peaceful authenticity are measured is the treatment of religious minorities within an Islamic state. Both Islamic and Western states, generally, claim to respect human rights, within the context of Islamic and democratic ideals, respectively. A Western nation-state's identity as a democracy will be measured not only against its own democratic ideals, but against an emerging body of international human rights law. Whether by national or international standards, the acid test of democracy is its treatment of minorities. The same holds true for Islamic states. For all of the rhetoric professing Islam's respect for human rights, human wrongs within the modern Muslim world must still be addressed, even if not redressed.

Not all religious minorities within predominantly Muslim countries are treated similarly. Comparatively speaking, Jewish and Christian minorities typically fare better than other minority faith-communities within Muslim societies functioning under Islamic law. But certain minority religions within Islamic states have experienced hardships of such proportions as to attract the attention of the international community. This chapter briefly looks at the Alevis, the Ahmadiyya, and the Bahá'ís and argues that Islamic majoritarian treatment of minorities – who are a problem for the majority because they hold unwelcome beliefs – reveals much about the real nature of particular claims to Islamic authenticity.

This chapter also suggests that Islamic identity and praxis must now withstand the scrutiny of the international community – a relatively new situation that certainly did not exist when Islam was the world's superpower during the so-called Dark Ages of Europe. Inevitably, Islamic law will be measured against international law, and will increasingly be constrained by it. More importantly, in the twenty-first century, the legal "right" of minority religions to an identity may be as important as the "truth" of their respective identities. The cosmopolitanism of human rights requires the right to an identity of a minority where that identity stands in tension with the identity of the majority.

Three of the most controversial religious minorities within the Islamic world will be examined in their respective socio-historical contexts: the Alevis in Turkey, the

Ahmadiyya in Pakistan, the Bahá'ís of Iran. These three faith-communities provide ideal subjects for a comparative study of the identities of religious minorities within the modern Muslim world. In an increasingly globalized world, Islamic identity is ultimately a legal as well as a religious issue. Characterizing the Ahmadiyya and the "Bahá'í Faith" as "Islamic minorities" is problematic in itself, as the Ahmadis profess themselves as Muslims while the Bahá'ís do not. Indeed, the distinctive identity of the Bahá'í Faith as an independent world religion is universally upheld by the Bahá'í scriptures, authorities, and adherents themselves, while the adamantine Islamic identity of the Ahmadiyya is universally upheld by the Ahmadiyya writings, authorities, and adherents with equal vigor. Where the self-identity of each of these two religious minorities is at issue within a given Islamic state offers a case-study in terms of Islamic claims to authenticity.

So, what is Islamic identity? More to the point is this question: Can an Islamic state tolerate a religious minority that has an alternative Islamic identity (as in the case of the Alevis), a rival Islamic identity (as in the case of the Ahmadiyya), or a post-Islamic identity (as in the case of the Bahá'ís)? The resolution of these vexed questions depends on which lens is used as a frame and focus. Here, the choice of the framework of analysis is critical, for it will largely determine the outcome. This study employs a three-faceted inquiry. The identities of religious minorities within Islamic states implicates 1) *etic* (outsider/majoritarian), 2) *emic* (insider/minority), and 3) *international* perspectives. Together, these three perspectives operate as a prism that works its own ideological optics, refracting claims to Islamic identity and breaking those claims into their constituent colors – the spectral measure of which is the treatment of religious minorities in an Islamic state.

Thus, this chapter explores Islamic and non-Islamic identities from multiple perspectives – external, internal, and international. External identity represents the perspective of dominant Islamic authorities. Internal identity emanates from the perspective of the faith-community itself. International opinion regarding the identity of both religious minorities and the majority of a given Islamic state is best viewed from the perspective of international human rights standards. In trying to make sense of all three vantage points, the connections between how Islamic authorities characterize certain religious minorities and how they treat them with respect to fundamental human rights will be explored. It is critical, then, to be clear throughout which perspective is being presented.

Islam, which has core beliefs and practices, lacks a central authority. Long before the abolition of the caliphate by Kemal Atatürk on March 2, 1924, the caliph had largely been a figurehead since 1258. Even before, the caliph was never a universal authority in Islam. Doctrinally, core Islamic beliefs and praxis were never reduced to a single creed or code. Sociologically, within the Muslim world, not only is the range of ethnicities, languages, and cultural traditions rich and variegated, there is a surprising range of Islamic identities as well. Ultimately, Islamic identity is as plural as it is plastic. Norms define and boundaries confine. These boundaries are in flux; they are as perceptual as they are conceptual. Whatever normative "Islam" is supposed to be is constantly being negotiated and renegotiated. As might be expected, Muslim questions surrounding the alternatively Islamic, rival Islamic, or post-Islamic identities of religious minorities within Islamic nation-states are vexing for Islamic orthodoxies.

The very notion of an Islamic "orthodoxy" is itself problematic. The concept is so theologically freighted that to speak of an Islamic orthodoxy begs the question. Heterodoxy is anything that departs from orthodoxy – that is, any belief that varies significantly from the perspective of the religious majority and is therefore objectionable to the dominant religion. Strictly speaking, notions of "orthodoxy" and "heterodoxy" are simply social realities. Here, and purely as a term of convenience, by Islamic "orthodoxy" we mean any establishment of "official" or "mainstream" Islam that, by dint of its dominance, has coercive power to render the existence of minorities problematic where such groups hold unwelcome beliefs. In pluralist societies committed to freedom of religion, even the religious majority has no coercive power over the religious minorities. But in a state where a particular formulation of "correct" Islamic belief is maintained *and enforced*, the existence of religious minorities whose beliefs and practices differ from the normative majoritarian position often tests the limits of the dominant religious leadership, which may have recourse in using the state's apparatus to suppress and, in some cases, to oppress a minority, with the goal of eventually marginalizing it out of existence.

Simply put, the Alevis are patently heterodox by normative Islamic standards, while the Ahmadiyya and the Bahá'ís are doubly heterodox due to their post-Islamic claims to revelation. All three of these groups are considered heterodox by their respective orthodox Sunnī (and Shīʿī) majorities. This is particularly problematic under *sharīʿa* law, which can theoretically accommodate non-Muslim minorities with some degree of egalitarianism, if not quasi-equality, but only if they fit within a prescribed religious framework. A religious minority that fits within that framework is afforded a degree of protection. This is the case with Christians and Jews – "Peoples of the Book" – who enjoy, in theory at least, recognition and protection within an explicit Qur'anic framework. Zoroastrians, Hindus, and other religious communities – such as the cluster of disparate groups that fell under the Qur'anic rubric of Sabians – have historically gained a certain measure of toleration within Islamic states as well. But a religious minority within an Islamic state that does not fit within that framework (such as the Alevis, the Ahmadiyya, and the Bahá'ís) is not afforded such protection. That is where the international human rights regime can, on a case-by-case basis, intervene – and does so with increasing frequency.

Under *sharīʿa* regimes in the past, the Alevis have, for the most part, historically adopted strategies of survival by secrecy, until secularization from within intervened, as in the case of modern Turkey, to secure their status as legally protected minorities. In the case of the Ahmadiyya in Pakistan and the Bahá'ís of Iran, the legal regimes of their respective countries bar full recognition and rights, leaving secularization – in the form of international law – as an ameliorative and constraining force. In so saying, this is not to suggest that religious minorities will fare better to the extent that Islamic governments abandon *sharīʿa* regimes. Yet some adjustment has to be advocated. While implementation of the International Covenant on Civil and Political Rights (discussed further in this chapter) will require such adjustments, it does not oblige the secularization of Islamic states.

The paradox of being heterodox is this: how can a religious minority either maintain its Islamic identity (as in the case of the Ahmadiyya) or maintain its independent, post-Islamic identity (as in the case of the Bahá'ís) where a dominant Islamic orthodoxy categorically rejects such self-defined identities as illicit, invalid, and illegal?

Simply put, the quasi-Islamic identity of the Alevis, the rival (revivalist) Islamic identity of the Ahmadiyya and the post-Islamic (independent) identity of the Bahá'ís all offend orthodox Islamic identities. These affronts – these offenses – while unintended, are variously taken as a real threat to traditional Islamic identities.

Times change, and so do Islamic identities. The Alevis have been branded in the past as heretics – and in 2007 as "pagans" for their musical religious ceremonies and liberal customs – but now enjoy a relative degree of state support in Turkey. More significantly, the Alevis constitute the ruling elite in present-day Syria (where they are known as Alawis). But the Ahmadiyya and the Bahá'ís are generally regarded as apostates. As will be seen, given the clash of religious identities within in the modern Muslim world, secularization is often superior to *sharīʿa* law in integrating religious minorities having quasi-Islamic, rival Islamic, and post-Islamic identities.

Minorities are defined by majorities (unless the minority is a ruling elite, as with the Alawis). Even an Islamic democracy may fail to equalize rights in a Muslim state. The modern Muslim Middle East demonstrates, time and again, that information management in the hands of a majority determines social policy and overrides the self-identity of the minorities. In Pakistan, for instance, the Ahmadis profess to be Muslims, while Pakistani law strips the Ahmadiyya community of the right to manifest its Islamic identity. To cite another instance, the Bahá'ís of Iran consider themselves to be an independent faith-community, while the Iranian regime is intransigent in its refusal to permit the Bahá'ís to practice their religion. Thus, the same group may have two distinct (even contradictory) identities: that defined by the prevailing Muslim majority, and that maintained by the minority group. Not only do these power disparities create formidable obstacles for scholarship in understanding these identities (especially in negotiating a middle ground between anti-minority polemics and pro-minority apologetics), they obviously pose problems for the minorities themselves.

Muslim majorities strenuously maintain that the rights of religious minorities are respected in an Islamic state. To varying degrees, this may be true, so long as those minorities do not pose any threat (real or perceived) to Islam. Put in different words, the way that Islamic minorities are treated within the Islamic world depends, to a large degree, on how the religious identities of these minorities are defined by the Islamic states in which they live. This, in turn, can lead to judgments about claims regarding Islamic identity by the surrounding, largely secular world.

To make matters worse, controversies within the modern Muslim world ignite controversies outside that world. While majority norms define Islamic identity within Muslim states, minority norms define Western valuations of those same Islamic identities. Clashes within the Muslim world exacerbate the clashes without. Social historian P. R. Kumaraswamy (2003: 244) notes that "discussions on minorities have often been controversial and politically loaded." States typically resent and resist "any outside criticisms over their treatment of their minority population and consider it to be a sovereign and inviolable subject." Yet, as Kumaraswamy observes, "they do not hesitate to use the treatment of minorities by their adversaries as a useful foreign policy instrument." In other words, minority issues within Muslim states are lightning rods for criticism by foreign states.

Not everything that affects the body politic is political in the sense that Kumaraswamy asserts. For instance, at a White House news briefing on March 28, 2006, a spokesman expressed President Bush's concern over worsening situation of the Bahá'ís in Iran. While such human rights concerns inform the policy of the USA, they are not determinative of it. Here, we see a triangulation of tensions between various Islamic orthodoxies, their constituent Islamic heterodoxies, and universal normative values, collectively defined by the human rights canons of international law, to which many Islamic states are signatories as well. There is a large body of literature on whether or not the human rights standards of international law represent Western values or universal values, and the view that they are Western is often advanced as an excuse for noncompliance.

Thus there are three competing sets of Islamic identities that act and react on any given religious minority in an Islamic state and these sets of identities will be examined here with the three groups in question: (1) the Alevis in Turkey, (2) the Ahmadiyya in Pakistan, and (3) the Bahá'ís in Iran. Of these three nations, Pakistan and Iran have been designated "countries of particular concern," "for ongoing, egregious violations of religious freedom" by the United States Commission on International Religious Freedom (2005). To label any Islamic state as a "country of particular concern" necessarily entails the interface of three identities: (1) the perceived identity of that religious minority within the broader framework of the group identity of the dominant Islamic majority; (2) the self-identity of the religious minority within an Islamic state; and (3) judgments made by the international community regarding these plural – and problematic – identities. A religious minority has its own moral compass and religious laws. These, in turn, are constrained by the overarching authority of the Islamic majority which, in turn, is constrained, at least in principle, under international law. Thus, concentric identities are layered within local, national, and international contexts that act and react on each other.

Outsider-majority views

The Alevis in Turkey

In 2002 the Alevis of Turkey numbered some twelve to fifteen million, comprising an estimated 20 to 25 percent of the total Anatolian population. The Turkish Alevis form a distinct religious and quasi-ethnic group. Alevis are the second most numerous ethno-religious minority of republican Turkey. The vast majority of Alevis are ethnic and linguistic Turks, although about 20 per cent of Alevis are Kurds, equal to about 25 per cent of the total Kurdish population of Turkey. Alevis live primarily in Eastern Turkey or Anatolia (the part of Turkey that lies in Asia).

Severely persecuted during Ottoman rule, Alevis adopted secrecy as a survival strategy, and so practiced dissimulation (*taqiyya*). Although Alevis have a distinct genealogy going back to early Shīʿī history, some of the outward identifiers of being Muslim – whether in the orthodox Sunnī or Shīʿī sense – are missing. For instance, Alevis do not observe the fast of Ramaḍān. Instead, they fast for 12 days during the month of Muḥarram. Neither do they perform their obligatory prayers five times daily, as Muslims are required to do. Nor do they make the pilgrimage to Mecca. The fact that fasting, prayer, and pilgrimage – three of the five "pillars of Islam" – are conspicuously absent raises serious questions about the identity of Alevis as Muslims.

The Alevis have reemerged in the past two decades as a largely secular, democratic community both in Turkey and in Europe. More important is Alevi identity in relation to what has been termed the "Turkish–Islam" synthesis that aims to transform inter-communal conflict into a sense of greater, particular Turkish, unity. Poyraz (2005: 512) argues that "the Turkish State uses the Alevis as a form of insurance against those who oppose secularism." The Turkish state has found an ally in the Alevis, who have proved useful as a bulwark against the encroachment of ultra-conservative Muslim clerics. But there is a more practical, immediate reason for recognizing the minority rights of Alevis, as Sahin explains: "Since the global discourse of identity as right has been accepted by the EU, Turkey is forced to promulgate laws to recognize its religious and ethnic minorities" (2005: 467). The question of the Islamic identity of the Alevi minority entails, in a positive form, an active state interest – an interest that we will see in the case of the Ahmadiyya of Pakistan and the Bahá'ís of Iran, but manifest in decidedly negative and oppressive ways in those instances.

The Ahmadiyya in Pakistan

The Ahmadiyya is a worldwide community, with Hazrat Mirzā Ṭāhir Aḥmad as its Supreme Head. The Ahmadiyya have around four million adherents in Pakistan (Khan 2003: 218). Perhaps the most well-known Ahmadi of recent times is Sir Muhammad Zafrullah Khan (d. 1986), former president of the International Court of Justice, Pakistan's first foreign minister, a translator of the Qur'ān and paternal grandfather of Ahmadi author Amjad Mahmood Khan, a 2004 graduate of Harvard Law School, who has published a legal analysis of the plight of the Pakistani Ahmadiyya in *Harvard Human Rights Journal* (2003).

In his article, Khan presents the official Islamic perspective of the government of Pakistan, of the Ahmadiyya community in Pakistan, and the international human rights regime. Khan notes that, in 1974, the orthodox Sunnī Muslim *ʿulamāʾ* successfully pressured then-Prime Minister Zulfikar Ali Bhutto to declare Ahmadis as non-Muslims. Accordingly, Bhutto oversaw the introduction into Pakistan's parliament of Articles 260(3)(a) and (b), defining the term "Muslim" in the Pakistani context and excluding groups that were, legally speaking, deemed to be non-Muslim. Effective as of September 6, 1974, this constitutional amendment explicitly stripped Ahmadis of their identity as Muslims. In 1984, the Government added Section 298(c) to its Penal Code, a section commonly referred to as the "anti-Ahmadi law." Used by the government and anti-Ahmadi religious groups to target and harass Ahmadis, the section prohibits Ahmadis from calling themselves Muslims or posing as Muslims, from referring to their faith as Islam, from preaching or propagating their faith, from inviting others to accept the Ahmadi faith, and from insulting the religious feelings of recognized Sunnī Muslims. The vague wording of the provision that forbids Ahmadis from "directly or indirectly" posing as Muslims has enabled mainstream Muslim religious leaders to bring charges against Ahmadis for using the standard Muslim greeting form and for naming their children Muḥammad. The constitutionality of Section 298(c) was upheld in a split-decision Supreme Court case in 1996. The punishment for violation of the section is imprisonment for up to three years and a fine.

This "excommunication" of the Ahmadiyya as Muslims by force of law was a clear extension of the hegemony that orthodox Muslim clerics wielded. Divesting the

Pakistani Ahmadiyya community of its Islamic identity was followed by legal entrenchment of the anti-blasphemy provisions in Pakistan's Penal Code. These provisions are systematically aimed at the eradication of every vestige of Islamic identity that the Ahmadiyya possessed. It is apparent that the Ahmadis in general are caught on the horns of a dilemma: while the Ahmadiyya see themselves as authentic Muslims, the theocratic force of Pakistani law endangers any visible manifestation of that identity. Here, the prevailing Islamic orthodoxy has, through the instrumentality of state law, legally barred the Ahmadiyya from openly practicing their faith as professed Muslims.

The Bahá'ís in Iran

The identity of the Bahá'í Faith is that of an independent world religion, and not as a sub-group within Islam. Given the longstanding, nearly universal and legally binding recognition of the independent status of the Faith worldwide, this is not merely a matter of internal Bahá'í claims versus those of certain Islamic authorities. However obvious this may be to the Bahá'ís themselves, the Iranian authorities have a contrary view based on Islamic doctrine that bars any religion from legitimately appearing after the time of Muḥammad. Absolutely fundamental to Islamic identity is the finality of Muḥammad, whom the Qur'ān dignifies as the "seal of the prophets" (Qur'ān 33:40) and thus the last of the prophets. Therefore it is an utter impossibility, from the strictly Muslim point of view, for any prophet to appear after Muḥammad. Since the Bahá'í Faith was established in the nineteenth century, its truth-claims are automatically rejected because of the doctrine of the finality of Muḥammad's prophethood (Buck 1995: 191–8; Buck 2007).

The idea that the Bahá'í Faith is a sect of Islam could brook no tolerance by Muslim authorities. This sectarian notion of Bahá'í origins is primarily a Western mischaracterization. The notion that the Bahá'í Faith has an Islamic identity and is an "Islamic minority" would, unless carefully contextualized, lend support to a pernicious misrepresentation of the Bahá'í Faith which is, after all, more aptly characterized as simply a religious minority within any given Islamic state. Simply put, the Bahá'í Faith has Iranian Islamic origins, and thus a great deal of continuity with Shī'ī Islam, yet emerged as an entirely independent religion, replete with its own scriptures, laws, and identity. In a word, the Bahá'í Faith is the daughter religion of Islam in much the same way as Christianity sprang from Judaism. In this respect, both Christianity and the Bahá'í Faith are secondary monotheisms, arising out of primary monotheisms. Although historically derivative, they are independent.

The Islamic Republic of Iran professes its support of human rights, arguing that Islam has long been the promoter and protector of human rights far in advance of Western secular formulations. Ironically, some of the United Nations human rights language has made its way into the Constitution of the Islamic Republic of Iran. Outlining the "General Principles" of the Constitution, Article 13 states: "Zoroastrian, Jewish, and Christian Iranians are the only recognized religious minorities, who, within the limits of the law, are free to perform their religious rites and ceremonies, and to act according to their own canon in matters of personal affairs and religious education." Members of these three religions are considered by Iranian clerics to be "People of the Book" and are therefore accorded Qur'anic protection. The effect of this provision is to deny Bahá'ís their freedom of religion. Bahá'ís are considered apostates, and their blood may be shed with impunity, perhaps even with clerical approval.

The vocabulary of human rights, which has been used in the Iranian Constitution, does not carry the universal application characteristic of international law. Elsewhere in the Constitution, under the rubric, "The Rights of the People," Article 20 adds: "All citizens of the country, both men and women, equally enjoy the protection of the law and enjoy all human, political, economic, social, and cultural rights, in conformity with Islamic criteria." Clearly, the Bahá'ís do not conform to these legal criteria. While the Iranian government has not denied that Bahá'ís are citizens of Iran, they do not enjoy equal rights.

In the years immediately following the 1979 Iranian revolution, clerics ordered the arbitrary arrest of Bahá'ís and the torture and execution of over 200 of them (particularly members of Bahá'í administrative bodies, sometimes with demands that their families pay for the bullets used to kill them). Other actions taken against Bahá'ís include confiscation of property, seizure of bank assets, expulsion from schools and universities, denial of employment, cancellation of pensions (with demands that the government be reimbursed for past pension payments), desecration and destruction of Bahá'í cemeteries and holy places, criminalizing Bahá'í activities and thus forcing the dissolution of Bahá'í administration, and pronouncing Bahá'í marriages as illegal acts of prostitution. In addition, there were relentless propaganda campaigns aimed at inflaming anti-Bahá'í passions to instigate mob violence and crimes against Bahá'ís. There are many documented instances of this state-instigated incitement to violence (see Ghanea 2002; Buck 2003). This phase of the anti-Bahá'í campaign has aptly been described as "civil death" – a cultural cleansing that collectively affects a community estimated to be 300,000 Iranians.

After 1985, with Iran having been scandalized for its violation of the rights of Bahá'ís and other religious minorities, the number of executions of Bahá'ís sharply dropped, and, in 1987 and 1988, most of the Bahá'ís being held in prison were released. While this may imply that improved treatment of Bahá'ís in Iran was due to the international attention focused on the issue, the cause of the improvement is not known and thus it should not be assumed that international pressure was a decisive factor. Yet there is more direct evidence of the efficacy of diplomatic recourse in partially restoring rights to education. In the early 1980s, a proportionally large number of Bahá'í children – probably most, but not all – had been expelled from public and private schools in Iran. But international pressure caused that policy to be rescinded, and, in the late 1980s, the Iranian regime adopted a new policy of concealment. This shift in anti-Bahá'í tactics masked a new and insidious strategy formalized in a secret 1991 memorandum from the Iranian Supreme Revolutionary Cultural Council on "the Bahá'í question." This document surfaced in 1993, first appearing in the report by Special Representative Reynaldo Galindo Pohl to the UN Commission on Human Rights. The policy recommendations of this document are still in force. Personally endorsed by Ayatollah Ali Khamenei on February 25, 1991 and written by Dr. Seyyed Mohammad Golpaygani, secretary of the Supreme Revolutionary Cultural Council, this document advises government officials, among other things, to expel Bahá'ís from universities, "once it becomes known that they are Bahá'ís." It further states: "Deny them employment if they identify themselves as

Bahá'ís." "Deny them any position of influence." The policy effectively denies Bahá'ís the right to higher education, a policy that had already been in effect since 1980. No Bahá'í can, in practice, attend university in Iran. As a result, Bahá'ís have organized the Bahá'í Institute for Higher Education (BIHE), popularly known as "Bahá'í Open University."

The Bahá'í International Community reports that Iranian Bahá'ís seeking to enter Iran's vocational and technical institutes are effectively barred from admission for the 2007–8 academic year, since the 2007 form for the entrance examination indicates that only one box may be marked for religion. Applicants are given three choices to self-identity as religious minorities – Zoroastrian, Jewish, or Christian. If none of these boxes is marked, the applicant will be considered Muslim. This is unacceptable to Bahá'ís as tantamount to a *de facto* denial of their faith.

As disturbing as this surely is to human rights advocates, it is not surprising. Bahá'ís are typically denied full freedom of religion throughout many states in the Muslim Middle East. There are two principal reasons for this: 1) Bahá'ís lack *dhimmī* (protected) status and are therefore excluded from Qur'anic protection; and 2) the Bahá'í Faith is a post-Islamic religion – a theoretical impossibility considering Muḥammad's ontological status as the "seal of the prophets." Apart from the day of judgment, Islam cannot conceive of a post-Islamic act of revelation, much less theologically tolerate a post-Islamic claim to revelation.

Insider-minority perspectives

The Alevis in Turkey

"Alevi" means "of ʿAlī" and thus comes to mean "follower of ʿAlī." Alevis revere ʿAlī ibn Abī Ṭālib (d. 661). Thus they have been called the "Deifiers of ʿAlī." This reflects ʿAlī's exalted station in Alevi theology. While Alevis claim a distinct identity, it is one that neither conflicts with Turkish national identity nor is inimical to the Turkish state. That identity kept at bay the threat of Alevi fusion into the Sunnī majority. According to David Zeidan:

> The resurgence of Sunni fundamentalism that began in the 1950s and has recently grown much stronger also pushed the Alevis to the political left. Many Alevis reacted by stressing their separate identity and reinterpreting Alevism in socialist and Marxist idiom that seemed to have an affinity to Alevi ideals of equality and traditions of revolt.
>
> (Zeidan 1999:77)

That "revolt" has gone full circle in Turkey, where the Alevi minority now enjoys the blessings of the moderate Sunnī majority. The Alevi question became one answer to countering the threat of Islamic fundamentalism in Turkey, where the former "Deifiers of ʿAlī" are now the reifiers of Turkish secularism.

The Ahmadiyya in Pakistan

The insider perspective is clear: Ahmadis consider themselves to be Muslims and observe Islamic practices. According to Khan (2003: 218, n. 4), the Ahmaddiyya are self-professed Muslims, and their claim to Muslim self-identity is valid and should be immune from exclusion by a Sunnī majority under the following rationale. As followers of the prophetic restorationist and messianic claimant, Mirzā Ghulām Ahmad (d. 1908) of Qadian, India, the Ahmadiyya profess what they consider to be the "true spirit" of Islam. They see their beliefs and practices as the restoration of pristine Islam. An orthodoxy may well define what and who is heterodox. But the arrow can quickly fly back at the archer, when one considers that orthodoxy and heresy are fluid notions that entail power relations. The irony is this: the Ahmadiyya, in their view, practice a more authentic form of Islam – one that is purified from 14 centuries of accretion. According to Pakistani authorities, the Ahmadiyya do have the freedom to practice their religion – but not as Muslims. So, while "might" makes "right" when the Sunnī orthodoxy in Pakistan proscribes the Ahmadiyya practice of the same religion under penalty of law, international religious human rights advocates see this as a clear breach of religious freedom.

The Bahá'ís in Iran

What kind of Islamic identity do Bahá'ís have? Are Bahá'ís, for instance, Muslims? The simple answer is no, since the Bahá'í Faith is an independent world religion. Bahá'ís do not, in fact, profess to be Muslim, although they recognize the divine station of Muḥammad. Because of the Islamic origins of their Faith, however, Bahá'ís have much in common with Muslims. What distinguishes the Bahá'í Faith from Islam is the revelation of Bahá'u'lláh (d. 1892), the socio-moral principles of which marked a major "paradigm shift" in what may be characterized as a paradigm of unity.

Explaining the relationship of the Bahá'í Faith to Islam raises the larger Bahá'í concept of "Progressive Revelation." Although the Faith has a close historical link with Islam, Bahá'í self-identity is intrinsically and intimately related to all of the world's great religions. Islam is seen as a major event in a series of decisive historical moments when great spiritual teachers appeared to catalyze the course of social evolution through renewed spiritual teachings and new social laws. To invoke the Western term, these Prophets are both "forth-tellers" (the literal meaning of the Greek *prophētes*) as well as foretellers. Each communicated a present message and future "prophecy." Prophecies converged in presaging the advent of Bahá'u'lláh, a world-messiah whose principles and spiritual influence would bring about world unity. As "World-Reformer," Bahá'u'lláh advocated world peace, parliamentary democracy, disarmament, an international language, harmony of science and religion, interfaith concord, gender and racial equality. From a historicist perspective, in precocious anticipation of a global society, Bahá'u'lláh's signal contribution was to sacralize certain secular modernist reforms, integrated within an irreducibly original paradigm of world unity in which peace is made sacred. From an emic perspective, Bahá'u'lláh's principles have a divine origin and, if carried out, promise the social salvation of society.

Designating his son ʿAbdu'l-Bahá (d. 1921) as interpreter, exemplar and successor, and by ordaining the eventual formation of elected councils, Bahá'u'lláh instituted his Covenant as the organizing principle of the Bahá'í community and guarantor of its integrity, safeguarding against major schism. Succeeding ʿAbdu'l-Bahá in 1921 as "Guardian" of the Bahá'í Faith, Shoghi Effendi (d. 1957) globalized and evolved Bahá'í administration as a system of Local and National Spiritual Assemblies, leading to the election of The Universal House of Justice in 1963, the international Bahá'í governing body, established on Mount Carmel in Haifa, Israel.

While Islamic sensitivities need to be respected, many would argue that they do not outweigh human rights considerations. Ironically, secular values can sometimes be more universal than religious ones. Consequently, in a clash of religious value systems, international law may be the only practical arbiter until the conflict is resolved. In the case of Iranian Islam, there is a considerable distance between the constitutional rhetoric of respect for minority rights and the prevailing sociopolitical reality. As a direct result of Iran's treatment of its Bahá'í minority, the ultimate injury-in-fact is refractory damage to the reputation of Islam in the eyes of a critical public that uncritically tends to see Islam as monolithic. By the yardstick of minority rights, Iran's efforts to preserve Islamic values have arguably had the effect of perverting them.

International perspectives

International law exerts external pressures on a given country. Religious human rights (i.e., freedom of religion) are a subset of human rights. Human rights watchers monitor inequitable legal/policy restrictions on religious minorities by governments in response to perceived religious threats. In 1998, the USA enacted the International Religious Freedom Act, making religious freedom a feature of its foreign policy. Passed by the Senate on October 9, 1998 and unanimously approved by the House by voice vote on the following day, President Clinton signed the International Religious Freedom Act of 1998 (IRFA) into law on October 27, 1998. That Act established an independent and bipartisan advisory Commission on International Religious Freedom, an office in the State Department, an Ambassador-at-Large for International Religious Freedom, and an Annual Report on International Religious Freedom. The President, moreover, is required to take defined actions against states that violate religious freedom.

Human rights standards encoded as international law serve as the secular norm for religious rights. Discrimination as to religion or belief is condemned and this proscription against religious discrimination is an essential feature of the United Nations human rights charters. Several instruments of international law have been adopted – with varying force of law – to protect freedom of religion. They are: 1) Article 1(3) and 13 of the United Nations Charter; 2) Articles 1, 2, 18, Universal Declaration of Human Rights (adopted December 10, 1948, GA Res. 217, UN Doc. A/810, 71); 3) Article 2, Convention on the Prevention and Punishment of the Crime of Genocide (1948); 4) Articles 2, 18, 26 and 27 of the International Covenant on Civil and Political Rights [ICCPR] (adopted 1966 and effective March 23, 1976) (see pp. 654–5) Declaration on the Elimination of All Forms of Religious Intolerance and of Discrimination Based on Religion or Belief (adopted November 25, 1981); 6) UN Declaration on the Rights of Persons Belonging to National or Ethnic, Religious and Linguistic Minorities (1992); and 7) Article 14, Convention on the Rights of the Child. Their language is strong but their enforcement is weak. This problem is nowhere better illustrated than in the unresolved problems affecting the Bahá'ís of Iran and the Ahmadiyya in Pakistan.

Article 18 of the ICCPR protects the right to "freedom of thought, conscience and religion" and the "freedom to have or to adopt a religion or belief" of one's choice. Article 18 is concerned only with one's right to profess and practice one's belief and not at all concerned with the "truth" of one's religious identity. Thus, what international law requires of Islamic states is not that they recognize religions *per se*, but that they recognize fundamental religious human rights. Of the instruments cited above, this article is the most directly applicable, legally binding provision on religious freedom. These complex distinctions among international covenants and conventions, however, are not decisive in and of themselves. In clarifying the legal distinction between international law and non-binding instruments, it should not be implied that the critical distinction is the legal status of the instrument (convention versus declaration), but rather the process of ratification by state parties. While international religious human rights law is evolving, it remains for member states to implement it.

Laws of religious freedom in Pakistan and Iran are vitiated by countervailing laws against Ahmadis and policies against Bahá'ís respectively. Technically, there are no "laws against" the Bahá'ís in Iran, but rather a lack of legal protection due to silence in the Iranian Constitution. Government action against Bahá'ís has been mandated not by laws but by government orders and instructions. While such laws, policies and directives may incorporate human rights language as a ringing endorsement of international covenants in theory, they may ring as a hollow echo in actual practice. Various United Nations resolutions have condemned these laws and their practices. Examples, where relevant, will be provided below.

The Alevis in Turkey

Turkey, of course, must satisfy the Copenhagen criteria in order to join the European Union, and this will act, in concert with Turkish secularism and the force of international law, as a further constraint against any reflex of repression. According to the *International Religious Freedom Report 2005* released by the Bureau of Democracy, Human Rights, and Labor, the Alevis have experienced relatively minor and isolated incidents of discrimination (US Department of State 2005a). Given the increasingly ideal Turkish state relations in recent support of the Alevi community as a bulwark against the perceived and real threat of radical Islam, however, these problems affecting the Alevis in Turkey are likely to resolve themselves.

The Ahmadiyya in Pakistan

According to the same *International Religious Freedom Report 2005* released by the Bureau of Democracy, Human Rights, and Labor, the situation of the Ahmadiyya is far most serious in terms of religious human rights concerns (US Department of State 2005b). Critics of Pakistan's anti-Ahmadi laws point out that Ordinance XX of Pakistan's Penal Code violates Article 18 of the ICCPR, under its provisions that "no one shall be subject to coercion which would impair his freedom to have or to adopt a religion or belief of his own choice." This analysis is borne out by United Nations

Resolution 1985/21. Under this analysis, international law is more concerned with the "right" of the Ahmadiyya to profess and practice Islam rather than with the "truth" of their Islamic identity. There are distinct advantages that will accrue if international law is more effectively enforced.

The Bahá'ís in Iran

In addition to the situation reported above, other recent actions in Iran against the Bahá'í community have been brought to light by the United Nations. On December 16, 2005, the United Nations General Assembly passed a resolution decrying human rights violations in Iran, citing

> escalation and increased frequency of discrimination and other human rights violations against the Bahá'í, including cases of arbitrary arrest and detention, the denial of freedom of religion or of publicly carrying out communal affairs, the disregard of property rights, the destruction of sites of religious importance, the suspension of social, educational and community-related activities and the denial of access to higher education, employment, pensions, adequate housing and other benefits.
>
> (Bahá'í World 2005)

The Iranian Bahá'ís have long been persecuted for their religious faith. Persecution entails a systematic policy of discrimination by a religious majority on the basis of heterodox beliefs of the oppressed minority. The *International Religious Freedom Report 2005* released by the Bureau of Democracy, Human Rights, and Labor specifies these human rights violations (US Department of State 2005c). This may partly be a symptom of a larger problem: Mohamed Eltayeb, an expert in the human rights field, points out that, in the aftermath of the 1979 revolution, a number of Muslim countries attempted "to construct alternative 'Islamic' human rights instruments," which, however, "have fallen far below the international standards" (cited in Buck 2003: 91–2).

The Bahá'í question is exacerbated by one particular problem in current international human rights standards: the UN's Declaration on the Elimination of All Forms of Intolerance and of Discrimination Based on Religion or Belief has yet to be raised to the level of an international convention, even though UN declarations on the elimination of racial discrimination and discrimination against women have already been codified as international law (Buck 2003: 91). At issue here is the difference between a declaration and a convention in the context of international law. The reason a convention takes the force of international law is that it operates as a multilateral treaty. The fact that the UN Declaration is an aspirational document and not law is not inherently a problem with respect to protecting the Bahá'ís in Iran, as Iran is already a party to the ICCPR and is thus bound by its Article 18. This is not to say that if the provisions of the Declaration became binding they would not be helpful, but Article 18 already requires Iran to protect the essential religious rights of the Bahá'ís.

Protection of the Bahá'ís in Iran (or of any religious minority anywhere), as a matter of international law, does not depend on recognition of the religion by the state government. Because of the religious identity of some Islamic governments, they could never, and could never be expected to, recognize the Bahá'í Faith as an independent religion. However, they can and they must be expected to permit all individuals to "have or to adopt a religion or belief of his choice" and "either individually or in community with others and in public or private, to manifest his religion or belief in worship, observance, practice and teaching" (International Covenant on Civil and Political Rights [ICCPR], art. 18). Thus the Bahá'ís are not seeking from the Iranian government a formal recognition of the independent identity of the Faith but rather the right to believe and to practice. The distinction may be fine, yet religious rights have a clear priority over religious recognition. The Bahá'í religion need not be "recognized," but the religious rights of the Bahá'ís must be recognized.

From the fact that various Islamic states and institutions have attempted to replicate international human rights language into their respective constitutions and legal codes, one may observe – and even predict – that international religious human rights will exert increasing pressures on Islamic regimes found to be in violation of international norms, to which most Islamic states are signatories and by which they are legally bound.

Conclusion

It has been shown that the Islamic identities of Islamic minorities are largely a matter of perspective. Where the legitimacy and rights of a controversial religious minority within an Islamic state are both in question and in peril, the interplay of what might be termed a "standpoint epistemology" must be taken into consideration. Like truth and beauty, Islamic orthodoxy is in the eyes of the beholder. More importantly, Islamic authenticity is in the hands of the powerful. Only the pressure of international human rights standards has the universal and even-handed potential needed to constrain Islamicate power-brokers from repressing their relatively powerless minorities.

Many in the field of international human rights feel that the Islamic world is the part of the international community least accepting of the international human rights regime. Clearly, what is needed is acceptance of international human rights laws, both in the enlightened self-interests of Islamic authorities, as well as in the interests of the religious minorities under their governance. Religious minorities that hold unwelcome beliefs within Islamic states – such as the Alevis of Turkey, the Ahmadiyya in Pakistan, and the Bahá'ís of Iran – continue to pose a challenge to the Islamic identity of its entrenched orthodoxies. This challenge is affrontive, not confrontive.

A test case in Egypt has recently drawn international attention: an Egyptian Bahá'í couple requested the Department of Passports and Immigration to add the names of their daughters to their passports. The department refused to return their passports and withdrew their ID cards – arguably in violation of their legal rights guaranteed by the Constitution of Egypt and the Universal Declaration of Human Rights. On April 4, 2006, a lower administrative court ruled that "[i]t is not inconsistent with Islamic tenets to mention the religion on this card even though it may be a religion whose rites are not recognized for open practice, such as Bahá' ism and the like." The Egyptian government has appealed this ruling. On December 16, 2006, the Supreme Administrative Court issued its final judgment in the case of Husam Izzat Musa and Ranya Enayat Rushdy, upholding the government's policy of allowing only affiliations of the three officially recognized religions – Judaism, Christianity, and Islam – on state ID cards and government documents. This ruling sets Egypt's religious human rights standards against international standards. However, on 31 March 2008, Egypt's official national newspaper, *Al-Akhbār* ("The News"), announced that Egypt's government-appointed National Council for Human Rights has just released its fourth annual report, recommending, *inter alia*, that the government allow the entry of "Bahá'í" as one of the choices in the religion field on official identity cards. Time will tell whether this recommendation will herald the dawn of a new era in the eventual freedom of oppressed religious minorities in Islamic states.

These and other recent events have reinforced the importance of sustained pressure by the international community on Islamic authorities to conform to international human rights standards. Accordingly, this chapter is not only about the identities of the minorities in emic, etic, and international perspectives, but about the perceived threat posed to the identity of the ruling majority, both by the existence of these minorities and by the requirements of international law that they be protected. International law bears on the right to choose and to practice a religion or belief. The right to religion as currently incorporated in international law is an individual right, not a group right, and is independent of the view of any state or people or even the international community itself as to the identity, nature or value of the belief or religion. What this has to do with the "identity" of a religious group is where Islamic states deny individual rights by denying group rights. In mustering the political will of states to advocate through international bodies and otherwise for the protection of the rights of members of a religious group, the political realities of efforts to implement human rights norms are challenging.

Since Islamic authorities are facing increasing pressure under international religious human rights law to allow religious minorities to maintain their own self-identities – whether as self-professed Muslims (as the Ahmadiyya maintain), or as self-professed religionists with a distinct identity separate from Muslims (as the Bahá'ís maintain), a full Islamicization of secular religious human rights standards is perhaps the most formidable challenge of all.

References and further reading

Bahai World (2005) "UN Calls on Iran to Stop Persecution of Bahá'ís," available online at http://www.bahaiworldnews.org/story.cfm?storyid=413.

Buck, C. (1995) *Symbol and Secret: Qur' an Commentary in Bahá' u' lláh's* Kitáb-i Íqán, Los Angeles: Kalimát Press; available online at http://bahai-library.com/books/symbol.secret.

—— (2003) "Islam and Minorities: The Case of the Bahá'ís," *Studies in Contemporary Islam* 5 (1–2): 83–106; available online at http://www.iranian.com/Opinion/2005/June/Bahái/Images/BuckBaháis2005Eng.pdf.

—— (2007) "Beyond the 'Seal of the Prophets': Baha'ullah's Book of Certitude (*Ketab-e Iqan*)," in C. Pedersen, F. Vahman, eds., *Religious Texts in Iranian Languages*, Copenhagen: Det Kongelige Danske Videnskabernes Selskab, 369–78.

Furman, U. (2000) "Minorities in Contemporary Islamist Discourse," *Middle Eastern Studies*, 36 (4): 1–20.

Ghanea, N. (2002) *Human Rights, the U.N. and the Bahá'ís in Iran*, Oxford: George Ronald.

Gualtieri, A. R. (1989) *Conscience and Coercion: Ahmadi Muslims and Orthodoxy in Pakistan*, Montreal: Guernica.

—— (2004) *The Ahmadis: Community, Gender, and Politics in a Muslim Society*, Montreal: McGill-Queen's University Press.

Khan, A. M. (2003) "Persecution of the Ahmadiyya Community in Pakistan: An Analysis Under International Law and International Relations," *Harvard Human Rights Journal*, 16: 217–44; available online at http://www.law.harvard.edu/students/orgs/hrj/iss16/khan.pdf.

Kumaraswamy, P. R. (2003) "Problems of Studying Minorities in the Middle East," *Alternatives: Turkish Journal of International Relations*, 2: 244–64; available online at http://www.alternativesjournal.net/volume2/number2/kumar.pdf

Poyraz, B. (2005) "The Turkish State and Alevis: Changing Parameters of an Uneasy Relationship," *Middle Eastern Studies*, 41: 503–16.

Rehman, J. (2000) "Accommodating Religious Identities in an Islamic State: International Law, Freedom of Religion and the Rights of Religious Minorities," *International Journal on Minority and Group Rights*, 7/2 (February): 139–66.

Sahin, S. (2005) "The Rise of Alevism as a Public Religion," *Current Sociology*, 53: 465–85

Shankland, D. (2003) *The Alevis in Turkey: The Emergence of a Secular Islamic Tradition*, London: Routledge.

United States Commission on International Religious Freedom (2005) *Annual Report of the United States Commission on International Religious Freedom*, Washington, DC; available online at http://www.uscirf.gov/countries/publications/currentreport/2005annualRpt.pdf.

United States Department of State (2005a) "Turkey: International Religious Freedom Report 2005," available online at http://www.state.gov/g/drl/rls/irf/2005/51586.htm.

—— (2005b) "Pakistan: International Religious Freedom Report 2005," available online at http://www.state.gov/g/drl/rls/irf/2005/51621.htm.

—— (2005c) "Iran: International Religious Freedom Report 2005," available online at http://www.state.gov/g/drl/rls/irf/2005/51599.htm

Yousif, A. (2000) "Islam, Minorities and Religious Freedom: A Challenge to Modern Theory of Pluralism," *Journal of Muslim Minority Affairs*, 20: 29–43.

Zeidan, D. (1999) "The Alevi of Anatolia," *Middle East Review of International Affairs* 3 (4); available online at http://meria.idc.ac.il/journal/1999/issue4/zeidan.pdf.

Zisser, E. (1999) "The Alawis, Lords of Syria: From Ethnic Minority to Ruling Sect," in O. Bengio, G. Ben-Dor, eds., *Minorities and the State in the Arab World*, Boulder, CO: Lynne Rienner Publishers, 129–48.

INTERNATIONAL COVENANT ON CIVIL AND POLITICAL RIGHTS

Adopted and opened for signature, ratification and accession by General Assembly resolution 2200A (XXI) of 16 December 1966

entry into force 23 March 1976, in accordance with Article 49

Article 4

1 In time of public emergency which threatens the life of the nation and the existence of which is officially proclaimed, the States Parties to the present Covenant may take measures derogating from their obligations under the present Covenant to the extent strictly required by the exigencies of the situation, provided that such measures are not inconsistent with their other obligations under international law and do not involve discrimination solely on the ground of race, colour, sex, language, religion or social origin.
2 No derogation from articles 6, 7, 8 (paragraphs 1 and 2), 11, 15, 16 and 18 may be made under this provision.
3 Any State Party to the present Covenant availing itself of the right of derogation shall immediately inform the other States Parties to the present Covenant, through the intermediary of the Secretary-General of the United Nations, of the provisions from which it has derogated and of the reasons by which it was actuated. A further communication shall be made, through the same intermediary, on the date on which it terminates such derogation.

Article 18

1 Everyone shall have the right to freedom of thought, conscience and religion. This right shall include freedom to have or to adopt a religion or belief of his choice, and freedom, either individually or in community with others and in public or private, to manifest his religion or belief in worship, observance, practice and teaching.
2 No one shall be subject to coercion which would impair his freedom to have or to adopt a religion or belief of his choice.
3 Freedom to manifest one's religion or beliefs may be subject only to such limitations as are prescribed by law and are necessary to protect public safety, order, health, or morals or the fundamental rights and freedoms of others.
4 The States Parties to the present Covenant undertake to have respect for the liberty of parents and, when applicable, legal guardians to ensure the religious and moral education of their children in conformity with their own convictions.

Article 26

All persons are equal before the law and are entitled without any discrimination to the equal protection of the law. In this respect, the law shall prohibit any discrimination and guarantee to all persons equal and effective protection against discrimination on any ground such as race, colour, sex, language, religion, political or other opinion, national or social origin, property, birth or other status.

Article 27

In those States in which ethnic, religious or linguistic minorities exist, persons belonging to such minorities shall not be denied the right, in community with the other members of their group, to enjoy their own culture, to profess and practise their own religion, or to use their own language.

Source: http://www.unhchr.ch/html/menu3/b/a_ccpr.htm

GLOSSARY

Abbasids dynasty of caliphs formally ruling 750 to 1258
adat customary or indigenous law
amīr commander or prince, frequently used in reference to the person who leads the community
Ashʿarī a theological school named after al-Ashʿarī (d. 935)
arkān the "pillars" of faith and practice (commonly numbered five)
aṣabiyya tribal or group solidarity
ashrāf plural of *sharīf*
basmala introductory phrase to each chapter of the Qur'ān (except *sūra* 9), "In the name of God, the Merciful, the Compassionate.
bidʿa disapproved innovation in legal or religious matters
Buwayhids dynasty of Shīʿī Persian military rulers 945 to 1055 (also spelled Būyids)
dār al-ḥarb the "house of war", the area of the world in which Islam does not dominate
dār al-Islām the "house of Islam" in which the religion of Islam dominates
daʿwa/dakwah propagation of Islam; missionizing
dhikr literally "mentioning" or "remembrance," used for the chant in Ṣūfī meditations.
dhimmī/dhimma a member of a protected community, especially referring to the Jews and Christians who live under Muslim rule
dīn religion; the word is used in the Qur'ān to refer to the specific beliefs and practices of people
dīwān register of government revenues such as land surveying, tax assessment, public health, etc.
dunyā the world
falsafa philosophy
fatwā a legal decision rendered by a *muftī*, who is a jurist qualified to make decisions of a general religious nature
fiqh jurisprudence, the science of religious law, as described by the jurists known as the *fuqahā'* (singular: *faqīh*)
ḥadd a group of offences and their punishment which are specifically defined in the Qur'ān (plural: *ḥudūd*) including unlawful intercourse, false accusation of sexual impropriety, drinking wine, theft and highway robbery
ḥadīth a tradition or written report, being the source material for the *sunna* of

Muḥammad, gathered together in the six books of authoritative traditions in Sunnī Islam

ḥajj pilgrimage to Mecca performed in the month of Dhū'l-ḥijja, one of the "Five Pillars" of Islam; a requirement for all Muslims, if they are able, once in a lifetime

ḥalāl permitted in Islamic law, often used referring to food

Ḥanbalī member of the Sunnī school of law named after Aḥmad ibn Ḥanbal (d. 855)

Ḥanafī member of the Sunnī school of law named after Abū Ḥanīfa (d. 767)

ḥijāb the veil or partition which prevents men from gazing at the "charms of women"

hijra Muḥammad's emigration from Mecca to Medina in the year 622; the date for the beginning of the Muslim *hijrī* calendar.

ʿīd al-aḍḥā the festival of sacrifice during the pilgrimage (*ḥajj*)

ʿīd al-fiṭr the festival of breaking the fast at the end of Ramaḍān

ifṭār the breaking of the fast at the end of Ramaḍān

ijmāʿ "consensus," one of the four sources of law for Sunnī law schools

ijtihād the use of one's "personal effort" in order to make a decision on a point of law not explicitly covered by the Qur'ān or the *sunna*; legal reasoning done by a *mujtahid*

Imām literally the "model," it can refer to a) the prayer leader in the *ṣalāt* who stands in front of the rows of worshipers, keeping their actions in unison during the prayer; b) a title of the revered early leaders of the Shīʿa who are the source of authority in that community, starting with ʿAlī ibn Abī Ṭālib; c) the founders of the Sunnī schools of law – Abū Ḥanīfa, Mālik ibn Anas, al-Shāfiʿī and Ibn Ḥanbal – and other significant religious figures

isnād the chain of authorities through whom a *ḥadīth* report has passed

isrāʾ Muḥammad's "night journey" to Jerusalem

Jaʿfarī legal school among the Shīʿa named after Jaʿfar al-Ṣādiq

jāhiliyya the "Age of Ignorance," often with a moral sense to ignoring Islam

jihād "striving for the faith" or "holy war," sometimes seen as a "sixth pillar" of Islam

jinn genies, another dimension of animate creation on earth

Kaʿba the sacred black cube building in the middle of the mosque in Mecca, focus of ritual prayer and the pilgrimage

kalām literally, "speech"; mode of theological discussion framed in terms of an argument and thence used for speculative theology as a whole

khalīfa Caliph, the leader of the Sunnī community, the "successor" to Muḥammad.

Khawārij group in early Islam who believed in absolute devotion as the mark of a true Muslim, all others being unbelievers (singular: Khārijī; also known as the Kharijites)

khulʿ divorce initiated by the wife by the agreement of her husband and repayment of the dowry

madhhab school of law (plural: *madhāhib*) formed around one of the four early figures significant in juristic discussions, Abū Ḥanīfa, Mālik ibn Anas, al-Shāfiʿī and Ibn Ḥanbal

madrasa school for religious education

Mahdī the awaited messiah-figure who will restore justice in the world prior to the judgment day

Mālikī the legal school named after Mālik ibn Anas (d. 795)
mawlid the celebration of the birthday of Muḥammad
miḥrāb prayer niche marking the direction of Mecca for prayer
miḥna the "inquisition," primarily under the Abbasid caliph al-Ma'mūn (ruled 813–33), which demanded that government officials and religious leaders adhere to the doctrine of the "created Qur'ān"
mi'rāj the "heavenly ascension" of Muḥammad
muftī a jurist who is authorized to give a *fatwā* or legal decision on a religious matter
mujtahid a jurist who is qualified to exercise *ijtihād* or personal effort in making legal decisions
Murji'a group in early Islam who held the "status quo" position in the debates over faith, generally connected to Abū Ḥanīfa (d. 767)
mut'a a marriage which is contractually limited in time
Mu'tazila a theological school of thought prominent in the eighth and ninth centuries, stressing human free will and the unity and justice of God, who employed rationalist modes of argumentation; also known as Mu'tazilites
Nawrūz celebration of the new year in the Persian (solar) calendar coming after the spring equinox
Pesantren Islamic religious school in Southeast Asian
Qadariyya group in early Islam who argued for free will in the theological debates; precursors of the Mu'tazila
qāḍī a judge who makes decisions on the basis of the religious law
qiyās "analogy", one of the four sources of law in Sunnī Islam, the others being Qur'ān, *sunna*, and *ijmā'*
riḥla journey
salaf the "pious ancestors," the first three generations of Muslims; in modern times, Salafis are those who consider the era of the *salaf* as embodying the ideal manifestation of Islam
ṣalāt the prescribed five prayers a day, one of the "Five Pillars" required of all Muslims
ṣawm fasting performed in the month of Ramaḍān, one of the "Five Pillars" required of all Muslims (also called *ṣiyām*)
Shāfi'ī the school of law named after al-Shāfi'ī (d. 820)
shahāda "witness to faith"; saying (in Arabic), "There is no god but God and Muḥammad is His messenger"; one of the "Five Pillars" required of all Muslims, indicating conversion to Islam but also a part of the ritual prayer (*ṣalāt*)
sharī'a the religious law derived from the four sources of law in Sunnī Islam (Qur'ān, *sunna, qiyās*, and *ijmā'*)
sharīf descendant of Muḥammad through his daughter Fāṭima and her husband 'Alī who are held in high respect; a title of honour
shaykh literally, "an old man"; a term of respect for a religious teacher and of a Ṣūfī master
Shī'a the religio-political party championing the claims of 'Alī ibn abī Ṭālib and his heirs to the rightful leadership of the community and to their status as Imāms
Sīra the biography of Muḥammad as found in written form
Ṣūfī an adherent to the mystical way of Islam, Sufism, *taṣawwuf*

sunna "custom"; the way Muḥammad acted which is then emulated by Muslims. The source material for the *sunna* is found in the *ḥadīth* reports. The *sunna* is one of the four sources of law for Sunnī Islam, along with Qur'ān, *qiyās*, and *ijmāʿ*

Sunnīs the majority form of Islam, those who follow the *sunna* (thus being called the *ahl al-sunna*), who do not recognize the authority of the Shīʿī Imāms

sūra a chapter of the Qur'ān

tafsīr interpretation of the Qur'ān

ṭalāq divorce by repudiation

ṭarīqa/ṭuruq "the way" of Sufism; a Ṣūfī order or brotherhood

tawḥīd the unity of God

ʿulamāʾ the learned class, especially those learned in religious matters (singular: *ʿālim*)

Umayyads the first dynasty of caliphs, ruling from 661 until the takeover of the Abbasids in 750

umma the community; the body of Muslims

Wahhābī the followers of Ibn ʿAbd al-Wahhāb (d. 1787); the official religious policy of Saudi Arabia

walī holy person, saint

waqf charitable endowment (plural: *awqāf*)

zakāt alms tax, one of the "Five Pillars" required of all Muslims

ziyāra grave visitation

GENERAL INDEX

Al- is ignored under alphabetizing; Arabic names are indexed under the full form found in the text except in cases where subsequent citations are under a partial form of the name or where people are known today under a certain part of the name. Titles are ignored.

Abaza, Mona 580
ʿAbbās Maḥmūd al-ʿAqqād 404
Abbasids 14, 26, 40, 73, 74, 75, 76, 77, 78, 86, 88, 89, 91, 165, 174, 184, 225, 226, 227, 232, 233, 237, 238, 241, 248, 249, 251, 252, 254, 255, 267, 271, 289, 290, 293, 329, 353, 354, 356, 374, 382, 423, 424, 425, 426, 427, 431, 432, 445, 446, 447, 451, 457, 458, 459, 467, 480, 490, 491, 492, 493, 511, 583, 585, 613
Abbott, Nabia 625
ʿAbd Allāh Anṣārī 356
ʿAbd Allāh Bihbahānī 81
ʿAbd Allāh al-Ḥabashī 367
ʿAbd Allāh ibn Ibāḍ 237
ʿAbd Allāh ibn Yaḥyā al-Kindī 237
ʿAbd Allāh Khān 96
ʿAbd Allāh Ṣāliḥ al-Fārisī 49
ʿAbd al-ʿAzīz al-Amawī 47
ʿAbd al-ʿAzīz al-Mahdawī 367
ʿAbd al-ʿAzīz al-Thaʿālibī 244
ʿAbd al-ʿAzīz, King, University 245
ʿAbd al-Bāsiṭ 516
ʿAbd al-Ghafūr Chishtī 221
ʿAbd al-Jabbār 344–9
ʿAbd al-Jalīl al-Qazwīnī al-Rāzī 355
ʿAbd al-Karīm al-Rāfiʿī 345
ʿAbd al-Karīm Hāʾirī 81
ʿAbd al-Karīm Surūsh: *see* Soroush, Abdolkarim
ʿAbd al-Laṭīf al-Baghdādī 301, 597
ʿAbd al-Majīd I 257
ʿAbd al-Malik ibn Marwān 40, 183–5, 237, 267, 289, 444, 490
ʿAbd al-Muṭṭalib 160
ʿAbd al-Qādir, Amīr 371
ʿAbd al-Qādir al-Jīlānī 216, 397
ʿAbd al-Quddūs Gangohī 370
ʿAbd al-Raḥmān I 480
ʿAbd al-Raḥmān al-Awzāʿī 171
ʿAbd al-Raḥmān Chishtī 370
ʿAbd al-Raḥmān ibn Rustam 238
ʿAbd al-Raḥmān Jāmī 370, 390
ʿAbd al-Raḥmān Shāghūrī 371
ʿAbd al-Raḥmān al-Saʿīd 30
ʿAbd al-Raḥmān al-Ṣūfī 296
ʿAbd al-Rāziq, ʿAlī 580–2, 603
ʿAbd al-Rāziq, Muṣṭafā 286
ʿAbd al-Razzāq Kāshānī 370
ʿAbd al-Salām ʿĀrif 406
ʿAbd al-Wahhāb al-Shaʿrānī 326, 368
Abdel Nasser, Gamal (Jamāl ʿAbd al-Nāṣir) 18, 19, 405–6, 557
ʿAbduh, Muḥammad 49, 107, 177–8, 243, 286, 312, 397, 567, 621
ʿAbdu'l-Bahá 647–8
Abdülhamid II, Sultan 64, 65, 397, 533
Abdülmecit I 63
Abdurrahman Tağī 396
Abortion 598–99
Abraha 39
Abraham 148, 149. 151. 157, 197, 199, 200, 203, 204, 207, 208, 209, 359, 396, 424, 450, 453, 502
Abū 'l-ʿAbbās al-ʿUraybī 366
Abū ʿAbd Allāh al-Baṣrī 345, 346
Abū ʿAlī al-Shādhān 352
Abū ʿAlī ibn Khallād 345
Abū 'l-Aswad al-Duʾalī 274
Abū Bakr 224, 225, 232, 234, 314, 348, 435, 630
Abu Bakr Baʾasyir 112
Abū Bakr al-Qaffāl al-Shāshī 91
Abū Bakra 631

INDEX OF QUR'ĀN CITATIONS